D1034376

CLASSICAL AND MEDIEVAL LITERATURE CRITICISM

Guide to Gale Literary Criticism Series

For criticism on	Consult these Gale series
Authors now living or who died after December 31, 1999	*CONTEMPORARY LITERARY CRITICISM (CLC)*
Authors who died between 1900 and 1999	*TWENTIETH-CENTURY LITERARY CRITICISM (TCLC)*
Authors who died between 1800 and 1899	*NINETEENTH-CENTURY LITERATURE CRITICISM (NCLC)*
Authors who died between 1400 and 1799	*LITERATURE CRITICISM FROM 1400 TO 1800 (LC)* *SHAKESPEAREAN CRITICISM (SC)*
Authors who died before 1400	*CLASSICAL AND MEDIEVAL LITERATURE CRITICISM (CMLC)*
Authors of books for children and young adults	*CHILDREN'S LITERATURE REVIEW (CLR)*
Dramatists	*DRAMA CRITICISM (DC)*
Poets	*POETRY CRITICISM (PC)*
Short story writers	*SHORT STORY CRITICISM (SSC)*
Literary topics and movements	*HARLEM RENAISSANCE: A GALE CRITICAL COMPANION (HR)* *THE BEAT GENERATION: A GALE CRITICAL COMPANION (BG)* *FEMINISM IN LITERATURE: A GALE CRITICAL COMPANION (FL)* *GOTHIC LITERATURE: A GALE CRITICAL COMPANION (GL)*
Asian American writers of the last two hundred years	*ASIAN AMERICAN LITERATURE (AAL)*
Black writers of the past two hundred years	*BLACK LITERATURE CRITICISM (BLC-1)* *BLACK LITERATURE CRITICISM SUPPLEMENT (BLCS)* *BLACK LITERATURE CRITICISM: CLASSIC AND EMERGING AUTHORS SINCE 1950 (BLC-2)*
Hispanic writers of the late nineteenth and twentieth centuries	*HISPANIC LITERATURE CRITICISM (HLC)* *HISPANIC LITERATURE CRITICISM SUPPLEMENT (HLCS)*
Native North American writers and orators of the eighteenth, nineteenth, and twentieth centuries	*NATIVE NORTH AMERICAN LITERATURE (NNAL)*
Major authors from the Renaissance to the present	*WORLD LITERATURE CRITICISM, 1500 TO THE PRESENT (WLC)* *WORLD LITERATURE CRITICISM SUPPLEMENT (WLCS)*

ISSN 0896-0011

Volume 111

CLASSICAL AND MEDIEVAL LITERATURE CRITICISM

Criticism of the Works of World
Authors from Classical Antiquity through the
Fourteenth Century, from the First Appraisals
to Current Evaluations

Jelena Krstović
Project Editor

GALE
CENGAGE Learning

Detroit • New York • San Francisco • New Haven, Conn • Waterville, Maine • London

GALE
CENGAGE Learning·

Classical and Medieval Literature Criticism, Vol. 111

Project Editor: Jelena O. Krstović

Editorial: Dana Ramel Barnes, Kathy D. Darrow, Kristen A. Dorsch, Jeffrey W. Hunter, Michelle Lee, Thomas J. Schoenberg, Lawrence J. Trudeau

Data Capture: Frances Monroe, Gwen Tucker

Indexing Services: Zott Solutions, Inc

Rights and Acquisitions: Jennifer Altschul, Timothy Sisler, Jhanay Williams

Composition and Electronic Capture: Gary Oudersluys

Manufacturing: Cynde Bishop

Associate Product Manager: Marc Cormier

For product information and technology assistance, contact us at
Gale Customer Support, 1-800-877-4253.
For permission to use material from this text or product,
submit all requests online at **www.cengage.com/permissions.**
Further permissions questions can be emailed to
permissionrequest@cengage.com

Gale
27500 Drake Rd.
Farmington Hills, MI, 48331-3535

LIBRARY OF CONGRESS CATALOG CARD NUMBER 88-641014

ISBN-13: 978-1-4144-3517-6
ISBN-10: 1-4144-3517-7

ISSN 0896-0011

Contents

Preface vii

Acknowledgments xi

Literary Criticism Series Advisory Board xiii

Preface

Since its inception in 1988, *Classical and Medieval Literature Criticism* (*CMLC*) has been a valuable resource for students and librarians seeking critical commentary on the works and authors of antiquity through the fourteenth century. The great poets, prose writers, dramatists, and philosophers of this period form the basis of most humanities curricula, so that virtually every student will encounter many of these works during the course of a high school and college education. Reviewers have found *CMLC* "useful" and "extremely convenient," noting that it "adds to our understanding of the rich legacy left by the ancient period and the Middle Ages," and praising its "general excellence in the presentation of an inherently interesting subject." No other single reference source has surveyed the critical reaction to classical and medieval literature as thoroughly as *CMLC*.

Scope of the Series

CMLC provides an introduction to classical and medieval authors, works, and topics that represent a variety of genres, time periods, and nationalities. By organizing and reprinting an enormous amount of critical commentary written on authors and works of this period in world history, *CMLC* helps students develop valuable insight into literary history, promotes a better understanding of the texts, and sparks ideas for papers and assignments.

Each entry in *CMLC* presents a comprehensive survey of an author's career, an individual work of literature, or a literary topic, and provides the user with a multiplicity of interpretations and assessments. Such variety allows students to pursue their own interests; furthermore, it fosters an awareness that literature is dynamic and responsive to many different opinions. Early commentary is offered to indicate initial responses, later selections document changes in literary reputations, and retrospective analyses provide the reader with modern views. The size of each author entry is a relative reflection of the scope of the criticism available in English.

An author or work may appear more than once in the series if they have been the subject of a substantial amount of criticism. Individual works or groups of works by an author may also be covered in separate entries. For example, Homer will be represented by three entries, one devoted to the *Iliad,* one to the *Odyssey,* and one to the Homeric Hymns.

CMLC continues the survey of criticism of world literature begun by Gale's *Contemporary Literary Criticism* (*CLC*), *Twentieth-Century Literary Criticism* (*TCLC*), *Nineteenth-Century Literature Criticism* (*NCLC*), *Literature Criticism from 1400 to 1800* (*LC*), and *Shakespearean Criticism* (*SC*).

Organization of the Book

A *CMLC* entry consists of the following elements:

- The **Author Heading** cites the name under which the author most commonly wrote, followed by birth and death dates. Also located here are any name variations under which an author wrote, including transliterated forms for authors whose native languages use nonroman alphabets. If the author wrote consistently under a pseudonym, the pseudonym will be listed in the author heading and the author's actual name given in parenthesis on the first line of the biographical and critical information. Uncertain birth or death dates are indicated by question marks. Single-work entries are preceded by a heading that consists of the most common form of the title in English translation (if applicable) and the author name (if applicable).

- The **Introduction** contains background information that introduces the reader to the author, work, or topic that is the subject of the entry.

- The list of **Principal Works** is ordered chronologically by date of first publication or composition and lists the most important works by an author. The genre and publication date of each work is given. In the case of foreign authors whose works have been translated into English, the Principal English Translations focuses primarily on twentieth-century translations, selecting those works most commonly considered the best by critics. For works originally written in Old or Middle English, the Principal English Editions section lists editions in modern English. Unless otherwise indicated, dramas are dated by first performance, not first publication. Lists of **Representative Works** by different authors appear with topic entries.

- Reprinted **Criticism** is arranged chronologically in each entry to provide a useful perspective on changes in critical evaluation over time. The critic's name and the date of composition or publication of the critical work are given at the beginning of each piece of criticism. Unsigned criticism is preceded by the title of the source in which it appeared. All titles by the author featured in the text are printed in boldface type. Footnotes are reprinted at the end of each essay or excerpt. In the case of excerpted criticism, only those footnotes that pertain to the excerpted texts are included. Criticism in topic entries is arranged chronologically under a variety of subheadings to facilitate the study of different aspects of the topic.

- A complete **Bibliographical Citation** of the original essay or book precedes each piece of criticism.

- Critical essays are prefaced by brief **Annotations** indicating the content of each piece.

- An annotated bibliography of **Further Reading** appears at the end of each entry and suggests resources for additional study. In some cases, significant essays for which the editors could not obtain reprint rights are included here. Boxed material following the further reading list provides references to other biographical and critical sources on the author in series published by Gale.

Cumulative Indexes

A **Cumulative Author Index** lists all of the authors that appear in a wide variety of reference sources published by the Gale, including *CMLC*. A complete list of these sources is found facing the first page of the Author Index. The index also includes birth and death dates and cross references between pseudonyms and actual names.

Beginning with the second volume, a **Cumulative Nationality Index** lists all authors and anonymous works featured in *CMLC* by nationality, followed by the number of the *CMLC* volume in which the entry appears.

Beginning with the tenth volume, a **Cumulative Topic Index** lists the literary themes and topics treated in the series as well as in *Nineteenth-Century Literature Criticism, Twentieth-Century Literary Criticism,* and the *Contemporary Literary Criticism* Yearbook, which was discontinued in 1998.

A **Cumulative Title Index** lists in alphabetical order all of the works discussed in the series. Each title listing includes the corresponding volume and page numbers where criticism may be located. Foreign-language titles that have been translated into English are followed by the titles of the translation—for example, *Slovo o polku Igorove* (*The Song of Igor's Campaign*). Page numbers following these translated titles refer to all pages on which any form of the titles, either foreign-language or translated, appear. Titles of novels, dramas, nonfiction books, and poetry, short story, or essay collections are printed in italics, while individual poems, short stories, and essays are printed in roman type within quotation marks.

Citing *Classical and Medieval Literature Criticism*

When citing criticism reprinted in the Literary Criticism Series, students should provide complete bibliographic information so that the cited essay can be located in the original print or electronic source. Students who quote directly from reprinted criticism may use any accepted bibliographic format, such as University of Chicago Press style or Modern Language Association style.

The examples below follow recommendations for preparing a bibliography set forth in *The Chicago Manual of Style*, 15th ed. (Chicago: The University of Chicago Press, 2006); the first example pertains to material drawn from periodicals, the second to material reprinted from books:

Sealey, R. J. "The Tetralogies Ascribed to Antiphon." *Transactions of the American Philological Association* 114, (1984): 71-85. Reprinted in *Classical and Medieval Literature Criticism.* Vol. 55, edited by Jelena O. Krstović, 2-9. Detroit: Thomson Gale, 2003.

Bourne, Ella. "Classical Elements in *The Gesta Romanorum.*" In *Vassar Medieval Studies* edited by Christabel Forsyth Fiske, 345-76. New Haven: Yale University Press, 1923. Reprinted in *Classical and Medieval Literature Criticism.* Vol. 55, edited by Jelena O. Krstović, 81-92. Detroit: Thomson Gale, 2003.

The examples below follow recommendations for preparing a works cited list set forth in the *MLA Handbook for Writers of Research Papers,* 6th ed. (New York: The Modern Language Association of America, 2003); the first example pertains to material drawn from periodicals, the second to material reprinted from books:

Sealey, R. J. "The Tetralogies Ascribed to Antiphon." *Transactions of the American Philological Association* 114. (1984): 71-85. Reprinted in *Classical and Medieval Literature Criticism.* Ed. Jelena O. Krstović. Vol. 55. Detroit: Thomson Gale, 2003. 2-9.

Bourne, Ella. "Classical Elements in *The Gesta Romanorum.*" *Vassar Medieval Studies.* Ed. Christabel Forsyth Fiske. New Haven: Yale University Press, 1923. 345-76. Reprinted in *Classical and Medieval Literature Criticism.* Ed. Jelena O. Krstović. Vol. 55. Detroit: Thomson Gale, 2003. 81-92.

Suggestions are Welcome

Readers who wish to suggest new features, topics, or authors to appear in future volumes, or who have other suggestions or comments are cordially invited to call, write, or fax the Associate Product Manager:

Associate Product Manager, Literary Criticism Series
Gale
Cengage Learning
27500 Drake Road
Farmington Hills, MI 48331-3535
1-800-347-4253 (GALE)
Fax: 248-699-8054

Acknowledgments

The editors wish to thank the copyright holders of the criticism included in this volume and the permissions managers of many book and magazine publishing companies for assisting us in securing reproduction rights. We are also grateful to the staffs of the Detroit Public Library, the Library of Congress, the University of Detroit Mercy Library, Wayne State University Purdy/Kresge Library Complex, and the University of Michigan Libraries for making their resources available to us. Following is a list of the copyright holders who have granted us permission to reproduce material in this volume of *CMLC*. Every effort has been made to trace copyright, but if omissions have been made, please let us know.

COPYRIGHTED MATERIAL IN *CMLC*, VOLUME 111, WAS REPRODUCED FROM THE FOLLOWING PERIODICALS:

Arthuriana, v. 14, summer, 2004. Copyright © 2004 *Arthuriana.* Reproduced by permission.—*Dalhousie French Studies,* v. 33, winter, 1995 for "The Pain of Reading Female Bodies in Marie de France's 'Guigemar'" by Suzanne Klerks; v. 61, winter, 2002 for "The End Game in Marie de France's *Lais*: The Search for a Solution," by Heather M. Arden. Both reproduced by permission of the publisher and the respective authors.—*French Studies,* v. 49, October, 1995 for "The Swan and the Nightingale: Natural Unity in a Hostile World in the *Lais* of Marie de France," by June Hall McCash. Copyright © 1995 Oxford University Press. Reproduced by permission of the publisher and the author.—*Germanisch-Romanische Monatsschrift,* v. 54, 2004. Copyright © 2004. Carl Winter Universitatsverlag. Edited by Conrad Wiedmann. Reproduced by permission.—*Journal of Early Christian Studies,* v. 10, winter, 2002. Copyright © 2002 The Johns Hopkins University Press. Reprinted by permission of The Johns Hopkins University Press.—*Medium Ævum,* v. 60, 1991. Copyright © 1991 Neil Adkin. Reproduced by permission.—*Romance Quarterly,* v. 49, winter, 2002; v. 53, winter, 2006. Copyright © 2002, 2006 by Helen Dwight Reid Educational Foundation. Both reproduced with permission of the Helen Dwight Reid Educational Foundation, published by Heldref Publications, 1319 18th Street, NW, Washington, DC 20036-1802.—*The Romanic Review,* v. 29, November, 2001. Copyright © 2001 by the Trustees of Columbia University in the City of New York. Reproduced by permission.—*Signs: Journal of Women in Culture and Society,* v. 25, winter, 2000. Copyright © 2000 University of Chicago Press. All rights reserved. Reproduced by permission.—*Studies in Medieval Culture,* v. 3, 1970. Copyright © 1970 by Western Michigan University. Reproduced by permission.—*University of Toronto Quarterly,* v. 64, spring, 1995. Copyright © 1995 University of Toronto Press. Reproduced by permission of University of Toronto Press Incorporated.

COPYRIGHTED MATERIAL IN *CMLC*, VOLUME 111, WAS REPRODUCED FROM THE FOLLOWING BOOKS:

Amidon, Philip R. From *The Church History of Rufinus of Aquileia: Books 10 and 11.* Translated by Philip R. Amidon. Oxford University Press, 1997. Copyright © 1997 Philip R. Amidon. Reproduced by permission of Oxford University Press.—Bloch, R. Howard. From *The Anonymous Marie de France.* The University of Chicago Press, 2003. Copyright © 2003 by The University of Chicago. All rights reserved. Reproduced by permission of the publisher and the author.—Calabrese, Michael. From "Controlling Space and Secrets in the *Lais* of Marie de France," in *Place, Space, and Landscape in Medieval Narrative.* Edited by Laura L. Howes. The University of Tennessee Press, 2007. Copyright © 2007 by The University of Tennessee Press. Reproduced by permission of The University of Tennessee Press.—Clark, Robert L. A. From "The Courtly and the Queer: Some Like It Not," in *'Cancon legiere a chanter': Essays on Old French Literature in Honor of Samuel N. Rosenberg.* Edited by Karen Fresco and Wendy Pfeffer. Summa Publications, Inc., 2007. Copyright © 2007 Summa Publications, Inc. Reproduced by permission.—Dionisotti, A. C. From "Walter of Châtillon and the Greeks," in *Latin Poetry and the Classical Tradition: Essays in Medieval and Renaissance Literature.* Edited by Peter Godman and Oswyn Murray. Clarendon Press, 1990. Copyright © 1990 by the individual contributors. Reproduced by permission of Oxford University Press.—Edwards, Robert R. From *The Flight from Desire: Augustine and Ovid to Chaucer.* Palgrave, 2008. Copyright © 2006 Robert R. Edwards. All rights reserved. Reproduced with permission of Palgrave Macmillan.—Guy-Bray, Stephen. From "Civilizing Sexuality: Marie de France's Lay with Two Names," in *Norbert Elias and Human Interdependencies.* Edited by Thomas Salumets. McGill-Queen's University Press, 2001. Copyright © 2001 McGill-Queen's University Press. Reproduced by permission.—Haidu, Peter. From *The Subject Medieval/Modern: Text and Governance in the Middle Ages.* Stanford University Press, 2004. Copyright © 2004 by the Board of Trustees of the Le-

.

Gale Literature Product Advisory Board

The members of the Gale Literature Product Advisory Board—reference librarians from public and academic library systems—represent a cross-section of our customer base and offer a variety of informed perspectives on both the presentation and content of our literature products. Advisory board members assess and define such quality issues as the relevance, currency, and usefulness of the author coverage, critical content, and literary topics included in our series; evaluate the layout, presentation, and general quality of our printed volumes; provide feedback on the criteria used for selecting authors and topics covered in our series; provide suggestions for potential enhancements to our series; identify any gaps in our coverage of authors or literary topics, recommending authors or topics for inclusion; analyze the appropriateness of our content and presentation for various user audiences, such as high school students, undergraduates, graduate students, librarians, and educators; and offer feedback on any proposed changes/enhancements to our series. We wish to thank the following advisors for their advice throughout the year.

Marie de France
c. Twelfth Century

French poet.

The following entry provides an overview of Marie de France's life and works. For additional information on her career, see *CMLC,* Volume 8.

INTRODUCTION

Marie de France is the earliest known French female writer. Considered one of the finest poets of her century, Marie benefited from a western European cultural renaissance that recognized the contributions of women among a growing class of intellectuals. Yet, from what little is known of her biography, it appears that her creativity was nonetheless restricted by the conventions of the aristocratic class to which she belonged and for whom she wrote. Especially in her best-known work, the short narrative poems entitled *Les Lais* (c. 1160-90; *Lays*), scholars perceive a tension between Marie's desire to expose the difficulties women faced under the medieval system of patrilineage and her duty as a member of the Norman aristocracy to uphold the rigid social and gender hierarchies demanded by that system. While critics agree that Marie was not a feminist in the modern sense of that word, they consistently discuss her subtle manipulation of source materials to present a distinctly female perspective. She is considered revolutionary in an age of predominantly anonymous authorship for her literary aspirations: in the epilogue to her *Les Fables d'Ysopet* (c. 1167-89; *Fables*), a collection modeled on Latin, Celtic, and English sources, Marie expressed fear that her works would be claimed by other writers and made a point of inserting her name into her text. In addition to the *Lays* and the *Fables,* her works include a translation from the Latin of the legend of St. Patrick, *L'Espurgatoire Saint Patriz* (after 1190; *St. Patrick's Purgatory*), and a translation, also from the Latin, of a biography of St. Audrey, *La vie seinte Audree* (after 1190; *Life of Saint Audrey*). It has only been in the last few years that scholars have confidently ascribed the *Audree* to Marie, largely because of its affinity with her other texts, especially in its expressed desire to document previous knowledge, and the assertion of its last three lines that "One is foolish indeed who forgets herself: / here I write my name 'Marie' / so that I may be remembered."

BIOGRAPHICAL INFORMATION

Since no details of Marie's life are known for certain, her biography, the extent of her body of work, and the order in which her writings were composed have all been subjects of intense debate However, scholars generally agree that Marie was born in France in the last half of the twelfth century and that she lived for many years in England. In each of her four works, the author names herself simply as "Marie." The name by which she is known today was coined by Claude Fauchet in 1581; while consulting a manuscript that included a collection of fables, Fauchet read in the epilogue, "Marie is my name and I am from France," and thereafter referred to the author as Marie de France. Since Marie claimed to have translated the fables from an English version by Alfred the Great, and since it would not have been necessary to declare herself from France had she been writing in her homeland, historians speculate that she was a French woman living in England—a conjecture borne out by the few other identifiers she provided, including her dedication of the *Lays* to a "noble king," widely thought to be Henry II. In addition, Marie's vocabulary, themes, and style, and her knowledge of Latin, French, and English indicate that she was probably of aristocratic, perhaps even noble, birth. The mention by Denis Piramus in his *Life of St. Edmund* (c. 1108-1200) of a "dame Marie" as the author of widely popular lays enjoyed by "counts, barons, and simple knights" also affirms her noble heritage. One commonly asserted theory about Marie's identity is that she was the natural daughter of Geoffrey Plantagenet, Henry II's father. This Mary, the half-sister of Henry II, was born in France and lived in England between 1181 and 1216 as the abbess of Shaftesbury, an abbey patronized by William Longsword, possibly the "Count William" to whom she dedicated the *Fables.*

TEXTUAL HISTORY

There are five extant manuscripts of Marie's *Lais,* thought to be her first work. The most complete text is the British Museum Harley 978 manuscript, which contains all twelve of the lays and Marie's prologue to that work. In the prologue, Marie states her intention and her source: she had heard Breton lays and decided to document them for posterity and for her own fame. Harley 978 also includes the whole of what scholars believe to be Marie's second work, *Les Fables d'Ysopet,* a collection of 103 fables she translated from English into French. The unusually large number of extant manuscripts (twenty-three exist from the thirteenth, fourteenth, and fifteenth centuries) indicates the popularity of the fables during her lifetime. The title of Marie's collection cites Aesop as her model, but in the epilogue she acknowledges Alfred the Great, whose fables have been lost, as her source. As with the *Lais,* the lack of extant literary antecedents makes it difficult to determine the level of Marie's originality. However, scholars have determined that the first forty fables closely correspond to the Latin *Romulus Nilanti,* while the others appear to be based on English and Celtic oral traditions. Henricus Salteriensis's Latin version of the legend of St. Patrick is the source of what many believe to be Marie's third work. Only one manuscript exists of her *L'Espurgatoire Saint Patriz,* a close translation of Salteriensis's work into French. Similarly, only one copy exists of what is now thought to be her last work, *La vie seinte Audree*—a British Library manuscript containing biographies of thirteen saints, probably recorded in the thirteenth or fourteenth century. Allegedly a translation from a single Latin text, it more likely represents a combination of three Latin sources documenting the life of the popular seventh-century English saint Etheldreda (known as St. Audrey). French scholars translated Marie's *Lais* into modern French long before the twentieth century, though the first English translation of this work did not appear until 1900, in a rendering by Jessie L. Weston of two of Marie's lays and two anonymous ones. Several recent English translations of the *Lais,* along with the first appearance in English of Marie's biographies of St. Patrick and St. Audrey—*St. Patrick's Purgatory* (1993) and *Life of St. Audrey* (2006)—attest to widespread and continuing interest in her work.

MAJOR WORKS

Considerable attention has been devoted to Marie's general prologue to the *Lais* as a source of information about her authorial intentions. As she explains in these opening verses, she wishes to preserve in writing the many *lais*—brief narrative tales of adventure and romance—that have been handed down to her generation. Historians speculate that Marie may have been the originator of the lay as a verse tale in octosyllabic couplets, but they concede that, since no original Breton lays survive (upon which she claims to have based the twelve poems in her collection), it is difficult to determine the extent of her creative input. Nonetheless, she was part of a generation of writers, among them Chrétien de Troyes, notable for inventing the French verse romance. In the prologue Marie makes bold

claims for the lay as she conceives it, placing her own vernacular enterprise within the tradition of the writings of the ancients: "When they wrote their books in the olden day / What they had to say they'd obscurely say / . . . future readers would gloss the letter / Add their own meaning to make the book better." Marie's belief that future generations will interpret her words beyond their literal meaning has been widely discussed in terms of her didactic intent, her economy of style, and her practice—avowed in all of her writings—of drawing on individual memory so that the collective memory of her predecessors will not be forgotten. In combination with her self-identification, Marie's prologue makes clear that she is proud of herself and her lays—a literary genre that she seeks to elevate to a position of respectability.

Marie's prologue to the *Lais* has also been seen as evidence of an understanding on her part of the self-reflexive nature of art. Her writings, especially the lays, are often interpreted as cultural translations for a medieval audience—including women—of myths and legends derived from classical and folkloric sources. The lays are unconnected in plot, but they are united by the theme of love, often involving chivalric episodes and set against a background of feudal politics. These stories of love describe power relationships such as rape, vassal-king bonds, and arranged marriages; consensual relationships, usually extramarital and secret; and parent-child relationships, generally described in terms of the system of patrilineage. Women are a presence in Marie's lays equal to that of men, and both sexes are represented as victims as well as perpetrators of genealogical politics. Scholars consider it bold on Marie's part to have even ventured to depict the treatment of women as objects of exchange in the service of arranged marriages, the cornerstone of the feudal system of patrilineage. Few of the marriages Marie depicts are happy. For example, in the lays "Guigemar" and "Yonec," jealous husbands imprison their wives, while in "Bisclavret," a suspicious wife punishes her husband for his presumed homosexuality by sentencing him forever to life as a werewolf. Many of Marie's characters live in a hostile world, trapped either literally by spiteful mates or figuratively by social and familial obligations, and they seek an ideal love as a means of escape. Marie depicts ideal love—loyal, generous, and pure—as attainable only between consenting parties. But for the most part, this type of love is beset by obstacles, either doomed to failure because it is exposed as extramarital, or dependent for its survival upon supernatural intervention, such as in "Milun," where a swan carries messages between separated lovers for twenty years, and "Lanval," where romantic bliss obtains in a fairy-tale world far removed from the realities of King Arthur's court.

Among Marie's other writings, only the *Fables* have attracted significant attention, though nothing approaching the critical interest in the *Lays*. The *Fables* are didactic, each closing with an epimythium, or moral teaching, adapted for a contemporary audience. According to the critic Judith Barban, the unifying theme of the fables is expressed in the twelfth-century colloquialism *lai estre* (let it be). Throughout the collection, Marie portrays the imprudence of seeking to alter one's preordained lot in life. Through her animal characters especially, she expresses the medieval belief in the permanence of the social class to which one is born. For example, in "The Affectionate Ass," the ass, jealous of his master's affection for the dog, is nearly beaten to death by the master's men when he paws the master in canine fashion. Yet Marie also expresses her disdain for the manipulative and the power hungry regardless of their social position, and she instructs readers to fight the oppression of the weak, to root out corruption and greed, and to choose a simple and free life over a luxurious but enslaved existence. And, as in the lays, the stories convey sympathy with women who are abused by men. In "The Monkey and the Bear," a male bear convinces a female monkey to show off her newborn baby, only to devour it in front of her; in "The Fox and the Bear," the male also cruelly tricks the female, in this case with designs of raping her. On the other hand, critics note that the closing lines of "The Peasant Who Saw His Wife with Her Lover" seem to share the misogyny so prevalent in the literature of the Middle Ages: "And so, forewarned all men should be / That women know good strategy / They've more art in their craft of lies / Than all the devil can devise."

CRITICAL RECEPTION

Judging from the numerous critical interpretations her stories continue to inspire, Marie's deceptively simple, timeless stories intrigue, in the words of R. Howard Bloch, by their "complicated opaqueness." The large body of recent criticism on the *Lais* has rendered anachronistic the once prevailing view that Marie's lays are charming in their simplicity but lacking in literary sophistication. As recent critics emphasize, Marie depicts an assortment of conflicts in the lays with unpredictable resolutions and, to use Peter Haidu's phrase, "situational morality." She is today considered daring in her efforts to present multiple perspectives on the conflicts she describes—not just the viewpoint sanctioned by the ruling aristocracy—and in her veiled attempts to subvert aspects of feudal politics, especially in her presentation of *mal mariées*, unhappy women forced into marriage to preserve the line of succession. Marie appears to have resisted the convention of arranged marriage by repeatedly portraying ideal love, yet she rarely allowed this type of love to triumph. As Robert M. Edwards notes, the lays are "stories of desire working within the constraints of twelfth-century baronial culture." Critic Robert W. Hanning remarks on the self-conscious nature of Marie's art, likening her to the Venus portrayed in the lay "Guigemar" who tosses Ovid's love poetry into the fire to express her disdain for the male-dominated strategies of courtly love: "Marie's representation of herself in this passage as a post-Ovidian female court poet, in whose sociopoetic situation . . . insight and victimization, willed authority and unwelcome restriction, radically interact, offers an important clue to a major project of the *Lais*: the depiction of women for whom creative or authoritative utterance is intimately connected with victimization, loss, and even destruction." It is generally agreed that Marie's lays continue to resonate with readers because of their expression of an independent, feminine spirit, albeit one constrained by the patriarchal culture in which she lived. The *Lais* presents rare contemporary insight into the female condition in Anglo-Norman England.

PRINCIPAL WORKS

Les Lais [*Lays*] (poetry) c. 1160-90
Les Fables d'Ysopet [*Fables*] (poetry) c. 1167-89
Espurgatoire Seint Patriz [*St. Patrick's Purgatory*] (poetry) after 1190
La vie seinte Audree [*Life of St. Audrey*] (biography) after 1190

Principal English Translations

Guingamor, Lanval, Tyolet, Bisclaveret (translated by Jessie L. Weston) 1900
Marie de France: Seven of Her Lays *Done into English* (translated by Edith Rickert) 1901
French Medieval Romances from the Lays *of Marie de France* (translated by Eugene Mason) 1911
Marie de France: Fables (translated by Alfred Ewert and R. C. Johnston) 1942
Marie de France: Lais (translated by Alfred Ewert) 1944
The Fables *of Marie de France* (translated by Mary Lou Martin) 1984
Fables (translated by Harriet Spiegel) 1987
Proud Knight, Fair Lady: The Twelve Lais *of Marie de France* (translated by Angela Barrett) 1989
St. Patrick's Purgatory: *A Poem* (translated by Michael J. Curley) 1993
The Honeysuckle and the Hazel Tree (translated by Patricia Terry) 1995

The Lais *of Marie de France* (translated by Robert Hanning and Joan Ferrante) 1998

The Lais *of Marie de France* (translated by Glyn S. Burgess and Keith Busby) 1999

Medieval Lays *and Legends of Marie de France* (translated by Eugene Mason) 2003

The Life of Saint Audrey: *A Text by Marie de France* (translated and edited by June Hall McCash and Judith Clark Barban) 2006

CRITICISM

Mary Lou Martin (essay date 1979)

SOURCE: Martin, Mary Lou. Introduction to *The Fables of Marie de France*, pp. 1-30. Birmingham, Ala.: Summa Publications, 1984.

[*In the following essay, originally published in 1979, Martin provides an overview of current scholarship on the* Fables, *offering sections on Marie's biography; her sources, including the oral tradition; the social and political context of the moral code presented in her tales; and the textual history of her entire output.*]

> Al finement de cest escrit,
> Qu'en Romanz ai traitié e dit,
> Me numerai pur remembrance:
> Marie ai num, si sui de France.[1]

Within these succinct lines penned by a French poetess sometime in the latter part of the twelfth century, the myth of Marie de France lies captive. Scholars of every succeeding century have attempted to unravel the mystery of her existence and to piece together from their reasoned conjectures the pattern of her literary production. Still she eludes identification, and the best of hypotheses concerning the dates of her compositions can only briefly illuminate the "vision légère et fugitive"[2] that she remains.

Marie's historical anonymity does not, however, preclude a long-accepted reputation as an established author. While her contemporary Denis Piramus acknowledged her popular success as the writer of *lais,* Marie's renown in later centuries was based not upon her authorship of the *Lais* but upon that of the *Fables.*[3] Until 1775 when Thomas Tyrwhitt named Marie as the author of the *Lais* and the *Esope,* all references to her work mentioned only the *Fables.*[4]

Yet if, from the early sixteenth to the late eighteenth century, Marie was indeed known and appreciated solely on the basis of her *Fables,* why has there been relatively little critical interest generated in them up to the present time? It would seem that they enjoyed a certain popularity during the thirteenth, fourteenth, and fifteenth centuries, having been preserved in twenty-three manuscripts, two of which contain all 102 fables of the collection, along with the Prologue and the Epilogue. By the time of the nineteenth-century renaissance in medieval studies, Marie had become generally accepted as the author of three works, the *Lais,* the *Fables,* and the *Espurgatoire seint Patriz*; so it was perhaps inevitable that the Romantic spirit of scholars who cherished such works as the *Tristan* and the romances of Chrétien de Troyes would single out the *Lais* as representative of Marie's production. The *Lais* do communicate the blend of symbolism and didacticism that is present in most of her work, but they are, in fact, of a more lyrical quality then the *Fables.* The poetic world of the *Lais* is that which modern tastes expect and prefer to the rustic didacticism of the *Fables,* and it may be for this reason that the *Lais* have had more appeal to readers and critics of the modern period.

The *Fables* themselves represent the ancient Aesopian tradition which was understandably quite popular in the Middle Ages, for it contained elements of two other favorite medieval genres, the animal tale and the didactic composition. The early medieval beast epics, such as the Latin *Ecbasis captivi* (c. 930), as well as the later *Ysengrimus* and *Roman de Renart* collections, showed obvious affinities with Aesop's fables, the same general source of Marie's work. A gift for persuasive exposition as demonstrated by authors such as Hélinand, in his *Vers de la mort* (1194-97), and Jean de Meun, in the *Roman de la Rose,* was also appreciated by medieval audiences. Marie's fables are thus highly representative of certain tastes for literature in the Middle Ages and should not be relegated, on the basis of modern literary preferences, to a position inferior to that of the *Lais.* Renewed interest and study in the *Fables* may, in fact, provide long-awaited clues to the mystery of their author, Marie.

MARIE'S LIFE AND WORKS

One basis assumption that has been generally accepted concerning Marie's identity is that she was a native French woman living in England. This idea is based on Marie's statement in the Epilogue to the *Fables* that she is "de France," a descriptive phrase that would have been unnecessary had she been writing in France. Furthermore, Marie claims to have translated the *Fables* from an English version by King Alfred, thus indicating her knowledge of English; the famous manuscript Harley 978, which contains the *Fables,* may have been copied at the abbey of Reading.[5] The *Espurgatoire seint Patriz* was also translated from a text believed to have been composed in England by a twelfth-century Cistercian monk named Henry of Saltrey.[6]

The tone of Marie's work and her choice of source material, reinforced by Denis Piramus' reference to her as "dame Marie," have led most scholars to believe that she was of noble birth. She has been identified variously as a countess (Marie de Champagne), the wife of a nobleman (Marie de Meulan), a nun (at Reading), or even an abbess (at Shaftesbury).[7] The opinion that Marie was indeed abbess of Shaftesbury from 1181 to 1216 and also half-sister to Henry II of England has gained some degree of acceptance.

Of key importance to the identification of Marie and to the dating of her works are the dedications of the *Lais* to an unspecified king and the *Fables* to a Count William. While some critics believed that the term "nobles reis" of the *Lais* was addressed to Henry the Young King, most assume the description of the king "a qui tute joie s'encline" to have reference to Henry II.[8] The identity of the *Fables*' Count William has been less precisely determined, since there was no dearth of chivalric Williams in twelfth-century England.[9] Count William has been linked with several prominent historical figures, among them William Marshal, William Longsword, William of Mandeville, William of Warren, and William of Gloucester (all of England), as well as Guillaume de Dampierre (of Flanders). Of this group, William Longsword, the natural son of Henry II and Rosamond Clifford, may have had the greatest connection with Shaftesbury, since he was a patron of the abbey and would have been the nephew of Marie the abbess. After 1196 he became the Earl of Salisbury, a district located about thirty kilometers northeast of Shaftesbury. On the other hand, both William of Mandeville and William Marshal were closely associated with the abbey of Reading and would likely have had contact with Marie if she was in fact connected with that abbey. Marie's description of the count "ki flurs est de chevalerie / d'enseignement, de curteisie" and who is "le plus vaillant de nul realme" might be applicable to William Longsword, whose tomb bears the inscription "flos comitum," as well as to William Marshal, whose valor has been preserved in legendary form in a 19,214-line biography dating from the thirteenth century.[10]

Since the identities of Marie's "noble reis" and "cunte Willalme" cannot be determined with absolute certainty, however, other criteria have been used to date Marie's works and to assign to them various orders of composition. Relationships between the *Lais* and other works such as the *Brut, Enéas, Ille at Galeron,* and *Guillaume de Dole* have placed the composition of the *Lais* between 1155 and 1199. On the basis of recent research indicating that Marie's *Espurgatoire* may have been written between 1208 and 1215, it seems highly improbable that this was her earliest work; if that were true, the period of her literary activity would have to be extended well into the thirteenth century.[11] Mall and

Warnke both remarked that the language of Marie's *Fables* closely resembled that of the *Brut* (1155); thus, to place this work in the thirteenth century would present difficulties with regard to the language of *Fables*.[12] Richard Baum hinted that, since a span of literary production of over fifty years would be quite unlikely, the same Marie may not have been responsible for all the works in question.[13] Without succumbing to this somewhat heretical intimation, it may be adduced that those theories which have placed the *Espurgatoire* as the last of Marie's compositions are the most substantial and the least anachronistic. Hypotheses concerning a later date for the *Lais* may also be of significance in limiting the supposed dates of Marie's production to a reasonable period of time. Ewert pointed out that in the prologue to the *Lais* Marie rejects the idea of translating stories from Latin into French, while in the prologue to the *Fables* she takes great pains to justify her translation, saying she was commissioned to do the work. These statements suggest the order *Lais, Fables, Espurgatoire,* indicating "a progression from entertainment through moralization to edification."[14]

Given the current lack of concrete evidence, any attempt to set precise dates from Marie's works must remain mere conjecture. It can be noted with certainty, however, that Marie's known texts come down to us from one of the most fruitful periods of medieval European society, that of the twelfth-century renaissance. Although her identity may be cloaked in anonymity, Marie herself is vividly present in her works, which depict in some detail the society of which she was an apt observer, and which confirm her deserved place of renown in a time of artistic reawakening.

THE SOCIAL BACKGROUND

At the end of the twelfth century, European society was marked by the transformation of its intellectual as well as its political makeup. While artistic, philosophical, and cultural activities blossomed in the new light of learning, political and economic affairs became more settled as the turbulence of the immediately preceding period diminished. In England, where Marie's fables were most likely composed, this earlier era had been dominated by the reign of Henry II, who, until his death in 1189, was considered the most powerful Western ruler. His reign was one of great turmoil, as evidenced by his quarrel with Thomas Becket and the revolt of Henry's own sons, instigated by their mother Eleanor of Aquitaine and aided by Louis VII of France. Richard the Lionhearted succeeded his father in 1189 and ruled until his own death in 1199. At this time his brother John acceded to the throne, inheriting a land beset with debts and rebellious barons, but eventually improving the administration by increasing revenues to the crown and by recognizing the supremacy of the law over the feudal monarchy in the Magna Carta of 1215.

In France, Marie's native country, the Capetian King Louis VII struggled to maintain the position of his dynasty following his former wife Eleanor's marriage to Henry II, but he could make little progress against the Plantagenet power that controlled such vast possessions in France. However, the accession of Louis' son Philip Augustus in 1180 marked the beginning of increasing authority and stability for the French throne, and by the end of 1205 Philip was master of Normandy, Maine, Anjou, Touraine, and most of Poitou.

The political restructuring in the last part of the twelfth century was reflected on the social level by a fundamental change in the development and organization of society. By the year 1200, such phenomena as the revival of trade and commerce and the growth of towns had greatly affected medieval society, chiefly through the creation of the middle class. The nobles were particularly annoyed by the financial position of the middle class; in France, laws were passed to maintain the status of members of the merchant class by limiting their ability to purchase land and luxury items.[15] The rise of the middle class, as well as the increasing new freedom of serfs in the twelfth and thirteenth centuries, created difficulties for the nobles, whose position became threatened, and for the members of the new social class, whose position was not always accepted.[16]

The continual political and social vicissitudes of the twelfth century altered attitudes and often brought about a reaction characterized by the inability to adapt, hostility towards change, and even withdrawal from the new society. This reaction can be seen in the works of authors who strive to find "the good old days," displacing the narrative into antiquity or far-off lands. Continued interest in the epic and the newly-acquired taste for the romance at this time reflect a desire to escape to a more perfect era, to an age when heroes were unquestioned and standards of behavior unchallenged. Whether seen in literature or in society, the attempt to circumvent change results in codification. In view of the social climate surrounding the composition of the *Fables,* then, it is likely that Marie's social observations and admonitions in her work represent an effort to codify modes of behavior at a time when the old codes were rapidly changing.[17] Marie simply reacted to the current of social change by presenting examples of contemporary behavior and evaluating them according to her own criteria. The resulting framework of moral and social values functions to unify the collection in spite of the diversity of subject and tone found in the individual fables.

Most of the 102 fables in Marie's collection end with an epimythium designed to draw a lesson from the narrative. These moral endings address themselves to various levels of society, ranging from peasant to king, but they may not always express the idea that one would expect to be derived from a given tale. In Fable 44, for example, a fabliau-like story of a husband who finds his wife with another man, the wife uses an imaginative ploy to convince her husband that seeing is not always believing. As a moral, one might expect to hear a warning about trusting and believing one's own eyes rather than the persuasive arguments of others; instead, Marie praises the wife for her creative thinking under pressure:

> Par cest essample nus devise
> que mult valt mielz sens e quointise
> e plus aide a meinte gent
> que sis aveirs ne si parent.[18]

In this case the satiric aspect preempts the conventional fable morality, highlighting the literary rather than the social role of the fable.

In most cases, however, the epimythium presents a logical comparison that is very much in keeping with the tone of the narrative. Marie's use of the animal characters becomes a code in itself, in that we come to recognize the lion as representative of government, royalty, or nobility; the fox as a symbol for the traitor or deceiver; the lamb as representing the weak and oppressed; the ass as a symbolic of the social incompetent, and so on. The list of stock characters, which includes man as well, comprises animals from the smallest and most insignificant to the greatest and most powerful. It is obvious that, in dealing with such a broad range of characters, Marie wishes to portray society on all levels, and not merely the knightly class.[19] It is also evident that these social classes represent clear, just, and ineradicable boundaries to Marie. Fable 15, **"The Affectionate Ass,"** illustrates Marie's position concerning individuals who would try to change their social standing. The ass, who is jealous of the little dog playing with his master, tries to imitate the dog by jumping up and pawing the master and braying at the top of his lungs. The master, terrified, calls his men, who are finally able to calm the ass by beating him nearly to death. In her closing statement, Marie justifies the treatment given the poor animal, saying that those who try to change their status in life often meet such a fate:

> Saveir poëz par ceste fable
> la maniere de meinte gent
> (mult le puet l'um veeir sovent),
> ki tant se vuelent eshalcier
> e en tel liu aparagier,
> ki n'avient pas a lur corsage,
> ensurquetut a lur parage.
> A meint en est si avenu
> cum a l'asne ki fut batu.

> *(Fabeln,* p. 56)

Marie's use of the word *parage* reflects the virtually universal conviction in the Middle Ages that one is born to a certain social class and should not try to overstep class boundaries.[20]

While Marie proposes an attitude of acceptance towards one's position in life, at the same time she calls for the just treatment of all individuals regardless of class. In several fables, she makes particular reference to the inequities of the judicial system. In Fable 2, **"The Wolf and the Lamb,"** the wolf accuses the lamb of muddying his drinking water, even though the lamb is drinking downstream. Despite the protests of the lamb, the wolf invents enough accusations to justify killing him. Marie's final observation is a clear indictment of the courts:

> Ço funt li riche robeur,
> li vescunte e li jugeur
> de cels qu'il unt en lur justise.
> False achaisun par els confundre;
> suvent les funt a plait somundre:
> la char lur tolent e la pel,
> si cum li lous fist a l'aignel.

> *(Fabeln, p. 10)*

The fable of **"The Dog and the Sheep"** (#4) tells a similar tale of a crafty dog who brought a lawsuit against a sheep, suing her for a fictitious loaf of bread he said he had loaned her. The dog brings in his friends, the kite and the wolf, to give false testimony against the sheep, who finally has to sell her wool to pay for the bread. The sheep then dies from the cold, and the three conspirators each get their share of her. Marie concludes:

> Cest essample vus vueil mustrer:
> de meint hume le puis pruver,
> ki par mentir e par trichier
> funt les povres suvent plaidier,
> fals testimoines avant traient,
> de l'aveir as povres les paient;
> ne lur chalt que li las devienge,
> mes que chescuns sa part en tienge.

> *(Fabeln, p. 20)*

These fables reflect Marie's obvious concern with the mistreatment of the poor and with the inequities of the court system; in addition, she warns that a ruler should not entrust his laws to the greedy.[21] Marie's sensitive awareness of the problems affecting the lower classes indicates that she was not the sheltered or frivolous individual one might imagine from reading the **Lais**. Her sympathy for the plight of the poor is a sentiment that is reiterated throughout the **Fables**, and it is this sense of concern as well as her honest appraisal of current social conditions that reveal the extent of her involvement with the real problems of the time.[22]

Marie is likewise concerned about justice in the general sense, in everyday dealings between people. She cites examples of treachery and deceit that victimize those of all classes and stations in life. Of particular significance are the terms *felun* and *felunie*, which appear quite often in the **Fables** and designate the especially reprehensible act of disloyalty and betrayal of faith. In Fable 12, for example, the eagle finds a shellfish beside the sea but doesn't know how to break open the shell to eat the fish. A crow comes up to him and tells him to fly high into the sky and drop the shellfish onto the ground. When the eagle does this, of course, the crow quickly eats the fish before the eagle can get to it. Marie's conclusion draws a perfect portrait of the *felun*:

> Par ceste fable del peissun
> nus mustre essample del felun,
> ki par aguait e par engin
> mescunseille sun bon veisin;
> tel chose li cunseille a faire,
> dunt cil ne puet a nul chief traire.
> Quant il unkes sunt mielz ensemble,
> par traisun li told e emble
> l'aveir que cil a purchacié
> par grant travail e guaaignié.

> *(Fabeln, p. 46)*

Here the feudal concept of loyalty between lord and vassal is given a more general and more basic application, as it involves interpersonal relationships on the individual rather than hierarchical level.

The hierarchical duties of men are nonetheless of key importance in the **Fables**. On the whole, Marie deals with three social domains: the political, the feudal, and the familial. On the political or governmental level, her favorite topic is that of the selection and duties of a ruler. One of the most amusing of the fables, No. 18, is the story of **"The Frogs in Search of a King."** The frogs want only one thing in life, and that is to have a king. So they beg and plead with their goddess to send them one, until finally she sends them a dead tree trunk floating into the middle of the pond. For a while, the frogs greatly revere the log, bowing to it and doing it much honor, but when it does not answer their requests or show any signs of life, they all climb upon it, curse it, and abuse it in various ways. They complain to their goddess, insisting that she give them a real king; she complies, sending them a huge adder that devours them all. Marie concludes that "many people do this to good lords, when they have them, and unless their lord keeps them in terror most of the time, people do not respect him" (**Fabeln,** p. 67). Thus her admonition is that they should appreciate a good and just king when they have one.[23]

On the other hand, the ruler must know how to maintain his position. Fable 14, **"The Lion Who Fell from Power,"** tells of the once-powerful lion who has grown old and feeble. His subjects, upon learning of his condition, come to see him and take advantage of his situation by stepping on him, striking him, biting him, and otherwise humiliating him. The lion remarks on this shameful behavior, saying "li nunpuissanz a poi amis." Marie continues the observation by adding:

> Ki qu'unkes chiece en nunpoeir,
> se pert sa force e sun aveir,
> mult le tienent en grant vilté
> nis li plusurs ki l'unt amé.

(Fabeln, p. 52)

This sad commentary could easily reflect the real situation surrounding the death of Henry II, who died with none of his family near to mourn him, and whose servants are even reported to have stolen the clothes from his body.[24]

The more specifically feudalistic relationship may be seen in several fables of the collection and is particularly well illustrated by Fable 27, **"The Stomach and the Members."**[25] This is the well-known story of the man who withholds food from his stomach because he believes the stomach has not earned it. He soon finds that his hands and feet become too weak to work. The interdependence of lord and vassal is described in Marie's epimythium:

> Cest essample puet hum veeir
> Chescuns frans huem le deit saveir:
> nuls ne puet mie aveir honur,
> ki hunte fet a sun seignur,
> ne li sire tut ensement,
> pur qu'il vueille hunir sa gent;
> se li uns a l'altre est failliz,
> ambur en ierent mal bailliz.

(Fabeln, p. 92)

Here the terms *frans huem*, *honur*, *hunte*, and *hunir* may be less significant from a moral point of view than from an ideological one, since to dishonor one's lord would have been, in this case, an infringement of the feudal code and would have led, in turn, to the disgrace of the serf as regards his social duty. Reciprocally, the lord as well as the serf would be *mal bailliz* if such dishonor occurred, because their roles in the social hierarchy would become less defined and would therefore be in danger of weakening. It is clearly this disintegration of the feudal model that Marie is attempting to circumvent through her codification of the social ethic.

On a second level of interpretation, however, Marie's advice may indeed be directed towards the moral duties of individuals in the new and developing social structure which characterizes a period of transition. The nuances of meaning in the term *frans huem* reflect the changing role of the man who is both honest in his social responsibilities and free to choose those responsibilities.

Obviously, if the structure of society crumbles, one can no longer rely on roles to define behavior, since those roles are either evolving or disappearing. Thus it is necessary to fall back on individual ethics in a time when the social ethic is no longer valid. As Erich Köhler notes regarding the **Fables,** "la transposition d'une problématique objective dans le comportement psychologique confère de plus en plus d'importance aux responsabilités de l'individu."[26] Clearly, the free man involved in a social contract is ultimately responsible to himself, whereas the serf's responsibility is to the feudal ethic. Viewed from this perspective, Marie's directive to the *frans huem* becomes an exhortation to individual responsibility as a means of recycling an outdated system and making it work successfully under new guidelines.

In the familial domain, Marie discusses two types of relationships: that between husband and wife, and that between mother and child. In both cases, Marie can be quite reproachful towards women concerning their roles in these relationships. Fable 45, for example, tells of the husband who sees his wife going off into the forest with another man. The husband, accompanied by his barons, confronts his wife, who says that she must be near death, since her mother and grandmother were also seen going into the forest with a man shortly before their deaths. Fearing that his wife has fallen victim to this dread congenital disease, the husband weeps and retracts his accusation. Marie remarks that it is shameful that women know how to deceive, for, as she concludes, "les veziëes nunverables / unt un art plus que li diables" (**Fabeln,** p. 152). This concluding statement stands in opposition to the immediately preceding fable of **"The Peasant and His Wife,"** in which Marie had commended the wife for quick thinking in outfoxing her husband; Marie's treatment of the same subject in two different ways is clearly satirical and underscores the literary nature of the fable here.

The willfulness of women is also criticized as being detrimental to the husband/wife relationship. In the fable of **"The Man and the Snake"** (No. 72), for example, a woman insists on advising her husband to do something he knows is unethical.[27] The husband had made a bargain with a snake that he would bring it milk and the snake, in turn, would tell him secrets about farming that would make him rich. The agreement worked well, until one day the man told his wife about it. She suggested that he kill the snake, since he had gotten what he wanted from it and would no longer fear the snake if it were dead. The man took his wife's advice and tried to kill the snake, but his axe missed its mark and the snake escaped. Following this, the snake killed all of the man's sheep and even his child in vengeance. Then the husband was forced to go to the snake and beg its forgiveness. According to Marie, the tragic outcome of the story was the fault of the wife for suggesting something that was harmful to another:

> Issi est suvent avenu:
> de plusurs femmes est seu,
> que si cunseillent lur seignur
> qu'il lur revert a deshonur;
> meinte femme cunseille a faire
> ceo dunt a plusurs nest cuntraire.
> Sages huem n'i deit pas entendre
> n'a fole femme cunseil prendre,
> cume fist icil par sa vileine,
> dunt il ot puis travail e peine.

(*Fabeln,* p. 243)

A woman's duty towards her children is the subject of Fable 21, **"The Wolf and the Sow,"** in which a wolf tries to steal some piglets that are about to be born, telling the mother-to-be that he will spare her if she will give him the piglets. The sow asks the wolf to go away from her while she delivers, saying that she is ashamed for him to see her at such a time. Once he has gone, the sow, of course, runs away. Marie's closing remarks here seem to be a rather grim indictment of motherhood in the twelfth century:

> Cest essample deivent oir
> tutes femmes e retenir,
> pur sulement lur cors guarir
> ne laissent lur enfanz perir!

(*Fabeln,* p. 74)

Here, as in Fable 32 where a lamb, deserted by its natural mother, is raised by a goat, the ideal mother is presented as one who remains loyal to her child even at the cost of her own life. Thus, Marie defines motherhood (on a somewhat feudal level) as a protective and steadfast loyalty towards the one who is weak; the moral responsibility of the mother, as that of a lord to his vassal, supersedes familial ties.

The traditional wisdom of Marie's portraits clearly applies to all levels of society. Upon close examination of the epimythia of the fables, the emphasis on various social divisions can be determined by the number of fables devoted to them. There are, for example, fifteen fables concerning the lord or king (authority) figure; nine having to do with the character of the fool; eight pertaining to the question of rich versus poor; six about women and children; three on judges and the law; and three concerning the working man. However, the largest group of fables, eighteen in number, pertains to the subject of *felunie* and the effect of the *felun* on the social environment. From this profile of society, then, the socioethical model with underlies and unifies Marie's work can be reconstructed.

It is evident that moral and behavioral deviations are a primary concern to Marie and that she views them as a danger to the system. Her emphatic condemnation of

the *felun* and of others who deviate from the norm (such as the social climber) is a clear indication of the value she placed on maintaining and upholding the social structure. Even the fool, so often portrayed in the **Fables,** may be seen as a social deviant, for in Marie's definition the fool is one who ignores the standards that society has set for him and whose expectations regarding a given situation are unrealistic in terms of the behavioral model. Many of the fables address themselves to particular behavior patterns which, while not representing a limited social category, do illustrate the moral problems of the individual functioning in society. The meek person who lets himself be controlled by others, the greedy man who is never content with what he has, the small person who finds himself continually scorned and underrated—all are characters in the moral drama of Marie's fables. Not all of them represent deviations *per se,* but they are a part of the behavioral model that Marie has drawn, a model that imitates and ultimately aspires to improve upon reality.

Superimposed upon the behavioral model in the **Fables** is the social model, whose parameters serve to define the limits of both moral and social acceptability for Marie. Inherent in this social construct are the roles which give it form and the hierarchy which gives it order. King and seneschal, lord and vassal, rich man and poor, and husband and wife are all quadrants on the plane of the social model. They occupy roles which cannot be changed without upsetting the balance of society. It is this balance, seemingly, that is of the ultimate importance in the **Fables.** Each participant in Marie's "ideal" society must play his role according to the directives, both moral and social, given by the creator of this model. In this manner each one is responsible not only for maintaining his role in the hierarchy but also for upholding the moral exigencies imposed on the individual. The seneschal, for example, must perform his duty appropriately as an appointee to the king and, at the same time, resist the greed that may tempt him as an individual.

All of Marie's characters are, in a very modern sense, held accountable for their actions as social and private beings. It is perhaps on this level that the communication of the **Fables** to their twelfth-century audience may be best understood by the twentieth-century reader. Writing during a time when values and structures were continually nuanced by change, Marie used reality as a point of departure to present two overlapping models of social and behavioral objectives. The social model, which defines the structure of society, superimposes itself upon the behavioral model, which serves as a basis for the ethics of society; together the two models form an historical matrix on which the reader sees the pattern of real and imagined existence: courts, kings, husbands and wives, both as they were and as they might have been. Marie mirrors faithfully the reality of twelfth-century society and holds it up to the individual for reflection, for it is ultimately the individual who must cope with a shifting social and ethical foundation. Her code in the *Fables* advocates acceptance first of one's place in society and then of one's individual responsibility as a part of the social hierarchy. While Marie's advice is directed primarily to the individual as a member of twelfth-century European society, its appeal is equally great to those for whom accountability and change are still constants of the social order.

FABLE AND FOLKLORE

To the extent that it mirrors society and culture, reflecting acceptable as well as forbidden modes of behavior, the fable is a forkloric genre. It is a part of that nebulous realm shared by songs, proverbs, *blasons populaires,* riddles, aetiological tales, fairy tales, animal tales, and other traditional manifestations of custom and belief known as the lore of the folk. Lore, which consists of the materials of folklore, and the folk, which may refer to any group of people sharing at least one common factor, are readily identifiable as characteristic of the fable, whose recording of beliefs, codes, or taboos of a defined group serves not only an historical and sociological purpose but a folkloric one as well.[28]

Folklore may derive from oral or non-verbal sources and may exist in variant forms which are recreated in face-to-face transmission. The question of an oral source for the *Fables* as a whole is, of course, unthinkable, in view of the close correspondence of the first forty of the fables with the well-known *Romulus Nilantii.* However, it may be that, for those fables listed as having an unknown source, as well as for those in which the motifs show variation from the pre-existing models, some influence or interference from oral tales circulating in Marie's time may have occurred. Among those fables whose sources are unknown are **"The Rich Man and the Serfs"** (No. 41), **"The Man Who Prayed for a Horse"** (No. 54), **"The Rich Man Selling His Horse and His Ox"** (No. 64), **"The Man and the Measure"** (No. 90), **"The Doe and Her Fawn"** (No. 91), **"The Crow and His Little One"** (No. 92), **"The Man and the Ship"** (No. 99), and **"The Old Man and the Knight"** (No. 100). These fables are all human anecdotes in one form or another, relating either stories of interaction between men, communication between men and God, or warnings against men. Although Warnke lists no known source for these fables, some of them do have parallels in oral tradition. The fable of the man who prays for a better horse but changes his mind when his old horse is stolen is similar in structure and theme to the tale numbered 1276 in the Aarne-Thompson index.[29] In this similar tale type, a woman rowing against the wind prays to have it change direc-

tion; when it does, she must row against it on her return. Both Marie's story and type 1276 are divided into two small episodes after the initial situation of the prayer, and both tales concern praying for a matter to be improved when actually it should have been left as it was. Likewise, other parallels may be seen between Marie's Fable 64 and type 1553, Fable 90 and type 1624, and Fables 91 and 92 and type 157. The similarities seen in these fables and tale types are obviously not sufficient to document a source for any individual fable, but they do point to certain motifs and structures which seem to be known in oral tradition and which surface in Marie's work. Warnke noted parallels in oral tradition for several of the fables in the second half of Marie's collection. Among these are No. 53, the story of **"The Man and the Hermit"**; No. 55, **"The Man Who Prayed Selfishly"**; No. 60, **"The Fox and the Rooster"**; No. 69, **"The Fox and the Bear"**; and No. 73, **"The Mouse Takes a Wife."** Of these fables, Nos. 53, 60, and 69 represent the oldest known versions of the tales, which can all be found in oral forms; thus it is possible that Marie's version of these fables may be an early documentation of the oral source.

Oral transmission also played a part in the formation of Marie's collection. According to Warnke, Fable 73, **"The Mouse Takes a Wife,"** is similar in form to a tale included in the Indian *Pañcatantra.* However, he feels that the story could only have arrived through oral transmission, since the Indian collection was not known in Europe during Marie's time.[30] Communication of the tales through oral rather than written means may also account for some of the details and motifs that are peculiar to Marie's version of certain fables. In Fable 5, **"The Dog and the Cheese,"** Marie uses the motif of the dog carrying cheese rather than meat or a bone as in the earlier versions of Phaedrus and Babrius. This variation in motif, which is seen for the first time in Marie's work and is later picked up by Berechiah in his Hebrew collection, could represent Marie's documentation of a tale that had been transmitted orally to her. In this sense, Marie herself might be seen as a folklorist recording the known versions of oral folktales circulating in her time. A similar case is that of Fable 61, **"The Fox and the Dove,"** which exists in other forms in Aesop, the *Berne Romulus* and the *Roman de Renart.* Marie, however, is the first to establish this animal joke using the dove rather than a little bird of non-specified type.[31] The change of motifs in such fables is very likely indicative of the oral means through which this material was ultimately transmitted to Marie and which links it inevitably to folklore.

The lore of the folk, as it applies to Marie's fables, can be rather specifically described. The folk, of course, designates that group to whom and about whom Marie was writing in this work: the society of twelfth-century

England and France. As has been discussed previously, this group was not limited to the aristocracy, although the *Fables* may have been written from an aristocratic perspective. The folk with which Marie concerned herself were not limited to a certain class, occupational division, age, or sex; thus, the lore that she recorded represents a documentation with wide application. Marie noted common beliefs, rituals, customs, and taboos belonging to the folk of the twelfth century. All of these forms of folklore work together to maintain the stability of culture, "to insure conformity to the accepted cultural norms, and continuity from generation to generation."[32] Marie's fables do function as a monitor of culture in that they attempt to codify the norms of twelfth-century society. They also fulfill in various ways four accepted functions of folklore: 1) to effect an escape in fantasy from the repressions imposed by society; 2) to validate culture by justifying its ritual; 3) to educate in nonliterate societies; and 4) to express social approval of those who conform.[33] The fable of **"The Fox and the Bear"** (No. 69) is a good example of a fantasy which allows a certain escape from social repressions. The fox's mischievous teasing and ultimate sexual triumph over the bear is representative of a common type of fantasy that permits an imagined escape from the limitations of a sexual code. Many of the fables are used to validate the feudal culture; No. 88, **"The Wolf and the Fox,"** for example, depicts the ideal lord, while No. 20, **"The Dog and the Thief,"** outlines the vassal's duty to the lord. The ritual of marriage is given approval in **"The Mouse Takes a Wife"** (No. 73), where Marie also makes the point that one should not marry outside one's class or social group. The *Fables* as a whole could, of course, have served to educate even nonliterates, since the fable genre itself has always been popular as a form of oral didactic literature. The retelling or reading aloud of Marie's tales was very likely a favorite pastime, in view of the large number of extant manuscripts as well as variations derived from her work. Finally, the social approval of conformity is a basic aim of the *Fables,* in that they represent a codification of socially acceptable behavior patterns. The bat, for example, Fable 23, should never have tried to be a bird but should have conformed to the norms of his own species in the animal community. Likewise, an honest man who wants to operate in court circles will never succeed until he learns to lie like everyone else at court (**"The Monkey King"**). The functions of folklore are thus amply illustrated by Marie's fables, which seek to uphold culturally-accepted models within the folk to which they have reference.

The structure of Marie's fables is another element relating them to folklore. According to Propp, all folktales have a certain paradigmatic structure that remains essentially the same in all forms of tales. Although the number of personages in folktales may be quite large, the number of functions or variants of structure is small. It is this combination of elements which accounts for the coexistent multiformity and uniformity of the folktale.[34] While Propp's study was particularly limited to the analysis of the fairy tale, his basic schema for the configuration of the tale may be applied to the fable as well. The skeletal form of Propp's paradigm may be represented as follows:

I. Initial Situation

II. Preparatory Section

III. Complication

IV. Donors

V. From Entry of Helper to End of First Move

VI. Beginning of Second Move

VII. Continuation of Second Move[35]

This organization is also seen in the fable, although some of the personages or moves may be omitted. In Marie's fables, there is often no donor or helper, and the second move is sometimes lacking. Such simplification can be explained by the fact that the fable is often missing the element of magic or the supernatural that is basic to the fairy tale; thus, a donor or helper who provides a magical agent is not generally needed. Because the encounters between personages in the fable may also be limited to as little as one exchange of dialogue, the second move may not be necessary. However, the fact that in many cases Propp's model does reflect the actual organization of Marie's fables is not mere coincidence but obviously underscores the close relationship of structure between forms of the folktale. While the fable has its own peculiar orientation as a succinct didactic form, its basic configuration shows it to be related to the family of folkloric narratives. This essential paradigm of the folktale is fundamentally a product of the repeated oral transmission of tales, although it may be documented and even fixed by written versions. Thus, Marie's fables, though largely literary by birth, are also of a folkloric lineage.

A recent structuralist analysis of Marie's fables is based on a simplified form of Propp's model and on what is termed "the constant fable cosmos," in which the functions of the personages are divided into archetypal "role constellations" such as Strong/Weak, Haves/Have Nots, or Worthy/Unworthy.[36] The following organizational schema differs from Propp's in that it telescopes the appearance of characters into the early part of the sequence, eliminating the element of the donor and the helper and reducing the two moves into one "interaction":

Starting Situation
Character-Intent-Frame
Role Constellation
Interaction Plot
Interaction Result[37]

In spite of, or perhaps because of, its simplicity, this paradigm seems to work for all of Marie's fables;[38] here again, the value of such analysis does not necessarily lie in the process itself but in the information that it provides as to the relationship of Marie's individual fables to each other and to other folkloric forms as well. The structuralist or hermeneutic method of analysis emphasizes the necessity of relating the roles and functions found in the fables to their sociological counterparts. Such a comparison is natural for a folkloric form, whose essence is to mirror culture. The reflection of the social code in Marie's fables underlines the folkloric aspect of her work and validates its place in the domain of folklore.

The Literary Tradition

It is the ultimate realism of Marie's fables that makes them succeed as both a literary and a folkloric genre. Literature and folklore are divergent arts which spring from convergent sources and, especially, from the persistence of the human spirit in its search for expression of the contradictory forces that animate it. The Aesopic genre as a whole and Marie's fables in particular inherit much from the rich folklore that precedes and surrounds them. This is not to say, however, that the influence of folklore has eclipsed the literary heritage of the fable. While the original fables of Aesop were circulated orally, it is through the written word that they came to the stability of form and style which makes them endure. The documentation of Aesop's work created the literary source from which all later derivations profited, directly or indirectly. As in most literary art forms, the fable operates through conventions of style, character, and form; its author is usually a practiced artist who is aware of his craft and of his public. Marie herself insists on her artistry and skill as a writer, taking pains to situate her work by discussing her source, Alfred, and by deferring to her patron, William, whose exigent tastes required her to be as authentic as possible in her translation. Through these opening and closing remarks on her art, Marie creates a conventional frame for her work that assures its identity as a literary form. A similar framing procedure is used at the beginning and ending of almost every fable, where Marie recalls to the reader first her source and finally the contemporary application of her material. Marie's consciousness of her art is a certain indicator that her work was destined to a reading public, perhaps limited, but critical and appreciative in its tastes for literature.

Apart from the traditional use of the animal characters and the repeated opening and closing stylistic devices,

Marie's fables are also conventional in their internal structure. When viewed from a literary perspective, the paradigmatic analysis of the fables as a folkloric form may be seen as little more than an updated interpretation of traditional dramatic structure. Each of Marie's fables is, in essence, a miniature drama, with its exposition, peripeteia, climax, and dénouement. While her tales rarely observe the classical unities one might associate with drama, they could easily be represented on stage through the use of medieval *mansions,* or simultaneous settings, since the action is often episodic and the time and place sometimes quite varied. In the inherent psychology of her characterizations, however, Marie does approach the modern idea of dramatic personages. The dog who is bribed to betray his master refuses, reflecting that he should not repay in such a way someone who has nurtured and cared for him. The wife who is caught with her lover in the forest by her husband distracts his attention from the situation by making him believe she is dying. The crow who has raised his little one and taught him to fend for himself insists that the little bird be self-reliant, saying that he has taught him all he can and must now take care of the others. These characters, like many others in the **Fables,** operate on a level that is always psychologically identifiable to the reader and that is thus realistic in spite of the possibly fantastic situation of the tale.

The question of verisimilitude lies at the heart of the meaning and interpretation of the term "fable," which derives ultimately from the Latin *fabula. Fabula (fari)* denotes those popular myths which, through oral transmission, have merged with the history of antiquity to form a body of legendary knowledge commonly believed to be true. The stories of Grecian and Scandinavian gods and heroes are examples of this use of the term. From *fabula* obtains the derivative *fabella,* a diminutive form referring to a type of literature in which the imagination rather than superstition is given creative sway and in which the inventions of the author, while recognized as fictitious by the reader, may be viewed as true when applied to corresponding circumstances in human life and conduct. Although it has been suggested that only *fabella* gave rise to the fable as we know it (*fabula,* in this view, having influenced rather the romance),[39] it seems probable that the two forms may have influenced one another, each having left its recognizable mark on the fable as it developed. Legendary figures as well as mythic deities were often present in fables of ancient times; much of what we know about the life of Aesop, for example, is related through fables that illustrate various aspects of his personality. It is, however, the "willing suspension of disbelief" that is crucial to the development of the fable as an allegorical form.

Whether a fable is viewed by its author as simply a narrative form destined to entertain or as a story meant to convey a second level of meaning, the presence of a moral in the form of a promythium or an epimythium serves to distinguish it from other, similar genres with less didactic intent. The promythium originally functioned to index the fable according to its subject, so that a would-be orator could easily locate exempla relative to his topic. Since the promythium also summarized the meaning of the text, however, it eventually came to be given after the fable, as an epimythium, to explain the moral symbolism.[40] Thus the original purpose of the promythium as an index was cast aside in favor of the consciously derived moral, or epimythium, following the narrative.

The earliest known collection of fables ascribed to Aesop was that which was compiled by Demtrius Phalereus, an Athenian orator and statesman of the fourth century B.C. Though no longer extant, this collection was well known until the ninth century A.D. and was considered the official Aesop. The oldest surviving collection of Greek prose fables comes from the first or second century A.D. and is known as the Augustana. The anonymous collector of these 230 fables ascribed them to Aesop. Both the collection of Demetrius Phalereus and the Augustana may have been sources for the 123 Greek fables known to have been written by Babrius in the second half of the first century A.D. A hellenized Italian and probably the great-grandson of King Herod, Babrius was the first to put the Aesopic fables into Greek verse; his Roman nationality has been deduced in part from his tendency to apply principles of Latin accentuation to the Greek iambic line. The work of Babrius inspired many imitators, among them the fourth-century Roman author Avianus and the ninth-century Ignatius Diaconus.

The chief Latin influence on the development of the Aesopic fable came from another Thracian, Phaedrus, an author of the first century A.D. who wrote in Latin. Though Greek by birth, he went to Italy early in his life and there studied the Latin authors who influenced his later writings. A member of the household of Augustus, Phaedrus, like the Aesop of legend, was at first a slave but was later freed. According to the testimony of Avianus, Phaedrus wrote five books of fables. These five books were published in 1596 by Pithou from the principal manuscript *P*; other, more recently-discovered manuscripts contain additional fables not included in the earlier codex *P*. The compilation of the fables included in all of the manuscripts resulted in a total of around 150 fables. Although he was mentioned by Avianus as an author of fables, Phaedrus received relatively little notice from his Latin successors, who freely made use of his work but ascribed their fables to Aesop. It was not until the publication of the *P* manuscript by

Pithou that Phaedrus came to be known, along with Avianus and Romulus, as one of the foremost names associated with fable. In fact, much of what we consider today to be in the Aesopic tradition is really "Phaedrus with trimmings."[41]

In the tradition of Phaedrus there exist both prose and verse adaptations. These fall into three major groups: 1) the prose *Aesopus* of Adémar de Chabannes, dating from the tenth century; 2) the *Aesopus* of Rufus, also known as the Wissemburg collection, written in prose in the early tenth century; and 3) the *Romulus,* a fourth-century work that is of particular interest because of its early popularity and its many redactions in prose and in verse. This collection was falsely ascribed to a certain Romulus, who, according to a prologue later added to the manuscript, had translated the fables from Greek for his son Tiberinus. The prose *Romulus* consists of three versions, the *Romulus ordinaire,* the *Romulus of Vienna and Berlin,* and the *Romulus Nilantii,* so called because of its publication by Nilant in 1709. Verse adaptations include the well-known *Romulus Neveletii,* an anonymous collection from the twelfth century published by Nevelet in 1610 and later ascribed to Walter the Englishman; and the thirteenth-century *Novus Aesopus* of Alexander Neckam. From these two verse translations came the French collections, the *Isopet de Lyon,* the *Isopet de Chartres,* and the *Isopet de Paris* I, II, and III.

It is the combination of the *Romulus* with other traditions that leads ultimately to the fables of Marie de France. In theory there may have existed at one time an Anglo-Latin Romulus which, judging from its extant derivations, the London, Brussels, and Gottingen fragments (LBG) and the *Romulus Robertii,* would have consisted of fables from the *Romulus,* other fables from Phaedrus, and animal tales in the same tradition as those of the later *Roman de Renart.* This Anglo-Latin Romulus would have been the model on which King Alfred, Marie's declared source, patterned his English adaptation.[42] However, it seems that Marie's fables contain various details which bring them closer on several points to the Greek fable tradition than to the Latin.[43] If indeed these Greek elements are taken from Alfred's version, it is theorized that they may have arrived through the Arabic tradition rather than the Latin, from the *Kalilah wa Dimnah,* or *Fables of Bidpai,* an eight-century Arabic transmission of the lost Sanskrit beast fables known as the *Pañcatantra.*[44] Ultimately this Arabic tradition goes back to the Indian *Jātakas,* a fifth-century B.C. collection of birth stories of the Buddha. . . .

The hypothesis that the source of Marie's fables was Arabic rather than Latin in origin has led to much varied speculation over her attribution of the English translation she used to King Alfred. Though known for his many translations realized for the instruction of his people, King Alfred preceded Marie by more than three hundred years, and it seems curious that no manuscript or mention of his translation of the fables is to be found prior to Marie. Marie's obvious misidentification of Aesop as the translator rather than the author of the fables has led some critics to believe that she may also have confused the name of the English translator, Alfred, with that of King Alfred.[45] Her use of several Middle English words for which a French equivalent did not exist has been cited as evidence that Marie's source text may have been composed in the beginning of the twelfth century in a Midland dialect.[46] Other scholars have theorized that Alfred was the compiler of the Latin collection rather than the English translator and have identified him with one Alfred the Englishman. This Alfred, a twelfth-century translator who did not know Arabic, may have worked with a Jewish dragoman at his side to aid in the translation into Latin and may therefore have had access to Arabic materials through his punctuator's familiarity with them.[47] The Jewish grammarian associated with Alfred the Englishman is Berechiah ben Natronai Ha-Nakdan, the author of a twelfth-century fable collection, the *Mishle Shu'alim,* or *Fox Fables,* comprising 107 fables, of which 53 are parallel with Marie's version. The known sources of the *Mishle Shu'alim* are the *Romulus,* Oriental and Arabic collections, popular fox tales, and Talmudic tradition; as in Marie's collection, there are diverse fables for which no source has been found.[48]

In spite of the affinities between Marie's fables and other existing collections, it has been thoroughly demonstrated that those collections resembling Marie's were patterned on her version and not vice versa. The Hebrew *Mishle Shu'alim* of Berechiah ben Natronai, the Latin *Romulus Robertii,* LBG fragments, and *Promptuarium Exemplorum* of Paris, as well as the Italian collection published by Rigoli in 1818, have all been shown to be adaptations or translations of Marie's work, rather than independent texts or even her source.[49] In view of the evidence showing that these translations contemporary with and parallel to Marie's work were in fact derived from it, and considering also the lack of proof for the existence of any similar fable collection prior to Marie, one might speculate that Marie had no English text as a model and that she herself was the compiler of the materials comprising the "Pseudo-Alfred." The use of a fictitious source was not uncommon in the literature of the Middle Ages; the popular *Ovide moralisé,* for example, was ostensibly a translation of the fifteen books of the *Metamorphoses* although its author used diverse sources, including texts written in the vernacular, such as *Philomena* and *Pyramus et Thisbé.* Given Marie's known tendency towards defensiveness and self-justification concerning her activities as an author,[50] it is not impossible that she could have invented a bogus source for her collection, choosing the name of a well-known and respected translator to lend status and instant acceptability to her work. Her knowledge of Latin, as attested by her translation of the *Espurgatoire seint Patriz,* would have made ancient and early medieval sources accessible to her, and her probable connection with the Church would account for the inclusion of popular monks' tales in her collection. The reason for the presence of twelfth-century Middle English words in her text is self-evident if one accepts the premise that Marie lived and worked in England in the twelfth century. Even if Marie were using an English text, for lack of an identifiable author she herself may have concluded, disregarding or ignoring the linguistic anachronisms, that it had been executed by King Alfred, whose name was often associated with proverbial wisdom in the popular tradition. Whatever the case may be, one must agree that the *Fables* of Marie de France constitute a unique addition to the Aesopic history, for whether the innovations of character and style found in Marie's collection are attributed to Marie or to her unknown textual model, it was Marie's work which popularized and thus legitimized them as a thenceforth integral and inseparable part of the fable tradition.[51]

THE MANUSCRIPT TRADITION

The popularity of Marie's fables is attested by the twenty-three manuscripts that have preserved them and have come down to us.[52] These manuscripts date from the early thirteenth to the sixteenth centuries and contain the *Fables* in whole or partial form. Karl Warnke's classification of all the manuscripts has been uniformly accepted, although the exact relationship that has been suggested among the individual manuscripts can be tentative at best. Through a detailed and erudite analysis of the order of the fables themselves, linguistic and scribal peculiarities, and parallel or derived textual forms, Warnke arrived at [a] . . . plan for the classification and provenance of the manuscripts.[53]

A NOTE ON THE TRANSLATION

This translation, intended to be as accurate and precise a rendering as possible of the Old French text, is based on Warnke's complete and authoritative edition, which is reproduced here without variants. While faithfulness to the original was a primary concern in translating, it was necessary to take certain liberties to produce a smooth English narrative; prose was chosen instead of verse, for example, to avoid the singsong effect of an English verse form comparable to the original. Paraphrase has been used with discretion, but it may be seen most often when the Old French passage contains a great economy of syntax which must be expanded by one or more clauses in order to create a logical English construction. The many relative clauses that appear, quite logically, in the most convenient position in the Old French text have also been restructured, for the most part, in the English version. Idiomatic expressions have been replaced by their appropriate English counterparts; *la char e la pel* becomes 'flesh and blood,' for example, and *querant folie,* 'asking for trouble.' The paired synonyms which Marie uses so often have been retained, as seen in Fable 12 in the expressions 'takes away and steals' and 'acquired and earned;' while it may seem unnecessary in English, this favorite device in Old French adds color to the narrative and, even in English, conveys something of the flavor of the original. The stylized openings and closings found in almost every fable, such as *ci dit* and *altresi est,* have been changed to an equivalent English commonplace ("once upon a time") or, in some cases, omitted. Shifts in tense sequence from present to past, so common in Old French narratives, have been largely eliminated in this translation to avoid confusion in English. Contractions appear most often in the English text where they seem to coincide with the register of language used in the original.

A few words have proven to be problematic in English because of their different significance to the medieval reader. *Felun,* for example, has been translated as 'treacherous' when used as an adjective and as 'betrayer' when used as a noun. The connotations of this word were obviously different for the medieval public, to whom it implied not merely betrayal but a breach of the social contract as well. A *vilein* could have been simply a man or, more specifically, a farmer, and this word has been translated according to its meaning in the individual fables. The word *sepande,* which Warnke felt was misunderstood by Marie, has been translated in all cases as 'goddess,' since it has reference here to the animal kingdom and its mythical overseer.

My intent throughout has been to produce a readable text that will communicate, insofar as possible, the engaging tone of the original and make Marie's fables more accessible to the modern reader.

Notes

1. *Die Fabeln der Marie de France,* ed. Karl Warnke, Biblioteca Normannica VI (Halle: Max Niemeyer, 1898), p. 328.

2. Ernest Hoepffner, ed., *Les Lais de Marie de France,* Bibliothèque de la Revue des cours et conférences (Paris: 1935), p. viii.

3. *La Vie Seint Edmund le Rei, poème anglo-normand du XIIe siècle,* par Denis Piramus, ed. H. Kjellman (Göteborg: 1935), vv. 35-48.

4. Thomas Tyrwhitt, *The Canterbury Tales of Chaucer,* 2nd ed. (Oxford: 1798), vol. I, pp. 99-102.

5. Emmanuel Mickel, *Marie de France,* Twayne's World Author Series (New York: Twayne Publishers, Inc., 1974), p. 16.

6. T. A. Jenkins, ed., *L'Espurgatoire seint Patriz,* rev. ed. (Chicago: University of Chicago Press, 1903), p. 2.

7. Emil Winkler, *Marie de France* (Vienna: Holder, 1918); U. T. Holmes, *A History of Old French Literature* (New York: Crofts, 1948), pp. 189-190; Ezio Levi, "Sulla cronologia delle opere di Maria di Francia," *Nuovi Studi Medievali* 1 (1923), pp. 41-72; and John C. Fox, "Marie de France," *English Historical Review* 25 (1910), pp. 303-306.

8. Mickel, p. 19.

9. At an extravagant Christmas Day banquet given by Prince Henry in 1172, reported Robert of Torigii, one room alone was filled with 110 knights named William.

10. *L'Histoire de Guillaume le Maréchal: Comte de Striguil et de Pembroke, Régent d'Anglerre de 1216-19,* ed. Paul Meyer (Paris: Société de l'Histoire de France, 1901).

11. F. W. Locke, "A New Date for the Composition of the *Tractatus de Purgatorio Sancti Patricii,*" *Speculum* 40 (1965), pp. 641-646.

12. Edouard Mall, "Zur Geschichte der mittelalterlichen Fabelliteratur, und insbesondere des Esope der Marie de France," *Zeitschrift für romanische Philologie* IX (1885), p. 162; Warnke, ed., *Fabeln,* p. cxxi.

13. Richard Baum, *Recherches sur les oeuvres attribuées à Marie de France* (Heidelberg: Carl Winter, 1968), p. 217.

14. Marie de France, *Lais,* ed. A. Ewert (Oxford: Blackwell, 1944), p. vii.

15. Sydney Painter, *A History of the Middle Ages,* 284-1500 (New York: Alfred A. Knopf, 1965), p. 239.

16. Painter, p. 240.

17. This idea is broached by Erich Köhler in his *L'aventure chevaleresque: Idéal et réalité dans le roman courtois,* trans. Eliane Kaufholz (Paris: Gallimard, 1974), pp. 29-32.

18. Warnke, ed., *Fabeln,* p. 147. Further references to individual fables appear in the text.

19. This is contrary to the theory of E. A. Francis in his article "Marie de France et son temps," *Romania* 72 (1951), pp. 78-79.

20. Other fables which treat the theme of social limits and mobility are numbers 9, 22, 26, and 76.

21. See also Fables 47 and 56.

22. Other fables dealing with the subject of the poor are numbers 10, 11, 16, 26, and 38.

23. See also Fable 46.

24. Aristide Joly, *Marie de France et les fables au moyen age* (Caen: 1863), p. 38.

25. See also Fables 7 and 20.

26. Köhler, p. 30.

27. See also Fable 95.

28. Alan Dundes, *The Study of Folklore* (Englewood Cliffs, N.J.: Prentice-Hall, Inc.), pp. 102.

29. Antii Aarne, *The Types of the Folktale,* trans. Stith Thompson, *Folklore Fellows Communications* No. 184 (Helsinki: 1961), p. 383.

30. Karl Warnke, *Die Quellen des Esope der Marie de France* (Halle: Max Niemeyer, 1900), p. 67.

31. Warnke, *Quellen,* p. 49.

32. William R. Bascom, "Four Functions of Folklore," in Dundes, *The Study of Folklore,* p. 297.

33. Bascom, pp. 290-295.

34. *Vladimir Propp, Morphology of the Folktale,* trans. Laurence Scott (Austin, Texas: University of Texas Press, 1968).

35. Propp, pp. 19-127.

36. Hans Gumbrecht, *Marie de France: Äsop* (München: Wilhelm Fink Verlag, 1973), p. 38.

37. Gumbrecht, pp. 37-38.

38. Gumbrecht, p. 40.

39. Thomas Newbigging, *Fables and fabulists, ancient and modern* (1895); rpt. Freeport, N. Y.: Books for Libraries Press, 1972), p. 102.

40. B. E. Perry, *Babrius and Phaedrus* (Cambridge: Harvard University Press, 1965), pp. xv-xvi.

41. Joseph Jacobs, *The Fables of Aesop as first printed by William Caxton in 1484 with those of Avian, Alfonso and Poggio* (London: Nutt, 1889), vol. I, p. 1.

42. Leopold Hervieux, *Les Fabulistes latins, depuis le siècle d'Auguste jusqu'à la fin du moyen age,* 2nd ed. (Paris: Didot, 1883-9), p. 731.

43. For example, in Fable 67, "The Crow in Peacock's Feathers," Marie uses a crow as the hero competing for the crown of beauty among the birds, as in the Greek tradition, rather than a jay as in the Latin Aesop. Also, in Marie's version of "The Dog and His Shadow" (5), the dog is crossing a bridge while holding a piece of cheese in his mouth instead of swimming in the river and carrying a piece of meat, as in Phaedrus. In "The Lion's Share" (11), Marie first depicts the lion's partners as being carnivorous, as is appropriate to the story, while in Phaedrus these characters are a cow, a goat, and a sheep, all herbivorous.

44. Jacobs, p. 163.

45. This misidentification appears in the Epilogue:

> Esope apelë um cest livre,
> kil translata e fist escrivre,
> de Griu en Latin le turna.
> Li reis Alvrez, ki mult l'ama,
> le translata puis en Engleis,
> e jeo l'ai rimé en Franceis,
> si com jol truvai, proprement.
>
> *(Fabeln, pp. 327-328)*

46. Warnke, ed., *Fabeln,* p. xlv.

47. Jacobs, p. 165.

48. Moses Hadas, trans., *Fables of a Jewish Aesop* (New York: Columbia University Press, 1967), pp. i-ix.

49. Warnke, ed., *Fabeln,* pp. xlvii-lxxx; and Hadas, *loc. cit.*

50. See particularly the Prologue to the *Lais* and the Epilogue to the *Fables.*

51. Jacobs, p. 159.

52. This large number of MSS seems curiously disproportionate when compared to the modern preference for the *Lais,* of which only six MSS are known to exist.

53. Warnke, ed., *Fabeln,* p. xliii.

Suzanne Klerks (essay date winter 1995)

SOURCE: Klerks, Suzanne. "The Pain of Reading Female Bodies in Marie de France's 'Guigemar.'" *Dalhousie French Studies* 33 (winter 1995): 1-14.

[*In the following essay, Klerks argues that, in the lay "Guigemar" Marie challenges the traditional gender hierarchy established by misogynistic medieval reading strategies and the discourse of courtly love.*]

"GUIGEMAR"[1]

Vouée à la violence, la «jeunesse» constitue, dans la société chevaleresque, l'organe d'agression et de tumulte. Mais elle se trouve par là offerte aux dangers. Agressive et brutale, la jeunesse est, par situation, un corps décimé.

(Duby 1964:839)

La façon qu'a l'homme de sortir de lui-même dans
celle qu'il prend non pour l'autre, mais pour sienne, le
prive, le saitil, de son propre territoire corporel. À se
confondre avec son pénis, et à se jeter à l'assaut, on
comprend qu'il ait le ressentiment et la crainte d'être
«pris» par la femme, d'être en elle perdu, absorbé, ou
seul.

(Cixous 40)

The systems which engendered the acts of violent aggression by men against men in late-medieval Western
aristocratic culture have been well-documented. What
seems to be less foregrounded are noblewomen's
cultural and especially literary relations to male
violence, their positions within the violent discursive
practises of the period.[2] The twelfth-century Anglo-
Norman writer Marie de France gives us the rare opportunity to explore female representation as a site of
male violence from an alternative perspective.[3] In her
lay **"Guigemar"** Marie exposes the antifemale violence
of two dominant discourses, the hermeneutic and the
courtly, when she critiques the ways in which both
systems naturalize or even romanticize rape. Before
turning to Marie's decoding of the violence endemic to
these discourses, the connection between reading and
rape in medieval poetics will first be briefly outlined.

Howard Bloch has recently noted that "to gloss or to
interpret" is always an eroticized experience in medieval
poetics, because of the sexualized relationship between
text and reader. He plots this relationship as follows:

it is the [poet] who introduces obscurities, gaps, or
holes in language (the trouvere), and is most capable of
attaining to the full word. . . . The reader or interpreter
desires access to the zone where . . . meaning is
imagined to come to rest and to be immutable.

(104)

In other words, the (male) reader is required and in fact
desires to fill the textual "holes" created by the trouvere. Bloch even reminds us of the etymological
relationship between the Old French *sens* and "seed" or
"semen" (103). Bloch refuses, however, to acknowledge
the violent effects of this reading paradigm. His refusal
stems in part from a reluctance to confront the fact that
it is not simply an ungendered "corporeal" (his term)
that represents the letter of a text in the hermeneutic
tradition. Conversely, Carolyn Dinshaw argues that the
routine association between women and carnality,
seduction and deceptive ornamentation, allows medieval
exegetes from Augustine to Boccaccio to equate the
female with the surface or letter of the text. This surface
must be undressed or unveiled by its male reader in
order to reveal the truth beneath.[4] Therefore, within this
epistemological framework, the act of reading becomes
a rape of the female text: the silent female text must be
stripped of its extraneous meanings—its rhetorical

adornments—in order that its truth/flesh may be
penetrated by the reader.[5] This reading paradigm carries
obvious implications for a woman writer, and I will
next explore how in **"Guigemar"** Marie de France challenges the antifemale violence of this paradigm.

In the mini-prologue to **"Guigemar"** Marie resists the
sexual violence implicit in hermeneutic discourse by
literalizing the reader's required task of raping a body/
text: she positions her own physical body within this
discourse. From this site, she problematically asks her
readers to perform these violent reading strategies on
her own body. At the same time she demonstrates her
unwillingness to be read by pointing out that a misreading of her body/text will cause her physical pain:

Ki de bone mateire traite,
Mult li peise si bien n'est faite.

(1-2)

If the author is the one who holds the key to meaning,
and this meaning is not divulged here, then these
introductory lines leave the lay's audience in an
extremely uncomfortable position, for how then can
"Guigemar" be read without causing its author pain?
And because this pain will be enacted on a female
body—that of the author—, as readers of the text we
are asked to rape this body if we want to *uncover* its
significance. The audience must participate in this pain-
fully literal process because of what Elaine Scarry calls
the "unsharability" of pain:

When one hears about another person's physical pain,
the events happening within the interior of that person's
body may seem to have the remote character of some
deep subterranean fact, belonging to an invisible
geography that, however portentous, has no reality
because it has not yet manifested itself on the visible
surface of the earth.

(3)

Marie cannot communicate her pain; instead she can
only make us self-conscious of our implication in its
production on the female body. The conception of the
female body and the vagina in particular as sites of
meaning is reiterated through the text's representation
of another female body, that of the iconographic Venus.

Embedded in Marie's account of the nameless heroine's
imprisonment are the frescoes adorning the walls of the
chapel that stands at the entrance to the lady's chamber:

La chaumbre ert peinte tut entur;
Venus, la deuesse d'amur,
Fu tres bien mise en la peinture;
Les traiz mustrout e la nature
Cument hom deit amur tenir
E lealment e bien servir.
Le livre Ovide, ou il enseine

Comment chascuns s'amur estreine,
En un fu ardant le gettout,
E tuz iceus escumengout
Ki jamais cel livre lirreient
Ne sun enseignement fereint.
La fu la dame enclose e mise.

(233-45)

When Venus burns what is presumably the *Remedia Amoris,* she displaces the male authority of Ovid and presents herself as an alternative, female authority on love. Venus, however, proffers no alternative text other than her own visual representation: her body accordingly becomes her text, for how else are we to read her meaning? Moreover, the fact that Venus is the goddess of love/sex/desire allows Marie to underscore the violent sexualization of the interpretive process within the raping/reading paradigm: there can be no mistaking how the silent Venus's holes are to be filled, or that a search for meaning requires the filling of holes. While this argument could be countermanded by recourse to Venus's sexuality, the universality of the goddess's insatiable desire is undermined by the possibilities afforded in her open-ended representation, when Marie replaces a description of the acts performed by the goddess on the chapel walls with a vague reference to Venus's "traits" and "nature." It is the traits or traces of this iconographic and therefore narrative visual body/text that I wish to examine. I have noted above that there is interwoven within the raping/reading paradigm an invocation of the etymology of "sens" as seed or semen: textual meaning depends upon the fallout from the ejaculation of this sense into female holes. Marie is here literalizing the consequences of probing a female body for meaning as she evokes an image of Venus dripping with seminal traces: the body/text of the goddess becomes like that of the cunt-covered wife in the Old French fabliau "Les quatres souhaits de saint Martin,"[6] as her body splits to accommodate more and more "sens." This iconographic relationship between Venus and the fabliau wife becomes even more powerful when we consider Jane Burns's connection between this fabliau wife and "the typcal medieval characterization of the libidinous woman" (51)—the sisters of Venus. I do not want to suggest that Marie does not allow for female desire, only that she is here complicating the arbitrary inscription of heterosexual male desire on women's bodies by marking the vagina as the site of that (violent) desire. Thus, female pain in **"Guigemar"** is equated with genital pain or rape.

Marie repeats her questioning of arbitrary inscription in her representation of a third female figure in **"Guigemar,"** the lay's heroine. First, she reinforces an alignment between her audience and those male characters who perform raping/reading exercises on the heroine's explicitly unwilling body, by making the suffering female body integral to the lay's narrative progression. Next, Marie repeats the deconstructive strategy of awareness she employed in the mini-prologue to the lay: she apprises us of the heroine's pain and then infuses this suffering body with its own subjectivity.

The suffering body of this heroine is inserted into the intricate narrative system, and in fact made integral to it, through the curse placed upon Guigemar by the androgynous hind he has wounded while hunting. This hind tells Guigemar that his wound will only be cured when he meets a woman who will suffer greatly for him:

E tu, vassal, ki m'as nafree,
Tel seit la tue destinee:
Jamais n'aies tu medecine,
Ne par herbe, ne par racine!
Ne par mire, ne par poisun
N'avras tu james garisun
De la plaie k'as en la quisse,
De si ke cele te guarisse
Ki suffera pur tue amur
Issi grant peine e tel dolur
K'unkes femme taunt pur li;
Dunt tuit cil s'esmerveillerunt
Ki aiment e ame avrunt
U ki pois amerunt apres.

(107-21)

Narrative action is precipitated by the suffering female body, and as readers of this text we participate through the very act of reading in the infliction of pain upon the lady's body, as we simultaneously inflict pain upon Marie's body. We are required to search this textual landscape for a woman we will make suffer more than any other, since it is this suffering that constitutes and ensures the narrative space, for now and for posterity. The pain inflicted on this body will be prolonged, enduring and eternal, and by seeking her we ensure this. I have indicated above that the genital nature of this suffering is implicated in the linguistic and iconographic echoes generated by Marie's representation of Venus. It is also implied in the type of wound written onto Guigemar's body. His castration by the hind requires a woman who will initiate healing desire in the hero. Once healed, Guigemar can spill the seed of meaning into the lady's holes, so that the *sens* of this text will drip onto its readers.

While Marie inserts us into this torturous position as the instigators of this rapacious search for meaning, she repeats her decoding strategy from the lay's prologue: she infuses the body of the lay's heroine with its own subjectivity. The lady's subject-position develops from her resistance to the repressive strategies set in place to control her.

When we first meet the lady, Marie devotes about forty-five lines to a description of the nearly impenetrable stronghold the lady's jealous old husband has constructed in an effort to "protect" his wife. This enforced enclosure of the wife is possible only by the *elided* premarital financial negotiations between the young woman's father and her husband, evoked for the medieval audience by the respective ages of the couple, since only an older man could afford to "buy" a young wife. This absent exchange of the woman between two sets of men—her father and her husband—reminds us that, in a culture where women are objects of exchange, "the relations of such a system are such that women are in no position to realize the benefits of their own circulation" (Rubin 174). Luce Irigaray suggests that this imbalanced exchange can only be remedied when a double system of exchange shatters the "appropriative power" of father-men (173). This shattering of male dominance—and the beginning and recognition of female desire and subjectivity—can occur in **"Guigemar"** only if the lady initiates and controls her own circulation. Her husband, aware that it is only through some form of sexual/textual circulation that the lady's body can begin to generate its own (as opposed to an inscribed) meaning, reinforces his position of power over his wife by assigning her as a guard an aged priest who has lost his "plus bas membres" (257)—presumably his testicles. Marie's famous doubling strategy here connects the castrated old priest and the lady's ancient husband, whose impotence is suggested by the couple's childlessness. This double impotence of priest and husband ensures that the lady remains untouched, silent and alone; in short, disempowered. It is Guigemar's arrival that sets in motion the lady's activity, that initiates her construction of a subject-position.

When Guigemar arrives on the shores of the island-fortress, the lady begins to transgress those boundaries set up by her controlling husband: she activates her voice and her desire. Until she is informed of the strange knight's presence on the boat, the lady is silent. It is her wish to see this knight which produces her speech:

> Respunt la dame: «Or i alums!
> S'il est morz, nus l'enfuirums;
> Nostre prestre nus aidera.
> Si vif le truis, il parlera».
>
> (287-90)

Speech, as Christine Froula argues, is one way that women can respond to the metaphysical violence inscribed against them in the literary tradition, and whereby they can regain a sense of their own identity (633). Male-gaze theory also offers a way by which women can construct their own subject-positions. When the lady sees Guigemar sleeping on the boat, she explores his body both visually and manually:

> Quant ele est en la neif entree,
> Devant le lit est arestee;

> Le chevalier ad esgarde,
> Mut pleint sun cors e sa beute
>
> . . . . .
>
> Desur le piz li met sa main:
> Chaut le senti e le quor sein,
> Ki suz les costez li bateit.
>
> (293-301)

The act of gazing on a female body is traditionally used by men to constitute their subjectivity, as Laura Mulvey has demonstrated. Consequently, the lady's study of the sleeping knight's body disrupts the normal gender hierarchy usually constituted by the gaze, as she appropriates the position of power allotted the traditionally heterosexual male gazer. Her visual objectification of Guigemar also establishes her own subject-position, as is usual in gaze theory, where the viewer defines his [sic] selfhood against an eroticized Other. As well, it is the lady's desire for Guigemar that finally allows her to escape from the island-fortress, through a door she hitherto believed locked (673-78). As I noted above, Guigemar's relationship to the lady is made dependent on her undergoing "issi grant peine e tel dolor / K'unkes femme taunt ne suffri." This female anguish is tempered—as it is not in the usual raping/reading paradigm—by Marie's emphasis on the couple's *mutual* desire, and mutual pain. Through this mutuality Guigemar can help the lady develop her own subject-position:

> La dame entent que veir li dit
> E li otreie sanz respit
> L'amur de li. . . .
>
> (527-29)

Thus, it is Guigemar—and not the invasive reader—who receives the fullest meaning from the lady because when the couple finally consummates their love, she willingly grants her body to him and to him alone:

> Bien lur coviene del surplus,
> De ceo que li autre unt en us!
>
> (522-34)

The word "surplus," with its dual meaning of excess and spilling of seminal fluid,[7] is also incorporated by Marie in the general prologue to the lays, as part of her discussion of reading strategies:

> Custume fu as anciens,
> Ceo testimoine Preciens,
> Es livres ke jadis feseient,
> Assez oscurement diseint
> Pur ceus ki a venir esteint
> E ki aprendre les deceient,
> K'i peussent gloser la lettre
> E de lur sen le surplus mettre.
>
> (9-16)

This linguistic duplication of "surplus" again underlines the sexualization of the interpretive process. As I contended above, if we read Guigemar's thigh wound as figuring castration, the physical joining of the couple not only gives the hero access to the lady's meaning, but also magically restores his ability to find that meaning. Guigemar's role as the apparently perfect reader/lover—the one who can perform without the violence that engenders the raping/reading paradigm—stands in contrast to the other male characters in the text who try to force meaning from the lady's body, as her husband and his men do when her adultery is discovered.

When the old husband is finally informed of the adultery, with the help of three of his men, he violently breaks down the door to his wife's chamber.[8] The sexual nature of this assault on the lady's body is again highlighted, this time by the punishment the hero wishes to impose on these transgressors:

> Il en ferat aukun dolent;
> Ainz ke il d'eus seit aprimiez
> Les avrat il tuz mainiez.

(598-600)

This desired punishment invokes the wounds already written on the body of the old guardian-priest (and Guigemar himself), the sexually-suggestive amputation of the "membres" that have made this man an acceptable warden of the lady.

We have thus far explored in **"Guigemar"** the implications of constructing a female body as the site of meaning: men wish to colonize this body to establish their own sense of self, their own identity, and—with the exception of Guigemar—can only do this through violence. Physical assault or its threat is not only a side-effect of traditional modes of gaining meaning; it is also an integral component of the discourse of courtly literature.

In her book *Ravishing Maidens: Writing Rape in Medieval French Literature and Law,* Kathryn Gravdal carefully documents both the pervasiveness of rape in medieval courtly literature and its disturbing romanticization there (67). Marie de France, as a woman in a culture desensitized to antifemale violence, rewrites women's position in courtly discourse. Rather than valorizing this violence, she reveals women's marginalized positions within courtly literature. This point is particularly valid when we consider, as Jo Ann McNamara reminds us, the status of Western European women in the twelfth century:

> excluded from the social mechanisms that define male identity and social status, women were relegated to the margins, not of life but of social consciousness. There they remained diffusely grouped not into categories based on their contributions to society or their own skills and achievements, but solely on gender. . . . In brief, women of the twelfth century were not silent and unprotesting victims, but they were victims of a vision of progress that defined civilization as a male preserve with no ground of enterprise for women.

(37)

Rape is part of this social context: Marie's contemporary, Andreas Capellanus, encouraged noblemen to "take [from peasant women] what you seek and to embrace them by force" (1.12); and Georges Duby has attested to the pervasiveness of rape in the aristocratic household (1983:220). Marie's most powerful critique of antifemale violence in courtly discourse is found in two superficially parallel yet dialogically engaged scenes in **"Guigemar"**: first, the hero's activities at his court, after he and his lover are separated, and then the lady's activities at the court of Meriaduc.

When Guigemar arrives at his court, languishing for his absent lover, women from all over Brittany come to him in an effort to untie his knotted shirt—so tied that only his love can undo it—but all fail (651-54). Guigemar is under no threat from the hordes of women who wish to untie his knot, because the physical dynamics involved in the women's attempt to undo his knotted shirt do not make him vulnerable: he is not exposed in any way during this process, nor is any weapon mentioned. In fact, when Guigemar's lady eventually does untie the knot, he is not even wearing the shirt (796-98). Furthermore, this comic colonization of Guigemar by the Breton ladies recalls the earlier, eroticized first encounter between the lady and Guigemar: once on board the boat that has brought him to her, the lady caresses the naked chest of the sleeping knight (299-301). But the brief encounter between Guigemar and the women of Brittany generates meaning most fully for Marie's gender politics when read dialogically with the lady's experiences at Meriaduc's court. The juxtaposition of these two episodes—Guigemar's encounter with the Breton ladies, and the heroine's encounter with Meriaduc and his knights—unmasks the very different positions of men and women in courtly discourse.

While harmless erotic undercurrents mark the women's attempts to disentangle Guigemar's knot, the heroine's encounter with Meriaduc is tinged with violence. Meriaduc, in fact, stands as an emblem of courtly aggression: his antifemale violence is connected to his position as a feudal lord. For instance: Meriaduc enters the narrative and espies the lady as he leaves his castle early one morning to engineer an attack on his neighbour (693-96). Violence also informs his first encounter with the lady:

Il la saisist par le mantel
Od lui l'en meine en su chastel.

(705-06)

Once inside his stronghold, Meriaduc informs her of his desire (721), although the violence which instigates this desire is deceptively hidden under cover of love. When the lady rejects Meriaduc's advances, he angrily accuses her of having another lover, whom he suspects to be Guigemar:

Quant il l'entent,
Si li respunt par maltalent:
«Autresi ad en cest pais
Un chevalier de mut grant pris:
De femme prendre en iteu guise
Se defent, par une chemise
Dunt li destre panz est pleiez;
Il ne peot estre despleiez
Ki force u cutel n'i metreit.
Vus feistes, jeo quit, cel pleit!»

(726-34; my emphasis)

This rage is a prerequisite for Meriaduc's next actions:

Il la receit entre ses braz,
De sun bliaut trenche les laz:
La ceinture voleit ovrir,
Mes n'en poeit a chief venir.
Puis n'ot el pais chevalier
Que il n'i feist essaier.

(737-42)

Marie replaces the eroticism of the parallel scene with the suggestion here of sexual violence: Meriaduc must first slice open her tunic and expose the lady publicly in order to reach the belt that she "dunt a sa char nue la ceint, / Par mi le flanc aukes l'estreint" (571-72). Meriaduc's aggressive, public stripping of the lady not only resonates as a violent action enacted against an unwilling female subject; it also reinforces Dinshaw's observation that medieval commentators from Jerome to Richard of Bury employ the specific metaphor of stripping the (female) textual body in order to discover its deeper meaning (41). Marie, therefore, deconstructs the language of this medieval hermeneutic paradigm by literalizing it, by playing it out before her readers and infusing the usually faceless textual body with life. Moreover, she does not limit her critique to misogynist medieval reading strategies: through her inclusion of an incremental pattern of violence in Meriaduc's behaviour—from warring with his neighbour, to seizing the lady and bringing her to his castle, to his attempted assault of her—Marie similarly exposes the complicity of a courtly culture predicated on aggression. This cultural complicity in antifemale violence is again literalized when the tableau of assault involving Meriaduc and the lady is temporally extended, and the lady is forced to endure the humiliating exposure (and the strange hands fumbling at her flesh) *until all the men in the region are (un)satisfied.* This attempted gang rape is similar to those exposed by the historian Jacques Rossiaud, in his study of such rapes in the southeastern French towns of the fifteenth century, where marauding clubs of unmarried men received little official censure. Yet these attempted rapes function in the narrative not only to demonstrate the horror of men's means to satisfy their violent desire. They also signify the process whereby narrative closure is to be enacted in the raping/reading paradigm. Closure can only be achieved by this dual filling of female holes for male pleasure and textual meaning. The violence endemic to this dual process is contrasted to Guigemar's own non-violent participation in the reading of the lady's body.

When he arrives at Meriaduc's court, Guigemar is unsure that the woman he meets there is his love, because "femmes se resemblent asaz" (779). Even after she has successfully untied his knotted shirt, he is still unready or unwilling to believe that it is she (810-14). He is only able to confirm her identity when he "reads" her body:

«Amie, duce creature,
Estes vus ceo? Dites mei veir!
Lessiez mei vostre cors veeir,
La ceinture dunt jeo vus ceins».
A ses costez li met ses meins,
Si ad trovee la ceinture.

(816-21)

Unlike Meriaduc and his men, Guigemar does not publicly undress the woman in an effort to open her belt; rather, he merely touches her to ensure that she is indeed wearing it. Guigemar's full reading of the lady's body will take place later on, when they reconsummate their relationship, because narrative closure in turn depends upon the sexual union of the couple. As Marie herself states at the end of the lay, only this union will assuage pain:

A grant joie s'amie en meine:
Ore ad trespassee sa peine!

(881-82)

This final excision of pain, however, is decidedly gendered: only Guigemar will be healed completely.

The marginalization of the heroine implicit in this final mention of pain in **"Guigemar"** seems to set up a contradiction in my essay: I have argued above that the love-relationship between the young couple is valorized by Marie because of its mutuality of desire, a mutuality that stands in contrast to the violence inherent in the text's other male-female relationships, and which also allows for the development of female subjectivity. What

I wish to suggest here is that throughout the lay Marie deliberately challenges the heterosexual union of Guigemar and the lady while simultaneously condoning it. For example, she insinuates that it is this very relationship that is the catalyst for the violence directed at the lady. Also, Guigemar's gift of a chastity belt to the lady places him on the same footing as her controlling husband: the belt inhibits the lady's desire. The androgynous hind, the monstrous horned mother who wounds and is wounded by Guigemar, and who demands suffering in compensation, can be read as a literal symbol for the unnaturalness and implausibility of a heterosexual love-relationship that issues from a courtly culture predicated on violence—such relationships cannot avoid engendering further aggressive acts.

The final painful lines of **"Guigemar"** recall for us another female body, and the questions which surround it: that is, it recalls Marie's initial insertion of her own body into the narrative, when she warned her readers that an incorrect interpretation of her text would cause her great suffering. This "painful" closure of the narrative therefore forces us to ask: have we as readers successfully performed our reading of **"Guigemar"**? This question, we discover, is unanswerable. Moreover, finding an answer is ultimately less important than the fact that we have interrogated this text in terms of its representations of gender, violence and poetics. But this seems to beg another question: if Marie is exposing the violent misogyny inherent in both the hermeneutic and courtly discourses, what does she posit as an alternative? The text of **"Guigemar"** apparently offers one solution: the unravelling of the "plaie," the knot in the shirt the lady hands Guigemar as a sign of her love. And yet the lay's juxtaposition of male and female positions in such an "untying" reveals the problematic status of such an action: to untie a knot leads to the undoing of a belt, which in turn leads to the enactment of a rape. I would argue, however, that the seed of the solution for antifemale violence is evinced elsewhere in **"Guigemar,"** although it does not come to fruition until **"Eliduc,"** as the final lay in the set.[9]

Marie's proposal in **"Guigemar"** of an alternative to the violence that she sees engendered by a heterosexual and therefore gender-hierarchical culture is contained in her representation of the iconographic Venus. In my above discussion of this representation, I provided one reading of the goddess's "traitz" as seminal traces encoded on her body, signifiers of her status as female text read by a heterosexual male audience. Yet "traitz," through its homonymic association with "traire," also signifies the act of drawing milk. Moreover, Howard Bloch has noted that "lai," as the generic space within which Marie locates her narratives, itself acts "as the word for another Marie's milk" (102).[10] Marie, then, moves towards a rejection of the language of a reading

strategy predicated on violence, which she replaces with the language of "maternal" nurturing.[11] She suggests that we characterize the search for meaning not as the raping of a text, but as the loving and nourishing relationship between a "mother" and child. While Marie's introduction of a maternal discourse for textual analysis prefigures the modern concept of an *écriture féminine,* her reliance on this maternal imagery is not necessarily linked to her sex, since motherhood—as Carolyn Bynum has observed—was a popular trope among twelfth-century Cistercians.[12] To Bernard of Clairvaux, for example,

> The maternal image is almost without exception elaborated not as giving birth or even as conceiving or sheltering in a womb but as a nurturing, particularly suckling. Breasts, for Bernard, are a symbol of the pouring out towards others of affectivity or of instruction. . . .
>
> (Bynum 115)

Marie's resistance to the heterosexual violence of both hermeneutic and cultural discourses in **"Guigemar"** is continued in **"Eliduc."**

In the prologue to **"Eliduc"** Marie tells us that the lay's title—the name of the male protagonist—is the older, now inappropriate one, and that its name has been changed to **"Guildeluec ha Gualadun,"** in honour of the two principle female characters. Marie explains the reason for the change, in lines charged with the maternal reading metaphor outlined above:

> Kar des dames est avenu
> L'aventure dunt li lais fu.
>
> (25-26)

This displacement of the male character in favour of the women—a gesture that recalls Venus's displacement of Ovid in **"Guigemar"**—is maintained throughout the text. As the story progresses, Eliduc's lecherous, deceitful and selfish nature is exposed, and his status as the hero of the story is recuperated for his forgiving wife and the pious young woman who, unaware of his marriage, had become his lover. This lay ends not with the traditional and problematic male-female love relationship which closes **"Guigemar"**; instead, another displacement occurs. The troublesome heterosexual couple is replaced with a powerful union between the two women Eliduc has betrayed, as they leave him to serve God together:

> [The wife] la receut cum sa serur
> E mut li porta grant honur.
> De deu servir l'amonesta
> E sun ordre li enseigna.
>
> (1167-70)

This substitution of a heterosexual relationship in favour of a same-sex one is not unique in the medieval literary corpus, even among women: one of the trobairitz, Bieiris de Romans, wrote a love poem in the early thirteenth century to a woman named Maria[13]; while John Boswell points out that there are extant "at least two erotic verse letters from one religious woman to another" (220).

In **"Eliduc"** Marie overturns not only the dominant heterosexual model, but also the traditional hermeneutic triptych of a male writer, male reader, and female text. She presents instead a female writer, literalized in this narrative as the wife who instructs her friend, a female reader. Theirs is a relationship based on love, without the threat of sexual violence that plagued the women in **"Guigemar."** While the text disseminated by the wife at first glance appears to be a masculine one—the ultimate patriarchal authority of Logos, God's word—, in the epilogue to **"Eliduc"** Marie subtly posits her own text as the third in her female reading triumvirate, when she inserts a reminder of the compositional process of the story:

> De l'aventure de ces treis
> Li auncien Bretun curteis
> Firent le lai pur remembrer,
> Qu'un hum nel deust pas oblier.
>
> (1181-84)

Furthermore, in the final lines of the lay, Marie reintroduces the concept of pain that pervaded **"Guigemar"**:

> Mut se pena chescuns pur sei
> De Deu amer par bone fei.
>
> (1177-78)

Pain here is reconstituted: it is transformed from an external weapon wielded by men to stop or redirect the circulation and desire of women, to an individual, internal condition that leads to love. This painful love of God is not constructed on a gendered hierarchy: men and women equally can participate, as they could not in **"Guigemar,"** where, at the conclusion of the lay, only *his* pain was now at an end.

My own text ends, as Marie's does, with a self-validation: in the course of my discussion of **"Guigemar"** and **"Eliduc,"** I have deliberately attributed to Marie herself the interpretive possibilities generated by the two lays' carefully constructed interplay between violence, reading and gender. I did this to emphasize the sophisticated fluidity of twelfth-century discursive practises, which can withstand the tension of subversive questioning.[14] This questioning of contemporary gender-spaces is echoed throughout Marie's lays, as women walk through locked doors, leap unharmed from windows, and escape from master narratives. Finally, as Marie herself points out in **"Milun"**:

> Nuls ne poet estre si destreiz
> Ne si tenuz estreitement
> Que il ne truisse liu sovent.
>
> (286-88)

Notes

1. An earlier version of this paper was given at the conference of the Canadian Society of Medievalists (Calgary) in 1994. I want to thank Sheila Delany, Betty Schellenberg and especially Mitchell Owens for their helpful comments at various stages in this study's conception.

2. The scholarly texts concerned with women and violence deal almost exclusively with saints' lives. The notable exception is Kathryn Gravdal's *Ravishing Maidens* (although Gravdal does not discuss Marie's lays).

3. I do not want to suggest that Marie's decision to explore antifemale violence stems from a biological imperative, or that her perspective is the only one available to women. Instead, I see her position as a deliberate and informed choice.

4. See Dinshaw's *Chaucer's Sexual Poetics,* especially chapter 1.

5. I want to stress here that the raping/reading paradigm that Marie is foregrounding is not the only one available to exegetes in the Middle Ages; it is one of several open to medieval readers. Therefore, every act of reading—then and now—is not implicitly a rape. This paradigm is simply the one that most explicitly condones violence against women, and it is for this reason that I believe Marie critiques it.

6. For an incisive reading of this fabliau see E. Jane Burns's *Bodytalk.*

7. Both Howard Bloch and Robert Hanning consider the implications of this etymology.

8. A final example that the pain to be suffered by the lady is of a sexual nature can be found in the architectural design of the island fortress, with its single entranceway. When the lady's husband and his men break into her bedchamber, they are symbolically engaged in a rape, a rape that the husband's impotence won't otherwise allow him to perform.

9. I have adopted the "Guigemar"-"Eliduc" ordering suggested by both Jean Rychner in his edition of the lays and more recently by Glyn Burgess.

10. Bloch mentions this sense of "lai" as milk only in passing, as part of his argument that the polyvalency of Old French complicates its reading.

11. I put "maternal" in quotations marks because nurturing, even breast-feeding, was not a position limited to medieval women. See Carolyn Bynum's *Jesus as Mother.*

12. My reading of Marie is influenced here by Suzanne Akbari's paper on maternity in Christine de Pizan, although Akbari argues that Christine relies on an early *écriture féminine* in order to construct a "specifically feminine basis of authorship." She does not mention the raping/reading paradigm detailed here.

13. See Meg Bogin, *The Women Troubadours.*

14. We can recall here the similar interrogation by Heldris of Cornwall in his *Roman de Silence.*

References

Akbari, Suzanne Conklin. 1994. "'Laict' and 'Lettre': Maternity and Authorship in Christine de Pizan." Unpublished essay.

Andreas Capellanus. See Parry 1969.

Bloch, R. Howard. 1991. "The Medieval Text—"Guigemar"—as a Provocation to Medieval Studies." *The New Medievalism.* Eds. Marian S. Brownlee et al. Baltimore: Johns Hopkins University Press. 99-112.

Bogin, Meg. 1980. *The Women Troubadours.* New York: Norton.

Boswell, John. 1980. *Christianity, Social Tolerance, and Homosexuality.* Chicago: University of Chicago Press.

Burgess, Glyn S. 1987. *The Lais of Marie de France: Text and Context.* Athens: University of Georgia Press.

Burns, E. Jane. 1993. *Bodytalk: When Women Speak in Old French Literature.* Philadelphia: University of Pennsylvania Press.

Bynum, Caroline Walker. 1982. *Jesus as Mother: Studies in the Spirituality of the High Middle Ages.* Berkeley: University of California Press.

Cixous, Hélène. 1975. "Le rire de la Méduse." *L'arc* 61:39-54.

Dinshaw, Carolyn. 1989. *Chaucer's Sexual Poetics.* Madison: University of Wisconsin Press.

Duby, Georges. 1964. "Au XIIe siècle: les jeunes dans la société aristocratique dans la France du nord-ouest." *Annales* 5:835-46.

———. 1983. *The Knight, the Lady and the Priest: The Making of Modern Marriage in Medieval France.* Trans. Barbara Bray. New York: Pantheon.

Froula, Christine. 1986. "The Daughter's Seduction: Sexual Violence and Literary History." *Signs* 2.4:621-44.

Gravdal, Kathryn. 1991. *Ravishing Maidens: Writing Rape in Medieval French Literature and Law.* Philadelphia: University of Pennsylvania Press.

Hanning, Robert W. 1991. "Love and Power in the Twelfth Century, with Special Reference to Chrétien de Troyes and Marie de France." *The Olde Daunce: Love, Friendship, Sex and Marriage in the Medieval World.* Eds. Robert R. Edwards and Stephen Spector. Albany: State University of New York Press. 87-103.

Irigaray, Luce. 1985. *This Sex Which is Not One.* Trans. Catherine Porter. Ithaca: Cornell University Press.

Marie de France. See Rychner 1966.

McNamara, JoAnn. 1989. "Victims of Progress: Women and the Twelfth Century." *Female Power in the Middle Ages.* Eds. Karen Glente and Lisa Winther-Jensen. Copenhagen: Reitzel.

Mulvey, Laura. 1975. "Visual Pleasure and Narrative Cinema." *Screen* 16.3:6-18.

Parry, John Jay, ed. 1969. *Andreas Capellanus: The Art of Courtly Love.* New York: Norton.

Rossiaud, Jacques. 1978. "Prostitution, Youth, and Society in the Towns of Southeastern France in the Fifteenth Century." *Deviants and the Abandoned in French Society.* Eds. Robert Foster and Orest Ranum. Baltimore: Johns Hopkins University Press. 1-46.

Rubin, Gayle. 1975. "The Traffic in Women: Notes on the 'Political Economy' of Sex." *Towards an Anthropology of Women.* Ed. Rayna R. Reitner. New York: Monthly Review.

Rychner, Jean, ed. 1966. *Les lais de Marie de France.* Paris: Champion.

Scarry, Elaine. 1985. *The Body in Pain: The Making and Unmaking of the World.* Oxford: Oxford University Press.

June Hall McCash (essay date October 1995)

SOURCE: McCash, June Hall. "The Swan and the Nightingale: Natural Unity in a Hostile World in the *Lais* of Marie de France." *French Studies* 49, no. 4 (October 1995): 385-96.

[*In the essay below, McCash analyzes the lays "Laüstic" and "Milun" to show how Marie combines symbolic and empirical approaches to nature in her work.*]

In an article published in 1980, Anne Tukey Harrison labelled Marie de France a 'pseudo-naturalist', arguing that she 'does not write from direct observation. She transmits the lore of others with no apparent concern for truth or accuracy'.[1] Elsewhere in the brief article, however, she contends that in the *Lais* Marie describes animals 'sparsely but accurately' (p. 251), and concludes that the poet has little interest in the animals themselves but merely places them in service to humankind. The fact is that Marie's animals will not fit conveniently into any single niche. There are those that are *féeriques,* playing a supernatural role and drawn largely from Celtic tradition, such as the white hind in **"Guigemar,"** those that are sculpted from symbolic lore such as the weasel in **"Guildeluëc et Guilliadun"** (known to scholars as **"Eliduc"**),[2] and those that seem merely to be animals living in a natural world, such as the swan in **"Milun."** Some have a knowledge that is transmitted to man, thereby helping to direct the action; others do not. All are intensely interesting. Within the last few years, a good deal of attention has been focused on animals in the *Lais,* yielding at least one doctoral dissertation and a number of articles.[3] These have tended to stress Marie's symbolic use of animals, as well as her tendency not to violate their natural capabilities unless, of course, they are given a clearly supernatural dimension. To my knowledge, however, no one has examined Marie's work within the context of her times and their prevalent and shifting attitudes toward nature. It is my contention here that Marie's use of animals, and especially birds, is deliberately varied, demonstrating the variety of techniques that she had at her disposal and chose to exercise.

Marie lived in an era in which philosophical/theological concepts of nature were in a state of transition. Hers was a time when the symbolic approach to the natural world, best illustrated by such works as bestiaries and lapidaries, was being challenged by a confrontation with what M. D. Chenu has called 'an external, present, intelligible, and active reality'.[4] The fabulous imaginary animals that adorned medieval architecture were 'now rivaled by naturalistic artists who [. . .] sculpted little scenes of animal or human life on the capitals of cathedrals'.[5] Artists who wished to satisfy the tastes of the day found it increasingly necessary to treat nature in a way that would not violate empirical evidence.

Marie had no doubt been schooled in the symbolic approaches to the natural world which are typical of the bestiaries, as her work clearly indicates, and she was very likely familiar with the Latin translations of the *Physiologus* and almost certainly with the one French bestiary then in existence, that of Philippe de Thaon which he had composed during the first half of the twelfth century. She could also have known the seventh-century *Etymologiae* of Isidore of Seville, Book XII of

which is entitled 'De animalibus', as well as Pliny's *Historia naturalis.* Her work reveals an awareness and understanding of at least some of these symbolic materials. However, it is also evident that she was conscious of the newer breezes emanating from the continent, especially from the school of Chartres, where we find a view of nature from a more objective and realistic perspective. She may also have known two works largely responsible for focusing renewed attention on nature and initiating this shift in thinking, Bernardus Silvestris's *De mundi universitate* (written between 1145 and 1156) and Alain de Lille's *De planctu Naturae* (composed between 1160 and 1170).[6] The work of Alain in particular is interesting as a possible influence on Marie's thinking, although, as we shall see, there are significant ways in which her attitudes differ from his. One is tempted to see in her general Prologue a reflection of the words that Alain puts in the mouth of Dame Nature: 'Poetry's lyre rings in the vibrant falsehood on the outward literal shell of a poem, but interiorly it communicates a hidden and profound meaning to those who listen. The man who reads with penetration, having cast away the outer shell of falsehoods, finds the savory kernel of truth wrapped within.' ('At, in superficiali litterae cortice falsum resonat lyra poetica, sed interius, auditoribus secretum intelligentiae altioris eloquitur, ut exteriore falsitatis abjecto putamine, dulciorem nucleum veritatis secrete intus lector inveniat.')[7] Marie has not mentioned the falseness of the shell, but she does suggest the need for intense study of the text to find its true meaning. However, as her authority she cites not Alain, but Priscian,[8] when she states:

> It was customary for the ancients [. . .] to express themselves very obscurely so that those in later generations [. . .] could provide a gloss for the text and put their finishing touches on the meaning. Men of learning were aware of this and their experience had taught them that the more time they spent studying texts the more subtle would be their understanding of them and they would be better able to avoid future mistakes.[9]

> Custume fu as ancïens,
> Ceo testimoine Precïens,
> Es livres ke jadis feseient,
> Assez oscurement diseient
> Pur ceus ki a venir esteient
>
> . . . . .
>
> K'i peüssent gloser la lettre
> E de lur sen le surplus mettre.
> Li philosophe le saveient
> Par eus meïsmes entendeient,
> Cum plus trespassereit li tens,
> Plus serreient sutil de sens
> E plus se savreient garder
> De ceo k'i ert, a trespasser.[10]

Obviously, it was not merely the ancients who held to this custom, as Marie was no doubt well aware. Whether or not she knew Alain's work directly, she would certainly have known his sixth-century model, Boethius's *De consolatione philosophiae,* and been aware of the newer ideas concerning nature that were in the air at the time she composed her **Lais.** As a consequence, her work in its portrayal of nature represents an intersection in time of the symbolic and mimetic currents of thought.

Like Alain, Marie personifies Nature as *genetrix rerum,* the generative principle of the material world. In **"Guigemar"** it is Nature who is blamed for creating the hero without any interest in love: 'De tant i out mespris Nature / Ke unc de nule amur n'out cure' (vv. 57-58); in **"Equitan"** we are told that Nature 'had spared no pains when fashioning [the seneschal's wife]' (p. 56): 'En li former uvrat Nature' (v. 34). In **"Fresne,"** it is Nature who forms her beauty: 'Quant ele vint en tel eé / Que Nature furme beuté, / En Bretaine ne fu si bele / Ne tant curteise demeisele' (vv. 235-38). For Alain, as for Marie, Nature is dependent upon God. He describes Dame Nature as *vicaria Dei,* the vicar of God. Like Alain, Marie depicts humankind as falling away from God, while both show how it can be restored by reason in harmony with nature to its original state of grace. The actions of Guildeluëc in the *lai* that Marie calls **"Guildeluëc et Guilliadun"** take love to a higher plane and show the proper subordination ordained by Dame Nature in Alain's work of the lower aspects of man (loins) to the higher (mind, wisdom), as well as Nature's subordination to God.

In one way, however, Marie's thinking differs significantly from Alain's. Alain de Lille rejected extra-marital love. Just as he attacks sodomy as an act of fruitless perversion *contra naturam,* so he attacks extra-marital coitus as a vicious satisfaction of the lust of the flesh. For Alain the only acceptable sexuality is within marriage, the holy bond in which Nature's call for procreation can be satisfactorily answered. Any other form of passion is condemned. Marie's **Lais** provide a clear and contrary response to Alain's rejection of passion, for she gives sympathetic treatment to extra-marital love, provided it is true, loyal, and mutual. Perhaps the difference can be accounted for in terms of Alain's male monastic perspective as opposed to Marie's clearly female point of view.[11] Whether or not Marie was a nun, as many have supposed, sufficient evidence in the text indicates that she was well familiar with the realities of medieval marriage and the painful experience it often brought to women. Marriage bonds were created for reasons of property, not love, and the woman was usually the pawn. Taking these conditions into consideration, Marie allowed her lovers their brief moments of happiness on earth. She does not condemn them, nor does she seem to see them, merely because of their extra-marital love, as sinful or unnatural. On the

contrary, nature seems to harmonize with true love, to support it, and to give the lovers comfort and even help at their time of grief and separation.

One could select a number of *lais* to demonstrate this point. I have selected two—**"Laüstic"** and **"Milun"**—for the variety of experience they include, the fruitfulness of one woman, the barrenness of another, the joyous ending for one, the sorrowful ending of the other, the fuller story of one, the brief moment in time of the other. Despite these differences, there are also fundamental similarities between the two. Both depict the plight of a married woman who loves someone other than her husband, and both use birds, the swan in **"Milun"** and the nightingale in **"Laüstic",** as message bearers that reinforce and comfort the lovers within a world that is hostile to their love. Marie is careful in both *lais* never to violate the natural function of the birds, but to use their natural state to enhance the love relationship. And in both, she uses birds that have a wealth of symbolic associations from which she may draw in order to render the image richer and more textured. Yet, as we shall see, in the final analysis, her treatment of the two is extremely different—one suggestive of the older symbolic approach, the other reflective of the more current trends espoused by the Chartrian school.[12]

The two *lais* are side by side in the Harley manuscript,[13] with **"Laüstic"** preceding **"Milun"**. **"Laüstic"** is probably the most anthologized of Marie's **Lais,** in large measure because of its denseness and brevity. In only 160 lines Marie has created a small gem, packed with meaning and intensity. The story of the two lovers who live in neighbouring fortified houses in St Malo is well known. They cannot meet in the garden that apparently lies between the two houses, because the lady is married to a cruel, jealous man. But they can gaze upon one another and exchange words from their windows, which they do at night when the husband is supposedly asleep. The husband awakens, however, to find his wife missing from the bed, and when he questions her about it, she says that she stands at her window to listen to the sound of the nightingale. Expressing symbolic truth beneath the surface lie, she waxes eloquent in describing her reaction to the nightingale's song, i.e. her lover's voice: 'So sweet is the song I hear by night that it brings me great pleasure. I take such delight in it and desire it so much that I can get no sleep at all' (p. 95);

> Tant ducement l'i oi la nuit
> Que mut me semble grant deduit;
> Tant m'i delit e tant le voil
> Que jeo ne puis dormir de l'oil.

(ll. 87-90)

The nightingale, constructed as symbol by the woman, is transformed, or 'deconstructed' in the terminology of Michelle Freeman,[14] by her jealous husband into his own ugly reality, for he captures the bird, breaks its neck with his bare hands and flings it at his wife. Her grief over the tiny nightingale reconstructs it once again into the symbol of her now-broken nocturnal love. She wraps it in a piece of cloth embroidered in gold in such a way as to tell the tale ('A or brusdé e tut escrit' (l. 136) and sends it to her lover. He, in turn, receives the nightingale's body as the symbolic embodiment of their love. In order to preserve it forever, he commissions a tiny golden casket, in which he seals the bird's body and carries it with him at all times.

Love poetry of the twelfth century is filled with nightingales, and Marie depends upon her readers' awareness of bestiaries, contemporary poetry, and classical works, such as the associations with death in Ovid's *Metamorphoses* or Pliny's *Historia naturalis,* to complete its meaning. Numerous critics have commented upon the symbolic associations with the nightingale, none more succinctly than Thomas Shippey, who points out its use in troubadour lyrics, particularly the works of Bernard de Ventadorn. Bernard uses the nightingale in ten of his more than forty extant poems 'to parallel his situation', thus associating the bird with the troubadour/lover himself.[15] The nightingale, a bird traditionally associated with spring, represents for the troubadours an integral part of the burgeoning landscape that brings love and joy. The poet's song is like that of the nightingale, his natural reflection aroused in the newly-green landscape. Pliny tells us in his *Historia naturalis* that the bird will literally sing itself to death.[16] In Ovid's work, as Shippey points out, the nightingale is also 'a piercing reminder of the *danger* of love' (p. 49). The story of Philomela, recounted by Ovid in the *Metamorphoses,* was well known in the Middle Ages and was retold by Marie's contemporary Chrétien de Troyes in a version with which Marie may well have been acquainted.[17] In Ovid's account, Tereus, king of Thrace, marries Procne but is overcome by desire for her sister Philomela. He rapes her, cuts out her tongue, and imprisons her, although he tells Procne that she is dead. But in her imprisonment Philomela weaves a tapestry that tells her story and sends it to her sister. Together the two sisters kill Tereus's and Procne's son and serve up his flesh in a 'ritual meal' to his father. On discovering the truth, an enraged Tereus pursues the two women and is transformed by the gods into a hoopoe (some translations give lapwing), a bird which, according to Hugh of Fouilloy's *Aviarium,* 'alights on human feces, and feeds on stinking dung' ('stercora humana consideat et fetenti pascatur fimo').[18] The two women become birds as well, their breasts spattered with blood from the murder becoming blood-coloured feathers.

That Marie intended her readers to recall this gruesome tale is evident from her careful attention to detail in describing the cruel slaughter of the helpless bird by the jealous husband. He breaks the neck of the fragile bird and flings it at his wife. Drops of blood spatter the woman's breast, recalling not merely the drops of blood that become red markings on the nightingale, but also the rape itself, the violence of Tereus against Philomela who is described by Ovid as being 'like a dove, which, with its own blood all [. . .] over its plumage, still palpitates with fright, still fears those greedy claws that have pierced it' ('utque columba suo madefactis sanguine plumis / horret adhuc avidosque timet, quibus haeserat, ungues').[19] To the lady in Marie's poem the nightingale is, at first, merely a convenient excuse for rising at night. Contemporary readers might have been expected to recall the words of Bernard de Ventadorn:

> During the night when I am asleep, I wake with joy at the nightingale's sweet song, all confused, troubled and pensive in love; for this is my best pastime, in which I always gladly take joy; and with joy my song begins.

> Pel doutz chan que.l rossinhols fai
> la noih can me sui adormitz
> revelh de joi totz esbäitz
> d'amor pensius e cossirans;
> c'aisso es mos melhers mesters
> que tostems ai joi volunters
> et ab joi comensa mos chans.[20]

Although the lady's words are less overt and seemingly intended to hide the lovers' tryst from her husband, the image symbolically embodies the truth. The song of the nightingale is, in essence, the words of her lover. However, the hapless woman has unfortunately underestimated her husband's understanding of the situation, for he not only hears her words. He reads their full meaning. To his understanding of *her* symbolic language, he adds another level of his own—the association of the nightingale with brutality and death. Marie has managed to conflate in a single brilliantly drawn image both the shattered joy of love and the violence and death which illicit love can bring. The husband's act of violence and cruelty is symbolically a double murder in which both the lover/troubadour, in his guise as nightingale, and the wife, in her association with the female image of Philomela, are slain. He has accomplished the base task that Tereus was about to complete at the moment the gods transformed him into a hoopoe.

The revenge of the husband, however, is ultimately defeated by the final symbolic victory of the wife and her lover. As Rupert Pickens has described it: 'Like Ovid's heroine, Marie's lady, violently silenced and held prisoner by an abusive man, creates a narrative tapestry recounting her misfortunes; her embroidered samite transmits a truthful text to her lover, and it becomes a shroud that enfolds the object of its discourse.'[21] The lover, in turn, encases the bird in yet another layer, the golden *chasse* he has carefully crafted. Scholars have suggested two possible interpretations that extend the image, and the medieval word *chasse*, which could mean either *coffre* or *reliquaire*, unlike its modern counterpart, *châsse*, which only carries the meaning of reliquary, allows for both possible interpretations.[22] On the one hand, the bird has now been transformed into a 'holy relic', and, the lover's passion, 'as in the act of transubstantiation, into a spiritual relationship'.[23] Alternatively it has been suggested that the nightingale as a male symbol, i.e., the lover/troubadour, has now been inserted into the *chasse*, the jewel case, an image of female sexuality, thereby symbolizing the consummation of the lovers' passion and their ultimate victory over the cruel husband.[24] Even if the latter interpretation is judged valid, it is clearly a sublimation of the sexuality which would in no way vitiate the more spiritual interpretations, which I believe are intended. In the final analysis, the husband is not victorious over the lovers, for the love is intact, even though its physical manifestation may be broken, for the lovers remain united in the preserved body of the slain bird. Nature, as *vicaria Dei* and in the form of the nightingale, has allied herself with the lovers to overcome to the extent possible the evils of a cruel and violent world and to provide them earthly solace.

The role of the swan in **"Milun"** is, as we have seen, similar in many respects to that of the nightingale in **"Laüstic"**. It, too, functions as messenger. It, too, consoles and provides unity through communication to the separated lovers. And in both lays Marie has chosen a bird that has a wealth of symbolic association on which the tale could draw. But, unlike the nightingale, the traditional symbolic associations with the swan are downplayed, even reversed, within the lay. Why, then, does Marie choose the image of the swan? She is, I think, using the swan, a bird with symbolic accretions even similar to those of the nightingale, to underscore her different treatment of the two tales. Symbolically swans, like nightingales, were also associated with singing and death, as they are in classical lore and in the *Etymologiae* of Isidore of Seville (xii. 7. 18), and they are said to sing most sweetly just prior to their death.[25] The swan might thus have prepared the reader for a love that would end tragically, as did the nightingale, but that is not the case. For Marie to have emphasized this aspect of the swan's symbolic association would, first of all, have been a violation of its nature, for as early as Pliny's *Historia naturalis*, this so-called swan-song has been judged as *contra naturam olorum*. Pliny writes 'a story is told about the mournful song of swans at their death—a false story as I judge on the strength of a certain number of experiences' ('olorum morte narratur flebilis cantus, falso, ut arbitror aliquot experimentis').[26] Second, it is precisely Marie's intent to

focus on the newer naturalistic approach to nature in this tale. We see in the two juxtaposed lays what appears to be a deliberate attempt to contrast the two approaches. Marie seems, in fact, to be signalling to her reader the newer, more current attitude toward nature in the exordial remarks of the *lai*: 'Anyone who intends to present a new story must approach the problem in a new way and speak so persuasively that the tale brings pleasure to people' (p. 97); 'Ki divers cuntes veut traitier / Diversement deit comencier / E parler si rainablement / K'il seit pleisibles a la gent' (ll. 1-4). Thus, the two bird images seem consciously paired within the work to emphasize two different approaches (these appearing alongside the third bird *lai*, **"Yonec"**, which demonstrates the supernatural treatment of birds with its shape-changing bird lover). Whereas in **"Laüstic"** Marie has created a densely conflated image of the nightingale, charged with symbolic meaning that expands and deepens the brief, simple story of separated lovers, in **"Milun"** she seems to have made a special effort to separate the natural swan from its symbolic associations. In her article 'The Love-Messenger in "Milun"', Constance Bullock-Davies demonstrates that 'the swan in **"Milun"** is neither a messenger of the gods nor a magnificent fairy bird lover whose snowy plumage dissolves in his loved-one's sight to reveal the customary irresistibly handsome young man. It is only a postman'.[27] Placed in service by Milun himself, who knows of no other way to communicate with his lady after her marriage, it flies back and forth delivering messages between the lovers for twenty years, fed by one lover immediately upon arrival, then starved so that it will fly back to the other lover, who again feeds it upon arrival, then starves it, etc. Marie not only does nothing to violate the physical reality of the swan, she seems also to make every effort to give it a natural function within a realistic, plausible setting. As Bullock-Davies has shown (pp. 22-24), swans did live in the precise region indicated by Marie, and they were under royal protection, as Marie takes pains to point out (see ll. 181-88).[28] The twenty-year relationship of Milun and his lady is not exceptional in terms of the life span of swans. 'Everything connected with the swan in **"Milun"**', Bullock-Davies concludes, 'can be accounted for in the realm of everyday reason and experience' (p. 25). Thus, while, like the nightingale, the swan has many possible symbolic interpretations, none of them seems particularly relevant here. We do not have here a metamorphosis, a transformation (in the manner of Leda and the swan) which is so common with the swan, particularly in classical and Germanic cultures, nor do we see in the swan with white feathers and black skin an indication of hypocrisy, as do some medieval moralists, or as a symbol of pride as does Hrabanus Maurus.[29] On the contrary, the swan is a simple creature, who flies for its supper, who is faithful to its task, and who, once the task is done and the lovers are reunited, disappears from the story without further mention. While the natural capabilities of the two birds in question are violated in neither story, Marie, using a more traditional approach, calls attention through intertextual allusions to the symbolic associations with the nightingale, while in **"Milun"** the swan is treated according to the fresher, more naturalistic approach toward observable reality that was beginning to make its way into both the art and the theology of the day.[30]

In the final analysis, the swan in **"Milun"** takes on a meaning of its own, for it becomes, in the course of the tale, emblematic of the loyalty of the two lovers. If it is under 'royal protection', it is the protection afforded true lovers in the works of Marie de France within the broader context of God's love. The swan, like the nightingale, functions within the domain of God's earthly caretaker Nature to keep the love alive despite the lovers' separation and to comfort each one in the absence of the other. In the end, the lovers' loyalty is rewarded, as they are reunited with their son and by their son within the bonds of marriage. The son, known only as Sanz Per in the *lai*, has expressed a willingness to kill his mother's legal husband in order to see that his parents are wed: 'Par fei, bels pere, / Assemblerai vus e ma mere! / Sun seignur qu'ele ad ocirai / E espuser la vus ferai' (vv. 497-500); however, the shadowy spouse, who is never described as brutal or jealous but merely represents an obstacle to the establishment of legal bonds between the lovers, conveniently dies without assistance. Thus, the lovers and their son are protected from the sin of taking the life of an innocent person, as we have seen Equitan try to do and as Guigemar did in his efforts to take back his lady. **"Milun"** is one of only two *lais* that end in the sacrament of marriage. The other is **"Fresne,"** which tells of another woman who loves truly and whose fidelity and *caritas* are rewarded with marriage.

While Marie does not condemn extra-marital love that is true and *fin*, she nevertheless sees marriage to be the rational consequence of mutual love and the highest form of community outside the love of God itself. Milun, his lady, and their son form, in their family harmony, if not a perfect union, the most perfect one that can be provided within the exclusive realm of *vicaria Dei*, Dame Nature.

Notes

1. 'Marie de France as Naturalist', *Romance Notes,* 21 (1980-81), 253. I am grateful to the research committee of Middle Tennessee State University for a summer research grant to prepare this article.

2. For a justification for using the title of *Guildeluëc et Guilliadun* rather than the more widely-known *Eliduc,* see June Hall McCash, 'The Curse of the White Hind and the Cure of the Weasel: Animal Magic in the *Lais* of Marie de France', *Literary Aspects of Courtly Culture,* ed. by Donald Maddox and Sara Sturm-Maddox (Cambridge, D. S. Brewer, 1994), pp. 199-209 (pp. 208-09), and Matilda Tomaryn Bruckner, 'Strategies of Naming in Marie de France's *Lais*: At the Crossroads of Gender and Genre', *Neophilologus,* 75 (1991), 31-40 (p. 38).

3. See, for example, Kathryn Isabelle Holten, 'Metamorphosis as Metaphor: The Animal Images in Six Lays of Marie de France', Ph. D. Diss., Tulane University, 1988; Leslie C. Brook, 'Guigemar and the White Hind', *Medium Aevum,* 56 (1987), 94-101; Matilda Tomaryn Bruckner, 'Of Men and Beasts in *Bisclavret*', *Romanic Review,* 82 (1991), 251-69; Pierre Jonin, 'Le Baton et la belette ou Marie de France devant la matière celtique', *Marche Romane,* 30 (1980), 157-66; June Hall McCash, 'The Hawk-Lover in Marie de France's *Yonec*', *Medieval Perspectives,* 6 (1991), 66-75; Sophie Quenet, 'Mises en récit d'une métamorphose: Le Loup-Garou', in *Le Merveilleux et la magie dans la littérature,* ed. by Gérard Chandes (Amsterdam, Rodopi, 1992), pp. 137-63.

4. M. D. Chenu, *Nature, Man, and Society in the Twelfth Century: Essays on New Theological Perspectives in the Latin West,* selected, edited, and translated by Jerome Taylor and Lester K. Little (University of Chicago Press, 1968), p. 5.

5. Ibid, p. 10.

6. James Sheridan in the introduction to his translation of the work dates it 1160-65, while Claude Luttrell argues for a much later date, 1178-80. See Sheridan, *Alan of Lille: The Plaint of Nature* (Toronto, Pontifical Institute of Mediaeval Studies, 1980), p. 35 and Luttrell, *The Creation of the First Arthurian Romance* (Evanston, Northwestern University Press, 1974), pp. 255-56. Most critics, however, have accepted the dates 1160-1170. Alain's *Anticlaudianus* was also an important text in influencing late twelfth-century views of nature, but it was written too late for Marie to have known it when she composed the *Lais*. It is also interesting to consider the possibility that Marie's attitudes toward nature may have been influenced by Boethius's *De consolatione philosophiae,* a work that also influenced Alain. Boethius contended that Nature, understood by Reason, is the best guide to the world and that what is natural is in accordance with an ordered world.

7. *Patrologia latina* CCX, 451c. Translated in Chenu, p. 99.

8. Emanuel Mickel contends that the allusion to Priscian, a sixth-century grammarian, is 'not correct within the context in which she was writing, yet her citation is specific enough to indicate that she may well have had firsthand knowledge of the text and that the reference was more than the simple use of a name for the sake of citing an authority'. See his *Marie de France* (New York, Garland, 1972), p. 22.

9. *The Lais of Marie de France,* translated by Glyn S. Burgess and Keith Busby (Harmondsworth, Middlesex, Penguin Books, 1986), p. 41. Subsequent quotations in English of Marie's *Lais* are from this translation and will be noted within the text.

10. *Les Lais de Marie de France,* ed. Jean Rychner (Paris, Honoré Champion, 1983), ll. 9-13, 15-22. Subsequent quotations will be from this edition, and line references will be noted within the text.

11. While Alain may not have been a monk at the time he wrote *De planctu Naturae,* he was certainly schooled by clerics in the ecclesiastical schools in Paris, and possibly in Chartres. He taught in Paris and probably in Montpellier. He may have been, at least for a time, a monk in the Benedictine monastery in Bec, and he ended his life as a Cistercian monk at Citeaux in 1202. See Sheridan, pp. 2-10.

12. If R. N. Illingsworth is correct in attributing *Laüstic* to the earlier grouping of Marie's works, which he dates between 1155-60, and *Milun* to the later grouping, which he believes were composed between 1160-65, precisely the dates Sheridan gives for the composition of *De planctu Naturae,* then it is logical that *Laüstic* would reflect the older symbolic tradition, while *Milun* would suggest approaches found in the newer naturalistic tradition. See Illingsworth, 'La Chronologie des *Lais* de Marie de France', *Romania,* 87 (1966), 433-75.

13. In fact, all three bird *lais* appear as a group within the text, with *Yonec* representing yet a third approach—the *féerique* or supernatural treatment of animals based largely on Celtic lore, which is not being considered in detail in this article.

14. 'Marie de France's Poetics of Silence: The Implications for a Feminine *Translatio*', *PMLA,* 99 (1984), 868. Freeman contends quite rightly that 'the Husband inverts the Lady's system as devised in the *Laüstic* explanation by corrupting the metaphor, that is, by thwarting, through his literalness, the possibilities of an exchange between two worlds of meaning' (p. 868).

15. 'Listening to the Nightingale', *Comparative Literature,* 22 (1970), 50.

16. For Pliny on nightingales, see *Natural History,* trans. by H. Rackham, Loeb Classical Library Edition (Cambridge, Mass., Harvard University Press, 1940), v. 3, Book x. 43. According to Pliny, nightingales 'compete with one another, and there is clearly an animated rivalry between them; the loser often ends her life by dying, her breath giving out before her song' ('certant inter se, palamque animosa contentio est; victa morte finit saepe vitam, spiritu prius deficiente quam cantu' (pp. 344-45)).

17. Chrétien de Troyes mentions in the prologue to *Cligés* that he has written 'de la hupe et de l'aronde / et del rossignol la muance', a clear allusion to a version of the Philomela story. Chrétien's version is presumably preserved in the *Ovide Moralisé.* See *Three Ovidian Tales of Love,* ed. and transl. by Raymond Cormier (New York-London, Garland, 1986), 183-281. Since he indicates in lines 3-4 that he has translated other works of Ovid, we can surely assume that his version of the Philomela tale was based on Ovid's *Metamorphoses.*

18. *The Medieval Book of Birds: Hugh of Fouilloy's Aviarium,* ed. and trans. by Willene B. Clark (Binghamton, NY, Center for Medieval and Early Renaissance Studies, 1992), pp. 238-39. According to Hrabanus Maurus, it 'symbolizes wicked sinners, men who continuously delight in the filth of sins' ('Haec avis sceleratos peccatores significat, homines qui sordibus peccatorum assidue delectantur'), *The Nature of Things,* 22.6 (Migne, *PL* 111:252). This is also cited by Hugh of Fouilloy, pp. 240-41.

19. Ovid, *Metamorphoses,* trans. by Frank Justus Miller, Loeb Classical Library Edition, 3rd ed. (Cambridge MA, Harvard University Press, 1977, reprinted 1984), vi, ll. 329-30. Interestingly enough, Ovid's version does not specify the types of birds that Philomela and Procne become, but other authors usually make of them a nightingale and swallow. Certainly throughout the Middle Ages, the nightingale was associated with Philomela. According to Michelle Freeman, the scene also recalls the stories of Piramus and Thisbe and of Vulcan's entrapment of Venus and Mars, both told in the *Metamorphoses.* See 'Marie de France's Poetics of Silence', p. 869.

20. *The Songs of Bernart of Ventadorn,* ed. by Stephen G. Nichols, Jr, et al. (Chapel Hill, University of North Carolina Press, 1965), #33, ll. 1-7, pp. 138-39. Sleeplessness because of the nightingale's

song is also found as a motif in canso 45: 'Alas, how I die of desire! I do not sleep day or night, for at night when I go to lie down, the nightingale sings or cries'; 'Ai las, com mor de talan. / Qu'eu no dorm mati ni ser, / que la noih can vau jazer / lo rossinhols chant' e cria' (ll. 8-11, pp. 173-75).

21. I am grateful to Rupert Pickens for allowing me to quote from his unpublished draft of 'The Bestiary of Marie de France', p. 32. See also Robert T. Cargo, 'Marie de France's *Le Laüstic* and Ovid's *Metamorphoses*', *Comparative Literature*, 18 (1966), 162-66. See also Freeman, p. 867, who describes 'the corpse prepared for burial, wrapped in an embroidered cloth that is [. . .] subsequently placed in the bejeweled reliquary, or *châsse*, which is sealed shut. The object, now devoid of song, is wrapped in a written or pictorial sign and inserted in another wordless object that attracts attention—an object, this time, that is symbolic of the hagiological'.

22. A. J. Greimas in his *Dictionnaire de l'ancien français jusqu'au milieu du XIVᵉ siècle* (Paris, Larousse, 1968), gives as his first definition 'Coffe', and as his second, 'Ecrin contenant des reliques', p. 108. Since a *coffre* could presumably contain anything, it is not illogical, given its small size, to extend its meaning to *coffret* (or *coffret à bijoux*, jewel case), although the greater body of evidence seems to weigh more heavily in favour of the interpretation of the word as 'reliquary'.

23. Glyn S. Burgess, 'Symbolism in Marie de France', *Bulletin bibliographique de la Société Internationale Arthurienne*, 33 (1981), 260. See also R. D. Cottrell, '*Le Lai du Laüstic*: From Physicality to Spirituality', *Philological Quarterly*, 47 (1968), 499-505; Holten, 'Metamorphosis as Metaphor', pp. 160-61.

24. Burgess, 260. See Robert B. Green, 'Marie de France's *Laüstic*: Love's Victory through Symbolic Expression', *Romance Notes*, 16 (1974-75), 695-99. He contends that 'culmination of love is reached through the masculine symbol of the nightingale contrasted first with the feminine symbol of a room and then with the jeweled case which explains the powerful image of permanent physical union with which the lay ends' (p. 696). He suggests that: 'Although the word *châsse* is used, a jewel case is suggested' (p. 698). See also Holten, 160. For a discussion of the sexual imagery of the nightingale, see Wendy Pfeffer, *The Change of Philomel: The Nightingale in Medieval Literature* (New York-Berne-Frankfurt, Peter Lang, 1985), pp. 157-68. We should also note at least one dissenting opinion. Emanuel

Mickel contends that the bird's body, thus preserved, is not a symbol of the lovers' triumph over the husband. 'What is being emphasized here is that the lover carries around with him always the agonizing memory of his lost love, and that never again would his suffering be assuaged by the sight of his loved one, represented by the bird.' See 'A Reconsideration of the *Lais* of Marie de France', *Speculum*, 46 (1971), 56.

25. See Isidore of Seville, *Etymologiarum sive originum libri XX.*, ed. by W. M. Lindsay (Oxford, Clarendon Press, 1911); Florence McCulloch, *Mediaeval Latin and French Bestiaries* (Chapel Hill, University of North Carolina Press, 1962), p. 176. Interestingly, Alain de Lille also mentions the swan's singing prior to its death in his *De planctu Naturae*. 'The swan, herald of its own death, foretold with its honey-sweet lyre of music the stopping of its life.' See *The Complaint of Nature*, trans. by Douglas M. Moffat (New Haven, Yale University Press, 1908; reprinted Hamden, CT, Archon Books, 1972), Prose 1, p. 11.

26. Book x, 32. 63.

27. Constance Bullock-Davies, 'The Love-Messenger in "Milun"', *Nottingham Mediaeval Studies*, 16 (1972), 21.

28. According to the tale fabricated by Milun's message-bearer, he wishes to give the swan to the lady in order to 'gain her support and protection' and thereby avoid being 'hindered and arraigned in this region', for he has captured the bird 'in a meadow beneath Caerleon', a well-known castle of King Arthur. Thus, according to Marie's account, the birds were protected by law in the region of the king's castle. See Burgess and Busby, p. 99:

> Jeo sui uns hum de tel mestier,
> D'oiseus prendre me sai aidier.
> Une archiee suz Karlïun
> Pris un cisnë od mun laçun.
> Pur force e pur meintenement
> La dame en voil fere present,
> Que jeo ne seie desturbez,
> En cest païs achaisunez
>
> (ll. 181-88)

29. See Beryl Rowland, *Birds with Human Souls* (Knoxville, University of Tennessee Press, 1978), p. 171. See also Hrabanus Maurus, *Patrologia latina* 112, col. 894.

30. If, as Harrison contends, animals are subservient to man, it may well suggest the microcosm/macrocosm idea developed by Bernard Silvestris.

Just as Nature is in the service of God and his universe, so animals, Nature's representatives, are in the service of man.

Laurie A. Finke and Martin B. Shichtman (essay date winter 2000)

SOURCE: Finke, Laurie A., and Martin B. Shichtman. "Magical Mistress Tour: Patronage, Intellectual Property, and the Dissemination of Wealth in the *Lais* of Marie de France." *Signs* 25, no. 2 (winter 2000): 479-503.

[*In the following essay, the authors argue that Marie's* Lais *reflects the attempts of the fringe aristocracy—court women and bachelor knights—to take advantage of the possibilities for social advancement inherent in the informal (but omnipresent) patronage system of Norman England.*]

The twelfth-century French poet we know as Marie de France may have been the greatest writer of short fiction before Boccaccio and Chaucer; arguably her best works—her *lais,* short, deceptively simple romances in octosyllabic couplets—rival even theirs. In these tales, Marie explores the situations of the most marginalized members of the Norman aristocracy, specifically women and bachelor knights, those younger sons dispossessed by the system of primogeniture through which the ruling class perpetuated itself. In so doing, Marie exposes the imbrication of artistic, political, economic, and legal activity in the production and reproduction of gendered (and classed) identities.

In the epilogue to her *Fables,* Marie gives her name "for memory" (pur remembrance) (1987, 256 [line 3]), so that her authorship will be remembered and appropriately rewarded: "My name is Marie; I am from France" (Marie ai num, si sui de France [line 4]). She names her patron as well, presumably also "for memory." The *Fables* are dedicated to, written for the love of ("Pur amur" [line 9]), a Count William, "the most valiant in any realm" (le plus vaillant de nul realme [line 10]). The epilogue seems almost another fable with its generic names—how many Maries and Williams were there in the French-speaking world of the twelfth century?—and it tantalizes us with the promise that these are historical personages associated with the Norman court of Henry II. A close analysis of the patron-client relationship implied in the epilogue illuminates the ways patronage regulated the formation and maintenance of gendered and classed subjectivities among the aristocracy of Norman England during the reign of Henry II. Patronage relationships dominated all aspects of social interaction during this period. Most

literary critics who study the role of patronage in the arts tend to isolate cultural patronage from the larger system of patron-client relations that organized social, political, and economic relations at every level of medieval society.[1] We believe, however, that during this period virtually all goods and services—whether manuscripts, military service, or political offices—circulated more or less interchangeably within an amorphous and informal system of patronage. In this article, therefore, we make no distinction between literary or artistic patronage and other forms of patronage—economic, political, military. One cannot fully understand how Marie's *lais* embody and reproduce the ideologies of class and gender held by the Norman ruling class without examining the wider cultural, economic, and political work that patronage performed.

Patronage relationships of all kinds were often structured as private erotic relationships with love as the medium for the distribution, exchange, and circulation of wealth (Finke 1992, 33-48). The first part of this article examines how the patronage system regulated aristocratic masculinity and asks why it was necessary to draw on the ideology and forms of heterosexual love to structure a social process—patronage—that was, with only a few exceptions, homosocial, a means of organizing relations between men through the exchange of women and wealth. But because women cannot so easily be reduced to ciphers—symbols of wealth—the second part of the article explores how, once they are no longer represented simply as prizes to be won by successful clients but become active participants in patronage networks, women might successfully negotiate these social networks to their own advantage. In a system whose very informality and lack of explicit institutionalization made it a suitable vehicle for the advancement of the marginalized, it is not surprising that Norman noblewomen would participate in the accumulation and distribution of capital as energetically as their husbands, fathers, and brothers.

We can begin to grasp the centrality of patronage to the social organization of the Norman aristocracy by speculating about the identity of the Count William named in Marie's epilogue. Scholars have proposed several possibilities, but the best arguments for each are no more conclusive than arguments that link the author of the *lais* with one of the various Maries associated with the Anglo-Norman court of Henry II.[2] Although we have no new evidence for this position, and it would require moving the date of the fables to after 1190 (Painter 1933), we would like to think that Marie's patron was William Marshal, Earl of Pembroke, marshal of England under Henry and guardian of his son and presumptive heir. William Marshal appeals to us because his career so strongly resembles that of the character Milun—and his son—in Marie's *lai* of the same name. The careers of both the historical William and of Marie's fictional characters—their success in manipulating the system of patronage to enhance their humble beginnings—demonstrate the workings of a system that organized male/male relationships, and hence masculine identity, through structured exchanges of women and wealth.

Georges Duby (1985) recounts the life of William Marshal based on the vita of an anonymous chronicler named Jean (Meyer 1891-1901).[3] William was one of the so-called new men, those men of the lower aristocracy who provided administrative and military services to the newly centralizing monarchies of Europe and who negotiated their relations to the aristocracy through patronage, often achieving significant power and prominence (Duby 1985, 58; Green 1986, 139-59). He was the fourth son of a minor Norman nobleman and, in a world in which inheritance was governed by the principles of primogeniture and nonpartition, a man with no prospects. Yet he eventually rose to become the marshal of England, regent for Henry's eldest son and heir, Henry Court Mantel, and one of the richest and most powerful men in the realm. He accomplished this by securing the "love" of increasingly more powerful patrons, including that of Henry II and his son, until he could acquire land, a wife, a title, and the position of a powerful patron.

While primogeniture and its attendant narrative, genealogy, would seem to produce a stagnant system of rigid class divisions that limited social mobility, patronage opened up spaces through which men disinherited and disadvantaged by birth might advance. While primogeniture created fictions of permanence and continuity, patronage created elaborate networks of male-male relations that emphasized discontinuity, change, and mobility. Individuals both within and outside Henry's government constituted their relationship to it through the exchange networks of patronage. Indeed, Henry's government was a product of these patronage relations and could not have functioned without them. Marshal differed from his contemporaries only in preferring military service to administration as a means of advancement, although his charters attest to his abilities as a businessman and estate manager.[4]

Patronage relations predominate when power in a society is to some extent centralized but relatively weak and when the power of the elite to control resources at the periphery is limited. Although the policy of the Norman kings since William the Conqueror had been to concentrate their power by holding their feudal prerogatives closely, avoiding the fragmentation and decentralization that plagued the monarchy in France, at the periphery of the kingdom they were forced to cede more power (Crane 1986, 7). As Earl of Pembroke, Marshal joined the ranks of the March lords who, because they controlled lands bordering hostile populations (in Marshal's case, the Welsh), were granted more power, wealth, and autonomy than Norman kings usually ceded to those barons more centrally located.

Marshal's career seems to have been not unlike that of Marie's characters in the *lai* **"Milun."** The title character is described as a knight of indeterminate origin who is "generous and strong, courteous and proud" (Francs e hardiz, curteis e fiers [line 14]).[5] He is beloved and honored by many princes, but he is clearly a bachelor knight who occupies the position of client to more powerful patrons. He falls in love with the daughter of a baron, and she becomes pregnant with his illegitimate child. Despite his martial abilities, however, Milun is not seen as an eligible match for the woman he loves, most likely because, like Marshal, he does not hold any land of his own. His lover is "given" by her father to "a rich lord of the region, / a powerful man of great repute" (Un mut riche humme del païs, / Mut esforcible e de grant pris [lines 125-26]), and the illegitimate child is secretly sent to Northumbria to be raised by Milun's sister.[6]

The division between married and unmarried men in the twelfth century, according to Duby, constituted a class division, a nearly insurmountable divide between men who could be patrons and those who were clients, between men who had land and wives to produce heirs and unmarried men who attached themselves as clients to more powerful men who bore the cost of their upkeep as part of their household or *mesnie*. Neither William Marshal, as a younger son, nor Milun, whose class status is unarticulated, is powerful enough to marry or to hold land—at least initially. Both seek their fortune by attaching themselves as bachelor knights to the households of increasingly more powerful patrons. Their success is measured primarily by success in tournaments, which is heavily rewarded by their patrons, often so much that they are themselves able to support clients of their own, bachelor knights less fortunate than themselves. In the case of Milun's son, who, like his father, begins his adventures as a bachelor knight, success in tournaments is so great that he is eventually able, without consulting anyone,[7] to give ("dona") his now-widowed mother to his father; he is able to act the part of the powerful patron, just as eventually Marshal was rewarded by the "gift" of a wife and, with her, the lands that would make him Earl of Pembroke. It is almost too much to hope that **"Milun"** is a thinly disguised biography of William Marshal—a medieval roman à clef.

Of course, this identification must remain highly speculative. For our purposes, however, it does not finally matter whether the Count William of the ***Fables*** was William Marshal or another of the king's powerful clients, say, William of Mandeville, the Earl of Essex (on Mandeville's career, see Keefe 1983, 112-15). Marshal's well-chronicled life helps us to understand the ways men of his status negotiated the patronage networks of Henry's court even if he was not one of Marie's patrons (and he certainly moved in the same court circles as Marie). The complexity of these networks is implied when Marie describes Milun's son's successes in Brittany:

> There he spent lavishly and tourneyed
> and became acquainted with rich men.
> In every joust he entered,
> he was judged the best combatant.
> He loved poor knights;
> what he gained from rich ones
> he gave to them and thus retained them in his service;
> he was generous in all his spending.
>
> (La despendi e turneia,
> As riches hummes s'acuinta.
> Unques ne vint en nul estur
> Que l'en nel tenist al meillur.
> Les povres chevaliers amot;
> Ceo que des riches gaainot
> Lur donout e sis reteneit,
> E mut largement despendeit.)

(Lines 321-28)

This passage illustrates several features of patronage relationships that are crucial to our arguments about Marie.[8] Patronage relations differ from other forms of exchange in that they are not one-time exchanges, but involve long-term obligation and credit. They are particularistic and diffuse rather than legal or contractual. Unlike other, impersonal forms of exchange that alienate individuals from one another, gift giving draws individuals together, establishing personal bonds between them, which is why terms such as *love,* applied above to Milun's son's relations with "poor knights," are often used to describe the relationship. Despite this affective dimension, however, patron-client relations are marked by extreme inequality, which in this passage is marked by the distance between the wealth of Milun's son and the poverty of the knights he supports. Nonetheless, patronage relations are entered into voluntarily and, as a result, are highly unstable; they can be terminated voluntarily by either party. For this reason, it would not be unusual for a client to seek out more than one patron or even to incur obligations on both sides of a conflict between two patrons. Because of the pervasiveness of patronage in twelfth-century England, all but the most powerful men would be patrons and clients simultaneously. (Even the king, who was the vassal of the king of France, was not excepted.) In the passage above, Milun's son gives to the poor knights who are his clients what he receives from rich ones who are his patrons. This economy of expenditure requires that gifts continually circulate; they cannot be hoarded. The circuit of the gift traces the complex web of relationships that crisscross the French and English aristocracies during the late twelfth century, as Marshal's well-documented career suggests.

Patronage relations always involve the exchange of different kinds of resources. These resources might be material and economic (such as the wealth Milun's son dispenses) or political and military (the support he receives from the knights who benefit from his generosity); often they were intangible, but no less vital, resources such as prestige, influence, and status. What facilitated the exchange of these different kinds of resources was symbolic capital—Pierre Bourdieu's term for those distinctions (honor, reputation, prestige) that in a precapitalist economy could be converted into material wealth (1977, 178). In a capitalist economy, money functions as a general symbolic equivalent, that is, it serves as an excluded bearer of value that establishes equivalences among commodities (Goux 1996). In precapitalist societies in which even money must bear the king's image so that its value is guaranteed by his prestige, symbolic capital would serve the function of general symbolic equivalent. For this reason, it is important to see the interrelationship between political forms of patronage, such as that enjoyed by William Marshal, and the literary patronage that Marie seeks in her prologue to the *Fables*. They circulated interchangeably. Literary patronage is but one specific instance of a social institution that organized social, political, economic, and cultural relations at every level of society.

Gender and class identities among the male English aristocracy at the end of the twelfth century, then, were produced through a homosocial arrangement in which relationships between men were marked by potent affective ties. The "hordes of younger sons" dispossessed by primogeniture who became bachelor knights may even, Carolyn Dinshaw suggests, have provoked anxieties about homosexual activity (1994, 222). There is some historical evidence to support Dinshaw's speculations that same-sex eroticism was widely feared where groups of bachelor knights congregated; several medieval writers associate the male aristocracy with homosexuality.[9] Although panic about sodomitical practices among knights did not reach its peak until 1307, with the trials and executions of the Templars, it is nonetheless already present in the twelfth century.[10] Saint Bernard, writing at roughly the same time as Marie, expresses disgust with the contamination of knighthood by feminine decoration: "You cover your horses with silks, and I do not know what hanging rags cover your breastplates; you paint your banners, shields and saddles; you decorate your bridles and spurs all over with gold and silver and precious stones, and with such pomp you hasten to death with shameful fury and impudent foolishness. Are these knightly insignia or are they rather ornaments for women?" (quoted in Barber 1978, 7). While this kind of effeminate profligacy was not invariably associated with same-sex eroticism, the two are linked often enough, especially by clerical writers. Orderic Vitalis, for instance, condemned the court of William Rufus, charging that "the effeminate predominated everywhere and revelled without restraint, while filthy catamites, fit only to perish in the flames, abandoned themselves to the foulest practices of Sodom" (quoted in Greenberg 1988, 292). The twelfth-century framers of the rule governing the Knights Templar expressed horror "when a brother was tainted with the filthy, stinking sin of sodomy, which is so filthy and so stinking and so repugnant that it should not be named" (quoted in Barber 1994, 227).

This panic specifically targeted bachelor knights, primarily because these "hordes" of young knights were bound together by the affective ties of gift giving—and receiving—which created personal relationships encoded in discourses about "love." Chivalric texts like Marie's *lais* must vigilantly guard against the slippage from the homosocial to the homoerotic that lurks in the semiotic structures of such relationships. Epithets describing social status, like those cataloged by Glyn Burgess (1985, 73)—*"proz," "hardi," "fier," "bel," "fort," "vaillant," "franc,"* and *"curteis"*—function interchangeably in the chivalric world to describe both martial and amatory prowess. The potential semantic confusion between the two domains requires the reassertion and policing of heteronormativity. Within this homosocial structure, women were required to mediate male-male intercourse; they did so by acting as "surrogate" patrons. One way these knights veiled their appeals for patronage to their lord was through erotic appeals to his wife. William Marshal, according to one story, was exiled from young Henry's court and nearly ruined because of rumors of an adulterous relationship with Henry's wife, Margaret.[11] Yet the competition for the favors of the lady of the castle, favors that were seen as conduits for the patron's favor, must have been just as keen among the knights as the martial competition of tournaments. By recasting the essentially homosocial relationships of patronage within the erotic fictions of heterosexuality, the twelfth-century aristocracy fashioned new political and economic roles for women, roles that Marie explores in the *lai* **"Lanval."**

The romances that propagated the ideologies of courtly love were primarily a means of articulating the hierarchical relations among men.[12] The bachelor knights celebrated in most of Marie's *lais,* however, stood at the center of several hierarchical and gendered structures of relationships—both male-male and male-female—whose coherence was sustained by the loyalty required

of the patron-client relationship. Marie's *lais* tend to romanticize the gender relations of patronage, while, as Duby argues, Jean's chronicle of William Marshal casts a "harsh light" on the relations between men and women at the end of the twelfth century and reveals the subordination of heterosocial relations to the homosocial relations between men (Duby 1985, 47). Reading Marie's literary text in relation to Duby's historical text enables us to explore the roles that gender plays in the distribution of wealth governed by the unspoken rules or "customs" of patronage. Burgess argues that Marie's heroes are predominantly from the class of "young, active well-connected knights in search of personal happiness," lords or potential lords (1985, 73). Yet many of Marie's *lais* focus on the hero's (Milun, Lanval, Tristan) initial distance from the centers of economic, political, and sexual power. The economic situation of Marie's heroes is more complex than Burgess suggests; we are interested in the possibilities for advancement that the patronage system of feudalism offered for less well endowed bachelor knights, particularly in their appeals for patronage through elaborate fictions of erotic love for the wives of their overlords. The remainder of this article, then, examines anxieties about women's necessary but dangerous participation in the networks of patron-client relationships that governed the distribution of wealth in twelfth-century England.

"Lanval," Marie's only Arthurian *lai*, offers a textbook view of these operations of patronage. It opens by calling attention to the lavish patronage dispensed in Arthur's court. Arthur, we are told:

> Gave out many rich gifts:
> to counts and barons,
> members of the Round Table—
> such a company had no equal in all the world—
> he distributed wives and lands,
> to all but one who had served him.
> That was Lanval.
>
> (Asez i duna riches duns
> E as cuntes e as baruns.
> A ceus de la Table Roünde—
> N'ot tant de teus en tut le munde—
> Femmes e teres departi,
> Fors a un sul ki l'ot servi:
> Ceo fu Lanval.)

(Lines 13-19)

Note the prominence in the opening verses of words about giving—"duns," "duna," "despendu," "departi"—which calls attention to the ways gift-giving organizes relationships among men. As it was in the historical account of William Marshal and in the *lai* **"Milun,"** the distribution of wives and lands is intricately linked, the one of necessity implying the other. Men deprived of wealth and status by the rigid hierarchies of genealogy and primogeniture can still attain both through gifts of women and land from more powerful men.

In this passage, only Lanval is untouched by Arthur's generosity, which raises questions about his place in the interlocking structures of genealogy and patronage that determine whether an individual knight inherited wealth or acquired it. We are told that "the king gave him nothing / Nor did Lanval ask" (li reis rien ne li dona, / Ne Lanval ne li demanda [lines 31-32]), but the *lai* never makes clear why Lanval needs patronage nor why he is passed by, even though his rank would seem to make him an attractive client, since "He was the son of a king of high degree" (Fiz a rei fu, de haut parage [line 27]). David Chamberlain sees Lanval as a royal heir with enormous prospects who foolishly abandons his legacy for the self-gratification of illicit fornication, but he overlooks Marie's emphasis on the knight's extreme poverty *before* his affair and the consequences of that poverty (1994, 19). Chamberlain's argument equates genealogy and wealth in twelfth-century Anglo-Norman culture, assuming that high birth necessarily implied wealth or at least the promise of wealth. But, as Susan Crane has argued, the Norman nobility saw a gradual deterioration in its economic and social position between 1066 and 1400. Moving out of baronial status was as easy as moving into it, so that individuals could not rely on ancestry or title alone to establish themselves (Crane 1986, 8). Marie is frustratingly ambiguous both about Lanval's expectations and the causes of his poverty; as in most of the *lais,* she offers little information concerning her protagonist's land holdings. She tells us only that Lanval has expended all of his wealth and hints that his distance from his father's lands may make him a stranger and thus someone suspicious, a "hum estrange" (strange man [line 36]), "luin ert de sun heritage" (far from his heritage [line 28]). Lanval has gambled on securing the patronage of a remote king apparently more powerful than his father, but because the pursuit of patronage requires expenditure, Arthur's subsequent neglect has serious consequences for Lanval, who can no longer support his own retinue of clients. As a failed client, he is unable to fulfill his responsibilities as a patron; he is in no position to give gifts.

In Marie's *lai,* then, a bachelor knight's survival in Arthur's court depends on the successful acquisition of patronage from other males. However, Marie also complicates the gender relations implied by this model of patronage, considering the aristocratic woman's ability to accumulate and dispense capital within such a homosocial world. She provides two paradigms of the woman as patron, one rooted in the erotic fictions of patronage and the other in the structure of exogamy and

intellectual property regimes. The first paradigm is represented by Arthur's queen, the second by the fairy woman Lanval meets when he leaves Arthur's court.

As a result of Lanval's social, political, and economic disenfranchisement as a failed client and patron, he is pushed to the geographic margins of Arthur's kingdom. Unable to take part in the exchange of capital and "depressed and very worried . . . a strange man, without friends" (Mut est dolenz, mut est pensis . . . Hum estrange descunseillez [lines 34-35]), Lanval leaves Arthur's court, traveling until he reaches the kingdom's outer boundary, a stream his horse refuses to cross. Having arrived some distance—metaphoric, if not literal—from Arthur's court, where he was apportioned neither women nor money, Lanval encounters an exceedingly beautiful damsel who proclaims her love for him. The love that Lanval would owe Arthur—if the king were a reliable patron—is transferred to a mysterious fairy mistress, and issues of economics become issues of courtly love, although the text never loses sight of the economic motives that fuel even extramarital love.

Lanval is first approached by two extraordinarily beautiful and "richly dressed" (Vestues furent richement [line 57]) women, one of whom is carrying finely made dishes of gold. He is led to a tent whose opulence is incalculable (lines 80-106). Over and over again, the poet asserts that there are no commodities on earth equivalent to the wealth of the smallest part of the tent. Marie examines the tent piecemeal; rather than being a single commodity, it represents a whole series of undifferentiated commodities. Neither Queen Semiramis nor the emperor Octavian "could have paid for one of the flaps" (N'esligasent le destre pan). The eagle on top is also priceless ("De cel ne sai dire le pris"); the bedclothes alone are worth a castle ("Li drap valeient un chastel"); and there is no king on earth who could buy even the cords and poles that hold the tent up ("Suz ciel n'ad rei kis esligat / Pur nul aveir k'il i donast). In describing the tent, Marie alludes to a rudimentary form of economic exchange in which money has not yet become the general symbolic expression of the value of all commodities (Goux 1996). Each commodity in this description both is and is not a part of the system of economic exchange that Marx in *Das Kapital* called the extended form of value, in which "for any one commodity there are numerous elementary expressions of value, according as it is brought into a value relation with this or that other commodity. . . . The value of any one commodity, such as linen [here we might think of the bedclothes], is expressed in terms of numberless other elements of the world of commodities [e.g., castles]. Any commodity you please to select may serve as mirror of the linen's value" (Goux 1996, 15).[13] This passage, with its elaborate denial of equivalency, serves to mystify the processes of economic transformation at work in twelfth-century England.

The form of primitive accumulation described in Marx's text bears more than a passing resemblance to the system of patronage networks that dominated Norman political life. On the one hand, "the exchange value of [a] single commodity is . . . fully expressed in the endless number of equations in which the use value of all other commodities forms its equivalents" (Goux 1996, 15), just as the client receives the value conferred by the patron (or even by multiple patrons who all give value to many different clients). On the other hand, "each type of equivalent commodity is itself involved in other relationships, where it in turn acts as relative form to an infinite number of equivalents" (Goux 1996, 15), just as in political relations clients become patrons and, in turn, confer value on their clients. Both describe articulated and disseminated networks of political and economic relations that were not yet centralized in twelfth-century England and France.

The tent's female occupant represents the promise of limitless wealth in the midst of Lanval's extreme need. Not only are her surroundings described as fabulously rich, her very body exudes wealth. Marie's descriptions both eroticize wealth (the lady somehow manages to be simultaneously dressed in sumptuous ermine and purple and almost completely naked) and commodify the body, highlighting the circulation between the discourses of desire and those of economics. In a gift-giving economy, such as the Norman court for which Marie produced her *lais,* exchange is erotic in the sense that it involves attraction, union, an affection that binds individuals (men as well as men and women) together, as opposed to the rationality and impersonality of market exchange (Hyde 1983, 60). The lady's studied nudity reveals a body that has been completely objectified. It is yet another marvelous and priceless artifact—another piece in the construction of the tableau of wealth that represents a projection of every bachelor knight's desire for prosperity and abundance. It alludes to a heteronormative sexuality specific to the romance, in which the circulation and exchange of women among men facilitates the circulation and exchange of wealth (see Krueger 1993, 39-50). Yet the tableau also carries a hint of danger because the lady's wealth appears to be entirely at her own disposal and not under the control of patriarchal property regimes (see Chamberlain 1994). Because she is, quite literally, a spectacle—something to be looked at—she is also powerful. She is a patron in her own right and not simply a vehicle for the patronage of wealthy men. Conventional feminist analyses of women's objectification are insufficient to understand this sort of spectacle. Passivity does not always or necessarily connote weakness and vulnerability to exploitation, as much feminist writing on the male gaze

suggests.[14] Within patronage systems, passivity or inactivity—as well as spectacle—often signals the power of the patron; others act on the patron's behalf. The fairy mistress's passivity, like Arthur's, is an expression of her power as a patron. She enables the activity of others.

Just as the mysterious maiden's wealth cannot be calculated because, while it can remind us of the extended form of value, it does not circulate within that system of economic exchanges, Lanval's worth as Arthur's client is unknown because he is excluded from the network of relationships that make up Arthur's court. Only after Lanval receives the patronage of the fairy woman—such extraordinary patronage that it enables him to act as a fairly conspicuous patron himself—does he become visible at Arthur's court. The text makes clear that the fairy mistress's "gift" of her love is also a gift of patronage. The exchange of wealth is chronologically and causally linked to the exchange of sexual love: "Afterwards she gave him a gift" (Un dun li ad duné aprés [line 135]). The gift she gives confers on Lanval inexhaustible wealth:

> Now Lanval is well cared for.
> The more lavishly he spends,
> the more gold and silver he will have.
>
> (Mut est Lanval bien assenez:
> Cum plus despendra richement,
> E plus avra or e argent!)

(Lines 140-42)

This largess makes Lanval in turn a powerful patron, able to dispense gifts and establish new relationships when he returns to Arthur's court:

> There was no knight in the city
> who really needed a place to stay
> whom he didn't invite to join him
> to be well and richly served.
> Lanval gave rich gifts,
> Lanval released prisoners,
> Lanval dressed jongleurs,
> Lanval offered great honors.
> There was no stranger or friend
> to whom Lanval didn't give.
>
> (N'ot en la vile chevalier
> Ki de surjur ait grant mestier
> Que il ne face a lui venir
> E richement et bien servir.
> Lanval donout les riches duns,
> Lanval aquitout les prisuns,
> Lanval vesteit les jugleürs,
> Lanval feseit les granz honurs!
> N'i ot estrange ne privé
> A ki Lanval n'eüst doné.)

(Lines 205-14)

His return to court is accompanied by a burst of activity, emphasized by all of the active verbs in the series of anaphoric parallels: he gives, releases, dresses, offers. It is as if only the circulation of gifts enables activity at court; failure to do so results in paralysis—the sleep that nearly overtakes Lanval when he lies down beside the stream. Lanval's earlier inactivity in the public sphere of homosocial relations at Arthur's court (he would not even ask for patronage), had the effect of feminizing him—at least in relation to other bachelor knights. However, once set into motion by his powerful female patron, he assumes the aggressive masculine position of the successful client who can dispense gifts of his own.

Only by assuming his place within the heteronormative order—by attaching himself to a woman—can Lanval acquire the capital to take on the role of patron. However, his acquisition of a lover also creates competition among patrons for Lanval's services as a client. The fairy mistress is more deserving than Arthur of Lanval's love both because she is physically attractive and because she possesses more wealth than the king. These two patrons' competition for Lanval as client is played out in the more overt contest between the fairy mistress and Arthur's queen for Lanval's love—which effectively displaces fears about homoeroticism by disguising the affective bonds of homosocial patronage as heterosexual love. The mediation of women is required in this process. Arthur's queen insists on her role as Lanval's lover and is infuriated when he refuses her, for her symbolic capital is derived not only through her relationship with her husband but through her participation in his patronage networks as well.

Only when Lanval has demonstrated his wealth and become a desirable client does the queen assert her right to his clientage by declaring her "love" for him:

> Lanval, I have shown you much honor,
> I have cherished you and loved you.
> You may have all my love;
> just tell me what you desire.
>
> (Lanval, mut vus ai honuré
> E mut cheri e mut amé;
> Tute m'amur poëz aveir.
> Kar me dites vostre voleir!)

(Lines 263-66)

Lanval's response, that he is unwilling to be the queen's lover because of his love for Arthur, demonstrates how very confused the situation can become when female patronage networks function via adultery. Moreover, the queen insists that Lanval refuses her largess not because of his appropriate love for his king but for altogether different, and dishonorable, reasons (a confusion not as surprising, we have been arguing, as it might at first glance appear):

> People have often told me
> that you have no interest in women.
> You have fine looking boys
> with whom you enjoy yourself.
>
> (Asez le m'ad hum dit sovent
> Que des femmes n'avez talent!
> Vallez avez bien afeitiez,
> Ensemble od eus vus deduiez.)

(Lines 279-82)

In effect, she accuses Lanval of the sodomy so repugnant to the framers of the Templar Rule that "it should not be named." If the courtly love tradition served as an elaborate code for disguising the economic operations of patronage, as we suggest, then it is possible that the queen is acting as a kind of surrogate for her husband and that the characteristic triangle of courtly love—Arthur, Lancelot, Guinevere; Mark, Tristan, Isolde—transforms what might otherwise appear a homosexual—or at least homoerotic—relationship into a heterosexual alliance. In rejecting the queen's love, Lanval, while not formally renouncing his vassalage (indeed the reason he gives is his loyalty to Arthur), calls into question the efficacy of Arthur's patronage and with it the whole facade of heteronormative sexuality that thinly disguises the homosocial—and even homoerotic—bonding on which the military culture depends.

The confusions in this scene reveal the contradictions at the heart of gender relations within the twelfth-century aristocracy, which required that a wife be simultaneously chaste (to ensure the legitimacy of her children) and sexually available to others (as a conduit for her husband's patronage). The queen's declaration of her patronage (as her love for Lanval)—and her competition with another woman for that patronage—places Arthur in the somewhat bizarre position of being betrayed and ultimately angered because Lanval refuses to be seduced by the queen. The actual charge for which Lanval is tried is not attempted rape or seduction of the queen; rather, he is accused of insulting the queen by boasting of another love:

> The king spoke against his vassal . . .
> he accused him of felony,
> charged him with a misdeed—
> a love that he had boasted of,
> which made the queen angry.
> No one but the king accused him.
>
> (Li reis parla vers sun vassal . . .
> De felunie le retta
> E d'un mesfait l'acheisuna,
> D'une amur dunt il se vanta,
> E ma dame s'en curuça.
> Nuls ne l'apele fors le rei.)

(Lines 437-43)

It does not reflect well on the king that his wife is not the most successful patron in the land, that Lanval is not willing to give her his love, is not glad to have her, despite all that she can offer. For the queen—and, indeed, for Arthur—there can be no possibility that some other person is better suited to be Lanval's patron.

The model of woman as surrogate patron, represented by the queen as well as by the great female patrons of the Anglo-Norman period (Eleanor of Aquitaine, Marie of Champagne, Adele of Champagne, Eleanor of Provence, and Eleanor of Castile)[15]—stands in opposition to another model, represented by the fairy mistress. Marie's use of the fairy mistress as a female patron able to control and dispense both her own sexuality and her own fortune, unconstrained by father, lover, or husband, represents a significant departure from routine marital arrangements of the twelfth-century aristocracy. To be sure, her existence holds out the prospect of exogamy, marriage outside of the group, as an opportunity for enrichment for those who have been disenfranchised by the institutions of primogeniture and patronage—the ultimate wish fulfillment for bachelor knights, who were among the most disenfranchised members of the Norman ruling class (Crouch 1990, 26-28). At the same time, however, her considerable largess suggests a model of empowerment (even if it is only a fantasy)[16] for women in medieval society, especially for learned women and artists like Marie. The fairy mistress is empowered by the magic she possesses, by her association with a supernatural world of fairy. This magic serves to mystify the means by which the maiden produces wealth and escapes the disciplines designed to control female sexuality. Michelle Freeman argues that, in a similar manner, Marie stresses in her prologue her own active role in formulating her *lais* themselves as gifts to be exchanged between a woman and a man, in this case her patron, Henry II (1984, 861). Like any client locked into an unequal relationship in which receiving a gift entails obligation and debt, Marie works to recast the relationship as one of equals or even to cast herself in the role of patron bestowing gifts. It does not seem surprising, then, that she creates a fairy mistress who has an inexhaustible power to give gifts.

In exchange for her patronage, Lanval is sworn never to divulge his lady's identity, never to speak of the magical source of his income or his love. The fairy mistress's magic and the secrecy required of Lanval as an initiate into her supernatural world may provide some insight into the anxieties of Marie and her audience about the competition for patronage and the circulation of intellectual property within the Anglo-Norman court. The systems of justice, finance, and administration created by Henry II required a cadre of bureaucrats who could gain access to information and to new technologies required for governing. Some of these bureaucrats came from the ranks of the so-called new men who came from outside the aristocracy and who were used by Henry to offset the power of the barons, although this distinction was never as rigid as some historians suggest and although all men in Henry's government—whether barons, bachelor knights, or bureaucrats—negotiated their relationship to the monarch through patronage, whatever their rewards (Keefe 1983, 93-96). However, while the mechanisms for rewarding warriors were well established, methods for compensating *ingenium* (intelligence or craft) were less highly developed.

Social structures had to be developed within informal patronage networks to govern the creation and dissemination of ideas. *Intellectual property* is the term used by legal scholars to refer to structures designed to regulate the value attributed to such intangibles as technological innovation, invention, and authorship and to distinguish it from the tangible products or devices produced by that knowledge (Long 1991, 846). However, because intellectual property has several characteristics that make it notoriously difficult to protect, it has been called the "law's stepchild" (Wincor 1962, 11). The most salient of these characteristics is that ideas, while often costly to develop, become valueless to their creator once they are revealed. This characteristic makes it difficult for innovators to capitalize on their ideas since investors cannot know the value of information until they have sampled it, but once they have done so, the incentive to buy is gone (Suchman 1989, 1267-69).

Most commentators identify intellectual property with "the document-intensive, governmentally administered" regimes typical of modern Western law (Suchman 1989, 1264) and, when faced with the absence of established patent, trade secret, and copyright law in early European legal history, have assumed that individuals at that time in history were not interested in protecting their rights in innovative ideas (Long 1991, 869). But it is specious to assume that because a culture does not have the same methods for protecting intellectual property as we do that it has no interest in such protection. Different regimes in different cultural contexts may accomplish much the same purpose. In cultures without established juridical procedures concerning intellectual property (and we have as yet found no evidence to suggest that Norman England had any established body of law in this area [see Pollock and Maitland 1968]), the creators of intellectual property—either individually or collectively—generally resort to other means to assure the profitability of their creations, whether literary or technological. For instance, they might "lock [the] idea into physical commodities" (Suchman 1989, 1269), as in the Middle Ages, when authors' ideas were inseparable from the manuscripts that conveyed them. But this mechanism was of only limited utility, for once those manuscripts began to circulate, authors had no control over how their ideas were used and appropriated, as Marie complains on several occasions.

Mark Suchman has argued that in preliterate cultures the invocation of magic may be more effective than law as a means of protecting intellectual property: "Because the value of magic derives purely from social construction, adding magical components to a new technology costs relatively little. At the same time, magic may be much easier to monopolize than the physical process that accompanies it" (1989, 1273). Because intellectual property was difficult to control and protect, precapitalist inventors who discovered some new technique could use it to earn material and social rewards only if they could monopolize it. Such monopolies are difficult to establish, especially if the benefits promised by the technology are great and the technique simple to replicate. Magical elements attached to the process are easier to monopolize. An intellectual property regime that relies on magic requires a dual dynamic of display and secrecy in which the display—the prestidigitation— serves as a distraction that hides processes that might be easily replicated if made public. This is not to suggest that such strategic calculations always would be made consciously; even the magician may not entirely distinguish between the effective and superfluous elements of the performance.

An understanding of enchantment as an instrument of economic protection may illuminate the presence of supernatural elements in Marie's *lai*. Before we proceed, however, a few caveats are in order. We are not arguing that the Arthurian world of **"Lanval"** is a simple reflection of the court of Henry II, and we are not positing the one-to-one correspondence characteristic of allegory in which the fairy mistress's magic mirrors something literal in Marie's world. Rather, the *lai* both represents and actively shapes the interests, tastes, and anxieties of the audiences it was written to entertain. Marie's culture was not preliterate, but it was a culture in which literacy itself was an innovation. Literacy was a new technology that afforded considerable power to its possessors and so was jealously guarded by an elite to which Marie belonged. A precedent for such a monopoly, Richard Wincor suggests, might be found in the Welsh bardic system, with its "system of secret information, magic spells, sacred verse, dramatic ritual, satiric parody and enciphered writing," although its early destruction, he argues, marked the end of literary property protection in England until the advent of copyright laws (1962, 31). The Anglo-Norman culture of twelfth-century England, however, did not need to look to preliterate Celtic cultures for models of occult and mystical practices designed to monopolize intellectual property (Wincor 1962, 22-31); there were examples nearer to hand. The Church, in its jealous guarding of its scripts and rituals in an arcane and dead language, its mystical transforma-

tions of bread and wine performed behind altar screens, and its celibate priesthood, was going about the business of protecting its intellectual properties every bit as energetically as any Celtic Druid, providing a ready-made model of an intellectual property regime.

With these caveats in mind, it may not be too far-fetched to suggest that the magic of Lanval's fairy mistress provides what Suchman calls a "host," a physical model, embodying Marie's own frequently expressed anxieties about her intellectual property—her writing. Marie's identification of the magician/patron/lover with a woman suggests her own social ambitions, hinted at both by the mention of Count William in the epilogue to the *Fables* and the fear, expressed in that epilogue, of having her work—which she clearly labels as her property—claimed by "clercs":

> I am from France, my name's Marie.
> And it may hap that many a clerk
> Will claim as his what is my work.
>
> (Marie ai num, si sui de France
> Put cel estre que clerc plusur
> Prendreient sur eus mun labur.)
>
> (*Fables*, p. 256; lines 4-6)

In this passage Marie proclaims her desire to protect her intellectual labor from those clerks who would appropriate it. In the prologue to the *lai* "Guigemar," she seems equally concerned with controlling the use of her tales once she has sent them forth; in particular she appears anxious that they be seen as her property:

> Whoever deals with good material
> feels pain if it's treated improperly.
> Listen, my lords, to the words of Marie
> who does not forget her responsibilities when her turn comes.
>
> (Ki de bone mateire traite,
> Mult li peise si bien n'est faite.
> Oëz, seignurs, ke dit Marie,
> Ki en sun tens pas ne s'oblie.)
>
> (*Lais*, "Guigemar," lines 1-4)

The prologue to Marie's collection of *lais* vacillates between the need to display her abilities and a desire for secrecy. At times she proclaims her desire for fame and recognition:

> Whoever has received knowledge
> And eloquence in speech from God
> should not be silent or secretive
> but demonstrate it willingly.
>
> (Ki Deus ad duné escïence
> E de parler bone eloquence
> Ne s'en deit taisir ne celer,
> Ainz se deit voluntiers mustrer.)
>
> (*Lais*, "Prologue," lines 1-4)

At other times she stresses the necessary obscurity of knowledge:

> The custom among the ancients—
> as Priscian testifies—
> was to speak quite obscurely
> in the books they wrote,
> so that those who were to come after and study them
> might gloss the letter
> and supply its significance from their own wisdom.

> (Custume fu as ancïens
> Ceo testimoine Precïens,
> Es livres ke jadis feseient,
> Assez oscurement diseient
> Pur ceus ki a venir esteient
> E ki aprendre les deveient,
> K'i peüssent gloser la lettre
> E de lur sen le surplus mettre.)

(*Lais,* "Prologue," lines 9-16)

In this passage, obscurity functions, alongside and in contradiction to display, to protect the monopoly of the learned few. Only initiates who have passed through a rigorous apprenticeship are allowed to "gloss the letter" and to understand the mysteries of old books. Old books do not yield their secrets to just anyone; they require the services of a mediator (in this case the poet) who possesses the necessary knowledge. In this sense, the creations of storytellers are not significantly different from the mysteries of Christianity: "Unto you it is given to know the mystery of the Kingdom of God; but unto them that are without all these things are done in parable: that seeing they may see, and not perceive, and hearing they may hear, and not understand" (Mark 4:11-12). Both require the services of a specialized knowledge monopolized by a few through obfuscation and mystery.

Henry's reliance on "new men," one of whom was William Marshal, to control the increasingly complicated technologies of government enhanced the value of intellectual property, including authorship. At the same time, it created new grounds for competition, which would ultimately be reflected in the management of patronage networks. The fairy mistress of **"Lanval"** and the survival of Marie's *lais* indicate the existence of something like a "new woman" in Henry's court, a woman who—like the new men—could break out of the confines of ascribed status (the ascribed status of gender as well as that of class) and transform intellectual property into capital, a woman who could, with her own abilities, accumulate sufficient capital to receive love as a patron in her own right and not only as a conduit for her husband's patronage.

The conclusion of **"Lanval,"** in which the fairy mistress arrives in a dazzling display just in time to save Lanval, who rides off with her to Avalon, may be understood in a number of different but potentially overlapping ways. One reading suggests that Lanval must leave Arthur's court (perhaps a residue of a more ancient form of exogamy in which the male becomes part of the female's kinship group rather than the reverse, which would have been more usual in Marie's experience). Lanval must leave, we would argue, not (or at least not only) because the purity of his love would be ruined by the sterility of the Arthurian world but because the kind of power that the fairy mistress possesses, a female sexuality unrestrained by a masculine sexual economy that requires the continual circulation of women and wealth, cannot be maintained for long within the Arthurian world without becoming subordinate to the sexual economy of feudalism. A second reading suggests that the kind of patronage represented in the queen has been supplemented by a new variety of women's patronage (and there is no reason to think that the historical Marie did not have considerable patronage of her own to dispense) that ultimately derives from the accumulation, exercise, and protection of women's intellectual property. With this reading, the fairy mistress, like Merlin in other Arthurian tales (see Bloch 1983, 1-2; Shichtman and Finke 1993, 28-35), becomes a paradigm for the artist, negotiating the circulation of capital between client and patron—and seeking to acquire for herself the status of patron. David Chamberlain has argued that Marie's magical mistress is a "succubus" determined to steal Lanval's soul (1994, 22). We believe, though, that she would simply like to be his boss.

Notes

1. The anthology edited by June Hall McCash (1996a) provides good examples of this approach.

2. The various candidates for Marie have included the Abbesses of Reading and Shaftsbury (Henry II's half sister) (Rychner 1983, viii), the daughter of Waleran II, Count of Meulan (Holmes 1932; Grillo 1988), and the daughter of King Stephen (Knapton 1978). Candidates for Count William have included Guillaume of Gloucester (Rychner 1983, ix), William Longsword, and Guillaume de Mandeville, Earl of Essex, as well as William Marshal (Painter 1933).

3. Crouch accuses Duby of being uncritical of Jean's *Histoire* and of ignoring pertinent historical facts (1990, 5). But Duby is quite specific that his purpose in writing about Marshal is not to establish a "history of events"—what really happened in William Marshal's life—but to examine the "culture of chivalry" through the eyes of the men who created it. He is less interested in establishing facts than in "the way they were created," that is, in understanding how the twelfth-century Anglo-Norman aristocracy fashioned

themselves through the histories they commissioned to advance their view of events (Duby 1985, 38). Jean's biases, then, are precisely Duby's point.

4. See Crouch 1990, 5. Both Duby 1985, 36, and Crouch 1990, 3, also point out that Marshal, unlike most of his contemporaries, was completely illiterate.

5. All references to Marie's *lais* are to the edition by Jean Rychner (Marie de France 1983); all translations are by Robert Hanning and Joan Ferrante (Marie de France 1978). Subsequent references to these texts will be by line numbers only.

6. Interestingly, Northumbria is march land, bordering Scotland. The hero and heroine come from South Wales. "Milun" is the most precisely localized of Marie's *lais,* situated in the very border lands that were England's buffers against its hostile Celtic neighbors.

7. "Unc ne demanderent parent: / Sanz cunseil de tute autre gent" (lines 525-26).

8. Our analysis draws on the work of S. N. Eisenstadt and Luis Roniger, who discuss social systems that combine elements of patronage with those of ascribed status (1984, 178-84).

9. This discussion follows Leonard Barkan's characterization of homosexuality as "erotic relations of any kind between those of the same gender, whatever mentality concerning psyche, society, or identity may accompany them" (1991, 22). This approach avoids the extreme positions of John Boswell (1980), who argues for the possibility not only of homosexuality during the Middle Ages but of a gay identity more or less continuous with modern gay identity, and David Halperin (1990), who argues that because sexual identity was an invention of the nineteenth century, seeking homosexuality in history is anachronistic. See also Dinshaw (1994, 207), who argues that we can and should speak of sexuality in the Middle Ages as long as we historicize it with regard to "psyche, society, and identity," and Greenberg 1988, esp. 255-60.

10. One of the most consistent charges against Knights Templar during the fourteenth-century trials was sodomy.

11. Significantly for our argument about the primacy of male homosociality among the Norman aristocracy, the prince ultimately banished his wife and brought William back to court as a favorite; see Duby 1985, 47-54, 119-20.

12. For a summary of arguments about male homosociality in medieval courtly literature, see Finke 1996, 355-58.

13. The translations from the German that Goux gives convey more clearly the proliferation of equivalences in Marx's text than does Fowkes's English translation of *Das Kapital* (see Marx 1976, 155-56).

14. For a critique of feminist theories of the gaze, see Stanbury 1997.

15. See McCash 1996a. While these women were certainly powerful literary patrons who controlled large fortunes in their own rights, none stood outside the system of exchanges of land and women by which aristocratic men perpetuated their class privilege. On the position of the great patron queens of this period, see the essays in McCash 1996 by McCash, Lois L. Huneycutt, John Carmi Parsons, and Miriam Shadis.

16. As Louise Fradenburg has argued, fantasy can be a potent carrier of social meaning (1996, 208-12).

References

Barber, Malcolm. 1978. *The Trial of the Templars.* Cambridge: Cambridge University Press.

———. 1994. *The New Knighthood: A History of the Order of the Temple.* Cambridge: Cambridge University Press.

Barkan, Leonard. 1991. *Transuming Passion: Ganymede and the Erotics of Humanism.* Stanford, Calif.: Stanford University Press.

Bloch, R. Howard. 1983. *Etymologies and Genealogies: A Literary Anthropology of the Middle Ages.* Chicago: University of Chicago Press.

Boswell, John. 1980. *Christianity, Social Tolerance, and Homosexuality: Gay People in Western Europe from the Beginning of the Christian Era to the Fourteenth Century.* Chicago: University of Chicago Press.

Bourdieu, Pierre. 1977. *Outline of a Theology of Practice.* Trans. Richard Nice. Cambridge: Cambridge University Press.

Burgess, Glyn. 1985. "Social Status in the Lais of Marie de France." In *The Spirit of the Court: Selected Proceedings of the Fourth Congress on the International Courtly Literature Society,* ed. Glyn S. Burgess, Robert A. Taylor, Alan Deyermond, Dennis Green, and Beryl Rowland, 69-78. Dover, N.H.: Brewer.

Chamberlain, David. 1994. "Marie de France's Arthurian Lai: Subtle and Political." In *Culture and the King: The Social Implications of the Arthurian Legend,* ed. Martin B. Shichtman and James P. Carley, 15-34. Albany, N.Y.: SUNY Press.

Crane, Susan. 1986. *Insular Romance: Politics, Faith, and Culture in Anglo-Norman and Middle English Literature.* Berkeley and Los Angeles: University of California Press.

Crouch, David. 1990. *William Marshal: Court, Career, and Chivalry in the Angevin Empire, 1147-1219.* London: Longman.

Dinshaw, Carolyn. 1994. "A Kiss Is Just a Kiss: Heterosexuality and Its Consolations in *Sir Gawain and the Green Knight.*" *Diacritics* 24(2-3):205-26.

Duby, Georges. 1985. *William Marshal: Flower of Chivalry.* Trans. Richard Howard. New York: Pantheon.

Eisenstadt, S. N., and Luis Roniger. 1984. *Patrons, Clients, and Friends: Interpersonal Relations and the Structure of Trust in Society.* Cambridge: Cambridge University Press.

Finke, Laurie A. 1992. *Feminist Theory, Women's Writing.* Ithaca, N.Y.: Cornell University Press.

————. 1996. "Sexuality in Medieval French Literature: 'Separés on est Ensemble.'" In *Handbook of Medieval Sexuality,* ed. Vern L. Bullough and James A. Brundage, 345-68. New York: Garland.

Fradenburg, Louise O. 1996. "'Fulfild of fairye': The Social Meaning of Fantasy in the Wife of Bath's Prologue and Tale." In *Geoffrey Chaucer: The Wife of Bath,* ed. Peter G. Beidler, 205-20. Boston: Bedford.

Freeman, Michelle A. 1984. "Marie de France's Poetics of Silence: The Implications for a Feminine *Translatio.*" *PMLA* 99(5):860-83.

Goux, Jean-Joseph. 1996. *Symbolic Economics after Marx and Freud.* Trans. Jennifer Curtis Gage. Ithaca, N.Y.: Cornell University Press.

Green, Judith A. 1986. *The Government of England under Henry I.* Cambridge: Cambridge University Press.

Greenberg, David F. 1988. *The Construction of Homosexuality.* Chicago: University of Chicago Press.

Grillo, Peter R. 1988. "Was Marie de France the Daughter of Waleran II, Count of Meulan?" *Medium Aevum* 57(2):269-74.

Halperin, David. 1990. *One Hundred Years of Homosexuality and Other Essays on Greek Love.* New York: Routledge.

Holmes, U. T. 1932. "New Thoughts on Marie de France." *Studies in Philology* 29(1):1-10.

Huneycutt, Lois L. 1996. "'Proclaiming her Dignity Abroad': The Literary and Artistic Networks of Matilda of Scotland, Queen of England." In McCash 1996a, 155-74.

Hyde, Lewis. 1983. *The Gift: Imagination and the Erotic Life of Property.* New York: Vintage.

Keefe, Thomas K. 1983. *Feudal Assessments and the Political Community under Henry II and His Sons.* Berkeley and Los Angeles: University of California Press.

Knapton, Antoinette. 1978. "A la recherche de Marie de France." *Romance Notes* 19(2):248-53.

Krueger, Roberta A. 1993. *Women Readers and the Ideology of Gender in Old French Verse Romance.* Cambridge: Cambridge University Press.

Long, Pamela O. 1991. "Invention, Authorship, 'Intellectual Property,' and the Origins of Patents: Notes toward a Conceptual History." *Technology and Culture* 32(4):846-84.

Marie de France. 1978. *The Lais of Marie de France.* Ed. and trans. Robert Hanning and Joan Ferrante. New York: Dutton.

————. 1983. *Les Lais de Marie de France.* Ed. Jean Rychner. Paris: Honoré Champion.

————. 1987. *Fables.* Ed. and trans. Harriet Spiegel. Toronto: University of Toronto Press.

Marx, Karl. 1976. *Capital: A Critique of Political Economy.* Vol. 1. Trans. Ben Fowkes. New York: Penguin.

McCash, June Hall, ed. 1996a. *The Cultural Patronage of Medieval Women.* Athens: University of Georgia Press.

McCash, June Hall. 1996b. "The Cultural Patronage of Medieval Women: An Overview." In McCash 1996a, 1-49.

Painter, Sidney. 1933. "To Whom Were Dedicated the Fables of Marie de France?" *Modern Language Notes* 48(6):367-69.

Parsons, John Carmi. 1996. "Of Queens, Courts, and Books: Reflections on the Literary Patronage of Thirteenth-Century Plantagenet Queens." In McCash 1996a, 175-201.

Pollock, Frederick, and Frederick William Maitland. 1968. *The History of English Law before the Time of Edward I.* 2 vols. Cambridge: Cambridge University Press.

Rychner, Jean. 1983. Introduction to Marie de France 1983, viii-xlv.

Shadis, Miriam. 1996. "Piety, Politics, and Power: The Patronage of Leonor of England and Her Daughters Berenguela of Leon and Blanche of Castile." In McCash 1996a, 202-27.

Shichtman, Martin B., and Laurie A. Finke. 1993. "Profiting from the Past: History as Symbolic Capital in the *Historia Regum Britanniae.*" *Arthurian Literature* 12:1-35.

Stanbury, Sarah. 1997. "Regimes of the Visual in Premodern England: Gaze, Body, and Chaucer's Clerk's Tale." *New Literary History* 28(2):261-90.

Suchman, Mark C. 1989. "Invention and Ritual: Notes on the Interrelation of Magic and Intellectual Property in Preliterate Societies." *Columbia Law Review* 89(6):1264-69.

Wincor, Richard. 1962. *From Ritual to Royalties: An Anatomy of Literary Property.* New York: Walker & Co.

Hans R. Runte (essay date 2000)

SOURCE: Runte, Hans R. "Marie de France's Courtly Fables." In *'Por le soie amisté': Essays in Honor of Norris J. Lacy,* edited by Keith Busby and Catherine M. Jones, pp. 453-62. Amsterdam, The Netherlands: Rodopi, 2000.

[In the following essay, Runte summarizes the findings of his research into the sources of Marie's Fables, *concluding that the best of them derive from Latin and French, rather than English, models.]*

"Au commencement étaient les *Sept sages de Rome.*" They figure in Norris Lacy's doctoral edition and study of "La femme au tombeau,"[1] and they were the subject of my own thesis, under his direction, five years later.[2] Unavoidably, his fabliau widow and my *vidua* lead to Marie de France's twenty-fifth fable; and Marie's "D'un hume [et de] sa femme"[3] was to lead me to the rest of her fables. Given this filiation, it pains me to conclude, after due consideration, that so many of Marie's fables are so bad that the better ones need a kind of "défense et illustration."

The indubitable unevenness of Marie's collection may possibly have something to do with the fact that it was commissioned: not only were her fables not a labor of love, but they were an inappropriate work to have commissioned in the first place. Indeed, what use could Count William and his court possibly have had for a collection of fables? Would he or any of his have profited from their self-evident, often platitudinous morals? Most of what Marie came up with to fill her collection of 104 stories belongs to a world far removed from courtly concerns and far removed from her own preoccupations, belongs, precisely, to the world in which she claims to have found her major source: the uneducated, low-class, English-speaking world of the elusive Alfred.

The need of the masses for a book of basic moral precepts is the most compelling argument yet for acknowledging the existence of Alfred's vanished work. But it is inconceivable that William should have asked Marie to make such a low-class work linguistically accessible to the French-speaking upper classes, unless he was looking for a snob's delicious *frisson* in finding out how the other half lives. In fact, William summoned Marie to "retraire plusurs paroles qui i sunt" ("Prologue"[4]), in other words, to edit her model or models, to leave things out, to replace them by others, in short, to put together a collection materially like Alfred's but ideologically intended for an un-Alfredian, courtly audience.

In twelve of the fourteen manuscripts which contain her "Epilogue," Marie is said to have "rimé" her stories, which is infinitely less restrictive and infinitely more consistent with William's commission than to have "translaté" them, and which should also have been, from the beginning, the first and last word on Marie as translator of Alfred.[5] Yet even so, to William's taste perhaps and certainly to mine, Marie has taken far too little liberty with Alfredian or Alfredesque material, excising too few passages from it, rejecting too little of it, and adapting some of it too imperfectly: there remain in her collection far too many stories spinning homespun truisms at which a courtly audience could only have scoffed.

Marie's is an atypically large collection which she may have found difficult to fill: making Alfred courtly where possible is one thing, but replacing his unsalvageable pieces with court-friendly new ones is quite another. Certainly Marie dipped into the Latin fable tradition, through and beyond Alfred, as well as into her own, continental, oral stock of wisdom stories, but lacunæ remained, which she filled with what was a hand: bits from, and from around, Alfred and his English milieu. If I seem to be implying that Marie's bad fables, as well as her humdrum ones, are of English provenance, and that the rest come from Latin and French stock, I mean to do just that, "à quelques nuances près."

Fully 70% (7 out of 10) of the fables I consider very bad (12, 21, 32 // 43, 55, 59, 66, 93, 94, 96) neither Alfred nor Marie could have gotten from the Latin Nilantius collection (corresponding to fables 1-40), for they are not to be found therein. Fable 66 represents this group well, its upshot being that a wolf will be a wolf will be a wolf: grey, mean, ugly, base and sly. So does fable 43, which teaches that the ignorant believe what cannot be, to wit, a peasant having been impregnated by a beetle which has crept up his "pertus [. . .] overt" (4) while he was sleeping naked in the sun . . . That Count William had such lessons in mind, and that such stories were part of Marie's cultural baggage I would find highly unlikely.

74% (20 out of 27) of the fables I consider excruciatingly platitudinous (9, 22, 24, 26, 31, 39, 40 // 42, 48, 54, 61, 64, 67, 74, 79-81, 83, 87, 90-92, 98, 100-103) are equally absent from the known Latin collection and may well have delighted the kind of audience for which Alfred wrote them down. Three examples will suffice:

"Pur ceo chastie le sené: / Que hum ne deie mal cunseil creire, / Ne mençuinge dire pur veire" (90: 22-24); "As prudes hummes e as leiaus / Avient suvent damage e maus / De la cumpainie as feluns; / Mauvais en est lur guerduns" (79: 39-42); and

Issi vet il des robeürs,
Des laruns e des tricheürs:
Quant il asemblent autri aveir,
Mut le peot hum sovent veer,
Qu'il n'en sunt gueres amendé;
Tuz jurz vivent en poverté.

(98: 13-18)

With the next group of fables the possibility that Marie side-stepped Alfred and took some of her inspiration directly from the Latin begins to increase. These are "real" fables in the traditional, universally understood Aesopian, Romulean, Phaedrian or La Fontainean sense, with useful, robust morals about greed (5, 52, 58, 63, 68), flattery (13), pretentiousness (15, 41, 77), pride (75), and so forth, and 38% (5 out of 13) are in Nilantius (1, 5, 13, 15, 28 // 41, 52, 53, 58, 63, 68, 75, 77). Of course, these successful fables may be what Alfred was capable of writing on good days, but his track record, as shown above, would militate against it, leaving Marie looking for models in Alfred's model and other non-English sources.

When Marie turns sociologist or social psychologist (in fables 4, 7, 8, 10, 11A, 11B, 38 // 49, 86, 88, 97), the possibility of Nilantian and French influences becomes a 63% likelihood (7 out of 11), William's ears prick up, as do ours, and it may be readily agreed that Alfred would have been incapable of penning such observations; the very notion of poor folk striving to "se [. . .] eshaucer" (97: 24), for example, may have been alien to him. Yet the rigid stratification of society into rich and poor, honest and wicked, haughty and humble, evil and good is precisely the theme of these eleven fables. Marie is brutally articulate in her condemnation of some of William's peers: the rich have no compunction about forcing the poor, by means of lies, trickery and false witnesses, to go to court (4); they value glory most and do not care if "li povres perdra s'amur" (11B: 46); and among the lords there are some so wicked that their subjects are grateful for not being killed for services rendered (7). Then, before displaying a few instances of social dialectics, Marie inserts a cautionary tale: the rich "Ja del povre n'avera merci / Pur sa pleinte, ne pur sun cri. / Mes si cil se pust dunc venger, / Sil verreit l'um tost suppleer" (10: 19-22). Play with opposition, contradiction and paradox is more fully developed in the story about those wicked, corrupt and evil folks who,

Quant uns produm les met avant
E par lui sunt riche e manant,

S'il surpuient meuz de lui;
Tuz jurs li frunt hunte e ennui.
A celui funt il tut le pis
Ki al desus les ad mis.

(49: 27-32)

William and his court would have derived intellectual enjoyment from this way of putting things, as they would have from the lesson of fable 86:

Issi fet del natre felun:
Quant il ad bien en bandun,
Vers les meillurs trop se noblee.
E de parole s'esrichee;
Par grant desdein les cuntralie.
Neis si nul est que bien li die
La verité de sun afeire,
En pleine curt, le(s) fera teire.

(21-28; see also fable 8)

Two noteworthily insightful lessons round out this group of fables: when the poor seek access to the wealthy, "Forment les quident curucier, / Damage feire e ennuier" (38: 17-18); and a reforming criminal's good intentions "turn askew" ("A mal en turne sun esper") if they are not recognized and praised (88: 36).

There are elements of rhetoric at work in these sociological fables, or echoes of courtspeak,[6] or at least hints of what was pleasing and elegant to courtly ears and minds. The search for stimulating turns of thought and phrase is carried over into the group of courtly fables proper, as in the story of the frogs who, unhappy with the log their king, drown it and replace it with an adder, who eats them: "A tel se pernent, quis destruit; / De lur aveir meine sun bruit. / Lores regretent lur bon seignur, / A ki il firent la deshonur" (18: 51-54; see also 6, 16). That this group of thirty-four fables (2, 6, 14, 16-20, 23, 25, 27, 29, 30, 33, 34-37 // 46, 47, 50, 51, 56, 57, 60, 62, 65, 70, 71, 76, 82, 85, 89, 99; 53% [18 out of 34] are also in the Nilantius) should be the largest in Marie's collection will not surprise us, for they are the very kind of fables Count William was looking for. If we interpret his commission liberally and include in it the eleven sociological fables as well as perhaps five stories on the "traitor betrayed" theme (3 // 69, 72, 78, 84) and four incipient fabliaux (44, 45, 73, 95), Marie achieves a 52% success rate (fifty-four fables) in terms of fulfilling her sponsor's wishes; not counting the fabliaux, that rate drops to 48%.

Inspired by Alfred, William wanted a how-to book for use by courtiers: how not to be a bad lord, how to be a good one, and how to behave and survive at court. Marie obliged him in half of her work, as we have seen, and her *miroir des princes* divides into those three categories. Bad lords, viscounts and judges make false charges out of greed (2), and the stronger they are, the less regard they have for their men (6). In fact, Marie's perspective in this first category is mostly that of a man choosing which lord to serve. Like the doves who elect as their king a hawk, only fools will swear allegiance to evil, cruel and villainous sovereigns (19); and unlike the animals who elect the wolf, any well-informed man will avoid a disloyal, "felun hume" as his "seignur" (29: 117).

Marie characterizes the ideal lord in **"Des oiseaus e del cuccu"** (46): he is

> [. . .] vaillant,
> Pruz e sage e enpernant.
> Reis deit estre mut dreiturers,
> En justise redz e fiers
> [. . .] ad bele grandur
> [. . .] Mut est sobres e atemprez.
> [. . .] Prince se deit bien reposer,
> Ne se deit mie trop deliter,
> Lui ne sun regné aviler,
> Ne la povre gent eissilier.
>
> (46: 51-68)

Many of these qualities receive detailed treatment in individual fables. The lion who gets butted, kicked and bitten teaches that he who is, or appears to be weak, is scorned (14), and he who dares not defy his enemies for fear of being defeated will get killed like the sheep in Fable 33. A smart prince should not want a seneschal or any other advisor who is arrogant, greedy and untruthful (62), but should he ever reject good advice, he will suffer the consequences (17). An honest, wise lord is impervious to bribery (20) and will always trip up a liar (99). In dealing justice, a good king or prince must not entrust his law to covetous people (56), and he must not avoid settling disputes, even if plaintiffs like the fox and the wolf are equally bad (89). He should indeed have "bele grandur," but should never be so swelled with pride that in overestimating his might he only does harm to himself (76). Finally, a good lord will not hate lesser ones than him (65), he will instead show his subjects charity (16), and it would be as shameful for him to disgrace his men as it would be for them to shame him (27).

Against this background of an idealized courtly milieu and the men who people it, Marie, no doubt herself no stranger to court life, observes an intriguing, pre-Machiavellian court etiquette, in the description of which she inverts and subverts the generic intent of her writing:

> Ki que unc se sent entrepris
> [. . .] bien deit *contreguaiter*
> Que en sa parole ait tel *cointise*—
> Par mi tute sa mesprisun,
> Que seit *semblable* a la reisun.
>
> (47: 53-60; emphasis added)

This moral, like the ten others in this category of courtly fables, moralizes about the immoral, or the amorally expedient; he who "en grant destreit / Turne suvent sun tort en dreit" (47: 61-62; see also 71) is a "sages hum," in the new, political way of courtliness as an art of survival at court, an art thanks to which the wise vanquish the honest by "schemes" ("cunsel") and stratagems ("engins") (70: 35-36).

Specifically, the courtier, like the wary fox who approaches the lion only half-way when summoned to court (36), will listen to what is happening in the corridors of power before entering. At the same time, he will not put too much trust in what he hears, which will mostly be beguiling speeches (57), for he has learned to believe only in what he sees, not "A fable, ke est mençuinge, / Ne a peinture, que semble sunge" (37: 61-62). In looking around, he will carefully control his body language, and especially his eyes, lest his glances give him away, just as the shepherd's eyes could have betrayed the wolf he was hiding from the hunter (30). More importantly still, men at court will check their tongues, for only fools speak when they should not (60). "La buche mustre le penser, / Tut deive ele de el parler" (82: 19-20). The cardinal rule is therefore: "ne devereit nul mustrer / Sa priveté ne sun penser. / [. . .] Par descoverance vient grant mals; / N'est pas li secles tut leals" (51: 25-30).

Marie's conception of "courtoisie" is thus double-edged, being based, on the one hand, on the ultimate etymon "cohors" and exemplified by the "honneur" and "loyauté" of the "courtois" knight in the fable about the Matron of Ephesus (25),[8] and reflecting, on the other hand, the new realities of "curia" and the "curiales" whom French, confusingly, could only designate by the same term, "courtois."[9]

These realities were in fact not so new anymore in Marie's time.[10] By the late twelfth century, writing about, and especially against, court life and the topos of "contemptus mundi" already have a long tradition;[11] Petrus Damiani's *Contra clericos aulicos* is a hundred years old. Court life has become grounded in moral relativism, and basic advice to any courtier is that he "adapt his words to places and times."[12] It will be said that those "who accommodate themselves to the times by simulating and dissimulating [. . .] never fail themselves. [. . .] O what a good thing it is to be able to cover up and veil your secret thoughts with astute artifice of smooth and false simulations."[13] Indeed, already in Proverbs it is said that "he that keepeth his mouth keepeth his life: but he that openeth wide his lips shall have destruction."[14] There are later echoes of this, as in Isocrates: "Take great care in what you say or do that you may fall into as few errors as possible,"[15] or as in: "When time and circumstances require silence about the truth [. . .] he who prudently keeps still certainly does not seem to be a liar."[16]

Such basic tenets of court culture were part of the education given to those who sought careers at ecclesiastical or secular courts,[17] as was Cicero's *De officiis.* In Cicero, they learned about *facetia,* a quality which "involves [a certain slyness and worldly-wise shrewdness,] a certain magicianship with words [. . .] deception and sleight of hand."[18] And in the *Facetus de moribus et vita* they could have read: "Retain your modest restraint even when speaking falsehoods. / For, always to speak the truth you may take to be wrong. / For the skilled man, it is often praiseworthy to conceal wrongdoings."[19]

This was the real purpose of Count William's commission, and it is not easily reconcilable with the traditional fable genre. How did Marie comport herself in the execution of her task?

Marie may have taken 53% of her courtly fables and 63% of the sociological ones directly from the only known Latin source, the Nilantius, by-passing Alfred; by the same token, she may also have taken many of the remaining courtly and sociological fables from other, unknown Latin sources. Can these possibilities be firmed up? I have experimented elsewhere[20] with a way of distinguishing, via syntax, between the English, Latin and French origins of Marie's fables and now dare superimpose that syntactic grid on the thematic grid developed here, assuring the reader that I did not reread my former analysis until after the completion of the current one! If I include the category of traditional fables in the corpus of the thematic grid (explaining that even, or especially, court people may still benefit from some solid moral teachings!), the overlap ratio is a respectable 77%: previously, I identified fables 1, 2, 6, 15, 17, 20, (25), 28, 58, 67, 75, 83 and 102 as being most likely of Latin stock, and it turns out here that only the "bad" fables 67, 83 and 102 should probably be assigned an English origin.

The result is even better (83%), although the sample is smaller, for fables of a likely French provenance as determined by syntactic analysis: of fables 5, 8, 33, 70, 77 and 94, only 94 should thematically be called English.

It grieves me considerably that three out of the four fables I called syntactically English (31, 50, 51, 76) now turn up in the thematically Latin or French categories. I console myself by noting that seven out of eight fables (87%) whose syntax I had to call simply "non-Latin," are traditional (68), sociological (7, 88) and courtly (18, 27, 36, 62) fables (101 is "platitudinous"), which may help me decide to call them henceforth syntactically French rather than English.

I cling therefore to the idea that many, perhaps most of Marie's bad fables have Alfredian and oral English roots, and that many, perhaps most of her good ones go back to known and unknown Latin and to oral French models.

In yet another study of Marie's collection[21] I attempted to determine which of the fables she designated specifically as her own, as more or less personal recreations of known models (1-40) or as more or less personal creations (41-104). Based on all manuscripts, Marie's "je" marks twenty fables as personalized recreations (1, 4, 5, 6, 8, 10, 11B, 12, 13, 18, 19, 20, 23, 27, 28, 30, 35, 37, 39, 40), and twenty-four as possibly of her own invention (43, 44, 45, 46, 47, 48, 52, 55, 56, 58, 60, 65, 66, 73, 75, 80, 81, 84, 90, 93, 95, 97, 101, 102).[22] Superimposing the personal-fable grid on the thematic grid yields the following results: 1. Marie seems to be claiming all four fabliaux as her own, which is, given their antifeminism, surprising; 2. of the twenty-seven very bad fables she "signs" only thirteen, which, while less than half, is still too much for a writer of her talent; 3. similarly, she signs only five of the eleven sociological fables, which, this time, is too modest for a keen observer of society like her; 4. seven of the thirteen traditional fables she claims as her own, which may be considered immodest, especially since four of them occur in Nilantius; 5. finally, she lays claim to only 44% of the courtly fables (15 out of 34), which is disappointing to me but indicates perhaps that she did not wish to be seen as too keen an advocate of a mind-set about which, after all, she wrote only under the duress of a princely commission.

Notes

1. "*La femme au tombeau*: Anonymous Fabliau of the Thirteenth Century." Diss. Indiana Univ. 1967, 164 pp. *DAI* [*Dissertation Abstracts International*] 28 (1968), p. 3676-A.

2. *DAI* 33 (1972), p. 2951-A. Published as *Li Ystoire de la male marastre: Version M of the* Roman des sept sages de Rome (Tübingen: Max Niemeyer, 1974).

3. Karl Warnke, *Die Fabeln der Marie de France* (Halle: Max Niemeyer, 1898), p. 85: 1, 3.

4. Harriet Spiegel, ed. and trans., *Marie de France: Fables* (Toronto: Univ. of Toronto Press, 1987), p. 30, vv. 28-29. Henceforth quotations from Marie's fables will be from Spiegel (by fable and verse).

5. See Hans R. Runte, "Marie de France, traite et retraite," *ALFA: Actes de langue française et de linguistique* (Halifax), 3-4 (1990-91), 129-35.

6. Cf. Hans R. Runte, "True Lies: From Speaking Courtly to Courtspeak," *Romance Languages Annual,* 7 (1995), 154-58.

7. See Frank Collins, "The Terms 'cortois', 'cortoise' and 'corteisie' in the Works of Chrétien de Troyes," *Vox Romanica*, 36 (1977), 84-92.

8. See Hans R. Runte, "'Alfred's Book,' Marie de France, and the Matron of Ephesus," *Romance Philology*, 36.4 (1983), 556-64.

9. See Hans R. Runte, "Lunete et Gaston Paris: Note sur le terme 'courtois,'" *ALFA: Actes de langue française et de linguistique* (Halifax), 2 (1989), 143-53.

10. See Runte, "True Lies."

11. C. Stephen Jaeger, *The Origins of Courtliness: Civilizing Trends and the Formation of Courtly Ideals: 939-1210* (Philadelphia: Univ. of Pennsylvania Press, 1986), pp. 54-66.

12. Allan H. Gilbert, *Machiavelli's* Prince *and its Forerunners:* The Prince *as a Typical Book "de Regimine Principum"* [1938] (New York: Barnes, 1968), p. 130.

13. Gilbert, p. 132.

14. Ibid., p. 130.

15. Ibid., p. 130.

16. Ibid., p. 127.

17. Jaeger, pp. 113-26.

18. Ibid., p. 167.

19. Ibid., p. 167.

20. "Marie de France's Fables as Trilingual Palimpsest," in *Meaning and Manner: From Marie de France to Marie-Claire Blais: Mélanges de littérature présentés à Rostislav Kocourek par ses collègues et élèves,* special issue of *Dalhousie French Studies,* 38 (1997), 17-24.

21. "Marie de France dans ses fables," *In Quest of Marie de France, a Twelfth-Century Poet,* ed. Chantal A. Maréchal (Lewiston, NY: Edwin Mellen Press, 1992), pp. 28-40.

22. Fable numbers in my "Marie de France dans ses fables" are Warnke's and have here been adjusted to Spiegel's.

Dolliann Margaret Hurtig (essay date November 2001)

SOURCE: Hurtig, Dolliann Margaret. "'I Do, I Do': Medieval Models of Marriage and Choice of Partners in Marie de France's 'Le Fraisne.'" *Romanic Review* 92, no. 4 (November 2001): 363-79.

[*In the essay below, Hurtig argues that Marie's lay "Le Fresne" subverts the feudal model of arranged marriage by portraying the eventual triumph of the ecclesiastical model, which is based on the mutual consent of the parties.*]

That Marie de France would choose to write a story about love and marriage with a happy ending is rather a surprise to readers mindful of the historical reality of the Middle Ages. The prospect of a woman having a happy, loving marriage in twelfth-century Renaissance France is bleak indeed. Georges Duby comments on how little historians do know about love between spouses: ". . . que savons-nous, en France, au XIIe siècle, de l'amour entre époux? Nous n'en savons rien, et nous n'en saurons, je pense, jamais rien pour l'immense majorité des ménages. . . ." ("Que sait-on de l'amour en France au XIIe siècle?" 5). Notwithstanding, the celebrated historian does mention Marie de France and how her depiction of love in the *Lais* seeks marriage as its ultimate goal: "In the poems attributed to Marie de France, ideal love is that which leads to marriage" (*The Knight, the Lady, and the Priest* 224).

Marie's notion of love as a constant presence creates among the poems a reciprocal harmony of lovers in love that makes for a unified collection. Jean Flori's insightful article on Marie's *Lais* points toward a commonality based on unconventional love: ". . . tous racontent une histoire d'amour contrarié et, dans tous les cas, les sympathies de l'auteur vont aux amants tant qu'ils vivent cet amour sans se soucier des convenances sociales" (19). Cynthia Ho in her stimulating essay from *Crossing the Bridge,* assigns monogamy in Marie's *Lais* a somewhat curious meaning, "defined as exclusive, committed love in disregard of marriage vows" (142). Robert Hanning in his reflective chapter from *The Olde Daunce* recognizes the various qualities of Marie's love ". . . in its many guises: married and adulterous, young and mature, successful and unsuccessful, idealized and degraded, comic and tragic" (95). Philippe Ménard in his essay "Marie de France et nous" insists upon the nature of love as shared: "Un aspect touchant de ces peintures tient au fait que l'amour vécu est réciproque" (12). Moreover, as evidence that Marie does not value the superficiality of courtly love games, Ménard judiciously comments upon Marie's penchant for authenticity in love: "En outre, loin d'accepter aveuglément les rites élégants, mais un peu artificiels de l'amour courtois . . . Marie préfère la spontanéité et les élans d'un cœur sincère" (14). Love in Marie demands equality between the sexes and thus defies the domination/submission precept of courtly love: "L'idée qu'il ne saurait y avoir de domination en amour, qu'aucun des partenaires ne doit commander à l'autre est éminemment étrangère à la doctrine courtoise" (15). For Donald Maddox in his provocative book *Fictions of Identity in Medieval France,* the tender and loving words of Tristan in **"Chievrefoil"** link the *Lais* together: "Bele amie, si est de nus: / Ne vus sanz mei, ne jeo sanz vus" (77-78). Maddox maintains that "this unadorned utterance is arguably the *umbilicus,* the key locus of the entire collection" (77). Yves Badel comments on how the brevity of the lays as a genre invites one lay to complement another: ". . . un texte court réussi appelle un supplément, demande à être repris, relancé en quelque manière . . . ainsi de récit en récit, narrateur et lecteur sont solidement contraints, par loi dure de la brièveté et d'une histoire à chaque fois nouvelle, à un face à face avec le réel de l'existence" (39). Thus, we can see how Marie's collection as a literary genre has been assessed by scholars as succinct yet compatible texts that like separate streams find their common source in Marie's abiding wellspring of true love.

While true love is everywhere present in Marie, are we able to generalize about love in the *Lais*? According to Burgess and Busby, generalization may be overly simplistic: "Love in medieval literature, as in any other period (indeed, in life itself), is too complex to be reduced to a single model which will not admit of variation" (Introduction 27-28). However, woven into the fabric of the *Lais,* we discover the fine thread of true love that embroiders one lay to another in a seamless tapestry where couples freely choose each other and enter into what we moderns would loosely designate as a "relationship". The story of the relationship of Le Fraisne and Gurun that would eventually culminate in a marriage of two hearts must have been looked upon at court as a charming fiction in view of the stark reality of the practice of arranged marriage among the aristocracy. Since true love among aristocrats is not likely to be found in the marriage bed, love is perhaps best discovered in art, in the delicately refined poetry of Marie de France.

If we were to consider what Marie values in love, a point of entry to our discussion would be the well-known verses in **"Guigemar"** where Venus, the goddess of love, casts Ovid's love poetry into the flames:

> Le livre Ovide, u il enseigne
> coment chascuns s'amur estreigne,
> en un fu ardant le getout,
> e tuz icels escumenjout,
> ki ja mais cel livre lirreient
> sun ne enseignement fereient.
>
> (239-244)[1]
> [In the painting, Venus was shown as casting
> into a blazing fire the book in which
> Ovid teaches the art of controlling
> love and as excommunicating
> all those who read this book
> or adopted its teachings.]

We are reminded that we are in the bedchamber of one of Marie's *mal mariées* whose jealous husband keeps her enclosed in a tower. Robert W. Hanning remarks upon the significance of the painting for Marie as poet:

> Marie's representation of herself in this passage as a post-Ovidian female court poet, in whose sociopoetic

situation (aptly figured as a beautifully decorated prison) insight and victimization, willed authority and unwelcome restriction, radically interact, offers an important clue to a major project of the *Lais*: the depiction of women for whom creative or authoritative utterance is intimately connected with victimization, loss, and even destruction.

("The Talking Wounded" 142)

Marie's voice will then be a voice from the edge, a voice to speak for women who make choices about whom they will love, who suffer in love or who derive joy in love because of their freely choosing, who ultimately win love on earth, or win love in another world or in the hereafter, or lose out because their love is not true after all. Hanning praises Marie's value as a female court poet: ". . . I believe, in her capacity as marginalized truthteller . . . that Marie makes one of her most significant contributions to twelfth-century Europe's post-Ovidian, vernacular discourse of desire" (142). What Marie dearly values in love is the story of love, in its telling and in its retelling.

In the love story **"Le Fraisne,"** a marginalized poet, Marie, chooses a marginalized heroine, Le Fraisne, and creates a lay about medieval models of marriage and the choice of partners, a poem highly suggestive of the dual notion that exists about marriage in twelfth-century France. What I intend to show is that Marie's text suggests a revolutionary concept of marriage. The traditional model of marriage, the *mariage de convenance,* a marriage most likely without love or the power of the couple to choose or the mutual consent of the spouses, represents the way feudal society maintains itself. A forlorn bride (*la mal mariée*) whose husband has been chosen without her consent, without her power to choose, is oftentimes the unhappy outcome. Alongside the secular model of marriage, an ecclesiastical model is beginning to take shape and definition. Medieval canonists like Gratian, theologians like Peter Lombard, and later, Alexander III, subject marriage to much examination and scrutiny. Notions of coercion without the consent of the couple about to be wed, questions about the right to freely choose a partner or mutual consent, the status of marital affection between the spouses introduce an enlightened way of regarding marriage. We will see how the religious model of marriage comes to interlace the secular one. **"Le Fraisne"** provides a forum for Marie to double the discourse on marriage and to balance family patriarchs with Church fathers.

The opening scene of the lay presents a fitting picture of the secular model of marriage:

> En Bretaigne jadis maneient
> dui chevalier; veisin esteient.
> Riche hum furent e manant

e chevalier pruz e vaillant.
Prochein furent, d'une cuntree.
Chescuns femme aveit espusee.
L'une des dames enceinta.
Al terme qu'ele delivra,
a cele feiz ot dous enfanz.

(3-11)

[There once lived in Brittany
two knights who were neighbors,
rich and wealthy men, worthy and
valiant knights from the same region.
They had both taken a wife and one
of the ladies conceived, giving birth
to two children when her time came.]

It is the twelfth century, and the feudal system is in full flower. Rich feudal lords and their ladies produce and offer heirs to a system that perpetuates itself. The core of feudal or lay society that ensures the social order is the *domus* (Duby, *Medieval Marriage* 3). One generation begets another, and the land passes on from father to son in a predictable rhythm that punctuates the undisturbed pattern of passing time.

In connection with this pattern, the title of the lay, **"Le Fraisne"** or **"The Ash Tree,"** becomes by extension a metaphor for the act of generation itself. An ash tree produces more and more branches as time passes. Its roots grow deep and it provides shade and protection. So, too, it is with families who through marriage extend their branches to offer protection to kinsmen, all the while remaining firmly rooted in the land. The French verb *enraciner* appropriately describes the dualism of the tree's connection to the soil and to the medieval family's love of the land. Thus, the birth of a male heir to a family is a joyous event.

In our lay, however, the birth of twin male heirs is one too many. In twelfth-century Brittany, a folkloric tradition prevails whereby a woman who gives birth to twins has received two seeds, not one, and as a consequence she is considered to be an adulteress (Thompson, T. 587.1). Consequently the barren noblewoman of the tale is quick to rush to judgment against her fruitful neighbor:

'Nus savum bein qu'il i afiert:
unques ne fu ne ja nen iert
ne n'avendra cele aventure,
qu'a une sule porteüre
une femme dous enfanz ait,
se dui hume ne li unt fait.'

(37-42)

[We know what is at issue here:
it has never occurred that a
woman give birth to two sons at
once, nor ever will, unless
two men are the cause of it.]

The moral code of the laity rigorously condemns adultery on the part of a woman. As *caput mansi* or head of the household, the husband of the mother of the twin boys, should he choose to repudiate his wife, would be following a convention deemed appropriate to protect the social order with respect to unfaithful wives:

Quant il l'oï dire e retraire,
dolenz en fu, ne sot que faire;
sa prude femme en enhaï
et durement la mescreï,
e mult la teneit en destreit,
senz ceo qu'ele nel deserveit.

(59-64)

[When he heard the account he was
saddened and did not know what to do.
For this reason he hated the worthy
woman and was highly mistrustful
of her, keeping her in close custody
without her having deserved it.]

While extramarital sex is rigorously condemned for a woman, for a bachelor to enjoy sexual pleasure outside the marriage bond is an accepted social practice. According to the lay model of marriage in the twelfth century, unmarried males had a right to female companionship or *contubernium*. The well-to-do landowner of our story, Gurun by name, therefore, freely chooses to take a mistress. To this end, he generously endows a nearby abbey with land in order to have access to it. He often sojourns there and woos the "niece" of the abbess whom he entreats to come live with him and be his love:

'Bele,' fet il, 'ore est issi
de mei avez fet vostre ami.
Venez vus ent del tut od mei!'

(287-289)

['Fair one, you have now made
of me your love. Come away
with me for good!']

The maid, whose name is Le Fraisne, freely accepts his offer; after all, it is not everyday that a girl abandoned under an ash-tree and brought up in a convent as the niece of the headmistress gets an invitation to live in a château:

Ensemble od lui en est alee,
a sun chastel l'en a menee.

(301-301)

[She granted him his request
and went away with him:
he took her to his castle.]

Here the text illuminates the concept of the choice of partners. Gurun and Le Fraisne freely consent to enter into a love pact, *l'union libre*. Gurun is comfortably entrenched in the system and works it to his best advantage. Marriage to Le Fraisne would have been an impossibility, for their uneven social status rules out any possibility of union. Le Fraisne can bring nothing to Gurun as his spouse, for she has no dowry. Her sole possessions are a piece of rich cloth to which is fastened a bejewelled ring. While these outward signs give rise to speculation that Le Fraisne is of noble birth, the apparent reality is that she has no birthright, no identity, nothing to offer Gurun. She does not have the opportunity given to fair ladies of noble birth to make a suitable *mariage de convenance*.

In the ecclesiastical model of marriage, the interdiction against concubinage is clear: sex outside of marriage is fornication and is forbidden. Yet the Church does recognize a clandestine or private marriage; that is to say, if a couple makes love with mutual consent outside the bond of marriage, they are considered as married (Sheehan, *Marriage, Family, and Law* 40). James Brundage comments upon Gratian's perspective on concubinage:

> Gratian ascribed to the concubinage relationship the quality of marital affection which the Roman jurists had reserved for marriage unions. As Gratian saw it, a concubine was a woman who united with a man in conjugal affection, but without legal formalities. Gratian, in other words, conceived of concubinage as an imperfect, informal marriage, a marriage which lacked legal formalities and full legal consequences, but which was nonetheless a true and valid marriage.
>
> ("Concubinage and Marriage" 3-4)

Thus, while in the ecclesiastical model of marriage Gurun and Le Fraisne may be considered as privately married, according to the secular model of the day, they are living openly as lovers, a feudal lord and his concubine.

It could well be argued that if Gurun and Le Fraisne had the power to choose a marriage partner for themselves, they would have chosen each other and the union of two hearts would have culminated in a love match, *un mariage d'amour*. Howard Bloch illuminates how dangerous for the patrimony a love match can be:

> The question of who may marry whom is, at bottom, that of the future of the paternal fief, or lineal *proprietas* and the propriety of lineage. . . . The prospect of individuals loving freely implies the possibility of their marrying freely; and this eventuality entails a concept of marriage in which the future of great family fortunes is increasingly removed from direct family control.
>
> (129)

The lords of the territory of Dol, in service to Gurun, exhort him to leave his mistress and make a suitable *mariage de convenance*:

> Soventes feiz a lui parlerent,
> qu'une gentil femme espusast
> et de cele se delivrast.
>
> (326-328)

[They often spoke to him saying
that he should take a noble wife
and free himself from Le Fresne.]

Their argument is a strong and sound one: without an heir, a power struggle for political control is bound to occur at Gurun's death:

> Lié sereient, s'il eüst heir
> ki après lui peust aveir
> sa terre e sun grant heritage;
>
> (329-331)

[They would be happier
if he had an heir
to inherit his land.]

The right to choose a suitable marriage partner is a family affair. Bloch provides ample clarity on the topic:

> The choice of partners was, for the aristocratic families of feudal France, a collective matter, since it carried with it a host of military, social, and economic considerations: obligations to vengeance and to armed service, political alliance, legal and financial responsibility.
>
> (162)

Their combined strength overpowers Gurun, who must yield to the threats that they will withdraw from his service:

> ja mes pur seignur nel tendrunt
> ne volentiers nel servirunt,
> se il ne fait lur volenté.
>
> (335-337)

[They would never more consider him their lord,
nor serve him willingly,
if he did not do their bidding.]

Gurun's only choice is to give in:

> Li chevaliers a graanté
> qu'a lur cunseil femme prendra.
>
> (338-339)

[The knight agreed to take
a wife on their advice.]

Those who work hard to make the feudal system viable preside over people, property, and behavior (Sheehan, *Marriage, Family, and Law* xix). To this end, the Council of Lords, the guardians of the feudal system, seeks a lady of equal social status to complement Gu-run. Then, too, that the lady of their choice is the sole heir to a great property has wide appeal:

> 'Sire,' funt il, 'ci pres de nus
> a un produme, per a vus.
> Une fille a, ki est sun heir:
> mult poëz terre od li aveir.'
>
> (341-344)

> ['Lord,' they said, 'close to us here
> is a worthy man quite your equal
> who has a daughter as his heir:
> much land will come with her.']

They arrange the marriage pact or *desponsatio* as is the custom among the nobility in twelfth-century France:

> Cel mariage unt purchacié
> e de tutes parz otrië.
>
> (353-354)

> [Thus they sought this marriage
> and assent was given by all parties.]

The twelfth-century French nobility locks its sons and daughters into a power structure controlled by the patriarchal family and the hierarchical social structure. A bride-to-be has no right to choose. She is a vessel to carry a child that will inherit the land from his father and thereby ensure the continuation of the line by means of a similar marriage. A fruitful wife is most desirable to maintain the health of the system. The vassals are eager to point out to Gurun how the bride of their choice, whose name La Coldre means "hazelnut tree," is a happy portent of the lady's potential for producing heirs. The hazelnut tree is associated with fertility while the ash tree carries with it the notion of barrenness:

> En la coldre a noiz e deduiz,
> li fraisnes ne porte unkes fruiz.
>
> (349-350)

> [On the hazel there are nuts to be enjoyed,
> but the ash never bears fruit.]

The lay model of marriage glorifies its stability and praises the fruitful couple to whom falls the careful husbanding of the patrimony (Duby, *Medieval Marriage* 4). Love between the parties contracting the marriage is not a consideration.

Among the aristocrats, as Sharon Kinoshita observes, "marriages contracted for political and familial gain excluded the possibility of true love, which by defini-tion had to be unconstrained and freely chosen" (33). However, the consensual theory of the Church canonists would have been attentive to and would have valorized "the freedom and autonomy of the individual in the crucial matter of marriage" (Murray 124). The Church

under Pope Gratian in 1140 is saying no to parentally compelled marriage (Noonan 424). Jacqueline Murray offers more on the topic: "Gratian . . . saw consent as essential to the formation of the union. In the *Decretum* (ca. 1140) he states plainly, 'Where they each do not consent, there is no marriage.'" (Murray 125). Sheehan remarks that "by the 1150s, the first syntheses, the one canonistic, the other theological, were available in the *Decretum Gratiani* and the *Libri IV Sententiarum* of Peter Lombard. In these works . . . a theory of marital consent was elaborated, the practical implications of which were to have immense social consequences—implications that may not be entirely unfolded to the present day" (91). Although Gratian's consensual theory is circulating about the time Marie wrote **"Le Fraisne,"** the marriage of Gurun and La Coldre does not stray from the feudal norm. The couple will make a *mariage de convenance* and not a *mariage d'amour*. After all, men carry out the act of arranging or making a mar-riage as Georges Duby aptly concludes: "Chose sérieuse, le mariage est affaire masculine" ("Que sait-on de l'amour en France au XIIe siècle?" 7). However, we have just seen that not all men concerned about marital issues are feudal lords!

The act and the meaning of marriage weigh heavily upon the minds of twelfth-century canonists. In the forefront is the question of what makes a marriage. The overwhelming answer to the question appears to be that consent makes marriage, and that *consensus* by clerics is not to be interpreted as consent of the parents whose children are to be wed, but of the partners themselves. Duby acknowledges the stance of the Church on consent: ". . . depuis le milieu du XIIe siècle, l'Eglise a fait admettre dans la haute aristocratie que le lien conjugal se noue par consentement mutuel . . ." (7). Historically, in medieval society, mutual consent by verbal commitment makes a marriage, as Duby relates: ". . . For Hugh of St. Victor, followed by Peter Lom-bard, it was the verbal pledge (*obligatio verborum*) that established marriage" (*Love and Marriage in the Middle Ages* 17). Irven Resnick's observation on the consent of the couple explains how the Church could use the theory to its best advantage: ". . . if consent—an internal disposition of the will—was the efficient cause of mar-riage, then to the extent that church authorities could reserve determinations of consent for ecclesiastical jurisdiction, they could extend their control over Christian marriage and society" (353). Once the consent theory had been worked out, the Church fathers then had to deal with the role of consummation in the act of marriage.

The Church looks to the marriage of Mary and Joseph, a marriage perceived by ecclesiastics as consensual but not consummated, for an answer. Church lawmakers soon found themselves in a dilemma as Resnick observes:

If the absence of sexual intercourse were to invalidate the marriage bond between Joseph and Mary, then Mary would suddenly appear as an unwed mother—a conclusion as unacceptable to the twelfth or thirteenth centuries as to our own! But if their relationship resulted in a chaste spiritual marriage, and if lay people were encouraged to realize this model too, then the distinction between a celibate clergy and a laity would be threatened.

(364)

What Gratian offers to ease "the tension between these two positions" (369) is a revolutionary stratagem to reconcile opposing views as John Perry comments:

In advancing the position that the married state begins with an exchange of uncoerced, sincere consent between bride and groom and becomes complete only by consummation, Gratian's *Concordia discordantium canonum* (c.1140)—or *Decretum,* as it became known—departs from both the Jewish and Roman traditions upon which the medieval Church has previously relied . . . the canonist managed to unite previously scattered sources in marshaling his model and to argue, from the Roman law, for consent based on 'marital affection.'

(137)

Gratian, doubtless following the tradition of churchmen since the ninth century, redefines the term "marital affection" as it relates to the act of marriage. Whereas the Roman Law assigns to the term "intent to get married," an emotive or affective quality is what the canonists now sought to convey (Noonan 425).

Finally, according to Christopher Brooke in his book, *The Medieval Idea of Marriage,* the *Decretum* of Gratian secures victory for the Church as the aristocrats embrace his definition: ". . . for the first time in the history of the Church, a single definition of what constituted a valid marriage was devised . . . What is astonishing is the degree of acceptance that it received from the lay aristocracy. . . ." (141). The question presents itself, then, as to how theology gave new meaning to marriage among the aristocracy. Brooke remarks that "the aristocratic societies of western Europe were increasingly concerned with the effective passage of landed estates and kingdoms by hereditary succession . . . you can not work a hereditary system at all unless the nature of inheritance is tolerably clear; . . . in the marriage market and the marriage games of medieval catholic Europe, the Church and the papacy acted as umpires, and were blessed and cursed accordingly" (142-43).

For the clergy, marriage acquired meaning as one of the seven sacraments. Among marriage legislators to succeed Yves de Chartres and Hugues of Saint-Victor emerges Peter Lombard who manages to frame a definition of sacrament. For Duby, the definition worked out

by Lombard in his *Livre des Sentences* ("A sacrament is an outward and efficient sign of grace"), carries with it the notion of the indissolubility of marriage (*The Knight, The Lady, and The Priest* 184). Duby describes how a privileged moment for the sacrament of matrimony occurs about midpoint into the twelfth century:

Placed at the intersection of the spiritual and the physical, it was the sacrament that most manifestly symbolized the mystery of the incarnation; it was trembling on the brink, in the middle ground, dangerous. . . . But the main thing is that by the middle of the twelfth century marriage had come to be sacralized without being disincarnated. The conflict between the ecclesiastical and lay models of marriage had become much less acute.

(185)

When we revisit Marie's story, the wedding of Gurun and La Codre, a binding and sacramental marriage, has taken place in a lavish manner:

Les noces tindrent richement;
mult i out esbaneiement.

(383-385)

[The wedding was richly celebrated
and there was much merrymaking.]

According to Neil Cartlidge, in marriages of the era, "the practice of using written records to assert the concrete existence of each marriage had yet to develop, and, in its absence, the more impressive the marital ceremony could be made to seem, then the greater the emphasis upon the finality of the union" (13).

When the ceremonies of the day are over, the Archbishop assumes an active role in the blessing of the couple and of the marriage bed, a ritual that will precede the couple's first night together:

kar l'erceveskes i esteit
purs els beneistre e seignier;
ceo afereit a sun mestier.

(416-418)

[The Archbishop was there
to bless them and make the sign
of the cross over them,
for this was part of his duty.]

Michael Sheehan remarks how clergymen were gaining more control of the institution of marriage to the extent that "marriage, hitherto, essentially an institution regulated by family custom and, to a certain extent, by Roman and barbarian civil law, passed more and more into the jurisdiction of the bishop" (91).

Le Fraisne, who remains silent about the marriage, prepares the bed and covers it with the fine cloth she was wrapped in as a babe. The mother of the bride ush-

　　　　　CLASSICAL AND MEDIEVAL LITERATURE CRITICISM, Vol. 111

ers in her daughter to the marriage chamber and spies the rich coverlet on the bridal bed. She examines a be-jewelled ring on the hand of Le Fraisne and recognizes the girl as the babe she had forsaken. The moment of recognition in the lay is considered by Donald Maddox as one of many "specular encounters" of which literature of the medieval ages is replete (58). For Maddox the specular encounter includes ". . . at least one locus in which action becomes contingent upon a primary personage's receipt of crucial information pertaining to the self and various aspects of its identity. The addressee of a specular disclosure . . . has in most instances been unaware of the degree and gravity of his or her prior ignorance" (11). Le Fraisne has now become aware of her birthright; she is orphaned no more. She has become the noble and marriageable daughter of a wealthy feudal lord. Le Fraisne's mother then tells her story to her husband, how many years ago she had given birth to twin girls and feared for her reputation, as it was she who had viciously maligned the mother of the twin boys. The feudal lord immediately sets about righting the injustice done to his daughter:

> Quant nostre fille avum trovee,
> grant joie nus a Deus donee,
> ainz que li pechiez fust dublez.
> 'Fille,' fet il, 'avant venez!'
>
> (495-499)

> ['I was never as happy as I am now
> that we have found our daughter.
> God has given us great joy rather
> than allowing the sin to be doubled.
> Daughter, come here!']

The father's reference to a sin "doubled" is somewhat puzzling. The most apparent sin that the text illumines is the abandonment of Le Fraisne by her mother. What the passage suggests is that to deny Le Fraisne her birthright a second time by refusing her the opportunity to make a suitable marriage as a daughter of a wealthy feudal lord would be a sin twice over.

The father of Le Fraisne summons the Archbishop to whom falls the responsibility of unmaking or annulling the *mariage de convenance* between La Coldre and Gurun. According to the Church model of marriage, a marriage that has not yet been consummated can be annulled (Brundage, *Sex, Law, and Marriage* 407). The annulment favors the Church and her consensual theory of marriage as Maddox observes: ". . . the annulment of La Codre's marriage of convenience in favor of her sister privileges conjugal reciprocity based on affective inclination" (59).

The father of the twins readily bestows upon his daughter Le Fraisne one half of his inheritance. As the *caput mansi*, he gives the bride in marriage to Gurun in a second public celebration amidst family and friends, feasting and much merriment:

> Granz noces refunt de rechief;
> a un riche hume sereit grief
> d'esligier ceo qu'il despendirent
> al grant convive que il firent.
>
> (521-524)

> [A grand wedding is celebrated once more in splendor,
> a wealthy man would be hard pressed
> to pay the expense
> of such a sumptuous feast.]

What occurs in this scene is a happy mingling of the two medieval models of marriage. Similar to other marriages among the nobility, Le Fraisne's marriage, as a *mariage de convenance,* creates a network of alliances to maintain the system's survival. Yet her marriage is also a love match, a *mariage d'amour.* And this marriage has the approval, the blessing of the Church fathers. **"Le Fraisne"** is circulating somewhere about the time of the Alexandrian synthesis (1163) when the Church, as has been stated earlier, strongly favors the consent of the couple to their union. To be good shepherds of the flock, it appears to be the duty of the Church to unite God's children in a marriage based on love, on Gratian's earlier assertion of "marital affection" (Noonan 425).

To duplicate the traditional model of marriage is not what the Church is about. The will of the heavenly Father for His children to be bound in marital affection prevails over the will of an earthly father's interest in the continuation of the patrimony. That the father in **"Le Fraisne"** aligns his will with that of the couple in love is no doubt favorable to the Church and to her consensual theory. And thus it comes about that the ecclesiastical model of marriage entwines the lay one without a hitch, and in its embrace foreshadows a revolutionary way of looking at marriage.

Finally, what is Marie saying about marriage and the choice of partners in the twelfth century? She presents two sides of the question and satisfactorily comes to terms with the duality of the poem's ending. In **"Le Fraisne"** the device of twins is a dynamic medium to present both the traditional and the ecclesiastical way of looking at marriage. Chantal Maréchal notes how the wedding of Fraisne to Gurun reconciles opposites: "Au terme de l'aventure, en accord avec l'évolution de la pensée religieuse du temps de Bernard de Clairvaux, l'amour humain spiritualisé n'est plus en conflit avec l'enseignement de l'Eglise—Gurun et Fresne peuvent être à la fois amants et époux" (137). Le Fraisne's *mariage de convenance* is a true *mariage d'amour.* It is as if by a miracle a branch from a tree begins a new growth, a new genealogy, implanted on free choice, imbedded in holiness and sacrament, yet nonetheless still rooted in tradition.

The final image we have of Le Fraisne is a noble one, that of a queen reigning over the festivities of her wedding day:

> Pur la joie de la meschine,
> ki de belté semble reïne,
> qu'il unt sifaitement trovee,
> unt mult grant joie demenee.
>
> (525-528)
>
> [The joy of the maiden,
> whose beauty rivaled that of a queen
> resonated the joy of her family
> who had found her as if by a miracle.]

From an abandoned child to the bride of a powerful feudal lord is a significant rise in feudal society. One wonders if Marie de France did not desire all young noblewomen to be queen of their own wedding days, freely choosing their marriage partners and bringing into their lives the magical dimension of fairy tale. In **"Le Fraisne"** she breaks through women's silent acceptance of the status quo by hinting at the way things ought to be, and thus, through her craft, ingeniously subverts twelfth-century marriage tradition.

Note

1. Quotations from Warnke (ed.), *Lais de Marie de France*; translations from *The Lais of Marie de France*, trans. Glyn S. Burgess and Keith Busby.

Works Cited

Badel, Pierre-Yves. "La brièveté comme esthétique et comme éthique dans les *Lais de Marie de France*." Dufournet 25-40.

Belmont, Nicole. *Les Signes de la naissance*. Paris: Plon, 1971.

Bloch, R. Howard. *Etymologies and Genealogies*. Chicago: The University of Chicago Press, 1983.

Brooke, Christopher Nugent Lawrence. *The Medieval Idea of Marriage*. New York: Oxford UP, 1989.

Brundage, James A. *Sex, Law and Marriage in the Middle Ages*. Brookfield, Vermont: Variorum, 1993.

———. "Concubinage and Marriage in Medieval Canon Law." *Journal of Medieval History* I (April 1975): 1-17.

Burgess, Glyn S. *The Lais of Marie de France: Text and Context*. Athens, Georgia: University of Georgia Press, 1987.

Burgess, Glyn and Keith Busby, trans. *Les Lais de Marie de France*. By Marie de France. Harmondsworth, England: Penguin, 1986.

Cartlidge, Neil. *Medieval Marriage: Literary Approaches, 1100-1300*. Rochester: D. S. Brewer, 1997.

Clifford, Paula. *Marie de France: Lais*. London: Grant & Cutler, 1981.

Coolidge, Sharon. "'Eliduc' and the Iconography of Love." *Mediaeval Studies* 54 (1992): 274-85.

Duby, Georges. *The Early Growth of the European Economy*. Trans. Howard B. Clark. Ithaca, N.Y.: Cornell UP, 1974.

———. *Guerriers et paysans*. Paris: Gallimard, 1983.

———. *Love and Marriage in the Middle Ages*. Trans. Jane Dunnett. Chicago: The University of Chicago Press, 1994.

———. *Medieval Marriage: Two Models from Twelfth-Century France*. Trans. Elborg Forster. Baltimore and London: 1978.

———. *The Knight, the Lady, and the Priest*. Trans. Barbara Bray. New York: Pantheon Books, 1983.

———. "*Que sait-on de l'amour en France au XIIe siècle?*" Oxford: Clarendon Press, 1983.

Dufournet, Jean, ed. *Amour et merveille: les Lais de Marie de France*. Paris: Champion, 1995.

Flori, Jean. "Amour et société aristocratique au XIIe siècle: L'Exemple des lais de Marie de France." *Le Moyen Age: Revue d'Histoire et de Philologie* 98.1 (1992): 17-34.

Foulon, Charles. "L'Ethique de Marie de France dans le lai de 'Fresne'; Offerts à Mademoiselle Jeanne Lods, professeur honoraire de littérature médiévale à l'Ecole Normale Supérieure de Jeunes Filles, par ses collègues, ses élèves et ses amis." *Mélanges de littérature: Du moyen âge au XXe siècle*. Paris: Ecole Normale Supérieure de Jeunes Filles, 1978. 203-12.

Goody, Jack. *The Development of the Family and Marriage in Europe*. Cambridge: Cambridge University Press, 1983.

Grimbert, Joan Tasker. "Love and Death? Reading Marie de France's 'Chievrefoil' against Bédier's *Roman de Tristan et Iseut*." *Bulletin Bibliographique de la Société Internationale Arthurienne* 52 (2000): 311-22.

Hanning, R. W. "Love and Power in the Twelfth Century, with Special Reference to Chrétien de Troyes and Marie de France." *The Olde Daunce: Love, Friendship, Sex, and Marriage in the Medieval World*. Ed. Robert Edwards and Stephen Spector. Albany: State University of New York Press, 1991. 87-103.

————. "The Talking Wounded: Desire, Truth Telling, and Pain in the Lais of Marie de France." *Desiring Discourse: The Literature of Love, Ovid through Chaucer.* Ed. Cynthia A. Gravlee. Selinsgrove: Susquehanna UP, 1998. 140-61.

Ho, Cynthia. "Words Alone Cannot Express: Epistles in Marie de France and Murasaki Shikibu." *Crossing the Bridge: Comparative Essays on Medieval European and Heian Japanese Women Writers.* Ed. Cynthia Ho and Barbara Stevenson. New York: Palgrave, 2000. 133-52.

Kinoshita, Sharon. "Two for the Price of One: Courtly Love and Serial Polygamy in the Lais of Marie de France." *Arthuriana* 8 (1998): 33-55.

Kunstman, Pierre. "Symbole et interprétation: Le Message de Tristan dans le 'Chèvrefeuille'." *Tristania* 13.1-2 (1987-88): 35-52.

Lombard, Peter. *Livre des Sentences, IV, 26.*

Maddox, Donald. *Fictions of Identity in Medieval France.* Cambridge: Cambridge UP, 2000.

Maréchal, Chantal. "Le lai de 'Fresne' et la littérature édifiante du XIIe siècle." *Cahiers de civilisation médiévale* 35 (1992): 131-41.

Marie de France. *Lais de Marie de France.* Trans. Laurence Harf-Lancner. Paris: Lettres Gothiques, 1990.

Ménard, Philippe. "Marie de France et nous." Dufournet 7-24.

McCash, June Hall. "The Hawk-Lover in Marie de France's 'Yonec'." *Medieval Perspectives* 6 (1991): 67-75.

Mickel, Jr. Emmanuel J. *Marie de France.* New York: Twayne Publishers, Inc., 1974.

Murray, Jacqueline. "Individual and Consensual Marriage: Some Evidence from Medieval England." *Studies in Medieval Culture* 37 (1998): 121-51.

Noonan, John T. Jr. "Power to Choose." *Viator* 4 (1973): 419-34.

Pontfarcy, Yolande de. "La Souveraineté: Du Mythe au lai de Guigemar." *Acta Litteraria Academiae Scientiarum Hungarica* 32.1-2 (1990): 153-59.

Perry, John H. "Opening the Secret: Marriage, Narration, and Nascent Subjectivity in Middle English Romance." *Philological Quarterly* 76 (1997): 133-57.

Potkay, Monica Brzezinski. "The Limits of Romantic Allegory in Marie de France's 'Eliduc'." *Medieval Perspectives* 9 (1994): 135-45.

Prior, Sandra Pierson. "'Kar des dames est avenu/ L'aventure': Displacing the Chivalric Hero in Marie de France's 'Eliduc'." *Desiring Discourse: The Literature of Love, Ovid through Chaucer.* Ed. Cynthia A. Gravlee. Selinsgrove: Susquehanna UP, 1998. 123-39.

Resnick, Irven M. "Marriage in Medieval Culture: Consent Theory and the Case of Joseph and Mary." *Church History* 69.2 (2000): 350-71.

Rothschild, Judith Rice. *Narrative Technique in the Lais of Marie de France: Themes and Variations.* Vol.1. Chapel Hill, North Carolina: University of North Carolina Press, 1976.

Sheehan, Michael M., C.S.B. *Marriage, Family, and Law in Medieval Europe: Collected Studies.* Ed. James K. Farge. Toronto: University of Toronto Press, 1996.

Sienaert, Edgard. *Les lais de Marie de France: Du conte merveilleux à la nouvelle psychologique.* Marseille: Librairie Honoré Champion, 1978.

Spence, Sarah. "Love and Envy in the Lais." *In Quest of Marie de France: A Twelfth-Century Poet.* Ed. Chantal Maréchal. Lewiston, NY: Mellen, 1992. 262-79.

Stapleton, M. L. "Venus Vituperator: Ovid, Marie de France and fin' amors." *Classical and Modern Literature* 13.4 (1993): 283-95.

Suard, François. "L'Utilisation des éléments folkloriques dans le lai du 'Frene'." *Cahiers de Civilisation Médiévale* 21 (1978): 43-52.

Thompson, Stith. *Motif Index of Folk Literature.* Bloomington, Ind.: Indiana University Studies, 1932-1936. T.587.1.

Tudor, A. P. "The Religious Symbolism of the 'Reliquary of Love' in 'Laustic'." *French Studies Bulletin* 46 (1993): 1-3.

Stephen Guy-Bray (essay date 2001)

SOURCE: Guy-Bray, Stephen. "Civilizing Sexuality: Marie de France's Lay with Two Names." In *Norbert Elias and Human Interdependencies*, edited by Thomas Salumets, pp. 149-58. Montreal, Quebec: McGill-Queen's University Press, 2001.

[*In the following essay, Guy-Bray maintains that Marie manipulates traditional literary codes in the lay "Le Chaitivel" to suggest her desire for greater independence within the male-dominated feudal system.*]

At the end of the epilogue to her *Fables,* Marie de France does something relatively unusual: "At the end of this text, which I have recited in French, I shall name myself so that you remember: Marie is my name; I am from France. It may be that many scholars will take my labour for themselves; I do not want anyone to do this" (1991, lines 11-17).[1] Of course, saying that your name is Marie and that you are from France is not particularly helpful, but the very presence of a woman's name in a literary text is significant. In any case, Marie's name is important not merely as a referent to an individual woman but as the origin of the works ascribed to her and, increasingly, as a figure for the writing woman in the Middle Ages. It is not easy to say what this distinction means. How can we tell that a literary work was written by a woman? How can we say that a text is feminine rather than masculine? In a recent essay on Marie, Sharon Kinoshita suggests that we can locate "the 'woman's voice' less at the stylistic or thematic level than in Marie's radical challenge to the structure of feudal society through her canny manipulation of literary codes" (1993-94, 268).

My concern in this essay is with Marie's highlighting of the literary code that governs the naming of texts. Names play an important part in the lays of Marie de France, as they do in much of medieval narrative verse. Often, for example, the narrator will withhold the main character's name until the point in the story where the character begins to be heroic. Sometimes the narrator will give the title of the story in more than one language, as Marie herself does in two of her lays. What I am interested in here is her decision to give a lay two titles, one connected to a feminine interpretation of the lay and the other to a masculine interpretation. Marie does this in two of her lays: **"Eliduc,"** which is the most famous of all her works, and **"Le Chaitivel."** I want to look at **"Le Chaitivel"** because what is at issue in this lay is not only the outcome of a romantic intrigue but also the status of women and of the role they play in an increasingly complex social organization. In this context, many of Norbert Elias's insights in *The Civilizing Process* are relevant. While most of this work is concerned with the later Middle Ages and with the centuries that followed them, he bases his work on his analysis of the consolidation of feudal power in the eleventh and twelfth centuries, or, in other words, on the time in which Marie wrote. Before going on to discuss **"Le Chaitivel"** itself, though, I shall briefly mention the points at which my and Elias's analyses overlap.

Elias does not devote much space in *The Civilizing Process* to the condition of women or the state of literature, but the few comments he does make on these subjects are instructive. He suggests that "the great feudal courts of the twelfth century . . . offered women special opportunities to overcome male dominance and attain equal status with men" (1994b, 326) and that "in this human situation what we call 'lyric poetry' evolves as a social and not merely as an individual event" (1994b, 327-8). Elias's concerns here are Marie's as well. Throughout her lays, she displays a keen interest in the connection between gender relations and issues of power and control within the society of the poems as a whole. At several points in her lays, she raises the

possibility of female autonomy, either in the real world or in some sort of feminine realm, such as a convent or an otherworldly kingdom. The opportunities for women that Elias describes are especially important to **"Le Chaitivel,"** in which the heroine turns out to be the author of the poem and the choice between titles becomes to some extent a question of who will own it. The lay demonstrates that women are subject to male control not only in their own persons but also in the products of their bodies.

We can approach the question of male control over women by invoking Elias's concept of monopolization: "a society with numerous power and property units of relatively equal size, tends under strong competitive pressures towards an enlargement of a few units and finally towards monopoly" (1994b, 341). In his analysis the monopoly takes the form of the gradual absorption of a formerly independent knightly class into the service of a few territorial magnates. This at least is how monopoly works in relations between men; in relations between men and women the term can describe the process by which a woman becomes the property of an individual knight. These two meanings come together in the world presented in **"Le Chaitivel,"** in which women seem to have replaced land as the objects over which a knight is expected to demonstrate his control and mastery.

Elias says that one of the necessary conditions for the development of the feudal system is a change in population which ensures "the formation of a human surplus . . . among the nobility" (1994b, 329). Although a surplus of knights may be advantageous to a feudal lord in his struggles with other lords, it may well give rise to problems in times of peace. Marie explores the consequences of this surplus in **"Le Chaitivel,"** which tells the story of a beautiful and courtly woman with whom all men are in love. This is, of course, a familiar situation, but Marie complicates the cliché by having the Lady loved by four knights and having her love them all in return. "They were all so precious that she could not choose the best. She did not want to lose three for one" (1991, lines 53-5).[2] The knights appear in the poem as a surplus because it is impossible for either the Lady or the reader to choose among them. "This group, which has in its number—that of the four seasons, the four winds, the four elements of the cosmos and of the human body—the sign of universality, constitutes a perfect group; but none of its members can have a distinct and individual life" (Mora-Lebrun 1986, 24).[3] The knights are introduced as a group: "In Brittany there were four barons, but I do not know their names" (1991, lines 33-4).[4] Although the female protagonist is not named either, it is remarkable that Marie draws attention to the fact that she does not know the knights' names. Furthermore, the knights are all equally wonderful: "they were very beautiful and valiant and brave knights, frank, courteous, and generous" (1991, lines 36-8).[5] There is no suggestion, here or elsewhere in **"Le Chaitivel,"** that one knight is better than the others.

This idea of surplus has a particular relevance to Marie's own work. In the prologue to her collection of lays, she speaks of the ideal readers of difficult classical texts as those "who can gloss the letter and give the surplus of the meaning" (1991, lines 15-16).[6] Most obviously, the surplus refers to the implications and significations that are not apparent at a first reading, but the word has its own hidden implications. Citing line 533 of Marie's lay **"Guigemar,"** Alexandre Leupin points out that "the word 'surplus' has a particular emphasis: it can denote sexual pleasure" (1991, 230). In my reading of **"Le Chaitivel"** the text that the Lady glosses is the social text which restricts female sexuality to one object. The Lady adds the surplus (in this case, more men and more pleasure than women are normally allowed) which, in Marie's theory of reading, is necessary to the proper understanding of a text. Furthermore, in transforming this text, the Lady does what Marie herself claims to do with the material she cites as her source for the lays: "In **"Chaitivel,"** Marie de France . . . presents a narrative example of her own double, the female creator of lays" (Faust 1988, 19). The Lady's glossing of the social text is the first movement towards her emergence as a writer.

The resulting surplus—the simultaneous possession of four highly impressive lovers—may not appear to present a serious problem, and in fact, Marie does not present it as one so far as the Lady is concerned. The problem lies in the potential for violent competition among the men in the story. One of Elias's major themes in the early part of *The Civilizing Process* is "the transformation of elementary urges into the many kinds of refined pleasure known to society" (1994b, 320). If knights are forced to spend much of their time not fighting and to be violent only at the command of their feudal superior, they must be provided with more peaceful diversions. Love is one of the obvious choices, as Elias points out: "encouraged above all by the presence of the lady, more peaceful forms of conduct become obligatory" (1994b, 323). He goes on to say that the change is not total and that the potential for spontaneous violence still exists. This potential violence is made more likely by the institution of the tournament, in which a knight's love for a lady and his skill as a fighter are supposed to reinforce each other: "At the tournament, each wanted to be first, to do well—if he could—to please the lady" (Marie de France 1991, lines 63-6).[7]

The four indistinguishable knights manage for some time to compete in tournaments without resorting to actual violence (as opposed to ritualized combat) and without disturbing their affairs with the Lady: "She loved and held all four until there was a tournament announced at Nantes after Easter. Men came from other countries to challenge the four lovers" (1991, lines 71-6).[8] Marie follows this passage with a list of all the areas of France and surrounding countries from which knights come to fight at the tournament. As Elias indicates, there are at this time a large number of knights who have no real wars to fight. Furthermore, these knights have only partially been brought under control: "even the *courtois* knight is first and foremost still a warrior, and his life an almost uninterrupted chain of wars, feuds and violence. The more peaceful constraints of social intertwining which tend to impose a profound transformation of drive, do not yet bear constantly and evenly on his life; they intrude only intermittently, are constantly breached by belligerence" (Elias 1994b, 468). In a tournament there is clearly always a danger that ritualized violence will turn into real violence, particularly when a knight's ability to joust is seen as connected with his status as a lover.

For some time, however, the tournament in the poem goes on without problems. The four knights cover themselves with glory as the Lady watches: "The Lady was in a tower; she could easily distinguish her knights and their men. She saw her lovers helping each other and did not know which one to value most" (1991, lines 107-10).[9] Although the Lady can tell her lovers and their retainers from all the other combatants, she is still unable to decide which of the four should be her favourite. Throughout the lay Marie is careful to obviate any possibility that a front runner will emerge. Although the Lady could still be said to have a certain power at this point in the lay, her spatial isolation from the scene of conflict is important. The narrative situation is reminiscent of Elias's comments about the position of women in an essentially martial society: "the men of the Middle Ages, when women were generally excluded from the central sphere of male life, military action, spend most of their time among themselves . . . The woman belongs in her own special room" (1994b, 326). The realities of the gender system are revealed in this tournament scene, as the mingling of the sexes typical of courtly society is replaced by the gender segregation that is necessary to the work of fighting which underwrites both courtliness and knightly identity.

As you might expect, the four knights fight brilliantly throughout the tournament. In fact, they fight *equally* brilliantly, and thus the narrative dilemma is prolonged. Like many other forms of narrative, the lay is supposed to end with a consummation. The unsuitable admirers must be dispensed with, leaving one knight who can be united with the Lady either in love or in death. In sexual terms, Elias's concept of monopoly refers to a man's undisputed possession of a woman. But rather than being the means for establishing this monopoly, the tournament has reconfirmed the impossibility of selection. It is clear that a drastic solution will have to be found: "Thus her four lovers did so well that they won the prizes; then night fell and they should have separated. They strayed too foolishly from their people, and they paid for it because three of them were killed" (1991, lines 115-21).[10] The knights suffer disaster because of their own recklessness in allowing themselves to be separated from their retinue. Furthermore, the men who struck the knights down are horrified: "They grieved greatly for them: they had not done it knowingly" (1991, lines 129-30).[11] Marie emphasizes that the situation is a tragic accident. Clearly, the potential for violence is still a real threat in courtly society. The tournament is intended to turn violence, which is the main preoccupation of the knightly class, into a ritualized activity performed in the service of romantic love.

Marie demonstrates that it is naive to think that violence can be kept under control. She illustrates how easily the pursuit of love, rather than civilizing warriors, can turn into war carried on by other means. Furthermore, she shows that violence is in fact necessary to at least some courtly narratives. Something, after all, has to be done to reduce the number of the Lady's lovers. The disaster at the tournament would seem to be the answer to the problem, but although three knights are killed off, the wedding still cannot take place: "the fourth was badly wounded; the lance went right through his thigh and his body" (1991, lines 122-4).[12] Even if we do not take the thigh wound as a periphrasis for castration, it is clear that the surviving knight is at least temporarily impotent. His impotency and the deaths of the three other knights are the necessary conditions for the Lady's assumption of agency in the poem: "I shall bury the dead, and if the wounded one can be healed, I shall willingly do it and I shall hire good doctors for him" (1991, lines 161-4).[13] Up to this point in the poem, the Lady, although Marie has described her as an admirable and accomplished woman, has been a largely passive figure. From this point on, she assumes a certain degree of control. The action has passed from the male to the female sphere, although it is of course significant that the female sphere is the place where women attempt to compensate for the destruction caused by male violence.

The Lady buries the dead knights magnificently and hires doctors for the wounded knight, whom she attempts to comfort. She is herself uncomforted, however, and her continuing sorrow leads her to what we can see as, in context, a powerful act of self-assertion: "Because I have loved you so much, I want my sorrows to be remembered. I shall make a lay about the four of you, and I shall call it The Four Sorrows" (1991, lines 201-4).[14] Elias sees medieval lyric verse as emerging from a new and more reverent attitude towards women. In **"Le Chaitivel,"** however, the woman is the poet rather than the object of the romantic impulses recounted in the poem; indeed, she becomes a poet as a result of functioning as a love object. The Lady is not content to be fictionalized as the object of masculine emotions, and she chooses to write a poem that has her own feminine emotions as its subject. The title neatly illustrates this situation, since the four knights are to be remembered, not for themselves, but for her response to them. The Lady's position in the tower, which I earlier described as an image of feminine isolation from masculine activities, is also the vantage point of the artist who, after all, has the final say in how events are remembered.

What the Lady produces and names need not simply be considered a text or even a comment on other texts, and she need not simply be considered an artist in the traditional sense. At the beginning of **"Le Chaitivel,"** when Marie summarizes what the lay will include, she mentions "where it was born" (1991, line 5).[15] Even before we hear the lay, then, we are invited to consider it a child. By suggesting this view of the lay and then telling us that the woman in the story has four lovers, Marie is perhaps setting up a reading of the text as a search to determine paternity. At the end of **"Le Chaitivel,"** the Lady's role in the production of the lay seems to be a traditionally feminine one. Michelle A. Freeman says that "Marie's work (1) explains an existing artifact by means of capturing the moment of inception and (2) depicts, in a celebratory manner, the artifact's subsequent existence as a private gift . . . between a man and a woman. In this sense, might not the gift represent a kind of sublimation of the child not borne by the woman for her lover?" (1984, 861). Inception, then, is a substitute for conception. The lay stands in for the child whom the knight is incapable of begetting.

Unfortunately, the wounded knight is well aware that a work's title is not simply descriptive, that it can also be taken as an instruction on how to read the text itself. By continuing the refusal to distinguish among the four knights, the Lady's title would commemorate her original independence and sexual freedom. When she tells him her plan, he quickly cries out, "Lady, make the new lay, but call it The Wretched Man" (1991, lines 207-8).[16] He tells her that the other knights' troubles are over while his continue, and he insists that the title should commemorate him: "If the lay is to be called after me, let it be called The Wretched Man. Whoever calls it The Four Sorrows will be changing its real name" (1991, lines 225-8).[17] A man's monopoly over a woman, his undisputed possession of her, extends not only to the woman herself but also to what she produces. Nevertheless, if the lay is a sort of child, then it is clear that the paternity is uncertain. In naming the lay, the knight attempts to set himself up as the father and to avoid the prospect of being declared a cuckold by the sexual pluralism evident in the lay's original title. But although he insists on naming the lay, there is no indication that he will write it or even that he will recite it. The parallels to childbirth and child-rearing could hardly be clearer. Thus the situation at the end of **"Le Chaitivel"** can be read as a narrative rendering of the fear that Marie expresses at the end of her fables: poems, like children, take their father's name, even though the woman has all the *labur.*

The poem does not end with the impotent knight's assumption of potency. Although the Lady gives in to him, Marie is careful to point out both at the beginning and at the end of the poem that either title is suitable. At the end she says that those who first recited the lay called it *Four Sorrows,* while *The Wretched Man* is the currently accepted title, thus giving the female title the claim of priority at least. In the very last lines of the poem, Marie draws attention to the lack of closure: "Here it ends; there is no more; I have heard no more; I know no more; I shall tell you no more" (1991, lines 238-40).[18] These lines can be read as an acknowledgment that the poem is unfinished because the story it recounts is unfinished. The couple in **"Le Chaitivel,"** alone of all the couples in Marie's lays, does not achieve narrative closure, which comes from union either in marriage or in death. The knight may at first be thought to have triumphed because the title of the lay suggests that his story is the central one in the poem, but this triumph is compromised by Marie's statements that his is only a possible title and by the fact that she ends the poem by calling attention to his impotence. His insistence on his singularity actually works against him: "this 'one' . . . is only produced by the text on the basis of exclusion of sexuality" (Huchet 1981, 429).[19]

The poem thus ends with a narrative impasse in which, as Samuel T. Cowling points out, "the narrator's commentary upon the naming of this *lai* explicitly restores in an unresolvable equilibrium the impulses that have been operating throughout" (1974-75, 687). This ending of the poem is hardly a triumph for the Lady, but neither is it a defeat. Although the violence that Elias reminds us is always just beneath the surface of courtly life has erupted, the man has been no more exempt from it than the woman, and the lay that remains to tell the story testifies to the woman's strength and skill. Marie has shown, to return to Elias's formulation, one of the ways in which women have "special opportunities to overcome male dominance." Although men may have a monopoly on the violence that underwrites the feudal system, a women who writes can at least ensure that they do not have the monopoly on how events are perceived and remembered.

Notes

1. Al finement de cest escrit,
    Qu'en Romanz ai treité e dit,
    me numerai pur remembrance:
    Marie ai num, si sui de France.
    Puet cel estre, que clerc plusur
    prendereient sur eus mun labur:
    ne voil que nul sur li le die.

2. Tant furent tuit de grant valur,
    Ne pot eslire le meillur.
    Ne volt les treis perdre pur l'un.

3. Ce groupe, qui porte dans son chiffre—celui des quatre saisons, des quatre vents, des quatre éléments du cosmos et du corps humain—réalise une sorte d'ensemble parfait; mais aucun de ses membres ne peut accéder à une existence distincte et individuelle.

4. En Bretaine ot quatre baruns,
    Mes jeo ne sai numer lur nuns.

5. . . . mut erent de grant beauté
    E chevalier pruz e vaillant,
    Large, curteis e despendant.

6. K'i peüssent gloser la lettre
    E de lur sen le surplus mettre.

7. A l'assembler des chevaliers
    Voleit chescuns estre primiers
    De bien fere, si il peüst,
    Pur ceo qu'a la dame pleüst.

8. Tuz quatre les ama e tint,
    Tant qu'aprés une Paske vint,
    Ot un turneiement crié,
    Pur aquointier les quatre druz
    I sunt d'autre païs venuz.

9. La dame fu sur une tur,
    Bien choisi les suens e les lur;
    Ses druz i vit mut bien aidier,
    Ne seit le quel deit plus preisier.

10. Si quatre dru bien le fescient,
    Si ke de tuz le pris aveient,
    Tant ke ceo vint a l'avesprer
    Que il deveient desevrer;
    Trop folement s'abaundonerent
    Luinz de lur gent, sil comparerent,
    Kar li treis i furent ocis.

11. Mut esteient pur eus dolent:
    Nel firent pas a escïent.

12. E li quarz nafrez e malmis
    Par mi la quisse e einz el cors,
    Si que la lance parut fors.

13. Les morz ferai ensevelir,
    E si li nafrez poet garir,

Volentiers m'en entremetrai
E bons mires li baillerai.

14. Pur ceo que tant vus ai amez,
    Voil que mis doels seit remembrez;
    Des vus quatres ferai un lai
    E *Quatre Dols* le numerai.

15. U il fu nez.

16. Dame, fetes le lai novel,
    Si l'apelez *Le Chaitivel.*

17. Pur c'ert li lais de mei nomez:
    Le Chaitivel iert appelez.
    Ki *Quatre Dols* le numera
    Sun propre nun li changera.

18. Ici finist, nen i ad plus,
    Plus n'en oï ne plus n'en sai
    Ne plus ne vus en cunterai.

19. ce "un" . . . n'est produit par l'écrit que sur fond
    d'exclusion de
    la sexualité.

Bibliography

Cowling, Samuel T. 1974-75. "The Image of the Turna-
ment in Marie de France's Le Chaitivel." *Romance
Notes* 16:686-91.

Elias, Norbert. 1994b. *The Civilizing Process.* Trans.
Edmund Jephcott. Oxford: Blackwell.

Faust, Diana M. 1988. "Women Narrators in the Lais of
Marie de France." In *Women in French Literature: A
Collection of Essays,* ed. Michel Guggenheim, 17-27.
Saratoga, Calif.: Anna Libri.

Freeman, Michelle A. 1984. "Marie de France's Poetics
of Silence: The Implications for a Feminine Translation." *PMLA* 99:860-3.

Huchet, Jean-Charles. 1981. "Nom de femme et écriture
féminine au Moyen Age: Les Lais de Marie de France."
Poétique 48:407-30.

Kinoshita, Sharon. 1993-94. "Cherchez la femme:
Feminist Criticism and Marie de France's Lai de Lanval." *Romance Notes* 34:263-73.

Leupin, Alexandre. 1991. "The Impossible Task of
Manifesting 'literature': On Marie de France's Obscurity." Trans. Judith P. Shoaf. *Exemplaria* 3:221-42.

Marie de France. 1991. *Les Fables.* Ed. Charles
Brucker. Louvain: Peeters.

Mora-Lebrun, Francine. 1986. "Marie de France
héritière de la lyrique des troubadours: L'exemple du
Chaitivel." *Travaux de linguistique et de littérature*
24.2:19-30.

Heather M. Arden (essay date winter 2002)

SOURCE: Arden, Heather M. "The End Game in Marie
de France's *Lais*: The Search for a Solution." *Dalhousie
French Studies* 61 (winter 2002): 3-11.

[*In the essay below, Arden speculates on Marie's motives for rejecting the peaceful solutions to love's dilemmas devised by her female characters in favor of the
antagonistic, often violent, resolutions conceived by the
males in the lays.*]

The endings of Marie de France's **Lais** raise the question: Who will decide the outcome, and thereby the
meaning, of the adventure? In some lais it is clearly the
male lover who determines the significance of the
adventure lived by the lovers, as we find in **"Chaitivel,"** a lai about a lady and her four admirers. After
the tournament in which three of the knights are killed,
the surviving lover wants to replace the lady's title,
"Quatre Dols" (**"[My] Four Griefs"** [l. 204]) by his
own, which commemorates their story: **"Le Chaitivel"**
(**"The Unfortunate One"** [208]).[1] Since the title of a
lai is assumed to summarize the adventure and point to
its meaning, the lady's remarkable adventure involving
her loss of four lovers becomes instead, with the change
in title, the story of the lover's adventure and his grief.
In many other lais it is the solution proposed by the
female protagonist which stands out: Fresne spreads her
blanket on her lover's marriage bed to prepare it for his
bride; Guildeluec retires to a nunnery so that her
husband can marry his beloved; Lanval's fairy mistress
comes to Arthur's court to clear her lover's name. If we
look more closely, however, we see that a masculine
solution replaces or rewrites the feminine one not
simply in one or two of the lais but in all of them,
thereby establishing the ultimate meaning of the
adventure as masculine. In this [essay] will explore the
ways in which Marie's female characters deal with their
difficulties, and how the ultimate resolution of the lais
are determined by their men. Finally, I will look at how
this remarkable pattern of male solutions taking
precedence over female ones may reflect Marie's pessimism about women's sphere of action in her society,
and even her uncertainty about the ultimate reception of
her own work in a society in which men traditionally
had the last word.

All of Marie's lais center on a love relationship, the
threat or obstacle to that love, and the resolution—
happy or tragic—of the situation, and in all the lais the
threat or obstacle that the lovers face is another person.[2]
In eight of the twelve stories, we find the traditional
love triangle in which the problem is caused by the
female lover's spouse or parent.[3] The other four lais
present multiple love relationships, either through the
situation of a male lover between two women, as in

"Fresne" (where the love relationship is threatened by the lover's impending marriage), "Lanval," and "Eliduc," or through the situation of a woman with four suitors, as in "Chaitivel." While it is true that some of the longer lais offer not one but a series of problems or crises, this article will focus on the final resolution brought about by the protagonists, to clarify the ways in which they attempt to overcome their difficulties and to discover whether a woman's or a man's solution ultimately determines the outcome—and the meaning—of the story.

Six of the twelve lais end with confrontational or violent acts by the male protagonists. In "Equitan" and "Bisclavret," the ending is written by men who violently punish a woman guilty of committing a crime. In each case the female protagonist has attempted not simply to maintain a relationship with her lover but to rid herself of an unwanted husband. Thus masculine violence (by the seneschal in "Equitan," by the werewolf and the king in "Bisclavret") simply responds to the women's aggressiveness by imposing a kind of socially sanctioned justice. While it is not surprising that when women are wicked, men will re-establish law and order, it is significant to find this pattern also in the lais in which women protagonists attempt a peaceful resolution to their problem.

In four of the six lais that end violently the agonistic ending imposed by men supercedes a woman's attempt to conclude the adventure non-violently, either through an effort to reunite the lovers or through the woman's act of communication with her lover. "Guigemar" is a striking example of this pattern. Guigemar's lady, sensing that she and her lover will be separated, devises a test to keep Guigemar faithful until they are reunited. After her husband causes their violent separation, she flees her imprisoning tower, finds the ship that takes her to her lover, and reaches him after danger and distress. Surprisingly he fails twice to recognize her. First, on seeing her again after their long separation, he doubts the evidence of his own eyes because, he says, "Femmes se resemblent asez" (779); she, however, does not have the same problem of recognizing him. Second, he refuses to believe that it is she even when she unties the knot in his shirt, that is, when she has passed the test she set for the woman he will love. It is only when he finds the girdle that *he* gave her that he recognizes her—by recognizing his object, the girdle. According to a common folktale pattern, the lovers should be reunited at this point, since they have passed the difficult tests. The lady does indeed ask Guigemar to take her away: "Amis, menez en vostre drue!" (836), but he must first fight and kill Meriduc, his competitor, who refuses to give her up. Thus the chivalric ending of "Guigemar," created by the two men, supersedes the lady's folktale resolution based on quest, test, and reward.

A similar pattern is found in the other lais in this category. "Yonec" presents a more somber story than that of "Guigemar," a story of attempted reunion which the male protagonist turns into a tale of vengeance. After her remarkable bird-lover is wounded by her jealous husband, the lady, like her counterpart in "Guigemar," makes a heroic attempt to rejoin her lover by fleeing her imprisonment and following the man she loves. When Muldumarec's beloved manages to reach him, after danger and distress, on his death bed, she continues to behave like a woman passionately in love: she is scripting a Tristanesque story of love and death. He however has other plans: the lady is "réduite à sa fonction procréatrice" (Harf-Lancner 106) when he gives her the sword with which he wants his yet unborn son to kill her husband. To further his plans, Muldumarec tells his beloved what she will say in the end and gives her a ring to protect her from her husband—he even gives her the clothes he wants her to wear: "Un chier bliaut li ad done; / si li cumandë a vestir" (438-39). Years later she carries out his instructions—and dies on his grave: the story ends as he has scripted it.

Another lai in which a woman attempts a peaceful reunion with her lover, only to be blocked by his aggressive intentions, is "Deus Amanz." The young woman in this lai, torn between the demands of her father and her lover, devises a conciliatory plan by which the lovers will be able to marry without causing pain to her father: she sends her lover to get help from her aunt in the form of a steroid-like potion that will allow the young man to accomplish the impossible task which her father has set for her suitors. But the young woman's plan fails simply because the young man refuses the cooperative solution she proposes in order to assert his own prowess: he sees the story as one of masculine valor, she sees it as one of mutual aid and cooperation.[4]

Finally, the lai of "Milun" follows the pattern of feminine attempts to maintain a loving relationship which is overridden by the masculine need for confrontation and retaliation, or by the violent assertion of the prerogatives of paternal lineage. The last act of Milun's lady, who does nothing in this lai but "communicate"—with her lover for twenty years and with her sister to whom she transfers their child—is to give Milun permission to seek their grown son, thus making possible the reunion of her menfolk. It is this son who decides, without consulting his mother, to kill her legal spouse and marry her to his father. For Marie's male protagonists, considerations of paternal lineage often come before all other questions. In these lais—"Guigemar," "Deus Amanz," "Yonec," "Milun"—at the moment of crisis, the heroine acts in a way aimed at bringing her beloved and herself together, or of maintaining their relationship, without harm to the person standing in their way. And these lais end in death—for the lovers or their adversary—due to the male protagonist's rewriting of the ending desired by his beloved.

While this first group of lais explicitly portrays masculine power and prerogative in medieval society, the other six lais also present masculine power and prerogative, but in a more subtle way, through men interpreting or appropriating a woman's experience—by adding "de lur sen le surplus" (16), a phrase from the prologue to the *Lais* to which we shall return.

In **"Chaitivel"** and **"Chievrefoil"** the male protagonists are ultimately responsible for the meaning of the lai which will recount their story. As described above, the surviving lover in the first lai reinterprets the lady's adventure by asking that *his* title—"Sun propre nun" (228)—be given to the lai she will compose. She defers to his request, although she recognizes that her adventure was unique:

> Jamés dame de mun parage,
> Ja tant n'iert bele, pruz ne sage,
> Teus quatre ensemble n'amera
> Ne en un jur si nes perdra,
> Fors vus tut sul ki nafrez fustes . . .[5]

(195-99)

While Marie concludes the lai by indicating that both names are appropriate, the scribe of Harley 978 gives it the lover's title (we will return to the question of titles later). Similarly Tristan will write a lai about his experience with Yseut in the forest ("Pur les paroles remembrer" ["Chievrefoil" 111]). Although it is not clear whose words he will record,[6] it is obvious that he sees the adventure as primarily his. He writes *his* name on the stick, when he could have written her name, since he is trying to attract her attention, or both of their names, since his point is that they cannot exist without each other. Tristan's lai will commemorate, then, "la joie qu'*il* ot eüe / De s'amie qu'*il* ot veüe" (**"Chievrefoil"** 107-08; my emphasis). Yseut, on the other hand, is more concerned with overcoming the rift between Mark and Yseut than in celebrating the fleeting joys of their love (see **"Chievrefoil"** 97-100).

The four remaining lais also portray how a masculine gesture closes the adventure and gives it its ultimate meaning. Like the lovers in **"Chaitivel"** and **"Chievrefoil,"** Lanval takes over the resolution—and the meaning—of the lai. His final act of leaping onto his fairy mistress's horse rewrites the ending she had intended, that is, the separation she had imposed after he broke her interdiction (she is not consulted about his desire to ride off with her). In contrast to the three lais just discussed, the final three lais in this category, **"Fresne,"** **"Eliduc,"** and **"Laüstic,"** present a strong, loving

heroine who seems to imprint her point of view on the adventure, but here too we find the final chapter written by the men in her life.

In **"Fresne"** and **"Eliduc"** the heroine acts in a selfless way to help the man she loves, without even expecting the reward of reunion with him. These are the strongest, most generous concluding gestures by Marie's heroines. Fresne makes a magnanimous gesture of support for her lover by spreading her beautiful blanket on his wedding bed, although she knows that he is about to marry someone else. Fresne's preparation of her beloved's nuptial bed results in her father learning about and pardoning her mother's sin; consequently the archbishop annuls Fresne's lover's marriage so that he can marry Fresne. In the end her father steps in to arrange it all:

> Sis pere ne volt plus atendre:
> Il meïsmes vet pur sun gendre,
> E l'erceveke i amena;
> Cele aventure li cunta.
> [. . .]
> El demain les departira,
> Lui e celë espusera.[7]

(493-96; 501-02)

And so the next day the newly-weds are indeed separated, Gurun marries his beloved ("Aprés ad s'amie espusee" [505]), and her father bestows half of his lands on his new son-in-law. There is no indication that Fresne was consulted. Her selfless act of love has thus become a family chronicle endorsed by the church.

The most generous gesture of all is undoubtedly that of Eliduc's remarkable wife, who withdraws into a convent to allow her husband to marry his beautiful *amie*. This ending of **"Eliduc"** parallels that of **"Fresne"** through the selflessness of the heroine who desires only the happiness of the man she loves. Although Guildeluec's withdrawal to a convent is one of the most memorable and moving endings in the lais, the story does not end with her taking the veil—it ends with Eliduc retiring to a monastery after years of happy marriage with his second wife, whom he sends to join the first one. Guildeluec's generous gesture is reabsorbed into Eliduc's adventure involving his relationship with two women—his serial polygamy and pious end. This tension between Eliduc's story and the women's is reflected (as in **"Chaitivel"**) in the competing titles for the lai: according to Marie, the lai should be named for the two women, "Kar des dames est avenue / L'aventure" (25-26). The scribe of Harley 978, however, adds his "surplus de sen" by reinscribing the title of **"Eliduc."**[8]

The most striking example of the hero's unilateral reinterpretation of the lovers' adventure is found in **"Laustic."** The heroine of the lai, who is carrying on a passionate but discreet love affair with her neighbor, invents one night, when her husband complains about the time she spends at the window, the excuse that she is listening to the nightingale—which thereby becomes a symbol of the love affair as well as being a real bird. This symbolic transformation of the illicit liaison is meant to preserve the lady's relationship with both her lover and her husband. The ensuing crisis is provoked by her husband's trapping and cruelly killing the nightingale, whose body he throws menacingly against his wife's chest. Wanting to inform her lover that she will no longer be able to come to the window at night, she wraps "le cors petit" (121), over which she has wept bitterly, in a piece of silk cloth embroidered with gold and written all over: "a or brusdé e tut escrit" (136). The dead bird and the cloth, the text suggests, are meant to convey "l'aventure" (134) to the lover— but already the heroine is fading from the picture. First, we are told simply that the cloth is "escrit": the passive verb hides the subject—did the lady "write" on the cloth? Is it her adventure that is conveyed by the writing?[9] Next, it is her male servant who recounts the adventure to the male lover, thereby making the lady's cloth irrelevant. Finally, the lover's fabrication of a beautiful golden box studded with jewels, in which he places the body of the bird, is a courtly gesture that leaves the lady out entirely. While he has the "chasse" ("reliquary" [155]) carried with him always, in an ostentatious gesture which makes their adventure public, she is left with the brutal husband ("trop vileins" [116]). She is left in the real world in which real nightingales are killed, while her lover displays the symbol of his love in a beautiful object of his making. The lady's attempt to convey a private communication to her lover has thus been transformed into a glittering public art object which expresses his interpretation of their adventure.

In all twelve lais, then, an ending proposed by the heroine is in some way rewritten by the male protagonist. While in **"Equitan"** and **"Bisclavret"** we do expect the men in authority to rewrite the murderous solution envisaged by the heroine, it is striking that men also do so in the remaining lais. Furthermore, this pattern of male-authored endings is significantly different from that of the endings proposed by females, which stress communication, aid, and union.[10] In contrast, the men write endings based on combat and competition, the fabrication of art objects, and royal or ecclesiastical authority. This end-game pattern incorporates the opposition between private relations and public authority which other scholars have seen in the *Lais* as a whole, for the women's solutions generally valorize the relations between a man and a woman, while the men valorize chivalric and patriarchal social structures.

Before considering the implications of this narrative strategy, let us ask whether the names of the lais clarify Marie's perspective. We have seen that the titles of two lais clearly reflect a man's interpretation of the adventure. In **"Chaitivel,"** it is the male lover who names the lai against the lady's **"Quatre Dols"**; in **"Eliduc,"** although Marie tells us emphatically that the lai's name is **"Guildeluëc ha Guilliadun"** (22), it is the scribe of MS. British Museum, Harley 978 (the only manuscript to contain **"Eliduc"**) who names the lai after its hero. This scribal naming reproduces the narrative palimpsest of masculine over feminine that I have described in the lais as a whole. While the original text of Harley 978 does not include titles for the lais (see Rychner 194), a second hand has added titles based on Marie's own indications: she refers more readily to the traditional name by which a lai was known, or the *aventure*[11] on which a lai is based, than to an eponymous hero. For example, **"Laüstic"** begins thus:

> Une aventure vus dirai
> Dunt li Breton firent un lai.
> Laüstic ad nun, ceo m'est vis,
> Si l'apelent en lur païs.[12]
>
> (1-4)

Nevertheless, given the repetitive pattern of male domination in the lais' endings, Marie most certainly intervened in the naming and telling of her stories in order to shape the lais to her understanding of her society, independent of the original titles.[13]

While the pattern of end-game resolutions is clear, its significance poses some intriguing questions, questions that challenge our understanding of Marie's literary endeavor. When Marie shows again and again how the male protagonist has the last word, is she simply recognizing the social reality of her time? For despite the influence, even the power, that noblewomen possessed in the twelfth century, they were ultimately subject to the authority of their male relatives or rulers. Is it possible to envisage a challenge to this state of affairs by the author, without reading too much into her "intentions"? While Marie recognizes the dominance of the chivalric social structure in which she lived, she also sees the possibility of another form of interaction, as shown most clearly in the lais of **"Fresne"** and **"Eliduc."** The confrontation of two value systems, one based on competition for hierarchical status, the other on cooperation for mutual fulfillment, underlies the contrasting endings created by Marie's female and male protagonists. Yet the endings of the lais also recognize the inevitable reestablishment of masculine value systems.

We therefore need to view this narrative pattern in the light of what modern scholars would like to see as her possible "feminism." Scholars have explored the possibility of a feminist reading of Marie's lais by focusing on the roles of her female characters, often seeing them as empowered by their female creator. For example, Michelle Freeman observes that in **"Fresne,"** "power rests in the hands of women" (1988:259). Furthermore, a number of scholars have suggested that Marie goes so far as to challenge the patriarchal structures of her society. "Marie's work," writes Jacqueline Eccles, "challenges the political and social structure of the time" (281). In an article in which she reviews various critical approaches to Marie's "femininity," Sharon Kinoshita concludes that it is "in this dissent from the fundamental premises of patriarchy that the 'feminism' of the *Lais* of Marie de France might ultimately reside" (272). While arguing that the "signs of women's power should be taken seriously in Marie's *lais*," Nora Cottille-Foley also recognizes that this power "is an area where [Marie's] writing entertains a tense relationship with the social reality of her time" (168). Other scholars have raised the difficulty of defining a "feminine voice" in the lais.[14] It now becomes clear, when we consider the complex way in which the lais reach their resolutions, that Marie's possible challenge to patriarchal society was an ambivalent one, and that she was ultimately realistic—even pessimistic—about the scope of women's sphere of action.

This ambivalence has important implications for Marie's conception of her own work. We find an indication of the personal value that this confrontation may have had for Marie in the striking parallels between the endings of the lais and the authorial concerns expressed in the prologue to the *Lais*.[15] Marie explains and justifies her project in a number of ways: beyond the necessity to use her God-given talents (1-4), she reveals an interest in making a name for herself as a writer. For this reason she rejected, she says, the idea of translating a Latin work (so many people are doing that, she tells us) in favor of the lais which she had heard, thus suggesting remarkable authorial confidence in this twelfth-century woman. It also suggests a desire to create a literary corpus more amenable to women's concerns than the clerical domain of translations from Latin.[16]

Another theme of the prologue deals with historical transmission and interpretation of texts.[17] In a difficult, much commented passage, Marie describes how subsequent generations reinterpret texts in their own way: "K'i peüssent gloser la lettre / E de lur sen le surplus mettre" (15-16).[18] Thus, as she is reinterpreting the stories she has heard, future audiences will reinterpret hers.

After this confident justification of her writing, Marie's tone changes in the envoi, that is, the dedication of her stories to the "nobles reis" (43), the paragon of chivalry: if he deigns to accept them, "Mult me ferez grant joie aveir" (52); do not consider me pushy ("surquidiee" [54]), she says, if I offer them to you. Thus, by presenting her lais to this first male reader, Marie is in effect in the position of the heroines of her lais—she must trust her story to the male-dominated society in which she lives.[19] Diana Faust believes that "one can only conjecture what changes her texts have undergone in order to please him" (21). The pattern of rewriting the lais' endings by the male characters which we have described suggests Marie's authorial anxiety about how her texts will be interpreted. While she feels compelled to transmit her texts to her own and future generations, and while she is confident of her creative abilities, she nonetheless feels apprehensive about how her texts will be received. Is this simply normal authorial anxiety, or is there the added element of concern about the possibility of divergent gendered readings of her texts? I believe that the pattern of male rewriting that we have seen in the endings supports the hypothesis that Marie is concerned about how men, in particular, will interpret her texts.[20] While other scholars have sensed Marie's anxiety about male rewritings of her texts, no one has yet observed the pattern of gendered endings which express this authorial anxiety. Andrew Cowell, for example, recognizes that Marie "takes a dangerous step as she releases her own lais into [. . .] a tradition where male desires may threaten to abuse both the woman and her texts" (355), while R. Howard Bloch sees a "deep desire on Marie's part for control over meaning, over intention [. . .] versus a heightened consciousness of the unmasterability of language" (42). While it would be naive to attribute to a medieval author a modern consciousness of gender issues in literary interpretation, I believe that we can glimpse Marie's perception of differences in how women and men respond to life's crises, and her realization that men and women will respond to her lais in strikingly divergent ways.

Notes

1. The edition used is that of Jean Rychner. All translations are mine.

2. A thorough analysis of love triangles in the lais can be found in Maddox. Lawson discusses narrative structure in the lais based on a Proppian approach. While helpful for understanding the structure of the lais, neither article discusses the gendered nature of their endings. Ménard suggests an approach to the endings based on the criteria of provisional vs. final, happy vs. unhappy, open vs. closed (61-99). The "conclusions fermées" (92) which he analyzes are forms of the masculine endings discussed in this article.

3. This pattern is found in "Guigemar," "Laüstic," "Deux Amanz," "Yonec," "Milun," "Chievrefoil," "Equitan," and "Bisclavret."

4. See Arden for a more detailed analysis of these gender-related value systems.

5. "Never will a lady of my breeding, / No matter how beautiful, valiant or wise, / Love four men together, / Nor lose them in one day, / Except for you who was wounded." See Faust's discussion of "Chaitivel" and other lais in which women "hope to convert their experiences to a solid and durable form" (27). For a perceptive analysis of the lady's role in "Chaitivel" see McCash.

6. See the note to line 110 of Marie's *Lais* in Rychner.

7. "Her father wanted to wait no longer: / He himself went to get his son-in-law, / And brought the archbishop there; / He recounted to them the adventure. / [. . .] / The next day [the archbishop] will separate them [Gurun and Fresne's sister], / He will marry him to her [Gurun to Fresne]."

8. The question of the lais' titles will be discussed below.

9. Scholars often interpret these lines as meaning that the lady embroidered an account of the nightingale's death on the silk, but there is no textual evidence for this idea (see, for example, Van Vleck 38-39). Faust points out a similar use of the vague passive voice in "Guigemar" (25).

10. Whitfield discusses this alternative morality further.

11. For a discussion of the significance of Marie's concept of "aventure," see Prior.

12. "I will tell you an adventure / About which the Bretons made a lai. / Its name is The Nightingale, I believe, / That is how they call it in their country."

13. For further discussion of names in the *Lais,* see Bruckner 1991.

14. See, for example, Huchet: "Pas trace [. . .] dans les *Lais* de la moindre conscience féministe" (408). Pickens argues against over-stressing the importance of women's roles in the lais: "La représentation de la production textuelle dans les récits de Marie est en effet bien plus riche et bien plus complexe que ne le suggère une lecture qui ne valorise que le rôle des personnages féminins" (1993:1121). It is interesting to note, however, that almost all of Picken's analysis of textual production in this article deals with the role of women characters. Pickens 1994 offers a masculinist perspective on the ambiguity of the lais.

15. Many scholars have offered interpretations of Marie's ideas in the general prologue and the prologue to "Guigemar." See in particular the discussions by Pickens 1978; Hunt; Foulet and Uitti. Cowell focuses on the opening lines, which refer to the biblical Parable of the Talents.

16. Bruckner 1995 argues that Marie's choice of oral material over texts suggests that she sees "un conflit potentiel à l'intérieur de la culture médiévale entre deux types d'autorité, l'une textuelle, l'autre de l'expérience" (7). I suggest that Marie also associates textual authority with masculinity, whereas she can use orally transmitted stories to focus more on women's experience.

17. Pickens argues that this is the central theme of each of her lais (1993:1122).

18. "[. . .] that they could gloss the letter / And add the additional measure of their interpretation." Burch analyzes the literal sense of the lines referring to the obscurity of the Ancients and the need to gloss their writings. Relevant to my argument here is simply the idea of successive interpretations of Marie's texts by subsequent generations.

19. Freeman 1984 focuses on parallels between Marie and her women protagonists.

20. Marie's concern about masculine appropriation of her work is expressed in the epilogue to her fables: "Put cel estre que clerc plusur / prendereient sur eus mun labur, / ne voil que nul sur li le die" (Brucker, ll. 5-7) ("It may be that several clerks / would take for themselves my work, / I don't want anyone to say that it is his.")

Works Cited

Arden, Heather M. "The *Lais* of Marie de France and Carol Gilligan's Theory of the Psychology of Women." *In Quest of Marie de France, a Twelfth-Century Poet.* Ed. Chantal A. Maréchal. Lewiston: Edwin Mellen Press, 1992. 212-24.

Bloch, R. Howard. "Other Worlds and Other Words in the Works of Marie de France." *The World and its Rival: Essays on Literary Imagination in Honor of Per Nykrog.* Eds. Kathryn Karczewska and Tom Conley. Amsterdam: Rodopi, 1999. 39-57.

Brucker, Charles, ed. *Marie de France: Les Fables.* Louvain: Peeters, 1991.

Bruckner, Matilda Tomaryn. 1991. "Strageties of Naming in Marie de France's *Lais*: At the Crossroads of Gender and Genre." *Neophilologus* 75:31-40.

———. 1995. "Conteur oral / recueil écrit: Marie de France et la clôture des *Lais*." *Op. Cit.: revue de littératures française et comparée* 5 (novembre):5-13.

Burch, Sally L. "The Prologue to Marie's *Lais*: Back to the *Littera*." *AUMLA* [*AUMLA: Journal of the Australasian Universities Language and Literature Association*] 89 (1998):15-42.

Cottille-Foley, Nora. "The Structuring of Feminine Empowerment: Gender and Triangular Relationships in Marie de France." *Gender Transgressions: Crossing the Normative Barrier in Old French Literature.* New York: Garland, 1998. 153-80.

Cowell, Andrew. "Deadly Letters: 'Deux Amanz,' Marie's 'Prologue' to the *Lais* and the Dangerous Nature of the Gloss." *Romanic Review* 88 (1997):337-56.

Eccles, Jacqueline. "Feminist Criticism and the Lay of 'Lanval': A Reply." *Romance Notes* 38 (1998):281-85.

Faust, Diana M. "Women Narrators in the *Lais* of Marie de France." *Women in French Literature* 58 (1988):17-27.

Foulet, Alfred, and Karl D. Uitti. "The Prologue to the *Lais* of Marie de France: A Reconsideration." *Romance Philology* 35 (1981):242-49.

Freeman, Michelle. 1984. "Marie de France's Poetics of Silence: The Implications for a Feminine *Translatio.*" *PMLA* 99:860-83.

———. 1988. "The Power of Sisterhood: Marie de France's 'Le Fresne.'" *Women and Power in the Middle Ages.* Eds. Mary Erler and Maryanne Kowaleski. Athens: University of Georgia Press. 250-64.

Harf-Lancner, Laurence. "La reine ou la fée: l'itinéraire du héros dans les *Lais* de Marie de France." *Amour et merveille: les* Lais *de Marie de France.* Ed. Jean Dufournet. Paris: Champion, 1995. 82-108.

Huchet, Jean-Charles. "Nom de femme et écriture féminine au Moyen Âge." *Poétique* 48 (1981):407-30.

Hunt, Tony. "Glossing Marie de France." *Romanische Forschungen* 86 (1974):396-418.

Kinoshita, Sharon. "Cherchez la femme: Feminist Criticism and Marie de France's 'Lai de Lanval.'" *Romance Notes* 34 (1994):263-73.

Lawson, Lise. "La structure du récit dans les *Lais* de Marie de France." *Court and Poet: Selected Proceedings of the Third Congress of the International Courtly Literature Society.* Ed. Glyn S. Burgess. Liverpool: F. Cairns, 1981. 233-40.

Maddox, Donald. "Triadic Structure in the *Lais* of Marie de France." *Assays* 3 (1985):19-40.

Marie de France. See Brucker, Rychner.

McCash, June Hall. "The Lady in 'Le Chaitivel': Villainous or Vilified?" *Medieval Perspectives* 14 (1999):140-51.

Ménard, Philippe. *Les* Lais *de Marie de France: contes d'amour et d'aventure du Moyen Âge.* Paris: Presses universitaires de France, 1979.

Pickens, Rupert T. 1978. "La poétique de Marie de France d'après les prologues des *Lais.*" *Lettres Romanes* 32:367-84.

———. 1993. "Poétique et sexualité chez Marie de France: l'exemple de 'Fresne'." *Et c'est la fin pour quoy sommes ensemble: hommage à Jean Dufournet.* Paris: Honoré Champion. III:1119-31.

———. 1994. "The Poetics of Androgyny in the *Lais* of Marie de France: 'Yonec,' 'Milun,' and the General Prologue." *Literary Aspects of Courtly Culture: Selected Papers from the Seventh Triennial Congress of the International Courtly Literature Society.* Eds. Donald Maddox and Sara Sturm-Maddox. Cambridge: D. S. Brewer. 211-19.

Prior, Sandra Pierson. "'Kar des dames est avenu / L'aventure': Displacing the Chivalric Hero in Marie de France's 'Eliduc'." *Desiring Discourse: The Literature of Love, Ovid through Chaucer.* Eds. James J. Paxson and Cynthia A. Gravlee. Selinsgrove: Susquehanna University Press, 1998. 123-39.

Rychner, Jean, ed. *Les* Lais *de Marie de France.* Classiques français du moyen âge. Paris: Honoré Champion, 1971.

Van Vleck, Amelia E. "Textiles as Testimony in Marie de France and *Philomena.*" *Medievalia et Humanistica* n.s. 22 (1995):31-60.

Whitfield, Pam. "Power Plays: Relationships in Marie de France's 'Lanval' and 'Eliduc'." *Medieval Perspectives* 14 (1999):242-54.

Judith Barban (essay date winter 2002)

SOURCE: Barban, Judith. "*Lai ester*: Acceptance of the Status Quo in the *Fables* of Marie de France." *Romance Quarterly* 49, no. 1 (winter 2002): 3-11.

[*In the following essay, Barban suggests that the* lai ester *(let it be) motif in Marie's* Fables *is the collection's unifying theme.*]

Although Marie de France's **Fables** have attracted much less critical attention than the **Lais,** they have engendered lively discussions concerning questions of patronage and audience—for whom and to whom they were written. Whether the author addressed them to the Plantagenet vassals at the behest of William Marshall, as Madeleine Soudée has suggested, or to princes and lords as a Mirror of Princes, which Karen Jambeck proposes, or to all of feudal society, as Léopold Sudre sustains, modern critics agree on two points: First, Marie did not write the **Fables** as a mere translation, but rather reworked material borrowed from more than one source, created her own versions, and generally adapted her original English or Latin texts, imbuing them with her personal stamp of individual creativity.[1] Second, she wrote the *Fables* to instruct her audience, whoever its members may be, for such is the nature of the fable genre. While each fable carries within itself a *micro*moral, usually explicit in the epimythium, Marie unifies her collection with implicit lessons, or *macro*morals, that embrace more inclusively the essence of her teaching.

In this [essay] I will examine the macromoral encapsulated in the colloquial expression *lai ester,* which I will show to be a motif that the authors [sic] uses to urge acceptance of one's physical, social, and financial limitations and, with guarded optimism, acceptance of the status quo, knowing that nature will inevitably take its course and that the Wheel of Fortune will turn.[2]

Lai ester, a colloquialism that appears early in twelfth-century texts and frequently throughout the thirteenth century, is translated variously as "Let it be," "Stop," or "Let well enough alone." It appears in a number of works before Marie's time, in the *Erec et Enide* (line 4233) of Marie's contemporary Chrétien de Troyes and in works of different dialects of Old French as well as Occitan.[3] The phrase, in one of its various forms, occurs five times in Marie's *Lais* and seven times in the *Fables,* in the latter always in a direct quotation from the mouth of one of the central characters. It is typically composed of the second person singular imperative form of the verb *laier* ("to leave, to abandon, to allow"), followed by the infinitive of the verb *ester,* a derivative of the Latin *stare* ("to be, to remain"). The verb *laier* is interchangeable with its synonym *laissier* and occasionally appears in the second person plural, *lessiez ester.* When used with a personal pronoun direct object, it is a command to go away and leave someone alone, normally the speaker: "lai mei ester" or "laisse m'ester." Without the direct object pronoun, *lai ester* does not signify a desire for the departure of the interlocutor but rather an exhortation to desist from questioning, seeking, or striving.

The idiom makes its first appearance in fable no. 31 in which a discontented peacock complains to the goddess of the animals that his voice is not suitable; he wants to sing like the nightingale.[4] The deity at first responds politely by asking him if he could not be satisfied with the beauty of his feathers. When the peacock pursues his complaint to the point of saying that he considers himself the vilest of all birds, the goddess dismisses him with a reproof: "Lai mei ester! / Bien te deit ta bealtez suffire" ("Leave me be! Your physical beauty should indeed be sufficient for you").[5] In this fable the *lai ester* expression seems to be the prelude to a lesson in acceptance of one's natural physical traits. There are

a number of similar fables in the collection. Closely related is the crow of no. 67 who pulls out his own feathers and tries to replace them with peacock feathers he has found, only to discover that he is then neither an acceptable crow nor a peacock, but rather a displaced person. In the fable of the hare and the stag, no. 96, the hare complains to the goddess of the animals that he has no horns like the stag. Annoyed with this foolish concern, the goddess replies, "Lai ester." In contrast to the peacock fable, the goddess grants the request, but the hare is unable to sustain the weight of the horns.

There are a number of animals in the *Fables* who wish to assume not the appearance but the behavior of another species. A donkey wants to behave like the master's dog to gain affection, but when he jumps up to greet his master he injures him and incurs his wrath. A beetle tries to soar high like an eagle and falls stunned to earth. A badger wants to be a pig and run with other pigs in the forest but realizes his error when he sees them being slaughtered. In all these fables the animals dissatisfied with their natural endowments are referred to as "fols" or "vezies" ("fools," "scoundrels") and suffer physically, or mentally as a result.

The problematic fable of the fox and the she-bear may be considered an illustration of the same theme. When threatened with rape by the fox, the bear tries first to outsmart the fox verbally, to beat him with a stick, then to outrun him, only to find her ranting, railing, and running to no avail. In this fable the reader is made clearly aware that the fox is being true to his nature: "jeo sui, fet il, tels cum jeo sueil" ("I am what I have always been"), he tells the bear, and he gets what he wants. The reader is left to surmise that the bear, had she followed her own nature more closely, perhaps by climbing a tree, or by using her claws rather than a *bastun* ("stick") to strike at the fox, may have avoided the rape.

The whole point of one short, eight-line fable about wolves is that they never change their nature: "[. . .] tuit li lou sunt enveilli / en cele pel, u il sunt ne; / la remainent tut lur eé / Ki sur le lou metreit bon mestre, / kil doctrinast a estre prestre, / si sereit il tuz dis gris lous, / fel e engrés, laiz e hisdous" ("All wolves are enveloped in the skin in which they were born. There they remain throughout their lives. No matter who should give a wolf a good master who might try to teach him to be a priest, he would still be a gray wolf, wicked and cruel, ugly and hideous"). In another fable a priest does try to teach a wolf the alphabet, but when asked to repeat "abc," the wolf remains true to his nature and cries "Aignel" ("lamb")!

Nowhere is the theme more clearly stated than in the fable of the little shrew who wants to wed outside his kind. He first asks the sun, then the cloud, the wind, and finally the tower, always seeking to find the most important and powerful mate possible. He learns that even the small mouse—his own kind—can destroy the strongest tower. The tower verbalizes the lesson to the shrew: "Va a maisun, e si retien / que ne vueilles pur nule rien / ta nature mes desprisie" ("Go home, and remember that you should not want for any reason to scorn your own nature"). The moral conclusion to the fable of the owls and the hawk states quite succinctly, "Sa nature puet hom guenchir, / mes nuls n'en puet del tut eissir" ("You can turn away from your nature, but you can never get completely out of it"). The importance of this aspect of the *lai ester* lesson in Marie's collection is confirmed by its reiteration in the final fable in which a woman's hen refuses to stop scratching the ground constantly for food even when promised to be supplied daily with an abundance of grain: "Par cest essample vuelt mustrer / que plusurs genz pueent trover / manaie e ceo qu'il unt mestier, / mes il ne pueent pas changier / lur nature ne lur usage: / tuz jurs avive en lur curage" ("This fable demonstrates that many people can find assistance and the answer to their needs, but they cannot change their nature or their custom, which always remains alive in their hearts," trans. Martin 251).

In addition to teaching acceptance of one's personality traits and physical endowments, the *Fables* demonstrate acceptance of social conditions. The frogs ask their "Destinee" (goddess) for a king; they are giving a floating log. Dissatisfied with that, they are given an adder who devours many of them. Elsewhere, the doves desire to have a king and are allowed to pick their own, but do so unwisely, for they choose a hawk who also devours them daily. In spite of the wise hare's warning that "folie ert que il quereient / a eissir de lur cunissance" ("It was foolish of them to desire to go out of familiar territory"), a group of foolish hares goes off in search of a better place to live and quickly learns that there are no utopias: "Ja mes regne ne troverunt / n'en cele terre ne vedrunt / que tut i seient senz pour / u senz travail u senz dolur" ("They will never find or see on this earth a kingdom where everyone lives without fear, without work, or without pain"). In one of the final fables the patience of a wise old man is provoked when he is asked a string of questions by a knight in search of an earthly paradise, a country where he could be sure that everyone would love him. The old man—and Marie—dismiss the knight as a fool. In other fables, the country mouse is not happy with the living conditions of the city mouse, nor can the powerful enticement of abundant food and comfortable shelter make the wolf accept to live like the dog with a chain around his neck.

Not only do the *Fables* urge readers to be content with their physical appearance, personality traits, and social conditions, they also clearly denounce dissatisfaction

with the state of one's material worth. When a man goes into a church to pray for a second horse, he loses the one he had to thieves who steal the horse while he is praying: "Pur ceo ne deit nuls huem preier / de plus aveir qu'il n'a mestier: / ceo guart que deus li a done, / si li suffise en leialté!" ("Thus no one should pray to have more than he needs. He should keep what God has given him, and it should be sufficient to him indeed," trans. Martin 153). Likewise, the dog who wants both the cheese in his mouth and the cheese reflected in the water ends up with no cheese at all.

Other characters in the *Fables* seek to possess that which is inappropriate or excessive. We have already mentioned the hare who wanted the horns of a stag. The fox, believing the reflection of the moon in the pond to be an enormous piece of cheese, laps so much water trying to eat the "cheese," that he drinks himself to death. The sun wants to take a wife, but all the animals protest that the sun needs no helpmate—it alone is hot enough, for in the summer "il ne lest rien fructifier" ("it allows nothing to flourish"). The deity agrees, declaring, "Laissum l'issi, / cum il a esté [. . .]" ("Let's leave it just as it has always been").

There is a variation on the theme of acceptance that may be viewed as a call to belief in the ultimate truth and beneficence of God the Creator of Nature, and thus an encouragement not to be anxious over matters that are beyond one's comprehension or control. In the fable just mentioned, the goddess reassures the animals that she will never let the sun become hotter. The man who questions the hermit about the doctrine of original sin wonders first why Adam would disobey God by eating the forbidden fruit, and second why God did not forgive Adam immediately. The hermit is able to prove the first point by hiding a mouse in an overturned bowl and instructing the man not to look under it, knowing full well that curiosity would prevail over the man's will. His kind words of remonstrance link this lesson to the macromoral: "'Amis,' fet il, 'or lai ester! / Ne vueilles mes Adam blasmer, / se le fruit de l'arbre manja / que nostre sire li vea'" ("'Friend,' he said, 'Now let it be! You should no longer blame Adam for eating the fruit of the tree which our lord forbade to him'").

In the fable **"The Crow and His Little One"** the parent crow has tried to explain to the nestling how to detect danger in human behavior—whenever a man stoops to pick up a stone or a stick it is time to fly away. When the little crow responds to this lesson with a question which in truth shows that he has not yet begun to understand, the parent sends him away from the nest: "Li cors respunt: 'Laisse m'ester! / Jeo ne te dei mais enseignier, / [. . .] / Vole par tei e si t'aie!'" ("Leave me alone! [. . .] Fly away by yourself and help yourself now"). The parent, by sending the little one away, is accepting the limits of instruction and expressing faith in the future effectiveness of its teaching efforts. The epimythium explains that the wise parent will trust that the good advice will be sufficient—"a sun cunseil le deit laissier / e puis les altres avancier" ("with this advice he should leave him and go on to instruct others"). The reappearance of the verb *laissier* in the epimythium underscores the *lai ester* lesson of "letting go" and leaving the situation to the working of providence. An illustration of the often repeated proverb of King Solomon, "Train up a child in the way he is to go and when he is grown he will not depart from it," this fable promotes faith in the fruition of one's labors and lack of anxiety over the future. The parent crow tells the young one: "Or sui senz dute de ta vie" ("Now I have no fear for your life").

The theme of acceptance, with its *lai ester* motif, is curiously counterbalanced by the repeated representations of the necessity and efficacy of the use of *engins* ("clever tricks"), particularly on the part of mothers and wives, to save their children, their marriage, their honor, or to provide food or shelter for their young. Yet the two themes are not in conflict: it is in following her natural instincts that the female resorts to her "engins." The pregnant sow, who is told by the wolf to give birth so that he might eat the piglets, instantly devises clever words to save her babies. The apologue urges all women to protect their children, even if it means telling a lie to do so: "Ceste essample deivent oïr / Tutes femmes e retenir: / que pur sulement mentir / Ne lassent lur enfanz perir!" ("All women should hear this tale and remember it well: Merely to avoid a lie, they should not let their children die!" text and trans. Martin 84-85). Thus circumstances alter cases. Whereas deception is condemned in many a fable, in this circumstance lying is admirable, for it saves innocent lives. Likewise, the nightingale uses her wits to keep a hawk from devouring her young. Elsewhere a pregnant hound convinces another dog to give her shelter to whelp her pups, and a swallow makes peace with her enemy the farmer, who then allows her to build her nest and raise her nestlings safely in his barn.

When confronted with a delicate situation and possible loss of honor and dissolution of their marriage, women in the **Fables** can be quite ingenious. Assessing the women of the **Fables,** Harriet Spiegel writes: "Especially shrewd are Marie's females; there is not one of them in these fables who does not outsmart her male counterpart. There are several *fabliau*-like tales in which a clever woman with quick tongue and keen thinking gets the last word on her befuddled husband. Where analogues in French *fabliaux* revel in sexual jokes and suggestions, Marie focuses instead on the woman's wit" (Spiegel 55). In the two consecutive poems that more resemble *fabliaux* than fables, adulterous wives use

very disparate "engins" to save their marriage and good name. In the first, a woman seen by her husband *in flagrante delicto* simply shows him his own reflection in a bowl of water and explains that since he is not really in the water, he should not always believe his eyes, and the husband naively concedes. The other wife, seen going into the forest with her lover, concocts an elaborate genetic explanation that entails her retirement to a convent and the division and distribution of her property to her relatives. It is precisely at that point in the dialogue—at the prospect of losing wealth and family connections—that the husband utters the words "Lessiez ester" and calls her "amie." Although not explicit in the text, the reader may assume that the cuckolded husband is willing to forget the whole affair (literally) to keep his wife's money and family connections. The author has prepared us for this interpretation in the epimythium of the preceding fable (the wife and the bowl of water) by explaining that many people get help from their own cleverness rather that from their money and relatives: "Par cest essample nus devise / que mult valt mielz sens e quointise / e plus aide a meinte gent / que sis aveirs ne si parent" ("By this example we learn that common sense and cleverness are worth more and are helpful to more people *than money or family*" [my emphasis]).

But money and good parental connections work well, too, as the second adulterous wife fable illustrates. In most manuscripts the epimythium condemns the wife of the second adultery fable; however, in the Chantilly, Musée Condé, ms. 474 a different view is offered, as Karen Jambeck has noted: "Por ce dit on en reprouier / Que fames seuent engignier / Les fox homes de faire croire / E tenir lor menconge voire" (133-34).

Yet Jambeck's translation of these lines omits a significant adjective that I now add: "For this reason, some say in reproach that women know how to deceive and to make *foolish* men believe what is false and to hold their lies as truth." By including the word "foolish" the fabulist is reproving foolish men, not necessarily the clever wife. Since the woman refers to the lover as a "bachelers," or young man, and since she alludes to her wealth, could she be another example of a young woman married off to an older man for socioeconomic purposes? This scenario would certainly be in keeping with the spirit of Marie's *lais* of **"Guigemar"** and **"Yonec,"** two stories of true love between a knight and a *mal mariée*.

Marie de France's fables are enveloped in the *lai ester* lesson, for the collection opens and closes with the theme illustrated by the image of a chicken scratching for food. In the first story a cock scratching in a dung heap "salunc nature purchaçot / sa viande, si cum il sot" ("according to nature was seeking food in his usual manner"). In the final fable the hen constantly scratching the ground for food responds to the woman's command of "lai ester" by saying that such behavior is "selunc ma nature e mun us" ("according to my nature and my custom"). Tracing the *lai ester* motif through the **Fables,** the reader discovers a major unifying theme of the collection, a macromoral that teaches that there is a natural order of things—order in the genetic distribution of physical and character traits, and order in the steady unfolding of the universe in time. Striving against this natural order, these fables instruct, is fruitless and often destructive. By accepting conditions beyond one's control, the individual is freed from needless anxiety. In contradistinction to Morten Nøgaard's idea that fables teach a person to "dominer ses instincts," Marie would find it appropriate to "*suivre* ses instincts." Women especially are endowed with an instinctive capacity for protecting their offspring and preserving the marital unit, the proper venue for production of children.

In her investigation of the images of women in the **Lais** of Marie de France, June Hall McCash's summation concerning Marie's female protagonists is in keeping with the *lai ester* motif of the **Fables**: "Life's options for women in the **Lais** are limited, and Marie explores them one by one, seeming to conclude in the final analysis that the least painful and least destructive strategy for women who find themselves in a negative position is, outwardly at least, calm acceptance and trust in Providence, since struggle against their fate seems futile" (108). McCash goes on to point out that "while her characters' outward options may be limited and their open resistance futile and even subversive, [Marie] points the way toward strong inner resources as a means by which women may maintain dignity and some degree of personal autonomy in repressive situations" (108-09). Like the *lai ester* lesson of the fables, the **Lais** also illustrate the fact that women are naturally equipped with certain "strategies" ("engins") that help them survive in difficult circumstances. One of these endowments, as McCash notes, is creativity (104). Time and again the **Fables** demonstrate a female's ability to create clever explanations, often on the spot, and to devise ingenious ways to preserve not only her dignity but also her marriage or the safety of her children.

Certainly the noble woman of the twelfth century felt the pull of varying and opposing forces: politically arranged marriages, the laws of the church and of the courts, which accorded little or no autonomy to women, and the emerging recognition of natural love as encouraged and propagated by André Chapelain, the Tristan legend, and troubadour poetry.[6] Within the framework of her *lai ester* concept, Marie presents a view of the female that, while not in conflict with the prevailing masculine perspective of women as quarrelsome, crafty,

and deceitful, subtly suggests that Nature has provided women a way to cope with these constraints and compulsions.

Through the use of the macromoral incorporated in the colloquialism *lai ester,* the **Fables** of Marie de France may be viewed as a work formulated to encourage both the great and the small to accept their circumstances, to be content with who they are and with what they have, to cease from fretting and striving in a world where, although there are seemingly many imperfections and obstacles, there is at the same time a grand design that endows each creature with what is needed to thrive. The lesson is simple, practical, and biblical, a belief expressed clearly in the Judeo-Christian tradition by the psalmist's faith that his life is in the hands of a higher power: "The Lord will watch over your going and coming now and forevermore," and by the admonition of Jesus to keep his followers from unnecessary worry: "See how the lilies of the field grow. They do not labor or spin."[7] During times of great political, social, and intellectual change the *lai ester* recommendation must have been most welcome and may in part explain the popularity of Marie de France's **Fables** throughout three centuries.[8]

Notes

1. For a brief summary of this scholarship, see Jambeck's "Reclaiming the Woman in the Book" (120 and note 8 on the same page).

2. In the introduction to her translation of the *Fables of Marie de France,* Mary Lou Martin mentions the theme but does not elaborate: "*While Marie proposes an attitude of acceptance towards one's position in life, at the same time she calls for the just treatment of all individuals regardless of class*" (7, my emphasis). Aristide Joly as early as 1863 sensed this call to the status quo, but gave it a negative connotation: "Il faut se résigner. [. . .] C'est le dernier mot du fabuliste, et la seule consolation qu'elle puisse donner aux pauvres gens: souffrir" (50).

3. The expression is found in the poetry of Bertrand de Born (Hill and Bergin 90, line 45). Marie's contemporary Guernes de Pont-Sainte-Maxence used the expression in his biographical poem (c. 1172-74) on the martyrdom of Thomas Becket (Kibler 206, example 17, line 38). It also appears in the *Chanson de Roland* (lines 265 and 2154), in the early thirteenth-century *Aucassin et Nicolette* (46, lines 29-30), and later in the *Roman de la Rose* (lines 3071, 10237, 11751, 16281). For more listings of this expression in its various forms throughout the literature of the medieval period, consult Godefroy and Tobler-Lommatzsch (s.v. "ester" and "laissier").

4. Fable numeration is that of the Warnke edition, *Die Fabeln der Marie de France.*

5. Unless otherwise indicated, the Old French quotations are from the Warnke edition, and, unless otherwise indicated, the English translations are my own.

6. For a discussion of the emergence of the concepts of love in the literature of the twelfth century, see Pernoud, part 2, ch. 4, "L'Amour, cette invention du XIIe siècle" (134-57).

7. Psalm 121.8, Matthew 6.28, and Luke 12.27, respectively.

8. For remarks concerning the popularity of Marie's *Fables,* see Mickel (34) and Spiegel's introduction to her translation of the *Fables* (3).

Works Cited

Aucassin et Nicolette. Ed. Mario Roques. Classiques Français du Moyen Age 41. Paris: Champion, 1965.

La Chanson de Roland. Ed. T. Atkinson Jenkins. Boston: D. C. Heath, 1924.

Chrétien de Troyes, *Erec et Enide.* Ed. Mario Roques. Classiques Français du Moyen Age 80. Paris: Champion, 1978.

Godefroy, Frédéric. *Dictionnaire de l'ancienne langue française du IXe au XVe siècles. 10 vols. Paris, 1880.* Kraus Reprints, New York, 1961.

Hill, Raymond, and Thomas Bergin. *Anthology of the Provençal Troubadours.* New Haven: Yale UP, 1941.

Holy Bible: New International Version. Grand Rapids: Zondervan, 1973.

Jambeck, Karen K. "The *Fables* of Marie de France: A Mirror of Princes." *In Quest of Marie de France, A Twelfth-Century Poet.* Ed. Chantal Maréchal. Lewiston, NY: Mellen, 1992. 59-106.

———. "Reclaiming the Woman in the Book: Marie de France and the *Fables.*" *Women, the Book and the Worldly.* Ed. Lesley Smith and Jane H. M. Taylor. Cambridge: Brewster, 1995. 119-37.

Joly, Aristide. *Marie de France et les fables au moyen-âge.* Caen: Legost-Clérisse, 1863.

Kibler, William W. *An Introduction to Old French.* New York: MLA, 1984.

Marie de France. *Les Lais de Marie de France.* Ed. Jean Rychner. Classiques Français du Moyen Age 93. Paris: Champion, 1981.

———. *The Fables of Marie de France.* Trans. Mary Lou Martin. Birmingham: Summa, 1984.

———. *Fables.* Ed. and trans. Harriet Spiegel. Toronto: Toronto UP, 1987.

———. *Die Fabeln der Marie de France.* Ed. Karl Warnke. Halle: Niemeyer, 1898.

McCash, June Hall. "Images of Women in the *Lais* of Marie de France." *Medieval Perspectives* 19 (1994): 96-112.

Mickel, Emmanuel J., Jr. *Marie de France.* New York: Twayne, 1974.

Pernoud, Régine. *La Femme au temps des cathédrales.* Paris: Stock, 1980.

Nøgaard, Morten. "La moralisation de la fable d'Esope à Romulus." *La Fable.* Ed. Francisco R. Adrados. Geneva: Vandoeuvres, 1984.

Le Roman de la Rose. Ed. Félix Lecoy. 3 vols. Classiques Français du Moyen Age 92. Paris: Champion, 1970.

Soudée, Madeleine. "Le dédicataire des *Ysopets* de Marie de France." *Lettres Romanes* 35.3 (Aug. 1981): 183-98.

Spiegel, Harriet. "The Woman's Voice in the Fables of Marie de France." *Quest of Marie de France, A Twelfth-Century Poet.* Ed. Chantal Maréchal. Lewiston, NY: Mellen, 1992.

Sudre, Léopold. "Les Fables." *Histoire de la France et de la littérature française.* Ed. Louis Petit de Juleville. Paris: Colin, 1896. 1.12-13.

Tobler, Adolf, and Erhard Lommatzsch. *Altfranzösisches Wörterbuch.* 12 vols. Berlin: Weidmannsche, 1925.

R. Howard Bloch (essay date 2003)

SOURCE: Bloch, R. Howard. "If Words Could Kill: The *Lais* and Fatal Speech." In *The Anonymous Marie de France,* pp. 51-82. Chicago: University of Chicago Press, 2003.

[*In the following excerpt, Bloch first describes in general terms how the language of the* Lais *actually mimics its themes. He then illustrates this thesis with respect to the elements of feudal love—loss, suffering, jealousy, suspicion, adultery, imprisonment, secrecy, betrayal, and tragedy—portrayed in specific lays.*]

We have seen by way of introduction the extent to which a drama of language is played out in the works of Marie de France with particular reference to the general prologue to the **Lais** and to **"Guigemar."** Defined as globally as possible, this drama involves a deep desire on Marie's part for control over meaning, over intention—over words, in a word—versus a heightened consciousness of the unmasterability of language, of the resistance of literary language in particular to any attempt to control its unpredictable effects. It can be seen on the one hand in her insistence upon the obligation to speak, to share one's knowledge, or to teach, and in the wish for wholeness captured in the project of "remembrement," both a remembering, an act of cultural reclamation, and a reassembling, and on the other hand in her awareness of the contingent, fragmentary, and fragmenting nature of linguistic expression, the tendency of words, once assembled, to move in unforeseen directions, to take on a life of their own. Such is, finally, the meaning of **"Guigemar,"** the tale of the arrow that returns to wound the one who launches it like a literary work, and of the hero whose quest for bodily wholeness takes him to the land of fiction and of love before returning in the end to the point of departure, and, finally, to conjugal union; the whole summed up in the knot to be undone without cutting.

Marie's language theater, which not only uses language as a poetic vehicle but makes of it an object of plotted scrutiny, places it on view in all its complicated opaqueness and infuses almost every aspect of her works on both a formal and a thematic level. The impulse toward wholeness manifests itself, in fact, in terms of a desire for structure in the most literal and concrete sense. Marie tends to frame her tales. In the **Lais** we find formal passages of entry and exit even when there is no independent prologue or epilogue; almost none are without markers of origin and of transmission, a showing of "how the lai was made," even when such points involve merely a vague allusion to source or a drawing of attention to the imposition of a name, a title, at beginning or end. Then too, as critics have noted for some time, the **Lais** tend to attract one another in pairs or in groups that can sometimes be defined even in terms of gender pairings—Lanval's feminine fairy benefactor, for instance, set against the dreams of rescue on the part of the imprisoned wives of **"Yonec"** and **"Guigemar."**[1] Unlike, say, the romances of Chrétien or the *Tristan* poets, unlike even the **Fables,** where much attention is paid to government and community, or the **Espurgatoire,** where Marie insists upon the spiritual fellowship of the saved and the damned, the couple is the operative social unit within the **Lais,** where the desire for wholeness is expressed in terms of love as a longing for union, a coupling, an appropriate—that is to say, equitable, decent, voluntary—love, which may even involve marriage.

Marriage, however, fails to satisfy the desire for wholeness on the part of a number of Marie's inevitably suffering heroes and heroines around the outer edges of these case studies in longing. At an extreme lurk those who, like Guigemar in the beginning, desire nothing more than to be beyond desire—autonomous, self-sufficient, entire unto themselves—or those who, as we shall see, confuse wholeness with abundance: Eliduc, who maintains two wives, and the lady of **"Chaitivel,"** who, when it comes to suitors, prefers not to choose and wants to keep them all.

Here we arrive at one of the defining dilemmas of the **Lais** and the subject of this chapter: that is, the constant tension between the recurrent desire to "have it all" and the necessity of choice, which amounts to an analogy between the material of the story, its *aventure,* and the making of narrative. Marie's **Lais** seem, where language is concerned, to perform that which they recount, to expose the architectonics of their own creation in a way that permits us to erect as a trait of her style, indeed as a productive principle, the fact that almost anything that can be said about the themes of the **Lais,** whether on the level of economics, erotics, or social institutions, can also be said about her conscious concretization of language itself. This is not a question of interpretation, but, I think, a matter of authorial intent. To repeat, words for Marie are not merely a vehicle, a transparent medium through which we glimpse the portrait of a world that is narratively reclaimed and contained, but a theme—perhaps the theme—of the **Lais** as well as the **Fables** and **Espurgatoire.** For no matter how a particular tale is resolved, whether it ends happily as in the case of **"Guigemar," "Lanval,"** and **"Le Fresne,"** or unhappily, as in **"Laüstic," "Deus Amanz," "Chaitivel,"** or **"Equitan,"** or in a mixed manner as in **"Yonec"** and **"Milun,"** or doesn't end at all as in **"Chevrefoil,"** the tension between a desire for wholeness and a sense of loss both experienced by the characters and thematized in terms of language itself is the inescapable hub around which everything turns. Language is a character, perhaps the main character, capable of eliciting all the emotions connected to the various figures depicted in the **Lais**—trust, love, fear, jealousy, betrayal. For there is no separating Marie's *contes* from their form; rather, there is no separating the themes they contain in language from the thematic performance of language as a constant threat to the wholeness that is the object of all human longing, and, as we shall see in the pages that follow, from language as fatal.

From the beginning Marie's readers have sensed something melancholic in the **Lais** that, as far back as the eighteenth century, conjures geographic associations. The Abbé La Rue, it will be remembered, claims that "the English muse seems to have inspired her. All her subjects are sad and melancholy; she appears to have designed to melt the hearts of her readers, either by the unfortunate situation of her hero, or by some truly afflicting catastrophe."[2] And while there is no reason to believe that the English were any more gloomy in the twelfth or thirteenth century than the

French or Anglo-Normans, the pioneering Abbé did sense something operative within Marie's text—that is, the extent to which the geographic sites of the *Lais* are infused with a sadness that seems often to be set in the soil, a sorrow out of which characters and situations seem to grow as if adapting to the depressive ecology of a dolorous natural habitat. The action of **"Le Fresne"** takes place in the land of "Dol" ("A Dol aveit un bon seignur" [v. 243, see also v. 362]), just as that of **"Yonec"** is situated on the river "Düelas" ("La cité siet sur Düelas" [v. 15]), both names carrying a sense of sadness, of "deuil" (from Latin *dolus*). The region of **"Yonec,"** of which the old, jealous man is the lord, is called, further, "Carwent" (or "Carüent" in other transcriptions) ("En Bretain[e] maneit jadis / Un riches hum viel e antis; / De Carwent fu avouez" [v. 11]), as if the realm itself, from the Latin *careo, carere,* signified "to be cut off from," "to lack." The lord of the region of "lack" is wanting. The couple lacks progeny ("Unques entre eus n'eurent enfanz" [v. 38]). Most of all, the lady of "Carwent" lacks: she is deprived of the outside world ("Ne fors de cele tur n'eissi, / Ne pur parent ne pur ami," "She did not leave the tower for either family or friend" [v. 39]); of male company ("N'i ot chamberlenc ne huisser / Ki en la chambre osast entrer," "There was neither chamberlain nor doorkeeper who would have dared enter the chamber" [v. 43]); of speech ("Mes ja la dame n'i parlast, / Si la vielle ne comandast," "The lady would never have spoken without the old woman's permission" [v. 35]); finally, she is robbed of her beauty because she lacks desire:

> Mut ert la dame en grant tristur;
> Od lermes, od suspir e plur
> Sa beuté pert en teu mesure
> Cume cele qui n'en ad cure.
>
> (v. 45)

The lady was in great distress, and she wept and sighed so much that she lost her beauty, like one who no longer cares.

"Lanval" takes place in the city of "Kardoel" (and in some transcriptions "Cardoel"), an allomorph of both *careokarere* and *duel/dol,* just as **"Laüstic"** is situated "En Seint Mallo," which resonates with the *malum/mal* that is its theme. The action of **"Les Deus Amanz"** occurs in "Neustrie," which, Marie tells is, "we call Normandy" ("Que nus apelum Normendie" [v. 8]); more precisely:

> Une cité fist faire uns reis
> Quë esteit sir des Pistreis;
> Des Pistreins la fist [il] numer
> E Pistre la fist apeler.
> Tuz jurs ad puis duré li nuns;
> Uncore i ad vile e maisuns.

> Nus savum bien de la cuntree,
> Li vals de Pistre est nomee.
>
> (v. 13)

A king had a city built which he named after the inhabitants and called Pitres. The name has survived to this day and there is still a town and houses there. We know the area well, for it is called the Valley of Pitres.

The site of the fatal love test of this particular lai is the "vals de Pistre," or the "valley of pity," an unavoidable semantic association with the Old French *pite* meaning "who has pity" or "worthy of pity" and *piteer,* "to have pity," "to pity." Then too, the valley that is in the moral geography of Old French literature linked to sadness is the place to which Lanval, despite the appearance of rescue, repairs at the end of the lai that bears his name—"Avalun," "in the direction of the little valley," "downhill."[3]

Indeed, the *Lais* often take us downhill, infuse in the reader a sense of loss and decline. The ways in which loss manifests itself do, of course, vary. We find, for example, a pattern of loss and recovery in **"Lanval,"** where the hero is swept off to Avalon by the fairy queen, in **"Guigemar,"** where, as we have seen, the lovers reunite in the end, in **"Milun,"** where the son joins his parents in marriage, and in **"Le Fresne,"** the lai with both the happiest and perhaps the most carefully plotted ending, in which true love triumphs, the malicious mother repents, and the parents who have consented to allow the archbishop to annul the marriage of their other daughter displaced by Fresne find her a rich husband in their own land. In each of these an initial state of fulfillment is interrupted by a temporary separation prior to recovery in the end, though sometimes, as in **"Lanval,"** the recovery is somewhat incredible and only in the nick of time; or, as in **"Le Fresne,"** somewhat accidental and, between the wedding ceremony and consummation of the marriage, none too soon; or, finally, as in **"Milun,"** where the death of the lady's husband allows the son to give his mother to his father—"Lur fiz amdeus les assembla, / La mere a sun pere dona" (v. 529)—suspiciously well timed. Only **"Guigemar,"** the first lai in the disposition of Harley 978, seems to enjoy a happy ending prepared narratively from the start or from somewhere around the middle, and not brought about by a sudden and factitious arrival of a rescuing fairy (**"Lanval"**), the accidental discovery of a piece of cloth dispensed with some twenty years earlier (**"Le Fresne"**), or the news of a liberating widowhood (**"Milun"**). After the first lai, it is, I am afraid, all downhill.[4]

From loss and recovery Marie quickly slides into a pattern of suffering and withdrawal from the world, as in **"Eliduc,"** or suffering and revenge. **"Equitan," "Bisclavret,"** and **"Yonec"** make it clear that there are certain losses that remain irrecuperable and that, when deliverance is no longer possible, getting even restores some sense of balance in the end. Even here, however, there are degrees. For the wronged husband of **"Equitan"** the death of his wife and her royal lover ("Issi mururent amb[e]dui" [v. 305]) is justified by a sense of distributive justice not unlike that meted out in the fabliaux—"[Anyone willing to listen] can take an example here: Evil can easily rebound on him who seeks another's misfortune" ("Ici purreit ensample prendre: / Tel purcace le mal d'autrui / Dunt le mals [tut] revert sur lui" [v. 308]). For the betrayed husband of **"Bisclavret,"** cutting off his wife's nose is sufficient revenge for her misdeed, but it does not prevent her from remarrying and producing a lineage of women, some of whom, Marie specifies, are "born without noses and live noseless" ("senz nes sunt nees / E si viveient esnasees" [v. 313]). Yonec's revenge is, however, more enduring: having heard the story of his father's death from his mother, who dies from the telling, he slays his father's killer, his mother's husband, on the site of his father's grave.

Where loss is not recuperated by withdrawal or revenge, it is pure, and nothing characterizes the *Lais* more than the irreversible sense of forfeiture and bereavement in **"Chaitivel,"** whose other name is **"Quatre Dols,"** **"Deus Amanz,"** the story of the fatal love ordeal, and **"Laüstic,"** where the death of the nightingale is synonymous with the death of love and, one assumes, the perpetual grief of lovers taken to be as good as dead. These are lais inscribed in the mood of loss, a mood hypostatized in **"Chevrefoil,"** the least resolved of the lais, in which the ash tree dies without the honeysuckle that surrounds it:

> Ensemble poënt bien durer;
> Mes ki puis les volt desevrer,
> Li codres muert hastivement
> E li chevrefoil ensement.
>
> (v. 73)
>
> The two can survive together; but if anyone should then attempt to separate them, the hazel quickly dies, as does the honeysuckle.

In **"Chevrefoil"** a lack of completion is both formal and thematic: a narrative fragment mirrors a state of suspended suffering without other resolution, as we know from other fragments, than love-death.

There is in the *Lais* a sense that love is tragic. Tragic not only for wives, but, it must be said, also for husbands, whose own sense of lack is more often than not expressed in terms of jealousy. We have already encountered the jealous old husband of **"Guigemar,"** who meets his match in **"Yonec"**: "Because she was so fair and noble, he took good care to watch over her and

locked her in his tower" ("De ceo kë ele ert bele et gente, / En li garder mist mut s'entente: / Dedenz sa tur l'ad enserree" [v. 25]). In **"Milun,"** we learn of the jealousy of the husband from the wife's point of view:

> "Mes jeo ne sui mie delivre,
> Ainz ai asez sur mei gardeins
> Veuz e jeofnes, mes chamberleins,
> Que tuz jurs heent bone amur.
> E se delitent en tristur."
>
> (v. 144)
>
> I am not free. I have my chamberlain and many guards, young and old, who hate to see a just love and who delight in sadness.

Nor are fathers immune from a version of jealousy that in **"Les Deus Amanz"** has all the earmarks of a sexual scenario according to which the daughter has merely replaced the dead mother in the psychic economy of the patriarch, who considers "how he could prevent anyone seeking his daughter's hand": "Cumença sei a purpenser / Cument s'en purrat delivrer / Que nul sa fille ne quesist" (v. 29). Alongside of the jealous old men, however, we find the merely suspicious mates of the *Lais*: the husband in **"Laüstic,"** who, "irritated," asks why his wife gets up so often at night ("Que ses sires s'en curuça / E meintefeiz li demanda / Pur quei levot e u ala" [v. 80]); the persistent wife of **"Bisclavret,"** whose curiosity about her husband's unexplained absences finally gets the better of her; the uncomprehending wife of **"Eliduc,"** who does not understand her husband's odd behavior (more later); the inquisitive Queen Guinevere of **"Lanval,"** who pushes for an explanation for the spurning of her advances.

Nor is jealously strictly sexual. As we saw by way of introduction, Marie accounts for the wicked behavior of her detractors in terms of a form of envy of her good works that is thoroughly analogous to the jealousy of lovers. So too, the *Lais* are filled with knights envious of the prowess of their peers, of lords envious of their vassals, of wives envious of one another, as if such envy were a negative navel from which narrative is born. Thus, the knights of **"Lanval"** are envious of the hero's valor, generosity, beauty, and prowess ("Pur sa valur, pur sa largesce, / Pur sa beauté, pur sa prüesce, / L'envioënt tut li plusur" [v. 21]), as are those of **"Milun"**: "He was widely known in Ireland, Norway, Gotland, England, and Scotland. Many people envied him" ("Mut fu coneüz en Irlande, / En Norweïe e en Guhtlande; / En Loengrë e en Albanie / Eurent plusurs de li envie" [v. 15]). Eliduc's lord, who originally retains him for his courage ("Pur sa prüesce le retint. / Pur tant de meuz mut li avint" [v. 35]), eventually becomes envious of his good deeds and chases him from the realm. Finally, Marie seems to suggest that if the gossipy wife of **"Le Fresne"** speaks ill of her neighbor's wife, it is because she is filled with an envy that, as we shall see, comes to haunt her: "Kar ele ert feinte e orguilluse, / E mesdisante e envïuse" ("For she was deceitful and arrogant, prone to slander and envy" [v. 27]).

MARIE MAL MARIÉE

The *Lais* in one respect represent a fantasy literature, a literature of evasion, a voyage to another land. In the case of **"Guigemar,"** to the land of the idyllic woman imprisoned in a tower lined with the fiction of a book of love waiting for the perfect lover—who turns out also to be a virgin—to arrive via a boat; in **"Yonec,"** to another tower where another woman waits for the ideal mate to slip in through the window; in the case of **"Lanval,"** to a fantasy land of women whose beauty is beyond comparison with even that of Queen Guinevere and who are the source of incomparable riches. This is a world of dream, of the marvelous—of rescuing fairies, magic animals, message-bearing swans, mysterious boats, curative weasels, enchanted chapels and swords, men metamorphosed into werewolves and hawks, not to mention the Otherworld of Avalon—even when the manifestations of "le merveilleux païen" are masked behind Christian trappings.

And yet a harsher reality lurks beneath the surface of the fantasy in the form of unhappy women. So prevalent is the theme of the unhappy wife that Marie is sometimes portrayed as the poetess of the "mal mariée," and, given the license with which she plays with names, one is even tempted to play upon her name—the Marie in whose work the husbands or "maris" are the source of a virtual class of "mal mariées."

The women of the *Lais* are unhappy, first of all, because they are imprisoned. Sometimes imprisonment takes the form merely of close surveillance, as in **"Laüstic,"** where the husband, who keeps a close watch on his wife when he is present, has her watched equally closely when he is away from home (v. 49). We have seen that the wife in **"Milun"** laments the extent to which she is under surveillance before, and the implication is also after, her marriage. So too, the husband of **"Guigemar"** has placed his wife in a maximum security prison de luxe:

> Il ne la guardat mie a gas.
> En un vergier, suz le dongun,
> La out un clos tut envirun;
> De vert marbre fu li muralz,
> Mult par esteit espés e halz;
> N'i out fors une sule entree,
> Cele fu noit e jur guardee.
> De l'altre part fu clos de mer:
> Nuls ne pout eissir në entrer.

>   (v. 218)

He did not take lightly the task of guarding her. In a garden at the foot of the keep was an enclosure, with a thick, high wall made of green marble. There was only a single point of entry, guarded day and night. The sea enclosed it on the other side, so it was impossible to get in or out.

The husband of **"Yonec"** seeks to contain his wife behind the castle walls:

> Dedans sa tur l'ad enserree,
> En une grant chambre pavee.
> Il ot une sue serur,
> Viellë et vedve, sanz seignur;
> Ensemble od la dame l'ad mise,
> Pur li tenir meuz en justise.

>   (v. 27)

He locked her in his tower in a large paved chamber. He had a sister, old and widowed, without a husband, and he placed her with the lady to keep her from going astray.

The imprisoned wife, the lady in a tower, is a leitmotif of the *Lais* that cannot be separated from the marital practices of France's nobility at the end of the first feudal age, or from the conflict between lay aristocratic and ecclesiastical models of marriage, or from what I have described elsewhere as a "biopolitics" of lineage.[5] The genealogical family implied, first of all, the exercise of a certain discipline with respect to marriage, the restriction of unions to the minimum necessary to assure the continuity of the family line. As Georges Duby and others have demonstrated for the regions of Mâcon and the northwest, noble families permitted the establishment of only one or two new households per generation, the rest of the unmarried sons being housed in monasteries and chapters, or simply remaining unattached and disenfranchised.[6] The noble family husbanded its reproductive resources so as to produce sufficient progeny to insure dynastic continuity without a surplus to deplete its wealth through the fragmentation of a patrimony divided among too many sons.

The constant tension between the drive toward consolidation and the tendency toward fragmentation of lands is one of the levels on which we can understand Marie's concern with wholeness and dispersion, the term *remembrement* surviving in modern French uniquely as a term referring to the realignment of scattered lands. Marie is concerned in an even more literal sense, however, with the question of inheritance, the production of heirs, proof positive of the proverb still current in French—"tout mariage est un héritage." Thus, Gurun in **"Le Fresne"** is motivated to marry out of his men's concern over succession: "They would be happier if he had an heir to inherit his land" ("Lié serei[en]t s'il eüst heir, / Quë aprés lui puïst aveir / Sa terë e sun heritage" [v. 319]). In **"Eliduc"** the Lord of Exeter seeks to marry his only daughter because he is old and has no male heir: "Vieuz hum e auntïen esteit. / Karnel heir madle nen aveit" (v. 93). The Lord of Carwent (**"Yonec"**), which I have identified with lack, is also old and lacks nothing so much as a successor:

> Mut fu trespassez en eage.
> Pur ceo k'il ot bon heritage,
> Femme prist pur enfanz aveir,
> Quë aprés lui fuissent si heir.
>
> (v. 17)

This man was very old and, because his inheritance would be large, he took a wife in order to have children, who would be his heirs.

Thus, if, as we have seen, Marie is concerned about cultural inheritance, about passing on a past that, unarticulated, is lost, the imprisoning old men in her works are themselves anxious about preserving a family line, passing on their property to a male heir. We see in Marie as good a representation of the feudal, aristocratic model of marriage as can be found in Old French literature.

And yet the rule of primogeniture alone—the concern for a "heir madle"—could not have insured the integrity of lineage if it had not been accompanied by a model of marriage appropriate to the unilateral transmission of the fief and to the organization of feudal society as a series of alliances between landholders with mutual obligations. Marriage represented in essence a treaty (*pactum conjugale*) to be negotiated between families. Such a complex web of kinship between the lineages of the postfeudal era depended, moreover, upon the careful surveillance of marital ties. In particular, it assumed a matrimonial system—possibly from Germanic tradition—involving early betrothal (often at age seven or ten), early marriage (often at puberty), and, above all, the choice of partners to be made by the family or feudal lord. A marriage was, under normal circumstances, concluded by the head of household (*caput mansi*) or the elders (*seniores*) of the lineage; in their absence, by the relatives (*amis charnels*), mother, brother, sister, or uncle; and when the potential spouse was an orphan, by the lord who exercised the right of wardship.[7] Under this "lay aristocratic model of marriage" (Duby), the consent of parties mattered minimally, while that of parents and guardians was the sine qua non of a legal union. The decision of who may marry whom was based upon a certain respect for canonical impediments and upon a careful husbanding of the paternal fief in accordance with an interlocking series of military, political, and social ties. The will of partners counted very little.

There is ample evidence of such practice in twelfth-century hagiography and romance, where it constitutes from the start a pervasive theme. Alexis's father in "La Vie de St. Alexis" chooses his son's bride; and it is his gaze upon her in the nuptial chamber that pushes him

toward sainthood. Iseult's first thought, upon awakening from the effects of the love philter, which I have maintained elsewhere is the equivalent of an awakening of social conscience, is that she should live in society "in order to give ladies away to noble knights."[8] It is in the **Lais,** however, that we find the most developed display of feudal marital practice, and the composite picture of marriage that emerges is surprisingly similar to that of the historians whose conclusions supposedly derive from extraliterary accounts. The choice of partners may vary from one lai to the next, but it is rarely that of the partners themselves. Indeed, only in **"Guigemar," "Milun,"** and **"Eliduc"** do lovers actually marry, the first example being a case of rapt, the second a case of well-timed widowhood (a "vidua ex machina"), and the third the result of a generous first wife's willing retreat from the world. It is true that **"Chaitivel"** offers the example of the dilemma caused by marital choice on the part of those involved. But in all other instances, the right to marry is exercised by the parents, the lord, or the vassals of those destined by others to be wed. In contrast to the numerous saints' lives in which parents try to force children to marry rather than to remain single or to enter holy orders, **"Les Deus Amanz"** is a tale that turns around a jealous father's refusal to allow his daughter to marry the man she loves or to marry at all:

> Li reis ot une fille bele
> [E] mut curteise dameisele.
> Fiz ne fille fors li nauoit;[9]
> Forment lamoit e chierissoit.
> De riches hommes fu requise
> Qui volentiers leussent prise
> Mes li rois ne la uolt donner,
> Car ne sem pooit consirer.
>
> (v. 21)

The king had a beautiful daughter, a most courtly damsel. He had no other son or daughter except her whom he loved dearly and cherished. Her hand in marriage was requested by rich men who willingly would have had her, but the king did not want to give her away since he could not do without her.

The greater part of **"Milun"** is predicated upon the imposition of a father's unhappy marital choice:

> Sis peres li duna barun,
> Un mut riche humme del païs.
> Al terme ke el fu donee,
> Sis sires l'en ad amenee.
>
> (vv. 126, 151)

Her father betrothed her to a nobleman, a very wealthy man from the region. . . . When the time came for her to be given in marriage, her husband took her away.

The suffering of the young wife of **"Yonec"** is, as she laments, the result of the marriage arranged by her relatives:

Malëeit seient mi parent
E li autre communalment
Ki a cest gelus me donerent
E a sun cors me marïerent!

(v. 81)

Cursed be my parents and all those who gave me to
this jealous man and married me to his person!

The people of **"Equitan"** put pressure upon their king
to marry against his desire to remain single in order to
carry on an adulterous affair with his seneschal's wife
("He did not wish to marry. . . . The courtiers thought
ill of him for this," "Il ne voleit nule espuser. . . . La
gent le tindrent mut a mal" [vv. 199, 201]). Finally, in
"Le Fresne," as in the Tristan legend, it is the barons
who pressure their lord to marry a woman of his own
class and to cast off the woman they consider inappropriate, a concubine ("suinant"):

Lungement ot od lui esté,
Tant que li chevaler fiufé
A mut grant mal li aturnerent:
Soventefeiz a lui parlerent
Que une gentil femme espusast
Et de cele se delivrast.

(v. 313)

After she had been with Gurun for some time, the
landed knights reproached him for it severely, and they
often spoke to him saying that he should take a noble
wife and free himself from Le Fresne.

The King Arthur of **"Lanval"** distributes not only the
booty of war but "women and lands" ("Femmes e tere
departi" [v. 17]).

To the extent to which the lay aristocratic marriages of
the *Lais* were arranged, they were unhappy. Thus the
theme, practically synonymous with the name of Marie,
of the "mal mariée"—the woman constrained or literally imprisoned and thus the structural gap between
marriage and love, between the inclination of lovers
and the constraints of the community, whether it is
represented by fathers, family, vassals, or lord. Which
is another way of saying that to the extent to which
love remains in courtly tradition outside of marriage, it
is against or outside of the law. That is why there are so
many lovers as outlaws (Tristan and Iseult, Lancelot
and Guinevere); for, as Eliduc recognizes in the lai that
bears his name: "If I were to marry my beloved, the
Christian religion would not accept it" "S'a m'amie es-
teie espusez, / Nel suff[e]reit crestïentez" [v. 601]). In
the series of lais in which marriage is imposed from the
outside against the will of partners, Marie seems to offer a casebook of medieval marital practice according
to Andreas Capellanus, who lays out the laws of love in
opposition to both secular and ecclesiastical authorities.
Andreas claims that only the rich, the beautiful, the

elegant, the generous, the eloquent, the clean, the courageous, and the young may love (under sixty for a man,
fifty for a woman, but not before fourteen for a man
and twelve for a woman). He describes the stages of
love in terms of sight, hope, a kiss, and finally the *com-
mixtio sexuum*. But most of all, he prescribes in the ruling of the countess of Champagne, who has, it will be
remembered, been identified, among others, as the real
Marie, that love is by definition adulterous:

We declare and we hold as firmly established that love
cannot exert its powers between two people who are
married to each other. For lovers give each other
everything freely, under no compulsion of necessity,
but married people are in duty bound to give in to each
other's desires and deny themselves to each other in
nothing. . . . Rightly, therefore, Love cannot acknowledge any rights of his between husband and wife. But
there is still another argument that seems to stand in
the way of this, which is that between them there can
be no true jealousy, and without it true love may not
exist, according to the rule of Love himself, which
says, "He who is not jealous cannot love."[10]

To the extent that marriages are arranged, love is
extramarital, against the law—"Kar n'est pas bien në
avenant / De deus espuses meintenir, / Ne la lei nel deit
cunsentir" ("For it was neither right nor proper to keep
two wives, nor should the law allow it" [v. 1128]), says
Eliduc. Yet, if the law (the "lei") does not allow it, the
lai certainly does; for no theme runs more rampant
throughout Marie's tales than that of adultery; coursing
as it does from the adulterous couples in **"Guigemar,"**
**"Bisclavret," "Equitan," "Laüstic," "Yonec," "Mi-
lun,"** and **"Chevrefoil,"** to Eliduc, the man with two
wives, and the adulterous queen of **"Lanval."** Moreover,
to the extent to which love is adulterous, it is hidden.
Thus the theme of discretion that we have already
encountered in **"Guigemar."** "Love, when discovered,
cannot last long"; "Thou shalt not be a revealer of love
affairs," warns Andreas Capellanus in passages that
might serve as a watchword of the *Lais*. Eliduc, for
example, is not only a courteous man, but, as Guilliadun's messenger reports, a hidden one, his discretion
being a surplus of character that confirms her willingness to speak of love: "I consider him courtly and wise,
and he knows well how to conceal his feelings" ("Jeol
tienc a curteis e a sage, / Que bien seit celer sun curage"
[v. 423]). Then too, the secret lovers of **"Guigemar"**
and **"Yonec"** are hidden in the towers that, intended to
sequester the wives of jealous old men, ironically also
serve to hide the very adultery they are meant to
prevent. Thus, in **"Yonec,"** when the old woman who is
supposed to guard the young wife locks her away for
the night, she unknowingly also seals in her lover:

Li chapeleins s'en est alez,
E la vielle ad les us fermez.

La dame gist lez sun ami,
Unke si bel cuple ne vi.

(v. 189)

The chaplain left and the old woman closed the doors.
The lady lay next to her beloved: I never saw so fair a
couple.

"Lanval" is in some extended sense about nothing other
than keeping love hidden, the discretion imposed by the
fairy lady echoing as it does Andreas's prescription
against revealing secret love affairs:

"Ne vus descovrez a nul humme!
De ceo vus dirai ja la summe:
A tuz jurs m'avrïez perdue,
Se ceste amur esteit seüe;
Jamés ne me purriez veeir
Ne de mun cors seisine aveir."

(v. 145)

"Do not reveal this secret to anyone! I shall tell you
the long and the short of it: you would lose me forever
if this love were to become known. You would never
be able to see me or possess me."

Tristan, who tries to pass unseen in **"Chevrefoil,"**
moves about alone and under the cover of night: "To
avoid being seen he took to the forest all alone, only
emerging after dark" ("En la forest tut sul se mist, / Ne
voleit pas que hum le veïst; / En la vespree s'en eisseit"
[v. 29]). Gurun and his lady (**"Milun"**) are closely
watched, yet they manage to meet several times, Marie
tells us, in the course of a twenty-year love affair carried on for the most part via correspondence:

Ensemble viendrent plusurs feiz.
Nul ne pot estre si destreiz
Ne si tenuz estreitement
Quë il ne truisse liu sovent.

(v. 287)

They came together on a number of occasions. No one
can be so imprisoned or so tightly guarded that he cannot find a way out from time to time.

And, of course, secretiveness is understood to be part of
the adulterous love depicted in **"Equitan," "Laüstic,"**
and, implicitly, **"Bisclavret."**

Now what is interesting about hidden love in the *Lais*
is that it is always sooner or later revealed." Or, to hone
the syllogism of love just a bit: if, to the extent to which
marriages are arranged, love is adulterous; and if, to the
extent to which love is adulterous, it is against the law;
and if to the extent to which it is against the law, it
remains secret; then to the extent to which it remains
secret, it is disclosed. So consistent is the exposure of
secret affairs that such exposure can be posited as
inevitable. Love in the *Lais* is, despite the necessity of

discretion, always revealed, lovers uncovered. Nor are
they unaware of the inevitability of betrayal. They
know, or at least they suspect. Thus the lady to Guigemar, "My fair, sweet friend, my heart tells me I am
about to lose you: we are going to be discovered"
("Beus duz amis, / Mis quors me dit que jeo vus perc: /
Seü serum e descovert" [v. 546]), before they are
"perceived, discovered, found, and seen" ("aparceü, /
Descovert, trové et veü" [v. 577]). Similarly, the bird
lover of **"Yonec"** is singularly nervous in responding to
his lady's pleas to visit her often:

"Dame," fet il, "quant vus plerra,
Ja l'ure ne trespassera.
Mes tele mesure esgardez
Que nus ne seium encumbrez;
Ceste vielle nus traïra,
[E] nuit e jur nus gaitera.
Ele parcevra nostre amur,
Sil cuntera a sun seignur.
Si ceo avi[e]nt cum jeo vus di,
[E] nus serum issi trahi,
Ne m'en puis mie departir,
Que mei n'en estuce murir."

(v. 199)

"Lady," he said, "whenever it pleases you, I shall be
with you within the hour, but observe moderation so
that we are not discomfited. This old woman will betray
us and keep watch over us night and day. When she
notices our love, she will tell her lord about it. If this
should happen as I say and we are betrayed in this
way, I shall have no way of preventing my death."

Which is, of course, exactly what happens. And happens in **"Yonec"** in a way that seems at once insidi-
ously fated and exemplary.

Secret love in **"Yonec"** reveals itself. For if the effects
of imprisonment upon the body of the wife are a loss of
beauty ("Sa beuté pert en teu mesure / Cume cele qui
n'en ad cure" [v. 45]), then love produces an equal and
opposite change upon her aspect so as to reveal that
which is to be kept secret:

Pur la grant joie u ele fu,
Que ot suvent pur veer sun dru,
Esteit tut sun semblanz changez.
Sis sires esteit mut veiz[ï]ez:
En sun curage s'aperceit
Que autrement est k'i[l] ne suleit.

(v. 225)

The great joy she often experienced on seeing her lover
caused her appearance to alter. Her husband was very
cunning and noticed that she was different from her
usual self.

The lovers are watched, a deadly formula as Marie
remarks in an aside: "Alas! how ill-served were they on
whom he wanted to spy in order to betray and trap
them" ("Allas! cum ierent malbailli / Cil ki l'un veut si

agaitier / Pur eus traïr e enginner!" [v. 254]). For the deadly combination of the changed appearance of a happy lover who is also observed leads to a sighting— "This one [the old woman] saw and took note of how he came and went" ("Cele le vit, si l'esgarda, / Coment il vient e il ala" [v. 275])—and the entrapment of yet another bird.

The entrapment of the lovers of **"Yonec,"** like that of **"Guigemar,"** is paradigmatic and allows us, finally, to complete the syllogism. For if, to the extent to which marriages are arranged, love is adulterous; and if, to the extent to which love is adulterous, it is against the law; and if, to the extent to which it is against the law, it remains secret; and if, to the extent to which it remains secret, it is disclosed; then, to the extent to which love is disclosed, it is tragic. To be more precise, with the exception of **"Le Fresne"** and perhaps **"Milun,"** a certain morbidity hovers in and around the love theme of the *Lais.* Love is conceived not only to involve suffering, to be a "wound in the body" (**"Guigemar,"** v. 483), but to be fatal. And to be fatal in the literal sense of the term—to be fated. To love in the *Lais* is to die or to risk death so inevitably as to suggest a link between adulterous love as a theme and some more deeply defining generic law that allows us to glimpse one of those moments in Old French literature where theory—a theory of literature—inheres in practice, and practice, like the lady's bearing in **"Yonec,"** discloses a wider rule of its own production and meaning.

What **"Yonec"** reveals about the revelation of secret love is that there is nothing the lovers can do to prevent discovery, since the very effects that love makes manifest in the body reveal its existence and therefore make it fatal; thus, the morbidity of the tale is, again as we saw in **"Guigemar,"** linked to the question of representation—a "semblance which kills," as the fantasy lover acknowledges:

> "Ma duce amie,
> Pur vostre amur perc jeo la vie;
> Bien le vus dis qu'en avendreit:
> Vostre semblant nus ocireit."
>
> (v. 319)

"My sweet beloved, for love of you I am losing my life. I told you what would come if it: your appearance would slay us."

Indeed, if love is by definition to be hidden, and if, at the same time, it shows itself inevitably on the body of the lover as a semblance or symptom, is there not something fatalistic not only about love, but, at least in the *Lais,* about the very act of representation? I have asserted in relation to **"Guigemar"** that the poet, in speaking of secret or courtly love, reveals that which is, by definition, to be hidden, and that in composing, s/he

does to the lovers exactly what the jealous husband does to his wife and her lover: s/he betrays by revealing, and thus destroys at the very moment s/he creates.

The morbidity that hangs over, lies at the core of, the *Lais* works, of course, in different ways, but of this there can be no doubt: that love is seen as fatal and that such fatalism is inextricably bound to the ways in which language, and poetic language in particular, is conceived to work to expose that which is abolished by becoming manifest. This is what occurs in **"Guigemar"** and in **"Yonec,"** and what is erected to the level of a law of exposure in **"Lanval"** and **"Laüstic."**

"LANVAL" AND "LAÜSTIC"

"Lanval" is the story of a knight of Arthur's court who, though he possesses all the qualities of the courtly lover and though he participates in the royal campaign against the Picts and the Scots, is forgotten when the time comes to distribute the booty of war.

> Asez i duna riches duns:
> E as cuntes e as baruns,
> A ceus de la table r[o]ünde—
> N'ot tant de teus en tut le munde—
> Femmes et tere departi,
> Par tut, fors a un ki l'ot servi:
> Ceo fu Lanval, ne l'en sovient,
> Ne nul de[s] soens bien ne li tient.
>
> (v. 13)

The king gave many rich gifts to counts and barons and to those of the Round Table: there was no such company in the whole world. He apportioned wives and lands to all, save to one who had served him: this was Lanval, whom he did not remember, and for whom no one put in a good word.

Given the economic theme, which is of a piece with that of the rivalry of Arthur's vassals for his attention ("Because of his valor, generosity, beauty, and prowess, many were envious of him," "Pur sa valur, pur sa largesce, / Pur sa beauté, pur sa prüesce, / L'envioēnt tut li plusur" [v. 21]), **"Lanval"** seems to summon its own historical/social context: The neglected knight, who also happens to be far from home ("He was the son of a king of noble birth, but far from his inheritance," "Fiz a rei fu de haut parage, / Mes luin ert de sun heritage" [v. 27]), is, in fact, about as pure an expression as can be found in Old French of the personal alienation of individual knights ("Now he was in a plight, very sad and forlorn," "Ore est Lanval mut entrepris, / Mut est dolent e mut pensis" [v. 33]), which Erich Koehler identifies with the alienation of an entire class—the twelfth-century lower nobility or squirarchy consisting in part of younger, unmarried sons.[12] Within the general crisis of aristocracy, menaced from above by the reconstitution of monarchy and from below by the rise of an urban bourgeoisie, the *bacheliers* or *jeunes* found themselves either without land or obliged to sell their holdings, and thus increasingly indebted to the caste of powerful feudal princes still possessed of the means (land, castle, and private armies) to rule. Lanval is impoverished not only because he has been neglected but because he has spent all he has: "Tut sun aveir ad despendu" (v. 30). Indeed, his situation can be understood as a projection of the material condition of both a class and a generation, whose dispossession, as Georges Duby has elaborated in a series of articles and books, is also the result of a matrimonial model that, as we have seen, works against the interests of women and younger sons. Under the rule of primogeniture, assuming that the first son survived to the age of marriage and reproduction, the younger branches were, in effect, left to wander far from home, were, like Lanval, "neglected."[13]

Thus seen within the context of the material condition of the lower nobility and within that of twelfth-century feudal marriage, Lanval's wandering off into the countryside and his encounter with the fairy lady represent a dream of possession. The lady has all that Lanval lacks. Where he is an exile at court, she leaves her own country to find him. Where he is neglected by Arthur, she prefers him to all other knights. Where Lanval is impoverished, she is so rich that "Queen Semiramis and the Emperor Octavian himself together could not buy the right panel of her tent" ("La reïne Semiramis, / Quant ele ot unkes plus aveir / E plus pussaunce e plus saveir, / Ne l'emperere Octaviën / N'esligasent le destre pan" [v. 82]). In the antithesis of Lanval's situation, and indeed in what could be read almost as a parody of the rescue of the damsel in distress by the valiant knight, the fairy lady promises eternal fidelity (in contrast to Arthur's neglect) and—more important—as much wealth as his heart desires:

> Ore est Lanval en dreite veie!
> Un dun li ad duné aprés:
> Ja cele rien ne vudra mes
> Qüe il nen ait a sun talent;
> Doinst e despende largement,
> Ele li troverat asez.
> Mut est Lanval bien herbergez:
> Cum plus despendra richement,
> [E] plus avrat or e argent!
>
> (v. 134)

Now Lanval was on the right path! She gave him a boon, that henceforth he could wish for nothing that he would not have, and however generously he gave or spent, she would still find enough for him. Lanval was very well lodged, for the more he spent, the more gold and silver he would have.

The fairy lady is the literary incarnation of a fantasized solution to the material problems of the class of unmarried, unendowed, and wandering younger knights, an heiress who is a source of unlimited riches—under one condition that we have already seen: that Lanval not reveal her existence. Even this prohibition can, again, be understood in the context of the reality of the aristocratic matrimonial model. For, as C. S. Lewis pointed out as early as the 1930s, to the extent that marriage is a matter of convenience and does not depend upon the choice of partners, there will be a gap between love and marriage, between desire and the law. Love is in this respect a legal necessity and not an elective affinity, which leads logically to the cardinal courtly rule of discretion.[14]

Here we are the witnesses to a happy marriage indeed! The Marxian fairytale of the fairy lady as the idealized solution to the material disenfranchisement of lower nobility, joined to the Cambridge Catholic's protopuritanical relegation of love to the secret dirty realm of adulterous passion. Neither, however, explains the one essential element of the rescuing woman's stipulation, which **"Lanval"** shares with a number of *lais*: that the revelation of love follows just as logically from the vow of discretion as discretion can be said to follow from love. The oath is taken to be transgressed. We know, in fact, that it will be violated the moment it is spoken.[15]

Like the stark world of repeatedly entwined broken promises of "La Chatelaine de Vergi," the universe of **"Lanval"** is one of necessity in which characters seem drawn along by an inescapable logic of articulation according to which each narrative element entails the next as part of a causal chain that can only partially be accounted for by any extratextual or historical explanation.[16] The first element is based upon the assumption, only later confirmed by events, that the reason for Arthur's original neglect is not so much the rivalry between his knights as his own jealousy of the Queen's interest in Lanval; which neglect inspires the daydream and the promise not to tell; which promise is kept only until Guinevere's interest becomes manifest and she requests Lanval's love; which request, rebuffed, produces the charge of homosexuality, the denial of which provokes the famous boast of loving someone whose humblest attendant is more beautiful than the Queen; which boast leads not only to Lanval's realization that he has lost his love ("Il s'est[eit] bien aparceüz / Qu'il aveit perdue s'amie: / Descovert ot la druërie!" [v. 334]), but, in yet another medieval rendering of the Potiphar's wife motif, to the denunciation before Arthur, who, like the Duke of "La Chatelaine de Vergi," puts the wronged knight in a position of either proving the truth of his boast—which, as boast, prevents its own proof—or being punished.[17]

If **"Lanval"** seems to turn fatalistically around a certain logic of the promise made to be broken and of the boast that denies the possibility of substantiation, it is because both speech acts are so thoroughly enmeshed in the poetics of the lai as to make the transgression rendered in terms of self-canceling vows and conceits mere thematizations of a broader paradox, which is that of fiction itself. Lanval, after all, not only uses his newfound wealth to dress jongleurs but is the very figure of the poet. He is depicted as the loner, a dreamer. The Queen's charge of homosexuality carried, as we know from Marie's contemporary Alain de Lille, an association with rhetoric.[18] But most of all, Lanval's dilemma is that of the poet who transgresses the unwritten rule of the courtly relation subsumed in the dictum "If you say it, you lose it," who violates, in other words, what is imagined to be the integrity of an orality present to itself—and the fairy lady is just one version of such a fantasy of plenitude—every time she speaks. Put in other terms, the voice associated with the presence of the body, or even of bodies, is transgressed by the lai, which is merely its trace, by the very act of articulation, transcription being merely the limit of such transgression.

There is no better example of the fatalistic mutual implication of articulation and betrayal than **"Laüstic,"** the story of two knights who are neighbors, one of whom, another "bacheler," is loved by the other's wife. It is unclear within the short narrative whether or not their love is consummated, whether or not, in other words, the body ever attains to a presence. Nonetheless, the lovers communicate by looking at each other from the windows of their respective homes. Asked by her suspicious husband why she gets up so often at night, the wife replies: "Lord, anyone who does not hear the song of the nightingale knows none of the joys of this world. This is why I come and stand here" ("Il nen ad joïë en cest mund, / Ki n'ot le laüstic chanter. / Pur ceo me vois ici ester" [v. 84]). And, as in **"Lanval,"** the lady has betrayed herself in the act of speaking. For the lie intended to cover her delight, to keep love secret, reveals that which it is supposed to hide in the very moment that it is pronounced. In fact, the fatality of the lie can be traced, I think, further back than the lady's fatal speech act to the husband's question—"E meintefeiz li demanda / Pur quei levot e u ala" (v. 81)—which is rooted, as in the love written on the altered face of the lady of **"Yonec,"** in the lover's bodily gestures at the window where she sits and looks when the lovers "were denied anything more" (v. 77). Despite the fact of hiding, love reveals itself. First in the body, which somatizes love's effects, and then in the language that speaks inevitably of that which is prohibited: in the moment that she speaks, the speaker destroys her own object of delight. Nor is Marie immune from the process of despoiling exposure she describes. The lai exposes that which is by definition intended to remain hidden: "This adventure was related and could not long be concealed. The Bretons composed a lai about it that is

called *Laüstic*" ("Cele aventure fu cuntee, / Ne pot estre lunges celee. / Un lai en firent li Bretun: / Le Laüstic l'apelë hum" [v. 157]).

The drama of language of **"Lanval"** is repeated in **"Laüstic,"** where the husband, jealous of his wife's pleasure, captures the nightingale by fashioning a "laz"—"There was no hazel tree or chestnut tree on which they did not place a snare or birdlime, until they had captured and retained it" ("N'i ot codre ne chastainier / U il ne mettent laz u glu, / Tant que pris l'unt e retenu" [v. 98])—as if, and the reference could not be more explicit, the nightingale as voice were caught in Marie's own trap, which is the "laz/lai." For the dead bird, thrown at the wife ("Sur la dame le cors geta, / Si que sun chainse ensanglanta / Un poi desur le piz devant" [v. 117]), makes a mark. The nightingale's body, the voice betrayed, is a form of writing upon the woman's body and a message to be read. Indeed, the lady sends it to her lover like a letter to inform him of betrayal:

> "Le laüstic li trametrai
> L'aventure li manderai."
> En une piece de samit,
> A or brusdé et tut escrit,
> Ad l'oiselet envulupé.
> Un sun vaslet ad apelé,
> Sun message li ad chargié,
> A sun ami l'ad enveié.
>
> (v. 133)

"I shall send him the nightingale and let him know what has happened." She wrapped the little bird in a piece of samite, embroidered in gold, with writing all around. She called one of her servants, entrusted him with her message, and sent it to her beloved.

The lover, in turn, has the dead bird enshrined in a reliquary, which he carries with him as long as he lives, as we realize that **"Laüstic,"** which is alternately spelled "L'Aüstic," resonates uncannily with audible sound—the acoustic, modern French *écouter* from the Latin *auscultare*, meaning "to hear," "to give attention to."[19]

We find in **"Laüstic,"** as in **"Lanval,"** the fantasy of a utopic plenitude or presence, here however explicitly identified with pleasurable orality.[20] For the supposed communication that the proximity of houses makes possible is equated with pleasure: "They took delight in seeing each other, since they were denied anything more" ("Delit aveient al veer, / Quant plus ne poeient aveir" [v. 77]). Here it is worth stopping a moment at the word "delit," since it is a key to the utopic presence associated with the body. The text *says* delight, but, one may ask, delight at what? Certainly not presence, since Marie is categorical: "They took delight in seeing each other, since they were denied anything more." The imagined pleasure of the body is a substitute for presence, a supplement, which is also synonymous with *délit* in the sense of the flagrante delicto in which the lovers are captured. For nowhere in the lai is the presence of a voice anything but a substitute for something else. The lovers are never present to each other, and the nightingale never sings to the lovers. It is itself nothing more than the sign of a ruse or lie told to calm the jealous husband's suspicions, an invention synonymous with the lai itself. In turn, the dead bird, encased—literally "embroidered and written" ("A or brusdé et tut escrit")—is sent like a poetic "envoi" to the lover once consummation or the presence of bodies is no longer even imaginable. Nor was it ever; for such presence in the lai is always deferred.

There is no language of presence either in **"Laüstic"** or anywhere else to represent the coupling of bodies, such coupling being, as we have seen in **"Guigemar,"** a surplus that never enters language. An excess that cannot be said, the presence of the body is excluded from the text. Which is not to imply that poets do not try all the time to capture the body or that such attempts do not constitute the very essence of the poetic instance. On the contrary, Marie makes this clear in the general prologue, an *art poétique* that prescribes the making of texts as a series of rewritings, which, no matter how perfect, always leave a "surplus of meaning."

What I am suggesting is that in the *Lais* Marie's understanding of the body (and the voice) is ultimately always deferred by the text that supplants it, transgresses it in a sense analogous to Lanval's betrayal of the fictional fairy and the self-betrayal of the lady of **"Laüstic."** For the theme of betrayal dominates not only **"Lanval"** and **"Laüstic"** but a great many other so-called courtly work as well. In the *chanson de geste* betrayal takes the form of broken oaths, apostasy, and treason, whereas in the courtly text it is to be found—from Béroul's *Tristan* and Chrétien's *Lancelot,* to the prose romances of the thirteenth century—in the theme of capture of the bodies of lovers in flagrante delicto. Betrayal is a structuring principle of the courtly lyric, whose stock of characters includes the *losengers,* liars, false speakers, and flatters, but also denouncers of adulterers. So widespread, in fact, is the theme of betrayal that the indiscretions of Lanval and the lady of **"Laüstic"** seem fated. The fatalism of the boast—whether of the most beautiful woman or of the greatest joy in the world—underscores the extent to which in medieval texts the poetic and erotic are embedded in each other. Even the word *traire,* like the word *lai,* is one of those polysemic markers that, in their semantic richness, transgress the premise of an assumed plenitude inherent to verbal signs, for the ear can never hear as much, make as many distinctions, as the eye can see.

"EQUITAN" AND "LE FRESNE"

If words come back to haunt and even to destroy those who speak in **"Lanval"** and **"Laüstic,"** their deadly effects seem even to precede speech in **"Equitan,"** where the King, who has never seen the wife of his seneschal, falls in love with her by hearsay:

> Li reis l'oï sovent loër.
> Soventefez la salua,
> De ses aveirs li enveia;
> Sans veüe la coveita.
>
> (v. 38)

The king, having often heard her praised, frequently sent her greetings and gifts. They had never met, but he conceived a desire for her.

Hearsay engenders the desire to speak directly with her: "E, cum ainz pot a li parla" (v. 42). In this the King is not alone. The lady of **"Laüstic"** falls in love with her neighbor because of "the good things she has heard about him": "Et tant par ot en lui grant bien / Qu'ele l'ama sur tute rien, / Tant pur le bien quë ele oï" (v. 25). Gurun falls in love with Fresne because of what has been said: "De la pucele oï parler; / Si la comença a amer" (**"Le Fresne,"** v. 247). Milun benefits similarly from the news of his reputation, which reaches the ears of the unnamed lady of Southwales: "Ele ot oï Milun nomer; / Mut le començat a amer" (v. 25). So too, Guilliadun falls in love with Eliduc because of that which is said about him: "La fille al rei l'oï numer / E les biens de lui recunter" (v. 273). And if the lady of Guigemar is a "mal mariée" in a tower, the lady of Eliduc is a "mal fiancée" whose father at first imprisons her in a tower to keep her away from the enemy who wants to marry her and then, upon Eliduc's arrival, sings his praises, thus inciting her desire (v. 496).

One of the great themes of Old French romance, love by hearsay takes on a special meaning in the *Lais,* where it functions as a precursor to, or alongside of, the dangerous speech acts that so define the linguistic universe of Marie. Indeed, as the example from **"Eliduc"** makes clear, the "good things that are told (*recunter*) about him" represent a form of narrative thoroughly analogous to the telling of the lai itself; and Marie often uses the verb *cunter* or *recunter*—"Dit vus en ai la verité / Del lai que j'ai ici cunté" (**"Chevrefoil,"** v. 117), "Plus n'en oï, ne plus n'en sai, / Ne plus ne vus en cunterai" (**"Chaitivel,"** v. 239), "Al recunter mut me delit" (**"Milun,"** v. 536)[21]—in order to describe the art of storytelling. Which inscribes a certain fatality into the relation of the body to its deeds, or rather into the relation between one's deeds, one's character, or one's beauty and what is said about them. The vicious cycle of reputation is such that the greater the prowess of a knight, as in the case of the neighbor in **"Laüstic,"**

"Milun," and "Eliduc," or the greater the beauty of the lady, as in the case of the seneschal's wife of "Equitan," the more appealing the words that are "recounted"; the more appealing the words that are "recounted," the more fated the attraction; and the more fated the attraction, the more fatal the seduction. The motif of love by hearsay represents an inscription within, and an embryonic form of, the art of storytelling itself. Once more, in the act of narration Marie spreads the word, creates the conditions of hearsay in her hearers, in a fashion thoroughly analogous to that which she describes as happening to the protagonists of the *Lais.* If language as an explicit theme of the *Lais* seems dangerous and often even fatal, it is because Marie performs in the very act of recounting that which she knows to be the impossible position of the poet who destroys by exposure.

"Equitan" is often represented as being more of a fabliau than a tale of love, and there is something uncourtly about the king who loves beneath his station, something comic about this bedroom farce that turns around the act of bleeding in order to keep love hidden, something farcical about the denouement in the bath tubs that belongs more properly to the tradition of the comic tale. Then too, to the extent to which the fabliaux can be considered to be didactic or to function according to a certain logic of distributive justice according to which "what A does to B, B will do to A, or what A does to B, C will do to A," "Equitan" can be considered to belong to the mode or the schema of the trickster tricked. Equitan is a king, Marie insists, whose role is to provide justice ("Sires des Nauns, jostis e reis" [v. 12]), and his very name is synonymous with equity. "Equitan" is in many respects about equity, as is obvious in the seneschal's wife's initial response that love is not worthy if it is not among equals—"Amur n'est pruz se n'est egals" (v. 137).

Where "Equitan" parts company with the fabliaux, however, is in the fatality of the ending, which is more cruel than most, and, more important, in the way in which the deaths of Equitan and of the seneschal's wife are inscribed in the language of love itself. Once engaged, speech in "Equitan," as in "Lanval," snowballs uncontrollably. Indeed, from the start, hearsay, speech in praise of the seneschal's wife's beauty, that which is said about her, leads to a desire to speak to her:

> Pur sei deduire e cunforter
> La fist venir a li parler.
> Sun curage li descovri,
> Saver li fet qu'il meort pur li;
> Del tut li peot faire cunfort
> E bien li peot doner [l]a mort.

(v. 111)

To please and comfort him the King had her come and speak with him, whereupon he disclosed his feelings to her, letting her know that he was dying because of her and that she was well able to bring comfort to him or to cause his death.

The desire to speak to the seneschal's wife for whom "he is dying" is automatically, almost syllogistically, connected to the desire for the seneschal's death. "Accept this as the truth and believe me," King Equitan promises his beloved to calm her fear of being deceived, "if your husband were dead, I should make you my queen and my lady. I should not be deterred from this for anyone's sake" ("Sacez de veir, e si creez: / Si vostre sire fust finez, / Reïne e dame vus fereie; / Ja pur [nul] humme nel lerreie" [v. 225]). This is a promise that comes to haunt him. For the words, once spoken, turn back upon the speaker and, like Guigemar's arrow, Lanval's promise, or the white lie of the lady of "Laüstic," rebound uncannily. The death planned for the seneschal is, in fact, reserved for Equitan—"His evil plan had rebounded on him, whereas the seneschal was safe and sound" ("Sur lui est le mal revertiz, / E cil en est sauf e gariz" [v. 299]). The dispenser of justice and king ("jostis e reis") ironically insures equity by his own death, as the lai in the end assumes its name.

"Le Fresne" differs from "Equitan" in the happily resolved quality of its ending. Indeed, it is in many ways the most carefully resolved of all the lais in that Fresne marries the man she loves, Gurun; and Fresne's sister Codre is given away richly in the parents' country: "Mut richement en lur cuntree / Fu puis la meschine donee" (v. 513). "Le Fresne" resembles "Equitan," then, in the justness of its ending, and in one other important aspect, that is, the extent to which it turns around an almost fatal speech act: the mother's derogatory remark about the neighbor's wife who delivers twins. Fresne's mother is, in a portrait in which character is captured as a mouth, "bad-mouthed and envious":

> Kar ele ert feinte e orguilluse
> E mesdisante e envïuse.
> Ele parlat mut folement
> E dist, oant tute sa gent:
> "Si m'aït Deus, jo m'esmerveil
> U cest produm prist cest conseil
> Que il ad mandé a mun seignur
> Sa huntë e sun deshonur,
> Que sa femme ad eü deus fiz.
> E il e ele en sunt hunis.
> Nus savum bien qu'il i afiert:
> Unques ne fu ne ja nen iert
> Ne n'avendrat cel' aventure
> Que a une sule porteüre
> Quë une femme deuz fiz eit,
> Si deus hummes ne li unt feit."

(v. 27)

She was deceitful and arrogant, prone to slander and envy. She spoke foolishly and said in front of the whole household: "So help me God, I am astonished that this worthy man decided to inform my husband of his shame and dishonor, that his wife has had two sons. They have both incurred shame because of it, for we know what is at issue here: it has never occurred that a woman gave birth to two sons at once, nor ever will, unless two men are the cause of it."

Nor does it take long for her judgment of her neighbor, which becomes notorious ("These words that were repeated became widely known throughout all Brittany" ["Asez fu dite e coneüe, / Per tute Bretaine seüe" (v. 50)]), to recoil upon herself:

> La dame que si mesparla
> En l'an meïsmes enceinta,
> De deus enfanz est enceintie;
> Ore est la veisine vengie.
>
> (v. 65)

The same year the slanderer herself conceived twins, and now her neighbor was avenged.

Marie may here hint that it is the husband's infidelity that has caused the neighbor to conceive twins, that in talking about another the wife is, in reality, speaking the truth about herself. There are only two possibilities: either the wife speaks the truth in slandering her neighbor, in which case she articulates unconsciously the possibility of her husband's unfaithfulness; or the slander is false, given the biological reality of her own pregnancy and birth. In either case, Marie insists upon the power of words to turn against those who pronounce them, as the gossipy wife of **"Le Fresne,"** in a phrase that resembles the return of the ill-intentioned speech act of **"Equitan"** ("Sur lui est le mal revertiz"), recognizes the danger of speaking ill of others: "Now I am paying the price. Whoever slanders and lies about others does not know what retribution awaits him" ("Sur mei en est turné le pis. / Ki sur autrui mesdit e ment / Ne seit mie qu'a l'oil li pent" [v. 86]).

The mother's slander of her neighbor is, however, only the first of two speech acts that rebound against her. For the wife who decides to cast one of her daughters out unknowingly encounters her again when she seeks to remove Fresne from the home of the man to whom she intends to marry Codre, the daughter she has retained: "She planned to cast her out of her own house and advise her son-in-law to marry her to a worthy man" ("De sa meisun la getera, / A sun gendre cunseilera / Quë a un produme la marit" [v. 369]). In the end it is Codre who leaves Gurun and is married to another.

The dangerous speech acts of both **"Le Fresne"** and **"Equitan"** seem to illustrate Marie's warning about language in the prologue to **"Guigemar."** That is,

words, like stories, once spoken, are "launched," sent out to find a meaning that not only is beyond the control of the storyteller or speaker but can also return to produce unforeseen effects. Indeed, Marie's drama of language, which pits the attempt to master meaning, to assemble, remember, and contain it, against an inherent unruly, entropic tendency for the meaning of words, once spoken, to escape, replicate, and to scatter, is nowhere more apparent than in the two names of the sisters of **"Le Fresne."** Codre, the sister who stays home and is raised under the parental roof, embodies the principle of union or "remembrement" in that her name is a homonym for *coudre*, "to sew."[22] **"Fresne"** (alternatively spelled "Freisne" or "Fraisne"), on the other hand, and this irrespective of the meanings that may in medieval folklore have been attached to the hazelnut and the ash tree, resonates with the Old French *fraindre* from the Latin *frango, frangere, fractum*, "to break, break in pieces, dash, break in two." Nor is it any accident that the sister who is cast out is accompanied by a signifying cloth, like the message-bearing samite of **"Laüstic"** or the message written on a stick of **"Chevrefoil":**

> A une pice de sun laz
> Un gros anel li lie al braz.
> De fin or i aveit un' unce;
> El chestun out une jagunce;
> La verge entur esteit lettree.
>
> (v. 127)

With a piece of ribbon, the lady attached to the child's arm a large ring made from an ounce of pure gold, with a ruby set in it and lettering on the band.

In the names of the sisters inheres the meaning of **"Le Fresne,"** which is about breaking apart and coming together, about a speech act that rebounds and comes to haunt, about a child who is cast out and returns, about a sister who is retained and later displaced.

"BISCLAVRET"

"Bisclavret," which begins with a problem of language and of naming ("*Bisclavret* is its name in Breton, while the Normans call it *Garwaf*," "Bisclavret ad nun en bretan, / Garwaf l'apelent li Norman" [v. 3]), is often classified and considered apart as deriving its material and interest from the world of folklore. Yet it is every bit as much a part of the problematics of dangerous language as any of the lais that we have seen thus far.[23] Speech is from the start characterized as worthy of caution when a wife expresses the same fear concerning a spouse's absence that is hinted at in **"Le Fresne"** and that is the source of disaster in **"Lanval":**

> "Sire," fait el, "beau duz amis,
> Une chose vus demandasse
> Mut volenters, si jeo osasse;

Mais jeo creim tant vostre curuz,
Que nule rien tant ne redut."

(v. 32)

"Lord," she said, "my dear, sweet love, I would gladly
ask you something, if only I dared; but there is nothing
I fear more than your anger."

If the rest of the lais are in some deep sense about
language as a flawed, uncontrollable, and sometimes
fatal medium, **"Bisclavret"** takes us even deeper into
the morass. For this tale is about the irresistibility of the
question, that is, about the wife's tenacious curiosity,
despite her fear of articulation, concerning that which
she knows will harm her. A curiosity that comes in
stages: first the question, met with a warning:

"Dame," fet il, "pur Deu, merci!
Mal m'en vendra si jol vus di,
Kar de m'amur vus partirai
E mei meïmes en perdrai."

(v. 53)

"Lady," he said, "in God's name, have mercy on me! If
I tell you this, great harm will come to me, for as a
result I shall lose your love and destroy myself."

Despite the warning, the wife's insistence elicits a
confession:

Suventefeiz li demanda;
Tant le blandi e losenga
Que s'aventure li cunta;
Nule chose ne li cela.
"Dame, jeo devienc bisclavret:
En cele grant forest me met,
Al plus espés de la gaudine,
S'i vif de preie et de ravine."

(v. 59)

She questioned him repeatedly and coaxed him so
persuasively that he told her his story, keeping nothing
secret. "Lady, I become a werewolf: I enter the vast
forest and live in the deepest part of the wood where I
feed off the prey I can capture."

And, as if confession weren't enough, the lady presses
for details concerning the clothes which, similar to the
rich swaddling cloth of **"Le Fresne"** or the inscribed
samite of **"Laüstic,"** are fetishized as the unmistakable
signs—like the *objets trouvés* of cubist and Dadaist col-
lages (a matchbook, a cut of newspaper or musical
score, a scrap of chair caning)—that the man's story,
like Fresne's origin, escapes fiction. (Which is a good
trick, for it guarantees, like Lanval's sudden departure
at the end, that fiction itself is true.) In any case, the
exchange between husband and wife has something
fated about it: the minute she asks, he resists; and the
minute he resists, she presses; in fact, the more she
presses, the more he resists, until, finally, the logic of
the question can yield nothing but an answer: "She

tormented and harried him so much that he could not
do otherwise but tell her" ("Tant l'anguissa, tant le suz-
prist, / Ne pout el faire, si li dist" [v. 87]). Language
that irresistibly, inevitably, reveals that which should be
kept secret has effects analogous to those provoked by
the lady's lie in **"Laüstic"** or by Lanval's indiscretion.
With, however, this essential difference: where the
revelation of a secret love results in its loss ("Say it and
you lose it"), revelation of a secret identity in **"Bisclavret"** results in condemnation to it ("Say it and you
will become it forever").

Bisclavret's wife's question is at bottom like Guigemar's arrow, which turns back upon the one who shoots,
like the lady of **"Laüstic"**'s treacherous lie or the wife's
slander in **"Le Fresne,"** in that language betrays the
one who uses it. Indeed, the reason that Bisclavret's
wife is so insistent is that she suspects that her
husband's regular disappearance means that he has a
mistress. And what could be worse than her husband's
infidelity? Few things. But one of those is surely the
fact that her husband is not just unfaithful to her, not
just amorously double, but unfaithful to his species.
And here there can be no doubt. The curious lady—a
sister of Eliduc's wife—might very well have settled
for learning that her husband were merely adulterous.
But she learns that he is perverse in the most literal
medieval sense of the term. He is a "bestourné," a
bestial, the truth of which, once disclosed, kills her
love, once said, once revealed, prevents the continuance
of their relation, their lying next to each other:

La dame oï cele merveille
De poür fu tute vermeille;
De l'aventure s'efrea.
E[n] maint endreit se purpensa
Cum ele s'en puïst partir;
Ne voleit mes lez lui gisir.

(v. 97)

The lady heard this remarkable revelation and her face
became flushed with fear. She was greatly alarmed by
the story, and began to consider various means of parting from him, as she no longer wished to lie at his
side.

Thus the species-traitor's worst fear in the beginning—
that he will lose his wife's love ("Kar de m'amur vus
partirai" [v. 55])—becomes true, as if saying it, once
again, made it so. So too with the wife's fear of her
husband's infidelity, which is no sooner said than it
causes her to become unfaithful, to marry the man who
has sought her love even before her husband's disappearance ("La dame ad cil dunc espusee, / Que lungement aveit amee," "Then the knight married the lady he
had loved for so long" [v. 133]), as if her desire (for the
knight) from the beginning were to discover her
husband's secret so that she might more fully live a

secret of her own. It is as if the question, once posed, leads inevitably to disaster, as with the husband's question in **"Laüstic,"** or, as if the origin of the wife's persistence resided in the ardent questions of her persistent suitor: "a knight who lived in the region and who had loved her for a long time, wooed her ardently, and served her generously" ("Un chevaler de la cuntree, / Que lungement l'aveit amee / Et mut preié' et mut requise / E mut duné en sun servise" [v. 103]).

There is much to be said about the signifying werewolf of **"Bisclavret,"** the way in which the King, like Guigemar's boat, or the swan of **"Milun,"** seems mysteriously drawn to it, as the werewolf seems drawn to the King,[24] and about the way, finally, a message passes between the two; but **"Bisclavret"** is also in some profound sense about the question of noses, which defines the ending of this curious lai about curiosity. The werewolf venges himself by relieving his treacherous wife of her nose: "He tore the nose right off her face" ("Le neis li asracha del vis" [v. 235]). Nor do things stop there, for the wife's dismorphism becomes hereditary: "Plusurs [des] femmes del lignage, / C'est verité, senz nes sunt nees / Et si viveient esnasee" (v. 312). On one level, of course, we could read these lines as "Many of the women in the family, I tell you truly, were born without noses and lived noseless." But a quick look at the Old French dictionary shows how tricky the nose is. For *nes,* also spelled *neis, neys, neiz, naes, nees, nes, nis, nois, neies, nedes,* is an adverb meaning *même, pas même, pas du tout*—"even," "not even," "not at all." The nose is, in other words, the equivalent of "noes," and **"Bisclavret,"** seen from this perspective, can be understood as the tale of a man who just can't say "no," or whose failure to say "no" to his wife's curiosity, a strange reenactment of the Fall, leads in effect to his wife's loss of her nose, exile, or expulsion ("[The King] banished the woman from the country, exiling her from the region," "La femme ad del païs ostee / E chacie hors de la cuntree" [v. 305]), and heritability of the lack of noes / nose. (I wouldn't presume to know which way to spell it.) The name **"Bisclavret"** again offers a key to Marie's fascination with tricky language and has not passed unnoticed by philologists. Joseph Loth claims that it derives from the Breton *bisc,* meaning "short," and *lavret,* "wearing breeches or short trousers." Heinrich Zimmer relates it to the Breton term *bleiz lavaret,* "speaking wolf." Th. Chotzen derives it from *bleidd llafar,* "the dear little speaking wolf" or *le bon loup fatidique.* H. W. Bailey explains the form *bisclavret* as *bleiz laveret,* "rational wolf." Finally, William Sayers proposes *bleiz claffet,* "wolf-sick, afflicted with lycanthropy," as the term "claff" is associated with leprosy.[25] However, if we were to take the name apart, **"Bisclavret"** can be divided into *bis,* "again," and *clavret,* which according to the dictionary is a "nail," a *clavreur* from the Latin *clavus,* or, alternatively, a *clavreüre,* a "key," from the Latin *clavis,* yielding, if we want to keep meaning open, or "supply surpluses of sense," as Marie suggests, either "again a nail," or "again a key." What I think I am saying is that we have again found the key to reading some of the most complex stuff the French Middle Ages produced, and it is not at all the simple, naive, spontaneous, artless creation it has been taken to be.

Notes

1. See S. Foster Damon, "Marie de France: Psychologist of Courtly Love," *PMLA* 44 (1929): 968-96; John A. Frey, "Linguistic and Psychological Couplings in the Lays of Marie de France," *Studies in Philology* 61 (1964): 3-18.

2. Of all her commentators, Milena Mikhaïlova is the only one of whom I am aware who links Marie's morbidity not only to the wound but to the sense of dispersion and loss defined as a linguistic drama as well. See *Le présent de Marie* (Paris: Diderot, 1996), p. 60.

3. Though her identification of a precise geographical site for the action of "Lanval" may seem overly literal, Elizabeth A. Francis nonetheless affirms the topographic association of the name and "down the valley" or "downhill." See "Marie de France et son temps," *Romania* 72 (1951): 87-88.

4. On the question of narrative structure and endings in the *Lais,* see Evelyn Birge Vitz, "The *Lais* of Marie de France: 'Narrative Grammar' and the Literary Text," *Romanic Review* 74 (1983): 396.

5. See R. Howard Bloch, *Etymologies and Genealogies: A Literary Anthropology of the French Middle Ages* (Chicago: University of Chicago Press, 1983), pp. 70-83.

6. See Georges Duby, *La société aux XIe et XIIe siècles dans la région mâconnaise* (Paris: Armand Colin, 1953), p. 280; "Structures de parenté et noblesse dans la France du Nord au XIe et XIIe siècles," in *Hommes et structures au moyen âge* (Paris: Mouton, 1973), p. 270; "Situation de la noblesse au début du XIIIe siècle," in *Hommes et structures,* p. 344.

7. See Georges Duby, *Medieval Marriage* (Baltimore: Johns Hopkins University Press, 1978), chap. 1; and *La société aux XI et XIIe siècles dans la région mâconnaise,* p. 436; Charles Donahue, "The Policy of Alexander the Third's Consent Theory of Marriage," *Proceedings from the Fourth International Congress of Medieval Canon Law* (Vatican: Biblioteca Apostolica Vaticana, 1976), pp. 256, 257; Michael M. Sheehan, "Choice of Marriage Partner in the Middle Ages: Develop-

ment and Application of a Theory of Marriage," *Studies in Medieval and Renaissance History* 1 (1978): 1-33; Juliette Turlan, "Recherches sur le mariage dans la pratique coutumière (XIIe-XIVe siècles)," *Revue historique du droit français et etranger* 35 (1957): 477-528.

8. R. Howard Bloch, "Tristan, the Myth of the State, and the Language of the Self," *Yale French Studies* 51 (1975): 61-81.

9. The following lines are not in the Harley 978 manuscript in the British Museum, but are to be found in BN fr. 2168. I have followed the transcription of the Warnke/Ewert/Burgess edition, p. 178.

10. Andreas Capellanus, *The Art of Courtly Love,* trans. J. J. Parry (New York: Columbia University Press, 1969), pp. 106-7.

11. For a discussion of the legal ramifications of the question of secrecy and exposure, see John M. Bowers, "Ordeals, Privacy, and the *Lais* of Marie de France," *Journal of Medieval and Renaissance Studies* 24 (1994): 1-31.

12. See Erich Koehler, *Ideal und Wirklichkeit in der Höfischen Epik* (Tübingen: Max Niemeyer, 1956), p. 25, and my *Medieval French Literature and Law* (Berkeley: University of California Press, 1977), pp. 220-38. Koehler's insight, from which I drew my own, is to be set against a whole tradition that considered Lanval to be merely homesick and such homesickness to offer proof that Marie was herself living at a foreign court. See Ernest Hoepffner, *Les Lais de Marie de France* (Paris: Boivin, 1935), p. 50; Paula Clifford, *Marie de France: Lais* (London: Grant and Cutler, 1982), p. 57.

13. See Georges Duby, "Les 'jeunes' dans la société aristocratique dans la France du Nord-Ouest du XIIe siècle," in *Hommes et structures,* pp. 213-26.

14. C. S. Lewis, *The Allegory of Love* (New York: Oxford University Press, 1958), p. 13.

15. The deepest discussion of the question of the broken promise is to be found in Shoshana Felman's *The Literary Speech Act: Don Juan with J. L. Austin, or Seduction in Two Languages,* trans. C. Porter (Ithaca: Cornell University Press, 1983).

16. For a comparison of the two *récits,* see Jean Rychner, "La présence et le point de vue du narrateur dans deux récits courts: Le *Lai de Lanval* et la *Châtelaine de Vergi,*" *Vox Romanica* 39 (1980): 86-103.

17. For a historically defined discussion of the judicial procedure of Lanval's trial, see Jacqueline Eccles, "Marie de France and the Law," in *Les Lieux In-* *terdits: Transgression and French Literature,* ed. Larry Duffy and Adrian Tudor (Hull: University of Hull Press, 1998), p. 17; Elizabeth A. Francis, "The Trial in *Lanval,*" in *Studies in French Language and Mediaeval Literature Presented to M. K. Pope* (Manchester: Manchester University Press, 1939), pp. 115-24.

18. See R. Howard Bloch, *Etymologies and Genealogies,* pp. 133-36; Alexandre Leupin, "Ecriture naturelle et écriture hermaphrodite," *Diagraphe* 9 (1976): 119-41; Eugene Vance, "Désir, rhétorique et texte," *Poétique* 42 (1980): 137-55; Jan Ziolkowski, *Alan de Lille's Grammar of Sex* (Boston: Medieval Academy of America, 1985), pp. 40-43.

19. Glyn Burgess suggests that *laustic* derives from the Breton form *éostic,* via *aostic, austic. The Lais of Marie de France: Text and Context* (Athens: University of Georgia Press, 1987), p. 10.

20. In the abutment of the lovers' houses we find the fantasy of presence: "Kar pres esteient lur repere, / Preceines furent lur maisuns / E lur sales e lur dunguns; / N'i aveit bare ne devise / Fors un haut mur de piere bise" ("Their houses, halls, and keeps were close by each other and there was no barrier or division, apart from a high wall of darkhued stone" [v. 35]). Because of such proximity oral communication is envisaged as possible: "Des chambres u la dame jut, / Quant a la fenestre s'estut, / Poeit parler a sun ami / De l'autre part, e il a li" ("When she stood at her bedroom window, the lady could talk to her beloved in the other house and he to her" [v. 39]).

21. "Cele aventure fu cuntee" ("Laüstic," v. 157); "Nul hum n'en oï plus parler, / Ne jeo n'en sai avant cunter" ("Lanval," v. 645).

22. Laurence de Looze has discussed the two names in terms of two family branches that correspond to separate manuscript families; see "Marie de France et la textualisation: Arbre, enfant, oeuvre dans le Lai de 'Fresne,'" *Romanic Review* 82 (1990): 396-408.

23. See Roger Dragonetti, "Le lai narratif de Marie de France," in *La musique et les lettres* (Geneva: Droz, 1986), p. 39; Jean-Charles Huchet, "Nom de femme et écriture féminine au Moyen Age: Les *Lais* de Marie de France," *Poétique* 48 (1981): 407-30.

24. First, Bisclavret, "De si qu'il a le rei choisi; / Vers lui curut querre merci" ("As soon as he saw the king he ran up to him and begged for mercy" [v. 145]); and then the King, "A grant merveile l'ot tenu / Et mut le tient a grant chierté. / A tuz les suens ad comaundé / Que sur s'amur le gardent

bien / E li ne meffacent de rien, / Ne par nul d'eus ne seit feruz; / Bien seit abevreiz e peüz" ("He considered the wolf to be a great wonder and loved it dearly, commanding all his people to guard it well for love of him and not to do it any harm. None of them was to strike it and plenty of food and water must be provided for it" [v. 168]).

25. Joseph Loth, "Le *Lai du Bisclavret*: Le sens de ce nom et son importance," *Revue Celtique* 44 (1927): 300-307; Heinrich Zimmer, "Histoire littéraire de la France, tome XXX," *Göttingische Gelehrte Anzeigen* 20 (1890): 800ff.; Th. M. Chotzen, "Bisclavret," *Etudes Celtiques* 2 (1937): 33-44; H. W. Bailey, "*Bisclavret* in Marie de France," *Cambridge Medieval Celtic Studies* 1 (1981): 95-97; William Sayers, "*Bisclavret* in Marie de France: A Reply," *Cambridge Medieval Celtic Studies* 4 (1982): 77-82. See also Burgess, *Lais of Marie de France*, p. 9.

William Sayers (essay date summer 2004)

SOURCE: Sayers, William. "Marie de France's 'Chievrefoil,' Hazel Rods, and Ogam Letters *Coll* and *Uillenn*." *Arthuriana* 14, no. 2 (summer 2004): 3-16.

[*In the following essay, Sayers focuses on the lay "Chievrefoil," discussing Tristan's encrypted message to Yseult—carved with a knife into a hazel rod—with reference to the Old Irish language and Celtic sources.*]

"Chievrefoil" is the shortest of Marie de France's *lais* and the event (*aventure*) around which it is built is no more than one lovers' meeting among many, yet it is replete with the terminology of communication and artistic creation.[1] In fact, the chiasmic effect of beginning and end,

> Del lai qu'hum nume chevrefoil,
> Que la verité vus en cunt,
> Pur quei fu fet, comment e dunt
>
> . . . . .
>
> Chevrefoil le nument Franceis.
> Dit vus en ai la verité
> Del lai que j'ai ici cunté[2]

(It pleases me greatly and I am eager to relate to you the truth of the lay called **"Chevrefoil,"** to say why it was composed and how it originated . . . The French call it **"Chevrefoil."** I have told you the truth of the lay related her.)[3]

suggests the permeable world of alloforms within, where we discover ingenuous tale and romance, written message and song, known story and new signification, in a variety of media: memory, ordinary speech, artistic language, writing on wood and on vellum.

Among these, critical attention has singled out the inscribed hazel rod and its message as the most problematic from a modern perspective, although this alone does not guarantee their centrality to Marie and her public. The evolution in narrative voice and shifts in style leave in question whether Tristan's declaration of love, longing, and interdependence was all contained on the dressed rod on which he had incised his name, was communicated to the queen from the forest by other means at some slightly early date, or simply expresses the mutual awareness of their love as encapsulated in a botanical image—the coterminous lives of the hazel and the entwining honeysuckle—an awareness later made explicit and given voice at the conclusion of this or a later encounter in a *lai* that Tristan composes at the queen's behest. As editor Jean Rychner observes of lines 53-78, 'Ces quelques vers . . . ont fait couler beaucoup d'encre' (these few verses have caused a great deal of ink to flow).[4] From the last century of scholarship we have no fewer than three summary reviews of the many critical stands taken on these issues.[5]

This essay defers comment on Tristan's message until the implications of its medium, the hazel rod, or rather media, rod and writing, have been explored. The starting point is Tristan's decision after returning to Cornwall from South Wales to communicate with the queen from a hiding place in the forest, when she passes with the royal party on the way to Tintagel.

> Le jur que li rei fu meüz,
> Tristram est el bois revenuz.
> Sur le chemin quë il saveit
> Que la rute passer deveit,
> Une codre trencha par mi,
> Tute quarreie la fendi.
> Quant il ad paré le bastun,
> De sun cutel escrit sun nun.

(47-54)

Illustrative of the generally accepted understanding of this scene is the prose translation offered by Burgess and Busby:

> On the day the king set out, Tristram entered the wood along the road he knew the procession would have to take. He cut a hazel branch in half and squared it. When he had whittled the stick he wrote his name on it with his knife.[6]

The hazel (*Corylus avellana*) is an important understory tree in the deciduous forests of much of Europe, where it shares space with the oak—and with the honeysuckle. A member of the birch family of trees, the hazel can grow to a height of thirty feet, although eighteen would be a better measure for the conditions of western Britain. Rather than having a single stem unbranched near the ground, the hazel typically has a number of shoots or trunks branching out at, or just above, ground level from a large base or stool, which can be up to two meters in diameter. This feature, plus the flexible, straight-grained and easily split wood, led to widespread coppicing in the Middle Ages and before. Hazel shoots were regularly harvested, typically after a six-year growth cycle, in late summer or during the dormant period. Each trunk was cut above the base and then trimmed of branches and foliage at the upper end for use as poles, staffs, crooks, in hurdles and mud-and-wattle walls, as inverted, U-shaped clamps to hold down thatch, split for basket-making and other applications. Male flowers, in the form of pale yellow catkins, open in February in Britain, when deciduous trees are still lifeless, and are then among the first signs of spring in the forest. Hazel leaves, among the last to fall in autumn, were used as cattle fodder. Hazelnuts or filberts, rich in fats and proteins, are important to the wood mouse, red squirrel, and dormouse, and have been prized in human diet, alone or ground in bread. The hazel has a symbiotic relationship with a variety of mosses, liverworts, lichens, and some fungi, but not with the honeysuckle, although coppicing, by letting more light reach the forest floor, would promote the growth of the climber. When a honeysuckle does twine around a hazel shoot, it leaves marks on the wood, still visible when the bark has been removed. Most or all of this would have been well known to Marie.[7]

We must recall the extent to which the medieval forest and woodland was managed and was not simply an impenetrable, sterile wilderness. Even in flight in the forest, Tristan and Yseult never seem quite beyond the reach of society and Mark's courtiers. Ownership and rights of exploitation were legally codified and game, timber, fruit and nuts were regularly harvested. *Sir Gawain the Green Knight,* for example, shows a landowner thinning out herds of fallow does. The hazel must then be seen as one among many resources in a largely controlled environment.

With that passion for categorization that characterized the learned stratum of early medieval Ireland, trees were classified in three groups.[8] The *coll* or hazel was included among the *airig fedo* 'nobles of the wood' and specific legal penalties were attached to its illegal cutting. The justification for this classification lay not in size but in 'a mes 7 a cáel' [its nuts and its rods]. One manuscript tradition includes honeysuckle in the third group, *fodla fedo* 'lower divisions of the wood.' Variant names for the plant were *féithlenn, fedlend, eidlenn,* and *uillenn.* This twining climber, like so many plants, may have had real or imagined pharmaceutical and charm-working properties but cannot have been of true economic importance. Its presence in the list may reflect the replacement of the relatively rare arbutus or strawberry tree by a better known plant.[9]

Hazel shoots were traditionally employed as divining rods and witching rods to locate buried treasure and valuable minerals and ores. Like the honeysuckle, the hazel was also employed by herbalists for various remedies. In Celtic tradition—the backdrop, however accurately discerned by Marie, against which we must situate the Tristan story—the hazel and its nuts were associated with wisdom and poetic inspiration, in particular with the very access to such preferential knowledge. In the legendary history of Finn mac Cumhail, hazelnuts drop into a stream and are then eaten by a salmon of knowledge that comes into the young Finn's hands. In parallel to other stories of novices winning insight, Finn burns his thumb when cooking the salmon, puts it in his mouth, and gains a greater awareness of the world. Here knowledge enters by way of the mouth, the means for its later communication to others.

Hazel and other light-colored wood was also employed as a medium for writing in early Ireland, if we may trust literary tradition on this count. But before recalling some legendary instances, we must consider the penetration of arboreal imagery into another important sphere, not that distant from the preferential knowledge afforded by hazelnuts. No later than in the fifth century, Irish scholars devised a signary specifically designed to transfer the Irish language to written form. Here it must be stressed that the Ogam alphabet, as it was known, was not part of a common Celtic learned or other heritage, was not the preserve of pagan druids, and was not magical in its principal applications, although, like other alphabets, it could be a medium for encrypted messages, prohibitions, curses, and other performative utterances in which Logos was strengthened by the Letter.[10] Used in monumental inscription, the signs consisted mainly of horizontal and diagonal strokes, and dots incised along the imagined stemline formed by a vertical edge or arris of an upright stone. Ogam was read from the bottom up. As in the Greek traditions, the letters of the Ogam signary had names (as well as a principal or generalized phonemic value). In Ireland these names continued as regular lexical elements of common speech and were thus still revelatory of their origins (cf. the loss of original meaning in the transfer from Phoenician of Greek *alpha, beta*). Since the majority of Ogam letters were composed of linear incisions out from the stemline, they bore some resemblance to twigs and tree imagery is basic to many (but not all) letter names and even to the very terms for the letters (*fid* 'wood') and constituent lines or strokes (*flesc* 'rod, wand' but also 'line, stroke'; cf. Modern Irish *flescín* 'twiglet' for the hyphen). While scholars have attempted to relate the tripartite taxonomy of the tree-list to the internal organization of the Ogam signary (initially grouped into four subsets) and to its nomenclature, this has not yielded results useful in determining the conditions or mindset in which the Ogam alphabet was devised and evolved.

Two letters will here retain our attention. The letter signifying /k/ was called *coll* or 'hazel' and its sign was four strokes out from the left of the stemline. *Coll* was one of twenty consonants and vowels in what is judged the original signary. Over time and perhaps when the alphabet was less used for monumental inscription and became the reserve of scholars more at home with parchment and antiquarian lore than with stone, wood or memorialization, five additions (*forfeda* 'supplementary characters') were made to the basic alphabet 'in particular to accommodate letters of the Latin and Greek alphabets not already matched by Ogam characters.'[11] One of these was *uilen,* introduced to represent Latin and Greek *y* and, perhaps later, the diphthongs *ui* or *úa.* Two signs—a curlicue and a double St. Andrew's cross to the right of the stemline—were alternately employed to represent it.

This has been the received view. Recently, it has been convincingly proposed that this supplementary letter initially designated geminate /l/ and its original name would have been *uillenn* 'honeysuckle.'[12] Since no words began with this labial geminate, the acrostic principle (*coll* for c) was not involved in the name, which may have rendered less stable its relationship with the phoneme.

As concerns the associated signs, the double St. Andrew's cross may be earlier than the curlicue, whose resemblance to a tendril of honeysuckle is nonetheless striking. The angular sign, on the other hand, may have contributed to the name of the letter being recast as *uilen,* a word that meant 'elbow, angle, corner' in Old Irish. But a multiple valence was still retained for the letter name, so that, while one of the kennings associated with the letter *uilen* was *cubat oll* 'great elbow' or 'cubit,' another, here with *uillenn* 'honeysuckle' in mind, was *túthmar fid* 'fragrant tree.'[13] In the meaning 'elbow' *uilen* was also used of the angular edge of a piece of wood or block of stone that could serve as the stemline for an Ogam inscription.[14] But this instance of learned Irish word-play cannot have been accessible to Marie de France, whatever awareness she had of non-Roman writing systems, and here it will be prudent to return to the concrete concerns of her *lai* and Tristan's hazel shoot.

> Une codre trencha par mi,
> Tute quarreie la fendi.
> Quant il ad paré le bastun,
> De sun cutel escrit sun nun.

It will not be profitable to comment in detail on the various, in my judgment all slightly inaccurate, ways in which this scene has been interpreted, due to insufficient knowledge of medieval forestry practices or Celtic writing tradition.[15] To cut to the heart of the matter and be rather categorical, Tristan does not cut a hazel branch 'in the middle' but rather cuts a central length from a stem, above the stool but below the twigs or branchlets at the top. He does not square off the two ends (for which *fendre* would be a poor verb) but axially splits off four half-round pieces of wood with bark, thus squaring the circular cross-section of the rod. The verb *parer* is then not to be read as 'peel' or 'pare,' since the bark has already been removed along with the quarter-rounds of external fibre, but rather as 'prepare.'[16] 'He cut out the central length of a hazel shoot and split it so that it was quite square in cross-section. When he had thus prepared the rod, he carved his name with his knife.' It must be emphasized that Tristan has not readied four flat surfaces for his inscription, the legibility of which might be better served by an incision directly into the retained bark of the rod, but has squared off the stick to yield four edges, stemlines for carving Ogam letters. The first of these will represent his name.[17]

We should not allow exclusively practical considerations to dictate our interpretation, but Marie is generally quite matter-of-fact, and the supernatural intervenes in her work in what we might call quite ordinary fashion. Thus, let us stay with familiar and realistic considerations, as far as they take us. Tristan counts on the queen recognizing his signal—if we view the rod as such in its initial function—because the two have used comparable means of communication in the past, unspecified in Marie but known as inscribed hazel chips floating on a stream elsewhere in the Tristan corpus. The rod cut out of season (just before Pentecost) and divested of its bark, but fixed vertically to permit the bottom-up reading of the name, would also be an anomaly by the roadside.[18]

> La reine vait chevachant:
> Ele esgardat tut un pendant,
> Le bastun vit, bien l'aparceut,
> Tutes les lettres i conut.
>
> (79-82)

(The queen rode along the way. She looked down the bank, saw the rod, and recognized it for what it was; she made out all the letters.)

I imagine the way through the forest to be elevated with reference to the roadside, where there may have been a hazel hedgerow or a stand of hazel on the slightly lower ground toward which the queen looks. At the side of a well traveled route, with easy transportation from the site, coppicing of the hazel would be expected. Planted upright, the rod would display only one (at best two) right-angled edges to a passerby, and thus we might assume that it is first the bright, bare wood of the squared shoot and then Tristan's name that comes to Yseult's attention. Had she been able to decipher a longer message from horseback, surely the staff if not its message, however encrypted, would have come to the attention of other members of the royal party. Let us settle, provisionally, for the fiction of the queen taking the staff with her as she and Brenguein go into the forest, turning it over for additional information.

All writing systems offer the possibility (but not the necessity) of compression over more or less spontaneous speech. Redundancies are resolved, accurate terminology replaces circumlocution, etc. Even considerations of effort and time may play a role in promoting economy, as in monumental inscription in stone. The desire to encrypt a message may also result in abbreviation, as in the Irish example cited by numerous scholars of Marie's opus in which Ogam *b* is repeatedly cut into a birch switch—the very first use of Ogam in fact—and the sequence can later be expanded by a qualified reader into an alliterative statement that Lug mac Ethlenn's wife would be abducted seven times unless the birch protected her.[19]

The most radical compression of Tristan's feelings or intended statement of waiting, longing, and interdependence that we can imagine would have been to carve next to his name or on another edge of the rod the letters *coll* and *uillenn,* hazel and honeysuckle. The letters could even have been juxtaposed on the left and right, respectively, of the stemline to suggest their intimate relationship (see the earlier figure). Interpretation would then require some astute 'glossing of the letter.'

But here we must pull up short and recall that there is no true symbiotic relationship between hazel and honeysuckle in the understory of the deciduous forests of western Britain, nor was one ever posited in Celtic tradition or story. A honeysuckle might well twine about a hazel shoot, leave its mark on it, and be materially damaged if the latter were cut, but this is not the conceit promoted by Tristan. How could such a notion have originally been advanced, against the evidence of direct observation?[20] The answer, I suggest, lies in both the natural physical circumstances of honeysuckle growing on hazel (among many other plants) and the wordplay subsumed in the name of the Ogam letter between *uillenn* 'honeysuckle' and *uilen* 'elbow, edge' (for inscription). That the honeysuckle literally inscribes itself on the hazel in nature, with marks visible beneath the bark, would have been a further incentive.

To turn now to Irish names for similarly Ogam-engraved wooden communications, Finn mac Cumhail's fool Lomnae discovers Finn's wife lying in stealth with Coipre. He prepares an allusive written statement that Finn will be able to interpret, in part because the

exceptional medium will promote mental acuity.[21] The bearer of this message is 'a four-cornered rod' *flesc cetharchuir* (*cethar* 'four' + *corr* 'projecting part') and thus the equivalent of Tristan's **bastun quarreie.* Another text mentions a *trosdán cetharuillennach* 'four-angled' or 'four-square staff' (four + *uillenn* + adjectival suffix).[22]

I propose that for the logocentric medieval Irish literati it was a short step from a 'quadrangular rod' to a 'honeysuckle-entwined rod,' especially when the wordplay was already active in the nomenclature for letters of the Ogam signary. If this explanation, and much of the foregoing concerning coppiced hazel, commands credence, the hazel/honeysuckle connection, its potential for extension to an amorous situation, and possibly the conceit of the two parallel forms of inscription (by twining tendril and with knife) would predate Marie in Irish (and conceivably Welsh) story-telling, and need have no literary antecedents in the Ovidian tradition of metamorphoses and vegetal unions.[23] The original learned wordplay in Irish would not have come down to Marie and only the circumstance of the natural co-occurrence of the two plants would have assured their continuing coherence as a literary motif. It is quite plausible that Marie was the first to associate the hazel/honeysuckle conceit with the Tristan story, perhaps prompted by knowledge of other incidents involving hazel chips, although in the fiction of the *lai* it is to Tristan himself that credit is due. This said, some knowledge of the Irish writing system is apparent in the *lai,* once we better understand the trimmed and squared length of hazel that is central to her poem and the Ogam inscription, of whatever length and degree of encryption, that is carved on one or more of its vertical edges.

On balance and largely for esthetic reasons, I judge that Marie wished us to believe that a rather full statement by Tristan was engraved on the rod, but that the very act of writing made this a *sume* in relation to his mental process or an imagined utterance and to the *lai* he subsequently composes.[24] To make this declaration the object of some prior communication with the queen, as some critics have done, is to deflate the *lai* to the prosaic and quotidian and, more importantly, would not authorize an equation between hazel rod and *lai,* composed at Yseult's request 'pur les paroles remembrer.' Here we should note that Tristan's *lai* is not a mnemonic device, an *aide-mémoire* to recall words exchanged between the lovers, but serves rather to commemorate these words in heightened artistic form, just as they had earlier been given similarly marked expression through the conventions of inscription on the dressed rod. It would now perhaps be prudent to review the opening claim that a lovers' meeting is the event on which the *lai* is spread and assign this function to the incision of the hazel message which, to adopt a useful modern image, 'morphs' into Tristan's harp-accompanied *lai* and—the circle now complete by the return to writing—into Marie's own *lai*.[25]

Much of earlier critical attention seems in my judgment misplaced in its fixation on the information in Tristan's message(s) to Yseult and on the sequence of his communications with her. Against this preoccupation with content and time, I would emphasize materiality, form, and the telescoping of time. What is illustrated and at issue in the lines following 'Ceo fu la sume de l'escrit . . .' is the creative process itself, the refinement of experience into art, a transformation which plays a role assigned to the supernatural in other poems by Marie. The author begins in the third person in the redundant, uneconomical discourse of real life: '. . . lunges ot ilec esté / E atendu e surjurné' (he had been there a long time and had tarried and waited). Marie then heightens the artistic stakes by moving to *style indirect libre*: 'D'eus deus fu il tut autresi / Cume del chevrefoil esteit / Ki a la codre se perneit . . .' (the two of them were just like the honeysuckle that twines itself around the hazel). She concludes not only with the immediacy of direct speech but also with a dense aphoristic turn of phrase marked by heightened emotionality, apostrophe, ellipsis, chiasmus, and parallelism: '"Bele amie, ci est de nus: / Ne vus sanz mei ne mei sanz vus"' ('Dear friend, the same is true of us: neither you without me nor I without you').

As in the medieval image of bark covering the pith of knowledge, the superfluous matter of experience, recollection, even of artless story itself, like the exterior of the hazel shoot, is pared away to its essentials, compressed as we assume the Ogam message was compressed, but at the same time given heightened expressivity through all the devices of poetry and music.[26] Tristan's transformation of his carved message and prior and later statements of love into a *lai* is replicated under Marie's more widely cast net, when she combines Celtic lore with conventional motifs from the Tristan story in a self-referential *lai* about *lai*-making.[27] Just as the hazel that became the medium of a message had a prior association in Celtic tradition with preferential knowledge, the *lai*, Tristan's and her own, is—to recall the terminology of her 'Prologue'—the further gloss on the letter of experience and story that assigns signification, and thus permits the possibility of permanence beyond vegetal and human life. But such transformation is always accompanied by cost: the honeysuckle indelibly marks the hazel that it embraces, the hazel shoot must be cut and trimmed, and any entwined climber sacrificed to permit the message. The separation of which the poem repeatedly speaks is not only of one lover from the other, it is also a separation, often violent, from prior form, from growing tree into fixed wooden letter, from declaration of love into song, from loving life into lovers' legend.[28]

Notes

1. This lexis includes, in addition to *lai, verité, sume*, references to oral and written stories, even corpora, in prose and verse, the vocabulary of royal and amatory decrees, and varied forms of communication such as authorial address of the public, hearsay, conversation, a rod incised with letters or words, and song.

2. In order to direct attention to the most recent edition of the *lai*, vv. 2-4 and 116-18 are quoted from *Le Lai du Chèvrefeuille*, ed. Mireille Demaules, in *Tristan et Yseult: Les premières versions européennes*, gen. ed. Christiane Marchello-Nizia (Paris: Gallimard, 1995).

3. *The Lais of Marie de France*, trans. Glyn S. Burgess and Keith Busby, 2nd ed. with two further lais in the original Old French (London: Penguin, 1999), pp. 109-10.

4. *Les Lais de Marie de France*, ed. Jean Rychner (Paris: Honoré Champion, 1966), notes to *Chievrefoil*, p. 276.

5. A first overview is provided in Rychner's edition of 1966 (276-79), completed by Maurice Cagnon, 'Chievrefueil and the Ogamic Tradition,' *Romania* 91 (1970), 238-55. Most recent is Demaules's summary and discussion from 1995 (1287-97).

6. *The Lais of Marie de France*, trans. Burgess and Busby, p. 109.

7. The term *coudrei* for a hazel thicket occurs in *An Anglo-Norman Brut* (Royal 13.A.xxi), ed. Alexander Bell, Anglo-Norman Texts 21-22 (Oxford: Blackwell, 1969), v. 6042. I am grateful to Ruth Timme and Erin Rentz for information on botanical matters.

8. See Fergus Kelly, 'The Old Irish Tree-List,' *Celtica* 11 (1976), 107-24.

9. Kelly, 'The Old Irish Tree-List,' 118f.

10. See Damian McManus, *A Guide to Ogam* (Maynooth: An Sagart, 1991).

11. McManus, *A Guide to Ogam*, p. 2.

12. Patrick Sims-Williams, 'The Additional Letters of the Ogam Alphabet,' *Cambridge Medieval Celtic Studies* 23 (1992), 29-75, at 74. Sims-Williams does not note the possibility of the letter name *uillenn* being associated with the honeysuckle, even though another of the supplementary letters, *pín*, seems based on the Latin tree name *pinus*. In apparent anticipation of Marie's *lai*, we then find that, like the honeysuckle inscribing the hazel in nature, the Irish word *coll* 'hazel' could, at one point, not be written in Ogam without the use of the letters *coll* and *uillenn*.

13. McManus, pp. 42f.

14. In a neat but unhistorical tie to Tristan the harper (*Chevrefoil*, v. 112), *flesc* was also used of a harper's plectrum. Leaving to one side the pairings of *fid/flesc* 'wood/twig' but also 'letter/stroke,' and harp/plectrum that are present only in the putative Irish matter, we could establish for Marie a varied set of pairs: origins and results, precedents and consequences: hazel-tree/shoot, hazel-rod/knife, hazel/honeysuckle, writer/reader, event/*lai*, memorized song/performance, performer/public. In this regard, we may entertain the notion that the plant symbolism that would equate Tristan with the hazel and Yseult with the honeysuckle, could, with the prompt of the feminine gender of *coudre* and masculine gender of *chievrefoil*, be reversed. Not only is the queen the tree- or statue-like object of attention, the skulking forest-dweller Tristan has affinities with the creeper and the very title of the *lai* foregrounds this plant; see Roger Dragonetti, 'Le lai narratif de Marie de France: "Pur quei fu fez, coment e dunt",' in *Littérature, Histoire, Linguistique: Recueil d'études offert à Bernard Gagnebin* (Lausanne: Age d'Homme, 1973), pp. 31-53, at 45.

15. A sampling of recent translations, in addition to that of Burgess and Busby (n. 6), will be illustrative: 'Il coupe une branche de coudrier, il la taille en baguette carrée. Puis quand elle est prête, il y écrit son nom avec son couteau et la plante au milieu du sentier,' *Lais de Marie de France,* trans. Paul Tuffrau (Paris: H. Piazza, 1959), p. 52f.; 'il y plante une branche de coudrier qu'il a fendu en deux et taillée en planchette. Quand il a preparé le morceau de bois, il y grave son nom avec son couteau,' *Les Tristan en vers,* ed. and trans. J.-C. Payen (Paris: Garnier, 1974), p. 300; 'He cut a hazel tree in half, then he squared it. When he had prepared the wood, he wrote his name on it with his knife,' *The Lais of Marie de France,* trans. Robert Hanning and Joan Ferrante (New York: Dutton, 1978), p. 191; 'Il coupe par le milieu une branche de coudrier, il l'équarrit et quand il a préparé le bâton de son couteau, il y grave son nom,' *Lais de Marie de France,* ed. and trans. Alexandre Micha (Paris: Garnier, 1994), p. 277; 'il coupa une branche de coudrier par le milieu, et la tailla pour bien l'équarrir. Une fois le bâton écorcé, avec son couteau il y grava son nom,' Mireille Demaules in T*ristan et Yseult: Les premières versions européennes* (1995), p. 214; 'Meanwhile, he cut down and squared A hazel branch. When it was pared, He signed it, using his knife to write', Patricia A. Terry, in *The Honeysuckle and the Hazel Tree: Medieval Stories of Men and Women*

(Los Angeles: The University of California Press, 1995), p. 90; 'He cut a hazel in half there, Shaped and trimmed it, neatly square. When he had prepared this staff, He autographed it with his knife.' *Chevrefoil,* trans. Judith P. Shoaf, http://web.english.ufl.edu/exemplaria/chev.html. Here it is appropriate to quote Brother Robert's rendering of Marie's *lai* into Old Norse: 'þa hio hann niðr einn hesli vonnd oc telgdi ferstrenndan með knifi sinum. ok reist nafn sitt a stavenom,' *Strengleikar,* ed. and trans. Robert Cook and Mattias Tveitane (Oslo: Norsk historisk kjeldskrift-institutt, 1979), p. 196. I would modify their translation as follows: 'Then he cut down a hazel wand and whittled it four-sided with his knife and carved his name on the rod.'

16. See, for example, *Altfranzösisches Wörterbuch,* ed. Adolph Tobler and Erhard Lommatzsch (Munich: Verlag der Bayerischen Akademie der Wissenschaften, 1965-), *s.v. parer,* one of whose meanings is given as 'einem Stab glätten (um darauf zu schreiben),' which extends a basic meaning of 'peel' toward one of specific preparation.

17. Milestones in the recognition that the Irish literary tradition and writing system are vital to our understanding of Marie are Gertrude Schoepperle, 'Chievrefoil,' *Romania* 38 (1909), 196-218, who quoted saga parallels but focussed on hazel chips not rods and did not imagine a non-Roman alphabet; Maurice Cagnon, '*Chievrefueil* and the Ogamic Tradition,' who brought Ogam into the picture, without, however, a consideration of letter names or the wooden medium of inscription; and Mireille Demaules in notes to her edition (n. 2), who introduced the additional important feature of inscription along the right-angled edge of the hazel staff. She errs (p. 1291), however, in stating that Marie claims a Breton source for this particular *lai,* and I judge the contention that Marie could have had first-hand knowledge of Irish tradition to be overstated. Nonetheless, some identities proposed for Marie and her later patron William do point to Britain's West Country and Ogam was earlier employed in the Irish colonies in South Wales. More recently, Thomas L. Reed, Jr. brings the discussion briefly to bear on the letter *coll* (but not *uillenn*) in 'Glossing the Hazel: Authority, Intention, and Interpretation in Marie de France's *Tristan,* "Chievrefoil",' *Exemplaria* 7 (1995), 99-143.

18. The king and his party are on their way to Tintagel for the Pentecost celebration. This corresponds roughly with Beltaine in the archaic Celtic calendar and from this perspective his voyage may be thought to represent part of an annual circuit of

royal territories, a circle now crossed by Tristan's inscribed rod and its angular message.

19. McManus, p. 159.

20. Admittedly, the idea of two entwined plants was a story-telling commonplace, documented from antiquity, and Reed (p. 127) calls attention to the Irish tale of Baile and Ailinn, which has very clear affinities with Marie's *lai*, even including poets' wooden tablets inscribed with tales of love and then sprouting tendrils.

21. The set of extended kennings for the betrayed Finn reads in translation 'a wooden stake in a fence of silver, hellebore among edible plants, husband of a wanton woman, a cuckold among the well-taught Féni, and heather on the Úalann of the Luigne,' in *Sanas Cormaic: An Old-Irish Glossary* compiled by Cormac úa Cuilennáin, ed. and trans. Whitley Stokes (Halle a.S.: Niemeyer and Dublin: Hodges, Figgis, 1912), item 1018, quoted in McManus, p. 159. For other examples in early Irish sagas of uses of Ogam unconnected with memorial inscriptions, see McManus, pp. 156-63. Several of these deal with injunctions, but it is the use of writing that lends them additional efficacy, not the specific deployment of Ogam. Other tales feature dressed rods used as a medium of record when memory might fail.

22. *Betha Maignenn* ('Life of St. Magnenn of Kilmainham'), in *Silva Gadelica,* ed. and trans. Standish O'Grady, 2 vols. (London: Williams and Norgate, 1892), I.44, cited in *Dictionary of the Irish Language,* gen. ed. E. G. Quin (Dublin: Royal Irish Academy, 1913-76), *s.v. uillennach.*

23. A connection promoted by Demaules in notes to her edition, p. 1294f.

24. Critical comment has, to the best of my knowledge, totally ignored the striking parallels to the *lai* offered by the Old English poem *The Husband's Message,* in which some unidentified wooden medium carries a message inscribed in runes between the couple; see, most recently, Lois Bragg, 'Runes and Readers: In and Around "The Husband's Message,"' *Studia Neophilologica* 71 (1999), 34-50.

25. If the carved message is seen as antecedent to the *lai,* the wood of the hazel rod may be seen as prefiguring that of Tristan's harp (although hazel itself was not so employed). The story then has affinities with tales of plants being witness to acts of violence and later revealing the truth when fashioned into musical instruments and played.

26. Consider, for example, Rabanus Maurus: 'What does it mean to place green rods of almond and plane before the eyes of the flock except to offer

to the people the lives and lessons of the ancient Fathers as they appear throughout the Scriptures? . . . And when from these the bark of the letter is taken away, the interior whiteness is shown allegorically,' discussed in D. W. Robertson, 'Allegory, Humanism, Literary Theory,' in his *A Preface to Chaucer* (Princeton: Princeton University Press, 1963), pp. 316-17.

27. From this perspective it may usefully be compared with *Le Chaitivel,* composed not under circumstances of joy but grief; see Alfred Ewert, *Marie de France: Lais* (Oxford: Blackwell, 1944), p. 184, but here the essential, 'shoot-like' message is repeatedly entwined by its various re-statings.

28. Marie's text seems intended to make a 'last word' difficult and *Chievrefoil* continues to attract scholarly attention. Recent studies relative to the concerns of this note, in addition to those listed above, are Pierre Kunstman, 'Symbole et interprétation: Le message de Tristan dans le *Chèvrefeuille,*' *Tristania* 13 (1987), 35-52; Keith Busby, '"Ceo fu la summe de l'escrit" (*Chevrefoil,* Line 61) Again,' *Philological Quarterly* 74 (1995), 1-15; Bernadette A. Masters, 'Involution of Meaning in the Harley *Cheuerefoil,*' *Parergon* 13 (1995), 81-115; June Hall McCash, '"Ensemble poënt bien durer": Time and Timelessness in the *Chevrefoil* of Marie de France,' ARTHURIANA 9 (1999), 32-44; and Anxo Fernández Ocampo, '*Tristan otiosus* dans le débat sur la traduction du *Chèvrefeuille,*' *Tristania* 21 (2001-2002), 1-12. The larger issues of the patronage of Marie's works and ambient political climate have recently been readdressed in Dinah Hazell, 'Rethinking Marie,' *Medieval Forum* 2 (2003), at http://www.sfsu.edu/~medieval/volume2.html. See, too, R. Howard Bloch, *The Anonymous Marie de France* (Chicago: University of Chicago Press, 2003).

William Sayers (essay date 2004)

SOURCE: Sayers, William. "Naval Architecture in Marie de France's 'Guigemar.'" *Germanisch-Romanische Monatsschrift* 54, no. 4 (2004): 379-91.

[In the essay below, Sayers examines how the craftsmanship of the magic boat in "Guigemar" reinforces the themes of the lay.]

The ship that the weary, wounded Guigemar boards is clearly a magical vessel, uncrewed, self-navigating, and, in the interests of plot, always on time. Yet the magical in Marie is often just a step away from the ordinary, like those walls of rock in Irish story that suddenly open to reveal sumptuous, well-lit caverns peopled with extraordinary beings.[1] Nevertheless even before the poet details the costly and lavish fittings we have an overall appreciation of the ship, perhaps Guigemar's own impression, that pulls us up short.

> *El hafne out une seule nef,*
> *Dunt Guigemar choisi le tref.*
> *Mult esteit bien apparillee;*
> *Defors e dedenz fu peiee,*
> *Nuls hum n'i pout trover jointure.*
> *N'i out cheville ne closture*
> *Ki ne fust tute de benus:*
> *Suz ciel n'at or ki vaille plus!*[2]

From this we learn that the ship had a sail, likely a single one, was well outfitted, and was caulked with pitch inside and out, so that no seams were visible.[3] Medieval ships were built of green timber so that warping and subsequent leakage were chronic problems, even on the most carefully assembled ships. Oakum was driven into seams and tar was applied, primarily on the outside. While small-scale tar production was possible anywhere with stands of birch or pine from which resin could be extracted and rendered, bituminous tar was also an important medieval trade commodity, with the major source being the tarpits of the Near East.[4] While a common enough substance, the lavish use of pitch on the magical boat underscores other luxurious and exotic details. *Chevilles* were treenails or wooden assembly pins, a common alternative to metal nails. The editor suggests that the rare word *closture* here means 'clameau' or a clamp of some kind; lexical affinities make it clear that some type of fastener or closing device is meant.

With these identifications, we must wonder what the treenails and clamps are holding together, since, if they had been used to assemble the planks of the hull—as seems a logical assumption from the immediate textual context—their heads or other external features would have been obscured by the caulkers' pitch. The important fact that they were made of ebony, a luxury wood, would not have been apparent. Before trying to penetrate further the basic naval architecture, it will be rewarding to review the other features and fittings of the ship, both their material nature and provenance.

One further detail, that the sail is of silk, is mentioned before Guigemar embarks and to his surprise finds no one aboard. And instead of the usual ship's gear, the central part of the vessel is taken up with a bed.

> *En mi la nef trovat un lit*
> *Dunt li pecul e li limun*
> *Furent a l'ovre Salemun*
> *Taillié a or, tut a triffoire,*
> *De ciprés e de blanc ivoire.*

(170-74)

This chiasmic sequence of bed parts and materials is to be resolved as the feet of the bed (*pecul*) being made of ivory and the side-pieces of the frame (*limun*) of cypress, with decorative elements in gold. So assigning materials and bed parts is in accordance with the likely size of the pieces to be worked, elephant ivory (rather than walrus) and cypress planks. The color scheme is gold, ivory and reddish-brown (cypress), against the black background of pitch and ebony. Cypress wood is extremely long-lasting and in the Middle Ages was viewed as the material of which the ark had been built. It thus points ahead to the issue of faithfulness in love and to agelessness in the Celtic Otherworld. In addition, Cyparissus in Book 10 of Ovid's *Metamorphoses*, grieving over the accidental death of a pet deer, is turned into a tree by the compassionate Apollo. The presence of the antlered hind in Marie's "Breton" source may then have prompted the author to complement this with a detail from the classical tradition.

Parallels with the bed or litter in the *Song of Songs* were noted in earlier studies of the *lai*, but, the wood aside, the immediate antecedent of these verses seems to be the description of Camille's saddle in the *roman d'Énéas*, a work which was trend-setting for medieval French romance in a number of respects (see below for another significant loan by Marie).

> *La sele ert bone, et li arçon*
> *furent de l'ovre Salemon,*
> *a entaille de blanc ivoire;*
> *l'entaille an ert a or trifoire.*[5]

The relative frequency of the combination of *trifoire* and *l'ovre Salemun* in other works led scholars to believe that this was a specific decorative technique, just as damascening, a technique for finishing sword blades, was named after the city, Damascus, where it was practiced.[6] This is as alternative to recognizing an extravagant elliptical simile, that the quality of the work was comparable to that in Solomon's era, even that deployed on the Temple. In his edition of the **Lais,** Jean Rychner explains *triffoire* as "œuvre d'incrustation" and concludes that "l'œuvre Salemun" referred to a bas-relief technique with which the gold was worked.[7] Nonetheless, the etymology of *triffoire* points to Latin *triforium* and thus a triple (or multiple) opening. I then judge *intaglio* might be a better description of the technique than *bas relief* and that the bed frame may have been thought to be decorated with fret-work, allowing the ivory and wood to show through. Further, *ovre Salemun*, like *opus Salomonis*, may well have suggested Solomon and the *ars notoria* and thus be a further reference to supernatural workmanship rather than a specific technique of carving.[8] In this reading, the special features of the ship's hull and bed-frame are then to be closed and open, respectively, in each case the mark of fine workmanship. Closure and aperture become central issues in the story that follows.[9]

The reference to Solomon is naturally programmatic in directing the public to associate further details of the ship with the marvelous east, the home of silk, ebony, and ivory.[10] Silk, used for the sail, is also woven with gold thread in the coverlet (*coilte*) on the bed. The pillow is so fine that a sleeper's hair would never turn white. The bed covering, the element to retain body heat, is of sable lined with Alexandrine purple. Sable reached western Europe directly from the North but could also have middlemen in the East and the dyed cloth suggests the purple color obtained from shellfish (called in Greek *porphura*) found in the eastern Mediterranean. Of less specific origin are the two candelabra with lighted candles in the prow of the ship, suggesting that wind and sail power may not the true means of locomotion.

Guigemar lies down on the bed and only later discovers that the ship has set sail in fine weather and with a gentle breeze. The ship makes port in an unknown city without incident and Guigemar's further adventure with the jealous lord of the castle and his fair lady pursues its course. The magical ship does not reappear until Guigemar and his lover have been exposed and he is threatened with death unless the details of his story—the encounter with the antlered hind, the wound from the ricocheting arrow, the punishment inflicted, the crewless ship—can be corroborated. As if summoned, the ship, now called *barge,* reappears and Guigemar is allowed to leave unharmed. Again without apparent direction, the vessel steers a true course to the harbor where Guigemar first discovered it, near his home in Brittany. But before his banishment, Guigemar and his lady have sworn faithfulness in love, exteriorized in a knot (*plet*) she ties in the tail of his shirt and in a belt (*ceinture,* what we would call a chastity belt) buckled around her loins next to her skin. They promise to give their love to none but the person who can untie the knot or open the belt with bare hands.

The lady is then imprisoned in a high tower which overlooks her lord's harbor. After two years of suffering, she manages her escape—the tower yielding where the belt later will not—and finds the prescient ship waiting. She is brought ashore near the castle of Meriaduc in Brittany, not distant from Guigemar's castle. With this the magical ship disappears from the *lai* as it had come, and the expected trials of the lovers and attempts to untie the knot and unbuckle the belt take their expected course. The role of the ship is however emphasized in the narrative through two recapitulations:

Guigemar's account to his lady's husband of his arrival in their territory, and his lady's account of her escape and arrival in Brittany, but in neither case is the ship again described.

With this summary, we return to the properties of the ship, or ferry as we might better call it. The kinds of ships that would have been best known to Marie, her patrons and public are those that we too know from the Bayeux Tapestry. These are of Norse design and incorporate multiple features, from single square sail to plank fasteners, that we know from Old Norse-Icelandic literature and now from recovered and restored wrecks, such as those housed in the Viking Ship Museum in Roskilde, Denmark, the Skuldelev wrecks.[11] Such ships are also known from Anglo-Norman literature where sailing scenes seem to have been a preferred set piece. The ample descriptions of ships and sailing in chronicles, saints' lives, and ancestral romances give a picture fully consonant with, and often usefully complementary to, what we know from other sources. In the departure of Arthur for Gaul that we find in Wace's *Brut* we have a description of the embarkation of a fleet that amounts to a narrativization of a list of ship's parts. No fewer than 25 discrete parts or sail-trimming activities are named and—strikingly—18 of these, roughly all those that do not reference basic parts such as mast and sail, are derived from Old Norse, e.g., *haubans* 'shrouds' <ON *höfuðbenda,* literally 'head rope.'[12] In Marie's **"Guigemar,"** on the other hand, the Norse-derived *hafne* 'haven, small harbor' <ON *hafn* stands alone and all subsequent nautical and marine terms are drawn from Gallo-Romance (but see below). This in itself invites us to see the craft as built on other than the imported Scandinavian model, something alien and potentially wondrous.

Early Norse ships were built on the clinker principle, which entailed that the hull was assembled before it was fitted with floor and other strengthening timbers. Starting from the keel, planks that would run the full length of the ship were mounted one on top of another, with the one above making a small overlap on that below, a stepped effect like a staircase seen from behind. Planks were joined one to another at the overlap by treenails fitted in holes drilled through both planks and secured on the inside with a wedge, often of willow that would expand in the humid environment, or by iron nail driven in from the outside with the point then clenched over a square iron rove on the interior of the hull. Wace records this stage of construction in the verse *"nés cheviller et nés cloer"* (v. 11,195). When timber supplies did not permit planks running the full length of the ship, lengths were scarfed together, again with nails or treenails to secure the tongue-and-groove or simpler scarfs. This assembly technique gave the Norse ships their characteristic studded look. Although animal hair, wool, moss, and other material was fitted in grooves running along the land or overlap of two planks and other caulking was later performed on the outside, the hulls, while sleek and clean-lined, were anything but smooth. Both the overlapping planks—the clinker effect—and the heads of the treenails or nails would remain in evidence. Thus, the craft that transports Guigemar is explicitly described as deviating from the Norse and Norman norm.

This was recognized by Brother Robert, an Englishman at the court of King Hakon of Norway, who translated Marie's *lais* into Old Norse. In *Guiamar* the hero spots the ship from the cliff and approaches it. But to his astonishment, and seemingly to Robert's:

> en þat skib var kynlegom haglœik gort þui at uttan borz ok innan matte œngi sía samfœlling borðanna ne nœgling naglanna nema sua var til synis sem œinn við vœre allt.

> The ship was constructed with amazing skill, for neither outside nor inside could be seen the joining of boards or the nailing of nails, but it appeared to the eyes as though it were all one piece of wood.[13]

Robert does not mention the thorough caulking with pitch, a feature that would have been less prominent on his patron's ships, but he expands on his source and is even more explicit than Marie is stating that the hull seemed to have been made of a single piece. Thus we have confirmation that the ship waiting for Guigemar was indeed exotic. But is it a ship pulled out of thin air by Marie as it seems to appear in the poem?

In contrast to the clinker construction characteristic of northern Europe, ships plying the medieval Mediterranean were built with a technique named after one of the most common ship types: carvel construction. Another name is skeleton construction. Here the planks of the hull were fitted edge to edge and were mounted on a pre-existent framework of ship's timbers. If fasteners were countersunk the overall effect would be of a very smooth surface, enhanced by a coat of tar. Somewhat greater precision would have been called for in fitting the edges together (rather than overlapping them) and to northern eyes this might well have suggested superior workmanship overall and thus a luxury vessel.

As trading networks expanded in the Middle Ages, carvel construction would come to be seen in northern ports, just as the residents of Acre in the Holy Land would have seen a clinker built ship when Earl Rögnvald of Orkney sailed from the Northern Isles across the Bay of Biscay, around the Iberian peninsula, and through the Straits of Gibraltar to participate in the second crusade in 1151.

Thus we have a historical antecedent for Guigemar's magical ship, one that accords well with its fittings and their origin in eastern luxury goods. This, of course, in no way diminishes the impact of the magical ship on Guigemar and on Marie's public but the jump from the real but exceptional to the magical is made from a known base. Could there have been other models, inherent to Marie's sources if not well known to her public?

Although the Irish *curragh* as immortalized in Robert O'Flaherty's documentary film, *Man of Aran,* is reasonably well known to a wider world, and the word *coracle* summons up images of single paddlers in round and round-bottomed leather-hulled craft, medieval Celtic ship-building techniques are now judged to have been capable of producing larger, ocean-going, as opposed to coastal, vessels. Construction of such vessels would involve a keel and wooden framework, the latter covered with a wickerwork shell, over which were stretched ox-hides that had been sewn together. To the observer, the hull would be smooth and when tarred would offer up no seams to the eye.[14]

But it is not only the construction of curraghs and related larger craft that may have underlain the conception of the ship that Marie encountered in her sources. Early Irish narrative tradition is also rich in magical vessels. The narrative genre of *immrama* or voyage tales was quite thoroughly christianized, so that ships that proceed without human intervention are actually being guided by God, usually toward marvelous islands, only a few of which recall the paradisiacal Otherworld of early Celtic story. Tales such as the voyages of Bran, Snedgus, Mael Dúin, and the Huí Corra have been cited in earlier studies of **"Guigemar"** and this correspondence need not be reviewed here. Rather, we may stay with naval construction and examine how in this respect too the wondrous boats of early Irish tradition differed from the ordinary.

A recurrent nautical motif is that the ships of the Otherworld or of supernatural beings are constructed of non-organic materials. In the *Wooing of Becfhola* (*Tochmarc Becfhola*) Diarmaid son of Aed Sláine held the kingship of Tara. He is approached by a beautiful young woman with all the attributes of an Other-world being, who offers herself as his consort. Later she seeks to elope with his foster-son Crimthann; when he refuses, she leaves the court and subsequently meets a warrior in the forest. After a meal he leads her to a lake where a boat of bronze ("*long crédumae*") is moored. They take the boat for a short crossing to an island where there was "a fine house, with both cubicles and bed" ("*amra an teg hí-sin itir irscartad 7 dérgudha*").[15] She learns that the warrior is named Flann and that he regularly does battle against another small party for control of the magical island. Although the woman Becfhola returns to the king, she is eventually reunited with Flann when he has won the island. In another short tale about the paramount Ulster hero Cú Chulainn, the warrior is performing martial exercises on the bank of the Boyne when he sees a tiny harper traveling the river in a bronze boat that does not require rowing. His musical abilities are equally magical.[16] Other tales feature boats made of crystal or glass.[17] In all these examples the hull either was or gave the impression of being made of a single piece, as in Marie's *lai*.

It is also in the context of trips to the Celtic Otherworld in a boat of bronze that we meet descriptions of luxurious halls with fine beds, used in dining, watching entertainment, etc.:

> *Cóeca lepad na leith dess*
> *7 chóeca airides,*
> *cóeca lepad na leth chlí;*
> *7 chóeca aeridi.*
> *Colba do lepthaib crónda,*
> *úatne finna forórda,*
> *is sí caindell ardustá*
> *in lía lógmar lainerdá.*[18]

> Fifty beds on the right side and fifty on the floor; fifty beds on the left side and fifty on the dais. Bedposts of bronze, white gilded pillars; the candle before them a bright precious stone.[19]

The detail of the lighted candle in conjunction with the decorated ship-borne bed may then also have remote Celtic origins.

Thus we have at least two antecedents for the boat with the smooth, apparently seamless hull in Marie's **"Guigemar"**: the tarred, leather-hulled craft of the Celts, which, in story, could be made of precious materials but retain their original construction principle, and the carvel-built hulls of the Mediterranean, whose edge-to-edge planking was also tarred. Fine woods and other precious materials are natural complements in the construction of such luxury vessels.

Sailing scenes are only rarely developed in Marie's *lais*. We see small harbors filled with ships as a sign of a town's wealth or Otherworld nature and the numerous Channel crossings are usually perfunctorily stated, occasionally with a reference to fair winds ("*Bon oré eurent e fort vent,*" **"Milun,"** v. 506, **"Eliaduc,"** v. 813). Only **"Eliaduc"** offers the otherwise popular Anglo-Norman motif of a storm at sea (vv. 815-68). Here the yard (*verge,* not the 'mast' as some translators would have it) and sail are lost and Eliaduc must throw overboard a reluctant sailor (*escipre* < ON *skipari*) and himself take the tiller (*estiere* < Old Norse *stýri* 'helm, rudder') in order to make the harbor (*hafne*). We should also recall that on the ships Marie knew best the huge single sail was the product of exclusively women's

work and the very considerable commitment of human resources in its weaving, assembly and treatment gave it a value comparable to that of the ship itself.

We had earlier deferred discussion of the word *closture*. The ships of the age that Marie would have known best had, as far as we can judge, nothing essential to their construction that we could call a clamp and other suggestions such as railing do not convince.[20] And we recall that Brother Robert elected not to translate this word directly. In the verses "*Nuls hum n'i pout trover jointure. N'i out cheville ne closture Ki ne fust tute de benus*" I judge that all elements relate to hull construction, that is, that the reference to *chevilles* and *closture* of ebony is part of the description of the seamless hull. As earlier noted, *cheville* would have been the standard term for one type of fastener employed to assemble the planks of the hull.

What has eluded earlier editors and translators addressing *closture* is that Marie has borrowed lexis and a rhyme from the *roman d'Énéas,* where we read of one of the ships in Énéas's fleet:

> *Devant lor roy ot une barje:*
> *son governail li ert brisiez.*
> *et mast et single en mer plongiez,*
> *.III. tors tourna en moult poi d'eure;*
> *un oraige li vint deseure*
> *qui se le fiert en l'un des lés*
> *les bors a frainz et desquasez;*
> *rompent chevilles et coustures,*
> *l'eve y entre par les jointures;*
> *emplie l'a soudeement:*
> *affondree est en .I. moment.*[21]

The second stage of damage to the ship, the shattered planking (*bors*) and treenails (*chevilles*), derives from these lines of Virgil: "laxis laterum compagnibus omnes / accipiunt inimicum imbrem rimisque fatiscunt." *Compagnes* means 'connection, joint, structure' and *rima* 'cleft, crack, fissure'. An authoritative modern translation renders the passage "with side joints loosened, all [three ships] let in the hostile flood and gape at every seam".[22] But this gives evidence of no great understanding of naval construction. What Virgil means is that the joins between the planks that make up the sides of the hull have opened and that water enters through the gaps, with *compagnes* and *rima* then making a neat antithetical pair. The poet of the *roman d'Énéas* has suppressed the fissures but duplicated the now opened joins in *coustures* and *jointures*. Marie, in turn, seems to have remembered the rhyming couplet and its terminology, but inverted the content so as to create a seamless, rather than shattered, hull. In the French of the time *closture/cousture* would appear to have referenced both something that effected closure and a joint, agent and object as it were.

I then believe that in *closture* Marie wished her public to understand a discrete ship's part. Several hull-related elements suggest themselves. One is the system of frames fastened to the interior of the hull, which would set off compartments in which ballast and trade goods would be stored. Another possibility is bulkheads, vertical partitions attached to floor timbers, similarly to compartmentalize the interior of the hull.[23] A bulkhead would have a functional resemblance to the chastity belt, if we were to equate the depths of the ship's hull with female pelvic anatomy (see below). We should not suppose Marie to have had detailed knowledge of ship construction and must then accept that in describing a largely Celtic-inspired magical ship and recasting the couplet from the *roman d'Énéas* she may have covered with pitch the very treenails that she claims were made of ebony-always assuming that a single focus is here on the hull.

In the *lai* of **"Guigemar"** Marie returns the supernatural boats of Christian hagiography to secular story-telling purportedly based on Breton *lais*. The masterless ship is initially in the service of the white hind's punishment, the thigh wounded by the returning arrow (punishing the sin of narcissism?) to be followed by the deeper wound and greater pain of unfulfilled love and longing.[24] Its magical properties, which are subsequently engaged to further the love of Guigemar and his lady, are first embodied in a construction feature—the seamless hull—which is singled out for emphasis. They are further exemplified in the propulsion and steering which derive from some unknown power, a power not identified as the Christian god. Guigemar's voyage is to be seen not so much in quantitative terms—the distance, say, from Brittany to Cornwall—as in qualitative terms, with the castle of his destination sharing many features with the Otherworld. After Guigemar's year of love and ease with the lady, whose lack of explicit name seems reminiscent of the nameless "fairy wives" of Celtic story, the external signs of faithful love take the form of the knot in Guigemar's shirt and the chastity belt thenceforth worn by his lady.[25] Both these embody semipermanent closure and it is perhaps not too far-fetched to see the motifs of the sail with its sheet (the line from the lower corner of the sail) and the seamless ship's hull in this exteriorization of the lovers' vow. The knot in the shirt-tail recalls the wounded thigh bandaged with the same cloth. We have the cluster of key- and often rhyme-words *jointure, closture, aventure, peinture, ceinture, sereure*. Similarly, the bed, the ship's one named accouterment, seems an allomorph of the ship itself, its rich frame and bedclothes replicating the vessel's hull and sail. Later the bed in the lady's chamber will dominate that space and be the prime site of love, under the programmatic sign of Venus.[26] Even here the ship, sail, and mast seem recalled in the chamber, bed, and pole used to suspend drying clothes, seized by Guigemar in self-defence.[27] Although Guigemar's admitted inability to navigate the ship is like the uncharted course of love, the prescient fairy- and ferry-like vessel shuttles back and forth on a linear course, suggesting the reciprocity of avowed love. At the same time, the lady moves among various forms of containment, willed and unwilled, as sequestered wife, lover, prisoner, and house guest in the various towers, chambers and hall, enclosed garden, belt, and boat. The concentric circles of castle enclosure, tower, and room give the lady's place of confinement a maze-like quality, accentuating the variant on the quest that is Guigemar's unwilled transportation by the ship and convalescence with the lady.

In **"Guigemar"** we see Marie's economy of means, prominence given to only a few features of the ship, which then return in the form of shirt and belt. Similarly, the Celtic Otherworld retains all its mystery since the poet is equally sparing in the deployment of its effects.[28] The *conjointure* realized by the ship's apparent lack of *jointure* along with the hermetic nature of knot and belt brings together nautical motifs from both the Irish Sea and the Mediterranean to introduce the unpredictable nature and force of love, then the internal and external signs that mark the pledge of faithfulness in love.[29]

Notes

1. See L. Rimpau, *Die aventure der escriture: Zu einem poetologischen Strukturprinzip des Lais von Marie de France*, in: *Das Wunderbare in der arthurischen Literatur: Probleme und Perspektiven*, ed. Friedrich Wolfzettel (Tübingen: Niemeyer, 2003), pp. 249-80, and Pierre Jonin: *Merveilleux et voyage dans le lai de Guigemar*, in: *Voyage, quête, pélérinage dans la littérature et la civilisation médiévales*, Senefiance 2 (Aix-en-Provence: CUER MA, 1976), pp. 273-86.

2. *Les Lais de Marie de France*, ed. Jean Rychner (Paris: Honoré Champion, 1966), vv. 151-58. Manuscripts consulted by the editor offer no variants that bear on the technical vocabulary here considered.

3. Rychner glosses *tref* with *mât*, but the term in Anglo-Norman always references either the sail (with the form traced to a Gmc root meaning 'woven material') or the sail-yard (<Lat. *trabs, trabis* 'beam'). Marie returns to boiling pitch among hell's punishment in *L'Espurgatoire seint Patriz*, ed. and trans. Yolande de Pontfarcy (Louvain: Peters, 1995), v. 1098.

4. In the later Middle Ages coniferous pitch was extensively exported from the Baltic; cf. *spruce* and Chaucer's *Pruce*.

5. *Eneas: roman du XIIe siècle,* ed. J.-J. Salverda de Grave, 2 vols (Paris: Honoré Champion, 1925), vv. 4075-78. The lengthy description of Camille's horse and weapons has only a brief antecedent at the close of Book 7 of Virgil's *Eneid,* where the saddle is not specifically mentioned.

6. Additional examples, from freshly edited works are, Thomas de Kent, *Le Roman d'Alexandre, ou, le roman de toute chevalerie,* ed. Brian Foster and Ian Short, trans. Catherine Gaullier-Bougassas and Laurence Harf-Lancer (Paris: Champion, 2003), v. 1033, and Robert d'Orbigny, *Le conte de Floire et Blanchefleur,* ed. and trans. Jean-Luc Leclanche (Paris: Champion, 2003), vv. 561f. Relevant studies are Nigel Abercrombie, *A Note on a Passage in 'Guigemar',* in: Modern Language Review 30 (1935), 353; G. D. West, *L'uevre Salemon,* in: Modern Language Review 49 (1954), 176-82; and F. Lyons, *Old French trifoire,* in: *History and Structure of French: Essays in Honour of Professor T. B. W. Reid,* ed. F. J. Barnett et al. (Totowa, N.J.: Rowland and Littlefied, 1972), pp. 152-69. Jean-Olivier Signoret, *Deo gubernante: navigations miraculeuses et miracles marins au Moyen Âge: l'union des cultures païennes et chrétiennes* (Paris: Presses universitaires du Septentrion, 2000), has a relevant section entitled "L'œuvre Salomon", but provides little in the way of analysis. The book as a whole is an interesting collection of motifs, but little more. Another doctoral thesis, with a rather better analysis of multiple motifs and a section, pp. 169-75, on "La nef sans équipage", is Brigitte Charles Lacombe, *Maroniers, notoniers et pescheors dans la littérature française des XIIe, XIIIe et XIVe siècles* (Villeneuve-d'Ascq: Presses universitaires du Septentrion, 2003).

7. *Lais,* 243, note to vv. 172-74.

8. Lynn Thorndike, *Solomon and the Ars Notoria,* Ch. 49 in his *Magic and Experimental Science* (New York, Columbia U P, 1958-60). In the century following Marie, Solomon would be ascribed his own ship and bed in *La queste del saint graal;* a recent appreciation of narrative strategies around the ship and bed is Nancy Freeman Regalado, *The Medieval Construction of the Modern Reader: Solomon's Ship and the Birth of Jean de Meun,* in: Yale French Studies 95 (1999), 81-108. The parallel with the ship and bed in Marie may be more than coincidental, since of the transversal guard of the sword to be placed on the bed, Solomon's wife dictates "*Et vos, qui conoissiez les vertus des pierres et la force des herbes et la maniere de toutes autres choses terrienes, si i fetes un pont de pierres precieuses si soutilment jointes qu'il n'ait aprés vos regart terrien qui poïst conoistre l'une de l'autre, ainz quit chascuns qui le verra que ce soit une meisme chose*"; *La queste del saint graal,* ed. Albert Pauphilet (Paris: Champion, 1923), p. 223. Is there some word play or echo between OFr. *pont* as 'sword guard' and 'bridge, deck of a ship'?

9. The preface to this *lai,* before turning to backbiters, stresses the artisanal side of literary creation: "*Ki de bone mateire traite, Mult li peise si bien n'est faite*" (vv. 1-2), preparing us for the well-built ship and bed.

10. For an overview see Carol F. Heffernan, *The Orient in Chaucer and Medieval Romance* (Rochester, NY, and Woodbridge, Suffolk: Boydell & Brewer, 2003). Also symptomatic of the renewed interest in eastern influence on medieval European culture is Catherine Gaullier-Bougassas, *La tentation de l'orient dans le roman médiéval: sur l'imaginaire médiéval de l'autre* (Paris: Champion, 2003).

11. *The Skuldelev Ships I: Topography, Archaeology, History, Conservation and Display,* ed. Ole Crumlin-Pedersen, Ships and Boats of the North 4.1 (Roskilde, The Viking Ship Museum, 2002).

12. Wace, *Le Roman de Brut,* ed. Ivor Arnold, 2 vols (Paris: Société des Anciens Textes Français, 1940), vv. 11, 190-238. Nautical lexis is studied in William Sayers, *Norse Nautical Terminology in Twelfth-Century Anglo-Norman Verse,* in: Romanische Forschungen 109 (1997), 383-426.

13. *Guiamar,* in: *Strengleikar: An Old Norse Translation of Twenty-one Old French lais,* ed. and trans. Robert Cook and Mattias Tveitane (Oslo: Norsk historisk kjeldeskrift-institut, 1979), pp. 16-17. See, too, Marianne Kalinke, *Gvímars saga,* in: Opuscula VII (Copenhagen: Reitzel, 1979), pp. 123f.

14. G. J. Marcus, *The Conquest of the North Atlantic* (New York: Oxford U P, 1981), pp. 8-15. In one voyage tale the hull is described as made of a triple layer of hides, "curach trecodhlaidi"; Whitley Stokes, *The Voyage of the Húi Corra,* in: Revue Celtique 14 (1893-94), 22-69, at 38f.

15. Máire Bhreatnach, *A New Edition of 'Tochmarc Becfhola',* in: Ériu 35 (1984), 59-91, at 74. Becfhola is a goddess of territorial sovereignty seeking a just and competent ruler for her land and then is not to be judged by conventional moral standards. Guigemar's lady is an attenuated reflex; see Yolande de Pontfarcy, *La Souveraineté: du mythe au lai de Guigemar,* in: Acta Litteraria Academiae Scientiarum Hungaricae 32 (1990), 153-59.

16. Charles Plummer, *The Combat of Cuchulaind with Senbecc, grandson of Ebrecc, from Seagais,* in:

Irish Miscellanies, in: Revue Celtique 6 (1883-1885), 162-92, at 183.

17. A "ship of crystal" in *The Adventure of Conla*; Kim McCone, *Echtrae Chonnlai and the Beginnings of Narrative Writing in Ireland* (Maynooth: National University of Ireland, 2000), 187ff.; a poet's boat of bronze with tin sail in Whitley Stokes, *81. Ess Rúaid,* in: *The Prose Tales in the Rennes Dindsenchas,* in: Revue Celtique 16 (1895), 31-83, at 31; another boat of bronze in Whitley Stokes, *45. Tond Clidna,* in: *The Prose Tales in the Rennes Dindsenchas,* in: Revue Celtique 15 (1894), 418-84, at 438.

18. *Serglige Con Culainn,* ed. Myles Dillon (Dublin: Dublin Institute for Advanced Studies, 1975), ll. 482-89; the boat of bronze at l. 152.

19. *The Wasting Sickness of Cú Chulaind,* in: *Early Irish Myths and Sagas,* trans. Jeffrey Gantz (Harmondsworth: Penguin, 1981), p. 167; the bronze boat at p. 159.

20. A sampling of modern renderings: "crampons" in *Les Lais de Marie de France,* trans. Paul Tuffrau (Paris: H. Piazza, 1959), *Lais de Marie de France,* ed. and trans. Alexandre Micha (Paris: Garnier, 1994), and *Marie de France, Oeuvres completes: les lais, les fables, le purgatoire de saint Patrick,* trans. Nathalie Desgrugillers (Clermont-Ferrand: Paleo, 2003); "deck-rail" in *Lais,* ed. Alfred Ewert (Oxford: Blackwell, 1944), and *The Lais of Marie de France,* trans. Robert Hanning and Joan Ferrante (New York: Dutton, 1978), "railing" in *The Lais of Marie de France,* trans. Glyn S. Burgess and Keith Busby (Harmondsworth: Penguin, 1986), "rails", in *Proud Knight, Fair Lady: The Twelve Lais of Marie de France,* trans. Naomi Lewis (New York: Viking Kestrel, 1989). "Closture" is rendered "attache" in a modern French version of *Le Roman d'Énéas,* trans. Martine Thiry-Stassin (Paris: Champion, 1985), p. 16. The presence of railings implies a raised deck area or castle, since the stretch of hull above the waterline would serve that end elsewhere on the ship, but there is no evidence for raised decks or sterncastles in Marie's time.

21. Vv. 141-51. On correspondences between Marie's *lais* and *Le roman d'Énéas,* see Sebastian I. Sobecki, *A Source for the Magical Ship in the Partonopeu de Blois and Marie de France's 'Guigemar',* in: Notes and Queries 48 (2001), 220-22.

22. *The Aeneid* in *Virgil,* ed. and trans. H. Rushton Fairclough, rev. ed. G. P. Goold, 2 vols (Cambridge, MA: Harvard U P, 1999-2000), Book I, vv. 122-23.

23. For evidence of bulkheads near the stems, see *The Skuldelev Ships I,* pp. 214-16. Finally, there is the remoter possibility that Marie ascribed this feature to the ship in a recall of the partitions of dining halls in Celtic story telling, where individual tables could be set off by dividers, daises, etc. in order to organize the interior space of the hall according to the rank of the diners. See William Sayers, *A Cut Above: Ration and Station in an Irish King's Hall,* in: Food and Foodways 4 (1990), 89-110.

24. See Leslie C. Brook, *Guigemar and the White Hind,* in: Medium Evum 56 (1987), 94-101. As in Celtic narrative, wounds to the thigh are symbolic of sexual dysfunction and thus a comment on fertility, that of human individuals or of a kingdom. In French romance, the Fisher King is the best known example. In *Guigemar,* the lady's supervision by a maimed priest seems symbolic of her unfertile union with the aged lord. Also part of the motif cluster is the seaside setting. A late example of this same motif may well be Gulliver's wound on an island shore after leaving the land of the Houyhnhnms, one of his last adventures and that which seems to determine his subsequent misanthropy and withdrawal from his family; see William Sayers, *Gulliver's Wounded Knee,* in: Swift Studies 7 (1992), 106-09.

25. See Nancy Vine Durling, *The Knot, the Belt, and the Making of Guigemar,* in: Essays: Critical Approaches to Medieval and Renaissance Texts 6 (1991), 29-53, and R. N. Illingworth, *Celtic Tradition and the Lai of Guigemar,* in: Medium Evum 31 (1962), 176-87.

26. On the iconography of the lady's chamber, see Logan E. Whalen, *A Medieval Bookburning: Object d'art as Narrative Device in the Lai of Guigemar,* in: Neophilologus 80 (1996), 205-11.

27. At the risk of a needlessly thorough classification we might venture the following correspondences, based variously on shape, function, symbolic value, etc., all under the general sign of male and female sexual characteristics: arrow and pelvis-shaped rack of antlers on the hind; wounded thigh and fabric bandage; the ship and all its features (bed, mast, sail) and the lady's chamber and its fittings; shirt tail and girdle; perhaps even *cheville* and *closture,* if the latter is identified as a bulkhead.

28. Six verses from the end of the *lai* we read: "*A grant joie s'amie en meine*" (881). As *joie* in French romance is a provisional and threatened state, or a terminal one because the tale ends, and thus a state always sought, it would be of interest to compare the "joy of the court" with the Irish

concept of *síd*, both 'peace' and the caves, islands, palaces of the Otherworld, a conception in which true peace meant harmony with the supernatural forces exteriorized in and inhabiting these extratemporal, extraspatial locales.

29. A complementary approach to the essential message of the *lai*, although with a more exclusive focus on containment and opening, is found in Jacques Ribard, *Le 'lai de Guigemar': conjointure et senefiance*, in: *Amour et Merveille: Les lais de Marie de France*, ed. Jean Dufournet (Paris: Champion, 1995), pp. 133-45. Ribard sees a parallel between the knot and belt in *Guigemar* and the hazel and honeysuckle of *Chievrefoil*; on the latter *lai* and these two motifs, see William Sayers, *Marie de France's 'Chievrefoil', Hazel Rods, and the Ogam Letters 'Coll' and 'Uillenn'*, in: Arthuriana 14 (2004): 3-16.

Karen K. Jambeck (essay date 2004)

SOURCE: Jambeck, Karen K. "'Femmes et tere': Marie de France and the Discourses of 'Lanval.'" In *Discourses on Love, Marriage, and Transgression in Medieval and Early Modern Literature*, edited by Albrecht Classen, pp. 109-45. Tempe: Arizona Center for Medieval and Renaissance Studies, 2004.

[*In the following essay, Jambeck studies the lay "Lanval," discussing Marie's manipulation of mythic and legal discourse to show the difference between private and public love in twelfth-century England.*]

> Speaking or writing in a variety articulates its own view of the world, and that articulation is a social practice, a conscious or unconscious intervention in the organization of society. Literature's cultural force has its origins in this property of language.[1]

"L'aventure d'un autre lai, / Cum ele avient, vus cunterai"[2]—with these words Marie begins the narrative known as **"Lanval."** Her account focuses on the "noble vassal," Lanval, who, having left his native Brittany, serves as a knight at King Arthur's court.[3] After a battle with the Picts and the Scots, Arthur rewards his vassals with wives and lands, but in so doing overlooks Lanval. Alone, without family or resources, the knight rides out to a remote meadow, where he encounters a nameless aristocratic woman from "another land," who offers love and abundance if he is worthy. Willingly, Lanval accepts the lady's love and in return promises absolute loyalty, which includes a vow of secrecy. Upon returning to Arthur's court, Lanval rejects the advances of Arthur's lustful queen. Although he refuses her, she insists, finally charging him with homosexuality;

nonplussed, he responds by praising the beauty of his beloved, thereby breaking his pledge. The vengeful queen accuses Lanval of misconduct, and the knight is brought to trial. Just as the verdict is about to be announced, Lanval's lady arrives; her appearance and words lead to his being adjudged innocent of the charge, and as she leaves Arthur's court, Lanval joins her.

The coexistence of apparently fabulous and demonstrably realistic elements in **"Lanval"**[4] has frequently led commentators to regard the *lai* either as an escapist fantasy[5] or as an historically accurate depiction of twelfth-century legal practice.[6] Such interpretations, while often insightful, tend to focus on static narrative blocks, placing some sections in the foreground while treating others as though they were irrelevant or merely fortuitous.[7] However, focusing instead on the dominant discursive modes that inform and shape **"Lanval"** reveals a dual-voiced narrative in which Marie deploys both legal and mythic discourse—described below—to examine and comment upon love, law, and marriage in the society of her time.[8]

LEGAL DISCOURSE:[9]

Monologic. Legal discourse is characterized by a "specialized lexicon, with fixed meanings; it attempts to map one-to-one equivalencies between signifier and signified." It is "monologic," "uniaccentual," and centripetal.

Intertextual. Legal discourse is "intertextual with other legal texts, usually written texts."

It "has its primary basis in custom and its vocabulary is correspondingly governed by doctrines of memory, recognition and usage, defined in textual terms by reference to extensive and obscure etymologies, inert and calcified meanings and procedures," and by its own "epistemology."

Institutionally Authorized. Legal discourse is "socially and institutionally authorised by a wide variety of highly visible organisational and sociolinguistic insignia of a privileged class." It functions in "a specialized context," a "highly restricted institutional setting" with a clear "legal and social hierarchy." The operations of legal discourse involve personnel of "elite character" and the "ritual trappings of trial."

Axiomatic and Rational. The function of legal discourse is to "prescribe, preserve, maintain social order by formulating and following normative codes." It is "institutional," "rational," and "axiomatic."

Authoritarian and Distanced. Legal discourse is a vehicle for the law, whose "source is always pre-existent," deriving, for instance, from a sovereign, legislature, or custom. It is "authoritarian," "distanced," "alien," "reified." It "restricts human actions" and it is characterized by "linguistic objectification," for "law fixes legal meaning to individual acts" in the context of "responsibility," ignoring human emotions and relationships. In law, the subject "is constituted" as a point of abstract equivalence and the ethical image of the speaking persona as a unitary and unique subjectivity comes to pervade legal discourse, as in testimony.

MYTHIC DISCOURSE:[10]

Polysemous and Metaphoric. Mythic discourse "describes and pictures," employing both language and symbolic images that are polysemous and tending to the centrifugal.[11] Myth and mythic discourse are metaphoric.[12]

Intertextual. Mythic discourse is intertextual: myths tend to resonate with other myths (whether as a consequence of mere resemblance or through attracting and absorbing features of other mythic narratives).[13]

Legitimating and Universal. Mythic discourse informs "legitimating narratives" that exemplify, justify, and validate cultural practices and human behavior. It has both personal and communal implications, providing models for "all significant human activities—diet or marriage, work or education, art or wisdom."[14] Mythic discourse can exist in a general, and even a universal, context; this mode of discursivity can be adopted, and even adapted, by all.[15] *Axiological.* Mythic discourse is axiological, illustrating moral and ethical values for living. Non-rational and affective, it "bypasses," exceeds, or transcends human logic.[16]

Transcendent and Interpellant. Mythic discourse participates in myth's "absolute authority," which is "implied rather than stated," its immediate and eternal "truth" emanating from "elsewhere, from an authority that is higher than human" (e.g., gods, ancestors, or some other transcendent source).[17] In communicating myths that account for the individual's participation with the universe, mythic discourse demonstrates how individuals fit into the natural scheme of things and why human beings are "constituted" in a particular way;[18] it is interpellant, requiring that humans "recognize themselves in this image."[19]

As these discursive modes function throughout Marie's narrative, the polysemic and metaphoric mythic discourse is reserved for the Lady and her relationship with Lanval. Once the knight leaves town and castle and enters a meadow near a stream, he encounters individuals and objects that exceed the significances normally assigned in everyday life. It is here, inside a magnificent pavilion, that he first meets the stunning, unnamed woman, who calls him by name and tells him she has come "Pur vus vienc jeo fors de ma tere" (l. 111). Here the straightforward connection between the term and place—the "tere de Loengre" (l. 9) or the "tere" (land or honors) presented by Arthur to his knights (l. 17)—dissolves into multivalence. Does she come from another "land" or "country," or an "other world"? After Lanval pledges his love to her, she makes an unexplained demand for his vow of secrecy (ll. 144-145). She brings Lanval limitless love, joy, and wealth (ll. 114-116). She tells Lanval that no other man will see or hear her ("Nul hum fors vus ne me verra / Ne ma parole nen orra" [ll. 169-170]). Moreover, this Lady, who has many servants, comes to and departs from Arthur's court at will, and even the King cannot retain her (ll. 630-632). In this discourse, not only lexical items[20] but also objects are charged with meaning: the "ewe curaunt" (ll. 45-46)]; golden basins and a "tuaile" borne by two richly-clad maidens who invite Lanval to a magnificent pavilion (ll. 61-64); and the Lady's palfrey, dog, and sparrowhawk (ll. 551-574). These and other images hint that they are more than they first appear.

Jean Rychner observes that Marie's lack of precision envelops the characters and action in a "halo de mystère, évocant l'autre."[21] In fact, the discourse portraying the Lady is infused with double meaning. All that surrounds her is of superior worth, items associated with sovereigns: she is draped with imperial purple, silk, and ermine (ll. 101-102); a golden eagle surmounts her tent (l. 87); the coverlets of her bed are worth "as much as a castle" (l. 98). However, a correspondence between the lady's possessions and some aspect of the material world once being established, each comparison subsequently negates the point of similarity. Her grand possessions, for example, exceed the grasp of the richest sovereign. Her pavilion is so resplendent that "no king under the sun could afford it" ("Suz ciel n'ad rei ki[s] esligast" [l. 91]). Her palfrey is "finer than any on earth," and the horse's tack and fittings are worth more "than a king's realm" (ll. 551-558). Even the lowliest of her maids-in-waiting is more beautiful than a queen (ll. 299-300).

The unnamed woman is always designated by human terms—"pucele," "dameisele," "meschine" ("girl" or "young woman") and "dame"—all appropriate for a young woman of noble birth; she is also referred to as Lanval's "amie."[22] And as Ernst Hoepffner has noted, the mysterious Lady is very much a woman.[23] On two separate occasions, the narrator describes the Lady's physical attributes. She is the object of Lanval's, and the audience's, gaze as she reclines upon a richly appointed couch inside her splendid pavilion:

Ele jut sur un lit mut bel

. . . . .

En sa chemise senglement.
Mut ot le cors bien fait e gent;
Un cher mantel . . .
Ot pur le chaut sur li geté;
Tut ot descovert le costé,
Le vis, le col e la peitrine;
Plus ert blanche que flur d'espine.

(ll. 97-106)

[She lay on a very beautiful bed . . . clad only in her shift. Her body was well formed and handsome, and in order to protect herself from the heat of the sun, she had cast about her a costly mantle. . . . Her side, though, was uncovered, as well as her face, neck and breast; she was whiter than the hawthorn blossom.]

The second time the Lady appears, she rides slowly into view of Lanval, the members of the court, and the townspeople. As she approaches, her natural beauty shines forth. She wears "a white tunic and a shift, laced left and right so as to reveal her sides" ("De chainsil blanc e de chemise, / Que tuz les costez li pareient, / Que de deus parz laciez esteient" [ll. 560-562]). Her figure is lithe and handsome ("le cors ot gent" [l. 563]); "her hips low" ("basse la hanche" [l. 563]); her eyes gray (l. 565); her face and neck "whiter than the snow on the branch" ("plus blanc que neif sur branche" [l. 564-565]); her brow and sculpted features fair (566-567); her hair golden (ll. 569-570).

However, even though she is depicted in terms of the physical world, she surpasses all to which she is compared, exceeding the capacity of worldly language and sense imagery to describe her. The similitudes used to portray her are marked by the comparative rather than the superlative, which is often associated with the hyperbolic; the result is a subtly understated quality that allows for the Lady's presence in Loengres, yet elevates her above her surroundings. She is more beautiful than the lily ("flur de lis") and the new rose ("rose novele") in the summer (ll. 94-96). Her skin is "whiter than the hawthorn" (l. 106); her "blond curls glisten more than a gold thread in the sun" ("E le chef cresp e aukes blunt; / Fil d'or ne gette tel luur" [ll. 568-569]). No mere ornaments, Marie's similitudes are central to the mythic theme, for the multivalent descriptions hover between the material world and an 'other' spiritual world, without decisively or explicitly committing to either. The result is an ambiguous suspension between the world of the senses and the world of affect and of spirit. These associations do indeed "bypass or transcend human logic," and they embody a "numinous quality [that] is compatible with the pervasive Celtic belief that the supernatural resided within the natural world."[24]

The discourse associated with the Lady also teems with mythic intertextuality, which scholars have investigated for more than a century. For example, the stream (l. 45), notable because Lanval's horse trembles as he approaches it and because the Lady is lodged nearby, has been identified with the *topos* of the sacred stream or spring that recurs throughout Celtic myth and legend.[25] According to Celtic tradition, streams, rivers, lakes, springs, and wells bear a close relationship to sacred powers and are often thought to offer access to the Other World, liminal spaces through which "humans might pass into the mysterious lands and realms of [supernatural] power." Especially sacred to the Celts, many aqueous sites were associated with "the life force" and attendant "female spirits."[26] Moreover, the golden basins and towel have been linked with ritual trappings and supernatural receptacles: cups, cauldrons, baskets, and cornucopiae of plenty.[27] So, too, critics have long noted the motif of the goddess or fairy who confidently and forthrightly announces her love for a human, presenting him with gifts.[28] Eithne O'Sharkey, for instance, has argued for the goddess Morgan[29] as the Lady's precursor. Constance Bullock-Davies links the tale's main characters to the god Lanovalus and the goddess Morgen.[30] Tom Peete Cross proposes the Welsh goddess Rhiannon, traditionally associated with the horse, as a model or analogue.[31] And yet another possible antecedent is the Romano-Celtic goddess Epona,[32] who is generally depicted riding on a horse, and accompanied by a dog and bird. Associated with fertility, abundance, and healing springs, Epona was the patroness of cavalrymen, the precursors of medieval knights like Lanval.[33] Similarly, the Lady's requirement and Lanval's pledge of secrecy have been explained in terms of the Celtic *geiš*, "a taboo or prohibition placed upon heroes in Irish narratives."[34] And, finally, some scholars have argued that Lanval's journey with the Lady to Avalon corresponds to mythic accounts in which a goddess or fée transports a mortal to an Other World.[35] Yet despite many valiant attempts to discover the origins of the Lanval tale, none has fully succeeded, and while the images, motifs, and themes are clearly reminiscent of various mythic components, no known extant tale has been identified as a source. Justifiably, then, Ménard rejects such attempts at uncovering sources as flawed because they are based on fragments from "une foule de textes hétérogènes."[36]

Still, viewed in the light of myth's tendency to attract and absorb a variety of traditional materials, such remnants and echoes are characteristic of mythic discourse. Additionally, these allusions and fragments may come from more than a single tradition, for instance, not only from Celtic but also from Greco-Roman antecedents. Thus as Marie describes the opulent pavilion, she observes that the right tent flap is worth more than either Semiramis at the peak of her power and wealth or Octavian would have been able to afford (ll. 82-86). In that both the Assyrian queen Semiramis

(Sammu-ramat)[37] and the Roman emperor Octavian (Augustus),[38] well-known rulers of the ancient world, had attained legendary, and even mythic, status as great sovereigns, conquering warriors, and persons of inestimable wealth, these allusions underscore the superiority of the lady, her metonymic tent far surpassing all worldly power and riches.

This allusion to Semiramis, moreover, further develops and calls attention to Marie's theme as it touches on love, for situated as it is immediately before Lanval's afternoon tryst with the Lady, Marie's reference to the Assyrian queen evokes a previously unnoticed correspondence with the fifth elegy of Ovid's *Amores* (Book I), in which the narrator describes his midday seduction, or perhaps rape, of a fair woman, Corinna, whose beauty is compared to that of Semiramis.[39] On a warm summer day, from the vantage point of his couch, the narrator sees Corinna, wearing only an ungirdled loosely-woven tunic ["ecce, Corinna venit, tunica velata recincta" (l. 9)].[40] Tearing the light tunic from her body, Ovid's narrator stops momentarily to observe the beauty of his prey:

> Quos umeros, quales vidi tetigique lacertos!
>   forma papillarum quam fuit apta premi!
> qua castigato planus sub pectore venter!
>   quantum et quale latus!
>
>   (19-22)

> [What shoulders, what arms did I see—and touch!
> How suitable for caress the form of her breasts!
> How smooth her body beneath the faultless bosom!
> What a long and beautiful side!]

Ultimately, despite her struggles against the narrator, the woman is "conquered."

Notably, Marie rewrites Ovid's scene. In an echo of the summer afternoon encounter, Lanval discovers the Lady, reclining on her couch and clad only in a "chemise"—a tunic or shift—and a lightly draped mantle that reveal her fair neck, breast, and side:

> Mut ot le cors bien fait e gent;
>
>   . . . . .
>
> Tut ot descovert le costé,
> Le vis, le col e la peitrine;
>
>   (ll. 97-105)

> [Her body was well formed and handsome,. . . . Her side, though, was uncovered, as well as her face, neck and breast; . . .]

In contrast to Ovid's predatory narrator, who overpowers Corinna in chilling silence, Marie's Lady warmly announces her love for Lanval, and after he responds with his declaration of love and fidelity, she willingly grants him "S'amur e sun cors" (l. 133). This intertextual connection also resonates with the *lai* of "Guigemar," where a mural depicts Venus throwing "le livre Ovide," perhaps Ovid's *Amores*, into the flames. As Marie explains, Venus is associated with "les traiz" and "la nature" of love: "Cument hom deit amur tenir / E lëalment e bien servir" [how one should observe love loyally and serve well]. Ovid's work, however, teaches "Coment chascun s'amur estreine" [how one dominates in love].[41] By contrasting such domination with the nature and true obligations of love, this allusion serves to accent Marie's delineation of love in "Lanval."

Thus mythic discourse here offers a model for human action and interaction with general and even universal applicability. Both the Lady and Lanval declare their love for each other (ll. 110-130), a love that is portrayed as reciprocal, entailing mutual fidelity and loyalty and mutual obligation.[42] Lanval and the Lady converse affectionately. The discourse conveying their words, actions, and existence permits communication between cultures and perhaps between worlds. Additionally, the Lady's maidens address Lanval and the King, directing the latter to prepare for their mistress (ll. 491-494; 535-537), issuing instructions as imperatives, not as requests marked by the interrogative or supplicative. Finally, the Lady and the King address each other and are heard by all at court. Like others of her time (e.g., Geoffrey of Monmouth, Wace, Gaimar), Marie appropriates mythic themes, and exploits them to communicate ideas about the origins and nature, both spiritual and physical, of shared love.

Inherently axiological, the mythic discourse of "Lanval" imparts transcendent values described in terms of truth: here the spiritual dimension of human love, which encompasses mutual respect, mutual obligation and loyalty, generosity, and freedom of choice. The Lady, her love, and her generosity inspire virtue in Lanval: if he is "pruz e curteis," she says, no emperor, count, or king could experience the joy that he will, for she loves him above all ("sur tute rien" [ll. 107-116]). And Lanval, in turn, acts with generosity when he returns to the town and court (ll. 205-215). These values are communicated in affective terms and center on sentiments and beliefs. Lanval's emotional, spiritual, and material well-being emanates from his relationship with his "amie." All at court sense the truth of Lanval's words when they see and hear the Lady. Moreover, the importance of loyalty and obligation is also highlighted by Lanval's profound contrition after he breaks his pledge to his "amie" (ll. 334-351).

More powerful than earthly sovereigns, the Lady embodies a transcendent force and supernal power that are signaled by her superiority over people and things of this world. Marie first highlights the significance of mythic truth when she introduces the maidens who invite Lanval to meet their mistress: "I will not fail to tell you the truth" ("Le veir vus en dirai sanz faile" [l. 63]). In this tale, the word *true* (*veir*) and its derivatives occur only in connection with the mythic discourse depicting the Lady and the love that she and Lanval share. The King and his vassals recognize the Lady's extraordinary beauty, and her words are acknowledged as truth by all at court (ll. 611-629). The truth encoded in the old story, the myth, still holds for Marie.

In **"Lanval,"** moreover, the mythic discursivity is inviting and interpellant, exemplifying the individual's place in the natural scheme of things, and reflecting timeless truths that explain human existence and human nature.[43] Just as Lanval is attracted to the Lady, ultimately joining her, so too the reader is drawn into the account of their mutual love, which is immediate, harmonious, and integral to life and well-being. From her tent in the meadow, in the heart of the natural world, the Lady, who is depicted in terms of nature, summons the "gentil" Lanval, who willingly pledges his love and loyalty (ll. 107-116). Their love is both in accord with nature and inherent in human nature. Affect is central, and psychological states, especially Lanval's, are placed in the foreground: his love for the Lady is spontaneous, and his joy overflows in the form of generous acts directed at all ranks of society. Similarly, after having heedlessly broken his pledge, his sense of loss and emotional pain (ll. 334-351; 375-378) so profound that the trial and impending punishment are of no consequence to him. These motivations and emotions are integral to Lanval's existence.

The tale also beckons to its readers and listeners; each is invited to see himself or herself in terms of this alluring and compelling love and to participate in the affective life of the lovers. Speaking to the individual, this mythic example of mutual love has captivated readers for centuries. According to her contemporary Denis Piramus, who describes the audiences of the time (e.g., "Li rei, li prince, e li courtur, / Cunte, barun, e vavasur"), Marie's *lais* held great attraction for the "Cunte, barun e chivaler" and especially the ladies, who recognized their own wishes and desires ("lur volenté") therein.[44] And the tale continues to invite readers to recognize human nature and even ourselves in it. So it is that some view the *lai* as an engrossing fantasy,[45] or as an account of discovering true identity.[46] Others extol Marie's engaging representation of "shared love," simultaneously as "an absolute right" and as "a true value,"[47] and her love ethic characterized by loyalty,[48] "une belle franchise et une noble élévation," and "une morale de la sincerité et de l'authenticité."[49] Still others point to Marie's language of "compassionate sensual-

ity,"[50] and her celebration of physical love, an "explosion of sexual energy" which produces cooperation between men and women.[51]

Marie's mythic discourse would have been appreciated and understood by a wide audience, especially the aristocracy, and the vestigial potency of Celtic myths and mythic elements would have been apprehended in many parts of Britain,[52] and indeed of the Angevin empire. During the twelfth century, oral Celtic tales persisted as a living tradition in Wales, Ireland, and Brittany. Constance Bullock-Davies maintains that such tales were transmitted by bilingual and trilingual *latimers,* or interpreters.[53] Marriages between the Anglo-Normans and the Welsh and Irish also provided spaces in which oral stories could circulate: some of the better-known alliances are those of Nesta, daughter of Rhys ap Tewdr, and Gerald of Windsor;[54] and Aiofe, daughter of Dermot, king of Leinster, and Richard de Clare (Strongbow).[55] In addition, marriages also linked the Angevin court to Brittany: the most prominent involved Henry's son Geoffrey, who became Duke of Brittany and who married Constance, heiress of Count Conan IV of Brittany.[56] Marie's appropriation of Celtic myth parallels a strategy popular with the Anglo-Norman and Angevin royalty, who utilized Celtic Arthurian materials (Welsh and Breton) for legitimating and political purposes.[57] While these myths may have become desacralized, thus losing some of their original coherence and spiritual significance, they still bore the traces of transcendent axiological truths. Additionally, some aspects of the belief system and cultural practices undergirding these myths were still in place in Wales and Ireland. For instance, in early Welsh and Irish custom and law, a woman "enjoyed a certain independence": she could not be married against her will; and there existed possibilities of choice in partner.[58] Such use of Celtic materials with deep cultural resonances and ties to individual psyche and spirit is also apparent in the hagiographical text ***Espurgatoire Seint Patrick,*** also attributed to Marie.

In **"Lanval,"** particularly in connection with the royal court, Marie also deploys a monologic legal discourse that represents the united voice of the king and the barons, the most powerful men in the realm, who endorse it, participate in it, and insist upon it. As has been amply demonstrated in previous commentaries, the trial scenes in Lanval are laced with legal terms of art (e.g. *acheisuner, felunie, garant, gager, jugement, respuns*).[59] William Rothwell convincingly argues that these terms are part of a specialized Anglo-Norman legal vocabulary that was formalized in speech and in written form soon after the Norman Conquest.[60] In that "legal meaning arrives after the event to reconstruct the discourse of others," the king and barons demand a legal trial, with a judgment based on *dreit* ("law," "legal rights," "justice"); Lanval's actions are to be defined and judged in accordance with the legal definition of "felunie." All, including the King and Lanval, agree to abide by the judgment of the barons (ll. 379, 625-626).

Notably, the legal vocabulary of "Lanval" resonates intertextually with legal texts of the time (the *Coronation Charter* of Henry I, Glanvill's *Treatise,* the *Leis Willelme*) and other texts that refer to law and legal practices (e.g., the Anglo-Norman *Alexander,* the *Tristan* of Thomas, Jordan Fantosme's *Chronicle,* Gaimar's *Histoire des Engleis*).[61] In addition, intratextual references occur throughout the legal discourse; the trial scenes focus on establishing whether or not Lanval is guilty of charges set forth first by the queen, then the king, and finally the Count of Cornwall, all in echoing terms. The spurned queen complains to the king of Lanval's purported offense: he brought shame upon her by attempting to seduce her ("l'ad hunie" [l. 316]), and subsequently he offended and dishonored her ("laidi" and "avila" [l. 319]). But it is the king who makes the official accusation: "Vassal, vus me avez mut mesfait! / . . . / De me hunir et aviler" (ll. 363-365) [Vassal, you have seriously wronged me . . . by shaming and dishonoring me]. Lanval denies bringing dishonor and shame to his lord ("defent la deshonur / e la hunte de sun seignur" [ll. 371-372]),[62] but he also acknowledges the truth of his boast about his beloved (l. 377). At the trial the Count of Cornwall explicates the charge as follows: "The king accused his vassal, whom I heard you call Lanval, of felony,[63] and charged him with a crime ('un mesfait'), about a love he boasted of which angered my lady" (ll. 439-442). Cornwall also asserts that a vassal owes appropriate honor to his lord: "a sun seignur / Deit hum par tut fairë honur" (ll. 447-448). And it is on this point that the judgment hinges.

In Marie's *lai* the institutionally authorized legal discourse is embraced by those of rank in the "legal and social hierarchy," and attendant "discursive techniques and sanctions" "delimit who may speak, on what topic, with what content," and in what "specific institutional settings." Thus it has the capacity to "exclud[e] and obscur[e] alternative or oppositional readings and meanings," thereby implying "ethical and political desirability while at the same time allowing highly refined manipulation."[64] Thus the king makes the formal accusation against Lanval, who is restricted to answering the charges in order ("de mot en mot, si cum il dist" [l. 373]). The king first commands his household vassals (those of his "maisne[e]" [ll. 359-394]) and then a larger assemblage of barons of the realm (l. 393) to deliver a judgment. Among these "jugeurs," the Count of Cornwall, perhaps an allusion to the esteemed and influential advisor of Henry II, Reginald de Dunstan-

ville (d. 1175),[65] has special authority. Notably, these men who share a linguistic code comprise an elite speech community.[66]

So too each of these trials follows established procedures of Marie's time.[67] In the first or preliminary trial, the king makes the accusation ("d'un mesfait l'acheisun" [l. 440]); Lanval then gives his legal answer ("respuns" [l. 500]), responding to each of the king's charges. In the first hearing, it is determined that Lanval must appear before an expanded *curia* ("la curz esforcie[e]" [l. 393]). Some of Lanval's fellow knights serve as guarantors ("li plegge" [l. 418]), offering their lands as security that Lanval will stand trial on the appointed day (ll. 415-419). During the deliberations, the Count of Cornwall restates the king's charge of "felunie" and specifies that only the sovereign can make such an accusation against a vassal (ll. 439-443). After directing the the knight to take a binding oath ("Un serement l'engagera" [l. 449]) in accordance with the law, Cornwall explains that the final judgment will turn on whether or not Lanval can produce his "guarant" (l. 451)—that is, "proof, justifying evidence" or "authority"[68]—in the form of his "amie," so that the court can determine the truth of his boast. If Lanval complies, he will be pardoned; if he fails, he will "lose the king's service and the king will banish him" ("Tut sun servise pert del rei, / E sil deit cungeer de sei" [ll. 459-460]). The trial concludes when the Lady appears; her presence and her formal statement confirm the truth of Lanval's legal declaration, and he is exonerated.

In this axiomatic and rational legal discourse, then, meaning is assigned "after the event to reconstruct the discourse of others and to rewrite the diversity of social language in terms of the purportedly neutral or artistic significances."[69] The barons are instructed to, and claim to, judge according to custom and law (ll. 434-460), and they must account for their decisions (l. 396). Lanval's words and actions are construed as a "felunie," which is punishable by law. At first the king threatens to burn or hang Lanval ("Il le ferat arder u pendre" [l. 328]). Later it is decided by the court that if Lanval is found guilty he will lose the king's service and be banished ("Tut sun servise pert del rei, / E sil deit cungeer de sei" [ll. 459-460]).

At Arthur's court, the legal discourse is both authoritarian and distanced, containing repeated references to *dreit* (i.e., "law" and "justice").[70] This emphasis on judgment according to law disregards situation and motivation. Thus, as the barons deliberate in regard to the king's charge and Lanval's "legal answer," or "declaration," the Count of Cornwall announces that they must abide by the law and do justice ("Le dreit estuet aler avant" [l. 436]). Similarly, at the conclusion of the trial the king grants that "it should be as the judges recommended, in accordance with law" ("Ceo qu'il en jugerunt par dreit / Li reis otrie ke issi seit" [ll. 625-626]). In contrast to mythic discourse, legal discourse "fixes legal meaning to individual acts." This reification of words and actions "obscures the real relations which form the context of such actions and the explanation of their motives," and transforms "human beings—the diffuse, complex and changing biographical entities of motivated interaction—into the ethical and political subjects of legal rationality and formal justice."[71] It is this discursive mode that restates and construes Lanval's actions and words. Focusing on such interpretations of actions and events, the legal discourse in **"Lanval"** ignores human affect and personal bonds. So, too, the context and motives behind his actions (e.g., the queen's offer of "druerie" and her angry taunting)[72] remain outside the legal deliberations. Once accused, Lanval is no longer free: he is summoned to court and he is allowed to leave only with bail ("plegges" [l. 390]); his words count only as responses to the charges; and his status as a loyal vassal hangs in the balance. When he is brought to trial, the barons order him to summon his "amie," but he declines, for he knows that because of his broken promise he has lost her. Publicly he asserts that he has been faithful to his lord and that he has spoken truthfully about his beloved, yet he suffers remorse (ll. 375-378). His personal obligations and private reasons for his actions, however, are irrelevant in the court of law, where his words and acts are judged exclusively within a legal framework. Lanval's very identity—as a loyal vassal of Arthur or as a *felun* who will be banned from the court—is to be determined solely by legal definitions, procedures, and judgments.

INTERSECTION AND TRANSGRESSION

Throughout **"Lanval"** mythic and legal discursivity coexist in parallel, except for a moment when the two discourses intersect, indeed, when the mythic discourse transgresses the boundaries of legal discourse. Three times the Lady's attendants and finally the "Dame" herself interrupt and confound the legal deliberations at court. On each occasion, Arthur presses the barons to state their verdict, but they fall silent each time a pair of maidens and finally the Lady herself come into view. At each of these three moments, the voices of the king and the barons are replaced by the voices of the maidens and their mistress.[73] When the Lady does appear, all who see her are transfixed by her radiant beauty. Confidently, she makes a formal statement, addressing each of the charges brought against Lanval: his boast, the queen's accusation, and implicitly the question of the vassal's loyalty to his lord and king. By thus proving the veracity of Lanval's boast and his subsequent legal statement, she exonerates and vindicates him.

In intersecting and transgressing the legal discourse, Marie's mythic discourse not only broadens the semantic range of previously restricted legal terms,[74] it also reformulates legal constructs of interpersonal and socio-political relationships, reconstituting concepts of mutuality, fidelity, and obligation. As the locus of public power, the king grants "femmes," "tere," and "riches duns" as recompense for service. Similarly, he requires that Gawain and the knights who serve as guarantors for Lanval "gage" their lands, which they hold from him, and he demands severe punishments for those who fail to uphold the vow of fealty: the escheating of lands, banishment, and even death. Thus on perceiving an affront on the part of his vassal, Arthur first threatens to hang or burn Lanval, and later announces that he will banish the knight if he is adjudged guilty. Conversely, the Lady generously bestows gifts out of love and generosity of spirit, a practice that Lanval subsequently adopts. Moreover, the Lady's loyalty to Lanval proves superior to that of the king to his vassal. Lanval's astonishment is clear when he discovers that his "amie" is in fact at Arthur's court: "'Par fei,' fet il, 'ceo est m'amie!'" (l. 597). This comment is, of course, doubly apt because it is precisely through faith and faithfulness that the Lady comes to redeem Lanval. It is clear that Lanval has found an enduring love, a private alliance that surpasses any public alliance. And in each case, the mythic construct surpasses the legal construct; the bonds forged by law fall short of the bonds born of love.

In Marie's *lai*, mythic discourse, underwritten by the authority of its ultimate source, portrays and constitutes love as deeply interiorized yet interpersonal, characterized by mutual respect, mutual loyalty, and mutual obligation. The love shared by Lanval and his "amie" then is an intensely private matter. From the time of their first interlude in the pavilion, the Lady explains that they will enjoy each other only in seclusion: "U nuls puïst aver s'amie / Sanz reproece, sanz vileinie" (ll. 165-166), and she exacts a pledge of secrecy, adding that she will not be seen or heard by others. This love, moreover, is intimately connected to virtue and spirit, for the Lady emphasizes the necessity of Lanval's being "pru" and "curteis," and there is an overflowing of the effects of love (e.g., well-being, joy, and generosity)[75] into the public sphere. Yet the exact nature of the love relationship is beyond the ken of any but the lovers. As the mythic discourse, with its emphasis upon human nature and its concern for values associated with human love, intersects the constraining legal discourse, private momentarily becomes public. Once the king and the people of the court perceive, however briefly and superficially, the manifestations of mutual devotion, they first recognize and then acknowledge the truth and rightness of the Lady's—and, in retrospect, Lanval's—words, which are manifestations of their love. While this love is known only to the two who share it, the onlookers discern it, albeit imperfectly, and experience an ineffable joy ("Il n'ot un sul ki l'esgardast / De dreite joie n'eschaufast / Cil ki le chevaler amoënt" [ll. 583-585]). Here, the concept of love thus fashioned through mythic discursivity is depicted as more powerful than the boundaries and limits established by legal discourse and law.

Apropos of the bond of love between Lanval and and his *amie*, it is worth noting that despite the absence of parental involvement, ceremony, lordly sanction, or ecclesiastical blessing, a union that was based on consent and consummation, or simply free consent, even if in secret—like the vows and acts of love that transpired in the privacy of the Lady's pavilion—would have constituted a valid marriage.[76] Thus, as the following discussion demonstrates, it is possible to see Marie's commentary as having noteworthy social significance and practical implications for her audience.

LAW, LAND, AND MARRIAGE IN TWELFTH- AND THIRTEENTH-CENTURY ENGLAND

In Europe, the late eleventh century through the twelfth century witnessed the burgeoning of legal systems, marked by increasing formalization and regularization of laws. So, too, twelfth-century England, especially during the reign of Henry II (1154-1189), experienced a striking growth in legal activity. By the time of *The Treatise on the laws and customs of the realm of England commonly called Glanvill* (1187-1189), the foundations of the common law had been established, "with a body of laws administered by a defined group of justices following a distinct procedure."[77] Notably, this legal activity emphasized landholding. Once a landholding relationship had been established, certain practices and customs had legal import, with perspectives regarding law and landholding dependent upon an individual's position in the landholding relationship. For the lord, land law was a means of "controlling key resources, his wealth, and his followers." For the tenant, land and custom or law was a way "to provide for himself, his family, and his followers, in his lifetime and beyond." Moreover, the tenant's family, his sub-tenants, and his peers also had a point of view on the landholding relationship and the laws associated with it. As John Hudson observes, people in Norman and Angevin England knew about the law and were "sensitive to its vocabulary."[78] In twelfth-century lawsuits, litigants would, for instance, enlist the aid of friends and family. Additionally, legal matters were discussed not only in the context of the trials but also in the retinue of Henry II and in all noble households. And legal proceedings also appear in many literary texts of the time.[79]

Women too, especially aristocratic women, had knowledge of the law. Tracing the changes in inheritance practices, Judith Green points out, "Women come into greater prominence in twelfth-century affairs" as a result of their importance in the transmission of land, as recipients of family land (the *maritagium* or marriage portion) when they married, and particularly as heirs. Significantly, in England at this time the number of heiresses and potential heiresses increased because of parceny (co-heirship).[80] John Gillingham has christened the twelfth century "the century of heiresses."[81] And J. C. Holt explains the importance of the heiress as "one of the fluid elements in the social structure": the heiress allowed sovereigns "to reward vassals, landless knights, and ambitious officials"; permitted "men to enter into the hierarchy of the noble elite"; enabled "families to form alliances with each other"; and helped "established lineages" to restore "their military reputation" or to enhance "their access to government circles."[82] During the twelfth century, then, a notable legal issue during the twelfth century is inheritance of land, especially as it pertains to women.

In his capacity as feudal lord, the king had the "right" of control over the marriages of his tenants' heiress daughters; this right could be exercised while the tenant was alive, and after his death the lord became the guardian of the daughter or daughters, even if they had reached majority. One of the early expressions of these rights occurs in the coronation charter of Henry I (1100). Throughout the early twelfth century, Henry I had considerable latitude in exploiting such royal rights.[83] Control of marriages not only prevented alliances between the king's enemies, but it allowed for the granting of rich heiresses as rewards to the king's men. Thus it was through marriage to aristocratic women, especially heiresses, that men could, and did, rise in status and wealth. Given the finitude of the royal demesne, granting heiresses as wives was also an important feature of royal patronage, and it was by such means that Henry I was said to have raised several of his men "from the dust."[84] Under Henry II prevailing practice is similarly defined by Glanvill's *Treatise*: "by the law and custom of the realm no woman who is heir to land may be married without the direction and consent of the lord."[85] To complicate matters further, lords and kings could "'sell marriages" (that is, "the right to control the marriage of an heiress") to those who might want to marry the ward, to give the ward to a family member, or to "resell" the marriage at a profit. This practice is documented for the reigns of Henry II and his sons, during which period there are records of sixty payments for permission to marry heiresses. Additionally, there are thirty-one instances of punishment for those who had done so without permission.[86]

According to law, then, daughters could marry only after gaining the lord's approval and satisfying his requirements. It is true that marriages that satisfied the rulings of the church but not the lord were "licit"; in the words of Glanvill, when there is a question of "lawful marriage," the "plea shall not proceed in the court of the lord king; and the archbishop or bishop of the place shall be ordered by the following writ to enquire about the marriage, and to inform the lord king or his justices of his judgment in the matter."[87] Nevertheless, violating the "lord's right to consent" might result in a strong reaction and heavy fines; under Henry II, for example, the average fine was £75, the equivalent of a knight's income for five years, and in some instances the offender's property might be seized.[88]

Aristocratic women participated in legal matters, both as wives and as widows, most notably in connection with their inheritance. While it is true that according to law a man had "extensive control" over his wife and over "her movable goods," and that by law a woman did "not control her own lands," Hudson argues that in practice women had "more control of the lands they brought to their marriage" than Glanvill indicates. For example, in instances "concerning lands she had brought to the marriage, a wife had to be sued jointly with her husband"; in addition, "women made grants in their own name with their husband's consent," and "a husband might vouch for his wife as warrantor." Moreover, widows are frequent litigants, "with numerous actions concerning dower" in litigation involving land.[89]

Virginie Greene has observed that Georges Duby's "pessimism about the condition of medieval women was reversed in one of his last books, *Dames du XIIe siècle* (1995), where he recognized that women can be visible as agents at least in the imaginary realm of romance."[90] The idea of women as "agents," moreover, extends beyond the boundaries of romance, for a growing body of historical evidence, much of which has gone unnoticed in regard to Marie's *lai*, indicates that women were not necessarily passive in connection with law, land, and marriage. One of the most famous examples of a marriage between an heiress and a landless knight is the case of Isabel, Countess of Striguil and Pembroke, and William Marshal. Having served Henry II long and faithfully, William was granted the hand, and the lands, of Isabel, the daughter of Richard of Clare (Strongbow), and Aiofe, or Eve, the daughter of King Dermot of Leinster (Ireland). At the time, William was forty-two, and Isabel between seventeen and twenty. Although the marriage seems to have been arranged,[91] some surviving details concerning the couple have relevance here.

David Crouch notes that the *Histoire* of William Marshal offers some brief insights into Isabel's role in this union. According to this account, councils of William Marshal's men deliberated about the countess's concerns on two occasions; once over her "doubts" about King John's "intentions" with regard to a trip that

the Marshal was to make to England, and once over her wish that her son Richard should not be "delivered to the King." These insights, Crouch points out, indicate that Isabel "was in reality no mere cipher in her husband's affairs"; indeed, she was "a great lady in a long line of powerful Norman aristocratic women; her advice and consent was both needed and sought."[92] Yet another telling passage from the *Histoire* describes a scene in 1207, when William Marshal was about to depart from Ireland for England, leaving the countess to defend her husband's, and her own, interests in Ireland.[93] As Crouch recounts the scene, having summoned his barons and knights of Leinster to his chief fortress of Kilkenny, the Marshal "made a dramatic entry, Isabel on his arm" and addressed his men as follows:

> Lords! See the countess, whom I here present to you; your lady by birth, the daughter of the earl who freely enfeoffed you all when he conquered this land. She remains amongst you, pregnant. Until God permits me to return, I pray you to keep her well and faithfully, for she is your lady, and I have nothing but through her.[94]

This account suggests that even in this arranged marriage mutual respect and cooperation could exist. Crouch's observation that Isabel was "a great lady in a long line of powerful Norman aristocratic women" is doubly significant. First, William Marshal respectfully acknowledges her importance in the transmission and retention of the land. Second, Crouch intimates that Isabel had inherited more than land from the women in her family. In fact, there is a pattern of medieval women passing down values and practices from mother to daughter (and grandmother to granddaughter), and such may well have been the case with Isabel, Eve, and those before her.[95]

So, too, many women took an active role in connection with their lands, and at least some also took an active role in regard to their marital status. Evidence, as is usually the case, is more abundant for widows than for single women and wives, whose legal identities were subsumed by those of their fathers or husbands. Extant documents indicate that not infrequently widows, particularly those wishing to remain single, tried to avoid arranged marriages. Their attempts encountered varied responses. For instance, Hawisa, the widow of the Earl of Essex and Countess of Aumale in her own right, refused (ca. 1194) to marry William de Forz, the husband chosen for her by King Richard; ultimately, however, she was forced to succumb when the king ordered her property to be confiscated.[96] And upon the death of Baldwin, the son and heir of the Earl of Devon, his young widow, Margaret de Redevers, a double heiress, was given in marriage to one of King John's Norman knights, Fawkes de Bréauté; she subsequently attempted to dissolve the union, maintaining that the marriage had occurred against her will.[97] In 1205 the widow Alice Belet refused to marry in accordance with King John's wishes. The king then seized her dower lands, but with the help of her father, who made the appropriate payments, she was able to recover her dower and live as a widow.[98]

When a widow did succeed in securing an exemption from "royal marriage," she gained "freedom" and "power over her inheritance, her dower, and her marriage-portion." Such was the case for Countess Lucy, who in 1130 after the death of her third husband, Ranulf le Meschin, Earl of Chester, paid 500 marks to avoid marrying for a period of five years; there is no evidence that she ever remarried. She was also successful in paying additional sums to enable her to "do justice in her court amongst her men" and to "recover her patrimony."[99] So too Margaret of Beaumont was widowed in 1119 and was still living as a widow in 1156.[100] In the following century, Margaret, heir to the earldom of Lincoln, which descended to her through her mother Hawise, the sister of Ranulf, Earl of Chester, married twice, and after the death of her second husband she lived as a widow for more than two decades, controlling not only her Lincoln inheritance but also her share of the Lacy lands and her dower settlement, which included entire counties.[101]

Historical records also provide examples of women who participated in and even shaped their own destiny. Scattered among the leaves and rolls of surviving documents are examples of couples who defied the laws and social conventions of the time. In the twelfth century, the widow of Hugh de Mount Pincon, Matilda de Grandmesnil, left her home, family, and friends in Normandy "to accompany her new love, a young knight called Matthew, on a journey to Jerusalem."[102] So, too, the well-born wife of Count Robert I of Meulun (d. 1118) was said to have left him for another earl.[103] Yet another example is Joan of Acre, daughter of Edward I and Eleanor of Castile. Joan had been married to Gilbert, Earl of Clare, who died in 1295. A wealthy widow at twenty-three, Joan avoided a second arranged marriage by secretly wedding Ralph de Monthermer, who had served her former husband as a squire. Joan was also foresighted enough to have Ralph knighted before she married him.[104]

Toward the end of the twelfth century and into the thirteenth century payment of such fines becomes more common. It is at this point that examples of some women exercising control over their marriages appear. Such seems to be the case for the heiress Philippa Basset, who was the widow of Henry de Newburgh, Earl of Warwick. In 1229 she paid 100 marks to the king in order to remain unmarried or to marry a man of her choice. Within a month she had remarried.[105] Furthermore, some women, and men, seem to have found a

way around the system by marrying first and paying a fine later. A fascinating example here is Elizabeth de Clare (1295-1360), who after the death of her husband John de Burgh, Earl of Ulster, was a widow at twenty-one. In this case King Edward I's plan to marry her to a favored vassal was thwarted when Theobald de Verdon abducted Elizabeth in 1316, wedding her without the king's license. Elizabeth's biographer, Francis Underhill, argues that since the payment of a fine, sometimes a high one, could usually secure the king's pardon for a marriage without previous royal approval, this appears to have been the situation with Elizabeth and Theobald. In fact, feigned abduction and clandestine marriages, a means by which women and men could exercise choice in marriage partners, became more common in the later Middle Ages.[106]

It is in the opening lines of "Lanval" that Marie begins to strike her theme: "femmes et tere departi." Law and legal practices assign wives to favored knights, and love is notably absent. This theme comes into high relief when Marie's text is compared to Wace's *Roman de Brut,* a work that has been sometimes been regarded as a source, sometimes as an analogue, for this section of "Lanval."[107] Both Marie and Wace describe the rewards for Arthur's loyal knights after the war with the Picts and the Scots. However, on the two occasions that Wace writes of such rewards, they are described as consisting of "enurs e terres," [honors and lands] or "enurs delivres," [escheated honors], whereas Marie announces that the rewards consist of "femmes et teres."[108] Significantly, the King grants these rewards on Pentecost (Whitsunday), a traditional time for the "king's crown-wearing" and a time associated with regnal authority and law.[109]

Early on, then, the *lai* establishes that the law sanctions the king's distribution of wives and lands. Moreover, Marie's narrative expresses concern about enacting and enforcing laws that can endanger or impede human relationships. In this context, courts and laws are antipathetic to individual volition;[110] additionally, laws that combine land and marriage have the potential of resulting in tenuous personal connections and uneasy alliances. Marie's dialogic conjoining of discourses allows for the contrast between public and private, and she demonstrates a keen awareness of interpersonal relationships within social and political matrices where law performs a central function. In this *lai* private and public exist in delicate balance: Lanval and the Lady honor social and legal obligations; they are generous to fellow human beings, and they acquit themselves responsibly in connection with the law and government. Yet Marie's *lai* also demonstrates that love functions most fully in private. According to "Lanval," the ethically-based love alliance emanates from two individuals; it is mutual and it is volitional; moreover, it is a requisite, in fact, a prerequisite, for a lasting union.

Relying on a dual narrative strategy, Marie appropriates the mythic discourse of Celtic inspiration—a source that had been so valuable to Norman and Angevin kings—and turns it to her own purposes. Simultaneously, she also appropriates legal discourse to vindicate the lovers and her approach to love. Having rendered the court speechless, the Lady, who is a myth-sanctioned representative of transcendent truth, expresses the verities of nature, and of human nature. Marie's freighted mythic discourse transgresses the twelfth-century legal discourse, which increasingly limited personal choices relating to love, marriage, and sexuality. The Lady's words and ways are contrasted with the restrictive laws and legal proceedings, some of which attempt to control the fates of women,[111] who were distributed along with land, and of men, especially landless knights and lesser vassals, who were rewarded, or not, according to the whim of a king or lord. Opposing the legal discourse of the feudal court with an oppositional mythic discourse, Marie demonstrates that attempts to constrain love are misguided.[112]

Although the conclusion of **"Lanval"** Marie's *lai* is notoriously open,[113] this *lai* undeniably centers on love. In fact, it presents a model of shared love and mutual commitment, an ideal for all women and men, and one with particular relevance to the heiress.[114] Here it is important to remember that many of Marie's contemporaries were vitally concerned about love and marriage, and not merely in connection with a first union. While it is true that the church promoted lifelong marriage, many medieval women and men married more than once because of the death of a spouse. As surviving legal documents from the period indicate, at first gradually and then with increasing frequency, women and men sought to marry partners of their own choosing.[115] Composing at a time when legal practices were encroaching upon one of the most intimate of human relationships, Marie offers practical observations on human nature, the limits of law, and a means of enriching the lives of men and women emotionally and materially. And, while it is perhaps too much to insist that **"Lanval"** also teaches socio-economic and political lessons, this thinly veiled but not overly subtle narrative illustrates a way to find love and even choice in marriage. Although normally marriage involved parental, lordly, and ever-increasing ecclesiastical involvement, a new option offered hope for some. Even though this option would have required determination, courage, planning, and cooperation, it was enabled, if not endorsed, by the church, which from the twelfth century on accepted as valid marriages based solely on free consent.[116] Marie's dedication of her *Lais* to a "noble reis," within

whose purview lay the enactment and enforcement of laws with significant implications for "femmes" and "tere," would have been especially apt. If Marie's dedication was in fact addressed to Henry II, the subject of the *Lais,* and especially **"Lanval,"** would no doubt have attracted his attention, for the Plantagenet king was most knowledgeable about wives, lands, and heiresses.[117]

Lai, Lei, *and* Conter

By deploying these two discourses in **"Lanval,"** Marie conjoins mythic lay and law. As Howard Bloch has observed in connection with his investigations of the "polysemic plasticity of Old French," there is in some dialects a homophonic relationship between *lai*—the "written residue," or "the trace of a pre-existing song,"—and *lei/loi,* in the sense of "justice" or "law."[118] In this context, it is significant that Marie begins and ends with the verb *cunter.* "L'aventure d'un autre lai, / Cum ele avient, vus cunterai" (ll. 1-2); and "Ne jeo n'en sai avant cunter" (l. 646) [I cannot relate any more]. Given the narrative's emphasis on legal register, the term *cunter* invites another reading. In her final statement, Marie switches to and integrates legal diction, with *cunter* functioning as an instance of *antanaclasis*: In the introduction to the *lai, cunter* has as its grammatical object "aventure" (ll. 1-2), and is equivalent to "telling a story or tale." In the concluding line, however, Marie incorporates the legal sense of the term, that is, "to make a [legal] declaration."[119] Thus, having set forth her account of Lanval and the Lady, and having illustrated the rightness of their cause through mythic discourse, Marie concludes, "I cannot declare any further," or "I cannot make a further legal declaration or pleading."[120]

Like the Lady, who at Lanval's trial directs her formal legal statement, or declaration, to the King and court, Marie too addresses her declaration, or pleading, to her audience, the "dames" and "barons" and "chevaliers," and also "li rei, li prince, e li courtur," that is, the kings, princes, and *curiales* who shaped and enforced the laws that affected women, marriage, and land. Marie's narrative, then, not only provides a social commentary, but also constitutes, in Fowler's terms, "an intervention in the organization of [her] society." She intercedes by offering her *conte*—her tale and her declaration—on behalf of Lanval and his "amie," and others like them who wish to choose a partner on the basis of mutual love and mutual enrichment.

Notes

1. Roger Fowler, *Literature as Social Discourse* (Bloomington: Indiana University Press, 1961), 8.
2. "Lanval" (ll. 1-2) [Just as it happened, I shall relate to you the story of another lay]. Unless otherwise noted, all French quotations are drawn

from Marie de France, *Lais,* ed. Alfred Ewert (Oxford: Blackwell, 1944; repr. London: Bristol Classical Press and Gerald Duckworth, 1995); and all English translations of Marie's text come from *The Lais of Marie de France,* trans. Glyn S. Burgess and Keith Busby, 2nd ed. (Harmondsworth: Penguin, 1999). In general see Roberta L. Krueger, "Marie de France," in *The Cambridge Companion to Medieval Women's Writing,* ed. Carolyn Dinshaw and David Wallace (Cambridge: Cambridge University Press, 2003), 172-83, esp. 176.

3. For the background, see J. E. Caerwyn Williams, "Brittany and the Arthurian Legends," in *The Arthur of the Welsh,* ed. Rachel Bromwich et al. (Cardiff: University of Wales Press, 1991), 249-72.

4. A tradition dating back to the eighteenth century attempts to account for the admixture of the fabulous and the historical by explaining that Marie de France medievalized her Breton story to suit the tastes of her audience. See the Abbé Gervais de La Rue, "Dissertation on the Life and Writings of Mary, an Anglo-Norman Poetess of the 13th Century," *Archaeologia or Miscellaneous Tracts Relating to Antiquity* 13 (1800): 35-67.

5. See, for example, S. Damon Foster, "Marie de France: Psychologist of Courtly Love," *PMLA* 44 (1929): 968-96.

6. See, for example, Jacqueline Eccles, "Marie de France and the Law," in *Les Lieux interdits: Transgression in French Literature,* ed. Larry Duffy and Adrian Tudor (Hull: Hull University Press, 1998), 15-30.

7. Ernst Hoepffner, for instance, found the trial scene irrelevant: *Les Lais de Marie de France* (Paris: Librairie Nizet, n.d.), 64.

8. It is generally accepted that Marie composed her *lais* in England in the latter part of the twelfth century, probably during the reign of Henry II. See, for example, Glynn S. Burgess, "Introduction," in *Marie de France, Lais,* ed. Ewert, vii-viii; and idem, *The Lais of Marie de France: Text and Context* (Athens, GA: University of Georgia Press, 1987), 1-34.

9. The following definition is drawn from Peter Goodrich, "Law and Language: An Historical Critical Introduction," *Journal of Law and Society* 11 (1984): 173-206.

10. Multiple meanings of *mythos* existed even in ancient Greece. From its original meaning, "anything delivered by word of mouth," it came to signify "design" or "plan" as in a narrative or dramatic plot, and, once associated with "tale" or "story," it began to connote a poetic or legendary tale as opposed to a historical account, and from there the semantic field broadened to include the sense of "something that is not true." See, for example, *A Lexicon Abridged from Liddell and Scott's Greek-English Lexicon* (Oxford: Clarendon Press, 1982), 454. Here *myth* can be considered as "a story or a complex of story elements taken as expressing and therefore as implicitly symbolizing certain deep-lying aspects of human and transhuman existence": *The Princeton Encyclopedia of Poetry and Poetics* (Princeton: Princeton University Press, 1974), 538. Following a different approach to some of Marie's *lais,* though not "Lanval," SunHee Kim Gerz considers Ovid's and Marie's "participat[ion] in the mythological process," which she defines in accordance with Cassirer as "the truth recreating and in so realizing itself": *Echoes and Reflections. Memory and Memorials in Ovid and Marie de France* (Amsterdam and New York: Rodopi, 2003), 31.

11. See, for example, *The Princeton Encyclopedia of Poetry and Poetics,* 539-40.

12. In myth there is "virtually no distinction between the literal and the figurative," between "psychic and linguistic amalgams"; mythic metaphor is based on a "prior semantic activity which operates, perhaps preconsciously, by fusing certain raw elements of experience—qualities, relationships, capabilities, emotional colorings . . .—into a unity of reference which some symbol is taken to represent": *The Princeton Encyclopedia of Poetry and Poetics,* 539. On *sign* and *myth,* see also Roland Barthes, *Mythologies,* trans. Annette Lavers (New York: Hill and Wang, 1972), 114-15, 131.

13. On the intertextuality of myth and the tendency of such discourse to attract elements from other mythic sources and to incorporate and absorb characters and features of other mythic and legendary strains, see Ken Dowden, *The Uses of Greek Mythology* (London and New York: Routledge, 1992), 8-16; Mircea Eliade, *Myth and Reality,* trans. Willard Trask (New York and Evanston: Harper & Row, 1963), 200; and Marie-Louise Sjoestedt, *Gods and Heroes of the Celts* (Dublin, Ireland, and Portland, OR: Four Courts Press, 1994), 25-36.

14. Eliade, *Myth and Reality,* 8.

15. Here *myth* is distinguished from "sacred story," which may be restricted to certain personnel (e.g., priests) and certain locations (e.g., temples or

churches). Eliade outlines the process by which a sacred tale "desacralizes," losing sacred meaning, yet "the mythical elements continue to play their functions": *Myth and Reality,* 111-13, 200. Dowden observes that even for the Greeks, "the old myths were there to be recycled," "reconceived," and "reformulated": *The Uses of Greek Mythology,* 22, 53.

16. Eliade, *Myth and Reality,* 140-42.

17. Eliade, *Myth and Reality,* 139, 75-91.

18. Eliade, *Myth and Reality,* 11, 92.

19. Barthes, *Mythologies,* 125, 155. In the following discussion, *interpellant* is used not in the strict Althusserian sense, but in the broader sense of "causing one to recognize the self in," or "identify with."

20. On the semantic range of terms like *herbergez, departir,* and *esgarder* in "Lanval," see, for instance, Emmanuel J. Mickel, "Marie de France's Use of Irony as a Stylistic and Narrative Device," *Studies in Philology* 71 (1974): 265-90, here 288-89; and Elizabeth Wilson Poe, "Love in the Afternoon: Courtly Play in the *Lai de Lanval,*" *Neuphilologische Mitteilungen* 84 (1983): 301-10. For fuller discussions of polysemy in Marie's *Lais,* see, for example, R. Howard Bloch, "The Dead Nightingale in the Tomb of Old French Literature," *Culture and History* 3 (1988): 63-78; idem, "New Philology and Old French," *Speculum* 65 (1990): 38-58; idem, "The Lay and the Law: Sexual/Textual Transgression in *La Chastelaine de Vergi,* the *Lai d'Ignaure,* and the *Lais* of Marie de France," *Stanford French Review* 14 (1990): 181-210; and most recently, although in a somewhat different direction, idem, *The Anonymous Marie* (Chicago and New York: University of Chicago Press, 2003), esp. 20-22, 32-50.

21. Jean Rychner, ed., *Les Lais de Marie de France* (Paris: Classiques Français du Moyen Age, 1966, 2nd ed. 1981), 235, note 61.

22. See, for example, Burgess, *Text and Context,* 105. While the term *pucelle* is most frequently used in "Lanval," the English honorific "Lady" ("dame," employed by her maidens and by Marie [ll. 536, 601]) is used in this analysis to indicate her elevated status.

23. See, for example, Hoepffner, *Les Lais,* 69.

24. On Celtic beliefs concerning the presence of the supernatural in the natural world; the perception of a spirit or divine force in trees, streams, mountains, and other natural objects; and the existence of the sacred on earth rather than in a separate realm, see Miranda Green, "Gods and the Supernatural," in *The Celtic World,* ed. eadem (London and New York: Routledge, 1995), 465-88, here 465; eadem, *Dictionary of Celtic Myth and Legend* (London: Thames and Hudson, Ltd., 1992), 22; and Sjoestedt, *Gods and Heroes of the Celts,* 92. For more on the Celtic connection, see the essay by Sharon Kinoshita in [Claussen, Albrecht, ed. *Discourses on Love, Marriage, and Transgression on Medieval and Early Modern Literature.* Tempe: Arizona Center for Medieval and Renaissance Studies, 2004], below, 147-62.

25. See, for example, Philippe Ménard, *Les Lais de Marie de France. Contes d'amour et d'aventure au moyen âge* (Paris: Presses Universitaires de France, 1979), 173.

26. See, for example, R. Stewart, *Celtic Gods, Celtic Goddesses* (London: Cassell, 1990), 40; and Miranda Green, *Celtic Goddesses* (London: British Museum Press, 1995), 90, 97-99.

27. See, for example, Jeanne Walthelet-Willem, "Le Mystère chez Marie de France," *Revue belge de philologie et d'histoire* 39 (1961): 661-86; Tom Peete Cross, "The Celtic Elements in the Lays of *Lanval* and *Graelent.*" *Modern Philology* 12 (1914-1915): 585-644, here 609; Ménard, *Lais de Marie de France,* 156; Jean Markale, *The Celts,* trans. C. Hauch (Rochester, VT: Inner Traditions, 1993), 267, 273-74; and T. G. E. Powell, *The Celts,* new ed. (London: Thames and Hudson, 1980), 153.

28. Cross, "The Celtic Elements," 609; Jacques Ribard, "Le Lai de Lanval: Essai d'interprétation polysémique," in *Mélanges de philologie et de littératures romanes offerts à Jeanne Wathelet-Willem,* ed. Jacques de Caluwecques, Mediaevalia 76 (Liege: Cahiers de l'A. R. U. Lg., 1978), 1:529-44, here 536.

29. Eithne M. O'Sharkey, "The Identity of the Fairy Mistress in Marie de France's *Lai de Lanval,*" *Trivium* 6 (1971): 17-25.

30. Constance Bullock-Davies, "Lanval and Avalon," *Bulletin of the Board of Celtic Studies* 23 (1969): 128-42.

31. Cross, "The Celtic Elements," 585-644.

32. On Epona, see Green, *Dictionary of Celtic Myth,* 90-92; and eadem, *Celtic Goddesses,* 186.

33. Celtic animal symbolism is abundant; see, for example, Stewart, *Celtic Gods,* 25; Green, *Dictionary of Celtic Myth,* 90-91; and on the Celtic connections of the sparrowhawk in Chrétien's *Erec and Enide,* Roger Sherman Loomis, *Arthurian Tradition and Chrétien de Troyes* (New York and London: Cornell University Press, 1949), 99-100.

34. Sjoestedt, *Gods and Heroes of the Celts,* 70-71. See also Cross, "The Celtic Elements," 609.

35. See Cross, "The Celtic Elements," 609; O'Sharkey, "The Identity of the Fairy Mistress," 60; Markale, *The Celts,* 285; James MacKillop, *Dictionary of Celtic Mythology* (Oxford and New York: Oxford University Press, 1998), 359. In the *Middle English Sir Launfal,* the destination is the island of Oleron off the coast of Brittany.

36. Ménard, *Lais de Marie de France,* 47.

37. Semiramis was known to the West largely through Greek sources in translation. On the Assyrian queen Semiramis (or Sammu-ramat), see William Hallo, *Origins: The Ancient Near Eastern Background of Some Modern Western Institutions* (Leiden and New York: E. J. Brill, 1996), 253-55. She was also famed for her building of cities and fortifications, which were said to include the walls and perhaps the hanging gardens of Babylon. See also Ekart Frahm, "Semiramis," in *Der Neue Pauly. Enzyklopädie der Antike* (Stuttgart and Weimar: Verlag J. B. Metzler, 2000), 11:378; and Wilhelm Eilers, *Semiramis. Entstehung und Nachhall einer altorientalischen Sage* (Vienna: Hermann Böhlau, 1971).

38. In addition to "his legal powers as magistrate, he was endowed with the divine right"; "he was a living god." He was also renowned for his monumental contributions to Imperial Rome: Gilbert Charles-Picard, *Augustus and Nero,* trans. Len Ortzen (New York: Thomas Y. Crowell, 1965), 16-17. Octavian had also attracted some of the qualities of Midas: Ewert, *Lais,* 174, note 82-86.

39. "qualiter in thalamos famosa Semiramis isse / dicitur" (ll. 11-12). The Latin quotations and English translations come from Ovid, *Heroides and Amores,* trans. Grant Showerman, 2nd ed. rev. G. P. Goold, Loeb Classical Library (Cambridge, MA: Harvard University Press; London: William Heinemann, Ltd., 1986), 332-35.

40. Showerman translates "draped in tunic girded round" (l. 9). However, *recingo* signifies "to ungird, loosen" as with *tunicas* in Ovid: *Cassell's Latin Dictionary* (London: Cassell & Company; New York: Macmillan, 1977), 503.

41. "Guigemar" (ll. 234-240); my translation.

42. On the pledge as obligation, see Ménard, *Lais de Marie de France,* 172.

43. Eliade, *Myth and Reality,* 92.

44. Denis Piramus, *La Vie Seint Edmund le rei. Poème anglo-normand du XIIe siècle,* ed. Hilding Kjellman (Göteborg: Wettergren & Kerber, 1935; repr. Geneva: Slatkine, 1974), ll. 42-50.

45. Foster, "Marie de France," 968-96; and William Calin, *The French Tradition and the Literature of Medieval England* (Toronto, Buffalo, London: University of Toronto Press, 1994), 28.

46. Michèle Koubichkine, "A propos du *Lai de Lanval,*" *Le Moyen Age* 78 (1972): 467-88, here 476-82.

47. Jean Flori, "Amour et société aristocratique au XIIe siècle: l'exemple des *Lais* de Marie de France," *Le Moyen Age* 98 (1992): 17-34, here 33.

48. Burgess, *Text and Context,* 134-78.

49. Ménard, *Lais de Marie de France,* 143.

50. Stephen G. Nichols, "Rewriting Marriage in the Middle Ages," *Romanic Review* 79 (1979): 42-60, here 59. Nichols also notes the similarities between Heloise's view of love as a binding force and that of Marie.

51. Rupert Pickens, "Poétique et sexualité chez Marie de France: l'exemple de Fresne," in *"Et c'est la fin pour quoy sommes ensemble": Hommage à Jean Dufournet: littérature, histoire et langue du Moyen Age,* ed. Jean-Claude Aubailly, Nouvelle Bibliothèque du Moyen Age 25, 3 vols. (Paris: Champion, 1993), 3:1119-131.

52. On Henry II and Wales, see W. L. Warren, *Henry II* (Berkeley and Los Angeles: University of California Press, 1977), 168-69. On the interchanges between the Irish and the Welsh in southwest Wales, from as early as the late third century, see Sioned Davies, "Mythology and the Oral Tradition: Wales," in *The Celtic World,* 785-91, here 787. And on Brittany, see Powell, *The Celts,* 203-4; and Williams, "Brittany and the Arthurian Legend."

53. Constance Bullock-Davies, *Professional Interpreters and the Matter of Britain* (Cardiff: Wales University Press, 1966), 24.

54. Nesta, or Nest, was also the mistress of Henry I: Robert Bartlett, *Gerald of Wales, 1146-1223* (Oxford: Clarendon Press, 1982), 113.

55. David Crouch, *William Marshal: Court, Career, and Chivalry in the Angevin Empire, 1147-1219* (London: Longman, 1990), 99-100.

56. Warren, *Henry II,* 563.

57. Henry was educated in the household of his maternal uncle Robert of Gloucester, the illegitimate son of Henry I and half-brother of Mat-

ilda and a dedicatee of Geoffrey of Monmouth's *Historia.* On the political dimension of Henry's interest in Arthur, see N. J. Higham, *King Arthur: Myth-Making and History* (London and New York: Routledge, 2002), 230.

58. See for example, Thomas Peter Ellis, *Welsh Tribal Law and Custom in the Middle Ages* (Oxford: Clarendon Press, 1926), 395. Green also points to the equality between males and females in Celtic myth: *Celtic Goddesses,* 117.

59. Hoepffner argued that the trial scene in "Lanval" was inspired by one in the *Roman de Thèbes* by Daire le Roux: see "Pour la chronologie des *Lais de Marie de France,*" *Romania* 59 (1933): 351-70; and idem, *Les Lais de Marie de France,* 64-65. The first close analysis of the *lai's* legal lexicon in the context of twelfth-century law appears in Elizabeth A. Francis, "The Trial in *Lanval,*" in *Studies in French Language and Mediaeval Literature Presented to Professor Mildred K. Pope* (Manchester: Manchester University Press, 1939), 114-24. Full accounts of the trial also appear in Jean Rychner, ed., *Marie de France. Le Lai de Lanval* (Geneva: Droz; Paris: Minard, 1958), 78-84; and esp. Yorio Otaka, "Le Vocabulaire de justice chez Marie de France," *Studies in Language and Culture* 6 (1980): 103-30. Eccles examines selected legal terms in relation to the Assize of Clarendon in "Marie de France and the Law," 15-30. William Rothwell provides a penetrating lexicographical analysis in "The Trial Scene in *Lanval* and the Development of the Legal Register in Anglo-Norman," *Neuphilologische Mitteilungen* 101 (2000): 17-36.

60. Rothwell, "The Trial Scene in *Lanval,*" 27-30; see also Otaka, "Le Vocabulaire de justice," 109-10.

61. See, for example, Rothwell, "The Trial Scene in *Lanval,*" 17-36.

62. My translations.

63. These repeated accusations of *felunie* resonate with several twelfth-century texts. Examples: The *Policraticus* of John of Salisbury, 6.25: "If we are bound by fealty (*fidelitas*) to anyone, we must not harm his soundness of body, or take from him the military resources upon which his safety depends, or presume to commit any act whereby his honor or advantage is diminished; neither is it lawful that that which is easy for him should be made difficult, or that which is possible impossible. . . .": *The Statesman's Book of John of Salisbury,* trans. John Dickinson (New York: Knopf, 1927, repr. New York: Russell & Russell, 1963), 261. See also the trans. by Cary J. Neder-

man (Cambridge: Cambridge University Press, 1990), 139. The *Leges Henrici Primi*: violations in respect to the sovereign include "injuring anywhere members of his household"; "unfaithfulness or treason"; "despis[ing] or speak[ing] badly of him [the king]," quoted in John Hudson, *The Formation of the English Common Law: Law and Society in England from the Norman Conquest to Magna Carta* (London and New York: Longman, 1996), 29. Glanvill: "The following [criminal pleas] belong to the crown of the lord king: The crime which the civil lawyers call *lèse-majesté,* namely the killing or betrayal of the lord king or the betrayal of the realm or the army; fraudulent concealment of treasure trove; the plea of breach of the lord king's peace; . . . all these are punishable by death or cutting off of the limbs": *The Treatise on the Laws and Customs of the Realm of England Commonly Called Glanvill,* ed. and trans. G. D. G. Hall (London: Thomas Nelson, 1965) (cited by book and paragraph), 1:1-2. See Glynnis M. Cropp, "Felony and Courtly Love," in *The Court Reconvenes: Courtly Literature Across the Disciplines,* ed. Barbara K. Altmann and Carleton W. Carroll (Woodbridge: D. S. Brewer, 2003), 73-80.

64. Goodrich, "Law and Language," 187, 190.

65. Ewert's edition reads, "li quoens de Cornwaille," following British Library MS. Harley 978; the four other manuscripts have "dus" or "dux." See, for instance, Rychner, *Le Lai de Lanval,* 58-59. After the earl's death in 1175 the earldom of Cornwall reverted to the King until 1189: Burgess, *Text and Context,* 19, 195, note 52.

66. On the composition the court of Henry II, see Warren, *Henry II,* 306-60.

67. See Francis, "The Trial in *Lanval,*" 114-24; and Otaka, "Le Vocabulaire de justice," 103-30.

68. *Lais,* ed. Ewert, 176.

69. Goodrich, "Law and Language," 189.

70. See lines 309, 383, 436, 625. In contrast with this emphasis on *dreit,* which prevails in the legal discourse, the mythic discourse emphasizes truth, "la verité."

71. Goodrich, "Law and Language," 190.

72. She asserts that he "has no desire for women" ("des femmez n'avez talent") and calls him "base coward" and "wicked recreant" ("Vileins cuarz, mauvais failliz" [ll. 180-183]). On eleventh- and twelfth-century ecclesiastical views of homosexuality as "a sin against nature," see James A. Brundage, *Sex, Law, and Marriage in the Middle Ages*

(Aldershot and Brookfield, VT: Variorum, 1993), 212-14, 250, 313; and R. D. Fulk, "Male Homoeroticism in the Old English *Canons of Theodore,*" in *Sex and Sexuality in Anglo-Saxon England,* ed. Carol Braun Pasternack (Tempe, AZ: MRTS, forthcoming).

73. Bernadine McCreesh points out "the progression from the long speech of Cornwall to the short speech of the barons, to the speechlessness of the courtiers": "The Use of Conversation in Medieval Literature: The Case of Marie de France and Her First Redactor," *Revue de l'Université d'Ottawa* 53 (1983): 189-97, here 192.

74. When the Lady's maidens appear at court, for instance, the verb *esgarder* expands from the sense of "judging" to include "seeing," and even "staring in amazement." See, for example, Poe, *Love in the Afternoon,* 301-10. Similarly, the term *fei* extends beyond that which is demanded by the feudal oath between lord and vassal.

75. For discussions of Marie's emphasis on love in connection with earthly happiness, see Albrecht Classen, "Happiness in the Middle Ages? Hartmann von Aue and Marie de France," *Neohelicon* 25 (1998): 247-74, here 256-64, and Flori, "Amour et société aristocratique," 33. Classen also makes an important link between such love and virtue and reason.

76. While a public ceremony, parental consent, or priestly blessing were considered desirable, they were not essential to a valid marriage: see, for example, Brundage, *Sex, Law, and Marriage,* 325; Michael M. Sheehan, "Choice of Marriage Partners in the Middle Ages: Development and Mode of Application of a Theory of Marriage," *Studies in Medieval and Renaissance History* n.s. 1 (1978): 3-33, esp. 9-15; J. Gillingham, "Love, Marriage and Politics in the Twelfth Century," *Forum for Modern Language Studies* 25 (1989): 292-303, here 294-95.

77. R. C. Van Caenegem, *The Birth of the English Common Law,* 2nd ed. (Cambridge: Cambridge University Press, 1988), 3. On *lex* as encompassing "all Law or laws, written or unwritten, or custom," in late eleventh- and twelfth-century England, see Hudson, *The Formation of the English Common Law,* 3. See also Harold J. Berman, *Law and Revolution: The Formation of the Western Legal Tradition* (Cambridge, MA and London: Harvard University Press, 1983), 253-81.

78. Hudson, *The Formation of the English Common Law,* 88, 6.

79. In addition, judicial and political processes often overlapped. See, for example, Robert Barlett, *En-gland under the Norman and Angevin Kings, 1075-1225* (Oxford: Clarendon Press, 2000), 187-90; Warren, *Henry II,* 306, 359-60; and R. Howard Bloch, *Medieval French Literature and the Law* (Berkeley, Los Angeles, and London: University of California Press, 1977).

80. Judith A. Green, "Aristocratic Women in Early Twelfth-Century England," in *Anglo-Norman Political Culture and the Twelfth-Century Renaissance. Proceedings of the Borchard Conference on Anglo-Norman History, 1995,* ed. C. Warren Hollister (Woodbridge: Boydell Press, 1997), 59-82, here 60-61. See also J. C. Holt, "Feudal Society and the Family in Early Medieval England: IV. The Heiress and the Alien," *Transactions of the Royal Historical Society* 5th ser. 35 (1985): 1-28, here 6-8; and Craig A. Berry, "What Silence Desires: Female Inheritance and the Romance of Property in the *Roman de Silence,*" in *Translating Desire in Medieval and Early Modern Literature,* ed. idem and Heather Hayton (Tempe, AZ: MRTS, forthcoming). See also Linda Paterson, "Women, Property and the Rise of Courtly Love," in *The Court Reconvenes,* ed. Altmann and Carroll, 41-55.

81. Gillingham, "Love, Marriage and Politics," 295. "Few maidens at their betrothal were heirs apparent. Some were heirs presumptive. All were heirs potential": Holt, "Feudal Society," 6.

82. Holt, "Feudal Society," 1-28.

83. Under William the Conqueror, who had vast lands with which to reward his men, the matter had not had great relevance; however, by the time of his son Henry I, concerns about depleting the royal demesne were apparent. Subsequently, Henry II was more cautious in exploiting these rights, but by the time of King John, the king's "rights" again became a matter of political contest. See Marjorie Chibnall, *Anglo-Norman England* (Oxford and New York: Blackwell, 1986), 72-76.

84. Judith A. Green, *The Aristocracy of Norman England* (Cambridge: Cambridge University Press, 1997), 266.

85. Glanvill, *Treatise on the Laws,* 7.12.

86. From 1130 the Pipe rolls begin to record information on the royal exploitation of the rights of wardship and marriage. On the "grubby characteristics" of this "marriage market," see Holt, "Feudal Society," 21-24.

87. Glanvill, *Treatise on the Laws,* 7.13. The church's role in legal decisions concerning marriage grew during the twelfth century and afterwards, as it

extended its jurisdiction over marriage and sexual affairs. See also Bartlett, *England under the Norman and Angevin Kings,* 547; and Scott Waugh, *Lordship of England: Royal Wardships and Marriage in English Society and Politics, 1217-1327* (Princeton: Princeton University Press, 1988), 87-88.

88. Waugh, *Lordship,* 87-88.

89. Hudson, *Formation of the English Common Law,* 235. Additionally, there are frequent examples of widows involved in litigation, several with considerable success.

90. See Virginie Green's contribution to this volume, "The Knight, the Woman, and the Historian: Georges Duby and Courtly Love," above, 43-63. On the limitations of Duby's "theoretical models of marriage in the eleventh century," see Brundage, *Sex, Law, and Marriage,* 194.

91. The marriage had been promised by Henry II; Richard I granted Isabel to William in 1189, just after his father's death.

92. Crouch, *William Marshal,* 99-100.

93. "Any great lady had to be ready to assume responsibility in her husband's time of need, and to defend her dower rights. Her interests and his were one": Marjorie Chibnall, "Women in Orderic Vitalis," *Haskins Journal* 2 (1990): 105-21, here 114.

94. Crouch, *William Marshal,* 99-100.

95. On intergenerational connections between women, see, for example, Eleanor Searle, "Women and the Legitimisation of Succession at the Norman Conquest," in *Proceedings of the Battle Conference on Anglo-Norman Studies,* 3, ed. R. Allen Brown (Woodbridge: Boydell Press, 1980): 159-70. For a later period, see Karen Jambeck, "Patterns of Women's Literary Patronage: England 1200-ca. 1475," in *The Cultural Patronage of Medieval Women,* ed. June Hall McCash (Athens, GA: University of Georgia Press, 1996), 228-65. On Isabel's possible patronage of *Dermot and the Earl,* see, for example, Paul Meyer, "Review of Orpen's edition of the *Song of Dermot,*" *Romania* 21 (1892): 444-51; and Evelyn Mullay, ed., *The Deeds of the Normans in Ireland: La Geste des Engleis en Yrlande* [*The Song of Dermot and the Earl*] (Dublin: Four Courts Press, 2002), 34-37.

96. Holt, "Feudal Society," 24.

97. The matter came to an end with the death of de Bréauté: Holt, "Feudal Society," 27.

98. Holt, "Feudal Society," 23-24.

99. Holt, "Feudal Society," 24. See also Green, *Aristocracy of Norman England,* 368-71.

100. Peter Coss, *The Lady in Medieval England* (Stroud, UK, and Mechanicsburg, PA: Sutton, 1998), 29.

101. Linda E. Mitchell, "The Lady as Lord in Thirteenth-Century Britain," *Historical Reflections/Reflexions historiques* 18 (1992): 71-97, here 87. Rowena Archer has argued that medieval widows who successfully managed their estates had had these abilities as wives; and even before they married, women learned by observing what occurred in their families: "'How ladies . . . who live on their manors ought to manage their households and estates': Women as Landholders and Administrators in the later Middle Ages," in *Woman Is a Worthy Wight: Women in English Society c. 1200-1500,* ed. P. J. P. Goldberg (Gloucester: Sutton, 1992), 149-81, here 152.

102. Holt, "Feudal Society," 24-25.

103. David Crouch, *The Beaumont Twins. The Roots and Branches of Power in the Twelfth Century* (London and New York: Cambridge University Press, 1986), 3-6.

104. Francis A. Underhill, *For Her Good Estate: The Life of Elizabeth de Burgh* (New York: St. Martin's Press, 1999), 6-7. As early as the twelfth century, there is evidence of wards' buying the freedom to arrange their own marriages, but the practice becomes more common in the thirteenth century and later. See, for instance, Sue S. Walker, "Free Consent and Marriage of Feudal Wards in Medieval England," *Journal of Medieval History* 8 (1982): 123-34; and Gillingham, "Love, Marriage and Politics," 295.

105. In 1242, she obtained an annulment, and thereafter she remained unmarried: Coss, *The Lady in Medieval England,* 121.

106. Noting that Theobald "testified that Elizabeth came to him freely," Underhill speculates that she may have had her mother's [Joan of Acre's] second marriage in mind: *For Her Good Estate,* 15-16. On clandestine marriages, see Brundage, *Sex, Law, and Marriage,* 250, 338.

107. Hoepffner, *Les Lais,* 58.

108. *Le Roman de Brut de Wace,* ed. Ivor Arnold, 2 vols. (Paris: Société des anciens textes français, 1940), 2:534, 555 (ll. 10169-10170; 10591-10592), and a variant in B.N. MS. fonds français 1416: "Enors et terres lor dona" (l. 10592).

109. Bartlett, *England under the Norman and Angevin Kings,* 128-29.

110. On Marie's *lai* as opposing general twelfth-century legal practices, see Don A. Monson, "L'idéologie du lai de Lanval," *Le Moyen Age* 93 (1987): 349-72. Jacqueline Eccles argues that Marie objected to laws that interfered with privacy during the reign of Henry II: "Marie de France and the Law," 21-22.

111. On the *lai*'s negative position in regard to feudal approaches to marriage, see Flori, "Amour et société aristocratique," 33; and Sharon Kinoshita, "Cherchez la femme: Feminist Criticism and Marie de France's *Lai de Lanval*," *Romance Notes* 34 (1993-1994): 263-73, here 272.

112. This concept of mutual love and loyalty is further highlighted through another contrast: Arthur's queen lacks not only the Lady's beauty but also her virtues. The Queen is portrayed as lustful and indifferent to the love and fidelity she owes to her husband and king, perhaps as a result of a marriage forged in a feudal environment. According to Geoffrey of Monmouth's *Historia,* Arthur marries Guinevere for her beauty: *The History of the Kings of Britain,* trans. Lewis Thorpe (Harmondsworth and New York: Penguin Books, 1966), 221.

113. See, for example, Ribard, "Le Lai de Lanval," 529-44; and M.-J. Walkley, "The Critics and *Lanval*," *New Zealand Journal of French Studies* 4 (1983): 5-23.

114. Howard Bloch has noted the similarity between the Lady and the heiress: "The fairy lady is the literary incarnation of a fantasized solution to the material problems of the class of unmarried, unendowed, and wandering 'jeunes'—an heiress whose riches are a reminder, as the French proverb still holds, that 'tout mariage est un heritage'": "The Lay and the Law," 201. Margaret Aziza Pappno links the Lady to Eleanor of Aquitaine, "the richest heiress in Europe": "Marie de France, Aliénor d'Aquitaine, and the Alien Queen," in *Eleanor of Aquitaine. Lord and Lady,* ed. Bonnie Wheeler and John Carmi Parsons (New York and Houndsmill, England: Palgrave Macmillan, 2003), 337-67, here 354.

115. On the growing importance of love and free choice as a prerequisite for marriage that was to be a lasting union, see, for example, Sheehan, "Choice of Marriage Partners," 3-33; John T. Noonan. "Marital Affection in the Canonists," *Studia Gratiana* 12 (1967): 479-509; and Gillingham, "Love, Marriage and Politics," 292-303.

116. Gillingham, "Love, Marriage and Politics." Additionally, a mechanism in secular law was also becoming increasingly viable, that is, the possibil-

ity of paying a fine in order to marry according to one's choice. See, for instance, Walker, "Free Consent and Marriage of Feudal Wards," 123-34.

117. In addition to being the husband and son of heiresses, Henry was much occupied with the marriages of his children. See, for instance, Christopher N. L. Brooke, "Marriage and Society in the Central Middle Ages," in *Marriage and Society: Studies in the Social History of Marriage,* ed. R. B. Outhwaite (London: Europa Publications Ltd, 1981), 17-34.

118. Bloch, "The Lay and the Law," 208. Additionally, these homophones can also be homographs (i.e., *lai* for both *lai* and *lei/loi,* though of differing grammatical gender) in Anglo-Norman, the dialect in which the *Lais* are recorded in British Library MS. Harley 978; see, for example, The *Anglo-Norman Dictionary,* fasc. 3:383.

119. J. H. Baker, *Manual of Law French,* 2nd ed. (Aldershot: Scolar Press, 1990), 79.

120. My translation. On the importance of the advocate (e.g., the *forespeca* and *conteur*) in connection with oral pleading in medieval English courts of law, see M. T. Clanchy, *From Memory to Written Record: England 1066-1307,* 2nd ed. (Oxford: Blackwell, 1993), 274-75.

Peter Haidu (essay date 2004)

SOURCE: Haidu, Peter. "'Marie de France': The Postcolonial *lais*." In *The Subject Medieval/Modern: Text and Governance in the Middle Ages,* pp. 121-41. Stanford, Calif.: Stanford University Press, 2004.

[*In the following excerpt, Haidu argues that Marie's economy of style in the* Lais *belies a complex system of signification that honors society's marginalized—especially women and those exiled by the Norman conquest of England.*]

IDENTITY

"Marie de France" is a battlefield of nineteenth-century constructs and twentieth-century deconstructions. Three works are attributed to her: a collection of *lais,* another of fables, and the ***Espurgatoire Saint Patrick.*** All name "Mary" as their author. The identification of these three Maries was the work of nineteenth-century scholars.[1] The tag "Marie de France" comes from the epilogue to the fables, where her pride at writing in the vernacular defies thieving clerics from stealing the product of her labor: "My name is Mary, and I'm from France." She's proud of the value of her work: "He's crazy who forgets himself!"[2]

A second stage of the debate was reached in a psycho-analytic denial of the very possibility of a medieval woman having written the texts in question.[3] It is technically true that attributing the *lais* to "Marie" in the grouping and the sequence that is the basis of modern editions occurs in only one manuscript.[4] A contemporary, however, surprisingly unmentioned in the debate, surveys contemporary writers and mentions, after others,

> Lady Mary wrote
> poetry, and composed
> measured verses in the *lais,*
> whose content is not quite entirely true.
> She garners much praise:
> the poetry is loved by all,
> counts, barons, and simple knights,
> they love her much, and hold her dear,
> they are enamored of her texts,
> and have them read for their delight,
> and have them oft retold.
> The *lais* also please the ladies,
> who listen joyfully, with gratitude,
> they follow their desire.[5]

This text does not specify by title the particular poems we know as the *lais* of Marie de France, nor does it provide their order. But it identifies "Lady Mary" as a woman of marked contemporary success and notes her particular appeal to women, to their taste and feelings, especially in the *lais.*

The identification of the three Marys is a scholarly conflation . . . but not an improbable one. There may have been three Francophone women, each named Mary, running about at the turn of the thirteenth century, engaged in forms of writing that stress cultural translation, insist on the duty of remembering the past, all in octosyllabic rhymed couplets. It is possible: it requires that numbers of women were writing at the time and that the distribution of literary talents among women was far wider than heretofore suspected. Identifying the three obeys a logic of parsimonious economy, a sense that leisure, education, the linguistic, stylistic, and narratorial skills displayed, were perhaps fairly rare. An alternative to one Mary is not a male writer, but three different women writers! The Harley manuscript does not identify the *lais'* author as "Marie de France," its order is not sacrosanct, though an excellent case has been made that it is the author's anthology of her own work and that the sequence is her own.[6] But the dismissal of the historical evidence for the woman writer's very existence seems an abrupt male abreaction to feminist claims. As to the variety of her texts, and the capacious multiplicity of the subject it marks, why impose a restrictive notion of unified subjectivity on this medieval woman's experiences of fragmentation?

Women were simultaneously enmeshed in relations of power and marginalized. Their promotions were ambiguous. Louis VII's imposition of "the King's Peace" was problematic, particularly in the anarchic south. Peter the Venerable, abbot of Cluny, said his region of southern Burgundy was "without king, without duke, and without prince." War raged among local chatelains. "Everything is consumed, devastated, soiled by fire, rapine, and murder," says another cleric, imploring the king's help, urging him to consider his kingdom a totalized body, even in areas not formally part of his dominion: what happens when one member of that body withers? Here as elsewhere, a negotiated peace fails. The king proceeds *manu militari. . .*

Toulouse is yet farther. The effort to impose the King's Peace is made: royal messengers and southern prelates promote a generalized pacification. The city calls on Louis: it is his, part of his kingdom, and its population is menaced. The problem is entangled in the feudal problematic of the king's relation to rear-vassals. He takes action in a case involving the Viscountess Ermengard of Narbonne. She wants to establish authority over Berenger of Puisserguier, who has established a new toll on the road between Narbonne and Béziers. On delicate ground, Louis moves cautiously. In spite of Roman law that forbids women to act as judicial powers, he cites the custom of "our kingdom," more generous, which allows women to replace "the better sex" when absent, in the administration of their heritage. Louis proclaims Ermengard's capacity to render justice: "*God made you woman as he might have made you a man*; in his good will, he has placed the regnum of the province of Narbonne in the hands of a woman; by virtue of our authority, let no one be allowed to subtract themselves from your jurisdiction under the pretext that you are a woman."[7] Men remain "the better sex," and yet women's equality is asserted and ascribed to God in the act of creation. The momentary assertion of equality hardly denies women's marginalization. It demonstrates that misogyny was not the exclusive medieval take on women.

Marie de France knew marginalization: to that of gender were added the geographical and the linguistic. Internal evidence of her *lais,* written in French but adapted from "Breton" antecedents, indicates she wrote and lived at least part of her life in England. We know *certainly* nothing of her subject position: she could have been a burgher's housewife, a lady-in-waiting, or a learned nun. She was *probably* associated with aristocratic life, possibly at court: she offers her *lais* to an unspecified "king"—perhaps Henry II, but "king" is sometimes used loosely as an honorific. Since she adapted both fables and the ***Purgatory of Saint Patrick*** from the Latin, she presumably knew that language. Most probably, she was a noblewoman, perhaps in that difficult position, a solitary woman in a patriarchal world of force and violence.[8]

Her texts often represent cultural, political, and even economic displacement. Falling in love, Guigemar greets his lady with consciousness of his own alterity:

> He dared not declare his love:
> Since he was of a foreign land,
> He feared, if he showed his feelings,
> She might hate and distance him.[9]

Marie renews the tag of the *Eneas—estranges hom, homme d'estranges terre—*thematizing the grief of solitary, friendless exile:

> without friends, a man, a foreigner
> grows sorrowful and grieves in an other land
> not knowing where to seek help.[10]

But self-pity is not at all Marie's game. On the contrary, not only is self-pity absent, her texts view a dreadful historical reality—the savage colonization of the island of England, the destruction of local culture and autonomy—with a haunting transcendence of marginalization into an actively hybrid multiculturalism, encompassing male and female, colonial subalternity and the colonizer. Her textual praxis constructs itself as a site of polymorphous traversals and imaginative equality, an appropriative self-extension to other marginalities. Her self-reflexivity elaborates the interconnections of multiple cultural codes, including a robust sexuality subtending the delicate verbal webs of mysterious texts, which incite theoretical reflection on narrativity and semiotics. Hypothetically, in some suprahistorical sphere, a man might have written these texts, either in France or in England. In the harsh realities of human experience, it is impossible to imagine their subtle putdowns of male phallocentrism issuing from a feather—a phallus—not a woman's.

How Marie acquired the cultural capital of the *ars* of writing (the technologies of letters, grammar, rhetoric, dialectic, and inscription) and developed them into writing in the aesthetic sense (structure, style, symbolic thought, their fusion), we have no idea: her identity, authorial and existential, is entirely defined by her texts. However those acquisitions were made, her strategy within the alternatives of the *ars* can too easily be termed "a woman's choice." Contemporary male writers show a preference for rhetorical *amplificatio.* Marie's texts are not only short, they are often minimalist, preferring the more "modest" *abbreviatio.* The lack of verbal ostentation too readily permits the critical elision of significance. But verbal "modesty" is a complex strategy. The subtraction of verbal rhetoric increases the importance of the remainder: narrative structure and symbolism. Marie's semiosis juxtaposes the dynamics of lithe narrative linearity with the radiating stasis of symbolism.

TEXTS

Social marginality is a site of cultural exploration where semiotic models are tried, tested, and fleshed out—as in the short, rhymed tales of Marie de France. The conclusion to the *Fables* demonstrates an author conscious of her production, its aesthetic value and its value as symbolic capital, subject to easy appropriation in a culture without copyright. She protects her production as she can, in a world where the extortion of value from producers is the normal way of doing business. Her semiotic reflection is elaborated around the imbrication of narrative and the self-reflexive sign. Such signs traverse Marie's texts, insistent on their enigmatic quality.[11] The texts' "phenomenological gaps" of signification between determinate communication and indeterminacy challenge the reader.[12]

It has been argued that the institution of the title does not exist at this period of the Middle Ages. The repeated internal use of titles in the *lais* offers counterevidence. **"Le Chaitivel"**—meaning, "Sad Sack," or "Schlemiel"—has been criticized as mediocre, stylistically muddled, having a tedious, disjointed plot, poor character motivation, and a reluctance to fictionalize.[13] In fact, the text's interest is not in narrative. Better than any other *lai,* it demonstrates Alexandre Leupin's point, that "the fiction of the lays is also a meditation on writing."[14] The *lai*'s interest is not in the narrative events, which are summarily recounted, but in the metadiscourse of two characters who survive their own story and assume it as already existing. Not narrative, not even narration, but textualized metaperspectivalism is the point.

The title itself is problematized as an element of signification. The story inverts the usual courtly scene. The knight and titular hero insists he hasn't got it any more, to the lady he loved and loves. It's not intense desire endured in frustration that blocks male potency, it's the permanent flaccidity, wound-induced in the wars of love, that preoccupies their sole male survivor, when the lady, ruing those wars, comes to visit. Three other suitors died in a tournament for love of her. It is the lady who prefers numerical self-glorification, in an argument about the title of "her" story. **"Le Chaitivel"** foregrounds her surviving lover; she prefers **"Les Quatre Deuils," "The Four Bereavals,"** counting her conquests . . . just like a man. She keeps entertaining him verbally: nothing else is possible. The epilogue plays with the text's identity, which endows it with an "*état civil.*"[15] Expanding on the perspectivalism already established, the narrator opines that either title would suit the story, but custom has chosen **"Le Chaitivel"!**[16] In the debate over the title and identity of the text that constructs their perspectival opposition, the two actors' subjectivities tend to be submerged. In fact, a complex, ironic chiasmus of cultural clichés is constructed: the woman counts her amorous triumphs . . . "just like a man"; the man wallows in his victimization . . . "just like a woman"!

In Marie's most telling texts, the alternatives of self-reflexive symbolism and narrative content are fused. **"Yonec"** might be either a first version of **"Laüstic,"** or an attempt to repeat its success: their intertextuality is unquestionable. A knight becomes the sign of his own presence, in his metamorphosis into a bird (as the hero in **"Bisclavret"** turns into a wolf). It is the discrepancy between signifier and signified that signifies: the shadow of the bird on the windowsill actually announces his presence. By dint of social and sexual intercourse with her new lover, the lady's appearance changes with pregnancy. Her face signals her new situation, in unintentional communication to her wealthy, older husband. Trapped and killed (as in **"Laüstic"**), the dying bird-lover gives the lady a double sign, a magic ring and a sword (in **"Laüstic,"** it is the lady who gives her lover a doubled sign), to communicate to his son as instruments of identitarian vengeance. Signs are integrated into the narrative structure: they serve the story, which functionalizes them perfectly.

"Fresne" makes use of the same doubled sign construction, but in a manner that emphasizes its integration into a story of, by, and for women. Neither sentimental nor gender-prejudiced, Marie limns a spiteful woman whose resentment encodes the trap in which she will be caught herself, a trickster tricked by her own trickery. When a neighboring woman has twins, the spiteful woman libels her as adulterous. But then she bears twins herself. Against the shame her own dictum would bring on her, one of the newborn girls is cast out and is given the doubled sign—a ring and a cloth. Left at a convent, hanging in an ashtree, she is adopted by the abbess who takes charge of her education and gives her the name Fresne—"Ashtree." Although a nobleman falls in love and takes her as mistress, his vassals insist he abandon Fresne in favor of another young woman of attested noble genealogy, who can give him proper noble heirs—in fact, Fresne's twin sister.

At the marriage, the new wife's mother comes upon a cloth that Fresne has laid out, in the abnegation of perfect humility, on the newlyweds' bed: the cloth that had accompanied her since birth, the sign of her unknown identity. The mother recognizes it, leading to the anagnorisis of mother and daughter, the reward of self-abnegation in the conversion of the evil mother, the accession to real identity, and the annulment that allows Fresne's marriage to her love. Recognition leads to reconciliation: a cognitive closing of the circle resolves the hanging conflict between mother and daughter. Narrative structure reveals a twelfth-century feminism

delicately sketching the working of a sisterly collective.[17] Would a man have drawn a world peopled almost entirely by women, acknowledging their potential for evil as well as good, in which a mother-daughter separation is recuperated by the daughter's loyal patience, as constituted by a sorority's collectivity? The problem of signification, functionalized by the narrative as in **"Yonec,"** veers into a specifically feminine problematics with **"Fresne,"** where humility and the mother's correct semiotic reading leads to the reintegration of subjectivity and identity.

The redoubled sign is functionalized in **"Yonec"** and **"Fresne"**: it is an instrument of storytelling and allows for different forms of resolution. In **"Milun,"** sign structures proliferate and lead more in the direction of a significatory problematics. Milun initially sends his lady-love a ring, to be hung around her son's neck. Fresne's cloth turns into a letter containing Milun's father's name, establishing an authenticating genealogy for claiming the heritage, accompanied by a silken purse furnished with coins: value is thematized both as sign and money. The sign structure here is not just doubled, it is tripled: there is a sign-sign, the ring whose shape is zero but which does signify: the explicatory, discursive text that spells out the sign-sign's meaning; and the purse of monetary signs. This set of signs will be replaced by another. When Milun and his lady-love are separated, they communicate in complicated and cumbersome ways. A courier-bird carries messages back and forth, not a pigeon but a swan. Not a merely functional messenger, it carries letters in its plumage, participating in both ornamental and signifying functions. The narrative naturalizes this messenger of love. The first time, the swan is bodily carried by a human supernumerary. Later, it is starved for days before each occasion, so that hunger impels its flight. Signs proliferate across the narrative landscape, with or without supplement.

The swan (*cisne*) is a *signe,* which the text terms an *[en]seigne* (l. 271): all three words might be pronounced identically. The swan-sign, more expansive than Mallarmé's, bears a complex sign in the form of a letter, signed and bearing the sign of a seal. Naturalizing the sign-messenger counterbalances a willful play of paradox with the dissemination of signs analogous to the proliferating signs whose texture constitutes a text. Narrativity itself becomes the sign of understanding and value. At the end of the tale, the narrative of combat between Milun and his bastard son is itself a sign of the antagonist's warrior excellence, of his *pris et valur,* so that Milun declares: You've bearen me at the joust; How much that makes me love you![18] As with Guivret and Erec, Yvain and Gauvain, fighting is sealed in friendship. In **"Milun,"** combat leads to the son's revelation of his identity, through recounted narrative and signs. Transposing the genders of **"Fresne,"** the play of conflict and signification leads to anagnorisis, reconciliation in love, and the reintegration of subjectivity and identity.

At this point, a distinction has been demonstrated, between a pure sign, a sign signifying nothing but signification—the multiple rings, the white swan—and the metonymic, contiguous series of signs, the missives that discursively explicate the solitary, polyvalent sign. Only in the string of signs, syntactically ordered, can articulated signification arise. The solitary sign alone signifies everything; hence it signifies nothing. Signification requires the analytic differences inherent to language, and only to language, hence pure signs that signify signification per se. They require the juxtaposition of discourse or narration to make sense and advance the anthropomorphic adventures of those pseudohumans called actors or characters.

The exact match of semiotic purity, narrative text, and symbolization occurs in **"Laüstic,"** the achieved fusion of story and the paradoxes of signification. The lady's husband, disturbed by her nightly risings from the marital bed, becomes suspicious of her cover story, that she goes to the window nightly to hear the nightingale sing. The reader knows she converses with the neighboring knight, in an amorous but nonsexual commerce of signs and unfulfilled desires. The "purity" of signification is anticipated by the "purity" of their narrative relationship. When the angry, brutal husband traps the bird, kills it, and throws it at his wife—its blood splatters her chest—she sends the dead bird to her "lover" and recounts the adventure by embroidering its story in brocade—fulfilling woman's function in a patriarchal society. Like Penelope and Philomena, she saves the small ground of independence within the patriarchal marriage by turning the activity which is the sign of her subjection into the sign of her narrative transcendence.[19] The lover will wrap the bird in texted cloth: encasing both within a reliquary, he carries it with him henceforth the length of his days.

Transcendence is achieved through the purity of love and the contiguity of the death of the symbol of their love with its narrative, wrapped in a transposition of religious adoration to a secular, passionate if unfulfilled love affair. The entire text builds toward the triumph of the signifying process over against repressive male violence: signification itself overcomes the rule of brutal patriarchy so as to maintain love's integrity. Does the lovers' noncarnal love suggest a secular spirituality, displacing the religious opposition of flesh and spirit?

In **"Laüstic,"** the doubled sign structure forms a *mise-en-abyme*: the small syntagm that reflects a narrative's totality. In the representational terms of modern

feminism, the tale is regressive, valorizing chastity's transcendence of the carnal. But the woman transforms the natural thing—the dead bird, the instrumental excuse for amorous conversations—into the sign of pure love, attaching its explicatory narrativization. The walls that surround, enclose, and imprison the woman are transcended by wit and ingenuity, as the weave that designates her submission to patriarchal power is transmuted into a play of signification. As with the trickster tricked, a victim transcends the master's power: she uses the powers of signification to overcome death, imprisonment, and separation, in the triumphant transcendence of the secularized relic. Subjectivity transcends the limitations imposed by social identity.

The delicate problematization of the feminine sign in the patriarchal order as its self-transcendence turns into a subtle and riotous explosion of the order of masculine signification itself. **"Chievrefeuil"** is named after the honeysuckle which, winding around the hazel tree, allegorizes Tristan and Iseut wrapped around each other in the natural "transcendence" of utterly carnal love. This is not a delicately cloying allegory; it resembles rather the analyticity of Chrétien de Troyes's occasional allegories, just more robustly and carnally vulgar. The lovers' brief narrative transcends all barriers by pure sexuality. For anyone who knew the fundamental story—and who, in the culture of the court, didn't know the twelfth century's universal myth of love, of Tristan and Iseut?—their story means the pain of separation, the heart-wrenching comings and goings that occupy the grievous space of adultery, the haunting, burning desire in the absence of the beloved who might satisfy it. The narrative crux is always, how to get Iseut away from her social context with Mark, so that she and Tristan can yield once more to their unending passion.

Tristan, alone in the forest, advertises his presence by waving his stick around, as Iseut passes by on horseback in the forest. Prearranged as a sign of recognition, Tristan's stick is also a sign of his own stick. It leads Iseut to leave her retinue in order to receive his stick in a good roll on the forest floor. The stick is a natural sign of itself. The sign, which normally supposes the absence of the signified, here signifies its presence. Tristan's stick is serviceable, as usual, and that's about all that is in question, aside from the deathless image of deathless love, the honeysuckle wound around the hazel tree as the icon of inseparability, figuring both the transcendence of deathless love and the lovers' limbs wrapped around each other against all effort at transcendence, in words that still resonate:

> Not you without me, nor me without you.[20]

But has the great discrepancy been noted, between the imaged inseparability of eternal love and the narrative of Tristan and Iseut? As is often the case, men's utterances, even moving, are unreliable. Here, the lovers, having taken their pleasure on the forest floor, talk the old talk of returning to the king, as if that would finally end the pain. But when it came time to part, both of them wept. The text witnesses their pain, their joy, and the truth of the *lai* he composed later in her absence,

> in memory of the joy he'd had,
> of the beloved he'd seen,
> and on account of what he'd written
> just as the queen had said,
> to remember the words.[21]

The discrepancy between the narrative and its purported *mise-en-abyme,* becomes a *différance* in the narratee's double reading. The discrepancy between the inseparability of eternal love and the narrative of Tristan and Iseut, inheres in the passage that gives the *lai* its title in free indirect discourse . . . a supposed invention of modernity.[22]

The most vulgar question about men's sticks is their length. The text asks the question, in a manner that confuses unwillingness to countenance the wrapping of Marie's honeysuckle discourse around its gross carnality. Tristan, waiting for Iseut, cut a hazel tree in half, split it square, and inscribed his name with his knife: the queen will recognize her lover's stick. That was the sum total of his writing:

> He cannot live without her.
> Like the honeysuckle wrapped around
> the hazelnut, enlaced and fastened
> all around the trunk,
> forever they stay together,
> but if separated,
> the hazel dies quickly,
> so does the honesuckle.
> Sweet love, so is it with us:
> Not you without me, nor I without you.[23]

The free indirect discourse leaves indeterminate whether it is Tristan's utterance or his author's that is unreliable and indeterminate. Its unreliability is attested by the scholarly debate it has occasioned and the long footnote the editor appends to this passage.[24] The linguistic crux is in the gap between lines 60 and 61. Does the demonstrative pronoun *ceo* of line 61 refer back to the preceding material, so that *la summe de l'escrit* would contain only Tristan's name carved into the stick? Or does the pronoun function proleptically, so that line 62 specifies in addition the facts recounted in the next sixteen lines, that he had sent Iseut a missive, in which he told her how much he missed her, that he could not live without her, that they were bound as the honeysuckle and the hazel tree, "not one without the other"?

The stick is a pure sign of purely sexual desire; the texted representation necessary to elucidate signification may circumcise the man's stick, waving in the air for

his lover's recognition. Some apply common sense to the passage: only Tristan's name is carved on the stick, the rest of his message having been sent earlier (by messenger? by Pony Express?). The editor insists that Marie's symbolism is never vague, but that she opts for "concrete and rational precision" (as a scholar should) within a self-sufficient (that is, modernist) text. Therefore, he concludes, Marie had Tristan write the entire message (translated above) on the hazelnut stick . . . at some expense to verisimilitude!

It is, in fact, impossible to delimit exactly the *summe de l'escrit.* The scholarly debate demonstrates that the passage is ambiguous, and that its ambiguity is indeterminable; I add only that it is likely intentionally so. It cannot but puzzle and lead to the reflection that, not only was Tristan's stick long indeed, but that even with the longest "inscription," it could not be brought under control and discipline. Marie's narrative—the briefest of the *lais*—is her hilarious put-down, not only of phallocentrism's deification of the male member, but of the Nietzschean theme of Tristan and Iseut's "eternal return." Is it about always coming back in the endless alternating pattern of presence and absence, or is it about coming again, and coming again, and singing, no matter the singer's veracity or mimetic consistency? It asserts the primacy of the carnal as against the pretense of idealism in the great myth of passionate love. It does so at the expense of verisimilitude: the text is a production of signification, for whose performance narrative is merely instrumental, not a watertight contract of mimetic exactitude. **"Chievrefeuil"** is both a repetition of the great medieval myth of love and its deconstruction.

Two of Marie's texts—**"Guigemar"** and **"Bisclavret"**—address directly the problematic of constitutive alterities: subjectivity's dependence on and grounding in alterity, or the alternative of Otherness and otherness. In **"Guigemar,"** a knight, well-loved by parents and the king who knights him, finds his social insertion in traveling to Flanders, "where there are always combats and wars," a well-formed male with one exception: like Hippolytus, he rejects love. In the course of a hunt, he encounters a peculiar alterity, a complex animal sign: a white animal, a doe by the presence of her fawn, a buck by its antlers. This is not a "real" animal: it is not presented as a "believable fiction" before which disbelief is to be suspended. It is a narrative sign, counterintuitive, counterfactual, complex, and paradoxical. Signaling the alternative between the two genders as totality and interdependence, it faces Guigemar with his lack: the desire for an O/other that would constitute him as subject. His sexual and class identity are given: he lacks the desire that makes a subject and encounters a complex sign whose fiction excludes lack. Only ideology claims to exclude lack.

This sign reflects back on Guigemar, as his critical Interpretant. The sign of androgyny, a totality lacking nothing, mirrors the hero's incompleteness in reverse: he lacks lack, the lack that impels desire. His hunter's arrow wounds the doe mortally, but bounces back to wound his thigh in symbolic castration (as with Perceval's father and the Fisher King). A wound (the word *plaie* is subject to multiple repetitions) is essential to the constitution of the subject: the cut constitutes being (see Yvain). The dying animal curses Guigemar: he will not recover from the wound until a woman suffers out love for him, and he for her; until he suffers his lack and his cut.

Desire is not willed. Abandoning himself to the contingency of a pilot-less boat, he arrives in the *antive cité*. The local lord is an old man, whose jealousy guards his desirable wife in a room decorated by the text's ideological *mise-en-abyme*. Rather than a "mandatory misreading," its rhetorical organization casts two signifying images as a complex emblem that demands attentive reading in its narrative context.[25] On the walls of her room are portraits of Venus and Ovid, the deity of Love and her opponent, complex signs that wander between visual aesthetics and the literary tradition. They repeat the alternative of the doe-buck, separating them as gyneco- and anthropomorphic figures. Venus shows *how* love is to be observed . . . as an art, a discipline. Ovid teaches how to repress love—exactly what Guigemar had been doing. The alternatives on love are framed as love's binarism: submission or rejection. The Latin poet represents the narrative subject's previous course, the goddess its future alternative. The first is decisively rejected by the emblem of an abyssal narrative, with no *vraisemblance* whatsoever, when Venus throws Ovid's book in the fire, the portrait climbing off the wall and turning into narrative agent against its opposite number.

The painted room in the *antive cité* is an Other World, the equivalent of Jehan's tower in *Cligés*, the location of a passionate but asocial love. The wounded lover and the Other's lady (the lover's Other) live their adulterous love there for a year and a half. The subject has overcome the ontological fault signaled by the white doe. Hypothetically, the initiating lack has been fulfilled. It has been done, however, at the expense of living that love in society. For the rejection of love, the rejection of a sociopolitical insertion has been substituted as lack. The junction of subject of desire and his object is faulty, in an encoding insistent on the interdependence of love and socialization. On this score, Marie and Chrétien are allied against Beroul and perhaps Thomas.

The "reality principle" by which the lovers and their affair are discovered by the jealous husband is not a realistic reality principle. The discovery is *preceded* by the woman's realization that discovery is inevitable:

consciousness precedes the event. It leads to oaths of fidelity and passional contracts: neither lover will accept love from any other. These contracts are materialized, symbolized, and narrativized by the knots that each ties into the other's clothing, to be untied only by the one who tied them: both will give their love only to that person who knows the shibboleth. The knots are both sign and instrument of fidelity, hence the ensuing flight from paradise, once the affair is discovered. Guigemar leaves first, the lady follows later, escaping from her prison when she finds her door surprisingly unlocked—a factoid asserted with narratorial imperturbability by a single verse in preemptive mockery of realistic *vraisemblance*.

Similar mockery attends the Meriaduc episode. He falls in love with Guigemar's lady, captures her and blithely organizes a tournament to which he expressly invites the hero. He realizes that his friend Guigemar and the lady of his desire share these peculiar knots, a test for whomsoever they are to love. He introduces them at his castle, both their rival and their Cupid. A fool, or a transparent narrative artifice? A bit of both, and something more. Guigemar's destiny aims at conjunction with a woman. Meriaduc is a good friend and instrument, doing everything required to reunite Guigemar and his lady. But triangular love determines that Guigemar will despatch him in spite of services rendered. Finding hospitality with Meriaduc's warring antagonist, he attacks and destroys Meriaduc's castle and kills him. His friend and rival killed off, he happily leads off his lady friend: the punishment (*peine*) inflicted by the magic doe-buck is ended. Achieving junction with the feminine principle, he discards the society of men through a complicated series of plot turns. It is the same conflict as is faced by both Erec and Yvain: gender and class identities are givens for both, but subjectivity must be found and constructed.

The discipline of love is dual. Ethically, it insists on the fidelity of an exclusive bond and does not tolerate multiplicities. Semiotically, it requires weaving together the signifying modes of the static but complex sign with the unfolding flow of narrative . . . itself a discipline of sequencing, of grasping how "one-thing-after-another" produces an ideational dialectic. But the narrative's cold, concluding words, just before the epilogue, give one the shivers:

> He's taken and destroyed the fortress,
> And killed the lord inside.
> In great happiness he leads off his lady.
> Now he's gone beyond his punishment.[26]

The coldly expedited ending yields nothing to the celebratory pleasure suggested by the well-told tale and its mimetically happy conclusion. Human happiness is not entirely joyous.

"**Guigemar**"'s trick is the knot of fidelity tied into clothing. In "**Bisclavret**," Marie adapts the oldest, the most widespread animal metamorphosis, figuring the fears of feral violence in the socialized subject.[27] Much has been made of Marie's use of folktales; she was once seen as a mere adaptor of folk legends and myths. In fact, her treatment of those tales is quite free: their material does not determine her structures or meanings. Hers is the only "literary" text in which the narrator adopts the werewolf's perspective in telling the tale.[28] She redeploys the tradition's projection of civilized fears onto the screen of a monstrous Other, in order to undermine the process of Othering in the creation of subjectivity, by transforming the Other into an anthropomorphic other. The werewolf is a self-conscious artifice, as was the mother-doe with male antlers. The werewolf is proffered, not as diegetic "reality," but as a complex, polyvalent sign in an ongoing discursive exchange: it is not the question of fictive belief that is raised, but that of reading.

The male protagonist alternates regularly between human and animal forms, between his "self" and its Other. The wife's uncomprehending fear of the Other leads her to steal the clothing that is the condition of his return to the human condition: he remains a wolf, unable to rehumanize, until the conundrum is resolved. That is achieved, but not by combat. The king recognizes true nobility even in wolf's clothing, from behavior that signals human subjectivity in spite of bestial identity. Like Arthur in the *Yvain*'s Blackthorn sisters' episode, the king exerts moral pressure on the evil woman to force her confession and the location of the clothing.

"**Bisclavret**"'s figuration of the subject's inherent splittedness, humanity's monstrous doubleness as *both* socialized *and* bestial, presents an option to those who would address werewolf humanity: address the good, or the evil?[29] The text does not hide the difficulty of the choice. The werewolf reveals human bestiality. Enraged at his wife, he avenges himself by tearing the nose off her face. The gelded nose is an established sign of sexual criminality, such as adultery and bigamy: his wife is guilty of both. Even the wise man who sides with the werewolf considers the act felonious, but the text stresses the appropriateness of the wife's punishment. As in Yvain's mad episode, clothing and language are the signs of properly socialized humanity: mute, nameless nudity signals the wildness that continues to inhere in man, hence the wolf's need to be alone to redress himself: the word "privacy" does not exist in either Old or Modern French, but its encoding is medieval.

Socialization is necessary for the question of identity to even surface; women and power are alternative means of male socialization. Yvain loses his mind, memory,

and identity along with his clothing, turning into an animal in human form; Bisclavret loses human form, remains forcibly caught in the inimical form of bestial alterity, but retains memory, identity, and a knowledge of social codes. Both texts address socialized humanity's incorporation of that which resists social incorporation: self and alterity are permanently joined in the human subject. We live with our constitutive Other and project it on the screen of real others.

SUBJECTIVITY

In Chrétien's novels, combat is the narrative coin of exchange, transformed from murderous scourge to social utility in serving the weak, the helpless, the exploited. With Marie, combat is less frequent: An embarrassment? A distaste for its endless repetitiveness? Awareness that its use plays into male phallicism? Does the choice of a "female" aesthetic of brevity rather than amplification produce lessened violence? In fact, if viewed with attention, not to the amplifications of violence, but to its occurrences, violence is as frequent in the Marie's discourse as in Chrétien's. A werewolf bites off a woman's nose; she is tortured; an adulterous couple is scalded to death in boiling water; a son avenges his father's death by killing his murderer; various symbolic animals are killed off in wanton violence; a jealous husband hurls a bird whose neck he has just wrung to bloody his wife's breast; female characters endure attempted rapes; a man-bird is impaled on a barbed spike; a thigh-wound stands for castration; a stripling's eager machismo explodes his heart, manuring hilltop grasses, herbs, and flowers with his blood; and so on. Violence is central to Marie's work: along with sexual ambiguity, it nourishes writing.[30] Marie metaphorizes both frequently. The writing subject constitutes itself at the edges of successive cuts: they perdure at its center. These violences are physical in nature; if focus is shifted to symbolic violence, nearly every narrative turn of the *lais* exemplifies it.

Subjectivity grows on internalized violence;[31] identity risks being destroyed by it. Identity, as might be expected of a writer of margins, is crucial in Marie's texts. The structure of "**Lanval**" is identical to the narrative model of romance: conjunction with the Fairy Princess, her love conditioned on secrecy, is destroyed by revelation of love's secret in self-defense against the queen's wrongful accusations of homosexuality, solicitation, attempted rape, and treason. The Fairy Princess no longer responds to the call of Lanval's desire. He is saved from certain death only by the grace she accords him, after a sequence in which his trial is interrupted by beautiful ladies on horseback arriving one after the other, each not yet the Fairy Princess herself, only messengers of her approach—courtly Johanna the Baptists, a fairy mistress as Christ? When her arrival finally demonstrates that her beauty is indeed greater than the queen's, the lovers are reunited, but with a bittersweet ending. She rides off, taking Lanval with her to Avalon, the beautiful island of the dead: transcendence achieved at the cost of an integrated social identity and existence.

Marie's art of *abbreviatio* is not quantitative merely. It contains as many rejections of dominant cultural models as incorporations: creativity operates by subtraction, division, and inversion as much as by addition. The brevity of her texts does not reduce them to simple, unpretentious realism, or delimit their theoretical import. Are a werewolf, a fairy mistress, a bird-man, or a female saint of abnegation, really "ordinary people coping with the problems of ordinary life"?[32] Her sign-characters track the satisfaction of emotional needs rather than status or "honor," needs that repeatedly lead to alterities of gender and culture, alterities that name so many identitarian interdependencies.

Reversing the usual order, Marie's authorial subjectivity is more accessible than her identity. Lacking all documentation, she is subject to so many identifications that she obviously has none. Her subjectivity is constructed entirely in and by her texts, outside any identifiable subject-position. It is that of borderlines, a marginal individual. Her texts locate her geographically at the Anglo-Norman colonial margin of French culture and semiotically at the borderlines of a male-dominated textual culture. Textual ontogeny displaces and stands for a possible biographical philogeny. Her textual "thresholds"—the margins of prologue and epilogue where authorial identity is conventionally given—signal their location at crossings, linguistic and geographic, repeatedly invoking the fiction of a prior subjectivity; they construct themselves as those crossings.[33]

Those thresholds most frequently give "Bretons" as Marie's sources. But what does that term mean? It is generally taken to refer to the modern French province of Britanny and its inhabitants. In fact, its meaning is less specific, more ambiguous, lacking the geographical basis it has in modernity. Chrétien has *"li Bretun"* identify his hero as Erec, whose kingdom is in Outer Wales (Estre-Gales), though he is crowned at Nantes in Britanny. He and his parents travel from Arthur's court to Erec's land and country, without crossing water, though *the romans antiques* offer many examples of sea voyages. After King Lac's death at Arthur's court in an unnamed town, Erec takes back his land in fealty from the king, who then declares it is time to go *"a Nantes en Bretaigne"* (6495). Erec has Enid's parents join them on the trip to Nantes. Each day, they travel a great distance, they ride a long ways, until they arrive at Nantes—again without mention of a sea crossing, from Arthur's domain to Bretaigne.

The distance from "Brit" to "Breton" is minimal. Bretun and Bretaigne are derived from Britonnum and could refer either to Britain or to Britanny. Throughout Wace's *Brut,* it refers to those from Britain, but retained both meanings in twelfth-century usage. Disambiguation was possible. Marie specifies *"Bretaigne la Menur,"* or adds a second geographical encoding: **"Laüstic"** locates its action near Saint Malo; **"Chaitivel"** takes place *"en Bretaine a Nantes."* But Marie also confounds meanings, as when she localizes **"Yonec"** in Carwent (Wales) at the River Duelas (Britanny).[34] **"Equitan"**'s emphasis on *"cil de Bretaine, li Bretun,"* refers to the Bretons of Britanny, but the Nauns whom Equitan rules may refer to a general "Celtic" legend rather than a specific geographical location. **"Milun"** distinguishes *"Bretun"* from *"Engleis,"* but that proves no more than the distinction between Norman and the French in the same passage. Bretan, the language, is associated with Kardoel (Carlisle) and Arthur's court in Logres.

Except where specified, the lexical family *Britaine, bretan,* and *Bretun,* referring to place, language, or people, is undecided between "Britain" and "Britanny," between "British" and "Breton." The distinction that remains stable in the *lais* is its opposition to "Norman": Bretun designates a Norman Other, the conquered Anglo-Saxons or the people of Britanny over whom Norman suzerainty was repeatedly reasserted by military expeditions.[35] The dominant semantic content of Bretun and Bretaigne was not geographical but genealogical: it expressed the notion of the transchannel Celtic unity of a people with a common ancestry, a single lineage. In the epilogue, Wace defines his *Brut* as "the history of the Bretons, and the lineage of the barons who descended from the lineage of Brutus"—whichever side of the Channel (or the Sleeve) they landed on.[36] What they shared in both locations was effective subjection to the Normans: they were the colonized. It is the memory of victims and enforced wanderers that Marie de France honors. It is with the "others" defined by and from her own subject-position that Marie knits a bond repeatedly, in prologues, in epilogues, in the bodies of the *lais* themselves.

In those liminal thresholds, the author defines herself as the site of multiplicities and transgressive traversals. Hers is a "minor literature" in a major language in which everything is political.[37] Although written in French multilingualism is omnipresent in the *lais*: other languages are named, terms are regularly translated. Marie's thresholds are concerned with the identities of the texts, not with the author's. The author functions as mere shifter, shifting adventure into *lai, lai* into poem, Breton into French, always reasserting the duty and necessity of memory: "to remember the words," "to remember lest it be forgotten."[38] Memory is the text's ideology. The first millennium may have been an age of forgetting, a mental clearing of the forest;[39] not so in the twelfth century. A complex dualism haunts Marie's relations to a constitutive past: though disappeared, it engenders identity. The general prologue asserts the extraordinary freedom and creativity of a modernity anchored in memory rather than oblivious erasure. The textual basis of **"Chievrefoil,"** of **"Fresne"** and **"Bisclavret,"** is literally enshrined in **"Laüstic."** Subjectivity is a site of constitutive disjunctions, a "margin of hybridity," where cultural differences, temporality, contingency, and conflictuality touch, to construct a "borderline experience" in the cultural and interpretive undecidability of the colonial moment.[40] This borderline experience is a space of encounters *"in-between* colonizer and colonized": silence or communication, concealment or revelation, essential narremes in the *lais,* make the difference of life or death.[41] It is a space that seeks to transcend identities of class, gender, age, or sex, requiring an extension of the subject beyond the boundaries of self: subjectivity as self-transcendence.

What is remarkable, even heroic in Marie de France's writing, is the appropriative generosity of spirit that extends skill, talent, and knowledge to rescue what can be captured and preserved of the colonized culture. Marie's narrator has an astounding ability to filter other voices through her own, safeguarding both the other's distinctiveness and her own narratorial "I."[42] The gesture toward the other proceeds as a re-creative fusion of personal disjunctions with those of the autochthonous, as authorial subjectivity cleaves to cultural alterity. How to distinguish appropriation from preservation? How to separate out the necessary subjective investment that energizes the rescue of a tattered culture? The wager of writing is to fuse binaries through the injection of new subjectivity. Recognizing the weaknesses of men and the continued dependence of at least some women on those very men, in the frequent vulgarity of both, it repeatedly posits transcendence of anger, resentment, suspicions, into spheres of recognition, forgiveness, or signification. A transcendence cognizant of vulgarity, of carnality and material fact, incorporates them in an equal reciprocity most gently, most nobly assumed.

Marie's recuperation of narratives that acknowledge their ground in other's voices, those of subalterns, models a subjectivity that insists that these scattered fragments constitute a relative but cohesive whole, a complex oscillation between self and Other as a constitutive contradiction: an early colonial hybridity. Her text suggests that one does not simply wait for the Other's arrival:[43] one goes to the encounter to negotiate the differences, in the representation of words if one has the talent, in a dual, coordinate, and always tragic invention of the Other's Real, out of one's own subjectivity.

Notes

1. Richard Baum, *Recherches sur les oeuvres attribuées à Marie de France* (Heidelberg: Carl Winter, 1968).

2. *"Marie ai num, si sui de France"* (Marie de France, *Fables,* ed. and tr. Harriet Spiegel [Toronto: Medieval Academy of America, 1987-94], p. 256); and "Epilogue," ll. 1-8.

3. Jean-Charles Huchet, "Nom de femme et écriture féminine au moyen âge: Les Lais de Marie de France," *Poétique* 48 (1981): 407-30.

4. Simon Gaunt, *Gender and Genre in Medieval French Literature* (Cambridge: Cambridge University Press, 1995), p. 335.

5. "E dame Marie autresi, / Ki en rime fist e basti / E compassa les vers de lais, / Ki ne sunt pas del tut verais; / E si en est ele mult loee / E la rime par tut amee, / Kar mult l'aiment, si l'unt mult cher / Cunte, barun e chivaler; / E si enaiment mult l'escrit / E lire le funt, si unt delit, / E si les funt sovent retreire. / Les lais solent as dames pleire, / De joie les oient e de gré, / Qu'il sunt sulum lur volenté" (Denis Piramus, *La Vie de Seint Edmund le rei,* ed. H. Kjellman [Göteborg: Elanders Boktryckeri Aktieholag, 1935]).

6. Matilda Tomaryn Bruckner, "Textual Identity, and the Name of a Collection: Marie de France's *lais,*" in *Shaping Romance: Interpretation, Truth, and Closure in Twelfth-Century French Fictions* (Philadelphia: University of Pennsylvania Press, 1993), pp. 157-205.

7. Yves Sassier, *Louis VII* (Paris: Fayard, 1991), pp. 354-68, 367f., emphasis added.

8. Michael J. Curley, ed., *Saint Patrick's Purgatory: A Poem by Marie de France* (Binghamton, N.Y.: MRTS, 1993), p. 5f.

9. "Il ne l'osot nïent requere; / Pur ceo qu'il ert d'estrange tere / Aveit poür, s'il li mustrast, / Qu'ele l'enhaïst e esloinast" (Marie de France, *Lais,* ed. Jean Rychner [Paris: Champion, 1983] ["CFMA" 93], ll. 477-80).

10. "Hum estrange descunseillez, / Mut est dolenz en autre tere, / Quant il ne seit u sucurs quere!" ("Lanval," ll. 36-38; ibid., p. 73).

11. Doris Desclais Berkvam, "La chose et le signe dans *Le Fresne*," in *L'imaginaire courtois et son double,* ed. Giovanna Angeli and Luciano Formisano (Salerno and Naples: Edizioni Scientifiche Italiana, 1991), pp. 235-44.

12. Robert Sturges, *Medieval Interpretation: Models of Readings in Literary Narrative, 1000-1500* (Carbondale and Edwardsville: Southern Illinois University Press, 1991), pp. 75-124.

13. Elizabeth Wilson Poe, "The Problem of the Tournament in *Chaitivel*," in *In Quest of Marie de France: A Twelfth Century Poet,* ed. Chantal A. Maréchal (Lewiston, N.Y.: Mellen, 1992), pp. 175-92.

14. Alexandre Leupin, "The Impossible Task of Manifesting 'Literature': On Marie de France's Obscurity," *Exemplaria* 3 (1991): 221-42, 225.

15. Marie de France, *Lais,* ed. Jean Rychner (Paris: Champion, 1983), p. 273.

16. Katharine Gingrass-Conley, "La 'Venue' à l'écriture de la dame dans *Le Chaitivel,*" *Romanic Review* 83 (1992): 149-60.

17. Michelle Freeman, "The Power of Sisterhood: Marie de France's 'Le Fresne,'" in *Women and Power in the Middle Ages,* ed. Mary Erler and Maryanne Kowaleski (Athens: University of Georgia Press, 1988).

18. "Tu m'as abatu al juster: / A merveille te puis amer!" (l. 443f.).

19. "Le laustic li trametrai, / L'aventure li manderai / En une piece de samit / A or brusde e tut escrit / Ad l'oiselet envolupé" (ll. 133-37).

20. "Ne vus sans moi, ne jeo sanz vus" ("Chievrefoil," l. 78).

21. Ibid., ll. 107-11.

22. Ann Banfield, *Unspeakable Sentences: Narrative and Representation in the Language of Fiction* (London: Routledge, 1982); against see Bernard Cerquiglini, "Le style indirect libre et la modernité," *Languages* 73 (1984): 7-16; and Matilda Tomaryn Bruckner, "Marie's Fusion of Voices," in *Shaping Romance: Interpretation, Truth, and Closure in Twelfth-Century French Fictions* (Philadelphia: University of Pennsylvania Press, 1993), pp. 184-89.

23. "Ne poeit vivre sanz li. / D'euls deus fu il tut autresi / Cume del chievrefoil esteit / Ki a la cordre se perneit: Quant il s'i est laciez e pris / E tut entur le fust s'est mis, / Ensemble poënt bien durer, / Mes ki puis les voelt desevrer, / Li cordres muert hastivement / E li chievrefoilz ensement / 'Bele amie, si est de nus: Ne vus sanz mei, ne jeo sans vus'" (ll. 67-78). I discard the editor's quotation marks, which partially resolve the question of (in)direct discourse.

24. Marie de France, *Lais,* ed. Jean Rychner (Paris: Champion, 1983), pp. 276-79.

25. Compare with R. Howard Bloch, "The Medieval Text—*Guigemar*—as a Provocation to the Discipline of Medieval Studies," *Romanic Review* 79 (1988): 63-73.

26. "Le chastel a destruit e pris / e le seignur dedenz ocis. / A grant joie s'amie en meine. / Ore a trepassee sa peine" (ll. 879-82).

27. Kathryn I. Holten, "Metamorphosis and Language in the Lay of *Bisclavret*," in *In Quest of Marie de France: A Twelfth Century Poet,* ed. Chantal A. Maréchal (Lewiston, N.Y.: Mellen, 1992), pp. 193-211, 193.

28. Kirby F. Smith, "An Historical Study of the Werewolf in Literature," *PMLA* 9 (1984): 2-3.

29. Matilda Tomaryn Bruckner, "Of Men and Beasts in *Bisclavret*," *Romanic Review* 81 (1991): 251-69.

30. Rupert Pickens, "Marie de France and the Body Poetic," in *Gender and the Text in the Later Middle Ages,* ed. Jane Chance (Gainesville: University of Florida Press, 1996), pp. 135-71, 138f.

31. Judith Butler, *The Psychic Life of Power* (Stanford, Calif.: Stanford University Press, 1997), p. 64.

32. Joan Ferrante, *To the Glory of Her Sex: Women' Roles in the Composition of Medieval Texts* (Bloomington: University of Indiana Press, 1997), p. 197.

33. On thresholds, see Gérard Genette, *Seuils* (Paris: Seuil, 1987).

34. See editor's footnote to ll. 13-16, p. 265.

35. John le Patourel, *The Norman Empire* (Oxford: Oxford University Press, 1976); François Neveux, *La Normandie des ducs aux rois, Xe-XIIe siècle* (Rennes: Ouest-France, 1998).

36. "La geste des Bretons / Et la lignee des baruns / Ki del lignage Bruti vindrent" (Epilogue to *Le Roman de Brut de Wace,* 2 vols., ed. Ivor Arnold [Paris: Société des Anciens Textes Français, 1940], ll. 14859-61).

37. Gilles Deleuze and Félix Guattari, *Kafka: Toward a Minor Literature,* tr. Dana Polan (Minneapolis: University of Minnesota Press, 1986), p. 16f.

38. "Pur les paroles remembrer" ("Chievrefoil"); and "pur remembrer / Qu'hum nel deüst pas oblier" ("Eliduc").

39. Patrick J. Geary, *Phantoms of Remembrance: Memory and Oblivion at the end of the First Millenium* (Princeton, N.J.: Princeton University Press, 1994), p. 29.

40. Homi K. Bhabha, *The Location of Culture* (London: Routledge, 1994), p. 206f.

41. Eva Rosenn, "The Sexual and Textual Politics of Marie's Poetics," in *In Quest of Marie de France: A Twelfth Century Poet,* ed. Chantal A. Maréchal (Lewiston, N.Y.: Mellen, 1992), pp. 225-42.

42. Bruckner, "Of Men and Beasts in *Bisclavret*," pp. 265ff.

43. Compare with Jacques Derrida, "L'invention de l'autre," *Psyché, Inventions de l'autre* (Paris: Galilée, 1987), p. 60.

Emanuel J. Mickel (essay date 2005)

SOURCE: Mickel, Emanuel J. "Marie's Use of Monologue and Dialogue in the *Lais.*" In 'De sens rassis': *Essays in Honor of Rupert T. Pickens,* edited by Keith Busby, Bernard Guidot, and Logan E. Whalen, pp. 467-89. Amsterdam, The Netherlands: Rodopi, 2005.

[*In the following essay, Mickel contends that Marie uses dialogue and monologue in the* Lais *for several purposes: to heighten the drama of urgent or dangerous situations, to enhance characterization, and to consider questions of love and ethics.*]

In both historical narrative and in romance, writers have long made extensive use of monologue and dialogue as narrative devices. In Book III of *The Persian Wars* Democedes the Crotoniat, a Greek skilled in medicine, cured Darius of his illness at Susa. When Atossa, the daughter of Cyrus and the wife of Darius, was afflicted with a boil on her breast, she called for Democedes to heal her discreetly. He did so, but he gained a promise that she would afterward return a favor. This favor was to speak to Darius about invading Greece. In the following few pages of direct discourse between Darius and Atossa, she persuades him that he should set aside his plans to invade Scythia for a much more important and advantageous invasion of Greece. This moment in the narrative was, in the mind of Herodotus, one of the most important of his entire history, for it was from this colloquy that the great conflict between Persia and Greece began. Scholars propose that Herodotus had received the details of Democedes' role in the events from descendants whom Herodotus had encountered in Magna Graecia. Clearly, though, no exact dialogue between Atossa and Darius could remain verbatim. Yet Herodotus chose, probably for dramatic purposes, to present the moment as if he had a copy of the precise language each speaker used.

Among historians such a practice became common. In his *Peloponnesian War* Thucydides often presented direct dialogue or a transcribed discourse as in the famous funeral oration of Pericles (Book II, Chapter VI) in which he praised the tradition of the citizen soldier of Athens as the great model for the current generation to emulate. In this panegyric one finds the leadership qualities of the renowned Pericles, but one

also finds a characterization of the best of Greek society. This speech is not so much a document purporting to be an exact witness to the very words Pericles used, but it captures the essence of what he said.

This method of reportage became standard among the best historians of the day. In his *Roman History* Appian, the Greek-born official from Alexandria, who wrote his book on Roman affairs in Greek in the first half of the second century A.D., used the technique frequently. In Book II, Chapter XI of the *Civil Wars* Appian takes advantage of the confrontation between Caesar and Pompey at Pharsalus to sum up in the commanders' respective speeches what he considers to be the essential characteristics of each man's position. Pompey speaks of his own desire to delay battle to cause Caesar to become depleted of supplies; he tells his men that fighting now is their desire so they should fight with hope and knowledge of their many previous victories. Contrarily, Caesar's direct address to his men emphasizes the importance of the immediacy of battle and the knowledge of their great fortune which has always allowed them to triumph over superior numbers and extreme adversity.[1]

Rome's best known historian, Livy, who wrote in the greatest years of the Roman Empire during the reign of Augustus, used direct address in his *Ab Urbe Condita* even in recounting the legendary tales of the ancient Roman past; hence he dramatizes the rape of Lucretia by Sextus Tarquinius in quoting his threats to her and her narrative of what transpired to her husband and Lucius Junius Brutus, the savior of the republic.[2]

One could easily trace this common historical practice through the Middle Ages in the *Historia* of Richer, written during the period when Gerbert was Archbishop of Reims (991-998),[3] or in the works of Ordericus Vitalis and William of Malmesbury, well known historians in the first half of the twelfth century and both particularly aware of French, Norman, and English affairs.

If the use of direct speech is common in historical writing from the earliest times to reveal the writer's interpretation of the situation, events, or character, a technique close to dialogue, monologue, is developed, often in debate form, to reflect the mental state of a given character in the fictional, historical narrative we call romance. In the greatly influential *Argonautica* Apollonius of Rhodes, the epic poet of Alexandria, Egypt in the late third and early second century B.C., recounts the first of the renowned love romances in the story of Jason and Medea.[4] When Cypris (Aphrodite) approaches Eros for help in the gods' plans, she acknowledges that he is an "unutterable rogue" and disobedient. Yet he is needed to overcome Medea, the devotee of Hecate. The arrow of Eros makes Medea look on dumbfounded as "speechless amazement seized her soul" (213). As Eros laughed loudly "her heart panted fast through anguish, all remembrance left her, and her soul melted with the sweet pain [. . .]" (215). Here one finds the characteristic speechlessness and amazement of the "traditional" lover, the loss of intellect through the loss of memory of what she had learned, and the antithesis ("sweet pain") which becomes the very means of defining this kind of love in future works. At night Medea has a dream in which her parents fall into contention with the stranger to whom she is so attracted. In the dream Medea chooses the stranger and neglects her parents, who were seized by "measureless anguish" (p. 237). After seeing her sister Chalciope, who pleads on behalf of "the stranger," Medea spends the night in anguish. She lies awake reflecting on her situation. Should she not leave Jason to his fate? If she helps him, she knows that the Colchians will mock her and she will become known as the maiden who yielded to a mad passion forsaking her parents for a stranger. She considers suicide to save her from disgrace and even takes the drug chest on her lap. But then she sets it aside and eagerly awaits the dawn when she can go to Jason.

Ovid made popular this form of debate within the character through the use of the inner monologue both in his *Heroides* and in the *Metamorphoses*. In Book VII of the *Metamorphoses* he retells the story of Medea to show how a person dominated by the passion of love can commit the most horrible crimes imaginable. Ovid takes up the story after Jason has arrived at Colchis and Medea has already seen Jason and become infatuated. He notes that she has tried to overcome her madness (*furorem*) by reason. Frustrated, she comes to the conclusion that some god must be opposed to her. Perhaps, she thinks, this is what is known as love. Medea is now torn between two arguments. Desire urges her one way, reason the other ("aliudque cupido, / mens alius suadet," 20-21). Verses 22-73 offer the conflicting arguments of *mens* and *cupido*. In this debate the pros and cons are presented in alternating statements. Medea asks herself why she should love a foreigner instead of someone her own country might offer her? Is his fate not in the hands of the gods? Against this seemingly harsh conclusion, Medea questions what he has done to merit such punishment. Clearly he will die without her help. She pities his youth and nobility. She would have to have a stone heart or be the child of a tigress not to help him. The conclusion to this argument is followed by another. Should she betray her father? Medea reflects that Jason will undoubtedly sail away and marry another, a Greek woman. This thought leads her to conclude that then he would deserve death. Yet she is persuaded that the loftiness and grace of Jason's soul will not permit him to be so deceitful and forgetful of the pledge he will make to her before the gods. An in-

ner voice urges her to act: Jason will marry her and take her to Greece where she will be celebrated. But, she asks, should she leave her father and native land? Another voice tells her that she will be going to a greater country renowned for its art and culture. Moreover, she will be with the man she loves and he will protect her in his arms. Again a voice warns Medea to look ahead, to see the great wickedness before her and to flee ("quin adspice, quantum / adgrediare nefas, et, dum licet, effuge crimen," 70-71). After Medea had spoken "ante oculos rectum pietasque pudorque / constiterant, et victa dabat iam terga Cupido" (72-73).

Medea's reason prevails in these arguments and she attempts to follow Ovid's principle that one must flee love to escape it. At that moment, however, she sees Jason and the flame within her rises up and effaces the arguments of reason. Ovid presents this inner debate within the monologue to show the clearly logical arguments in favor of supporting her own father and people and not thwarting the will of the gods as opposed to the illogical arguments supported only by her own desire that she would find acceptance among the Greeks and that Jason would not leave her for a woman of his own country.

Ovid especially uses the monologue to advantage in the cases where there is a conflict between reason and desire. In Book X he develops the painful inner debate that Myrrha undergoes in her growing incestuous love for her father Cinyras. In Book IX Byblis emerges from a deceitful erotic dream of incestuous desire for her brother, Caunus. In the inner debate that follows Byblis' desire sweeps away every argument her reason presents against her unnatural desire even to the extent that she pursues her pious brother across Asia Minor. In the *Heroides* Ovid presents the famous love of Ariadne for Theseus. Like Medea she helps Theseus overcome her father and homeland by revealing to him the way to overcome the labyrinth and the Minotaur. She too discovers the folly of following her desire when Theseus abandons her to die alone on the island of Naxos.[5] Ariadne awakens to find that Theseus has left her on the desolate island. She climbs the mountain and glimpses the sails of his ship on the horizon. Her "monologue" is really a kind of address to Theseus, but it is essentially a monologue of her thoughts and anguish about what she has done for Theseus and how her love is costing her the love of family and homeland.

The monologue and dialogue came by way of Ovid and Virgil into the vernacular narrative of the mid-twelfth century in France. In the Old French version of Virgil's Aeneid, the *Roman d'Eneas,* the author embellishes Virgil's narrative concerning the encounter between Lavinia, the Latin Princess, and Eneas, the Trojan hero destined to found the new Latin people. Lavinia's mother wishes her daughter, Lavinia, to marry the indigenous prince, Turnus, and give him her lands. She argues that Turnus nobly fights for Lavinia because of love, whereas for Eneas the marriage will be merely a convenient way to acquire the land. But in making this argument, Lavinia's mother must explain to an enquiring Lavinia "what is this thing called love." In an amusing dialogue drawn from Ovid's *Ars Amatoria, Remedia Amoris,* and the *Amores,* the queen tries to interest her daughter in love, this encounter which mingles so much pain with pleasure. There is here the same irony as in Marie de France's **"Guigemar,"** in which the old husband has painted the walls of his wife's bedroom with Venus burning Ovid's book (it must be the *Remedia Amoris*) and excommunicating anyone who would reject love. In this he presumably means love for himself and not the newcomer. Just so here. Because Turnus loves Lavinia, the queen speaks on behalf of love. But to Lavinia, who is not in love with Turnus, her mother's description is uninteresting: "Onc de bon mal n'oï parler," says Lavinia. Her mother answers: "Amors n'est pas de tel nature / com autres maus." Lavinia replies: "Ge n'en ai cure."[6] But shortly thereafter Lavinia is looking down from the walls of the city on the Trojans. There she sees Eneas and discovers what her mother has been instructing her about: "Quant voit que eschiver n'en puet, / vers Eneam a atorné / tot sun corage et son pansé" (8062-64). The text (8047-81) describes how love has struck Lavinia and has her in his power. Then follows Lavinia's long monologue (8083-399) in which she affirms that she is indeed caught by the love of which the queen spoke. She laments her infortune and determines to hide her love from the queen. Lavinia reproaches herself for her folly and yet recognizes that she can do nothing.

Both the dialogue between the queen and Lavinia and the monologue of Lavinia became staples of the romance narrative of the twelfth century. Chrétien de Troyes used both devices for dramatic purposes and for exploring in monologue the most important questions of his narrative. One need only think of *Erec et Enide,* Chrétien's first extant romance, and the dialogue that follows Enide's meditation on the slanderous accusations being made against Erec's reputation as a knight. In the crisp exchange that follows Erec's question to Enide concerning what she had said Enide lies to Erec in trying to evade his enquiry. It is Enide's lie that makes Erec wonder what she really thinks herself. Does she in fact secretly fear that the slanderers may be right? Other dialogues of great importance occur later in the romance. In Erec's reconciliation with Enide he confirms that he was testing her and that he now knows that she loves him (despite her repeated disregard of his request that she not speak). Moreover, he makes what may be the most important statement of the romance in declaring that they can now return to the way they had

been before. Here one finds no indication that Erec has learned some kind of correction for his previous conduct. In fact Erec does not even allow that there was anything wrong with their previous manner. This dramatic moment, as significant as it is, is often ignored by scholars who cling to the idea that Erec is somehow at fault here and learns as much during the quest.

But even more important than the significant dialogues in Erec's first romance are the many monologues of Enide. It is safe to say that the most important analysis of *Erec et Enide* comes in Enide's own self-questioning reflections. To be sure the individual encounters Erec has are important for establishing his prowess and for the conflict between his prohibition and her inner debate about obeying him or not. But even more significant are Enide's self-reflective monologues on her relation with Erec and what she had done. As Enide stays awake in the woods or awaits the dawn, her own self evaluation focuses on her original reaction to the remarks of the slanderers and what it indicated about Enide's blame in what happened between her and Erec.[7]

Before considering the use of dialogue and monologue in Marie's **Lais,** one should note the vastly different restrictions of the short *lai* (between little more than 100 to just under 1200 lines) in comparison with the six-thousand-line or more romance narrative of Chrétien. One might think that Marie's need to cut her narratives would all but eliminate dialogue and monologue in favor of the narrative. Contrarily, one is struck by the fact that Marie devotes so much attention to these moments. If anything, her narratives give greater emphasis to dialogue than do the longer romance works.

Whereas the longer romance often has its moments of great resolution in decisive narrative action, Marie tends to use dialogue to bring to life significant turning points in the narrative. Not unlike the historian's use of the commander's speech to his troops before battle to bring to the fore the reasons for the battle, the great importance of the outcome, and the urgency of their situation, Marie halts the narrative drive of the text to dramatize a particular moment. In **"Le Fresne"** the wedding between Fresne's sister Codre and Gurun has been arranged. Fresne, who has been Gurun's concubine, has just spread her own blanket on the bed in the wedding chamber because she found the bedclothes unworthy of Gurun and the event. When the mother of Fresne brings Codre into the bedchamber to prepare for the wedding night, she sees the blanket and it recalls to her the one she gave to her baby the day she abandoned her many years earlier. Instead of narrating the dramatic moment, Marie has the mother address the chamberlain and then Fresne directly about the blanket. In her answer, Fresne also notes the ring that she had received from "l'abeesse" her aunt. When the mother sees the ring, the confirming second piece of evidence, she loses consciousness in her emotion.

Another excellent example of Marie's use of dialogue in this dramatic manner is in the two hundred forty-four line *lai*, **"Les Deus Amanz."** In line 184 the young woman feels her lover weakening as he carries her up the mountain and urges him to drink the restorative potion: "'Amis,' fet ele, 'kar bevez! / Jeo sai bien que vus [a] lassez: / Si recuvrez vostre vertu!'[8] This is the turning point of the narrative. The young man rejects her plea in his desire to reach the summit as soon as possible.

In **"Milun"** Marie reserves the moment of significant dialogue until Milun confronts the young knight whose great renown has eclipsed his own. When Milun is unhorsed, the young knight perceives his white beard and courteously and apologetically asks him to remount. Milun sees the distinguishing ring on the young man's finger and asks where he obtained it. In the next twenty-five lines the young man tells the story of his life and is united with his father after twenty years.

In **"Lanval"** Marie describes Lanval's unfortunate situation in Arthur's realm and his encounter with the fairy mistress. Now Lanval's life and situation are completely changed as he has the funds to exercise largesse. But the queen's approach to him changes his life immediately. The queen's offer of love and his rejection of her occupy more than thirty lines of the narrative. By quoting their interview verbatim Marie captures the drama of the queen's offended pride and her insult of Lanval. Moreover, only by quoting Lanval's words directly can one appreciate the virulence of his response to her and the excessive language "Dunt il se repenti sovent" (290). Not only does Lanval declare his love more beautiful than the queen,

> 'Une de celes ke la sert,
> Tute la plus povre meschine,
> Vaut meuz de vus, dame reïne,
> De cors, de vis et de beauté,
> D'enseignement et de bunté.'

(298-302)

It is these precise words of excess, of course, that will structure the remainder of the *lai* and the trial that follows, for Lanval now must not only produce his lady, something she had warned him about, but he must prove that even her lowliest servant is more beautiful than the queen to prove the truth of what he said and thus avoid the charge of slander.

Marie rarely uses dialogue in unimportant situations. On two occasions she has a character recapitulate events that the reader already knows. The instance in **"Guige-**mar,"** when Guigemar is asked to tell his story to the young woman, seems the most gratuitous. The reader has already been through the narrative so it hardly seems necessary for Guigemar to spend twenty-six lines (311-36) recounting what the reader already knows. But in the instance in **"Eliduc"** one can see the reason for Marie having Guilladun tell of Eliduc's deception and her own innocence in following him abroad:

> 'Dame, jo sui de Logres nee,
> Fille a un rei de la cuntree.
> Mut ai amé un chevalier,
> Eliduc le bon soudeer;
> Ensemble od lui m'en amena.
> Peché ad fet k'il m'enginna:
> Femme ot espuse; nel me dist
> Në unques semblant ne m'en fist.
> Quant de sa femme oï parler,
> De duel kë oi m'estuet paumer.
> Vileinement descunseillee
> M'ad en autre tere laissee;
> Trahi[e] m'ad, ne sai quei deit.
> Mut est fole quë humme creit.'

(1071-84)

By her words and unaware that Guildeluec is Eliduc's wife, one can see the effectiveness of having Guilladun proclaim her ignorance and hence innocence. What is fascinating here is the twist Marie places on the usual Ovidian scenario of a young woman who foolishly leaves her own country and family for love only to be betrayed by the man. It helps explain the unusual conclusion of Marie's narrative. Whereas Eliduc does lead Guilladun astray, he does not do so merely for his own pleasure. Unlike Ovid's mythical male characters, Eliduc acts with conscious concern for Guilladun and does not simply abandon her. It is this that allows Marie not to bring harsh judgment on him despite his betrayal of Guildeluec. Guildeluec does not seem to blame Eliduc for having fallen in love with another woman. Marie also seems to judge him for his conduct and not his emotional attachment. In fact, after Guildeluec hears Guilladun explain her situation, it is she who defends Eliduc's conduct to the grief-striken girl.

Marie also uses dialogue for moments in which there is a significant warning that defines the narrative. In **"Les Deus Amanz"** the king's daughter explains to the young man that she knows that he is not strong enough to carry her to the top of the hill without special assistance (84-87). And she explains that she loves her father too much simply to run off with her lover and cause her father such grief (88-92). Instead she proposes that he go to her aunt in Salerno for the strength-giving medicine (93-116). This moment provides a potentially happy ending for the *lai*, but we know that the young man's lack of *measure* when on the hill undoes the young woman's thoughtful preparation.

In **"Guigemar"** the hero receives a warning from the dying doe after she has been fatally wounded by Guigemar during the hunt. Until this scene in the story Guigemar's life has been defined by his lack of interest in marriage even to the extent that many suspected that he had no interest in women. Now the wounded doe warns him that he cannot be cured from his own wound unless he does fall in love:

> 'Oï, lase! jo sui ocise!
> E tu, vassal, ki m'as nafree,
> Tel seit la tue destinee:
> Jamais n'aies tu med[e]cine!
> Ne par herbe ne par racine
> Ne par mire ne par pocium
> N'avras tu jamés garisun
> De la plaie ke as en la quisse,
> De s[i] ke cele te guarisse
> Ki suffera pur tue amur
> Issi grant peine e tel dolur
> Ke unkes femme taunt ne suffri;
> Et tu ref[e]ras taunt pur li,
> Dunt tut cil s'esmerveillerunt
> Ki aiment e amé avrunt
> U ki pois amerunt aprés.'

(106-21)

At this point the narrative changes in that Guigemar realizes that he must leave his own country (he knows that he loves no woman there) and go "en aventure."

In **"Lanval"** the fairy mistress changes Lanval's life entirely in providing him with the means to become a popular knight in Arthur's court, but she also warns him (143-50) that he may not ever let anyone know about her or he will lose her forever. This, of course, also foreshadows what will happen and defines the remainder of the narrative.

In **"Yonec"** the hawk-lover gives the young woman an explanation that is not unlike that of the fairy-mistress in **"Lanval"**: "'Dame,' fet il, 'quant vus plerra, / Ja l'ure ne trespassera.'" Thus she can see him whenever it will please her. But he warns her of the potential consequences:

> 'Mes tele mesure esgardez
> Que nus ne seium encumbrez:
> Ceste vielle nus traïra,
> [E] nuit e jur nus gaitera.'

(199-204)

In the case of the hawk-lover, however, the foreshadowing is of his death and not just the end of their seeing one another. Just as he feared, the lovers are discovered and the lover is killed.

Marie also uses dialogue to present conflicts and crises in her narrative. In **"Lanval"** we have looked at the scene between the queen and Lanval in which they insult one another. And we have seen the confrontation between Milun and his son and the resolution of the *lai* which follows immediately upon the conclusion of their encounter. In **"Laüstic,"** the shortest of Marie's *lai* after **"Chevrefoïl,"** the narrative turns on the subtle confrontation between the wary husband and his wife. When she has told him her reason for getting up at night, an insult to him because of its implication that he does not know "joïe" and that her love lies elsewhere, the angry husband not only traps the bird but sarcastically addresses her wakefulness as if he were concerned for her welfare:

> 'Dame,' fet il, 'u estes vus?
> Venez avant! Parlez a nus!
> J'ai le laüstic englué,
> Pur quei vus avez tant veillé.
> Desor poëz gisir en peis:
> Il ne vus esveillerat meis.'

(105-10)

Marie might have told us about the husband's anger and how he responded. But a third person narrative once removed, no matter how well and vigorously reported, could never equal the powerful, emotion-filled violence of these few lines in which the husband pretends to be answering her comment about hearing the *laüstic* as if he were doing her a kindness.

For the most part poets reserve the discussion and debate over love for the monologue. But Marie twice uses the dialogue to examine the question of love. In this amusing exchange between Guigemar and the lady, the young man tries to persuade the lady that she need not resist his sexual advances long. Only a loose woman ("Femme jolive de mestier") must make the man wait a long time to emphasize that she is not accustomed to being an easy conquest. But the lady "de bon purpens" and who has both "valur" and "sens" will not remain too reserved when she has found a man "a sa manere." Then the couple will take their pleasure privately without anyone knowing of it or having heard about it: "Bele dame, finum cest plait!" (526)

This is a curious argument set against the background of the debate over love at the time. It is clearly in the young man's amorous interests to persuade the lady to accept his love, but his logic naturally places the emphasis on the free granting of love once the woman has found a man to her liking. It is amusing that she is so easily persuaded that delay is unnecessary to her honor:

> La dame entent que veirs li dit,
> E li otreie sanz respit
> L'amur de li, e il la baise.
> Desore est Guigemar a aise.

(527-30)

In another important dialogue, this time in **"Equitan,"** the king and the seneschal's wife discuss the possibility of having love between two people of different stations in life. The king discloses his love for her but she argues that she would be ill advised to enter into such a relationship with him because he is so wealthy and powerful and her husband is his vassal (117-36). The king would naturally think that this love was in his possession and at his command. She continues her argument by stating that love is of no value if the parties are not equal:

> Amur n'est pruz se n'est egals.
> Meuz vaut un povre[s] hum lëals,
> Si en sei ad sen e valur,
> [E] greinur joie est de s'amur
> Quë il n'est de prince u de rei,
> Quant il n'ad lëauté en sei.
>
> (137-42)

The idea that love must be freely given reminds one immediately of the logic of Héloïse who proclaimed love incompatible with marriage because the marriage contract requires love to be given. Because love can only be given freely, it cannot exist in marriage. The twist on this argument is that it does not concern marriage, but substitutes the requirement from rank. Here he would consider her love his by right of rank and so, she argues, love is only worthy if between equals.

The king cleverly turns her argument to his own advantage by telling her that such calculations really are beneath love, that such considerations are only a "bargaine de burgeis" (152). The king tries to take the high ground. Love has nothing to do with position and wealth. Clearly a "riches princes de chastel" would love a poor woman even if she had only "sun mantel" as long as she were "curteise e franche de curage" (156). To prove himself to be of this generous and noble cast of mind, the king says: "Ma chiere dame, a vus m'otrei! / Ne me tenez mie pur rei, / Mes pur vostre hum e vostre ami!" (169-71). The king's "high-minded" argument and his willingness to become not just her equal but her vassal is punctuated by his condemnation of base people who deceive: "Cil ki de amur sunt nov[e]llier / E ki se aturnent de trichier, / Il sunt gabé et deceü" (163-65). Although it is difficult to imagine how the king does not see the self-condemnation in his assertion, one can see that the king's new position as the "vassal" of the seneschal's wife will lead to disaster. The discussion of love probes the question whether there can be love between unequal partners. The king rejects his title to superiority, but the result is not equal partners but an upside down relationship in which the king becomes the underling and accepts the dominant role of the seneschal's wife.

Another significant use Marie makes of dialogue is in revealing a person's character. It should be noted here that Marie's characters often show their flaws or good qualities in what they say, perhaps even more than in what they do. In **"Les Deus Amanz"** the young lover, so prudent in following the king's daughter's advice in going to Salerno for the necessary strength-enhancing potion, nonetheless reveals his youthful lack of *mesure* in contradicting the girl's urgent insistence during his climb up the hill: "'Amis,' fet ele, 'kar bevez! / Jeo sai bien que vus [a]lassez: / Si recuvrez vostre vertu!'" In this crucial moment the young boy rejects the girl's advice to drink the potion answering her common-sense urgency with a spurious response that pausing to drink would delay their joy unnecessarily while he drank the potion.

In **"Le Fresne"** Marie uses dialogue to reveal the mother's own uncharitable nature. When she hears that her neighbor has had twins, she maliciously implies that no woman can have twins unless she has had sexual relations with two men. Marie has the woman's words spoken in open court in front of everyone. This makes the damage of the slanderous remarks even greater as the lady of the court speaks with a certain authority. Her husband makes it clear that such an opinion is not believed by the enlightened person, but the damage has been done. The fact that Marie has the woman speak in front of people rather than privately to her husband reveals her poor judgment. Later, when she has twins herself, she expresses her remorse that she condemned herself in open court when slandering her neighbor. But at this point she is unwilling to accept the shame and even considers killing one child: "'Un des enfanz m'estuet murdrir: / Meuz le voil vers Deu amender / Que mei hunir e vergunder'" (92-94). But those who served her refused to allow her to make such a catastrophic mistake: "De hummë ocire n'est pas gas." (98) At the *lai*'s conclusion the mother recognizes the blanket and ring she had given to her daughter nearly twenty years earlier. Here she could have remained silent and hidden her crime, but her emotional response to her bereft daughter's plight no longer allows her to hide her guilt. Marie not only makes her confess her crime in open court, "Oiant tuz, dist, ne ceil [e] mie" (449), but she has her acknowledge her unjust accusation against her neighbor:

> 'Sire, quant parduné l'avez,
> Jel vus dirai; si m'escutez!
> Jadis par ma grant vileinie
> De ma veisine dis folie;
> De ses deus enfanz mesparlai:
> Vers mei meïsmes [mes]errai.'
>
> (465-70)

When one says that Marie reveals character in her use of dialogue, one must understand this in the medieval sense of character. All men have free will to choose to do good or evil. When they choose to oppose God, that decision and their actions establish their character. In the *Conquête de Constantinople* Villehardouin takes great care to record the promises made by the men representing the crusade in negotiations with the Venetians for naval passage to the Holy Land. Promises are the formal decisions made to support an agreement. If men follow their good promises with deeds, then there is harmony between the world of thought and action. When they did not fulfill their promises, the Fourth Crusade went astray. In the Christian perspective redemption allows the human being an opportunity to erase his past and set a new course in eternity. This the mother does in her confession with her husband's guarantee of pardon and the mother's crime, though it caused her daughter much pain, is removed. The father's own statement expresses it all with no hint of recrimination:

> '[. . .] De ceo sui liez;
> Unques mes ne fu [i] si haitiez;
> Quant nostre fille avum trovee,
> Grant joie nus ad Deu donee,
> Ainz que li pechez fust dublez.'

(485-89)

Neither Fresne nor the husband questions how the mother could have done what she did. Man's capacity to act selfishly is well established. What matters is repentance and the willingness to confess, to bear the burden of one's sin. Yet, in Christian terms, those that are "heavy laden" find rest. The father's answer focuses not on the pains of this life but on the gift that God had restored to them their daughter in time to save the family from a real grief of permanent alienation.

In **"Eliduc"** Marie presents one of the more complicated *lais* in the collection. It is interesting that Marie names the work not after Guildeluec, Eliduc's wife, and the figure in the *lai* whose good character and understanding restore life to Guilladun and happiness to all, but after Eliduc, the man who betrays his wife, lies to the foreign king he serves, and deludes the king's daughter. Each of these deceptions is underscored by Marie in having them "acted out" in dialogue form. In other words, Eliduc must voice his own lies and not merely have them mentioned.

After Eliduc has left his wife (because some have slandered him to the king) and has been serving a foreign king, he falls in love with the king's daughter. Marie describes how the daughter confesses her love for Eliduc and asks for his response:

> 'Dame,' fet il, 'grant gre vus sai
> De vostre amur, grant joie en ai;
> [E] quant vus tant me avez preisié,
> Durement en dei estre lié.'

(519-22)

There is no doubt here that Eliduc has the perfect opportunity to reveal his marriage to Guilladun but he chooses not to do so. Rather he leads her to believe that he returns her love. He goes on to say that he can do nothing until he has served his pledge to her father. She then offers herself completely to Eliduc and, Marie says, "Bien s'esteent aseüré" (537) though "A cele feiz n'unt plus parlé" (538). Eliduc has accepted an unspoken commitment that he cannot keep. Earlier, in monologue, he had professed his desire to maintain loyalty. Although he could not keep himself from loving her:

> ja ne li querra amur
> Ke li [a]turt a deshonur,
> Tant pur sa femme garder fei,
> Tant pur ceo qu'il est od le rei.
> En grant peine fu Elidus.

(473-77)[9]

But Eliduc's private vow to keep faith with his wife was belied by the open dialogue in which he made an avowed commitment. This leads to his later return to Guilladun, even though he is married, and to open lies to his wife about why he must return to the foreign territory and leave her again. He must feign to her that his grief and morose attitude are not her fault but he is grieved that he has promised the foreign king to return to his service (727-32). When he returns to Guilladun, he tells her that they must leave together in the evening—no discussion with her father and no marriage for her. They are in the position of proscribed lovers, the lovers of the *alba*, the adulterous lovers Tristan and Iseut or Abelard and Héloïse. Their love is an outlaw existence outside the ban of society. On the ship Guilladun learns her true situation and falls unconscious. She is not dead nor can she live in her current status. Eliduc cannot move forward in life in his current dilemma: he cannot continue to love Guilladun and not betray his wife if life is to go on. Guilladun might be his concubine in another setting (**"Le Fresne"**), but she cannot live with Eliduc in society. It is as if she were in suspended animation.

This situation can only be resolved by Guildeluec. If she acts in the way one would expect an ordinary human being to react, the situation must end in grief for all three of them. If Marie had chosen to remove her from the story by death, the moral dilemma would remain unresolved. Only Marie's focus on a love of another dimension removes the obstacle and resolves the dilemma in happiness for all. Guildeluec's love for Eliduc transcends her mortal love for him in that she wishes to see Eliduc and Guillandun happy. As discussed earlier, it is she who understands Eliduc's dilemma and defends his actions to Guilladun. One can only say here that Eliduc is pardoned. His sin of thought, never quite translated into open betrayal of his wife, has led to the impasse. It is interesting that he never confesses and repents as did the mother in **"Le Fresne,"** he is merely granted "grace." He is saved despite his sins as man is saved without really meriting it. And his "salvation" depends on the greater understanding of Guildeluec and her love for him. Marie pauses on Guildeluec's reflection and has her express her thoughts openly to her valet:

> 'Veiz tu,' fet ele, 'ceste femme,
> Que de beuté resemble gemme?
> Ceo est l'amie mun seignur,
> Pur quei il meine tel dolur.
> Par fei, jeo ne me merveil mie,
> Quant si bele femme est perie.
> Tant par pité, tant par amur,
> Jamés n'avrai joie nul jur.'
>
> (1021-28)

By using direct dialogue to express the wife's character through her own words, Marie lays emphasis on the moment and underscores the woman's compassion and love.

In the *Metamorphoses* and the *Heroides* Ovid makes popular the use of the monologue for inner debate on ethical questions concerning love and its power over the individual's ability to reason. He also uses the monologue as a meditation on love and the effects it has on the individual. As mentioned above, Marie's shorter narrative form probably limited her use of the longer monologue as found in Chrétien or in the *romans d'antiquité*. However, she does use the monologue to describe the effects of love in a classic instance in **"Guigemar."**

Guigemar has awakened after his voyage in the unmanned boat and he looks into the eyes of the "dame" of the castle. He is so struck by love that "Tut ad sun païs ublïé" (382) and "De sa plaie nul mal ne sent" (383). He realizes that this must be the love spoken of by the doe. When he is left alone, Guigemar suffers the classic "passio" described by Ovid in the *Ars Amatoria*. He is "pensif" and "anguissus." If this lady does not cure him, then he is surely destined to die. Marie's use of description here lapses into free indirect discourse as the words seem to reflect Guigemar's thoughts:

> Ne seit uncore que ceo deit,
> Mes nepurquant bien s'aparceit
> Si par la dame n'est gariz,
> De la mort est seürs e fiz.
>
> (395-98)

Marie then slides from the free indirect discourse into direct citation:

> 'Allas!' fet il, 'quel le ferai?
> Irai a li, si li dirai
> Quë ele eit merci e pité
> De cest cheitif descunseillé.
> S'ele refuse ma prïere
> E tant seit orgoilluse e fiere,
> Dunc m'estuet [il] a doel murir
> E de cest mal tuz jurs languir.'
>
> (399-406)

The doe had told him that the lady must also suffer for him in love or his wound cannot be cured. This is, of course, the classic love wound which only requited love can cure. Then his obsession or *passio* causes him to recall her words, her features, her eyes and mouth (as the god of Love tells the *Amant* in the *Roman de la Rose*). These thoughts bring joy but pain: "Entre ses denz merci li crie" (417). His pain is so intense that he almost calls out her name even though he is alone. Had he known that she too was suffering because of love, he would have found some "rasuagement" that might have relieved somewhat the "dolur" that caused him such pallor.

But more often Marie uses the monologue to reveal an inner debate of an ethical nature closely tied to the dialogues which reveal character. In Ovid's monologues the character's inner debate often concerns the wisdom of leaving one's country or family to follow the stranger. Or in the case of Byblis and Myrrha the debate is over a moral issue: the desire for incestuous love and the reasons against it. Because these monologues contain a conflict between reason and love, it is reason that suffers. Normally the character adopts the point of view of his emotions pretending that it is the more reasonable view—as Byblis does in arguing that there would be nothing wrong with her love for her brother if he did not happen by chance to be her brother.

In **"Equitan"** the king reflects on his love for the seneschal's wife and the conflict there is between his love and duty. He realizes that love has struck him and that he will do great harm if he makes love to the seneschal's wife:

> 'E si jo l'aim, jeo ferai mal:
> Ceo est la femme al seneschal.
> Garder li dei amur e fei,
> Si cum jeo voil k'il face a mei.'
>
> (71-74)

The king knows that much depends on the loyalty he expects from the seneschal and the loyalty he owes his vassal. One might say that such obligations made and kept are the basis of civilization. Moreover, he also perceives what great personal injury he would do his loyal vassal: "Si par nul engin le saveit, / Bien sai que mut l'en pesereit." Thus both from a public and private viewpoint the king's conduct would be very injurious. He understands this, yet in the next breath his desire invents a spurious argument in support of his love:

> 'Mes nepurquant pis iert asez
> Que pur li seïë afolez.
> Si bele dame tant mar fust,
> S'ele n'amast u dru eüst!
> Que devendreit sa curteisie,
> S'ele n'amast de druërie.'
>
> (77-82)

The king's first conclusion can be seen either as a most selfish choice of oneself over someone else or one might imagine that it would be, according to rank, worse for the king to suffer than his vassal. His next argument is a pretense of concern for the seneschal's wife and, perhaps, Marie's sarcastic remark against certain attitudes at court which might be considered sophisticated in some circles. Were she not to have "druërie," the poor woman would be deprived of her "curteisie"! The king's next argument is that every man would act as he is: "'Suz ciel n'ad humme, s'ele amast, / Ki durement n'en amendast'" (83-84). If every man would return love to this woman if she loved him, can he be blamed for having fallen in love with her? And, finally, the seneschal himself cannot be so selfish as to think that he can keep such a woman all to himself:

> Li seneschal, si l'ot cunter,
> Ne l'en deit mie trop peser;
> Sul ne la peot il nient tenir:
> Certes jeo voil od li partir.'
>
> (85-88)

He concludes his argument by returning to the earlier reference to the pain he knows that his actions would cause the seneschal. But this time he concludes that the seneschal should not be so unreasonable to be hurt. Surely he cannot think that he could keep his wife selfishly to himself.

In **"Yonec"** Marie uses the monologue to express the "imprisoned" wife's predicament and her thoughts (67-104). She laments her "destinee" that has her locked up in a room never to be free unless death should relieve her ("Ja n'en istrai si par mort nun," 70). She questions the old man's jealousy that keeps her even from going to hear mass. He must have been baptized in the "flum d'enfern," she speculates. She even curses her parents for having married her to him. At this point one might expect her to meditate some crime for her deliverance. Rather she wishes for the kind of magic escape to which ladies of old could resort in her country when "aventure" brought them "chevaliers" for lovers that only they could see:

> 'Si ceo peot estrë e ceo fu,
> Si unc a nul est avenu,

> Deu, ki de tut ad poësté,
> Il en face ma volenté!'
>
> (101-04)

This can only be the *lai* version of the "epic prayer" where the *chevalier* prays for his miracle citing biblical precedent as proof that it can be if God wills it. It is curious that the lady prays to God for a lover and even stranger when her hawk-lover appears. Aware of the extraordinary event and now frightened that the shape-changing hawk was not sent by God, the lady makes the hawk-lover go through a ceremony of the Eucharist to prove that he is not a fiend.

In **"Chaitivel"** the lady's ethical lament is of quite a different order. After she has watched her four lovers in the tourney and realizes that three are dead and the other wounded in such a way as to be a lover no longer, the lady laments:

> 'Lasse,' fet ele, 'quei ferai?
> Jamés haitie ne serai!
> Ces quatre chevalers amoue
> E chescun par sei cuveitoue;
> Mut par aveit en eus granz biens;
> Il m'amoënt sur tute riens.
> Pur lur beauté, pur lur prüesce,
> Pur lur valur, pur lur largesce
> Les fis d'amer [a] mei entendre;
> Nes voil tuz perdre pur l'un prendre.
>
> (147-56)

What Marie brings out most strikingly in the monologue is the subject of the lady's lament. She expresses no pity for the three that are dead and nothing for the wounded survivor. Her lament is that her great loss means that she will never be happy again.

In **"Eliduc"** the ethical question follows the Ovidian models rather closely. After revealing her plight to the chamberlain (337-50)—that she has fallen in love with the new mercenary of her father and must have him for a husband or die from grief—she sends word by her servant to Eliduc. During his absence she meditates on her situation:

> 'Lasse, cum est mis quors supris
> Pur un humme de autre païs!
> Ne sai s'il est de haut gent,
> Si s'en irat hastivement;
> Jeo remeindrai cume dolente.
> Folement ai mise m'entente.
> Unques mes ne parlai fors ier,
> E or li faz de amer preier.
> Jeo quid kë il me blamera;
> S'il est curteis, gre me savra;
> Ore est del tut en aventure.
> E si il n'ad de m'amur cure,
> Mut me tendrai [a] maubaillie;
> Jamés n'avrai joie en ma vie.'
>
> (387-400)

She laments that her heart has been taken over by a man from another country, the classic Ovidian situation. She does not even know if he is of the high nobility. If he leaves her quickly, she will remain in grief. She has set her heart on him even though she first spoke to him "ier." Now she is seeking his love actively! If he has no interest in her, she will be miserable the rest of her life.

This monologue reveals to the reader the state of mind of Guilladun. Clearly she is ready to give up everything for Eliduc. Like the women in Ovid's *Heroides* and *Metamorphoses* she can see that her decision is precipitate and unwise, placing her life's happiness in the power of someone who may not even be of her own station. Having this information revealed in monologue not only heightens the dramatic moment but it prepares one better for Guilladun's collapse. We understand the potential impact on her from the monologue and her expressed feeling that she would no longer have a reason to live without Eliduc.

At first glance one might expect to find more use of monologue and dialogue in the longer romances of the period. They are more imitative of history and they follow in the love traditions of Virgil and the medieval *Eneas*. But it has long been accepted that the *lai* differs from the *roman* in the quality of *aventure* that we encounter in each form. In the *roman* the hero seeks *aventure* and often succeeds in his *aventure* through his prowess and use of arms. The amorous theme of the *roman* is often closely linked to the knight's *aventure* and is dependent on the outcome. In Marie's *lais* the principal character, often a woman, has the *aventure* come to him (or her). The *aventure* is always closely linked to love and the outcome of that love is dependent upon the resolution of the *aventure*. But the resolution of the *aventure* does not depend on feats of arms; rather it is the result of personal decisions the characters make or of turns of event that reveal or force personal decisions. Because of this the monologue and dialogue have a much larger role proportionately in the *lai* than in the *roman*. Curiously, however, we have seen that Marie used the dialogue much more frequently than the monologue. This may well be the result of the brevity of the form. The greatest use of monologue is in the longest *lai*, "**Eliduc.**" But the use of dialogue for dramatic purpose and as a conclusive device is everywhere in the *lais*. This is probably attributable to the fact that the principal action of the *lai* often involves decisions made by someone that affects the life of another character. The resolution of both lives is effected by the decisions that are made. What better way for Marie to underscore and vivify the result and at the same time cause that moment to stand out than to have it played live before the reader as if it were transpiring then, as if we were hearing the voices of the characters at that very moment. Marie's narratives have long been

applauded for their timeless observations on human nature and for the fact that they seem timeless in their appeal. It is appropriate that Marie found a narrative technique that would give her works an immediacy of impact without divorcing them from that charming larger narrative frame listeners and readers have always loved, "Il y avait une fois [. . .]."

Notes

1. Appian, *Roman History,* trans. Horace White, 3 (Cambridge: Harvard Univ. Press, 2000; 1913), Book II, Chap. XI, pp. 361-65.

2. Livy, *Ab Urbe Condita,* trans. B. O. Foster, I (Cambridge: Harvard Univ. Press, 1988; 1919), Book I, Chap. LVIII, pp. 201-203.

3. Richer, *Histoire de France* (888-995), ed. and trans. Robert Latouche (Paris: Champion, 1930-37).

4. Apollonius of Rhodes wrote the first version of the *Argonautica* in Alexandria without much success. He gave a successful revised edition after he left Alexandria for Rhodes. He later returned to Alexandria as librarian at the famous Library of Alexandria in 196 B.C. The story of Jason and Medea inspired Virgil's narrative of Aeneas and Dido and various love stories in Ovid.

5. Ovid, *Heroides et Amores,* trans. Grant Showerman (Cambridge: Harvard Univ. Press, 1986), *Heroides* X, 1-152.

6. J. J. Salverda de Grave, ed., *Eneas. Roman du XIIe siècle,* 2 vols. (Paris: Champion, 1968), vol. II, 7938-40.

7. See my article, "Mercury's Philologia and Erec's Enide," *Romance Philology,* 56 (2002), pp. 1-22.

8. Marie de France, *Lais,* ed. Alfred Ewert (Oxford: Blackwell, 1965; 1944), vv. 185-87. All future citations of the *Lais* are from this edition.

9. It is noteworthy here that Marie innovates in having the man have the inner debate in monologue, something more often given to the woman in the Ovidian tradition.

Logan E. Whalen (essay date 2005)

SOURCE: Whalen, Logan E. "Marie de France and the Ancients." In "De sens rassis": *Essays in Honor of Rupert T. Pickens,* edited by Keith Busby, Bernard Guidot, and Logan E. Whalen, pp. 719-28. Amsterdam, The Netherlands: Rodopi, 2005.

[*In the essay below, Whalen suggests that Marie was like other writers of medieval French romances in her appropriation of ancient sources—in her case especially Roman rhetorical texts.*]

The three extant narrative texts of the twelfth-century Anglo-Norman poet, Marie de France, are marked with references that reveal a literary technique steeped in the tradition of classical rhetoric.[1] As Douglas Kelly has pointed out in *The Art of Medieval French Romance,* classical influence on medieval poets came through their training in the arts of poetry and prose: "The medieval arts of poetry and prose draw on learned and scholastic traditions of ancient, and especially Roman, origin. These traditions linked poetics to one or more of the Liberal Arts, especially grammar and rhetoric."[2]

Given the apparently important role that training in the arts of poetry and prose played in the development of twelfth- and thirteenth-century vernacular literature, an understanding of such instruction sheds light on the poetics of medieval authors who learned to write through their study of the "ancients" as appropriated by medieval grammarians, rhetoricians, and glossators. Moreover, such a study makes it possible to identify which parts of the grammatical or rhetorical paradigm a particular poet may have privileged over others, and the ways in which that aspect may have become essential to her or his own literary program. In the case of Marie de France, for example, certain textual references, especially throughout her prologues, suggest a propensity for the arts of *memoria* (memory) and *descriptio* (description).

The rhetoric of antiquity was available to medieval students through a broad selection of sources, but the surviving manuscripts from the period point to a privileged status for certain authorities such as the works of Cicero, the *Rhetorica ad Herennium,* and Priscian, to name but a few. If authors of literature in the Middle Ages were interested in keeping a textual tradition alive by assuring the transfer of material from a prior time to their own period, medieval compilers of the arts of poetry and prose were concerned with developing an instruction based on the classical divisions of rhetoric, while at the same time adapting it to fit the literary needs of their own students. What medieval authors gleaned from this instruction steeped in Roman tradition was an ability to gather material from pre-existing sources, shape that material in their imaginations, combine it with other previously collected material in the storehouse of memory, and mesh the disparate parts into a new work that was suitable for their audience. This process of medieval *inventio* may have found its fullest expression in the romances of Chrétien de Troyes and specifically through the technique of *conjointure,* his own word for the art of combining source material in a way that reveals the *ingenium* of the author. This poetic craft is present from the beginning of his literary career in his first work, *Erec et Enide.* But in this area, he must share the stage with his contemporary, Marie de France, as she exhibits the same talent, though within the textual boundaries of a significantly shorter genre, the *lai.*

While a detailed analysis of the *artes poeticae* as they existed in Antiquity and throughout the Middle Ages is beyond the scope and limits of this article,[3] a brief summary of the development of classical rhetoric and grammar and its eventual transmission into the treatises that codified the stages of medieval topical invention will nonetheless sketch the tradition from which Marie developed a unique mnemonic system of narrative. As the first woman to write in the French language, insofar as we know from the surviving evidence, she received training in the arts of poetry and prose rivaling that of her male counterparts, and commanded a marked apprehension of the use of elaborately constructed descriptions to ensure the memory of both textual and cultural artifacts.

Ciceronian rhetoric of Antiquity embodied five basic parts as outlined in the author's *De inventione*: invention (*inventio*), arrangement (*dispositio*), style (*elocutio*), memory (*memoria*), and delivery (*pronuntiatio*).[4] All of these divisions are included a few years later in the *Rhetorica ad Herennium,*[5] which James Murphy calls "one of the most influential books on speaking and writing ever produced in the Western world," adding that it can be regarded as "a complete textbook of rhetoric" (pp. 18-19). The *ad Herennium* also contains material not found in the *De inventione* such as the complete listing of "figures" (*exornationes*) of speech and thought,[6] and, as Murphy notes that "the section on *memoria* is the oldest extant treatment of the subject" (p. 19).

Memoria, though not first in the series of faculties listed, merits particular attention since without it the speaker would not be capable of *pronuntiatio* of the other faculties.[7] Indeed, the author stresses the significance of memory to the entire rhetorical process, suggesting that all other parts of composition fall into its domain.[8] This emphasis on memory may help to explain the importance allocated to it during the thirteenth century as treatises on the subject began to appear in significant numbers.

In the *ad Herennium,* memory is divided into two facets, natural and artificial.[9] Natural memory is that with which we are born, while artificial memory is that which we create through the use of figures and backgrounds. These backgrounds are mental grids in which images are arranged as though placing them within the rooms of an imaginary building. The author explains that the two systems work together, natural memory being used to call forth from the storehouse of artificial memory the images or figures that have been created and placed there, and artificial memory, in its turn, sharpening the innate ability of the person to remember material through training and discipline in the invention and placement of such images. The image functions as a marker of the object we wish to remember and must be placed in a background that will facilitate its recall.[10]

In light of this type of mnemonic exercise that is extolled in one of the best known works of ancient rhetoric that came down to the Middle Ages, it is not surprising that medieval authors should be concerned with creating narratives that exploit the association of images, often in the nature of the *merveille,* with ideas or lessons that they wished their audiences to remember. The popularity of the *Rhetorica ad Herennium* and the *De inventione* during the twelfth century makes it likely that an educated author like Marie de France, who was evidently well versed in the arts of poetry, as her works bear witness, had knowledge of them.[11] Her implementation of the technique is apparent on many occasions throughout her narratives, such as in the case of the androgynous hind that utters a prophetic discourse to the wounded knight in the *lai* of **"Guigemar."** In fact, this entire *lai* is an assembly of different stories that all revolve around the lovesick condition of the hero: the hunt for the stag, the episode where he discovers the lady enclosed in the castle by her jealous husband, and his separation from and eventual reuniting with his new love. Reading between the couplets, as it were, one can imagine that these episodes may have existed somewhere in past works before they were discovered by Marie, tucked away into her memory, and later brought forth and adapted to satisfy the preferences of her courtly public. Much in the same way that Chrétien ties together different episodes of his romances into a symmetrical whole, she meshes the segments of her tale into a congruous textual unit. By all accounts of its structure and themes, the *lai* of **"Guigemar"** wants to be a romance; it is, for all intents and purposes, a romance waiting to happen, in need only of *amplificatio* to free it from the aesthetic confines of its genre.

Grammar, another division of the Liberal Arts that was ultimately important to the development of vernacular literature in the Middle Ages, appears first in the list of the Trivium, with rhetoric often appearing in second place. Just as memory was vital to the discipline of rhetoric, it played a crucial role in the instruction of grammar. Martin Irvine has signaled a common preface to grammatical commentaries in which memory was indeed listed as one of the keys of wisdom.[12] He notes the significance of *grammatica* to the preservation of a written tradition from Antiquity through the medieval period: "Rather than one discipline among many, *grammatica* had an essentially constitutive function, making a certain kind of literacy and literary culture possible *per se.* Both the textual objects defined or constructed through grammatical discourse and the social relations

enacted and replicated through the institutional practice of the discipline are inscribed everywhere in medieval culture."[13] In its classical and then later medieval context grammar is not solely the study of language, as in the university classroom of our day; rather, as Murphy suggests, "it is first of all the science of speaking and writing correctly (*recte loquendi*),[14] and then the art of interpreting the poets (*enarratio poetarum*)."[15]

During the transitional period between Late Antiquity and the early Middle Ages, the study of grammar began to enjoy privileged expression as a tradition of its own, separate from that of rhetoric, beginning with the *Ars poetica* of Horace between 23 and 13 B.C., and then with the *Barbarismus* of Donatus around A.D. 350.[16] This tradition reached its apogee in the sixth century with Priscian's *Institutionum grammaticae,* of which there are over one thousand extant manuscripts. Murphy underscores the importance of this movement in relation to the epoch in which Marie composed her narratives by pointing out that "Donatus, Priscian, and their imitators, copyists, and commentators dominate grammatical instruction during the period up to A.D. 1200" (p. 139). It is no coincidence then that Marie de France mentions Priscian by name in her prologue: "Custume fu as anciëns, / ceo testimoine Preciëns" (Pr 9-10).[17]

The debt that medieval theories of grammar and rhetoric owe to the classical tradition is significant. The preceding account demonstrates the manner in which certain precepts within these first two branches of the Trivium made their way into the medieval practice of vernacular literary composition. Classical *artes poeticae* in general were adapted by, and found expression through, medieval grammarians and rhetoricians to accommodate the needs and usage of their contemporary literary practitioners, and certain aspects of classical grammar and rhetoric eventually became codified *mutatis mutandis* as medieval literary theory. The resulting Ciceronian-based theory as expounded in various treatises was the foundation of instruction for poets in the twelfth century, such as Marie de France, who not only perfected its implementation *in toto,* but also advanced certain elements of composition over others, developing a personal style of *inventio* that would be imitated in the following centuries.

Though the medieval rhetorical and grammatical paradigm of literary composition that developed from the epideictic art of the "ancients" represents a rather complex and somewhat diverse body of writing, the art of literary topical invention (*inventio*) as it was expressed in the Middle Ages can best be summed up by what Kelly has recognized as three primary stages: "First, the author has an idea or mental conception of a subject. Second, material is sought and identified through which the initial conception may find appropriate statement and elaboration. Third, the mental conception and the *materia* are meshed as the subject matter of the work" (p. 38).

As previously mentioned, *memoria* was an integral part of *inventio* as it was understood and practiced in the Middle Ages since the second stage of this process, the search for subject matter, depended heavily on the author's storehouse of memory. When quoting Alcuin's dialogue with Charlemagne, Mary Carruthers notes: "*Memoria* is a storehouse, custodian of invention and cogitation, of 'things' and 'words,' and without it, even the most eminent of the speaker's other talents will come to nothing."[18] This sentiment reflects that of the author of the *ad Herennium.*[19]

Within the context of the preceding remarks, it comes as no surprise that the General Prologue to Marie's *Lais* begins with an encomium of the act of literary composition. Like her reference to Priscian a few lines farther in the same prologue, these opening remarks justify her own poetic endeavor and place her squarely in the company of those who share the gift of eloquent composition:

> Ki Deus ad duné escïence
> E de parler bone eloquence
> Ne s'en deit taisir ne celer,
> Ainz se deit voluntiers mustrer.
> Quant uns granz biens est mult oïz,
> Dunc a primes est il fluriz,
> E quant loëz est de plusurs,
> Dunc ad espandues ses flurs.

(Pr 1-8)

Her own awareness of the arts of medieval poetry is evidenced by the juxtaposing of two of the most fundamental qualities of medieval literary invention as outlined earlier: the acquisition of material from acquired knowledge ("escïence" in the Old French), and the capacity to organize it and communicate it to an audience in "true eloquence" ("de parler bone eloquence").

The significance of verses 1-2 from the prologue of the *Lais,* most likely the earliest extant work composed by Marie de France,[20] cannot be overemphasized as it relates to the entire corpus of the poet. Not only do these verses recall the process of literary invention in general, but they also invoke two of the most salient aspects of her own poetics: memory and description. The reference to "escïence," or knowledge, points to *memoria,* for Marie clearly and consistently demonstrates that it is through her storehouse of memory that she has gained the knowledge necessary to create her own version of the tales that she assembles. One

example is her constant reference to the stories that she remembers from the Bretons, and which she in turn draws upon as sources to compose her *Lais,* short narrative texts that reveal a concern for creating images that will be easily retained in the imagination of her audience.

Likewise, the expression "de parler bone eloquence," or "to speak eloquently," refers not only to the technique of literary *inventio* as a whole, but in Marie's case it alludes especially to the art of *descriptio,* the rhetorical device that will permeate her narratives to follow. In essence, memory and description, two elements of medieval topical invention inherited from classical rhetoric by means of medieval training in the arts of poetry, are the hallmark of her style.

Certainly, though, Marie was not the only medieval poet of the twelfth century to make use of narrative description. The technique is fairly common in the *romans d'antiquité,* one example being the lengthy description of Carthage in the *Roman d'Eneas,* a twelfth-century French *translatio* of Virgil's *Aeneid.*[21] Furthermore, descriptions are ubiquitous in Chrétien's romances. His descriptive talents are evidenced in several ways: by the descriptions of persons such as the beauty of Cligés, or the ugliness of the hideous peasant in *Yvain*; by the descriptions of events like that of the knights' appearance in the "gaste forest" at the beginning of *Perceval*; and by the descriptions of objects such as Erec's coronation robe at the end of *Erec et Enide.*[22]

However, the striking feature of description in Marie's narratives that distinguishes her from her predecessors such as the authors of the *romans d'antiquité,* and from her contemporaries like Chrétien, is the amount of textual space allocated to its use in proportion to the rest of the narrative. Though she wrote in two of the shortest genres of the twelfth century, the *lai* and the fable, she nonetheless devoted significant segments of her texts to detailed descriptions. These textual embellishments are not mere aesthetic adornments, but rather become a crucial part of Marie's poetic design, as she deliberately uses the art of *descriptio* to construct a narrative architecture of memory that will facilitate the future recollection of important moral and didactic lessons posited in her texts.

Just as the works of the sixth-century grammarian Priscian bear witness to the literary "customs of the Ancients," Marie's corpus bears the transparent markings of a classical rhetoric inherited through training in the medieval arts of poetry and prose. Her own art of *inventio* intricately links *descriptio* and *memoria* through well-developed descriptions that are strategically intended to give substance to her thoughts, to create a visual representation no less significant than that of the written word. Her narrative art preserves the literary aesthetics of an ancient cultural tradition, while at the same time it fashions a new poetic voice for posterity.

Notes

1. I presented a preliminary version of this study as a paper in 2001 at the 58th Annual Convention of the South Central Modern Language Association in Tulsa, Oklahoma. My interest in Marie de France and rhetoric grew from independent studies with Rupert T. Pickens who advised me during my MA program at the University of Kentucky from 1989-92. I am honored to publish the article in this collection dedicated to my mentor, dear friend, and "plus que père."

2. Douglas Kelly, *The Art of Medieval French Romance* (Madison: Univ. of Wisconsin Press, 1992), p. 32.

3. For a detailed study on the development of rhetoric from Greece to Rome, to medieval Europe, and to the Renaissance see James Murphy, *Rhetoric in the Middle Ages* (Berkeley: Univ. of California Press, 1974). Edmond Faral offers a thorough investigation of the arts of poetry and prose in the twelfth and thirteenth centuries in *Les arts poétiques du XIIᵉ et du XIIIᵉ siècle: recherches et documents sur la technique littéraire du moyen âge* (Paris: Champion, 1924). For the most detailed analysis of the development of medieval French literary invention, stemming from the arts of poetry and prose as learned and implemented by medieval authors, see Kelly, *The Art of Medieval French Romance.*

4. See H. M. Hubbell, trans., *De inventione. De optimo genere oratorum. Topica,* Loeb Classical Library (Cambridge: Harvard Univ. Press, 1949). "Quare materia quidem nobis rhetoricae videtur artis ea quam Aristoteli visam esse diximus; partes autem eae quas plerique dixerunt, inventio, dispositio, elocutio, memoria, pronunciatio. Inventio est excogitatio rerum verarum aut veri similium quae causam probabilem reddant; dispositio est rerum inventarum in ordinem distributio; elocutio est indoneorum verborum ad inventionem accommodatio; *memoria est firma animi rerum ac verborum perceptio*; pronunciatio est ex rerum et verborum dignitate vocis et corporis moderatio" (I.vii.9; my emphasis here and throughout).

5. See Harry Caplan, trans., *[Cicero] Ad C. Herennium de ratione dicendi,* Loeb Classical Library (Cambridge: Harvard Univ. Press, 1954). "Oportet igitur esse in oratore inventionem, dispositionem, elocutionem, memoriam, pronuntiationem. Inventio est excogitatio rerum verarum aut veri similium quae causam probabilem reddant. Dispositio est ordo et distributio rerum, quae demonstrat quid quibus locis sit conlocandum. Elocutio est idoneorum verborum et sententiarum ad inventionem adcommodatio. *Memoria est firma animi rerum et verborum et dispositionis perceptio.* Pronuntiatio est vocis, vultus, gestus moderatio cum venustate" (I.ii.3). See also James Murphy, *Rhetoric in the Middle Ages* (Berkeley: Univ. of California Press, 1974) p. 19. He has pointed out that, "the discussion of *inventio* [in the *Ad Herennium*] is essentially the same as Cicero's, a fact that may account for the widespread medieval belief that Cicero was the author."

6. For a useful chart listing these figures and tropes see Murphy, p. 21.

7. *Ad Herennium,* "memoria est firma animi rerum ac verborum perceptio" (I.ii.3).

8. *Ad Herennium,* "Nunc ad thesaurum inventorum atque *ad omnium partium rhetoricae custodem,* memoriam, transeamus" (III.xvi.28).

9. *Ad Herennium,* "Sunt igitur duae memoriae: una naturalis, altera artificiosa. Naturalis est ea quae nostris animis insita est et simul cum cogitatione nata; artificiosa est ea quam confirmat inductio quaedam et ratio praeceptionis" (III.xvi.28).

10. *Ad Herennium,* "Imagines sunt formae quaedam et notae et simulacra eius rei quam meminisse volumus; quod genus equi, leonis, aquilae memoriam si volemus habere, imagines eorum locis certis conlocare oportebit" (III, xvi, 29).

11. See Murphy, p. 109. He records their appearance in medieval library catalogues during the twelfth century: thirteen times for the *Rhetorica ad Herennium* and thirty-two times for Cicero's *De inventione.*

12. Martin Irvine, *The Making of Textual Culture: 'Grammatica' and Literary Theory, 350-1100* (Cambridge: Cambridge Univ. Press, 1994), p. 461. "Quot sunt claves sapientie?.V. Que? Assiduitas legendi, *memoria retinendi,* sedulitas interrogandi, contemptus diviciarum, honor magistri."

13. Irvine, p. xiv. For the development and divisions of *grammatica,* ca.350-ca.1150, see the chart in Irvine, p. 6.

14. Murphy uses the term *loquendi* to refer to both reading and writing because Quintilian explains that the two are connected: "Nam et scribendi ratio coniuncta cum loquendo est [. . .]" (I.iv.3).

15. Murphy, pp. 24-25. See H. E. Butler, trans., *The Institutio Oratio of Quintilian,* Loeb Classical

Library, 4 vols. (Cambridge: Harvard Univ. Press, 1920-22). Quintilian's *Institutio oratoria* makes this distinction in A.D. 92: "Haec igitur professio, cum brevissime in duas partes dividatur, recte loquendi scientiam et poetarum enarrationem" (I.iv.2). See also Murphy, pp. 22-26 for a thorough discussion of Quintilian as he relates to the art of grammar.

16. See Murphy, pp. 42-88. He discusses in detail the transition of rhetoric and grammar from their classical expressions to their medieval manifestations.

17. Unless otherwise noted, all references to the *Lais* are from the edition of Jean Rychner, *Les Lais de Marie de France* (Paris: Champion, 1983). I adopt his abbreviation for the title of the General Prologue: Pr.

18. *The Book of Memory: A Study of Memory in Medieval Culture* (Cambridge: Cambridge Univ. Press, 1990), p. 144.

19. See note 8.

20. Although it has not been possible to date with certainty the three extant works of Marie de France—*Lais, Fables,* and *Espurgatoire Saint Patrice*—it is commonly accepted scholarly opinion that they were all composed during the last half of the twelfth century in that order.

21. See verses 407-548 in J.-J. Salverda De Grave, ed., *Le Roman d'Eneas* (Paris: Champion, 1925-29).

22. Claude Luttrell and Stewart Gregory, eds., *Cligès* (Cambridge: D. S. Brewer, 1993), beginning at 2741. Wendelin Foerster, ed., *Yvain. Le chevalier au lion* (Manchester: Manchester Univ. Press, 1942; rpt. 1967), 288-326. Keith Busby, ed., *Le Roman de Perceval ou Le Conte du Graal* (Tübingen: Niemeyer, 1993), beginning at 69. Wendelin Foerster, ed., *Erec et Enide* (Halle: Niemeyer, 1934), beginning at 6713.

H. Marshall Leicester, Jr. (essay date 2005)

SOURCE: Leicester, Jr., H. Marshall. "The Voice of the Hind: The Emergence of Feminine Discontent in the *Lais* of Marie de France." In *Reading Medieval Culture: Essays in Honor of Robert W. Hanning,* edited by Robert M. Stein and Sandra Pierson Prior, pp. 132-69. South Bend, Ind.: University of Notre Dame Press, 2005.

[*In the following essay, Leicester contends that Marie's lays sequentially and cumulatively demythologize romance through the intrusion of medieval social convention and public opinion in the "voice of the hind"—representative of female discontent and counter to male fantasy. The critic traces this voice from its first appearance in "Guigemar" throughout the lays, illustrating Marie's emphasis on women's attempts to escape male solidarity, manipulation, and domination.*]

In this essay I want to suggest some protocols for a way of reading the *Lais* of Marie de France. I will focus on a certain voice that can intermittently be found in them, and an anamorphosis, or displaced angle of viewing/reading, that is, I think, potentially transformative for the interpretation of the individual *lais* and the collection as a whole. In keeping with my title, I call the perspective I have in mind "the voice of the hind" and begin the analysis with an examination of that curious magical figure, at once central and marginal to the action, in **"Guigemar" ("G.")**.

I

Immediately after we have been introduced to the hero of the *lai,* his country, lineage, upbringing, and unnatural indifference to love ("G." 1-68), he is seized by a desire to hunt; and in the course of his hunting, he encounters the game that will change his life: "Tute fu blaunche cele beste, / Perches de cerf ont en la teste" ("G." 91-92; A completely white beast, / With deer's antlers on her head). Firing at her, Guigemar is himself wounded by the rebound of his arrow; and as both hunter and prey lie wounded, the hind begins to speak:

> "Oï! Lase! Jo sui ocise!
> E tu, vassal, ki m'as nafree,
> Tel seit la tue destinee:
> Jamais n'aies tu medecine,
> Ne par herbe, ne par racine!
> Ne par mire, ne par poisun
> N'avras tu jamés garisun
> De la plaie k'as en la quisse,
> De si ke cele te guarisse
> Ki suffera pur tue amur
> Issi grant peine e tel dolur
> K'unkes femme taunt ne suffri,
> E tu referas taunt pur li;
> Dunt tuit cil s'esmerveillerunt
> Ki aiment e amé avrunt
> U ki pois amerunt aprés.
> Va t'en de ci, lais m'aveir pés!"
>
> ("G." ["Guigemar"] 106-22)

"Alas, I'm dying!
And you, vassal, who wounded me,
this be your destiny:
may you never get medicine for your wound!
Neither herb nor root,
neither physician nor potion
will cure you
of that wound in your thigh,
until a woman heals you,
one who will suffer out of love for you,

pain and grief
such as no woman ever suffered before.
And out of love for her, you'll suffer as much;
the affair will be a marvel
to lovers, past and present
and to all those yet to come.
Now go away, leave me in peace!"

It is striking that, after this dense and extended presentation, noticeable in so relatively short a poem from a
writer typically committed to bald statement and narrative economy, the hind disappears, never to be seen
again. She is an early example of what might be called
"conspicuous *surplus*," a richly suggestive source of
potential signification that is linked (in Marie's Prologue
to the ***Lais***) to what the ancients left undeveloped in the
matiere they handed down to us, and linked as well (in
the lovemaking of Guigemar and his lady) to the *jouissance,* as well as the *solas,* of eros. Though, as I'll
argue, her voice resonates throughout the collection,
narratively the hind is the merest device to move the
plot of the *lai* forward, killed off, as she herself notes,
to set the hero on the path to love. As a magic talking
animal, she is a marker of Romance, one of those
manifestations from the Other World who tell us that
our lives are allegories of love. She is there to take a
complex but determinate part in Guigemar's self-
reflexive wounding, the stalking-deer of what will turn
out to have been his discovery of desire; and she is
there to tell him the kind of story he is in, the particular
bundle of romance clichés about faithful love and suffering that will turn out to have made him memorable
to the *Bretun.* The hind is burdened with and occluded
by the Symbolic, the discourse that has always already
structured our experience of the Real; and she is
therefore a hapless bearer of the future anterior, the
known-before-it-happens.

What I find most interesting about the hind, however, is
her resistance to being made the vehicle of so much
portentousness, whether of the romantic *Bretun* or of
poststructural psychoanalytical me. The resistance is
most concentrated, perhaps, in her final bitter dismissal
of Guigemar, "Va t'en de ci, lais m'aveir pés!" Hovering somewhere between relief at the discharge of her
obligatory message and a need to be alone with the
pain her involvement in this man's affairs has caused
her, the comment adds a different sort of *surplus,* a tone
of what we now call "attitude," to her narrative function, stressing her detachment from it, her dislike of it
and of those responsible for it, and her independence in
a kind of suffering the message itself does not declare.
It is a sentiment that can be heard to echo behind situations as superficially diverse as those of the lady in
"Yonec" and of Guildeluec in **"Eliduc,"** although it is
only glancingly relevant to anyone else in **"Guigemar"**.[1]

But once we begin to attend to it, the ways the hind
exceeds her place in this *lai* begin to multiply. Her
horns and her fawn mark an instability of gender
identity at once powerfully tempting to interpretation—
I'll resist for now—and difficult to bring home very
clearly to the story of Guigemar. More immediately
productive is the fact that her prediction of what will
happen to the hero does not quite jibe with the course
of the story. At a very general level, the question of
whether the love and suffering Guigemar and his lover
feel and undergo for each other are really such as were
never seen before and a marvel to lovers for all time is
at least subject to debate and interpretation. To take it
seriously, rather than as an instance of the general
romance category into which adventures of this kind
fall, would need at least as much interested contestation
as, say, the question of whether a given woman is really
better—"De cors, de vis e de beauté, / De enseignement
e de bunté" (**"Lanval"** 301-2)—than Guenevere or not.
More immediately, however, the abduction of the hind
and her wound into the Symbolic is marked by the
bodily *surplus* the change of register leaves behind.
That is, the hind and Guigemar both begin with real
physical injuries, however framed by marvels, and the
hind is left, as far as we know, to die of hers. For Guigemar, however, his injury is quite rapidly transformed
into the wound of love, a metaphorical illness whose
physical register ("plaie dedenz cors / E si ne piert
nïent defors": "a wound in the body, / and yet nothing
appears on the outside," **"G."** 483-84) enters into
discourse and is subject to its processes, like the boasting of "vilain curteis" and the laws of feudal service
(**"G."** 485-95). Though it takes several hundred lines
for this transformation to be completed in the plot of
the *lai,* Guigemar already has it fully under rhetorical
control by the time he first wakes up to tell his story to
the lady of the tower. He has received such a wound, he
tells her:

> Jamés ne quid estre sané.
> La bise se pleinst e parlat:
> Mut me maudist, e si urat
> Que ja n'eüsse guarisun
> Si par une meschine nun,
> Ne sai u ele seit trovee.
>
> (**"G."** 320-24)

. . . I've given up hope of being cured.
The hind complained and spoke to me,
cursed me, swore
that I'd never be healed
except by a girl;
I don't know where she might be found.

The leading nature of this recital is confirmed a moment later with the mock-innocence of Guigemar's
conclusion, "Bele dame, pur Deu vus pri, / Cunseillez
mei, vostre merci!" ("Beautiful one, I beg you for God's
sake, please advise me!" **"G."** 533-34). The lady shows

that she has understood the message behind the narrative by launching at once into an impassioned denunciation of her husband (**"G."** 336-58). She then conceals Guigemar from the husband and his agents using surplus food saved from her own meals (**"G."** 375-79), and waits for him to heal.

"De sa plaie nul mal ne sent" (**"G."** 383). Henceforward the healing of the physical wound takes a back seat to the developing love between the two protagonists, a process the *lai* follows with loving attention to the psychological and rhetorical skill the lovers use in deploying their affecting conventional laments to themselves and each other, and the "brief debate," whose "delightfully spurious reasoning," as Hanning and Ferrante note (p. 57), brings them together. I mean this disenchanted summary to suggest the extent to which the *lai* attends to its characters less as innocent embodiments of an experience of "falling in love," which happens to be expressed in the conventional forms and style of twelfth-century romance, than as knowledgeable users and performers of those conventions. Guigemar is, of course, looking for shelter and for tending for his wound, but he is aware of where such things are likely to lead in the circumstances; he may well be aware also, since he is used to being propositioned ("Plusurs l'en [d'amer] requistrent suvent" **"G."** 63), that his charms—"sages e pruz" (**"G."** 43) as he is—are his strongest cards in winning help. The lady, similarly, at least knows that this pitiable and handsome young man is more interesting than anything else going on in her life at the moment.[2] It is not necessary to make these people deliberately calculating in order to register the deftness of their practical consciousness of how to "go on" in conventionally recognizable situations. One might put it rather that, like Le Fresne, they can make effective improvisatory use of the signifying resources of their world and its furniture, and, like Equitan, can put themselves in the way of occasions of desire without having to take full note of their own agency in the matter.

Such a perspective, one that attends to various forms of narrative and descriptive *surplus* in the *lais* as traces of the material interests and agency of the social actors within them, allows one of the central themes of the collection: the examination of the uses of stories, to be read as Marie de France's psychology and socioanthropology of her culture's technologies of desire. The conventions, narremes, and tropes, the exquisite pains and elegant marvels of *fin amor* and romance are represented in the poem as techniques people use to negotiate their interests in the register of desire and to negotiate their desires in accordance with their interests. What justifies my characterization of Marie's project in such general and abstract terms is precisely the systematic and cumulative character of the representation; and this will bring us back to the hind.

Guigemar and his lady build their romance by a kind of Freudian *Anlehnung* on a real physical wound that is symbolized and transcended, leaving its literal and bodily character and consequences back with the hind. The pattern is a general one in the *lai*, a pattern set up even before the hind appears in it, insofar as the poem begins with an extended account of historical, geographical, genealogical, and political detail—King Hoel of Leonnais and his vassal Oridial; the mother and sisters, education and travels of the latter's son Guigemar—which is never used again. One effect of making the episode with the hind the point of transition for the journey to the Other World (which is to say the abstraction into romance of what might otherwise be, say, a story about a problem of feudal succession and the provision of an heir)[3] is that it sets up the borderline between the Real of the body and its Symbolic representations as the site of a *gendered* differentiation in the experience of eros and its difficulties, which is then played out in the rest of the *lais*. That is, the difference I have been developing between the hind's real experience of bodily rupture and Guigemar's complex interpretive engagement with an increasingly symbolized lack, is the first instance in the **Lais** of a consistently developed difference in the way the structuring of desire weighs on women and on men.

Many of the Francophone writers of the early courtly period,[4] in taking notice of the derangements, in both fields, that arise from linking the circulation of economic resources to the vicissitudes of erotic life—the aspect of arranged marriage as the main material source of *fin amor*—take note as well of the fact that the burdens of these derangements fall more heavily on women. In **"Guigemar,"** this differential appears most plainly in the careers of Guigemar and his lady after their affair is discovered and he is expelled by her husband. It is not simply that she must wait and he must seek, in accordance with general romance stereotypes. To begin with, it is noticeable that Guigemar does *not* seek for her, and it is made more noticeable by the energy with which he engages in the politics of renouncing his fealty, raising an army, and conducting a siege to regain her once his hand has been forced by her rediscovery and the issues of male and feudal competition imported into the story by Meriaduc (**"G."** 840-80). The knotted shirt that is the sign of his attachment to her is, unlike the knotted belt from him that she wears, detachable. Guigemar has a special officer, "Un chamberlenc . . . / Ki la chemise ot a garder" ("A chamberlain . . . / who was in charge of the shirt," **"G."** 796-97), who produces it on demand (I imagine a silken pillow) for the widely famed social occasions when "Il n'i ad dame ne pucele," throughout Brittany, "Ki n'i alast pur asaier" ("all the women and girls came to try their luck," **"G."** 652-53).[5] One cannot help noticing that this ritual supplies Guigemar with a perfect excuse for continuing to live in the way that he did before he met the hind, but now without the criticisms for indifference to love that he received before, and apparently without pressure to marry. The possibility that the shirt has more significance for him as a convenient symbolic defense against unwanted involvements in the present than as a living trace of the lady herself is strengthened by the fact that Guigemar does not recognize her when she does turn up, even after she has successfully undone the knot (**"G."** 801-14).

In order to convince himself that it is really she, Guigemar invokes a signifier of identity that sticks to the lady the way the wound sticks to the hind—and it is not a belt: "'Lessiez mei vostre cors veeir!'" ("'Let me see your body!'" **"G."** 818). This "request" is made in open court, and not for the first time.[6] The lady wears Guigemar's belt under her clothes, and it apparently serves as a physical warden of her chastity, since it frustrates Meriaduc's attempt to rape her:

> Il [Meriaduc] la receit entre ses braz,
> De sun bliaut trenche les laz:
> La ceinture voleit ovrir,
> Mes n'en poeit a chief venier
>
> (737-40)
>
> He took her in his arms,
> cut the laces of her tunic.
> and tried to open the belt.
> But he didn't succeed.[7]

If this assault is, as one hopes, at least conducted in private, the brief but startling account of Meriaduc's reaction to his failure sounds like an all-too-public way of socializing his losses: "Puis n'ot el païs chevalier / Que il n'i feïst essaier" (**"G."** 741-42), "There wasn't a knight in the region / Whom he didn't summon to try his luck." The *lai* consistently focuses on both the invasive publicity of the lady's exposure and the apparent failure of the characters to remark it.

In **"Guigemar"** the insistence of a woman's body as a marker for the actuality of female oppression, begun in the episode of the hind and kept running in the adventures of the belt, is not directly acknowledged. Along with the other forms of more realistic political violence that start to push through the surface of a happy ending—delayed just a little too long—the situation of Guigemar's lady remains mostly tacit, a *surplus* that presses on the margins of the romance plot. The further progress of the **Lais** can be read as the gradual explicit rendering of this theme in the central characters and action, thereby giving body and voice in the tales

to a perspective we first bruited in the hind. **"Guigemar"** already suggests Marie's sense of the unbalanced construction of gender roles in her society, such that the dominant (or in our current jargon, hegemonic) view of feminine protest, where it is not simply disregarded, is negative. The practical consequence in the early **Lais** is that the voice of the hind is given to what are, in conventional terms, "bad girls": the seneschal's wife in **"Equitan,"** the mother in **"Le Fresne,"** the werewolf's wife in **"Bisclavret,"** and Guenevere in **"Lanval."** I will attempt to move quickly through the first three of these, before looking more closely at the queen.

II

One implication of male ideological domination of romance as a technology of desire is that the *Bretun* who supplied Marie with her material were, mostly unconsciously, male chauvinists, and this prejudice is nowhere more evident than in **"Equitan"** (**"Eq."**). The basic story of the plot by a wife and her lover to kill her husband is close enough to modern tales like *Double Indemnity* and *The Postman Always Rings Twice* to warrant its characterization as a *lai noir*, especially when that plot is enacted in an atmosphere of obsessive and slightly perverse sexuality. The poem concentrates on powerful bodily sensations in a way unique in medieval literature, first in its association of the lovers' sexual trysts with Equitan's practice of being bled, and then by the *amour fou* of their impulsive sexual embrace on the husband's bed when the latter steps out of the room,[8] leading, on his return, to the immediate deaths by scalding that their action courts. Equitan is a pursuer of intense experiences at the boundaries of pleasure and pain, and he does so in the company of what looks like a classic *femme fatale*. Hanning and Ferrante take note of the "doggedly didactic tone" of the *lai* (p. 69); and though most of their paraphrase of the poem's stern moralizing concentrates, quite properly, on Equitan, the poem begins by sketching a recognizably *noir* apportionment of blame. Equitan is one whose love "n'unt sen ne mesure" (**"Eq."** 18, is "without sense or moderation"), but everyone knows that it is the nature ("mesure,") of love "Que nuls n'i deit reisun garder" (**"Eq."** 20, "that no one involved with it can keep his head"); and if we are looking for the cause of the great public damage that arose from this affair, "Femme espuse ot li seneschals / Dunt puis vint el païs granz mals" (**"Eq."** 29-30: "This seneschal took a wife / through whom great harm later came to the kingdom"). After all, before that unlucky marriage and its exciting consequences, Equitan pursued his hunting and hawking in peace, and the seneschal took—the poem spends four lines on it—excellent care of the kingdom.

I take this moralized plot and its lesson to be the *lai* the *Bretun* made of the *aventure* they heard. In the virtual origin the poem projects, the story takes both its didactic tendency and its covert prurience from the guilty fantasies of the folk imagination; and the structure it gave to those events was relayed to Marie, though she heightens both tendencies to the point of discomfort as a way of stressing them. Her own *relais,* however, presses back against the overt moralizing of the official surface of the tale to reimagine the *aventure* in the discursive detail of its dramatization. As with Meriaduc and Guigemar, Equitan's homosocial relationship with the seneschal (which in this case, as noted, predates the advent of the wife) is foregrounded, first by the fact that the king desires her ("la coveita," a word the Decalogue itself applies to a neighbor's goods as well as his wife) sight unseen ("**Eq.**" 41). The *lai* next focuses on the deliberation with which Equitan plans his hunting trip to put himself in the way of an encounter with his vassal's wife ("**Eq.**" 43-50), so that when he begins his stock love-soliloquy with "'Allas, fet il queils destinee / M'amenet en ceste cuntree?'" ("**Eq.**" 65-66: "'Alas,' he says, 'what destiny / led me to these parts?'"), its performed and self-serving character is evident. This framing context brings forward, as well, how much more the soliloquy is focused on the seneschal than on the lady, and the extent to which it is transgression and the prospect of its discovery rather than her actual erotic attractions that excite him, since that prospect is its main theme. By the end of the passage, it is clear that if the *Bretun* were inclined to blame the lady for this *aventure,* they took their cue from Equitan, who is the first (in this story anyway) to blame the insatiable sexuality of a woman he knows nothing about for his own desire: "'Suls ne la peot il pas tenir[9] / Certes, jeo voil a li partir!'" ("**Eq.**" 87-88: "'he certainly can't hold her all by himself, / and I'm happy to share the burden with him!'").

It is this persistent concentration on the aggressive agency that Equitan cloaks in the performance of abject *fin amor,* that makes the lady's responses to him into the voice of the hind rather than the cold calculation of a *femme fatale.* She registers with complete clarity the power differential between them, the freedom it gives to his situation, and, with the hind's savvy about how things go, the anxieties that must beset hers:

> "Vus estes reis de grant noblesce;
> Ne sui mie de teu richesce
> Qu'a mei vus deiez arester
> De druërie ne d'amer.
> S'aviez fait vostre talent,
> Jeo sai de veir, ne dut nïent,
> Tost m'avrïez entrelaissiee
> J'en sereie mut empeiriee."
>
> ("**Eq.**" 121-28)
>
> "You're a king of high nobility,
> and I'm not at all of such fortune
> that you should single me out
> to have a love affair with.

> If you get what you want from me
> I have no doubt of it:
> you'll soon get tired of me,
> and I'll be far worse off than before."

Her assessment is entirely correct. Because we know that he does not really mean it, Equitan's counter to her appraisal of the class (and gender) difference between them—"Ne me tenez mie pur rei, / Mes pur vostre humme e vostre ami. . . . Vus seiez dame e jeo servanz, / Vus orguilluse e jeo preianz" (*Eq.* 170-71, 175-77: "Don't think of me as your king, / but your vassal and your lover. . . . You be the lord and I'll be the servant—You be the proud one and I'll be the beggar")—sounds like his fantasy of a role-reversal sex game. I suggested earlier that Equitan's intensest *jouissance* (with typical concentration on sensation, the text notes what makes him "trembler," 69, and his "friçuns," 109) comes from self-dramatizing his transgressions, in a flirtation with discovery. The lovers' exchange of rings after the wife gives in ("**Eq.**" 181), surely likely to be noticed by her husband, continues this practice, as does the king's aggressive refusal to wed, which draws—which is *meant* to draw—the attention and protest of his people ("**Eq.**" 197-201).[10] Thus, by the time she speaks again, the text's concentration on her anxiety brings out, in a situation where she must make the best of a coerced intimacy with no other resource than the king's pleasure, how little of her own pleasure the wife gets from it, as opposed to the complex pleasures Equitan does:

> Quant ele pout a lui parler
> E el li duit joie mener,
> Baisier, estreindre e acoler,
> E ensemblë od lui juer,
> Forment plura e grant deol fist.
>
> ("**Eq.**" 205-9)
>
> So when she next had the chance to speak to him—
> when she should have been full of joy,
> kissing and embracing him
> and having a good time with him [od lui juer][11]—
> she burst into tears, making a big scene.

The plot to murder the husband that arises from the wife's statement of her anxiety is proposed to her by Equitan: "'Si vostre sire fust finez, / Reïne e dame vus fereie'" ("**Eq.**" 226-27, "'If your husband were dead, / I'd make you my lady and my queen'"). When she dutifully comes up with the details, the exchange between them reads as a series of attempts on her part to gain the security of some admission of complicity from him ("Legier serait a purchacier [her husband's death], / Pur ceo k'il li vousist aidier" "**Eq.**" 236-37, emphasis added: "It would be easy to arrange / *if he were willing to help her*"). However, she is frustrated by the bland cruelty of his refusals of complicity: "Ja cele *rien ne li dirrat* / Que il ne face *a sun poeir,"* ("**Eq.**" 238-39, "there was *nothing she could demand of him* / that he wouldn't do, *if he possibly could*," emphasis added); and "Li reis li ad tut *graanté* [as if she had asked him a favor] / Qu'il en ferat *sa volonté*" ("**Eq.**" 261-62, "The king promised her / that he'd do *just as she wished*," emphasis added).[12]

At the end of the *lai,* Equitan engineers the culmination of his pleasure in dramatizing his malfeasances, his hatred and contempt of himself for doing these things and of others for letting him get away with them, his delight in taking chances and in intense sensations, and the power of his love and hatred for the seneschal—all bound up in the advance planning and controlled improvisation that sends him into the tub of boiling water. In tending so carefully to his own poetic justice, Equitan would seem to have evoked from the *Bretun* pretty much the response he sought: "Tels purcace le mal d'autrui / Dunt tuz li mals revert sur lui" ("**Eq.**" 309-10, "he who plans evil for another / may have that evil rebound back on him"), making himself into an example for the ages of a wickedness to savor and denounce.[13] What escapes this wrap-up in Marie's telling, and in the oddly suspended last line of the *lai,* is the sense she develops of the wife as the stalking-horse and victim of the king's project, made so by his power, his malice, and his indifference to her, "la dame ki tant l'ama" ("**Eq.**" 314, "the lady who loved him so much").

III

Both of the women who carry the voice of the hind in the next two *lais* in the collection share with the wife in **"Equitan"** this feeling of being caught out on a limb, surrounded and overwhelmed by the forces of social convention and public opinion. Indeed, the lady who will become the mother of Le Fresne brings about her own humiliation through her ill-judged invention, "oant tute sa gent" ("**Le Fresne**" ["**LeF.**"] 30, "for all her household to hear"), of an improbable and slanderous sex-fact that is also sufficiently compelling as gossip to circulate throughout Brittany ("**LeF.**" 49-52). As a result, "Mut en fu la dame haïe" ("**LeF.**" 53, "The slanderous wife was hated for it") by every woman who heard the story, and by her husband as well.

This instance of Marie's interest in how stories get started and how they circulate is glossed by the circumstances of her story's invention and reception. The imprudent factoid—that the conception of twins is caused by intercourse with more than one man—is generated by the very public generosity of a neighbor knight whose wife has just borne twin boys and who sends a messenger to tell his neighbor, surrounded by his household at dinner, that he will name one of them after him and give it to him to foster. The neighbor's way of announcing his good fortune, "Que sa femme ad

deus fiz eüz: / *De tant de force esteit creüz*" ("that his wife had had two sons— / *by so much was his power increased,*" translation altered and emphasis added), is crucial to understanding the situation. This is a *don contraignant* or prestation, an aggressive gift that enforces social subordination and imposes an obligation, as the receiver-lord's immediate attempt to hold his place in the potlatch by rewarding the messenger with a "bel cheval" confirms ("**LeF.**" 23-24).[14] It is another instance of the way men in the world of these poems use their women to play power games with each other; and the wife's attack on the other messenger of this aggression, the neighbor's wife—because it strikes indirectly but powerfully at the imputedly cuckolded husband—*blows the cover* of a social transaction everyone else is trying to keep tacit. Her own husband's potential difficulties with his neighbor are reason enough for his response; but the hostility of "tutes les femmes" is testimony to their awareness of the social power of even so implausible a tale. Thus their hostility is readily traceable to the way the wife's story threatens to make them even more vulnerable than they already are to the unpredictability of their own bodies and to the rumor-mill in the game of shame and dishonor. The wife notes as much, in the voice of the hind, in the complaint she delivers when, conceiving twins in her turn, she is betrayed by her own biology to the consequences of her story: "'Mis sire e tuz sis parentez / Certes jamés ne me crerrunt, / Des que ceste aventure orrunt'" ("**LeF.**" 76-78, "'My lord and all his kin / will never believe me / when they hear about this bad luck'").

The rest of the *lai* details the steps that are taken over the course of a generation to contain the effects of this too-open-speaking and to return the management of conflict to the level of the tacit. The poem is in large part about noble female support networks and the manipulation of symbolic objects, and it celebrates the cultural resources—everything from a convenient wet nurse to a bishop in one's pocket—that allow the negotiation of interests and desires through deals and exchanges of real and symbolic capital.[15] This is not the place for a full reading of the *lai*; let it suffice to note the most complex moment in the poem: when Le Fresne places the unique birth-garment, whose provenance her guardian-abbess has told her, on the marital bed that is about to receive her lover Gurun and his new bride, her unacknowledged sister La Codre. As the text makes clear, this is a triumph of practical consciousness. Le Fresne need tell herself and others no more than that the coverlet the servants had placed there "N'ert mie bons, ceo li sembla" ("**LeF.**" 401, "it seemed to her poor stuff"). The rest can be left to luck, supported by the powerful network of significations the cloth carries and participates in.

Nor is it only her mother and sister who are potentially to be caught up in the weave of this symbolic nexus. What if Le Fresne has shared something of what she knows about the cloth—whatever that is—with Gurun? What message will it carry to him when he brings his bride to bed and finds it there? Does not the coverlet hang suspended between moral blackmail, reminding him and others of how he has treated the previous occupant of this bed, and the veiled threat of how much trouble might still be made by the woman, intimate enough in his life to have put the cloth there, who has—so far—chosen not to make it?"[16] The aggressive deployment of innocence and virtue shadowed here is, like the other instances of potential conflict in the tale, not allowed to emerge into the open scandal Fresne's mother incautiously provoked.[17] But Fresne's garment barely covers the world of such things as marital tension and status competition, the disposal of inconvenient daughters, the collusion of guardians in the sale of mistresses, and the expedient annulment of inexpedient marriages. One might put it that the garment is a cover story that allows the appearance of moral resolution in an objectively amoral world. It is Fresne's ability to keep the insistent pressure of this world both present and tacit that enables her to manipulate it so brilliantly, since, as her mother's rash sounding of the voice of the hind shows, it is just such carefully maintained universal silence about what they are really doing that allows everyone to keep on doing it.

IV

Marie's reading of women's situation in the *Lais* emerges sequentially and cumulatively. The meaning of the fate of the werewolf's wife in **"Bisclavret"** (**"Bisc."**) comes clear in the light of the demythologizing context supplied for its romance events by the previous poems in the collection. The surface of the tale is implacably stacked against her; but, as early as her initial questioning of her husband's absences, we can find some intertextual support for a more mundane, and more interesting, reading of her situation. Hanning and Ferrante note that the *lai* "prompts our initial sympathy with the wife's reaction of fear and loathing when she learns that her husband is [a werewolf]" (p. 101); and certainly her reported reaction—"Ne voleit mes lez lui gesir" (**"Bisc."** 102, "she never wanted to sleep with him again")—supplies one of the *lai*'s characteristically infrequent but telling touches of emotion and action connected to the immediacy of the body; although one notes, as well, its purchase in domestic rather than public life.

This response to her husband's potential savagery, however, is balanced by the implications of his more domesticated inflection of wolf nature.[18] When her husband informs her that what he does in wolf-form is

to go hunting, we have at a minimum the previous examples of Guigemar and Equitan to remind us that men in the world of these poems do not need the impetus of lycanthropy to absent themselves for days on end from the society of their women. We can even suspect that the wife's discontent might not be hers alone: "Mes d'une chose ert grant ennui, / Qu'en la semeine le perdeit / Tres jurs entiers, qu'el ne saveit / U deveneit ne u alout" (**"Bisc."** 24-27: "but one thing was very vexing to her: / during the week he would be missing / for three whole days, and she didn't know / what happened to him or where he went").[19]

I find one of the most striking features of this *lai* to be the considerable time it spends narrating the initial conversation between the couple, in which both announce themselves reluctant to speak their true feelings to the other for fear of losing love (**"Bisc."** 29-62). I see the passage as a recuperation of many of the odd silences, conspicuous omissions, and unexplained bits of pregnant behavior throughout the *lais* that are so characteristic a feature of Marie's laconic style, because, if we let the scene speak beyond its immediate place here, it allows us to bring these gaps home to the characters whenever they occur. Things that might otherwise have to be ascribed to ineptitude or the conventions of fable and romance become more compelling if they are seen as the symptoms of a world in which people have fairly good, if not fully formulated, practical intimations of what they are doing to one another and even better reasons for not acknowledging these intimations to themselves or others. Such a perspective, for example, adds further complexity and bite to the already complex political reasons for Eliduc's continuing refusal or inability, in the final *lai* of the collection, to reveal to Guilliadun that he is married. That said, **"Bisclavret"** demonstrates in spades the uneven distribution of pressures and consequences for men and women of acting on one's feelings. "If I told you who I really am or how I really feel, you would leave me" needs to be qualified by the realities of social power to include the rider "if you could." The balance of the story is given over to a demonstration of just how hard it is for a woman to escape a husband with whom she can no longer bear to sleep.[20]

From this perspective, it is not so much the particular details of the mechanism that will strand her husband in werewolf form that ask for attention, suggestive though those are, as it is the alliance the wife has to accept in order to carry them out. It is true that **"Bisclavret"** shares with **"Le Fresne"** a world of latent cultural resources that can be activated at need: there is always a courtly lover pining in the wings for his turn. However, the way the poem spends time on the wife's dealings with a man—"Ele ne l'aveit unc amé / Ne de s'amur aseüré" (**"Bisc."** 107-8, "She'd never loved him at all, / nor pledged her love to him"), not only offering him her body and her love but extracting an oath from him and then, as it were in return, marrying him,[21]—stresses how much trouble she has to take, and how much she has to agree to in an attempt to feel secure. A committed and socially embedded treachery is the first price of her body's safety.

One consequence of the initial domestication of the *bisclavret* in the poem is the consistent displacement of violence away from the werewolf, though just enough of the *frisson* attached to violence is allowed to show through to make the displacement conspicuous. Thus the hounds who first detect the *bisclavret* in the woods when they are loosed, run him down "Tant que pur poi ne l'eurent pris / E tut deciré e maumis" (**"Bisc."** 143-44, "Until they were just about to take him / and tear him apart"), at which point his timely obeisance to the king rescues him and finds him a place at court. When the knight who has married his former wife appears at court, the werewolf attacks "As denz li prist, vers lui le traït. / Ja li eüst mut grant leid fait" (**"Bisc."** 199-200, "sank his teeth into him, and started to drag him down. / He would have done him great damage"), only to be frustrated by the Old French equivalent of "*bad* doggie!": "Ne fust li reis ki l'apela, / D'une verge le manaça." (201-2, "if the king hadn't called him off / and threatened him with a stick").[22]

The third instance of displaced violence of this sort is both edgier and more illuminating, because it makes clear where the violence displaced *from* the wolf is displaced *to*. Rather than follow the displacement line by line, let me just narrate it in an impersonal—though perhaps not an entirely impartial—voice: (1) a woman is attacked by a usually tame, but occasionally unruly, pet wolf, and her nose is bitten off. (2) Rather than kill the wolf—or at least threaten to punish it, as has been done on previous occasions—an explanation for the incident is sought by torturing the victim until, "Tant par destrece e par poür" (**"Bisc."** 265, "out of fear and pain"), she confesses that the wolf is her former husband, a werewolf, whom she has imprisoned in wolf form by hiding his clothes, with the help of her present husband.[23] (3) On the basis of this likely story, the clothes are sent for;[24] but when they are offered to the animal, it pays no attention to them (**"Bisc."** 275-80). (4) Undeterred by this seeming disconfirmation, the men of the court conduct the wolf, along with the clothes, to a private chamber in order to spare him the shame of public nudity should he be moved to change into a man. I do not mean to ignore the "facts" of the *bisclavret's* situation—what was indeed done to him by his wife, though I have tried to suggest that the human situation might have more than one reading—but it does seem to me that the events of the end of the *lai* make eminently clear the lengths to which the king and court are prepared to go in his behalf, and their lack of concern for the wife, in circumstances where they have far less information than we.

The conclusion of the poem, with its account of the fate of the wife and her descendents, once again benefits from an intertextual reading. Banished with her husband, she lives on to have many descendents who were

> . . . bien cuneü
> E del semblent e del visage:
> Plusurs des femmes del lignage,
> C'est veritez, senz nes sunt neies
> E sovent ierent esnasees.
>
> (**"Bisc."** 310-14)
>
> . . . widely known
> for their appearance:
> several women of the family
> were actually born without noses,
> and lived out their lives noseless.

Though the myth of the werewolf lends itself generically to the individual and psychological thematics of the wolf within—what Hanning and Ferrante call "the forces of bestiality that exist within human nature" (p. 101)—the actual violence in the tale is predominantly social and judicial, and, in the narrow sense, rational. The wife is not directly subjected to further bodily harm in these terms, but her extended punishment is conducted in this register; and to trace its connections with other moments in the *Lais* is to gain a more precise measure of its costs as well as a clearer idea of Marie's sense of the social meanings of stories. The voice of the hind proposes a darker inflection of Hanning and Ferrante's benignly inflected, but by no means inaccurate, contention that "In **"Bisclavret"** Marie argues that human beings are defined not by their inherent potential for good or evil but also by their fellow humans' responses of trust or fear" (p. 104). In my hearing of her, the hind might say that human beings are defined by the way people choose to take them *regardless* of their inherent potential for good or evil or any other "true nature" they may have, that audiences control the stories that they get themselves told. The wife's punishment itself has certain similarities to the imprudent sex-fact invented by Le Fresne's mother, in that it is the sort of improbable but titillating and memorable tale about generation that is ready-made for popular oral transmission. Marie frequently registers this kind of improbability by overprotesting its veracity, as here, or by distancing herself from the received traditional *lai* as the source of otherwise unattested events "ceo m'est avis, si cum j'entent" (**"Bisc."** 220), perhaps "as I understand from what I'm told." This is the kind of thing a family (and indeed women in general, if they are thinking about their husbands along certain lines) can be tarred with where it really counts—in the realm of gossip and entertainment beyond the reach of judicial punishment *or* its redress. It is a fate feared by Fresne's mother and actually suffered by the seneschal's wife in **"Equitan,"** she of the "neis bien asis" (**"Eq."** 36, "well-shaped nose"); and the strongest image for it is an intertextual extension of one of the moments of apparently arrested violence in **"Bisclavret."** I have in mind the brief mention of the king's dogs, who are just prevented from tearing the *bisclavret* apart (143-44, see above). The pack connects back to the opening of **"Guigemar,"** where a similar image, which is associated with the poet's defense of her own activity and which is not used again in that *lai,* lies dormant until energized in this new context. Men or women of great *pris,* says Marie, attract envious slanderers, backbiters who "comencent le mestier / Del malveis chien coart, felun, / Ki mort la gent par traï-sun." (**"Guigemar"** 7-14, "Thus they act like / vicious, cowardly dogs / who bite people treacherously").

Werewolves are not common, but there are more ordinary ways in which people behave like beasts, and worse, to other people by turning them into the prey of feral imaginings. It is Marie's particular gift to identify and extract from the dreams and nightmares of the folk imagination their more mundane, more persistent (and therefore more terrifying) sources in everyday experience. The most existentially powerful sequence in the tale is the initial conversation between husband and wife as they try to negotiate their need for, and fear of, each other. Marie's telling, with its pervasive structure of conspicuous displacements, identifies the *lai,* as she has it from *li Bretun,* as itself a defensive displacement into romance and magic of such needs and such fears. Her conclusion identifies, as well, how much easier it is to make women rather than men the scapegoats of the process—and to keep on doing it.

V

Among the many services that Hanning and Ferrante have done the criticism of the *Lais,* an important one is their identification of the level of conspicuous fantasy in **"Lanval"** (**"Lanv."**). I want to begin by emphasizing two things about it. The first is that certain details of the fairy lady and her entourage mark the fantasy she embodies as gendered male, the most important being the slightly prurient edge imparted by brief but pointed references to their revealing costumes. This begins with the handmaids who first greet Lanval, wearing purple tunics "laciees mut estreitment" (**"Lanv."** 58, "tightly laced"); continues with the Playmate-of-the-Month pose of the lady herself (**"Lanv."** 97-106); and is perhaps most amusingly noted near the end of the *lai,* when the handmaids appear to announce their mistress's approach, once again dressed in purple, "*tut senglement a lur chars nues. / Cil les esgardent volentiers*" (**"Lanv."**

476-77, "*and nothing else* over their bare skin. / The men looked at them with pleasure"; translation altered and emphasis added). When the lady grants "sun amur e sun cors" (**"Lanv."** 133, "her love and her body") to Lanval, the term she uses, "de mun cors seisine aveir" (**"Lanv."** 150, "to have seisin of my body"), would, in a *lai* that is centrally concerned with female power, seem to stress her independence, since what she grants is a feudal term of *usufruct,* the possession in the sense of enjoyment, plainly extending here to the *jouissance, of* herself, but reserving *to* herself her ownership and final disposal. Nonetheless, what that use gives is the ideal life of a courtly male, satisfying not only his needs for erotic satisfaction and sustenance appropriate to a nobleman,[25] but allowing him to fulfill his chivalric spirit in generosity of a public, indeed kingly sort, giving hospitality, patronage, and rich gifts to all (**"Lanv."** 203-15).

The second thing that might be noticed about the ideal quality of Lanval's dream lady is that she not only (no doubt) deserves and gets his undivided attention, but that she makes it possible precisely *because* she takes such good care of everything else. It is true that he remains faithful to her in adversity, of which more anon; but some odd details at the beginning of the poem work to bring out the way her care obviates a certain heedlessness on the hero's part. When Lanval rides into the woods to brood on his neglect by the king and court, he ignores the steed's trembling (presumably at the proximity of the Other World and its fairy mistress), unsaddles it, and leaves it to roll in the meadow (**"Lanv."** 45-48). When the lady's maidens summon him to her, Marie takes time to mention that "Li chevaliers od eles vait, / De sun cheval ne tient nul plait, / Ki devant lui pesseit el pré" (**"Lanv."** 77-79. "The knight went with them; giving no thought to his horse / who was feeding before him in the meadow"). After he has reached his accommodation with the lady, this bit of minor neglect is pointedly repaired at her unsolicited behest: "Quant del mangier furent levé, / Sun cheval li unt amené; / Bien li eurent la sele mise" (**"Lanv."** 189-91, "When they finished dinner, / his horse was brought to him. / The horse had been well saddled").

The poem's pause to notice here is itself noticeable, but it would mean little if it did not connect to other places in the text **"Lanval"** is the only one of the *Lais* set overtly and specifically at the court of King Arthur, and this move has several functions. To begin with, it allows Marie the use of a world that is the quintessence of Romance: it is discursively presupposed as the idealized and exemplary space of the celebration of chivalric virtue and the noble life, as Auerbach's analysis of Chrétien's *Yvain* in *Mimesis* long ago demonstrated. Everybody knows that Arthur's court was the gathering-place of the best, the bravest, and the most courtly knights who had ever been. In keeping with the demythologizing thrust of the **Lais,** however, Marie's opening description of Arthur's court identifies a conspicuous neglect that parallels Lanval's:

> A Kardoel surjurnot li reis
> Artur, li pruz e li curteis,
> Pur les Escoz e pur lis Pis,
> Ki destrueient le païs;
> En la tere de Logre entroent
> Et mut suvent la damagoent.
> A la Pentecuste en esté
> I aveit li reis sujurné;
> Asez I duna riches duns. . . .
>
> ("Lanv." 5-15)

> Arthur, the brave and courtly king
> was staying at Cardoel,
> because the Scots and the Picts
> were destroying the land.
> They invaded Logres
> and laid it waste.
> At Pentecost, in summer
> the king stayed there.
> He gave out many rich gifts. . . .

Despite the conventional formula in the second line, there is not much *proece* showing just now at this court. This framing helps to identify it as a place of *escape* from feudal/national politics and war, a retreat from such concerns to more relaxed and courtly pursuits that, for the moment, pointedly ignores the things it is escaping. The word *esbanier,* which Marie uses repeatedly to characterize the leisure of the inhabitants of the world of the *lai,*[26] catches the overall effect nicely. It refers to the condition of being unbound from *ban,* its cognates and extensions, whether that be taken to mean the feudal levy, the banner under which men fight, or the worlds of public proclamation and public order.[27] Marie's presentation focuses from the beginning on the attempted exclusion of real-world concerns that threaten the courtly ideal and identifies the knights and ladies of King Arthur less as exemplars of those ideals than as imperfect aspirants to them. As in the other *lais,* stories of the Other World and of Ideal Chivalry, like those of Arthur's Court, do not form the stable backdrop of these poems but occupy their foreground as social technologies that the characters use for evading whatever would trammel their comfort and self-esteem. Especially, given the other difficulties that emerge in the course of the *lai,* the characters are best seen as Camelot wannabees who *aspire* to their station as Arthurians, and the plot of the poem can be seen as a study in the art of covering up.

There is thus a metonymic relationship between Lanval and the Arthurian court: both turn away from the problems of the everyday world to fantasy. The *surplus* of human conflict that remains in the court—even after

it has escaped from epic strenuousness to the re-*lax*ation of romance, exemplified in just such things as the unworthy treatment of Lanval by Arthur that is the hero's initial impetus—is further refined and repressed by and for him into the ideal love of a perfect mate who makes the trammels of social existence unnecessary while surreptitiously mastering them. He lives a purified core of ideal individual courtly existence (right at the edge of making that phrase an oxymoron), whose structure of displacement reveals what it has in common with the court he flees.[28] In both cases, the remainder of the Real that disturbs and questions the evasive fantasy is concentrated in the antitype and dark sister of the fairy mistress, perhaps the most articulate and powerful bearer of the voice of the hind in the **Lais,** Queen Guenevere.

As with the wife in **"Bisclavret,"** the queen's function as a voice for the suppressed of the system emerges best when her speeches and actions are given their full intertextual force, which here includes the wider Arthurian context as well as the other poems in Marie's collection. This context is pointedly evoked as the poem shifts from Lanval's private joys to the court scene at line 219: the famous knights are named (Gawain, Yvain), thirty of them gathered in the orchard beneath the tower[29] to amuse themselves. They invite Lanval to join them, at which the queen enters with thirty of her maidens, sees Lanval standing alone to one side, and propositions him with the offer of her *amur* and *druërie* (237-68).[30] The advantage Marie derives from the Arthurian setting in this case comes from our knowledge of the queen's erotic history. It is not clear from the text of **"Lanval"** whether Lancelot is already the queen's lover. In either case, however, his presence in the background of the story enforces the persistence of the queen's discontent and of her determination to find a lover: if not Lanval, then Lancelot; if Lancelot already, then Lanval as well; in either case, not Arthur.[31] Some sense of the precise bearing of this discontent is also conveyed in a remark Marie makes about Lanval immediately prior to the queen's approach, as an explanation for the way he holds himself apart from the festivities even when he has at last been invited to them: "L'autrui joie prise petit, / Si il nen ad le suen delit" (**"Lanv."** 257-58, "he thought little of others' joys / If he could not have his pleasure"). In line with the metonymic relationship suggested above, the remark applies not just to Lanval but much more broadly to the men of the world of this *lai,* and indeed to all the other absent male lovers in Marie's larger poem. It applies with particular force here to Arthur, especially when, after Lanval has refused the queen and she has left him, "Li reis fu del bois repeiriez; / Mut out le jur esté haitiez" (**"Lanv."** 311-12, "The king returned from the woods, / he'd had a very good day"). Arthur joins the ranks of Guigemar, Equitan, and Bisclavret in a context in which the impact of male absence on women's pleasure is given its full sexual force. Everything about the situation stresses its specific relation to female rage and resentment at the deeply embedded social denial of women's right even to *legal* orgasms.[32]

That anger also drives the queen's explicit sexualization of the equivocal aura that surrounds male bonding. She begins with an accusation that reflects back upon (and brings out a tacit possibility in) a common situation in earlier *lais,* marking the turn that social disapproval of a man who shows no interest in women can take if the observer is angry or malicious enough to make it:

> Vallez avez bien afeitiez,
> Ensemble od eus vus deduiez.
> Vileins cüarz, mauveis failliz,
> Mut est mis sires maubailliz,
> Ki pres de lui vus ad suffert,
> Mun escïent que Deu en pert.
>
> ("Lanv." 281-86)

> You have fine-looking boys
> with whom you enjoy yourself.
> Base coward, lousy cripple,
> My lord made a bad mistake
> When he let you stay with him.
> For all I know, he'll lose God because of it.

The language of the passage allows a slippage in its last three lines from Lanval to Arthur in particular and the wider world of masculinity in general. The condemnation of Arthur for "countenancing" Lanval's behavior implicates the king in Lanval's putative sin to a degree hard to specify,[33] since its apparent hyperbole invites the question of just what would put Arthur's soul in such danger. It is a question appropriately voiced in the shadow realm of social disapproval, whose protean perils Marie is so good at evoking: the world of "asez le m'ad hum dit sovent." Once this sexual reading of homosocial behavior is broached, the run of its reference is hard to contain; and though the other *lais* have no one who will quite broach it in the way the queen does here, her anger—echoing the hind's "a plague on your desire!"—adds a certain bite to the question of how the women in these poems may be feeling about the behavior of their men. That it is this imputation that stings Lanval to his near-fatal revelation of the existence of his mistress suggests that he feels that bite too.[34]

When the queen carries her dealings with Lanval into the public sphere by complaining of him to Arthur, the subsequent action of the poem gives us the most fully developed picture in the *Lais* so far of the complex behind-the-scenes negotiations, improvisations, and contestations that are involved in the increasingly precarious maintenance of the male *status quo*. To begin with, it is interesting that her complaint is two-pronged, comprising accusations of sexual harassment on the one

hand and *lèse majesté* on the other ("Lanv." 315-24). Whatever her motives for this, the reactions of Arthur and the court are more interesting still. If the first accusation of an indecent proposal to his wife is true, one supposes that Arthur would be within his rights, or at any rate within his power and its justification, to simply have Lanval killed. From the beginning, however, the king's response is a curious blend of expressed emotions proper to the first accusation and actions more appropriate to the second. In the presence of the queen,

> Li reis s'en curuçat forment;
> Juré en ad sun serement,
> S'il ne s'en peot in curt defendre,
> Il le ferat ardeir u pendre
>
> ("Lanv." 325-28)

> The king got very angry;
> he swore an oath:
> if Lanval could not defend himself in court
> he would have him burned or hanged.

Though the slight weaseling in the third line mars the effect a bit, the pattern of strong talk and cautious action is only fully established when the king leaves the presence of his wife ("Fors de la chambre eissi li reis," "Lanv." 329. "The king left her chamber"), calls three of his barons, and summons Lanval. When the latter appears, the king maintains his vehemence ("'Vassal, vus m'avez mut mesfait,'" "Lanv." 363. "'Vassal, you have done me a great wrong!'"); but his statement of the charge does not mention the more serious crime at all.[35]

When the king passes the problem on to his feudatories ("ses humes," 382), he does so in part to get a verdict that will silence the affair, something no one can question.[36] Though part of this aim requires that the judgment not come too directly or too personally from the king (which is presumably one reason the formal and legal language of feudal duties—for example, the interpellation of Lanval as "Vassal!"—comes to dominate the situation so quickly), the feudatories are equally reluctant to commit themselves. Their first council results in a decision to postpone Lanval's day in court until the full baronage is assembled, since only the king's household is currently present at court (394). As the matter snowballs, the roles of the participants become more clearly established. The king continues to press for justice and a resolution (the queen's agency is always mentioned in this, stressing the extent to which Arthur's hand is forced here), but in such a way as to continue to avoid taking direct action himself. The barons continue to stall, seeking excuses to postpone a verdict five times, by my count, before the matter is at last resolved. Most of them are at pains to indicate that their sympathies lie with Lanval. Gawain and his companions offer themselves as pledges for the hero, since he has no kin or friends at court (395-405); and

Marie notes, "Jeo quid k'il en i ot teus cent / Ki feïssent tut lur poeir / Pur lui sanz pleit delivre aveir"[37] ("**Lanv.**" 420-23, "I think there were a hundred / who would have done all they could / to set him free without a trial"). A bit later, the Count of Cornwall, who is apparently newly arrived and a stranger to the case, since he does not know Lanval (436), articulates what the reader as well as the participants may well have felt: that the case for *lèse majesté* is a flimsy one.[37] He goes on to declare the conditions of trial—that Lanval shall provide proof that his mistress and her entourage are superior in beauty and worth to the queen.

To take a larger view of these events in the light of the rest of the **Lais** is to see that we are dealing here with another instance of the way, by now familiar, that male interests close ranks to protect their own. But what are they protecting? It may well be that the maneuvering here arises from knowledge or suspicion of the injustice of the queen's complaint, but what such a reading ignores is the striking fact that, by the time the beauty issue is made the basis of the legal decision, the sexual charge has been read out of the situation. Part of what the long delay accomplishes is precisely the burying of this issue, which is kept marginally alive only by the increasingly tacit presence of the queen and by Arthur's increasingly *pro forma* exhortations to speedy justice. The fact that the delay and the maneuvering are so extensively portrayed marks the difference between the situation in this *lai* and previous ones, because it puts a new spin on the kind of casual and confident male solidarity we see in, say, **"Bisclavret,"** which here appears more defensively motivated. The same is true of Lanval's exemplary loyalty to his mistress. Once the magnificently, if scantily, attired maidens have started to appear, Lanval may well suppose his fairy lady cannot be far behind; and, in any case, claiming the wrong lady patently opens him to easy denunciation if, as he hopes for many reasons, the right one appears. His persistent, steadfast refusal to take the suggestion of the other knights, "Ici vienent deus dameisles, / Mut acemees et mut beles: / C'est vostre amie veirement!" ("**Lanv.**" 521-23, "Here come two maidens, / well adorned and very beautiful; one must certainly be your love.") says less about him than about the eagerness of the barons to jump on any plausible excuse to acquit him and, beyond that and more importantly, to do so on the issue of *lèse majesté* alone, now further refined into the issue of comparative beauty and worth; that is, into a matter not of fact but of consensus. What needs attention is not that the participants figure out how to get Lanval off, but that they work so hard to avoid having him tried for trying to seduce the queen. They do so because admitting the question of his desire cannot avoid raising the question of hers; and this is what the whole performance is dedicated to covering up.

On the surface, the story of this *lai* is a tale of the defeat of the queen's unjust abuse of her power by the superior power of true love, as embodied in the uncoerced generosity of the fairy mistress and her willingness to break her earlier behest for Lanval's sake. The queen is silenced and her desire suppressed, for the last hundred lines of the poem, in favor of the celebration of an ideal love too good for this world. But the framing of this happy ending, as I have tried to show, continually stresses the continuing power of what is being evaded in the pressure it exerts on the evasion; and the queen's last appearance as the voice of the hind makes that power and its continuance echo with devastating force:

> [Li reis] ad tuz ses baruns mandez,
> Que li jugemenz seit renduz:
> Trop ad le jur esté tenuz;
> *La reïne s'en curuçot,*
> *Que trop lungement jeünot*
>
>   ("**Lanv.**" 542-45, emphasis added)[38]
> [The king] summoned all his barons
> to render their judgment;
> it had already dragged out too much.
> *The queen was getting angry*
> *because she had already fasted so long.*

Hanning and Ferrante, in a note to this passage, report Ewert's emendation of *jeünot* to *atendeit*, "waited," "which is not as callously selfish" (p. 120, note 6).[38] I take the editorial fuss here to reflect the editors' sense of the *surplus*, the excess of the line, which they demonstrate by trying to mitigate it rather in the manner of the knights of the court. They want to edit it into decorum (those who do) because they can sense that she is not just talking about missing brunch.

In fact, the power of the line arises as much from its metaphorical indirection, which allows it to function as a metonymy for the whole cumulative portrayal in the *Lais* of the blockage of feminine desire, as it does from its immediate context in **"Lanval."** An intertextual reading of the kind of allegorical figure or personification of love the *queen* (as opposed to the fairy lady) makes, enforces the general and persistent character of what it is the men don't want to have come out—what they don't want to know. To suppose that giving the queen a day in court over the issue of her desire would reveal something of the order that she is an adulteress and/or that Arthur is impotent, is a misplaced concretion—not only because there is no real evidence for such things in the text, but because it would confine the trouble the queen *is* and the trouble she *has* to the merely individual, and therefore genuinely marginal, case. What **"Lanval"** shows is not the queen's marginality but the laborious and conspicuous (and therefore unsuccessful) attempted *marginalization* of a character who carries the entire structure of gender relations and the gendered organization of desire, which the *Lais* as a whole has developed, into the center of the poem. Insofar as the queen speaks for the silenced, in trying to silence her the men in this *lai*, like those in the others before it, are trying to keep the voice of the hind from being heard, are trying not to hear it.

The complex of feminine discontents that I have been calling the voice of the hind emerges gradually through the first half of the *Lais*. I have argued for its prominence in **"Lanval"**; and its emergence has a further consequence for the reading of the representation of feminine power in the poem as a whole. I have suggested that the cover story of the *lai* is the victory through love of a powerful, independent "good" woman over the attack on the proprieties, and on love itself, by a "bad" one. The latter's attempt to abuse her own position of power by working behind the scenes, through the men she coerces and deceives, is brought to naught in open court by unforced public recognition of the gifts and virtues, as Lanval has it, "de cors, de vis e de beauté, / D'enseignement, e de bunté" (**"Lanv."** 301-2: "in body, face, and beauty, / in breeding and in goodness") of the former. But if, as I have argued, the queen represents the deeper truth of women's situation in the poem, then the allegorical pretensions of the figure of the fairy lady are revealed as what they are—a fiction, a male fantasy—and this origin is manifested and played out in practical form in the *lai*'s conclusion. There is no real question of a decision on the "merits" of the case; it has been made fully clear by the time the fairy mistress appears that the barons were ready to declare any reasonable-looking woman the winner, and they were only blocked from doing so by Lanval's refusal to be acquitted too quickly.[39]

In these circumstances, the extended description of the procession of ladies leading up to the final one becomes a legal *surplus,* a description of what amounts to the bodily rhetoric that can be used to justify (in later accounts like this *lai,* for instance) the decision the barons were going to make anyway. This understanding of the situation gives a further twist to the bearing, and especially the dress (or lack of it) of the fairy and her servants. Besides giving a summary of the case that gets all parties except the queen off the hook (**"Lanv."** 615-24), Lanval's lady also appears dressed "De chainse blanc e de chemise, / Que tuit li costé li pareient" (**"Lanv."** 560-61, "in a white linen shift that revealed both her sides").[40] This, and the fact that, just before speaking her defense of Lanval, "Sun mantel ad laissié cheeir, / Que mieuz la peüssent veeir" (**"Lanv."** 605-6, "she let her cloak fall so they could see her better"), focus us on the *kind of persuasion* that is being brought to bear here. What it stresses is that the fairy herself recognizes, at least in practical terms, the extent to which her apparent independence and power are, like

the queen's, dependent on men and on her ability to appeal to their desire. The point is perhaps clearer if we reflect that, in order to clinch the win, these women put themselves in the position of promising, with the stipulation that they will not give it,[41] what the queen started the trouble by offering to give in deed. The good girls and the bad ones are closer together than might have been imagined.

The final outcome of the *lai,* in which Lanval exits the court—and, with it, what Sharon Kinoshita, following Roberta Krueger, calls "the project of primogeniture"[42]— shows the same structure of similarity underlying apparent difference. On the surface it appears that Lanval quits a world too corrupt to sustain the ideals of love and faithfulness he embodies; but at the very end there is a teasing detail, the hero's place of escape: "Od li s'en vait en Avalun, / Ceo nus recuntent li Bretun, / En un isle ki ut est beaus" (**"Lanv."** 641-43, "With her he went to Avalun, / so the Bretons tell us, / to a very beautiful island"). Once again there is a convergence: Arthur too, after all the trouble the queen's adultery with Lancelot brings on internally, and after all the political/feudal strife, whose marker in this text might well be the almost-excluded Picts and Scots, will end up in dreamtime on the island of Avalon. "Pur," says the *Brut,* "ses plaies médiciner": to heal his wounds, whence the *Bretun* still await his return.[43] If this is a rejection of conventional masculine values, it is one, it seems to me, in the service of those values. The metonymy I argue earlier still holds: what the hyper-idealized image of love, fidelity, and a guaranteed income achieves now, the merely idealized though equally fictional Arthur will reach later; which is to say that the Arthurian world is constituted over a desire to escape itself. Given what it takes in the effort of domination and its cost in guilt, to be a "man" in these poems—a Bisclavret or Equitan, to say nothing of a Yonec or Eliduc—might well be something that the subjects in men's bodies on whom that masculinity is laid might want to escape. The *Bretun* built that escape into the limits of their favorite fantasy. They did so, moreover, in a way that insures—is meant to insure— that the healing they dream of is entrusted to a woman of a certain sort, one whose image blocks that of the woman they are always going hunting to avoid.

VI

Thus, a retrospect, from the vantage of **"Lanval"** back to the *lais* of the first half of the collection, brings out the extent to which the distinction between "good" and "bad"—in general, but, for starters, in women—has been progressively redefined as a distinction between "successful and unsuccessful in the generation and control of the future anterior"; that is, in the management of self-presentation and reputation. The effect of

morality depends on the ability to influence the definition of what will have been, through control of the
stories that will be told about oneself and one's actions.
The poem has further established the ongoing practices
of the gendering that structure this struggle for one's
history: good girls are the ones who have submerged
their own desire in order to create socially effective
simulacra of the desires of men. In doing so, they have
produced (or been forced to produce) a *surplus* of
feminine discontent that shadows and whispers—the
voice of the hind—to men and women alike. This is
perhaps another reading of the hind's androgyny as a
surrogate for the poetess: she must don male drag, the
chivalric values that shape the stories the *Bretun* have
left her, in order to be heard at all, though she also
gains the option of telling those stories with a difference.

I do not wish to make the poet sound too polemical
here; that is not her tone. In common with her mentor
Ovid and his blank-faced dissection of the *mores* of the
Roman singles-bar scene (and the mythological stories
of the rapes and revenges of goddesses and heroines
that are told in it), and along with her closest modern
kinswoman Angela Carter, the mistress of X-rated fairy
tales for grown-ups,[44] Marie shares what I think of
(following William Burroughs) as the cold eye that
registers the nakedness of lunch—what's on the end of
the fork. It is her ability to see and show that this is
what people *do,* without giving way too quickly or too
often to the rage and sorrow that may well be appropriate to the perception, that allows her to trace the *workings* of the generation and perpetuation of stories as
richly and as deftly as she does. What she sees, in fact,
is not simply that men oppress women and that women
fight back by turning the instruments of their oppression to their own purposes. One of the things that makes
"Lanval" a culmination, but also a turning point in the
Lais, is the clarity and tenacity with which it portrays
the ongoing *politics* of representation in courtly life and
especially the way that politics is *persistently* shaped as
much by what the actors try to escape as by what they
try to affirm. This is why the *lais* in the second half of
the collection become more fragmented, their endings
less apparently conclusive, their meanings more
evidently contested within the poems themselves.
"Laüstic" is everybody's favorite instance of this, a *lai*
in which what is remembered is not the meaning of the
nightingale but the struggle of the three characters to
give it one; but the double-named *lais,* **"Chaitivel"/**
"Quatre" "Deuls," and **"Eliduc"/"Guildeluëc ha Guilliadun,"** which Marie also passes on to us as not-yet-
finished because not yet securely titled, turn in their
different ways on the same interest in the ongoing
processes of storymaking.

Another of the meanings of the androgyny of the hind
and her voice is that it speaks to the cultural/social/
anthropological situation in which both sexes find
themselves and with which, in their various ways, they
have to do and be done by. Neither the hind nor Marie
seems much taken with the choices and opportunities
offered to men *or* women, though Marie at least is
clearly fascinated by the variety, deviousness, and skill
with which they make and take them. Though the playing field is scarcely level for both sexes, everyone can—
must—play, and Marie is above all the poet of that
game.

Notes

As the reader will discover, I do not follow the practice
in this essay of citing published criticism in support of
points I make or to acknowledge specific anticipations
of my formulations. Though I have done my homework,
I felt on reflection that for good or ill, the perspective
developed here was sufficiently different, especially in
its systematic nature, from what I found elsewhere to
justify proceeding as I do. Nonetheless—indeed,
precisely for that reason—I ought here to declare my
indebtednesses; and it is a pleasure to begin with the
one that is both deepest and most appropriate to the occasion. That Bob Hanning is a close friend and Joan
Ferrante a friendly acquaintance is much to me. But, in
thinking about the *Lais* of Marie de France, what counts
is my sense, developed over years of teaching the poems
in most of the available translations, that their translation and commentary is the single best assemblage of
criticism of the work in English or French, both because
I find the translation itself continually rewarding and
suggestive, a coherent act of criticism as a good translation should be, and because the commentary is one of
the few (and in my estimation easily the best) attempts
to deal with all the *lais,* both individually and as a
group. If I have quibbled with a translation or disagreed
with a reading in what follows (and if such things did
not happen there would be nothing to write or think
about in literature), I have done so because they made it
possible. The old saw about the shoulders of giants may
seem grandiose in such a context, but it has its point
here too. Therefore I have made *The Lais of Marie de
France,* translated and with an introduction and notes
by Robert Hanning and Joan Ferrante (New York: E. P.
Dutton, 1978), the translation of reference in this essay.
I cite it in the text, after the Old French, not only in aid
of readers who may find it useful linguistically, but to
keep the voices of these excellent critics, in the detail
of critical choice that a translation is, constantly before
us. I have, of course, also consulted Ferrante's *Woman
as Image in Medieval Literature, from the Twelfth
Century to Dante* (New York and London: Columbia
University Press, 1975), and Hanning's other critical
writings on the *Lais,* especially "The Talking Wounded:

Desire, Truth Telling and Pain in the *Lais* of Marie de France," in *Desiring Discourse, The Literature of Love, Ovid through Chaucer,* ed. James J. Paxson and Cynthia A. Gravlee (Selinsgrove, Pa.: Susquehanna University Press, 1998), 140-61. For the original text I have used the edition of Jean Rychner, *Les lais de Marie de France* (Paris: Champion, 1969). I cite each *lai,* by an abbreviated title with line numbers, parenthetically in the text. In thinking about the poem over the years and again recently, I have drawn special benefit from the following. The discourse on Marie's work in the light of feminist theory and interpretation has been consistently illuminating, first in conversations with my former colleagues, Linda Lomperis, Kristine Brightenback, and Cécile Schreiber, and in the work and talk of my friend Roberta Krueger, and then in other published writings, especially E. Jane Burns, *Bodytalk, When Women Speak in Old French Literature* (Philadelphia: University of Pennsylvania Press, 1993); Michelle A. Freeman, "Marie de France's Poetics of Silence: The Implications for a Feminine Translation, *PMLA* 99 (1984): 860-83; and, most recently, in the article by my present colleague, Sharon Kinoshita, "Cherchez la Femme: Feminist Criticism and Marie de France's *Lai de Lanval,*" *Romance Notes* 34 (1994): 263-73, whose project is close to my own. I have also used the articles of Rupert T. Pickens, "Marie de France and the Body Poetic," in *Gender and Text in the Later Middle Ages,* ed. Jane Chance (Gainesville: University Press of Florida, 1996), 135-71; and "The Poetics of Androgyny in the *Lais* of Marie de France: Yonec, Milon, and the General Prologue," in *Literary Aspects of Courtly Culture,* ed. Donald Maddox (Rochester, N.Y.: Boydell and Brewer, 1994), 211-19. Many of the articles in Chantal A. Maréchal, *In Quest of Marie de France, A Twelfth-Century Poet* (Lewiston, N.Y.: Edwin Mellen, 1992) have aided me; the most suggestive were concerned with *Yonec,* and so escape citation here. However, I must single out for special mention Robert M. Stein's "Desire, Social Reproduction, and Marie's *Guigemar,*" 280-94 in that volume. Like many others, I have learned from R. Howard Bloch, both in his work on the treatment of misogyny in the *Lais* in *Medieval Misogyny and the Invention of Western Romantic Love* (Chicago: University of Chicago Press, 1991) and in the more deconstructively oriented articles: "The Lay and the Law: Sexual/Textual Transgression in *La Chastelaine de Vergi,* the *Lai d'Ignaure,* and the *Lais* of Marie de France," *Stanford French Review* 14, (1990): 181-210, and "The Voice of the Dead Nightingale: Orality in the Tomb of Old French Literature," *Culture and History* 3, (1990): 63-78. (Yet I am bound to say that Bloch is less willing to consider the texts as themselves deconstructive than I am.) Finally, I have tried to keep myself, probably in vain, from missing important recent work

by consulting the valuable review article by Chantal A. Maréchal, "Marie de France Studies: Past, Present, Future," *Envoi* 8 (1999): 105-25.

1. Guigemar's lover might be supposed to feel something like this at times, perhaps especially when Meriaduc summons "el païs chevalier" to essay the belt she wears next to her skin (*G.* 741-42), but in this *lai* she does not speak at such times.

2. Her first sight of Guigemar tends to stress the extent to which she takes him as an occasion of emotional indulgence at the expense of more precise observation: "Le chevalier ad esgardé, / Mut pleint sun cors et sa beauté, / Pur lui esteit triste e dolente / E dit que mar fu sa juvente" (*G.* 295-98). Only then does she check more closely: "Desur le piz li met sa main: / Chaut le senti e le quor sein" (*G.* 299-300). That she is not a close observer and tends to prefer romance, the more dramatic the better, to other styles of interpretation is later confirmed by her ability to mourn her desperate situation for two years after Guigemar's departure before trying the door (*G.* 655-77).

3. This issue is a persistent one in the collection, at least as a device to drive plots. It is raised as a concern of the anxious subjects of lords who are too content with their mistresses in *Le Fresne* and *Equitan,* and again as the husband's motive for immuring his wife in *Yonec,* to mention only the most explicit instances. See the discussion of *Lanval* below.

4. I specify Francophone because such writers—for instance Marcabru, whom she may not have known, and Chrétien, whom she surely did—form Marie's extended literary community, the vernacular texts and discourses of reference, imitation, criticism, and competition for her work. Of course Italian, German, and English writers notice, too, to say nothing of Ovid.

5. Hanning and Ferrante's translation here does not quite register the likelihood that the distinction between "dame" and "pucele" is one of marital status as well as age and sexual experience. This characterization of the contestants takes on even greater interest when the happy ending of the *lai* neglects to inform us that Guigemar married his lover: "A grant joie s'amie en meine" (*G.* 881), which they translate in a way that catches the implication of "amie" admirably: "Guigemar led away his mistress with great rejoicing" (54).

6. The lady herself is the first to be put in the position of displaying her body; she presumably further incites Meriaduc to lust in the attempt to

fend him off: "Il la requiert, el n'en ad cure, / Ainz li mustre de la ceinture" (*G.* 721-22). This is complicated, because it eventually leads to Guigemar getting wind of her presence; but whatever her motives, the lady has literally to expose herself in a way he does not.

7. Marie's line, "but he could not come to the head of the matter," is a little rawer than the translation.

8. "Pur *deduire* fu fors alez" (*Eq.* 278), which suggests that there is something at work in the room, even before the wife enters, from which he feels the need for relief, literal "diversion."

9. The use of *tenir* here is interesting because it is a feudal term for the usufruct (or *jouissance*) of land, thus echoing the similar use of it by Meriaduc against Guigemar's claim to his lady: "Jeo la trovai, si la tendrai / E cuntre vus la defendrai!" (*G.* 851-52).

10. Perhaps the most striking instance of this theme in the poem is our belated discovery that the lovers' final embrace is being watched over by a servant girl *from inside the chamber* where they are making love: "L'us firent tenir e garder; / Une meschine i dut ester. / Li senescals hastis revint; / A l'hus buta, cele le tint. / Icil le fiert par tel haïr, / Par force li estut ovrir." (*Eq.* 285-90). How long has this practice been going on? *Somebody* must have brought in the boiling water ("L'ewe buillant feit [the wife] aporter," 275). Who *else* (the king's physician, or whoever bleeds him?) has been privy to the affair?

11. I'd like to press the possibility that this phrase means "and coming with him," in the light of my reading of Guenevere in *Lanval*.

12. Billy Wilder's 1944 film of *Double Indemnity*, by the way, responds well to a similar line of analysis. When Phyllis tells Walter of the unexpected love for him that renders her unable to carry out, to the *coup de grace*, the role of *femme fatale* he has assigned her throughout the movie ("I just couldn't fire that second shot"), she is rewarded by having him shoot her—twice.

13. Equitan seems to be one of the first to sexualize the representation of this particular form of *accedia*, prefiguring, if perhaps not influencing, the importance of the theme in Jean de Meun's Fals Semblant and in Chaucer's Pardoner.

14. See Marcel Mauss, *The Gift*, trans. Ian Cunnison (New York: Norton, 1967), especially the section on potlatch, 31-45; and Harry Berger, Jr., and H. Marshall Leicester, Jr., "Social Structure as Doom: The Limits of Heroism in *Beowulf*," in *Old English and Norse Studies in Honor of John C. Pope*, ed. Robert B. Burlin and Edward B. Irving, Jr. (Toronto: University of Toronto Press, 1974), 37-79.

15. The clearest example is the tacit bargain Gurun makes with the abbess who is the girl's warden: endowment of the abbey with lands in return for access to Fresne (*LeF.* 250-70); but this is just the tip of the iceberg. A more interesting, because better-covered, instance is the mother's horrifying decision at the end of her lament, "Pur mei defendre de hunir, / Un des enfanz m'estuet murdrir (*LeF.* 91-92). It is only after the lament is over that we are told it was made in the presence of the servants, "Celes ki en la chambre esteient" (*LeF.* 94), converting what looked like a despairing private resolve into the opening bid of a request to the Noblewomen's Network for help in solving the problem—which is at once forthcoming.

16. Since it is common knowledge that Fresne has been Gurun's mistress up to now, this message, with a few additional twists, might also reach both Codre and her mother, whether they discover who Fresne is or not. The servants, after all, at least know where the cloth came from; and Fresne's mother has reason to know what such folk are capable of.

17. That tone will have to wait for Chaucer's depiction of Le Fresne's descendent Griselde in the Clerk's Tale (*CT*):

> "My lord, ye woot that in my fadres place
> Ye dide me streepe out of my povre weed,
> And richely me cladden, of youre grace.
> To yow broghte I noghte elles, out of drede,
> But feith, and nakednesse, and maydenhede;
> And heere agayn youre clothing I restoore,
> And eek youre weddyng ryng, for everemoore

> ". . . But yet I hope it be nat youre entente
> That I smokelees out of youre paleys wente.

> Ye koude nat doon so dishonest a thyng,
> That thilke wombe in which youre children leye
> Sholde biforn the peple in my walkynge,
> Be seyn al bare; wherfore I yow preye,
> Lat me nat lyk a worm go by the weye. . . .

> "Wherfore, in gerdon of my maydenhede,
> Which that I broghte, and noght agayn I bere
> As voucheth sauf to yeve me, to my meede,
> But swich a smok as I was wont to were,
> That I therwith may wrye the wombe of here
> That was youre wyf. And heere take I my leeve
> Of yow, myn owene lord, lest I yow greve."

(*CT* IV.862-68, 874-80, 883-89)

I cite from *The Riverside Chaucer,* 3rd ed., gen. ed., Larry D. Benson (Boston: Houghton Mifflin, 1987).

18. The ethnic joke that begins the *lai* sets out the conditions of the Norman *garwaf,* or EC horror-comic reading of the plot, The Return of the Thing in the Woods (which the the rest of the poem mostly avoids) in order to contrast it, a touch bathetically, with the more everyday Breton *bisclavret* world of noble pursuits that will occupy it thereafter: "Garvalf, ceo est beste salvage; / Tant cum il est en cele rage, / Humes devure, grant mal fait, . . . Del Bisclavret vus voil cunter" (*Bisc.* 9-11, 14).

19. From this point of view, the language used to describe the *bisclavret*'s downfall is significant— "Issi fu Bisclavret trahiz / E per sa femme maubailiz" (*Bisc.* 125-26)—because "maubailiz," ("badly served, in the way a bailiff would misman-age an estate") suggests the caretaker role the wife was left in before she found out why.

20. It should be noted that Guildeluëc in *Eliduc* is one of the few women in the *Lais* who may be thought to manage this.

21. "La dame ad cil dunc espusee / Que lungement aveit amee" (*Bisc.* 133-34). Hanning and Ferrante translate "The wife later married the other knight," but Marie's "dunc," "thereupon" adds stress to the aspect of conditional exchange of value for service in a matter whose aspects of mutual blackmail, sustained by public commitment, are evident enough.

22. Hanning and Ferrante translate the following line, "Deus feiz le vout mordre le jour!" as "twice that day he tried to bite the knight"; but it seems to me that the French must mean "twice *a* day," which also seems to me to increase the bathetic and comic effect by further stressing the futility of the werewolf's behavior.

23. Marie is careful to note that, even under torture, the most the wife can confess is "l'aventure qu'il [*scil.* her husband] li cunta" (*Bisc.* 269)—she has not seen him change.

24. Why did she keep them?—or did she? He might be supposed to have more than one set, if indeed he really needs clothing with a personal stamp to transform. Many of the casual details of the *lai* have the quality, when examined closely, of what Pooh Bah in *The Mikado* calls lending an air of verisimilitude to an otherwise bald and unconvincing narrative, of which more below.

25. Hence the magical transformation of his retinue, "Il est a sun ostel venuz, / Ses humes treve bien vestuz" (*Lanv.* 201-2).

26. Of Lanval in the meadow, "Si s'est alez esba-neier," 42; of the knights of the court: "s'ierent alé esbanier," 222; of the queen and her entourage in the same scene, "li s'irrunt esbanïer," 245.

27. See the Larousse *Dictionnaire de l'ancien français,* s.v. *ban.*

28. Kinoshita, "Cherchez la Femme," 269-70, follow-ing Bloch, *Medieval Misogyny,* sees Lanval as feminized, and there is a lot to this idea. For the reasons given in the text, however, the move seems best viewed as a strategic or *faux* feminin-ity, playing a female role in order to gain male ends. It should be clear that a phrase like "false femininity" does not entail the possibility of a "real" one, if that is construed as some sort of female essence. It ought to be evident by now, from situations like the one described here, that Marie understands "male" and "female" as dis-courses and roles that can be played by anyone with a motive, conscious or unconscious, for do-ing so, and that they can be mixed and matched as well. This is one reflection of the hind's an-drogyny: that "she," "Marie, elle" can write as s/he does, with an understanding of the different *functions* of the same fantasies in the plural col-locations of "masculinities" and "femininities." None of this, by the way, precludes noticing how the subjects who are forced or persuaded to be "women" are treated, the *political* logic of the structure called "femininity." I develop some of this further at the end of this section.

29. I take this tower, for reasons given immediately below, to be a slightly displaced allusion to Chre-tien's *Chevalier au charette,*

30. The language and the situation here are sufficiently parallel to the similar proposition made to Lanval by the fairy mistress to suggest that the queen again fills in the real-life effort, the labor and preparation women have to take in order to play the game of eros—the alertness to opportunities, the attention to the work of self-staging (for example, the deployment of the thirty ladies)—of which only the onstage effect is manifest with the former lady.

31. See Rychner, *Le lais,* 256, note to line 259.

32. Lines 257-58 just cited, about Lanval's attitude to the pleasure of others, thus also describe in inverted form the queen's feelings as well.

33. The range of "Ki prez de lui vus ad suffert" is uncertain, but it might be glossed by the wife in *Bisclavret,* whose fear of her husband manifested itself as a desire not to lie "lez lui" any more. It is at least interesting that Marie uses the same word,

"maubailliz," to describe Lanval's relation to Arthur (or the queen's version of it) and the werewolf's wife to her husband in *Bisclavret*. See note 19 above.

34. I do not wish to be understood as maintaining that the queen is accusing Lanval and the king of sleeping together, or even of sharing a taste for boys, much less that they or anyone else in the poem actually does these things. She is implying *something* about the two of them that carries resonances with other places in the *Lais*. The precise reference, if there is one, is almost certainly irrecoverable historically, and she herself may well be uncertain of it. If so, though, the men involved are more than likely to be equally uncertain of the precise justice of the imputation. One is reminded of Eve Kosofsky Sedgewick's marvellous analysis of the "coercive double bind" of male homosocial desire: "the tendency toward important correspondences and similarities between the most sanctioned forms of male-homosocial bonding, and the most reprobated expressions of male homosexual sociality. . . . To put it in twentieth-century American terms, the fact that what goes on at football games, in fraternities, at the Bohemian Grove, and at climactic moments in war novels, can look, with only a slight shift of optic, quite startlingly 'homosexual,' is not most importantly an expression of the psychic origin of these institutions in repressed or sublimated homosexual genitality. . . . For a man to be a man's man is separated only by an invisible, carefully blurred, always-already-crossed line from being 'interested in men.'" *Between Men: English Literature and Male Homosocial Desire* (New York: Columbia University Press, 1985), 89. Marie's poem offers a number of situations where the tension of the double bind might be invoked, and she here offers a kind of *point de capiton* to organize a certain reading of them in the person of a woman with a reason for shifting the optic. At the very least, she shows that this possibility is present in the text as an option for its characters: and Lanval's response suggests further that the characters have to take it seriously even when it is not true, precisely because its social reality is discursive, independent of individual psyches and sexualities.

35. This puts Lanval, a few lines later, in the curious position of denying an accusation that has not been made: "Que la reïne ne request" (*Lanv.* 374). The fact that he seems to expect it foregrounds the extent to which Arthur is conspicuously avoiding something that is common knowledge.

36. "C'um ne li puisse a mal retraire" (384). The verb is from Latin *retractare*, perhaps "so no one could *reconsider* it in a bad light," though "a mal" might carry the sense "maliciously."

37. Contextually it is not hard to remember here that in this culture, any man is entitled by convention to insist, in poetic public performance before the court, that his lady is the fairest in the land. There is something conspicuously wrongheaded or deliberately obtuse from the beginning about the queen's insistence on pulling rank over this question, which makes the court's hustling to address it look more awkward and adds force to the count's comment.

38. Rychner, *Le lais,* 259-60, *ad loc.,* similarly reports a like emendation suggested by Burger.

39. This is the point of their reaction to the second pair of ladies: "Mut les loërent li plusur / De cors, de vis e de colur: / N'i ad cele mieuz ne vausist / Qu'unkes la reïne ne fist" (*Lanv.* 529-32).

40. The lines preface a more conventional romance-courtly *blason* of her face (563-74), ending with the information that she has a cloak, "les pans en ot entur li mis" (572). To ask the question, "In that case, how do we know you could see her sides?" is to see the particular range of courtly voyeurism this passage is working, consistent with the general trope of the not-quite-covered-up that pervades the *lai*.

41. "Look but don't touch.—or you will blow the cover story that we are just talking about facts here by revealing the facts we are actually talking about." The extent to which this *lai* and the *Playboy* cultural phenomenon continually illuminate one another is a source of continual inspiration and bemusement.

42. Kinoshita, "*Cherchez la Femme,*" 270 and 272.

43. Cited in Rychner, *Les lais,* 261, note to line 641.

44. For Ovid I have in mind, of course, the itinerary that runs from the *Amores* through the *Ars amatoria* to the *Remedia amoris*; for Angela Carter, the short tales, especially those collected in *The Bloody Chamber.*

K. Sarah-Jane Murray (essay date winter 2006)

SOURCE: Murray, K. Sarah-Jane. "The Ring and the Sword: Marie de France's 'Yonec' in Light of the *Vie de Saint Alexis.*" *Romance Quarterly* 53, no. 1 (winter 2006): 25-42.

[*In the following essay, Murray compares Marie's lay "Yonec" with the eleventh-century French poem* Vie de saint Alexis, *noting their shared themes: the chivalric code vs. Christianity, lineage and paternity, marriage, truth vs. the supernatural, and disguise.*]

In the tale of **"Yonec"** (ca. 1165), Marie de France recounts the tragic love affair of a young and cruelly treated *malmariée* who falls in love with a marvelous shape-shifting Christian knight. The heroine's great joy turns to bitter sadness when her lover, Muldumarec, who flies in through her bedroom window in the shape of a hawk, is trapped and mortally wounded by her jealous husband. In a touching scene, moments before his death, the hawk-knight entrusts to the lady his ring and his sword. This episode bears a striking similarity to a decisive and equally moving scene from the Old French *Vie de saint Alexis* (ca. 1040). On the night of his wedding, before abandoning his beautiful bride, St. Alexis gives her his ring and his sword for safekeeping.

Stories involving the gift of a ring abound in Old French literature of the twelfth century (see Ruck, Guerreau-Jalabert).[1] The simultaneous gift of a ring *and* a sword, however, is much rarer.[2] The similarity of the episodes in **"Yonec"** and *Vie de saint Alexis* merits exploration. To be sure, the two works belong to very different genres. The *Vie de saint Alexis (Vie)* constitutes a vernacular life of the romanized St. Alexis, translated from a tenth-century Latin *Vita* and issued from a lengthy and complex textual tradition (Uitti, "Old French" and "Life"). Marie's *lai,* on the other hand, is a short, predominantly Celtic narrative, that claims its roots within the oral traditions of the *matière de Bretagne*.[3] Nonetheless, a close reading of the two poems reveals that they share many themes and motifs and poetic ways of expressing them. Both works possess an undeniably Christian character. From the outset, however, they are dominated by earthly concerns. In keeping with the Old French *Vie,* Marie's *lai* underlines the importance of lineage and paternity, which are closely associated with the idea of worldly position and the necessity of securing an heir. The second part of my study addresses the question of marriage. Indeed, the framework provided by the *Vie de saint Alexis* suggests that the focus of **"Yonec"** is not an adulterous relationship. Rather, by giving his ring and his sword to Marie's heroine, Muldumarec effectively marries her. The new relationship, sanctioned by God, transcends the lady's purely social (and barren) wedding to a jealous *vieillard*. Finally, the ending of **"Yonec"**—centered on the concealment and subsequent revelation of the hero's identity—continues to build on (and gloss) Alexis's story while emphasizing, once again, the truth revealed by the saint to his bride on their wedding night: that there is no happiness in this world. Throughout **"Yonec"**, Marie de France echoes a wide number of texts and traditions (see Johnston) both sacred and profane: the Annunciation (Freeman), the *Song of Songs,*

the legends of *Tristan et Iseut,* and references to Celtic faery lore (Cross, *Celtic*; Illingworth; Mickel 88). But it is Alexis's *Vie*—the principal echo or allusion—that imparts the overarching unity and coherence to Marie's poetic enterprise.

If, as Philippe Ménard is careful to remind us, it is extraordinarily difficult in Marie's *Lais* to discern between the marvelous and the real (151-89), scholars have not hesitated to observe the especially supernatural and symbolic qualities of **"Yonec"** (Damon; Hœpffner; Clifford 968-96). The tale possesses an overt Christian and marvelous character (Depres; Nelson; Ribard). For example, when Muldumarec first appears, responding to the heroine's plea for help, the mysterious knight is presented to the audience as a savior figure (Burgess 163). He reveals to Marie's lady that he has loved her for a very long time, but could not come to her until she called for him (vv. 134-37).[4]

This passage, in particular, recalls the setting of the *Song of Songs,* in which the voice of the lover responds to the bride only after she professes her love for him (1.1-7). Biblical elements continue to set the stage for the *lai* when, in order to reassure Marie's heroine—and her audience—of his Christian identity and charitable intentions, Muldumarec recites the Credo (vv. 153-58) and takes communion (vv. 190-91).[5] Finally, the scene depicting the hawk-knight's death, a direct consequence of the lovers' betrayal by the lady's husband and his widowed sister, recalls in many ways Christ's own sacrifice. Although he displays foreknowledge of the plot (vv. 209-14), Muldumarec, motivated by love, nevertheless goes to meet his beloved and his doom. As he flies through the window, his flesh is pierced by iron (spearlike) stakes, and his blood, in a *clin d'œil* to the Tristan legends, stains the white bedsheets (v. 320). Muldumarec's story effectively imitates Christ's and identifies the hawk-knight as a saintly figure. In **"Yonec"**, the theological and courtly realms are closely intertwined (Freeman 243-61). Within this context, Marie's allusion to the *Vie de saint Alexis* is certainly not out of place.

Like the Old French *Vie,* Marie's *lai* strongly emphasizes the importance of lineage and paternity. This theme extends to the very title of the *lai,* which has often puzzled scholars. Michele Freeman has stated critics' major objection to it in a most compelling manner: "One is tempted to question this choice of title. After all, why should Marie select as the subject of her poem a male character who makes but a fleeting appearance at its close, who speaks no lines, and who performs only one action described in a single couplet?" (243). The rubrications in MSS. Harley 978 and B.N.F. fr. 24432 attest, nevertheless, that such a title was favored by the scribes of the manuscript tradition.[6]

Readers of these codices are invited to look backward through time and understand Marie's *lai* as the story of Yonec's lineage and origin. This is precisely what the poetess urges in the prologue to her tale. After explicitly addressing her audience in the first person (*vus die*), she then introduces Yonec by name, invokes the circumstances of his birth, and finally, reveals the identity of his father:

> En pensé ai e en talant
> que d'Yonec vus die avant
> dunt il fu nez, e de sun pere
> cum il vint primes a sa mere.
> *Cil ki engendra Yonec*
> *aveit a nun Muldumarec.*

(vv. 5-10; emphasis added)

"It is my intention and my desire henceforth to tell you about Yonec, under what circumstances he was born and how his father, whose name was Muldumarec, first met his mother."

Nowhere else in her **Lais** does Marie "insist so strongly on the issue of paternity" (Freeman 243). The author presses into her service the rhyme scheme of two successive octosyllabic couplets to implicitly draw her audience's attention to, on one hand, the relationship between Yonec's parents (*pere/mere*), and on the other, the association of the son and father (*Yonec/Muldumarec*).[7] Marie's *lai* is presented poetically, from the outset, not only as a tale of love but as a story "whereby [Yonec] can be legitimately accepted" as the ruler of his father's kingdom (Freeman 257).

Similar dynastic concerns are central to the *Vie de saint Alexis* (Durling). A closer examination of the opening lines of the *Vie* reveals several striking analogies between the hagiographical narrative and Marie's *lai*. Even before Alexis is named by the author of the *Vie*, the holy youth is presented, like Yonec, in relationship to his father, Count Eufemien:

> Si fut uns sire de Rome la citet;
> Riches om fut, de grand nobilitet:
> Pur çol vos di d'un suen fil vueil parler.

(*Vie,* vv. 13-15)[8]

"There was a lord in the city of Rome: he was a powerful man, of high nobility. I am telling you this, because I wish to speak about a son of his."

Eufemien's presence is even more overwhelming in the prologue to the St. Alban's Psalter's copy of the *Vie*. This passage, relegated to an appendix by Gaston Paris, is frequently ignored by modern editors of the work.[9] To be sure, linguistic evidence suggests that the piece was not composed by the poet responsible for the *Vie*, yet in the manuscript, both the prologue and Alexis's story have been copied in the same hand:

> Ici cumencet amiable cancun e spiritel raisun d'iceol noble barun eufemien par num, e de la vie de sum filz boneuret del quel nus avum oit lire e canter. [P]ar le divine volentet il desirrables icel sul filz angendrat [. . .].

"Here begins the pleasant song and spiritual account of that noble baron named Eufemien, and of the life of his blessed son about whom we have heard readings and song. By the divine will and his own wish he [Eufemien] begat this one son [. . .]."

The above passage does not name Alexis. As Margaret Jubb has noted, "the writer purports to be introducing the story of the father Eufemien and only by extension the life of his blessed son" (n.p.). In so doing, the St. Alban's prologue effectively glosses the *Vie de saint Alexis* (especially vv. 13-15), and brings to light the poem's central themes of paternity and *lignage*. Marie employs a similar technique when she introduces the character of Yonec to her audience for the first time. Although the poetess announces her desire to tell us of Yonec (vv. 5-6), the main focus of the narrative will be the story of his parents and, in particular, his father (vv. 7-10). In other words, whereas the Old French *Vie* begins by presenting Alexis's father Eufemien and focuses on the story of his son, Marie's *lai* reverses this paradigm and introduces the son, Yonec, only to subsequently devote much of her narrative to the story of his father. At the same time, Yonec, who is the first character to be named by Marie, remains in the mind of the audience throughout the presentation of her tale, just as St. Alexis is present, through his unexpected absence, to the reader or auditor of the St. Alban's prologue to the *Vie*.

Questions of lineage continue to play an important role throughout **"Yonec."** Within the first lines, the narrator introduces us to a powerful and elderly man ("uns riches huem, vielz e antis" [vv. 12-13]), who lived in Brittany long ago. Stressing once more the age of the character, Marie tells us how he took a young and noble wife, so that he might have children who would one day inherit his fortune:

> Mult fu trespassez en eage.
> Pur ceo qu'il ot bon heritage,
> femme prist pur enfanz aveir
> ki aprés lui fussent si heir [. . .].

(**"Yonec,"** vv. 17-20)

"He was very old and because his inheritance would be large, he took a wife in order to have children, who would be his heirs [. . .]."

Once again, the poetess pays special attention to the rhyme scheme to underline the husband's social status (*eage/heritage*) and motivations (*enfanz aveir/heir*). From the outset, the *vieillard* is presented as a practical man, who is preoccupied (like Eufemien) with the material world and his earthly legacy. Eufemien, in the Old French *Vie,* is dearly beloved by the emperor and as a result enjoys a life of privilege. In the past men looked toward God for love, but now the emperor has taken his place. This is especially evident when the following symmetrical verse lines are considered side-by-side:

Et al David, cui Deus par *amat* tant
. . . . .

Sour toz ses pers *l'amat* li emperedre [. . .].
(*Alexis,* vv. 7 and 18, emphasis added)
"And [in the time] of David, whom God loved so much
. . . . .

Above all of his peers the emperor loved him [. . .]."

Within this new way of envisioning man's place in the world, the question of lineage becomes extraordinarily important. Eternal life is a gift bestowed by God on those who follow him, yet mortal men may aspire to perpetuate their name, and their place in this world, by arranging a suitable marriage and having children (especially a son). And so Eufemien, who by far surpasses all other nobles in the eyes of the emperor, takes as his wife a woman who appropriately surpasses all the women of the region because of her grace and noble birth: "Donc prist moillier vaillant et onorede, / Des mielz gentilz de tote la contrede" ("And so he took a noble and honorable wife, who came from one of the most well-respected families of all of the land"; *Alexis,* vv. 19-20). For Alexis's father, as for Marie's *vieillard,* worldly position is all-important. Yet from the very beginning of the *Vie de saint Alexis,* Eufemien earns the sympathy and understanding of the audience: the author paints, as Patrick Vincent states, "a warm picture of a good, upright, successful man, devoted to his temporal lord and of exemplary piety. [. . .] He embodies, albeit somewhat ideally, the joys, cares and aspirations common to most fathers" (531). Marie's *vieillard,* however, is a particularly unsympathetic character, who is attracted to his youthful wife because of her ability to bear children and who loves her only for her physical appearance: "Pur sa bealté l'a mult amee" ("He loved her very much because of her beauty"; v. 24). The jealous *vieillard* does not possess the noble and charitable character of Alexis's father: he locks his wife up in a tower, cares little for her well-being, forbids her from seeing friends or family (vv. 43-44), and does not allow her to attend church (vv. 79-80). (One suspects that a number of Marie's female auditors would have sympathized and identified with the plight of the heroine.) The *vieillard*'s so-called marriage to the lady is quickly and overtly condemned by Marie as sinful: "Grand pechié fist ki la dona" ("A great sin was committed by the person who gave her to him"; v. 28). Furthermore,

that barren, loveless, and forced relationship stands in stark opposition to the fruitful marriage of Alexis's parents in the *Vie de saint Alexis.* We recall that, as the years go by, Eufemien and his wife (who remains unnamed[10]) are still without a child. Good Christians, they pray to God that he might grant them a son according to His will (*Alexis,* v. 25); their prayers are fulfilled shortly thereafter. In contrast, the lady's marriage to the *vieillard,* although "official" according to the rules of society, remains childless. This is not, apparently, for lack of physical encounters between the lady and her husband. Although the lady is locked up in a tower for more than seven years, Marie subtly hints at the consummation of their relationship when the heroine, initially referred to as a "pulcele" (v. 21), becomes a "dame" (vv. 35, 39, 49, et al.). The absence of a child can be understood, in turn, as a sign that the union—which has failed to produce the earthly heir the *vieillard* so desperately desires—is not recognized by God as a truly Christian marriage.

The circumstances surrounding Alexis's birth suggest yet another similarity between Marie's **"Yonec"** and the *Vie de saint Alexis.* To a great extent Yonec is, like Alexis, a miracle child. There is no doubt in the reader's mind that Marie's heroine and her lover have experienced, as did Alexis's parents, all the joys that love brings: "Ensemble funt joie mult grant / e par parole e par semblant" ("Together they made great joy, both by talking and by appearance"; **"Yonec,"** vv. 275-76). It is nevertheless puzzling that the knight himself reveals to the lady her sudden pregnancy (of which she apparently has no knowledge): "Il la cunforte dulcement / e dit que duels n'i valt niënt. / De lui est enceinte d'enfant, / un fiz avra pruz e vaillant: / icil la recunfortera. / Yonec numer le fera" ("He comforted her tenderly, saying that grief was of no avail, and telling her she was with child by him and would have a worthy and valiant son who would comfort her"; vv. 329-34). In this scene, which vernacularizes within a courtly setting the Annunciation to Mary by the angel Gabriel (Freeman 250), Yonec's birth is presented as miraculous to the heroine of the tale and to Marie's audience.[11] Formerly confined to a marriage without love and without children, Marie's heroine is suddenly blessed with both. The model provided by Eufemien's marriage to Alexis's mother, which is blessed by God with a child (in answer to the couple's prayers), suggests that the relationship between Marie's heroine and her lover Muldumarec, which also leads to the birth of a miraculous son as a result of the lady's own courtly prayer (vv. 107-08), is sanctioned by God.

The audience's sympathy for the lovers is further increased when the cruel *vieillard* and his widowed sister, who prepare a trap for the hawk-knight, are described as treacherous criminals: "Deus, qu'il ne set la traïsun / que apareillent li felun!" (vv. 299-300). In other words, throughout the first half of her story, Marie leads us to understand that the people doing wrong are not the lovers. In **"Yonec"** the poetess does not condemn the (seemingly) adulterous couple as she will, for example, in **"Equitan."** This does not mean, however, that Marie approves of adultery in **"Yonec."** Rather, she invites us to reflect on the true nature of marriage. Has the *vieillard,* through his cruel, unjust and unchristian treatment of Marie's heroine, forfeited—as will the bumbling Arthur in Chrétien de Troyes's *Chevalier de la Charrette*—all rights to his wife? The *Vie de saint Alexis* offers an interesting context in light of which readers of **"Yonec"** might explore Marie's definition of marriage.

When Alexis grows up, his parents wish him to wed according to his rank and assume an important role in the service of the emperor. Although the youth shows little interest in worldly honors or possessions, count Eufemien finds his son a beautiful, noble, young—and, likely, fertile—wife. The maid is a perfect match: "Fut la pulcele de molt halt parentet, / Fille ad un comte de Rome la citet" (vv. 41-42).[12] But when Alexis beholds his bride in the nuptial chamber, his love for her reminds him of his calling to serve God:

> Com vit le lit, esguardat la pulcele;
> Donc lui remembret de son seignour celeste,
> Que plus at a chier que tote rien terrestre [. . .].
>
> (*Vie,* vv. 56-58)

> "When he sees the bed, he looked at the maiden; he then remembers his Heavenly Lord, whom he holds dearer than any earthly thing [. . .]."

In the saint's eyes, his wife's beauty is a temptation to sin: "'E! Deus!' dist il, 'si forz pechiez m'apresset'" ("'Oh, God!' he said, 'how greatly sin aflicts me!'"; v. 59). By coupling with her in the flesh, he fears that he will lose God—"'S'or ne m'en fui, molt criem que ne t'en perde'" ("'If I do not flee now, I am very afraid that I will lose you!'"; v. 60)—and eventually her as well. The *clerc*'s choice of the verb *remembret* (v. 57) is central to understanding the passage. Alexis sees the young woman (*esguardat*; v. 56), and then remembers his heavenly Lord. When Alexis sees his beautiful bride, he experiences a love of the flesh, and as a response to her beauty, immediately turns his love toward God (Uitti, "Old French" 281-92; Uitti, "Life" 45-40). Alexis's reaction thus illustrates and exemplifies the words of Bernard of Clairvaux in *On Loving God*:

> [. . .] Since we are carnal and are born of concupiscence of the flesh, our cupidity or love must begin with the flesh, and when this is set in order, our love advances by fixed degrees, led on by grace, until it is consummated in the spirit, for not what is spiritual

comes first, but what is animal, then what is spiritual [1 Cor. 15.46]. It is necessary that we bear first the likeness of an earthly being, then that of a heavenly being.

> (ch. 15)

True love, according to Alexis, is not of this world. Our mortal lives are fragile and nothing lasts. Any joy humans may experience quickly turns (as it will for Marie's heroine) into great sadness. But through God, man and woman truly become one for all eternity. Alexis asks his bride to become the spiritual bride of her Savior rather than serve her worldly husband in the flesh:

> "Oz mei, pulcele? Celui tien ad espous
> Qui nos redemst de son sanc precious
> An icest siecle nen at parfite amor;
> La vide est fraiele, n'i at durable onour;
> Ceste ledece revert a grant tristour."
>
> (*Vie,* vv. 66-70)

> "'Do you hear me, maiden? Consider him as your husband who redeemed us with his precious blood. In this world there is no perfect love. Life is frail, there is no lasting honor in it; this joy turns back into great sadness.'"

The model of such a love relationship is provided, according to St. Bernard, by the *Song of Songs*. It is therefore interesting that, while Alexis asks his youthful wife to become the *sponsa* of the canticle, Marie's heroine will reenact the very actions of Solomon's passionate bride. In a marvelous (or miraculous?) passage of the *lai*, the lady leaps through her window; the narrator immediately remarks that it is a *merveille* ("marvel") that she does not kill herself (v. 342).[13] Dressed only in her nightshirt (like Dané in the Old French *Narcisus et Dané*[14]), she follows the trail of Muldumarec's blood along a path (vv. 345-49), through a mysterious entrance that leads under a hill (vv. 350-59), across the fields (vv. 360-63), and throughout a foreign city (vv. 364-96). Nothing, not even the darkness (v. 357), prevents her from seeking out and eventually finding he whom she loves. It is as though she performs, before the readers' very eyes and within the setting of the marvelous Celtic and courtly faery world, the actions of the *Song of Songs*:

> By night on my bed I sought him whom my soul loveth: I sought him but I found him not. I will rise now, and go about the city in the streets, and in the broad ways I will seek him whom my soul loveth: I sought him, but I found him not. [. . .] But I found him whom my soul loveth: I held him, and would not let him go.
>
> (3.1-4)

Such is, to borrow the words of the Old French *Piramus et Tisbé*, the courage that love gives to Marie's heroine: "Tel hardement li done Amour!" (Baumgartner, v. 609).[15]

Although Alexis is pressed to leave his bride behind in the nuptial chamber, he does not forsake her. Karl Uitti has convincingly argued that, in giving his ring and sword to the bride, Alexis celebrates and renews his wedding vows (Uitti, "Life" 40). The solemnity of the scene is carefully emphasized by the illustrator of the Alexis quire in the St. Alban's Psalter (ca. 1123).[16]

To the far left of the tripartite image preserved on fol. 57r, Alexis and his bride stand facing one another, as the young woman accepts her husband's gifts. Above the image is the following caption: "Ultima pudice donantur / munera sponse anulus et / remge verboru[m] finis / et ave" ("Final gifts are given to the chaste bride. A ring and a swordbelt, the end of words, and hail"). The gift of the ring and the sword establishes a new covenant, a new form of marriage between the spouses, which transcends and takes the place of the old. At the center of the same image, the emotional bride, clutching her face in her hands, watches alone as Alexis departs from his parents' home. To the right of the tripartite image, Alexis sails away.

Like Alexis, Muldumarec must leave his beloved physically alone in this world. But, before dying, he, too, gives to her his ring and his sword. (The latter is entrusted to the lady in safekeeping for Muldumarec's unborn son.)[17] If read in light of the *Vie*, then, we see that with his own "final gifts" Muldumarec effectively marries the heroine of Marie's story. The spiritual bond established between the lady and the hawk-knight supercedes her artificial and purely social union to the cruel *vieillard*.[18]

In the *Vie de saint Alexis*, the holy man returns to Rome and lives, unrecognized and in secret, under his parents' stairs, where he eventually dies. A letter written by the saint moments before his death is read aloud in public and reveals his identity. Heartbroken, Alexis's *pulcele* expresses her profound grief: "si grant dolor ui m'est apareude / mielz me venist, amis, que morte fusse" ("such great grief has now come upon me! It would be better for me, my beloved, if I were dead"; *Alexis*, v. 484-85). Marie transforms the words spoken by Alexis's *pulcele* into a dramatic scene, whereby we witness, firsthand, the grief of the heroine: "Si tost cum ele l'a veü, / le chevalier a cuneü. / Avant ala tute esfreee; / par desus lui cheï pasmee" ("As soon as she saw the knight, she recognized him and approached in alarm, falling over him in a swoon"; vv. 397-400). As she leans over the body of her dying lover, Marie's lady also exclaims, "Amis / Meilz veuil ensemble od vus murir" ("Beloved, I should rather die together with you"; **"Yonec,"** v. 414-15). Neither of the young women is destined, however, to be reunited with her loved one until she lives out the rest of her natural life. Alexis's bride shows her love for the saint by devoting her life

to the service of God. Muldumarec's lady (and here is the twist or *sen* of Marie's tale) must raise her son in secret after returning to the cruel *vieillard*, who will surely kill her: "S'a lui revois, il m'ocira" ("If I go back to him, he will kill me"; v. 417). Fortunately, Muldumarec's ring has the power to make the old man forget—or more precisely, to not remember ("n'en memberra")—everything that has happened as long as the lady wears it on her finger (vv. 420-22).[19] This constitutes an interesting play on the properties of the ring in the *Vie*. The saint entrusts the ring and sword to his bride, whose beauty makes him remember ("remembret") God. In turn, the objects serve as a physical reminder to the bride of her loving husband.[20] In **"Yonec,"** the comfort provided by the ring and sword to the heroine is rendered explicit by the author, who adds, "Ele s'en vet; l'anel en porte / e l'espee ki la cunforte" ("She went away wearing the ring and carrying the sword that comforted her"; vv. 445-46). Thus, the power of Alexis's ring is both preserved and reversed in Marie's tale: it simultaneously reminds the lady of Muldumarec and magically prevents the *vieillard* from remembering anything that has happened.

For many years, the identity and lineage of Yonec are carefully concealed. The youth lives, like Alexis, as a stranger in his own home.[21] Marie's heroine shares in this alienation: as she presumably goes through her daily routine, her history is kept secret by the magical ring's power. Thus, the remainder of the *lai* is marked by the themes of disguise and nonrecognition that dominate the second half of Saint Alexis's story: no one sees the lady or Yonec for who they truly are. It is not, as one might expect, until the end of the *lai* that the truth is revealed. In the days preceding the feast of St. Aaron, the *vieillard*, Yonec, and the lady visit an abbey near Caerleon in Wales. There they discover a sumptuous tomb, where the body of a noble knight is laid to rest in great honor (see Burgess 160-61). The local people tell the story ("recunte"; v. 518) of how their lord died for the love of a lady (v. 526). Since that day, they have been without a king; they await, as instructed by the dead knight, the coming of his son (vv. 525-30). Immediately on hearing the tale, the lady understands that the knight buried in the abbey is her beloved Muldumarec. The brief oral account of Muldumarec's life and death serves a similar function, in Marie's story, as does Alexis's letter in the Old French *Vie*: both histories—oral and written—reveal the identity of the dead protagonist to those who love him. In the *Vie*, a written document furnishes the explanation. In a manner befitting Marie's own goal to record the Celtic stories she has heard ("des lais pensai qu'oï aveie" [general prologue, v. 33]), the oral tradition takes precedence in **"Yonec."** In addition, the heroine proves herself, like the author, not only to be an inventive poet and storyteller (Freeman 257), but also a talented glossator, who brings to light the *sen* of the oral tradition passed onto her. Throughout the *lais,* Marie interprets and adapts the content of the *matière de Bretagne* for her courtly audience while appealing, in **"Yonec,"** to the *Vie* of the St. Alexis. In a similar fashion, the heroine of *Yonec* interprets and explains to her son the importance of the strange story she hears in front of the tomb in the abbey: "'Beals fiz', fet ele, 'avez oï / cum Deus nus a amenez ci! / C'est vostre pere ki ci gist, / que cist villarz a tort ocist. / Or vus comant e rent s'espee; / jeo l'ai asez lung tens guardee'" ("Fair son, you have heard how God has brought us here! It is your father who lies here, whom this old man unjustly killed. Now I commend and hand over to you his sword, for I have kept it long enough"; vv. 533-38). And so Marie's heroine fulfills the duty entrusted to her by the hawk-knight moments before his death (vv. 425-39). The lady's speech to her son, when read alongside Muldumarec's final words, imparts to the *lai* a symmetrical structure that emphasizes the fulfillment of the promise she made to her dying lover.

> Quant il sera creüz e granz
>
> . . . . .
>
> A une feste u ele irra
>
> . . . . .
>
> Iluec li baillera l'espee[22]
> *L'aventure li seit cuntee*
> *cum il fuz nez, ki l'engendra;*
>
> . . . . .
>
> "*C'est vostre pere ki ci gist*
> *que cist villarz a tort ocist.*
> Or vus comant e rent s'espee;
> *Jeo l'ai asez lung tens guardee.*"

(**"Yonec,"** vv. 429, 431, 437-39, 535-38)

"When he had grown up [. . .] at a feast to which she will go [. . .] there she would give the sword to his son who was to be told the story of his birth and who his father was; [. . .] 'it is your father who lies here, whom this old man unjustly killed. Now I commend and hand over to you his sword, for I have kept it long enough.'"

The heroine's speech to Yonec actualizes and brings to life Muldumarec's words. Although her lover is dead, the lady responds to him. Through this symmetry, Marie's *lai* takes on a central poetic structure closely analogous to that of the *Vie de saint Alexis.* In that tale, when Alexis's bride beholds the body of her dead husband, her touching *planctus* responds to the request made by him so many years before: with her last words, she devotes the rest of her life to the service of God. An elaborate symmetry—the poetic symbol of the couple's spiritual union—transforms the words spoken by St. Alexis and his bride into a passionate dialogue:

> "Oz mei, pulcele? Celui tien ad espous
> Qui nos redemst de son sanc precious
> *An icest siecle nen at parfite amor;*
> *La vide est fraiele, n'i at durable onour;*
> *Ceste ledece revert a grant tristour."*
>
> . . . . .
>
> *Ja mais ledece n'avrai, quer ne puet estre,*
> *Ne charnel ome n'avrai ja mais an terre*
> Deu servirai, le rei ki tot governet:
> Il nem faldrat, s'il veit que jo lui serve."

(*Alexis,* vv. 66-70 and 492-95)

"Do you hear me, maiden? Consider him as your husband who redeemed us with his precious blood. In this world there is no perfect love. Life is frail, there is no lasting honor in it; this joy turns back into great sadness. [. . .] Nevermore will I have any joy, that cannot be; nor will I take a man again in the whole earth. I will serve God, the king who governs everything; He will not fail me, if He sees that I serve him."

Hence, in both of our tales the narrative achieves closure, and poetically comes full circle, thanks to the words spoken by the (unnamed) female protagonists. As the respective compositions come to an end, each of the faithful young women obtains that which she most deeply desires: in death, she is reunited with her spiritual husband. No sooner does Marie's heroine reveal the truth to her son then she faints, never to wake again: "Sur la tombe cheï pasmee; / en la pasmeisun devia: / unc puis a hume ne parla" ("On the tomb she fell into a faint; while unconscious, she died. She never spoke again"; vv. 544-46). Although her dead body does not fall immediately over the knight's but lies, instead, on top of his tomb, the audience (and readers) of **"Yonec"** will not fail to recognize the author's allusion to such *liebestode* as *Piramus et Tisbé, Narcisse,* or *Tristan et Iseut.* Ironically, just as Alexis's parents received from God exactly what they had asked for (a son according to his will who, consequently, showed little concern for the material world), so, too, is the prayer of Marie's heroine fulfilled to the very letter: she has become the heroine in an *aventure* resembling the stories she had once heard (vv. 95-97).[23] Like Heloise—and the bride of St. Alexis in the Middle High German version (*Das Leben de hl.*) of the saint's life—Yonec's mother is laid to rest alongside Muldumarec, in the same tomb: "a grant honur la dame unt prise / e el sarcu posee e mise / delez le cors de sun ami; / Deus lur face bone merci!" ("they took the lady in great honor and laid her in the tomb beside the body of her beloved; God have mercy on them"; vv. 553-56).[24] Unable to be together in this life, the couple is finally reunited in death for all eternity. Presumably they experience, as do Alexis and his bride, an abundance of joy: "Ne vos sai dire com lour ledece est grande" ("I cannot express how great their joy is"; *Vie,* v. 610).

And, yet, the ending of **"Yonec"** deviates from the *Vie*. After the revelation of truth, Yonec cuts off the head of his evil stepfather with his father's sword. In so doing, the son has avenged both his father and his mother: "Quant sis fiz veit que morte fu / sun parastre a le chief tolu. / De l'espee ki fun sun pere / a dunc vengié lui e sa mere" ("When her son saw she was dead, he struck off his stepfather's head. With his father's sword he thus avenged both his father and his mother"; vv. 547-50). Whereas the *Vie de saint Alexis* ends with a message of forgiveness, peace, and love, the conclusion of the *lai* is bathed in bloodshed and revenge. Yonec's actions bear a close resemblance to a passage from the Gospel of St. Matthew that records Jesus's warning to his followers:

> Do not think that I have come to bring peace on the earth; I have not come to bring peace, but a sword. For I have come to set a man against his father, and a daughter against her mother, and a daughter-in-law against her mother-in-law; and a man's foes will be those of his own household. He who loves father or mother more than me is not worthy of me; and he who loves son or daughter more than me is not worthy of me.

(10.34-37)

According to the Gospel, the idea of holiness is directly opposed to the concept of lineage. This is one of the central themes of both the *Vie de saint Alexis* and **"Yonec"** (Durling 451-54, cf. Gourian). In Marie's *lai*, the eponymous hero is effectively "set against" the man he believed to be his father. True to the words recorded by Saint Matthew, the *vieillard*, who desired a son only to ensure the perpetuation of his wealth and influence in this world, has been punished. At the same time, Marie's tale comes full circle by returning to the worldly considerations of lineage, power, and prowess with which it had begun. Yonec, whose lineage is now established, is accepted as lord of his father's lands: "Lur seignur firent d'Yonec, / ainz que il partissent d'ilec" ("They made Yonec their lord before leaving this place"; vv. 557-58). The *translatio imperii*, represented by the transfer from father to son of the rule over Muldumarec's kingdom, is complete. Yonec has become, like Muldumarec before him (and in a manner that eerily recalls the presentation of the *vieillard* at the beginning of the *lai*), a powerful man. There is no indication at this point, however, that the transfer of knowledge (or *translatio studii*) has been equally successful. Will Yonec (and Marie's audience) understand the story entrusted to him by his mother? In a final effort to reveal the meaning—and truth—of her fabulous narrative to her auditors and readers, the author reminds us that the tale was primarily recorded so as to commemorate the pain and suffering endured by the two lovers: "Cil ki ceste aventure oïrent / lunc tens après un lai en firent, / de la peine e de la dolur / que

cil sufrirent pur amur" ("Those who heard this story long afterwards composed a *lai* from it, about the sorrow and grief that they [the lovers] suffered for love"; vv. 559-62). In other words, Marie entrusts to her readers, once more, the crux of Alexis's message to his young bride on the night of their wedding: there is no happiness in *this* world ("Ceste ledece revert a grant tristour"; *Alexis*, v. 70).[25] Those who hear the *lai* are invited, at each performance, to understand this foundational teaching of the *Vie de saint Alexis*. Thus Marie's courtly and Celtic narrative takes on the didactic and exemplary quality of the Old French saint's *Vie*. It remains to be seen if we, in the real world, and Yonec, in the storybook realm, will be able to apply this lesson to our own lives in the future. We, too, must wait and see what Yonec will do: "asez verrunt qu'il en fera" (v. 440).

In conclusion, Muldumarec's gift of the ring and the sword to Marie's heroine invites readers to understand **"Yonec"** in light of the popular eleventh-century *Vie de saint Alexis*. Indeed, the two vernacular compositions share much in common: the authors' preoccupation with lineage at the beginning of both poems; the miraculous circumstances surrounding the births of Alexis and Yonec; the centrality of the anonymous female protagonists, who embody the determination and courage of the *sponsa* in the *Song of Songs*; the themes of disguise and nonrecognition that loom over Alexis's homecoming and the lady's return to the *vieillard*'s castle; finally, the revelations of truth that occur on the discovery of Alexis's body in the Old French *Vie* and of Muldumarec's tomb in Marie's tale. Furthermore, the framework provided by the *Vie de saint Alexis* suggests that the focus of **"Yonec"** is not, as it will be in her **"Equitan,"** an adulterous relationship. Instead, Marie presents to her audience a careful and thoughtful meditation on the true nature of marriage. The lady's barren wedding to the cruel *vieillard*, devoid of love and not sanctioned by God, clearly opposes the fruitful and loving relationship of the heroine with Muldumarec. Through the gift of the ring and the sword, the mortally wounded hawk-knight marries the heroine of the Celtic poem, just as St. Alexis reaffirms his wedding vows to his youthful bride before leaving Rome.[26]

"Yonec" is a tale about pain and suffering; it is also a story of love and hope. Marie's poem teaches us (as does the Old French *Vie*) that happiness in this world is transient, yet joy is everlasting in the life to come. **"Yonec"** thus demonstrates how the *matière de Bretagne*, which Jean Bodel will soon qualify as "vain and pleasing" in the *Chanson des Saisnes* (ca. 1200), is capable of serving a purpose as "learned and wise" as the *matière de Rome*—if only we, as auditors and readers of the *lai*, are astute enough to gloss its letter. The birth of Yonec reminds us, however, that the *lai* is not a simple rewriting, within a Celtic and courtly setting, of St. Alexis's *Vie.* The true subtlety of Marie's storytelling resides in her ability to allude to multiple literary and cultural backgrounds without anchoring her composition in, or limiting it to, any one distinct tradition. Marie crafts an astonishingly rich web of allusions, bound together like the images of an intricate tapestry, to works that form a corpus in light of which the educated reader can begin to appreciate the complexity of her humanistic and highly vernacular poetic gloss. One would be hard-pressed to find a more poignant example of what Chrétien de Troyes calls, in his prologue to *Érec et Énide,* "une moult bele conjointure" ("a most beautiful conjoining"; v. 14).

Notes

I would like to thank Matthieu Boyd, Peter F. Dembowski, Norris J. Lacy, Maud Simon, Raymond Cormier, and the reviewer for *Romance Quarterly,* who read and commented in detail on this article. It is all the better for their thoughtful suggestions. I would also like to thank the Biblioteca Apostolica Vaticana, British National Library, and Bibliothèque Nationale de France for providing me with access to their manuscript collections during the summers of 2001 and 2004. A section of this article was presented in a session sponsored by the International Marie de France Society at the fortieth International Congress on Medieval Studies in Kalamazoo, Michigan, on May 7, 2005.

1. Lancelot in *Le Chevalier de la Charrette* owns a magic ring given to him by the Lady of the Lake that has the power to reveal to its wearer enchantments that would otherwise not be seen. Rings are commonly exchanged as love tokens: in *Érec et Énide,* for example, the beautiful Énide gives a ring to her husband Érec, sealing her promise to remain faithful to him while he is away, provided that he agree to return within the year. (Énide promptly sends her maiden to recuperate the ring when Érec does not honor that promise.) The list of examples is endless; Marie's *Lais* alone offer several further cases in point: *Guigemar, Laüstic, Fresne, Chaitivel, Milun,* and *Eliduc.* Quotations are from Marie de France's *Lais,* ed. Karl Warnke; English translations, slightly modified, are by Glynn S. Burgess.

2. No further examples of the simultaneous gift of a ring and a sword are noted in the indexes compiled by Thompson; Cross, *Index*; Pickford and Last; Ruck; Guerreau-Jalabert; or Tusach. The closest analogous example in Old French literature survives perhaps in Béroul's *Tristan,* when Mark places a sword between the lovers sleeping in the forest and slides his own ring onto Iseut's hand. (On the theme of the sword of chastity, see

Brockington.) At least one instance of the motif survives in an ancient Irish tale, *The Battle of Mag Mucrama (Cath Maige Mucrama).* The possible influences of that work on Marie's *lai* demands further investigation. It is also worthy of note that rings and swords both figured prominently in medieval marriage ceremonies; in medieval Germany, for example, there are accounts of a ring being handed to the bride on a sword hilt (see Davidson 962).

3. M. B. Ogle opposed the Celtic provenance of *Yonec,* insisting that all of the motifs found in the *lai* of *Yonec* survive in classical literature. One thinks, for example, of the many instances in Ovid's *Metamorphoses* when Jupiter takes on the form of an animal to sleep with (or in Europa's case, rape) a beautiful mortal woman who then gives birth to a semi-divine child. As Judith Shoaf comments in her online translation of *Yonec* (2, n. 3), the situation of Marie's imprisoned heroine closely resembles the classical story of Danae, who was locked in a tower by her father to prevent her from conceiving a child. Ovid adds in the *Amores*: "Si nunquam Danaen habuisset aenea turris / non esset Danae de Jove facta parens" ("If the bronze tower had not held Danae, Danae would not have been made a parent by Jove") *Ovid: Metamorphoses,* ed. G. P. Goold, trans. F. J. Miller, 2 vols., Loeb Classical Library, Cambridge: Harvard UP, 1984. The Christian St. Barbara was also held captive in a tower by her father—because (like St. Alexis) she did not wish to marry—and was fed by God's messengers. In any case, Marie's adventure is colored by an undeniably Celtic setting, as suggested by the place (Caerleon) and character names (Muldumarec, Yonec) she chose.

4. I'm using the Laurence Harf-Lancner edition for quotations from the *Lais* in Old French; the translations (slightly modified) are based on Keith Busby's Penguin translation.

5. Jean d'Arras's Mélusine (ca. 1390) also reassures Raimondin by reciting the Credo (Harf-Lancner 381-90).

6. Marie's tale *Milun* bears an equally curious title. This *lai,* which constitutes a sort of mirror image of *Yonec,* is also the story of an unnamed *mal-mariée* who gives birth to her lover's son. The young man is raised by his aunt, far from his mother, and his identity concealed until he is old enough to learn the truth. When the time comes, his aunt gives him a letter, written by his mother, in which the young man's true origins are revealed. He also inherits his birth father's ring. Finally, the

protagonist is reunited with his father and mother. In a striking contrast to the end of *Yonec,* it is he who performs, in this world, the marriage ceremony between his parents. Whereas *Yonec* ends on a note of sadness ("pur rappeler la peine et la douleur"; v. 561), *Milun* joyfully celebrates love victorious ("De leur amour et de leur bonheur"; v. 531). Also, whereas *Yonec* bears the name of an absent son, *Milun* bears the name of an equally absent father.

7. In addition, throughout these verses, Yonec himself is associated with both his parents by a chiasmus: "Yonec / sun pere / sa mere / Yonec."

8. Quotes from the Old French *Vie de saint Alexis* are from the edition by Gaston Paris (1980).

9. It is included by Storey in his edition of the Hildesheim manuscript (L), but is not even mentioned by Perugi in his edition.

10. In the Latin *Vita,* however, Alexis's mother is given the name Aglaes.

11. Yonec—whose name signifies "comforter" (Holmes)—will take over his father's role at his mother's side as suggested by the *adnominatio* in v. 329 ("cunforte") and 334 ("recunfortera"). Yonec's identity as "the comforter" is also suggested by the following chiasmus: "Il la cunforte dulcement / e dit que duels n'i valt niënt. / De lui est enceinte d'enfant, / un fiz avra pruz e vaillant: / icil la recunfortera" (vv. 329-34).

12. The bride, like Alexis's mother and Marie's heroine, remains anonymous throughout the saint's tale and is defined only in relationship to her husband. Furthermore, Marie's presentation of the heroine in *Yonec* is virtually identical to the *Vie's* poet's description of the bride. Indeed, when introducing her female protagonist for the first time, Marie writes, "De halt gent fu la pucele" (*Yonec,* v. 21).

13. Old French *merveille* (like Eng. "marvel") derives from Latin *mirabilia* 'wondrous things,' which is closely related to Latin *miraculum* 'miracle.'

14. From Baumgartner's edition of *Narcisus et Dané,* vv. 430-32: "Tote nue fors de chemisse, / Et affublee d'un mantel; / Aloeuc atent le jovenciel" ("Wearing only a shift, and with a cloak around her shoulders; there she waits for the youth").

15. Also from the edition by Baumgartner (see *Pyramus et Thisbé* in the bibliography).

16. Thanks to the *St. Alban's Psalter Project,* scholars now have access to high-quality color images of the entire manuscript online. This valuable resource, provided by the University of Aberdeen, also features simple transcriptions and translations of the materials within the codex, as well as detailed commentaries on the illuminations and several informative scholarly essays.

17. Shoaf has underlined the similarity between the room in which Muldumarec lies and the description provided in the Middle English Corpus Christi Carol, preserved in Oxford MS Balliol 354.

18. In a scene that Marie carefully separates from the giving of the ring and the sword, Muldumarec also gives the lady a dress, so that she might return to the *vieillard*'s home in proper clothing (she had left wearing only her nightshirt): "Quant tut li a dit et mustré, / un shier blialt li a doné; / si li comandé a vestir. / Puis l'a faite de lui partir" ("When he had explained everything to her, he gave her a costly tunic, and ordered her to put it on. Then he made her leave him"). The dress constitutes a seal and a veil on what Muldumarec has just told the lady. By giving her his ring, the hawk-knight has effectively revealed to her the secret of their love and death and future life beyond the grave. This promise is given shape and form with the child who grows within the lady's womb. The secret and the promise, so to speak, live within her body and are of her body. The dress Muldumarec gives to her seals them and veils them as it covers her body itself. Can we not imagine that, years later, when the lady presents the sword to Yonec, she takes it from under that very same dress?

For an Old Irish antecedent of the gift of the dress, see the *Battle of Mag Mucrama.* It is possible that Marie simultaneously drew on that source as well as the *Vie de saint Alexis,* combining Celtic and Mediterranean-centered motifs in her *lai.*

19. A magic ring also causes forgetfulness in the *Merveilles de Rigomer* (vv. 6109-6412).

20. In a similar fashion, the ring in Marie's *Milun* serves as an agent of recognition or remembering. The lady sends the child, with his father's ring and a letter, to her sister. Much later, when the boy is fully grown, the ring allows the father to recognize his son.

21. It is interesting to note that Alexis lives in secret for seventeen years in his parents' home. By the time Yonec's true lineage is revealed, Marie tells us he is fully grown and has been knighted. He is presumably, therefore, close to sixteen or seventeen years old.

22. The corresponding parts of the symmetrical construction are highlighted by the use of bold and italics.

23. Another chiasmus, based on the *adnominatio cunter/cuntee,* binds together the lady's original request and the telling of Muldumarec's and, consequently, her own story (or adventure): "Mult ai sovent oï cunter, / que l'em suleit jadis trover / aventures en cest païs / [. . .] L'aventure li a cuntee . . ." (*Yonec,* vv. 95-97 and 543). Cf. Sturges: "The unnamed heroine, locked in a tower by her jealous husband, wishes that she might gain her freedom by becoming what the author and the reader know her to be: the heroine of a *lai*" (245).

24. In Ovid's *Metamorphoses,* Pyramus and Thisbe's ashes are placed in the same urn—"una requiescet in urna" (4.165). In the Old French version of the legend, Tisbé glosses what this means: in her final plea, she insists that her body be placed alongside Piramus's in the same tomb: "Que nous contiengne .i. seulz tombliaux / Andeus nous recoive .i. vesseaux . . ." (*Piramus et Tisbé,* vv. 856-57).

25. This does not mean that Marie's *lai* displays what Payen has referred to as a "pessimisme assez radical" (63). Instead, Marie's story is imbued, like the Old French *Vie de saint Alexis,* with a profound message of hope.

26. Interestingly, just as Marie's *lai* borrows from the *Vie de saint Alexis,* so, too, does the hagiographical work take on more and more romance characteristics as it evolves over time. Thus, in the thirteenth-century MS *S* (Paris B.N.F. fr. 12471), Alexis no longer gives the ring and the sword to his bride, but, like the hero in the Arthurian romance of *Yder,* draws his sword and splits the golden ring in two. Each spouse safeguards one half of the ring as a promise of their future reunion. (When placed together, the matching halves will allow the lovers to recognize one another.) This narrative development constitutes a compelling illustration of the dynamic and even symbiotic relationship of vernacular hagiography and romance narrative during the twelfth and thirteenth centuries. The mixing of genres in the Old French *Vie de saint Alexis* makes it an example of what Robertson calls a "hagiographical romance" (200-52).

Works Cited

Bernard of Clairvaux. *On Loving God.* Trans. Emero Stiegman. Kalamazoo, MI: Cistercian, 1995.

———. *On the Song of Songs.* Ed. E. Rozanne Elder. Trans. K. Walsh and I. M. Edmonds. Kalamazoo, MI: Cistercian, 1979.

Bodel, Jean. *La Chanson des Saisnes.* Ed. Annette Brasseur. Geneva: Droz, 1989.

Brockington, M. "The Separating Sword in the Tristan Romances: Possible Celtic Analogues Reexamined." *Modern Language Review* 91 (1996): 281-300.

Burgess, Glynn. *The Lais of Marie de France: Text and Context.* Athens: U of Georgia P, 1987.

Cath Maige Mucruma: The Battle of Mag Mucrama. Ed. Máirín O Daly. Dublin: Irish Texts Society, 1975.

Chrétien de Troyes. *Le Chevalier de la Charrette.* Ed. Alfred Foulet and Karl D. Uitti. Paris: Bordas, 1989.

Clifford, Paul. *Marie de France: Lais.* London: Grant and Cuttler, 1982.

Cormier, Raymond. *Three Ovidian Tales of Love: Piramus et Tisbé, Narcisus et Danaé, and Philomena et Procné.* New York: Garland, 1986.

Cross, Tom P. "The Celtic Origin of the *Lay* of *Yonec.*" *Studies in Philology* 11 (1913): 26-60.

———. *Index of Early Irish Literature.* Bloomington: U of Indiana P, 1952.

Damon, Foster. "Marie de France: Psychologist of Courtly Love." *Publications of the Modern Language Association of America* 44 (1929): 968-96.

Das Leben de hl. Alexius von Konrad von Würzburg. Ed. Richard Henczynski. Berlin, 1898.

Davidson, Hilda Ellis. "Sword." *Medieval Folklore.* 2 vols. Santa Barbara: ABC-CLIO, 2000.

Depres, Denise. "Redeeming the Flesh: Spiritual Transformation in Marie de France's *Yonec.*" *Studia Mystica* 10.3 (1987): 26-39.

Durling, Nancy Vine. "Hagiography and Lineage: The Example of the Old French Vie de saint Alexis." *Romance Philology* 40 (1987): 541-69.

Freeman, Michelle. "The Changing Figure of the Male: The Revenge of the Female Storyteller." *In Quest of Marie de France, A Twelfth-Century Poet.* Ed. Chantal A. Maréchal. Lewiston: Mellon, 1992. 243-61.

Gouiran, Gerard. "Les saints et leurs familles dans les vies de saints occitanes." *Les relations de parenté dans le monde médiéval. Senefiance* 26 (1989): 471-86.

Guerreau-Jalabert, Anita. *Index des motifs narratifs dans les romans arthuriens français en vers, XIIe-XIIIe siècles.* Genève: Droz, 1992.

Harf-Lancner, Laurence. *Les fées au Moyen Âge.* Paris: Champion, 1984.

Hoepffner, Ernest. *Les Lais de Marie de France.* Paris: Boivin et cie., 1935.

The Holy Bible: Authorized King James Version. Nashville: Cornerstone, 1999.

Illingworth, R. N. "Celtic Tradition and the *Lai* of *Yonec*." *Études Celtiques* 9 (1960-61): 501-20.

Johnston, Oliver M. "Sources of the *Lay of Yonec*." *PMLA* 20.2 (1905): 322-38.

Jubb, Margaret. "The Old French Life of Saint Alexis." *The St. Alban's Psalter Project.* 2003. June 17, 2004. <http://www.abdn.ac.uk/stalbanspsalter/english/essays/alexisquire.shtml>.

Marie de France. *Lais.* Ed. Karl Warnke. Trans. Laurence Harf-Lancner. Paris: Librairie générale française, 1990.

————. *Lais.* Trans. Glynn S. Burgess. London: Penguin, 1986.

Ménard, Philippe. *Les Lais de Marie de France.* Paris: PUF, 1935.

Mickel, Emmanuel. *Marie de France.* New York: Twayne, 1974.

Nelson, Deborah. "*Yonec*: A Religious and Chivalric Fantasy." *University of Southern Florida Language Quarterly* 16 (1978): 33-35.

Ogle, M. B. "Some Theories in Irish Literary Influence and the *Lay* of 'Yonec.'" *Romanic Review* 10 (1919): 123-48.

Payen, J. C. *Le lai narratif.* Turnhout: Brepols, 1975.

Pickford, Cedric E., and Rex Last, eds. *Arthurian Bibliographies.* Cambridge: Boydell and Brewer, 1981-2002.

Pyrame et Thisbé, Narcisse, Philomena. Ed. and trans. Emmanuelle Baumgartner. Paris: Gallimard, 2000.

Ribard, Jacques. "Le lai d'Yonec est-il une allégorie chrétienne?" *The Legend of Arthur in the Middle Ages: Studies Presented to A. H. Diverres by Colleagues, Pupils, and Friends.* Cambridge: Brewer, 1983. 160-69, 248-50.

Robertston, Duncan. *The Medieval Saints' Lives: Spiritual Renewal and Old French Literature.* Lexington: French Forum, 1995.

Ruck, E. H. *An Index of Themes and Motifs in Twelfth-Century French Arthurian Poetry.* Cambridge: Brewer, 1991.

Shoaf, Judith. *Yonec.* 1993. June 1, 2004. <http://www.english.ufl.edu/exemplaria/marie/yonec.pdf>.

Sturges, Robert. "Texts and Readers in Marie de France's *Lais*." *Romanic Review* 71 (1980): 245.

The St. Alban's Psalter Project. 2003. June 1, 2004. <http://www.abdn.ac.uk/stalbanspsalter/english/index.shtml>.

Thompson, Stith. *Motif-Index of Folk Literature: A Classification of Narrative Elements in Folktales, Ballads, Myths, Fables, Mediaeval Romances, Exempla, Fabliaux, Jest-books, and Local Legends.* Bloomington: Indiana UP, 1955-58.

Tubach, F. C. *Index Exemplorum, A Handbook of Medieval Religious Tales.* Helsinki: Academia Scientiarum Fennica, 1969.

Uitti, Karl D. "The 'Life of Saint Alexis'." *Story, Myth, and Celebration in Old French Narrative Poetry. 1050-1200.* Princeton: Princeton UP, 1973. 3-64.

————. "The Old French *Vie de saint Alexis*: Paradigm, Legend, Meaning." *Romance Philology* 20 (1967): 263-95.

La Vie de saint Alexis, poème du XIe siècle. Ed. Gaston Paris. Classiques Français du Moyen Âge, 4. Paris: Champion, 1980.

La vie de saint Alexis: édition critique. Ed. M. Perugi. Geneva: Droz, 2000.

La vie de saint Alexis: poème du XIe siècle et renouvellements des XIIe, XIIIe et XIVe siècles. Ed. Gaston Paris and L. Pannier. Paris, 1872.

La vie de saint Alexis: texte du manuscrit de Hildesheim (L). Ed. C. Storey. Geneva: Odenkirchen, 1978.

Vincent, Patrick. "The Dramatic Aspect of the Old French *Vie de saint Alexis*." *Romance Philology* 40 (1987): 451-69.

Robert R. Edwards (essay date 2006)

SOURCE: Edwards, Robert R. "Marie de France and *Le Livre Ovide*." In *The Flight from Desire: Augustine and Ovid to Chaucer,* pp. 85-103. New York: Palgrave, 2006.

[*In the following excerpt, Edwards explores the influence of Ovid on Marie's lays, showing how she reconstitutes Ovid's third phase of lovemaking—keeping the lover—into a discourse of frustrated desire for courtly audiences.*]

The *Lais* recounted by Marie de France are stories of desire working within the constraints of love in twelfth-century baronial culture. Marie insists that her stories originate in tales recounted by the Bretons to preserve adventures within cultural memory. Certainly the prominence of folk motifs, themes, and structural patterns argues for the origin of her courtly subject matter (*matiere*) in traditional narratives. Yet, as Marie makes clear in her Prologue, her own authorial grounding is in Latin—which is to say, written—literary culture. The *Lais* depend fundamentally on established traditions of writing, reading, and commentary. Marie says that she takes on the project of composing the *Lais* as a conscious alternative to translating "aukune bone estoire" ("Some good story" [prologue 29]) from Latin to

French.[1] As she shifts her topic from history (*res gesta*) to romance (*aventure*), a signature topic for the vernacular, her approach to the stories nevertheless remains the same as it would be to a Latin text. She follows the model of the ancients who, according to Priscian, composed their works obscurely ("oscurement") so that later readers can gloss them and provide the supplement ("surplus") that completes their meaning within a community of schooled readers: "K'i peüssent gloser la lettre / E de lur sen le surplus mettre" (prologue 15-16). This "surplus," as R. Howard Bloch points out, directs the tales toward the future, not the originary past, toward an audience of readers moved by their own desires, at the same time that it presents reading—glossing the literal body of *aventure* and supplying something beyond what it possesses—as both hermeneutic and erotic.[2]

Marie makes a bold literary claim for her *matiere,* one as ambitious as Dante's assertion over a century later in the *De vulgari eloquentia* that the illustrious vernacular has a coherent and independent poetic tradition. Stephen G. Nichols contends, "she makes the first explicit canon revision in European literary history."[3] At a theoretical level, Marie argues that vernacular stories of love and desire function within the compositional and interpretive procedures of literary culture and that they carry the same exemplary and allegorical value as Latin texts. Like Latin texts, they can bear the attention and scrutiny of moral reflection, which is the possibility for meaning that they hold out for their readers to supply. Such readers, as Robert W. Hanning points out, are a constitutive element of Marie's authorship.[4]

For the *Lais,* scholars generally approach the influence of classical works as a source for specific borrowings, for material gathered discretely from other texts and then inserted into the narrative skein of her stories of *aventure.* They cite narrative parallels from Ovid's *Metamorphoses,* in particular, such as the influence of the tale of Piramus and Thisbe on **"Les Deus Amanz"** and **"Laüstic,"** or of the Philomela story on **"Laüstic,"** and, more generally, the impact of the Narcissus story as a model for narratives on the power of beauty or the *Metamorphoses* as the model for a thematically integrated collection.[5] In this [essay], I want to examine a different facet of Ovid's influence. I begin by focusing on the ekphrasis of Venus in **"Guigemar"** and the apparent repudiation of Ovid implied by that description. It is in Ovid's erotodidactic poems, I contend, that Marie finds a topic and conceptual frame for serious poetic invention rather than rhetorical adornment and learned allusion. Ovid's *Ars amatoria* and *Remedia amoris* furnish a way for Marie to imagine the workings of love and desire within a courtly sphere. She focuses on transforming a complex phase of Ovid's program—maintaining a love affair—into a social form

of stable devotion and service. In **"Eliduc,"** which ends the *Lais* in the only complete medieval arrangement of her stories, she ostensibly turns to an Augustinian transcendence of desire that nonetheless continues to serve some of its demands.

THE PAINTED ROOM AND OVID'S BOOK

In **"Guigemar,"** Marie introduces Ovid's erotic teaching as part of an elaborate architectural description. The aging lord of the city to which the wounded Guigemar is carried by a mysterious ship protects the chastity of his young wife by placing her in an green marble enclosure situated beneath the donjon of his castle. The enclosure has a single, guarded entry and contains inside it a room where the wife is accompanied only by the lord's niece. The key to the gate of the enclosure is held by a castrated old priest who says mass in the chapel at the entrance to the room and serves meals to the wife. The sexual imagery of the phallic donjon looming over the enclosure translates immediately into the symbolism of male power seeking to contain and dominate female sexuality. It is an assertion of control that also reveals the anxiety at the heart of baronial power. For there is a mordant irony in an impotent old man acting as unlikely gate keeper, spiritual warden, and domestic staff in place of a vigilant and jealous old husband, driven now by envy rather than lust. The *senex amans* ("old lover") has accidentally and comically produced a sterile version of himself as the support staff in his wife's love story. The most striking detail of Marie's description, however, is her account of the paintings that adorn the inside of the room:

> La chaumbre ert peinte tut entur;
> Venus, la deuesse d'amur,
> Fu tres bien mise en la peinture;
> Les traiz mustrout e la nature
> Cument hom deit amur tenir
> E lealment e bien servir.
> Le livre Ovide, ou il enseine
> Comment chascuns s'amur estreine,
> En un fu ardant le gettout,
> E tuz iceus escumengout
> Ki jamais cel livre lirreient
> Ne sun enseignement fereint.
> La fu la dame enclose e mise.

(233-45)

[The walls of the chamber were covered in paintings in which Venus, the goddess of love, was skilfully depicted together with the nature and obligations of love; how it should be observed with loyalty and good service. In the painting Venus was shown as casting into a blazing fire the book in which Ovid teaches the art of controlling love and as excommunicating all those who read this book or adopted its teachings. In this room the lady was imprisoned.]

Jean Rychner confidently glosses "Le livre Ovide" as the *Remedia amoris.*[6] For other commentators, the literal and figurative meaning of Marie's citation of Ovid remains a topic of critical debate and uncertainty. Herman Braet points out that a case can be made for identifying the Ovidian book as either the *Ars amatoria* or the *Remedia amoris*. Hanning sees a comprehensive reference: "Not just the *Remedia amoris* but the whole Ovidian system (*Ars* and *Remedia* alike), which seeks to control the force and course of love by artfulness and strategy, stands condemned by Venus and by Marie, for whom the goddess here stands surrogate."[7] He suggests elsewhere that Marie displaces Ovid and offers a "vernacular discourse of desire" in which writing gains its authority from pain and provides truthtelling from the margins.[8] SunHee Kim Gertz finds a "dissonant relation" between the description of the mural and the rest of the *lai*.[9] Marie's visual evocation of Ovid discloses its meaning, I believe, through the structure of his program, to which she gives a new configuration and revised content.

. . . Ovid sets out an erotic program with four distinct phases across the *Ars amatoria* and *Remedia amoris*: finding, capturing, keeping, and abandoning a lover when she becomes tedious or troublesome. The medieval *accessus ad auctores* describes the first three phases as the method of exposition in the *Ars amatoria*: "Modus istius operis talis est, ostendere quo modo puella possit inveniri, inventa exorari, exorata retineri" ("The mode of this work is such that it shows how a girl can be found, captured after she is found, and kept after she is captured").[10] The visual details in **"Guigemar"** show that Marie's concern is with the third phase—how a woman can be retained after she has been induced to take a lover ("exorata retineri"). The paintings reveal the nature of love and demonstrate how a man can extend and protract the duration of his love affair: "Cument hom deit amur tenir" (237). The burning of Ovid's book on controlling love ("Comment chascuns s'amur estreine" [240]) effectively cancels out the final stage of the Ovidian program contained in the *Remedia amoris*. It incidentally demolishes a book whose writing Cupid fully sanctions in a scene from Ovid's poem (*Remedia amoris* 40: "Et mihi 'propositum perfice' dixit 'opus'").

The wife is immured, then, within a visual program whose topic is the maintenance of love after hunting and capture but before pleasure, satisfaction, and fulfilment erode. Marie transforms the erotic project from servicing Ovidian appetite against the decaying arc of gratification to sustaining courtly devotion ("lealment e bien servir" [238]). M. L. Stapleton argues that Marie, in effect, "domesticates" Ovid, divesting him of deceit and cynicism.[11] Donald Maddox contends that the scene portrays the need for "intersubjective *reciprocity*," which informs all of Marie's *Lais*.[12] R. Dubuis finds in Marie's *druërie* ("love") an innovative theory of

reciprocal love.[13] Certainly, the emphasis on fidelity in love is expressed consummately later in **"Guigemar,"** in the two knots that only Guigemar and his lady can untie and elsewhere in permutations of the phrase *amer lëalment* ("to love loyally").[14]

In the painted room in **"Guigemar,"** Marie's transformation of eros is expressed in the contrast between the husband's obsessive desire to control his wife by layers of containment ("La fu la dame enclose e mise" [245]) and the devoted lover's task of drawing out and extending the duration of love within those walls and constraints. As Gertz notes, one point of critical debate is whether and how the paintings on the wall bear out the intentions of the husband who presumably authorized their execution in the chamber.[15] Do they represent what he hopes for himself or fears from his wife? Stapleton argues that we must separate the prescription about preserving love faithfully from its mode of representation.[16] To focus on the husband's intentions as a defining source for meaning is, however, to ignore the "surplus" that Marie makes an element of reading in her prologue to the *Lais* and the condition of desire in her writing.[17] It is the lover hovering in the future, the embodiment of husbandly anxiety and wifely desire, who will interpret and perform the scene painted on the walls of the wife's chamber.

"MUT FU DELITUSE LA VIE"

The *ekphrasis* in **"Guigemar"** serves as a poetic emblem for one of the central concerns in the *Lais*—the fragile interim of pleasure which lovers cooperate on constructing for themselves. By canceling the *Remedia*, Marie truncates the four-step Ovidian project to direct the narrative focus to the problem of erotic dilation, to the interval of stolen pleasure unfolding in a joint venture of ingenuity and dedicated, clandestine betrayal. Distinguishing Marie's portrayal of love from both courtly love and romance chivalry, Philippe Ménard stresses its indulgence and *otium*: "In Marie knights hardly look for adventure and glory. By preference, they remain at home to savor untroubled loves at their leisure."[18] Marie's topic, put another way, is the enjoyment and maintenance of reciprocal pleasure operating against time and contingency. In **"Guigemar"** (537) and **"Milun"** (277), Marie uses the word *vie* ("life") to demarcate this erotic interval within the larger narrative. In **"Eliduc,"** the *terme* ("fixed date" [550, 689]) of his military service overseas to the king of Exeter corresponds to his first erotic interval with Guilliadun.

Marie's poetic invention of Ovid builds on the point of greatest vulnerability for the teacher and students of love. As we have seen, the emergence of desire as a force beneath appetite and gratification threatens to disable Ovidian erotodidaxis. Desire is, however, already the starting point for Marie's lovers. Though pleasure and jouissance lead Equitan to chivalry (**"Equitan"** 15-16), he falls in love with the seneschal's wife without seeing her: "Sanz veüe la coveita" (41). So, too, does Milun's beloved, moved as she is by mention of his name. Marie thus poses the question implicit but largely suppressed in the *Ars amatoria*: how do lovers maintain and protract an erotic interim based on desire rather than appetite and simple gratification? The Ovidian lover draws out his liaison by subtrefuge and manipulation and finds a momentary resolution in the equity of sexual exhaustion. Marie explores an interval of erotic reciprocity that varies in time yet remains strikingly constant in structure and intensity. **"Chievrefoil"** recounts a brief meeting of Tristan and Iseut in the forest that encompasses satisfaction, intimacy, and pleasure: "Entre eus meinent joie mut grant. / A li parlat tut a leisir / E ele li dit sun pleisir" ("They shared great joy together. He spoke freely to her and she told him of her desire" [94-96]). The faery mistress of **"Lanval"** promises a succession of these encounters:

> "Quant vus vodrez od mei parler,
> Ja ne savrez cel liu penser
> U nuls puïst aveir s'amie
> Sanz repreoce e sanz vileinie,
> Que jeo ne vus seie en present
> A fere tut vostre talent . . ."

(163-68)

["Whenever you wish to speak with me, you will not be able to think of a place where a man may enjoy his love without reproach or wickedness, that I shall not be there with you to do your bidding."]

Separated from external shame and internalized censorship ("Sanz repreoce e sanz vileinie"), this is the imaginary site of erotic plenitude, the fantasy of a libidinal object fully available and compliant to the lover's demands: "present / A fere tut vostre talent."[19] Sarah Kay points out that the tale turns paradoxically on what is not there—on the substitutions of fetishistic objects and the loss marked by language.[20] Structurally and thematically, Marie sets this illusory presence against the denials and omissions of favor at Arthur's court, which Lanval gladly abandons for Avalon at the end of his tale.

Some of Marie's stories portray the interval of pleasure as real but unreachable. The couple of **"Deus Amanz,"** ostensibly bound in a committed love for each other ("s'entreamerent lëaument" [72]), perishes in their effort to meet the letter but circumvent the constraints imposed by the lady's father, who decrees that anyone seeking his daughter must be able to carry her up the high mountain outside the city of Pitres. What fails them in a practical sense is "mesure" (189), the self-possession and internalized discipline of the Ovidian

lover (*modus*), for the lover resists drinking the potion that will assure success in his trial. The lady of **"Chaitivel"** proves a better Ovidian lover than her suitors, playing all four of them against each other but then losing three to the chance slaughter of a tournament designed to show their prowess. The survivor faces the prospect of endless service without pleasure. He is granted the company of his mistress but no comfort: "Si n'en puis nule joie aveir / Ne de baisier ne d'acoler / Ne d'autre bien fors de parler" ("I cannot experience the joy of a kiss or an embrace or of any pleasure other than conversation" [220-22]).

"Deus Amanz" and **"Chaitivel"** are stories of predicament, in which narrative action is contained by the governing fictional premise (an impossible task or choice), and their stasis reveals a key element of Marie's portrayal of desire. The conditions imposed by the father on his daughter's suitors in **"Deus Amanz"** scarcely conceal his incestuous desire. His unwillingness to suffer the loss of her comfort and proximity ("Pres de li esteit nuit et jur" [30]) provokes widespread censure: "Plusur a mal li aturnerent, / Li suen meïsme le blamerent" ("Many people reproached him for this, and even his own people blamed him" [33-34]). In some measure, the daughter seems to accept and ratify his desire. When she rejects her lover's plea to flee with him, her sympathies lie with her father, and she imagines his response to her flight as that of a rejected lover:

> "Si jo m'en vois ensemble od vus,
> Mis pere avreit e doel e ire,
> Ne vivreit mie sanz martire.
> Certes tant l'eim e si l'ai chier,
> Jeo nel vodreie curucier."

(96-100)

["But if I went away with you, my father would be sad and distressed and his life would be an endless torment. Truly, I love him so much and hold him so dear that I would not wish to grieve him."]

The surviving lover of **"Chaitivel,"** whose wound may be a sign of castration, faces the kind of predicament posed by a love question (*demande d'amour*): is it better for a lover to face rivals with the prospect of consummation, or to have no rivals yet no chance of pleasure?[21] Moreover, his lady's continued deferral after chance has produced a single result represents a flight from desire and from the interim of pleasure that other lovers seek in Marie's tales. These tales of predicament forestall the lovers' consummation precisely because the couple's erotic attachments are uncertain and contested from within. It is a critical commonplace that Marie's lovers must be committed to each other, even in a problematic case like **"Equitan,"** where a lord wrongly desires his vassal's wife. But as **"Deus Amanz"** and **"Chaitivel"** demonstrate, reciprocity demands in turn a commitment to desire (hence **"Equitan"** as a monitory example, a critique not just of lordship blinded by lust but of desire as the condition of unforeseeable reversal).

In stories where Marie goes beyond predicaments to create a richly imagined and potentially unstable fictional world, the dilation of eros finds a complex and highly nuanced treatment. For Guigemar, this period begins with treatment for the wound ("la plaie" [113]) to his thigh caused by the ricocheted arrow during his hunt in the forests of Brittany. The external symbolic wound ("Sa plaie" [370]) healed by the lady in her chamber becomes the indwelling metaphorical wound of love ("Amur est plaie dedenz cors" [483]). When he discloses his love, Guigemar asks the lady not to act like a manipulative Ovidian lover or the conflicted lady of **"Chaitivel."** His request centers on the ethics of managing the erotic interim:

> Femme jolive de mestier
> Se deit lunc tens faire preier
> Pur sei cherir, que cil ne quit
> Que ele eit usé cel deduit. . . .
>
> (515-518)

[A woman who is always fickle likes to extend courtship in order to enhance her own esteem and so that the man will not realize that she has experienced the pleasure of love.]

Glyn Burgess finds in this passage a prescription for loyal service in love.[22] Hanning sees it as an example of Marie's using love casuistry against itself.[23] Jacques Ribard believes that it shows a natural and spontaneous love opposed to calculation and conferring liberty and selfhood.[24] The Ovidian background reminds us how closely Marie links temporality and desire. Ovid recommends that women use delay as a tactic for control, consolidation, and amusement: "Quod datur ex facili, longum male nutrit amorem: / Miscenda est laetis rara repulsa iocis" ("What is easily given ill fosters an enduring love; let an occasional repulse vary your merry sport" [*Ars amatoria* 3.579-80]). Delay (*mora*) hovers between two forms in Ovidian doctrine—*tuta* (safe) and *brevis* (short-lived). The *praeceptor* advises slow lovemaking to his male disciple (2.717-718). He counsels women to time their public entrances to their greatest advantage, adducing a proverb with larger applications to the management of eros: "maxima lena mora est" ("a great procuress is delay" [3.752]). Guigemar condemns the mystification of such tactics; they are, he says, a means for leveraging esteem while obscuring desire. He argues instead for the lady to act on her pleasure: "Ainz l'amerat, s'en avrat joie" ("she should rather love him and enjoy his love" [523]). Revealing desire produces the erotic "surplus" (533) of **"Guigemar."** What fol-

lows from that disclosure is a year-and-a-half interlude replete with sensual pleasure: "Mut fu delituse la vie" ("their life gave them great delight" [537]).

The acknowledgment of desire, such as Guigemar urges, is the precipating event of the parallel story **"Yonec,"** where the aging husband isolates his wife within a paved chamber in his tower, attended by his sister. Here the patriarchal anxieties over lineage, inheritance, and cuckoldry in **"Guigemar"** and other tales are made explicit. The lady laments the isolation forced on her by her husband. The remedy she seeks lies in *aventure* as a social and discursive form, for she turns to stories like her own as they are memorialized within aristocratic culture:

> Chevalier trovoent puceles
> A lur talent, gentes e beles,
> E dames truvoent amanz
> Beaus e curteis, pruz e vaillanz,
> Si que blasmees n'en esteient
> Ne nul fors eles nes veeient.
>
> (95-100)

[Knights discovered maidens to their liking, noble and fair, and ladies found handsome and courtly lovers, worthy and valiant men. There was no fear of reproach and they alone could see them.]

This story she acknowledges as the object of her wish and will ("ma volenté [104]). It is a textualized model of erotic subjectivity. Muldumarec, the princely lover who immediately arrives in the form of a hawk, reports that he has already desired her but could not come to her until her she has made her self-disclosure, until she has read and applied the story and so made possible the narrative and erotic surplus. Once the lady is reassured of her lover's belief in God, which adds no apparent scruple of conscience about adultery, the couple commits itself to the erotic plenitude of laughter, play, and intimacy ("unt asez ris e jué / E de lur priveté parlé" [193-94]). This period, Marie makes clear, is a dimension of time enclosed on itself: "E nuit e jur e tost e tart / Ele l'ad tut a sun pleisir" ("Night and day, early or late, he was hers whenever she wanted" [222-23]). The phrase *avoir tut a sun pleisir* echoes the promise of erotic repletion given by the faery mistress in **"Lanval"**: "present / A fere tut vostre talent" (167-68). As in **"Equitan,"** this period is punctuated and given an shape only by the comings and goings of the lady's husband, even though discovery and vengeance wait in the background.

In **"Milun,"** Marie reformulates the periodicity of erotic fulfilment from **"Lanval"** into an incremental narrative structure. Milun and the lady who summons him as her lover enjoy their first interval of pleasure in her garden and bedchamber: "La justouent lur parlement / Milun e ele bien suvent" (51-52). This period ends with her pregnancy, the sending away of the child to Milun's sister, and the lady's subsequent arranged marriage to a local nobleman, as Milun leaves for paid service as a warrior. His return begins a second interval, in which the lady's husband replaces the father as the obstacle to pleasure, just as Meriaduc serves as a rival but unwanted suitor to replace the jealous husband in **"Guigemar."** The swan who serves as a messenger between Milun and the lady is the sole mechanism for sustaining a twenty-year love affair (277-88). Marie makes the swan a figure for the ingenuity of erotic craft: "Nuls ne poet estre si destreiz / Ne si tenuz estreitement / Que il ne truisse liu sovent" ("No one can be so imprisoned or so tightly guarded that he cannot find a way out from time to time" [286-88]). The starvation and feeding of the bird as it shuttles between the lovers carrying their messages symbolizes the epicycles of separation and plenitude.

The final interval in **"Milun"** begins as the lovers' son, who has unknowingly proved the chivalric equal of his father by unhorsing him at a tournament, prepares to kill the lady's husband, and a sealed message arrives announcing the husband's death. The son's betrothal of his mother to his father—done on his own authority ("Sanz cunseil de tute autre gent" [526])—fulfills his Oedipal desires and circumvents the anxieties of that desire by restoring the man he has mastered as his mother's partner. Reunited and freed from obstacles, Milun and the lady resume their roles as an erotic couple: "En grant bien e en grant duçur / Vesquirent puis e nuit e jur" ("Thereafter they lived night and day in happiness and tenderness" [529-30]). They live the life of pleasure in south Wales that Lanval finds by removing himself from Arthur's court to Avalon.

In portraying the interval of erotic plenitude for her lovers, Marie borrows and transforms structural devices from Ovid. The husbands and guardians—*vafer maritus* and *vigil custos* (3.611-612)—who stand as obstacles to the lover in the *Ars amatoria* have their counterparts in the *senex amans* of **"Guigemar"** and **"Yonec,"** the seneschal of **"Equitan,"** the violent husband of **"Laüstic,"** the incestuous father of **"Deus Amanz,"** the husband who replaces the father in **"Milun,"** King Mark in the Tristan episode of **"Chievrefoil,"** the retainers ("chevalier fiufé") of **"Le Fresne,"** and even Guildeluëc, the wife of Eliduc. These figures simultaneously block the lover's satisfaction and bring the pressures of time and contingency that give definition to the lovers' shared erotic interlude. Lovers outwit these obstacles and communicate through intermediaries who function like the maids and go-betweens who must be cultivated in the *Ars amatoria*. In the *Lais*, they are not, however, as in Ovid, potential objects of seduction themselves. The old husband's niece in **"Guigemar,"** assigned as a

companion to the captive lady, becomes a collaborator in the love plot in a way that redounds to her credit and stature: "Mut ert curteise e deboneire" ("she was most courtly and noble" [464]). The abbess who raises Le Fresne abets her concubinage with Gurun. The chamberlain in **"Eliduc"** negotiates Guilliadun's cautious approach to her lover. The nightingale in **"Laüstic"** and the swan in **"Milun"** are devices for arranging the lovers' encounters.

In the *Ars amatoria,* the space for finding and capturing a lover is the Roman cityscape, but the site of desire and pleasure is the bedchamber (*thalamus*). The Ovidian teacher proclaims, "Conveniunt thalami furtis et ianua nostris" ("Chambers and a locked door beseem our secret doings" [2.617]). The obstacle of a barred door, he advises later, can be a stimulus to desire: "Adde forem, et duro dicat tibi ianitor ore / 'Non potes,' exclusum te quoque tanget amor" ("add but a door, and let a doorkeeper say to you with stubborn mouth, 'You cannot'; once shut out, you too, sir, will be touched by love" [3.587-88]). The bedchamber is a stronghold under siege by the recruits and veterans ("vetus miles") of the *militia Veneris* (3.559-74) whose tactics differ while their objective remains the same. Access to the chamber is thus a metaphor for access to the lover's body, and admission to the private space is a form of sexual penetration. Submerged under Ovid's pretext of harmless pleasure and displaced from the teacher's consciousness is the additional sense that entry to the chamber is also trespass on another man's household. It is here that Marie, imagining a baronial rather than cosmopolitan world, rejects Ovid's governing premise: "Nos venerem tutam concessaque furta canemus, / Inque meo nullum carmine crimen erit" ("Of safe love-making do I sing, and permitted secrecy, and in my verse shall be no wrong-doing" [*Ars amatoria* 1.33-34]). For her the erotic interim is framed not just by obstacles (all potentially comic in Ovid) but by violence within a militarized society, always potentially at war among and within its patriarchal households.

In the *Lais,* Marie exploits the Ovidian equation of bed, body, and property for its nuances as well as its basic structure. Guigemar is brought into the lady's chamber to be healed, and it is there that the wound in his thigh becomes the hidden wound of love. Equitan and his lover are discovered on the seneschal's bed, as he bursts into his chamber to discover his wife's betrayal and the means she has prepared to murder him. Le Fresne recovers her identity and her lover in Gurun's bedchamber, where she presides over the preparations for consummation that become, by chance disclosure and happy substitution, her own marriage. Lanval's lady has a portable chamber in the richly appointed pavillion where he first encounters her. The lady's bedroom window opens on her lover's house in **"Laüstic,"** granting him a visual display of his otherwise unattainable beloved. The garden where Milun meets his lady is next to her bedchamber. Eliduc and Guilliadun disclose their love to each other in the bedroom that he enters with the king's encouragement, interrupting her chess lesson with another knight but securing access to her person in the most intimate space of the castle.

Marie's most striking use of the Ovidian *thalamus* occurs in **"Yonec."** Muldumarec, the shape-shifting lover who appears immediately after the lady's self-disclosure of desire, enters by a narrow window ("Par mi une estreite fenestre" [107]) that represents both her jealous husband's constraint and the sexual organs he seeks to protect and employ to assure himself of an heir, without success. The first interlude with the lover restores the lady's beauty, fuels her desire, and gives her a new appreciation of solitude: "Sun ami voelt suvent veeir / E de lui sun delit aveir" ("she wanted to see her beloved often and to take her pleasure with him" [219-20]). The old woman charged with guarding her, herself widowed and barren like the castrated priest of **"Guigemar,"** remarks that the lady now remains alone more willingly than before (239-40). In this way, the chamber is transformed from a site of privation, where the lady is removed from society and conversation by a sterile marriage.[25] The lover provides a "surplus" to its desolation, and this supplement is pleasure, sociability, intimacy, and progeny.

When the husband discovers the cause of his wife's restoration, he acts to prevent her body from penetration by rendering the space of her chamber lethal. The *engin* he prepares is both a deadly trap and a clever assertion of his right of seigneural possession:

> Broches de fer fist granz furgier
> E acerer le chief devant:
> Suz ciel n'ad rasur plus trenchant!
> Quant il les ot apparailliees
> E de tutes parz enfurchiees,
> Sur la fenestre les ad mises,
> Bien serreies e bien asises,
> Par unt li chevaliers passot,
> Quant a la dame repeirot.
>
> (286-94)

[He had large iron spikes forged and the tips more sharply pointed than any razor. When he had prepared and cut barbs in them, he set them on the window, close together and well-positioned, in the place through which the knight passed whenever he came to see the lady.]

This fortified barrier does not simply defend the aperture that grants the lover entry to the lady and her body, nor does it make the passage inaccessible or forbidding. It is an aggressive, inverted phallic display designed to inflict a wound ("sa plaie" [334]) on the trespasser in

vengeance for his transgression of household, property, and patriarchal ambitions. The symbolic aim of the sharply honed spikes is to castrate the lover, to reverse the sequence of wounds in **"Guigemar"** and to make Muldumarec as impotent as the lover in **"Chaitivel."** Muldumarec impales himself on the barrier, seemingly unaware of the trap, but enters the room and seats himself on the bed. His flow of blood on the sheets ("tuit li drap furent sanglent" [316]) represents his insemination of the wife, just as her tracking him by the trail of his blood back to his ornate chamber symbolizes the eventual succession of their son Yonec as lord of the city, after he beheads the lady's husband at the site of his father's tomb.

IMPOSSIBLE DESIRE

In her most richly plotted *Lais,* Marie transforms the interim of pleasure into some form of stable consolidation, often marriage or restitution. Guigemar destroys Meriaduc's castle, kills his rival, and goes off with his lover to a place beyond threat: "A grant joie s'amie en meine: / Ore ad trespassee sa peine" ("With great joy he took away his beloved. Now his tribulations were over" [881-82]). The love triangle of Gurun, Le Fresne, and La Codre is resolved by La Codre's marriage to another man when she returns with her parents to her country. Lanval and his faery mistress retire to Avalon. Milun and his lover are married by their son. Where erotic transformation fails, restitution prevails. Bisclavret, the werewolf betrayed by his wife out of fear, is restored to his land and possessions, while his wife goes off with the knight who had since married her. Yonec buries his mother at his father's tomb and becomes lord of Muldumarec's city before returning to the fief in Caerwent held by the stepfather he has murdered. The narrative mechanism that produces these transformations is disclosure. Disclosure forces the narrative crisis that brings *aventure* to closure, thence to public memory and literary form. The ending of **"Le Fresne"** plots the dual trajectories of closure and disclosure from fiction to writing and performance: "Quant l'aventure fu seüe, / Coment ele esteit avenue, / Le lai del *Freisne* en unt trové" ("When the truth of this adventure was known, they composed the lay of *Le Fresne*" [515-517]).

Marie writes other tales, however, that significantly resist the transformation of desire within narrative fiction and readerly understanding. **"Deus Amanz"** leaves its two dead lovers in a sepulchre on the mountain as a memorial to unconsummated desire. **"Chaitivel"** oscillates between two names (the other is **"Les Quatre Deuls"**) to show the undecidability of its underlying love question. Both names signify thwarted desire, and the answer to the *demande* posed by the story is that neither tragic rivalry nor barren possession is preferable. **"Chievrefoil"** promises a future reconciliation between Tristan and King Mark, but its tradition tells us that the "acordement" ("peace" [98]) promised during their encounter is a device for deferred consummation. In **"Eliduc"** and **"Laüstic,"** to which we now turn attention, Marie goes beyond desire as stasis to examine the Ovidian interim in perhaps its most radical terms.

"Eliduc" in fact begins with the stable erotic interim that is the point of closure for Marie's stories of couples who overcome obstacles to achieve sustained fulfillment at the end of their *aventure*. In her opening summary of the tale, Marie locates Eliduc and Guildeluëc exactly at the point where nothing more can be told in **"Guigemar,"** **"Lanval,"** and **"Milun"**: "Ensemble furent lungement, / Mut s'entreamerent lëaument" ("They lived together for a long time and loved each other with great loyalty" [11-12]). The intervening force in their happiness is external in the opening summary ("soudees," paid military service [14]) and internal in the narrative ("l'envie del bien de lui" [41]), yet in both cases it calls into question whether the erotic interim can be sustained within social structures based on a network of implicit allegiance and feudal loyalties: "amur de seignur n'est pas fiez" ("a lord's love is no fief" [63]). Eliduc's conflicted loyalty to his wife and mistress duplicates the competing claims that his Breton lord and English employer hold over his services. Terms like *fiance, fei,* and *leauté* apply equally to political allegiance and love.[26]

Though Eliduc's military service structures time and contingency, the poem's narrative concentrates on a series of erotic intervals. When Guilliadun falls in love with Eliduc, her chamberlain assures her that she can operate within the period of Eliduc's contracted service to her father: "Asez purrez aveir leisir / De mustrer lui vostre pleisir" ("Thus you will have enough opportunity to show him your desire" [453-54]). She accepts those limits in her ensuing interview with Eliduc (532-36), and there follows an interim of pleasure notable for its absence or suppression of sexual appetite:

> Mes n'ot entre eus nule folie,
> Joliveté ne vileinie;
> De douneier e de parler
> E de lur beaus aveirs doner
> Esteit tute la druërie
> Par amur en lur cumpainie.
>
> (575-80)

[There was no foolishness between them, nor fickleness, nor wickedness, as their love consisted entirely of courting and talking, and exchanging fair gifts when they were together.]

Marie sets this restraint and sublimation against the desire that her characters so intensely experience. The circulation of words and gifts displaces but stands for

sexuality. Sandra Pierson Prior observes that at the start of these exchanges Guilliadun becomes "the desired Ovidian female," while Eliduc's feelings are those of "the desired object rather than of the desiring subject."[27] A second interval—Eliduc's temporary return to Brittany to aid his lord—repeats the first. Limited again by a promised term of service, Eliduc rejoins his wife and retainers but remains alienated from their joy and isolated within his concealed desire: "Mut se cuntient sutivement" ("He behaved most secretively" [717]). When Guideluëc discovers Guilliadun after another return journey, she recognizes "la verité" (1017) of his withdrawal in a scene where she views Guilladun's body, ironically adopting the lover's gaze and cataloguing the features it beholds (1010-1016). Motivated "[t]ant par pitié, tant par amur" (1027), Guildeluëc removes herself as an obstacle, taking the nun's veil and founding a religious community with thirty other women.

Guildeluëc's removal permits the kind of unforeseen closure we see at the end of **"Milun,"** where the husband suddenly dies so that the son can marry his parents. This device returns the story to the erotic consolation with which it began, though with a different couple. Eliduc and Guilladun marry and resume the life of apparent plenitude in a conscious echo of the restored couple in **"Milun"**: "Ensemble vesquirent meint jur, / Mut ot entre eus parfite amur" ("They lived together for many a day and the love between them was perfect" [1149-50]; cf. **"Milun"** 530). Unlike **"Milun,"** however, in **"Eliduc"** this new form of erotic interval, secured by trial, suffering, and generous resignation, is as untenable as the first. The life of plenitude that Eliduc and Guilliadun lead centers on charity and good works, which lead to religious conversion. In most modern readings of the poem, this final step demonstrates a movement from earthly to spiritual love.[28] Guildeluëc receives Guilladun as a sister in her community; the two pray for "lur ami" (1171), the shared husband turned patron who prays for them in return. The "bone fei" that Eliduc first pledges Guildeluëc when he leaves Brittany for England (84) presumably finds its proper object in their collaborative enterprise—a spiritual *amicitia* of rivalry in devotion and prayer: "Mut se pena chescuns pur sei / De Deu amer par bone fei / E mut par firent bele fin" ("Each one strove to love God in good faith and they came to a good end" [1177-79]). Placed in the final, emphatic position in the sequence of *Lais* in British Library MS Harley 978, the mid-thirteenth-century English manuscript that offers the only medieval disposition of the full collection, **"Eliduc"** seemingly gives Marie's last word on the Ovidian project of amplifying pleasure. In its portrayal of monastic flight from worldly attractions and the presence of an erotic other, it also effects the closure of spiritual conversion that Abelard seeks to impose on Heloise's irreducible desire.[29]

But if **"Eliduc"** follows a trajectory toward spiritual transcendence (*mut bele fin*), its narrative closure leaves open an interpretive "surplus" for Marie's readers. Marie says at the beginning that the poem used to be called *Elidus* but is now called *Guildeluëc ha Guilliadun* (21-28); at the end, she says that the Bretons made a lay "De l'aventure de ces treis" (1181). The undecidability of the title points toward the undecidability of the *matiere*. Is **"Eliduc"** about a knight who finds salvation after securing worldly pleasure? Is it about two women who eschew rivalry and become spiritual sisters? Is it about a love triangle transformed by something other than removing the obstacle or devising a double marriage?[30] The *aventure* all three share comes at the end to mean separation as well as reconciliation. Lodged in their monastic houses and communicating through messengers, the characters inhabit a sanctified version of the chambers holding unhappy wives elsewhere in the *Lais*. Their exchange of messages is a benevolent form of the "druërie" that sustains lovers.

The shift from worldly contentment in the Ovidian interval to spiritual transcendence marks the paradox of desire in **"Eliduc"**—its simultaneous impossibility and persistence. Throughout the poem, the erotic intervals cannot be sustained within the social structures where Marie locates human action, will, and gratification. Eliduc and Guildeluëc lose their happiness to envy and court rivalry. Eliduc and Guilladun cannot consummate their love during Eliduc's service to the king of Exeter. When they are legitimized as a couple, charity ("Granz aumoines e granz biens" [1151]) replaces eros in their "parfite amur" ("perfect love").[31] When they undergo conversion, they reenact their courtship, safely beyond the threat of pleasure and consummation, its intimacy now fully contained in language.

"Eliduc" ends, then, with sublimation, not reconciliation, and its closure is perhaps more apparent than real. The husband and his two wives commit themselves to prayer as a form of exchange, a means of continuing transactions. The late conversion of Eliduc and Guilladun shows that Guildeluëc has failed or miscalculated in her gesture of resigning marriage for the nun's veil so that Eliduc can take his lover ("Elidus ad s'amie prise" [1145]). The problem of the poem is not to find the right couple but to find an arrangement for all three. This they discover in the exchange of messages, whose topic is the exposure of female emotion and affect ("Pur saveir cument lur estot, / Cum chescune se cunfortot" [1175-76]). Separated by agreement rather than jealous husbands, politics, or social constraints, Eliduc and his wives devise what we might call a spiritual Ovidianism.

The messengers he sends to Guildeluëc and Guilladun continually pose the lover's demand that his beloved reveal herself fully to him. Eliduc has appropriated Heloise's demand for erotic presence and her means of securing it through letters.

The demand for such disclosure is what constitutes the Ovidian interim of **"Laüstic."** Marie adapts the Piramus and Thisbe story for her fictional premise and evokes the story of Philomela at the point of narrative crisis. Yet the differences from Ovid's mythographic narratives are as important as the parallels. **"Laüstic"** is the story of adults, not children thwarted by their fathers; and it goes to the heart of baronial culture, not Semiramis's Babylon, by showing the contradiction of a social order centered simultaneously on rivalry and identity.[32] St. Malo, Marie's locale for the story, enjoys its reputation "Pur la bunté des deus baruns" ("Because of the fine qualities of the two men" [11]). Their two fortified houses opening onto each other, with no barrier except a wall, are the social core of the city. The wife whom one of the noblemen marries is the obstacle who disrupts their chivalric identification with one another and generates their rivalry. She accedes to her neighbor's importuning for all the qualities that he implicitly shares with her husband: "grant bien" ("so many qualities" [25]), reputation ("Tant pur le bien qu'ele en oï" [27]), and proximity. (The only difference that emerges between the men is the husband's later cruelty in strangling the nightingale.[33])

As this roster of qualities suggests, desire operates in **"Laüstic"** through language. The Ovidian interim made possible by the architecture of the houses is a traffic in signs and performance conducted through the lover's prudence and ingenuity. Conversation and gifts move across the wall and enter through the window of the lady's bedchamber, much as Muldumarec penetrates the window of his lover's room in **"Yonec."** Nothing impedes the lovers' display for each other in their facing windows: "Nuls nes poeit de ceo garder / Qu'a la fenestre n'i venissent / E iloec ne s'entreveïssent" ("no one could prevent their coming to the window and seeing each other there" [54-56]). Marie makes it clear that all these signs are linguistic substitutes for erotic consummation:

> N'unt gueres rien ki lur despleise,
> Mut esteient amdui a eise,
> Fors tant k'il ne poent venir
> Del tut ensemble a lur pleisir . . .
>
> (45-48)

[There was scarcely anything to displease them and they were both very content except for the fact that they could not meet and take their pleasure with each other. . . .]

What she also demonstrates is that symbolic exchange not only replaces but comes to constitute desire. As

Michelle Freeman points out, the lady finds an alternative to the role of the *mal mariée* under conditions not for lovemaking *"but for dialogue."*[34] The interim for maintaining the love affair ("Lungement se sunt entreamé" [57]), as Paul Zumthor observes, is the sole marker of time in the poem.[35] It lasts until the lady exceeds the moderation (*modus*) of Ovidian craft and uses the nightingale as a pretext for their meetings. Asked by her husband why she rises in the night, she indirectly but fatefully speaks her dissatisfaction, the distance between him and the joy she finds in her nightly meetings: "Il nen ad joïe en cest mund / Ke n'ot le laüstic chanter" ("anyone who does not hear the song of the nightingale knows none of the joys of this world" [84-85]).

The husband's capture and killing of the nightingale is the transgression (*vileinie*) that differentiates him morally and socially from his baronial double and reorders the economy of desire in **"Laüstic."** Thomas A. Shippey proposes that the nightingale stands for the "ideal love" sought by the lovers.[36] Emanuel J. Mickel, Jr. glosses the dead bird subsequently carried by the lover as the "agonizing memory of his lost love."[37] The wife describes the nightingale to her husband as desire that stands beyond him: "mut me semble grant deduit; / Tant m'i delit e tant le voil / Que jeo ne puis dormir de l'oil" ("it brings me great pleasure. I take such delight in it and desire it so much that I can get no sleep at all" [88-90]). When the husband breaks the nightingale's neck and splatters its blood on her tunic in an oblique echo of **"Yonec,"** the crisis for the lady is hermeneutic. Deprived of her pretext for nightly display, she wonders how her lover will interpret her absence at the window. Her problem, in other words, is to control the interpretive "surplus" of possible meanings: "Il quidera ke jeo me feigne" ("He will think I am faint-hearted" [or dissumulating or that I have abandoned him, 131]). She solves her problem by generating her own surplus. The dead bird is transformed into a funerary artifact, wrapped in a rich silk cloth embroided with gold and writing. To assure the right reading of this overwrought sign, she sends with it a messenger as glossator to explain her intended meaning ("sun message" [143]) to her lover, who nonetheless adds his own surplus to what the messenger says and shows ("tut li ad dit e mustré" [145]).

The dead bird, as Bloch remarks, is sent to the lover as a poetic envoi that marks the impossibility of desire.[38] Without the pretext of the nightingale's song, the erotic exchanges between the wife and lover are no longer possible, and the Ovidian interim closes down under violence to the symbol of love lyric. The lavish reliquary that the lover orders made for the bird represents, however, a double, even contradictory meaning. At one level, the entombment equates death and

desire, for the nightingale is not just placed inside the reliquary but the casket is sealed ("Puis fist la chasse enseeler" [155]), as the final act in the lovers' erotic exchanges. At another level, this fixing of desire is what allows desire to persist. The lover always carries the reliquary with him, as a memorial presence. Though sealed (*enseelee*), what the object represents cannot be concealed (*celee*): "Cele aventure fu cuntee, / Ne pot estre lunges celee" ("This adventure was related and could not long be concealed" [157-58]). In ordering the reliquary, the lover has shown that, unlike the husband (116), he is not "vileins" (148), and the object that contains impossible desire makes sure that desire persists and circulates in the lai preserving the *aventure*.

The reliquary of **"Laüstic"** inevitably recalls the marble tomb of **"Deus Amanz."** But the lovers of **"Laüstic"** do not have the unreachable desire of the young couple who possess the means but not the wisdom to overcome the obstacle placed in their way. The more revealing comparison is with **"Eliduc."** In **"Eliduc,"** the Ovidian interval seemingly transforms into religious conversion. Similar interpretations have been made for **"Laüstic,"** arguing that the reliquary retains its religious symbolism and that entombing the dead bird amounts to a transubstantiation of earthly love into "an ideal spiritual bond."[39] Whether spiritual, idealized, memorial, or morbid, love in **"Laüstic"** remains desire only partially transformed. The dead bird is not a metaphor but a metonymy for the lovers' Ovidian interval, the symbol of sustained pleasures arbitrarily brought into the economy of signs and performance when the wife improvises an excuse for her nightly displays. It is preserved in the vessel ordered by the lover, just as the three converts in **"Eliduc"** are situated in the houses and rules they create for themselves. Though the lady sends her message, the lover's continual possession of the reliquary ("Tuz jurs l'ad fete od lui porter" [156]) acts out Eliduc's demand that the women separated from him continue to reveal themselves by telling how they feel.

Marie engages "Le livre Ovide" imaginatively at the phase of the Ovidian project that demands the greatest craft and artfulness. In her rewriting of the *Ars amatoria,* keeping love is neither a domestic or harmless enterprise. Though the Ovidian interim in her stories remains somehow beyond moral condemnation, it still belies Ovid's claims to commit no trespass (*nullum crimen*) and to celebrate love without penalties (*venus tuta*). Resituated in a context of baronial power, the erotic interval is all about consequences. Only in the fantasy of **"Lanval"** does Marie approach something like the licensed intrigues (*concessa furta*) that Ovid claims to extoll. At the same time that she represents the Ovidian interim under time and contingency, Marie also discovers that the transformations of desire to marriage, restitution, and mourning offer provisional answers to its urgent demands. **"Eliduc"** and **"Laüstic"** suggest that in Marie's fictive realm the fixing of desire only masks its continuing circulation.

Notes

1. I quote from *Les Lais de Marie de France*; the translation is by Burgess and Busby.

2. Bloch, *The Anonymous Marie de France*, pp. 42-48. Fitz, "Desire and Interpretation" traces the dialectic of exegesis and eros in Marie's Tristan episode. For desire as the supplement operating through the social sphere, see Stein, p. 289. Pickens observes that Marie as a feminine poet effectively inseminates her audience and patrons.

3. Nichols, "Marie de France's Commonplaces," p. 135.

4. Hanning, "The Talking Wounded," p. 144.

5. Discussion in Segre, Cargo, Gertz, and Brightenback.

6. *Les Lais de Marie de France,* p. 244.

7. Hanning, "Courtly Contexts for Urban *cultus,*" p. 45.

8. Hanning, "Talking Wounded," pp. 141-42.

9. Gertz, p. 382.

10. *Accessus ad auctores,* p. 33.

11. Stapleton, p. 294.

12. Maddox, p. 36.

13. Dubuis, p. 397.

14. Burgess, pp. 147-58.

15. Gertz, p. 382; Whalen.

16. Stapleton, p. 293.

17. Fitz, "The Prologue to the *Lais* of Marie de France and the *Parable of The Talents,*" p. 563.

18. Ménard, *Les Lais de Marie de France,* p. 237; translation mine.

19. For Marie's contemporary Walter Map, author of the antimatrimonial tract "Dissuasio Valerii ad Ruffinum," the women who bestow this plenitude are sources of fear and demonic power; see *De nugis curialium* 2.12-14, 4.8-9, 11.

20. Kay, pp. 202-203.

21. For the reading of castration, see Bloch, *The Anonymous Marie de France,* p. 93.

22. Burgess, pp. 135-36.

23. Hanning, "Courtly Contexts," p. 51.

24. Ribard, pp. 143-45.

25. Paupert, pp. 177-81, notes the equivalence of love and speaking for the heroines of the *Lais.*

26. Burgess, pp. 152-57.

27. Prior, p. 129.

28. Nelson, and Howard S. Robertson.

29. Brook, pp. 15-16, conveniently sets the textual against the historical evidence.

30. Kelly, "'Diversement comencier' in the *Lais* of Marie de France," p. 109, notes that the triangle is not just a fundamental or inherited structure in the *Lais* but also the point from which Marie begins the process of rhetorical invention that connects her to Latin literary culture.

31. Mickel, "A Reconsideration of the *Lais* of Marie de France," p. 64.

32. In this respect, the story addresses its audience directly, the "Cunte, barun e chivaler" and the aristocratic ladies whose pleasure with the *Lais* is mentioned by the twelfth-century Anglo-Norman writer Denis Piramus; quoted in Ménard, "Marie de France et nous," p. 7.

33. Cottille-Foley, pp. 157-61, suggests that the husband's killing the nightingale removes him from the love triangle and substitutes the entombed bird; in a further substitution, the bird comes to represent Marie's story itself.

34. Freeman, p. 868.

35. Zumthor, p. 389.

36. Shippey, p. 51.

37. Mickel, "A Reconsideration of the *Lais* of Marie de France," p. 56.

38. Bloch, *The Anonymous Marie de France*, p. 73.

39. Tudor, and Cottrell, p. 504.

Works cited

PRIMARY TEXTS

Map, Walter. *De nugis curialium; Courtiers' Trifles,* ed. and trans. M. R. James, rev. C. L. N. Brooke and R. A. B. Mynors. Oxford: Clarendon Press, 1983.

Marie de France. *Les Lais de Marie de France,* ed. Jean Rychner. Paris: Champion, 1971.

———. *The Lais of Marie de France,* trans. Glyn S. Burgess and Keith Busby. 2nd ed. London: Penguin, 1999.

Ovid. *The Art of Love and Other Poems,* trans. J. H. Mozley. Cambridge, MA: Harvard University Press, 1969.

CRITICISM AND SCHOLARSHIP

Bloch, R. Howard. *The Anonymous Marie de France.* Chicago: University of Chicago Press, 2003.

Brightenback, Kristine. "The *Metamorphoses* and Narrative *Conjointure* in 'Deuz Amanz,' 'Yonec,' and 'Le Laüstic.'" *Romanic Review* 72 (1981): 1-12.

Brook, Leslie C. "A Note on the Ending of *Eliduc.*" *French Studies Bulletin* 32 (1989): 14-16.

Burgess, Glyn S. *The Lais of Marie de France: Text and Context.* Athens, GA: University of Georgia Press, 1987.

Cargo, Robert T. "Marie de France's *Le Laustic* and Ovid's *Metamorphoses.*" *Comparative Literature* 18 (1966): 162-66.

Cormier, Raymond J. and Urban Tigner Holmes, eds. *Essays in Honor of Louis Francis Solano.* Chapel Hill: University of North Carolina Press, 1970.

Cottille-Foley, Nora. "The Structuring of Feminine Empowerment: Gender and Triangular Relationships in Marie de France." In *Gender Transgressions: Crossing Normative Barrier in Old French Literature,* ed. Karen J. Taylor. New York: Garland, 1998. Pp. 153-80.

Cottrell, Robert D. "*Le Lai du Laustic*: From Physicality to Spirituality." *Philological Quarterly* 47 (1968): 499-505.

Dubuis, R. "La notion de *druërie* dans les *Lais* de Marie de France." *Le Moyen Age* 98 (1992): 391-413.

Dufournet, Jean, ed. *Amour et Merveille: Les "Lais" de Marie de France.* Paris: Champion, 1995.

Fitz, Brewster E. "The Prologue to the *Lais* of Marie de France and the *Parable of The Talents*: Gloss and Monetary Metaphor." *MLN* 90 (1975): 558-64.

Freeman, Michelle A. "Marie de France's Poetics of Silence: Implications for a Feminine *Translatio.*" *PMLA* 99 (1984): 860-83.

Gertz, SunHee Kim. "Echoes and Reflections of Enigmatic Beauty in Ovid and Marie de France." *Speculum* 73 (1998): 372-96.

Hanning, Robert W. "Courtly Contexts for Urban *cultus*: Responses to Ovid in Chrétien's *Cligès* and Marie's *Guigemar.*" *Symposium* 35 (1981-82): 34-56.

———. "The Talking Wounded: Desire, Truth Telling, and Pain in the *Lais* of Marie de France." In Paxson and Gravlee, *Desiring Discourse.* Pp. 140-61.

Kay, Sarah. *Courtly Contradictions: The Emergence of the Literary Object in the Twelfth Century.* Stanford, CA: Stanford University Press, 2001.

Kelly, Douglas. "'Diversement comencier' in the *Lais* of Marie de France." In Maréchal, *In Quest of Marie de France.* Pp. 107-122.

Maddox, Donald. *Fictions of Identity in Medieval France.* Cambridge: Cambridge University Press, 2000.

Maréchal, Chantal A., ed. In *Quest of Marie de France, A Twelfth-Century Poet.* Lewistown, NY: Mellen, 1992.

Ménard, Philippe. *Les Lais de Marie de France: Contes d'amour et d'aventure du Moyen Age.* Paris: Presses universitaires de France, 1979.

———. "Marie de France et nous." In Dufournet, *Amour et merveille.* Pp. 7-24.

Menocal, María Rosa. *Writing in Dante's Cult of Truth From Borges to Boccaccio.* Durham, NC: Duke University Press, 1991.

Mickel, Emanuel J., Jr. "A Reconsideration of the *Lais* of Marie de France." *Speculum* 46 (1971): 39-65.

Nelson, Deborah. "Eliduc's Salvation." *The French Review* 55 (1981): 37-42.

Nichols, Stephen G. "Marie de France's Commonplaces." *Yale French Studies,* Contexts: Style and Values in Medieval Art and Literature (1991): 134-48.

Paupert, Anne. "Les femmes et la parole dans les *Lais* de Marie de France." In Dufournet, *Amour et Merveille.* Pp. 169-87.

Paxson, James J. and Cynthia A Gravlee, eds. *Desiring Discourse: The Literature of Love, Ovid through Chaucer.* Selinsgrove, PA: Susquehanna University Press, 1998.

Prior, Sandra Pierson. "'Kar des dames est avenu/ L'aventure': Displacing the Chivalric Hero in Marie de France's *Eliduc.*" In Paxon and Gravlee, *Desiring Discourse.* Pp. 123-39.

Ribard, Jacques. "Le *Lai de Guigemar: Conjointure* et *Senefiance.*" In Dufournet, *Amour et Merveille.* Pp. 133-45.

Robertson, Howard S. "Love and the Other World in Marie de France's *Eliduc.*" In Cormier and Holmes, *Essays in Honor of Louis Francis Solano.* Pp. 167-76.

Segre, Cesare. "Piramo e Tisbe nei *Lai* di Maria di Francia." In *Studi in onore di Vittorio Lugli e Diego Valeri.* 2 vols. Venice: Pozza, 1961. 2: 845-53.

Shippey, Thomas A. "Listening to the Nightingale." *Comparative Literature* 22 (1970): 46-60.

Stapleton, M. L. "*Venus Vituperator*: Ovid, Marie de France, and *Fin'Amors*." *Classical and Modern Literature* 13 (1993): 283-95.

Tudor, A. P. "The Religious Symbolism in the 'Reliquary of Love' in *Laustic*." *French Studies Bulletin* 46 (1993): 1-3.

Whalen, Logan E. "A Medieval Book Burning: *Object d'art* as Narrative Device in the Lai of *Guigemar*." *Neophilologus* 80 (1996): 205-211.

Zumthor, Paul. *Essai de poétique médiévale*. Paris: Seuil, 1972.

Sharon Kinoshita (essay date 2006)

SOURCE: Kinoshita, Sharon. "Colonial Possessions: Wales and the Anglo-Norman Imaginary in the *Lais* of Marie de France." In *Medieval Boundaries: Rethinking Difference in Old French Literature*, pp. 105-32. Philadelphia: University of Pennsylvania Press, 2006.

[*In the following essay, Kinoshita studies the lays "Yonec" and "Milun," both of which are set in South Wales and focus on illegitimate children, to illustrate the tension between Anglo-Norman feudal politics and native Welsh marriage and inheritance practices.*]

[I] read the Welsh setting of two *lais* of Marie de France as what Mary Louise Pratt calls a contact zone: an area of "the spatial and temporal copresence of subjects previously separated by geographic and historical disjunctures, whose trajectories now intersect" in ways that reveal "the interactive, improvisational dimensions of colonial encounters so easily ignored or suppressed by diffusionist accounts of conquest and domination."[1]

Though illicit love is central to medieval romance, these adulterous affairs rarely result in illegitimate children. Adulterous queens like Iseut and Guenevere remain barren because, in a society so strongly based in genealogical politics, the threat of illegitimacy was regarded as "too serious to be treated lightly in literature."[2] The *lais* of Marie de France, however, present two exceptions: **"Yonec,"** the classic tale of a *mal-mariée* who finds solace with a lover who comes to her in the form of a bird; and **"Milun,"** in which an unmarried maid takes a poor but valiant knight as her lover. Each affair results in the birth of a son who grows up to vindicate the secret love shared by his parents. Despite variations in plot and tone, these two *lais* dare to imagine what more traditional romance cannot: the genealogical consequences of *fin'amor*. In **"Yonec"** and **"Milun,"** the birth of an illegitimate son is the point where courtly desire runs up against the limits of the feudal politics of lineage.[3]

Why these exceptions? The answer, I suggest, lies in the other thing the two *lais* have in common. Both are set in South Wales: **"Yonec"** in Caerwent and Caerleon, and **"Milun"** in "South Wales" (Suhtwales) as well as on the Continent.[4] Generally, this setting has been ignored or, at best, taken as adding a touch of "local color."[5] Yet in the twelfth century, South Wales was a "contact zone" where the shared culture of post-Carolingian Europe met the so-called Celtic fringe which, though Christian, remained outside the bounds of this nascent imagined community. When the Normans arrived in the wake of their conquest of England, they found a distinctive and, in their eyes, alien culture—pastoral, seminomadic, and highly decentralized, in contrast to the manorial and increasingly rationalized feudal system characteristic of eleventh-century Normandy. Clerics were particularly scandalized by indigenous marriage and inheritance practices, persistently condemning the Welsh for "taking a cavalier attitude towards the bonds of matrimony, choosing partners within the prohibited degrees, keeping mistresses, divorcing their wives, and treating legitimate and illegitimate children as equals."[6] Such customs had long been common in other parts of Latin Christendom as well. But as the reformist church began insisting on exogamy and the indissolubility of marriage, and as the feudal nobility began practicing primogeniture, Welsh traditions of endogamy, partible inheritance, and "trial marriage" came increasingly to exemplify Welsh deviance.

Recent criticism has suggested the relevance of postcolonial theory to the medieval Welsh context. Most such studies have centered on the work of Gerald of Wales (Giraldus Cambrensis), the twelfth-century author whose own lineage exemplified the hybridity of "Cambro-Norman" Wales.[7] But cross-cultural interactions are an abiding feature of Marie's *lais* as well, from the project of *translatio* thematized in the prologue to the bi- and trilingual titles given **"Bisclavret"** and **"Laüstic."**[8] In this chapter I read Marie's two Welsh *lais* as alternating visions of the colonial encounter. From the common plot of the illegitimate son who seeks out the biological father he has never known, **"Yonec"** and **"Milun"** present distinct visions of the relationship of the indigenous past to the Anglo-Norman present. In **"Yonec,"** the *mal-mariée*'s dissent from the feudal politics of lineage is at once an erotic fantasy and an allegory of native resistance to colonial rule, figured as the romantic desire for a scion of the occluded civilization. In **"Milun,"** traces of the conflict between colonizer and colonized are erased, giving way to a larger feudal world bound together by common chivalric practices. Customs associated with the feudal politics of lineage are represented as atavistic and, in the twenty years it takes the plot to unfold, displaced by the utopian vision of a new Cambro-Norman society based on conjugal love. As recent analyses have shown, colonial encounters are always messier than dominant ideologies imply. Beneath the surface of these two charming *lais,* Marie affords us a glimpse of the political and cultural complexity of post-conquest Wales.[9] We begin with a brief overview of that complexity.

* * *

The Norman colonization of Wales began soon after the conquest of 1066. In the river valleys of the southeast, progress was rapid: Norman knights quickly overwhelmed the lightly armed Welsh infantry. Like the Anglo-Saxons, however, they soon learned that Wales was easier to conquer than to hold. In the highlands, the mountainous terrain produced a fragmented and localized culture whose basic political unit was the kinship group (*tref*) and largest institutional structure the *commote,* ruled by a prince (*tywysog*) who held court (*llys*) in great timbered halls. Since anyone could become *tywysog* by overthrowing the incumbent, plotting and sedition were endemic. The same political fragmentation that made Wales so easy to conquer meant that (in contrast to Anglo-Saxon England) there were few institutions through which power could be exercised and maintained. Thus even the most crushing military victory could prove indecisive.[10] To compensate for the instability of the frontier, William the Conqueror created the Marcher earldoms of Chester, Shrewsbury, and Hereford, entrusted to loyal vassals given exceptional powers.[11] Still, colonization remained partial and uneven. Like the Anglo-Saxons before them, the Normans dominated the lowlands (well-suited to their manorial economies), building castles on the lands seasonally vacated by seminomadic indigenous pastoralists. Above six hundred feet, where Norman knights lost whatever advantages they otherwise enjoyed over Welsh archers and infantry, the highlands remained in native hands.[12]

At first, colonizers and colonized faced each other across a great cultural divide. In the late eleventh century, the Normans were in the vanguard of what historian Robert Bartlett has called "the making of Europe": the consolidation and diffusion of a set of institutions and practices, emerging in the heartland of the old Carolingian empire, that included a standardized Roman liturgy, the international religious orders, the minting of coins, court chanceries, the use of the Carolingian miniscule, universities, and chivalry—even the preference for universal Christian names (like John or Henry) over local ones (like Duncan or Pribislaw).[13] As these institutions and practices became increasingly normative, cultural differences and misunderstandings arose between groups like the Normans and those, like the Welsh, who were indisputably Christian but not yet (in Bartlett's sense) "European." To Norman knights

accustomed to open-field skirmishes, the highlanders' reliance on infantry and guerrilla warfare was literally unchivalrous. Clerical marriages and inheritable ecclesiastical benefices were "calculated to give deep offence to anyone conversant with the norms and teaching of the post-Gregorian church."[14] As is often the case, markings of difference clustered around perceived sexual transgressions: Welsh practices of endogamy, concubinage, trial marriages, and the inheritance rights accorded to illegitimate children provided ready-made targets for Anglo-Norman nobles and churchmen.

At the same time, the conquest brought colonizer and colonized together in a shared process of accommodation and acculturation. At the highest social levels, their disparate systems were, in a sense, superimposed: Marcher lords began behaving like native princes (*twysogion*), while *twysogion* became royal vassals.[15] Henry I (ruled 1100-35) established feudal ties with native Welsh princes to curb the power of his father's border earls; "overlordship" became a flexible means of controlling geographically distant areas where "existing patterns of authority were fluid."[16] Meanwhile, communication was facilated by professional interpreters (*cyfarwyddiadid* and latimers)—often high-ranking men granted fiefs in exchange for their service.[17] By the mid-twelfth century, the two systems had begun to merge: several generations of alliances and intermarriage had produced a hybrid Cambro-Norman elite, exemplified by the historian Gerald of Wales.[18]

When Henry I died, however, native princes capitalized on the succession wars between Mathilda and Stephen to revive the kingdoms of Gwynedd (north-northwest Wales), Powys (center-east), and Deheubarth (south). In Welsh political geography, these traditional kingdoms existed in name only; with no permanent institutional structures to support them, they "expanded, contracted, fragmented, and even disappeared, as military fortunes ebbed and flowed."[19] Any strong and charismatic *tywysog* might claim the title of king. In the tenth century the king of Deheubarth, Hywel Dda (d. 950), even succeeded in uniting all of Wales. Once the king died or was overthrown, however, his kingdom simply disappeared. The obverse was that when conditions were once again favorable—as they were during the political turmoil of the Norman wars of succession—such kingdoms could suddenly reappear, as if by magic.[20]

When Henry II became king in 1154, he assiduously set out to recover the royal prerogatives wielded by his grandfather, Henry I. Among these was control over Welsh marcher barons and native princes alike.[21] Early in his reign, Henry (sometimes identified as the "nobles reis" to whom Marie dedicated her *lais*) was faced with numerous native revolts, particularly by Rhys ap Gruffydd—the formidable "Lord Rhys" who became king of Deheubarth (South Wales) in 1155.[22] Lands Henry captured from the Welsh were returned to their hereditary Anglo-Norman lords. In 1171, however, Henry inaugurated a new policy, naming Rhys justiciar for South Wales as part of a new balance of power between the Marcher lords and the native princes of *pura Wallia*.[23] Through all these shifts, Caerleon (where the conclusion of **"Yonec"** is set) remained, as we shall see, a site of particular contest.

This political turmoil notwithstanding, the kaleidoscope of shifting power relations had produced "a distinctive Cambro-Norman society. . . . [n]either purely Welsh nor wholly Norman."[24] South Wales, where Anglo-Norman colonization was heaviest, emerged as a "social space of subaltern encounters" in which geopolitically distinct peoples "manufacture new relations, hybrid cultures, and multiple-voiced aesthetics."[25] The communities that grew around Anglo-Norman settlements were culturally diverse, but faced a "chronic lack of manpower, the necessity of accommodating large numbers of native Welsh within the social order, the constant threat of encroachments by unconquered Welsh tribesmen, the desire not to stray too far from the mainstream of life of Anglo-Norman society, the desire to prevent royal and ecclesiastical domination, the goal of exploiting the frontier through further conquests."[26] Meanwhile, in the castles of the Welsh Marches, French, Welsh and English minstrels came together in a cultural mix exemplified in the trilingual prologue to **"Laüstic."** The result was the matter of Britain: Celtic (hi)stories "translated" into Latin by Geoffrey of Monmouth, and then into Old French by Wace, Marie de France, and Chrétien de Troyes.[27]

In the opening scene of Chrétien de Troyes's *Conte du Graal,* Perceval encounters five knights who perceive him through the standard tropes of the Norman imaginary. In their eyes, "gallois" is synonymous with rustic, and Perceval's ignorance of courtly forms is a natural consequence of his "ethnicity": "All Welshmen are, by nature, more irrational than animals in the field" (243-44) (Galois sont tuit par nature / Plus fol que bestes an pasture). When Perceval later sets out for court, his mother persuades him to leave two of his three javelins behind, "because it looked too Welsh" (609) (Por ce que trop sanblast Galois).[28] Marie, in contrast, transforms such denunciations of Welsh difference into visions of the multiform ways the Celtic past haunts the Cambro-Norman present. In **"Yonec"** and **"Milun,"** transgressive aspects of Welsh sexuality provide not simply variants on the plot of courtly love but meditations on the complexity of twelfth-century Cambro-Norman relations.

"Yonec"

In the guise of a conventional tale of courtly love, **"Yonec"** narrates a crisis in the feudal politics of lineage. As the story opens, the aged advocate of Caerwent takes a wife, explicitly "to have children who would be his heirs" (19-20) (pur enfanz aveir, / Ki aprés lui fuissent si heir). He chooses a young and beautiful girl of noble birth, but after their marriage he grows jealous and locks her in a tower, where she pines away under the guard of his old widowed sister:

> He kept her like this *more than seven years.* They never had any children, nor did she ever leave that tower, neither for family nor for friends. (37-40, emphasis added)

> (Issi la tint *plus de set anz.*
> Unques entre eus n'eurent enfanz
> Ne fors de cele tur n'eissi,
> Ne pur parent ne pur ami.)

One day she suddenly starts dreaming of the way things used to be, when beautiful ladies took handsome lovers. Wishing that she, too, might enjoy such an adventure, she is startled when a magnificent hawk (*ostur*) flies in through the window, turns into a handsome knight, and pledges her his love. The two conduct a secret affair, with the bird-man, Muldumarec, appearing to the lady whenever she wishes. Soon, however, her new radiance triggers her husband's suspicions; he lays a trap, catching and wounding the bird-man. Dying, Muldumarec tells his sweetheart she is pregnant with their son, Yonec, who will some day avenge them. Then he flees. She follows, tracking him through a magical landscape to a great castle within a fabulous walled city. Inside, her dying lover gives her a ring to erase her husband's memory and a sword to give their son when he is grown. Returning to Caerwent, the lady bears a son—a handsome, brave, strong, and generous youth whom the advocate rears as his own. When it is time for Yonec to be knighted, all three journey to Caerleon for the feast of Saint Aaron. In the castle's abbey, they are shown the magnificent tomb of a former king of the land who, they are told, was killed in Caerwent "for the love of a lady" (522) (Pur l'amur d'une dame ocis). The lady reveals that the king was Yonec's father, then falls dead in a swoon. Grabbing Muldumarec's sword, Yonec kills his stepfather—thus avenging his mother's sorrow. In this version of a happily-ever-after ending, Yonec is acclaimed king of the land.

That the advocate should marry "to have children" (19) (pur enfanz aveir") is perfectly understandable. Nowhere was the feudal politics of lineage more important than in Wales where, during the twelfth century, several major earldoms established by William the Conqueror twice passed, "through marriage or gift," to new lineages when ruling families failed in the male line.[29] Such marriages—contracted for political advantage—took little account of personal inclinations. (The disastrous ending of Marie de France's **"Equitan"** serves as a cautionary tale to anyone foolish enough to value elective affinities over genealogical expediency.[30]) From the late eleventh century, such dynastic politics were threatened (admittedly more in theory than in practice) by reformist churchmen's insistence that marriage could be contracted only with the consent of both partners.[31] In **"Yonec,"** the lady is clearly married in the old fashion, shared by the Anglo-Norman and Celtic kin nobility alike.[32] Later, when she finally breaks her silence, she rails first against those who had "given" her to the old man in marriage: "A curse on my family, and on all the others who gave me to this jealous man, who married me bodily!" (81-84) (*Maleeit seient mi parent / E li autre communalment / Ki a cest gelus me donerent / E de sun cors me marïerent!*). Her powerlessness in her marriage is pointedly contrasted to the agency she exercises in her secret affair with Muldumarec, where she only has to think of him for him to appear. The advocate, for his part, is caught between the feudal politics of lineage and the church's increasing insistence on the indissolubility of marriage. Dynastic expediency might dictate that he repudiate his childless wife, but reformist churchmen would threaten him with excommunication if he did.

In **"Yonec,"** however, the familiar courtly plot of the *mal-mariée* is inflected by its Welsh setting. By the late twelfth century, the "heroic days of conquest and colonization" had given way to a distinctive Marcher society governed by its own law and custom.[33] Nevertheless, certain Welsh marriage and inheritance patterns persisted—among them the tradition of trial marriage. The law code of Hywel Dda (assembled under Rhys ap Gruffyd in the late twelfth century and recorded in the early thirteenth) stipulated that marriages became fully official only after seven years.[34] This is echoed in Gerald of Wales's report that the Welsh "will only marry a woman after living with her for some time, thus making sure that she will make a suitable wife, in disposition, moral qualities *and the ability to bear children.*"[35] The impulse to judge a marriage's success in genealogical terms was of course common among Latin Europe's ruling elite. But as reformist churchmen began insisting ever more stringently on the indissolubility of marriage, it was easy for the Anglo-Norman clergy to take trial marriages, along with other Welsh customs, as proof of their deviance.[36]

After seven childless years, the advocate's marriage clearly counts as a failure. In courtly terms, the couple's sterility confirms the unnaturalness of their May-December union. In the Welsh context, a man who had married expressly to have children would surely, after

seven years, be expected to dismiss the wife who had failed to provide them. The lady, in turn, might plausibly have taken her loveless and barren marriage to the old *gelos* to be a terrible but temporary misfortune. But as the seven-year deadline comes and goes, the advocate's failure to repudiate her marks him as either remarkably compliant with reformist church dictates or unusually uxorious, sacrificing genealogical expediency to a possessiveness now overtly pathological. Little wonder if the lady, newly deprived of all hope of liberation, chooses this moment to break her silence:

> "Alas," she says, "that I was ever born! My fate is very hard. I'm imprisoned in this tower and I'll never get out of here except by dying. What is this jealous old man afraid of that he keeps me so imprisoned? He's completely mad and out of his senses! They always fear being betrayed!"
>
> (67-74)

> ("Lasse," fait ele, "mar fui nee!
> Mut est dure ma destinee!
> En ceste tur sui en prisun,
> Ja n'en istrai par mort nun.
> Cist vielz gelus, de quei se crient,
> Qui en si grant prisun me tient?
> Mut par est fous e esbaïz!
> Il crient tuz jurs estre trahiz!")

Trapped in a loveless marriage, imprisoned by her jealous husband, abandoned by family and friends, the lady begins to dream compensatory dreams of the way things used to be:

> I've often heard that one could once *find* adventures in this land that brought relief to the unhappy. Knights might *find* young girls to their desire, noble and lovely; and ladies *find* lovers so handsome, courtly, brave, and valiant that they could not be blamed and no one else would see them. If that might be or ever was, if that has ever happened to anyone, God, who has power over everything, grant me my wish in this! (91-104, emphasis added)

> (Mut ai sovent oï cunter
> Que l'em suleit jadis *trover*
> Aventures en cest païs
> Ki rehaitouent les pensis.
> Chevalier *trovoent* puceles
> A lur talent, gentes e beles,
> E dames *truvoent* amanz
> Beaus e curteis, pruz e vaillanz,
> Si que blasmees n'en esteient
> Ne nul fors eles nes veeient.
> Si ceo peot estrë e ceo fu,
> Si unc a nul est avenu,
> Deus, ki de tut ad poësté,
> Il en face ma volenté!)

Like Marie de France herself, the lady has been listening to indigenous tales of *aventure*; instead of *translating* them, however, she seeks to *relive* them—her amorous aspirations linked to Marie's literary ones by the repetition of the verb *trover*. In her wistful evocation of the adventures "formerly found in this land," the desire for escape is fused with a nostalgia for and sympathy with the indigenous past.

Welsh history provided spectacular examples of women exercising sexual agency, like Nest—the daughter of Rhys ap Tewdwr (prince of Deheubarth) and maternal grandmother of Gerald of Wales. By her marriage (c. 1100) to Gerald of Windsor, the Norman castellan of Pembroke, she had three sons and a daughter (Gerald of Wales's mother, Angharad).[37] In the meantime, she also produced three illegitimate sons by three different fathers: Henry FitzHenry (by King Henry I of England), Robert FitzStephen (by Stephen, constable of Cardigan), and William FitzHai (by Hait, the sheriff of Pembroke).[38] The most dramatic episode in her sexual history, however, occurred in 1109, when she captured the attention of her second cousin, Owain of Powys. In a description reading less like history than romance, historian J. E. Lloyd recounts how Owain, having "heard much" of Nest's beauty,

> resolved to pay a visit to the castle of Cenarth Bychan, where she was at the time in residence with her husband, and see with his own eyes the graces of form and feature which were the occasion of so much eloquence. He found them not a whit less marvellous than they were reported, and left the castle with the determination, in spite of all laws and regardless of risk, to become possessor of the fair one who had been not inaptly styled the "Helen of Wales." One dark night he and some fifteen companions stealthily worked their way into the stronghold by burrowing under the threshold of the gate; directly they were within the wall they rushed with wild cries upon the sleeping inmates and added to the alarm and confusion by setting fire to the buildings. By the advice of his wife, Gerald attempted no resistance, but made a hurried escape through a garderobe; thus the raiders found their task an easy one, and, having burnt and dismantled the castle, Owain carried off Nest and her children to Ceredigion. The story suggests that the heroine did not play an altogether unwilling part in the affair; at any rate, she did not disdain afterwards to use her influence over her lover to bring about the return of Gerald's children to their father's roof. None the less, the outrage was a challenge to the king, of which Henry [I] did not fail to take prompt notice.[39]

The political stakes here are unmistakable. Inflamed by secondhand accounts of his cousin's beauty, the native Welsh prince launches a raid that results in the burning and destruction of a Norman castle and the flight of its garrison. Nest's complicity—the suspicion that she may not have played "an altogether unwilling part in the affair"—registers Anglo-Norman anxiety over both the political and sexual promiscuity of the native noblewomen through whom the new hybrid Cambro-Norman society was being produced. Owain and Nest's kinship, making any sexual relationship between them incestuous, further confirms Welsh deviance.[40] No wonder the outrage they generate touches not just Gerald of Pembroke, but the king and the whole Anglo-Norman colonial order.

For Marie's heroine, "adventure" arrives in the shape not of an ardent cousin who burrows under a wall but of a great bird that flies in the window, morphs into "a handsome and noble knight" (115) (*Chevaliers bels e genz*), and boldly declares his love:

> I have loved you for a long time and desired you in my heart. I've never loved any woman except you and will never love another. But I couldn't come to you or leave my palace if you hadn't requested it. Now I can be your lover!
>
> (127-34)

> (Jeo vus ai lungement amee
> E en mun quor mut desiree;
> Unkes femme fors vus n'amai
> Ne jamés autre n'amerai.
> Mes ne poeie a vus venir
> Ne fors de mun paleis eissir,
> Si vus ne n'eüssez requis.
> Or puis bien estre vostre amis!)

Like Owain, he has nursed his passion from afar. His ability to come to her, however, is entirely dependent on *her* will—completely reversing her powerlessness in her marriage to the advocate. Taken by the bird-man's beauty, she nevertheless hesitates on one important count:

> She answered the knight and said she would make him her sweetheart, if he believed in God (and if their love were thus possible), for he was very handsome. Never in her life had she seen such a handsome knight nor would she ever see one as handsome.
>
> (137-44)

> (Le chevalier ad respundu
> E dit qu'ele en ferat sun dru,
> S'en Deu creïst e issi fust
> Que lur amur estre peüst,
> Kar mut esteit de grant beauté:
> Unkes nul jur de sun eé
> Si bel chevalier n'esgarda
> Ne jamés si bel ne verra.)

Ostensibly, she wants to prove to herself that Muldumarec (who has after all just flown in the window) is a man and not a demon come to seduce her. She is a good Christian: this much we know from her distress that her husband's jealousy had prevented her from attending mass: "I can't go to church nor hear God's service" (75-76) (*Jeo ne puis al mustier venir / Ne le servise Deu oïr*). Now she needs to know the handsome knight is a believer before she will grant him her love.

Within the colonial allegory, however, the lady's question may be read as an expression of skepticism concerning Welsh Christianity. As we have seen, Anglo-Norman churchmen coming to Wales in the wake of the conquest found much in the native church to "cause amazement and prompt condemnation." Religious life, like political life, was highly decentralized: each district had a mother church (*clas*) consisting of an abbot and a group of canons, many of whom married and transmitted their offices to their children. Bishoprics (essentially federations of daughter churches linked by their common cult of a local saint) were fluid, with no hierarchy or metropolitian structure. With no standardized usages and no diocesan structure, practices varied from "the excessive asceticism of the holy hermits to the secularism and corruption of monks scarcely distinguishable from the tribesmen about them."[41] For Norman churchmen, such idiosyncracies might be explained "in terms of isolation and archaism; at worst they had to be condemned as the deviations of a local church which had ignored the norms and categories of the church universal and surrendered itself entirely to the ethos and practices of a secular, aristocratic, and heroic society."[42] In response, they "Normanized" the Welsh church by literally reterritorializing it: the land was divided into parishes grouped into dioceses administered by Norman bishops subordinate to the archbishop of Canterbury. In South Wales, churches devoted to local saints were displaced by Benedictine abbeys dedicated to universal saints whose increasing popularity exemplified the "europeanization of Europe" and were frequently located "in the shadow of the new Norman castles" dominating the lowlands.[43] The ecclesiastical colonization of Wales, in other words, was as visible as and even more systematic than the political.

In this light, Muldumarec's declaration of faith reads not simply as assurance that he is no demon, but as a vindication of Welsh Christianity:

> "Lady," he says, "you've spoken well. Not for anything would I wish for there to be any accusations, doubts or suspicions about me. I believe in the Creator who brought us out of the sorrow that our father Adam got us into by biting into the bitter apple; He is and will be and has always been life and light to sinners. If you don't believe me, ask for your chaplain . . . I will take your form and will receive the Lord's body; I will spell out my belief to you: nevermore will you doubt it!"
>
> (145-64)

> ("Dame," dit il, "vus dites bien.
> Ne vodreie pur nule rien
> Que de mei i ait acheisun,
> Mescreauncë u suspesçun.
> Jeo crei mut bien el Creatur,
> Ki nus geta de la tristur
> U Adam nus mist, nostre pere,
> Par le mors de la pumme amere;

> Il est e ert e fu tuz jurs
> Vie e lumiere as pecheürs.
> Si vus de ceo ne me creez,
> Vostre chapelain demandez . . .
> La semblance de vus prendrai,
> Le cors Damedeu recevrai,
> Ma creance vus dirai tute:
> Ja mar de ceo serez en dute!")

In asserting that he is a good Christian, Muldumarec speaks not only for himself but for all his people, affirming the orthodoxy of an occluded indigenous culture sometimes suspected of being less than fully Christian. By offering to take communion in her place, he both assuages her fear and interpellates God as a witness and complacent supporter of their adulterous love; in assuming her own form, he embodies the possibility of transgressing the binary oppositions subjugating her to the possessive old *gelos*.[44]

In the adulterous tales of Tristan or Lancelot, the lady's illicit lover is a prominent member of her husband's court. In contrast, Muldumarec (like Lanval's fairy mistress) remains hidden, in accordance with the indigenous model of ladies who took lovers "no one else could see" (100) (nul fors eles nes veeient). But if he is invisible, *she* is not: her new radiance arouses her husband's suspicion, leading to his discovery of her secret affair. In Welsh tradition, a woman caught in adultery might hope for a happy resolution: "Goronwy ap Moriddig [author of a Welsh lawbook] used to say that a man who lies with another man's wife is not bound to pay anything while the woman approves the act; but if the deed becomes known, the woman should pay *sarhaed*, 'insult-price' to her husband, or else the husband may freely repudiate her and let her turn away from him."[45] The advocate, however, is not so complacent. Instead, he booby-traps his wife's window and snares the bird-man on his next visit. Though mortally wounded, Muldumarec tells the lady not to grieve and, in a curious variation on the Annunciation,

> He comforted her gently, said that sorrow would do no good, but that she was pregnant with his child. She would have a son, brave and strong, who would comfort her; she would call him Yonec. He would avenge both of them and kill their enemy.
>
> (325-32)

> (Il la cunforte ducement
> E dit que dols n'i vaut nïent:
> De lui est enceinte d'enfant.
> Un fiz avra, pruz e vaillant;
> Icil la recunforterat.
> Yönec numer le ferat.
> Il vengerat e lui e li,
> Il oscirat sun enemi.)

In asserting his paternity and instructing his mistress to name their son Yonec, Muldumarec explicitly claims him for indigenous rather than Anglo-Norman culture.[46]

By emerging European standards, the baby the lady carries is feudal society's worst nightmare: an illegitimate child passed off as her husband's son and heir—a scenario so explosive that, at we have seen, romance writers typically refused to touch it.

In Wales, on the other hand, children born out of wedlock could be legitimized for purposes of inheritance:

> Welsh law differed fundamentally from the law of the Church and of England in that it knew no sharp antinomy between legitimate and illegitimate children: what mattered was a child's affiliation to his father. If the child's parents lived together, there was a natural presumption in favour of paternity. If they did not, a formal procedure of affiliation might be necessary: if successfully affiliated, a son born outside wedlock in *llwyn a pherht*, "bush and brake," could inherit a share of his father's land.[47]

The contrast between Welsh and Anglo-Norman attitudes appears in a colorful story Gerald of Wales tells about a Welsh princess named Nest (granddaughter of Grufydd ap Llewelyn). Married to Bernard of Neufmarché, one of William's early Marcher barons,[48] Nest

> fell in love with a certain knight, with whom she committed adultery. This became known, and her son Mahel assaulted her lover one night when he was returning from his mother. He gave him a severe beating, mutilated him and packed him off in great disgrace. The mother, disturbed by the remarkable uproar which ensued, and greatly grieved in her woman's heart, fled to Henry I, King of the English, and told him that her son Mahel was not Bernard's child, but the offspring of another man with whom she had been in love and with whom she had had secret and illicit intercourse. This she maintained rather from malice than because it was true, confirming by an oath which she swore in person before the whole court. As a result of this oath, which was really perjury, King Henry, who was swayed more by prejudice than by reason, gave Nest's eldest daughter, whom she accepted as Bernard's child, in marriage to a distinguished young knight of his own family, Milo FitzWalter, constable of Gloucester, adding the lands of Brecknock as a marriage portion. Later on Milo was made Earl of Hereford by Matilda, Empress of Rome and daughter of Henry I.

In this astounding example of what Jeffrey Jerome Cohen calls the "deployment of Welshness," Nest admits not just to one lover but two, and falsely declares her *legitimate* son a bastard in order to disinherit him. Paradoxically, however, the main beneficiary is Henry I's kinsman, Milo FitzWalter: in the end, the perfidy and promiscuity of highborn Welsh ladies works to the advantage of the king.[49] Conversely, in **"Yonec"** our heroine returns home to bear her son, then lives "many days" (456) (meint di e meint jur) with her husband, creating the "natural presumption" that Yonec is his

son, the heir he had specifically married to procure—not the illegitimate son of the ruler of a mysterious and occulted indigenous kingdom.

In his *Journey through Wales*, Gerald of Wales tells of a Swansea priest who as a young man had been taken by small people "through a dark underground tunnel and then into a most attractive country, where there were lovely rivers and meadows, and delightful woodlands and plains. It was rather dark, because the sun did not shine there. The days were all overcast."[50] When the heroine of **"Yonec"** jumps from her tower to pursue her wounded lover, the bloody trail leads her to just such an otherworld:

> She set out to track the blood that the knight was shedding on the road she was traveling. She wandered on this path and held to it until she came to a hill. There was an entrance in this hill that was wet with blood. She couldn't see anything ahead of her but she was convinced her lover had gone in. Hurriedly, she entered: she found no light within. She continued on the straight path until she exited the hill and came to a very beautiful field. She found the grass moist with blood, which distressed her a lot. She followed the track through the field.
>
> (342-59)

> (A la trace del sanc s'est mise
> Ki del chevalier degotot
> Sur le chemin u ele alot.
> Icel sentier errat e tint,
> De si qu'a une hoge vint.
> En cele hoge ot une entree,
> De cel sanc fu tute arusee;
> Ne pot nïent avant veeir.
> Dunc quidot ele bien saveir
> Que sis amis entrez i seit:
> Dedenz se met a grant espleit.
> El n'i trovat nule clarté.
> Tant ad le dreit chemin erré
> Que fors de la hoge est issue
> E en un mut bel pré venue.
> Del sanc trovat l'erbe moilliee,
> Dunc s'est ele mut esmaiee.
> La trace ensiut par mi le pré.)

On the other side she finds a walled city enclosing silver buildings, surrounded by marshes and a port harboring more than three hundred ships. Following the trail of blood to the inner chamber of the palace, the lady finds her dying lover. He gives her a ring to erase the advocate's memory and a sword that she is to pass on to their son when he is grown. Then he sends her home, back through the hill, to her own land.

Accessible only through the magical tunnel, Muldumarec's kingdom—like Gerald's magical realm—occupies nearly the same space as the prosaic world, as if in anamorphic alternation with it.[51] Later, Muldumarec's subjects relate that at his death, his kingdom had fallen into abeyance: "Since then we have had no lord, but have waited many days, just as he told and commanded us, for the son the lady bore him" (523-26) (Unques puis n'eümes seignur, / Ainz avum atendu meint jur / Un fiz qu'en la dame engendra, / Si cum il dist e cumanda). In feudal Europe, a kingdom thus held in abeyance would be a fantasy indeed: the death of a ruler without a legitimate heir was sure to produce a scramble for power among rival claimants. In Wales, on the other hand, such a disappearing kingdom evokes the transitory realms of the *twysogion,* ready to be revived by a new charismatic prince. Like Gwynedd or Deheubarth, Muldumarec's land disappears at his death, only to await a propitious moment to reemerge. Here the messianic overtones of the son's anticipated return merge with the geo-temporal "fluidity" of Wales's political geography.

In Marie's colonial tale, the Welsh king's illegitimate son becomes the perfect realization of Anglo-Norman chivalry. As Muldumarec had predicted, Yonec grows up to be "a brave and valiant knight" (426) (chevaliers pruz e vaillanz), an exemplar of courtly values: "In all the kingdom you couldn't find one so handsome, brave, or strong, so generous, so munificent" (462-64) (El regné ne pot hum trover / Si bel, si pruz ne si vaillant, / Si large ne si despendant).

The dénouement is set years later when the advocate, his wife, and son journey to Caerleon to celebrate the feast of Saint Aaron "according to the custom of the land" (474) (a la custume del païs). Strategically located at the crossing of the old Roman road and the Usk River, Caerleon was a significant site in both history and fiction. In the *Domesday* accounts of 1086, it marked the edge of the Norman frontier.[52] In the twelfth century, it was the center of the Anglo-Norman lordship of Careleon-and-Usk, held by the earls of Pembroke.[53] During the wars following Henry I's death, the native prince Morgan ab Owain seized Usk castle and made Caerleon a Welsh lordship.[54] Though Henry II later reestablished control of the lowlands, upland Caerleon remained under native rule. Tensions remained acute.[55] In 1171, Henry took Caerleon castle from Morgan's brother, Iorwerth.[56] Two years later, during the Great Revolt against Henry II, Iorworth's son Hywel captured all Gwent Iscoed (Lower Gwent) except the castles.[57] Then in 1175, Henry II forced Richard Strongbow, the Norman earl of Lower Gwent, to restore Caerleon to Iorwerth ab Owain. The following year, Richard died without male heirs; his lands remained under royal control until 1189, when a newly crowned King Richard gave Strongbow's daughter Isabel in marriage to the loyal family retainer, William Marshal. Meanwhile, Caerleon remained independent but "moved increasingly in the orbit of the greater kingdoms."[58] In

contemporary literature, on the other hand, Caerleon connotes not political turmoil but Arthurian grandeur—the site of King Arthur's plenary court in Geoffrey of Monmouth's seminal *Historia Regum Britanniae* (late 1130s), Wace's *Roman de Brut,* in Chrétien de Troyes's *Perceval.*[59]

Marie's account of Caerleon features two buildings characteristic of Anglo-Norman colonial settlements: a castle, the "visible expression and guarantee of conquest," and an abbey, "spiritual arm" of the military conquest.[60] "They came to a castle; in all the world there was none more beautiful! There was an abbey within with many monks" (481-84) (viendrent a un chastel; / En tut le mund nen ot plus bel! / Une abbeïe i ot dedenz / De mut religïuses genz). The importance of the ecclesiastical establishment is signaled by the pride the abbot takes in showing his visitors around: "He entreated them to stay, showing them his dormitory, chapter house, and refectory" (492-94) (Mut les prie de surjurner: / Si lur musterrat sun dortur, / Sun chapitre, sun refeitur).

Curiously, Saint Aaron, whose feast day they have come to celebrate, was not one of the international saints in whose favor so many Welsh churches had been disendowed but an indigenous saint, a local third-century Romano-Briton martyr.[61] This discrepancy reflects the fact that in the later twelfth century, a native Welsh church had begun to reemerge in Cistercian guise. In 1179, Hywel ab Iorwerth—the native ruler who challenged the Anglo-Norman earls of Pembroke for control of Caerleon—endowed Llantarnam abbey as a daughter house of Strata Florida, which was strongly identified with Welsh interests.[62] Such foundations served as venues for native assemblies and mausolea[63]—perhaps like the magnificent tomb the abbot shows the advocate and his family:

> They found a large tomb covered with silk, a band of precious gold running from one side to the other. At the head, the feet, and at the sides were twenty lighted candles. The candle holders were pure gold, the censers which perfumed that tomb during the day to do it great honor were of amethyst.
>
> (500-508)

> (Une tumbe troverent grant,
> Coverte d'un palie roé,
> D'un chier orfreis par mi bendé.
> Al chief, as piez e as costez
> Aveit vint cirges alumez;
> D'or fin erent li chandelier,
> D'ametiste li encensier
> Dunt il encensouent le jur
> Cele tumbe par grant honor.)

When the visitors inquire who is buried there, the locals respond with the tale of their king who died for love:

They began to cry and, as they cried, to tell how it was the best knight—the strongest and proudest, handsomest and best loved—ever born in this world. He had been king of this land; no king had ever been as courtly. He had been caught at Caerwent and killed for the love of a lady.

(513-22)

(Cil comencierent a plurer
E en plurant a recunter
Que c'iert li mieudre chevaliers
E li plus forz e li plus fiers,
Li plus beaus e li plus amez
Ki jamés seit el siecle nez.
De ceste tere ot esté reis,
Unques ne fu nuls si curteis.
A Carwent fu entrepris,
Pur l'amur d'une dame ocis.)

Recognizing the story as her own, the lady turns to her son and, in quick succession, reveals that the king was his father, slain by the advocate, gives him Muldumarec's sword, then falls dead on his tomb.

Like the historical Nest, the lady here robs her husband of his son and heir by revealing his paternity and her infidelity. Acting on the Welsh imperative that a "slain man's kinsfolk" avenge his death in order to "remove the dishonour it had caused them," Yonec takes up Muldumarec's sword and beheads the man he had always considered his father in order to avenge a dead man he has never known.[64] "He took his stepfather's head off with the sword that had belonged to his father: thus he avenged him and his mother" (544-46) (Sun parastre ad le chief tolu; / De l'espeie ki fu sun pere / Ad dunc vengié lui e sa mere). In this highly condensed scene, the transfer of Muldumarec's sword to his son functions as a kind of posthumous *cynnwys,* affiliating Yonec to the father he had never known and legitimizing him for purposes of inheritance. Moreover, by slaying his stepfather in the abbey church, Yonec symbolically adduces ecclesiastical approval for his act—exemplifying the Welsh "assimilation of lay and ecclesiastical values" by which "the right of vengeance" could be "jealously upheld in the name of the saint."[65] Where Muldumarec had taken pains to prove he was a good Christian, his son openly vindicates native practices of inheritance and vengeance.

The advocate's concern with dynastic continuity thus ends, ironically, in the resurgence of Muldumarec's kingdom: endowed with his father's sword, Yonec is acclaimed king by his late father's subjects. In wistfully evoking the way things used to be, the lady unleashes the return of the (autochthonous) repressed, not only as erotic fantasy but as political revenge. In this version of the colonial allegory, both father and stepfather die violently. By slaying his stepfather, Yonec not only avenges his father's death and his mother's unhappiness but restores the old, occulted order: the advocate's murder is the "surplus"—the constitutive excess—that enables the reimposition of traditional rule.[66]

"MILUN"

Like **"Yonec," "Milun"** takes place in South Wales and turns on an illegitimate birth. A baron's daughter falls in love, sight unseen, with a famous knight named Milun. Taking him as her lover, she bears a son, whom she sends to her sister in Northumbria. Married off to a local lord, she secretly corresponds with Milun over the next twenty years. When their son reaches adulthood, he receives his father's ring and a letter disclosing his parents' identity. Proud of his father's reputation, he makes his way to Brittany, where his chivalry wins him the epithet Peerless (Sanz Per). Milun, not suspecting this brilliant young man is his son, meets him at a tournament at Mont Saint Michel. As they are about to clash, Milun recognizes the young man's ring, which leads to an emotional reunion between father and son. Happy to hear that his parents still love each other, Sanz Per decides to bring them together by slaying the stepfather he has never met. At that moment, word arrives of the stepfather's death. Father, mother, and son enjoy a happy reunion, with Sanz Per presiding over the marriage of his parents.

"Born in South Wales" (9) (de Suhtwales nez), Milun seems to inhabit the hybrid Cambro-Norman society of the late eleventh and twelfth centuries. Unlike Yonec or Muldumarec, he (like Gerald of Wales) bears a name that marks him as culturally if not ethnically Norman.[67] A simple knight who makes his living by his sword, Milun becomes a star on the wide circuit of European chivalry. Making his way to Brittany, he builds a reputation not through the kind of adventures found in the *matière de Bretagne* but in tournaments that attract a mixed crowd of "Normans and Bretons, Flemings and Frenchmen" (386-87).[68] That Milun should go abroad to gain fame is ironic, since historically Wales was one of the places chivalric "youth" might realize their aspirations in fact rather than fiction.[69] On the politically unstable Cambro-Norman frontier, "the vassal's obligations of military service . . . were never in danger of becoming archaic." It was a land of opportunity for the disenfranchised: for younger sons of great families, as well as for poor but valiant knights who "had everything to gain and nothing to lose by pursuing their careers in Wales, for there they would have military adventure in abundance and possibly a territorial fortune as a reward."[70] Still, by the last quarter of the twelfth century, "the age of rapid Anglo-Norman advance in Wales had drawn to a close"[71]—a constriction that propelled members of the new mixed-blood nobility to seek new frontiers, as in the Cambro-Norman conquest of Ireland.

MARIE de FRANCE *CLASSICAL AND MEDIEVAL LITERATURE CRITICISM, Vol. 111*

Milun, however, chooses to make his way in the world of international chivalry. His skill, we are told, is famous as far away as Ireland, Norway, Gothland, Logres, and Scotland (15-17), earning him the esteem of the powerful: "Because of his prowess he was much loved and honored by many princes" (19-20) (Par sa pruësce iert mut amez / E de muz princes honurez). It also earns him the heart of a young girl,[72] who falls in love with him through hearsay:

> In his country there was a baron—I don't know his name. He had a beautiful daughter who was a very courtly maid. She had heard Milun spoken of and began to love him very much.
>
> (21-26)

> (En sa cuntree ot un barun,
> Mes jeo ne sai numer sun nun;
> Il aveit une fille bele
> E mut curteise dameisele.
> Ele ot oï Milun nomer,
> Mut le cumençat a amer.)

Concealing the girl's (and her father's) identity under a protestation of ignorance, Marie intimates the social impossibility of an affair between a baron's daughter and a landless knight.[73] Nevertheless, the liaison is conducted with exemplary courtesy: the girl sends Milun a message offering him her love; he happily acquiesces and, sending her his ring in return, promises to come to her whenever she wishes. Before long, Milun is a frequent visitor to her courtly enclosure.

The sunny tale of love turns dark, however, when the girl finds herself pregnant:

> She sent for Milun and made her lament, and told him what had happened: she had lost her honor and her worth, when she'd gotten mixed up in such a situation. She would be put to the sword or sold abroad. *Such was the custom of the old ones* as they held at that time.
>
> (56-64, emphasis added)

> (Milun manda, si fist sa pleinte,
> Dist li cument est avenu:
> S'onur e sun bien ad perdu,
> Quant de tel fet s'est entremise;
> De li ert faite granz justise:
> A gleive serat turmentee
> U vendue en autre cuntree.
> *Ceo fu custume as ancïens,*
> Issi teneient en cel tens.)

In the general prologue to Marie's *Lais,* "the custom of the old ones" (9) (custume as ancïens) refers to classical authors' penchant for speaking obscurely, so that those coming after them might "gloss the letter" (15) (gloser la lettre) of their texts "and add the surplus of their understanding" (16) (E de lur sen le surplus mettre). Here, in contrast, "custume as ancïens" designates the atavistic punishment meted out to unwed mothers. Where in **"Yonec"** the olden days evoked ladies with handsome and courteous lovers, in **"Milun"** they signify instead the intolerance of a staunchly patriarchal society.

Despite the menace hanging over her, the girl energetically takes charge of her own fate. Where Fresne's mother anonymously disposes of her incriminating child, the lady summons Milun and details her plan:

> "When the child is born," she says, "you will take it to my sister, who is married in Northumbria—a rich lady, worthy and wise. You will send word to her, in writing and orally, that this is her sister's child, on whose account she has endured many pains. Now take care that it is well brought up, whatever it is—daughter or son."
>
> (67-76)

> ("Quant li enfes," fait ele, "ert nez,
> A ma serur le porterez
> Ki en Norhumbre est marïee,
> Riche dame, pruz e senee,
> Si li manderez par escrit
> E par paroles e par dit
> Que ceo est l'enfant sa serur,
> S'en ad suffert meinte dolur.
> Ore gart k'il seit bien nuriz,
> Queil ke ço seit, u fille u fiz.")

In an interesting variation on Welsh practices, the illegitimate child is "affiliated" in advance not with its father but with its mother through a secret complicity among sisters that circumvents the strictures of the feudal politics of lineage. Where Yonec's identity is conserved in a ring and a *sword*, Milun's unborn child is dispatched to his mistress's sister along with a ring and a *letter*. "I will send her a letter; in it will be written the name of [the baby's] father / and his mother's adventure" (78-80) (un brief li enveierai; / Escriz i ert li nuns sun pere / E l'aventure de sa mere).[74] Milun, the child's biological father, becomes the messenger who conveys the newborn to its maternal aunt and delivers these tokens of its identity. His inability to decide the fate of his own son (in contrast, for example, to Muldumarec) underscores the power gap separating a baron's daughter from a simple knight, however exalted his reputation. After discharging his mission, Milun goes abroad to earn his way as a knight-for-hire: "he went outside his land, seeking wages for his valor" (121-22) (eissi fors de sa tere / En soudees pur sun pris quere).

Meanwhile, his mistress is betrothed to "a very powerful man from the region" (125) (un mut riche humme del païs). In the brief delay before her wedding, missing Milun and fearful that her illicit pregnancy will be discovered, she falls prey to a kind of desperation the heroine of **"Yonec"** experiences only after seven years:

"Alas," says she, "what shall I do? I am to have a husband? How can I take him? I'm no longer a virgin. I'll be a servant all my life. I didn't know it would be like this, but thought I would have my friend. [I thought] we would conceal this affair between us, that I would never hear it told anywhere. It would be better for me to die than to live! But I am not free, but have many guards, old and young, around me: my chamberlains, who always hate good love and delight in sorrow. So I will be made to suffer. Alas! that I can't die instead!"

(133-48)

("Lasse," fet ele, "que ferai?
Avrai seignur? Cum le prendrai?
Ja ne sui jeo mie pucele;
A tuz jurs mes serai ancele.
Jeo ne soi pas que fust issi,
Ainz quidoue aveir mun ami;
Entre nus celisum l'afaire,
Ja ne l'oïsse aillurs retraire.
Mieuz me vendreit murir que vivre!
Mes jeo ne sui mie delivre,
Ainz ai asez sur mei gardeins
Vieuz e jeofnes, mes chamberleins,
Ki tuz jurz heent bone amur
E se delitent en tristur.
Or m'estuvrat issi suffrir,
Lasse! quant jeo ne puis murir!")

Her distress is a useful reminder that the Welsh tolerance of illegitimate children did not mean that their attitude to marriage "was in any way cavalier." It was "the solemn duty of the girl's kinsfolk to guard her virginity until she was given in marriage; it would be no small public shame for them, as well as for her, if they were found to have failed in their duty."[75] In the end, however, her worries are groundless: on the appointed day, she is married, and no one notices anything amiss.

The *lai*'s best-known feature is the twenty-year exchange of letters the protagonists maintain by hiding their correspondence in the feathers of a white messenger-swan. Feeling "very sad and pensive" (152) (mut . . . dolenz e mut pensis) without his beloved, Milun soon devises a way to contact her: "He wrote his letter and sealed it. He had a swan he loved very much. He tied the letter to its neck and hid it in its plumage" (161-64) (Ses lettres fist, sis seela. / Un cisne aveit k'il mut ama: / Le brief li ad al col lïé / E dedenz la plume muscié). He then commends the swan to a messenger, with instructions to deliver it to his lady.

"Milun" is the third of three consecutive *lais* in which birds play central narrative functions. After **"Yonec,"** in which Muldumarec takes the form of a goshawk (*ostur*), comes **"Laüstic,"** in which a nightingale singing outside a lady's window provides a pre-text for her secretly to meet with her lover. In **"Milun,"** the swan serves as the

medium of the lovers' ongoing communication, the near homophony of the words "cygne" (swan) and "signe" (sign) highlighting the *lai*'s fascination with the materiality of the word.[76] If the message Milun had delivered to his lady's sister "in writing and in speech" (71-72) (par escrit / E par paroles e par dit) was characterized by its built-in redundancy, the letters he sends her trigger a metonymic fetishization of writing itself, as the girl lavishes on the parchment all the affection she is unable to show her absent lover:

Under [the swan's] plumage she felt the letter. Her blood stirred: she knew well it came from her lover. . . . She [and her maid] disengaged the letter, and she broke the seal. At the top she found "Milun." Recognizing her lover's name, she kissed it a hundred times, weeping, before she could speak any further!

(218-30)

(Desuz la plume sent le brief;
Li sancs li remut e fremi:
Bien sot qu'il vint de sun ami . . .
Le brief aveient deslïé,
Ele en ad le seel brusié.
Al primier chief trovat "Milun";
De sun ami cunut le nun:
Cent feiz le baisë en plurant,
Ainz qu'ele puïst dire avant!)

In the twelfth century's two great adulterous romances, writing remains marginal: Béroul's Tristan and Iseut communicate through hushed tones, secret signs, and ambiguous language, while Chrétien's *Chevalier de la Charrete* shows writing to be blatantly deceptive, always already susceptible of forgery.[77] In **"Milun,"** on the other hand, literacy is no longer the monopoly of clerics. The energy and imagination Tristan and Iseut expend arranging clandestine trysts our heroine devotes to finding ways of writing to Milun: "she tried so hard that, by art and strategem, she obtained ink and parchment" (253-54) (Tant quist par art e par engin / Ke ele ot enke e parchemin).[78] Through the medium of writing, the protagonists maintain an extraordinary twenty-year affair, translating the volatility of courtly passion into a sustained, long-term devotion—a prosaic variation of the lyric theme of *amor de lonh*. In Marie's calculus, true love seems to flourish in inverse proportion to physical proximity, with **"Chaitivel"** at one end of the scale and **"Milun"** at the other. Though it is Milun's prowess that first catches his sweetheart's attention, it is his faithful correspondence that nurtures and retains her affection.

The ending of **"Milun"** closely parallels that of **"Yonec"** but completely rewrites it. Like Yonec, the couple's illegitimate child grows up to be a brave and valiant knight. When he comes of age, his aunt gives him his mother's ring and letter, telling him his father was the best knight in the land. Wishing to prove himself, the young man heads to Brittany, where his prowess and largesse earn him the name "Sanz Per"—peerless, but also a homophone for "sanz pere," fatherless. Meanwhile, Milun sets out to defeat the newcomer, never suspecting he is his son. When the two come face-to-face in a tournament at Mont Saint Michel, Sanz Per knocks his father from his saddle. At that moment, Milun recognizes his assailant's ring: "'Friend,' he says, 'listen to me! By God Almighty, tell me, what is your father's name? What is your name? Who is your mother?'" (433-36) ("Amis," fet il, "a mei entent! / Pur amur Deu omnipotent, / Di mei cument ad nun tis pere! / Cum as tu nun? Ki est ta mere?"). Despite the superiority of his maternal lineage, Sanz Per seeks to identify himself with the father he has never known:

> I'll tell you as much as I know about my father. I think he was born in Wales and his name is Milun. He loved the daughter of a rich and powerful man, and secretly engendered me in her.
>
> (445-50)

> (Jo vus dirai
> De mun pere tant cum j'en sai.
> Jeo quid k'il est de Gales nez
> E si est Milun apelez.
> Fillë a un riche humme ama,
> Celeement m'i engendra.)

Overjoyed, Milun reveals his identity and recounts how he and the boy's mother have continued to love each other and exchange messages despite her marriage. For Sanz Per, the solution is simple: "By my faith, fair father, I'm going to bring you and my mother together! I will kill her husband and have you marry her" (497-500) (Par fei, bels pere, / Assemblerai vus e ma mere! / Sun seignur qu'ele ad ocirai / E espuser la vus ferai). Fate, however, spares Sanz Per from this displaced patricide: landing in South Wales, father and son receive the news that the lady's husband has died; in an inversion of the conclusion of **"Yonec,"** "the father-lover remains alive and the husband dies conveniently instead of being killed by a vengeful stepson."[79]

In **"Milun,"** the happily-ever-after consists not in the return of an occluded past but in the opening of a new, utopian future. After meeting his mother, who is delighted to find him so "pruz e gentiz" (524), Sanz Per in effect legitimates himself by presiding over the marriage of his parents: *They never asked their kin: without anyone else's counsel,* their son brought the two of them together: he gave his mother to his father" (525-28, emphasis added) (*Unc ne demanderent parent: / Sanz cunseil de tute autre gent / Lur fiz amdeus les assembla, / La mere a sun pere dona*).[80] In contrast to the lady's first marriage, in which "her father gave her a lord" (124) (Sis peres li duna barun), this union is

consistent with the reformed model of marriage, whose sole requirement is the mutual consent of the partners—except there is no priest to sanctify the proceedings. It is a remarkable inversion of the feudal politics of lineage.

Falling outside all recognizable models of medieval marriage, this match legitimizes both Sanz Per (now no longer fatherless) and Milun as well, uniting him with the woman previously beyond his reach. In a sense, the belatedness of this marriage mocks the chivalric ideal: the valiant knight fulfills the *joven*'s dream—but twenty years late and through the intervention of his own illegitimate son. At the same time, this resolution signals the emergence of a new Cambro-Norman meritocracy in which the kinship group (*tref*) no longer plays the dominant role. Simultaneously the progeny and progenitor of this plot, Sanz Per parlays his illegitimacy into a utopian family—and chivalric—romance.

In **"Milun,"** Marie ironically takes pains to conserve a tale thematizing the erasure of the past. As elsewhere, she emphasizes her own work of transcription: "Of their love and fortune the ancients made a *lai*, and I, *who have put it down in writing,* take great pleasure in retelling it" (531-34, emphasis added) (De lur amur e de lur bien / Firent un lai li aunciën, / E jeo, *ki l'ai mis en escrit,* / Al recunter mut me delit). Two things, however, set this epilogue apart from that of **"Yonec."**[81] First, given the protagonists' twenty-year correspondence, Marie's claim to have transcribed a traditional *lai* overwrites her tale's most distinctive feature, its thematization of writing. Second is the pleasure Marie derived from her task. Elsewhere, Marie likes to highlight her fidelity to her source: "I have told you the truth [la verité] about the *lai* I've recounted here" (**"Chievrefoil,"** 117-18).[82] Here, her emphasis on her own pleasure—"I took great pleasure in retelling [it]" (534) (Al recunter mut me delit)—forms a striking contrast to the "surplus of their *intellect*" (16, emphasis added) (de lur *sen* le surplus) invested by those still engaged in translating texts from the Latin.

* * *

For Marie, the project of glossing the letter of her predecessors is both a creative intellectual act and a moral imperative. In **"Yonec"** and **"Milun"** it is also a political commentary on the uses of the past—a matter of particular importance in the borderlands and in transitional cultures. The two *lais* offer radically different representations of the relations between an indigenous past and a colonial present. In **"Yonec,"** the past is a repository of nostalgia and desire that promises escape from the harsh demands of the feudal politics of lineage. Figuratively buried in the person of Muldumarec, it is resurrected in his son, Yonec, who violently slays his curmudgeonly stepfather to restore the old order to power. In **"Milun,"** the past is represented as a merciless patriarchal regime that sells wayward daughters into bondage. Both for noblewomen and for outstanding knights, hope lies not in the atavistic past but in an idealized future exemplified by Sanz Per. In contrast to the violence that in **"Yonec"** is at once revenge and ritual sacrifice, this transition comes as a peaceful withering away of the old. In place of the conflictual model of colonizer versus colonized, **"Milun"** proposes a new Cambro-Norman society that functions as a chivalric meritocracy. Spun out over the years, the protagonists' transgressive love results in a new social order transcending the divisions between the native and the colonial past, between high lineages and landless knights. Under the sign of chivalry, Sanz Per—no longer haunted by the political and familial violence "formerly found" in the land (**"Yonec,"** 92) (que l'em suleit jadis trover)—becomes the champion of a bright and peaceful future.

Notes

1. Mary Louise Pratt, *Imperial Eyes: Travel Writing and Transculturation* (London: Routledge, 1992), 6-7.

2. Duby, *The Knight, the Lady and the Priest,* 222.

3. Among Marie's *lais,* "Guigemar" and "Equitan" feature married women who commit adultery but remain childless. In "Bisclavret," the lady remains childless within the tale itself, but we are told that her descendants all bear the snub-nose of their ancestress's punishment for her disloyalty. In "Fresne," the protagonist's first marriage goes unconsummated; the day after the wedding, he divorces his wife and marries her twin sister. See Kinoshita, "Two for the Price of One."

4. Marie de France, *Les Lais,* ed. Rychner, l. 9. Moreau, in "La Citez," argues for the *lais'* deep connection to a Celtic world speanning Brittany, Cornwall, and Wales. Rupert Pickens also links these two *lais* but with a focus on the alternation between the voices of male and female internal narrators. See Pickens, "The Poetics of Androgyny in the Lais of Marie de France: 'Yonec,' 'Milun,' and the General Prologue," in *Literary Aspects of Courtly Culture: Selected Papers from the Seventh Triennial Congress of the International Courtly Literature Society, University of Massachusetts, Amherst, 27 July-1 August 1992,* ed. Donald Maddox and Sarah Sturm-Maddox (Cambridge: D. S. Brewer, 1994), 211-19.

5. Ernest Hoepffner, for example, minimizes the significance of Celtic proper names in "Yonec" and "Milun." In *Les Lais de Marie de France,* ed.

Hoepffner (Paris: Nizet, 1971), 79, 109-10, cited in Moreau, "La Citez," 497, 503.

6. R. R. Davies, *Age of Conquest,* 127.

7. On his mother's side, Gerald was descended from both Gerald of Windsor, the Norman castellan of Pembroke, and Rhys ap Tewdwr, the powerful eleventh-century king of Deheubarth (South Wales). Examples of this criticism include Cohen, "Hybrids, Monsters, Borderlands"; Rollo, *Historical Fabrication,* chap. 11; and M. Warren, *History on the Edge.*

8. In the prologue to "Laüstic," for example, Marie names the *lai* in three languages: "Its name is 'Laüstic,' I think; That's what they call it in their country; That's 'russignol' in French and 'nightingale' in pure English" (3-6) (Laüstic ad nun, ceo m'est vis, / Si l'apelent en lur païs; / Ceo est "russignol" en franceis / E "nihtegale" en dreit engleis).

9. Peter Haidu situates Marie "geographically at the Anglo-Norman colonial margin of French culture and semiotically at the borderlines of a male-dominated textual culture," seeing her *lais* as a "minor literature" in (for example) their play on "double sign construction" (in numerous *lais,* including "Yonec" and "Milun") and "constitutive alterities" (as in "Guigemar" and "Bisclavret"). See *The Subject Medieval/Modern,* chap. 6.

10. R. R. Davies, *Age of Conquest,* 92.

11. These were Hugh of Avranches, Robert of Montgomery, and William Fitz Osbern, respectively. They were accorded rights—generally retained by the king—to found boroughs, wage war, administer justice, keep chanceries, and exploit the forest. See R. R. Davies, *Age of Conquest,* 28, and Nelson, *Normans in South Wales,* 24.

12. "The history of the area for the next 150 years was to be one of transient political hegemonies established across this line by one side or the other. It was also to be the story of the complete failure of Anglo-Norman society to establish itself in the highland moors" (Nelson, *Normans in South Wales,* 117). On the division between mountains (*mynydd*) and lowlands (*morfa*) in the Welsh imaginary, see R. R. Davies, *Age of Conquest,* 11-12.

13. Bartlett, *The Making of Europe.*

14. In contrast, the Norman church was strongly marked by eleventh-century reforms, including the spread of the universal monastic orders and the strict delincation between clerical and secular spheres. R. R. Davies, *Age of Conquest,* 176.

15. Nelson, *Normans in South Wales*, 159. In 1081 Rhys ap Tewdwr paid homage to William the Conqueror at Saint David's, in exchange receiving Deheubarth as a feudal "fief." From this moment, the Welsh chronicle *Brut y Tywysogion* styles William "king of the Britons" (brenhin y Brytanyeit) (Nelson, *Normans in South Wales*, 35, 39). The ensuing stability allowed Rhys to reconstitute Deheubarth as a political power. R. R. Davies, *Age of Conquest*, 33-34.

16. R. R. Davies, "Henry I and Wales," 138.

17. Royal "latimers" included Bledhericus Latemeri, prince of Dyfed, who served Henry I, and Iorwerth ap Maredudd ap Bleddyn ap Cynfan, prince of Powys, who served Henry II. Bullock-Davies, *Professional Interpreters and the Matter of Britain*, 18.

18. See above, note 7. For examples of Norman-Welsh marriages, see R. R. Davies, *Age of Conquest*, 102.

19. R. R. Davies, *Age of Conquest*, 59.

20. Nelson, *Normans in South Wales*, 9-14.

21. On Henry's use of his grandfather's reign as a point of reference, see W. L. Warren, *Henry II*, 62-63.

22. R. R. Davies, *Age of Conquest*, 41-51. Earlier in the century, Deheubarth was eroded by Norman advances. The success of Lord Rhys (ruled 1155-97) resulted in part from the diversion of Anglo-Norman attention to Ireland in 1170. Allied by marriage with both Anglo-Normans and the native Welsh, Rhys presided over a cultural renaissance, exemplified by the great assembly (*eisteddfod*) of poets and musicians held at Cardigan in 1176 to demonstrate the cultural preeminence of his court. After Henry's death (1189), Rhys and his sons launched raids on Anglo-Norman South Wales, culminating in their victory at Radnor (1196), on the border of England itself (ibid., 217, 221-23).

23. Walker, *Medieval Wales*, 50. Justiciar was an honorary title signifying Rhys's jurisdiction over all the princelings of the south—often bound to him by ties of kinship and matrimony. R. R. Davies, *Age of Conquest*, 51-55, 213, 217, 222.

24. Nelson, *Normans in South Wales*, 6.

25. This is José David Saldívar's description of *la frontera* between the United States and Mexico, inspired in part by Raymond Williams's work on the Welsh-English border (*Border Matters: Remapping American Cultural Studies* [Berkeley: University of California Press, 1997], 13-14, 202n. 3).

Compare Cohen's call for "an alliance . . . between medieval studies and . . . borderlands theory," focusing on the "overlap among a multitude of genders, sexualities, spiritualities, ethnicities, races, cultures, languages" ("Hybrids, Monsters, Borderlands," 86).

26. Nelson, *Normans in South Wales*, 152.

27. Tales traveled in the other direction as well. The early thirteenth-century Welsh translation of the *Chanson de Roland* survives in ten manuscripts. It appears as chapter 22 of the Welsh translation of the *Pseudo-Turpin Chronicle* (possibly from Llanbadarn Fawr in Ceredigion) made for Reginald, king of Man and the Western Isles (1188-1226) (Annalee C. Rejhon, *Can Rolant: The Medieval Welsh Version of the Song of Roland*, University of California Publications in Modern Philology 113 [Berkeley: University of California Press, 1984], 68-69, 88-89).

28. Chrétien's patron, Count Philip of Flanders, was Henry II's first cousin, their interests linked by the Flemish cloth industry's dependence on English wool. Flemish immigrants settled in southwest Wales from the time of Henry I (R. R. Davies, *Age of Conquest*, 98-99, 159-60). On anti-Welsh sentiment, see J. Davies, *History of Wales*, 131.

29. The new men who came to power under Henry I (1100-35) included Robert of Gloucester (the king's illegitimate son), Miles of Gloucester, Brian Fitz Count, and (in Caerleon and Usk) Gilbert of Clare; by 1200, these families had all failed in the direct male line, bringing to power yet another group, including William Marshal (R. R. Davies, *Age of Conquest*, 84).

30. See Kinoshita, "Royal Pursuits."

31. Duby, *The Knight, the Lady and the Priest*, chaps. 9-10.

32. On the role traditional Welsh kinship groups played in marriage (*o rodd cenedl*, kin investiture), see R. R. Davies, *Age of Conquest*, 125.

33. R. R. Davies, *Age of Conquest*, 214.

34. Its name derives from the early tenth-century king of Deheubarth, to whom it was attributed (Pryce, *Native Law and the Church*, 89, 93). On the Welsh tradition of legal writings, see R. R. Davies, *Age of Conquest*, 133-34, 221.

35. Gerald of Wales, *Journey through Wales*, 263 (emphasis added).

36. R. R. Davies, *Age of Conquest*, 127-28.

37. William and Maurice FitzGerald played important roles in the Cambro-Norman conquest of Ireland; David (d. 1176) became bishop of Saint David's, in Pembroke.

38. Henry FitzHenry was killed during Henry II's 1157 expedition against Owain of Gwynedd. Robert succeeded his father as constable of Cardigan. Taken captive by his cousin Rhys ap Gruffydd, he was released three years later on promising to support Rhys's campaigns against Henry II. Caught between his oath to his Welsh kinsman and his allegiance to the Anglo-Normans, Robert solved this "problem of divided loyalties" by enlisting in the Irish expedition of 1169. Nelson, *Normans in South Wales*, 135; Lloyd, *History of Wales*, 499, 502; Gerald of Wales, *Journey through Wales*, 189.

39. Lloyd, *History of Wales*, 418.

40. Gerald of Wales attributes the political defeat of Dafydd of Gwynedd and his brother, Rhodri, to the fact that both were "born in incest" to Owain Gwynedd and his first cousin, Cristin. Owain died excommunicate for refusing to relinquish this "incestuous" wife. *Journey through Wales* II.8 (192-94).

41. Davies, *Age of Conquest*, 173-74, 177; Nelson, *Normans in South Wales*, 161. Clerical marriage and clerical dynasties were common across western Europe before the Gregorian reforms of the late eleventh century; however, their persistence in Wales became a mark of Welsh otherness.

42. R. R. Davies, *Age of Conquest*, 177.

43. Ibid., 181-82. The highlands, in contrast, were dominated by the Cistercians, whose introduction of sheep raising created a viable economy that helped incorporate them into the European mainstream. Cistercian monasticism "became the first institution fully shared between the Cambro-Normans and the native Welsh" (Nelson, *Normans in South Wales*, 160-64).

44. See Kinoshita, "Two for the Price of One," 50.

45. Pryce, *Native Law and the Church*, 93. On the manuscript tradition of the Welsh lawbooks, see *The Law of Hywel Dda: Law Texts from Medieval Wales*, ed. and trans. Jenkins (Llandysul: Gomer, 1986), xxi-xxiii.

46. Yonec is a Cornish or Breton diminutive of the popular Welsh name Iwon or Iwein. See Moreau, "La Citez," 497-98. On the importance of names in the "europeanization of Europe," see Bartlett, *The Making of Europe*, 270-72

47. Pryce, *Native Law and the Church*, 97. This custom, called *cynnwys*, survived in parts of Wales until the end of the Middle Ages (R. R. Davies, *Age of Conquest*, 128). The Welsh tolerance of illegitimate children undoubtedly played a part in the Angevins' dynastic alliances with two princes of Gwynedd: Dafydd, who married Henry II's illegitimate sister, Emma (a reward for supporting Henry in the civil wars of 1173-74), and Llewelyn ab Iorwerth, who married John's illegitimate daughter, Joan, in the early thirteenth century. W. L. Warren, *Henry II*, 167, and Walker, *Medieval Wales*, 53.

48. On Grufydd ap Llewelyn (d. 1063), who briefly united all of Wales just before the Norman Conquest, see R. R. Davies, *Age of Conquest*, 24-27; on Bernard of Neufmarché, see p. 86.

49. Gerald bears a grudge against Earl Milo's son Mahel for his treatment of Gerald's maternal uncle David, bishop of Saint David's. See Gerald of Wales, *Journey through Wales* II, 2, 89, 90-91, 94n. 99, 94-95, 100, 109.

50. Years later, he still claimed to remember the language of the little people (Gerald of Wales, *Journey through Wales*, I.8). Other curiosities paralleling elements in Marie's *lais* include the antlered doe (as in "Guigemar"), shot and sent to Henry II (I.1); the pharmaceutically inclined weasel (I.12), as in "Eliduc"; the preoccupation with the metropolitan status of Dol (II.1), as in "Fresne"; and the chance accident that becomes an inherited trait (II.7), as in "Bisclavret."

51. On anamorphosis, see Stephen Greenblatt, *Renaissance Self-Fashioning from More to Shakespeare* (Chicago: University of Chicago Press, 1980), 18-23.

52. Nelson, *Normans in South Wales*, 76.

53. These were Walter of Clare (d. 1138), granted the lordship in 1119; Walter's nephew Gilbert Fitz Gilbert (d. 1148); and Gilbert's son Richard Strongbow. R. R. Davies, *Age of Conquest*, 41 and 278 (diagram 6).

54. R. R. Davies, *Age of Conquest*, 467.

55. Ibid., 100.

56. Iorwerth raided the town in retaliation, but the castle withstood the siege and was specially provisioned against further attacks. Lloyd, *History of Wales*, 540-41.

57. R. R. Davies, *Age of Conquest*, 93. The previous year, Hywel's brother Owain had been killed by the earl of Gloucester's men, in an example of the Norman-on-Welsh violence that threatened Henry II's peace with the native princes (Davies, *Age of Conquest*, 291). For the relationship between Morgan ab Owain and Hywel ab Iorwerth, see Walker, *Medieval Wales*, 31, figure 2A.

58. R. R. Davies, *Age of Conquest,* 217, 271, 275, 277.

59. Geoffrey of Monmouth, *History of the Kings of Britain,* trans. Lewis Thorpe (Harmondsworth: Penguin, 1966), 226-27; *La Geste du roi Arthur,* ed. and trans. Emmanuèle Baumgartner and Ian Short, Bibliothèque Médiévale (Paris: 10/18, 1993), 100-120; and Chrétien de Troyes, *Perceval, Oeuvres complètes,* 4003, 4606.

60. R. R. Davies, *Age of Conquest,* 181. On the role of castles in the Norman conquest of Wales, see ibid., 89-92.

61. Contrast Caerwent, where the cult of Saint Stephen had replaced that of Saint Tathan (R. R. Davies, *Age of Conquest,* 179-82). Saint Aaron's feast day is July 3. In Gerald of Wales's time the church of Saint Aaron's had a "distinguished chapter of canons" (*Journey through Wales* I.5, 115). The church of Caerleon is still dedicated to him (Moreau, "La Citez," 495).

62. The community of Strata Florida was endowed in 1164 as part of the "triumph of Cistercian monasticism in Wales" between 1131 and 1201. It soon attracted the patronage of the Lord Rhys, king of Deheubarth, and became the center of the tradition of Welsh historical writing that produced the *Brut y Tywysogyon* (R. R. Davies, *Age of Conquest,* 197, 273, and Walker, *Medieval Wales,* 81-82). Contrast the nearby abbey of Margam—also Cistercian but associated with Anglo-Norman interests. Cowley, *Monastic Order in South Wales,* 26-27.

63. R. R. Davies, *Age of Conquest,* 201.

64. Ibid., 123-24.

65. Ibid., 175.

66. This supersedes my previous view of "Yonec" (in Kinoshita, "Cherchez la femme") as a normative tale in which even adultery is conscripted to serve the feudal politics of lineage.

67. Compare the Count Milon (2433) (le cunte Milun) mentioned in the *Chanson de Roland* or Milon de Nanteuil, the dedicatee of Jean Renart's *Roman de la Rose ou de Guillaume de Dole.* In Marie's "Chievrefoil," Tristan is also described as having been born in "Suhtwales" (16).

68. Compare the "internationalism" in "Guigemar," whose titular hero proves himself in wars in Flanders, Lorraine, Burgundy, Anjou, and Gascony (51, 53-54), and "Chaitivel," in which a tournament held at Nantes draws knights from France, Normandy, Flanders, Brabant, Boulogne, Anjou, and Hainault (77-79, 92).

69. On youth, see Duby, "Les 'jeunes' dans la société aristocratique."

70. R. R. Davies, *Age of Conquest,* 85-86, 95. Compare Gerald of Wales's grandfather, the younger son of the constable of Windsor, who demonstrated his prowess in defense of Pembroke castle (1096) before marrying the daughter of Rhys ap Tewdwr. Gerald of Wales, *Journey through Wales* I.12, 148-49.

71. R. R. Davies, *Age of Conquest,* 271. For the dating of Marie's *lais,* see Glyn Burgess, introduction to *Lais,* ed. Alfred Ewert (Oxford: Blackwell, 1965), ix.

72. Throughout this discussion of "Milun," I use "girl" rather than "lady" to translate Marie's designation "dameisele" (ll. 24 et passim), indicating that she, unlike the heroine of "Yonec," is unmarried.

73. Contrast the alternate reality of a romance like Chrétien de Troyes's *Erec et Enide,* where a king's son weds the daughter of an impoverished *vavassor.*

74. Since Milun makes his living with his sword, he can ill afford to leave it behind. Compare "Fresne," in which the foundling girl is abandoned with a ring and blanket of Byzantine silk. The fact that the lady's sister is married in Northumbria confirms the family's Anglo-Norman connections. In 1136, the ancient kingdom of Northumbria was revived as an earldom for the son of King David of Scotland; in 1149, during the English civil war, David seized it for Scotland. After David's death, his great-nephew Henry II reclaimed it for England—part of his campaign to recover the prerogatives held by his grandfather, Henry I. See W. L. Warren, *Henry II,* 180-82.

75. R. R. Davies, *Age of Conquest,* 128. Reparations included the payment of a "virginity fine" (*amobr*) for a daughter's sexual lapses—its amount determined by the status of the family in question (116).

76. The messenger claims to have captured the swan "outside Caerleon" (183), providing an intertextual link to "Yonec."

77. Tristan and Iseut resort to writing only once, in seeking to return to court: a hermit takes down Tristan's dictated message; Marc, in turn, summons a clerk to read the letter once he receives it. There is no indication the protagonists themselves are literate (*Tristan et Iseut,* ed. Lacroix and Walter, ll. 2355-2434, 2510-2620). Contrast Marie's "Chievrefoil," in which Tristan (from Suhtwales, like Milun) makes an inscription on a branch of hazelwood and Iseut successfully

decodes it. See also Chrétien de Troyes, *Lancelot ou le chevalier de la Charrete, Oeuvres complètes,* 5338-51.

78. The diffusion of court chanceries is associated with the "europeanization of Europe." Using "European-style Latin charters" as an index of degree of "europeanization," twelfth-century Wales (with 60 extant) falls between Ireland (with 10) and Scotland (with 160). See Pryce, *Literacy in Medieval Celtic Societies,* 3. On clerks and literacy in native Wales, see R. R. Davies, *Age of Conquest,* 263.

79. *The Lais of Marie de France,* trans. Hanning and Ferrante, 180.

80. Illegitimate children were typically legitimized by their parents' subsequent marriage, except in England, where Henry II rejected church policy. See Pryce, *Native Law and the Church,* 98, 101.

81. "Cil ki ceste aventure oïrent / Lunc tens aprés un lai en firent / De la pitié de la dolur / Que cil suffrirent pur amur" (555-58).

82. "Chievrefoil," as noted earlier, is also set in South Wales. Its epilogue names the *lai* in French and in Anglo-Saxon—"The English call it Goatleaf" (115) (Gotelef l'apelent Engleis)—but not in Welsh.

Selected Bibliography

PRIMARY SOURCES

Chrétien de Troyes. *Oeuvres complètes.* Ed. Daniel Poirion. Paris: Gallimard, 1994.

Gerald of Wales. *The Journey through Wales/The Description of Wales.* Trans. Lewis Thorpe. Harmondsworth: Penguin, 1978.

Marie de France. *Les Lais.* Ed. Jean Rychner. Paris: Champion, 1983.

————. *The Lais of Marie de France.* Trans. Robert Hanning and Joan Ferrante. New York: Dutton, 1978.

Tristan et Iseut: Le poème français—La saga norroise. Ed. and trans. Daniel Lacroix and Philippe Walter. Lettres Gothiques. Paris: Livres de Poche, 1989.

SECONDARY SOURCES

Bartlett, Robert. *The Making of Europe: Conquest, Colonization and Cultural Change, 950-1350.* Princeton, N.J.: Princeton University Press, 1993.

Bullock-Davies, Constance. *Professional Interpreters and the Matter of Britain.* Cardiff: University of Wales Press, 1966.

Cohen, Jeffrey Jerome. "Hybrids, Monsters, Borderlands: The Bodies of Gerald of Wales." In Cohen, *Postcolonial Middle Ages,* 85-104.

Cowley, F. G. *The Monastic Order in South Wales, 1066-1349.* Cardiff: University of Wales Press, 1977.

Davies, John. *A History of Wales.* London: Allen Lane, 1993.

Davies, R. R. *The Age of Conquest: Wales, 1063-1415.* Oxford: Oxford University Press, 2000.

————. "Henry I and Wales." In *Studies in Medieval History Presented to R. H. C. Davis,* ed. Henry Mayr-Harting and R. I. Moore. London: Hambledon Press, 1985, 133-47.

Duby, Georges. "Les 'jeunes' dans la société aristocratique dans la France du Nord-Ouest au XIIᵉ siècle." In *La Société chevaleresque: Hommes et structures du Moyen Age.* Paris: Flammarion, 1988, 129-42.

————. *The Knight, the Lady and the Priest: The Making of Modern Marriage in Medieval France.* Trans. Barbara Bray. New York: Pantheon, 1983.

Haidu, Peter. *The Subject Medieval/Modern: Text and Governance in the Middle Ages.* Stanford, Calif. Stanford University Press, 2004.

Kinoshita, Sharon. "Cherchez la femme: Feminist Criticism and Marie de France's *Lai de Lanval." Romance Notes* 34:3 (1994): 263-73.

————. "Royal Pursuits: Adultery and Kingship in Marie de France's *Equitan." Essays in Medieval Studies* 16 (2000): 41-51.

————. "Two for the Price of One: Courtly Love and Serial Polygamy in the *Lais* of Marie de France." *Arthuriana* 8:2 (1998): 33-55.

Lloyd, John Edward. *A History of Wales from the Earliest Times to the Edwardian Conquest.* 3rd ed. Vol. 2. London: Longmans, 1939.

Nelson, Lynn H. *The Normans in South Wales, 1070-1171.* Austin: University of Texas Press, 1966.

Pryce, Huw, ed. *Literacy in Medieval Celtic Societies.* Cambridge: Cambridge University Press, 1998.

Pryce, Huw. *Native Law and the Church in Medieval Wales.* Oxford: Clarendon Press, 1993.

Rollo, David. *Historical Fabrication, Ethnic Fable and French Romance in Twelfth-Century England.* Lexington: French Forum, 1998.

Walker, David. *Medieval Wales.* Cambridge: Cambridge University Press, 1990.

Warren, Michelle R. *History on the Edge: Excalibur and the Borders of Britain, 1100-1300.* Minneapolis: University of Minnesota Press, 2000.

———. "The Noise of Roland." *Exemplaria* 16:2 (2004): 277-304.

Warren, W. L. *Henry II.* Berkeley: University of California Press, 1973.

Robert L. A. Clark (essay date 2007)

SOURCE: Clark, Robert L. A. "The Courtly and the Queer: Some Like It Not." In *'Cançon legiere a chanter': Essays on Old French Literature in Honor of Samuel N. Rosenberg,* edited by Karen Fresco and Wendy Pfeffer, pp. 409-27. Birmingham, Ala.: Summa Publications, Inc., 2007.

[*In the following essay, Clark studies "discordant sexuality" in "Lanval" by reevaluating the text in light of medieval history, which, according to the critic, has been mediated by a tradition of literary response that tends to exclude homosexuality from its discourse.*]

Many years ago when, as an undergraduate, I first read Marie de France's **"Lanval,"** I was struck by the passage, as I'm sure many others have been, in which the Queen angrily accuses Lanval, who has rejected her amorous advances, of preferring *vallez,* or "young men," to women:

> La reïne s'en curuça;
> Iriee fu, si mesparla:
> "Lanval, fet ele, bien le quit,
> Vus n'amez gueres cel deduit.
> Asez le m'ad hum dit sovent
> Que de femmes n'avez talent!
> Vallez avez bien afeitiez,
> Ensemble od eus vus deduiez.
> Vileins cüarz, mauveis failliz,
> Mut est mis sires maubailliz,
> Ki pres de lui vus ad suffert,
> Mun escïent que Deu en pert."
> Quant il l'oï, mut fu dolenz;
> Del respundre ne fu pas lenz.
> Teu chose dist par maltalent
> Dunt il se repenti sovent.
> "Dame, dist il, de cel mestier
> Ne me sai jeo nïent aidier.
> Mes jo aim e si sui amis
> Cele ki deit aveir le pris
> Sur tutes celes que jeo sai."[1]

(vv. 275-95)

Years later, my interest in the passage was rekindled by a discussion in 1992 on MEDFEM-L, the electronic forum for medieval feminists, on recent English translations of the **Lais.** In that discussion, the record of which has not survived, the above-quoted passage was, as I recall, the only one to receive close scrutiny.[2] And it was suggested that, given the inevitable loss of semantic

richness and subtlety in even the most excellent translations of Marie's text, the ambiguity of the Queen's speech in this passage was 'lost in translation.' At the time I argued that it is perfectly clear from Lanval's response that he understands the Queen quite well, but upon further reflection I realized that Marie's treatment of this episode is in fact rife with ambiguities and silences. It thus seems appropriate that in the current context, in which we honor one of our most accomplished editors and translators of medieval texts, we should return yet again to this passage and the lai of **"Lanval,"** a text that is emblematic of the voicing and silencing of discordant sexuality, the sort of queer saying and unsaying, the talking and yet not talking about sexual relations between members of the same sex, that one finds in certain courtly texts and in the scholarship on those texts.

My project here is to offer a queer reading **"Lanval"** and of *fin'amors* more generally. By 'queering' I mean a reevaluation that seeks to understand how discordant sexual practices were represented (or not) in specific, historically situated discourses. Such a reevaluation cannot be limited to a rereading of the texts—in this instance, courtly texts—in which these representations occur. It must also include a reexamination of the critical tradition through which our understanding of these literary texts is filtered. The goal of such a rereading is, quite simply, to gain a fuller understanding of transgressive sexualities in the past, and by this I emphatically do not mean a past that would be of interest only to those who wish to reclaim a queer history, a gay and lesbian past, a "history of our own," however laudable those enterprises may be. For discordant sexuality was, in the medieval period as it is now, part of the fabric of human existence. By suppressing one part of the historical record—or trying to recuperate it in the name of heteronormativity, that is, the representation of heterosexuality as the norm—we not only falsify the whole but also perpetuate the past's misprisions in the present.[3] By listening carefully to what the texts say, which includes listening for their silences, and by confronting texts of different kinds, we can discover, and at least partly recover, the ways in which discordant sexualities were discursively constructed in a particular cultural setting.[4]

In the electronic discussion evoked above, one participant said of the Queen's remarks that surely the context leaves little "wiggle room." This is all the more true if one considers that two of the four manuscripts, S and C, have *amez* instead of *avez* in line 281, an unequivocal medieval reading that suggests that any subtlety in the Queen's speech as it appears in manuscripts H and P probably did not make her meaning more ambiguous for medieval readers than the more explicit rendering.[5] Earlier translators did, however, try to wiggle their way around this problematic passage. Two squeamish translators, both anglophones, simply dodged the issue by cutting or drastically modifying the Queen's speech. Edwin B. Williams, who reprinted the fairly faithful rendering into modern French by Paul Tuffrau (Appendix, III), simply cut the Queen's entire speech from his edition (Appendix, IV). This deletion must have made Lanval's reference to the "vilenies" with which he has been charged something of a cipher for Williams's readers. Eugene Mason, on the other hand, opted for innuendo in place of the Queen's bald-faced charge, following the fairly straightforward, "Well I know that you think little of woman and her love," with the insinuating, ambiguous trope: "There are sins more black that a man may have upon his soul" (Appendix, V). Perhaps a sharp reader could have drawn the conclusion that the sin here is literally the one that dare not speak its name. Oddly enough, Mason felt compelled then to add the phrase, "Neither am I a despiser of women," to Lanval's assertion that he does not, as Mason has it, "belong to the guild" that the Queen is talking about, a rendering of *mestier* which finds an echo in Burgess and Busby's "profession."

Now, it should certainly come as no surprise to us that a couple of prudish translators who were producing translations for a non-specialist public that may well have been used as school texts, should have cut a passage containing an unambiguous reference to sexual relations between men, although their strategies for avoiding any but indirect reference to homosexuality is nothing but the editorial equivalent of less dignified exercises in rumor, calumny, and blackmail, as I have suggested. But I think that we must ask: what was it exactly that these "school texts" were teaching? It is my contention that they were, quite simply—and rather blatantly—presenting a veritable recoding of Marie's text, one that in its alteration of the original serves to uphold heteronormativity. Through the suppression of references to sexual relations between members of the same sex, all sexuality becomes heterosexual, which is clearly not the case in Marie's text.[6] Yet, while the Queen's meaning seems clear enough, it is less easy to say just what such an accusation *meant,* what its implications were. Marie's text, at least on the face of it, is of little help here: despite the Queen's vague reference to court gossip—"on m'a dit"—there has been nothing in the text to prepare the reader for her claims.[7] Her slanderous assertions thus have the effect of catching both Lanval and the reader off guard. And just as the Queen's allegation seems to come out of nowhere, in Marie's text it goes nowhere. There is no further reference to sexual impropriety in the form of sexual relations between men after the private exchange between Lanval and the Queen. In short, her claim seems totally gratuitous, which has the effect of making it all the more unsettling. At this crucial moment,

however, this is but the first of two accusations: the second is, of course, the Queen's claim that Lanval made amorous advances to *her* (the "Putiphar's wife" motif) and that, when she rejected him, he shamed her by saying that the least of his lover's servants surpassed the Queen in beauty and breeding. Thus, we have a double accusation involving sexual impropriety, the first made privately, to Lanval's face, and the second, to Arthur. In the rest of the lai, the first accusation is totally overtaken by the second. It is the second charge, to which the Queen adds Lanval's disparaging remarks about the her beauty, that will be played out at length in the text, as Lanval is cleared in a trial that concludes with a highly dramatic public vindication of his innocence and, perhaps not incidentally, of his love for women. But what, we may well ask, of the other accusation, the first one? What was *that* all about? Certainly, the reader is given to understand that that claim is as unfounded the other, coming as they do from the same source and both unsupported by anything in the text. But can one say that the nullification of the second charge has the same effect with regard to the first?[8] This textual working out of the altercation between Lanval and the Queen, so clamorous regarding the possibility of adultery, so silent regarding same-sex relations, raises a number of questions, among which: 1) what, if any, is the relation between the Queen's accusations, involving, as they both do, allegations of sexual offense? 2) what are the broader implications of the first charge? what suppositions about sexual conduct underwrite it, what constructions of the field of sexual behavior? and, most important for our purposes here, 3) what does the silencing effect imply, the effect that is created when such charges are blurted out and then receive no further mention? Why is there *silencing* instead of just *silence* on the question of same-sex love? These are, I believe, very important questions that challenge our understanding of **"Lanval"** and the culture that produced it.

The silencing that I have noted in Marie's text and the elisions in the early translations tend, not surprisingly, to be repeated in the criticism on **"Lanval,"** although the passage in question has certainly not been completely ignored by scholars. Both Ewert and Rychner, in the notes to their respective editions of the *Lais,* point out that in the *Roman d'Enéas*—which Marie certainly knew—Lavine's mother makes the same accusation against Enéas. And Ewert remarks: "This charge was commonly levelled at men who repulse the advances of women," adding "The Celts were frequently accused of this vice by ancient writers."[9] The scene between Lanval and the Queen has, to be sure, been the focus of a good deal of commentary. Michèle Koubichkine, in an influential piece on the psychology of **"Lanval,"** maintains that Lanval's violent response to the Queen can be attributed to his being torn between the necessity of being faithful to Arthur, on the one hand, and to his beloved, on the other.[10] Surely, Lanval's position of being torn between the world of the court and the Other World is a difficult one, but it is not, as Koubichkine claims, the motivation of his anger. For Lanval responds twice to the Queen. The first time, when she offers him her love, he responds firmly, if rather too bluntly. But it is only the second time, when she accuses him of loving boys, that he loses his composure and answers her angrily and rudely. Koubichkine's reading, though compelling in many respects, sidesteps the issue of the alleged sexual relations between members of the same sex. Don A. Monson, in an important article on the ideology of **"Lanval,"** also devotes an extended analysis to the "scène capitale" of the confrontation between Lanval and the Queen, noting that the accusation of "pédérastie" (Monson's word) can indeed be explained by Lanval's perceived indifference to women.[11] Now that Lanval's fairy mistress has granted him unlimited wealth in addition to her love, he no longer needs to compete with the other knights of the court for the gifts, including women, which it is Arthur's prerogative to distribute. Having thus disposed of the accusation by offering a plausible motivation for it, Monson, like Marie, turns his attention to the Queen's second charge. His piece thus effectively repeats the text's pattern of accusation and silencing by suggesting that the Queen's charge is, one might say, only natural given Lanval's observable behavior at court.

The relative lack of interest on the part of critics in the accusation that Lanval loves boys cannot, in my opinion, be completely justified by saying that the second charge is, after all, the one that becomes public and is adjudicated. Rather, this critical indifference may be attributed to the fact that, until very recently, scholarship on courtly literature has been underwritten by the assumptions of heteronormativity, the assumption (despite evidence to the contrary) that heterosexuality was, if you will, the only game at court. The striking negation of this assumption in the Galehout episode of the *Lancelot en prose* and the recent critical interest in this text do not seem to have altered the commonly held notion that erotic love, *fin'amors,* "courtly love"— call it what you will—can only exist between a man and a woman.[12] In this connection I would like briefly to evoke two classic formulations of *fin'amors* that show that the ideology of heteronormativity constructs itself of necessity through the negation of queer sexuality.[13]

The first of these classic formulations of *fin'amors* is a modern one, the opening chapter on "courtly love" in C. S. Lewis's *The Allegory of Love*. Certainly Lewis's text no longer enjoys the authority that it once did, although I find rather persuasive his discussion of the primacy of male-male relationships in the Middle Ages. But it is precisely in this construction of medieval ho-

mosociality, to use Eve Sedgwick's term, that one can see an unmistakable anxiety about homosexuality in Lewis's discussion.[14] Early on in the chapter, Lewis evokes the notion of Platonic love as developed in the *Symposium* in order to contrast it with courtly love, and he remarks:

> In the *Symposium,* no doubt, we find the conception of a ladder whereby the soul may ascend from human love to divine. But this is a ladder in the strictest sense; you reach the higher rungs by leaving the lower ones behind. The original object of human love—who, incidentally, is not a woman—has simply fallen out of sight before the soul arrives at the spiritual object.[15]

The offhandedness of this remark should not, I think, fool us, for Lewis will once again evoke the spector of homosexuality in his discussion of male friendship in the pre-courtly literature of the Middle Ages. He writes:

> Ovid, too, was known to the learned; and there was a plentiful literature on sexual irregularities for the use of confessors. Of romance, of reverence for women, of the idealizing imagination exercised about sex, there is hardly a hint. The centre of gravity is elsewhere—in the hopes and fears of religion, or in the clean and happy fidelities of the feudal hall. But, as we have seen, these male affections—though wholly free from the taint that hangs about 'friendship' in the ancient world—were themselves lover-like; in their intensity, their willful exclusion of other values, and their uncertainty, they provided an exercise of the spirit not wholly unlike that which later ages have found in 'love'.[16]

This is a curious text, to be sure, in which male affections are first purged of erotic desire only to be likened to heterosexual love!

Lewis is, of course, only following the other classic formulation of *fin'amors,* this one medieval, to which I will refer and which he himself evokes a little further on in his discussion: Andreas Capellanus' *Treatise on Love,* or *De arte honeste amandi*. I quote from Book I, chapter II in John Parry's translation:

> Now in love, you should note first that love cannot exist except between persons of the opposite sex. Between two men or two women love can find no place, for we see that two persons of the same sex are not at all fitted for giving each other the exchanges of love or for practicing the acts natural to it. Whatever nature forbids, love is ashamed to accept.[17]

It is striking how closely Andreas's condemnation of sexual acts between members of the same sex resembles those to be found in other clerical writings on sexuality. To cite another contemporary formulation, Peter Abelard rearticulates Saint Paul's injunction from Book V of Romans as follows: "Against nature, that is, against the order of nature, which created women's genitals for the use of men, and conversely, and not so women could cohabit with women" [Contra naturam, hoc est contra naturae institutionem, quae genitalia feminarum usui virorum praeparavit, et e converso, non ut feminae cohabitarunt].[18] Thus, we have the same kind of formulation being used, in Andreas's text, nominally to extol love outside of marriage, and in Abelard's, to promote the Church's definition of legitimate sexuality, that is to say, within marriage. What the two formulations have in common, of course, is that in order to establish heterosexuality, whether within marriage or without, as "natural," they must first posit the unnatural so as to condemn it. The norm cannot exist without the co-existence of the queer.

Andreas's move is interesting for another reason. He is not, as we have noted, championing marriage, that is, sanctioned sex for the purpose of procreation, in this, the first section of his treatise. For this reason he must eliminate from the field that other form of nonprocreative *fin'amors,* that is, sexual relations between members of the same sex. Andreas will, of course, defend marriage in the third book of his treatise, but its blatant misogyny suggests why he also needed that initial hedge that allowed him to distance himself from male-male sexuality, which also implies a rejection of women. Needless to say, it was also an accusation that was frequently leveled at the clerical class.

A similar tactic can be seen in the *Livre des manières,* an estates poem by Etienne de Fougères, who served as chaplain to Henry II Plantagenet before becoming Bishop of Rennes.[19] His work is thus chronologically very close to Marie's, and indeed both works may have been intended for Henry, although Etienne's is dedicated to a certain countess of Hereford. Etienne's poem is violently misogynistic and, like Andreas in book III of the *De amore,* he holds up as the ideal a life free from the cares of sexuality. This is the consolation he offers to his dedicatee, who has outlived all of her children. Like Andreas, Etienne defends marriage as the only legitimate arena of sexuality, and to do so he must first attack what he clearly saw as the two most serious rivals to the Church's campaign to promote marriage: sexual relations between members of the same sex and *fin'amors.* Etienne sees both as endemic to the court, and he attributes both to the ladies. For, curiously, he makes no mention of sexual relations between men although he devotes 28 lines to the sin against nature, a game, he says, practiced by "ces dames."[20] It is curious that Etienne has nothing to say about sexual relations between men—perhaps it was too close to home—but it is difficult not to read this as a subtext in the above-mentioned passage, which fairly bristles with phallic symbols. Having dispatched the "sin against nature," Etienne turns his attention to the adulterous wife, that is, the courtly *amie,* and once she has been dealt with,

he appropriates the word *joie* from courtly discourse to champion the virtues of matrimony.

These texts contemporary with Marie's begin to point us in the direction of an understanding of the stakes in the Queen's dangerous game with Lanval and in our interpretations of it. In the construction of sexuality in the twelfth century, sexual relations between members of the same sex and *fin'amors* were structurally in a similar position as forms of sexuality that were seen as rivals for the way they challenged the institution of marriage. As a young, desirable man who is not a cleric and who exhibits no apparent interest in women nor in marriage, Lanval finds himself occupying this structural position. Hence, the Queen's double accusation. It should be noted that sexual relations between members of the same sex and adultery have another structural feature in common, also brought out in Marie's text: they are seen as specific threats to the feudal lord, that is to say, to the social structure.[21] For Marie condemns adultery when it involves a betrayal of the trust between lord and vassal, as she does in **"Lanval"** and **"Equitan."** Sexual relations between members of the same sex are also perceived to threaten social structure in that they have the potential of taking men and women out of the sanctioned arrangements of the sex-gender system (marriage and the family) without necessarily bringing them into the fold of the Church and, presumably, under its control. Nothing is more alarming to Etienne de Fougères, at least in the sexual realm, than the idea of women of gentle birth doing without men and without the Church. But the violence of the medieval condemnations of *fin'amors* and sexual relations between members of the same sex should, of course, alert us to the fact that these were in fact potential sexual options that were seen as rivals of the Church's new pro-marriage sexual ideology.

It makes little sense to wonder what Marie may have thought herself about same-sex relations per se. But it is clear that, like adultery—or, indeed, any kind of love in the *Lais*—the imputation of same-sex relations in **"Lanval"** cannot be separated from the social context in which it occurs: the court. In this light, the Queen's accusations are but another variety of the envy and attendant slander that is endemic in that milieu. In **"Lanval"** they are the complement of the homosocially driven envy that his fellow knights feel towards the valorous young foreigner, just as Arthur's slighting of Lanval in the distribution of "femmes et teres" (v. 17) finds a double complement in the love of his fairy mistress and the unwanted advances of the Queen. To a great extent, Marie's plot is structured by this play of complements, but it is important to note that these structural elements are based on the social dynamics of life at court: lord-vassal relations, with their attendant machinations and intrigues.

In a witty and insightful article, Elizabeth Poe argues that in **"Lanval,"** Marie creates an "topsy-turvy world where delays, reversals, and other departures are the order of the day."[22] Poe notes the elaborate word play that Marie uses to create her ironic and ludic representation of the court, commenting that the cleverest word play is on the verb *esgarder,* with its differing meanings of "to regard attentively," "to gaze upon," but also "to pass judgment."[23] It is indeed striking the extent to which gazing drives the plot of **"Lanval,"** in which the protagonist finds himself at the center of what one could term an "ocular plot."[24] Gazing in **"Lanval,"** as Poe suggests, is never simply erotic; it is, rather, charged with economic and political implications. In **"Lanval,"** looking serves as both reward (as when Lanval gazes upon the body of his fairy mistress, who promises him limitless wealth) and punishment (when that gift is taken away); it constitutes betrayal (as when the Queen gazes on Lanval) and vindication (when his lover appears before the adoring eyes of the court). Looks, in Marie's courtly world, can both kill and exonerate.[25]

At the beginning of the text, Lanval's very existence has been called into question, threatened by Arthur's failing to cast his eye upon him and remember him in the distribution of his bounty. Denied both arms and women—that is, the means of maintaining his social and sexual status at court—he becomes, in effect, an outcast, a fact underscored by his physical isolation before the encounter with the fairy mistress. Shunned and symbolically castrated by the king (who is his surrogate father, as well, since Lanval is a young foreigner at court), he is granted a boon by his lover that compensates for both lacks, material and sexual. The latter is figured in the text by the passage in which Lanval gazes upon the (as-yet-unpossessed) body of the fairy, which Marie spreads before him and us in a highly erotic *blason.*[26] Her gift, with its infantile illusion of plenitude, though, comes at a price: he must recognize her as lord ("Jeo ferai voz conmandemenz," he says; "pur vus guerpirai tutes genz," vv. 127-28). But, as the proverb says: "Don de seigneur n'est pas fief." In swearing allegiance to his lover, he also must recognize that she can take all away if he does not respect her commands and reveals his secret to anyone. She not only supplants Arthur as lord (and also as lover and surrogate mother), she also possesses the power to punish him for his negligence, the way that Arthur punished him through being negligent. The third figure who fills this function of rewarding/punishing is the Queen, who fatefully spies Lanval from her window ("Lanval conut et esguarda," v. 243). Just as Arthur and the fairy mistress before her have done, she simultaneously offers and denies rewards of a sexual and presumably material sort. The repetition of this pattern in the *lai* is highly suggestive, for the ever-present power to punish suggests an equally ever-present and primordial injunc-

tion against transgression, but curiously, the result of the transgression (Arthur's failure to reward Lanval's service, the fairy mistress's command that Lanval in effect betray his loyalty to Arthur, the Queen's infidelity), is that it is always Lanval who is punished, emasculated, feminized—in short, queer. Why should this be? Perhaps, on one level, this is a working out of Marie's rueful commentary in the *lai*'s preface on the vagaries of being a foreigner at court (vv. 36-38). On another level, however, it functions as a symptom or sign of the hero's struggle, most often thwarted, to free himself from psychical and social bonds of domination.[27]

What solution, if any, does Marie offer her hero? The text's structure here offers another clue as we move from public humiliation (Arthur's snub) to private rewards (the fantasy world of plenitude) to further private humiliation (the Queen's insult), to public accusation and, finally, exoneration. The structure is strikingly similar to that of *Erec et Enide,* as analyzed by Sarah Stanbury, where Enide moves from the private realm to the public world of the court, followed by the couple's expulsion from court due to Enide's "transgression" and their final reintegration at the end of the romance. Stanbury reads the romance as signifying an ultimate mastery of the feminine (Enide is elevated, but she has also learned her place).[28] Reading **"Lanval"** against *Erec et Enide* reveals a rather different conclusion, for the ending of the former does not possess the closure of Chrétien's romance. It remains open-ended as Lanval, ever passive, is spirited away by his lover, as if to suggest the impossibility (or undesirability?) of assimilating this oddly feminine couple into courtly society. And, in a final, ironic twist in the cycle of reward and punishment, Lanval's final reward looks strangely like the banishment he stood to suffer if found guilty in the trial.[29] Marie's wistful conclusion is that in her world, ultimately, the courtly cannot assimilate the queer.

Notes

1. *Les Lais de Marie de France,* ed. Jean Rychner (Paris: Champion, 1983), 80-81. All translations are given in the Appendix.

2. The two translations in question were those of Ferrante and Hanning (1978) and Burgess and Busby (1986). See Appendix, I-II [Rychner, 1983]. Unfortunately, the archives of MEDFEM-L currently available go back only as far as December, 1996.

3. On the dangers of assuming a transhistorical category of heterosexuality against which the queer is defined, see James A. Schultz, "Heterosexuality as a Threat to Medieval Studies," *Journal of the History of Sexuality* 15 (2006): 14-29.

4. Beginning with the publication of John Boswell's *Christianity, Social Tolerance, and Homosexuality: Gay People in Western Europe from the Beginning of the Christian Era to the Fourteenth Century* (Chicago and London: University of Chicago Press, 1980) and well into the 1990s, most of the scholarship on the history of "homosexuality" fell, for better or for worse, on either side of a fault line separating the so-called essentialists from the cultural constructionists. For a somewhat revised statement of his position, see Boswell, "Revolutions, Universals, and Sexual Categories," Hidden from History: Reclaiming the Gay and Lesbian Past, ed. Martin Duberman et al. (New York: Meridian, 1989), 17-36; for the cultural constructionist position, see in the same volume David M. Halperin, "Sex before Sexuality: Pederasty, Politics, and Power in Classical Athens," 37-53. This debate has been largely surpassed with the emergence of queer theory, in which sexuality identity—be it medieval or modern—is seen as less fixed and more open and fluid.

5. See Jean Rychner's *Lai de Lanval,* Textes Littéraires Français (Genève: Droz; Paris: Minard; 1958) in which his critical edition is presented with all four manuscript versions of the lai in parallel columns. In the notes to his later edition of the *Lais,* Rychner remarks that this variant "n'a guère d'importance," except perhaps in the inflexion given to the meaning of *afeitiez*: with *amez,* the second word could take on the meaning of "bien soignés," as opposed to the more standard one of "dressé, formé" (256).

6. Peggy Maddox notes that Mason's translation expunges not only the accusation of homosexuality but also mutes the frank eroticism of Marie's text ("Ravishing Marie: Eugene Mason's Translation of Marie de France's Breton Lai of *Lanval,*" *Translation Review* 63 [2002]: 31-40). My argument here is that suppressing the reference to same-sex sexuality has an altogether different and quite specific effect, the establishment of heteronormativity, which is not diminished by Mason's bowdlerization of Marie's text.

7. In his *Anonymous Marie de France* (Chicago: U of Chicago P, 2003), R. Howard Bloch suggests that "the reason for Arthur's original neglect is not so much the rivalry between his knights as his own jealousy of the Queen's interest in Lanval" (70), a reading which, despite its plausibility, is not supported by Marie's text.

8. The charge of *felunie,* or treason, due to Lanval's alleged attempt to seduce the Queen, is settled by having him swear an oath denying the claim. The trial itself regards the lesser charge, that of slandering the Queen's beauty. On the trial, see E. A. Francis, "The Trial in *Lanval,*" *Studies in French Language and Mediaeval Literature Presented to Professor Mildred K. Pope* (1939; Freeport, NY: Books for Libraries P, 1969), 115-24; Rychner, "Explication du jugement de Lanval," *Lanval,* 78-84; John M. Bowers, "Ordeals, Privacy, and the *Lais* of Marie de France," *Journal of Medieval and Renaissance Studies* 24 (1994): 1-31, esp. 21; Jacqueline Eccles, "Marie de France and the Law," Les Lieux Interdits: *Transgression and French Literature,* ed. Larry Duffy and Adrian Tudor (Hull: U of Hull P, 1998); Katherine Kong, "Guilty as Charged? Subjectivity and the Law in *La Chanson de Roland* and "Lanval," *Essays in Medieval Studies* 17 (2000): 35-47.

9. Marie de France, *Lais,* ed. Alfred Ewert (Oxford: Blackwell, 1976), 174 (note the curious tension in Ewert's statement between past tense "levelled" and present tense "repulse"). The key text in the *Eneas,* prolix and rich in gastronomic metaphors, makes Marie's text seem understated in comparion: "Cil cuiverz est de tel nature / qu'il n'a gaires de femmes cure; / il ne prise plus lo ploin mestier; / il ne velt pas biset [femelle du pigeon?] mangier, / molt par aimme char de maslon; / il priseroit mialz un garçon / que toi ne altre acoler; / o feme ne set il joër, / ne parlerast pas a guichet; / molt aime fraise [tripes] de vallet; / an ce sont Troïen norri" (*Eneas,* ed. J.-J. Salverda de Grave, 2 vols. [Paris: Champion, 1983-85]), ll. 8567-77, 2: 81. Further on Lavine repeats the accusation in a monologue, noting that "il voudroit deduit de garçon, / n'aime se males putains non. / Son Ganimede a avec soi . . ." (ll. 9133-35). For a rendering into idiomatic English that captures the nuances and vulgarity of this diatribe, see William E. Burgwinkle, *Sodomy, Masculinity, and the Law in Medieval Literature: France and England, 1050-1230* (Cambridge: Cambridge UP, 2004), xi-xii.

10. Michèle Koubichkine, "A propos du Lai de Lanval," *Le Moyen Age* 78 (1972): 467-88, esp. 477-78: "En fait, Lanval est écartelé entre le monde arthurien où il vit et l'Autre-Monde dont il tire son existence et sa Joie. Il y a, pour lui, antinomie irréductible entre les devoirs eux-mêmes complexes, sinon contradictoires, de la courtoisie et l'emprise d'un amour étranger. Ces incompatibilités et la suprématie contraignante de l'amour expliquent la violence des réponses de Lanval à la reine."

11. Don A. Monson, "L'Idéologie du lai de Lanval," *Le Moyen Age* 93 (1987): 349-72, esp. 359: "Cette

indifférence apparente à l'égard du beau sexe est d'autant plus inexplicable que maintenant Lanval a visiblement les moyens matériels de s'établir et de prendre femme et que le nouveau prestige qui provient de ses profusions de largesse, en s'ajoutant aux qualités de valeur, de beauté et de prouesse qu'on lui connaissait déjà, le rend d'autant plus désirable aux yeux des femmes. C'est ce mystère qui provoquera l'intervention désastreuse de la reine et qui explique aussi l'accusation de pédérastie qu'elle proférera contre lui (v. 277-86) lorsque sa proposition d'amour sera refusée."

12. On the Galehout episode, see Christiane Marchello-Nizia, "Amour courtois, société masculine et figures du pouvoir," *Annales: Economies, Sociétés, Civilisations* 36 (1981): 974-81; and Reginald Hyatte, "Recoding Ideal Male Friendship as *fine amor* in the *Prose Lancelot*," *Neophilologus* 75 (1991): 505-18.

13. See Carolyn Dinshaw's reading of the opening lines of the General Prologue of Chaucer's *Canterbury Tales,* in which she argues that the author naturalizes a normative heterosexuality that is, none the less, haunted by a "sodomitical shadow—in the figure of the feminized man" (*Getting Medieval: Sexualities and Communities, Pre- and Postmodern* [Durham: Duke UP, 1999], 116-21, here 121). For critiques of Dinhshaw's reading (also included in her earlier article, "Chaucer's Queer Touches/A Queer Touches Chaucer," *Exemplaria* 7 [1995]: 76-92), see Allen J. Frantzen, *Before the Closet: Same-Sex Love from* Beowulf *to* Angels in America (Chicago: U of Chicago P, 1998), 18-19; and Schultz,, 23-26.

14. On homosociality, see the introductory chapter of Eve Kosofsky Sedgwick's *Between Men: English Literature and Male Homosocial Desire* (New York: Columbia UP, 1985).

15. C. S. Lewis, *The Allegory of Love: A Study in Medieval Tradition* (1936; Oxford: Oxford UP, 1953), 5.

16. Lewis, 10.

17. Andreas Capellanus, *The Art of Courtly Love,* trans. John Jay Parry (1941; New York: Columbia UP, 1990), 30.

18. As translated in Louis Crompton, "The Myth of Lesbian Impunity: Capital Laws from 1270 to 1791," *Journal of Homosexuality* 6.1/2 (Winter 1980-81), 14, from Peter Abelard, *Commentarium super S. Pauli epistolam ad Romanos libri quinque,* PL 178: 806.

19. Etienne de Fougères, *Le Livre des manières,* ed. R. Anthony Lodge, Textes Littéraires Français

(Geneva: Droz, 1979). For a fuller version of the argument offered here, see Robert L. A. Clark, "Jousting without a Lance: The Condemnation of Female Homoeroticism in the *Livre des Manières,*" *Same Sex Love and Desire among Women in the Middle Ages,* ed. Francesca Canadé Sautman and Pamela Sheingorn (New York: Palgrave, 2001), 143-77. See also, in the same volume, Sahar Amer, "Lesbian Sex in the Military: From the Medieval Arabic Tradition to French Literature," 179-98.

20. Etienne de Fougères, ll. 1097-1124.

21. Regarding Lanval's alleged love of boys, the Queen says: "Mon escient, que Deu en pert" (l. 286), as if to suggest that Arthur's very salvation is threatened by his lord-vassal relationship with Lanval. As for the charge of seduction, if proven it would have constituted treason in the form of acting against the interests of one's lord.

22. Elizabeth Wilson Poe, "Love in the Afternoon," *Neuphilologische Mitteilungen* 84 (1983), 301-10 (citation on p. 305). Poe's analysis of the ludic and ironic elements in *Lanval* is highly convincing; I am less persuaded, however, by her conclusions, in which she suggests that we should "take the *Lai de Lanval* lightly . . . as an essentially humorous piece, which pokes gentle fun at certain paradigms of courty literature (e.g., hospitality, adulterous love, justice by tribunal) and which makes no claim to profundity" (309-10). The stakes in *Lanval* strike this reader as being considerably higher than Poe's analysis would seem to allow.

23. Poe, 308.

24. The term is Sarah Stanbury's. See her article, "The Virgin's Gaze: Spectacle and Transgression in Middle English Lyrics of the Passion," *PMLA* 106 (1991), 1083-93 (citation on 1088). In a series of articles, Stanbury has explored the relevance for medieval textual and visual culture of feminist and psychoanalytic film theory. Her goal, as she puts it an article on Chrétien de Troyes' *Erec et Enide,* is "not of imposing the culture of Hollywood on the European Middle Ages, but of allowing us to examine the sight lines of visual desire within medieval culture and medieval texts," Sarah Stanbury, "Feminist Film Theory Seeing Chrétien's Enide," *Literature and Psychology* 36.4 (1990): 47-66 (citation on 49).

25. My interpretation here shares some features with R. Howard Bloch's in the chapter in his recent book bearing the title "If Words Could Kill: The *Lais* and Fatal Speech." Bloch argues that the accusation of homosexuality carries with it an as-

sociation with rhetoric, as in the *De planctu naturae* by Marie's contemporary, Alain de Lille. Likening Lanval to a poet, he sees in the lai's pattern of transgressions "mere thematizations of a broader paradox, which is that of fiction itself." In his reading the "voice associated with the presence of the body, or even of bodies, is transgressed by the lai, which is merely its trace, by the very act of articulation, transcription being merely the limit of such transgression" (Bloch, 71).

26. The highly explicit eroticism of this passage (ll. 94-106) is unique in the *Lais*.

27. William E. Burgwinkle notes similarities between Lanval, the Narcissus of a contemporary Old French version of the Ovidian tale, and Marie's own Guigemar: "All three prefer to be alone; they all declare their indifference to love; and they develop fantasy relationships in response to the strong pressure put upon them to make love to women and, presumably, to procreate" (162).

28. Stanbury, 60-61.

29. Burgwinkle, noting that Lanval is *raviz,* that is, raped or kidnapped, argues that "[t]he strong connection between death, disappearance, and heterosexuality is ominous and alerts us once again to the signs of a persecutory mentality at work" (164).

Michael Calabrese (essay date 2007)

SOURCE: Calabrese, Michael. "Controlling Space and Secrets in the *Lais* of Marie de France." In *Place, Space, and Landscape in Medieval Narrative,* edited by Laura L. Howes, pp. 79-106. Knoxville: University of Tennessee Press, 2007.

[*In the following essay, Calabrese argues that the themes of the prologue to the* Lais, *especially Marie's implied need to hide behind "learned obliqueness," are mirrored in the tales, where true love seeks "secrets and secret places" far removed from societal judgments.*]

Right from the beginning of her *Lais,* in two prologues, Marie de France makes it clear that her enemies are never far behind, the *gangleür* and *losengier* whose biting slanders constantly snap at the heels of anyone who has distinguished herself. Where, this makes us ask, can the poet and her reputation be safe from such attacks, once she has spoken her mind and expressed her poetic gifts? Marie confronts this problem head on, insisting throughout that there are stories to tell—"they will not stay hidden for long," as she often reports—and that she is the one to tell them:

> Ki Deus ad duné escïence
> E de parler bone eloquence
> Ne s'en deit taisir ne celer,
> Ainz se deit volunters mustrer.
>
> (Whoever has received knowledge
> and eloquence in speech from God
> should not be silent or secretive
> but demonstrate it willingly.)[1]

("Prologue" 1-4)

Marie respects God's gift and will speak openly and fearlessly, but oddly, she must at the same time follow the classical principle of speaking obscurely so as to inspire glosses and sharpen the minds of both author and reader:

> Custume fu as ancïens,
> Ceo testimoine Precïens,
> Es livres ke jadis feseient,
> Assez oscurement diseient
> Pur ceus ki a venir esteient
> E ki aprendre les deveient,
> K'i peüssent gloser la lettre
> E de lur sen le surplus mettre.
>
> (The custom among the ancients—
> as Priscian testifies—
> was to speak quite obscurely
> in the books that they wrote,
> so that those who were to come after
> and study them
> might gloss the letter
> and supply its significance from their own wisdom.)

("Prologue" 9-16)

Through this the philosophers and, we presume, the evolving readership throughout time, not only became "plus . . . sutil de sens" (20) but also learned how to guard themselves from things "that should be avoided" ("de ceo k'i ert a trespasser") (22). Marie's opening manifesto thus signals not only her refusal to "conceal" ("celer") what she knows but also, paradoxically, her need to reveal things "oscurament" in accord with a legacy of learning and glossing that best supports both tradition and the individual talent ("lur sens") of the ongoing readership.[2]

To accomplish all she sets out to do, Marie must embrace this paradox of at once unsealing and concealing, both showing (*mustrer*) and hiding (*celer*) together. Through this she finds safe space for herself in the learned tradition, whose borders will justify and protect her endeavor through time, as it has protected the ancients before her. For Marie serves at an ancient alter, safe then as it will be for Pope over five hundred years later, from "sacrilegious hands" (Pope 280). But in Marie's case the enemies are less hands than mouths, the sniping dogs addressed in her second "Prologue" preceding the first *lai,* **"Guigemar":**

Mais quant il ad en un païs
Hummë u femme de grant pris,
Cil ki de sun bien unt envie
Sovent en dïent vileinie:
Sun pris li volent abeissier;
Pur ceo comencent le mestier
Del malveis chien coart, felun,
Ki mort la gent par traïsun.
Nel voil mie pur ceo leissier,
Si gangleür u losengier
Le me volent a mal turner:
Ceo est lur dreit de mesparler!

(But anywhere there is
a man or woman of great worth,
people who envy their good fortune
often say evil things about them;
they want to ruin their reputations.
Thus they act like
vicious, cowardly dogs
who bite people treacherously.
I don't propose to give up because of that;
If spiteful critics or slanderers
wish to turn my accomplishments against me
They have a right to their evil talk.)

(7-18)

The envious force her into the paradox of open obscurity, force her to brave their slander while hiding within a learned obliqueness that they cannot penetrate with their envy. This obscurity, as Augustine and Aquinas had argued for Scripture and as Boccaccio would later for poetry, prevents the unworthy from grasping its truths, for we should not cast pearls before swine, or before curs in this case.[3] With dogged and mordant confidence, then, Marie defies her potential detractors, crafting a safe space from which to exercise her learning free from envy, free from vice and from whatever "grant dolur" ("Prologue" 27) they might bring the anxious poet. The prologues are a success.

But within the *Lais* themselves, Marie's lovers are not always so easily successful, and throughout them Marie wonders where the young lover or the noble knight can be safe from the envy of husbands, fathers, courts, comrades, and anyone who takes pleasure in ruining the happiness of others. Rumor and slander run wild in the *Lais,* as we know, for example, from **"Fresne,"** where a jealous woman accuses her twin-bearing neighbor of having slept with "dui humme" (43). The rumor spread till it was known all over Brittany ("Par tute Bretaine seüe") (52). In varied manifestations, the *Lais* are all about the concealing and revealing of information by, from, and about both the noble and the villainous. I therefore agree with Sarah Spence that though we customarily see "love" as the common theme in the *Lais,* we can make just as strong a case for "envy."[4] Thus the very search for safety that animates Marie's "Prologue" animates the stories themselves, and the poet's conflict with slander and envy is replicated anew

in each fictive world she summons out of "Briton." Marie's enemies are the lovers' enemies too, those who snipe and snip at the heals of freedom and of love. Marie will show often in the *Lais* that with a kind of natural law on their side, the lovers will defeat the plans of the envious, just as Marie will defeat the *gangleürs* and follow her muse. The "Prologue" prepares us for this conflict and sets up the forthcoming battles between the intrusive, envious slanderers and the open-hearted lovers who try to honor their own muse, not of poetry but of love. This neither makes Marie a lover nor the lovers poets but rather unifies the struggles between the two, exposing the parallel dangers that hamper each, stemming from the common causes of envy and intrusion.[5] Marie was aware of the constant dangers of slander, exposure, and judgment faced by poets, wives, knights, young lovers, and werewolves, even when they practice *mesure* and love honestly. Thus in her *Lais* she constantly explores the search for a secret, private space where, if only fleetingly, love and honor can be free, if it meets with her high standards, that is, if it deserves a home either in time or in memory.

Much of the *Lais,* thus, is about the search for what Lanval's mythic lady calls a place "U nuls puïst aveir s'amie / Sanz repreoce e sanz vileinie" (165-66) ("where a man might have his mistress without reproach or shame"). And yet the conflict is not so rigidly structured nor contrived, for not all lovers are the same and not all are entitled to the same protection, either by natural or societal law. All Marie's lovers, good and bad, young and old, sympathetic or scurrilous, seek safety from their envious enemies, yet not all find surety and safety, and some even meet death for their efforts, as in **"Equitan"** and **"Bisclavret."** Success in love depends on the deft use of secrets and secret places, a control and manipulation of the physical world, the artificial landscape of love. Those who use it well will thrive and find security; those overcome by foul lust and envy will suffer when space betrays them. In some cases, further, secret loves can finally be revealed and publicly enjoyed by the persevering couple. Thus, as Marie takes us through the secret places of love, she simultaneously conducts a moral inquiry of its spatial poetics. And, as is usually the case with Marie, the poetics that emerges is not without its ambiguities and aporias.

Spence notices such ambiguities, studying what she calls the "ever-changing qualities of life of the individual in a changing spatio-temporal frame," which leads to a kind of situational morality in the *Lais*: "What is right for X in situation Y is not right for X in situation Z or for W in situation Y" (*Texts* 124). This fluidity is crucial to the *Lais,* but I agree less with Spence's conclusion that amid all this confusion love asserts itself as a medicine. Spence says of **"Guigemar"** that "the love between Guigemar and his lady, and the true love Marie writes of in all her stories, is both the cure for envy and the empowerment of *caritas*" (*Texts* 130).[6] Marie is ever playful and ambiguous, for though lovers battle envy, seldom are any characters "cured" of envy in the *Lais*; more often they are cuckolded, mutilated, or killed for their envy. And sympathetic lovers, furthermore, often prosper without displaying anything close to *caritas*. For often space helps the lovers throughout the work—if they are noble, and even if they commit acts of violence and callous vengeance, as Renée L. Curtis has observed.[7] I agree with Spence, therefore, if I may synthesize her different formulations, that there is a force of love that animates the *Lais,* sometimes remotely but sometimes not at all related to *caritas*. And in this [essay] I will argue that secrets and space play important roles in serving the aims of this love, when neither *caritas* nor any other abstract virtue is always at hand. To put it differently, and I hope provocatively, space helps the lovers that we and Marie like—those we feel for as victims of envy or of imprisoning encumbrance. Because restraint and space are at the center of all Marie's dramas, love can succeed, and the noble can reclaim their right and honors by using the spatial world deftly, even if treachery and violence are needed.

In order to understand more about the use of space in Marie's romantic universe, I want to trace her depiction of the strategies, games, and devices that lovers employ to protect themselves from exposure and woe, often involving the use of secret spaces and private places, away from the watchful eyes of authority and custom.[8] Marie enacts her study of space variously, and our discussion could embrace all twelve *Lais,* but I will focus on six stories: **"Guigemar," "Equitan," "Yonec," "Milun," "Laüstic,"** and **"Eliduc,"** which collectively display the varied, and sometimes confusingly mercurial, role of space and secrecy in the *Lais*.[9] How, indeed, does Marie use space? Often Marie's theme is escape from confinement, as young lovers combat the imprisonment brought on by jealousy, envy, and old grasping men who try to confine women behind walls, as in **"Guigemar," "Yonec,"** and **"Milun."** In other instances, specifically enclosed spaces often provide secrecy and security, as in the case of Milun's swan, Bisclavret's hollow rock, Guigemar's well-caulked ship, and the haven of Lanval's lady's tent where he finds freedom from the slander and political persecution of Arthur's court. Further, when finally the real world will not deliver, Lanval flees to yet another, imaginary space and pulls it in around him, finding there inviolable surety that no one can penetrate or expose. On the other hand, spatial poetics can punish vicious lovers who do not take proper secretive precautions and who treacherously misuse space, as in **"Equitan"** and **"Bisclavret."** In **"Yonec,"** similarly, the *Jaloux* who treacherously traps a noble lover is himself later killed at the man's

tomb by his son, proving that he could not use a spatial trap to kill or confine the force of love and justice. Marie depicts a wholly different kind of private place in **"Laüstic,"** where the bachelor neighbor has an elegant gold vaisselet made for the dead nightingale—a personal memorial to a love and disaster barely averted. **"Eliduc,"** we will see, far from wrapping up the collection neatly or confirming a clear moral paradigm, explodes the issues of the previous poems, in a festival of mock-comic secrecy and lies. **"Eliduc"** is the longest *lai,* the feistiest, most persistently episodic and picaresque, Marie's final flourish, where the outcome is kept secret from the reader in an extended tease until all the lovers mysteriously retreat into holy orders, safe behind sacred walls.[10] Just as Marie must survive as an artist by controlling both the surface and the hidden treasures within her words, her characters too must control the secrets and the hidden spaces that ensure the survival of love.

Marie launches her collection with **"Guigemar,"** a tale of secrecy and of spaces that ultimately protect and exult its lovers, while the restraints of evil fail and the enclosures of the envious betray their masters. Throughout the *lai,* acts of concealing and revealing, of entering and exiting, and of opening and closing animate the amorous drama, as Marie crafts a complex landscape of spatial poetics. The first intrusion is by Guigemar's hunting dogs, which flush out the white stag, which, in turn, flushes Guigemar himself out of sexlessness and solitude, cursing him and condemning him to both love and to fame (119-21). The stag wishes, finally, to be left in peace ("lais m'aveir pés" [123]). As Marie begins the *Lais,* she wants us to recall the forces of intrusion and persecution with which she began, and so Guigemar's hunting dogs imagistically—if subtly—recall the yelping curs who pursue Marie in her "Prologue." Like Marie, Guigemar cannot hide; he now enters public life, and from now on the dogs will be chasing him, Actaeon-like. So exposed, like the "hummë u femme de grant pris" (8) in Marie's "Prologue," for the rest of the *lai* Guigemar must search for safety and security from his enemies, but at the same time he must do so without withdrawing from the world, for he must bravely confront his amorous, as Marie does her artistic, destiny.

After his wounding, he finds refuge first in one of the central images of enclosed space in the *Lais,* the ship that ferries him to his destiny: "Defors e dedenz fu peiee, / Nuls hum n'i pout trover jointure" ("caulked outside and in— / no one could discover a seam in its hull") (154-55). Marie's emphasis on the carpentry stresses surety and protection, and her observation that Guigemar did not think boats could land in that harbor (161ff.) underlines this boat's unique abilities to penetrate risky enclosures in pursuit of its odd amorous mission. The boat's appearance, though unexplained, is no accident, because Guigemar does indeed need it to help him circumvent his future lover's imprisonment in the walled garden and tower where she is held by the *Jaloux,* for, as Hanning and Ferrante aptly render it, "the watch he kept over her was no joke" ("Il ne la guardat mie a gas") (218). Since the grove is "clos tut envirun" (220) and the marble walls are "espés e halz!" (222), and the other side of the grove is "clos de mer" (225), this boat is the lovers' only means of subverting these restraints. As we will see so often in the **Lais,** success in love comes to those who, either through craft or magical fortune, can master the spatial poetics of entry and exit, of "conceal" and "reveal."

And once he meets the lady, Guigemar, despite his Hippolytus-like beginning, wants love and knows how difficult is it for a woman to find a man as worthy as herself ("a sa maniere") (521) and to be safe from public scrutiny and invasion. He tells his hesitant savior that when a woman "de bon purpens, / Ki en sei eit valur ne sens" ("of good character, sensible as well as virtuous") (519-20) finds a man of worth, she should not "treat him too disdainfully" ("Ne se ferat vers lui trop fiere") (522) because love only allows a brief period of safety:

> Ainz l'amerat, s'en avrat joie.
> Ainz ke nuls le sachet ne l'oie
> Avrunt il mut de lur pru fait!
>
> (Rather she should love him and enjoy him;
> this way, before anyone knows or hears of it,
> they'll have done a lot that's to their advantage.)
>
> (523-25)

Here Marie creates not physical but temporal space; love exists in this brief moment, as a coveted secret "before anyone hears of it," before it is revealed and ruptured by the envious. The lady quickly agrees, and the lovers unite, though Marie gives them their privacy and only implies that they enjoyed the sorts of things that people do in this situation: "Bien lur covienge del surplus, / De ceo que li autre unt en us!" (533-34). The poet sets up walls herself, over which she will not peer, but she lets us witness just enough to celebrate a love fulfilled. Yet knowing how fragile such space is, the lovers sense something is wrong and fear that they will be exposed by the husband.

Thus, to protect themselves from the ruin of exposure, the lovers seal off and take control of their own secret spaces, as they essentially enclose each other's bodies for private use through the devises of the knot and the belt that each alone can unravel and unlock and thus "reveal." We might say both these enclosures are "well caulked" like the stout ship; no man can find a seam, that is, no one can penetrate these seals, except the lovers themselves. She makes the knot then puts the belt

on none too soon, as Marie underlines the urgency of the pact by having them discovered immediately after they seal their plan:

> Ki la bucle purrat ovrir
> Sanz despescier e sanz partir,
> Il li prie que celui aint.
> Puis la baisë, a taunt remaint.
> Cel jur furent aparceü,
> Descovert, trové e veü
>
> (Whoever could open the buckle
> without breaking it or severing it from the belt,
> would be the one he would urge her to love.
> He kissed her and left it at that.
> That day they were discovered—
> Spied upon and found out.)¹¹
>
> (573-78)

Somehow, even before the lock and knot come into play, this plan works like a charm, for the next time space tries to encumber the lovers, it fails to do so. For once the lovers are caught and the Lady is imprisoned by the *Jaloux,* for some reason, the cell is not particularly confining. One day, while apostrophizing her lover,

> Dunc lieve sus;
> Tute esbaïe vient a l'hus,
> Ne treve cleif ne sereüre,
> Fors s'en eissi; par aventure
> Unques nuls ne la desturba.
> Al hafne vint, la neif trova.
>
> (She got up:
> In astonishment she went to the door
> and found it unlocked;
> by good fortune, she got outside—
> no one bothered her
> She came to the harbor, and found the boat.)
>
> (673-78)

The door is not locked, and no one "disturbs" her (an important word in the **Lais,** from the Latin *turba,* a swirl or disturbance but also an assembly); we might say "she went privately" to the magic ship. As one friendly open enclosure frees her, another, well sealed and safe, welcomes her and takes her to her lover.

In this *lai* a genuine love cannot be undone by jealous restraint, for just as the *Jaloux* uses space ineffectively, just so does the hapless Meriaduc, the next man who attempts to enclose Guigemar's love but who, of course, cannot open her belt. Guigemar, claiming the lady and her sealed body as his own, besieges Meriaduc's castle and kills him, for the last edifice in this *lai* yields, as all others have done, to the will of the lovers. Despite the fortified castle's resistance ("Mes forz esteit, al prendre faillent" [874]), the final assault underlines the charmed spatial life Guigemar and his lady have led. Thus this *lai,* we see, is a series of intrusions, entrances and exits prevented or facilitated, a flow inward and out, the making and the unmaking of what Chaucer will later call "privitee."[12] Marie, as Bloch argues, may at one point participate as the author of the lovers' discovery, betraying and revealing them, but that moment is fleeting, for throughout the *lai* Marie makes sure that the lovers enjoy a series of safe and private spaces (see Bloch 72-73). Ships ferry the lovers; locks and doors open for them at will, while, with a little perseverance, strong castles finally yield to their authority and might. And in the lovers' wake lie the failed, fallen forces of envy: "Le chastel ad destruit e pris / E le seignur dedenz ocis" (879-80) ("the castle he seized and destroyed; the lord inside he killed"; my translation). For although the lovers endure much and live in constant danger, **"Guigemar"** is a clear triumph for love and a defeat for the dogs of envy and espionage. We cannot find a seam in it.

"Equitan" provides immediate contrasts to **"Guigemar,"** and though the moral framework here may be more broad than in other *lais,* as Hanning and Ferrante note (see their commentary, 69ff.), Marie nonetheless enacts the drama of love and of justice again through a series of physical spaces and enclosures. The focus in this *lai* is not only on how the envious plot against the good but also on the treacherous abuse of secrets and space, the misuse of the arts of concealing and revealing. The lovers here look for all the same things as in **"Guigemar"**: surety, privacy, freedom from control and intrusion, but they do not earn or deserve it. Equitan has merely heard the seneschal's wife praised for her beauty and covets her without seeing her, evidently envious of the love between this "Bon chevalier, pruz e leal" (22) and his wife, "bele durement / E de mut bon affeitement," with "gent cors" and "bele faiture" (31-33). This appetite and covetousness leads to a series of secret, private trysts for the glib king Equitan and his seneschal's all-too-willing wife, all set behind the king's closed doors: "Li us des chambres furent clos" (191; see 185ff.). But finally, the profane secret space of treachery is ruptured, for the adulterous lovers pursue their secret love rather sloppily and without adequate precautions against being exposed, discovered, and revealed. For just as Guigemar's lady's prison door is easily opened, so too is the door guarding these adulterous lovers, letting the truth out and the avenging husband in, in the *lai's* steamy, final scene:

> Pur la cuve, ki devant fu.
> L'us firent tenir e garder;
> Une meschine i dut ester.
> Li senescals hastis revint;
> A l'hus buta, cele le tint.
> Icil le fiert par tel haïr,
> Par force li estut ovrir,
> Le rei e sa femme ad trovez
> U il gisent, entr' acolez.

> Li reis garda, sil vit venir;
> Pur sa vileinie covrir
> Dedenz la cuve saut joinz piez;
> E il fu nuz e despuillez,
> Unques garde ne s'en dona:
> Ileoc murut e escauda.
> Sur lui est li mals revertiz
> E cil en est saufs e gariz.

> (Because the tub was right before them,
> they set a guard at the bedroom door;
> a maidservant was to keep watch there.
> Suddenly the seneschal returned,
> And knocked on the door; the girl held it closed.
> He struck it so violently
> That he forced it open.
> They he discovered the king and his own wife
> Lying in each other's arms.
> The king looked up and saw him coming;
> To hide his villainy he jumped into the tub feet first,
> Stark naked.
> He didn't stop to think what he was doing.
> And there he was scalded to death,
> Caught in his own evil trap,
> While the seneschal remained safe and sound.)

("Equitan" 284-300)

Some secrets ought not to be kept, and space becomes permeable not to aid the lovers but to expose and in fact destroy them, as the seneschal easily bursts through the young girl's absurd buttressing. Guigemar and his lady had been discovered, but that was a temporary setback to a destined love, whereas here the revelation brings the base to justice. The bathtub serves as the final, ridiculous attempt to conceal what has been revealed in the *lai,* an enclosed space that provides neither privacy nor security but frantic death. Readers are left feeling that the king and the wife got what they deserved not so much for their adultery but for their blundering use of space. Equitan cannot have thought to be safe on the cuckolded husband's bed with only a door and "une meschine" (286) protecting them, and he cannot have thought to be protected by the boiling tub with which he planned to kill his own man. But in his nakedness and shame he was not thinking clearly, and this thoughtlessness here stands in stark contrast to his earlier rhetorical seduction of the wife, in which he artfully reverses their power relationship; as he puts it: "Vus seiez dame e jeo servanz" ("you be the lord and I'll be the servant") (175). Marie thus uses physical space to strip the king, literally and figuratively, down to his essential nature, weak, frightened, shameful, and artless, as he desperately seeks a security that he himself has squandered through his own vice. The tub, no doubt, welcomes him, as the caulked ship does Guigemar, and it too holds water all too well.

Another of Marie's naked men is more thoughtful than Equitan in his use of space and secrets, for though Bisclavret's wife and her lover attempt to betray him, he ultimately masters space in his own struggle for justice. The noble werewolf is thus in the parallel position of Equitan's seneschal—the victim of secretive betrayal who, finally, by his own control of space and of the art of concealing and revealing, defeats his duplicitous enemies. Bisclavret's own secret, of course, generates the central drama in the *lai*: he is a werewolf who hides his clothes in a hollow rock, an enclosure that protects him, because without his clothes, without concealing himself after a bestial episode, he cannot transform himself back into a man, exposed ("aperceüz") and trapped as a werewolf forever "a tuz jurs" (74-75). He continues to explain to his inquiring wife how his security depends on maintaining his secret and his secret space: "Ja nen avreie mes sucurs / De si k'il me fussent rendu. / Pur ceo ne voil k'il seit seü (76-78) ("I'd be helpless / until I got them back / That's why I don't want their hiding place to be known").

The object that protects him from exposure and enslavement to the werewolf form is the "piere cruose e lee . . . dedenz cavee" (93-94) ("a big stone / hollowed out inside"), a convenient and friendly enclosure left, like Guigemar's ship, unexplained. But the wife coaxes the secret out of him with verbal craft, much as Equitan glibly wins the wife of the seneschal and betrays him. Bisclavret was not anxious to reveal himself because secrets, he knows, preserve not only his humanity but also, therefore, the love he fears to lose: "Mal m'en vendra si jol vus di, / Kar de m'amur vus partirai / E mei meïsmes en perdrai" (54-56) ("Harm will come to me if I tell you about this, / because I'd lose your love / and even my very self"). He begs her, for love, to stay away from his secret space, but by pretending to ask for love's own sake herself (80 ff.), she tricks him into revealing it, all the while planning "Cum ele s'en puïst partir: / Ne voleit mes lez lui gisir" (101-2) ("how she might get rid of him; / she never wanted to sleep with him again"). Her treacherous violation of space, a space her husband imbues with the power to preserve their love, leads ironically to her own downfall, for one revelation leads to another here, and the wife's infidelity is exposed in the process. Bisclavret was simultaneously and unknowingly preserving not only his dark side but hers too, and one could argue that the real monster in the tale is the treacherous wife, who ends up the mutilated mother of deformed, noseless children, as the beast himself is restored to humanity, civilization and honor. Her secret would not stay hidden for long, as Marie might say, because it is extracted from her, not with sly rhetoric but with torture (255ff.) in moments of violence that recall the end of Equitan. And like Equitan, the wife here proves herself no master of the arts of concealing and revealing, for her actions serve only to unmask herself, all too literally as it turns out.

Significantly, Marie draws much attention to the final private space in the *lai*, the inner chambres where Bisclavret changes clothes.[13] The king's councilor advises giving the beast private time and space to allow the proposed retransformation; it all occurs behind firmly shut doors:

> "En tes chambres le fai mener
> E la despoille od lui porter;
> Une grant piece l'i laissums.
> S'il devient hum, bien le verums."
> Li reis meïsmes le mena
> E tuz les hus sur lui ferma.
> Al chief de piece i est alez,
> Deus baruns ad od lui menez.
> En la chambrë entrent tuit trei;
> Sur le demeine lit al rei
> Truevent dormant le chevalier.

> ("Have him lead to your chambers
> and bring the clothes with him;
> then we'll leave him alone for a while.
> If he turns into a man, we'll know about it."
> The king himself led the way
> and closed all the doors on him.
> After a while he went back,
> taking two barons with him;
> all three entered the king's chamber.
> On the king's royal bed
> they found the knight asleep.)

("**Bisclavret**" 289-99)

The episode reflects the return of privacy, and the proper use of space, in this case the king's own chambers which facilitate and signify the beast's reintegration into society, just as the dense wood and the hollow rock had earlier hidden him and his secret from observation. But now he has moved from that exilic landscape to the king's own bed, in a wonderful reversal of the profane bed in "**Equitan.**" Marie shows in this *lai* that space serves not only deserving lovers but also a just and isolated man, for Bisclavret, like the seneschal in "**Equitan,**" loses his treacherous wife but keeps his honor and his place. The animated spaces in the *Lais* can protect Marie's lovers from treachery and can protect the "Hummë . . . de grant pris" ("**Guigemar**" 8) too, punishing, in the process, the secretive lovers who sought to benefit from betraying the just. These last two *lais* do not feature a woman imprisoned by an old jealous husband or father but rather a man as the victim of secrecy and lies; yet nonetheless, just as in "**Guigemar**" and in the other *lais* to follow, Marie manipulates the physical world to alternately rupture and conceal secrets in a series of violations, intrusions and reclamations, exposing the base and protecting her heroes, bringing everyone, finally, to a place of justice.

In "**Yonec**" we see a similar use of enclosures to mete out justice, this time as a *Jaloux* both imprisons his wife and uses a trap window to ensnare her magical, birdman lover, Muldumarec, the father of the yet unborn title character. As in **"Guigemar," "Equitan,"** and **"Bisclavret,"** the evil once again try to manipulate secret space to further their control over the protagonists, but Marie depicts the marriage here as a particularly severe form of isolation and deprivation:

> De ceo ke ele iert bele e gente,
> En li garder mist mut s'entente;
> Dedenz sa tur l'ad enserreie
> En une grant chambre pavee.
> Il ot une sue serur,
> Veille ert e vedve, sanz seignur:
> Ensemble od la dame l'ad mise
> Pur li tenir mieuz en justise.
> Autres femmes i ot, ceo crei,
> En une autre chambre par sei,
> Mes ja la dame n'i parlast,
> Si la vielle nel comandast.
> Issi la tint plus de set anz.
> Unques entre eus n'eurent enfanz
> Ne fors de cele tur n'eissi,
> Ne pur parent ne pur ami.
> Quant li sires s'alot cuchier,
> N'i ot chamberlenc ne huissier
> Ki en la chambre osast entrer
> Ne devant lui cirge alumer.
> Mut ert la dame en grant tristur,
> Od lermes, od suspir e plur;
> Sa beuté pert en teu mesure
> Cume cele ki n'en ad cure.
> De sei meïsme mieuz vousist
> Que morz hastive la preisist.

> (Because she was beautiful and noble
> he made every effort to guard her.
> He locked her inside his tower
> in a great paved chamber.
> A sister of his,
> who was also old and a widow, without her own lord,
> he stationed with his lady
> to guard her even more closely.
> There were other women, I believe,
> in another chamber by themselves,
> but the lady never spoke to them
> unless the old woman gave her permission.
> So he kept her more than seven years—
> they never had any children;
> she never left that tower,
> neither for family nor for friends.
> When the lord came to sleep there
> no chamberlain or porter
> dared enter that room,
> not even to carry a candle before the lord.
> The lady lived in great sorrow,
> with tears and sighs and weeping;
> she lost her beauty,
> as one does who cares nothing for it.
> She would have preferred
> death to take her quickly.)

(25-50)

Though the *Jaloux* wanted children to pass on his lineage, Marie hints at his impotence, making this space not only a prison of silence and deprivation but also a dead and sterile place, bound to be ruptured, with the approach of spring, by love, by life, and by procreation. As Ferrante puts it, concerning the **Lais** as a whole, "Possessive love brings sterility, shame, frustration, even death, but generous love heals, brings joy, wealth, and honor in the world" ("French Courtly Poet" 66). The evil and artificiality of her confinement is worsened by the fact that she cannot even hear mass (75-76). Thus, not only does he fail to love and to impregnate her, but he also strips her of her religious rights, cutting her off from both nature and from spirit. From what we have seen so far in Marie's poetics of space, we recognize here a corrupt, even unholy space, watched by the envious eyes of the impotent *Jaloux* and his lordless sister, forces eager to prevent all love and joy from flourishing. The bird lover himself describes their constant surveillance, as he promises his love to return at her will:

> "Mes tel mesure en esgardez
> Que nus ne seium encumbrez.
> Ceste vielle nus traïra,
> E nuit e jur nus gaitera;
> Ele parcevra nostre amur,
> Sil cuntera a sun seignur.
> Si ceo avient cum jeo vus di
> E nus seium issi trahi,
> Ne m'en puis mie departir
> Que mei n'en estuce murir."

> ("But you must make certain
> that we're not discovered.
> This old woman will betray us,
> night and day she will spy on us.
> She will perceive our love,
> and tell her lord about it.
> If that happens,
> If we are betrayed,
> I won't be able to escape.
> I shall die.")

(201-10)

Like Bisclavret, Muldumarec knows that betrayal can lead to doom and thus that a secret is a fragile thing in the world of suspicion, envy and treachery. "Encumbrez" (202) indicates not merely discovery but also dishonor and harassment (*encumbrance*), which will destroy both the love if it is "perceived" and the lover himself. His fears are of course all too justified, as the envious successfully plot his death.

Marie, sworn enemy of the envious, accordingly lashes out at the conspiracy launched against the handsome couple, as she recounts the *Jaloux*'s instructions to his old sister:

"Fetes semblant de fors eissir,
Si la lessiez sule gisir;
En un segrei liu vus estez
E si veez e esgardez
Que ceo peot estre e dunt ço vient
Ki en si grant joie la tient."
De cel cunseil sunt departi.
Allas! Cum ierent malbailli
Cil ke l'un veut si agaitier
Pur eus traïr e enginnier!

("Let her lie alone;
You stay in a hidden (secret) place
And see and look
For what it can be and from whence it comes
That holds her in such great joy."
They broke off their meeting.
Alas, how mistreated will be
Those whom someone wants to spy upon
In order to betray and deceive them!)[14]

(247-56)

The exclamation indicates Marie's hatred, but it also displays how the envious use secrecy to try to undo the lovers, who are of course keeping secrets themselves to protect their love. Marie is thus here crafting a battle for control of both space and of secrecy, with love, and life itself, at stake.

The battle continues when, after the lover is wounded, the lady defies her prison by leaping from the window—a more perilous escape than that of Guigemar's lady through the unlocked door (337), and in may ways **"Yonec,"** is an intensified version of **"Guigemar,"** more dire and violent. She follows the trail of blood through an "entree" in a hill; then to a city "De mur fu close tut entur" (361), but luckily, "La porte aval fu desfermee" (371); she then enters one chamber and then a second and finally a third (382), where she finds her love, dying but able to give her the ring that protects her from her husband's wrath. Just as the lady escapes an enclosure, she at once takes control of space in seeking out her man, leaping out of and penetrating into a series of places. The ring may reflect the renewed power she has over her captor, since she has willed herself free from his encumbering control by planning her and her lover's ultimate revenge. But in any case, all motion out of and through enclosures in this *lai* helps to bring about justice. Those who use space to spy and trap and to kill, making space not only a prison but an animal trap, will suffer for their envy and treachery. Fittingly, the lover's ornate tomb is the *lai's* final locus; here in front of memorialized space, the son learns the story of his parents and kills his evil stepfather. The lady, fleeing confinement for most of her life, now dies and is placed in the coffin together with her dead lover, in a final act of spatial and romantic justice.[15]

The tomb here foreshadows the jeweled box of the next *lai*, **"Laüstic,"** where the killing of another bird

chastens loving neighbors who were toying with dangerous spaces and secrets as they conduct an extramarital flirtation. The description of their situation is rich with the vocabulary of space, enclosure, surveillance, and secrecy that informs and animates the drama here and in so many other of the *lais*:

Sagement e bien s'entreamerent,
Mut se covrirent e garderent
Qu'il ne feussent aparceü
Ne desturbé ne mescreü;
E il le poeient bien fere,
Kar pres esteient lur repere:
Preceines furent lur maisuns
E lur sales e lur dunguns;
N'i aveit bare ne devise
Fors un haut mur de piere bise.
Des chambres u la dame jut,
Quant a la fenestre s'estut,
Poeit parler a sun ami
De l'autre part, e il a li,
E lur aveirs entrechangier
E par geter e par lancier.

(They loved each other discreetly and well,
concealed themselves and took care
that they weren't seen
or disturbed or suspected.
And they could do this well enough
since their dwellings were so close,
their houses were next door,
and so were their rooms and their towers;
there was no barrier or boundary
except a high wall of dark stone.
From the rooms where the lady slept,
if she went to the window
she could talk to her love
on the other side, and he to her,
and they could exchange their possessions,
by tossing and throwing them.)

("Laüstic" 29-44)

Here neighbors flirt, loving each other "discreetly and well," "conceal[ing] themselves" and "tak[ing] care that they weren't seen or disturbed or suspected," all facilitated by the physical proximity of their homes. Thus, though the woman is "estreit gardee" (49) when her husband is in town, the lovers can communicate through and around the impeding wall. Marie's lovers, as we will see emphasized in **"Milun,"** always find a way, no mater how awkward or bizarre it now seems. The lady's husband thwarts the affair by killing the nightingale, her excuse for waking at night and going to the window to see her lover. At the end of the failed love and failed adultery, we learn that the affable but thwarted lover has enshrined (*enseeler* [155]) the dead nightingale in a lavish, bejeweled box:

Un vaisselet ad fet forgier;
Unques n'i ot fer ne acier,
Tuz fu d'or fin od bones pieres,
Mut precïuses e mut chieres;

Covercle i ot tres bien asis.
Le laüstic ad dedenz mis,
Puis fist la chasse enseeler.
Tuz jurs l'ad fete od lui porter.

(He had a small vessel fashioned,
with no iron or steel in it;
it was all pure gold and good stones,
very precious and very dear;
the cover was very carefully attached.
He placed the nightingale inside
and then he had the casket sealed—
he carried it with him always.)

                              (149-56)

The killing of the bird, therefore, does not bring justice to evil doers per se but hints at the potential violence that would occur if the married lady and her neighbor were to concretize their illicit love—a love that has no sanction because, in contrast to **"Yonec,"** the lady here has suffered no severe imprisonment or deprivation beyond the basic demands of marriage. The violence here is actually a gift to the lady, who makes it a gift to her would-be lover, a jeweled memorial sublimating their love and representing disaster averted, for as the *Lais* clearly depict, foolish lovers are just as likely to suffer violence as are the envious enemies of love. Thus the box here constitutes not so much the death of love as it embodies a safe space for a love unfulfilled but keenly felt and perpetually remembered. The husband conceals well, for he does not reveal openly his knowledge of the incipient affair, communicating instead in secret signs, just as the wife had when she claimed it was the bird who drew her nocturnal attention. In fact, all three conceal danger craftily, and in the jeweled box the potential for both love and death remain forever hidden. Perhaps, as readers have noticed, no other image in the *Lais* reflects Marie's own art as pointedly as does this elegant box enclosing the tuneful bird.[16] For three lines after describing the sealed, concealing box, Marie reports, in one of her customary celebrations of tale telling, that the story she has just told would not stay hidden for long ("Ne pot estre lunges celee" [158]). Marie thus juxtaposes these images of concealment and revelation (here carried by *enseeler* and *celer*) in **"Laüstic"** just as she does in her "Prologue," where she will not hide her abilities, although she must offer them forth obscurely, as if in a splendid *chasse,* a bejeweled *integumentum* that hides a secret truth within. For though a sinful love is thwarted, here it can be enclosed, encased, and enshrined within walls, where it remains forever an obscure object of scrutiny that we may gloss, becoming, one would hope, "plus sens" in the process. This *lai* displays well that the labor of gloss, more than the comfort of *caritas,* is Marie's legacy to her readers.

In **"Milun"** we witness another kind of concealing *integumentum,* as Marie conducts a battle between secrets and intrusions and lovers again use concealed spaces to further their love and to defeat the encumbrances of the envious and wicked. This time Marie offers not a jeweled case but a feathery swan that ferries secret missives between the lovers, well concealed from the lady's husband, a rich and powerful lord. The *lai* recalls **"Guigemar"** and **"Yonec,"** for here again our protagonists combat surveillance and female constriction, first under the rule of the lady's father and then of the husband. As soon as the love begins, Milun knows that it must be kept secret, because if their *cunseil* were revealed, all will be lost, as he tells a trusty companion: "Amis, fet il, or t'entremet / Qu'a m'amie puisse parler / E de nostre *cunseil* celer" (36-38) ("My friend," he said, "please undertake / to help me to speak to my beloved / and to keep our communications secret"). As in **"Yonec,"** this *lai* revolves around an extramarital birth, which itself betrays the double nature of concealing and revealing. Giving birth is the most powerful kind of revelation, expressing the strength and historicity of a noble love, yet it also provides the ultimate challenge for Marie's masters of concealing secrets. Pregnancies often are "writ," as Shakespeare would put it, "with character too gross" (*Measure for Measure* 1.2.136) on the mother, yet Milun's girl manages to hide both pregnancy and birth from her father with the help of a trusty old servant and friends of Milun who take the child to his sister. No one ever knew. Despite this success, the lady's troubles are not over, for she fears that she will not be able to conceal the unsealing, as it were, of her virginity. Her words before her wedding night depict her awareness of the plight of lovers exactly as we have been tracing it in the *Lais*:

"Lasse, fet ele, que ferai?
Avrai seignur? Cum le prendrai?
Ja ne sui jeo mie pucele;
A tuz jurs mes serai ancele.
Jeo ne soi pas que fust issi,
Ainz quidoue aveir mun ami;
Entre nus celisum l'afaire,
Ja ne l'oïsse aillurs retraire.
Mieuz me vendreit murir que vivre!
Mes jeo ne sui mie delivre,
Ainz ai asez sur mei gardeins
Vieuz e jeofnes, mes chamberleins,
Ki tuz jurz heent bone amur
E se delitent en tristur."

("Alas," she said, "what can I do?
Must I be married? How can I?
I am no longer a virgin,
I'll have to be a servant all my life.
I didn't know it would be like this;
rather I thought I could have my love,
that we could keep it secret between us,
that I'd never hear it bruited about.
Now I'd rather die than live,
But I'm not even free to do that,

Since I have guardians all around me,
Old and young; my chamberlains,
Who hate a noble love,
And take their delight in sadness.")

(133-46)

Like Lanval, she looks for the place where lovers can be free from slander and intrusion, imagining that this is how she thought things should be, that love is a private matter, "celisum" and "entre nus." And like Marie herself in the "Prologue," she knows that the envious are always present, armed with gossip and savoring the suffering of the wise and noble. Marie perseveres, as the *Lais* themselves illustrate; some force drives her on and protects her from the bite of the curs who can never really stop her from revealing, one after the other, these children of her imagination and learning. Oddly, the girl here enjoys some similar success. She keeps the secret of her motherhood into her marriage, for though she fears being discovered as less than a virgin, we never hear report of the husband's discovery. The lady has somehow mastered the art of concealment. Like the open door in **"Guigemar,"** this is one of Marie's oddly magical moments, and so somehow the lover's secret is safe, safe with Marie and safe with us, allowing Milun and his lady to continue the affair, employing at this point the hidden letters. The whole plan ends, finally, in reunion, unity and family—vital, creative, and redemptive principles that flourish in the wake of the sterile, jealous husband's death. Marie is not writing allegorically; the lovers do not merely represent the writer, but both lover and poet face similar trials in their aspirations to live free, to create, and to survive the onslaught of the envious who live to undo the renown and the happiness of others.

As the lovers engage in this combat, we witness continuous images of sealing and secretiveness: Milun writes the first letters and "sis seela" (161), hiding them in the feathers ("E dedenz la plume musció") (164). Thus his lover extracts it and opens the seal: "Ele en ad la seel bruise (226)," completing the secret process of communication.[17] The scene recalls the mutual knotting and locking of their private bodies by the lovers in **"Guigemar,"** as the lovers here too control the private spaces of intimacy by sealing and unsealing secrets. Even seemingly incidental exposition in **"Milun"** reveals the language of secrecy, as the very tone and texture of the poem reflects a struggle against exposure and confinement. Milun's messenger who brings the girl the swan claims as his pretense that he wants to show his respects so that he will not be "desturbez" (187) while visiting in the country. The porter then brings him in "in such a way that he wasn't seen or disturbed by anyone," "Celui ameine en teu maniere / Que de nului n'i fu sceüz, / Desturbez ne aparceüz" (200-202), just as Guigemar's lady escapes her room

and heads for the ship "undisturbed" (677 and see above). A girl opens the door to the chamber to let the porter in, an image opposed to the scene in **"Equitan"** where a girl holds the door fruitlessly against the seneschal as he discovers the king with his adulterous wife. Marie tends to describe all the processes of love as spatial negotiations, a series of articulated movements that lead to freedom and love for those who can master the art of concealing and revealing. And the entire process mediated by the swan leads in fact to many intimate encounters between the lovers because nothing can stop love:

> Nuls ne poet estre si destreiz
> Ne si tenuz estreitement
> Que il ne truisse liu sovent.
>
> (They met together several times.
> (No one can be so closely constrained
> or so closely guarded
> that he can't find a way out.))

(286-88)

Marie here recognizes a force that has nothing to do with *mesure* or with *caritas*. My argument here thus supports Spence's historical hypothesis that "[w]hat we now call courtly love-which Marie and her contemporaries were engaged in exploring—developed at least in part as a response, an answer, a solution even to the growing court vice of envy" ("Double Vision" 267). This force, call it anachronistically "courtly love" or not, breaks through all barriers of restraint and confinement. With what result in **"Milun"**? This extramarital love, sanctioned in Marie's moral economy, brings forth not a jeweled box but a good son, and when father and son are reunited, Marie makes a family out of the revealed secret, as the *lai* moves toward order, family, and an open and just love. Milun, just as Muldumarec does in **"Yonec,"** reports to his lover that she holds his life in her hands (237-38). Yonec's mother fails, sadly, to protect her lover and must await distant but sure revenge, dying herself, nonetheless, when it is at hand. **"Milun,"** as a companion piece to **"Yonec,"** depicts a similar struggle but one that yields greater success. In opposition to the tragic failure of the hawk, the delightful feathers of the swan keep both murder and tragedy away: Milun lives, and, unlike in **"Yonec,"** the son here need not kill his mother's husband to unite his parents, for the husband conveniently dies. Despite these differences in degree, in both *lais,* the mastering of space and secrecy brings forth final justice against the enemies of love and ensures the perpetuity of family, embodied in two strong sons, loyal to their amorous parents and sworn enemies of the envious. Like Marie's many *lais* themselves, these children, swords in hand if needed, could not stay hidden for long.

After twelve poems in which lovers combat or utilize enclosed spaces in their quest for love and safety, Marie ends the whole affair by putting all three lovers from **"Eliduc,"** the final *lai,* behind sacred walls, where presumably they will be safe from all the dangers at hand and no longer be a bother to poet or reader. But before they reach safe haven, they participate in adventures of love and space that allow Marie to recapitulate the *Lais'* themes of secrecy, slander, envy, adultery, and privacy, all informed by the paradoxical imperative to at once conceal and to reveal. As Eva Rosenn rightly observes, "[I]ssues of concealment and revealment provide a recurrent theme throughout the *Lais,*" and "[s]ecrets are at the heart of ten of the twelve *Lais*" (226). These issues run through the prologues and all the *lais* because the good and noble, once others hear of their happiness or fame, become vulnerable to the envious machinations of others. To reveal one's own worth is to expose oneself to attack, but worth is difficult to conceal.[18] Accordingly, **"Eliduc"** opens by echoing Marie's own troubles in the "Prologue," for the accomplished knight, like our talented poet, is attacked by envy and slander:

> Pur l'envie del bien de lui,
> Si cum avient sovent d'autrui,
> Esteit a sun seignur medlez
> E empeiriez e encusez,
> Que de la curt le cungea
> Sanz ceo qu'il ne l'areisuna.

> (But envy of his success,
> which often happens among people,
> caused trouble between him and his lord.
> He was slandered and accused
> until the lord sent him away from his court
> without a formal accusation.)

(41-46)

But **"Eliduc"** is not only the story of a man dishonored, recalling, in addition to Marie herself, **"Lanval"** and **"Bisclavret,"** but also the story of a man with two loves, both noble, beautiful, and as he is, deserving of happiness. To put the problem into spatial terms, too many doors are open for Eliduc. In the absence of a *Jaloux* and with his mistress's father encouraging the love (see 492ff.), the married Eliduc thus becomes his own worst enemy. Marie intentionally paints him and herself into a corner: without prison walls and a tormented or closely guarded woman, in **"Guigemar,"** **"Yonec,"** and **"Milun,"** and without the evil treachery that dooms foolish lovers as in **"Equitan"** or **"Bisclavret"** (**"Laüstic"** more innocently works its own justice), this situation in **"Eliduc"** is difficult to adjudicate by Marie's standards.

And yet, as in the other *lais,* the drama here revolves around secrets concealed and revealed, and such imagery and vocabulary saturates the text. For example,

when Guilliadun becomes interested in Eliduc, she sends a chamberlain who approaches the knight "a cunseil" ("in secret") (404); when he returns with news of her suit, she commands him, "nel me celer" ("don't hide anything from me") (419), for though she acted secretly, she wants nothing hidden from herself. But things *are* hidden, for Guilliadun "ne saveit pas que femme eüst" (584) ("didn't know he had a wife"), and, at the same time, Eliduc hides the very affair from his own wife to whom he has promised fidelity and return. The *lai,* then, is a complex game of concealing and revealing. The great truth of love must be revealed, but all revelations, like Marie's own expression of art, bring vulnerability and danger to their "author." Since Eliduc does keep the affair chaste, he is always only on the verge of sin. And yet, with two noble loves, Eliduc is trapped in an unhealthy concealment, and he must "behave very secretly" ("Mut se cuntient sutivement") (717). He makes his entourage pledge and swear "De tut sun afaire celer" (758) ("to keep the whole affair secret"), and as he returns to Guilliadun, "Ne voleit mie estre veüz / Ne trovez ne recuneüz" (765-66) ("he didn't want to be seen, / or found or recognized"). As she plays with the concealed and the revealed, Marie offers us many such pregnant situations, and thus by this final *lai* we know that this is not the kind of secret that can remain hidden under a rock or in a swan's feathers for twenty years. According to the private laws of the heart that Marie has been forging, all these lovers have just claims. What can be done with them?

Before the finale, one odd option presents itself when Guilliadun seems to die at sea, shocked from learning Eliduc's secret. His men prepare to dig a grave for her, a final, private resting place, but "Mes il les fist ariere traire" (922) ("he made them hold"), for he wants to see how he might "le liu eshaucier / U d'abbeïe u de mustier" (927-28) ("glorify a place with an abbey or a church"). That is, he wants to construct a more elaborate tomb, to create worthier, memorial space, so he can mourn perpetually: "Sur vostre tumbe chescun jur / Ferai refreindre ma dolur" (949-50) (each day on your tomb / I shall make my grief resound). The proposed tomb continues Marie's fixation on memorial space; it recalls that of **"Deus Amanz,"** where place and time remember the two dead lovers, and also the tomb of **"Yonec,"** where tragedy and justice converge, and finally the jeweled box of **"Laüstic,"** that *lai's* elaborate shrine to lost love. Yet it is not this lai's fate to end in such an enclosure, and Eliduc's delay luckily defers the dénouement until all can find shelter in Marie's final, glorious construction, the *Lais's* last enclosure, the sacred space behind the walls of the cloister.[19] Guildeluec first takes the veil; then Marie describes Eliduc's preparation for himself and Guilliadun:

Pres del chastel, de l'autre part,
Par grant cunseil e par esgart
Une eglise fist Elidus.
De sa terë i mist le plus
E tut sun or e sun argent;
Hummes i mist e autre gent
De mut bone religïun
Pur tenir l'ordre e la meisun.
Quant tut aveit appareillé,
Si nen ad puis gueres targié:
Ensemble od eus se dune e rent
Pur servir Deu omnipotent.
Ensemple od sa femme premiere
Mist sa femme que tant ot chiere.
El la receut cum sa serur
E mut li porta grant honur.
De Deu servir l'amonesta
E sun ordre li enseigna.
Deu priouent pur lur ami
Qi'il li feïst bone merci,
E il pur eles repreiot.

(Near the castle, on the other side,
after great care and deliberation
Eliduc founded a church
To which he gave most of his land
And all his gold and silver.
To maintain the order and the house,
He placed his men in it, and other people,
Devout in their religion.
When he had prepared everything,
he delayed no longer;
with the others he gave and rendered himself up
to serve almighty God.
With his first wife he placed the wife whom he so
  cherished.
She received her as her sister
And gave her great honor;
She encouraged her to serve God
And instructed her in her order.
They prayed to God for their friend—
That He would have mercy on him—
And he prayed for them.)

(1153-73)

Marie's decision is a crafty one here, confusing and perhaps ironic in its implications, an act that undoes all the picaresque trials of love in **"Eliduc"** and in all the *Lais.* If the chaste cloister and mutual prayer are the best safe haven for the conflicting claims of love, why recount love's trials at all, unless to display love's folly? But in other *lais,* love brings marriage, happiness, and children, in the spirit of natural justice. The cloister is the final, but not the authoritative option, Marie's way of playfully escaping, like Lanval, pulling the world in after her and her lovers, entering a safe, sacred space beyond both romance and reproach.

As Marie builds toward this artfully ambiguous climax in **"Eliduc,"** she leaves us with a number of questions. What makes things work in the *Lais*? What sort of moral or romantic universe has Marie created? Does

her treatment of slander, surveillance, and confinement reflect how Marie saw marriage or poetry in the twelfth century—or both? Whoever she may have been, was she trying to undermine the social paradigms and institutions of marriage in favor of some notion of what we might call "romantic love," based on private feelings, the secrets of the heart, as revealed by the noble lovers of the *Lais,* beyond the reach of fathers, husbands, and all forces of envy and joylessness? Mikhaïlova calls this "amour *absolu,*" arguing that "Marie de France plaide pour un amour pur et naturel qui doit être la seule loi justifieé dans le monde" (152). Yet in **"Equitan"** and **"Laüstic"** we see that "free love" is constrained by violence when necessary. Marie was aware that some lovers deserve a world free of envy, where, in Lanval's quotable formulation, "U nuls puïst aveir s'amie / Sanz reproece e sanz vileinie" (165-66).[20]

Further, how does her work here relate to the rest of her corpus? How can we connect the drama of conceal and reveal to the world of craft and reason offered in the *Fables* or in the mystical, visionary adventures into the unknown in the *Espurgatoire Seint Patriz*? This latter is interesting, for it is itself a work about the revelation of secret places of torment and of joy, the inner sanctums of divine justice, concealed from sinners but revealed to the penitent. As **"Eliduc"** ends with the building of a cloister, this poem features the Saint's erection of an abbey at the sight of his revelations. This abbey is well sealed and becomes the entryway for many who come to witness the truth of St. Patrick's preaching. We recognize here the spatial vocabulary we know so well from the *Lais*:

De mur l'enclost, portes i fist,
e bone fermeüre i mist,
pur ceo qu'um n'i peüst entrer,
se par lui nun, ne la aler . . .
El tens seint Patriz, par licence,
pristrent li plusur penitence.
Quant il esteient absolu,
si vindrent la u li us fu.
Enz entrerent seürement.
Mult sufrirent peine e turment
e mult virent horrible mal
de la dure peine enfernal;
aprés icele grant tristesce
virent grant joie e grant leesce.
Ço qu'il voldrent cunter e dire
fist seinz Patriz iluek escrire.

(He closed it with a wall and made gates,
And placed good locks on them,
So that one could not go or enter there
Without his permission . . .
In the time of Saint Patrick,
Many entered with permission, and did penance there.
When they were absolved of their sins,
They came to the place where the gate was,
And entered securely.

They suffered great pain and torment,
And witnessed much of the horrible agony
Of bitter infernal pain;
After this great sorrow,
They witnessed great joy and happiness.
Whatever they wished to recount and tell,
Saint Patrick had written down on the spot.)

(*Espurgatoire* 343-46 . . . 351-62)

And here, too, in the *Espurgatoire,* just as in the *Lais,* we see that the spatial drama creates narrative, for the Saint and the canons who follow him write down what the visitors witness, "pur edifiér altre gent / e qu'il n'en dutassent niént" (431-32) ("to edify other people and to leave no doubts about purgatory"). These stories thus recall the *Lais* themselves, which will sharpen the minds and the morals of those who hear, interpret, and gloss them throughout time. These striking connections between the *Lais* and the *Espurgatoire* clearly display that space and the complex drama of entering, sealing, and revealing is central to an understanding of Marie, her moral universe, and her art, whether her subject be chivalric love or divine justice. I hope in this chapter to have sparked future study of these thematic and imagistic relations in these two poems about different kinds of "revelations."

Finally, how does our study relate to critical understanding of Marie specifically as a woman and as a woman writer?[21] I have resisted this particular focus here, but I hope to have shown that in whatever gendered or political context we want to embrace Marie, any understanding of the *Lais* must consider Marie's deep treatment of space and secrecy in love. As lovers flee from spaces of confinement and seek places of privacy and freedom, the artificial and natural landscapes, including ships, towers, chambers, tubs, tombs, rocks, birds, and cloisters, all open and close as good lovers require. As if animated by Orpheus's song, or, should we say, Marie's, they themselves move to serve love and to combat envy. How can lovers ensure that the natural and artificial landscape will support their cause, and what has Marie shown us about space, secrets, and the search for privacy in the *Lais*? In part, she shows that those who can master the paradox of concealing and revealing, who can most artfully modulate the two, will thrive and find safety and freedom from envy. As I noted, Marie will often report that the story at hand must be told, that some force is driving her on to reveal the past and to succeed as a learned artist. In her surrogates she replays the drama of her own struggle, punishing the envious *gangleür* and *losengier,* who pry and penetrate, and rewarding the lovers who hide what they must but persevere to reveal the great truth of love, which, like Marie's own "escïence," is a gift from God that emboldens lovers to brave slander, surveillance, time, shame, and death as they seek freedom, privacy, and peace. When all else fails or is exhausted and the priorities of love become nebulous, the sacred walls to the community of heaven on earth are always there to receive the weary lover, who, like an aging troubadour, hears the divine calling.

Writing a "final word' on Marie is difficult, for it is impossible to decide whether to end on a note celebrating concealment or perhaps revelation, *celer* or *mostrer.* Marie's playfulness has shown us that we should not be too bold in any claim to have unlocked the mystery of the *Lais.* Whenever we try to do so, we are thwarted, because Marie's moral, ethical, and gendered frameworks are offered "oscurement," leaving us the obligation of supplying the "surplus" as best we can. Thus, though I hope to have revealed something of her art, I would argue that Marie, finally, seals herself in a private space of art and imagination that we have not yet penetrated.[22] And yet, as master of *celer* and *mostrer,* she has at the same time revealed all the *Lais,* just as promised, in defiance of her envious enemies, and has forged for herself not an open, public love, nor a husband and a child, but rather a place in literary history as heir to the "custume . . . as ancïens" ("Prologue" 9). For like a noble man, a gentile woman, and a worthy love, a wise poet and her "escïence" will not stay hidden for long.

Notes

1. All references to Marie are to the Rychner edition, and all translations, except where noted, are from Hanning and Ferrante. For a basic and thorough introduction to Marie's literary culture and themes, see Mickel and see Burgess; concise studies of Marie, with emphasis on her status as a woman writer, are offered by Ferrante ("French Courtly Poet" and *To the Glory* 195-204); see also here Sankovitch. For a concise historical survey of awareness and attitudes toward Marie, see Maréchal 1-21. Linda Georgianna is currently working on Marie's relations to history, truth, and historiography in preparation for the forthcoming "The Literary Cultures of Early England" (*Oxford English Literary History,* Vol. 1, Georgianna and K. O. O'Keeffe). After composing this chapter, I attended her presentation "Marie de France and the *Aventures* of History" on 25 October 2003 at a conference in honor of Robert W. Hanning, held at Columbia University.

2. On Marie's "Prologue," see Spitzer's influential study of its exegetical dimensions; see Robertson and see Leupin on the same subject and also on the "inexhaustible readership of the future" (241). See Rosenn on the relations of Marie's obscurity to male literary tradition; on textual and editorial problems in relation to meaning and translation,

see Burch; and see Bloch 61. See also Cowell, who, in studying "Deus Amanz" specifically, highlights the importance of secrecy to lovers in the *Lais*; his excellent point complements my arguments in this chapter: "['Deux Amanz'] thematizes a desire for silence, or at the very least for strictly guarded private communication. . . . [This creates] a seeming fundamental contradiction between Marie's Pro[logue] and its use of the Parable of the Talents on the one hand, and the content of many of her tales on the other" (341).

3. See Augustine, *De Doctrina*, especially 6.7, and Boccaccio, *Genealogia* 14.12 et passim.

4. As Spence puts it. "All the tales, it can be argued, are about envy and the problems that stem from it" (*Texts and the Self* 127 and note); on publicity and on the audience's participation in it, see Sturges, who studies the characters' need for symbols and interpretive skills, 94-100: "Publicity, we learn over and over again in the tales themselves, can destroy the love-relationship" (94). See also Spence, "Double Vision," for an important and useful study of envy and love in the context of Patristic and vernacular conceptions of "invidia."

5. In his study of "Deus Amanz," Cowell notes the ways in which the *Lais* often recapitulate the drama of particularly female authorship, offering that "Deus Amanz" "is not the only one of Marie's narratives which can be read as the story of the origin of her texts" (339).

6. Though Spence discusses "Guigemar" when making this observation, her idea applies perfectly to "Fresne," where the slandering neighbor repents, now cured of her envy, when happily reunited with her daughter; see "Fresne" 465 ff. But the issue is complex: Spence elsewhere, discussing "Eliduc," not "Guigemar," writes that "aside from this *lai*, however, *caritas* does not play a large part in Marie's work" ("Double Vision" 265). Her ultimate position might found in her comment that there is in Marie a love that is a *"tertium quid* between *caritas* and *invidia"* ("Double Vision" 268) Spence is not interested in secret spaces per se but in the relations among text, self, and reality; thus "Guigemar," is, for example, "clearly the story of the self as a duality which, discovered in the transgressive space outside the court and within the body, is played out in the vernacular written text" (*Texts and the Self* 131). And elsewhere: [Marie] "explores a space in which the causes of envy, the increasingly visualized and reified world, can be manipulated in a different setting to produce different results. This new found

land is the land of love, its means of expression, the written text, and its inhabitants, the individual or self. The model the written word offers speaks to the elevation of the signifier and its new visibility which, in turn, reflects a similarly autonomous understanding of the self" ("Double Vision" 275-76).

7. See Curtis's study of the oddly casual violence that pervades the *Lais,* committed by both villainous and heroic characters.

8. My interest in this topic was initially sparked by observing the use of space in the plastic arts, specifically the Metropolitan Museum of Art's *Casket, with Scenes from the Romances* (17.190.173), discussed in the Metropolitan Museum's *Secular Spirit* 26, no. 10, with an illustration. The fourteenth-century ivory depicts various scenes of privacy, fortification, and surveillance, including one panel of Mark observing Tristan and Isolde. See Barnet for further study of such objects, especially the chapters, "Popular Romances Carved in Ivory" and "Secular Objects and the Romance Tradition," which includes discussion of the Metropolitan's *Casket with Scenes from La Châtelaine de Vergi,* recounting thirteenth-century romance about love, secrecy, and death. Such works provide compelling analogues to the *Lais* and invite further interdisciplinary study.

Mikhaïlova provides a compelling analysis of space, openings, and closures in the *Lais,* often focusing on the boundaries and passages between the social, court world and the "other" world of the marvelous. In the first half of her essay (145-49), Mikhaïlova examines water, forests, windows, and prisons as spaces of boundary and transgression; she is particularly insightful about the ambivalence of space in the *Lais,* and my chapter here hopes to complement some of her fine insights: "La clôture de l'espace est associée à une situation tragique, sans issue, et l'ouverture se présente comme la solution, l'evasion, l'élan vers l'imaginaire. Mais en dehors de cette connotation qui relève d'une symbolique humaine universelle, l'espace dans les *Lais* apparaît ambivalent. Ainsi, à côté de l'espace clôturé comme prison, recontre-t-on également le traitement de la fermeture comme asile, repliement, cachette, lieu de protection de la vie, de l'amour ou d'un secret. Inversement, a côté de l'ouverture-libération, on trouve l'ouverture-chute, l'ouverture-trahison ou déchirement" (147). The rest of her essay explores the complex, geometric structure of the *Lais,* relating the themes of openings and closures generally to Marie's narrative art and language, which she sees reflecting a movement, "vers les une ouverture d'ordre plotonicien" and "vers valeurs transcendantales comme l'amour absolu, l'art et la foi dans l'éternal" (153). Mikhaïlova does not study envy, privacy, and control per se but rather the power of words as they variously activate the amorous drama: "L'univers des *Lais* est un monde de la porole, d'une parole ambivalente: dite, entendue ou écrite, elle peut tuer, mettre fin à l'amour et à la vie, mais aussi engendrer l'amour, le prolonger, le sauver" (155).

9. I omit a study of the fascinating "Chievrefoil," which has drawn much commentary; see Spence, "Double Vision" 270ff. and n.18.

10. On the ways "Guigemar" and "Eliduc" thematically frame the collection and on themes of love and social integration in these *lais,* see McCash, "The Curse of the White Hind." For a study of love in "Guigemar," as it relates specifically to the notion of *surplus* established in the "Prologue" and as it reflects Maris's complex Ovidianism, see Adams.

11. See Bloch's use of this passage in his study of how to read "Guigemar" in relation to Marie's complex and even eroticized "programmer for the writing and reading of medieval literature," (67) in her "Prologue." Bloch studies the relations between the poet and the lovers in the *lai* and explicates the complex imagery of knots, pleats, and the unfolding of narrative; he offers a dramatic and important assessment (though much different from mine) of Marie's relation to her creation: "the poet, in composing, does to the lovers exactly what the jealous husband does to his wife and her lover: she betrays by revealing, and thus destroys at the very moment she creates" (73).

12. On this notion of *privitee,* a Chaucerian theme of interest and importance to readers of Marie, see Hanning.

13. Mikhaïlova notes the importance of the hollow stone and of the king's inner chambers; see 148.

14. The translation is my own with help from Professor M. Roy Harris.

15. For a study of family, parentage and female narratology in the *lai,* see Freeman, "Changing Figure."

16. Freeman sees "Laüstic" reflecting Marie's concerns as a female artist in the "Prologue" and sees the encased bird as a layered symbol that encloses and sanctifies the events of the tale and the characters: "This final object engenders the narratives that retell its origins . . . until finally sealed in the *lai* entitled *Laüstic*" ("Poetics of Silence"

871). Following Freeman, Pickens studies the chasse and notes its relations to the creation of the story itself (144). See also Mikhaïlova: "L'impossibilité de vivre l'amour charnel mène à la sublimation d'un amour qui s'efface au profit de la beuté, de l'art, à la pérennite de l'Amour" (153).

17. The lady here calls a serving girl for assistance, and the text is ambiguous as to who detaches the letter and who opens it. I believe the meschine detaches the letter but that the "ele" of 226 refers to the lady, the subject of "ad brusié."

18. See Matthew 25:14-32 and consider Rosenn's comment that Marie is beginning the "Prologue" "with an allusion to the parable of the talent" (225). Working from Brian Stock, Rosenn is interested in how the *Lais* "can be seen . . . as a reaction to the social strategies of containment that would deny [Marie] access to the power of speech" (227). See also Wilson and McLeod on the parable as it relates to authorship, responsibility, and dynamic reciprocity, specifically developed by Marie in "Lanvall" and "Yonec," which the authors study comparatively as "male and female fantasies of love" (3).

19. On the relations between religious houses and heaven, see Duby 38ff. See Mikhaïlova 153 for a survey of critical reactions to this religious moment in "Eliduc."

20. On the varieties and complexities of love in the *Lais,* see the thorough survey by Burgess in chapters 6-7, "Women in Love" and "The Vocabulary of Love" (100-178); among Burgess's several solid conclusions is the stark observation that "life for those lovers able to enjoy each other's company is one of constant delight" (178). For a useful study of Marie's women in twelfth-century, sociological context, seeing her treatment of women as "profoundly sympathetic and pragmatic" (107), see McCash, who concludes, however, that "Marie is not a reformer" ("Images of Women" 108).

21. For treatments of Marie's gendered literary consciousness, see Freeman, "Poetics of Silence" 878; Pickens 135; Rosenn 225; Arden 215; Sankovitch 10; and Ferrante, "French Courtly Poet" 67.

22. Mikhaïlova's conclusion is noteworthy here, concerning Marie's rhetorical play: "Cette dynamique de la parole . . . symbolise enfin le côté ouvert, infini de la glose, auquel tous les nouveaux venus apporteront un surplus de sens" (157).

Works Cited

Adams, Tracy. "'Arte Regendus Amor:' Suffering and Sexuality in Marie de France's lai de Guigemar." *Exemplaria* 17.2 (2005): 285-315.

Arden, Heather. "The Lais of Marie de France and Carol Gilligan's Theory of the Psychology of Women." *Maréchal* 213-23.

Augustine. *De Doctrina.* Trans. D. W. Robertson Jr. Indianapolis: Bobbs-Merrill Educational, 1958.

Barnet, Peter, ed. *Images in Ivory: Precious Objects of the Gothic Age.* Princeton: Detroit Institute of the Arts and Princeton UP, 1997.

Bloch, R. Howard. "The Medieval Text— 'Guigemar'—as a Provocation to the Discipline of Medieval Studies." *Romanic Review* 79 (1988): 63-73.

Boccaccio, Giovanni. *Genealogia Deorum Gentilium.* Trans. Charles G. Osgood. Indianapolis: Liberal Arts, 1930.

Burch, Sally L. "Prologue to Marie's Lais: Back to the Littera." *AUMLA: Journal of the Australasian Universities Language and Literature Association* 89 (1998): 15-42.

Burgess, Glyn S. *The Lais of Marie de France: Text and Context.* Athens: U of Georgia P, 1987.

Cowell, Andrew. "Deadly Letters: 'Deus Amanz,' Marie's 'Prologue' to the Lais and the Dangerous Nature of the Gloss." *Romantic Review* 88.3 (1997): 337-56.

Curtis, Renée L. "Physical and Mental Cruelty in the Lais of Marie de France." *Arthuriana* 6.1 (1996): 22-25.

Duby, Georges, ed. *A History of Private Life.* Vol. 2, Revelations of the Medieval World. Cambridge: Belknap P of Harvard UP, 1988.

Ferrante, Joan. "The French Courtly Poet: Marie de France." *Medieval Women Writers.* Ed. Katharina M. Wilson. Athens: U of Georgia P, 1984. 64-89.

———. *To the Glory of Her Sex: Women's Roles in the Composition of Medieval Texts.* Bloomington: Indiana UP, 1997.

Freeman, Michelle A. "The Changing Figure of the Male: The Revenge of the Female Storyteller." *Maréchal* 243-61.

———. "Marie de France's Poetics of Silence: The Implications for a Feminine Translatio." *PMLA* 99.5 (1984): 860-83.

Hanning, R. W. "'Parlous Play': Diabolic Comedy in Chaucer's Canterbury Tales." *Chaucer's Humor: Critical Essays.* Ed. Jean E. Jost. New York: Garland, 1994. 295-319.

Leupin, Alexandre. "The Impossible Task of Manifesting 'Literature': On Marie de France's Obscurity." *Exemplaria* 3.1 (1991): 221-42.

Maréchal, Chantal, ed. *In Quest of Marie de France: A Twelfth-Century Poet.* Lewiston, N.Y.: Edwin Mellen, 1992.

Marie de France. *Fables.* Ed. and trans. Harriet Spiegel. Toronto: U of Toronto P, 1987.

———. *Les Lais de Marie de France.* Ed. Jean Rychner. Paris: Champion, 1983.

———. *The Lais of Marie de France.* Trans. Robert Hanning and Joan Ferrante. Durham: Labyrinth, 1978.

———. *Saint Patrick's Purgatory.* Ed. and trans. Michael J. Curley. Binghamton: Medieval & Renaissance Texts & Studies, 1993.

McCash, June Hall. "The Curse of the White Hind and the Cure of the Weasel: Animal Magic in the *Lais of Marie de France*." *Literary Aspects of Courtly Culture.* Selected Papers from the Seventh Triennial Congress of the International Courtly Literature Society. Ed. Donald Maddox and Sara Sturm-Maddox. Rochester: Boydel and Brewer, 1994. 211-19.

———. "Images of Women in the Lais of Marie de France." *Medieval Perspectives* 11 (1996): 96-112.

Metropolitan Museum of Art. *The Secular Spirit: Life and Art at the End of the Middle Ages.* New York: Dutton, 1975.

Mickel, Emanuel J., Jr. *Marie de France.* New York: Twayne, 1974.

Mikhaïlova, Miléna. "L'espace dans les Lais de Marie de France: lieux, structure, rhétorique." *Cahiers de Civilisation Médiévale* 40 (1997): 145-57.

Pickens, Rupert. "Marie de France and the Body Poetic." *Gender and Text in the Later Middle Ages.* Ed. Jane Chance. Gainesville: UP of Florida, 1996. 135-71.

Pope, Alexander. "An Essay on Criticism." *Critical Theory Since Plato.* Ed. Hazard Adams. Fort Worth: Harcourt Brace Janovich, 1992.

Robertson, D. W. "Marie de France, *Lais,* Prologue 13-15." *Modern Language Notes* 64 (1949): 336-38.

Rosenn, Eva. "The Sexual and Textual Politics of Marie's Poetics." *Maréchal* 225-42.

Sankovitch, Tilde. "The French Woman Writer in the Middle Ages: Staying Up Late." *Essays in Medieval Studies* 7 (1990): 1-12.

Spence, Sarah. "Double Vision: Love and Envy in the Lais." *Maréchal* 262-94.

————. *Texts and the Self in the Twelfth Century.* Cambridge: Cambridge UP, 1996.

Spitzer, Leo. "The Prologue to the Lais of Marie de France and Medieval Poetics." *Modern Philology* 41 (1943): 96-102.

Sturges, Robert S. *Medieval Interpretation: Models of Reading in Literary Narrative, 1100-1500.* Carbondale: Southern Illinois UP, 1991.

Wilson, Katharina, and Glenda McLeod. "Wholism and Fusion: Success in/of the Lais of Marie de France." *Arachne* 5.1 (1998): 3-30.

Logan E. Whalen (essay date 2008)

SOURCE: Whalen, Logan E. "The *Espurgatoire seint Patriz* and *La vie seinte Audree*." In *Marie de France & the Poetics of Memory,* pp. 137-73. Washington, D.C.: Catholic University of America Press, 2008.

[*In the excerpt below, Whalen stresses the importance of the medieval rhetorical strategies of memory and description in all of Marie's works, studying in particular the opening and closing lines of her writings and her emphasis on secular language and the adventures characteristic of the medieval court. For Whalen, the appearance of these techniques in the* La vie de seinte Audree, *studied in relation to Marie's better-known writings, is sufficient to establish her as its author.*]

Marie de France's **Lais** and **Fables** reveal a poetics of memory through vocabulary that implicitly or explicitly evokes this aspect of literary topical invention, and through a plan of detailed descriptions that render objects and events visible to the imagination, helping the audience later to recall the narrative sequence. Both of these texts demonstrate her creative art of finding preexisting material, committing it to memory, embellishing it with descriptive detail, and arranging it in an order that generates a new conception of the work.

Like the two narrative texts before them, the **Espurgatoire seint Patriz** and **La vie seinte Audree** display literary characteristics that are meaningful to Marie. In the **Espurgatoire** the reader or listener navigates a story in which successful linear development of the narrative depends on the ability of a character to remember past information during his journey through an underworld rich in the *merveille* of vividly described objects, people, and places. The **Audree,** while not as rich in vivid, energetic descriptions as the **Espurgatoire,** nonetheless bears the mark of the author's ability to adorn her source through her own poetic craft. Her ver-

sion of the story depends on a discursive construction and vocabulary that stress the necessity of memory to preserve the celebration of one of medieval literature's most venerated female saints, St. Etheldreda.

To our understanding, the **Lais** and the **Fables** represent Marie's reworking of material largely through her own imagination. The works she adapts in the former apparently came to her from oral sources. In the latter, the first forty fables are rewritten from the *Romulus Nilantii,* but the majority of them are derived from sources that have not been sufficiently identified for comparison with her renditions of them. By contrast, the **Espurgatoire seint Patriz** and **La vie seinte Audree** are translations of known Latin texts that have come down to us in manuscript form: H. of Saltrey's *De Purgatorio Sancti Patricii* for the **Espurgatoire,** and, for the **Audree,** a text close to a tripartite *Vita sancte Ætheldrede, De secunda translatione,* and *Miracula* (hereafter collectively referred to as *The Life of St. Etheldreda*).[1]

Marie's shift of approach at this point in her life seems significant in light of what we know about her stated purpose in earlier prologues, but one wonders to what extent it would be so notable if we did not possess the two sources she translates to compare with her own versions of the texts. The **Espurgatoire** and the **Audree** suggest that Marie's focus as author changes from literary to hagiographic, but a close reading shows that her vernacular training in the arts of poetry and prose still informs the narratives, and even clearly manifests its presence at times as she brings these two stories to a lay audience. For reasons of thematic unity, I have chosen to discuss these works together in this final chapter, beginning with the **Espurgatoire seint Patriz.**

THE *ESPURGATOIRE* AND THE ART OF *TRANSLATIO*

Marie's translation of the monk of Saltrey's text consists of 2,302 lines arranged in octosyllabic rhymed couplets and is preserved in a single manuscript dating from the end of the thirteenth century, Paris, BNF, fr. 25407.[2] It is likely that she wrote the **Espurgatoire** sometime between 1190 and the turn of the century.[3] The legend of St. Patrick's discovery of Purgatory is the source of H. of Saltrey's text and eventually of Marie's translation.[4] According to the legend as developed by H. of Saltrey, St. Patrick has a church and monastery built in an attempt to evangelize the area around Lough Derg in Ireland. After the local inhabitants fail to heed his admonitions to lead a purer life, he prays for God's assistance, which arrives in the form of revelation of the entrance to Purgatory. He makes the journey there and sees both the torment of sinners and the eventual bliss of those who enter the celestial paradise. He returns, has a wall constructed around the entrance, and leaves the area in the charge of the monastery. The monks later record various accounts of Purgatory provided by others who made the journey and returned safely. Emanuel J. Mickel Jr. has shown that the story of St. Patrick's Purgatory enjoyed great success in medieval literature for more than three hundred years, and that references to it appeared in literature that followed.[5]

The theme of journeys to the underworld dates back at least to the Greek and Roman epics of Homer and Virgil. The innovation of medieval literature of the twelfth century is that the visits to the Other World begin to become the core narrative of the entire story rather than a mere interpolation in it, as Peter Dewilde notes: "A cette époque la visite de l'au-delà, cessant de s'intégrer dans le récit hagiographique ou historique, accède au statut de genre autonome" (During this period, the visit to the Other World became an autonomous genre, ceasing to be integrated in hagiographic and historical texts).[6] In the legend of St. Patrick's Purgatory, an example of the newly developed autonomous otherworldly literature of this period, H. of Saltrey's original contribution is his account of the adventures of an Irish knight named Owein who enters the underworld passage. According to Mickel, H.'s version of this tale enjoyed great success during the Middle Ages and is the first of its kind to appear in the Purgatory tradition, since its theme of knightly adventure is absent from contemporary narratives about Purgatory.[7] Attesting to the literary success of this tale, Yolande de Pontfarcy has recorded more than 150 extant manuscripts of H. of Saltrey's version of the *Purgatorio*.[8]

There are two versions of H.'s *Purgatorio*, a long version and a short one, which represent two groups of manuscripts. Marie translated the shorter version of the legend, but since her text contains elements from both the long and short versions, Warnke and editors following him—Thomas A. Jenkins and Pontfarcy—have held that she worked from an exemplar containing a combination of the two versions.[9] Surprisingly, scholars have neglected the possibility that she could have used manuscripts from both the long and the short versions as she was translating. This method of treating her exemplars would mirror the process of *inventio* through which material was gathered from disparate sources and given form in a single new conception. In any case, hers was apparently the first translation of the *Purgatorio* into French among at least six other French verse translations, and Michael Curley notes that there were many French prose translations, as well as translations of the tale into many other languages during the Middle Ages.[10]

Apart from Marie's own prologue, epilogue, and a few other original lines, her version of the tale follows the events in H.'s diligently, but she distinguishes herself by the narrative energy she brings to the tale. In this way, her creative method places her squarely in the tradition of *translatio studii,* the retelling of a preexisting story in her own words to transfer knowledge from one culture to another, as in the case of the *Lais* and the *Fables.* The exemplar from which she copied is now lost, but H.'s Latin elements for the majority of her lines can be identified in manuscripts of his *Purgatorio*.[11] Mickel notes that a close comparison of certain passages of Marie's text with corresponding ones found in a manuscript of the monk of Saltrey's text, London, BL, Harley 3846, reveals that "when she departs from the text, it is to clarify an ambiguous Latin passage or to develop clearly what is implied in the original."[12] This is true for lines 185-88, discussed below, in which she evokes the process of *inventio* through her arrangement of rhetorical vocabulary belonging to the arts of poetry and prose at a point in the text where her source states the matter rather simply.

Why Marie chooses at this point to turn her attention to projects that embrace translation more closely than her previous two collections did is impossible to determine conclusively from the surviving textual evidence. Indeed, her decision appears to refute her stated desire, found in the General Prologue to the *Lais*:

> Pur ceo començai a penser
> D'aukune bone estoire faire
> E de latin en romaunz traire;
> Mais ne me fust guaires de pris:
> Itant s'en sunt altre entremis!
>
> (28-32)

For this reason I began to think of working on some good story and translating a Latin text into French, but this would scarcely have been worthwhile, for others have undertaken a similar task.

It should be remembered that Marie did not wait until the *Espurgatoire* to depart from this position. As mentioned above, the first forty fables from her *Isopet,* which was composed after the *Lais,* are taken from the Latin text of the *Romulus Nilantii*.

Was Marie simply tired of continuing in the same generic direction, and was she searching for a new type of literary challenge, or did she expressly begin to think of material that was more religious in theme than her previous selections had been? Whatever her reasons may have been—edification, entertainment, both, or something entirely different—her eventual purpose is to make this Latin story available to her audience in the vernacular:

> Jo, *Marie,* ai mis, en memoire,
> le livre de l'Espurgatoire
> en Romanz, qu'il seit entendables
> a laie gent e convenables.
>
> (2296-300)

I, Marie, have put
The Book of Purgatory into French,
As a record, so that it might be intelligible
And suited to lay folk.

A telling part of her stated purpose is that she put the story "en memoire." In fact, the significant emphasis on memory in hagiographic texts could have been one of the reasons, among others, that inspired Marie to compose vernacular versions of H. of Saltrey's text and of the *Life of St. Etheldreda,* instead of other Latin texts that contained religious themes, such as bestiaries or certain chronicles.

That Marie's religious concerns have become more transparent in this work should not be surprising given her possible ecclesiastical ties. Moreover, her interest in Purgatory was timely. As Curley remarks, the doctrine of the Church concerning Purgatory was very much in transition at this time, being reevaluated and conveyed by philosophers and theologians such as Bernard of Clairvaux, Hugh of St. Victor, Peter Lombard, and Gratian: "The period from 1170-1200 in particular saw the doctrine of purgatory assume what would remain for centuries its canonical form. The *Tractatus de Purgatorio Sancti Patricii* by the English Cistercian H. of Saltrey, the source of Marie's *Espurgatoire,* figured prominently in the dissemination of the concept of purgatory during the Middle Ages."[13] While one cannot neglect the role that the religious milieu played in attracting Marie to this legend,[14] it is likely that H.'s original contribution to the tale, namely, the descent of a knight into Purgatory, played at least an equal role in the appeal of his version to a poet writing for the court of England.

Indeed, it may have been the combination of elements that prompted Marie to bring this text to her lay audience, both the religious and didactic aspects, as well as the dimensions of *aventure.*[15] Curley notes that "Marie's *Espurgatoire* served not only to transmit this image of Purgatory to a French-speaking public, but also to refashion the story of Owein's experiences into the idiom of the *conte d'aventure,* which she and her contemporaries, Chrétien de Troyes and Wolfram von Eschenbach, did so much to popularize."[16]

The *Espurgatoire* and a New Audience

When Curley refers to Marie's putting the story into the "idiom of the *conte d'aventure,*" what must be understood is the way in which she omits certain monastic elements at times in the narrative to emphasize the adventurous elements and to make the story more appealing to her lay audience.[17] Her reference to the knight by name seven times stands in striking contrast to H.'s single mention of Owein's name at the beginning of his text.[18] They [sic] way she describes the scene in which Owein consults the king in making a decision to remain a knight and not to enter holy orders also highlights the courtly over the monastic. However, H. of Saltrey's version of the story is already partly "courtly" ipso facto: as Mickel observes, some fifteen hundred of the twenty-three hundred lines deal with the adventures of the knight.[19]

By engaging her audience through courtly discourse, Marie makes it clear in the *Espurgatoire* that she is an author of vernacular training, and that she has not abandoned her original regard for *descriptio* and memory prevalent throughout the first two texts she composed, works that the same audience undoubtedly knew well. She keeps the consideration of memory before her public through repeated references to this cognitive act, usually through the specific mention of the term "remembrance" or "memoire." The prologue to the *Espurgatoire* puts such an emphasis on the act of memory that it uses both of these terms within a single line of the text, "en remembrance e en memoire" (5).[20] The focus in her prologue to the *Espurgatoire* is not on the eventual bliss of paradise that will be encountered in the story, but rather on the "peines" to be portrayed along the purgatorial voyage. She wants to ensure that her audience does not forget the sufferings that are about to be depicted.[21]

Literary representations of Hell through graphic descriptions of suffering were found in texts from antiquity, such as those in Book 6 of Virgil's *Aeneid* and in Book 10 of Ovid's *Metamorphoses.* These texts were popular throughout the Middle Ages and were accessible to authors as early as the twelfth century.[22] In addition to these texts, Marie would also have had access to other works that vividly recounted sufferings in an underworld context, as in the *Dialogues* of Pope Gregory the Great, the *Vision of Saint Paul,* and Benedeit's *Voyage of Saint Brendan,* among others.[23] The important role that description and memory played in purgatorial literature raises the possibility that their design is one reason, combined with the other courtly and religious ones, that she chose to adapt H. of Saltrey's *Purgatorio* for a lay audience.

Memory in the Journey through Hell

As the lines from the prologue and epilogue indicate, the *Espurgatoire,* like the *Lais* and the *Fables* before it, begins and ends by calling attention to memory. The cognitive process of remembering is associated with writing, and more specifically, in both instances, with a book. Not only does the juxtaposition of memory and books call to mind Chaucer's similar association in the prologue to the *Legend of Good Women,* discussed in the previous chapter, it also recalls Dante's famous opening phrase in the *Vita nuova,* quoted in the Introduction.

Memory, as we have seen, is not only necessary to preserve material from the past and to create new literature to transfer from one generation to the next, it is also useful for future moral reference and self-edification through the recall of precepts drawn from the material in question. Marie achieves the same results as she did in her previous works by handing down to a vernacular public a literature that can be "seen" with the mind's eye as easily as it can be read or heard.

It is significant that Marie focuses on the faculty of memory in most of the lines that can be considered entirely original with her. Apart from four couplets—1019-20, 1053-54, 1119-20, and 1667-68—Marie's additions consist of the prologue (1-8) and the epilogue (2297-302).[24] Both of these passages center on remembering the work at hand. In this way, Marie envelops H.'s text in the act of memory by reminding the audience of its importance, both at the beginning of the narration and again at its conclusion.

For his part, at a strategic moment in his prefatory comments just before the opening of the narration proper, H. indicates that he tells this story from memory: "Quam quidem narrationem, si bene memini, ita exorsus est" (If I remember correctly, the story certainly begins in this manner) (II, 14).[25] Marie's text renders the Latin original as follows:

> Se j'ai bien eü en memoire
> ço que j'ai oï en *l'estoire,*
> je vus dirrai veraiement,
> en *ordre,* le comencement.
>
> (185-88, emphasis added)
>
> If I have well retained in memory
> What I have heard in the story,
> I shall truly recount to you
> The beginning, in an orderly fashion.

Marie's terms "remembrance" and "memoire" in line 5 of the prologue cited above are echoes of H.'s expression of the same idea in his phrase "si bene memini," which she translates at this point in the text as "Se j'ai bien eü en memoire."

Another point about Marie's translation in lines 185-88 centers on her use of the terms "estoire" and "ordre," for both belong to the paradigm of medieval topical invention as *historia* and *ordo.* Marie explicitly emphasizes the technique of *inventio* through her choice of rhetorical vocabulary. While the monk of Saltrey simply announces that he will relate the tale in an orderly fashion, Marie, as a vernacular poet well trained

in literary composition, reveals an understanding of how this process works when she names specific stages in *inventio: memoria, historia,* and *ordo,* as posited in the art of rhetoric.

Historia, taken in its rhetorical context, refers to the first part of medieval literary invention in which source material is located, namely, the *materia* that will inform the new conception of the work.[26] *Historia,* in a broader medieval understanding, was passed down through annals, chronicles, biographies, and hagiography, and regardless of whether this material was accepted as truth, its value to the art of poetry was appreciated by medieval authors, as Kelly notes: "The historical paradigm, although by and large an illusion, was apparently taken quite seriously by medieval authors and audiences. It contributed to the romancer's conception of *conte,* and thus to the art of inventing *matiere* and *sen.*"[27]

Ordo in the rhetoric of medieval literary composition is associated with *figura,* "the stamp of auctorial conception on the work's *materia.*"[28] There were two types of order in the Middle Ages, natural and artificial, the former referring to a chronologically correct sequence of narration, the latter meaning that the order of the narration was not bound by chronology, such as in the account in Chrétien's *Yvain* that Kelly cites as an example: "Calogrenant's presence at Arthur's court precedes the chronologically earlier adventures he relates there about his defeat at the fountain."[29] When Marie uses the terms "estoire" and "ordre," she assures her audience that H.'s text is coming to them, through her own version of it, by a technique analogous to the process of *inventio.* Her reference here takes on even greater significance if she indeed copied his story from two or more manuscripts at the same time, instead of using a single exemplar, a method that would mirror the art of *inventio.*

The role of memory in the **Espurgatoire** is not limited to authorial exhortation or invocation at the outset or end of the narration, both for H. in his text and for Marie in her version, but is also instrumental in the linear development of the story. Owein's journey into the underworld includes passage through ten different torments, in which he is taunted and tortured by devils and during which he witnesses souls undergo various forms of punishments for their earthly sins. Upon his entrance into the pit of Purgatory, he is greeted by fifteen holy figures, one of which appears to be a Prior, who instructs him in the importance of memory throughout his journey: "'Ferme creance aies en tei! / Retien ço que tu oz de mei'" (Keep your faith strong within you: / Remember what you have heard from me) (729-30). He tells Owein that his only hope in Purgatory will be to remember God: "'E aiez tuz jurs en memoire / Deu ki est sire e reis de gloire'" (Always remember God, / Who is Lord and King of Glory!) (771-72).

The Prior tells Owein that he will be approached by devils who will not only torture him but will also attempt to deceive him:

> "Grant multitudine i verras
> des diables, n'en dute pas,
> ki granz turmenz te musterrunt,
> de greignurs te manacerunt.
> Se en lur cunseil vus metez
> e se creire les en volez,
> il vus prometrunt veirement
> que hors vus merrunt salvement
> a l'entree, dunt vus venistes
> quant dedenz cest clos vus mesistes;
> si vus quiderunt engignier."
>
> (733-43)

> "You will see, have no doubt,
> A huge crowd of devils
> Who will show great suffering to you,
> And threaten you with greater suffering;
> If you show trust in their advice
> And believe what they say,
> They will promise solemnly
> To lead you back safely
> To the gate by which you entered
> When you first placed yourself inside this enclosure.
> Thus they will think they have fooled you."

The admonition to avoid believing plausible-sounding lies recalls Marie's moral to the fable **"Del lëun e del vilein"** **"The Lion and the Peasant,"** in which she addresses her audience in a similar way:

> Par essample nus vuelt aprendre
> que nuls ne deit niënt entendre
> a fable, ki est de mençunge,
> n'a peinture, ki semble sunge.
>
> (59-62)

> From this fable we should learn not to believe anything from a lying story or a dreamlike painting.

At this point in the narrative, Marie must have remembered her own words, which were an original addition to the Latin source of her fable.

Owein's need for a reliable memory is further stressed by the Prior because it is the only way in which he will be able to overcome the torment of the devils and resist putting faith in their deceptive words:

> "En quel liu que seiez menez
> e quel turment que vus sentez,
> le nun Ihesucrist apelez:
> guardez que vus ne l'obliëz!
> Delivres serrez par cel nun,
> par la Deu grace le savum."
>
> (777-82)

> "In whatever place where you are led,
> And whatever torment you will experience,
> Call on the name of Jesus Christ.
> Take care that you do not forget,
> For you will be delivered by his name.
> We know this through the grace of God."

At the end of each of the ten torments that Owein must endure throughout his journey in Purgatory, he remembers to call on God's name and is saved from the torture and deception of the devils.

It is significant that Marie makes one of her completely original additions to H.'s text precisely at one of the moments when memory serves Owein and saves him from perdition. At the end of his fifth torment, the halfway mark of the trials in Purgatory, and just after Owein has saved himself by remembering to invoke his Lord's name, Marie addresses her audience and reminds them that "mult est cist nuns bons a nomer, / par quei um se puet delivrer" (This name is a very good one to name, / For by this act one can deliver oneself) (1119-20). Through her textual interjection and descriptive embellishment in this couplet, Marie depicts the power of God's name in the struggle of good and evil, while at the same time implicitly highlighting the role that memory plays in this battle.

The art of memory operates on at least two levels in this text. On a narrative level, the story can progress because the knight faithfully remembers to invoke God's name at the end of each torment and is thereby delivered from suffering at the hands of the devils. Likewise, the lay audience of Marie's *Espurgatoire,* who could not read the Latin of the monk of Saltrey's text, are encouraged to remember the images of suffering that they will encounter on their own journey through Purgatory, horrible images that Marie describes in detail, including burning bodies, people nailed to the ground by their hands and feet, people being devoured by dragons, serpents and toads tearing out the hearts of those being tormented, people hanging by various parts of their bodies from burning chains and hooks (even by their eyes and genitals), people attached to burning wheels, and people being boiled alive in liquid metal. These are precisely the types of highly charged descriptions that easily register in the audience's memory.

DESCRIPTION AND *MERVEILLE* IN THE *ESPURGATOIRE*

If the primary role of memory throughout the *Purgatorio* that Marie translates reflects its importance in her first two narrative works, the elaborate descriptions found at the beginning and end of the purgatorial journey recall similar descriptions from the *Lais.* Whereas the vivid depictions of torture are designed to remind us of the importance of avoiding sin, the beautiful accounts of the entrance to Purgatory and to the celestial city of paradise are intended to recall the rewards for living a righteous life.

Marie's choice of vernacular vocabulary at this point makes the objects under consideration visible to our imagination through her descriptive art. When Owein first enters the pit of Purgatory he is struck by the marvel of a house and wall that he discovers there:

> Tant a erré par desuz terre
> qu'il vint al champ qu'il alout querre.
> Une maisun vit bele e grant,
> dunt il oï parler devant.
> Tel lumiere a iluec trovee
> cum est d'yver en l'avespree.
> Icist palais aveit en sei
> en tur une entiere parei;
> faiz fu a piliers e a arches
> a volsurs e a wandiches.[30]
> Cloistre resemblout envirun
> cum a gent de religiün.
> Li chevaliers s'esmerveilla
> de l'ovraigne qu'il esguarda.
> Quant le palais out esguardé
> dehors e tut en tur alé,
> hastivement dedenz entra.
> Asez plus sei esmerveilla
> de ço qu'il a dedenz veü.
> A tant s'assist, loant Ihesu.
> Ses ueilz turna e sus e jus;
> merveilla sei, ne poeit plus:
> ne quida pas, c'en est la sume,
> que cele uevre fust de main d'ume.
>
> (681-704)

> He wandered far underground
> Until he came upon the field that he sought.
> He saw a large and lovely house
> Which he had heard spoken of before.
> The light he saw there
> Was like winter light at dusk.
> The palace had all around it.
> One continuous wall,
> Constructed of columns, arches,
> Vaults and *wandiches*.
> It resembled a cloister,
> Suited for men of religion.
> The knight marvelled
> At the work he observed.
> When he had looked the place over
> From without, and had gone all around it,
> He went inside quickly.
> There he marvelled even more
> At what he saw,
> And sat down praising Jesus.
> Casting his eyes up and down,
> He could not have marvelled more,
> Nor could he believe, to sum it up,
> That this was the work of human hand.

If her audience was familiar with Marie's **Lais,** this descriptive passage would remind them of her depiction

of the castle, its wall, and the painting of Venus from **"Guigemar,"** as well as the marvelous description of the ship, both discussed in chapter 4. In lines 675-704, some form of the Latin *mirabilis* appears four times, rendered in the vernacular by Marie as *merveille, s'esmerveilla, esmerveilla,* and *merveilla.* Descriptions of the marvelous, as we know, represent a fundamental thematic element in courtly literature, as in the genres of romance and *lai,* for example.

Marie does not limit her choice of *merveille* to scenes of beauty but employs the term in unpleasant contexts as well. In the eighth torment, Owein marvels at the pain he sees before him, "Li chevaliers s'esmerveilla / de cele gent qu'il esguarda" (The knight marvelled at those / He now gazed upon) (1235-36), and in the ninth torment he stands in awe of the dangerous situation in which he finds himself, "Une piece suls i estout; / mult s'esmerveilla u il fu" (Where he paused for a moment, / And marvelled at where he was) (1306-7).

Marie also uses the term strategically to add energy to her description of the suffering that sinners endure during several of the ten torments that occupy nearly five hundred lines of the **Espurgatoire.** At the beginning of the first torment, the devils set fire to the house in which Owein awaits their arrival: "Un feu firent demeintenant / en la maisun, merveilles grant" (And immediately [they] set / A huge fire in the house) (887-88). Her use of "merveilles grant" in this couplet is absent from H.'s account, and it serves to underscore the seriousness of the scene she describes as the devils launch their program of torture. She uses the same expression fewer than one hundred lines later in the story, when she recounts a horrible torment that Owein witnesses:

> Crapolz i vit, merveilles granz,
> ço li ert vis, trestuz ardanz.
> Sur les piz des alquanz seeient;
> od lur bes, qu'orribles aveient,
> a grant force erent ententis
> de traire les quers des chaitis.
>
> (1007-12)

> He also saw huge toads,
> Burning fiercely, and perched
> On the breasts of some of these people.
> With enormous force they attempted
> To tear out the hearts of their captives.

Although her passage conveys the same idea as the Latin exemplar, Marie's choice of "merveilles granz" differs from H.'s vocabulary and makes the scene more vivid than it is in the source. She repeats this same construction later, in the sixth torment:

> Un torment vit, merveilles grant:
> une roe ardant e fuïne;

desuz ert la flame sulphrine.
A la roe, u li rai sunt mis,
ot cros de fer ardant asis;
fichié furent espessement.
Sur cez cros pendeient la gent.

             (1122-28)

A terrible punishment: he saw a fiery wheel,
Burning with sulfurous flame.
On the rim of that wheel where the spokes touch
Were flaming irons hooks,
Affixed thickly all around.
On these hooks people were impaled.

Here again, her vernacular expression renders the torment more lively than it appears in her source, while its use also accommodates a lay audience accustomed to hearing the term in regard to the description of spectacular events.

Likewise, during the fifth torment, Marie uses the word "merveille" to interrupt the narrative and to interject a line that is entirely absent from her model in the scene that depicts people hanging from flaming hooks:

Li un pendeient cruëlement
a cros ardanz diversement:
par ueilz, par nes et par oreilles,
—de cels i aveit il merveilles—
par col, par buche et par mentun
e par mameles, ço trovun,
par genitailles, par aillurs,
e par les joues les plusurs.

             (1083-90)

Others were hung cruelly
From flaming hooks:
Some by their eyes, others by their noses or ears
(This was a great wonder),
Or neck, or mouth, or jaw,
Or by their breasts we find.
Some were hung by their genitals,
And many others by their cheeks.

One has the impression that the events in this scene were so striking to Marie herself that she felt the need to express her own wonder.

After Owein successfully passes through the torments of Purgatory, he arrives at the gates of the celestial paradise. Like the account of the house he discovered at the beginning of his journey, the narration of this scene calls to mind the earlier descriptive passages from Marie's **"Guigemar"**:

Devant lui vit un mur si grant,
halt de la terre, en l'air a munt.
Les merveilles ki del mur sunt
ne purreit nuls cunter ne dire,
ne l'ovraigne ne la matire.
Une porte a el mur veüe,
bien l'a de loinz aparceüe.

De preciüs metals fu faite
e gloriusement portraite:
porsise esteit de bones pieres,
mult preciüses e mult chieres.
Li chevaliers s'esmerveilla
de la porte, qu'il esguarda,
pur la clarté qu'ele rendeit,
ki des chieres pieres eisseit.

             (1488-1502)

And he came to a huge
Wall rising high up from the earth.
No one could recount
The marvelous nature of this wall,
Or its design or material.
He saw from afar
That the wall had a gate
Made of precious metals
Splendidly inlaid,
Containing lovely, rare,
And very costly stones.
The knight marvelled
At the door he was observing,
On account of the brightness
Given off by its costly stones.

Again, the treatment of the *merveilleux* is emphasized in these lines as in the lines discussed above, not only by the repetition of the word itself but also by the magical quality that the door seems to possess in giving off radiant light from its precious stones. As in the **Lais**, the use of the term "merveille" here has special significance to the act of remembering. Tobler and Lommatzsch attest that the etymology for the Old French "merveille" is Latin *mirabilia*, or German *Wunder*, that which is marvelous, unusual, or wonderful to behold. By giving an object unusual qualities, an author assists the audience in the process of creating a lasting image in the faculty of memory.

In addition to the ability of these descriptive lines to help us create a picture of the scene in our imagination and then enter it into our storehouse of memory, much like the medieval student would have done from the pictureless descriptions in the *Bestiaire* of Philippe de Thaon, these passages also serve a structural function within the text. Just as the lines that speak of the act of memory in Marie's prologue and epilogue enclose the memory-oriented narrative of the **Espurgatoire** in a general sense, so too do the descriptive scenes of the marvelous objects at the beginning and end of the journey in Purgatory frame the episode of the ten torments and Owein's repeated victory through the act of memory.

The courtly and religious dimensions of H. of Saltrey's account of St. Patrick's Purgatory were no doubt important considerations for Marie, but she was equally interested in presenting her lay public with a text that reflected her own poetics, one that incorporated detailed descriptions of events and objects and privileged the act of memory. When Marie translates H.'s *Purgatorio,* she not only takes literature from one language to another and passes it along to a new audience, she also transfers memory, what I would call a *translatio memoriae,* as she brings to her public a text that accentuates the significance of this faculty.

LA VIE SEINTE AUDREE AND THE QUESTION OF AUTHORSHIP

I originally intended to include a chapter on each of the three narrative texts that scholarship, through general consensus over the years, has confidently attributed to Marie de France. In the July 2002 issue of *Speculum,* however, June Hall McCash revived a debate over authorship that had lain dormant for several years when she revisited the long-accepted attribution of a late twelfth-or early thirteenth-century French narrative text, *La vie seinte Audree,* to an author known simply as "Marie."[31] Through a cogent linguistic and stylistic argument that compares this text to the *Espurgatoire seint Patriz* discussed above, and through reconsidering the dating of the *Audree,* McCash presents a convincing case that both narratives are the work of the same author, France's first known feminine voice of the Middle Ages, whom we traditionally know as Marie de France.

Based on McCash's evidence, on Pickens's recent research, and on my own subsequent reading and analysis of the text and its manuscript in light of her poetics of memory, it is now my conviction that *La vie seinte Audree* merits inclusion in her corpus, as the discussion to follow seeks to demonstrate. Indeed, Pickens declares that, "thanks to June Hall McCash, no one can pretend any more to write comprehensively on Marie de France while ignoring the *seinte Audree.*"[32] It is not my intention here to argue for Marie's specific identity as a nun or otherwise, and this issue has been exhaustively debated for many years.[33] Rather, I suggest that the evidence continues to come forth in support of including the *Audree* among the three other texts in which she identifies herself simply as Marie, and once as Marie de France. Much has in fact been made of her anonymity, most recently by Bloch's book, *The Anonymous Marie de France,* in which the author argues that she was intentionally anonymous. As an author in early medieval culture, however, Marie is much less anonymous than others writing during her period, owing to the very fact that she names herself in all four works—many, if not most, authors at this time do not, and as such they remain truly anonymous. She is, in fact, no more anonymous than her contemporary, Chrétien de Troyes, who also names himself in his texts.

As with Chrétien, it is true that we have very few details of her life, and even those about which we are relatively confident have been debated—she was a woman from France and she wrote for the court of Henry II in England. Nonetheless, in the true sense of the word she is not anonymous, and the fact that the author of these four texts showed remarkable concern that we record her name in memory remains significant.

To begin, a brief summary of the theories associated with the authorship of *La vie seinte Audree* clarifies the position of McCash and others, including myself, who share her view and who currently work on Marie de France. The controversy over Marie de France's possible authorship of the *Audree* dates back at least to Richard Baum's 1968 study,[34] in which Baum actually challenges her authorship of the three texts from the end of the twelfth century that are now confidently ascribed to her: the *Lais,* the *Isopet* (*Fables*), and the *Espurgatoire.* Baum's assertions—and a dubious view posited by Jean-Charles Huchet in 1981 contending that the *Lais* were composed by a man rather than a woman—have now been largely discredited.[35] Baum's most lasting contribution to the recently reborn question may in fact be his contention that the *Audree* deserves to be reckoned with, alongside the three other texts, in any consideration of their authorship.[36]

A few years after Baum's study, Mickel, in his book on Marie de France published in the Twayne Series in 1974, proposed the need for a close linguistic investigation of the *Audree* and stated that it may have "as much right to be placed among Marie [de France]'s work as any of the other three."[37] Likewise, Curley refers the reader to lines 4624-25 in the epilogue of the *Seinte Audree*—"Ici escris mon non Marie / Pur ce ke soie remembree" (Here I write my name "Marie" / so that I may be remembered)—and he notes that "both the sentiments and the language expressed here closely parallel passages in Marie's *Fables* and in [the] *Espurgatoire,* which raises the possibility that Marie de France was the author of four works rather than three."[38] The corresponding passages in both texts are lines 3 and 4 from the epilogue of the *Fables* and lines 2297 and 2298 from the epilogue to the *Espurgatoire,* quoted above. The years following Curley's comments saw little discussion about Marie de France's possible authorship of *La vie seinte Audree* until McCash's sound argument on the subject in *Speculum.*[39]

La vie seinte Audree is recorded in a single thirteenth- or early fourteenth-century manuscript, London, BL, Add. 70513, and has only recently been edited again since the edition in 1955 by Östen Södergård.[40] The story recounts various events associated with the life and death of the saint, including her two marriages, the founding of Ely Cathedral, the second translation of her body, and a series of miracles.[41] The manuscript contains exclusively thirteen lives of saints in its 265 folios, the life of St. Etheldreda of Ely (St. Audree) occupying folios 100v-134v.[42] Of the thirteen texts presented in the collection, six of them open with a small miniature of a portrait of the saint whose story follows.[43] In the case of St. Audree, one of these six decorated opening initials, the 30 × 30 mm illumination on folio 100v, depicts the saint standing in frontal pose and reading from a book on a podium in front of her. She holds a small cathedral (Ely) in her right hand and gestures toward it with her left hand. Virginia Blanton-Whetsell has noted that iconography up to that time had portrayed St. Audree with a crozier, highlighting her role as abbess. She points out that the substitution here of the miniature church for the crozier underscores her role as founder of the Ely Cathedral, and that it represents her "telling her own story as patron of religious institutions."[44] Interestingly, the iconography here, specifically the way in which St. Audree is positioned, recalls the author portraits of Marie de France from some of the *Fable* manuscripts discussed in chapter 4.[45] Although purely speculative in nature, this similarity invites us to consider whether or not the illuminator of BL, Add. 70513, or the scribe who left instructions for the illumination, was familiar with Marie de France's *Fables* manuscripts, from roughly the same period, that contain her portrait. Even though Marie de France, or at least the female figure depicted in the *Fables* manuscripts in question, is presented as the author of the text, whereas the woman shown in Add. 70513 is obviously the saint whose subject is recounted in the narrative, it is nevertheless possible to imagine that the scribe or illuminator associated the Marie who names herself at the end of the *Audree* with the Marie of the *Fables*, at least from an iconographical perspective.

With this brief summary in mind, the following analysis treats the use of rhetorical memory in the *Audree* to demonstrate the discursive relationship between it and Marie's other works, especially the *Espurgatoire.* While McCash's article has already dealt with several stylistic and thematic similarities that I highlight in this discussion, I focus on the author's use of rhetorical memory and the medieval art of *inventio,* an aspect of her narrative art that she emphasizes in the texts discussed [elsewhere].

THE *AUDREE* AND MARIE'S POETICS OF MEMORY

Marie exhibits an accomplished understanding of the medieval arts of poetry and prose in the *Espurgatoire,* as is evidenced by her references to rhetorical terms from the paradigm of literary invention. In the *Audree* she employs a similar rhetorical vocabulary when she brings her version into the vernacular, and the terms she chooses are sometimes absent from the source material, as we have already seen in the *Espurgatoire.* One passage in particular from the *Audree* confirms this occurrence toward the beginning of the text, where she enlists the expressions *venir a la matere, trovom en escrit,* and *mostre l'estoire,* terms that are designed to give credibility to the work at hand through the rhetorical implications of *captatio benevolentiae* and *auctoritas*:

> Pour la grant bonté de ceo roy
> Et pur s'onesté et sa foy,
> Com il fu bon rei et bon pere
> Et pur venir a la matere,
> Avom de li parlé et dist
> Ceo que nos trovom en escrit.
> De Kenewal, un roy puissant,
> Mostre l'estoire ici avant.
>
> (525-32)[46]

> In order to get to the main story
> we have told at length
> what we find in the written record about this king
> because of his goodness,
> his honor, and his faith,
> and because he was a good king and a good father.
> Now I will tell the story
> of Cenwald, a powerful king.

This narrative strategy is particularly apparent in regard to the use of words associated with memory where Marie uses terms that her source does not.[47] In fact, throughout the *Audree,* she seems quite intent on conveying to her audience the importance of memory by invoking this faculty at least sixteen times in the 4,625 lines in the text with expressions like "mettre en memoire," "remembrer/membrer," and "faire la memoire."[48]

Reading the prologues and epilogues of Marie de France's *Lais, Isopet,* and *Espurgatoire* against the exordial and closing lines in the *Audree* reveals a shared rhetorical discourse among the four narratives. The author pays particular attention throughout the prologues and epilogues of her works, discussed earlier, to the techniques of *descriptio* and *memoria,* both fundamental parts of *inventio* that imbued the medieval arts of poetry and prose.[49] She also opens the *Audree* by invoking the faculty of memory:

> An bon hovre e en bon porpens
> Devroit chascun user son tens.
> Pur sage devroit hon tenir
> Celui ke porroit *sovenir*
> Dont il est fait, qui le cria,
> Et quel part il *revertira.*
>
> (1-6, emphasis added)

For a good work and for a good purpose
should each person use his time.
It would be wise
for everyone to remember
what he is made of, who made him,
and whither he shall return.

Both of the verbs *sovenir* and *revertir* are etymologically related to memory, the latter of which in Old French can mean to return, to come back, or to return to one's senses, in other words, to *remember* who you are. Indeed, the noun based on the verb—*reverteure*—indicates a "souvenir" or "memory" of something. As I have shown in chapter 2, Marie de France's *exordia* consistently express a concern with memory. It should also be noted that the first two lines of the *Audree*— "An bon hovre e en bon porpens / Devroit chascun user son tens" (For a good work and for a good purpose / should each person use his time)—are very close to those that open the General Prologue to the *Lais*: "Ki Deus ad duné escïence / E de parler bone eloquence / Ne s'en deit taisir ne celer" (Anyone who has received from God the gift of knowledge and true eloquence has a duty not to remain silent), evoking the rhetorical device of *causa scribendi*.

Furthermore, Marie ends the *Audree* with an epilogue that also points to the importance of memory by syntactically juxtaposing her name with the past participle *remembree* and with the verb *obliër* (or its negation, as the encouragement is not to forget), a strategy similar to that found in the epilogues to her earlier works:

> Issi ay ceo livre finé
> En romanz dit et translaté
> De la vie seintë Audree
> Si com en latin l'ay trové,
> Et les miracles ay oÿ,
> Ne voil nul mettrë en obli.
> Pur ce depri la gloriuse
> Seinte Audree la precïeuse
> Par sa pité k'a moy entende
> Et ce servise a m'ame rende,
> Et ceus pur ki ge la depri
> K'el lur aït par sa merci.
> Mut par est fol ki se oblie.
> Ici escris mon non Marie
> Pur ce ke soie remembree.

(4611-25)

Now I have finished this book,
told and translated into French
the life of Saint Audrey
just as I found it in Latin,
along with the miracles I have heard.
I do not wish to let anything be forgotten.
Therefore I beseech glorious,
precious Saint Audrey
to hear me out of compassion

and give aid to my soul,
as well as to those for whom I pray:
may she help them through her mercy.
One is indeed foolish who forgets herself:
here I write my name "Marie"
so that I may be remembered.

Although the *Lais* do not contain a formal epilogue, "Eliduc," the last text in the collection, ends with its own epilogue, which serves to frame the entire work: the opening references to the faculty of memory in the General Prologue and the prologue of "Guigemar" function as one "bookend," and the direct appeal to this faculty in the epilogue of "Eliduc" functions as the other.

In addition to the affinity of opening and closing material in the four texts under consideration here, a stylistic comparison of the narrations themselves in the two texts that are most thematically alike, the *Espurgatoire* and the *Audree*, reveals a shared concern with the application of *memoria* as it is expressed in the art of literary composition. McCash has already exposed the significance of this similarity by pointing to the paucity of references to memory in other hagiographic texts of the same period: only three times in Clemence of Barking's *La vie de Seinte Catherine d'Alexandrie* and only four times in the anonymous Nun of Barking's *Vie d'Edouard le Confesseur*, for example.[50] By contrast, the *Audree* offers numerous mentions of memory. McCash is quick to acknowledge that vernacular hagiographic writers use memory to a slightly different end than do authors of secular romance narratives, the former focusing more on "the celebration of shared memory" of a saint who already exists "en memoire," the latter desiring to preserve the memory of the past through rhetorical devices that included, but were not limited to, such techniques as *translatio studii* and *imperii, ordo, descriptio*, and *amplificatio*; in sum, they were more interested in the process of "mettre en memoire," or putting the material into memory, both for their own audiences and, as Marie de France makes explicit, for posterity.[51]

In the *Espurgatoire* and the *Audree* Marie's comprehension and implementation of this process shows that she was an author accustomed to secular vernacular narrative, even though she is now working in the domain of hagiography in translating the lives of the saints from their Latin models into Old French.[52] Lines 185-88 of the *Espurgatoire*, as discussed above, reveal her understanding of *inventio* as it emerges from her interpretation of the source material, H. of Saltrey's *Purgatorio*. Likewise, the *Audree* demonstrates her training and knowledge in the arts of poetry and prose. She states clearly in line 318 that she will leave aside the *matere* of her narrative digression and pick up again the *historia* of her source material so that she will not transgress the order (*ordo*) of the work at hand that she is putting "en memoire":

> Ceste matere lais issi,
> Kar revertir voil a l'estoire
> Dont en romanz fas la memoire.
> Sainte Audree dont nos parlon
> Fu mut de grant religion.
>
> (318-22)
>
> But I will not pursue this subject,
> for I wish to return to the main story
> which I am recording in French.
> Saint Audrey, of whom we are speaking,
> was devoutly religious.

In fact, numerous passages throughout the *Audree* reveal a certain obsession on the part of the author with *estoire* and *matere*.[53]

It is worth mentioning that the *Espurgatoire* and the *Audree* share yet another resemblance, apart from the design of memory, in their common use of courtly language. By putting the story "en memoire" for her lay audience, as she states in the epilogue of the *Espurgatoire,* Marie de France has helped her readers and listeners understand its message by means of the *aventure* to which they are accustomed.[54] Curley's observations on her method of putting the religious story of the *Espurgatoire* into the "idiom of the conte d'aventure" can be extended to the *Audree,* in which Marie generously and consistently employs the word *aventure* throughout the entirety of her text. In comparable fashion, both texts narrate the importance of the role that holy names play in acts of deliverance from peril. For the *Audree,* the very memory of the name of the saint represents assurance: "Digne chose est a remembrer / La seinteté et recorder / De la roïne sainte Audree / Ke a Deu out s'amur donee" (It is well worth remembering / her righteousness and recalling / how queen Saint Audrey / had given her love to God) (1443-46).[55] In the *Espurgatoire,* memory assures Owein of a means of escaping difficult circumstances, as he is encouraged to remember the name of Jesus Christ.[56] The vocabulary in these passages is similar to vocabulary in several other passages throughout both texts in which the author adopts a strikingly parallel discourse in bringing her Latin sources into the vernacular.

DESCRIPTION AND *MERVEILLE* IN THE *AUDREE*

In both works a similar strategy is used for describing objects that will help the audience remember key episodes and themes in the story. The knight in Marie de France's **"Laüstic"** creates a small and decorative container to house the dead nightingale that is wrapped in a precious samite cloth embroidered in gold, which will serve as a memorial of the love of his lady. In like fashion, and with much the same vocabulary, the two decorative *objects* that St. Audree makes, the elaborate stole and maniple for priestly service, are associated with the act of remembering, as the author informs us that these items are kept in Durham in God's honor *par remembrance*:

> D'or et de saie sainte Audree
> Fist une estole bien ovree
> Et un fanon k'el li tramist;
> Pieres precïeuses i mist.
> Ces aornemenz sont gardé
> A Durthaim par [mut] grant chierté;
> En l'onor Deu par remembrance
> L'eglise fait une monstrance.
> L'amur des deus ert covenable,
> Kar ele ert a Deu acceptable:
> Virges furent et chastement
> Tindrent lur vie et seintement;
> Li uns avoit l'autre en memoire
> Ke Deus le menast en sa gloire.
>
> (1097-110)
>
> Saint Audrey made a finely worked stole
> and maniple out of gold and silk,
> adorned it with precious stones
> and gave it to him.
> These adornments are still kept
> with great affection in Durham.
> To honor God in memory of Saint Cuthbert
> the church made a monstrance for them.
> The love between these two [Cuthbert and Audrey]
>   was proper
> and acceptable to God
> for they were both virgins who led
> chaste and holy lives.
> One was always mindful of the other,
> [praying] that God would bring each of them into His
>   glory.

Whether *eros* for the knight-lover in the *lai* of **"Laüstic,"** or *caritas* for the *Audree,* these passages demonstrate the author's desire to adorn objects descriptively and render them more accessible in our memory.

Moreover, Marie employs the term *merveille,* as she did in the *Espurgatoire,* when describing scenes that are particularly important to her. Here again, her audience would be used to hearing this expression in vernacular descriptions of people, places, objects, and events. She uses it in the beginning of her narrative to enhance her description of St. Audree's virginity:

> Sainte Audree dont nos parlon
> Fu mut de grant religion
> Pur Deu garda virginité
> Et toz jurs menoit en chasté:
> Ceuz ke la virge conoiseient
> A grant merveillie le teneient

K'ele gardoit en mariage
Virginité et pucelage.

(321-28)

Saint Audrey, of whom we are speaking,
was devoutly religious.
She kept her virginity for God
and lived a chaste life daily.
Those who knew the virgin
marveled at her,
for though she was a married woman, she kept
her virginity and maidenhood.

The *grant merveillie* of line 326 recalls the use of the same expression throughout the *Espurgatoire* and calls attention to her description at this point. She chooses this construction again, later in the text, when she speaks about the virginity of the saint: "Grant merveillie fu de la foy / K'ele garda a Jhesu Crist / A cui virginité promist" (It was a great miracle of faith / that she remained faithful to Jesus Christ, / to whom she had promised her virginity) (1258-60). In fact, as in the *Espurgatoire,* she uses *merveille* regularly throughout the story to add descriptive energy to the scene.[57] Virginia Blanton has shown that Marie's focus on St. Audree's virginity and sexual desires from her daily life is original and cannot be found in sources prior to her vernacular version of the life.[58]

Marie consistently embellishes her version of the events from the Latin model with descriptions rich in vocabulary belonging to secular literature. At another point in the narrative in which St. Audree's chastity is emphasized, the author uses the same construction she has employed twice earlier to address the subject of virginity, but this time with yet another discursive dimension her audience would have no doubt known:

Une haute roche i avoit
Ke un de[s] costés aceignoit,
Entaillié ert la pere dure:
C'estoit merveillieuse aventure;
Et la mer ke desouz estoit
Ou ele au tertre se tenoit
En pes se tint sanz departir
Si ke hom ne poet avenir.

(1355-62)

There was a high rock
that formed part of the coastline.
The hard stone had been hollowed out.
This was a miraculous occurrence,
the water at the base
of the hill where she stood
stayed there without moving,
so that no one could come near her.

To the term *merveillieuse* Marie has added the element of *aventure* in this account of a miracle that saves the saint from the advances of King Egfrid. The juxtaposi-

tion of these two terms, which belong to the discourse of courtly literature, cannot be coincidental, and they betray the talents of an author well trained in the art of literary composition.[59]

The preponderance of references to memory and the act of remembering in the *Espurgatoire* and the *Audree,* the way in which Marie frames her works in these references, her demonstration of competence in the process of medieval literary *inventio* and its vocabulary, the regular occurrence of the courtly register in the descriptions, and the fact that the author syntactically associates her name in the epilogues with memory, represent more than mere artistic coincidence. These characteristics reveal an author with training in the vernacular, someone well versed in the arts of poetry and prose as they were understood during the last quarter of the twelfth century, an artist accomplished in *translatio studii,* in bringing preexisting material to a new, lay audience through her own conception of the work. Whether we call her simply Marie or Marie de France, the poetics of memory that emerge from the *Lais,* the *Isopet,* the *Espurgatoire,* and the *Audree* point rather convincingly to the same author, not an anonymous ghost hiding in her narratives, but a poet who wants to be remembered.

Notes

1. For an updated and thorough study of the *De Purgatorio Sancti Patricii* and its relationship to Marie's text, see Pontfarcy's edition of the *Espurgatoire,* 1-70. She notes that the word "tractatus" does not appear in any of the extant manuscripts of this work, so I have omitted it in my references to the full title of the work. Pickens has studied closely the source for the *Audree* in its manuscript context. In a paper read at the 2003 International Medieval Congress, University of Leeds, UK, July 16, 2003, he offered a thorough analysis on this subject, on which he provided a detailed handout. Marie's exemplar is very close to the text in BL, Cotton, Domitian A xv, fols. 9v-75r (a transcription of this manuscript served as the basis for St. Etheldreda's Life in the *Acta sanctorum*). As this book was going to press, he had significantly expanded his commentary on these sources as part of a forthcoming larger project on *La vie seinte Audree.* See the introductions to Östen Södergård's edition, *La vie seinte Audree: Poème anglo-normand du XIIIe siècle,* Uppsala Universitets årsskrift 11 (Uppsala: Lundequistska Bokhandeln, 1955), and to McCash and Barban's edition of *The Life of Saint Audrey,* in which they cite the work of Pickens mentioned above. See also chapter 4, "'La gloriuse seint Audree / Une noble

eglise a fundee': Chastity, Widowhood, and Aristocratic Patronage (ca. 1189-1416)," in Virginia Blanton, *Signs of Devotion: The Cult of St. Ethelthryth in Medieval England, 695-1615* (University Park: Pennsylvania State University Press, 2007).

2. For descriptions of this manuscript, see Pontfarcy's *Espurgatoire*, 19-22, and Warnke's *Espurgatoire*, 65.

3. See Bruckner, "Marie de France," in Kibler and Zinn, *Medieval France*; Emanuel J. Mickel Jr., *Marie de France* (New York: Twayne, 1974), 41; and Pontfarcy's edition of the *Espurgatoire*, 4-10. For dating that differs considerably from the commonly accepted view, see Eduard Mall, *De aetate rebusque Mariae Francicae nova quaestio instituitur* (Halle, 1867). Though he held the same sequence of composition that was later accepted by most scholars—*Lais, Fables,* and *Espurgatoire*—he offered much later possible dates of composition: for the *Lais*, 1245; for the *Fables*, 1248; and for the *Espurgatoire*, 1250. For a different sequence, and an earlier date of 1185 for the *Espurgatoire*, see Ezio Levi, "Sulla cronologia della opera di Maria di Francia," *Nuovi Studi Medievali* 1, no. 1 (1923): 41-72. Levi proposes that the *Espurgatoire* was written after the *Lais* but before the *Fables*.

4. The brief résumé of the legend and of H. of Saltrey's and Marie's versions that I make here owes much to Mickel, *Marie de France*, 41-49.

5. Ibid., 42.

6. See Peter Dewilde, "Le système descriptif des visions de l'autre monde dans le *Purgatoire de saint Patrice*," in *La description au Moyen Âge: Actes du Colloque du Centre d'Études Médiévales et Dialectales de Lille III, Université Charles-de-Gaulle-Lille III, 25-26 septembre 1992*, ed. Aimé Petit Villeneuve d'Ascq (Université de Lille III, 1993), 144.

7. Mickel, *Marie de France*, 42.

8. See Michael Haren and Yolande de Pontfarcy, *The Medieval Pilgrimage to St. Patrick's Purgatory: Lough Derg and the European Tradition* (Enniskillen, Ireland: Clogher Historical Society, 1988), 212-14. They list fifty-four manuscripts and incunabula of the *Purgatorio*. In Pontfarcy's edition of the *Espurgatoire*, 11n, she has increased the list of extant manuscripts of the *Purgatorio* legend to more than 150, the same number that appears in the works of Robert Easting, *St. Patrick's Purgatory: Two Versions of Owayne Miles and The Vision of William of Stranton Together with the Long Text of the Tractatus de Purgatorio Sancti Patricii* (Oxford: Oxford University Press, 1991), lxxxiv-lxxxvii, and in Curley's translation, *Saint Patrick's Purgatory*, 14. See Mickel, *Marie de France*, 42, where he puts the number of extant manuscripts at more than thirty, but the more recent works of Curley and Pontfarcy were not available to him at the time.

9. See Pontfarcy's *Espurgatoire*, 2-4. She notes, "Marie traduit le texte de la version courte et donne la plupart des additions de la version longue" (2). For the correspondence of segments of Marie's text with segments in different manuscripts of H.'s text, see the chart in Mickel, *Marie de France*, 43, which he reproduces from Thomas A. Jenkins, ed., *The Espurgatoire Seint Patriz of Marie de France with a Text of the Latin Original* (Chicago: Decennial Publications of the University of Chicago, 1903).

10. Curley's translation, *Saint Patrick's Purgatory*, 2. For a study of the French verse translations, see Kurt Ringger, "Die altfranzösischen Verspurgatorien," *Zeitschrift für romanische Philologie* 88, nos. 4-6 (1972): 389-402. See also Haren and Pontfarcy, *Medieval Pilgrimage to St. Patrick's Purgatory*, 83-98, and D. D. R. Owen, *The Vision of Hell: Infernal Journeys in Medieval French Literature* (Edinburgh: Scottish Academic Press, 1970), 51-141.

11. For a study of the manuscript tradition of H.'s *Purgatorio*, see Lucien Foulet, "Marie de France et la légende du Purgatoire de Saint Patrice," *Romanische Forschungen* 22, no. 4 (1908): 599-627; Jenkins's *Espurgatoire*, 236-327; Pontfarcy's *Espurgatoire*, 11-14; and Warnke's *Espurgatoire*, 7-9.

12. Mickel, *Marie de France*, 47.

13. Curley's translation, *Saint Patrick's Purgatory*, 1.

14. See Jeanette M. A. Beer, *Narrative Conventions of Truth in the Middle Ages* (Geneva: Droz, 1981), 69. Beer states that "Marie's translation *L'Espurgatoire Seint Patriz* was dedicated exclusively to Christian truth." Since Marie's narrative interventions in H.'s text privilege a lay perspective over an ecclesiastical one, this position exaggerates the poet's religious intentions.

15. See Owen, *Vision of Hell*, 66: "It seems fair to conclude that if one quality that drew Marie's attention to the *Tractatus* was its salutary moral tone, another was its value as an adventure story.

This would be in keeping with her personality as it emerges from her other works."

16. Curley's translation, *Saint Patrick's Purgatory*, 2. H.'s addition of a knight in the legend and its rapport with medieval courtly society has been noticed by most critics. See especially Mickel, *Marie de France*, 48-49, where he compares Owein's various encounters in Purgatory with the themes found in the *roman* and the *chansons de geste*. He specifically recalls the *Joie de la Cort* and sword-bridge episodes from Chrétien for romance, and Owein's struggle with the enemies of God for the *chansons de geste*. See also Curley's translation, *Saint Patrick's Purgatory*, 33-34, where he compares Owein's adventures in Purgatory to the adventures of Lanval, Muldumarec, and Eliduc in Marie's *Lais*.

17. For a discussion of Marie's creative art as translator, especially her use of rhetorical techniques that render her version of the tale more concise than that of the source, see Rupert T. Pickens, "Marie de France: Translatrix," *Le Cygne: Journal of the International Marie de France Society*, n.s., 1 (fall 2002): 7-24.

18. Curley's translation, *Saint Patrick's Purgatory*, 24. H. uses Owein's name only once. Otherwise, he refers to him as *vir* or *miles*.

19. Mickel, *Marie de France*, 48.

20. See [Whalen, Logan E. *Marie of France and the Poetics of Memory*. Washington, DC: Catholic University of America Press, 2008] chapter 1, in which I discuss the terms "memoire" and "remembrance" in Old French as treated by Stefenelli.

21. See Bonnie H. Leonard, "The Inscription of a New Audience: Marie de France's *Espurgatoire Saint Patriz*," *Romance Languages Annual* 5 (1993): 57-62. Leonard stresses Marie's role in bringing a religious message to a French-speaking audience.

22. Owen, *Vision of Hell*, xi.

23. For a discussion of the impact of these texts on French literature of the Middle Ages, see ibid., chapters 1-4.

24. Ibid., 65. He refers to these couplets as "quite commonplace pious interjections," adding that, "as for the omissions and discrepancies between Marie's text and the *Tractatus* as we know it, these are very small matters and contribute in no way to our knowledge of the authoress or her text." The four couplets are "Chaitis est cil ki en tel peine / pur ses pechiez se trait e meine!" (1019-20), "A

las, se nuls deit deservir / que tel peine deie sufrir!" (1053-54), "mult est cist nuns bons a nomer, / par quei um se puet delivrer" (1119-20), and "Or nus doint Deus ço deservir / qu'a cez joies puissuns venir!" (1667-68). In relation to my study, the first three couplets hold more significance than Owen ascribes to them, and they all occur within the context of the ten torments, a passage of the *Espurgatoire* that Marie would have particularly wanted her audience to remember.

25. All references to H. of Saltrey's *Purgatorio* are taken from Warnke's edition of the *Espurgatoire*, which also reproduces the Latin source on the page facing the Old French text. The translation here is my own.

26. Kelly, *Art of Medieval French Romance*, 44.

27. Ibid., 86.

28. Ibid., 61.

29. Ibid., 264-69. For a full discussion of *ordo* as a division in the medieval literary paradigm, see 263-305.

30. "Wandiches" is a *hapax legomenon*. See the note in Curley's translation, *Saint Patrick's Purgatory*, 81.

31. The discussion at this point, and throughout the rest of the chapter, owes much to June Hall McCash, "*La vie seinte Audree*: A Fourth Text by Marie de France?" *Speculum* 77, no. 3 (2002): 744-77.

32. See note 1 above.

33. The articles devoted to the subject of Marie de France's identity are too numerous to cite. See Burgess, *Analytical Bibliography*. However, a recent study worth highlighting broadens our understanding of traditional arguments surrounding her identity: see Rupert T. Pickens, "*En bien parler* and *mesparler*: Fecundity and Sterility in the Works of Marie de France," *Le Cygne: Journal of the International Marie de France Society*, n.s., 3 (fall 2005): 20n23.

34. Baum, *Recherches sur les œuvres attribuées à Marie de France*.

35. McCash, "A Fourth Text," 745n.

36. Ibid., 744-45.

37. See ibid., 745, where McCash quotes Mickel.

38. Curley's translation, *Saint Patrick's Purgatory*, 7.

39. See McCash, "A Fourth Text," 745. She notes that Jocelyn-Wogan Browne and Virginia Blanton-Whetsell have worked on the provenance and patronage of the *Audree* manuscript.

40. Södergård's edition of *Vie seinte Audree*. The manuscript that measures 250 × 170 mm, with a ruled text area of 190 × 135 mm, was formerly Welbeck Abbey MS. I.C.1. The most recent edition is McCash and Barban, *Life of Saint Audrey*.

41. See the beginning of this [essay] and note 1.

42. I thank Mr. Joe Maldonado and Mr. Michael J. Boggan of the Manuscripts Reading Room at the British Library in London for their assistance during my consultation of this manuscript and for providing valuable information about it. The lives of the saints appear in the following order: fols. 1r-4r, St. Elizabeth of Hungary; fols. 4r-5v, St. Paphnutius; fols. 6r-8r, St. Paul the Hermit; fols. 9r-50v, St. Thomas Becket; fols. 50v-55v, St. Mary Magdelen; fols. 55v-85v, St. Edward the Confessor; fols. 85v-100r, St. Edmund, Archbishop of Canterbury; fols. 100v-134v, St. Etheldreda of Ely (St. Audree); fols. 134v-147v, St. Osyth; fols. 147v-156v, St. Faith; fols. 156v-222r, St. Modwenna; fols. 222r-244v, St. Richard of Wych, Bishop of Chichester; fols. 246r-265v, St. Catherine of Alexandria.

43. Edward the Confessor, fol. 55v; St. Etheldreda (St. Audree), fol. 100v; St. Osyth, fol. 134v; St. Modwenna, fol. 156v; St. Richard de Wych, fol. 222r; St. Catherine of Alexandria, fol. 246r.

44. See Virginia Blanton-Whetsell, "*Imagines Ætheldreda*: Mapping Hagiographic Representations of Abbatial Power and Religious Patronage," *Studies in Iconography* 23 (2002): 74-80. She describes the image in detail and provides two reproductions, one as it appears in relation to the entire manuscript folio, fig. 11 (76), and one enlargement of the illumination alone, fig. 12 (76).

45. See [Whalen, 2008] chapter 4, and my article, "*Ex Libris Mariae*," for a discussion of the images in question: Paris, BNF, fr. 2173, fol. 93r.; BNF, fr. 1446, fol. 88v; Paris, Arsenal 3142, fols. 256r and 273r. The author portrait in Vatican, BAV, Ottob. Lat. 3042, fol. 235r, is most probably later than BL, Add. 70513. Furthermore, her position in the Vatican manuscript illumination is slightly different than it is in the *Isopet* manuscripts that precede it, in that she is sitting at a covered desk and leaning forward before four male figures. See Busby, *Codex and Context*, 478.

46. Other passages where Marie includes these and similar terms not found in her source are lines 315-16, 484, 562, 603, 636-38, 811, 919, 1799, 1992-94, 2899, 2905-6, 3637-38.

47. Marie records the term, while her source does not, in the following lines from the *Audree: memoire* (rhymed with *estoire*) in 399-400, 855-56; *remembrance* in 1103-6; *recorder* in 1444; *remembra* in 3427-31. At times, Marie uses a form of *remembrer* where her source uses *memoria*: 1129, 1443.

48. "Membra lui par religion," 113; "Ceste matere lais issi, / Kar revertir voil a l'estoire / Dont en romanz fas la memoire," 318-20; "Ky en chercha la veire estoire / Pur mestre la vie en memoire," 399-400; "De cui vie et de cui victoire / En cel livre mis en memoire," 657-58; "En cel tens, si com ge recort," 778; "Ou quart livre de ceste estoire / Dont seint Bede feit la memoire," 855-56; "A la mateire revendrons," 919; "En l'onor Deu par remembrance / L'eglise fait une monstrance," 1103-4 (these lines are marked in the margin on fol. 108v, line 19, of the manuscript with a large plus symbol [+]); "Li uns avoit l'autre en memoire," 1109; "Ky poet remembrer en corage," 1129; "Digne chose est a remembrer / La seinteté et recorder / De la roïne sainte Audree," 1443-45 (cf. *Espurgatoire*, 771-82); "Si com nos reconte l'estoire / Ke saint Bede mist en memoire," 2381-82; "En son quer prist a remembrer / De seinte Audree et de sa vie," 3302-3; "En ses tormenz li remembra / De Brustan ke Deu delivra," 3427-28; "Li sovint et ad remembré / De seinte Audree la roïne," 3572-73; "Ne voil nul mettrë en obli," 4616; "Mut par est fol ki se oblie. / Ici escris mon non Marie / Pur ce ke soie remembree," 4623-25.

49. See [Whalen, 2008] chapters 1 and 2.

50. See McCash, "A Fourth Text," 752. McCash refers to Clemence of Barking's *La vie de Seinte Catherine d'Alexandrie*, 384, 483, and 2608, and the anonymous Nun of Barking's *Vie d'Edouard le Confesseur*, 2079, 2797, 2844, and 6385.

51. Ibid., 752.

52. Ibid., 753.

53. See notes 47-49, above.

54. See Leonard, "Inscription of a New Audience," 57-62, as discussed earlier in this [essay].

55. This theme recurs often throughout the text: 1129-30, 3337-38, 3427-29, 3572-73, and 3838-40. See also notes 46-48, above.

56. See, for example, 771-72 and 1119-20 of the *Espurgatoire*.

57. Similar uses of *merveille* are found in lines 1358, 1430, 1532, 2058, 2105, 2187, 2241, 2273, 2283, 2317, 2332, 2498, 2564, 2715, 2744, 3052, 3455, and 4279.

58. Blanton, *Signs of Devotion*, chapter 4.

59. In fact, Marie uses *aventure* and the verb *avenir* numerous times throughout the *Audree,* especially when she recounts the miracles, to which she often refers as *aventure.*

Bibliography

Baum, Richard. *Recherches sur les œuvres attribuées à Marie de France.* Heidelberg: Carl Winter, 1968.

Blanton, Virginia. *Signs of Devotion: The Cult of St. Ethelthryth in Medieval England, 695-1615.* University Park: Pennsylvania State University Press, 2007.

Burgess, Glyn S. *Marie de France: An Analytical Bibliography.* London: Grant and Cutler, 1977. Supplement no. 1, 1986. Supplement no. 2, 1997. Supplement no. 3, 2007.

Busby, Keith. *Codex and Context: Reading Old French Verse Narrative in Manuscript.* 2 vols. Amsterdam: Rodopi, 2002.

Haren, Michael, and Yolande de Pontfarcy. *The Medieval Pilgrimage to St. Patrick's Purgatory: Lough Derg and the European Tradition.* Enniskillen, Ireland: Clogher Historical Society, 1988.

Kelly, Douglas. *The Art of Medieval French Romance.* Madison: University of Wisconsin Press, 1992.

Leonard, Bonnie H. "The Inscription of a New Audience: Marie de France's *Espurgatoire Saint Patriz.*" *Romance Languages Annual* 5 (1993): 57-62.

Levi, Ezio. "Sulla cronologia della opera di Maria di Francia." *Nuovi Studi Medievali* 1, no. 1 (1923): 41-72.

Mall, Eduard. *De aetate rebusque Mariae Francicae nova quaestio instituitur.* Halle, 1867.

Marie de France. *The Espurgatoire Seint Patriz of Marie de France with a Text of the Latin Original.* Ed. T. A. Jenkins. Chicago: Decennial Publications of the University of Chicago, 1903.

———. *Das Buch von Espurgatoire S. Patrice der Marie de France und seine Quelle.* Ed. Karl Warnke. Halle: Niemeyer, 1938.

———. *Marie de France, L'Espurgatoire Seint Patriz: Nouvelle édition critique accompagnée du De Purgatorio Sancti Patricii (ed. de Wernke), d'une introduction, d'une traduction, de notes et d'un glossaire.* Ed. and trans. Yolande de Pontfarcy. Louvain: Peeters, 1995.

McCash, June Hall. "*La vie seinte Audree*: A Fourth Text by Marie de France?" *Speculum* 77, no. 3 (2002): 744-77.

Mickel, Emanuel J., Jr. *Marie de France.* New York: Twayne, 1974.

Owen, D. D. R. *The Vision of Hell: Infernal Journeys in Medieval French Literature.* Edinburgh: Scottish Academic Press, 1970.

Whalen, Logan E. "*Ex libris Mariae*: Courtly Book Iconography in the Illuminated Manuscripts of Marie de France." In *Courtly Arts and the Art of Courtliness,* ed. Keith Busby and Christopher Kleinhenz, 745-53. Woodbridge, UK: Boydell & Brewer, 2006.

FURTHER READING

Criticism

Bruckner, Matilda Tomaryn. "'Le Fresne''s Model for Twinning in the *Lais* of Marie de France." *MLN* 121 (2006): 946-60.

Examines the literal and metaphoric meanings of the motif of twins in the *Lais,* also relating these to Marie's understanding of her craft as a writer.

Burgwinkle, William E. "Queering the Celtic: Marie de France and the Men Who Don't Marry." In *Sodomy, Masculinity, and Law in Medieval Literature: France and England, 1050-1230,* pp. 138-69. Cambridge: Cambridge University Press, 2004.

Explores the theme of homosexuality in Marie's *Lais,* especially "Guigemar," "Lanval," and "Bisclavret"; Burgwinkle attributes this motif partially to Marie's use of Celtic sources and partially to the suspicion surrounding the male-male bond reinforced by the chivalric code.

Howie, Cary. "Nothing Between." In *Claustrophilia: The Erotics of Enclosure in Medieval Literature,* pp. 123-38. London: Palgrave, 2007.

Brief treatment of the theme of enclosure in "Yonec" and "Guigemar" within a lengthier discussion of the same motif in the *Revelation* of Julian of Norwich, a fourteenth-century female mystic.

Maréchal, Chantal, ed. *The Reception and Transmission of the Works of Marie de France, 1774-1974.* Lewiston, N.Y.: Edwin Mellen Press, 2003, 360 p.

Collection of Marie scholarship, with each chapter dedicated to a critic or editor who made a significant contribution to the development of Marie de France studies, from the eighteenth century onward. Essay writers include Karen K. Jambeck, R. Howard Bloch, Emanuel J. Mickel, Jr., June Hall McCash, and Hans R. Runte.

Mickel, Emanuel J., Jr. *Marie de France.* New York: Twayne Publishers, 1974, 188 p.

   Critical and background study of Marie widely praised for making her works accessible to general readers. Mickel comments on unresolved questions concerning Marie's biography and sources; focusing on the *Lais,* he regrets the lack of critical attention accorded her other writings because of their classification as "translations."

Sansone, Giuseppe E. "Some Poetical Structure in the *Lais* of Marie de France." *Esperienze Letterarie* 25, no. 2 (April-June 2000): 3-13.

   Describes the salient features of Marie's *Lais,* including elements of realism supernaturalism, didacticism, and themes of courtly love and predestination.

Spiegel, Harriet. "The Male Animal in the Fables of Marie de France." In *Medieval Masculinities: Regarding Men in the Middle Ages,* edited by Clare A. Lees, with the assistance of Thelma Fenster and Jo Ann McNamara, pp. 111-26. Minneapolis: University of Minnesota Press, 1994.

   Illustrates how Marie provides a personal, feminine, and medieval slant on classical fables.

Additional coverage of Marie's life and career is contained in the following sources published by Gale: *Classical and Medieval Literature Criticism,* **Vol. 8;** *Dictionary of Literary Biography,* **Vol. 208;** *Feminist Writers*; *Literature Resource Center*; *Poetry Criticism,* **Vol. 22; and** *Reference Guide to World Literature,* **Eds. 2, 3.**

Rufinus

c. 345-410

(Also known as Rufinus of Aquileia and Tyrannius Rufinus) Italian translator and religious writer.

INTRODUCTION

As one of the best known translators of early Christian texts from Greek to Latin, Rufinus exerted considerable influence on the shaping of Western theological thought. His religious orthodoxy was challenged by Jerome, a onetime friend and fellow translator; the resulting controversy ended their friendship and tarnished the reputation of Rufinus for centuries. In addition to his translations, Rufinus wrote a historically significant commentary on the Apostles' Creed and various treatises in defense of his theological integrity.

BIOGRAPHICAL INFORMATION

Rufinus was born in Concordia, near Aquileia (in present-day Italy), around 345; his parents are believed to have been Christians. At the age of fifteen he was sent to Rome to be educated. While there he became acquainted with Jerome, who would become a friend and colleague until personal and theological conflicts turned the two into bitter adversaries. Rufinus returned to Aquileia some years later, where he was baptized around the year 370. He and Jerome were both part of a group of ascetics guided by Chromatius, Bishop of Aquileia, until 372. After the group disbanded, Rufinus traveled to Egypt, where he became acquainted with other ascetics in the desert and heard lectures given by Didymus, who taught the early Christian doctrines of Origen. Around 378 Rufinus traveled to Palestine, gathering other monks to form a monastery in Jerusalem, where he studied Greek religious texts and lived a contemplative life. In 386 Jerome arrived in Bethlehem and the friendship between the two men was renewed. Ordained a priest in 390 by John, Bishop of Jerusalem, Rufinus soon found himself involved in the controversy over Origenism that would cause a lifelong breach between himself and Jerome.

The ecclesiastical teachings of Origen of Alexandria were considered heretical by the influential Bishop Epiphanus of Salamis, in Cyprus, who demanded in 393 that the bishops in Palestine refute and condemn Origenism. Both Rufinus and Jerome had been admirers of Origen, but Jerome now turned against his teachings, opening a rift among religious scholars in Palestine. Some sided with Rufinus and John, Bishop of Jerusalem; others were allied with Jerome and his followers. In 397 Theophilus of Alexandria negotiated a fragile truce among the theologians; shortly thereafter, Rufinus left to return to Aquileia, carrying with him a collection of Greek manuscripts containing Eastern Christian writings. During a sojourn in Rome, he began translating these into Latin. In 399 he arrived in Aquileia, where he remained until 407, when he fled to Rome to escape the Gothic invasions. He migrated several more times, settling finally in Sicily, where he died in 410.

TEXTUAL HISTORY

During the fourth century, translations of works from one language to another were not expected to be literal. Instead, translators were allowed significant interpretive liberty, but critics often charged that the essential meaning of an ecclesiastical work was deliberately misrepresented or altered inappropriately by the translator. Concerns over defining and maintaining orthodoxy during the first centuries of Christendom frequently led to theological infighting, and campaigns of polemic and intrigue were mounted to promote or suppress teachings set forth by competing factions. By the time Rufinus began translating ecclesiastical writings, the Greek language was becoming less important in the West, so many of the teachings of the Christian patriarchs were not known to scholars until they became translated into Latin. As multiple translations were produced to meet growing interest, vehement arguments arose over orthodoxy and accuracy.

MAJOR WORKS

Although Rufinus is best remembered as a translator, he likely began his literary work around 397 with the original treatise *De adulteratione librorum Origenis*, a defense of Origen's doctrines. The work, which was published along with a translation of Pamphilus's *Apologia* in defense of Origen, is significant among Christian ecclesiastical writings because it preserves the only record of one of Origen's letters in his own defense. Much of Rufinus's work was devoted to the works of Origen, from the doctrinal text *De Principiis* (*On First Principles*), which he translated in 398, to the various teachings categorized as homilies, the translation of which occupied Rufinus until his death. Rufinus's original writings include his *Commentarius in symbolum Apostolorum* (404; *Commentary on the Apostles' Creed*), which is considered noteworthy as a historical marker of fourth-century religious practice as well as an influential document in shaping church theology during the following century.

Rufinus translated Eusebius's multivolume *Historia Ecclesiastica* (*Ecclesiastical History*) and added sections to cover events that occurred between 324 and 395. This work was used by scholars for centuries following Rufinus's death. Some of his translations of lesser works were later found to have been erroneously attributed, although the errors appear to be traceable to faulty oral transmission of the day, which later scholarship has been able to correct, rather than to any deliberate failure by Rufinus to properly credit the original authors. As well, the *Historia Monachorum in Aegypto sive De vitis patrum* (c. 398), long attributed to Rufinus as an original work, is now known to be his translation of the writings of an anonymous monk.

CRITICAL RECEPTION

In an 1892 essay covering the life and works of Rufinus, Philip Schaff and Henry Wace wrote that he was known to scholars of that era primarily because of his ill-fated relationship to fellow translator Jerome. While Jerome survived the Origenist controversy with his reputation for orthodoxy intact, Rufinus was never able to fully rehabilitate his theological standing with the patriarchs of the church during his lifetime. In the centuries that followed, when independent scholarship on ecclesiastical matters simply didn't exist, the rhetoric of church historians and patriarchs depicted Rufinus as a scoundrel and a heretic. Yet, as Schaff and Wace pointed out, neither they nor later scholars of church history would have had direct knowledge of many of the early works of Christendom if Rufinus had not translated them. They suggest, too, that the survival of Rufinus's translations through the Dark Ages and the Middle Ages may have been due to the very lack of critical scholarship that left his reputation tarnished through those centuries: if church historians had known that the texts they were using were attributable to Rufinus, they likely would have been destroyed. Calling it a "curious and important fact," Schaff and Wace note that all the works of translation prepared by Rufinus did survive to modern times. The same cannot be said of all of his original works, including letters referred to in the writings of his contemporaries.

In the mid-twentieth century, Francis X. Murphy wrote that Rufinus's value to the history of the church is in "the part he played in the promotion of western monasticism" and in his role in "the preservation of the works of Origen, while being principally responsible for making them available to the West." Noting that Rufinus was overshadowed by Jerome's personality and style, Philip J. Amidon asserts that while Rufinus possessed "an equally thorough mastery of Greek and a better sense of historiography," his historical original writings were weak due to a lack of source citation and an "unparalleled capacity for chronological errors." Critics, therefore, generally consider Rufinus's translations a greater contribution than his original writings, lauding his role in having preserved works of Greek antiquity.

PRINCIPAL WORKS

Apologia [translator; from Pamphilus's defense of Origen] (treatise) c. 397

De adulteratione librorum Origenis (treatise) c. 397

Instituta Monachorum and Homilies [translator; from the writings of Basil of Caesarea] (theology) c. 397-400

Opuscula [translator; from writings of Gregory of Nazianzus] (theology) c. 397-400

De Principiis [translator; from Origen's *On First Principles*] (treatise) c. 398

Historia Monachorum in Aegypto sive De vitis patrum [translator; from the writings of an anonymous monk] (history) c. 398

Apologia pro Fide Sua ad Anastasium Pontificem (treatise) c. 400

Homilies [translator; from the Homilies of Origen] (theology) c. 400-10

Sententiae [translator; from the writings of Sixtus] (theology) 400

Apologia s. Invectivarum in Hieronymum Libri II (treatise) c. 401

Historia Ecclesiastica [*Church History*] [translator; from the writings of Eusebius of Caesarea] (history) c. 402

Commentarius in symbolum Apostolorum [*Commentary on the Apostles' Creed*] (theology) 404

Recognitions [translator; from writings of Clementine] c. 406

De benedictionibus XII patriarchum libri II (preface) c. 408

Principal English Translations

Nicene and Post-Nicene Fathers, Series 2, Vol. 3 (edited by Philip Schaff and Henry Wace; contains translations of Rufinus's works except *Historia Monachorum in Aegypto*, *Historia Eccleistica*, and *De benedictionibus XII patriarchum*) 1892; reprinted 1979

The Lives of the Desert Fathers: Historia Monachorum in Aegypto (translated by Norman Russell) 1981

The Church History *of Rufinus of Aquileia* (edited by Philip R. Amidon) 1997

CRITICISM

Philip Schaff and Henry Wace (essay date 1892)

SOURCE: Schaff, Philip, and Henry Wace. "Prolegomena on the Life and Works of Rufinus." In *A Select Library of Nicene and Post-Nicene Fathers of the Christian Church (second series), Volume III—Theodoret, Jerome, Gennadius, Rufinus: Historical Writings, etc.,* edited by Philip Schaff and Henry Wace, translated by W. H. Fremantle, pp. 405-13. Grand Rapids, Mich.: Wm. B. Eerdmans Publishing Company, 1979.

[*In the following essay, originally published in 1892, Schaff and Wace present an overview of the life and works of Rufinus in their introduction to a nineteenth-century English translation of several of his works.*]

Tyrannius Rufinus is chiefly known from his relation to Jerome, first as an intimate friend and afterwards as a bitter enemy. The immense influence of Jerome, through all the ages in which criticism was asleep, has unduly lowered his adversary. But he has some solid claims of his own on our recognition. His work on the Creed, besides its intrinsic merits, must always be an authority as a witness to the state of the creed as held in the Italian churches in the beginning of the 5th century, as also to the state of the Canon and the Apocrypha at that time. And it is to his translations that we are indebted for our knowledge of many of the works of Origen, including the greatest of them all, the Περὶ Ἀρχῶν. We are the more grateful for his services because they were so opportune. The works of Origen, which had been neglected in the West for a century and to such an extent that the Pope Anastasius says (433) that he neither knows who he was nor what he wrote, came suddenly into notice in the last quarter of a century before Alaric's sack of Rome A.D. 385-410: and it was at this moment that Rufinus appeared, according to his friend Macarius' dream (439) like a ship laden with the merchandize of the East, an Italian who had lived some 25 years in Greek lands, and sufficiently equipped for the work of a translator. Through his labours during the last 13 years of that eventful time a considerable part of the works of the great Alexandrian have floated down across the ocean of the Dark Ages, and, while lost in their native Greek, have in their Latin garb come to enrich the later civilization of the West.

Rufinus was born at Concordia (Jer. Ep. v. 2. comp. with Ep. x. and De Vir. Ill. § 53) between Aquileia and Altinum, a place of some importance, which was destroyed by the Huns in 452 but afterwards rebuilt. His birth was about the year 344 or 345, he being slightly older than Jerome. Nothing is known of his education or the events of his youth; but that he was early acquainted with Jerome and was interested in sacred literature is seen from the fact that in 368 when Jerome went with Bonosus to Gaul, Rufinus begged him to copy for him the works of Hilary on the Psalms and on the Councils of the Church (Jer. Ep. v. 2). His mother did not die till the year 397, as is seen from Jerome's mention of her (Letter LXXXI, 1), and it would appear that both his parents were Christians. But he was not baptized till about his 28th year. He was at that time living at Aquileia, where he had embraced the monastic state, and was a member of the company of young ascetics to which Jerome and Bonosus belonged. The presence among them of Hylas (Jerome Letter III, 3) the freedman of Melania, the wealthy and ascetic Roman matron, shows that that relation had already begun which was afterwards of such importance in the life of Rufinus. It must have been just before the breaking up of that company that he was baptized, for Jerome, writing of him (Ep. iv. 2) in 374 from Antioch says "He has but lately been washed and is as white as snow." He himself gives a full account of his baptism in his Apology (436).

When this company of friends was scattered, Rufinus joined the noble Roman lady, Melania, in her pilgrimage to the East (Jer. Letter iv. 2). He visited the monasteries of Egypt, and apparently desired to remain there; but a persecution arose against the orthodox monks from Lucius the Arian bishop of Alexandria, seconded by the governor, both being prompted by the Arian Emperor Valens: the monasteries were in many cases broken up (Sozomen, vi, 19, Socrates iv, 21-3, Rufinus Eccl. Hist. ii, 3), and Rufinus himself for a while suffered imprisonment and was then banished from Egypt (430 Eccl. Hist. ii, 4). Rufinus probably on coming out of prison joined Melania who had then settled at Dio Cæsarea (Pallad. Hist. Laus. § 117) on the coast of Palestine for the purpose of making a home for the Egyptian exiles on their way to their various destinations. He states in his Apology (466) that he was 6 years in Egypt, and that he returned there again, after an interval, for two years more. He was a pupil both of Didymus, then head of the catechetical school, who wrote for him a treatise on the death of infants (534), and of Theophilus, afterward Bishop of Alexandria (528), and that he saw many of the well-known hermits

(466), such as Serapion and Macarius, whom he describes in his History of the Monks. Whether Melania returned with him to Egypt, or whether she went to Jerusalem, we do not know: it is also uncertain whether a journey which he made (Eccl. Hist. ii. 8) to Edessa was undertaken at this time. The date of the settlement of Melania on the Mount of Olives according to Jerome's Chronicle is 379, or, according to our present reckoning of dates, 377. We may suppose that Rufinus joined her in 379. This was his home for eighteen years, till the year 397.

Rufinus was ordained at Jerusalem, probably about the time when John, with whom he was closely connected, succeeded Cyril in the Bishopric (A.D. 386). The great resources of Melania were added to his own which seem to have been not inconsiderable. He built habitations for monks on the Mount of Olives, and employed them in learned pursuits, and in copying manuscripts. On the arrival of Jerome at Bethlehem, the old friendship was renewed, though not apparently with all its former warmth. Jerome certainly at times visited Rufinus and once at least stayed with him (465), and he and his friends brought MSS. to be copied by the monks of the Mount of Olives (465). He gave lectures on Christian writers and doctrine, of which a satirical account is given at a later period by Jerome[1] in his letter to Rusticus (cxxv, § 18). The nick-name Grunnius which he there gives him was probably caused by some trick of the voice. But we may gather from Jerome that he read the Greek church writers diligently and lectured upon them, a study which enabled him to do much good work at a later time. It is probable that he lectured in Greek, since he says in 397 that his Latin was weak through disuse (439). We may set against Jerome's depreciatory description the account given by Palladius (Hist. Laus. § 118). "Rufinus, who lived with Melania, was a man of congenial spirit, and of great nobility and strength of character. No man has ever been known of greater learning or of gentler disposition." Palladius also speaks of the princely hospitality of Melania and Rufinus: "They received," he says, "bishops and monks, virgins and matrons and helped them out of their own funds: They passed their life offending none and being helpers of the whole world." It is said by Palladius that he had heard from Melania that she had been present at the death of Pambas in Egypt which took place in the year 385, and it is probable that Rufinus accompanied her on this occasion. He himself records[2] a journey which he made to Edessa and Charrhoe, when he saw settlements of the monks like those which he had previously seen in Egypt. But the date of this journey does not appear. It may have been undertaken in order to visit some of the exiles from Egypt before his establishment on the Mt. of Olives. He records also the visits of the remarkable men who were entertained by him; Bacurius, who had been king of the Ubii, and afterwards count of the

Domestics under Theodosius, and was governor or duke of Palestine when Rufinus settled there; and Ædesius the companion of Frumentius the Missionary to the tribes in the N. W. of India. But his chief interest and occupation throughout seems to have been with his monks at Mt. Olivet with perhaps some connection with the diocesan work of his friend John, the Bp. of Jerusalem. Palladius records that Rufinus and Melania were the means of restoring to the communion of the church 400 monks. What was this schism, which Palladius describes as being "on account of Paulinus"? It is probable that the words relate to the monks of Bethlehem whose alienation from the Church of Jerusalem had been due to the ordination of Paulinian, Jerome's brother, by Epiphanius. We know that Rufinus before leaving Palestine was reconciled to Jerome (Jer. Ap. iii. 26, 33); and we know also that Jerome's book against John, Bishop of Jerusalem, which describes the schism was suddenly broken off;[3] and that he remained from that time forward at one with his Bishop. We may be allowed to believe that the influence of Melania as well as Rufinus had been exerted for some time previously to bring about this happy result.

Rufinus' part in the controversy thus terminated is partly known and partly the subject of inference. The original source of discord is not known. It is possible that Rufinus, who had been mentioned by Jerome in his Chronicle (A.D. 378) as being, together with Florentius and Bonosus, a specially distinguished monk, did not find himself included in his friend's Catalogue of Church writers (De Vir. Ill.) published at Bethlehem. When Aterbius began the Origenist troubles at Jerusalem, Rufinus, who treated him with merited scorn (Jer. Ap. iii, 33) probably felt some resentment at Jerome who, by "giving satisfaction" to the heresy hunter, had countenanced his proceedings. Rufinus appears as Bishop John's adviser during the visit of Epiphanius (Jer. Letter li, 2, 6), as the chief of a chorus of presbyters who applauded their own bishop and derided Epiphanius as a "silly old man;"[4] and as present when Epiphanius remonstrated with his brother-bishop. He is also mentioned by Epiphanius in his letter to John (Jer. Letter li. 6) as holding an important place in the Church, "May God free you and all about you, especially the presbyter Rufinus, from the heresy of Origen, and all others." This sentence will suggest to all who are familiar with church-controversies a whole series of scenes in the schism which continued between Bethlehem and Jerusalem during the next five years. Jerome believed Rufinus to have injured him at every turn, to have procured the abstraction of a Manuscript of his from the house occupied by Fabiola on her visit to Bethlehem (Apol. iii, 4) perhaps to have been in league with Vigilantius (Comp. Jer. Ep. lxi, 3 with Apol. iii, 4, 19). But such insinuations have the appearance rather of the suspicions prompted by anger than of actual fact.

In any case they were condoned when the two old companions who had been so long parted by ecclesiastical strife met together at the Church of the Resurrection at a solemn eucharistic feast, and joined hands in token of reconciliation, and when Jerome accompanied his friend some way on his journey before their final parting (Jer. Vol. iii, 24).

He arrived in Italy, in company with Melania, early in the spring of 397. They were there received by Paulinus of Nola with great honour.[5] Melania went on at once to Rome; but Rufinus stopped at the monastery of Pinetum near Terracina. His welcome by the Abbot Urseius and the philosopher Macarius, and their request to him to translate various Greek books, amongst others the Περὶ Ἀρχῶν of Origen, are described in his Prefaces to the Benedictions of the Patriarchs, the Apology of Pamphilus and the translations of Origen (417, 418, 420, 439). The preface to Origen's chief work (427) had the worst and most lasting results. He says that, being aware of the odium attaching to the name of Origen, he had feared to translate the work: but that the example of Jerome (whom he does not name but whose great ability he extols) in translating Origen encourages him to follow in his steps. This Preface, with this translation of the Περὶ Ἀρχῶν, was published in Rome early in the year 398, Rufinus having moved there to stay with Melania. At Rome he lived in the circle of Melania, her son Publicola and his wife Albina, with their daughter the younger Melania and her husband Pinianus, to whom we may probably add the Pope Siricius, and certainly Apronianus, a young noble whom he speaks of as his son in the faith (435, 564). Jerome's friend Eusebius of Cremona was also in Rome, and on friendly terms with him (445). But on the appearance of the work of Origen with Rufinus' Preface, a great ferment arose leading to the violent controversy between Rufinus and Jerome which is described in the Preface to their Apologies (434, 482).

Meanwhile, Rufinus had left Rome probably in 398, having obtained the usual Literæ Formatæ from the Pope Siricius, who died that year, to introduce him to other churches.[6] We hear of him at Milan, where in the presence of the Bishop, Simplicianus,[7] he met Eusebius of Cremona, and heard him read out a letter of Theophilus containing some passages from the Περὶ Ἀρχῶν, against which he vehemently protested (490). He then, having probably visited his native city of Concordia, where his mother,[8] possibly his father also (430, 502) was still living, took up his abode at Aquileia. There he was welcomed by the bishop, Chromatius, by whom he had been baptized some 26 or 27 years before. Rufinus probably arrived at Aquileia in the beginning of 399, and remained there 9 or 10 years. It was during this period that all his principal works except the Commentary on the Benedictions of the patriarchs, the

translation of the Περὶ Ἀρχῶν and Pamphilus' Apology, and the book on the Adulterations of Origen were composed. It was soon after his settlement at Aquileia that he heard from Apronianus of the letter of Jerome to Pammachius and Oceanus[9] expressing his anger against him for the mention he had made of Jerome in the Preface to the Περὶ Ἀρχῶν. The conciliatory letter to Rufinus which accompanied this and which was an answer to a friendly one from Rufinus[10] was not sent on by Jerome's friends (489); and Rufinus, thinking that his old friend had completely turned against him, composed his *Apology* (434-482) which drew forth Jerome's reply (482-541). This controversy is placed in full before the reader of this volume in an English translation, with prefatory notes. It may therefore be treated very shortly here.

> Rufinus' *Apology* is an answer to Jerome's letter to Pammachius and Oceanus. It is addressed to Apronianus of Rome. He makes a profession of his Christian standing and faith, especially on the points raised by the Origenistic controversy; he describes the circumstances which had led him to translate the books of Origen, and defends his method of translation, which, he says, has been misrepresented by men sent from the East to lay snares for him. His method, he declares, was the same which had been used by Jerome, who boasted that through him the Latins knew all that was good in Origen and nothing of the bad. Where he found passages in Origen's writings, in flagrant contradiction to the orthodox opinion he had maintained elsewhere, he concluded that the passage had been falsified by heretics, and restored the more orthodox statement which he believed to have been originally there. He then turns round upon Jerome and points out that, in his Commentaries on the Ephesians, written some 10 years before, to which he specially referred in his Letter as showing his freedom from heresy, he had practically adopted the opinions now imputed to Origen as heretical, such as the fall of souls from a previous state into the prison house of earthly bodies, and the universal restoration of spiritual beings.

> In the second book he clears himself from the imputation of following Origen and Plato in believing in the lawfulness of using occasional falsehood in the government and training of men. But he imputes to his adversary a systematic use of falsehood in reference to his reading heathen authors, while he professed in his letter to Eustochium (Jer. Ep. xxii) to have solemnly promised never even to possess them. He then takes a wider view of Jerome's writings, showing how, in this Letter to Eustochium, his books against Jovinian, etc., he had by his satirical pictures held up to ridicule the various classes of Christians, clergy, monks, virgins: how he had praised Origen indiscriminately as a teacher second only to the Apostles: how he had defamed men like Ambrose, and therefore his present accusations were little worth: how he boasted of having taken as his teachers not only Origenists like Didymus or heretics like Apollinarius, but heathen like Porphyry, and had made his translation of the Old Testament under the influence of the Jew Baranina (whose name

Rufinus perverts into Barabbas). He concludes by summarizing his accusations and calling upon the reader to choose between him and his opponent.

This *Apology* was only sent to a few friends of Rufinus (530); but portions of it became known to Jerome's friends and his brother Paulinian (493) carried them to Bethlehem, together with Rufinus' *Apology* addressed to Pope Anastasius. Jerome had also before him the letter of Anastasius to John Bishop of Jerusalem (509) showing his dislike of Rufinus' proceedings. On these he grounds his own *Apology*, which was originally in two books and was addressed to Pammachius and Marcella A.D. 402.

In the first book he blames Rufinus' breach of friendship after the reconciliation which had taken place at Jerusalem; he then shows that he was compelled to translate the Περὶ Ἀρχῶν in order to show what it really was. He declares that the *Apology of Origen* translated by Rufinus as the work of Pamphilus was really written by Eusebius; that Origen had been condemned by Theophilus and Anastasius, by East and West alike, and by the decree of the Emperors. He defends himself for having used heathen and heretical teachers, and help of a Jewish scholar in translating the Old Testament. As to his Commentaries on the Ephesians he declares that he merely put side by side the opinions of various commentators, indicating at times his knowledge that some were heretical: and as to his anti-Ciceronian dream, he ridicules the idea that a man can be bound by his night visions.

In the second book he criticizes Rufinus' *Apology* addressed to Anastasius as to both its style and its matter, and blames him for his treatment of Epiphanius, and endeavours to implicate him in the imputation of heresy. He then defends his translation of the Old Testament, showing by copious quotations from the Prefaces to the Books that he had done nothing condemnatory of the Septuagint, whose version he had himself translated into Latin and constantly used in familiar expositions.

This Apology was brought to Rufinus at Aquileia by a merchant who was leaving again in two days (522). Chromatius no doubt urged him, as he urged Jerome (520) not to continue the controversy and he yielded. He wrote, however, a private letter to Jerome, which has been lost, sending him an accurate copy of his *Apology*, and while declining public controversy, yet declaring that he could have said even more than before, and divulged things which would have been worse to Jerome than death. Jerome in his answer written A.D. 403, which forms B. iii of his Apology, declares that the controversy is Rufinus' fault, and defends his friends for their conduct towards him, even in holding back the conciliatory letter written in 399; but shows how a way might still be open for friendship. He touches again upon most of the points dwelt on in the previous books, defending himself and accusing Rufinus, and ends by declaring that his bitter reply was necessitated first by Rufinus' threats, and secondly by his abhorrence of heresy, from all complicity with which he must at any price clear himself.

This book closed the controversy. Rufinus did not reply, Jerome did not relent. Nothing in Rufinus' subsequent writings reflects on Jerome; but Jerome is never weary of expressing his hatred of Rufinus, speaking of him after his death as "the Scorpion"[11] and writing malignant satirical descriptions of him like that in his letter to Rusticus.[12]

It may be observed, however, that notwithstanding the violent words used on both sides, it was possible for eminent churchmen to esteem and befriend both parties. Augustine, on receiving Jerome's Apology, laments, in words which must have been felt by Jerome as a severe reproach, that two such men, so loved by the churches, should thus tear each other to pieces. Chromatius, while he kept up communications with Jerome, and supplied him with funds for his literary work, was also the friend and adviser of Rufinus.

Rufinus' friends at Aquileia, like those at the Pinetum and at Rome, were anxious to gain from him a knowledge of the great church-writers of the East, and especially of Origen. No one at Aquileia seems to have known Greek. He makes excuses in his Prefaces (430, 563, 565, etc.) for the difficulty of the task and his own short-comings which seem to be partly conventional, partly genuine. But he did a work which he alone or almost alone at that period was qualified to do. His translations of Origen and Pamphilus were already known. We learn from Jerome (536) that Rufinus had translated parts of the LXX. He now translated Eusebius' Church History, and added to it two books of his own; he translated the so-called Recognitions of Clement, which till then were almost unknown in Italy. He wrote a History of the Monks of the East, partly from personal knowledge, partly from what he had heard or read of them. And he translated the Commentaries of Origen upon the Heptateuch or 1st seven books of Scripture, except Numbers and Deuteronomy; and those on the Epistle to the Romans. He also wrote his exposition of the Creed (541-563), and probably some other works which have not come down to us.

The first part of his stay at Aquileia was troubled by the controversy with Jerome. He also received from his friends at Rome the intelligence that his Preface and translation of the Περὶ Ἀρχῶν had been brought to the notice of the Pope Anastasius, by Pammachius and Marcella (430); and probably the letter of the Pope to Venerius Bishop of Milan, which is quoted in Anastasius' letter to John of Jerusalem (433) was also brought to his knowledge. Though there is no reason to suppose, as has been often done, that the Pope passed sentence upon him, still less that he summoned him to Rome. Rufinus was so far affected by what he heard of the adverse feeling excited in the Pope's mind toward him that he thought it desirable to write an explanation or apology (430-2) vindicating his action in the translation of Origen, and giving an exposition of his own belief on some of the principal points dealt with in the Περὶ Ἀρχῶν. From the letter of Anastasius to John of Jerusalem we gather that John had written to him in the interest of Rufinus, and had blamed Jerome's friends at Rome, perhaps also Jerome himself, for the part they had taken in reference to him. It is a curious fact that this letter was known to Jerome but not to Rufinus during the controversy (509); but it can hardly be inferred with any certainty from this that John had changed sides and favoured Jerome at Rufinus' expense.

After 8 or 9 years at Aquileia Rufinus returned to Rome. His friend Chromatius of Aquileia had died in 405. Anastasius of Rome had also passed away A.D. 402), and his successor Innocentius was without prejudice against Rufinus. Melania was either there or with Paulinus at Nola. Her son Publicola had died in 406, but his widow Albina was with her, and her granddaughter the younger Melania with her husband Pinianus. The siege of Rome by Alaric was impending, and the whole party were starting by way of Sicily and Africa, in both of which Melania had property, intending eventually to reach Palestine. He joined their "religious company" as he tells us in the Preface to Origen on Numbers (568) which, according to Palladius (Hist. Laus. 119) formed a vast caravan with slaves, virgins and eunuchs; and he was with them in Sicily when Alaric burned Rhegium (568) the flames of which they saw across the straits.

This translation of Numbers was his last work. He was at that time suffering in his eyes; and he died soon afterwards in Sicily, as we learn from Jerome's malicious words "The Scorpion now lies underground between Enceladus and Porphyrion."[13] The undying hatred of Jerome towards him has unduly lowered him in the estimation of the Church. He was far below Jerome in literary ability, but in their great controversy he displayed more magnanimity than his rival, being willing to forego a public answer to his provoking apology. He was highly esteemed by the eminent churchmen of his time and the Bishops near whom he lived. Chromatius of Aquileia was his friend; for Petronius of Bologna he wrote his monastic history, for Gaudentius of Brixia he translated the Clementine Recognitions, for Laurentius (perhaps of his native Concordia) he composed his work on the Creed. Paulinus of Nola continued his friendship for him to the end. Above all Augustine speaks of him as the object of love and of honour; and, in his reply to Jerome[14] who had sent him his Apology, says: "I grieved, when I had read your book, that such discord should have arisen between persons so dear and so intimate, bound to all the churches by a bond of affection and of renown."

We may conclude this notice by two quotations from writers who lived shortly after the death of Rufinus; the first of which shows how unfairly the fame of Jerome

has pressed on the memory of his antagonist, while the second may be taken as the verdict of unprejudiced history. Pope Gelasius, at a Council at Rome in 494, drew up a list of books to be received in the church, in which he says of Rufinus: "He was a religious man, and wrote many books of use to the Church, and many commentaries on the Scripture; but, since the most blessed Jerome infamed him on certain points, we take part with him (Jerome) in this and in all cases in which he has pronounced a condemnation." (Migne's Patrologia vol. lix. col. 175). On the other hand Gennadius, in his list of Ecclesiastical writers (c. 17) says: "Rufinus, the presbyter, of Aquileia, was not the least of the church-teachers, and showed an elegant genius in his translations from Greek into Latin;" and, after giving a list of his writings, he continues: "He also replied in two volumes to him who decried his works, showing convincingly that he had exercised his powers through the might which God had given him, and for the good of the church, and that it was through a spirit of rivalry that his adversary had employed his pen in defaming him."

WORKS OF RUFINUS

I. ORIGINAL WORKS WHICH STILL SURVIVE

1. **A Commentary on the Benedictions of the 12 Patriarchs.** This short work was composed at the monastery of Pinetum near Terracina during Lent in the year 398, at the request of Paulinus of Nola. Rufinus had stayed with Paulinus on his first arrival with Melania in Italy (Paulinus. Ep. xxix, 12.) and Paulinus wrote to him (417) after he had gone to Pinetum begging him to give an explanation of the blessing of Jacob in Judah. Rufinus, though not replying for a time, sent his exposition, and afterwards, on a second request from Paulinus, added the exposition of the rest of the blessings in the Patriarchs, like the son in the parable (as he explains in a graceful letter prefixed to the work) who said "I go not," but afterwards repented and went.

The exposition is well written and clear; but it is not in itself of much value. The text on which he comments is very faulty: for instance, in the Blessing of Reuben, instead of the words "the excellency of dignity and the excellency of power," it has "*durus conversationc, et durus, temerarius.*" When Rufinus adheres to the plain interpretation of the passage his comments are sensible and clear; but he soon passes to the mystic sense: Reuben is God's first-born people, the Jews, and the couch which he defiles is the law of the Old Testament; and the moral interpretation is grounded on the supposed meaning of Reuben, "the Son who is seen," that is the visible, carnal man, who breaks through the law. So, in Judah's "binding his foal to the vine," the explanation given, as he says, by the Jews, that the vines will be so plentiful that they are used even for tying up the young colts, is dismissed. The foal is the Christian Church the offspring of Israel which is God's ass, and is bound to Christ the true vine.

2. *A Dissertation on the Adulteration of the Works of Origen by Heretics,* subjoined to his translation of Pamphilus Apology for Origen. This will be found in [Freemantle, W. H. *A Select Library of Nicene and Post-Nicene Fathers of the Christian Church,* Vol. III. Grand Rapids, MI: Eerdmans, 1979] pp. 421-427.

3. *An Apology Addressed to the Pope Anastasius.* See the introductory note prefixed to the translation of this work (429) now first translated into English.

4. *The Apology for Himself against the Attacks of Jerome.* See the introductory statement prefixed to the translation (434-5).

5. *Ecclesiastical History in Two Books,* being a continuation of the History of Eusebius translated by Rufinus into Latin. This work was composed at Aquileia at the request of the Bishop, Chromatius. The date is probably 401, since in the Preface Rufinus says that he had been requested to translate Eusebius at the time when Alaric was invading Italy. This must allude to the first of Alaric's invasions, in 400, since the second invasion (402) would have been marked by some word such as "Iterum," and at the 3d in 408 Chromatius had already died. The history does not attempt to give more than the chief events, and these are told with little sense of proportion, the Council of Ariminum occupying about 20 lines, while the story of the right arm of Arsenius which Athanasius was accused of cutting off takes up five times that space. Some documents of great importance, however, are given, such as the canons of Nicæa, and the Creed as it issued from the council. But there is much credulity, as shown in the account of the Discovery of the True Cross by Helena mother of Constantine, and the stories of the death of Arius and the attempted rebuilding of the Jewish Temple under Julian. Rufinus has none of the critical power needed for a true historian. We may add that all that is valuable in his history is incorporated into the works of Socrates (translated in Vol. iii. of this Series). See especially B. ii, c. 1.

6. *The History of the Monks* which is a description of the Egyptian Solitarier appears to have no mark of its date: But it was, no doubt, composed at Aquileia between 398 and 409, probably in the later part of that period. It was written in the name of Petronius Bishop of Bologna, and records his experiences, which he says he had been often requested by the monks of Mt. Olivet to commit to writing. It is full of strange stories like those in Jerome's Lives of the Hermits Hilarion and

Malchus.[15] There is often a verbal resemblance between this book and the Lausiac History of Palladius; indeed, they at times record the same adventures (compare the story of the crocodiles, Ruf. Hist. Mon. xxxiii. 6 with Pall. Hist. Laus. cl., where even the same prayers and texts are put into the mouths of the two narrators.) But it is probable that in these cases Palladius is indebted to Rufinus.

7. *The Exposition of the Creed* is described in the note prefixed to the Translation (541).

8. *The Prefaces to the Books of Origen,* translated by Rufinus, and to the *Apology of Pamphilus for Origen,* together with the *Book on the Adulteration of Origen's Writings* are given in this volume (420-427). That to the Περὶ Ἀρχῶν (427) is the document on which the great controversy between Jerome and Rufinus turns. That to Numbers gives personal details of importance, while the Peroration to the Ep. to the Romans exhibits the method used in translating. The Preface and Epilogue to the work of Pamphilus are of great importance in connexion with the controversy between Jerome and Rufinus.

II. TRANSLATIONS FROM GREEK WRITERS

1. *The Rule of St. Basil,* translated at Pinetum for the Abbat Urseius in 397 or 398. This was the first work written by Rufinus of which we have any knowledge.

2. *The Apology of Pamphilus for Origen.* This formed the 1st book of an Apology for Origen's teaching in 6 books, which were composed by Eusebius and Pamphilus during the latter's imprisonment at Cæsarea previous to his martyrdom. Eusebius speaks of this work in a general way (H. E. vi. 33) as written by himself and Pamphilus. The last book, however, was written by Eusebius alone after the death of Pamphilus. The part translated by Rufinus is only the 1st book, and this he believed to be by Pamphilus alone. Jerome in his Apology (487, 514) asserted that the whole was by Eusebius alone. But his bitter feeling led him astray in this. The Apology for Origen has perished with the exception of this 1st book which survives in Rufinus' Translation. The Preface which he prefixed to the work, and the Epilogue which he subjoined to it under the name of *The Book Concerning the Adulteration of the Works of Origen* are given in our translation (420-427). This work was written at Pinetum near Terracina at the request of Macarius, to whom the Preface is addressed, in the end of 397 or the beginning of 398. For the questions relating to the authorship of the Apology the reader is referred to the Apologies of Jerome and Rufinus (esp. pp. 487, 514), to Lightfoot's Article on Eusebius in the Dict. of Eccl. Biography, and the Prolegomena to the Translation of Eusebius in this Series, p. 36.

3. *Origen's* Περὶ 'Αρχων. This translation was also made at the request of Macarius, and was finished as the Preface to B. iii. shows in the Lent of 398. The questions raised by this Translation are discussed in the Introductions to the Works of Jerome (Vol. vi of this Series), and of Rufinus in this Volume; and the controversy itself is developed in their Apologies (434-540). The greater part of the Περὶ 'Αρχων is known to us only through this translation.

4. *Origen's Homilies.* Those on *the Books of Moses and of Joshua* were translated at various times during the last 10 years of Rufinus' life. He had intended, as he states in his Preface to the Book of Numbers, to translate all that had been written by Origen on the Pentateuch: he accomplished this as regards the first three books, and also as to the book of Joshua, at the request of Chromatius; the book of Numbers he only finished in Sicily, just before his death; and the Commentaries on Deuteronomy he did not live to translate. In these translations, as he tells us (567), he did not scruple to supply what he found to be omitted in the Greek, the Homilies being of a hortatory kind, whereas Rufinus' object was an exposition of the text.

The Translation of the *Homilies on Judges,* though there is no Preface to it, is ascribed to Rufinus by Fontanini, who maintains that in this case, the name of Rufinus being discredited on account of Jerome's diatribe against him, the editors have suppressed the Preface, while in some other cases they have substituted the name of Jerome for that of Rufinus.

The Translation of **Origen's** *Commentary on the 36th, 37th and 38th Psalms* is unquestionably by Rufinus; it is dedicated to Apronianus, and may have been written in Rome (Fontanini col. 188, beginning of ch. viii). The Preface is given by us in this volume. Fontanini also gives to Rufinus a Translation of Origen's Homilies on 1 Kings and on Canticles. The books on Joshua and Judges he translated as he found them (567), but in the next he adopted a different method.

The works of Origen on the Ep. to the Romans were very long, and Rufinus did not scruple to condense them (reducing the 25 books of Origen to 10), as he clearly states in his Peroration (567). This work he addressed to Heraclius, and it was composed during his stay at Aquileia.

Rufinus had hoped, as we learn from the same Peroration (567), to translate some at least of the Commentaries of Origen upon the other Epistles of St. Paul; but he first determined to finish those upon the Pentateuch, a task in which, as we have seen, he was overtaken by death.

5. *The Translation of 10 Tracts of St. Basil and 8 of Gregory Nazianzen.* These are to be found in the works of Basil and Gregory, but without Prefaces; they are, however, mentioned by Rufinus himself in his Eccl. Hist. ii. 9, and in a letter to Apronianus quoted by Fontanini Vit. Ruf. II., viii, I. col. 189.

6. *The Sentences of Xystus,* which have been variously attributed to a philosopher who flourished in the reign of Augustus, and is quoted by Seneca, and to Xystus, or Sixtus, Bp. of Rome, who suffered martyrdom in 258. They are called the Annulus ('εγχειρίδιον) as inseparable from the hand. Rufinus speaks of them in his Preface, translated in this volume, as being traditionally ascribed to the Bishop; he does not pledge himself to this opinion, but does not deny it; and recent research has shown that, though they may have a basis in heathen philosophy, they are in their present form the writings of a Christian. Jerome, however, scoffs at Rufinus again and again, as either through ignorance or heterodoxy ascribing to a Christian Bishop and martyr the work of a Pythagorean (See Jerome ad Ctesiphontem (Ep. cxxxiii. c. 3), Comm. on Ezek. B. vi. ch. 8, on Jerem. B. iv. ch. 22. The whole matter is fully discussed in Dict. of Christian Biog. Art. Xystus.)

7. *The Sentences of Evagrius Ponticus (or Iberita or Galatus)* in three treatises, (1) *to Virgins,* (2) *To Monks,* (3) *On the Passionless State.* These are described with bitter depreciation as heretical works by Jerome (Ad Ctes. Ep. 133 c. 3. Pref. to Anti-Pelagian Dialogue and to B. iv. of Comm. on Jerem.) but approved by Gennadius (c. 9.) who issued an amended version of Rufinus' translation. Rufinus' translation is said to be in the Vatican library by Fontanini (Vita Rufini Lib. II. c. iv. in Migne's Patrologia Vol. 21 col. 205.)

8. *The Recognitions of Clement* supposed to have been written by Clement Bishop of Rome, but now known to be a work of 50 or 60 years later. The translation of it was asked for by Silvia sister of Rufinus the Prætorian Prefect, and was unsuccessfully attempted by Paulinus of Nola (see his letter to Rufinus in Fontanini as above, col. 208.) After the death of Silvia, Gaudentius Bp. of Brixia where she died as a saint, urged Rufinus to make the translation (Peror. to Ep. to Rom. 567) Preface of Rufinus.)

9. The translation of *Eusebius' Eccl. History* in 9 books, a work much valued in Gaul, and often reprinted in later times. The Preface (Migne's Rufinus col. 461) is addressed to Chromatius, and says that it was demanded by him at the time of Alaric's invasion of Italy (A.D. 400) as an antidote to the unsettlement of men's minds. Rufinus speaks humbly of himself as having little practice in Latin writing. He says that he has

compressed the 10th book which contained little of real history, and added what remained of it to Book 9. See Prolegomena to Eusebius in this Series Vol. i p. 54.

It is a curious and important fact that all the translations known to have been made by Rufinus have survived. This is due no doubt to their being the only translations extant in the Middle Ages of great writers like Origen and Basil, and to the impossibility of procuring others. The uncritical spirit of the time may have been favourable to them. Had they been recognized as the works of Rufinus, they might have been destroyed; but it was possible, even after the revival of learning, to attribute many of them to Jerome.

Gennadius mentions a series of Rufinus' letters, which have not survived, amongst which were several of special importance addressed to Proba, a lady who is highly commended by Jerome in his letter to Demetrias.[16] Jerome also mentions (537) some translations of Rufinus from Latin into Greek, but his allusion is somewhat vague; and some translations from the LXX (536). A translation of Josephus, and a Commentary on the first 75 Psalms, and on Hosea, Joel and Amos, a Life of St. Eugenia and a Book on the Faith have been attributed to Rufinus but are believed not to be his. These, with the exception of the translation of Josephus, are given by Vallarsi in his edition of Rufinus. Besides these, translations of Origen's Seven Homilies on Matthew and one on John, and of his treatises on Mary Magdalen and on Christ's Epiphany have at times been attributed to Rufinus.

We do not propose to go minutely into the Bibliography of Rufinus' Works. Some of them were among the earliest printed books. The Editio Princeps of the **Commentary on the Creed,** bears date *Oxford, 1468,* but is commonly believed to be really of 1478; that of the **Ecclesiastical History,** *Paris, 1474*; that of the **History of the Monks,** undated, is believed to be of 1471; that of the *Commentaries of Origen* is of 1503 (Aldus Minutius); that of the *Sayings of Xystus* of 1507, and of the Περὶ Ἀρχῶν is of 1514 (Venice). They continued to be reprinted up to 1580; but, with the exception of the *Sayings of Xystus,* no further editions were published till the edition of Vallarsi (Verona, 1745), and the Life by Fontanini (Rome, 1742). Since that date, though various editions and translations of the **Expositions of the Creed** have appeared, no attempt has been made to give the whole of Rufinus' writings. Migne (Patrologia, Vol. xxi., Paris, 1849) is contented to reprint Vallarsi without alteration.

No complete edition of Rufinus' Works, therefore, exists. The volume of Migne's Patrologia (21) contains the Life by Fontanini (Rome, 1742), the Notice by Schœnemann (Leipzig, 1792), and Vallarsi's edition (Verona, 1745) of Rufinus' chief works, viz. The **Benedictions of the Patriarchs,** the **Commentary on the Creed,** the **Monastic History,** the **Ecclesiastical History,** the **Apology against Jerome,** and the **Apology Addressed to Anastasius.** Vallarsi had intended to edit the Translations from Greek writers, but did not accomplish this. The Prefaces to these translations, some of which are of great importance, have therefore to be sought by the student in the editions of the writers to whose works they are prefixed. They are collected and translated in this Volume for the first time.

We have in the present work not attempted to translate all the original works of Rufinus. We have omitted the **Exposition of the Benedictions of the Twelve Patriarchs,** the **Ecclesiastical History** and the **History of the Monks.** The rest we have given. They include his Apologies, together with the Letter of Pope Anastasius about him to John of Jerusalem, the Prefaces to the Περὶ Ἀρχῶν and the Apology of Pamphilus, and the Epilogue to the latter work, called the Dissertation on the adulteration of the Works of Origen, together with the Prefaces which are still extant to his Translations of Origen's Commentaries and his Peroration to Origen on Romans. We have also included his best-known work, his **Commentary on the Creed,** a translation of which has kindly been placed at our service by Dr. Heurtley, Lady Margaret Professor of Theology at Oxford.

Notes

1. "He came in with a slow and stately step; he spoke with a broken utterance, sometimes with a kind of disjointed sobs rather than words. He had a pile of tomes upon the table; and then, with a frown and a contraction of the nostrils, and his forehead wrinkled up, he snapped his fingers to call the attention of his audience. What he said had no depth in it; but he criticized others, and pointed out their defects, as though he would exclude them from the Senate of Christian teachers. He was rich, and entertained freely, and many flocked round him in his public appearances. He was as luxurious as Nero at home, as stern as Cato abroad; as full of contradictions as the Chimæra."

2. *Hist. Eccl.* ii. 8.

3. For the date of this work, see the Note prefixed to it in the translation of Jerome's works, Vol. vi. of this series.

4. See Jerome's expressions in his book "*Against John of Jerusalem*" c. 11, which evidently refer to Rufinus: "grinning like a dog and turning up his nose."

5. Paulinus Ep. xxix, 12.

6. Jer. Ep. cxxvii, 9 Ap. iii. 21.

7. Successor of Ambrose, and Bishop A.D. 397-400. See the Letter of Anastasius to him. Jer. Ep. xcv.

8. She died soon after. See Jerome Ep. lxxxi, 1.

9. Jer. Ep. lxxxiv.

10. See Jer. Ep. lxxxi, 1.

11. Jer. Ep. cxxvii. 10.

12. Jer. Ep. cxxv.

13. Jer. Pref. to Comm. on Ezek. B. I.

14. Aug. Letter 73 (In Jerome's Letters No. 110).

15. See those Lives translated in Vol. vi of this Series.

16. Letter cxxx, 7.

Francis X. Murphy (essay date 1945)

SOURCE: Murphy, Francis X. "Historical Preoccupations." In *Rufinus of Aquileia (345-411): His Life and Works,* pp. 158-85. Washington, D.C.: Catholic University of America Press, 1945.

[*In the excerpt below Murphy offers commentary on four historical works attributed to Rufinus: the translation of Eusebius's* Church History *plus its two-volume continuation by Rufinus, the* Historia monachorum in Aegypto sive devitis partum *and the* Commentarius in Symboum Apostolorum *(Commentary on the Apostles' Creed).*]

The Origenistic troubles, including the quarrel with Jerome, do not seem to have dominated the actual life of Rufinus, as they have overshadowed his place in history. At least they did not interfere with the quantity of the literary production, both original and translation work, that he had been engaged upon since his return to the West in 397, and which kept him occupied until his death in 410. Thus we find him late in 401[1]—probably not long after the completion of his *Apologia*—embarking upon a very important piece of translation: the *Ecclesiastical History of Eusebius.*[2] He undertook the work at the request of his own bishop, Chromatius of Aquileia. Then evidently grown interested in the endeavor, he decided to continue the history itself from midway in Constantine's reign, down to the death of Theodosius in 395; but first he abridged the tenth book of Eusebius, and inserted a long note on Gregory Thaumaturgus.[3]

Rufinus heads the work with a comparatively short but informative preface:

> It is said to be the custom of competent physicians, when they perceive an epidemic threatening their cities or countryside, to provide some medicine or (kind of)

drink whereby men may protect themselves from the impending destruction. Now you, my beloved father Chromatius, searching for some species of medicament at the moment when the gates of Italy have been broken through by Alaric, the commander of the Goths, and a pestiferous disease has poured in upon our fields and cattle and men, raising havoc throughout the land—you have sought a remedy against this cruelty and destruction. This you have done by enjoining upon me a Latin translation of the ecclesiastical history which was written in the Greek language by that most learned man, Eusebius of Caesarea. You believed that the minds of those who heard it read to them might be held so fast by it that, in their eager desire for the knowledge of past events, they should to a certain degree become oblivious of the evils taking place about them.

> When I tried to excuse myself from the task, as being rather weak and unequal to it and as having in the course of years lost use of the Latin tongue, I reflected that you demanded these things of me not without a certain right due to the apostolic institution (of your office).[4]

Rufinus goes on to compare this command of his bishop to the incident in the Gospel where our Lord, taking compassion on the hungering multitude, ordered the Apostles to "Give them to eat." He feels the comparison is quite apt in as far as he is about to feed the multitude with Philip's "twice-told five loaves"—the ten books of Eusebius—as well as with his own "two fishes."[5]

He then explains the course he has pursued in producing the work:

> It should be known that I have joined the tenth book of this work (since in the Greek it has little to do with the course of events, and almost all the rest of it is devoted to the panegyrics of bishops, adding nothing to our knowledge of facts) to the ninth, there embodying what little history it contained and omitting all that was superfluous: thus I have brought the narrative of Eusebius to a close.

> The tenth and eleventh books I myself have composed, partly from the traditions of our forebears and partly from facts within my own memory; and these I have added to the previous books, as the two fishes to the loaves. . . . The whole work now contains the events enacted in the Church from the Ascension of the Savior and then on; my own two books, those from the days of Constantine when the persecution came to an end, down to the death of the Emperor Theodosius.[6]

A comparatively recent attempt has been made to deny that Rufinus composed the last two books of the *Ecclesiastical History* which he claims as his own. In a monograph written in 1914[7] Anton Glas enunciated the theory that Rufinus had merely translated a work of Gelasius of Caesarea, enlarging upon it and publishing it in his own name. Glas' thesis seemed to receive all but general acceptance.[8] However, the Bollandist Paul

Peeters disposed of it somewhat summarily in 1932[9] and quite recently F. Diekamp has devoted to it what amounts to a definitive refutation.[10]

Among the principal proofs advanced by Glas was the hypothesis that the Bishop of Caesarea, Gelasius, had died in 395.[11] As various evidences of a Greek version of the two books of the *Ecclesiastical History* manifesting undeniable interdependence with the Latin books of Rufinus have come down to us under the name of Gelasius,[12] Glas naturally concluded that Rufinus' work, which was not produced before 402, must have been a translation.[13] In support of this chronological argument he adduced further proofs by pointing out the small value to be attributed to the literary tradition claiming the work for Rufinus;[14] by denying that Rufinus had ever produced an original work;[15] and by a long dissertation, comparing the Latin text with the Greek of both Gelasius of Caesarea and with two other Greek writers who made use of it, Georgius Monachos and Gelasius of Czyicos.[16]

Fortunately, in 1930 there appeared a monograph on the life of St. Porphyry, Bishop of Gaza, by H. Grégoire and M. A. Kugener,[17] which completely destroyed Glas' chronological argument by proving that the Vita *Porphyrii* of Mark the deacon, upon which the date of the death of Gelasius had been computed as of 395, was a sixth-century revision of the original *Vita* and completely unreliable.[18] Diekamp points out the fact that it is only in 405 that there is evidence of a new bishop in Caesarea, a certain Eulogius, to whom John Chrysostom then addressed a letter from exile, not knowing that this new bishop was on the side of the opposition.[19] Thus it appears that Gelasius lived on until 404, giving him ample time to have translated Rufinus' own history, which was produced in 402.

Beginning with Rufinus' own testimony, Diekamp next defends the literary tradition attributing the work to him,[20] and devotes considerable time to vindicating both the Commentary on the *Symbolum Apostolorum*[21] and the *Historia Monachorum*[22] as original productions of Rufinus. Finally he takes up the matter of the comparative study of the texts, demonstrating that the evidence produced can be used to indicate that Gelasius was the translator, and Rufinus the original author, just as easily as it can be made to prove the opposite.[23]

There can be little doubt now that Rufinus actually wrote books X and XI of the *Ecclesiastical History* as he claims he did. In this connection, Diekamp points out an interesting indication of the character of the man, Rufinus. He quotes Rufinus' own sentiments in the matter of literary pilfering from his prologue to Origen's *Commentary on St. Paul's Epistle to the Romans*:

Even though I am seen to add some things—I still do not think it right to steal the title from the one who has laid the foundations of the work and provided the material for constructing the edifice.[24]

As has been pointed out in earlier chapters of this work, Rufinus was very careful in this regard in his translation of Origen, protesting to Jerome again and again that his alterations and omissions were all provided for by his introductions.

On the face of it, the claim that Rufinus produced nothing original is rather absurd: his two *Apologiae* (to Anastasius and to Jerome) are well-constructed, original pieces of writing. No one can doubt their authenticity.[25] Certainly his preface to his rendition of the *Ecclesiastical History,* though somewhat simple and strange to modern literary tastes, is, despite Rufinus' own modest protest, a representative piece of Latinity, straightforward and highly informative. As G. Bardy has indicated in a similar connection, even Cicero once complained that his long familiarity with Greek had impaired his use of Latin.[26]

In the introduction to his edition of Rufinus' Latin of the *Ecclesiastical History,* Theodore Mommsen was unnecessarily severe in his strictures regarding both the historical and the literary value of Rufinus' work. He remarks that the worth of the Latin version of the incomparably important Greek work is small, as far as it goes, apart from its elucidation of the hitherto neglected text. He complains of the arbitrary and often very curtailed treatment of the original;[27] but in passing, refers to a few places in which Rufinus draws upon independent sources of information, among which he mentions the Apology of Lucian of Antioch,[28] the stories relating to Gregory Thaumaturgus—"incomparably absurd miracle stories, which at least in this setting, the Greek sources do not seem to vouch for"[29]—and two places where Rufinus supplies the original Latin of Tertullian.[30]

But as Mgr. Batiffol once remarked, Mommsen "était né insolent."[31] In connection with his part in translating the *Ecclesiastical History* of Eusebius into English, J. E. L. Oulton has recently published a comprehensive article, vindicating in many respects the historical value of the insertions to be found in Rufinus' version.[32] As Oulton points out, the most notable of his additions are connected with the life and work of Origen;[33] but his knowledge extended also to details connected with the writings of the other great Alexandrian, Clement.[34] As for matters of a topographical or historical character, Rufinus often records an additional fact connected with some place or country where at one time or another he had lived, as for example, Rome, Jerusalem, and Caesarea Philippi.[35] It is rather significant that he amplifies

Eusebius' account of the martyrdoms that took place in Caesarea, and Tyre, in Antioch, Egypt, and Mesopotamia[36]—places of which Rufinus from his travels might be supposed to have had some local knowledge.[37] In one instance at least, he quotes directly—almost *verbatim*—from documentary evidence in the shape of acts of the martyrdom.[38] Doubtless he had similar evidence to go on in other passages where we are unable to trace the source from which he drew his details. His word-for-word account of what the martyrs said points in this direction.[39]

Regarding most of the omissions, additions, and modifications which Rufinus is guilty of in translating Eusebius, Oulton maintains that they are dictated in good part by his desire to avoid expressions that were theologically suspicious; and this, in view of the difficulties he was then going through at the hands of the anti-Origenist group in Italy.[40] Oulton gives three main indications of this phenomenon: Rufinus' translation of the introductory chapter of Eusebius, where he is at great pains to cover up the latter's Arian or semi-Arian learnings; his omission from the tenth book of Eusebius of the Panegyric delivered by Eusebius at Tyre; and finally the passages that deal with the canon of the New Testament. The argument is plausible enough; Rufinus must have begun his translation shortly after receiving the first two books of Jerome's Apology (late in 401), for in the personal letter whereby he had then replied to Jerome he made mention of the barbarian incursion.[41] Hence the various points at issue with Jerome and his partisans would be very fresh in his mind. This is particularly striking in the first case that Oulton cites:

> H. E. 1, 2, 2. Eusebius: "For in truth neither did any one know the Father, save the Son; nor, on the other hand, did ever any one worthily know the Son, save only the Father who begat Him."
>
> Rufinus added: 'et sine dubio, exclusit ceteros a discutienda notitia, qui ad unum solum patrem filii scientiam revocavit.'[42]

It is not hard to pick out an echo here of his difficulties with Eusebius of Cremona at Milan and the interpolation into the Rufinian text of the *Periarchon* made at this very passage.[43] No wonder he treaded gingerly. However, in this and in the various other passages that Oulton cites, there is no need to attribute all Rufinus' care to his fear of the suspicions of his enemies: the man had a very good theological training, and, as his writings prove, he was conscientious about being orthodox as a matter of principle. There is too the matter of style and his interest in vividness of expression that possibly account for some minor variations.

Oulton attributes his failure to translate the *Panegyric at Tyre* to a similar desire to avoid the Arian difficulties to be met with in that eulogy, though he does give some

credit to Rufinus' own expressed reason for the omission.[44] Finally, regarding his handling of the passages in Eusebius referring to the canon of the New Testament, Oulton believes "that the attitude of Rufinus towards statements" recording the doubtful character of certain of the books "seems to have been somewhat similar to his attitude towards dangerous theological language. He appears anxious to water down any remarks of Eusebius that tend to cast doubt upon the canonicity of a New Testament book."[45] This can be interpreted as an indication of his fear to offend the Hieronymite group. But it can also be taken as evidence for the fact that he had some rather strong opinions of his own regarding the canonicity of the books of the New Testament, and, as in other matters, did not hesitate to correct Eusebius. His somewhat decided rejection of the *Epistle to the Hebrews* might be considered a confirmation of this; as well as the fact that he differed from Jerome's views on the subject.[46]

It was almost with pained surprise that Rufinus had come to realize that Eusebius omitted all but the mention of Gregory Thaumaturgus from his *History*. Hence in the chapter dealing with Pontus and Cappadocia during the first half of the third century, he halted the narrative and inserted several of the more famous incidents connected with the sainted martyr's career which he had apparently gathered from hearsay.[47] He thus introduces his insertion:

> Because indeed the text of this history has made mention of the blessed Gregory, I think it most proper to insert for the memory of posterity the deeds of so great a man, which are celebrated in the speech of all under the Eastern pole as well as in the West, but which have been omitted, I know not why, from this narrative.[48]

He then tells three stories of a legendary character, which Mommsen has pounced upon rather savagely, but which are quite in keeping with a whole literary genre devoted to the heroic *gesta* of the saints. Besides he expressly mentions that he is merely reporting the popular lore connected with the great 'Miracle-worker' for the edification of posterity.[49] His fourth item in connection with Gregory is an exposition of his faith, a subject in which Rufinus had a special interest. These notes on Gregory, then, were in keeping with the purpose Rufinus had in presenting the people in the neighborhood of Aquileia with the history of the Church; they are a vivid narration, highly edifying. They serve further to indicate the man's own interests in asceticism and theology.

Tillemont has been very hard on Rufinus' own two books in which he continued Eusebius' history from the rise of Arius down to the death of Theodosius; his adverse judgment has been concurred in rather generally.[50] Mommsen, however, has paid this first Christian attempt at historical composition in the West a well-tempered tribute:

> "That the two books (X and XI) added by Rufinus are an important source for both the ancient Christian legends as well as for contemporary happenings needs no further amplification. In the matter of vividness or reliability, for example, there is not much in this period that is comparable to his report on the destruction of the temple of Serapis in Alexandria.[51] In his notes on Athanasius he has used the latter's own writings; but beyond this, he appears not to have used the written sources that have come down to us for either the Council of Nicea nor for other matters.[52]

While it is perfectly true that Rufinus is responsible for the preservation of many of the legends connected with the history of the fourth century, in passing judgment on his unreliability or on his credulity account must be taken of his stated purpose in setting out to write; likewise, he must be judged in accordance with the ideas and productions along historical lines of his contemporaries. But even beyond this, a fair case can be made out for his accuracy and reliability when reporting things of which he was able to obtain first hand knowledge.[53]

Immediately preceding his continuation of Eusebius, Rufinus inserted a brief prologue:

> Thus far has Eusebius handed down to us a record of the activities carried on in the Church. For subsequent events until the present time, in the order in which they have taken place, I have added those things which I have found in the writings of our forebears or which pertain to my own memories, briefly, and obeying, in as far as I have been able in this, the command of my father in religion.[54]

In his narration of the events that took place at the Council of Nicea, Rufinus—though given credit as a witness for the text of the Creed and the anathematizations that accompanied it—has been accused of inventing out of whole cloth many of the otherwise unrecorded scenes that he connects with the council.[55] The accusation goes a bit too far. While several of the incidents that he presents are incredible, he is usually careful to point out that he is merely recording a tradition; thus he introduces the presence of the pagan philosophers at the Council with the words: "Quantam vero virtutem habeat simplicitas fidei, etiam ex his, *quae inibi gesta referuntur,* agnoscimus."[56] He narrates the story of Spyridon, the bishop of Cyprus, qui "ex eorum numero . . . *fuisse dicitur* etiam . . . vir unus ex ordine profetarum. . . ."[57]

He does not mention the source of the details he gives regarding Helena, the mother of Constantine, and particularly of the story of the finding of the Cross. But it is obvious that he is recording a story then current in the East.[58] Later on he tells us that he is passing over the account of St. Anthony the hermit, because his life is contained in the book, "which has been written by Athanasius and is already translated into Latin," for he does not feel called upon to narrate those matters which have already been recorded. He confines himself to deeds long past, the memory of which is growing dim.[59]

In many instances he cites the actual person from whom he received his information. Thus in the case of the conversion of "India"—Ethiopia—by Frumentius and Edesius, he says explicitly: "These things we know to have been so done, not by way of common hearsay—*opinione vulgi*—but upon the narration of Edesius himself, who had been the companion of Frumentius and afterwards was made a priest at Tyre."[60] He received the account of the conversion of Iberia—modern Georgia—from Bacurius, "rex ipsius gentis" who was serving as a "Comes domesticorum" in Palestine at the time, and actually stayed with Rufinus at the monastery in Jerusalem.[61] He mentions the fact that he got many of the details concerning the early life of Athanasius from people who knew the great bishop in Alexandria, and he cites his writings for the account of his various political and religious activities.[62]

Quite recently J.-R. Palanque has vindicated the account Rufinus has devoted to the life and activity of St. Ambrose, pointing out the fact that he obtained his information, in all probability, from Bishop Chromatius himself, who was an intimate friend of the Bishop of Milan.[63] We know of Rufinus' own intimacy with Didymus in Alexandria and the great admiration he had for the Cappadocians; hence his information in their regard is first hand. The same holds for most of the material he records in his second book, much of which he either witnessed himself or obtained from those who had been on the scene.[64]

There is in general no particular plan of narration perceptible in his story beyond a rather rough chronological frame; nor does he give evidence of a philosophy, or of a thesis even, guiding his selection, as do Augustine and Orosius. As he indicated in his general preface, his purpose was to carry on the narration of events in the history of the Church from the end of Eusebius' recordings. He does touch most of the salient happenings, including the Arian troubles, the spread of the Church in the frontier provinces, the beginnings of the ascetical movements, and an account of the most outstanding ecclesiastical figures of both the eastern and the western Church. In all this, he proves himself worthy of Paulinus of Nola's admiration expressed when he wrote to Sulpicius Severus who had requested of him information regarding "the annals not of one nation alone but of the whole human race." "If Rufinus," replied the presbyter of Nola, "has not published the subject-matter of this history that is lacking (*hiantis historiae*) . . . I am afraid that we seek it in vain in anyone else in these regions."[65] This is high praise, coming from a man of such parts as Paulinus.

All things considered, his *History* is, then, a competent piece of work, admirably suited to the purpose he had in mind. It certainly is a vivid, well-written narrative, making use of various literary devices admired by the people of his times. The story is enlivened by frequent recourse to direct discourse,[66] as well as to figures of speech, of sound, and of word-order,[67] And though, unlike his great contemporary and opponent, Jerome, he does not introduce citations from pagan authors, he does resort to frequent direct and indirect quotation of the Scriptures.[68]

That his history was well appreciated in his own day is evident from the use made of it by his contemporaries, Augustine, Paulinus, Orosius, Gennadius of Marseilles. It was one of the very few Latin works then translated into Greek—attaining that distinction within two years after its composition; and was then used copiously by Socrates, and the other Greek church-historians.[69] The number of manuscripts that have preserved the contents are an eloquent testimonial to its popularity during the middle ages. It is not without great value today for the history of the all-important fifth century.

The most notable work connected with the name of Rufinus—certainly the most read throughout the Middle Ages, and even up to modern times—is again a piece of historical composition: the *Historia Monachorum in Aegypto sive de vitis patrum.*[70] Just before the close of the last century, it proved a hotbed of excitement for the extreme rationalism of such critics as Weingarten and Lucius, until its value as history received well-merited and all but definitive vindication at the hands of Preuschen, Ladeuze, and particularly, of Cuthbert Butler.[71] Yet it still presents an historical problem of considerable intrigue: for it has come down through recent centuries as the original work of Rufinus—and we have testimony of Jerome witnessing thereto[72]—, yet the Latin text has all the earmarks of a translation.

The *Historia Monachorum* tells the story of a pilgrimage made through Egypt in the winter of 394 by a group of seven monks from Rufinus' own monastery on the Mount of Olives.[73] It records the life story and the deeds of some thirty-four of the desert fathers, and of various others, living in the Thebaid and in Lower Egypt. The narrative is enlivened with a wealth of legendary and miraculous happenings that proved immeasurably precious to subsequent ages; and just as immeasurably disconcerting to the nineteenth-century historian. Yet it is a document all but indispensable for the history of early monasticism.[74]

The difficulties surrounding its authorship are manifold. Though it possesses a preface describing the occasion and reason for its composition, the author there remains anonymous. It is not mentioned by Gennadius among the works of Rufinus, though Gennadius does attribute a similar work to a Petronius, Bishop of Bologna.[75] The chief problem arises however from our inability to establish definitively the priority of either the Greek or the Latin version, although the majority of modern scholars have accepted Butler's thesis in favor of the Greek text as the primary document.[76] But just previous to the appearance of Butler's work, E. Preuschen, in editing the Greek text, had decided in favor of the priority of the Latin; in this he has been supported by R. Reitzenstein, and most recently, by F. Diekamp.[77] However, the general consensus of opinion still favors the evidence in support of the Greek as the original and the Latin as a slightly amplified translation.

What appears certain in all this, however, is the fact that the current Latin text is from the hand of Rufinus; this is a thesis ably demonstrated by the eminent seventeenth-century editor of the *Vitae Patrum,* the Bollandist Rosweyd.[78] That Rufinus produced his part of the work sometime after the appearance of his *Ecclesiastical History* is likewise certain from the fact that in the end of the chapter of the *Historia Monachorum* having to do with Macarius the Alexandrian (c. 29), he expressly refers the reader to the eleventh book of his History for further wondrous details concerning the work of that saint.[79]

As has been said, the problem concerning the original version of this work is a complicated one: no new attempt will be made to settle it here. However, the general tenor of the preface, though it does contain self-depreciatory passages regarding the author's stylistic competence as do Rufinus' prologues, gives the impression that it was written by one still in the Monastery at the Mount of Olives being continually pressed by his brethren for an account of his conversations with the desert fathers; likewise there is an indication that the journey described was the only contact the writer had with the desert fathers.[80] Neither of these circumstances fits in well with what we know of Rufinus; for he had left Jerusalem by the early part of 397, and, on his own relation, had spent the better part of six, if not eight, years in Alexandria in frequent contact with the monks of the desert. There is the fact too that at the time of the journey Rufinus was certainly a priest: but the narrative expressly states that all they had with them was a deacon.[81] Were Rufinus actually a member of the pilgrim party in 394, then in his own *Apologia* and in his *History* there is a surprising omission of several of the more famous desert fathers whom the author of the

Historia Monachorum describes at length—of these the most noteworthy being John of Lycopolis and Apollonius of Hermopolis Magna.[82]

The strongest argument in favor of the Rufinian authorship seems to be the fact that Jerome attributes this work to him. But as has been pointed out, Jerome had a rather meager knowledge of what was going on in the West, and particularly in regard to the activities of Rufinus. Hence he probably heard of this work in connection with Rufinus' name. Then in the midst of an attack upon Evagrius of Ponticus, whom he considered a fellow Origenist along with Rufinus and Melania, he naturally vented a little of his ill humor on his former friend and enemy, now dead some four years (314).[83] But at least Jerome considered Rufinus capable of a work of this caliber.

Due to the fact that the work lacks its own proper preface in Latin, we do not know the occasion or the reason for Rufinus' translation or adaptation. It is but natural to conjecture that it was done in accordance with his practice of supplying his friends and followers in Italy with a more intimate description of the ascetical life as it was practiced in Egypt, the source of many of the monastic currents then prevalent in Italy. Unfortunately, there is no immediate trace of the work in the contemporary literature beyond its use by Sozomen, who attributes it to Timotheus of Alexandria. However, that bishop was dead by 385. Butler has suggested that Sozomen might possibly have had in mind an archdeacon Timotheus mentioned by Socrates; but this was sheer conjecture, as Butler was quick to point out.[84] However, the ***Historia Monachorum in Aegypto,*** whoever the original author may have been, is a lively, basically accurate account of a phenomenon of primary interest in the history of the Church in the fourth and the fifth centuries. It is only fitting that it should be connected with the name of Rufinus.[85]

About this time (*ca.* 402), Rufinus was engaged upon another work with an historical as well as a theological bearing, his ***Commentarius in Symbolum Apostolorum.***[86] It is dedicated to a Bishop Laurentius, of whom we know nothing, beyond the fact that he had requested the Commentary of Rufinus. The work is really a theological tract based in good part upon the *Catechesis* of Cyril of Jerusalem.[87] It gives a detailed explanation of each article of the Creed then recited in Aquileia, as well as an account of the supposedly Apostolic origin of the Roman creed and a résumé of the accepted canon of the Sacred Scriptures.

Rufinus embarks on the work modestly enough, as is his usual fashion. He says quite explicitly that he is acquainted with the treatises of some of his predecessors, though he mentions by name only the heretic Photinus.[88] His purpose in writing is to record the Apostolic tradition and to supply whatever explanation seems to have been omitted by those who preceded him.[89] Thus he begins with an account of the composition of the Creed by the apostles on the eve of their setting out to convert the world. He makes special mention of the fact that this story is a matter of tradition—*tradunt majores nostri.*[90] He stops to offer an explanation of the word "*Symbolum*" which, he says, was properly applied to the formula of the Apostles, since it stands in Greek for both "*indicium,*" "sign" or "indication," and for a "*collatio,*" or, "a joint contribution made by several." He compares the use of the word as an '*indicium*' to the pass-word employed by army units in a civil war as a means of identification; and he contrasts the agreement of the apostles in the '*collatio*' despite their gift of tongues with the confusion surrounding the tower of Babel.[91]

Besides being a most important witness to the text of both the Roman and Aquileian creeds of the fourth century, Rufinus' ***Commentary*** is an interesting and competent theological treatise, ranging over the whole doctrinal field in a manner at once instructive and adequate to his subject matter. He records, of course, the body of doctrine with its ramifications as it has been taught to him by his contemporaries; he makes frequent and good use of the *Catechesis* of Cyril of Jerusalem; but he embodies notations stemming from his own personal interests as well as incidental explanations that reveal in him a constant awareness of possible difficulties—an essential preoccupation of a good teacher.[92]

He proceeds through the Creed, then, article by article, clarifying and explaining. In regard to our belief "*in God the Father Almighty,*" he prefaces his remarks with the note that in some Churches additions are made to this article by way of dispelling possible heresy; but that in Rome, no accretions are permitted, the reason being, as he expressly supposed, "that no heresy has had its origin there," while the custom of having the one about to be baptized recite the creed aloud before the whole congregation has been retained so that "the addition of one syllable even is not permitted."[93] He justifies the necessity of faith, "that the path of understanding may be laid open before the believer."[94] He then launches into a metaphysical appreciation of the nature of God "*sine initio, sine fine, simplicem, sine ulla admistione, invisibilem, incorporeum, ineffabilem . . .*" as well as of the divine paternity and omnipotence, that does him credit as a theologian. He closes by justifying the addition in the Aquileian Church of the words "invisible and impassible" as a counterthrust against the heresy of Sabellius, which "among us is called Patripassianism."[95]

Concerning belief *"in Christ Jesus His only Son, our Lord,"* it is well to know that Jesus is a Hebrew word meaning 'Savior'; and that Christ comes from 'chrism' and refers to the 'Anointed One.' He then justifies these names for our Lord by means of Scriptural allusions and prophecy.[96] Pointing to the inadequacy of illustrations and analogy, he discusses the eternal generation of the Son, thus leading into a consideration of the divine dispensation regarding man's salvation: *"Qui natus est de Spiritu Sancto ex Maria virgine."* He defends the perpetual virginity of the blessed Virgin, offering as a counter to the disbelief of the pagans their credulity in regard to the many irrationalities connected with their own gods.[97]

In discussing the crucifixion, the burial and the descent into hell, he extols the cross as a sign of triumph, explaining at length, and with copious reference to scripture and prophecy, the economy of Salvation.[98] He gives a running commentary on each act of the Savior's passion from the betrayal by Judas to the descent into hell. On the Resurrection, the Ascension and the Judgment to come, he glories in the copiousness of Scriptural prediction, closing with a caution concerning the coming of the anti-Christ.[99]

In speaking of the Holy Ghost, he again refers to the nature of the Trinity, and expressly states that it is from both the Father and the Son (*ab utroque*) that the Holy Ghost proceeds, sanctifying all things.[100] He makes a distinction regarding the use of the preposition *"in"* reserving it for reference to persons. The next article of the creed reads: *"the holy church, the forgiveness of sin, and the resurrection of this flesh."* For, he maintains, by the omission of this preposition when referring to things, "the Creator is distinguished from the creature, and things divine are separated from things human."[101]

Referring back to the previous articles concerning the Holy Ghost, he feels obliged to enumerate the books of the Old and the New Testament, "as we have received them from the *Monuments* of the Fathers."[102] He distinguishes between those books which are canonical and those which are ecclesiastical, classifying among the latter the *Book of Wisdom,* and *Ecclesiasticus,* as also *Tobias, Judith* and the *Machabees*; together with *Pastor Hermes,* and the Book of the *Two Ways* or the *Judgment of Peter.* Finally he mentions the apocrypha, which he says should not be read in the churches.[103]

In discussing the *"sanctam ecclesiam"* he gives a brief summation of various heresies: that of Marcion, Valentinian, the Ebionites, the Manicheans, and that of Arius.[104] He justifies belief in the forgiveness of sins, pointing out the distinction between the act and the intention in the commission of a crime; demonstrating that there is nothing unreasonable about forgiving, once a person's will has been changed from bad to good.[105]

In his discussion of the Resurrection of "this flesh," there is no reference whatever to his former troubles; he seems to direct his explanations against the Valentinians. He concludes the treatise with a recapitulation, praying that "if . . . we have logically followed out all these things in accord with the rule of tradition outlined above, we pray that the Lord may concede to us, and to all those who hear these words, that having kept the faith . . . finished our course—we may await the crown of justice. . . ."[106]

There is no certain reference whereby the work may be definitely dated. It does seem to have come after his profession of faith to Anastasius, and after his Apology against Jerome.[107] Hence Bardenhewer puts it down as written about 404.[108] That the work was well appreciated in its day is evident from the use of it made by Cassian, Gaudentius of Brescia, Fortunatus, etc., as well as from the way in which Gennadius speaks of it.[109] Though not original in any real sense, it is a competent theological tract, witnessing to the solid training its author had once received in the schools of Alexandria.

Notes

1. In his preface, Rufinus says that he wrote: "tempore quo diruptis Italiae claustris Alarico duce Gothorum se pestifer morbus infudit et agros armenta viros longe lateque vastavit" (ed. T. Mommsen, p. 951—see following note). Alaric twice invaded Italy, in 401-402, and in 408 (cf. O. Seeck, *Regesten der Kaiser und Päpste,* Stuttgart, 1919, pp. 304 and 314). As Bishop Chromatius, who requested the work, was dead by 407, the History must have been undertaken upon the occasion of Alaric's first invasion. Cf. L. de Tillemont, *Mémoires . . .* XII, 656 f.; E. Preuschen, *Palladius und Rufinus* (Giessen, 1887), 203 f.

2. Edited by E. Schwartz and T. Mommsen, *Eusebius Werke,* II Band, Teil I-III: *Die Kirchengeschichte* (Leipzig, 1903-1909). Teil I contains Eusebius' Greek and Rufinus' Latin of books 1-5; Teil II, the Greek and Latin of books 6-10, as well as Rufinus' note on Gregory Thaumaturgus, pp. 953-956, and his continuation of the history in books 10 and 11 (pp. 957-1040). Teil III is made up of several introductions and studies, as well as indices. The "Einleitung zu Rufin" is on pp. CCLI-CCLXVIII; it is the work of T. Mommsen, who likewise provided the Rufinian text, and consists principally in a consideration of the manuscripts and the text. Hereafter, references to Rufinus' own books 10 and 11 will be cited under Mommsen's name, and the page references will refer to Teil II.

3. This is explained in Rufinus' preface (Mommsen, pp. 951 f.).

4. Mommsen, p. 951.

5. *Ibid.,* 951-952.

6. *Ibid.,* 952.

7. A. Glas, *Die Kirchengeschichte des Gelasios von Kaisareia* (Leipzig, 1914: *Byzantinisches Archiv.,* Heft 6).

8. Cf. O. Bardenhewer, *Gesch. der altk. Litt.* IV (Leipzig, 1924), 146; B. Altaner, *Patrologie* (Freiburg-im-Breisgau, 1938), 147, 250. However, H. Grégoire ("La christianization de la Géorgie," *Byzantion,* 7 (1932), 737) has pointed out that Glas' thesis "avant même de naître était démoli par M. van den Ven"; and he quotes the latter's "Fragments de la récension grecque de l'Histoire ecclésiastique de Rufin dans un texte hagiographique," *Le Muséon* 2 (1915), 92-115.

9. P. Peeters, "Les débuts du christianisme en Géorgie," *Anal. Bolland.* 50 (1932), 5-58. The refutation of Glas' theory (pp. 27 ff.) was accepted by H. Grégoire (*op. cit.,* above).

10. F. Diekamp, "Gelasius von Caesarea in Palaestina," *Orient. Christ. Analecta* (OCA) 117 (1938), 16-32.

11. A. Glas, *Die Kirchengesch. des Gelasios,* 1-2. Gelasius of Caesarea in Palestine was the nephew of Cyril of Jerusalem, son of the patriarch's sister. His uncle obtained for him the see of Caesarea in 367, but he was unable to take possession of it until 381, when he received the assistance of Theodosius, the emperor. He was present at the councils of Constantinople held in 381 and 394. According to Glas, he died in 395.

12. Glas gives an account of this data (pp. 2-3). The work was mentioned by Photius (codex 89: PG 103, 293). There is a further note on Gelasius and his work in an epitome of church history which has been edited by I. A. Cramer (*Anecdota graeca e codd. manuscriptis Biblio. regiae Parisiensis,* II, Oxford, 1839, 91, 8). C. de Boor had already pointed out that there was evidence for the fact that Gelasius had continued the work of Eusebius in the *Chronographia* of Theophanes (ed. C. de Boor, Leipzig, 1882, I, 11, 17-18); cf. T. Mommsen, *Eusebius Werke* II, Teil III, CCLVII-CCLVIII. Likewise in the sections of the *Church History* of Gelasius of Cyzicus that have survived, there is direct mention of both Gelasius of Caesarea and of Rufinus. F. Diekamp (Gelasios, OCA 117, 1938, 21 f.) gives an account of further evidence recently unearthed supporting de Boor (e.g. P. Heseler, *Hagiographica II: Byzant.-neugriech. Jahrbücher* 9, 1932, 320-337, who found evidence for the use of Eusebius of Caesarea in a fifteenth-century Greek legendary life of Constantine and Helena). Heseler considers this material as supporting Glas' thesis (cf. his notes in BNJ 12, 1936, 347-351, and *Byzantion* 10, 1935, 438-442); but Diekamp dismisses this claim as unfounded.

13. Photius is the one responsible for the story that Cyril had encouraged his nephew to continue the work of Eusebius and that both Cyril and Gelasius had translated the work of Rufinus (Photius, *codex* 89: PG 103, 293 and 296). Cf. Glas, 3-10; Diekamp, 19-20. In the whole discussion thus far, no consideration has been given to determining just what might be the probability that Gelasius knew enough Latin to have translated the work. Certainly Rufinus was bi-lingual; but it seems that few Greek-speaking Orientals knew much Latin at this time.

14. Glas: "Geringer Wert der literarischen Tradition," *Die Kirchengeschichte des Gelasios,* 13-15.

15. *Ibid.,* 15-16.

16. *Ibid.,* 74-78 for his conclusions.

17. H. Grégoire et M.-A. Kugener, *Marc le diacre: Vie de Porphyre, évêque de Gaza* (Paris, 1930).

18. Grégoire et Kugener, *op. cit.,* p. xxxix.

19. Diekamp, "Gelasius von Caesarea," OCA 117 (1938), 18.

20. Rufinus himself starts the literary tradition in favor of his authorship, as we have seen in his preface above. Augustine next mentions his continuation expressly in a note on Eusebius of Caesarea "cui Rufinus a se in linguam latinam translatae subsequentium etiam temporum duos libros addidit" (Aug., *De haeresibus,* 83: PL [*Patrologia Latina*] 42, 46). Gennadius next records: "historiae etiam ecclesiasticae, quam ab Eusebio scriptam et ab ipso interpretatam diximus, addidit decimum et undecimum librum" (Gen., *De viris inlus.* 17: ed. E. Richardson, Leipzig, 1896, p. 68).

Among the Greeks, Socrates attributes the two books to Rufinus (Soc., *Hist. eccl.* [*Historia Ecclesiastica*] I, 12; II, 1; III, 19: PG 67, 103; 183-186; 427). So does Gelasius of Cyzicus (*Hist. eccl.* I, 2, 1 and 11, 17: ed. G. Loeschcke and M. Heinemann, Leipzig, 1918, GCS 19, p. 7, 13) and Georgios Monachos (*Chronicon*: ed. C. de Boor, Leipzig, 1904, I, LXXV) who make use of the Greek of Rufinus at great length (cf. A. Glas, *Die Kirchengeschichte des Gelasios,* 18 ff.).

F. Diekamp ("Gelasius . . . ," OCA 117, 1938, 19 f.) offers an explanation for Photius' mistake (cited in n. 12, above) in saying that both Cyril and Gelasius had translated Rufinus; Cyril was dead by March 18, 386.

21. F. Diekamp, *op. cit.,* 27.

22. *Ibid.,* 22-27; cf. below, n. 75 ff.

23. *Ibid.,* 28-31.

24. Ruf., *Peroratio in explanationem Origenis super epistolam Pauli ad Romanos* (PG [*Patrologia Gracea*] 14, 1293): "malevolae mentes vigiliis nostris contumelias reddant. . . . Novum quippe apud eos genus culpae subimus. Aiunt enim mihi: 'in his quae scribis, quoniam plurima in eis tui operis habentur, da titulum nominis tui. . . .' Hoc ego, qui plus conscientiae meae quam nomini defero, etiam si addere aliqua videor et explere quae desunt aut breviare quae longa sunt, furari tamen titulum ejus qui fundamenta operis jecit et construendi aedificii materiam praebuit, rectum non puto. Sit sane in arbitrio legentis cum opus probaverit operis meritum cui velit ascribere. Nobis enim propositum est non plausum legentium sed fructum proficientium quaerere."

25. See [Murphy, Francis X. *Rufinus of Aquileia.* Washington, DC: Catholic University of America Press, 1945], chapter 5, n. 83.

26. G. Bardy, *Recherches sur l'hist. du texte et des versions du De Principiis d'Origène* (Paris, 1922), 119, esp. n. 2.

27. *Euseb. Werke,* II, 3, p. CCLI.

28. *Ibid.* See however, G. Bardy (*Recherches sur s. Lucien d'Antioche et son école,* Paris, 1936, 133-163) for a complete appreciation of the service rendered by Rufinus in preserving this Apologia of Lucian.

29. Mommsen, *loc. cit.*: "Er ergänzt die Angaben des Eusebius über Gregorius von Neocaesarea, den Thaumaturgus, durch einige unvergleichlich absurde Wundergeschichten welche weningstens in dieser Fassung die griechischen Quellen nicht aufzuweisen scheinen." Tillemont (*Mémoires* . . . IV, p. 328) is of similar sentiments. On these matters, however, it is well to keep in mind the sensible observations of the Bollandist, H. Delehaye in his *Les passiones des martyrs et les genres littéraires* (Brussels, 1921), and in his *Sanctus* (Brussels, 1923).

30. Eusebius quotes Tertullian's *Apologeticus* (in H. E. II, 2, 5-6); Rufinus supplies the original Latin (Mommsen, I, 111-112); Eusebius quotes *Apolog.* 5 (in II, 25, 4); Rufinus again gives the original (Mommsen, I, 177).

31. P. Batiffol, *S. Grégoire le Grand* (Paris, 1928).

32. J. Oulton, "Rufinus's Translation of the Church History of Eusebius," *JTS* 30 (1929), 150-174.

33. Oulton, 160-164. Rufinus fills in many of the details connected with various incidents in the life of Origen. He explains, for example, the assistance that Origen rendered the martyrs at Alexandria; the passages in Eusebius narrating the manner in which Origen disposed of his library and the remittance he received for it, which was just sufficient to satisfy his sustenance-needs. He clears up the history of Origen's relations with Bishop Demetrius of Alexandria, and gives the source of the Bishop's jealousy, which led him to reveal Origen's youthful indiscretion. He gives a clear account of the *Hexapla,* evidently describing the work as he himself had seen it (cf. his account of this work in his *Apol.* II, 36: PL 21, 614-615). He supplies the reason for Origen's journey to Greece and Achaia, corroborated by a letter of Origen's that Rufinus had already quoted in his *De adulteratione* (PG 17, 625). He gives a summary of another letter of Origen to Africanus, which Eusebius merely mentioned, concerning the genuineness of the story of Susanna in the book of *Daniel.* This matter concerning the canonicity of Daniel had come up before in his *Apologia* (II, 32: PL 21, 613-615). Oulton supplies the references to the passages in Eusebius and Rufinus.

34. *Op. cit.,* 159-160.

35. *Ibid.,* 165-168. Rufinus describes the *splendidissima monumenta* erected to the memory of the apostles Peter and Paul by Constantine on the sites of their original burial places on the Ostian Way and in the Vatican. He supplies topographical details concerning the site of the tomb of Queen Helena of Adiabene "pro portis Hierosolymorum." He offers details surrounding the election of Pope Fabian, but remarks that the very same story concerning the dove settling upon the shoulder of the one to be elected was also told of Pope Zephyrinus. He amplifies the account given of the choice of Alexander as Bishop of Jerusalem; and the manner in which he clears up the account of the local miracle that took place annually at Caesarea Philippi indicates that he must have witnessed the actual happening at some time—perhaps in connection with the trip he made to Edessa in *ca.* 380 (cf. chapter 2, pp. 49 f., [Murphy, 1945]).

36. Oulton, 168-170. For the martyrs at Caesarea, Rufinus supplies various incidents connected with the processes of martyrdom including a conversation with the judge, precise names, and the types of suffering undergone (H. E. VII, 12 and 15; VIII,

3, 1-4). For the happenings at Tyre, Rufinus' account is extremely vivid, including a description of the incitation of the beasts before sending them into the arena and the fury that overtook the spectators, etc. (VIII, 7, 2-5). In his description of the martyrdom on the way to Antioch of a pious mother and her two virgin daughters, he introduces the exhortation of the mother in *oratio recta*, and adds a very lucid account of how they avoided contamination (VIII, 12, 3-4). In detailing the enormous number of victims in Alexandria and in the Thebaid, he incorporates many details not mentioned by Eusebius (VIII, 9, 4-8; 14; 15). Finally, his enlarged and clarified account of the sufferings of the martyrs in Mesopotamia (VIII, 12) has been enhanced by the finding of the *Acts* of three martyrs there, Shmona, Guria, and Habbib (cf. F. C. Burkitt, *Euphemia and the Goth, with the Acts of Martyrdom of the Confessors of Edessa,* London, 1913), though these *Acta* are now considered legendary for the most part; cf. B. Altaner, *Patrologie,* p. 134-135.

37. Cf. [Murphy, 1945], chapter 2, p. 50.

38. J. Oulton, 171. This is the account Rufinus gives of the martyrdom of Phileas and Philoremus at Alexandria (VIII, 9, 6-8). The *Acta* are printed in T. Ruinart, *Acta Primorum Martyrum sincera et selecta* (Regensburg, 1859), 494 ff. Cf. J. Knipfing, "The Date of the Acts of Phileas and Philoremus," *HThR* 16 (1923), 198-203.

39. From the general manner of Rufinus' procedure, it would seem that he was dependent upon the local stories in this matter rather than that he made up such *oratio recta* merely for the enlivenment of his narrative. For a case in point, see G. Bardy (*Recherches sur s. Lucien d'Antioche et son école,* 133-166). Bardy gives considerable credit to Rufinus' elaboration upon Eusebius' text (IX, 6), showing at great length that Rufinus must have been using the *Acta* of the martyrdom of Lucian, so well do the sentiments expressed in the *Credo* he puts into the mouth of Lucian agree with what a martyr might very well have said at the beginning of the fourth century. Bardy demonstrates this by numerous citations and parallels.

40. Oulton, 152-156. This is also the contention of E. Kimmel's dissertation (*De Rufino Eusebii interprete,* Gerae, 1838).

41. Jer., *Apol.* III, 21: PL 23, 472.

42. Oulton, 153.

43. See [Murphy, 1945], chapter 5, p. 127.

44. Oulton, 155-156.

45. Oulton, 156-159. In passages touching upon the New Testament, Rufinus, following Eusebius, deals with *James* and *Jude* (II, 23; 25); 2 *Peter* (III, 3, 1-4; VI, 25, 7-14); St. John's *Gospel,* his *First Epistle,* and the *Apocalypse* (VII, 25, 8 ff.). Finally he gives a classification of the various books with claims to apostolicity (III, 25). See below n. 102.

46. Oulton, 157-158. Thus where Eusebius remarks (III, 3, 5), "Some have rejected the Epistle to the Hebrews," Rufinus says, "I know that among the Latins doubt is entertained concerning the Epistle to the Hebrews." And where Eusebius says (IV, 20, 3), "Even to this day among the Romans, some do not consider it to be the Apostle's," Rufinus is emphatic, "even now among the Latins it is not thought to be the Apostle Paul's."

47. Edited by T. Mommsen, *Eusebius Werke* II, 2, 952-956. The insertion is made in bk. VII, 28, 2.

48. Mommsen, 952.

49. As for the sources of Rufinus' insertions, see the recent conclusion put forth by W. Telfer ("The Latin *Life* of St. Gregory Thaumaturgus," *JTS* 31 (1930), 142-155) who agrees with the older study of P. Koetschau ("Zur Lebens-Geschichte Gregors des Wundertäters," *Zeit. f. wiss. Theol.,* 41, 1898, 240 ff.) against A. Poncelet ("La Vie latine de Saint Grégoire le Thaumaturge," *RSR* 1, 1910, 132-160; 567-569), that the life in the eleventh-century legendaries was based upon Rufinus for at least one of the anecdotes there reported. Rufinus himself, though apparently acquainted with Gregory of Nyssa's Panegyric on the "Wonder-Worker" (PG 46, 893-958) also drew on an independent source. Eucher of Lyons, d. 450-455. (*Ep. paraenetica ad Valerianum:* CSEL 31, 2), Gregory the Great (*Dialogi* I, 7: PL 77, 183), and Bede (*In Marcum,* XI: PL 92, 247), all allude to these anecdotes. Cf. W. Telfer, "The Cultus of St. Gregory Thaumaturgus," *HThR* 29 (1936), 283.

50. L. de Tillemont, *Mémoires* . . . XII, 304-305: "Rufin mérite peu de croyance, ayant fait son histoire avec peu de soin, non sure les actes et les monuments authentiques, mais sure des narrations fabuleuses et sure des bruits populaires. (Il n'aurait) suivi que sa memoire sans consulter aucune pièce, tant tout y est rapporté avec négligence et sans soin." Bardenhewer's judgment is more tempered: "Rasch hingeworfen, ohne gründliche Vorstudien, ohne ausreichende Gewissenhaftigkeit in einzelnen, lässt er sich mit seinem morgenländischen Vorbilde nicht vergleichen . . . aber . . . ist er eine wertvolle Quelle" (*Gesch. der altk. Litt.* III, 556).

51. On the destruction of this cult and temple at Serapis, see O. Seeck, *Gesch. des Untergangs der antik. Welt*, V, 218; 233-234.

52. Mommsen, "Einleitung zu Rufin," *Eusebius Werke*, II, 3, cclii.

53. A good example of this is Rufinus' account of the battle at the Frigidus in 395 (H. E. XI, 33-34), in which Theodosius practically annihilated the army of Arbogast. Rufinus evidently visited the battleground which was not far from Aquileia, and got an eyewitness account of the whole battlefield. Cf. O. Seeck and G. Veith, "Die Schlacht an Frigidus," *Klio* 13 (1913), 451-467; also A. Jülicher, "Ein Wort zugunsten des Kirchenhistorikers Rufinus," *Klio* 14 (1914), 127-128.

54. Mommsen, p. 957.

55. Cf. P. Batiffol, "Les sources de l'histoire du concile de Nicée," *Echos d'Orient* 24 (1925), 400-402.

56. Ruf., H. E., X, 3 (Mommsen, 961-963). Cf. M. Jugie, "La dispute des philosophes paiens avec les péres de Nicée," *Echos d'Orient* 24 (1925), 403-410.

57. Ruf., H. E., X, 5 (963-965).

58. On this whole story, and the part Rufinus played in spreading it, see H. Leclerq, "Croix, Invention de la," DACL 3² (Paris, 1914), 3131-3137; I. Straubinger, *Die Kreuzauffindunglegende* (Paderborn, 1913: Forschungen zur. Lit.-und Dogmengeschichte), 15-49.

59. Ruf., H. E., X, 9 (Mommsen, 971).

60. *Ibid.*, X, 10 (973). Cf. E. W. Budge, *A History of Ethiopia* (2 vols., London, 1928), I, 147-151.

61. *Ibid.*, X, 11 (973-976). Cf. P. Peeters, "Les débuts du christianisme en Géorgie," *Anal. Bolland.* 50 (1932), 5-58. P. Peeters maintains that Rufinus' recital of the story told him by King Bacurius, buttressed as it is with legend, is still a good historical source. The events Rufinus narrates could easily have taken place during the reign of Constantine in the capital of the kingdom of Iberia, which faced the Roman fortress at Harmozica on the river Kur. P. Peeters likewise demonstrates that all the other narratives detailing this event depend on Rufinus: thus Moses of Khoren used the *Eccles. Hist.* of Socrates, which had been translated into Armenian by Philon de Tirak. C. Toumanoff, however ("Medieval Georgian Hist. Litt.," *Traditio* 1 (1943), 151-152), seems to believe that Rufinus and Moses represent independent accounts possibly springing from a common

source. In this he is following J. Karst, *Litt. géorgienne chrét.* (Paris, 1934), 66-67. But see the review of Karst by M. van Custem, *Anal. Bolland.*, 54 (1936), 170-171.

62. Ruf., H. E., X, 15-20; 34-35 (Mommsen, 980-987; 995). In this connection, it is interesting to note that when telling of the return of Pope Liberius after his exile under Constantius for having refused to sign the formula of the third Synod of Sirmium (358), Rufinus expressly says that he has not been able to find out for certain (*pro certum conpertum non habeo*), whether or not the Pope had signed the formula thus facilitating his return. Evidently then, he had made enquiries. He had previously been interested in this question in regard to the forged letter of Hilary, of which he spoke in his *De adult. librorum Origenis*. Cf. chapter 4 [Murphy, 1945], p. 87.

63. Cf. J.-R. Palanque, *Saint Ambrose et l'empire romain* (Paris, 1933), 407-421.

64. A. Jülicher, "Ein Wort zugunsten des Kirchenhistorichers Rufinus," *Klio* 14 (1914), 127-128, for a further estimate of the man's honesty and reliability as an historian.

65. Paulinus of Nola, *Ep.* 28, 5.

66. See in particular the recitation of the lives of the martyrs, and note 36 above.

67. Cf. H. Hoppe, "Rufin als Übersetzer," *Studi ded. allà memoria di Paolo Ubaldi* (Milan, 1937), 133-150. Hoppe points out what is quite obvious in the matter of Rufinus' striving to achieve rhetorical "delectare" as well as "prodesse." He frequently employs figures of sound. As might be expected, he abounds in alliteration.

He makes frequent use of Gorgianic figures and allied devices of parallelism. For his use of rhymed prose and of the clausulae, see Hoppe, 146-147. For a general discussion of his translation method, see E. Kimmel, *De Rufino Eusebii interprete* (Gerae, 1838); but better, Sr. M. Monica Wagner, *Rufinus the Translator* (Washington, D. C., 1945).

68. See the frequent annotations in Mommsen's edition.

69. For its use by Augustine and Orosius, as well as, probably, by Paulinus of Nola (*Carm.* 19, 98 ff.), consult A. Jülicher, "Ein Wort zugunsten . . . ," *Klio* 14 (1914), 128. Gennadius mentions the H. E. in his continuation of Jerome's *De viris inlus.*, 17. For its use by Socrates and the Greek authors, see [Murphy, 1945], pp. 162 f.

70. Edited in PL 21, 387-462. The Greek text has been put out by E. Preuschen, *Palladius und Rufi-*

nus (Giessen, 1897), 1-131. There are several Syriac versions of the work; on the relations between the various recensions, see C. Butler, *The Lausiac History* I, 268-276.

71. H. Weingarten, *Ursprung des Mönchtums* (Gotha, 1877); *id.* "Mönchtum," *Encyc. f. prot. Theol.,* X (1882), 758 ff. E. Lucius, "Die Quellen des älteren ägyptischen Mönchtums," Breiger's *Zeit. f. Kirchengesch.* 7 (1885), 163-198. P. Ladeuze, *Étude sur le cénobitisme Pakhomien* (Louvain, 1898). C. Butler, *The Lausiac History of Palladius* (Cambridge, 1898-1904). For a good summation of the routing of the extreme rationalist positions in regard to the origin of Christian monasticism, see P. Gobillot, "Les origènes du monachisme chrétien et l'ancienne religion d'Égypte," *RSR* 10 (1920), 303-354; 11 (1921), 29-86; 168-213; 328-361; 12 (1922), 214-235. For the more recent bibliography, see chapter 2, [Murphy, 1945], n. 9.

72. Jer., *Ep.* 133, 3 (CSEL 56, 246): "(Rufinus) librum quoque scripsit quasi de monachis multosque in eo enumerat qui nunquam fuerunt. . . ."

73. The date of the journey is set by the fact that the party was staying with John of Lycopolis when Theodosius gained his victory over Eugenius (September, 394); Macarius of Alexandria was already dead when they reached Nitria—he died at the end of 394 (cf. Butler, I, 10).

74. Butler, I, 198-203.

75. Gennadius, *De viris inlustribus* 42 (ed. E. Richardson, Leipzig, 1896, p. 77).

76. Cf. O. Bardenhewer, *Gesch der altk. Litt.* III, 555; E. Schwartz, "Palladiana," *ZntW,* 36 (1937), 164, n. 6.

77. *Palladius und Rufinus,* 176-220; R. Reitzenstein, *Historia Monachorum und Historia Lausiaca* (Göttingen, 1916), 1-11; F. Diekamp, "Gelasios von Caesarea," *Analecta Patristica,* OCA 117 (Rome, 1938), 22-27.

78. *Vitae Patrum,* Prolegomena iv, 10 (PL 73, 35); cf. Butler, HL I, 11, n. 1.

79. *Hist. Monachorum,* 29 (PL 21, 455): "sed et multa, ut diximus, alia de operibus sancti Macarii Alexandrini mirabilia feruntur, ex quibus nonnulla in XI libro ecclesiasticae historiae inserta, qui requirit inveniet."

80. *Ibid.,* Prologus (389-390); c. 1 (394).

81. *Ibid.,* 1 (394): "Septem fuimus simul comitantes. . . . Interrogabat ergo, si quis in nobis esset clericus . . . intellexit esse inter nos quem-

dam, qui hujus erat ordinis sed latere cupiebat. . . ." On the accuracy of the account concerning John of Lycopolis in the *Hist. Monachorum,* see P. Peeters, "Une vie copte de S. Jean de Lycopole," *Anal. Bolland.* 54 (1936), 375-377.

82. Cf. C. Butler, *The Lausiac History,* I, 10-12; Appendix I, 257-277, where he gives a long technical justification of his position. This is answered summarily, and to my way of thinking, indecisively, by F. Diekamp, "Gelasios von Caesarea," OCA 117 (1938), 23-27. Butler had already vindicated his original position in "Palladiana," *JTS* 22 (1921).

83. See note 72, above.

84. Butler, II (appendix viii), 261.

85. There is no indication that Rufinus attempted in any way to have the work connected with his name: hence Glas' charge (p. 13) that he was attempting to pass off the work as his own is rather futile. The same may be said of a similar objection in E. Schwartz's "Palladiana," *ZntW* 36 (1937), 164, n. 6.

86. PL 21, 335-386. There is an Eng. transl. by E. F. Morison, *A Commentary on the Apostles' Creed by T. Rufinus* (London, 1916). For the date of the original, see F. Kattenbusch, *Das apostolische Symbol* (Leipzig, 1894-1900), I, 104-105; II, 435, n. 6. Kattenbusch points out the fact that the similarity between the passages in this Commentary (c. 43), relating to the 'resurrection of the body' and that in Rufinus' *Apologia* (I, 5) can only indicate that the Commentary was written after the *Apologia*—hence about 404.

87. D. Vallarsi, *Praefatio in Rufini operum editionem* (PL 21, 57-58); Kattenbusch, *Apost. Symbol* I, 105-106; II, 434 f.; F. Diekamp, "Gelasios von Caesarea," OCA 117 (1938), 27, n. 1. Diekamp mentions that there is sufficient similarity between the Commentary and Gregory of Nyssa's *Oratio catechetica* to postulate dependence: (Rufinus, *Comm.* 14 on Gregory, *Orat. Catech.,* 32: PG 45, 81; Ruf., 15 on Greg., 6; PG 45, 28). But he defends Rufinus from the charge of plagiarizing, such as is made by Glas (*Kirchengesch. des Gelasios . . .* 10 and 14-15). Diekamp maintains that there is no source thus far unearthed for the first thirteen chapters of Rufinus' Commentary; the rest but for the last chapters is taken from Cyril's *Catechesis* 13, 7 ff. and 14-18. In this opinion, he agrees with Kattenbusch.

88. On Photinus, see O. Bardenhewer, *Gesch. d. altk. Litt.* III, 123-124.

89. Ruf., *Comm. in Symb. Apost.* (CSAp.) 1 (PL 21, 335): "Equidem comperi nonnullos illustrium trac-

tatorum aliqua de his pie et breviter edidisse. Photinum vero haereticum scio eatenus scripsisse, non ut rationem . . . explanaret. . . . Nos ergo simplicitatem suam vel verbis Apostolicis reddere et signare tentabimus, vel quae omissa videntur a prioribus, adimplere." He makes no claim at being original.

90. Ruf., CSAp. 2 (337-339). Rufinus is, of course, quite wrong on the story of the actual Apostolic origin of the creed as he gives it; however, he is here but recording a tradition then current. Practically the same story is told by St. Ambrose (*Explanatio symboli ad initiandos*: PL 17, 1155-1158), and by Niceta of Remesiana (ed. A. Burn, Cambridge, 1905).

There is a considerable literature devoted to the origin of the Creed, cited in B. Altaner, *Patrologie* (1938), 22-23. The original confession of faith, as of apostolic times, seems early to have crystalized into an eight- or nine-sectioned formula. It is to be met with in the Roman baptismal liturgy about 200; it is witnessed to by both Tertullian and Hippolitus. This early Roman creed is also found in the letter written by Marcellus of Ancyra to Pope Julius I (*ca.* 340); it is practically the same as the creed given by Rufinus and Niceta, except for the omission of the article on the 'forgiveness of sins.' The form of the Apostle's Creed that we are acquainted with today reached its present state in the 6th century; it is to be found almost word for word in Caesarius of Arles and in the later liturgy of both the Gallican and the Roman church. On the early creed, see especially, D. B. Capelle, "Les Origines du symbole romain," *Recherches de theol. ancienne et mediévale* (RTAM), 2 (1930), 5-20. For a different viewpoint, cf. F. Badcock, *The History of the Creeds* (London, 2nd ed., 1938).

91. Cf. F. Kattenbusch, *Das apost. Symbol,* II, 4 ff. He stresses the fact that Rufinus does not elaborate upon the legend: he does not even stop to point out which were the twelve articles of the Creed. Rufinus' main preoccupation is with pointing out the *Symbolum* as a monument safeguarding orthodoxy: hence his contrasting it with the Tower of Babel. His belief that the Apostles themselves referred to the creed as a *Symbolum* (CSAp. 2) is of course unfounded: the word is probably first used by Cyprian (cf. Kattenbusch, II, 4 n. 1).

92. The references to military institutions and to the circumstances of the tower of Babel (c. 2: PL 21, 337 f.) are a good indication of this. There are similar references scattered through the work; e.g., in c. 3, there is a fine exemplification of the

epistemological and psychological approach to the background of an act of faith; Rufinus links it with the experiences of every day life, such as boarding a ship, contracting marriage, etc. In c. 42-43, he compares the resurrection of the body to the renewal of plant and animal life, etc.

93. While his witness to the creed and the procedure then in vogue in Rome is valuable, he is mistaken in believing that the creed-formula there remained stable. See D. B. Capelle, "Les origines du symbole romain," *RTAM* 2 (1930), 5-20; J. Badcock, *The Hist. of the Creeds,* 122 ff.; H. Carpenter, "Creeds and Baptismal Rites in the first four Centuries," *JTS* 44 (1943), 1-11.

94. CSAp. 3 (PL 21, 540): "Ut ergo intelligentiae tibi aditus patescat, recto primo omnium te credere profiteris . . ." and he justifies this by citing daily experiences: "Nihil denique est, quod in vita geri possit, si non credulitas ante praecesserit."

95. Cf. Kattenbusch, I, 86-87.

96. CSAp. 6 (PL 21, 345). Rufinus is here drawing on Cyril's *Catechesis,* 14. See Kattenbusch, II, 554-562 for a long discussion of the problem relating to the use of the names Jesus and Christ and their collocation in the creeds.

97. CSAp. 9-13 (348 ff.). Rufinus maintains that Mary remained a virgin *ante et post partum,* but not *in partu.* He defends a natural birth for the Savior from any suggestion of its being unworthy. For his ideas on the death of Christ, see R. Favre, "Credo in Filium Dei, mortuum et sepultum," *RHE* 33 (1937), 709-712.

98. CSAp. 14-17 (352-356). He speaks of the cross as the "tropaeum triumphi Salvatoris." Cf. Kattenbusch (II, 638, n. 255) for his possible dependence upon Origen here.

99. CSAp. 31-34 (367-371).

100. CSAp. 35 (372-373).

101. CSAp. 36. This idea is not in Cyril's *Catechesis*; but it is to be found much later in Faustus of Riez (d. 490/500), *De Spiritu Sancto* (CSEL 21, p. 102 ff.). See F. Kattenbusch, II, 481-485; 510-515; J. Oulton, "The Apostles' Creed and Belief concerning the Church," *JTS* 39 (1938), 239-243. Oulton indicates the influence of this use of 'in' upon the Gallican and Irish creed formulas.

102. CSAp. 37-38 (PL 21, 373-374). Cf. E. Magenot, "canon," DThC 2^2 (Paris, 1905), 1577, for a consideration of Rufinus' witness to the canon of both the Old and the New Testament. Rufinus defends the fragments of Esther and Daniel against

St. Jerome (*Apol.* II, 33: PL 21 611). He cites Baruch, Wisdom, and Ecclesiasticus, even by way of a confirmation of his faith (CSAp. 5, 46: PL 21, 344, 385; *De bened. patriarch.*: PL 21, 326, 332, 333). On the New Testament Magenot gives him credit for quoting a full canon (c. 1591).

103. Rufinus is here dependent upon Athanasius (*Ep. fest.* 39); cf. O. Bardenhewer, *Gesch. der altk. Litt.* II, 266 f.; A. Krawutzcky, "Über das altk. Unterrichtsbuch 'Die zwei Wege oder die Entscheidung des Petrus,'" *Theol. Quartalschrift* 64 (1882), 359-445.

104. CSAp. 39 (PL 21, 375-377).

105. CSAp. 40 (377-378).

106. He gives a long rational explanation of the possibility of the resurrection from the standpoint of each man's receiving his own body after its disintegration; he compares it to the processes involved in plant life (c. 42-43); he disclaims the charge that St. Paul was enunciating a new doctrine in speaking of the resurrection (c. 44). His summation is in c. 48.

107. See above, note 86.

108. Bardenhewer, III, 556.

109. Joh. Cassian, *De incarnatione Domini* VII 27 (ed M. Petschenig, CSEL 17, 385): "Rufinus quoque . . . ita in expositione symboli de domini nativitate testatur. . . ." Cassian then incorporates a verbatim quotation from c. 13. On the possible use made of Rufinus' Commentary by Gaudentius in his *Tractatus 10* (in *Exodi lectione octavus*; ed. A. Glueck, CSEL 68), see Kattenbusch, I, 105, n. 6. The *Expositio Symboli* of Venantius Fortunatus (ed. F. Leo, MGH, Auct. Antiq. IV, 1) is merely a polished version of Rufinus—thus Kattenbusch, I, 130-132. Gennadius is a witness to the Rufinian authorship (*De viris inlus.* 17: ed. E. Richardson, TU 16, 46): "Proprio labore . . . exposuit idem Rufinus Symbolum, ut in eius conparatione alii nec exposuisse credantur." Cf. Bäumer, *Das apostolische Glaubenkenntnis* (Mainz, 1893), 65. The work was handed down through the middle ages principally under the names of Cyprian and Jerome; but there can be no doubt that it is Rufinus' (cf. Kattenbusch, I, 105 f.).

Bibliography

ABBREVIATIONS

AB—Analecta Bollandiana, Brussels.

ASS—Acta sanctorum bollandiana.

BLE—Bulletin de littérature ecclésiastique, Paris.

CSEL—Corpus scriptorum ecclesiasticorum latinorum, Vienna.

DACL—Dictionnaire d'archéologie chrétienne et de liturgie, Paris.

DHGE—Dictionnaire d'histoire et de géographie ecclésiastiques, Paris.

DSp—Dictionnaire de Spiritualité, Paris.

DThC—Dictionnaire de théologie catholique, Paris.

GCS—Griechische christliche Schriftsteller, Leipzig.

HThR—Harvard Theological Review, Cambridge (Mass.).

JTS—Journal of Theological Studies, London.

LThK—Lexikon für Theologie und Kirche, Freiburg.

PG—Migne, Patrologia, series graeca.

PL—Migne, Patrologia, series latina.

NRTh—Nouvelle revue théologique, Tournai.

PW—Pauly-Wissowa-Kroll, *Realencyklopädie der klassischen Altertumswissenschaft,* Stuttgart.

Rev Bened.—Revue Bénédictine, Maredsous.

RHE—Revue d'histoire ecclésiastique, Louvain.

RSR—Recherches de science religieuse, Paris.

TU—Texte und Untersuchungen, ed. Gebhardt-Harnack-Schmidt, Leipzig.

ZKG—Zeitschrift für Kirchengeschichte, Stuttgart.

ZntW—Zeitschrift für neutestamentliche Wissenschaft.

ZThK—Zeitschrift für Theologie und Kirche, Tübingen.

PRIMARY SOURCES

Baehrens, W. A., *Origenes Werke VI-VII, Homilien zum Hexateuch in Rufins Übersetzung,* Leipzig, 1920-1921.

———, *Origenes Werke VIII, Homilien zu Samuel I, zum Hohelied und zu den Propheten, Kommentar zum Hohelied,* Leipzig, 1925.

Batiffol, P. et Wilmart, A., *Tractatus Origenis,* Paris, 1900.

Butler, C., *The Lausiac History of Palladius,* 2 vols., Texts and Studies VI, Cambridge, 1898-1904.

Conybeare, F. C., *The Ring of Pope Xystus* (Eng. transl.), London, 1910.

Dalton, O. M., *The Letters of Sidonius Apollinaris,* 2 vols., Oxford, 1915.

Elter, A., *Gnomica I: Sexti Pythagorici, Clitarchi, Evagrii Pontici Sententiae,* Leipzig, 1892.

Engelbrecht, W., *Tyranni Rufini Orationum Gregorii Nazianzeni novem interpretatio,* CSEL 46, Vienna, 1910.

Fritzsche, O. F., *Epistola Clementis ad Jacobum ex Rufini interpretatione,* Zurich, 1873.

Gildemeister, I., *Sexti sententiarum recensiones,* Bonn, 1873.

Glueck, A., *Gaudentii tractatus,* CSEL 68, Vienna, 1932.

Koetschau, P., *De Principiis Origenis, Origenis Werke* V, GCS, Leipzig, 1914.

Hennecke, E., *Neutestamentliche Apokryphen,* 2nd ed., Tübingen, 1924.

Hoffman, H., *Augustini De civitate Dei,* 2 vols., CSEL 40, Vienna, 1899.

Lake, K., and Oulton, J. E. L., *Eusebius, The Ecclesiastical History,* 2 vols., Loeb series, 1926-1932.

Lommatzsch, C., *Origenes Werke,* 12 vols., Berlin 1830-1848.

Mynors, R., *Cassiodori Institutiones divinarum et humanarum lectionum,* Oxford, 1937.

Richardson, E., *Hieronymus, Liber de viris inlustribus, TU* 14, 1, Leipzig, 1896.

———, *Gennadius, Liber de viris inlustribus, TU* 14, 2, Leipzig, 1896.

Rufinus, Tyranius, *Ad Heraclium peroratio in explanationem Origenis super Epistolam Pauli ad Romanos,* PG 14, 1291 ff.

———, *Sancti Basilii regulae ad monachos interpretatio,* PL 103, 485-554.

———, *De Adulteratione librorum Origenis,* PG 17, 615 f.

———, *Praefatio ad Gaudentium,* CSEL 68, Vienna, 1932.

———, *Praefatio in Epistolam Pauli ad Romanos,* PG 14, 831 f.

Sacchini, F., *Divi Paulini ep. Nolani opera cum notis,* Antwerp, 1622.

Schenkl C., *Ambrosii de Patriarchis,* CSEL 32, 2, Vienna, 1897.

Schwartz, E., und Mommsen, T., *Eusebius Werke*: Die Kirchengeschichte, 3 vols., Leipzig, 1903-1909.

Schwartz, E., *Epistula Anastasii Romanae urbis Episcopi ad Johannem episcopum Jerosolymorum, Acta conciliorum oecumeniorum,* I, 5, Berlin and Leipzig, 1927.

Vallarsi, D., *T. Rufini Opera omnia,* Verona, 1742: reprinted PL 21.

Van den Gehyn, J., La lettre du pape Anastase I à S. Venerius, évêque de Milan sur la condemnation d'Origène, *Revue d'histoire et de litterature religieuses,* 4 (Paris, 1899), 1-12.

Van de Sande Bakhuyzen, W. H., *Der Dialog des Adamantius,* Leipzig, 1901.

Zycha, J., *Augustini Contra Faustum,* CSEL 25, Vienna, 1891-1892.

SECONDARY WORKS

Alexander, Natalis, *Selecta historiae ecclesiae capita,* 9 vols., Lucca, 1749 ff.

Amann, E., "Aprochryphes du Noveau Testament," *Dictionnaire de la Bible, Supplément I,* Paris, 1928.

———, "Chronique d'ancienne littérature chrétienne," *Revue des sciences religieuses* 12 (1932), 220-238.

Babut, C., "Paulin de Nole, Sulpice Sévère, saint Martin," *Annales du Midi* 20 (1908), 5-28.

Baehrens, W. A., *Überlieferung und Textgeschichte der lateinisch erhaltenen Origeneshomilien sum alten Testament, TU* 42, 1, Leipzig, 1916.

Bardenhewer, O., *Geschichte der altkirchlichen Literatur,* 5 vols., Freiburg im Breisgau, 1914-1932.

Bardy, G., "Les citations bibliques d'Origène dans le De Principiis," *Revue biblique* 16 (1919), 106-135.

———, "L'église et l'enseignement au quatrième siècle," *RSR* 14 (1934), 525-549; 15 (1935), 1-27.

———, "Faux et fraudes littéraires dans l'antiquité chrétienne," *RHE,* 32 (1936), 5-23; 275-302.

———, "Gélase (décret de)," *Dictionnaire de la bible: Supplément III* (1938), 579-590.

———, *Recherches sur l'histoire du texte et des versions latines du De Principiis d'Origène,* Paris, 1923.

———, "Rufin d'Aquilée," *DThC,* 14 (Paris, 1939), 153-160.

———, *Saint Athanase,* Paris, 1914.

———, "Saint Athanase," *DHGE* 3 (Paris, 1930), 1321-1325.

———, "Sur la patrie des évêques dans les premières siècles," *RHE* 35 (1939), 217-242.

———, "Le texte de l'épitre aux Romains dans le commentaire d'Origène-Rufin," *Revue biblique* 29 (1920), 229-235.

Baronius, C., *Annales ecclesiastici,* 12 vols., Rome, 1588-1607; Venice, 1738.

Basnagius, S., *Annales politico-ecclesiasticae,* 3 vols., Rotterdam, 1706.

Bauernfeind, O., *Der Römerbrieftext des Origenes, TU* 44, 3, Leipzig, 1923.

Baynes, N. H., "The Dynasty of Valentinian and Theodosius the Great," *Camb. Med. Hist.* I (New York, 1911), 218-248.

Brochet, J., *Saint Jerome et ses ennemis,* Paris, 1906.

Burn, A., *Niceta of Remesiana,* Cambridge, 1905.

Butler, C., "Monasticism," *Camb. Med. Hist.* I (New York, 1911), 521-542.

Caspar, E., *Geschichte des Päpsttums,* 2 vols., Tübingen, 1930-1933.

Cavallera, F., *Saint Jérôme, sa vie et son ouevre,* 2 vols., Louvain, 1922.

————, *Le schisme d'Antioch,* Paris, 1905.

Cave, G., *Scriptores ecclesiastici,* 2 vols., Geneva, 1693.

Chapman, J., "On the date of the Clementines," *ZntW* 9 (1908), 21-46; 147-159.

————, *Saint Benedict and the Sixth Century,* London, 1929.

Cullman, O., *Le problème littéraire et historique du roman pseudo-clémentin,* Paris, 1930.

D'Alès, A., "Baptême selon les pères," *Dictionnaire de la bible, Supplément I* (Paris, 1928), 864-871.

DeBruyne, D., "La correspondance échangée entre Augustin et Jérôme," *ZntW* 31 (1932), 233-248.

Diekamp, F., "Gelasius von Caesarea," *Orientalia christiana analecta* 117 (1938), 16-32.

Duchesne, L., *Histoire ancienne de l'église,* 3 vols., 1910-1929.

————, *Les origines du culte chrétien,* 3 ed., Paris, 1903.

Dzialowski, G. v., *Isidor und Ildefons als Litteraturhistoriker,* Kirchengeschichtliche Studien IV, 2, Münster, 1898.

Eberding, H., "Pammachius," *LThK* 7 (1935), 911-912.

Ebert, A., *Allgemeine Geschichte der Literatur des Mittelalters,* 3 vols., Leipzig, 1889.

Fliche, A. et Martin, V., *Histoire de l'église,* vols. III and IV, Paris, 1936-1937.

Fontanini J., *Historiae literariae Aquileiensis libri V,* Rome, 1742.

Freemantle, W., "Rufinus," *DCB* IV (London, 1887), 555-561.

Glas, A., *Die Kirchengeschichte des Gelasios,* Leipzig, 1914: Byzantinisches Archiv, Heft 6.

Grégoire, H. et Kugener, M.-A., *Marc le diacre: vie de Porphyre, évêque de Gaza,* Paris, 1930.

Grégoire, H., "La christianization de la Géorgie," *Byzantion* 7 (1932), 737-739.

Gorce, D., *Les voyages, l'hospitalité et le port des lettres dans le monde chrétienne des IV et V siècle,* Paris, 1926.

Goyau, G., *Sainte Mélanie,* Paris, 1908.

Grützmacher, G., *Hieronymus, eine biographische Studien zur alten Kirchengeschichte,* 3 vols., Berlin, 1903-1909.

Gwynn, J., *Roman Education from Cicero to Quintillian,* Oxford, 1926.

Harnack, A., *Die Chronologie der altchristlichen Literatur bis Eusebius,* 3 vols. (I-II, 1 and 2), Leipzig, 1904.

————, *Die kirchengeschichtliche Ertrag der exegetischen Arbeiten des Origenes, TU* 42, 3 and 4, Leipzig, 1918-1919.

————, *Marcion, das Evangelium des fremden Gottes,* 2nd ed., Leipzig, 1924.

Heussi, K., *Der Ursprung des Mönchtums,* Tübingen, 1936.

Hilpisch, S., "Die Doppelklöster: Enstehung und Organization," *Beitrage zu Geschichte des alten Mönchtums,* 15 (ed. I. Herwegen), Münster, 1928.

————, *Geschichte des benediktinischen Mönchtums,* Munich, 1929.

Hoppe, H., "Rufin als Übersetzer," *Studi dedicati alla memoria di Paolo Ubaldi* (Milan, 1937), 133-150.

Hörle, G., *Frühmittelalterliche Mönchs-und Klerikerbildung in Italien,* Freiburg, 1914.

Jülicher, A., "Ein Wort zugunsten des Kirchenhistorikers Rufinus," *Klio* 14 (1914), 127-128.

Kattenbusch, F., *Das apostolische Symbol,* 2 vols., Leipzig, 1894-1900.

Kimmel, E., *De Rufino Eusebii interprete,* Jena, 1838.

Kirsch, J., *Die römische Titelkirchen in Altertum,* Münster, 1924.

————, *Kirchengeschichte I: Die Kirche in der griechischen-römischen Kulturwelt,* Freiburg, 1930.

Koetschau, P., "Zur Lebens-Geschichte Gregors des Wundertäters," *Zeits. für wissensch. Theologie* 41 (1891), 240 ff.

Krumbacher, K., *Geschichte der byzantinischen Literatur,* 2nd ed., Munich, 1897.

Ladeuze, P., *Étude sur le cénobitisme pakhômien pendant le IV siècle et la première moitié du V,* Louvain, 1898.

Leclercq, H., "Celius," *DACL* 2 (Paris, 1925), 2836-2870.

———, "Croix, Invention de la," *DACL* 3 (Paris, 1914), 3131-3137.

———, "École," *DACL* 4 (Paris, 1921), 1730-1883.

———, "Monachisme," *DACL* 11 (Paris, 1934), 1774-1947.

Lübeck, E., *Hieronymus quos noverit scriptores et ex quibus houserit,* Leipzig, 1872.

Marzuttini, J., *De Turani Rufini presbyteri Aquileiensis fide et religione,* Padua, 1835.

Monceaux, P., *S. Jérôme, sa jeunesse, l'étudiant et l'ermite,* Paris, 1932.

Moricca, U., *Storia della litteratura latina christiana,* III, Rome, 1934.

Moretus, H., "Les Bénédictions des Patriarches," *BLE,* 1909, 405-411.

Murphy, F., "Foil for the Irascible Hermit: Rufinus of Aquileia," *Catholic World* 150 (1940), 556-564.

Noris, H. Cardinal, *Historia Pelagiana* I, 2nd ed., Verona, 1729.

Oulton, J., "Rufinus' Translation of the Church History of Eusebius," *JTS* 30 (1929), 150-174.

Palanque, J.-R., *Saint Ambroise et l'empire romain,* Paris, 1933.

Paschini, P., "Chromatius d'Aquilée et le commentaire ps.-Hieronymien," *Rev. Bénéd.* 26 (1909), 469-475.

Pasté, R., "Un orientali latinista presso S. Eusebio di Vercelli: Evagrio di Antiochia," *Scuola catolica* 3 (1932), 341-358.

Peeters, P., "Les débuts du christianisme en Géorgie," *Anal. Bolland.* 50 (1932), 558.

———, "Une vie copte de S. Jean de Lycopole," *Anal. Bolland.* 54 (1936), 369-375.

Pètursson, P., *Symbolae ad fidem et studia Tyranii Rufini presbyteri Aquileiensis illustranda, e scriptis suis petitae,* Havniae, 1840.

Philipp, M., *Zum Sprachgebrauch des Paulinus von Nola,* Erlangen, 1904.

Preuschen, E., *Palladius und Rufinus: ein Beitrage zur Quellenkunde des ältesten Mönchtums,* Giessen, 1897.

Ramsbotham, A., "The Commentary of Pelagius on Romans compared with that of Origen-Rufinus," *JTS* 20 (1919), 127-177.

Reinelt, P., *Studien über die Briefe des hl. Paulinus von Nola,* Breslau, 1904.

Reitzenstein, R., *Historia Monachorum und Historia Lausiaca,* Göttingen, 1916.

Richard, P., "Aquilée," *DHGE* 2 (Paris, 1924), 1114-1115.

Salonius, A., *Vitae Patrum, kritische Untersuchungen über Text, Syntax und Wortschatz der spätlateinischen Vitae Patrum,* Lund, 1920.

Schanz, M., *Geschichte der römischen Literatur,* IV Teil, 1 Hälfte, Munich, 1914.

Schmidt, C., *Studien zu den Pseudo-Clementinen, TU* 46, 1, Leipzig, 1929.

Schoenemann, C., *Bibliotheca historico-literaria Patrum latinorum,* 2 vols., Leipzig, 1792.

Schwartz, E., "Palladiana," *ZntW* 27 (1936), 161-204.

———, "Unzeitgemässe Beobachtungen zu den Clementinen," *ZntW* 31 (1932), 151-199.

Seeck, O., *Die Briefe des Libanios, TU* 30, Leipzig, 1906.

———, *Geschichte des Untergangs der antiken Welt,* V, Leipzig, 1924.

———, *Regesten der Kaiser und Päpste,* Stuttgart, 1919.

———, und Veith, G., "Die Schlacht an Firgidus," *Klio,* 13 (1913), 451 467.

Stilting, J., "De S. Hieronymo presbytero et doctore ecclesiae in Bethleem," *ASS,* 48, September VIII, Antwerp, 1762.

Telfer, W., "The Cultus of St. Gregory Thaumaturgus," *HThR* 29 (1936).

———, "The Latin *Life* of St. Gregory Thaumaturgus," *JTS* 31 (1930), 142-155.

———, "The Trustworthiness of Palladius," *JTS* 38 (1937), 379-

Tillemont, S. LeNain de, *Mémoires pour servir à l'histoire ecclésiastique des dix premiers siècles,* 16 vols., Paris, 1693 ff.

Villain, M., "Rufin d'Aquilée, l'étudiant et le moine," *NRTh* 64 (1937), 5-33; 139-161.

———, "La querelle autour d'Origène," *RSR* 37 (1937).

Westcott, B., "Origenes," *DCB* IV (London, 1887), 96-142.

Wagner, Sr. M. Monica, *Rufinus the Translator,* Washington, in press.

Philip R. Amidon (essay date 1997)

SOURCE: Amidon, Philip R. Introduction to *The Church History of Rufinus of Aquileia: Books 10 and 11,* translated by Philip R. Amidon, pp. vii-xix. Oxford: Oxford University Press, 1997.

[*In the following essay, Amidon offers an overview of twentieth-century scholarship on Rufinus.*]

What is known of the life of Tyrannius (or Turranius) Rufinus is well set out on F. X. Murphy's authoritative biography.[1] He was born around 345 C.E. in Iulia Concordia (west of Aquileia). His parents were noble and wealthy, to judge from his education, which he completed in Rome. While a student there he became close friends with Jerome.

Athanasius had popularized montasticism in the West during his long exile there, a year of which was spent in Aquileia around the time of Rufinus's birth. By 370 there was an ascetic community in Aquileia that Rufinus joined upon his return to Rome. He was baptized in 369 or 370. His enthusiasm for the monastic life inspired him, as it did other Western Christians, to visit its birthplace, and he made his way to Egypt at the end of 372 or early in 373.

It was about the same time, in November of 372, that Anthonia Melanio, a widow of the highest nobility who had likewise taken up the ascetic life, sailed from Rome to the East. She arrived in Alexandria at about the same time as Rufinus (although there is no reason to suppose that they traveled together), just in time to witness the oubreak of the Arian persecution that followed Athanasius's death (in May of 373). She decided to follow a group of exiles from the persecution to Diocaesarea in Palestine, and from there went on to Jerusalem in 375.

Rufinus, meanwhile, stayed in Egypt to continue his studies for six years under Didymus the Blind and others; it was Didymus who introduced him to Origen's works. He spent 378(?) visiting the other homeland of monasticism, in Palestine and Syria, and then returned to Alexandria for a final two years of study with Didymus.

Melania, meanwhile, had founded a monastery in Jerusalem, where Rufinus joined her perhaps in 380. It was a double monastery, for women and men, the first such Latin foundation in the Holy Land, and it included a guest house for pilgrims. Rufinus, in his part of the monastery, directed the copying of books (including the Latin classics, for which there would have been some demand in the new Latin colonies of the Near East). He must have been ordained presbyter about this time.

Jerome arrived in 385 to tour the Near East, and in 386 his friend Paula began work on a double monastery in Bethlehem after the example of Melania and Rufinus. His relationship with Rufinus, however, cooled for a number of reasons,[2] until it was finally disrupted by the outbreak of the Origenist controversy. Both of them had admired Origen greatly, but Epiphanius of Salamis's attempt (in 393) to get John of Jerusalem to condemn Origen as the forerunner of Arius drew different responses from them. Rufinus followed John in refusing to do so, while Jerome agreed to the condemnation. The two of them, together with their monks, were divided over the issue, which dragged on for years. Jerome and Rufinus were finally reconciled in 397, the same year Rufinus returned to Italy, taking his books with him.

He found, when he landed in Rome, that rumor of the Origenist quarrel had far outrun him. It was not long before he was asked to translate **Pamphilus's Vindication of Origen.** To it he added his own **The Falsification of Origen's Works,** in which he explained that the heterodox views found in Origen's books were the falsifications and interpolations of his enemies.

He spent the fall of 397 and spring of 398 at the monastery of Pinetum, near Terracina, where he translated **Basil's Rules** for Abbot Ursacius. It was also in 398 that at the instance of the noble scholar Macarius he undertook his fateful translation of **Origen's First Principles.** In his preface he repeated his view that the text had been corrupted by Origen's enemies, and he explained that he had therefore altered or replaced statements of doubtful orthodoxy with other, sounder ones taken from Origen's other works. He also said that in doing so he was simply following Jerome's lead, both in translating Origen into Latin and in suppressing suspect passages in him (he did not mention him by name but alluded to him so clearly that the reference was unmistakable). Word of his project got around Rome, and the anti-Origenist party denounced him and complained to Jerome.

His translation of the letter to St. James the Apostle attributed to Clement of Rome may perhaps also be dated to around this time, but by the second half of 398 Rufinus had had enough of the Origenist controversy; he left Rome for the more peaceful atmosphere of Aquileia after writing Jerome an apparently amicable letter explaining his move. Jerome, meanwhile, stung by his friend's public reminder of his own earlier infatuation with Origen, made a literal translation of the *First Principles* and sent it to Rome, together with an angry open letter to his friends there in which he practically accused Rufinus's translation of fostering heresy. He also wrote a private letter to Rufinus explaining the apologetic purpose of the open letter; he evidently hoped to avoid a public break. But Jerome's friends in

Rome withheld the letter from Rufinus and drummed up a campaign against him throughout Italy.

Once settled in Aquileia, Rufinus continued producing translations: of Basil's homilies and Gregory's discourses, the **Sentences of Sextus,** Adamantius's *De recta in Deum fide,* the **Commentary on the Apostles' Creed,** and Origen on Joshua, Judges, and Psalms 36-38.

Pope Siricius died in November of 399 and was succeeded by Anastasius, who proved more sympathetic to Rufinus's anti-Origenist foes. Theophilus of Alexandria now took the field against Origen, presiding over a council which condemned him in 400. The emperor confirmed its sentence and proscribed Origen's works; Theophilus communicated this in a letter to Anastasius. The pope in turn confirmed the council's sentence and communicated his decision to Simplician of Milan, inviting him and his colleagues in northern Italy to add their own confirmation. But Simplician died that year, so Anastasius wrote to his successor Venerius repeating his invitation. Rufinus, by now feeling himself under increasing pressure, composed the **Apology to Anastasius.** Anastasius made no direct answer, but to John of Jerusalem, who had expressed concern about his old friend, he replied condemning Origen but adding that he wished to know nothing about Rufinus, neither where he was nor what he was about.

Rufinus, worried and resentful at having received no reply to his letter to Jerome (as he thought), replied to Jerome's criticisms in 401 with his **Apology against Jerome.** In it he defended himself against the imputation of heresy and furnished massive evidence of Jerome's own earlier devotion not only to Origen's exegesis but to his speculative theology as well. It was the final break; Jerome replied the same year with his ferocious *Apology against Rufinus,* and although the latter, after one final personal letter, discontinued the public argument thereafter, Jerome pursued him with vitriolic pen even beyond the grave, much to Augustine's dismay.

It was in November of this year that Alaric and his Goths marched into Italy and in 402 laid siege to Milan. With his city under threat, Chromatius of Aquileia asked Rufinus to translate Eusebius of Caesarea's **Church History,** the reading of which he thought might divert his people's attention from their danger. Eusebius's work had, since its publication in 325, acquired an extensive and well-deserved reputation for its learned and edifying survey of Christian history from its beginning to the end of the pagan persecutions. Rufinus agreed to Chromatius's request and in 402 or 403 published an abridged translation of the original,

together with his own continuation of it to carry it forward to the year 395 (the date of Theodosius's death).

By then the Gothic threat had receded, and Rufinus may well have left Aquileia for Rome at this time; he was almost certainly there by the middle of 406 and probably earlier. The atmosphere there had become more congenial to him since the return of his powerful patroness Melania in 400, the succession of Innocent I in 402 following the death of Anastasius, and the new antipathy many people felt for the anti-Origenist party due to the exile of John Chrysostom, the most celebrated victim of Theophilus's campaign against the Origenist monks. It cannot be proved beyond all objection that he left Aquileia before 407, but the circumstantial evidence is strong.[3] The years 403-406, at any rate, saw him back at work on translations of Origen: his commentaries on Genesis, Exodus, and Leviticus, and the Letter to the Romans. He also translated the **History of the Monks in Egypt,** perhaps as a contribution to the campaign in favor of John Chrysostom, and the pseudo-Clementine *Recognitions.* Pelagius, also in Rome at this time, was put into fateful contact with Origen through his translations. He laid Origen/Rufinus under heavy tribute in forming his own doctrine on free will and grace, being influenced in particular by the Commentary on Romans.

The Elder Melania left Italy to return to the Holy Land in 406 or early 407. Rufinus also thought of returning there, but for some reason he put it off, and in 408 he was forced to join the great caravan of his fellow Romans fleeing to Sicily before a new invasion of Goths. There, from across the strait, he watched Rhegium go up in flames under Alaric's assault, and there he died in 410 or 411, still at work translating (Origen on Song of Songs, I Samuel, Numbers, and perhaps Deuteronomy).[4]

Rufinus was a person of unquestionable impoftance in the turbulent history of the church in the late fourth and early fifth centuries. He can hardly match Jerome's colorful personality and brilliant style, but together with him he introduced the Latin-speaking church to a trove of important Greek Christian literature that had hitherto been practically inaccessible to it. He had little of the other's acuteness in exegesis, but he had an equally thorough mastery of Greek and a better sense of historiography.[5]

Whatever may have been his at least professed initial hesitation in acceding to Chromatius's request for a translation of Eusebius's **Church History,** his execution of the project shows a keen appreciation of the narrative power of the original, clumsily dressed though it was in the author's infelicitous style. It is true that he translated freely, at times to the point of paraphrasing.

But he viewed the history of the church of his own time as a reproduction in miniature of the vast canvas of the first centuries of its life painted by Eusebius, on which the pattern of mission, persecution, division, and salvation stood out so clearly. Just as the earliest church in its deprivation and suffering, the seedbed of its mission, had been aided by God's power working through His servants and been securely established by the pious emperor Constantine, so that of his own time had seen God's power equally at work in the lives of its holy ones to extend its mission in the midst of suffering and to reestablish its safety with the accession of the orthodox emperor Theodosius. The reproduction was not exact, for this time most of the persecutors were Christian (and therefore much more dangerous). But for Rufinus, this is the secret of church history: the power of God revealed in weakness. The weakness is evidenced in persecutions and in the divisions of heresy and schism, but the power shows forth in the lives of holy Christians through whom God continues to work the kind of wonders recorded in previous times in the Scriptures. For Rufinus there is but one people of God, with one continuous history in which this pattern is revealed. That is what he set out to offer the Western Church in his translation and continuation.[6]

His history was an instant and lasting success. It was the first Latin Christian history and, as such, exerted great influence over both his contemporaries and later generations. Augustine relied on it in composing the historical sections of the *City of God*. Paul Orosius implicitly challenged its outlook in his *Historiae adversus paganos* (417). But the Byzantine church historians Socrates and Sozomen as well were deeply (and not always happily) influenced by it; Socrates (at least) evidently read it in the original Latin. He later had to rewrite the first two books of his history in order to correct Rufinus's chronology. He continued to use him nonetheless, and his and Sozomen's works won for Rufinus a place among the few Latin Christians to affect the course of Greek Christian literature. Even more important, perhaps, was his influence in the later Western Church right through the Middle Ages, when Greek was forgotten and his translation/continuation offered it the only available view of its earliest formative history.

In the prefaces to the translation and to the continuation, Rufinus distinguishes between the methods he used in the two. He says that he shortened Eusebius's original as he saw fit. In fact, he abridged freely and often drastically, smoothing out inconsistencies and irrelevancies (as he saw them), simplifying the style, and expunging any tinges of heterodoxy (about which he was by this time quite sensitive). "He felt himself justified in replacing imprecise words and phrases in Eusebius with expressions which were clear and unambiguous. Nor

did [he] hesitate to rewrite or add explanations of his own if this would aid understanding."[7] He also occasionally added items from his own experience. His additions to the martyrdom accounts square with the extant Acts and show that he took the trouble to consult documents for fuller information.[8]

For the continuation of the history, Rufinus says that he relied upon records and his own memory: "on what has come down from those before us, and . . . on what we remembered," as the preface to the translation puts it, or as he repeats in the preface to the continuation, "[the material that] we either found in the writings of those before us or we remembered." But here we come upon the controversy surrounding his relationship with the first continuer of Eusebius's history: Gelasius of Caesarea.

In his influential monograph of 1914,[9] Anton Glas noted that Greek texts paralleling most of Rufinus's continuation can be assembled from Gelasius of Cyzicus's *Syntagma* (fifth century) and from the *Chronicle* of George the Monk (ninth century). But the passages where Gelasius explicitly cites Rufinus are not in fact from him; they deal with a time before his continuation begins. As for George, he was (all agree) incapable of translating Latin (at least into the kind of Greek where he parallels Rufinus). Nor did he copy from the *Syntagma*; much of his text is not found there, and even where their texts run parallel in content, one is not a copy of the other. From this Glas inferred that there existed a Greek history which early became attributed to Rufinus for some reason. Now the *Syntagma* in one place (1.8.1) refers to "Rufinus or Gelasius" as a source. Glas therefore concluded that Rufinus's continuation had at some point become confused with that of Gelasius of Caesarea (well attested but long since vanished). The independence of Gelasius's is shown both by the fact that it began before Rufinus's and by a comparison of passages where its Greek is preserved: Rufinus's is clearly a translation of the other. Therefore, whatever he may have claimed in his prefaces, Rufinus did little more in his continuation than translate Gelasius without attribution.

In the following year Paul van den Ven independently suggested the existence of a Greek version of Rufinus's continuation, attributed to Gelasius of Caesarea, from which later sources drew.[10] He wrote without reference to Glas, but his article was viewed as a defense of Rufinus's honor, and from then on the battle lines between German- and French-language scholarship were drawn up in almost perfect order.

In 1932 Peter Heseler, accepting Glas's conclusions without discussion, presented as excerpts from Gelasius of Caesarea texts from the *Life of Metrophanes and Alexander* and the *Life of Constantine and Helena*.[11]

In 1938 Franz Diekamp, in the only German-language article to oppose Glas's thesis overall, protested that a comparison of Rufinus's Latin with the parallel Greek passages would not yield more securely the conclusion that the Latin was a translation than the converse.[12] It might be true that he had translated the **History of the Monks in Egypt** without attribution and that his commentary on the creed depended in great part on Cyril of Jerusalem's *Catecheses,* but in the former case he simply translated an anonymous work anonymously, while in the introduction to the latter he admitted his debt to others. Thus neither case proves that his claim to independent authorship in the preface to his continuation should not be taken seriously.

In 1946 Van den Ven published his agreement with Diekamp: Rufinus's work was the original, and Gelasius had translated him with additions of his own.[13]

Felix Scheidweiler came to Glas's defense in 1953, rejecting Diekamp's attempt to save Rufinus's integrity.[14] Rufinus's continuation, whatever he claimed, was mainly a translation of Gelasius's with a few additions of his own. The reason that the credit later went to Rufinus was that both Socrates and Gelasius of Cyzicus cite him as a source, and their later readers, noticing the parallels between Rufinus and Gelasius of Caesarea, must have assumed, on Socrates' authority, that Rufinus was the original whom he had consulted. But Rufinus's text bears all the earmarks of translation, in contrast to the Greek parallels.

Ernest Honigmann advanced the debate the following year with the observation that according to the address of Letter 92 in Jerome's collection, Gelasius of Caesarea must have died in or before the year 400. Thus his work is independent of Rufinus's, which was published afterward. But later readers of Gelasius of Cyzicus may have been misled by his claim that Rufinus attended the Council of Nicaea (*Syntagma,* Proem. 1.21-22) and may have thought of Rufinus as older than Gelasius of Caesarea. They may also have thought that he wrote only of that council, if all that they knew of his work came from Gelasius of Cyzicus. Honigmann proposed that someone during the fifth century composed a kind of *historia bipartita* or *tripartita* in Greek covering the Council of Nicaea or perhaps the reigns of Constantius Chlorus and Constantine. It may have borne a title which made readers think that Rufinus and Gelasius were the same person. That would explain why passages not in the Latin Rufinus were later attributed to him. He also conjectured that during this period there was as well a Greek text corresponding closely to the Latin Rufinus; perhaps Rufinus himself composed it. He did admit that Rufinus had probably used Gelasius's history.[15]

Scheidweiler welcomed Honigmann's proof of Gelasius of Caesarea's priority, but rejected his hypothesis about a "Greek Rufinus." Rufinus remained for him little more than the translator of Gelasius's history.[16]

In 1962 Ernest Bihain made the little noticed but useful suggestion that attention be paid to how Cyril of Jerusalem, Gelasius of Caesarea's uncle and patron, shows up in passages supposedly deriving from his nephew, as in the critical notice in Socrates 2.38.2.[17]

In a series of publications from 1964 to 1982, Friedhelm Winkelmann surveyed the ground gained and yielded by either side in the debate. The priority and therefore independence of Gelasius of Caesarea's history had been established, but not its extension; though two of the ancient sources mentioned that it reached back into Diocletian's reign,[18] none of them said how far forward in time it extended. If one assumed that Rufinus had done little more than translate Gelasius, then the latter must have been the original author of the lengthy narratives of events in Egypt which take up so much of Rufinus's Book 11. But it was Rufinus who spent years in Egypt and who could be supposed to have had firsthand knowledge of what had happened there; Gelasius may never have visited it. Winkelmann accepted this point, and he also disagreed with Scheidweiler that Rufinus's Latin looked like a translation. He did, however, agree with him that it was Gelasius who had moved the Council of Tyre which condemned Athanasius to Constantius's reign; Rufinus had merely followed his chronology. All things considered, then, he marked Rufinus's Book 10.1-15 as certainly an abridged and slightly modified translation of Gelasius, and he thought the same could probably be said of the following chapters up to and including 11.3 (about half to two-thirds of the whole). As for Socrates' complaint about having to revise and correct Rufinus's chronology, Winkelmann boldly claimed that Socrates was telling an untruth; it was really Gelasius he had been using for his first draft. And as for the difficult fact that there are Greek parallel texts to Rufinus even after 11.3, from which point he is certainly the original author, Winkelmann hypothesized that someone had translated him into Greek from the point where Gelasius left off, in order to provide a continuous Greek church history down to the death of Theodosius. But a careful study of the topography of Rufinus's history could, he thought, make possible the exhumation of at least the skeleton of Gelasius's.[19]

In 1987, however, Jacques Schamp cancelled the exhumation order after a close study of Photius's remarks about Gelasius of Caesarea, in which he argued persuasively that according to the patriarch, not only did his history end with Arius's death, but it placed that death (in contrast to Rufinus) in Constantine's reign.[20]

Both observations reduce the possible extent of Rufinus's dependence on Gelasius to the point where all hope of using the Latin history to reconstruct the Greek one vanishes.

Françoise Thelamon, meanwhile, in the introduction to her magistral study of Rufinus, *Païens et chrétiens au IVᵉ siècle* (Paris, 1981), dismissed the whole discussion as a misguided attempt to compare a still extant work with one now entirely lost, and she proceeded to treat Rufinus's history as an original work.[21]

The results of the debate may be summed up as follows. Gelasius of Caesarea certainly wrote a continuation to Eusebius's *Church History,* and he certainly completed it before Rufinus set to work on his; the ancient authorities leave no doubt on either point. It apparently began with Diocletian's reign and ended with the death of Arius. Rufinus probably consulted it and may have translated or paraphrased some passages without attribution. The conventions of his day were different from ours; as Manlio Simonetti remarks, "The custom of publishing under one's own name works which were essentially nothing more than paraphrases of Greek originals was by then wide-spread in the Christian world,"[22] and both Jerome and Rufinus engaged in this activity.

Schamp's investigations, however, show that this is not the way he used Gelasius, whose history ended with Arius's death in 335. Rufinus's own work continued on to the death of Theodosius in 395. He does not name his other sources, so we cannot tell how he employed them. But as Thelamon has so clearly shown, he wrote according to a definite plan; however deeply he drew from his sources, the final arrangement and form of his history are his own.

The hypothesis, put forward by various parties on either side of the debate, of a Greek translation of Rufinus's continuation, seems to have gained widespread acceptance. The influence he exercised upon the course of Greek church history through the lawyer-historians who could read him in the original is already considerable, but a Greek translation would have extended that influence immeasurably.

His work has been variously assessed over the past century. By modern historical standards it fares badly when compared with Eusebius's *Church History,* which is impressive in its discrimination of sources and nothing short of revolutionary in its citation of them. The revolution does not continue in Rufinus. He does not name his sources, with one or two exceptions, and he shows little of Eusebius's wariness of miraculous tales. He also displays in his continuation an almost unparalleled capacity for chronological errors, some of which

appear to be deliberate. If judged by its purpose, however, which was to buck up the beleaguered faithful of Aquileia, it may be said to be "a competent piece of work, admirably suited to the purpose he had in mind. It certainly is a vivid, well-written narrative."[23] It may be added that the continuation is also of considerable importance as a source for ancient and modern scholarship alike. Great was his authority among the Byzantine historians (Gelasius of Cyzicus believed he had attended the Council of Nicaea in person, as we have seen), and he will often be found to be the first source for the events they record (and the origin of the errors they repeat).

Rufinus condensed the ten books of Eusebius's history into nine in translation, so that the additional two books of his continuation are entitled Books 10 and 11 in the Latin work as a whole. These are the two books that are translated here. This is the first English translation of them. There is also an Italian translation in the *Collana di testi patristici* series.[24] The Latin edition used is that of Theodor Mommsen in the *Griechische Christliche Schriftsteller* series.[25] Special mention must also be made of Thelamon's work, cited earlier; it has become the standard reference for all modern studies of Rufinus's continuation, and the extent to which the present commentary is indebted to it will be easily apparent.

Notes

1. *Rufinus of Aquileia* (345-411): *His Life and Works* (Washington, 1945). See also C. P. Hammond's indispensable article, "The Last Ten Years of Rufinus' Life and the Date of His Move South from Aquileia," *JTS,* N.S., 28 (1977), 372-429. Cf. as well G. Fedalto, "Rufino di Concordia. Elementi di una biografia," *AAAd,* 39 (1992), 19-44.

2. Cf. J. N. D. Kelly, *Jerome* (New York, 1975), 196.

3. Cf. Hammond, "The Last Ten Years of Rufinus' Life," note 1.

4. Not all of Rufinus's works are covered here, and the dates of composition of many of them must remain conjectural. For a complete list cf. ibid., 428-429.

5. On Jerome's adaptation of Eusebius's *Chronicle,* see Kelly, *Jerome,* 72-75.

6. Cf. F. Thelamon, "Rufin historien de son temps," *AAAd,* 31 (1987), 1.41-59, and "Apôtres et prophètes de notre temps,'" *AAAd,* 39 (1992), 171-198.

7. T. Christensen, *Rufinus of Aquileia and the "Historia Ecclesiastica,"* Lib. VIII-IX, *of Eusebius* (Copenhagen, 1989), 333.

8. J. E. L. Oulton, "Rufinus's Translation of the Church History of Eusebius," *JTS* 30 (1929), 150-174.

9. *Die Kirchengeschichte des Gelasios von Kaisareia* (*Byzantinisches Archiv* 6, 1914).

10. "Fragments de la recension grecque de l'histoire ecclésiastique de Rufin dans un texte hagiographique," *Le Muséon* 33 (1915), 92-105.

11. "Hagiographica I" and "Hagiographica II," *Byzantinisch-Neugriechische Jahrbücher* 9 (1932), 113-128 and 320-337.

12. "Gelasius von Caesarea in Palaestina," *Analecta Patristica* (*Orientalia Christiana Analecta* 117 [1938]), 16-49.

13. "Encore le Rufin grec," *Le Muséon* 59 (1946), 281-294.

14. "Die Kirchengeschichte des Gelasios von Kaisareia," *Byzantinische Zeitschrift* 46 (1953), 277-301.

15. "Gélase de Césarée et Rufin d'Aquilée," *Académie royale de Belgique. Bulletin de la classe des lettres et des sciences morales et politiques* 40 (1954), 122-161.

16. *Byzantinische Zeitschrift* 48 (1955), 162-164, and 50 (1957), 74-98 (critical reviews of Honigmann's article in note 15).

17. "La source d'un texte de Socrate (HE 2.38.2) relatif à Cyrille de Jérusalem," *Byzantion* 32 (1962), 81-91.

18. Cf. Honigmann, "Gélase de Césarée," 159-160.

19. "Das Problem der Rekonstruktion der Historia Ecclesiastica des Gelasius von Caesarea," *Forschungen und Fortschritte* 38 (1964), 311-314; *Untersuchungen zur Kirchengeschichte des Gelasius von Kaisareia* (*Sitzungsberichte der deutschen Akademie der Wissenschaften zu Berlin,* Klasse für Sprachen, Literatur und Kunst 1965.3); "Charakter und Bedeutung der Kirchengeschichte des Gelasios von Kaisareia," *Byzantinische Forschungen* 1 (1966), 346-385; "Die Quellen der Historia Ecclesiastica des Gelasios von Cyzicus (nach 475)," *Byzantinoslavica* 27 (1966), 104-130; "Zu einer Edition der Fragmente der Kirchengeschichte des Gelasios von Kaisareia," *Byzantinoslavica* 34 (1973), 193-198; "Vita Metrophanis et Alexandri," *Analecta Bollandiana* 100 (1982), 147-184.

20. "Gélase ou Rufin: un fait nouveau," *Byzantion* 57 (1987), 360-390; "The Lost Ecclesiastical History of Gelasius of Caesarea," *The Patristic and Byzantine Review* 6.2 (1987), 146-152.

21. Thelamon *PC* 20.

22. "L'attività letteraria di Rufino negli anni della controversia origeniana," *AAAd* 39 (1992), 91.

23. Murphy, *Rufinus of Aquileia,* 174.

24. L. Dattrino, *Rufino. Storia della chiesa* (Rome, 1986).

25. *Eusebius Werke* 2.2. *Die Kirchengeschichte,* ed. E. Schwartz and T. Mommsen (Leipzig, 1908).

Abbreviations

AAAd: *Antichita altoadriatiche*

CCL: Corpus Christianorum, Series Latina

JTS: *Journal of Theological Studies*

Thelamon *PC*: F. Thelamon, *Païens et chrétiens au IVe siècle* (Paris, 1981).

Bibliography

GENERAL

Bihain, Ernest, "La source d'un texte de Socrate (HE 2.38.2) relatif à Cyrille de Jérusalem," *Byzantion* 32 (1962), 81-91.

Dattrino, Lorenzo, *Rufino. Storia della chiesa* (Rome, 1986).

Diekamp, Franz, "Gelasius von Caesarea in Palaestina," *Analecta Patristica* (*Orientalia Christiana Analecta* 117 [1938]), 16-49.

Fedalto, Giorgio, "Rufino di Concordia. Elementi di una biografia," *AAAd* 39 (1992), 19-44.

Glas, Anton, *Die Kirchengeschichte des Gelasios von Kaisareia* (*Byzantinisches Archiv* 6, 1914).

Hammond, C. P., "The Last Ten Years of Rufinus' Life and the date of His Move South from Aquileia," *JTS,* n.s., 28 (1977), 372-429.

Heseler, Peter, "Hagiographica I" and "Hagiographica II," *Byzantinisch-Neugriechische Jahrbücher* 9 (1932), 113-128 and 320-337.

Honigmann, Ernest, "La liste originale des Pères de Nicée," *Byzantion* 14 (1939), 17-76.

———, "Gélase de Césarée et Rufin d'Aquilée," *Académie royale de Belgique. Bulletin de la classe des lettres et des sciences morales et politiques* 40 (1954), 122-161.

Kelly, J. N. D., Early Christian Creeds (London, 1972).

———, *Jerome* (New York, 1975).

Murphy, F. X., *Rufinus of Aquileia (345-411): His Life and Works* (Washington, 1945).

Schamp, Jacques, "Gélase ou Rufin: un fait nouveau," *Byzantion* 57 (1987), 360-390.

————, "The Lost Ecclesiastical History of Gelasius of Caesarea," *The Patristic and Byzantine Review* 6.2 (1987), 146-152.

Scheidweiler, Felix, "Die Kirchengeschichte des Gelasios von Kaisareia," *Byzantinische Zeitschrift* 46 (1953), 277-301.

Schwartz, Eduard and Theodor Mommsen (ed.), *Eusebius Werke 2.2. Die Kirchengeschichte* (Leipzig, 1908).

Simonetti, Manlio (ed.), *Tyrannii Rufini Opera* (CCL 20, 1961).

Thelamon, Françoise, *Païens et chrétiens au IVe siècle* (Paris, 1981).

————, "Rufin historien de son temps," *AAAd* 31 (1987), 1.41-59.

————, "'Apôtres et prophètes de notre temps'," *AAAd* 39 (1992), 171-198.

Van den Ven, Paul, "Fragments de la recension grecque de l'histoire ecclésiastique de Rufin dans un texte hagiographique," *Le Muséon* 33 (1915), 92-105.

————, "Encore le Rufin grec," *Le Muséon* 59 (1946), 281-294.

Winkelmann, Friedhelm, "Das Problem der Rekonstruktion der Historia Ecclesiastica des Gelasius von Caesarea," *Forschungen und Fortschritte* 38 (1964), 311-314.

————, *Untersuchungen zur Kirchengeschichte des Gelasios von Kaisareia* (*Sitzungsberichte der deutschen Akademie der Wissenschaften zu Berlin,* Klasse für Sprachen, Literatur und Kunst 1965.3).

————, "Charakter und Bedeutung der Kirchengeschichte des Gelasios von Kaisareia," *Byzantinische Forschungen* 1 (1966), 346-385.

————, "Die Quellen der Historia Ecclesiastica des Gelasios von Cyzicus (nach 475)," *Byzantinoslavica* 27 (1966), 104-130.

————, "Zu einer Edition der Fragmente der Kirchengeschichte des Gelasios von Kaisareia," *Byzantinoslavica* 34 (1973), 193-198.

————, "Vita Metrophanis et Alexandri," *Analecta Bollandiana* 100 (1982), 147-184.

Works on Rufinus's Translations

Christensen, Torben, *Rufinus of Aquileia and the "Historia Ecclesiastica," Lib. VIII-IX, of Eusebius* (Copenhagen, 1989).

Oulton, J. E. L., "Rufinus's Translation of the Church History of Eusebius," *JTS* 30 (1929), 150-174.

Simonetti, Manlio, "L'attività letteraria di Rufino negli anni della controversia origeniana," *AAAd* 39 (1992), 89-107.

Winkelmann, Friedhelm, "Einige Bemerkungen zu den Aussagen des Rufinus von Aquileia und des Hieronymus über ihre Übersetzungstheorie und -methode," in *Kyriakon. Festschrift Johannes Quasten,* ed. P. Granfield and J. Jungmann (Münster, 1970), 532-547.

G. W. Trompf (essay date 2000)

SOURCE: Trompf, G. W. "The Man in the Middle: Rufinus of Aquileia between East and West." In *Early Christian Historiography: Narratives of Retributive Justice,* edited by G. W. Trompf, pp. 158-84. London: Continuum, 2000.

[*In the following essay, Trompf provides a historiographical context for identifying and understanding the perspectives of early Christian historical writings, focusing on the role played by Rufinus in translating numerous important Greek texts into Latin, the language of the Roman Empire.*]

> There's no human history in the world which has not got its ups and downs.
>
> Cervantes, *Don Quixote* (1614), II, 3

Eusebius of Caesarea initiated both a new way of writing history and a new tradition of political legitimation. It is no secret that the great orthodox ecclesiastical historians of the fourth and fifth centuries were purveyors of the new Christian imperial ideology. They as much as any group of writers laid the foundations of Byzantinism, by demonstrating from the course of events how it paid for emperors to be pious according to the prescriptions of the Catholic tradition, or how much better it was for the security, prosperity and destiny of the Roman empire when the state and the (true) Church were consonant and false religion abandoned. So successful was the campaign in which they were engaged that by the sixth century, even though virtually all the western provinces had fallen into barbarian hands, a clash between Church and State had become unthinkable, and no other 'single hope for the permanency of the Empire' had become possible but 'the favour of God Himself', as Justinian, the energetic champion of reunification, proclaimed to all his successors.[1] Such sentiments were in large measure the results of the works of those who had created attractive historical images of good Christian rulers.[2] It was above all the ecclesiastical historians—Eusebius Pamphili himself, Tyrannius Rufinus, Socrates 'Scholasticus', Salaminius Sozomen, Theodoret of Cyrrhus and Gelasius of Cyzicus—who bequeathed to future generations an unblemished, idealized picture of *Pax Constantiniana,* a paradigm also buttressed by other Christian recorders such as Lactantius and Athanasius.[3] It was Rufinus who set the tone for a comparable enshrinement of Theodosius the Great's principate (379-395 CE), while the three writers of the Tripartite History—Socrates, Sozomen and Theodoret—all magnified the piety of the younger Theodosius, under whose rule they had each been writing, at a time when they believed they could celebrate another (relatively) happy 'ending' in the ongoing affairs of the empire and of Church-State relations.[4]

What has been less well perceived, however, is that there was an intimate connection between voicing this kind of *Geschichtsapologetik,* whether we find it above or below the surface in these orthodox ecclesiastical histories, and the actual business of structuring and presenting credible works of historiography. The connection has a great deal to do with the logic of retribution, because in the prevailing imperial ideology of the fourth and fifth centuries, and in the concerns of contemporary practising historians familiar with both Biblical and Graeco-Roman historiography, the fundamental importance of interpreting retributive principles through time was virtually taken for granted.

CONTINUING EUSEBIUS: THE HERMENEUTICS OF RETRIBUTION

. . . [The] logic of retribution as the reason-supported disposal of blame and praise is an apparently universal structure of human thinking; and it is thus obvious that in any crisis situation (and there were many grounds for inter-group hostility in the history of the later Roman Empire), large numbers of people would have been looking for reasons why any side they adopted was the right one and ought to win in a given conflict, and why 'the wrong' ought to lose, even as a defeated 'enemy'. What imperial courts and historians had in common was an interest in providing people with convincing reasons, from both past example and present achievements, why their cause did indeed merit victory and their opponents' cause opprobrium. Certainly it was often the most crucial task for imperial chanceries in this period to draw a strong and public demarcation line between the acceptable and the unacceptable. During intense ideological struggles this typically meant highlighting the piety (εὐσέβεια) of one's emperor and the impiety and unwisdom of those taking oppositional stances. From 312 to 435 this was never more clearly illustrated than in the rescripts of the pagan Maximin Daia (see Chapter 3), the official correspondence of the Christian Constantine (I) the Great, the diatribes of the pagan revivalist Julian, and the anti-apostate or anti-heretical decrees of Theodosius the Great.[5]

The Constantinian ideology, as the most determinative of all for later antiquity, surely has its *locus classicus* in a letter attributed to the emperor by means of which he hoped to dissuade Sapor II, king of Persia, from any further persecution of Christians beyond the eastern boundaries of the Roman domain (*c.* 337).[6] 'I hold to the holy religion [θρηϰεία]', the letter begins, 'which teaches the knowledge of the most holy God.' It is this God who has brought Constantine victory, and yet He is a God who has no desire for blood sacrifice and who shuns 'the godless and shameful pollutions of "the nations"'.

> For above all God does not permit the gifts he has supplied for human needs by his providence [πρόνοια] to be perverted according to individual desire. He only requires men with a pure mind and spotless soul, and by these he assesses their actions of virtue and piety [τῆς ἀρετῆς ϰαὶ εὐσεβείας]. He is pleased with gentleness and modesty; He loves the meek. He hates those who create contention [ταραχώδεις]; He loves faith, but unbelief He chastises [ϰολάζων]; He breaks all power of boasting, and punishes the insolence of the proud [ὕβριν ὑπερηφάνων τιμωρεῖται].

Conscious that it is this God who brings to just kingship the blessings of peace, Constantine drew Sapor's attention to the lessons of the past: 'for many who preceded me upon the imperial throne were so deluded by error as to attempt to deny this God, but the end issuing on them all was such a punishment [τιμωρός] that all humanity can be deterred by the example [παράδειγμα] of this dreadful calamity [συμφορά] from going the same way'.

And who was a better example of this than Valerian, who had been captured in the unsuccessful campaign against the Persians in 254, and whose death at their hands Constantine puts down to divine retribution?[7] And what better way of clinching his argument than by asserting that he himself had personally witnessed the 'manifest punishment' (τιμωρίαν περφανῆ) of those who persecuted the people of God (and where more clearly than at the defeat of Maxentius at the Milvian Bridge)?[8]

The basis on which this letter rests has the simplicity of Deuteronomic retributive logic. There is an immense confidence in its advocacy of the right way of life and the true basis of kingship, with promised rewards for those who espoused the correct path and penalties for those who despoiled them. Legal, dare I say constitutional, implications automatically arise from this orientation, and indeed are referred to at the conclusion of this very letter, where the work of providence, the restoration of peace, and the security (cf. ἀσφαλέστατα) of the empire are directly connected to the observance of the θεῖες νόμος and the true θρησκεία. This νόμος, by inference, now justifiably includes Constantine's imperial edicts (προστάγματα), which are safeguarded from being unlawful/godless (ἀθεμίτοι) like those of his persecuting predecessors.[9] Integral to this ideology, moreover, as phrases earlier in the letter indicate, and as imperial Christian usage confirms during subsequent reigns, is the vilification of 'tyranny'. The polemical application of this epithet by the Constantinians was not unrelated to an older usage in Latin reflection on Roman constitutional history,[10] but we have already shown it to owe much more to Hellenistic eastern Mediterranean depreciations of unjust rule or usurpation as they had come to affect Roman thinking by Diocletian's time.[11] Under the new order, 'tyrants' came to cover enemies of the people of God, in the form of emperors or powerful personages, and included usurpers, whether they were believers or not, who threatened the integrity of the Christian principate.[12]

The very mention of this propaganda against tyrants should immediately remind one of Lactantius, who may well have been its initiator (see Chapter 3). Yet it especially recalls the later writings of Eusebius, because more than any other spokesman it was he who popularized the notion that, by divine providence, the pious Constantine had succeeded 'against the most impious tyrants [κατὰ τῶν δυσσεβεστάτων τυράννων]', first against Maxentius and Maximin Daia, and eventually against Licinius, whose later defection earned him the same dishonourable title.[13] And one is tempted to conclude from the conciliatory letter to Sapor that Eusebian historiographical principles have been stamped upon it. Considering Eusebius' intense interest in early Christianity at Edessa and beyond Rome's eastern frontiers, Eusebius was probably the very rhetorician asked to frame the epistle, or at least prepare the official Greek version of it for Persian readership.[14] Already we begin to discover just how important historical perspective could be for political ideology in this setting, and how writing a history, even what is termed an ecclesiastical one, can be a political act, and nowhere more political than in the discussion and apportionment of praise and blame.

Significantly, the earliest extant 'complete version' of the imperial letter to Sapor we have in our possession stands strategically towards the end of Book I of Theodoret's well-known *Historia ecclesiastica*, written while in exile in an obscure eastern monastery in 450. Together with Constantine's long appeal for peace and an end to doctrinal disputes sent to the ecclesiastical Council of Tyre (335), the epistle to Sapor serves Theodoret's purposes perfectly in conveying the meaning of his whole history, not just in relaying his admiration for Constantine and the orthodox dynasts.[15] Just to reveal how crucial the discourse of retribution could be,

moreover, Theodoret appears to have put two distinctive touches of his own upon the letter, the original and more hurried nature of Eusebius' Greek being better preserved by Gelasius of Cyzicus.[16] What was originally a reference to 'enslaving tyrants of the nations' in general becomes an allusion to the specific tyrants introduced at the beginning of Theodoret's whole work (Maxentius, Maximin and Licinius), while the terrible death of the persecutor Valerian at the Persians' hands is put down to the divine vengeance (ἡ θεία μῆνις) rather than to the (characteristically Eusebian) ἡ θεία δίκη of the original.[17] Being a pastor to Christians near the border between Roman and Sassanid domains, to explore these points further, Theodoret provided a definite, if chronologically misplaced, setting to the letter. He treats it as Constantine's vigorous response to Sassanid attempts to persecute Persian Christians, an effort at contextualization ignored in Eusebius' *Vita Constantini*. In unifying his ecclesiastical history, Theodoret also quite appropriately finishes his whole history with a graphic account of Persian persecution in his own times, in fact with the most detailed descriptions of torture and the courage of martyrs to be found in his work.[18] At that last juncture he cannot forbear from reflecting on how Constantine managed to save the churches after 'all the Roman emperors' had persecuted 'the friends of the truth', and how Diocletian especially was destroyed (ἀπέσβη) on account of his impiety (δυσσέβεια) (*Hist. eccles.*, v, 39 [24-25]). In Theodoret's case, then, we can see at a preliminary synoptic glance that the handling of the principles of retributive logic was of critical importance in his historiography, even to the extent that documents central to the unity of his narrative could be slightly amended to give them the appropriate ideological accents.

By now we will hardly be surprised by historiographical attention to the human experience of rewards and penalties. After all, the past was full of altered circumstances and conflict, and the ancient historians' perception of pattern, contour and resolution, which provided the impetus to attempt a historical work in the first place, had to do with assessing along 'a narrative route' the worth and outcome of impressive careers, significant courses of action, let alone the effects of whole institutions or peoples.[19] What the modern empirical historian has to be constantly reminded of here, however, is the real possibility that significant retributions will be pointedly noticed as very important for the original narrator (in the building up of a whole picture), but that these same references can be easily overlooked as rather tangential, or belonging to 'byways of narrative', by moderns who are bent on getting straight the facts and order of socio-political events. The suggestion that Theodoret chose to use a stronger language of divine vengefulness against the pre-Constantinian persecutors will quickly recall to mind that extraordinary piece of historical imprecation *De mortibus persecu-torum,* with Lactantius' 'shrill voice of implacable hatred', as Arnaldo Momigliano provocatively puts it, sounding out from the West against the looming prospect or the very beginnings of the Licinian persecu-tion (*c.* 314-315).[20] Was it not after all Lactantius, a writer deeming all persecuting emperors tyrants, who made up for the brevity of Constantine's (or Eusebius') allusions to Valerian's fate in the letter to Sapor? For Lactantius provides us with the only substantial (and gory) account of Valerian's appalling end as sacrificial meat on the altars of Persia.[21] There are among the orthodox other examples of gloating over the deaths of imperial persecutors, the protracted, exultant hymn by Brother Ephrem the Syrian to celebrate the end of Julian the Apostate (on his retreat from Persia in 363) being truly remarkable among them.[22] But we must not forget that, since the construction of an appropriate retributive logic was grist to virtually every ancient historian's mill, the variations can range from the rough-textured and abrupt to the muted and subtle.

We have to take stock. The classical heritage was being transformed, but when it came to the rhetorical and explanatory devices of historiography, we cannot say the transformation was revolutionary. If the language and procedures of the imperial court, with its panegyrics, triumphal processions, administrative and legal ap-paratus, witnessed only step-by-step and sometimes quite superficial changes,[23] the discourse and hermeneu-tical approaches of historians, which were often conditioned by 'official expectations' of the continuing Roman empire, were bound to reflect a special conserv-atism, and to see a mixing of familiar pagan conceits or terminology with intruded Biblico-Christian mean-ings. Romano-Hellenistic historians, we remember, typi-cally addressed ethical issues, illustrating for their read-ers not just the difference between good and bad deeds, but the consequences of them.[24] When Dionysius of Halicarnassus shared a faith with

> those who do not absolve the gods from the care of hu-man affairs, but, after looking deeply into history, hold that they are favourable to the good and hostile to the wicked.

> (*Archaeol.,* II, lxviii, 2)

was he not appealing to the same sort of 'reference structure' that Christians applied, even if on behalf of their 'one true God'? During the fourth and fifth centuries pagan thinkers continued to be comforted by the traditional role of history as praising the worthy and blaming the wicked.[25] It does not take long to discover, as well, that most of those biographies of later antiq-uity—all those writings *de viris illustribus* in the wake of Plutarch—were written with a view as much to evok-ing admiration and emulation of individual great figures

or, in the case of evildoers, posthumous opprobrium and aversion, as to providing a record.[26] Christians were willing to 'baptize' the quest for appropriate retributive principles, while their own vocabularies of reward and punishment would become 'acculturated' into phraseolo-gies familiar across the empire.

Still using the Constantinian letter to Sapor II as a touchstone, for it was an official document, no mean fascination lies in the potential which some of the key ideologically-loaded terms of the epistle possessed for historical *Bedeutungsbildung,* indeed for bridging two traditions of historiography. Had not moralizing historians from both Biblical and pagan backgrounds already extolled πρόνοια before Eusebius?[27] Had not they ascribed Rome's success to its ἀρετή, and also already noted, as did Polybius, that 'all ἀσέβεια towards God and all savagery towards men' brought 'the due penalty' (τὴν ἀρμόζουσαν δίκην), albeit, in his opinion, at the hands of Tyche?[28] Enough histories were already woven with various examples of τιμωρίαι, and συμφοραί, these to punish (κολαζεῖν) persons of ὕβϰις and creators of ϰαϰία or ταραχή, and presented in paradigmatic fashion with a recognition of measured or appropriate δίϰη (or μῆνις), if one may pick out all the favourite verbal devices of Hellenistic symptomatol-ogy—which also happen to appear in Constantine's let-ter![29] The discourse of retribution, most surely, is one in which ancient Mediterranean historiography lived, and moved, and had its being.

A crucial task of the modern hermeneutist of ancient historiography, it has become clear, is to distinguish one style of applied retributive logic from another, because it was precisely through illustrating how principles of rewards and punishments came into play in human af-fairs that a historian could impress a whole memorial with a special stamp. Formulating a characteristic ac-count of retribution, and using it to guide readers' evalu-ations and endows events with meaning, was one among an essential cluster of conventions for ancient narrators to exploit, and one means of leaving a 'trademark'. Historians were often reinforcing a prevailing or presumed ideology, yet it is in the *stylistic applications* of retributive logic that one locates a crucial index to both the historiographical individuality and the socio-intellectual positioning of any given writer.

We see all this at its clearest as soon as we try to unravel what we may call 'the second synoptic problem' of ancient Christianity, that of the comparable ecclesiasti-cal histories of the fifth century. The Tripartite History, as it has been referred to by tradition since Theodorus Lector and Epiphanius Scholasticus,[30] is, however, in good measure quadripartite, for we should not forget Rufinus, the main subject of this chapter. And matters are made still more complex by the work of the

'Eunomian' historiographer Philostorgius. Modern critical interpreters have thus far been greatly interested in the *Quellenproblematik* of this body of literature, although not so much for the sake of showing who was dependent on whom (and who independent) as for the purpose of deciding what actually happened during the events themselves, and also what were actually the doctrinal beliefs of various parties.[31] More recently, admittedly, a few scholars have taken to asking why these ecclesiastical historians believed most of the miracle stories they told, but this concern still has much to do with reliability and the old question of *wie es eigentlich gewesen ist.*[32] The amount of redaction-critical analysis applied to these Church historians, on the other hand, has been rather meagre, certainly from a comparative point of view.[33] And yet it is of immense significance that Christian historians, learned men who had apparently been sensitized to the problems of passing judgement on others from the teachings of the New Testament, made so much of cultural and literary inheritances which could compromise the Gospel with power-broking and partisan spirit.

The methods of Eusebius, of course, were highly determinative for any exercises in Church history essayed in the two centuries after him, and the preceding chapter suggests its own sequel, beckoning us to apply a comparable analysis to authors who in one way or another saw themselves as continuing his remarkable enterprise.[34] Being a continuator, as has already been noted, did not mean replicating the Eusebian style or annotative technique, but rather expressing new interpretations within the same literary genre. Eusebius' precedent of quoting documents at length had to be followed, but that did not prevent selections and adaptations being made to suit a 'historiographical stance'. This is true, we shall now argue, even in the case of the most likely exception, Rufinus, who, while he is usually thought of as a would-be, some might say uninspired, mediator of Greek theological thought to the West,[35] was actually engaged in the creative Latinization of Eastern hermeneutical conceits. His powers of adaptation are nowhere more interesting than in his assessments of the course of events from the time of the Great Persecution to the reign of Theodosius the Great, and the work of detecting his special touches, we shall show, is of crucial relevance for interpreting subsequent historiographical texts.

Latinizing Retributive Logic for Church History

In the spring of 402, in his home city of Aquileia, the large Roman base at the head of the Adriatic which was then greatly threatened by the north Italian incursions of Alaric the Visigoth, the presbyter Rufinus finished the gratifying task of translating **Eusebius' History** into Latin. Perhaps he was trying to escape the tirades of Jerome for his defence of the suspect theologian Origen, while taking some comfort in the fact that the great Eusebius himself was an 'Origenist'.[36] Be that as it may, Rufinus performed a singular service for the West and for his sponsor, Bishop Chromatius, by translating everything except Eusebius' lengthy panegyric (because it was not in the second-last [or 313/314] Eusebius edition he was using? or because it detracted from a continuous narrative?) and by appending two further books on his own account—'two fishes supplementing the five loaves [or Eusebius' nine(-ten) books]' (cf. *Hist. eccles., prolog.*)—to bring the narrative down to the reign of Theodosius the Great.[37] Relying on his 26 years' experience in the eastern provinces, and thus in an environment familiar to his celebrated predecessor, he consciously limited his role to that of a kind of intellectual subordinate, choosing to be conditioned by the framework and themes of the 'master' and thus to produce an appendix rather lacking in independence, let alone idiosyncrasy, for the sake of an overall congruence.[38]

On the other hand, the translation, taken with the additional two books, ought to be considered as a literary whole, with the relative freedom and quite distinctive style of his Latin version being continued without unevenness into his own proportionately small collection of vignettes at the end.[39] Rufinus' accomplishment ought to be viewed, then, as a treatment of Church affairs from Jesus to Theodosius, with the presbyter ready to preserve much the same kind of Eusebian balance of materials, structural unity and interpretative comment throughout the entire work. When it comes to the addenda, Rufinus is a classic case of the continuator. *Inter alia,* he documents at least two more persecutions over and above Eusebius' ten or so—one under Julian (x, 28, 32-6) and one centring on Bishop Lucius of Alexandria during Valens' reign (xi, 3-6),[40] and he shows in each book how pious defenders of the true faith bore with the troubles (especially x, 26; xi, 7-9 . . .). His continued interest in the problems caused by heresies; his comparatively greater emphasis on the events and episcopal continuity in Alexandria and Rome; his interest in the Holy Land and holy relics, as well as in Edessa and the eastward expansion of the Church; his quotations *in extenso* and referencing of sources of information; his appeal to the miraculous (although much less critical); and so forth, are in accord with Eusebian patterns.[41] In terms of the unity of the whole, the space devoted to the monks (especially xi, 4) nicely relates back to Eusebius' account of the Therapeutae (*Hist. eccles.,* II, xvii) and thereby continues an undeveloped theme; while if any wilful removal of Eusebius' protracted panegyric on Constantine did take place, its absence is redeemed by Rufinus' own highly condensed encomium for Theodosius I, and by the quotation of the emperor's impressive prayer to God for victory over the tyrant Eugenius (in 394) (xi, 33-4).

As for applying principles of retributive logic, Rufinus remains true to Eusebius in proclaiming the divinely supported mission of the Church. To complete each of his own two books he emphasizes God's removal of obstacles: when Julian gives orders to the Jews to re-erect the Temple, as a means of undermining the Christians' faith, the builders have to contend with fire from the earth itself and the strange appearance of *sig-naculum Crucis* on their clothes (x, 38-9; cf. 38), while it is the tyrant Eugenius who, *Deo adverso,* must fall before the most pious Theodosius' feet and remove the barrier to a united Christian empire (xi, 32; cf. 33).[42] In the first case, at the end of Book x, it is both *Judaei atque Gentiles* whose works are given up for naught, this revealing the cunning means by which Rufinus yet again picked up an apparently discontinued theme about divinely ordained κακά befalling the Jews (from *Hist. eccles.,* IV, ii, 1; vi, 4; xv, 29). In the second case, to conclude the whole work, the triumph of 'the true religion' over 'the opinions of the pagans' and 'the glorious victory of the emperor' over the impious tyrant couples the two interwoven, compelling motifs of Euse-bius' original finale, where one finds εὐσέβεια under Constantine overcoming 'all tyranny', and also a confidence in the imperial succession (*Hist. eccles.,* X, ix, 9 [cf. 7-8]; Rufinus, x [= i], 9[8], and then paralleled to Rufinus, xi [= ii], 33, *finis;* cf. 34).[43] Thus Eusebius' optimism and general providentialism are upheld, despite the threat of barbarians at Rufinus' own door;[44] and this naturally brings with it a selective, even constrained or lessened, emphasis on adverse retribu-tion in Rufinus' own appended *libri.*

To understand his orientation, we need to analyse the manner in which Rufinus sought to preserve a Eusebian principle of organization, or more correctly what he evidently perceived as such: namely an alternation between the consolidated and the more troubled times for the true religion. In one of the most painstaking of all Patristic commentaries, the Danish scholar Torben Christensen has systematically exegeted Rufinus' translation of the eighth and ninth books of **Eusebius' Ecclesiastical History,** two crucial books in which the great bishop, as we have already seen, was the least organized and the most prone to make 'scissors and paste' revisions.[45] Christensen did not live long enough to draw any more general conclusions about Rufinus as a translator except that he took more liberties in tidying up Eusebius' narrative in these books than has hitherto noticed. In giving the Greek text greater clarity, flow and literary organization Rufinus often departed from the sense of the original, and he also tended to stress the retributive motif.[46] Whether or not Christensen perceived it, however, his extremely detailed study also

helps to reveal one other Rufinian touch: he evidently interpreted events as oscillating from a state of adversity for the Church to one of security, and took this to be how Eusebius viewed the whole *cursus historiae* from Christ's ministry until Constantine's time.

Reflecting on the details, Rufinus accentuates a mount-ing crisis in Church affairs before the outbreak of Dio-cletian's persecution (and it was with this troublesome situation that Eusebius probably ended his first edi-tion—not accessible to Rufinus).[47] According to Euse-bius the Church's security at this time is offset by its own spiritual weakness, which receives ἡ θεία κρίσις (*Hist. eccles.,* VIII, i, 7); for Rufinus the Christian faith *in quantum sublimitatis ascenderit* (VIII, ii, 4 [737.6-7]), and while he concurs that persecution comes as God's salutary purification of sin (VIII, i, 8 [739.18-19]), one is left with the definite sense of a downswing of affairs following this acme of *sublimitas.* The move-ment into crisis under Diocletian and his appointees, moreover, is deep and barely qualified in Rufinus, hav-ing the impress of 'a new phase'.[48] The cruelties and the extent of the persecution are made more pronounced by his embellishments.[49] He reinforced the point about God's castigation of sinful Christians (especially at viii, 13 [9-11]) without any Eusebian textual mandate.[50] He apparently found it disruptive to the flow of the narra-tive to reflect on times of peace between the emperors and the Christians, and to give too much favourable press to Constantius I (Constantine's father), as Euse-bius had done (in *Hist. eccles.,* VIII, xiii, 9, 12-13). This disinclination arose because events were proceed-ing towards the most serious low point for the Chris-tians, so that Rufinus condensed and glossed over such matters, accentuating instead the crimes of Galerius, Maximian, Maximin Daia and Maxentius, as well as the terrible fates to befall them, more so than his source re-ally warranted (*Hist. eccles.,* VIII, xiii, 11—xvii, 1; IX, vii, 1-2, 16; viii, 1—x, 15).[51] He possibly excluded Eu-sebius' account of Constantius I's happy death (VIII, xiii, 13) because he preferred another account which made the demise shameful.[52]

In Christensen's view, Rufinus intends Maxentius' be-haviour to reach 'a veritable crescendo' of destructive-ness against the faith,[53] but rightly implies a slow release of the tension after this peak. Unlike Eusebius, to il-lustrate the climb back, Rufinus does not say im-mediately that Galerius was forced to call off the persecution (as Eusebius did in (*Hist. eccles.,* VIII, xvi, 1), but lets his readers wait, writing only that God 'sent mitigation to the faithful whom he had tested in the fire' (VIII, xvi, 1 [788.15]).[54] Then, when Galerius falls grieviously ill, Rufinus interprets the turn of events with 'a clear Christian tone . . . nowhere to be found in Eusebius, for Galerius realizes he cannot find a remedy unless he allows prayers to the true God, and so he (and Constantine) come to promulgate the edict of recantation which halts the persecution (VIII, xvi, 3—xvii, 4)'.[55] Even with such a dramatic change of policy, however, the process towards the liberation of the Church still remains slow, since Maximin is reluctant to publish the edict in the East, and Rufinus continues to plot a gradual ascent by softening the Eusebian stress on Maximin Daia's tyrannical rule (IX, i, 1 [802.1-11]; vi, 1 [807.19-20]),[56] and thereafter by making the victory at the Milvian Bridge a decisive high point, with the worst of tyrants, Maxentius, removed (IX, ix, 1—ixa, 12).

The import that 'God again granted the Christians salvation' through the eradication of tyranny is powerfully underscored in Rufinus because there is no mention of a battle bringing about Maxentius' downfall: God acts to deliver Rome without Constantine shedding blood.[57] Events subsequent to this, furthermore, including the submission and death of Maximin and Constantine's eventual subjection of Licinius (IX, x, 1—xi, 8), appear more as appendages and as of lesser moment than this miracle of liberation under God's guiding hand. Rufinus apparently had no access to the fourth and final edition of Eusebius, or the *Vita Constantini,* in which Licinius had to be defeated as the last tyrant (cf. Eusebius-Rufinus, X, viii, 2; Rufinus, x, 12), such insufficient information unfortunately affecting Latin Christian histories to come (e.g., Sulpicius, *Chron.,* ii, 35; Orosius, *Hist. adv. pagan.,* VII, 28). Yet in any case the treatment is consistent with the focus of Rufinus' retributive logic in translating ***Hist. eccles.,*** VIII-IX. He has taken Eusebius' cue from the beginning of Book VIII, that the sins of the Christians bring on persecution as a deserved punishment, and he applies this belief more consistently than Eusebius until the final *Pax Constantiniana* wipes the slate clean. God was thus using the emperors 'as his tools to chastise the Christians', although once the Caesars overstepped their 'mandate', by bloody persecution, God 'intervened against them and punished them'.[58] This is an orientation different from, even if not necessarily inconsistent with, the one prevailing in Eusebius' earlier books. In these books, we remember, the sinners (at first Jewish and then pagan) are those who force a wholly undeserved suffering upon the martyrs, and who pay heavily for their crimes in so doing. Rufinus' rendering, however, commonly links the retributive theme with motions of *alternatio,* a connection sustained enough throughout his whole enterprise to show that he took the Eusebian reading of historical change as a seesaw-like pattern between respite and trouble. Such was his trademark, the hermeneutical signature through which patterned process and morally significant outcomes are interwoven, and whereby Greek concepts of cyclical *metabolē* and deserved justice are Latinized into meaningful *fluctiones* and *poenae.*

Now these fluctuations are reckoned by Rufinus to apply down to his own time. In the concluding books, though, written as his own historiographical creations, the major problem is with the Arian-orthodox conflict, and the prior stress in Books VIII-IX on the sins of the Church should be seen as prefacing this dire divisiveness. Thus—to detail the uniquely Rufinian appendages—we find that despite Arius' teaching, Constantine's reign is marked by *gratia,* including the anti-Arian credal formulary of Nicaea,[59] while for the succeeding period, Rufinus concentrated on Constantius II's sponsorship of the Arian *perfidia,* not on Constans' attempts at succour. Further on, however, Constans' reinstatement of Athanasius foreshadows the first, acceptable 'half' of Julian's reign, during which the exiled orthodox bishops are recalled, the right faith returns *ad sanitatem,* and the Church is virtually united and renewed.[60] Rufinus is alone among the Church historians in accentuating this interim of consolidation before the storm of apostasy breaks.[61] Julian certainly brings persecution and thus a nadir (in the face of which the Church stands firm), yet Rufinus' first book (= x) nonetheless ends on a triumphant note (with the failure of the attempt to reconstruct the Temple at Jerusalem).

At the beginning of his Book ii (= Eusebius-Rufinus, xi), he prolongs the sense of crescendo by highlighting the *pax et lux* of Jovian's all too short rule and by noting how Valentinian I was then rewarded with the purple for upholding the faith against Julian (xi, 1-2), before the *multaque nefanda et crudelia in Ecclesiam Dei* which come when Valentinian relinquishes control over the East to his brother Valens (2). The transition from good to bad in this next case is distinctly marked by the death of the great Athanasius. Athanasius is allowed to die quietly in peace despite all previous attempts to persecute him (xi, 3; cf. x, 14), and it is only after his death, in Rufinus' somewhat arbitrary construction, that Valens' persecutions begin (xi, 2). The 'wolf' Lucius, Athanasius' 'illicit successor', is just around the corner with unprecedented exiles, killings and destructions which affect the lives of up to 3000 monks (xi, 3-4).[62]

Valens' reign is singled out as the beginning of evils (*initium mali*) as far as the Roman empire's vulnerability to outside powers is concerned, since during his fourteen-year rule his fruitless wars against the Goths and Thracians were the first in a series to come (xi, 13). From this assessment, however, one cannot fairly turn Rufinus into a proponent of a general Roman *degeneratio.* He was simply noting the mounting barbaric pressures which inhabitants of the empire were forced to bear. Besides, Valens' defeat and the exposure of Rome's flanks are taken as the consequences of his earlier, far worse, crimes: those of persecuting the orthodox. Referring to the latter half of Valens' reign, in fact, Rufinus notes some respite for the faithful. An upward turn begins when Gratian and (the four-year-old!) Valentinian II are appointed to the purple in the West after Valentinian I's death (xi, 12), and Valens himself, when pressed by his military problems, allows the exiled orthodox bishops to return (xi, 13). With his death and Gratian's reign of 'piety and religion' a small peak has been reached, but already there are signs of a downturn in Gratian's immature personal indulgences, and although he is the one who calls Theodosius to be his partner and ruler in the East, a crisis looms out of Britain in the West with the tyrant Maximus (xi, 13-14). After Gratian's murder (unexplained), the crisis deepens with the attempts of the empress-dowager Justina—who has the infant Valentinian II under her influence—to impose the *impietas* of Arianism on the West, and with the persistence of Maximus' 'infamous tyranny' (xi, 15-16). The accentuation of these Arianizing tendencies in the Roman court is surreptitiously polemical, and not corroborated by other evidence.[63]

The first upward step comes with Rufinus' brief description of Theodosius' actions to restore the Catholic faith and overcome the usurper (xi, 17). The presbyter could have made much of the extraordinary events in 388, near his own city of Aquileia, when Theodosius surprised Maximus with an almost bloodless victory.[64] But Rufinus declined to do so. Characteristically, he plotted an upward gradient, not a surge. Before the greatest achievements for the faith could be realized, Theodosius had two 'seditions' to contend with, one at Thessalonica, which he put down too vehemently, and the other among pagans at Alexandria, which is intriguingly traced back to the perfidy of Constantius II (and thus to a link between Arianism and the heathens: xi, 18, 22-3). By treating the perpetrators of this latter sedition as tyrannical, typical of pagan *audacia* and appropriately requited by the destruction of the Serapion at Alexandria, Rufinus' account then reaches a final crescendo.[65] Thus three tyrants are repulsed one after the other. First, Maximus' removal marks the all-embracing significance of Theodosius' reign; second, with exposure of the (symbolic) priest of Saturn's cult (conveniently named Tyrannus) as a fraud (xi, 25; cf. 26); then, when Theodosius has overcome Eugenius, the collective phenomenon of ousted tyranny reinvokes the great Constantinian victories of the preceding generation.[66] The very amplitude of the true religion and its justifiable condemnation of pagan errors (cf. xi, 24) is clinched by the finding of the *signum Dominicae Crucis* (as an ancient pagan prophecy of Christ's dominion) among the hieroglyphics of the despoiled Serapion (xi, 29; cf. x, 39), by the prophecies of the holy Egyptian monk John that tyranny would be defeated and peace return (xi, 32; cf. 19); and by the answered prayer of the most pious Theodosius himself, who calls on the Lord for vindication and thereafter defeats Eugenius (xi, 33; cf. Eusebius-Rufinus, IX, ix, 3 on Constantine).

By emphasizing and detailing only one of Theodosius' two great victories in the West, moreover, Rufinus evidently seeks to balance his work with accounts of affairs in both East and West, so that Theodosius' effect over the whole empire is made clear, and the Eusebian apportionment of interests maintained. Like other authors—Gelasius of Caesarea, Ambrose and Augustine—Rufinus evidently did not know of Constantine's vision of the Holy Cross before the campaign against Maxentius (in Eusebius' still unpublished *Vita*), but the presbyter's stories about appearances of the Cross at the end of each of his two books (and his work as a whole) produce a unifying effect. In obvious contrast, too, the Arian Constantius II is not simply treated as a pious emperor who similarly and successfully reduced two tyrants (Vetranio and Magnentius) at an earlier stage.

For Rufinus to have stressed *alternatio* as the underlying pattern of change in human affairs, however, would have meant writing at variance with Eusebius' providentialism and sense of overall direction, and running counter to that welcome tendency toward consummation at the tail-end of the Eusebian narrative (at least in its second to fourth editions). And the same contrariety would have arisen if each work of evil along the zigzag-like course was to be requited by God. In any case, it was not in the spirit of Eusebius' instancing of retribution (and this would have been a more obvious datum to Rufinus) that all acts considered worthy of divine punishment would be satisfied in accordance with some pattern or principle of recurrence.[67] Admittedly Rufinus paid careful attention to Eusebius' explicit references to ἡ θεία δίκη and its analogues and tended to turn his predecessor's somewhat varied usages into a more uniform Latin vocabulary—with a greater stress on God's *poenae* and applying the harsher *ultio* and *vindicta* where deemed appropriate.[68] Right from the start, however, Rufinus had felt the weight of Eusebius' proclamation that the great turning-point had already arrived at the Milvian Bridge (*Hist. eccles.*, IX, viii, 15-ix, 11), and that God, by *patientia* and *clementia*, works things out in His good time.[69] Thus the desire to celebrate the blessing at the whole story's finale, with a general vindication of the faithful and the martyrs being gathered up in the overall betterment of affairs from Constantine's victories to the 'Theodosian age', was more instrumental, in Rufinus' perspective, than any stage-by-stage documentation of fitting penalties along the way.

We are now in a position to explain why it was that, for all their apparent deservedness of God's negative judgement (cf. x, 15, 19, 32-9; xi, 1, 22), Rufinus passes no pointed comments on the fates or deaths of the emperors Constantius and Julian (x, 26; xi, 1).[70] In the first of his own books the death of the heresiarch Arius alone merited special, if indirect, assessment, with the realization by the great Constantine himself that, since Arius perjured himself, the heretic's death was nothing else but God's revenge (*neque aliquid quod [quam] Dei vindictam indicare videretur*) (x, 13).[71] It is only towards the middle of the second book, when the strong stress on the overcoming of impiety and tyranny also begins (xi, 13-17, 31-4), that Rufinus avails himself more of the retributive principles one might have expected of him earlier. According to his account, Valens finds himself surrounded by enemies at the end of his reign—because of his war on the Church—and has to recall the exiled orthodox high clergy (xi, 13). Whether a recall actually occurred or not,[72] it suits Rufinus to mark this action as a turning-point from a bad to a good phase (just as Julian's earlier recall was used to signify a time of consolidation before a low point), because Valens dies very soon at the hands of the Goths, punished for his impiety (*impietatis suae poenas*), and makes way for Gratian's welcome principate. The suggestion is clearly there that Valens had brought on evils never before experienced by the Roman empire, but it is unwarranted to turn Rufinus into a proto-Gibbon, especially since Gratian is shown to have addressed himself to the relevant problems immediately (xi, 13), and Theodosius is eventually portrayed overcoming all obstacles.[73] Through Theodosius the Arianizing of Justina is annulled and two tyrants removed. The first, Maximus, is challenged by the faithful bishop Ambrose, and in remarking on the removal of this evil, Rufinus does not characterize it as Theodosius' revenge for the death of his co-emperor Gratian (as did Orosius, for instance),[74] and also declines to describe either the remarkable military victory involved or the fates of Maximus and his promoter Andragathius (cf. xi, 15, 17). When the second tyrant, Eugenius, is toppled, and a great wind is sent against his army because of Theodosius' prayer (xi, 16, 33),[75] we are left with a strong sense of 'blessed outcomes' issuing from 'true religion'. God's intervention is all the more accentuated in this latter victory, since Eugenius' superstitious deference to pagan rites comes to naught, and although Theodosius loses so many of his barbarian (Gothic) auxiliaries at the enemy's hands, that only confirms that his victory was by God's hand, not *per barbaros*.[76]

Rufinus' own two books make him very much the historian of 'blessed outcomes'. At first sight, his work is largely made up of episodic segments strung together, each intended to foster Christian piety. We are meant to admire the persecuted, tested as they are in the fire, or marvel at the providence by means of which opposition to the true faith is thwarted.[77] It is as if, to follow Peter Brown's recent suggestions,[78] readers have to be reconciled to the outcome of each episode, resolved in God's favour, especially to the upshot of 'civil wars' within the Empire, and to accept them as 'finishing matters' without need of recrimination, However, we

have shown here that each paradigmatic or exemplary scenario in Rufinus is set in a process, and when viewed together they are neither a series of dislocated addenda to Eusebius nor out of keeping with Eusebius' own methods—for Eusebius was a past master of the strategic arrangement of historical building-blocks. He has plotted fluctuations but they still move towards a finale.

The *Historia* of Rufinus, therefore, somewhat neglected and still untranslated, remains basically true to the Eusebian paradigm. Rufinus, to be sure, was no Lactantius. Of the two culprits singled out as persecutors, neither Julian nor the hated Lucius personally experiences *ira Dei* (xi, 1, 4, 6). In being so restrained, one might add, Rufinus was also no Athanasius. Athanasius? We would do well to remember that Rufinus was a near contemporary of the great hero of the Homoousian cause, probably keeping abreast of Athanasius' relations with Rome during the 360s and himself being in the East two years before Athanasius' death in 373. Athanasius' is the only death, moreover, which Rufinus views with any really positive significance; Jovian's is sad, but Athanasius rests *in pace* after his many troubles (xi, 3; cf. 1, 10, 14). And Athanasius is significant for Rufinus not only for personal reasons, nor only because the episcopate he held was as pre-eminent as Rome's, but also on account of the great man's writings, certain tracts by Athanasius presumably providing one set of sources for his chronicling (and quotations?) in Book x.[79]

Theologically, we must hasten to note, Rufinus was not domesticating a 'worriedly Arianizing' Eusebius to the Nicene cause. He has no apparent knowledge of Eusebius' special views concerning the Nicene creed (which is reproduced by Rufinus himself in its earliest known Latin version at x, 6), and he leaves no suggestion that there were any tensions between Eusebius, the historiographer he continued, and Athanasius, his own latter-day ecclesiastical hero.[80] In this connection, significantly, there is no clear evidence that Rufinus knew the *Vita Constantini* (cf. Chapters 3 and 5), and thus he was translating a pre-Nicene historical text in which Eusebius' Arian tendencies were not manifested.[81] Besides, Rufinus, who knew Eusebius would have joined him in defending Origen's theology,[82] did not see any clash between Origen's and Athanasius' theologies, or between Origenism and the Nicene faith.[83] Though he came to know all too well Jerome's vehement opposition to Origen's doctrine of the immortality and persistence of souls, he had no knowledge of Epiphanius' campaigns in the East to discredit Origenism as a heresy (*Adv. haer.*, lxiv) or even for that matter his sniping at John Chrysostom in Constantinople.[84] Thus theologically as well as historiographically Rufinus was the 'man in the middle', and if in his wrangle with Jerome he might not have conformed well to his own principle that 'he who avenges himself cannot claim vindication from the Lord' (*Apol.*, iii, 1), in his history he restrained himself against too retributive an emphasis—in imperial as well as ecclesiastical matters. By the time he put together the *Historia* the advice of the holy monk Macarius may have had a guiding effect: 'It is enough for me that the innocent goes free; it is not for me to betray the guilty' (*Hist. monach.*, xxviii).

In showing such restraint, Rufinus did not pick up on Athanasius' well-known tendentiousness. We are left supposing, in fact, either that he had only limited access to the body of Athanasian 'publications', or that he deliberately chose to avoid writing narrative in a comparable vein, for if there was ever a Christian historical writer in the second half of the fourth century who set great store by the uncompromising demands of divine justice, Athanasius was the one. As we shall soon see, Rufinus was also the man in the middle, chronologically at least, of a process in which retributive logic was deployed in active polemicism, first by Athanasius against Arianism, by the pagans Julian, Libanius and Eunapius against the Christians, by the Eunomian Arian Philostorgius against orthodoxy, and, as if to settle matters for the Byzantine establishment, by the Tripartite ecclesiastical historians, Socrates, Sozomen and Theodoret, against all who threatened the orthodox truth and the 'Theodosian succession'.[85] This process, which carries with it polemics to do with such *causes célèbres* as Chrysostom and Nestorius along the way, is largely to do with the Eastern empire. . . .

The East, more theologically literate, with more lay involvement in debate, and rapidly declining paganism, was already promising to be a stormier sea of theological difference and controversy than the West.[86] Rufinus, though, was a Latin, and is very much a watershed figure for mediating Eastern thought to his side of the empire. Upon its dedication in 402, Rufinus' translation and supplementation of Eusebius' master-work was the only Latin Church history in circulation in the western provinces up to that time (apart from pre-Vulgate versions of Acts),[87] and stood alone in this respect for another century. We learn that, by 415 at least, the great North African bishop Augustine had in his possession **Eusebius' *Historia Ecclesiastica*,**[88] and one can safely assume that it was in Rufinus' translation, with the latter's two additional books. As we shall confirm [elsewhere], Augustine developed his own understanding of retributive logic, which is somewhat more subtle than, and over some basic points at odds with, the norms of Christian historiography from Constantine's time onwards. One is tempted to conclude, however, that his picture of human affairs as the arena of *vicissitudines*—of constant ups and downs—was very much affected by Rufinus' rendering of Eusebius and of events

as far as Theodosius I's reign. Admittedly, the usage of *vicissitudo* to denote instability in human affairs has a long history—in Cicero for one—and like *fluctio* it was an older term to convey alternation.[89] Yet with the extraordinary prolongation of Roman imperial rule, the notion of oscillation between good and bad rulers, or between collective prosperity and affliction, often came to the fore (as we saw with the Latins 'Vopiscus' and Ausonius).[90] That Rufinus structured his translation and whole narrative along these lines is probably of significance for Augustine's *De civitate Dei*; and that his conveyance of the Eusebian achievement was there at all in the West meant that views of the past in other important Christian historians, such as Sulpicius and Orosius, were to be conditioned by him as their source. . . .

Notes

1. [Justinian I] *Corpus Juris Civilis*, ed. R. Schoell and W. Kroll, Berlin, 1928, iii, 517; A. Gerostergios, 'The Religious Policy of Justinian I and His Religious Beliefs' (Doctoral dissert., Boston University School of Theology) (University Microfilm Internat.), Ann Arbor, 1974, p. 210.

2. Among other authors, Theodorus Anagnostes/ Lector, taking his own account to the beginning of Justinian's reign (527), sought to appeal to these earlier images in his predecessors' works to reinforce the imperial ideals of the sixth century: H. G. Opitz, in RECA, ser. 2, vol. 5a(2), cols 1869-81.

3. To this list one might safely add Gelasius of Caesarea (d. 395), and Philip Sidetes (early fifth century), although only fragments of their ecclesiastical histories remain. Other Christian historians, such as Sabinus, Orosius and Gennadius of Marseilles, should not be forgotten.

4. Rufinus, *Hist. eccles.*, xi (= ii), 17-34; Socrates, *Hist. eccles.*, vii, 22, 34, 47-8, and also v, 18, 25; Sozomen, *Hist. eccles.*, prolog., ix, and also vii, 10-17 (though for qualifications, see Chapter 6 [Trompf, G. W. *Early Christian Historiography*. London: Continuum, 2000]); Theodoret, *Hist. eccles.*, v, 36, and also 5-8, 17, 24-5.

5. Eusebius, *Hist. eccles.*, IX, xii, 8-14 and *Vit. Const.*, ii, 12.8-14 (Chapter 3 [Trompf, 2000]); Julian, e.g., *Epist. ad Sacerd.*, 293A. On Theodosius: see N. Q. King, *The Emperor Theodosius and the Establishment of Christianity* (LHD), London, 1961, ch. 3.

6. Versions of which are in Eusebius, *Vita Const.*, iv, 9-13; Theodoret, *Hist. eccles.*, i, 25 [5-6] (squarebracketed divisions and lines from L. Parmentier's

edn, GCS, Leipzig, 1911); Gelasius (Cyzicenus), *Hist. eccles.*, iii, 11 [3-4] (square-bracketed divisions and lines from G. Loeschcke and M. Heinemann edn). On the question of 'original' versions, see note 16 below. On dating, Theodoret's positioning of the letter would have it very late in Sapor's reign, but others do not see why it should not be placed earlier: see Sozomen, *Hist. eccles.*, ii, 15; recently: W. Eilers, 'Iran and Mesopotamia', in E. Yarshater (ed.), *Cambridge History of Iran*, Cambridge, 1983, vol. 3/l, p. 485; M.-L. Chaumont, *La christianisation de l'empire iranien des origines au grandes persécutions du IVe siècle* (CSCO, 499, subsid. 80), Louvain, 1988, pp. 56-70; T. Barnes, pers. comm., 1988.

7. See also p. 136 [Trompf, 2000]. The reference is a pointed concession, since the Persians were known to have made much of this victory; but the loser is now being looked back on as impious. For background: G. Fowden, *Empire to Commonwealth*, Princeton, 1993, p. 23 (Persian iconography), 93-4.

8. Eusebius, *Vita Const.*, iv, 11; Theodoret, *Hist. eccles.*, i, 25 [5-6; cf. 1, 8]; Gelasius, *Hist. eccles.*, ii, 11 [3-4].

9. Theodoret, *Hist. eccles.*, i, 25 [8-9; cf. 3]; Gelasius, *Hist. eccles.*, iii, 11 [7-9]. On how Constantinian pronouncements became embedded in the Theodosian code: see King, 'The Theodosian Code as a Source for the Religious Policies of the First Byzantine Emperors', NMS, 6 (1962): 14-15.

10. Thus Trompf, *Idea of Historical Recurrence*, pp. 266-7 (esp. on Livy, *Ab urb. cond.*, III, 36 [2, 5]; 37; IV, 13 [1]-16 [8], and Cicero, *De Amicit.*, viii, 28, etc.).

11. See Chapter 3 [Trompf, 2000] (esp. on *Script. Hist. Aug.*). For various key background references: see Plato, *Resp.*, VIII, 562a-576a; Wisd 6:9; Eccles 11:5; Polybius, *Hist.*, II, xlvii, 3; VI, vii, 5-7; VIII, xxxii, 33; XIII, vi, 2, etc.; 4 Macc 8:15; 9:15, etc.; Josephus, *Bell. Jud.*, I, 70 [10-11]; Cornelius Nepos, *Miltiad.*, viii; Plutarch, *Tib. et Gai. Gracch.*, xiv, 3; Herodian, *Hist.*, e.g., I, iv, 4; cf. also Diodorus, *Bibliot.*, XIV, etc.

12. Theodoret, *Hist. eccles.*, i, 25 [1, l. 6]). That this usage is official and not a device of ecclesiastical historians is confirmed by Ammianus Marcellinus [?], e.g., *Excerpta*, 12; cf. Eutropius, *Breviar. ab urb. cond.*, x, 3 (on Maxentius' *seditio*); Zosimus, *Hist. nov.*, VI, i (yet, see IV, xxxv, 3; xxxvii, 13; liv, 1; V, xl for an implicit rebuttal of this ideology). For usages in connection with Theodosius I's victories over Western usurpers, such as

Eugenius: see note 66 below. Note also Augustine, *Civ. Dei.*, V, 25-6; Orosius, *Hist. adv. pagan.*, V, 22; VII, 17.

13. See Chapter 3 [Trompf, 2000]; cf. Eusebius, esp. *Hist. eccles.*, IX, viii, 15-ix, 1; X, vi-ix; *Vit. Const.*, i, 1. Remember that Lactantius wrote too early to cover the Licinian persecutions.

14. Note also the ethical terms which have a prior Biblical usage in the epistle (at *Vita Const.*, iv, 11; Theodoret, *Hist. eccles.*, i, 25 [5]). For Eusebius on Edessa: see *Hist. eccles.*, I, xiii, 2-36; II, i, 6; cf. *Onomast.*; and on the Eusebius-Constantine connection: see H. A. Drake, *In Praise of Constantine*, pp. 4-8, 59-60, 75-9; T. Barnes, *Constantine and Eusebius*, pp. 226, 231, 261.

15. On the provenance of Theodoret's history, esp. his *Epist.*, 119, 123, and on the location of his retreat at Nicerte: P. P. Naaman, *Théodoret de Cyr et le monastère de Saint Maroun*, Beirut, 1971, p. 38. For the apparently surprising historical priority of Theodoret's extant version: see next note. On the context of the letter, see Theodoret, *Hist. eccles.*, i, 25-34; and for Sozomen's paraphrasing of Constantine in *Hist. eccles.*, ii, 15 in a comparably significant way: see B. Grillet in the introduction to the SC edn, Paris, 1983, p. 70.

16. After a detailed comparative textual analysis, referred to in my 'Rufinus and the Logic of Retribution in Post-Eusebian Church Histories', *JEH*, 43/3 [1992]: 355, n. 17), I have concluded that Gelasius (Cyzicenus)—rather than the present edition of Eusebius' *Vita Const.*—contains a virtually complete original of Eusebius' epistolary draft or translation from an official Latin prototype. Our present version of the *Vita Const.*, as I have acknowledged in Chapter 3, was edited long after Eusebius' death, probably at the end of the fifth century (and thus in a post-Theodoretan situation). The editor(s) of *Vita Const.*, in attempting to complete Eusebius' unfinished historiographical enterprise (see esp. F. Winkelmann, *Die Textbezeugung der Vita Constantini des Eusebius von Caesarea* [TU, 84], Berlin, 1962, pp. 70ff., 142ff.), apparently possessed a version shorter than the original by seven lines, but nonetheless incorporated into their version some apparently unprecedented phrases (corruptions? PG, vol. 30, col. 1153, n. 36), and some of what they had of Theodoret's phraseology. The latter's renowned Church history and his use of Constantine's correspondence were known to these editors, as also Sozomen's paraphrase, but they were evidently unaware that they themselves had a shorter version of the letter, for their text actually does not

permit the conclusion that they abbreviated a longer original. Now we can see from his quoting it (*c.* 450) that Theodoret possessed a complete Greek, Eusebian, original, while slightly 'doctoring' it. He touched it most noticeably in connection with retribution against Valerian, and did so not only because he thought Sozomen's use of the strong phrase θεία μῆνις for this punishment better suited the situation (and the kind of point he himself wanted to make toward the end of his first book) (see [Trompf, 2000] Chapter 6), but also because he assumed that the phrase better reflected Constantine's Latin prototype. Gelasius faithfully reproduced the most complete version (*c.* 480), and it was probably the original, as it contains characteristically Eusebian phrases and stylistic touches. Gelasius' reproduction was a (witting?) textual corrective to Theodoret, but in his *Church History* he developed a *Bios* of Constantine curiously not used by—perhaps not available to—the later editors of Eusebius' *Vita Const.* Cf. Winkelmann, *op. cit.*, p. 88 (by implication).

It should be made clear here that these assessments are derived from examining differences and minutiae in *whole* texts, not just the phrase referring to God's vengeance. Taking this one phrase alone, one might deduce that it goes back to Eusebius himself, even though he does not use it elsewhere; and that it was reproduced by Sozomen, Theodoret and the editors of the *Vita,* only to be changed by Gelasius. But with the whole texts considered, I have put the priority of the use of this phrase with Sozomen, my analysis of his retributive logic in [Trompf, 2000] Chapter 5 corroborating my decision.

17. Theodoret, *Hist. eccles.*, i, 25 [1, l. 6; and 7, l. 15]; Eusebius, *Vita Const.*, iv, 11, cf. Gelasius, *Hist. eccles.*, iii, 11 [1, ll. 6 and 7]. Be warned that B. Jackson's translation of Theodoret at i, 25 [7] (NPNF, N.S. 3) reads Gelasius' sense back into the text.

18. *Hist. eccles.*, v, 39 (sect. 40 is a kind of appendix). On the question of chronological misplacement see note 6 above, noting that Theodoret locates Constantine's letter prior to the Council of Tyre in 335 (i, 27).

19. See Trompf, *Recurrence,* esp. pp. 94-7, 147-8 (Herodotus, Thucydides, etc.).

20. For the argument that Lactantius did not write this work from Nicomedia as usually supposed: see J. Stevenson, 'The Life and Literary Activity of Lactantius', in K. Aland and F. L. Cross (eds), *Studia Patristica,* Berlin, 1957, vol. 1, pt 1, pp. 675-6; J. L. Creed, 'Introduction', to his edn of

Lactantius, *De mort. pers.,* pp. xxxiii-xli. For the quotation, see A. Momigliano, *The Conflict Between Paganism and Christianity in the Fourth Century,* p. 79.

21. Lactantius, *Mort. pers.,* v, 3-7. The τρόπαιον in *Vita Const.,* iv, 11 [40] and Theodoret, *Hist. eccles.,* i, 25 [7] is probably a sarcastic allusion to this sacrifice: Lat. *tropaeum.* That Eusebius knew only of Valerian's captivity and not the details of his death is suggested by *Hist. eccles.,* VII, xiii, 1, but there is no reason why he was not made better informed at a later stage—perhaps even through the Lactantius-Constantine connection? See Barnes, *Constantine,* pp. 14, 43, 47, 74-5.

22. Ephrem, *Hymni contr. Jul.,* i, 2, 10-11, 27; iii, 1-3, 9, 14; iv, 5-8.

23. For background: E. Nixon, *In Praise of Later Roman Emperors, op. cit.*; J. van der Spool, *Themistius and the Imperial Court: Oratory, Civic Duty and* Paideia *from Constantius to Theodosius,* Ann Arbor, 1995; M. McCormick, *Eternal Victory,* Cambridge and Paris, 1986, chs 2-3.

24. For background: esp. W. Jaeger, *Paideia: the Ideals of Greek Culture,* trans. G. Highet, Oxford, 1947, ch. iii, and 1944 edn, vol. iii, *passim.*

25. Thus Trompf, *Recurrence,* p. 242; cf., e.g., Ammianus Marcellinus, e.g., *Rer. gest.,* XIV-XVI (on corruption); Zosimus, *Hist. nov.,* VI, iii; cf. III, xxxff. (comparing Julian's rule with others), pagan historians becoming fewer and farther between.

26. E.g., among Greek writers, Diogenes Laertius, *Vit. philos.* (third century); Philostratus, *De sophist.,* and *Apoll. Tyan.* (third century). The Latin collections *de viris illustribus* go back to Cornelius Nepos (his work being also known under the title *De excell. ducib. ext. gentium*) (first century BCE); Valerius Maximus, *Fact. et dic. memorabilium* (first century CE, after Plutarch) and Suetonius (with a work under this title now surviving only in fragments) (first to second century CE); cf. Aelianus, *Varia hist.* (third century). Jerome and Gennadius Christianized this tradition in the fourth and fifth centuries, although their approach is surprisingly one of a subdued chronicle in which they write supportively of Christian learning and exclude important heretics.

27. E.g., the Delphic maxim: πρόνοιαν τίμα (1 Kyzik., II, col. 1 [Schwertheim edn, IGSK, 26/2]); Herodotus, *Hist.,* III, 108; Diodorus, *Biblioth.,* I, i, 1, 3; X, xx, 13, etc. (on fortune as providential overlord); LXX Dan 6:19; 4 Macc 9:24; 13:19; Wisd 14; 17, etc., cf. Philo Judaeus, *De immut.,* ii, 8-14. For the most obvious philosophical back-

ground: A. P. Bos, *Providentia Divina: The Theme of Divine* Pronoia *in Plato and Aristotle,* Amsterdam, 1976.

28. Thus Polybius, *Hist.,* XV, xx, 4-5. See Trompf, *op. cit.,* esp. pp. 97-104, for the most relevant references. For cultural-political background: Momigliano, 'Empietà ed Eresia nel Mondo Antico', RSI, 73 (1971): 771-91.

29. Cf. esp. Trompf, *op. cit.,* pp. 93-101, 164-74, etc. On συμφοραί: note also G. F. Chesnut, *The First Christian Histories, op. cit.,* p. 49.

30. As well as by Cassiodorus, of course, using Epiphanius; cf. also Evagrius on his fifth-century predecessors: *Hist. eccles., prolog.* What J. G. Dowling wrote of these matters a century and a half ago still holds good (*An Introduction to the Critical Study of Ecclesiastical History,* London, 1838, pp. 44-5, 51-3); see also Aftermath below.

31. For use of the relevant works in different types of historical studies: see H. Lietzmann, *History of the Early Church, op. cit.,* esp. vol. 3; A. von Harnack, *Lehrbuch der Dogmengeschichte,* Freiburg, 1894-7, esp. vol. 3; J. N. D. Kelly, *Early Christian Doctrines,* London, 1960, pp. 239-40, 406-8; P. Meinhold, *Geschichte der kirchlichen Historiographie* (OA), Munich, 1967; and more recently, R. A. Markus, 'Church History and the Early Church Historians', in D. Baker (ed.), *The Materials, Sources and Methods of Ecclesiastical History* (EHS), Oxford, 1975, pp. 1ff.; yet for shifts of interest towards historiographers' conceptual life, Y.-M. Duval, *Les métamorphoses de l'historiographie aux IVe et Ve siècles,* Budapest, 1984 [note new book, see Bibliography]; I. E. Karagiannopoulos and G. Weiss, *Quellenkunde zur Geschichte von Byzanz (324-1453)* (SGOE, 14), Wiesbaden, 1982, pp. 69-70 and *passim*; P. Allen, 'Some Aspects of Hellenism in the Early Greek Church Historians', Trad, 43 (1987): 368ff. For comments on Church history as a genre: e.g., E. Schwartz, 'Über Kirchengeschichte', in his *Gesammelte Schriften,* Berlin, 1938, vol. 1, pp. 116ff.; J. Nirschl, *Propädeutik der Kirchengeschichte,* Mainz, 1888.

32. E.g., R. M. Grant, *Miracle and Natural Law in Graeco-Roman and Early Christian Thought,* Amsterdam, 1952; M. Meslin, *Le Christianisme dans l'empire romaine,* Paris, 1970, esp. p. 168; L. C. Ruggini, 'The Ecclesiastical Histories and the Pagan Historiography: Providence and Miracles', Ath, N.S. 1-2 (1977): 107ff.; F. Thélamon, *Païns et Chrétiens au IVe siècle; l'apport de l'*'Histoire ecclésiastique' *de Rufin d'Aquilée* (EA), Paris, 1981, pt 3.

33. The work of Chesnut and G. Downey notwithstanding. See esp. Downey, 'The Perspective of the Early Church Historians', GRBS, 6 (1965): 57-70.

34. For this self-perception: Gelasius of Caesarea, *Hist. eccles.* [lost; yet cf. Fabricius, *Bibliotheca Graeca,* Hamburg, 1727, vol. 5, col. 24]; Rufinus, *prolog.* (Schwartz-Mommsen edn of Eusebius, GCS, 9/2, vol. 2, p. 951); Philostorgius, *Hist. eccles.,* i, 2; Socrates, *Hist. eccles.,* i, 1; Sozomen, *Hist. eccles.,* i, 1; Theodoret, *Hist. eccles.,* i, 1; and even Evagrius, *Hist. eccles.,* i, *prolog.* (and by implication the lost Eustathius of Epiphaneia, whom he knows), as well as the Monophysite Zachariah of Mitylene (cf. *Syr. chron.,* ii, 1), whom he rebuts. On these last two, see Aftermath below.

35. For background: A. di Berardino (ed.), *Patrology,* Rome, 1986 [follows Quasten, as vol. 4], pp. 247-8, 250.

36. See esp. F.-X. Murphy, *Rufinus of Aquileia (345-411): His Life and Works* (CUASMH, N.S. 6), Washington, 1945, chs 3-5; C. P. Hammond, 'The Last Ten Years of Rufinus; Life and the Date of His Move South of Aquileia', JTS, 28/2 (1977): 372ff.; cf. Eusebius, *Hist. eccles.,* VI, ii; viii; xix-xxvi; xxx; xxxii; xxxvi, etc. The Jerome-Rufinus conflict was very bitter, Jerome rejecting Rufinus' acceptance of Origen's teaching that all human souls were pre-existent, and eventually accusing Rufinus of conspiring to kill him! See Rufinus, *Apol.,* i; Jerome, *Apol.,* iii, 1; cf. i, 11; ii, 4ff., and *passim*.

37. Schwartz-Mommsen, p. 951, ll. 23-4; cf. 6ff. Note that Mommsen and Schwartz have chosen to present *two* tenth books of Rufinus, the first of these inserted beside Eusebius' Greek whenever an attempt at translation appears to apply (thus pp. 859-63, 893-903, before Rufinus' own Book x, pp. 937ff.). The text-form Rufinus is likely to have used in MSS BD has the doxology of X, i, 1 to complete Book IX (for discussion: R. Lacqueur, *Eusebius als Historischer, op. cit.,* p. 190; cf. H. Emonds, *Zweite Auflage im Altertum* [KSU, 14], Leipzig, 1941, pp. 25ff.); though Rufinus does imply he is rendering a truer Book X to Eusebius with the expression *decimum vero* (*prolog.* [Schwartz-Mommsen, p. 952, l. 9]); and for discussion of Rufinus' possible decision not to translate Eusebius' panegyric: see J. E. L. Oulton, 'Rufinus's Translation of the Church History of Eusebius', JTS, 30 (1928): 152.

38. Here we accept Rufinus, not Gelasius of Caesarea, as the author of the two additional books, following especially P. Peeters, 'Les débuts du christian-

isme en Géorgie', AnB, 1 (1932): 5-58; F. Diekamp, 'Gelasius von Caesarea in Palaestina', OCA, 117 (1938): 16-32; and Murphy, *op. cit.*, pp. 160-3, rather than A. Glas, *Die Kirchengeschichte des Gelasios von Kaisareia*, Leipzig, 1914, pp. 1-3; and more recently (but ambiguously) Momigliano, *The Classical Foundations of Modern Historiography*, Berkeley, 1990, p. 143. Photius (*Cod.*, 89 [67a, ll. 35-9]) held that Gelasius merely translated Rufinus' history: W. T. Treadgold, *The Nature of the Bibliotheca of Photius*, Washington, DC, 1980, p. 63; but such a translation would be impossible, since Gelasius died at least six years before Rufinus completed his work (cf. E. Honigmann, 'Gélase de Césarée et Rufin d'Aquilée', BAB, 40 [1954]: 122-61). For other possibilities: see Chapter 5 below, note 38.

39. Rufinus, *Hist. eccles.*, x, 1 actually follows on very neatly from Eusebius' conclusions at *Hist. eccles.*, VII, xxxii, 30-1. Whereas Eusebius, VIII-X (= Rufinus, viii-ix) was treated as a special block of material covering Eusebius' own day, Rufinus might have perceived a major binding theme of his predecessor to be ecclesiastical διαδοχή (see Eusebius, *Hist. eccles.*, I, i, 1; VII, xxxii, 32; VIII, *prolog.*); he immediately picks this up with his reference to *successio* in *Hist. eccles.*, x, i.

40. For all the major Eusebian references to persecution: Chapter 3 [Trompf, 2000], pp. 125-30. On the stereotype of between five and ten identified from the complexities of Eusebius' material: see Trompf, *Recurrence*, p. 219, n. 83. As for Rufinus, I do not take *Hist. eccles.*, x, 1 or 14 to refer to distinct persecutions.

41. *Hist. eccles.*, x, 1, 16, 21, 25; xi, 3, 20; cf. Eusebius, *Hist. eccles.*, II, i, 13; III, xxvi-xxxii; IV, xxii-xxiv; V, iv, 13-19, etc. (heresies); Rufinus, x, 1, 12-14, 22, 28; xi, 3, 10, etc.; cf. Eusebius, esp. II, ii; iv, 19-20; V, vi; VI, xxxiv-xlvi (Alexandria and Rome); Rufinus, x, 7-9, 37-9; xi, 5, 20; cf. Eusebius, I, ix-xiii; III, v-x; IV, vi; V, xii; VI, viii-ix; VII, xxii, 29, etc. (Holy Land, Edessa, etc.); Rufinus, x, 6, 14 (Alexander on Athanasius as a youth), 17 (parts of a report on interchange in council proceedings), 29; Eusebius, I, xi, 13; II, xvii; xxiii-xxv; III, xxxvii-xxxix; IV, xv; V, i; VI, xli-xlv, etc. (easily identifiable quotations); Rufinus, x, 5, 8-10, 35, 37-9; xi, 4, 29-30; cf. Eusebius, esp. V, iv, 4; VIII, vii, 2-6 (the miraculous). For further background: see R. M. Grant, *Eusebius as Church Historian*, chs 6-10.

42. See his uses of *deterriti* in x, 39 and *frustratio* at xi, 33, the end of each book. Note that Theodosius

died unexpectedly in January 395, four months after his victory over Eugenius in September 394. Rufinus' work appears seven years after the death but omits mention of it, on a high note of *praemia meritorum* equivalent to Eusebius' IX, xi, 9. For historical background to Julian's rebuilding the Temple: see, e.g., C. R. Phillips III, 'Julian's Rebuilding of the Temple: a Sociological Study of Religious Competition', in P. J. Achtemeir (ed.), *Society of Biblical Literature 1979 Seminar Papers*, Missoula, 1979, vol. 2, pp. 167ff.; M. Avi-Yonah, *The Jews under Roman and Byzantine Rule*, New York and Jerusalem, 1984 edn, ch. 8. On the phenomenon of the Cross in this context: see Chapter 6 [Trompf, 2000], note 35.

43. Rufinus omits references to the δυσσέβεια of the tyrants at the end of Eusebius' work (*Hist. eccles.*, IX, vii, 2; X, viii, 2) and thus transfers the emphasis on overcoming tyrannical impiety to the end of his work instead. He also knows by hindsight that the confidence Eusebius expresses in Constantine's sons (Eusebius, *Hist. eccles.*, X, ix, 9) is ill-founded and leaves the phrase καὶ τοῖς αὐτοῦ παισίν untranslated. On the other hand, while surely aware of Theodosius I's untimely death, he transposes the notion of imperial foresight to this emperor instead (*Hist. eccles.*, xi, 34), and declines reporting his death even though, as most sources tell, Theodosius had to make *ad hoc* arrangements from his deathbed: Socrates, *Hist. eccles.*, v, 36; Sozomen, *Hist. eccles.*, vii, 29; Theodoret, *Hist. eccles.*, v, 24. [Note: to distinguish referencing between Eusebius and Rufinus *once Rufinus ceases translation*, I refer to the latter's appended two books as lowercase Books x-xi (=i-ii), unless conceptualizing Eusebius-Rufinus as a whole.]

44. According to J. Straub, who has made too much of comments in *Hist. eccles.*, xi [=ii], 13, interpreting them as a statement of Rome's decline: 'Christliche Geschichtsapologetik in der Krisis des römischen Reiches', Hist, 1 (1950): 55. Note, too, that Rufinus did not always translate Eusebius' πρόνοια as *providentia* but sometimes as *clementia* (e.g., *Hist. eccles.*, III, vii, 8), and also, as at VIII, i, 7-8, translates ἡ θεία κρίσις as *divina providentia*. For significant uses of *providentia* in his own history see xi [=ii], 19, 28; and also ii, 1 (*divina clementia*), 29 (*Dei favor*).

45. Christensen, *Rufinus of Aquileia and the Historia Ecclesiastica Lib. VIII-IX of Eusebius*, (HM, 58), Copenhagen, 1989, p. 9; cf. E. Schwartz in Schwartz-Mommsen edn of *Hist. eccles.*, vol. 2/3, pp. xlvii-lxi; R. Lacqueur, *op. cit.*; H. Janne, 'Schwartz et Lacqueur comme les Dioscures de la

critique eusébienne', Byz, 8 (1933): 749; Lietz-mann, *Geschichte*, vol. 3, ch. 6, on difficulties and signs of revision in the Eusebian text of Books VIII-IX. See also Christensen, 'The so-called *Appendix* to Eusebius' *Historia Ecclesiastica* VIII', CeM, 38 (1983): 177ff.

46. Christensen, *Rufinus*, pp. 10, 333-6 and *passim*, and 'Rufinus of Aquileia and the *Historia Ecclesiastica, lib. VIII-IX,* of Eusebius', StTh, 34 (1980): 129ff.

47. See Chapter 3 [Trompf, 2000], following (with caution) esp. Barnes, 'The Editions of Eusebius' Ecclesiastical History', *loc. cit.*

48. Christensen, *Rufinus,* p. 28, and also pp. 17-19, 21.

49. For the details, *ibid.*, pp. 24-36, 41-6, 52-4, 58-78, 89-103, 108-12. More precise section identifications here derive from Christensen.

50. *Ibid.*, pp. 127-8.

51. *Ibid.*, pp. 127-32. See also Christensen, *C. Galerius Valerius Maximinus,* Copenhagen, 1974, pp. 103ff.; cf. B. Leadbetter, *Galerius and the Tetrarchy,* Ann Arbor, 1998.

52. Cf. Lactantius, *Mort. pers.,* xxiv. Christensen suggests that Rufinus and Lactantius both used a common 'imperial' source here: *Rufinus,* p. 130.

53. *Ibid.*, p. 140 and also pp. 142-3.

54. *Ibid.*, p. 192.

55. Christensen, *Galerius,* ch. 5; *idem, Rufinus,* pp. 194-6 (p. 194 for the quotation). Cf. Lactantius, *Mort. pers.,* xxxiii, where, as in Eusebius, this tone is entirely weaker still, Galerius turning just to *Deus,* while in Eusebius he supplicates 'the God of the universe' (VIII, xvii, 1). On the other hand, see Orosius, *Hist. adv. pagan.,* VII, 28, who is apparently following Rufinus.

56. In Rufinus' account, Maximin's persecution appears to be more geographically limited than in Eusebius: Christensen, *Rufinus,* p. 242.

57. *Ibid.*, pp. 280 (quotation), 294-8; but see Eusebius, *Hist. eccles.,* IX, ix, 3; *Vita Const.,* i, 2; Lactantius, *Mort. pers.,* xliv; *Panegyr.,* ix, 17; Anon., *Vales.,* iv, 12; and H. J. Lawlor and J. E. L. Oulton (ed. and trans.), *Eusebius,* vol. 2, p. 299.

58. Christensen, *Rufinus,* p. 127.

59. *Hist. eccles.,* esp. x [=i], 2, 7-8, 11; for *gratia* see also x, 9.

60. Thus x, 30, *erga instaurandas ecclesias,* referring mainly to the work of Hilary and Eusebius of Vercelli.

61. See Philostorgius, *Hist. eccles.,* vii, 1; Socrates, *Hist. eccles.,* iii, 11 (the closest to Rufinus in this: see Chapter 5 [Trompf, 2000]); Sozomen, *Hist. eccles.,* v, 1-3; Theodoret, *Hist. eccles.,* iii, 1 (more emphasis on 'concealed impiety for a considerable time').

62. The use of *lupus* here also has a unifying effect on his whole enterprise in both translating and continuing Eusebius: *Hist. eccles.,* I, i, 2. On the element of arbitrariness in Rufinus' phrase *sed haec omnia post Athanasii obitum* in xi, 2: note that Athanasius died in 373, in the middle of Valens' reign (364-378), which was more generally known for its persecutions (see, e.g., Socrates, *Hist. eccles.,* iv, 6; Theodoret, *Hist. eccles.,* iv, 5; Hilary of Poitiers, *Hist. frag. (Collect.), apud* Jerome, *De vir. illustrib.,* 100). Lucius figures in Valens' reign in Socrates, *Hist. eccles.,* iv, 24; Sozomen, *Hist. eccles.,* vi, 20, yet given apparently less stress.

63. Cf. *Chron. Pascal.,* 364-75 (trans. and ed. M. and M. Whitby, TTH, 7, Liverpool, 1989, pp. 45-8); and see Chapter 8 [Trompf, 2000] on Sulpicius Severus.

64. Cf. Orosius, *Hist. adv. pagan.,* VII, 35. See also Zosimus, *Hist. nov.,* IV, xlvi; Socrates, *Hist. eccles.,* v, 14; Sozomen, *Hist. eccles.,* vii, 14.

65. Rufinus probably develops a parallel here with Eusebius' account of the Christian *seditio* and its tyrannical elements, which emerged before Constantine conquered the three tyrants (*Hist. eccles.,* VIII, i, 7-8) (see also notes 12, 13 above).

66. For other Christian Latins extolling Theodosius' victory over tyranny: see esp. Paulinus of Nola, *apud* Gennadius, *De script. eccles.,* 49; Prudentius, *Contr. Symmach.,* i, 410ff.; Ambrose, *De obit. Theod.* (PL, vol. 16, cols 1385ff.). See also King, *Emperor Theodosius, op. cit.,* pp. 90-2.

67. Trompf, *Recurrence,* p. 235; cf. Chapter 3 [Trompf, 2000] on Eusebius.

68. See esp. Eusebius-Rufinus, *Hist. eccles.,* I, viii, 8; II, i, 12; vii; III, v, 6; vii, 1, 8; V, i, 26; IX, x, 14 (*poena*); I, viii, 3; II, vi, 8; IX, xi, 1 (*ultio*); II, x, 1; III, v, 3; V, i, 60 (*vindicta*).

69. Thus Eusebius-Rufinus, *Hist. eccles.,* I, i, 2; III, vii, 8-9; xi, 1. See also note 39 [Trompf, 2000], and Chapter 3 on Eusebius.

70. Yet see Socrates, *Hist. eccles.,* iii, 1, 21; Sozomen, *Hist. eccles.,* vi, 2; Theodoret, *Hist. eccles.,* iii, 8-9. Note also Philostorgius, *Hist. eccles.,* vi, 5; vii, 15 for comparisons.

71. I owe the suggested Latin emendation to my colleague Professor Dexter Hoyos.

72. In his favour see R. Snee, 'Valens' Recall of the Nicene Exiles and Anti-Arian Propaganda', GRBS, 26 (1985): 395-419, although she does not consider these historiographical points. Orosius, *Hist. adv. pagan.*, VII, 33 agrees with Rufinus on the recall. Note also the discussion [Trompf, 2000] in Chapter 5 and note 35.

73. Note that neither Rutilius Namatianus nor Theodoret mentions Alaric's sack of Rome in the West! Zosimus evidently did not get to it (before he died?), although he follows Eunapius in seeing religio-cosmic significance in Alaric's despoliation of Greece: cf. Momigliano, 'Popular Religious Beliefs and the Late Roman Historians', SL, 135 (1975): 83. See also note 44 above.

74. *Hist. adv. pagan.*, VII, 35.

75. Long before comparable accounts by the Greek continuators Socrates, Sozomen and Theodoret, Augustine provides a variant of this incident in *Civ. Dei*, V, 2 [6]; cf. Orosius, *Hist. adv. pagan.*, VII, 35. Dust storms affecting military outcomes were not unheard of: cf. Plutarch, *Vit. Sull.*, xxvii, 15-16 (and note the servant's divine prophecy in this context! 12-13), but the pagan Zosimus (deliberately?) omits the occurrence (*Hist. nov.*, IV, lviii), and it intriguingly has no place in the later Nestorian Chronicle of Séert (*Hist. Nest.* [*Chron. de Séert*], XVI, Ap. 7 [using A. Scher edn, PO, vol. 4/3]).

76. Both emphases at xi, 33. Rufinus characterizes Eugenius as a pagan when he was probably a Christian with pagan supporters (King, *Emperor Theodosius*, p. 83); and is vague about the losses incurred against Theodosius' Gothic auxiliaries. See, e.g., Zosimus, *Hist. nov.*, V, lviii; Socrates, *Hist. eccles.*, v, 35; Sozomen, *Hist. eccles.*, vii, 34.

77. Thélamon, *op. cit.*, esp. pp. 468-72 and *passim*.

78. P. Brown, 'The Problem of Christianization', unpublished seminar paper, 9 April, Dept of History, University of Sydney, 1991.

79. See *Hist. monach.*, 29-30; *Hist. eccles.*, x, 8 (*Life of Antony* quoted), and then x, 2-5, 11-21, 27-9, 33-4 with Athanasius' *Apol., De Synod.*, etc. in mind, with the wolf image looking a possible Athanasian conceit, as in *Epist. encycl.*, i; yet cf. also Acts 20:29. In Socrates (*Hist. eccles.*, ii, 1), however, lies the accusation that Rufinus does not have enough information about Athanasius' career (see Chapters 5 and 6 below). Note also the quotation (x, 6) of the Nicene decisions. Perhaps Sabinus was more important than Athanasius as a source of documents for Rufinus: Socrates, *Hist. eccles.*, i, 8; and W. A. Löhr, 'Sabinus of Hera-

clea: a Reassessment of the Scope and Tendency of His Work' (unpublished paper, Tenth International Conference on Patristic Studies, Oxford, 28 August 1987).

80. For this tension, see Chapter 3 [Trompf, 2000] (on the exchanges between the two at Tyre and Constantinople).

81. This means also that Rufinus lacked most of the material in Eusebius, *Hist. eccles.*, X that is parallel to *Vita Const.*, i, 49-51, 54-6; ii, 10-13 (largely on the lapsing of Licinius).

82. See note 36 above. Soon after Rufinus translated Origen's *De principiis* and what he took to be Origen's (in this case 'Adamantius'), *De recta in Deum fide*, he was translating Eusebius and Origen's Biblical commentaries at the same time: see Hammond, *loc. cit.*, p. 428.

83. See esp. R. Sträuli, *Origenes der Diamantene*, Zurich, 1994, ch. 15 ('Rufinus im Schatten des Athanasius'); cf. E. A. Clark, *The Origenist Controversy*, Princeton, 1992. Significantly, the 'Adamantius' dialogue defended the usage *homoousios* before Nicaea (Trompf, 'Significance of the Adamantius Dialogue', in R. A. Pretty [ed.], *Adamantius*, p. xviii), and so Origen could be rendered theologically 'clean'; yet cf. V. Buchheit, 'Rufinus von Aquileia als Fälscher des Adamantiosdialogs', BZ, 51 (1958): 314-28.

84. See Quasten, *Patrology*, vol. 3, pp. 384-5, and see Chapter 7 [Trompf, 2000].

85. From Theodosius I, under whom Rufinus wrote, to Theodosius II (408-450), under whom Philostorgius, Socrates, Sozomen and Theodoret all wrote, the first Theodosius' two sons Arcadius and Honorius reigning in between in the first stage of this succession (cf. this last usage in McCormick, *Eternal Victory*, ch. 3).

86. Remaining so for centuries ahead: S. Runciman, *The Eastern Schism*, London, 1970 edn, ch. 1.

87. Jerome, another great mediator of Eastern theological insights to the West, published his Latin translation of the Gospels by 383, and of the Old Testament by 405. His translation of Acts revised older versions only in a minor way. As for his completion of the Eusebian *Chronicorum* (in 380), it was not strictly Church history.

88. Start with B. Altaner, 'Augustinus und Eusebios von Kaiserea. Eine quellenkritische Untersuchung', BZ, 44 (1951): 1ff.

89. E.g., Terence, *Eunuch.*, ii, 2, 44; Cicero, *Tusc. Orat.*, v, 26 [69]; *Fain.*, v, 12 (*vicissitudo*); Augustus *apud* Suetonius, *Claud.*, 4 (*fluctio* as

alternation); cf. Diodorus Siculus, *Bibliot.*, I, ii, 5 (περιστάσεις). While also recalling 1-2 Chronicles (on the monarchs) (Chapter 1 [Trompf, 2000]), a possible Jewish (extra-)Biblical base lies in Jubilees; cf. J. T. Milik, 'De vicissitudinibus notionis et vocabuli jubilaci', VDom, 38 (1950): 162-7; and for the paradigm of 'recurrent crests and hollows' in Rev 4-22: see J. G. Gager, 'The Attainment of Millennial Bliss Through Myth: the Book of Revelation', in P. D. Hanson (ed.), *Visionaries and Their Apocalypses* (IRT, 4), Philadelphia and London, 1983, pp. 150-1.

90. See Chapter 3 [Trompf, 2000]; not to forget that the Alexandrian conceptions of history as a process of ἄνω καὶ κάτω may lie behind both the Eusebian and Rufinian methods (thus Chapter 2 [Trompf, 2000], esp. on Philo).

Abbreviations

AA: *Acta Archaeologica*

AARSR: *American Academy of Religion: Studies in Religion*

AB: *The Anchor Bible*

AbSa: *Abba Salama*

AC: *Acta Classica*

AGRL: *Aspects of Greek and Roman Life*

AHDLMA: *Archéologie, histoire, doctrines et littérature du Moyen Âge*

AHR: *American Historical Review*

AJBI: *Annual of the Japanese Biblical Institute*

AJP: *American Journal of Philology*

AJPH: *Australian Journal of Politics and History*

AJS: *American Journal of Sociology*

Akk: *Akkadica*

AKPAW: *Abhandlungen der Königlichen Preussischen Akademie der Wissenschaften*

AnBibl: *Analecta Biblica*

AnBoll: *Analecta Bollandiana*

ANCL: *Ante-Nicene Christian Library*

ANET: *Ancient Near Eastern Texts* (ed. J. B. Pritchard) (1969 edn)

AnGreg: *Analecta Gregoriana*

Ant: *Antichthon*

Antiq: *Antiquity*

ANTJ: *Arbeiten zum Neuen Testament und Judentum*

ANYAS: *Annals of the New York Academy of Sciences*

ARCA: *ARCA: Classical and Medieval Texts, Papers and Monographs*

ARID: *Analecta Romana Instituti Danici*

AS: *Anatolian Studies*

ASOR: *American School of Oriental Research*

ASPACL: *Australian and South Pacific Association for Comparative Literary Studies*

ASS: *All Souls Studies*

Ath: *Athenaeum*

BAB: *Bulletin de la Classe des Lettres de l'Académie Royale de Belgique*

BZ: *Byzantische Zeitschrift*

CeM: *Classica et Mediaevalia*

CSCO: *Corpus scriptorum Christianorum orientalium*

CUASMH: *The Catholic University of America Studies in Medieval History*

EA: *Études augustiniennes*

EHS: *Ecclesiastical History Society, Papers*

GCS: *Griechischen christlichen Schriftsteller*

GRBS: *Greek, Roman and Byzantine Studies*

IRT: *Issues in Religion and Theology*

JTS: *Journal of Theological Studies*

NMS: *Nottingham Mediaeval Studies*

OCD: *Oxford Classical Dictionary* (ed. N. G. L. Hammond and H. H. Scullard) (1970 edn)

OChA: *Orientalia Christiana Analecta*

OCM: *Oxford Classical Monographs*

PG: *Patrologiae cursus completus; series Graeca* (ed. J. P. Migne)

PO: *Patrologia Orientalis* (ed. R. Griffin, F. Nau *et al.*)

RECA: Pauly's *Realencyclopädie der classischen Altertumswissenschaft* (rev. ed. G. Wissowa)

SC: *Sources Chrétiennes*

SGOE: *Schriften zur Geistesgeschichte des östlichen Europa*

StTh: *Studia Theologica*

TTH: *Translated Texts for Historians*

TU: *Texte und Untersuchungen zur Geschichte der altchristlichen Literatur*

VD: *Verbum Domini*

Select bibliography

Chesnut, G. F., *The First Christian Histories: Eusebius, Socrates, Sozomen, Theodoret, and Evagrius*, Macon, 1986 edn.

Christensen, T., *Rufinus of Aquileia and the Historia Ecclesiastica Lib. VIII-IX, of Eusebius* (Historisk-filosofiske Meddelelser, 58), Copenhagen 1989.

Duval, Y.-M., *Histoire et historiographie aux IVe et Ve siècles* (Variorum Collected Studies Series, CS577), Aldershot, 1998.

Thélamon, F., *Païens et Chrétiens au IVe siècle; l'apport de l''Histoire ecclésiastique' de Rufin d'Aquilée* (Études augustiniennes), Paris, 1981.

Richard A. Layton (essay date winter 2002)

SOURCE: Layton, Richard A. "Plagiarism and Lay Patronage of Ascetic Scholarship: Jerome, Ambrose, and Rufinus." *Journal of Early Christian Studies* 10, no. 4 (winter 2002): 489-522.

[*In the following essay, Layton explains the workings of the patronage system by which literary and scholarly pursuits were financed and given social status during the fourth century. In this light he examines the writings, teachings, and arguments of Rufinus's one-time friend Jerome—particularly those which stood in contrast to the arguments Rufinus made on the topic of plagiarism.*]

In the middle of the 380s, Jerome leveled a charge of plagiarism against Ambrose of Milan. Few literary indiscretions in late antiquity produced more rancor. Jerome found himself responding to reciprocal allegations in the 390s and his arch-rival Rufinus adduced the accusation against Ambrose as an act of unprincipled malevolence. The dispute faded in the first decade of the fifth century, without resolution but not without impact. Its effects rippled through aristocratic Roman Christian society and imprinted the remainder of Jerome's contentious literary career. The full extent of the plagiarism dispute, nevertheless, has not been the subject of a study. The few discussions that have raised the issue have attempted either to adjudicate individual allegations or to explain the personal enmity prompting Jerome's attack on Ambrose.[1] These piecemeal explanations of individual complaints do not enable a probing of the aims that Jerome might have pursued, of the

tactics he adopted to achieve these aims, and the enduring consequences of this controversy. By expanding the scope of the investigation, it may be possible to discern an underlying unity to the disparate charges, and bring greater clarity to the potential benefits that Jerome perceived in his conduct of the dispute. Accordingly, I propose to shift the focus from individual allegations to the controversy as a whole, and from the specific content of these accusations to the rhetorical framework in which they were prosecuted.

This essay aims to delineate a link between the plagiarism dispute and Jerome's quest for lay patronage. I contend that Jerome crafted his attack on Ambrose, and the ensuing defenses against reciprocal charges, to appeal to a well-defined set of readers. These readers were ascetics from the Roman nobility who would be conditioned by longstanding traditions of literary patronage to recognize the implicit invocations of the reciprocal duties of patron and author. This approach to the controversy, if successful, bears significant implications for understanding Jerome's aims in his rivalry with Ambrose and more generally for defining the role of patronage relationships in the production of a body of learning dedicated to ascetic ideals. Before developing this argument, it is necessary to address the two central, and problematic, terms: "patronage" and "plagiarism."

PATRONAGE AND PLAGIARISM IN ROMAN LITERARY PRODUCTION

R. P. Saller's definition of Roman patronage provides a useful point of departure.[2] In Saller's model, patronage was a relationship of exchange marked by reciprocity, endurance and asymmetry. Patronage, that is, facilitated a transaction of goods between two persons of different social status over a prolonged time, so that both parties planned to maintain this relationship. There is little dispute that literary relationships in ancient Rome exhibit features of an exchange between poet and patron, of which both parties occasionally demonstrated frank awareness.[3] Financial considerations were the most prominent, but by no means only, support that authors sought from their benefactors. An influential patron could offer his prestige—what Peter White dubs a "loan of status"—to a writer. This reflected glory could be of immense value to a poet, ensuring that audiences at recitations were receptive and that his reputation would be diffused through the interconnecting social networks in which both poet and patron circulated. The poet, in return, provided the "great friend" with companionship, amusement, and, it was hoped, both extended notoriety in the present and lasting fame beyond the patron's lifetime. As Saller and others have observed, the terminology of patronage was avoided in describing such exchanges, especially between members of the Roman elite, in favor of the affective, and ambiguous, language of "friendship."[4] The term *amicitia* could describe a wide spectrum of associations, extending to relationships of strictly utilitarian, or even exploitative, quality. While the powerful and influential patrons of literature came from elite families, the authors could come from a wide range of the social scale, and the support they required, and dependence they would have on a patron, would naturally vary.[5] Poets could form part of the regular entourage of the powerful, and take part in the routinized displays of dependence of the *amicus inferior,* including the morning *salutatio.* On the other hand, poets were distinguished from other members of the coterie by the pursuit of mutual interests with their benefactors, a commonality that might lessen the disparity in social prestige. Patrons and protégés, moreover, did not form exclusive attachments. A writer who entered into a patronage relationship became part of a wider society of fellow writers and other potential patrons. In these wider networks, there were abundant opportunities for reciprocity in the activity of writing, reciting, and receiving criticism.[6]

Was the social world of the Augustan poets sufficiently intact at the end of the fourth century to support traditional patronage? A thorough study of fourth-century literary relationships remains a desideratum, but at least some significant divergences can be identified. The patronage system in the early empire flowed downward from the emperor, a centralizing element conspicuously absent from fourth-century Rome, which drew upon competing senatorial families to sustain the production of literature.[7] While these families actively supported literary pursuits, it is less clear that they produced cohesive literary circles that brought together a stable network of patrons and protégés. Symmachus, for example, clearly took pride in promoting literary efforts among the elite of Roman society, but attempts to define a "circle of Symmachus" have collapsed.[8] Moreover, significant components of Augustan literary society model were difficult to transfer to circles that promoted ascetic ideals. The society celebrated by the poets was sustained by dinner entertainment frequented by both writers and patrons, which provided a showcase for writers and a safe, even if competitive, arena to encounter rivals. Ascetic practice replaced the conviviality of the symposium with the intimacy of Bible study. Face-to-face relationships among competing writers were replaced by the solitary quest of the ascetic, and even friendships among ascetic writers were conducted at long distance, by the exchange of letters rather than the familiar intercourse of colleagues. These shifts were accompanied by an altered relationship between patron and protégé, which became merged with that of teacher and student. Patrons of ascetic causes might still crave enduring social recognition, but this was not the

medium of exchange in which an ascetic teacher could traffic.[9] Instead of poetic fame, the teacher proffered access to esoteric knowledge. The viability of the patronage relationship turned on the confidence of a patron that her or his teacher had access to the richest deposits of knowledge, and minted from these stores the genuine coin of the realm. Despite these significant differences, it is equally clear that the rhetorical conventions of patronage persisted at least until the end of the fourth century. Jerome, for example, frequently employs many of the traditional motifs of literary patronage, including dedicatory prefaces, acknowledgments of gifts, and responses to requests by supporters. It is especially useful to consider how two fourth-century writers, the rhetor Ausonius and the poet Claudian, thought it appropriate to address prospective patrons from the senatorial class. Although from vastly different backgrounds, both parlayed expertise in literature into spectacular social distinction. Both Ausonius and Claudian, moreover, left works addressed to the family of chief concern for Christian writers: the *Anicii,* headed by Sextus Claudius Petronius Probus.[10]

Probus stemmed from one of the first aristocratic families in Rome publicly to adopt Christianity. His formidable career included four prefectures and the honor of holding the consulate jointly with the emperor Gratian in 371. Probus also adroitly managed the patronage system, placing family members in influential offices in provinces where they might look after the interests of family landholdings. His effectiveness as a patron was respected, even if resented, by his rivals.[11] Much of the family's largess supported Christian causes. Anicia Faltonia Proba, the wife of Petronius, bequeathed substantial revenues from her estates in Asia to the support of clergy and monasteries, and for the relief of the poor.[12] When her husband died, she received letters of consolation from writers as distant as John Chrysostom, then a presbyter in Antioch, and the newly elevated bishop of Hippo, Augustine.[13] Beyond their direct relationships to protégés, the *Anicii* could shape the view of other senatorial families.[14]

During his service in the imperial court in Milan as the tutor of Gratian, Ausonius obtained the friendship of Probus. In the single extant piece of his correspondence to the senator, the rhetor forwarded to Probus a copy of books he considered suited for his children's education. Ausonius enclosed with this gift a long poem, addressed to the proffered volume, in praise of its recipient. "Go forth, little book," the poet commissions his gift, to "enjoy boundless happiness" in the halls of Probus. What fortune for this *libellus felix,* "which so great a man shall unroll upon his lap, nor shall he complain when his welcome time of leisure is filled." This encomium continues at length, gracefully comparing Probus to epic heroes canonized by Virgil and Ovid.

The address to his volume recalls the benedictions that Martial pronounced upon the epigrams that he sent to prospective patrons.[15] Moreover, the imagined tableau of Probus musing over the fables echoes a long past golden age of literary leisure. Ausonius depicts the powerful aristocrat as "unrolling" (*evolvet*) his book, an incongruous action in the age of the codex that had replaced the scrolls of Augustan *literati*. Ausonius even excuses his flattering verse to Probus with an anecdote drawn from the Augustan age. Should Probus not be pleased with his poem, the author reminds him that "since I have copied Choerilus in his madness, you must pardon me with the generosity of Alexander." The excuse appeals to the actions of a poet whose uncouth verses were repaid by the king with a "royal coin." Ausonius takes for granted that his reader would recognize the previous use Horace had coyly made of this *exemplum* in addressing Augustus, and perhaps also hoped that Probus would appreciate the analogy drawn to the poet's supplication of the emperor.[16]

In 371, when Ausonius sent Probus this volume of fables with its versified dedication, the teacher had no immediate need of support from the *Anicii* and their extensive connections. The rhetor, however, would be prudently aware of the swift reversals that imperial courtiers could suffer, and would cultivate a network of support to insure against the whims of the emperor.[17] The case was different for the young poet, Claudian, when he offered a panegyric on the joint consulate of two sons of Probus, Olybrius and Probinus. An émigré from Egypt, the poet had wandered through the eastern Mediterranean, and arrived in the Eternal City around 394.[18] By this time, Probus had died, and the emperor Theodosius was battling the usurper Eugenius. The Roman aristocracy had been placed in an awkward situation when Theodosius crushed this rebellion, as significant members of the senate, especially those with pagan commitments, had backed the cause of Eugenius.[19] In part to mend this rift, and also to provide a clear signal of the preference for Christianity, Theodosius appointed Olybrius and Probinus, the surviving male leaders of the conspicuously Christian *Anicii,* as consuls for the year 395.

Claudian's *Panegyric on the Consuls Probinus and Olybrius*—the first preserved speech of the poet after his arrival in Italy—provides an excellent measure of how an outsider to Roman society might craft a suitable address to potential patrons. Claudian waxes eloquent on the accomplishments of the *Anicii*, whom he celebrates as the premier family in a city "thronged with senators." In the poet's verse, Theodosius fondly recollects the service of Probus, who led the "war-weary peoples" of Italy to an era of prosperity (166-68).[20] Proba is depicted as the very personification of Modesty; "worthy is she of Probus for a husband, for he surpasses

all husbands as she all wives" (195-200). The panegyric also taps the still vital spirit of *Romanitas*. Adorned in the guise of the virgin goddess Minerva, a "chaste beauty armed with awe," Rome herself petitions Theodosius to name the young scions of Probus to the consulate. She celebrates both the heritage of the city and the fortunes of the *Anicii*, incongruously comparing the young sons of Probus to the great heroes of Rome's past (147-49).[21] Claudian suitably affects an epic tone throughout this recollection of Rome's proud history, recombining the evocative phrases of Virgil, Ovid and Statius in dense allusions. In a city awash with Virgilian quotations on its monuments, Claudian could expect the majority to appreciate the epic tone he struck.[22] The elites in his audience, who had assimilated the poets in their grammar-school curriculum, probably would recognize the echoes of Virgil.[23] Claudian most certainly gauged the sensibilities of the *Anicii* correctly, as had the citizens of Venice and Istria when they listed at the head of Probus' accomplishments that their patron excelled "in letters and speech."[24]

Both Claudian and Ausonius accurately judged that prospective patrons would respond favorably to appeals that celebrated the continuing vigor of the Roman spirit, including its literary accomplishments. Jerome also deemed it appropriate to define the events in the lives of senatorial families in terms drawn from the city's epic past. In a eulogy of Fabiola dedicated to Oceanus, Jerome celebrated the noblewoman's pious accomplishments as a triumph more glorious than those of the same storied Roman generals adduced by Claudian in his panegyric. In the midst of a consolatory letter to Pammachius, Jerome inserted congratulatory words praising the senator's establishment of a hospice in Rome. As had Aeneas, Pammachius was now "tracing the outlines of a new encampment," which would surpass even that of the ancient founder of Rome.[25] In Jerome's letters, the Christian order may supplant the foundations of Aeneas, but the senators would yet measure this accomplishment by that yardstick.

As did Ausonius and Claudius, Jerome encouraged Roman aristocratic families to identify with the glory of the Augustan age and to emulate its literary accomplishments. As noted above, literary patronage encoded friendship as the "moral archetype"—regardless of how accurately that ideal defined any individual patronage relationship—that regulated interactions among the various participants of literary society.[26] Unlike the relationship of *patronus* and *cliens,* legal sanctions did not maintain or reinforce the obligations between writer and patron, or among the diverse constituents of literary society. Ancient conceptions of plagiarism developed in this context of the governing obligations of *amicitia* rather than in an impersonal legal system. Ancient writers nevertheless defined plagiarism as a literary "theft" (*klopê* or *furtum*).[27] This juridical analogy, despite its ready intelligibility, had signficant limitations in the social world created by patronage. Those who suspected that a rival had advanced through literary fraud had no judicial remedy available. The only relevant court was that of public opinion, more specifically, whatever literary circles a plaintiff and defendant might share. As there was no legal process, so also there was no fixed standard to adjudicate an alleged theft, rendering a charge all but undemonstrable. Moreover, many ancient plagiarism charges concerned misuse of a deceased predecessor. Such allegations might be coupled with the contention that the thief was incompetent as well as dishonest, having sold a cheap imitation of the genuine item. The identified victim in such cases was not the plaintiff, but the unsuspecting reader, who risked being deceived by fraudulent claims. Plagiarism allegations were necessarily presented as a review of past indiscretions. The aims of an allegation, however, were future-oriented, meant to influence authorial practices of contemporaries, and less explicitly, the reputation of the plaintiff and the defendant in select, well-targeted circles.

This anomalous application of legal categories outside of a judicial framework calls attention to the wide variety of purposes the plagiarism *topos* could serve. In crafting an allegation of plagiarism, an author had the opportunity to project his self-conception to a number of separate, but intersecting, circles: current and prospective patrons, rivals, disciples, and wider circles not immediately known to the author. When Martial suspected a rival of parroting his epigrams, he retaliated by instituting his own judicial proceedings in print: "my books need neither evidence nor judge," he accused, "your page takes the stand against you and calls you 'thief.'"[28] The poet might have recited this epigram when he arose from a convivial dinner at his host's house to regale the guests with his latest work. Before reaching this dramatic charge, he perhaps read a few examples from both his own and his rival's works. This exposure obtained compensation for the alleged injustice by employing the poet's wit to devastate his opponent in the public arena established by the host and his guests.

Martial's ritual of ridicule vividly reflects the performative aspect of a plagiarism charge, but the nature of that performance could vary. Porphyry recalled a dinner party his teacher, Longinus, gave for a few literary friends. Longinus raised the question whether the poet Ephorus should be condemned as a plagiarist, and worse yet, as a hack. This jury quickly returned the guilty verdict, and each guest topped each other by ferreting out other literary thieves. Longinus held the final card and trumped everyone by supplying a bibliography of his predecessors who had treated the subject of plagia-

rism.[29] In this case, the accused were all safely entombed in the remote past, and the question of literary deceit focused the attention of the symposium onto the expertise of the host. The detection of plagiarism showcased the learning of the scholar rather than policed the crimes of literary fraud.

One more well-known appeal to the plagiarism *topos* shows the use of *furtum* to buttress other authorial aims. In a prefatory letter dedicating his *Natural History* to the caesar Titus, Pliny professed that he—unlike his predecessors, who cribbed unapologetically from other authorities—would identify the sources used for the facts his book contained. It was the mark, he asserted, of a "dishonorable spirit" to be "apprehended in theft" rather than voluntarily to "repay the loan."[30] He made good on this debt by devoting the first book to an index of authorities for each of the thirty-six book-length subjects upon which he would subsequently expound. In the topical investigations themselves, the author also frequently identified an authority, enabling some cross-referencing between the books and the preceding index. Nonetheless, in a detailed examination, Filippo Capponi exposes significant inconsistencies between Pliny's professed method of research and the actual structure of the *Natural History*. Capponi judges that the author clandestinely reproduced a list of authorities appropriated from an earlier bibliographer (probably Varro), and that this vaunted display of authorial integrity is itself not "genuinely Plinian."[31] It is not necessary to question the candor of Pliny's index of authorities to call attention to the rhetorical force of his high-minded declaration. The entire preface places the scholar in a relationship of sincere and open friendship to Titus, the future Augustus of the empire.[32] The historian adopts a confidential tone with the emperor, alluding at one point to his faithful service to Titus in military campaigns they had shared. Within this rhetorical context of faithful service to the man who was at once ruler and reader, the plagiarism *topos* serves a positive, rather than prosecutorial, function. As the entire preface concerns the credibility of the author, the modest acknowledgment of his predecessors invites the reader's trust.

From the examples of Martial, Longinus, and Pliny, it is evident that there was no administrative procedure for prosecuting an allegation of plagiarism, no standard to adjudicate the complaint, and consequently, no single aim in lodging a charge. These three examples also point to a close relationship between the requirements of patronage and the concept of plagiarism. The various uses of the rhetoric of plagiarism exposed one of the vulnerabilities in literary patronage—the dependence of the patron on the trustworthiness of his or her protégé. With the exception of Martial, the specter of plagiarism typically identified the patron—the unsuspecting reader—as the victim of unscrupulous vendors of fraudulent literature. The exposure of fraud purported to protect the integrity of the intellectual and literary resources shared by the patrons. With these considerations in mind, we turn now to the individual charges in Jerome's controversy to examine how the author defined his position with various constituents of the literary world.

STOLEN FEATHERS AND MENACING OMENS:
HORATIAN ALLUSIONS IN THE INITIATION OF THE
PLAGIARISM CONTROVERSY

The first item in the plagiarism docket comes from the preface of Jerome's translation of a treatise by Didymus of Alexandria that defended the divinity of the Holy Spirit. Jerome lodged this charge from his new home in Bethlehem sometime during the year that elapsed between the middle of 386 and the end of 387.[33] Jerome addressed the translation to his brother, Paulinian, and his patronesses, Paula and Eustochium, explaining in his preface that he originally intended to dedicate the work to bishop Damasus, a plan left unfulfilled by the bishop's death and Jerome's own precipitous departure from Rome to escape the "senate of pharisees." Jerome contrasted his own frankness in acknowledging the work as a translation with the duplicity of an unnamed rival:

> And as I have confessed the name of the author in the title, I have preferred to stand forth as the translator of the work of another, rather than to adorn myself as some do with foreign colors, as some deformed little crow. I read not long ago the slight books of a certain author concerning the Holy Spirit and I saw, in keeping with the opinion of the comic, bad Latin made from good Greek. There was nothing in these books of dialectic, nothing manly and rigorous, which even in difficult points draws the reader to assent, but everything was weak, soft, yet refined and beautiful, embellished here and there with painted colors.

After lauding the spiritual vision of "my Didymus," Jerome closes the preface with the conclusion he expects every reader to reach: "Surely, whoever reads the work of Didymus will recognize the plagiarism of the Latins (*Latinorum furta*), and will condemn the trickle when he has begun to drink from the spring."[34]

Ambrose, whose own treatise on the Holy Spirit had appeared a few years earlier, is the thinly veiled target of this complaint. Why did Jerome level the charge of plagiarism at this particular juncture in his career, and why did he choose Didymus' treatise *On the Holy Spirit* to raise the allegation? During his residence in Rome during the 380s, Jerome certainly was aware of Ambrose's reliance on Greek sources. Ambrose had published *On the Holy Spirit* in the early 380s; Jerome knew of at least some of Didymus' writings at this time and probably had opportunity to voice his complaint while still in Rome.[35] Moreover, as Neil Adkin has ad-

duced, Jerome found several means in his treatise on virginity (*ep.* 22) of 384 to disparage an earlier book of the bishop, *Concerning Virgins*.[36] Jerome offered a lukewarm commendation of Ambrose's text in comparison to the "distinguished volume" of Cyprian, and it is to be expected that his readers recognized the faintness of the praise. Jerome further disavowed the praise of virginity which was an acknowledged subject in Ambrose's treatise. While such flattery might be charming, it would be more likely to cultivate vanity than to arm the reader for the strenuous rigor of the ascetic life. A "flatterer is a charming enemy," and the true friend of the virgin should not shrink from challenging the novice to higher levels of achievement.[37] Finally, Jerome remarked that the bishop had "investigated, arranged, and expressed" (*exquisierit, ordinarit, expresserit*) all things pertaining to the praise of virginity.[38] Jerome may have intended this observation, which he emphasized with rhetorical flourish to bring to the reader's attention the derivative nature of Ambrose's work.[39] Ambrose had drawn on Athanasius' letter to virgins, and Jerome likely knew of this use, and had also employed Athanasius' text for his own use.[40] On the other hand, none of these verbs are synonyms for "plagiarism." "Searching out" or "investigating" and "arranging" are normal procedures for the writing of learned treatises. The only term that can point to plagiarism is the final verb, *expresserit,* which can be applied to the process of translation. If Jerome did intend such a play on the verb *exprimo,* he would be insinuating that Ambrose's treatise represented, at least in some elements, an unacknowledged translation. I have found no other context, however, in which an author makes a charge of plagiarism by this means, and Jerome elsewhere uses the term innocuously.[41]

Even granting that such an extended meaning of *exprimo* is present, it should not be presumed that every claim that a work is derivative is tantamount to an accusation of plagiarism. There is a wide difference between an inference that a reader might draw from ambiguous expressions and an allegation that forces the reader to reach a determination. On their own terms, the concatenation of verbs could be construed as warm praise for the bishop and it is only in the wider context of Jerome's persistent hostility toward Ambrose that a less congenial reading emerges. The most powerful evidence for construing *ep.* 22 as covertly attacking Ambrose as a plagiarist is the *open* charge that Jerome makes in the subsequent preface to *On the Holy Spirit.* This is a vital point, as the question that the Didymus preface poses is not the cause for Jerome's antipathy toward Ambrose, but rather the motivation that prompts Jerome to move from oblique criticism to open accusation. Jerome takes little pain to disguise his scorn for Ambrose, but such animus does not shed light on what he hoped to achieve by forcing the public to acknowledge and respond to this hostility. The plagiarism charge is not intended only to settle a score with a perceived rival, it is also meant to evoke a reaction from present and potential supporters. For this reason, it is all the more striking that Jerome made his accusation when highly disparate fortunes separated the two protagonists.

Jerome had moved to Rome in the early 380s after an extended tenure in the East, bringing with him an ambitious plan to translate the biblical scholarship of the Greeks, especially that of Origen, for Latin readers. This wide-reaching program for developing Latin Christian scholarship required substantial patronage, a constraint of which Jerome was highly conscious.[42] Jerome had won meager support in his previous residences of Antioch and Constantinople, and he hoped to have more success in the highest circles of the Roman elite.[43] While in Rome, Jerome coupled his translation efforts with regular study with supporters, primarily wealthy women—teaching them not only the Bible, but also the importance of critical tools, especially Greek and Hebrew. He edited his early historical compilation, a chronicle of world history following Eusebius, to expunge a critical reference to Probus.[44] The *Chronicon* also included a laudable entry to the widow Melania, praising this "noblest of Roman women" as a second Thecla.[45] Jerome had deposited a copy of the *Chronicon* in Rome, where it would be easily available for senatorial families to peruse.[46] Jerome's literary diplomacy had only grudgingly begun to yield fruit. His rival, Rufinus, earned the firm backing of Melania. Jerome gained entry into the family of the *Anicii* only after many decades, when in 414 he was able to send a treatise on virginity to Proba's granddaughter, Demetrias.[47] At the time of the Didymus preface, Jerome's most important success was with the family headed by the widow Paula. Paula controlled a substantial amount of property, but neither her social station nor her wealth approached that of Melania or Proba. Melania was the granddaughter of a consul, and if, as is possible, her husband was Valerius Maximus, she was also the wife of a former prefect of the city.[48] By contrast, Paula could not lay claim to high distinction, as is underscored by Jerome's vague claims that she descended from the ancient lineage of the Gracchi and Scipios.[49] Paula's resources were insufficient for the demanding enterprise of Jerome's Bethlehem monasteries, and the cash-strapped scholar found it necessary to divest himself of his own family properties to add to the largess she had bestowed upon him.[50] Jerome's abrupt departure from Rome in 385, under a cloud of suspicion, had put at risk even the modest success he had obtained.

Ambrose, on the other hand, had already established a formidable presence among devout senatorial families by the time Jerome arrived in Rome. His sister, Marcellina, had taken the veil in a ceremony celebrated by bishop Liberius—himself a favorite of the Roman aristocracy[51]—and remained in the city the rest of her life. Ambrose had obtained governmental appointments through the patronage of Probus, including the consular position from which he ascended to the episcopal throne in Milan.[52] Ambrose continued to influence Roman aristocratic circles from Milan. In 384, he had persuaded Valentinian to reject the appeal of Symmachus to restore the statue of Victory to the altar in the Roman senate house. This diplomatic triumph may have been of marginal significance to the religious policies of the regime as a whole, but it was of intense local interest to the Roman aristocracy.[53] Roman Christian senators had protested the initial *relatio* of Symmachus, and the aged Damasus had dutifully placed their protest in the hands of his more vigorous colleague in Milan. The Christian aristocracy of Rome could have little doubt that it had been the energetic Ambrose who had looked after their interests. If any question of the bishop's authority remained, they could read the lengthy letters Ambrose sent to Marcellina narrating his triumphs in Milan, including a dramatic standoff with Justina and the discovery of the relics of Gervasius and Protasius.[54] Even in his absence, the influence of Ambrose was palpable among the senatorial class, attested by the petitions the bishop received from the nobility, such as Symmachus, for favorable treatment in cases affecting their interests.[55] Among the aristocratic society of Rome, no Christian figure in the middle of the 380s matched Ambrose's prominence. Jerome might have regarded the bishop with envy and malice, but these dispositions do not explain what the scholar would have expected to accomplish by this attack on one so intertwined with the Roman nobility.

To understand Jerome's aims in this preface, we can begin by observing that he frames his allegation in terms that recall the competition of poets in the golden age of Roman literature. He invokes the advice given by Horace to a young writer to rely more on his own powers than copying the style of the ancients, lest when "the flock of birds comes back to reclaim their feathers, the little crow, denuded of stolen colors, should provoke laughter."[56] Horace presents himself as a fatherly figure, seeking to preserve the fledgling poet from ridicule. Jerome's appropriation of the poet's counsel substitutes a prosecutorial accusation for this tone of paternal benevolence. The charge is especially useful to Jerome in allowing him to bring other insinuations in tow. He contrasts his own frankness with his rival's duplicity, and the vigor of Didymus' prose with the flaccid and unmanly quality of Ambrose's treatise. This last complaint echoes the previous criticism Jerome had made of *Concerning Virgins* in his letter on virginity. The flatterer, he had warned Eustochium, is a *blandus inimicus,* instilling in the virgin "pride" instead of the "fear" necessary to enable the "weak flesh" to overcome its enemies (*ep.* 22.2-4). In both cases, Jerome criticizes Ambrose in terms that draw upon longstanding models for defining *amicitia,* which anxiously sought to discern the flatterer in the midst of the circle of friends.[57] For Jerome the flatterer embodies the antithesis of the friend.[58] In raising the specter of the *adulator* Jerome has in mind the office of the friend as a teacher, whose frank criticism is vital to the moral development of the adept. The praise of the flatterer cultivated a complacency that encouraged indolence when unflinching courage was necessary.[59] In connecting Ambrose to both plagiarism and flattery, Jerome frames the issue of fraud as one of grave moral risk to those who might fall under the bishop's spell. He presents himself as the genuine *amicus,* addressing his readers with blunt honesty and willing to confront even the powerful bishop to protect his friends against unscrupulous conduct.

Jerome constitutes the author and his readers as the proverbial "flock" of birds, a literary circle based on Christian wisdom rather than the ornament of Latin poetry. He posits the allegation as an address to the reader, rather than as a complaint made directly against the alleged wrong-doer, establishing a collusive relationship with his audience and appealing to a collective sense of responsibility to expose the fraud. In advertising his own frankness, Jerome inclines the reader as "judge" to accept the veracity of his claims, and more generally to present himself as the trustworthy mediator of Greek learning to Latin readers. In using the plagiarism allegation to preface the translation, Jerome turns the entire publication into an aggressive instrument, providing the appearance of hard "evidence" to support the allegation. In attaching the translation to the plagiarism charge, Jerome nevertheless aims at more than providing evidence of Ambrose's wrongdoing. Jerome contrasts the bishop's paltry treatise to that of "my Didymus" (*meus Didymus*). This passing, proprietary reference to the scholar hints at an intimate connection to the Alexandrian teacher and suggests that Jerome had an exclusive access to the author which was not shared by Didymus' imitator.[60] The exposure of Ambrose thus aimed to inspire among potential readers in Rome an increased desire for the vast learning that Jerome—and Jerome alone—could mediate for them. This consideration can help to explain the timing of the attack. With his removal to Bethlehem, Jerome obtained access to the great collection of Origen in Caesarea, which made the Latin scholar judge himself to possess the wealth of Croesus.[61] While visiting Didymus in Alexandria, Jerome also had petitioned the blind scholar to complete what "Origen had not done," and commissioned from him commentaries on Hosea and Zachariah.[62] The translation provides a sample of the fare that Jerome could now serve Roman readers.

Throughout the preface, Jerome touches in various ways upon the ideals of *amicitia,* championing his own defense of literary friendship. Jerome identifies the victim of the fraud as the potential reader, and assumes himself the role of the dutiful protégé. He impresses upon his Roman readers the need for a trustworthy broker of the theology of the East, who can represent this learning in all its vigor and manliness. As the faithful protégé, Jerome positions himself both as the protector of the integrity of the new literary venture and as the sole mediator of Greek learning to the Roman reader. The plagiarism accusation brings the individual elements of Jerome's appeal into high relief. This attack focused the attention of potential patrons in the sharpest possible terms on the qualities of trustworthiness, frankness, and expertise. It is with these broader associations of the plagiarism *topos* that we should consider the reappearance of several of these themes in the preface to a translation Jerome subsequently made of Origen's *Homilies on Luke.*

In this prologue, Jerome asserts that he had undertaken the translation in response to the urgent petitions of Paula and Eustochium, who were disappointed in another exposition that "sported in word, but slept in thought," Ambrose's *Expositions on the Gospel of Luke.* Jerome put aside other pressing tasks to meet the request of his patronesses:

> I have set aside for a short while the books on *Hebrew Questions,*[63] to dictate, in accordance with your judgment, these words of a useful work, such things as belong to someone else and not to myself. I say this, since I may hear from the left the oracular raven croaking, who strangely laughs at the colors of all other birds, although he is himself completely dark. I confess therefore, before he might be able to object, that in these sermons, Origen played with the subject as if he were a child. There are other works of his maturity and serious things of advanced age, which should it be agreeable, should I be able, should the Lord give respite and should I have completed the earlier, interrupted work, I will translate into Latin. Then through your agency, the Roman language will know of how much good it had earlier been ignorant and has now begun to learn.[64]

Jerome concludes the preface with a promise to forward to Paula and Eustochium the commentary of Hilary of Poitiers on the gospel of Matthew to replace another unsatisfying work. This last remark conveys to more distant readers that had a competent Latin commentary on Luke been available, the scholar would gladly have foregone the effort of translation.

A reader familiar with Jerome's translation of *On the Holy Spirit* would readily detect the recurrence of the motifs of frankness and competence, albeit in an altered form and with a different tone. The candid admission made by the translator concerns the value of the work, which he characterizes as suited for children. This apparent slight of his own effort is yet more condescending to the exposition of his unnamed rival; even Origen's lightest works are of more substance than the superficial exegesis of Ambrose. The critique of Origen allows Jerome to make a tantalizing claim. While his rival has contented himself with the play-things of Origen's youth, Jerome knows of more profound works of the Alexandrian exegete that Ambrose has overlooked or neglected. As in the earlier preface, the exposure of Ambrose's inadequacies positions Jerome as the trustworthy guide to the spiritual gems of the Orient.

The dominant image in the preface also contributes to a revised posture. The fledgling crow (*cornicula,* a diminuitive of *cornix*), mocked in the previous preface, is replaced by an "oracular raven" (*corvus*), which Jerome apprehensively views croaking at the "left." Who is this raven and for what reason is it the object of Jerome's opprobrium? The two species of bird were not always distinguished in Latin writing, so Jerome's readers would have reason to identify both with Ambrose.[65] Rufinus asserted that "everyone knows" that Jerome directed this blow against Ambrose, and claimed to possess a letter to substantiate his complaint.[66] Angelo Paredi, and in his train a number of others, have built on this assertion to discern in this preface a repetition of the charge of plagiarism against Ambrose.[67] This argument can draw not only on the similarity of the two birds in the respective prefaces, but also on suggestions made by Jerome himself. In a subsequent defense against his own use of Origen, Jerome protested that in "translating" the works of Origen he had followed the example set by "Victorinus, Hilary, and Ambrose."[68] The most obvious writing of Ambrose that could fit this description is the bishop's *Exposition on Luke.* This position nevertheless faces serious obstacles. It requires that not only must Ambrose be seen as lurking under the figure of the raven, but that the bird's action must also be identical with that of the unfortunate *cornicula* of the earlier preface. Paredi accordingly paraphrases the bird's demeanor as "strutting with the colorful feathers of other birds," a translation that has since been widely adopted.[69] This translation depends, however, on construing the verb *ridere,* which normally means simply "to laugh at," as to "adorn oneself with," a use for which neither Paredi nor any other translator can supply a parallel.[70] Neil Adkin has convincingly demonstrated that the verb here must carry its usual meaning, and therefore the behavior of the unfortunate *cornicula* of the earlier preface cannot be equated with that of the *corvus* in the Luke homilies.[71] Adkin proposes that while Jerome still has Ambrose in view, the provocation for the attack has shifted.[72] He holds that Ambrose was among those who criticized Jerome's controversial use of Hebrew as the basis for the retranslation of Scripture and the foundation for biblical exegesis. Adkin understands the allusion to the raven in this fashion: he laughs at (*ridere de*) the colors of all the birds, even though he is completely ignorant ("dark," *tenebrosus*).[73] It is not the bishop's appropriation of Greek scholarship that Jerome has in view, but the bishop's own "mockery" of Jerome's Hebrew scholarship. I am unconvinced by this explanation,[74] but adopt the two major premises of Adkin's argument: that Jerome does intend Ambrose as the target of his complaint, and that he does not make a *repetition* of the plagiarism charge. The precise motivation for attacking the bishop, however, remains in doubt. We can, perhaps, make progress on this problem by focusing attention on Jerome's concern for the omen that the raven croaks.

As discussed above, the entirety of this preface echoes the motifs of frankness and competence at the heart of the attack on Ambrose in the earlier preface. It is also striking that Jerome pins his complaint, as he does in the earlier preface, to an allusion from Horace. The fledgling crow, an object of ridicule, gives way to the menacing presence of the oracular raven, which ominously croaks "from the left." Jerome obtains this *oscinem corvum* from a poem Horace composed to dissuade a lover from leaving the poet to undertake a trip. Horace declares that while wicked individuals might deservedly receive bad omens before a journey, he will exercise all his power to summon a good omen "for whomever I feel fear." He promises to summon the *oscinem corvum* to arise and fly "from the east" before it has the opportunity to appear from the "stagnant marshes," which would presage bad weather.[75] Jerome alters Horace's augury by adding the phrase "from the left" and specifying that it is the "croaking" of the raven, rather than its flight, which provides the omen. The guttural call of the *corvus* or *cornix* was widely considered as an omen of an adverse turn of events.[76]

Jerome changes the poet's promising invocation into a menacing admonition, and calls attention to the disturbing effect upon himself of the raven's guttural cry. Jerome's specification of the left side as the source of the raven's warning is sometimes taken to refer to a general belief that evil omens came from the left.[77] The truth of the matter, however, was more complex, and Roman augurers detected auspicious and evil omens from either side.[78] Perhaps Jerome sought to recall for his readers another famous omen by a crow that took place "on the left." In his ninth *Eclogue,* Virgil presents a dialogue between two shepherds, Moeris and Lycidas, directly after Moeris had been evicted from his fields. Moeris informs his friend that he had almost perished in the struggle: "had not a crow on the left warned me from the hollow oak to break off, however I might, from new disputes, neither your Moeris nor Menalcas himself would live."[79] The salient characteristic of the omen of the crow was its timely intervention with a sign that the shepherd could recognize as certain.[80] By recognizing the sureness of its omen, the shepherd (taken in antiquity as the poetic representative of Virgil himself)[81] immediately ceased from a quarrel with more powerful opponents. Moeris insists that justice lay on his side even though the crow's counsel dictated the prudent course. In specifying the raven's oracle as coming "from the left," Jerome might declare, as had the wronged shepherd, his reluctant removal from an engagement with a more powerful adversary.[82] His wariness about the "oracular raven" would in this case express an effort to forestall an escalation of the conflict. At about the same time as his translation of the Luke homilies, Jerome found it necessary—as will be discussed below—to respond to accusations of plagiarism against himself.[83]

As a whole, the preface to the Luke homilies obliquely continues the dispute with Ambrose while avoiding a repetition of the plagiarism charge. The verbal play on *corvus/cornicula* recalls the previous allegation, but Jerome skillfully mutes the directly aggressive challenge of the Didymus translation. Paula and Eustochium assume the responsibility for the initiative of the translation project, for which Jerome reluctantly interrupted more serious endeavors. Jerome also emphasizes the superficiality, rather than the derivative nature, of Ambrose's *Expositio* as the defect that rendered necessary his actions. By these means, the second preface adapts the plagiarism *topos* to achieve the same aim of positioning Jerome as the scholarly authority and genuine friend of pious Roman aristocrats seeking to expand their knowledge of the intellectual foundations to ascetic practice.

Framed as direct addresses to current patrons, both prefaces enabled Jerome to make several claims designed to appeal to readers from Roman ascetic circles. He deprecated the writings of Ambrose in comparison to the achievements of previous Greek writers, and urged serious Latin readers to aspire to these loftier regions. Ambrose's treatises were a paltry "trickle," and the thirsty reader would naturally seek for the genuine "springs." Ambrose's writings, he intimated, were not merely inadequate, but were also dangerous. The bishop flattered and charmed his readers, domesticating the original sources to the point of soft refinement. Such efforts might be sufficient for the "childish" who were content to play with the Bible, but did not hone the virile mind essential to ascetic progress. The plagiarism allegation bluntly and aggressively focused these various deprecations, advancing Jerome's claim to possess access to untold treasures of knowledge, while posing as the honest broker who exposed a dishonest and incompetent rival. By introducing these allegations through prefaces to the translations, Jerome invited the reader to discern from the subsequent translation the

richer storehouse of Greek learning that could be made available to the Latin reader. I have suggested that the Luke preface represents an effort to deflect criticism, while still effectively drawing on the plagiarism *topos*. Evidence of hostility generated by the initial charge against Ambrose comes from responses by Jerome, drafted at roughly the same period, to plagiarism allegations leveled against himself.

WIELDING THE CLUB OF HERCULES: JEROME'S DEFENSE AGAINST PLAGIARISM CHARGES

The bishop of Milan never deigned—at least publicly—to acknowledge the persistent criticism he received from Jerome. Ambrose's honor, however, did not go unavenged. Rufinus defended the bishop: even if Ambrose had used Greek sources, and "quoted some of their words," nevertheless, it was truly his own work, written both in the bishop's own words and with the blood he "offered to the persecutors."[84] As I noted above, Jerome penned the translation to the Luke homilies during the same period when he was composing the *Hebrew Questions*. In prefaces to the *Hebrew Questions on Genesis* and to a contemporary work, his *Commentary on Micah*, Jerome responds to accusations of *furtum* against himself. These two prologues ought to be treated in tandem, and translations of the relevant portions of each can draw out their close connection. First, the preface from the *Hebrew Questions*:

> Although I should have set forth at the beginning of a book the subjects to be addressed in the work, I am compelled first to respond to slanderers, following up on a custom of Terence, who, for his own defense, put on stage the prologues of the comedies. For Luscius Lanvinus had been pressing him hard—similarly to our own Luscius—and accused the poet as if he were a thief of the public treasury. The Mantuan poet suffered the same thing from his rivals, that, when he had translated some verses of Homer literally (*ad verbum*), he was called a plunderer of the ancients (*conpilator veterum*). To which he responded that it took great strength to wrest the club of Hercules from his hand. Even Cicero, who stood at the pinnacle of Roman eloquence, the king of orators and the most distinguished speaker of the Latin language, is accused of extortion by the Greeks. Therefore I am not surprised if against me, who am but a lesser man, unclean pigs grunt and trample pearls under foot, since spite blazed up also against the most learned men, who should have conquered envy with glory.[85]

Next from the preface of book two to the *Commentary on Micah*:

> Moreover, I warn the fat bulls who have surrounded me to cease and desist from slandering, lest they read about their own misdeeds, which will be publicly disclosed, if they persist in their attacks. For they say that I plunder (*compilare*) the books of Origen, and that it is not fitting for the writings of the ancients to

be corrupted (*contaminari non decere veterum scripta*). What they regard as a violent curse, I receive as the greatest praise, since I desire to imitate that man, whom I do not doubt finds favor with all the wise, and you as well. If, moreover, it is reprehensible to translate the good writings of the Greeks, let Ennius and Maro, Plautus, Caecilius and Terence, even Cicero and other eloquent men stand accused, who translated not only verses, but many chapters and extremely long books and entire plays. Let even our Hilary be accused of plagiarism (*reus furti*), for in the commentaries on forty psalms he translated in substance (*ad sensum*) almost a thousand lines of the aforesaid Origen.[86]

Both works were published between 391 and 393, shortly before the eruption of the Origenist controversy.[87] The two prologues reflect strong similarities both in the framing of the accusation and in the tactics Jerome employs in response. In both Jerome responds to abusive statements (*maledictis*) made by envious critics, who charge that Jerome had committed plagiarism and "plundered" (*compilare*) and "spoiled" (*contaminari*) the writings of the "ancients." Jerome invokes the pantheon of Latin writers who faced similar charges, and casts himself in the role of the comic playwright Terence, whose prologues Jerome cites in both prefaces.[88] Given the similarity of the structure of both accusations and response in works that are roughly contemporary, it seems necessary to treat the two apologies as responses to the same set of critics in defense against the same charges.[89]

Jerome does not identify either his accuser(s) or the works that give rise to the complaints. He satirizes the opposition—labeling them "grunting pigs" and "fat bulls"—and surrounds himself with the company of literary giants who fended off the attacks of the envious. He multiplies the charges that have been leveled against him, holding that his critics have variously accused him of "plagiarism" (*furtum*), "spoiling" (*contaminatio*), and "plundering" (*compilatio*). Jerome ties the first two of these accusations to complaints Terence faced from rival playwrights. In the Roman theater, the charges of *furtum* and *contaminatio* referred to separate forms of wrongdoing. A playwright was guilty of "spoiling" if he interpolated elements from two separate Greek plays to construct a single Latin comedy. This procedure violated informal operational codes of conduct among playwrights by reducing the stock of Greek plays available for use by Latin dramatists. The charge of "plagiarism" concerned the appropriation of material that had already been crafted by a playwright's predecessors on the Roman stage. The prohibition of this practice also had a practical aim, that of preventing the depletion of stock by borrowing too quickly upon itself.[90] The final charge of "plundering" does not appear among the disputes of Roman theater, and was used by contemporaries of Jerome as synonym of "pla-

giarism."[91] Noting the specific application of the concept of *furtum* in the production of Latin plays, C. T. R. Hayward has suggested that in the *Hebrew Questions* prologue Jerome addresses criticisms relating to unacknowledged use of a previous Latin translation in a work he had recently published, *On the Location and Names of Hebrew Places.*[92] Hayward, however, does not explain the recurrence of these charges in the Micah prologue, which specifically adduces Jerome's use of Origen as the issue. Moreover, the presumption that Jerome had in mind a technical distinction between *furtum* and *contaminatio* is greatly weakened by the explicit application of Macrobius and Jerome's own teacher, Donatus, of the allegation of *furtum* to illicit appropriation of *Greek* sources.[93] The effort to discern a defense by Jerome of his use of sources in producing any individual publication seems doomed to failure. Jerome combines all these allegations precisely to create the impression that he has been persecuted by wild and indiscriminate accusations, and to cloud the ability to examine the merits of any one charge.

In his defense, Jerome draws on a shared literary and commentary tradition that shaped the Roman elite. The central figures in his rebuttal are Terence and Virgil, staples of the elementary education of Roman schoolboys. The Mantuan poet had been deprecated by critics as being derivative of Homer, and Donatus conveyed Virgil's rejoinder: "He was accustomed to defend himself against this accusation in this fashion, saying, 'Why don't they attempt the very same theft (*eadem furta*)? Indeed, then they will know that it is easier to steal the club of Hercules than a verse of Homer.'"[94] The poet's retort was widely taken as a denial of his illicit appropriation of Homer, as a youthful interlocutor in the *Saturnalia* of Macrobius exclaims, "There are three things that are judged to be equally impossible: to rob Jupiter of his thunderbolt, Hercules of his club, and Homer of a verse."[95] Jerome alludes to this famous anecdote, but his declaration that "it took great strength to wrest the club of Hercules" might suggest a different claim. He does not meekly assert the inimitability of the accomplishments of the Greeks, but rather touts that he now wields the club of Hercules.

Is it possible that in the heat of polemic Jerome forgot the lesson he had learned from Donatus? It would be a highly uncharacteristic slip. Jerome may have demurred that "I can barely recall as in a dream" what had been drummed into him in his boyhood education,[96] but he cites Virgil repeatedly with an acute ear for both the cadence and the imagery of the poetry.[97] Even in his latest commentaries, Jerome is able to cite a grammatical point from Donatus, complete with its Virgilian prooftext.[98] In his *Commentary on Galatians*, written a few years previously, Jerome accurately adduces another anecdote of Virgil taken from Donatus' *vita*.[99] Finally,

Jerome makes a second, less direct allusion to his wielding the club of Hercules in concluding his defense against plagiarism accusations in the Micah prologue, vowing to crush the heads of the hydra with the "prophetic *rhopalôi*," leaving the Greek term for "club" untranslated. In light of this parallel usage and the firm grasp of the Virgilian canon attested elsewhere in Jerome's writings, it is best to take this twist of the poet's retort as fully intentional. Jerome's seizure of the "club of Hercules" defiantly turns Virgil's saying to address both rivals and patrons. If his accusers hold that his achievements are stolen from the writings of Origen, let them be aware that no one before him has accomplished this feat—indeed, let them attempt the very same theft! In his previous attacks on Ambrose, Jerome had championed his access to the genuine springs of biblical wisdom, and here again Jerome turned these allegations into evidence of his superiority as the mediator of Greek learning to Latin ascetics.

Jerome caricatured his opponents under the figure of Luscius Lanvinus, the hapless critic who fell into obscurity while Terence's plays achieved fame, urging his readers to see the allegations he faced as repetitions of the sterile criticism voiced against the comic's genius.[100] In the *Hebrew Questions* prologue, Jerome satirized his own "Luscius" as a grunting pig, and one suspects, as the "fat bull" of the Micah prologue, whose own wrongdoing he threatened to expose. The identity of this Luscius redux is uncertain, but he may have been Rufinus, Jerome's most persistent opponent, whom he subsequently identified as "Grunter" and as a second "Luscius."[101] In any case, within a few years the charges that "Luscius" had made in private, Rufinus declared in public. At the end of 393, after Jerome published the *Hebrew Questions* and the *Commentary on Micah*, controversy erupted over Origen, whose voluminous commentaries and theological treatises were widely circulated among learned ascetics. The focus of controversy of Jerome's use of Origen shifted away from his scholarly practices and on the more dangerous point of his orthodoxy. Rufinus, however, did not let the question of plagiarism vanish completely. He translated Origen's *On First Principles,* which he published along with a separate treatise defending the theologian's orthodoxy. This short treatise, **On the Falsification of the Writings of Origen,** advanced the thesis that objectionable content in the writings of Origen resulted from the interpolation of heretics. In the midst of this argument, Rufinus complained about the hypocritical attitude toward Origen displayed by his detractors. Origen's critics "write books, in which they either speak or write wholly from Origen." For this reason, "they deter the uneducated from reading him, lest the majority come to know of their plagiarism (*ipsorum furta*)—which surely would not appear a matter of reproach were they not ungrateful to their teacher."[102] One target of this

complaint was Epiphanius, but in light of the prior suspicions about Jerome, readers would have no difficulty including the Latin scholar in this indictment.

Rufinus identified the chief fault in plagiarism in its denial of honor due to the original author, which he characterized as "ingratitude." He offered to readers an alternative to Jerome's definition of plagiarism; the victim was not the unsuspecting reader, as Jerome had declared, but the original author. In the absence of ancient theories of the offense of plagiarism and the damage it inflicted, which construction of the case would be more persuasive to the adversaries' readers is open to speculation. It seems probable, however, that Rufinus could expect the scholar's patrons to be sensitive to the fault he attributed to Jerome.[103] Ausonius, for example, held that ingratitude (*ingrati crimen*) was rooted in a general disposition of maliciousness (*malevolentia*): failure to recall the benefits one has received revealed a spiteful will.[104] In his astrological treatise, Firmicus Maternus repeatedly identified the *ingratus amicus* as one of the primary misfortunes that could befall the ill-starred.[105] In attacking Jerome as *ingratus* toward Origen, Rufinus pointed to a basic character flaw that he hoped would not be lost on his adversary's patrons. Where Jerome appealed to their desire for progress in ascetic practice, Rufinus reminded them of the obligations of friendship. Rufinus insinuated that the hypocrisy of his behavior toward his teacher was the measure by which he would act toward his contemporary benefactors. It is fitting that this concluding volley in this acrimonious exchange should return the dispute to its origins in the anxieties and ambiguities of patronage and *amicitia*.[106]

CONCLUSIONS: PLAGIARISM AND LAY
PATRONAGE IN ASCETIC CIRCLES

In assessing the plagiarism controversy, there is little to be gained by determining whether one work or another represents an instance of "plagiarism." I have argued that Jerome's conduct of the plagiarism controversy is best viewed in the context of an ongoing effort of the scholar to secure and to maintain the patronage vital to his program. Jerome's definition of the offense of plagiarism was determined by the rhetorical conventions of literary patronage. Jerome couched the detection and exposure of plagiarism in terms of protecting the value of the literature shared by a defined circle, which could be damaged by the fraudulent appropriation of another writer's efforts.

Linking these allegations to the pursuit and defense of patronage suggests a different framework for their evaluation. The allegation against Ambrose aimed at a well-defined goal, and did not simply vent the scholar's frustration and bitterness against a perceived rival. The storm raised by this accusation, while not directly related to the subsequent controversies, helped to shape the social contours of the disputes that divided Roman ascetic society.[107] Ambrose skillfully maintained social ties even when he opposed significant Roman families, as is evident from the courteous correspondence he held with Symmachus after opposing the senator on the contentious issue of the Altar of Victory. Jerome's tactics, by contrast, explicitly promoted factionalism—a "holy arrogance"—that hardened family divisions. It is possible that Jerome did not expect his attack on Ambrose to widen his own support. The plagiarism allegation and defenses can be read as efforts to consolidate a base of support, rather than to expand it, and to fortify a sense of being "outsiders" in the midst of Roman aristocracy. If this were Jerome's aim, he experienced a high degree of success. The families that were at the heart of his support before his depature for Bethlehem remained his core patronage base for the rest of his life. In his prefaces addressing the plagiarism charges, Jerome calibrated the positions he assumed, from satiric criticism to defiant bluster, suited to the position of an outside critic, and which aggressively asserted his independence from the most prominent Roman supporters of Christian asceticism.

Jerome correspondingly promoted the authorial virtue of expertise that rivaled the traditional protégé's qualities of fidelity, gratitude, and discretion. Horace, to whom Jerome alluded in the two prefaces discussed above, mastered the subtle vocabulary of traditional patronage, making necessary gestures of deference to his patrons, assertions of confidence in his own authority, and finding the perfect pitch in defining his position with respect to his rivals.[108] Unlike his model, the most apparent tone Jerome struck was an aggressive manifestation of his scholarly and teaching authority. In contrast to Horace, Jerome emphasized the qualities, brashly and stridently, that he deemed would earn the trust of a distant Roman patron. He presented himself as the skilled arbiter of ascetic wisdom, protecting his readers from the attractive, but counterfeit writings of those in power. Jerome promoted his own expertise at conveying the reader to the true fountain of spiritual knowledge, and defended this ability at the expense of the delicate balance of self-assertion and self-deprecation cultivated by Horace and his peers. Rufinus labeled Jerome's behavior with an unerring ear for the anxieties of aristocratic patrons. The "ingratitude" of Jerome summed up for his critics the hubris of the scholar who refused to give due recognition to the honor of a teacher, and perhaps, as well, to the perogatives of the patron.

The appeal of both Jerome and Rufinus to the embedded moral codes of patronage betrays the subtle shifts in the social institutions that resulted in a new configuration of the literary world. In this way, the plagiarism dispute offers a glimpse into the emergence of intriguing new possibilities in literary relationships, but the vituperative exchange of accusations effectively foreclosed any dispassionate reassessment of authorial integrity and authenticity. The plagiarism dispute, however, was not simply a tempest produced by the conflict of personalities, and its occurrence reveals the anxieties of both readers and writers in ascetic literary society.

Notes

1. For judgments on the validity of the allegations, see, e.g., O. Faller, Prologomena 17*-21*, in *Sancti Ambrosii Opera*, 7 (CSEL [Corpus Scriptorum Ecclesiasticorum Latinorum] 79) on *De Spiritu Sancto*; G. Tissot, *Ambroise de Milan: Traité sur l'Evangile de S. Luc*, SC 45 (Paris: Cerf, 1956), 33; C. T. R. Hayward, *Saint Jerome's* Hebrew Questions on Genesis (Oxford: Clarendon Press, 1995), 88-92. Occasionally, scholars have ventured more global assessments concerning an author's work. See, e.g., C. Bammel, "Origen's Pauline Prefaces and the Chronology of his *Pauline Commentaries*," in *Origeniana Sexta: Origen and the Bible. Actes du Colloquium Origenianum Sextum. Chantilly, 30 août-3 septembre 1993*, ed. G. Dorival and A. Le Boulluec (Leuven: University Press, 1995), 495-513, who asserts, 496, that Jerome's Pauline commentaries were "largely plagiarised from Origen," and alludes, 505, to "Jerome's habits in plagiarising from Origen." See also H. Hagendahl, *Latin Fathers and the Classics: A Study on the Apologists, Jerome and Other Christian Writers* Studia Graeca et Latina Gothoburgensia 6 (Göteborg: Elanders Boktryckeri Aktiebolag, 1958), 308: "Jerome is a thorough-paced compiler and plagiarist."

   The literature treating Jerome's antipathy to Ambrose is extensive. For the primary alternatives, see N. Adkin, "Jerome on Ambrose: The Preface to the Translation of Origen's Homilies on Luke," *RBen* [*Revue benedictine*] 107 (1997): 5-14; idem, "Ambrose and Jerome: The Opening Shot," *Mnemosyne* 46 (1993): 364-76; P. Nautin, "Le premier échange épistolaire entre Jérôme et Damase: Lettres réelles ou fictive?" *Freiburger Zeitschrift für Philosophie und Theologie* 30 (1983): 331-44; G. Nauroy, "Jérôme, lecteur et censeur de l'exégèse d'Ambroise," in *Jérôme entre l'Occident et l'Orient: XVIe centenaire du départ de saint Jérôme de Rome et de son installation à Bethléem*, ed. Y.-M. Duval (Paris: Etudes Augustiniennes, 1988), 173-203.

2. See R. P. Saller, *Personal Patronage under the Early Empire* (Cambridge: Cambridge University Press, 1982), 7-40. Saller's model has recently

been appropriated for explicating literary relationships by P. L. Bowditch, *Horace and the Gift Economy of Patronage* (Berkeley: University of California Press, 2001), esp. 19-27, and R. R. Nauta, *Poetry for Patrons: Literary Communication in the Age of Domitian,* Mnemosyne Suppl. 206 (Leiden: Brill, 2002), esp. 11-34. In several discussions of literary relationships, but especially *Promised Verse: Poets in the Society of Augustan Rome* (Cambridge: Harvard University Press, 1993), Peter White seems to assume Saller's definition of patronage, even while contesting its applicability to literary relationships. As this study is concerned with rhetorical structuring of literary relationships, the continuing problem of determining the actual significance of patronage in shaping economic and social relations need not be resolved. See S. F. Silverman, "Patronage as Myth," in *Patrons and Clients in Mediterranean Societies,* ed. E. Gellner and J. Waterbury (London: Duckworth; Hanover: Center for Mediterranean Studies of the American Universities Field Staff, 1977), 7-19; A. Wallace-Hadrill, "Patronage in Roman Society: from Republic to Empire," in *Patronage in Ancient Society* (London: Routledge: 1989), 63-87.

3. White, *Promised Verse,* 14-27. Bowditch, *Horace and the Gift Economy,* 19-27, offers the idea that reliance on the language of "friendship" by both patron and protégé sought to cultivate an "ideology of voluntarism" intended to make palatable the necessity of the transaction.

4. R. P. Saller, "Patronage and Friendship in Early Imperial Rome: Drawing the Distinction," in *Patronage in Ancient Society,* 49-62; cf. D. Konstan, "Patrons and Friends," *CP* [*Classical Philology*] 90 (1995): 328-42.

5. Pliny, as J. Garthwaite, "Patronage and Poetic Immortality in Martial, Book 9," *Mnemosyne* 51 (1998): 161-75, shows, accorded Martial a special status of *cliens.* At the other end of the social and chronological spectrum of antiquity, Paulinus of Nola, *carm.* 10.96, a man of senatorial birth, could address his grammar teacher Ausonius as "patron, teacher and father." See White, *Promised Verse,* 5-14, 212-22, on the social status of poets. For a critical assessment of White's conclusions, see Bowditch, *Horace and the Gift Economy,* 21.

6. For the contributions of the literary circle to the process of publication, see H. Y. Gamble, *Books and Readers in the Early Church: A History of Early Christian Texts,* (New Haven: Yale University Press, 1995), 84-85, and R. Starr, "The Circulation of Literary Texts in the Roman World,"

CQ [*Classical Quarterly*] 37 (1987): 213-23. For a fourth-century example, see D. Trout, *Paulinus of Nola: Life, Letters, and Poems* (Berkeley: University of California Press, 1999), 57f., who provides an insightful discussion of such collaboration and reciprocity between Paulinus and Ausonius.

7. The case of the poet Claudian, who entered into the court of Honorius, might represent an exception. Claudian, however, was closely attached to Stilicho, rather than to the emperor. His verse also differed from that of Horace or Virgil (however one assesses their support of imperial aims) in being explicit propaganda produced for specific occasions.

8. See A. Cameron, "The Roman Friends of Ammianus" *JRS* [*Journal of Religion Studies*] 54 (1964): 15-28; idem, "Paganism and Literature in the Fourth Century," *Christianisme et formes littéraires de l'antiquité tardive: Entretiens sur l'antiquité classique* XXIII (Geneva: Fondation Hardt pour L'étude de L'antiquité Classique, 1977), 1-30.

9. J. Matthews, *Western Aristocracies and Imperial Court,* A.D. 364-425 (Oxford: Clarendon Press, 1975), 362-69, documents the continuing appeal to the emerging Christian senatorial class of monumental foundations with dedicatory inscriptions.

10. On the career of Probus and his family, see D. M. Novak, "*Anicianae domus culmen, nobilitatis culmen,*" *Klio* 62 (1980): 473-93; W. Seyfarth, "Sextus Petronius Probus: Legende und Wirklichkeit," *Klio* 52 (1970): 411-25.

11. Ammianus Marcellinus, *hist.* 27.11.2. Cf. Symmachus, *ep.* 7.66 to Faltonius Probus Alypius, requesting protection of Symmachus' property interests during his tour of duty in Africa. This request from a rival of the *Anicii* provides grudging testimony to the effectiveness of Probus' efforts to secure influence.

12. On Proba's support of Christian clergy, see *PLRE* [*Private Libraries in Renaissance England*] 1:732f.

13. John Chrysostom, *ep.* 169; Augustine, *epp.* 130, 131.

14. See generally, and also specifically on the *Anicii,* P. Brown, "Aspects of the Christianization of the Roman Aristocracy," *JRS* 51 (1961): 1-11; and "The Patrons of Pelagius: The Roman Aristocracy between East and West," JTS [*Journal of Theological Studies*] n.s. 21 (1970): 56-72.

15. Martial, *ep.* 3.4, 3.5, 8.1.

16. Horace, *ep.* 2.1.232-34, cf. Ausonius, *ep.* 10.5.

17. See Matthews, *Western Aristocracies and Imperial Court,* 56-87.

18. On Claudian's career before his arrival in the West, see A. Cameron, *Claudian: Poetry and Propaganda at the Court of Honorius* (Oxford: Clarendon, 1970), 1-29.

19. Matthews, *Western Aristocracies,* 238-47.

20. Contrast this assessment of Probus to Ammianus, *hist.* 30.5.4-10, who criticizes his tenure as governor of Illyricum as thoroughly corrupt and oppressive.

21. See Cameron, *Claudian: Poetry and Propaganda,* 33, on the scant qualifications of the two consuls, who had yet to reach their twentieth birthdays.

22. A survey of the contribution of Virgil, as well as other Augustan poets, to Roman inscriptions is provided by R. P. Hoogma, *Der Einfluss Vergils auf die Carmina Latina Epigraphica* (Amsterdam: North-Holland Publishing Co., 1959), who provides examples from both Christian and pagan inscriptions. For Virgilian reminiscences in an epigraph dedicated to Probus by his wife Proba, see M. G. Schmidt, "Ambrosii Carmen de Obitu Probi. Ein Gedicht des Mailänder Bischofs in epigraphischer Überlieferung," *Hermes* 127 (1999): 99-116, esp. 111f.

23. See S. MacCormack, *The Shadows of Poetry: Vergil in the Mind of Augustine* (Berkeley: University of California Press, 1998), esp. 1-44.

24. *Litterarum et eloquentiae lumini, ILS* 1265 = *CIL* [*Corpus Inscriptionum Latinarum*] 6:1751; text in Novak, "Anicianae domus culmen," 475. Cf. *ILS* 1266, *tatis disertissimo atque omnibus rebus eruditissimo.*

25. Jerome, *epp.* 77.11, 66.11.

26. I owe the phrase "moral archetype" to C. Damon, *The Mask of the Parasite: A Pathology of Roman Patronage* (Ann Arbor: University of Michigan. 1997), 3 (with further bibliography), who addresses the phenomenon of the "parasite" as a deformation in the ideology of patronage. "Plagiarism" might similarly be regarded as an instance of transgressive actions within the context of the entire social world constructed by the codes appealed to in literary patronage. As will be seen below, Jerome connects both violations of the trust of *amicitia* in his attack on Ambrose.

27. On the terminology of plagiarism allegations, see K. Ziegler, "Plagiat," *Paulys Realencyclopädie der classischen Altertumswissenschaft* 20.2, cols. 1956-97.

28. Martial, *ep.* 1.53; cf. *ep.* 1.29, 1.66, 7.51.

29. Porphyry, *phil.* ap. Eusebius, *p.e.* 10.3, 467d.

30. Pliny, *nat. hist.,* pref. 23.

31. F. Capponi, *Le fonti del X libro della "Naturalis Historia" di Plinio* (Genova: Istituto di Filologia Classica e Medievale, 1985). Capponi does not include among his aims a judgment on the veracity of Pliny's claims as an author. Nevertheless, he does conclude (13, 26) that Pliny's index of "foreign authorities" is derivative.

32. I have relied on the analysis of Pliny's prefatory dedication in J. Isager, *Pliny on Art and Society: The Elder Pliny's Chapters on the History of Art* (London: Routledge, 1991), 18-31, who summarizes the earlier discussion of G. Pascucci, "La lettera prefatoria di Plinio alla 'Naturalis Historia,'" *Invigilata Lucernis: Rivistia dell' Università di Latino* 2 (1980): 5-39.

33. In my view, the precision of the date of 387 assigned by P. Nautin, "L'activité littéraire de Jérôme de 387 à 392," *Revue de Théologie et de Philosophie* 115 (1983): 247-59, esp. 257-58, exceeds the evidence available for determining an absolute chronology of Jerome's writings.

34. Jerome, *did. spir.,* prol. (ed. Doutreleau, SC 386:138-41).

35. Jerome twice mentions Didymus in works previous to his tenure in Rome: *chron.* 372e (Helm, GCS [Griechieschen christlichen Schriftsteller] 24:246) and in his preface to the translation of Origen's *Homilies on Ezekiel* (GCS 33:318). In the latter, Jerome cites Didymus' opinion of Origen as *alterum post Apostolum ecclesiarum magistrum.* The source where Jerome located this judgment is uncertain, but it might have been Didymus' now-lost apology for Origen's *On First Principles,* which was known to both Jerome and the historian Socrates.

36. N. Adkin, "Ambrose and Jerome: The Opening Shot," *Mnemosyne* 46 (1993): 364-76. Adkin successfully challenges, in my view, the hypothesis posited by Angelo Paredi and subsequently developed by Pierre Nautin, that the Didymus preface represents the initiation of Jerome's hostility toward Ambrose. For this reason, it will not be necessary to treat Nautin's correlative theory that Jerome lodged the plagiarism accusation in order to obtain some measure of revenge for a perceived injustice he suffered from the bishop. For another discussion of Jerome's early criticism of Ambrose, see S. M. Oberhelman, "Jerome's Earliest Attack on Ambrose: *On Ephesians,* Prologue (ML

26:469D-70A)," *TAPA* [*Transactions of the American Philological Association*] 121 (1991): 377-401.

37. Jerome, *ep.* 22.2.2 (CSEL 54:146): *adulator quippe blandus inimicus est,* quoting Seneca *ep.* 45.7. Both Hagendahl, *Latin Fathers,* 111, and Adkin, "Ambrose and Jerome," 372, recognize the hostile use Jerome makes of this citation.

38. Jerome, *ep.* 22.22.2 (CSEL 54:175).

39. Nautin, "Activité littéraire de Jérôme," 258, Adkin, "Ambrose and Jerome," 365-68.

40. On Ambrose's use of Athanasius, see Y.-M Duval, "L'originalité du *De virginibus* dans le mouvement ascétique occidental: Ambroise, Cyprien, Athanase," in *Ambroise de Milan: XVIe centenaire de son élection épiscopale,* ed. Duval (Paris: Etudes augustiniennes, 1974), 9-66. For Jerome's use of both Ambrose and Athanasius, see N. Adkin, "Athanasius' *Letter to Virgins* and Jerome's *Libellus de Virginitate Servanda,*" *Rivista di Filologia e di Istruzione Classica* 120 (1992): 185-203.

41. Cf. Jerome, *epp.* 18.15.9 (CSEL 54:95), 20.3.1-2 (54:106), 21.29 (54:131), 26.1 (54:221), and *ep.* 57 frequently.

42. See, e.g., Jerome's prefatory letter to his translation of Origen's homilies on Ezekiel, with the insightful discussion of P. Nautin, "La lettre *Magnum est* de Jérôme à Vincent et la traduction des homélies d'Origène sur les prophetes," in Duval, ed., *Jérôme entre l'Occident et l'Orient,* 27-39. The importance of patronage to Jerome is also indicated by the prominence he gives to Ambrose, Origen's patron, in his catalogue of Christian writers, *vir. ill.* 56.

43. For an excellent discussion of Jerome's efforts, largely unsuccessful, to cultivate support in Antioch and Constantinople, see S. Rebenich, *Hieronymus und sein Kreis: prosopographische und sozialgeschichtliche Untersuchungen,* Historia Einzelschriften 72 (Stuttgart: Franz Steiner Verlag, 1992), 98-127.

44. See Rebenich, *Hieronymus und sein Kreis,* 136.

45. Jerome, *chron.,* ann. 374 (GCS 24:247).

46. Paulinus of Nola, *ep.* 3.3, refers to the "great universal history of Eusebius, the venerable bishop of Constantinople [*sic*]" as being in the possession of "our most holy father, Domnio," in Rome. Paulinus most likely has Jerome's translation of Eusebius in the *Chronicon* in mind, as Jerome, *ep.* 47.3, names Domnio as one the Roman retainers

of his writings, and also names Marcella as keeping an archive of Jerome's writings. See also *ep.* 126.1.3 (CSEL 56:143), mentioning Oceanus as able to provide a copy of Jerome's apology against Rufinus. On the practice of depositing authoritative copies with friends and patrons, see Gamble, *Books and Readers,* 132-39.

47. Jerome, *ep.* 130.

48. See *PLRE* 1:582 (Maximus, 17), 592 (Melania, 1).

49. Jerome, *ep.* 108.1.

50. Jerome, *ep.* 56.14.

51. See Theodoret, *h.e.* 2.17.1-6.

52. Paulinus, *vit. Amb.* 8.3. M. G. Schmidt, "Ambrosii Carmen de Obitu Probi," mounts a credible case for attributing to Ambrose one poem in the epitaph to Probus. If so, this would provide evidence for the continuing connection of the bishop with his erstwhile patron.

53. See Matthews, *Western Aristocracies,* 203-11 on the limited impact of the debate on the religious policy of the imperial court.

54. Ambrose, *epp.* 60, 61.

55. Symmachus, *epp.* 3.30-37; cf. M. Forlin Patrucco and S. Roda, "Le lettere di Simmaco ad Ambrogio," in *Ambrosius episcopus: atti del Congresso internazionale di studi ambrosiani nel XVI centenario della elevazione di sant'Ambrogio alla cattedra episcopale, Milano, 2-7 dicembre* 1974, ed. G. Lazzatie (Milan: Vita e pensiero, 1976), 284-97. A detailed discussion of *ep.* 3.36 is provided by P. Bruggisser, "Orator disertissimus: A propos d'une lettre de Symmaque à Ambroise," *Hermes* 115 (1987): 106-15. Matthews, "Symmachus and His Enemies," *Colloque genevois sur Symmaque à l'occasion du mille-six-centième du conflit de l'autel de la Victoire* (Paris: Les Belles Lettres, 1986), 163-75 and N. McLynn, *Ambrose of Milan: Church and Court in a Christian Capital* (Berkeley: University of California Press, 1994), 263-75, vary from Patrucco and Roda in detecting carefully measured threats and hostility, rather than courteous friendship, in Symmachus' letters.

56. Horace, *ep.* 1.3.18f. See further, Hagendahl, *Latin Fathers and the Classics,* 116-17.

57. See D. Konstan, "Friendship, Frankness and Flattery," in *Friendship, Flattery, and Frankness of Speech: Studies on Friendship in the New Testament World,* ed. J. T. Fitzgerald (Leiden: Brill, 1996), 7-19.

58. Jerome, *Gal.* 2.4.15f (PL 26:409, Vallarsi 462-63).

59. Ambrose's own passing reference to flattery, *offic.* 1.209, ed. Testard (Paris: Les Belles Lettres, 1984), echoes this sentiment: the "softening" that takes place by flattery (*emolliri adulatione*) prevents the exercise of courage. Jerome's and Ambrose's view of flattery, and the contrasting virtue of frankness, would seem to derive from Stoic and Epicurean scholastic traditions on the necessity of frankness in teacher-student relationships. See Konstan, "Friendship, Frankness, and Flattery," 12-14, and C. E. Glad, "Frank Speech, Flattery, and Friendship in Philodemus," in Fitzgerald, *Friendship, Flattery, and Frankness of Speech,* 21-59.

60. Jerome's personal acquaintance with Didymus was based on a brief visit to Alexandria in 386. See Jerome, *Eph.* 1.prol. Rufinus, *apol.* 2.12, later complained about the presumptuousness of Jerome's claim to a special relationship with Didymus.

61. Jerome, *vir. ill.* 75.

62. Jerome, *Os.* 1. prol.

63. The identity of this work is uncertain. Jerome may refer to his *Hebrew Questions on Genesis*. That book, however, consisted of one volume, and in this preface, Jerome seems to anticipate several books (*libros*). It is possible either that Jerome did not realize this plan to extend the *Hebrew Questions* beyond Genesis, or that he simply used the plural in this preface in an inexact sense. See A. Kamesar, *Jerome, Greek Scholarship and the Hebrew Bible: A Study of the* Quaestiones Hebraicae in Genesim (Oxford: Clarendon Press, 1993), 74-75; Hayward, *Jerome's* Hebrew Questions, 23-27.

64. Jerome, *Orig. Luc.* pref. (GCS 49:1-2).

65. F. Capponi, *Ornithologia Latina* (Genoa: Istituto di filologia classica e medievale, 1979), 190-202. The *corvidae* do not figure prominently in the common stock of epithets that Jerome applies to his many opponents, which also encourages an identification of the two birds in these related prefaces. I have found only one other instance of an enemy of Jerome labeled as *cornicula* or *corvus* (*ep.* 40.2 [CSEL 54:310]).

66. Rufinus, *apol.* 2.26 (CCL [Corpus Christianorum, Series Latina] 20:101). Schenkl, *Sancti Ambrosii Opera* 4 (CSEL 32.4), praef. xvi; J. Steinmann, *Saint Jerome and his Times,* tr. R. Matthews (Notre Dame: Fides Publishers, 1959), 186 have contested the trustworthiness of this attribution. The former identifies the "oracular raven" with Jerome himself, while the latter holds that Rufinus was the target of this complaint.

67. See A. Paredi, "S. Gerolamo e S. Ambrogio," *Mélanges Eugène Tisserant* 5, Studi e Testi 235 (Città del Vaticano: Biblioteca Apostolica Vaticana, 1964), 183-98, with further bibliography at 188 n. 6. Rufinus, *apol.* 2.28 (CCL 20:103), however, carefully limited the allegation of plagiarism to the treatise on the Holy Spirit.

68. Jerome, *Ruf.* 2.14, 3.14 (CCL 79:47, 86).

69. Paredi, "S. Gerolamo e S. Ambrogio," 187-88: corvo di malaugurio che crocida e si pavoneggia con le penne iridescenti degli altri uccelli. Cf. the translations of H. Crouzel, F. Fournier, P. Périchon, *Origène: Homélies sur S. Luc,* SC 87 (Paris: Cerf, 1962), H.-J. Sieben, *Origenes: in Lucam Homilie* (Freiburg: Herder, 1991), J. T. Lienhard, *Origen: Homilies on Luke,* FC 94 (Washington: Catholic University of America Press, 1996). For a full review, see N. Adkin, "Jerome on Ambrose: The Preface to the Translation of Origen's Homilies on Luke," *RBen* 107 (1997): 5-14, 6 n. 5.

70. The *Sources Chrétiennes* translators, 70-71 n. 4, assert that Jerome uses the expression *ridere coloribus* in a "sens figuré et poétique," and claim that "*ridere,* au sens de *se moquer de,* exige un complément à l'accusatif." This objection can be dismissed. The construction of *ridere de* with the ablative is not uncommon. Three examples of the form in the meaning of "to laugh at" can be cited from Jerome, *ep.* 40.2 (CSEL 54:310), *Ezech.* 11.37.1-14, 13.pref. (CCL 75:512, 605).

71. Adkin, "Jerome on Ambrose," esp. 6-7, 13-14.

72. G. Grützmacher, *Hieronymus: Eine biographische Studie zur alten Kirchengeschichte* (Leipzig: 1901-1906), 2:75 offers the same translation Adkin proposes, which I have adopted, and also concludes that Ambrose was the intended target of the complaint against the "raven."

73. Adkin, "Jerome on Ambrose," 11, rightly calls attention to Jerome's surprising description of the *corvus* as "dark" (*tenebrosus*), rather than, as usually labeled, "black" (*niger*). It might not be accidental that Ambrose, *Noe* 17:62 (CSEL 32.1:458) also characterizes the raven released by Noah as symbolizing the "dark" nature of the wicked.

74. Adkin's case depends on the assumption that Ambrose in fact attacked Jerome's use of Hebrew in biblical scholarship, citing four earlier works of Jerome as the target of possible criticism. Two of the works, *On the Interpretation of Hebrew Names* and *On the Location and Names of Hebrew Places,* were simple etymological studies, which were not subject to this kind of attack. Jerome excited criticism for the translation of Old Testament scriptures

from the Hebrew, rather than the compilation of etymological dictionaries. A third work that Adkin adduces is the book of *Hebrew Questions on Genesis,* the preface of which will be discussed below. Relying on Nautin, "L'activité litteraire de Jérôme," Adkin asserts that this book was published "in the year before" the translation of the Luke homilies. As noted below, the dating of the *Hebrew Questions* is far from certain, and the preface to the Luke homilies might suggest that the volume was still in progress, and not yet published. Nautin's chronology for Jerome's publications depends on the highly questionable assumption that Jerome only published one of his works in each year from 387 to 392. This leaves the *Commentary on Ecclesiastes,* which undoubtedly was earlier than the Luke translation and in which Jerome did profess to correct misinterpretations by reference to the Hebrew text, as the only reliable basis for the kind of criticism Adkin detects. This is a slender reed from which to mount his case.

75. *Carm.* 3.27.11. See G. Williams, *The Third Book of Horace's Odes* (Oxford: Clarendon Press, 1969), 137f.

76. Pliny, *nat. hist.* 10.33, holds that the "strangled" call is a bad omen. Ridicule of this popular view in Augustine *Civ.,* 4.30 and Sozomen, *h. e.* 4.9 attests to the broad appeal of attributing oracular significance to the call of the *corvidae.*

77. H. Hagendahl, *Latin Fathers and the Classics,* 117; G. Grützmacher, *Hieronymus,* 2:75.

78. See the informative notes by A. S. Pease, ed., Cicero, *de Divinatione* (Darmstadt: Wissenschaftliche Buchgesellschaft, 1963), to 1.12 (*cornix* and *corvus*) and to 2.82 (*laevum*). For instances of the left as the side of good omens, see Varro, *ling. lat.* 7.97, Pliny, *nat. hist.* 2.142.

79. Virgil, *ecl.* 9.14f.

80. Cicero, *div.* 1.85 held that a raven from the right and a crow from the left provided certain omens (*a dextra corvus, a sinistra cornix faciat ratum*).

81. Cf. Macrobius, *sat.* 4.6.18, citing a speech of Moeris as made *ex poetae persona.* Christian readers would not be disturbed by an identification of Jerome with Virgil. Cf. M. Roberts, "Paulinus Poem 11, Virgil's First *Eclogue,* and the Limits of *Amicitia,*" TAPhA [*Transactions of the American Philological Association*] 115 (1985): 271-82, esp. 277-80 for the assumption of the persona of the shepherd Tityrus (likewise identified with the poet in antiquity) by Paulinus and other Christian writers.

82. This would be, admittedly, a condensed allusion for Jerome's readers to recognize. While contemporary poets frequently composed by splicing such fragments of verses, it is not widely attested elsewhere in Jerome. For some examples, identified by Hagendahl (137, 190), see Jerome *ep.* 58.7.2 (CSEL 54.537), and Hagendahl's discussion, 137f. of Jerome's Micah prologue (see further below) as a "fine specimen of tesselated work."

83. The translation of the Luke homilies cannot be precisely dated, but belongs in general to the period of 391-93. See Sieben, *Origenes: in Lucam Homilie,* 34-36; Lienhard, *Origen: Homilies on Luke,* xxxiv-xxxv.

84. Rufinus, *apol.* 2.28 (CCL 20:103).

85. Jerome, *qu. hebr. Gen.* prol. (CCL 72:1).

86. Jerome, *Mich.* 2.prol. (CCL 76:473).

87. The *terminus ante quem* for both works is set by *vir. ill.* 135, completed in the first months of 393, which includes both titles among Jerome's completed works. After reviewing the complex evidence for the date of the *Hebrew Questions,* Hayward, 26, concludes that the completion of the work can be dated no closer than "between the latter part of 391 and the early months of 393," a judgment substantially in agreement with Kamesar, *Jerome, Greek Scholarship and the Hebrew Bible,* 73-76. For dating of the Micah commentary, see Y.-M. Duval, *Jérôme: Commentaire sur Jonas,* SC [Sources chrétiennes] 323 (Paris: Cerf, 1985), 18-22; idem, "Jérôme et les prophètes. Histoire, prophétie, actualité et actualisation dans les Commentaires de Nahum, Michée, Abdias et Joël," *Actes du Xⁱᵉ Congrès international sur l'Ancien Testament (Salamanaca, 1983),* Vestus Testamentum suppl. 36 (Leiden: Brill, 1985), 108-31, esp. 114-21.

88. Jerome, *Mich.* 2.prol. *contaminari non decere veterum scripta,* cf. Terence, *an.,* prol. 1.15-16: *contaminari non decere fabulas*; Jerome, *qu. heb. Gen.* prol.: *et quasi publici aerarii poetam furem criminabatur*; Terence, *eu.,* prol. 22f.: *exclamat furem, non poetam fabulam.. . .*

89. It is difficult to determine which was written first, but the first sentence of the Micah prologue suggests that Jerome had previously addressed this "envy," and points to the priority of the prologue to the *Hebrew Questions.* The complex preface to the latter work also contributes to the confusion. Jerome responds first to the charge of plagiarism, and then subsequently defends his advocacy of the "Hebrew Truth" against biblical exegesis that

relies on the Septuagint. This sequence creates the impression that Jerome's critics are primarily opposed to his use of earlier writing to undermine the authority of the LXX. Jerome, however, distinguishes these two sources of opposition in his first sentence to the prologue, alerting the reader that he must *first* respond to *maledictis* brought forth by "Luscius Lanvinus" *before* setting forth the primary intent of the work (*operis argumenta*).

90. On the separate nature of the charges of *furtum* and *contaminatio,* see S. M. Goldberg, *Understanding Terence* (Princeton: Princeton University Press, 1986), 91-122.

91. Jerome, *ep.* 84.7 (CSEL 55:130), *nuper Ambrosius sic Exameron illius conpilavit* (regarding use of Greek sources); Macrobius, *sat.* 6.2.33, asserting that Virgil had "plundered" [*conpilando*] from Cicero, a parallel, a critic asserts, to his "thefts" from Homer (5.16.12-14). On *compilatio* as "plagiarism," see N. Hathaway, "Compilatio: From Plagiarism to Compiling," *Viator* 20 (1989): 19-44.

92. Hayward, *Jerome's* Hebrew Questions, 88-89.

93. Donatus, Ter. *eu.* (Wessner, 275), explained as follows the exact line of *Eunuchus* cited by Jerome: *adhuc nulla reprehensio, siquidem licet transferre de Graeco in Latinum.* For the accusation of theft against Virgil, see Macrobius, *sat.,* 5.16.12-14 (*subripere*), and Donatus, *vita Virg.* (cited below). In the Micah prologue Jerome holds that Hilary could be subjected to allegations of *furtum* for his use of Greek, not Latin, sources. On the relationship of Jerome and Donatus, see G. Brugnoli, "Donato e Girolamo," *VetC* [*Vetera Christianorum*] 2 (1965): 139-49.

94. Donatus, *vita Virg.* 186-92, ed. C. Hardie, *Vitae Vergilianae Antiquae* (Oxford: Oxford University Press, 1966), 18.

95. Macrobius, *sat.* 5.3.16.

96. Jerome, *ep.* 70.3 (CSEL 54:703).

97. Cf. Jerome, *ep.* 20.5.2 (CSEL 54:109) to Damasus explaining the pronunciation of Hebrew poetry in comparison to Virgil; for effective use of the imagery of the poet, see, e.g., *epp.* 49.20.2 (CSEL 54:385), and 52.1.2 (CSEL 54:414).

98. Jerome, *Dan.* 3.11.17 (CCL 75:911) cites the same texts of the *Aeneid* used by Donatus (*ars gramm.* 3.3) as examples of pleonasm; cf. *Ezech.* 9.30.1-19 (CCL 75:422) adducing the *Aeneid* to supply an example of *prolepsis.* The most plausible explanation for this recall, more than four decades after

his own schooling, is that Donatus' grammar books accompanied Jerome on his removal to Bethlehem. If such were the case, it would support Rufinus's complaint (*apol.* 2.11 [CCL 20:92]) that Jerome conducted grammatical education of young boys in his monastery, and provide further indication of Jerome's financial constraints.

99. Jerome, *Gal.* 3.prol (PL [Patrologia Latina] 26:400B, Vallarsi 485-86).

100. Jerome also derives this information from Donatus, commenting on Terence, *an.,* prol. 1.4; *eu.,* prol. 1.4.

101. Jerome, *epp.* 119.11; 125.18; *Ruf.* 1.30; *Ezech.* 10.33.23-33; *Hier.,* 1.pref., 4.pref, 4.61, 5.61, 5.66, for allusions to Rufinus as a "grunting pig" (*Grunnius*). The possible identity of the "enigmatic Luscius" with Rufinus is considered by Hayward, *Jerome's* Hebrew Questions, 91.

102. Rufinus, *De adulteratione* 14 (CCL 20:16). Cf. Jerome, *Ruf.* 2.22 (CCL 79:58).

103. On the social significance of the charge of ingratitude in the early empire, see Saller, *Personal Patronage,* 14.

104. Ausonius, *grat. act.* 41 (Green, 152). Cicero had identified the foundation of friendship in *benevolentia,* a good nature that was the antithesis of *malevolentia.* See C. White, *Christian Friendship in the Fourth Century* (Cambridge: Cambridge University, 1992), 32, 116, who also discusses the appropriation of the concept of benevolence by Ambrose.

105. Firmicus Maternus, *math.* 5.1.2, 5.1.29, 5.1.34, 8.29.15 (horoscopes for Aries, Aquarius, and Pisces), and frequently.

106. Rufinus made the final complaint, but he did not have quite the last word. Jerome, *Ruf.* 2.21-22, closed the dispute by calling his adversary's charges of plagiarism hopelessly exaggerated, and conveniently focusing on the charge against Epiphanius.

107. On the reciprocal influence of theological dispute and competition among the elite families of Rome, see the series of seminal articles by Peter Brown, "Aspects of the Christianization of the Roman Aristocracy," *JRS* 51 (1961): 1-11; "The Patrons of Pelagius: The Roman Aristocracy between East and West," *JTS* n.s. 21 (1970): 56-72; and "Pelagius and His Supporters: Aims and Environment," *JTS* n.s. 19 (1968): 93-114: For an analysis that recognizes that even the most distinguished families participated in wider "elite networks," see Elizabeth Clark, *The Origenist Controversy: The*

Cultural Construction of an Early Christian De-bate (Princeton: Princeton University Press, 1992), 11-42.

108. See E. Oliensis, *Horace and the Rhetoric of Authority* (Cambridge: Cambridge University, 1998).

Mark Vessey (essay date 2004)

SOURCE: Vessey, Mark. "Jerome and Rufinus." In *The Cambridge History of Early Christian Literature*, edited by Frances Young, Lewis Ayres, and Andrew Louth, pp. 318-27. Cambridge: Cambridge University Press, 2004.

[*In the following essay Vessey discusses the respective works and scholarly contributions of Jerome and Rufinus, both of whom were translators of biblical texts and early Christian teachings in the fourth century.*]

JEROME

Jerome obliged all future historians of Christian literature by compiling the first chronological list of Christian writers and their works, beginning with St Peter and ending with himself. His catalogue *De Viris Illustribus* ('On Famous Men') or *De Scriptoribus Ecclesiasticis* ('On Ecclesiastical Writers') was published in 'the fourteenth year of the Emperor Theodosius' (AD 392/3) when he was in his mid-forties and had been living for several years in Bethlehem. His principal generic model was a biobibliography of Roman literature by C. Suetonius Tranquillus (d. AD 160), while for his knowledge of ante-Nicene Christian literature he relied heavily on the *Ecclesiastical History* of Eusebius of Caesarea. Where Suetonius divided his subjects into separate sequences by profession (grammarians, rhetoricians, poets, etc.), Jerome makes one sequence of all who had 'left something on record about the Holy Scriptures (*de scripturis sanctis*)' (*Vir. Ill. prol*). And where Eusebius aimed to recall those 'who in each generation were the ambassadors of the word of God either by speech (*agraphos*) or writing (*dia sungrammaton*)' (*HE* 1.1), he attends mainly to written performance. 'Christian literature', as he conceives and presents it for the first time, is defined in three ways: negatively as a class of writing distinct from the corpus of pagan literature (*litterae gentiles*), positively as an elaboration of the Bible (in the first instance, of the Old Testament), and practically as the life's work of Jerome himself.

In the concluding chapter (135) of the *De Viris Illustribus* Jerome tells us that he was the son of a certain Eusebius and that he was born (probably *c.* 347) at Stridon near the border between the Roman provinces of Dalmatia and Pannonia. He then lists his works to date.

Since the underlying structure of the list is chronological, by combining its details with other autobiographical information we can make out the course of a literary career. In so doing, however, we risk overestimating the ease with which this author took his place in literary history. No Latin writer before Petrarch had a finer sense than Jerome of his own life as a work of art. By obvious design, his many letters, prefaces and personal digressions present a strikingly consistent profile of the character, formation and activity of a Christian *literatus*.

The main stages of Jerome's 'life in letters' are well marked: grammatical and rhetorical education in Rome, where he was also baptized; the beginnings of a secular career, terminated by ascetic conversion; sojourn at Aquileia in the company of fellow ascetics; removal to Antioch in Syria and then, after a trial of his monastic vocation in the 'desert' of Chalcis, to Constantinople (by 381); journey to Rome on business of the Antiochene Church, in which he had been ordained presbyter; residence in Rome, in the entourage of Pope Damasus, until shortly after the latter's death in 384; pilgrimage to Palestine and Egypt; final settlement (386) in a monastery at Bethlehem funded by his patron and companion of many years, the noble Roman widow Paula, where he spent his remaining twenty-five years in a round of study interrupted only by ill-health and the grief occasioned by events such as the Gothic capture of Rome in 410 or Paula's death.

Although few of the facts of this autobiographical narrative can now be independently checked, there is no reason to doubt its general reliability. Matters become more complicated when we begin to correlate biography and bibliography. Much of Jerome's entry in the *De Viris Illustribus* is devoted to works of biblical scholarship published or undertaken after his move to Bethlehem in 386, broadly divisible into the three categories of *translation* (Latin versions of the Old Testament from Greek and Hebrew, extending his earlier work as reviser of the Latin New Testament), *exegesis* (commentaries on St Paul, Ecclesiastes, and the Minor Prophets; tractates on the Psalms; translation of Origen's homilies on Luke; 'Hebrew Questions' on Genesis), and *aids to study* (dictionary of Hebrew names, biblical gazetteer). If we add the commentaries on the Major Prophets and on Matthew begun after 393, a picture emerges of the Christian writer *de scripturis* that exactly answers the implicit prescriptions of the *De Viris Illustribus*. The creation of that role or literary persona is Jerome's masterpiece, as Augustine and Erasmus among others were quick to appreciate and as artists of the Later Middle Ages and Renaissance remind us at every turn. At this distance, it is instructive to realize how little there was of inevitability about it. For a traditionally educated upper-class Roman of the late Empire to make a name (and, within existing structures of patronage, a living) for himself as a *scriptor de scripturis sanctis* required a significant adjustment of cultural assumptions on the part of his readers and a vast labour of improvisation by the writer himself. If the nature of the evidence precludes our reconstructing all the processes behind Jerome's consummate production of his life-and-work, a modern literary history can at least point to his more startling initiatives.

Jerome is the protomartyr of Latin literature. Until he travestied himself as an incorrigible Ciceronian and Christ the Judge as a persecuting magistrate,[1] few would have taken it for granted that a Christian man of letters should suffer for his art. Among the Greeks, a contemporary like Basil of Caesarea could calmly recommend the study of pagan authors to well-born Christian youth. For the Latins, Lactantius, Juvencus and Hilary had already provided models of a confident adaptation of classical norms to the gospel teaching. Even Tertullian, whose polemical opposition of Greek philosophy to biblical revelation Jerome twists in a literary-aesthetic sense,[2] had not made the deceptions of pagan poetry and rhetoric into a stumbling-block for the would-be Christian writer. The illusion of a conflict between classical and Christian literary values in the late fourth-century West may be very largely of Jerome's making. He himself never gave up his favourite Roman authors.[3] Plautus, Cicero, Virgil, Horace and their fellows are always on hand in his work and, on the strength of his reading in the Alexandrian theologians, he can provide an elegant justification for their presence there when called upon to do so.[4] When he chastens his naturally luxurious style—as, for example, in interpreting Scripture—he does so for effect and according to a programme.

It was no part of Jerome's purpose to prescribe a new Christian rhetoric, still less to overturn the classical literary canon. The opposition which he makes between the party of Cicero and that of Christ is contrastive and emulative, calculated to assert the heteronomy of Christian literature—its conformity to a distinct set of rules associated with the Bible—, even as it invites comparisons between the works of Christian writers and the most cherished products of the classical literary system.[5] Classical literary theory taught that writers should seek to outdo their predecessors in particular genres. Jerome generalized the principle, conceiving an entire 'anti-literature' based on Scripture. It is perhaps in this sense that we should construe his otherwise unfathomable comparisons, such as the remark that Hilary of Poitiers in his work *On the Trinity* 'imitated the twelve books of Quintilian both in style and number' (*Ep.* 70.5).

Jerome's biblicism is the other side of his classicism. Like his Constantinian precursors Lactantius and Juvencus or such contemporary classicizing poets as Proba and Paulinus, he was interested in mediating the Bible to a public of cultured Roman readers and conscious that the scriptural text, in its Old Latin versions, was an affront to their sensibilities. However, whereas Juvencus and the centonists seem to have denied the Bible intrinsic 'literary' value by recasting it in classical genres, Jerome contrived to dignify it as the master-text of a separate literature. Now and again he points to 'correspondences' between the genres of the biblical books and those of the classical canon,[6] but this is neither his most original nor his most productive line of thought. The ideal writer *de scripturis* is not an imitator of biblical forms, any more than, strictly speaking, he is an imitator of classical forms. He is an interpreter (*interpres*) of the biblical text itself, one who cleaves to its letter and fastens on its sense. Although previous Latin writers had essayed close and consecutive biblical commentary, Jerome is the first to theorize the art and to make its practice the main burden of the Christian *literatus*.

The inspiration to do this came chiefly from Origen, whose biblical scholarship Jerome encountered as early as *c.* 380 and whose life's work furnished a fateful model for his own. From Origen he learnt three things which through him would powerfully affect the later Christian culture of the West: a strongly ascetic conception of Bible study as part of a regime of Christian life; a text-centred biblical philology in the exacting tradition of the Hellenistic grammarian-critics; and an ethical hermeneutic which set a premium on spiritual meanings obtained by allegorical exegesis. Convinced by his perusal of Origen's multicolumn recension of the Old Testament (the Hexapla) that the 'received' Latin text of the Bible did not—and, even if revised, would still not—convey the plenitude of divine meanings consigned in Scripture, Jerome took it upon himself to provide a kind of hypertextual edition for Latin readers, the components of which (translation, exegesis, study aids) have been listed separately above but demand to be considered together.[7] To think of Jerome principally as 'the author of the Vulgate' is to miss the intricate interdependence of his literary undertakings. The commentaries on the prophets exemplify his approach: lemma by lemma, in strict obedience to the sequence and supposed logic of the original, painstaking collation of the Hebrew and Greek texts (Septuagint and *recentiores*) prepares the way for one or more attempts at translation-and-interpretation.[8] Commentary, as Jerome announces it, is less a genre than a job (*opus commentariorum*),[9] a literary activity subordinate to the Bible as a signifying whole, one which claims neither style nor artistic unity of its own. Any writing that would count as 'Christian literature' in Jerome's book had to be of a piece with the Bible itself.

Jerome's forging of a new 'biblical' literary persona was not his only innovation. Nor would it have succeeded so well without the publicity created by his performances as historian, hagiographer, controversialist and letter-writer. Generic inventiveness is the keynote of Jerome's writings before 386. These include the first Latin universal history (adapting and continuing Eusebius' *Chronicle*), the first original Latin *Life* of an ascetic hero (the *Life of Paul the First Hermit*, designed to outdo the Athanasian *Life of Antony* recently translated by his friend Evagrius), a polemical dialogue (the *Altercation between a Luciferian and an Orthodox*, prelude to more vehement and declamatory exchanges with Helvidius, Jovinian, Rufinus and others), and a series of exegetical essays on problems arising from the Hebrew of the Old Testament (to be found among the letters to Damasus and Marcella). The project of revising the Latin New Testament, for which Jerome claimed a commission from Damasus, belongs with these experiments. Some early schemes, such as those for a history of his own times and more extensive translations from Origen, were quietly dropped in favour of the biblical opus.

Yet even after committing himself to his main task, Jerome continued to be an extraordinarily versatile writer. During the 380s he discovered that one literary form, the published 'familiar' letter, was particularly well suited to his purposes as freelance scholar, moralist and occasional dogmatist. His extant correspondence (over 150 items) includes matter of every kind: exhortation, instruction, consolation; satire, complaint, polemic; biography, panegyric—and more. The familiar letter was also his preferred medium for editorializing upon his work-in-progress, and as such a vital means of contact with his newly constituted public. When Jerome addressed letters to well-placed individuals in Africa, Italy, Spain and Gaul, he conscripted them as collaborators in a large-scale literary-religious enterprise. Thus, astonishingly, was he able for a time to make the town of Christ's nativity the centre of the Latin-reading Christian world.

RUFINUS

If patristic confirmation were needed of Samuel Johnson's principle that literary judgments are by their nature comparative, the fortunes of Jerome and the companion of his youth, Rufinus, would provide it. When the first Christian *De Viris Illustribus* appeared in 392/3, the latter had still to make his literary début, else he might have received flattering mention in it. The notice given of him by Gennadius of Marseille, continuer of Jerome's catalogue in the second half of the fifth century, is carefully tilted in his favour, as if to redress a balance. 'Rufinus, presbyter of the church at Aquileia,' it begins, 'not least among the doctors of the

Church, had an elegant talent for translating Greek into Latin and made a great part of Greek [Christian] literature accessible to Latin readers.'[10] The accompanying list of translations, which is not complete, refers in broad terms to works by Basil of Caesarea (monastic *Rule,* select *Homilies*), Gregory of Nazianzus (select *Sermons* or *Speeches*), Eusebius of Caesarea (*Ecclesiastical History,* with two-book continuation by Rufinus), Pamphilus (book 1 of the *Apology for Origen*), Evagrius of Pontus (*Sentences* for monks and virgins), 'Clement of Rome' (pseudepigraphic *Recognitions* and *Letter to James*), 'Sixtus' (*Sentences,* the work of a pagan philosopher, Sextus, misattributed to a martyr-pope), and, reserved for last because of the number and importance of Rufinus' translations of this writer, Origen. 'Not all' of the Latin Origen is Rufinus' work, says Gennadius, but versions with translators' prefaces are his—unless they are by Jerome! As original works of Rufinus he lists a **Commentary on the Apostles' Creed,** an explanation of Jacob's **Benedictions of the Patriarchs** 'in the threefold sense, that is, the historical, moral and mystical', 'many letters exhorting to the fear of God' (not extant), and a two-volume **Apology** in response to a detractor. Gennadius tactfully omits the name of the detractor, whom he certainly knew to be Jerome.

For many years Jerome of Stridon and Rufinus, a native of nearby Concordia in northern Italy, led parallel lives. Schooled together in Rome by the best masters, both became adepts of an oriental-style Christian asceticism in the early 370s, briefly shared the monastic milieux of Aquileia, then pursued their vocations in the East. After eight years in Egypt, visiting the desert monks and studying in Alexandria where he listened to Didymus the Blind and read Origen, Rufinus moved to Jerusalem in 380, there to found a monastery on the Mount of Olives with the financial help of Melania the Elder, an aristocratic widow who befriended and patronized him as Paula did Jerome. As a place of hospitality for pilgrims arriving in the Holy Land from the West and others returning from Egypt, the Latin community on the Mount of Olives quickly became a vital site of Christian cultural exchange. It would have been a natural model for the similar community set up by Jerome and Paula in Bethlehem a few years later. Relations between the two establishments seem to have been cordial until 393 when Jerome, caught in the whirlwind of anti-Origenist propaganda unleashed by Epiphanius of Salamis, decided that his friend and fellow monk was not fierce enough against the works and ideas of a theologian whom they had both long venerated, and denounced him. Their quarrel was patched up in 397, only to break out again even more rancorously when Rufinus, having returned to Italy, claimed Jerome's translations of Origen as a warrant for his own version of that writer's treatise **On First Principles.**

As his friend and rival had eventually found fortune as an exile in the land of the Bible, so Rufinus now aimed to make himself useful as an importer of foreign stuffs into the West. The most precious commodity he could bring home with him, albeit already devalued by Jerome's panicky sale of stock, was the literary heritage of Origen. To explain why he translated the **Apology for Origen,** he tells the story of a Roman friend who dreamt that a ship came to port with answers to certain vexed questions on fate and divine providence; the next day, hearing that Rufinus had arrived from the East, he asked him for Origen's views, which were found conveniently excerpted in the *Apology*.[11] We are told that the translation of **On First Principles,** Origen's classic attempt to mark the limits for a biblical philosophy of creation and human destiny, was motivated by this friend's desire to read more from the same source.

Rufinus may in fact have needed little prompting to pursue an 'edition' of Origen which, even at this awkward juncture, would secure part of his work as a resource for Western theology. Unhappily for him, the editorial principles on which he chose to proceed—that Origen's texts had been interpolated by heretics, and that where he appeared to hold contradictory opinions, the 'orthodox' alternative alone was to be considered his[12]—were too easily ridiculed, and his appeal to Jerome's example in support of his practice too inflammatory, for the latter not to become involved. The ensuing polemics of Rufinus **Against Jerome** and Jerome *Against Rufinus,* in which neither party (certainly not Jerome!) precisely weighed the other's case, witness to the strength of feeling aroused among Latin readers by the contested legacy of Origen.[13] Nowadays they can be read as a disjoint commentary on the hazards of Christian literary activity at a time when episcopal and monastic zeal for orthodoxy, encouraged by the legislation of the militantly Christian emperor, Theodosius I, was threatening to narrow the scope of theological discourse to the hard-won certainties of the Nicene creed. By precipitating controversy over the terms on which Latin Christian writers adapted the texts of their Greek precursors, Rufinus ensured that his enterprise would not be mistaken for a simple extension of Jerome's. Versions from the Greek, adjusted where necessary for intelligibility or doctrinal respectability, were to be the staple of his literary production. In these works, as in those for which he claimed an author's rights,[14] he exhibits a many-sided literary personality. Exponent of the biblical theology of Origen before all else, he is also a skilful moralist in his own fashion and an imaginative narrator of Christian history.

Despite all difficulties, Origen claimed the lion's share of Rufinus' literary labour. In the decade from 400, he translated sets of this teacher's homilies for the whole Heptateuch except Deuteronomy, and others on selected psalms, the Song of Songs and 1 Samuel. Taken with Jerome's commentaries on the prophets, themselves heavily indebted to Alexandrian exegesis, these texts furnished a substantial Latin library on the Old Testament. At the same time, Rufinus' translation of Origen's great commentary on St Paul's Epistle to the Romans (*c.* 405-6) gave fresh stimulus to discussions of destiny and free will that had been going on in Roman circles since the mid-390s and would shortly come to an issue in Augustine's clash with Pelagius.[15]

These and other literary works were carried out with the support of friends and patrons in Italy, notably in Rome and Aquileia, the two places where Rufinus chiefly resided in the years 397-408, before heading south in flight from Alaric's Goths.[16] Like Jerome, but with a less obvious regard for the processes of literary dissemination and publicity, he regularly gives the appearance of writing to commission or with a local readership in mind. Several of his minor translations, including Origen's homilies on Psalms 36-8 and the collection of moral maxims known as the *Sentences of Sextus,* are commended to women readers as instruction in Christian living. The 'moral' sense is likewise favoured in the threefold exposition of the **Benedictions of the Patriarchs,** written for Paulinus of Nola, as naturally it is too in the translations of Basil's monastic *Rule* (made for the monastery of Pinetum, near Rome) and the Evagrian *Sentences* for monks and virgins. If Jerome in his paraenetic writings at times displays an excessive flair for satire and pathos, the moralist Rufinus—like the dogmatist Rufinus of the **Commentary on the Apostles' Creed**—is invariably lucid, practical and compendious. Had they survived, his 'many' letters would doubtless have confirmed his proficiency as a teacher of ascetic piety.

The emphases and originality of Rufinus' activity as a purveyor of Greek cultural products to Latin Christian readers are well displayed in three narrative works, two of them histories. His translation of Eusebius' **Ecclesiastical History,** undertaken in 401 at the request of Bishop Chromatius of Aquileia as an antidote to the terror caused by the Gothic incursions into Italy, was the first significant addition to the Latin store of Christian historiography since Jerome's pioneering version of the *Chronicle* two decades earlier and would stand almost alone until joined by the *Tripartite History* compiled by Cassiodorus. Rufinus omits much of Eusebius' tenth book and compresses what remains of it into book 9; he also retouches the narrative in several places and adds two books of his own to bring the account down to the death of Theodosius the Great (395). His personal experience and concerns are reflected in the prominence given to events in Alexandria and to the trials and triumphs of Athanasius, whom he revered as confessor of the faith and successor of the martyrs.

Rufinus was as keen to associate the figure of the martyr with the office of Christian writer as Jerome had been, but is content as a rule to leave the association implicit. Stories of Antony and the desert monks in book 11 of the *Ecclesiastical History* provided a natural cue for the translation made soon afterwards of the *History of the Egyptian Monks,* a work which must have sharpened, where it did not cloy, the Western appetite for ascetic miracles whetted by Jerome's hagiography (already followed by Sulpicius Severus) and soon to be exploited to different effect by John Cassian, a fellow enthusiast with Rufinus for the Origenist monasticism of Evagrius of Pontus. As Latinized texts, both Rufinus' histories attest the desire to domesticate an ideal of dedicated, even heroic, Christian spirituality that he himself could claim to have seen realized in foreign lands. That the heroes of the histories were to be regarded as perfectly orthodox, even in cases where doubt was possible (e.g., the Egyptian monks expelled during the recent anti-Origenist purge), goes without saying. A similarly elevated and expansive view of orthodox Mediterranean Christianity commands the translation (c. 407) of the *(Pseudo-) Clementine Recognitions,* an elaborate disquisition on cosmology, theodicy and ethics, thinly disguised as sentimental romance. The preface speaks of the laborious transfer of 'goods from overseas', while the story of the future Pope Clement's journey to Caesarea in Palestine and his instruction there by St Peter would have offered at once a reassuring myth of Christian unity in doctrine and a satisfying analogue for the translator's own trade and travel beween Rome and the East.

Notes

1. *Ep.* 22.30 (addressed to the virgin Eustochium at Rome, *c.* 384). The scene is recounted as a vision experienced years earlier, at the outset of the writer's ascetic life.

2. *Ep.* 22.29 ('What has Horace to do with the Psalter, Virgil with the Gospels, Cicero with the Apostle?'), echoing Tertullian, *Praescr.* 7. Where Tertullian asks, 'What has *Athens* to do with Jerusalem?', his successor sets the Bible against three founders of the 'classical' Latin literature of Rome, itself a triumph of Roman Hellenism. As an exceptional Hellenist among westerners of his time, Jerome was conscious—more acutely than Ambrose, in advance of Rufinus—of the possibility of creating a 'classical' Christian literature in Latin by emulation of the Greeks.

3. H. Hagendahl, *Latin Fathers and the Classics: A Study on the Apologists, Jerome and Other Christian Writers,* 91ff.

4. *Ep.* 70 (to the Roman orator Magnus, *c.* 397), a model for many later such defences in the West. The use made by Jerome of the image of the cap-tive woman of Deut. 21:10-13 as a figure for Christian appropriation of pagan learning would become standard, alongside Augustine's preferred image of the spoils of the Egyptians. Both images already served this purpose for Origen.

5. Reinhart Herzog, *Die Bibelepik der lateinischen Spätantike. Formgeschichte einer erbaulichen Gattung,* Bd. 1, 167ff.

6. E.g., *Ep.* 53.8, 17 (the Psalmist as 'our Simonides, Pindar and Alcaeus, our Horace, Catullus and Serenus'); E. R. Curtius, *European Literature and the Latin Middle Ages* (Princeton: Princeton University Press, 1953), 447.

7. H. F. D. Sparkes, 'Jerome as biblical scholar', *Cambridge History of the Bible,* I, ed. P. R. Ackroyd and C. F. Evans (Cambridge: Cambridge University Press, 1970), 510-41.

8. Pierre Jay, *L'exégèse de saint Jérôme d'après son Commentaire sur Isaïe.*

9. *Commentarius in Epistula Pauli ad Galatos* 3, praef. (*PL* 26, 427D). For the formal requirements of Jerome's notion of 'commentary', see Yves-Marie Duval's introduction to the commentary on Jonah (SC 323, 1985).

10. Gennadius, *Vir. Ill.* 17.

11. *Apol. c. Hier.* 1.11.

12. This is the position set forth in the prefaces to the translations of Pamphilus' *Apology* and of *On First Principles,* and in a monograph *On the Adulteration of the Books of Origen* appended by Rufinus to the former work. Jerome's rationale for a selective approach to Origen's oeuvre is first outlined in his *Epp.* 61 and 84.

13. The same context can be assumed for Rufinus' version of the anti-heretical *Dialogue of Adamantius,* falsely ascribed by him to Origen. For particulars, see E. Clark, *The Origenist Controversy: the cultural construction of an early Christian debate,* 121ff. (Jerome) and 159ff. (Rufinus).

14. For the distinction, see the epilogue to his translation of Origen's commentary on Romans (CCSL 20, ed. Simonetti (1961), 276-7), an important statement of his principles and programme as a translator.

15. Further versions of Origen's commentaries on St Paul were projected but never made.

16. For a detailed chronology, see C. P. Hammond, 'The Last Ten Years of Rufinus' Life and the Date of His Move South from Aquileia', *JTS* n.s. 28 (1977), 372-429. Rufinus died in Sicily in 411.

Abbreviations of patristic and other texts

Apol. c. Hier. = Apologia contra Hieronymum

Ep(p). = Epistulae

HE = Historia Ecclesiastica

Vir. Ill. = De Viris Illustribus

Other Abbreviations

These abbreviations are used in the notes, and in the bibliographies, where publication details can be found.

CCSL: Corpus Christianorum. Series Latina

JTS: *Journal of Theological Studies*

PL: *Patrologia Latina*

VigChr: *Vigiliae Christianae*

Works Cited

No critical edition of Rufinus; critical edition of Jerome in CCSL (in progress).

J. Brochet, *Saint Jérome et ses ennemis: étude sur la querelle de Saint Jérome avec Rufin d'Aquilée et sur l'ensemble de son oeuvre polémique* (Paris: Fontemoing, 1906).

D. Brown, *Vir Trilinguis: a study in the biblical exegesis of Saint Jerome* (Kampen, The Netherlands: Kok Pharos, 1992).

E. Clark, *The Origenist Controversy: the cultural construction of an early Christian debate* (Princeton: Princeton University Press, 1992).

G. Fedalto, *Rufino di Concordia (345 c.-410/411): tra Oriente e Occidente* (Rome: Città Nuova, 1990).

Harald Hagendahl, *Latin Fathers and the Classics: A Study on the Apologists, Jerome and Other Christian Writers* (Göteborg: Almqvist & Wiksell, 1958).

C. P. Hammond Bammel, *Origeniana et Rufiniana* (Freiburg: Herder, 1996).

Pierre Jay, *L'exégèse de saint Jérôme d'après son Commentaire sur Isaïe* (Paris: Études Augustiniennes, 1985).

B. Jeanjean, *Saint Jérôme et l'hérésie* (Paris: Institut d'Études Augustiniennes, 1999).

J. N. D. Kelly, *Jerome. His Life, Writings and Controversies* (London: Duckworth, 1975).

P. Lardet, *L'Apologie de Jérôme contre Rufin: un commentaire*, Supp. *VigChr* 15 (Leiden: Brill, 1993).

F. X. Murray, *Rufinus of Aquileia (345-411): his life and works* (Washington, DC: Catholic University of America Press, 1945).

S. Rebenich, *Hieronymus und sein Kreis: prosopographische und sozialgeschichtliche Untersuchungen* (Stuttgart: Steiner, 1992).

Rufino di Concordia e il suo tempo, 2 vols (Udine: Arti grafiche friulane, 1987).

Storia ed esegesi in Rufino di Concordia (Udine: Arti grafiche friulane, 1992).

M. Wagner, *Rufinus, the Translator: a study of his theory and his practice as illustrated in his version of the Apologetica of St. Gregory Nazianzen* (Washington, DC: Catholic University of America Press, 1945).

Walter of Châtillon
c. 1135-c. 1202

(Also Gautier de Châtillon) French poet.

INTRODUCTION

A poet who flourished during Europe's cultural flowering in the twelfth century, Walter of Châtillon is best known for his epic poem in the classical style, the *Alexandreis* (1184), which relates the exploits of the Macedonian conqueror Alexander the Great. Comprising 5,464 hexameters in ten books, the poem is written in Latin and draws heavily from the *Historiae Alexandri Magni* by the Roman historian Quintus Curtius Rufus, with additional references to Christianity that made the poem more relevant to its medieval reading audience. In its time the *Alexandreis* was widely admired and was used as a schoolbook to teach Latin and history. Later falling into relative obscurity, it was not a subject of study again until the nineteenth century, when German and Italian scholars translated it.

BIOGRAPHICAL INFORMATION

Walter was most likely born at or near Lille, France, around the year 1135. Not much else about his early life is known with any certainty. He studied at Paris and Reims under Stephen of Beauvais, a canon of the northern French town of Beauvais and a strong presence in the court of Henry I of Champagne. After completing his studies, Walter became a teacher in Laon. He then worked as headmaster of a school in Châtillon, where he began writing poetry and with which he became most closely associated. But Walter found teaching an unrewarding and poorly paid profession, so he moved to Bologna, in what is now Italy, to study canon law. Afterward he secured the patronage of the Archbishop of Reims, Guillaume des Blanches Mains, whose influence was extensive. Guillaume's brother-in-law was King Louis VII, and his nephew was Philip Augustus, who would later rule France as Philip II. Walter's *Alexandreis* is dedicated to Guillaume. Scholars surmise that the dedication may have been an attempt to curry Guillaume's favor after one of Walter's satirical poems made reference to Guillaume's homosexuality. Walter's attempt to appease Guillaume appears to have been successful, as the latter made him a canon, probably at Amiens. Walter is believed to have died of the plague, leprosy, or self-flagellation in Amiens sometime around 1202.

MAJOR WORKS

During his lifetime Walter was known for his satirical poems, in which he criticized the often scurrilous behavior of the clergy. He published one known prose work, the *Tractatus contra Judaeos* (late twelfth century; *A Treatise against the Jews*), a refutation of Judaism written as a dialogue between Walter and Canon Baldwin of Valenciennes. Such written tracts favoring Christianity over Judaism—often virulently—were typical in Walter's time. He also is believed to have composed numerous hymns and poems describing the lives of the saints. These, however, are considered ephemera compared with his epic poem, the *Alexandreis*. Most likely composed at some point between 1171 and 1181 and published in 1184, the *Alexandreis* draws heavily from classical Latin texts, including those of Vergil, Ovid, Lucan, Juvenal, and Horace, at times repeating lines from those poets, but in Walter's own verse hexameter—not an unusual technique for writers in the Middle Ages, who valued received literary and historical knowledge over originality. Walter's stated purpose in writing the *Alexandreis* was to correct what he considered the great omission of classical literature: that no poet of that period had written an epic account of Alexander's exploits. But despite his debt to earlier material, Walter's version of Alexander's life is considered a work of great creativity and even curiosity for its inclusion of post-classical biblical themes, elements of New Testament Christianity, and anachronistic allusions to political and ecclesiastical events of Walter's France. Of particular importance is evidence of Walter's understanding of the major tenets of medieval Christianity, including the salvation of humanity by Christ's sacrifice, the nature of heaven and hell, and the duality of body and soul.

TEXTUAL HISTORY

There are more than two hundred extant manuscript copies of the *Alexandreis* in existence, making it one of the most-copied works of the twelfth century. Each has its own editorial commentaries and glosses explaining and interpreting the poem and demonstrating its widespread use as a textbook for Latin and vernacular grammar, as well as history and literature. As R. Telfryn Pritchard writes in the introduction to his seminal 1986 English translation of the poem, the *Alexandreis* is also notable for the number of early printed editions in existence—a 1480s edition by Guillaume Le Tailleur of Rouen, a 1513 edition printed by J. Adelphus of Strasbourg, a 1541 edition by Alexander Weissenborn of Ingolstadt, and a 1558 edition printed by Robert Granjon of Lyons—all of which testify to the work's ongoing influence for several centuries after Walter's death.

CRITICAL RECEPTION

The popularity of the *Alexandreis* during the late twelfth and thirteenth centuries is well documented. With the exception of Walter's contemporary Alain de Lille, who—unhappy with Walter's use of his text *De planctu naturae* (*On the Plaint of Nature*) in Book 10 of the *Alexandreis*—complained in his *Anticlaudianus* that Walter's muse was "slow and listless," Walter's work was widely hailed as a great poetic achievement in its time and it spawned numerous vernacular imitations across Europe. The work was even translated into Icelandic by Brand Jonsson around 1260 and into Czech around 1290-1300. At some point, however, after the beginning of the widespread use of the printing press after the mid-1400s, the *Alexandreis* fell out of favor in medieval literary and historical scholarship. Compared with such works as Guillaume de Lorris's later *Roman de la Rose* and Geoffrey Chaucer's fourteenth-century *Canterbury Tales*, Walter's *Alexandreis* has not, in general, been regarded by modern audiences as exemplary of medieval poetry. In Europe the work began to regain its reputation in the nineteenth century after it was translated into German and Italian. Marvin L. Colker published a new Latin edition of the work, *Galteri de castillione Alexandreis*, in 1978, sparking the interest of contemporary scholars. The *Alexandreis* is now considered one of the most important works of the twelfth-century French renaissance. According to translator David Townsend, "Readers today can still find in the poem, and often find easily and intuitively, an extraordinary subtlety, a keen intelligence, a beauty in turns lyrical and outlandish, and at times even an uncanny postmodernity. [The *Alexandreis*] rewards the reader as richly as do many of the better-known texts we think of as the heart of medieval European literature."

PRINCIPAL WORKS

"Propter Zion non tacebo" (poetry) c. 1170
Alexandreis (epic poem) 1184
Tractatus contra Judaeos (theology) late 12th century

Principal English Translations

The Alexandreid *of Walter of Châtillon: A Translation and Commentary* (translated by W. T. Jolly) 1968

The Alexandreis (translated by R. Telfryn Pritchard) 1986

The Alexandreis *of Walter of Châtillon, a Twelfth-Century Epic* (translated by David Townsend) 1996

CRITICISM

Laurence Eldredge (lecture date 1966)

SOURCE: Eldredge, Laurence. "Walter of Châtillon and the *Decretum* of Gratian: An Analysis of 'Propter Zion Non Tacebo.'" In *Studies in Medieval Culture, Vol. III*, edited by John R. Sommerfeldt, pp. 59-69. Kalamazoo, Mich.: Medieval Institute, Western Michigan University, 1970.

[*In the following essay, originally presented as a lecture in 1966, Eldredge discusses how Walter of Châtillon viewed twelfth-century developments in canon and theological law in his poem "Propter Zion non tacebo."*]

If there is any truth in William Blake's contention that poets are prophets, then Walter of Chatillon in the heaven reserved for poets must derive a measure of satisfaction from the prophecy in **"Propter Zion."** One can even go so far as to envision Walter, again in his heaven, deriving a certain delight from reading Charles Schulz's comic strip, *Peanuts*. Several autumns ago a *Peanuts* strip showed Linus writing a letter to the Great Pumpkin. "Dear Great Pumpkin," he wrote, "Now that Hallowe'en is coming again and you will rise out of the pumpkin patch to bring presents to all the good boys and girls, I want you to know that I have been a good boy all year and I hope you will bring me lots of presents." As he wrote, his skeptical sister Lucy stood by, interjecting such comments as "preposterous," "absurd," "ridiculous," and she followed him all the way to the mailbox, uttering similar imprecations. But after Linus had mailed his letter and walked away, Lucy called to him, "Did you tell him I've tried to be good too?"

A frivolous illustration perhaps, but not a trivial one. For the exchange of material rewards for good behavior seems so much a part of our culture that even a skeptic is hard put to maintain his skepticism. In fact it seems so much a part of our culture that one hardly pauses to question its origins, mutely assuming that such a *quid pro quo* in ethics has always been the case. But in fact it has not always been the case, as anyone knows who has seen a tragedy or considered the question of grace.

I think today we know that certain developments in canon law and theology in the Middle Ages had a deep and lasting effect on our moral thought, and what I should like to do here is not to present any startling new theory on the origins of this thinking, but only to describe how one sensitive and intelligent man regarded some of these developments while they were in their earliest stages. Walter of Chatillon, whose active life spanned the second half of the twelfth century, studied law at Bologna, that center of legal studies which gave birth to Gratian's *Concordia discordantium canonum* around 1140. Some thirty years later, during the pontificate of Alexander III, the first of a long line of popes to come from the ranks of canon lawyers, Walter wrote his major statement on canon law and theology, **"Propter Zion non tacebo."** It proved to be his most popular poem, both in medieval and modern anthologies, but its significance, its *sententia,* appears to have been elusive.

Editors of the two most scholarly modern editions of the poem, Karl Strecker, and Alfons Hilka and Otto Schumann,[1] approach the poem in a similar fashion, by providing detailed explanatory notes on each stanza. But neither set of editors has very much to offer on the problem of the sum of all the stanzas. Indeed, Strecker states the problem in reverse fashion when he claims that the general intent of the poem is clear enough, but the details are confusing. However, Strecker's notes indicate clearly that the details are not in themselves confusing; it is their relations to one another, their general intent, that eludes the editor.

But an editor's job is textual criticism, not contextual criticism, and my remarks are not intended to slight the monumental work of three superb scholars. They are, however, intended to refocus attention away from editorial concerns and onto concerns of structure. How is the poem put together and what *sententia* emerges from it? However, I should be less than candid if I did not acknowledge my large debt to the careful work of Strecker and Hilka-Schumann. Indeed, much of what I have to say depends heavily on their annotations, and anyone who is at all familiar with medieval Latin satire will easily note how much of Walter's poem falls into the convenient category of "standard satirical topos." But I hope, nevertheless, that I can make a case for Walter's infusing new meaning into these topoi by treating them in a manner not altogether typical of his contemporaries. One may note the analogous case of Renaissance sonnets, where we know in advance that the poet will complain of his lady's cruelty, but we read on to see how his skill with form and rhetoric can charge his commonplace theme with new meaning.

And now to **"Propter Zion."** The poem is made up, I believe, of two large parts, stanzas 1 through 8 and stanzas 9 through 30. Stanzas 1 through 8, written in the style of the Old Testament prophets, comprise a prophetic criticism of Rome, and the remainder of the poem is an exegesis of this pseudo-prophecy. In the first eight stanzas Walter writes with the authority of one who bears the sacred mission of the prophets, to speak God's message. In the last twenty-two stanzas the style changes markedly and the poet assumes the intellectual authority of the exegetical scholar.

The first eight stanzas are then of paramount importance for the poem. They are comparable to the Biblical text on which the scholar works, and thus assume a semi-sacred character in relation to the second part of the poem. Since their interpretation occupies the greater part of the work, their imagery and metaphor dominate the whole. Therefore, let us begin as the exegete would begin, with a literal understanding of the text.

For an educated man of the twelfth century, like Walter, Rome was the center of two worlds. Twelfth-century interest in the classics inevitably drew attention to pagan Rome, and the city had, of course, long been the center of the Christian world. Walter saw this duality in Rome, and for him, as for many others, it was not a mutually exclusive division into pagan and Christian. The imagery of these opening stanzas reflects an idea of Rome as one city with two kinds of greatness. The Bible provides the tone, some of the rhetoric, and the attitude of moral condemnation, but the central image is drawn from classical sources. Thus Rome is judged by the two standards intrinsic to it, classical and Christian.

Walter wastes no effort in getting things under way. The first two lines of the poem embody the dual imagery, and the first stanza establishes not only the theme but also the poet's prophetic authority:

> Propter Sion non tacebo,
> set ruinas Rome flebo,
> quousque iustitia
> rursus nobis oriatur
> et ut lampas accendatur
> iustus in ecclesia.

(St. 1)

The opening line is quoted directly from Isaiah 62:1, where the prophet expresses a desire for the new Jerusalem, traditionally associated with Christianity and by implication with Rome.[2] Rome, as the center of Christianity, is the new Jerusalem, the fulfillment of Isaiah's prophecy. However, in its turn the fulfillment of the prophecy has become the basis of a new prophecy. The quotation from Isaiah also helps to establish the poet's prophetic authority—perhaps that of Isaiah himself—and of setting in motion the Biblical machinery of the poem. The second line, with its allusion to the ruins of Rome, sets in motion the classical imagery.

Walter continues to echo Isaiah in the remainder of the stanza, and his additions to the Biblical text provide the shade of meaning that reorients the passage to the Christian church in another historical period. Isaiah does not, of course, mention "ecclesia" (line 6), and the adverb "rursus" (line 4) is also the poet's addition. This adverb, which connects with the idea of the "new Rome" implied in the first line, suggests that the "new Rome" has existed in the past and will exist again, but the suggestion is not merely the cry of decline, standard among satirists. Walter nowhere recommends a return to the simple organizational principles of the early church, and an explanation more consistent with his moral concern and his vision of possibility might be that the spirit of the early church should inform the "new Rome." Precisely what sort of spirit the poet had in mind should become clear as we move on.

In the second stanza Walter continues to echo phrases from the prophets, both Isaiah and Jeremiah, with emphasis on the former:

> Sedet vilis et in luto
> princeps, facta sub tributo;
> quod solebam dicere,
> Roman esse derelictam
> desolatam et afflictam,
> expertus sum opere.

(St. 2)

The notion of a thing's being low, worthless, and filthy is found in both Isaiah and Jeremiah (Is. 3:26, 47:1; Jerem. 2:36. Also Sap. 15:10), and the "princeps" (here to be taken as an adjective) brought under tribute is from the Lamentations of Jeremiah (Thren. 1:1). Of the adjectives applied to Rome, "derelictam" and "desolatam" are found in Isaiah 62, once again accompanied by an exegetical tradition that applies them to the church.[3] These allusions strengthen the impression of prophetic writing, but the most important parts of the stanza are lines 3 and 6 where Walter interjects two comments in the first person. Both of these imply earlier writing and experience, and the most obvious interpretation of them, and the one followed by the editors, is that they refer to Walter's earlier work, especially since the polished skill of the poem presupposes previous attempts. But Ovidian asides in such a context are grossly out of place. I would suggest that a better understanding is achieved if one sees that Walter is again speaking as a prophet. Not only does such an interpretation acknowledge Walter's ability as a skilled poet, but it also suggests the dimensions of this prophetic fragment. What we are led to see is that the fragment should be understood as just that, a fragment, standing in a synecdochic relation with a larger body of prophecy. It is as if Walter were establishing for himself a position as the continuer of the Old Testament prophetic tradi-

tion, with all the experience and authority of an Isaiah or Jeremiah incorporated into the fragmentary prophecy of these first eight stanzas.

Stanzas 3 through 8, which complete the prophecy, do not depend upon Biblical allusion for their efficacy. What is at work is a combination of the impetus of prophetic authority from the first two stanzas and a prophetic use of the rhetorical device of *repetitio*. Throughout these six stanzas Walter uses the word "ibi" eight times at the beginning of lines.[4] Sometimes two lines together begin with "ibi," and sometimes the word occurs without being repeated immediately. But the cumulative effect of this echo is unmistakably reminiscent of Isaiah, Jeremiah, and Ezechiel.[5] The imagery of these stanzas is, however, predominantly classical. Rome is called the "caput mundi" (Lucan 2, 136, and 655) and is compared to the Strait of Messina, the traditional location of Scylla and Charybdis. Instead of their usual capacity for ships, however, these two figures are eager for gold, an eagerness reinforced by a reference to Crassus. Then the poet adds the Syrtes and Sirens to the strait as images of shipwreck; these are characterized as having some exterior human qualities but interior demonic ones. With stanza 6 there is an abrupt shift in imagery. Here the poet introduces an unidentified Franco as an equivalent of just such a strait. This Franco has all the characteristics of the Strait of Messina: he is voracious, he neither spares nor pities anyone, he attracts others to him, and, finally, he is in love with money.

As prophecy, these eight stanzas represent a careful poetic imitation of the Old Testament. As is the case with many prophecies, there is here no pretense to historical completeness nor chronological accuracy. It would also appear that, like many Old Testament prophets (Dan. 8:27, 12:8; Zach. 6 *passim*. Also Augustine, *De civ. Dei*, 7, 32.), Walter does not wholly understand his own prophecy, or at least he tries to give that impression; for example, in stanza 4, 6, the pirates are said to be cardinals, but this is not in complete accord with the exegetical section. Most important of all is the anagogical view that the lack of historical perspective implies. This is a vision, however ironical, and it is seen from a mythopoeic point of view. The type and the anti-type exist simultaneously in Scylla, Charybdis, the Syrtes, and the Sirens, although the exegetical section is necessary to prove it.

From an iconographical point of view, Walter has chosen his imagery carefully and apparently with an eye to traditional typology. The sea, or any water, is traditionally a type of baptism, which itself signifies a rebirth into a new life. This may be understood as an analogue to the ironic vision of a new Rome no better than the old, but on a deeper level it demands serious consideration as an expression of hope for genuine rebirth of the church into new vigor. It is important here to recall that the only trip through the Strait of Messina recorded in the Bible is that of Paul on his last voyage. It was this voyage that brought Paul to Rome, an event of some significance for the early history of the church, and perhaps Walter implies that a similar great event is in store for the twelfth-century church. Moreover, the sea imagery sets the scene for a ship, which Walter introduces in the nineteenth stanza. The ship has traditionally been symbolic of the church, a symbolism that has been preserved in some of the terms of church architecture.

Thematically, the first eight stanzas center on the sin of *avaritia,* one of Walter's favorite themes. Walter sees *avaritia* as the basis of the ruin of Rome and, by implication, as a more serious sin than *superbia.* Such an attitude toward the relative gravity of sin may be seen as no more than a reflection of medieval values, but I think we may also note that a more carefully planned theme is here introduced. The rise of trade in the previous century had given money, a kind of immaterial wealth, a new value and a basis of power that had formerly been the exclusive value of land. Just as the landholding nobility had become more and more dependent on the wealth of the merchant-banking class, so too the church had to adjust its economic procedures and policies in order to finance its activities. It devised and adopted methods of obtaining funds that might well have seemed avaricious to many observers. Walter gives no indication in his poem that he understood the social and economic basis for the increase in *avaritia,*[6] but he recognizes the fact and, more important, he recognizes some of its implications.

In turning now to the second section of the poem, the gloss, we need first to note that it too divides into two principal sections. The first section, stanzas 9 through 19, are an allegorical interpretation of the prophecy, and the second section, stanzas 20 through 29, are an anagogical view of the whole. The last stanza is a tongue-in-cheek ending in which the poet claims to be putting a guard on his mouth so that he too will not be shipwrecked in the strait. This stanza is not to be taken seriously, because actually the poem says everything that is necessary.

Generally, the allegorical section, stanzas 9 through 19, concentrates on the image of the Strait of Messina. The fact that no reference is made to the first two stanzas of the poem confirms the interpretation, made earlier, that those stanzas serve mainly to establish the theme and confer prophetic authority on the poet. Two stanzas each are given to Scylla and Charybdis, while Syrtes and the Sirens are considered together and are treated in two stanzas, 13 and 18. Stanzas 14 through 17, which

quote the flatteries of a typical cardinal, are, I believe, an interpretation of the unknown Franco of stanzas 6 through 8 of the prophecy. Stanza 19 provides a kind of peroration to the allegorical section.

In the ninth stanza Walter concentrates not on Scylla but on the dogs that grew out of her. These dogs are the lawyers, the enemies of truth, whose falsehoods are compared to the dogs' barking. A general impression of the barking is given in stanza 10, where Walter takes up the lawyers themselves:

> Iste probat se legistam,
> ille vero decretistam
> inducens Gelasium;
> ad probandum questionem
> hic intendit actionem
> regundorum finium.
>
> (St. 10)

The first three lines suggest the presumption of both civil and canon lawyer. The verb "probare," used reflexively, implies that no one asked them to do this, but they, like Gelasius, who named himself pope on the grounds that every call to Rome was valid, insinuate themselves into the Roman curia. The last three lines, rich with legal phrases, illustrate the kind of noise the barking lawyers engage in: instead of applying themselves to the solution of the problem at hand, they expend energy in determining which tribunal is competent in a particular case.

From the point of view of imagery, the introduction of lawyers at this point is appropriate, since they are connected with Charybdis, the gold swallower. Walter seems to suggest here that the relation between lawyers and avarice is not accidental, and in the next stanza he confirms this view. Here he takes up the figure of Charybdis, that is, the chancellery, whose activities are scornfully summed up in the verb "debachatur."

> Nunc rem sermo prosequatur:
> hic Caribdis debachatur,
> id est chancellaria;
> ibi nemo gratus gratis
> neque datur absque datis
> Gratiani gratia.
>
> (St. 11)

There is some deft, though commonplace, punning on *gratus-gratis-gratia,* but the reference to Gratian adds a level of penetrating observation to the standard pun. If grace is thought of as Gratian's grace, then it has moved from the area of theology into the province of law. This translation means that grace, of whatever sort, is no longer a matter of God's mercy freely given, but rather of man's paying for it. Here Walter claims that money is the unit of exchange, but the important point to note,

I think, is the idea that an actual exchange of grace for something else takes place. And we may also note that the traditional hallmark of canon law, and of its direct forebear Roman civil law, is the formalizing of exchange into contract. This characteristic of canon law is so well known today as to appear almost a cliché. But it is startling, I think, to see how firmly, and how soon after Gratian, Walter grasped the theological implications of legal contract. What the poet suggests is that, through Gratian's influence, grace has become a commodity, subject, like any other commodity, to a contractual arrangement between two parties. Walter sees the church transformed, as it were, from Christ's vicar to Christ's huckster, through the influence of canon law. The road from here to the late medieval morality play *Everyman* is clearly marked: man and God are signatories to a mutually binding contract, and when man can show evidence of having fulfilled his obligations, God must then fulfill his and grant the ultimate grace of salvation.

Clearly, then, the papal chancellery, with the justification of the curial lawyers, has transformed the Christ-given power of the keys into an economic enterprise, the sale of grace. Little wonder, then, that in stanza 12 these dispensers of grace are said to value lead, from which they make the seal of their authority, more highly than gold and silver. Walter describes an imaginary figure, "equitatis fantasia," sitting on the leaden seal, and calls upon Zachariah as a witness:

> equitatis fantasia
> sedet teste Zacharia
> super bullam plumbeam.

> (St. 12, 3-6)

These three lines have caused editors considerable difficulty, and I refer you to the notes to Hilka-Schumann's edition of the *Carmina Burana* (*II, Kommentar,* #41, p. 74) for substantiation of the interpretation that the "equitatis fantasia" here means a "duplex iniquitas," a double injustice. I take this double injustice to be the activities of the lawyers and chancellors just described. But Hilka-Schumann run into difficulty in explaining why this figure should sit "super" the lead seal. Since Zachariah described a figure in a bottle stoppered with lead, they believe that Walter's figure would make better sense if it were somehow placed under the lead seal. But I think Walter is suggesting here that the genie has escaped from its bottle and that the situation Zachariah described has been reversed. In other words, a double force of injustice has been let loose by lawyers and chancellors.

The opening line of stanza 13 asks, "Qui sunt Sirtes vel Sirenes?" The remainder of the stanza goes on to add further qualifiers, and the question itself, as Strecker

notes, is not answered directly until the first line of stanza 18, "Cardinales, ut predixi." The question and its answer form a frame around a discussion, apparently of a typical cardinal.

The cardinals are charged, like the lawyers and chancellors, with avarice, but it is their suaveness and flattery that receive the most attention. Their speech is characterized as "blando," but they feign gentleness only to get the better advantage of the purse. Stanzas 14 through 16 are a skillful example of *sermocinatio,* the flattering speech, presumably addressed to a suitor at the papal curia, of a typical cardinal. The opening remark of this speech, "Frare, ben je te cognosco," is partly in French, and the word "Francia" occurs in the last line of the stanza. Surely the verbal echoes here are intended to recall the Franco of the pseudo-scriptural passage. When the poet introduces Franco in stanza 6, he cautions, "quod ne credas frivolum,'" and the passage in stanzas 14 through 16 is, it seems to me, an interpretation of stanzas 6 through 8. Just as the prophetic passage establishes the greed, but only infers the duplicity, of Syrtes and the Sirens, so the Franco passage reveals the avarice of a typical cardinal but needs this interpretive *sermocinatio* to show the fraud.

Stanza 17 continues against the cardinals in the same vein. Notice that the rape of the purse threatened metaphorically in stanza 13 is accomplished at the end of this stanza. Stanza 18, however, is the climax of the allegorical interpretation and combines the two themes emphasized up to this point, avarice and law.

> Cardinales, ut predixi,
> novo iure crucifixi
> vendunt patrimonium;
> Petrus foris, intus Nero,
> intus lupi, foris vero
> sicut agni ovium.

> (St. 18)

The cardinals' avarice is not merely incidental: it has become a new law by which they sell the forgiveness of Christ. As the chancellery had brought grace into the province of law, so here we find that the cardinals have moved the forgiveness of Christ from the area of theology to that of economics by using that new law. The cardinals are also identified with the false prophets of Matthew 7:15. They seem to be like Peter, like the lamb among the sheep, but inwardly they are Nero and wolves, the legendary harbingers of doomsday.

Stanza 19 is both a summary of the allegorical section and a transition to the following section. In summary, the stanza points out that the officials who have been described are in charge of the church and of the spiritual welfare of the people. By way of transition, the stanza does two things. First, it introduces the ship image, "Petri navem," that dominates the remainder of the poem; and second, it begins the shift in point of view from allegory to what I have called anagogy. Where the allegorical section concerned itself with the operations of those within the church, this section examines the church from a greater distance. No longer do we see the specific affairs of Scylla, Charybdis, Syrtes, and the Sirens; instead we see the course of the ship of the church through the world. A certain inconsistency of image can be observed as we move from one vantage point to another. For example, the cardinals, we have just been told, are Syrtes and the Sirens, but as we move on we find that the cardinals become pirates. This shift should not cause difficulty. Anagogy, as I shall use the term here, means a view of the whole and implies a view from a distance. From a close vantage-point, church officials appear to prey upon passing ships, but from further away Walter notes that these same officials threaten the safety of their own ship too.

Stanza 20 presents a rather obsure image, but clearly an image of an ecclesiastic:

> In galea sedet una
> mundi lues inportuna,
> camelos deglutiens;
> involuta canopeo
> cuncta vorat sicut leo
> rapiens et rugiens.

(St. 20)

The key phrase here, it seems to me, is "in galea." If this is taken to mean "at the helm," as Strecker suggests, then it can only refer to Pope Alexander III, whom Walter later praises. A reading that makes better sense is "on the boat," as Hilka-Schumann interpret; not only does this interpretation avoid the difficulty over Alexander, but also, taken in context, it forms a consistent part of an image of "clergy." The figure on the ship, a plague that afflicts the world, is devouring camels, a reference to Matthew 23:24, where the scribes and pharisees are so described. Scribes and pharisees are traditionally associated with hypocrisy, in the modern sense of the term, their interest lying as it does in lip-service rather than belief. The descriptive phrase, "involuta canopeo," is best understood, I think, as a general description of clerical garb, an interpretation that is in accord with the reference which follows to the roaring and rapacious lion. There are three Biblical sources for this latter reference (Ps. 21:14, Ezech. 22:24, I Peter 5:8), all of which use the comparison to emphasize the nature of an enemy.

In the pun of the following stanza, the identification of the figure as a cleric is made more definite. This stanza opens, "Hic piratus principatur / et Pilatus[8] appellatur,"

and surely the "piratus-Pilatus" pun functions as an echo of "prelatus." The remainder of stanza 21 adds further description to sharpen, but not to alter, the picture. This description is drawn primarily from Juvenal and calls to mind once again the second of the two standards, Christian and classical, by which Rome is to be judged.

With stanzas 22 and 23, the poet further broadens the scope of the vision to include the goddess of the sea on which the ship of the church sails:

> Maris huius non est dea
> Thetis, mater Achillea,
> de qua sepe legimus,
> immo mater sterlingorum,
> sancta soror loculorum,
> quam nos bursam dicimus.
>
> Hec dum pregnat, ductor ratis
> epulatur cum piratis
> et amicos reperit;
> set si bursa detumescit,
> surgunt venti, mare crescit
> et carina deperit.

(St. 22-23)

This goddess, who is introduced with a series of descriptive epithets, clearly represents *avaritia*. The elliptical structure of stanza 23 has prompted Hilka-Schumann to offer two interpretations,[9] but actually neither is in strict accord with the point Walter is making. In this anagogic view the ship is the church, and the sea, on this level of meaning, can only be the environment surrounding the church, that is, the world. The goddess Bursa is pregnant with money. As long as this condition prevails, the ship is buoyed up and the going is smooth; pope (ductor ratis) and prelates (piratis) dine together as friends. But if the purse becomes flat, as it must since birth naturally follows pregnancy, then serious economic trouble ensues and the ship is wrecked. It is here, I believe, that the climax of the poem lies. Walter has already noted that the intrusion of legal formulas has transformed the church into an economic enterprise. Here he makes clear the secular nature of church economics: the church is no longer the type of Noah's ark, a bulwark against a threatening environment; it has now become part of the secular world, and, as such, dependent upon secular economics for its continued existence. The implications of Walter's charge against the church are now clear: the internal confusion and corruption caused by the intrusion of law into theology has weakened the church as an institution, so that its very survival depends upon those forces against which it was formerly poised.

Now the effect of the earlier imagery can be more fully understood. The apparent confusion over whether the cardinals were to be pirates or Syrtes and the Sirens is a device necessary for Walter to show the ironic reversal of roles. From a close vantage point, the curia seems to be hurting others, but within a larger perspective, the damage is actually seen to be to the church itself. Moreover, I think we are also in a position to see some hint of what Walter's vision of the "new Rome" may entail. A detailed picture would of course be impossible on so little evidence, but at least we can say that the new Rome would not be characterized by the confusion of law and theology Walter notes as a basis for ruin of the present Rome.

The climax of the poem is now over, and with stanza 24 the critical analysis begins to fall back into the commonplace. There is also a partial shift in point of view. Walter continues with his holistic approach to the church, and he continues in anagogic fashion to expand the limits of his vision. But the identification of types no longer depends upon complex and consistent metaphor; instead, we find a one-for-one correspondence of type and antitype, the same sort of device that was used in the earlier allegorical section. It would seem to me that the poem has been carefully built to embody, and at the same time to disguise, a serious criticism of the church. This is not the standard anticlerical criticism, which blames clerics for their faults but rarely questions the clerical institution. Walter has, in fact, been daring enough to find fault with the church itself, and perhaps he felt that such a criticism should be disguised and placed in a context, if the poet is both to make the charge successfully and to avoid difficulties for himself. Hence, the slackening of the attack is part of the plan to embed serious theological criticism in clever commonplaces, so that not every casual reader will understand.

Stanzas 24 and 25 deal with the rocks, that is, the gate-keepers of the papal curia. They are the ones who deprive all of both money and clothing, and only the traveler with empty pockets, as Juvenal says (10, 22), and naked too, adds Walter, can sing among thieves. They are compared to beasts in their savagery; and only the rich man can get past them into the curia. The poet does not criticize the gate-keepers *per se*, however. The point is that curial avarice has spread to those who serve the curia, and the servants can cause as much havoc through their avarice as the clergy themselves.

Stanzas 26 through 29 are a further softening of the attack; in fact they actually contribute a note of hope to all that has preceded. They describe the two harbors, the two refuges, for those little ships (presumably individual churches or perhaps clerics) that have been wrecked in the sea. The first is Peter of Pavia and the second Pope Alexander III. Only two things need to be noted in these stanzas, since they are quite straightforward and need little explication. First, Peter of Pavia

was elected bishop of Meaux in 1171 but never took the position and was commanded by Alexander III to give up his claims to the bishopric in 1175. Since Walter refers to Peter as "electus . . . Meldensis," we can conclude that **"Propter Zion"** was written between 1171 and 1175. Second, although Walter praises Alexander III as an excellent man who encourages scholars, he does not shrink from criticizing him for allowing an economic standard to usurp the theological basis of the church. Hilka-Schumann[10] praise Walter for his courage in this criticism of the pope, but actually the poet has shifted the blame for the greater evil from the pope's shoulders and accused him only of having reprehensible counselors around him.

The last stanza of the poem is a tongue-in-cheek refusal to continue. But the point has already been made and it is unnecessary to go on. The stanza, then, is once again a device for concealing criticism in commonplaces. Here the poet tries to make the reader believe that he has not yet said what he had intended to say, but the poem is complete as it stands.

Notes

1. Karl Strecker, *Moralisch-satirische Gedichte Walters von Chatillon* (Heidelberg, 1929). "Propter Zion" is number 2 in this collection [Sommerfeldt, John R. *Studies in Medieval Culture,* Vol. III. Medieval Institute, Western Michigan University, 1970]. Alfons Hilka and Otto Schumann, *Carmina Burana,* I, 1, *Die moralisch-satirischen Dichtungen* (Heidelberg, 1930); I, 2, *Die Liebeslieder* (Heidelberg, 1941); II, 1, *Kommentar* (second edition; Heidelberg, 1961). "Propter Zion" is number 41 (I, 1, pp. 65-76) of this collection.

2. Isaiah 62:2 goes on to say: ". . . Et vocabitur [Sion] tibi nomen novum, quod os Domini nominabit," which Jerome glosses as follows: "Denique nequaquam vocabitur Jerusalem et Sion, sed nomen novum accipiet, quod ei Dominus imposuerit, dicens ad apostolem Petrum: 'Tu es Petrus et super hanc petram aedificabo ecclesiam meam, et portae inferi non praevalebunt adversus eam.' (Matt. 16:18). Quod vocabulum a nomine Domini derivavit, ut dicatur Dominicum. Et populus illius nequaquam veteri nomine appelatur Israel, sed novo, id est Christianus." J. P. Migne (ed.), *Patrologia Latina,* 24, col. 628B. ". . . Pro Sion et Jerusalem vocaberis Ecclesia, et Dominicum: pro Judaeis appellabuntur Christiani." (*Ibid.,* col. 628C). This collection will hereafter be referred to as P.L.

3. Isaiah, 62:4. Jerome comments: "Sive hoc ipsum [the entire verse] referamus ad Ecclesiam, quae possessa primus ab idolis, deserta fuerat a Deo." P.L. 24, col. 629B.

4. This count accepts Hilka-Schumann's reading of 4, 4. Strecker prints: "fit concursus galearum," Hilka-Schumann: "ibi cursus galearum." In addition to the improved rhetoric, Hilka-Schumann's "cursus" seems more applicable to a strait.

5. See, for example, Isaiah 13:20-22, 22:18, 27:10, 28:10, 34:12-15. Jeremiah 42:14-17. Ezech. 32:22-30.

6. Several scholars have noted that emphasis on *avaritia* increases in the late Middle Ages. See, for example, J. Huizinga, *The Waning of the Middle Ages* (New York, 1954), p. 27 ff. See also M. W. Bloomfield, *The Seven Deadly Sins* (Lansing, Mich., 1952), chapter iii *passim* and pp. xiv, 74-75, 90, 95-96. See also Rudolph Sohm, *Das altkatholische Kirchenrecht und das Dekret Gratians* (Leipzig, 1918), whose thesis on the transformation of the church from a sacrament to a corporation need not be accepted in order to appreciate the carefully documented analysis of the role of canon law in church history.

7. Strecker interprets: "Don't make any unjustified comparison." Hilka-Schumann translate: "Don't take this as a joke," which seems to me the better interpretation.

8. Strecker gives several MS variants for this name, one of which, "Spurius," is adopted by Hilka-Schumann. "Pilatus" is the reading most often found and best suited, I think, to the context.

9. See *Carmina Burana,* II, 1, p. 77.

10. See *Carmina Burana,* II, 1, p. 79.

R. Telfryn Pritchard (essay date 1986)

SOURCE: Pritchard, R. Telfryn. Introduction to *Walter of Châtillon: The Alexandreis,* translated by R. Telfryn Pritchard, pp. 1-30. Toronto: Pontifical Institute of Mediaeval Studies, 1986.

[*In the following introduction to his translation of the* Alexandreis, *Pritchard provides an overview of Walter's life, a historical overview of the text, and a synopsis of the poem.*]

WALTER OF CHÂTILLON

The twelfth century witnessed an astonishing renewal of interest in the Latin classics, both prose and verse.[1] A more orderly form of government, secularization of learning, closer relations between East and West, economic expansion and the growth of towns all combined in various degrees to produce an age of wealth, taste and refinement. No longer satisfied with works destined for the cloister, the educated were now driven by the classical spirit of the Renaissance to emulate the poetic techniques of the ancients themselves. With other literary genres epic, too, experienced a revival as Joseph of Exeter took up once again the theme of the Trojan War or Hugh of Orleans that of the return of Ulysses. This revival of interest in the classics during the twelfth century is represented by a number of distinguished poets and scholars, among whom the North French cleric Walter of Châtillon is a major figure.

Our information about his life, however, is somewhat nebulous, being gleaned for the most part from the biographical notes that accompany the numerous manuscripts of the **Alexandreis.** These tell us that he was born at Lille, probably in the second quarter of the century, and that he studied at Paris and Reims under the popular teacher Stephen of Beauvais, before becoming a teacher himself at Laon and Châtillon.[2] However, he found teaching to be 'a matter of much toil and little profit' and gave it up to study canon law at Bologna instead. He was fortunate enough to secure the patronage of William of the White Hands, archbishop of Reims (1176-1202), who invited him back to Reims as a kind of notary and public orator. It was with William's encouragement that the **Alexandreis** was written,[3] and the poet expresses his gratitude to his patron in fulsome terms in the poem, each book beginning with a letter of the Latinized form of William's name Guillermus. For his pains, Walter was rewarded with a canonry, but the location of that canonry is uncertain, for Reims, Amiens, Tournai and Beauvais have all been suggested.[4]

The biographical notes also maintain that he died either of leprosy or as a result of the continual scourgings which he inflicted upon himself.[5] But it may well be that the wording 'by the scourge of leprosy' in an early gloss such as that found in Laon Bibl.mun.401 was later misconstrued, thereby giving rise to a separate tradition about his death. Veiled or specific references, however, to a serious illness curtailing the poet's work are to be found both in the **Alexandreis** (10.442 ff.) and in Walter's rhythmical poetry, e.g. **"When Walter Was Ill . . ."** (**"Dum Gualtherus egrotaret"**) or **"Walter's Lyre Has Turned to Grief"** (**"Versa est in luctum / Cythara Waltheri"**).[6] The discovery of 116 lines of a poem entitled *"The Georgica of Walter of Châtillon"* in Paris Bibliothèque Nationale 15155 led some scholars to believe that, towards the end of his life, Walter began another epic, and that it was this poetic activity that was suddenly cut short by illness and death. But the *Georgica* in question has been shown to be the *Georgica spiritualia* of John of Garland.[7]

There is yet another mystery if one considers Walter's links with the English court. Despite the general silence of the biographical notes in the manuscripts, it is often asserted that Walter spent some time in the Chancery of Henry II, thereby gaining access to the brilliant circle of scholars gathered round Theobald, archbishop of Canterbury (1139-1162). The evidence depends mainly on certain references in John of Salisbury's correspondence to a Walter of Lille and to a Walter who is clerk to the lord of Reims.[8] This Walter is clearly a trusted servant of the king having been sent by him to England with important documents from the Chinon conference in the spring of 1166. It has been generally accepted, too, that the poet renounced his court position following Becket's murder in 1170, in view of his sympathy with the archbishop's case and his friendship with John of Salisbury. Presumably, it would be around this time that he studied canon law in Bologna and visited the Roman Curia, before returning to his literary pursuits in France. Walter is certainly interested in England, and in his rhythmical poetry he disapproves of the tyranny of Henry II.[9] But the name Walter is so common at this time in documents that confusion is always possible, and a number of scholars have challenged the widely held assumption.[10]

As a writer, Walter was in many ways a child of his age. His interest in religion inspired him to compose both theological tracts in prose, especially the **Tract against the Jews (Tractatus contra Iudaeos)**, and many outspoken poems criticizing the Church of his day in verse.[11] He could compose with relish a masterly satire, lyric or *pastourelle* in the new metres, but, above all, he reflected a conscious effort to imitate the great Latin poets of antiquity. He was deeply versed in Latin literature, and his manner and method were to influence a large number of other contemporary Latin writers, so much so that Strecker propounded the existence of a 'school' of Walter of Châtillon. Clearly, his authority was based on first hand acquaintance with the classical authors themselves and not on florilegia.

The lyric poems have already attracted fair attention during the course of this century. Karl Strecker published valuable editions, first of the St. Omer poems in 1925 and then of Walter's moral and satirical poems in 1929, and his pioneering work in this field has been maintained in subsequent years by H. Spanke, Dom A. Wilmart, F. J. Worstbrock and, more recently, P. G. Walsh.

Walter's major work, however, and the one that he himself wished to be remembered by in his self-composed epitaph, was undoubtedly the **Alexandreis.**

The epic comprises ten books of over five thousand hexameter lines, each book being preceded by a metrical summary, usually of ten lines and acting as a kind of index in accordance with the author's stated intention in his prose prologue. The theme was an old one. Caesar, Caligula, Trajan had all admired Alexander. But for all the admiration of the Romans, no Roman poet had attempted a full-scale epic on Alexander's exploits. In Walter's own opinion, the theme was considered too demanding. It was therefore left to a twelfth-century poet to repair the deficiency, and in the opinion of most scholars, Walter of Châtillon's **Alexandreis** is a highly creditable attempt to do justice in verse to Alexander's great achievements.

THE DATE OF THE *ALEXANDREIS*

The date of the poem is subject to a controversy that is evident as early as the thirteenth century. From the poet's preface, clearly authentic, we learn that he spent five years on the poem and that he hesitated a long time before publishing it. Aware, no doubt, that Vergil had spent eleven years on his unrevised epic, he requests the more fastidious of his readers to regard as extenuating circumstances both the brief period of composition and the loftiness of a theme unattempted by the ancients. We do not know whether the five year period would include the necessary prior research as well as the actual writing. But the **Alexandreis** is an impressive work of erudition, and sifting through the sources, selecting and arranging appropriate episodes for inclusion, would no doubt be time-consuming.

Several manuscript glosses maintain that Walter began the work in the very year that Thomas Becket was murdered, i.e. 1170. If this were true, the poem occupied the poet during the years 1170-1175. Unfortunately, such a dating does not accord with the known details of the career of Walter's patron William of the White Hands, who was bishop of Chartres 1167-1169, archbishop of Sens 1169-1176, and finally archbishop of Reims 1176-1202. Unless we assume that passages such as 1.12-26, 5.520 and 10.461-469 belong to the period of final revision before publication, and are thus later insertions, the **Alexandreis** must be dated post 1176 and pre 1202.

The references to contemporary historical events in the poem do not help us very much. Often quoted are the three lines in Book 7 (7.328 ff.) which deplored the fact that two archbishops had 'recently' been murdered, Becket in 1170 and Robert of Cambrai near Valenciennes in 1174. Despite its vagueness, the passage is clearly post 1174 and, unless it, too, was a later insertion, again suggests a later quinquennium than 1170-1175. In the absence of clearer evidence, Christensen's quinquennium 1178-1182 for the poem's composition, with publication a few years later, seems as good as any. What is fairly certain is that the **Alexandreis** was well enough known by 1189 for Henry II's epitaph to bear a striking resemblance to Book 10.448 ff. with the inclusion of the same reference to the grave sufficing "for the man who had previously found the whole world insufficient."[12]

THE POPULARITY OF THE *ALEXANDREIS*

Few epic poems of the Latin Middle Ages can have been so extensively copied and so enthusiastically studied and annotated as the **Alexandreis.** The remarkable number of over two hundred extant manuscripts listed in Colker's edition is in itself convincing proof of its popularity.

The literature of the late twelfth and thirteenth centuries soon attests this popularity, most writers being fulsome in their praise. Alan of Lille, however, is a noteworthy exception. Alan, it seems, was aware that Walter had made use of his *On the Plaint of Nature* (*De planctu naturae*) for **Alexandreis** Book 10.1-167 and, as a result, speaks in scathing terms of the epic in his *Anticlaudianus*: "There Maevius, daring to raise a dumb mouth to heaven, tries to portray the exploits of the Macedonian leader in a dark and shadowy ode; tired he is slowed down at the very beginning of the course and complains that his muse grows slow and listless."[13]

Such derogatory remarks are exceptional. Manitius[14] cites the prominent place given to the poem in Hugo of Trimberg's *Register of Many Authors* c.1280 and the appearance of several lines in the *Distinctiones Monasticae*[15] and thirteenth-century florilegia.[16] Some lines soon became proverbial, especially 5.301 which is sometimes referred to as 'the line': "Wishing to avoid Charybdis, you fall upon Scylla."[17]

The importance of the **Alexandreis** in the thirteenth century is further attested by the number of vernacular Alexander-books that were based upon it.[18] These include:

1. The *Alexanders Geesten* of Jakob van Maerlant—a middle Dutch poem in twelve books, written between 1256 and 1260 in rhymed couplets. The poem is a very close translation of the **Alexandreis.**

2. The Spanish *Libro de Alexandre*—a mid-thirteenth-century Spanish poem in four-line rhyming stanzas. R. S. Willis,[19] in establishing the relationship of the poem to the **Alexandreis,** has shown that the author has changed the atmosphere of the original into a medieval romance by skilful inclusion of material from the *Historia de preliis* and the *Roman d'Alexandre,* and by excluding the heroic and mythological episodes in the original.

3. The *Alexander* of Ulrich von Eschenbach—the longest medieval Alexander poem of 28,000 lines written in Middle High German rhyming couplets. As in the case of the original, the poem is divided into ten books, but Ulrich, though borrowing most of his material from Walter, adds much from other sources.

4. Icelandic and Czech versions of the **Alexandreis.** The **Alexandreis** was translated into Icelandic prose by Brand Jónsson c. 1260 and into Czech verse probably about 1290-1300.

In addition, there are striking reminiscences of the **Alexandreis** in a number of late twelfth- and early thirteenth-century Latin poets, and here consideration of textual similarities may well assist Walter's editor, assuming, of course, that the textual transmission of these authors is reliable. These poets include a. Albert of Stade who treated in elegiac verse the tale of Troy, from the sailing of Jason to Colchis down to the founding of Rome by Aeneas, in his *Troilus,* (dated c. 1249);[20] b. the author of the adventures of Duke Ernest of Swabia in epic form, dated between 1206 and 1233;[21] c. Henry of Settimello, who composed in Italy, around 1192-1194,[22] an elegy *The Inconsistency of Fortune and the Consolation of Philosophy* (*De diversitate fortunae et philosophiae consolatione*); d. William the Breton who composed his *Philippis,* either between 1214 and 1224 (Baumgarten), or c. 1225 (Raby);[23] and e. Nicholas de Braye who imitated William the Breton to honour his own patron, Louis VIII; in a similar way, not long afterwards.[24]

Not surprisingly, the **Alexandreis** became a favourite set text in the curriculum of the medieval schools, and the comment of Henry of Ghent[25] is significant: "Walter of Châtillon, a native of Lille . . . composed *The Achievements of Alexander the Great* in elegant verse. This book today enjoys such standing in the schools of the grammarians that, in comparison, the reading of the ancient poets is being neglected"—praise indeed for a twelfth-century poem.

Further testimony to the fortunes of the **Alexandreis** in the French schools and universities of the thirteenth century is provided by Henri d'Andeli's satirical poem *Bataille des Sept Arts.* The Norman troubadour writes of the dispute between Paris and Orleans concerning the relative merits of logic and grammar, and describes (282-288) how Parealmaine (a personification of Aristotle's peri Hermēneias) kills with a blow of the hammer the representatives of the popular school texts of the period—Jean d'Hauteville's *Architrenius,* Matthew of Vendôme's *Tobias,* the *Aurora* of Peter Riga and the **Alexandreis** of Walter of Châtillon.

The same is true of other scholastic texts and commentaries where the **Alexandreis** is frequently mentioned, for example the thirteenth-century commentary on Ovid's *Metamorphoses* in Paris Bibliothèque Nationale lat. 8010, or the fourteenth-century *Scholastic Miscellany* (*Miscellanea scolastica*) in Paris Bibliothèque Nationale lat. 8653A, or the metrical tract (*Tractus artis metrice*) in Paris Bibliothèque Nationale lat. 8175.

In the scholastic context, the glosses and commentaries that accompany the *Alexandreis* in so many of our manuscripts are particularly instructive. Not only do they assist the interpretation of the poem, but they also shed valuable light on the use of the vernacular in the schools, as well as emphasizing the popularity of the *Alexandreis* as a school text. They were, no doubt originally, dictated reproductions of a lecturer's notes, and in many cases were further expanded by the student himself when he, in turn, became a teacher. These commentaries were circulated, and when they came into the possession of university, cathedral or monastic libraries they underwent further allegorical or exegetical explications.[26]

It is therefore difficult to trace with any degree of confidence the origins of the commentary on the *Alexandreis.* Colker draws attention to a couplet in the thirteenth-century Oxford manuscript Corpus Christi College 211 which suggests that the author of the commentary was an otherwise unknown Geoffrey of Vitry. And since another thirteenth-century Oxford manuscript, Exeter College 69, mentions a certain Peter the Hermit correcting that book from the 'great Orleans glosses,' Colker suggests Orleans as the place of origin.[27]

The *Alexandreis* was to retain its popularity even in the face of the advent of the printing press and the Renaissance bias towards the masterpieces of antiquity. Four early printed editions of the poem exist, the earliest being that by Guillaume Le Tailleur of Rouen c. 1487, and this was followed in turn by those of J. Adelphus (Strasbourg 1513), Alex. Weissenborn (Ingolstadt 1541), and Robert Granjon (Lyons 1558). Significantly, too, in Welsh Literature, it is from the Renaissance period that we find Welsh translations of popular *Alexandreis* passages.

WALTER'S SOURCES[28]

Medieval accounts[29] of Alexander the Great are based on two principal sources, the Alexander Romance and the historical-romance of the early Roman imperialist, Quintus Curtius Rufus. From the former are derived several Latin works, including:

a. Julius Valerius' *The Achievements of Alexander of Macedon* (soon after 300 AD).

b. The *Epitome* of Julius Valerius (probably ninth century).

c. Archbishop Leo's *Nativity and Victory of Alexander the Great* (sometime after 952) which has become known as *The History of the Battles* (*Historia de preliis*).

Among supplementary texts to the Alexander Romance may be listed:

a. *The Letter of Alexander the Great to his teacher Aristotle about the geography and marvels of India* (composed in late imperial times but much expanded in or before the ninth century).

b. *Palladius' Letter of Instruction,* relating Alexander's contacts with the Brahmins of India (late imperial).

c. *The Correspondence of Alexander the Great with Dindimus King of the Brahmins about Philosophy* (late imperial).

d. *The Secret of Secrets,* a book of counsel on statecraft allegedly written by Aristotle for Alexander (compiled in Syriac in the eighth century and first translated into Latin in the twelfth century).

Apart from Quintus Curtius Rufus, the historical tradition is represented by Orosius' *Seven Books of Histories against the Pagans* (fifth century) and by the unknown Justin's *Epitome of the Macedonian Histories of Pompeius Trogus* (probably third century).

It was from Curtius' highly-coloured and romanticized biography of Alexander[30] that Walter drew his main inspiration for the *Alexandreis,* even though extant twelfth-century library catalogues contain surprisingly few references to this popular author.[31] Many *Alexandreis* passages reveal a particularly close dependence, where Walter very skilfully reproduces the exact wording of his Curtius text[32] within the strictures of a hexameter line. The sequence of events, too, generally follows Curtius.

But Walter selected his material to suit his purpose, which was not to write a history but an imaginative, poetical biography of Alexander as man, king, and general. Hence, for example, the events which followed the king's death, while clearly appealing to Curtius, are omitted by Walter. Campaigns, too, are given less prominence. In the Indian section, only that against Porus and the capture of the stronghold of the Sudracae are treated with any detail, whilst no mention is made of contemporary events in Greece included by Curtius.

Omitted, too, are incidents that would tarnish the hero's reputation. The dragging of Betis, governor of Gaza, around the walls of the captured city[33] is not mentioned, nor is Curtius' statement that Persepolis was sacked to satisfy the whim of the drunken courtesan Thais.[34] No detailed account is given of the deaths of Clitus,[35] Hermolaus[36] and Callisthenes,[37] nor of Alexander's adoption of Persian customs and his soldiers' displeasure.[38]

Omitted, too, are events that would prove tedious or that would interrupt the smooth flow of the poet's account. Here may be included, for example, the detailed struggles in Bactra and Sogdiana,[39] the capture of Susa,[40] the struggle with Satibarzanes satrap of the Arii,[41] or the murder of Spitamenes by his wife.[42] The siege of Tyre is abridged[43] as is the conspiracy and trial of Philotas,[44] and little is said about Alexander's visit to the temple of Jupiter Ammon.[45] Military details, too, are given less prominence. Hence the battles of Issus and Arbela are treated in Vergilian style with single combats,[46] whilst the Granicus, described in the lost second book of Curtius, is dismissed in but a few lines.[47] There is no mention of the arrangements made by Alexander to rule the subdued areas, and, compared with Curtius, Walter's geographical descriptions are few, only Asia and India, the major theatres of war, being described in any detail.

But Walter was clearly happy to borrow Curtius' moral tone and rhetorical embellishments. Most of Curtius' speeches in those parts used by the poet are reproduced, and often, for more graphic effect, an indirect speech in Curtius is converted into a direct speech in Walter. But here, too, we find abridgements to help the flow of the poem, as in the case of Darius' conversation with Patron, leader of the Greek contingent, at the end of Book 6.[48]

But Curtius is not the only source. Indeed, there had to be others, for there are several lacunae in the Curtius text, and of the ten books the first two were already lost in the archetype of all the surviving manuscripts. Hence Walter was forced to turn to Justin for many of the early events.

It is Justin who supplies the details for Alexander's enlistment of both young men and veterans, noting that the sixty-year-olds chosen as leaders resembled a Senate.[49] The only difference is that Walter dates the events to Alexander's Greek expedition and not to the Asian expedition as in Justin. Details of the comparative military strength of the Macedonian and Persian armies are also derived from Justin.[50] Among other borrowings from this author in Book 1 may be included the note of admiration that Alexander resolved to conquer the world with so few men,[51] the sedition of Athens,[52] the abandonment of the less gifted soldiers to protect the homeland,[53] Alexander's marking his landing in Asia with a javelin throw,[54] the sharing out of Alexander's possessions among his acquaintances (though this was before the fleet left home in Justin),[55] and Alexander's command to his men not to lay waste Asia.[56]

Book 7 shows further borrowing from Justin, for there was another lacuna in Curtius regarding the discovery of the dying Darius by the Macedonian soldier Polystratus. Though the name Polystratus is not found in Justin, nevertheless, Darius' consolation that his final words will be understood by the Macedonian is clearly from Justin, as is Alexander's honourable burial of the Persian king.[57] In Book 10, where there is yet another lacuna in the Curtius text, it is Justin who supplies the names of the countries which sent envoys to Babylon, though the gifts they brought are Walter's own invention.[58] Finally, the designation of Alexander as descendant of Aeacus is also probably from Justin.[59]

Among the non-historical sources consulted, there is one clear borrowing from the influential Pseudo-Aristotelian *The Secret of Secrets,*[60] namely the exhortation speech of Aristotle to his twelve-year-old pupil in Book 1.82 ff. Here, in the only reference to Alexander's childhood in the poem, the philosopher advises the young prince on the delicate art of statecraft, stressing the virtues that characterise the successful ruler and the vices he should avoid. The poet has freely adapted his source material at this point, but the reference to the philosopher's drawn and haggard look may well be an original addition by Walter himself.

Walter also turned to the Alexander Romance when a historical source let him down. It was Julius Valerius[61] rather than Leo's adaptation that he consulted, and that, as we should expect, in an abbreviated form. At the same time, Walter wisely resisted the temptation to insert some of Alexander's strange adventures recorded in the Romance. But he was clearly aware of the myth that Alexander's father was Nectanabus, for he refers to it no less than three times in the course of the poem.[62] Alexander's lament at the beginning of the first book that Greece is subject to Persia also comes from the Romance,[63] and material from the Romance is combined with Justin for the poet's account of the siege and sack of Thebes.[64] It is the Romance that supplies details of the means adopted to attack the city, and if the subject-matter of Cleades' intercession is from Justin, the idea of the singer, the direct form of address, and even individual phrases recall the Romance.

Walter, likewise, turned to this work for the site of Alexander's landing in Asia. Curtius' account was lost and Justin mentioned no specific region. But the *Epitome* stated that it was Alexander's intention to go against the barbarians "through Cilicia," hence Walter's Cilician references in Book 1.[65] However, this leads to inconsistency, for in the next book Walter, oblivious of the contradiction, brings Alexander back to Tarsus in Cilicia.[66]

Curtius had mentioned, but without giving details, an arrogant letter sent by Darius to Alexander. Walter, wishing to underline the vanity of the Persian king, again turned to the Romance for details both of this letter and the gifts which Alexander received. Even the letter's title is the same: "Darius, King of Kings, kinsman of the gods to his servant Alexander." Similar, too, is the way Alexander interprets the envoys' gifts.[67]

Then, in the last book, Alexander discloses to his men his intention to lead them against rebellious Rome. This submission of Rome, clearly not historical, is attested by the Romance, and it is there that we find the consul Aemilius offering Alexander a golden crown as proof of friendship.[68]

Isidore of Seville is another author used by Walter. His *Origins*[69] supplied the necessary details for the description of Asia, whilst his *Chronicle*[70] provided both the time span of 4,868 years from creation to Alexander's conquest of Persia and probably the reference to Darius as the descendant of Arsamus.

A Latin version of Josephus, in turn, provided the poet with details of Alexander's meeting with the Jewish High-priest in the first book.[71] The story naturally appealed to a Christian author, and Walter very skilfully recounts the incident in the form of a speech of exhortation delivered by Alexander to his men at the tomb of his kinsman Achilles.

In the final book, Walter combines material from several sources as he cites the portents witnessed at Alexander's birth.[72] From Justin he draws the story of the two eagles on the palace roof, except that they were sitting not fighting in Justin.[73] Walter, however, clearly wishes to underline his hero's warlike nature. The hail of real stones comes from Orosius,[74] while the snake born of a hen recalls the *Epitome* story of the snake emerging from an egg and dying, which was interpreted as foretelling the rise to power and early death of Alexander.[75] The speaking lamb seems to come from Isidore's *Chronicle*[76] (which, in turn, was taken from Jerome's *Chronicle*), but it is Walter who links the portent with Alexander.

The above sources demonstrate clearly the breadth of Walter's reading, and they explain why the poet spent five years on the *Alexandreis*. At the same time, one should not overlook Walter's original contribution. Several speeches are clearly his own invention, such as that of Darius to his generals (2.325 ff.); Darius' monologue before his capture (7.17 ff.); Fortune's monologue (2.190 ff. with its recall of Boethius); those of Alexander to his troops before his death (10.398 ff.); to the foreign envoys (10.283 ff.); to his faithful Macedonians (10.301 ff.); and, especially, the speeches of Nature, Leviathan and Treachery in the final book.

The many similes introduced into the poem to clarify and embroider the narrative are drawn mostly from the animal or natural world. But even here, although the technique and general outline are clearly classical, there are still traces of originality in the poet's presentation. Perhaps the animal at the centre of the simile differs from the one in the Vergilian parallel, or a historical dimension may be added. A good example is the Rhone simile in Book 2.318 ff. There is nothing new about the overflowing river, but the allusion to the martyrdom of the Theban legion of Christians at Agaunum in 285 AD gives an attractive new twist to a conventional theme.[77]

Clearly original, too, are the numerous references to contemporary ecclesiastical events and issues, whether they be the murders of important church dignitaries or the vices besetting the Church of Walter's time. For we are not allowed to forget that the author of the **Alexandreis** is a committed Christian whose poetry affords a classic example of the fusion of sacred and profane in the later Middle Ages. Hence, as well as echoes from Vergil,[78] Ovid, Statius, Lucan or Juvenal, we have reminiscences of the Christian Latin poets, especially Prudentius. The numerous biblical allusions, too, reveal Walter's thoughts on some of the central issues of the Christian faith: the relationship between body and soul, sin and its consequences, heaven and hell, God and Satan, and, above all, the triumphant power of Christ's salvation.

The poet's profound biblical knowledge is well exemplified by the account of Darius' shield and the tombs of the Persian king and his queen. In 2.494 ff. the poet describes Darius' arms, especially the scenes depicted upon his shield, and the classical models for the ecphrasis are clearly Hephaestus' shield for Achilles in *Iliad* 18 and Vulcan's shield for Aeneas in *Aeneid* 8. Walter regards the Persian kings as descendants of the kings of Assyria and Babylon and thus skilfully introduces the role played by these kings in the Old Testament, as well as the subsequent overthrow of the Babylonian empire by Cyrus the Persian. Some details, however, are not biblical, for example the building of the Tower of Babel as a refuge against a renewal of the flood, which is a view found in Josephus' *Antiquities* and the *Scholastic History* of Walter's contemporary Petrus Comestor.

Then in 4.176 ff. we have a detailed account of the biblical scenes carved on the Persian queen's tomb by the Jew Apelles. The poet begins with creation and traces in detail the subsequent story of the patriarchs, the judges, the kings of Israel, the two kingdoms of Israel and Judah, and the Old Testament prophets and their message. Though impressive for its knowledge of the Old Testament, this section is poetically perhaps the weakest part of the whole poem, for there were obvious difficulties in trying to fit a catalogue of biblical names into hexameter lines. Little attempt is made to develop a periodic style, and the overall effect is rather stilted and pedestrian. The honouring of a Persian queen's tomb with scenes from Jewish history is highly unrealistic and tends to detract from the general unity of the poem.

The same Apelles is also made responsible for Darius' tomb which is described in 7.382 ff. On it are depicted the countries of the world with their particular characteristics—a popular topic in Walter's day. There are clearly many anachronisms with the mention of England, Normandy and even Arthur. But the inscription is biblical, recording Daniel's vision of the he-goat breaking the ram's two horns which the prophet interpreted as the overthrow of the twin kingdoms of Media and Persia by the Greek warrior-king.

Finally, Walter's presentation of Alexander's death is imaginative with several original touches, even if there are distinct echoes of earlier Latin poets. The general idea, no doubt, came from Alan of Lille's *Anticlaudianus* Book 8, where Rumour spreads abroad the news of the making of the New Man by Nature. Allecto, hearing this, calls the Vices and their retinues together and urges them to make war on the New Man. But Alan himself was much indebted to Prudentius and, especially, to Claudian's *In Rufinum,* where Allecto, angry at the growth of Virtue on earth, calls together an assembly of the Vices to devise a worthy crime. Thereupon Megaera promises to conduct the arch villain Rufinus into the imperial palace so that he can embark on a career of deceit and disruption. As well as giving Walter an opportunity to propound his views on hell and its torments, the whole section is noteworthy for the poet's powers of graphic description and dramatic presentation.

SYNOPSIS OF THE *ALEXANDREIS*

The poem is preceded by the author's prose prologue. The introduction and dedication are followed by Aristotle's long speech of advice on statecraft to the young Alexander. Thus encouraged, Alexander, as soon as he is of age, takes up arms and, having been elected commander of the Greeks at Corinth, musters his troops (336 BC). The Athenians break faith but soon repent of their hasty action and are spared. Thebes, however, rebels and is punished (335 BC). Alexander's fleet sets sail against Darius and arrives in Asia (334 BC). The poet describes the geography of Asia and Alexander's reaction to its sight. Alexander proceeds to visit Troy and reflects on the posthumous fame of his kinsman Achilles. He encourages his men by recounting his strange encounter with the Jewish High-priest. (Book 1)

Darius sends a proud dispatch, bidding Alexander desist from his foolish undertaking, and receives a fiery reply.

The Persian king reviews his troops, whilst Alexander cuts the celebrated Gordian knot and hastens to meet Darius (333 BC). The strength of the Persian army is described. Alexander comes to Tarsus, bathes in the Cydnus and falls gravely ill. He places implicit trust in Philip, despite the slanderous accusations of the doctor's personal enemies, and, regaining his strength, discharges the vows pledged for his recovery. Issus is captured, and the generals debate the strategy to be adopted. Sisenes is killed for not revealing the letter sent to him by the Persians, urging him to kill Alexander. The Greek contingent under Thymondas unsuccessfully urges Darius to retreat and fight in the spacious Mesopotamian plains, or else divide up his troops. Darius encourages his generals and prepares for battle. Alexander is overjoyed at the sight of the advancing Persian army. Panic now grips the Persians as Alexander draws up his battle-lines and encourages his men. The poet describes Darius' shield. (Book 2)

The battle of Issus is described in epic manner. The Macedonians prove victorious and proceed to collect the booty. While his soldiers insult the Persian womenfolk, Alexander himself shows signal generosity towards Darius' family. The poet contrasts this clemency with its later subordination to arrogance. The governor of Damascus, where Darius' treasure is stored, treacherously betrays the city to Parmenion but is slain by a loyal Persian. The celebrated siege of Tyre is carried on with great courage and skill on both sides (332 BC). Undeterred by wounds, the victorious Alexander proceeds to capture Gaza, and foils an attempt on his life. He visits the oracle of Jupiter Ammon in Egypt, but an intended expedition into Ethiopia is thwarted (331 BC). Darius summons the Persians once more into battle and, after Alexander crosses the Tigris and Euphrates, unsuccessfully adopts a scorched earth policy. When Alexander encamps near Arbela, a lunar eclipse alarms the Macedonians, but Aristander's favourable interpretation rouses them to battle. (Book 3)

Darius' wife dies in captivity and is mourned by Alexander. Darius, suspicious of the circumstances, is reassured by his slave who recounts the admirable self-control shown by Alexander. Accordingly, moved by Alexander's generosity, Darius offers new conditions of peace. Parmenion urges acceptance, but Alexander declines them. The poet describes in detail the scenes of biblical history carved on the tomb of Darius' wife by the Jew Apelles. Alexander sends Menidas to explore the enemy position, whilst Darius resolves to fight in the open plains. The apprehensive Macedonians prepare for battle. Parmenion urges a night attack on the numerically superior Persians, but Alexander rejects a victory gained by unfair tactics. Darius' troops are ready and confident. Alexander, however, cannot sleep as he ponders over which tactics to adopt, but with the aid of the God of Sleep he finally falls into a deep slumber. He has to be awoken by Parmenion and surprises his men by asserting that he has slept free from care. The armour of Alexander is described, and, confidently rousing his men, the Macedonian leader instructs them in the tactics to adopt. A Persian deserter warns him of the traps laid by Darius on the battlefield. Alexander harangues his men, and battle is commenced. (Book 4)

The poet describes the battle of Arbela, concentrating on individual contests in epic style. Defeated, Darius flees, and the retreating Persians find themselves in desperate straits. As he pursues them, Alexander repels an attack by a squadron of enemy cavalry. The surviving Persians join Darius at Arbela, and he encourages them to accompany him to Media to collect fresh forces. Alexander, he insists, will find his newly won booty more of a burden than an advantage. But to the listening Persians his speech lacks conviction. Alexander makes his way to Babylon where its governor Mazaeus surrenders both himself and the city. Alexander enters the city in triumph to the general acclaim of the Babylonians. The poet concludes with an impassioned plea for the appearance in his own day of a second Alexander to re-establish Christian authority over the world. (Book 5)

Babylon corrupts the Macedonians, and Alexander, moving to the region of Satrapene, reforms camp rules to reward valour. After capturing Susa, he meets strong resistance from the Uxii and is exposed to danger. Medates and the townsfolk are spared through the intercession of Darius' mother. Alexander, now in pursuit of Darius, crosses the Araxes, and his greedy soldiers sack Persepolis (330 BC). Alexander encounters three thousand Macedonian captives horribly mutilated by the Persians and offers them a choice between staying where they are or returning home. Euticion argues for the former course, Theteus for the latter. They decide to stay, and Alexander makes generous provision for them. In Ecbatana Darius exhorts his unenthusiastic men to fight on. Bessus and Nabarzanes now conspire against their king, Nabarzanes urging him to hand over the reins of government for the time being to Bessus. Having almost killed Nabarzanes, Darius retires to his tent alone. The next day, the traitors feign loyalty, but Patron and his men guard the king and vainly warn him of the impending treachery. (Book 6)

Darius soliloquizes upon his unfair treatment. If he has been unjust he deserves to die; otherwise let the guilty be punished. In despair, he almost commits suicide. The traitors place him bound with gold fetters in a chariot and flee. Alexander, in hot pursuit to rescue Darius, takes a shorter route and has the enemy in sight. The traitors in panic mortally wound Darius and escape, Bessus to Bactra, Nabarzanes to Hyrcania. The Mace-

donians overtake the main body of Persians and massacre those in their path. After the carnage, the thirsty Polystratus finds the dying Darius by a stream and catches his final words of gratitude to Alexander. If Alexander punishes the parricides and gives Darius proper burial, the Persian king will willingly concede world dominion to the Macedonian. The poet muses on the confinement of a man's soul by his corrupt body. Alexander grieves for Darius and buries him with royal pomp in a pyramid adorned with biblical scenes by Apelles. After Alexander has rewarded his gallant troops, a rumour pervades the camp that he intends to return home. Alexander wins the support of his officers and addresses his men, stressing that more time is required to establish the newly won empire and to punish the parricides. The troops respond with enthusiasm. (Book 7)

Alexander conquers Hyrcania but spares Nabarzanes. Talestris, the Amazon queen, visits Alexander, desiring to have a child by him, and is allowed to stay thirteen nights. To enable the army to overtake Bessus more quickly, Alexander orders all the possessions of the Macedonians, including his own, to be burnt. Philotas suppresses knowledge of a conspiracy against the king and he and his father Parmenion are accused of complicity. After demanding vengeance, Alexander leaves the council. Philotas, who gains sympathy until Amyntas rekindles the men's anger, seeks to defend himself, stressing his loyalty and urging pity for his aged father. Finally, the distraught Philotas is threatened with torture and immediately confesses his guilt. The poet reflects on the changed fortunes of a man who was once so powerful. Six days later, Alexander proceeds against Bessus and, capturing him, allows Darius' brother to torture the parricide to death by crucifixion (328 BC). Alexander arrives at the river Tanais where he is met by twenty Scythian envoys whose leader urges Alexander not to cross the Tanais but to accept the warlike Scythians as allies. The king rejects their advice and, crossing the river, defeats the Scythians, whose sudden overthrow strikes terror into the hearts of neighbouring tribes. (Book 8)

The geography of India is described, especially its rivers. Several Indian princes submit to Alexander, but not the proud Porus. Alexander confronts him at the Hydaspes (326 BC), but crossing the deep river proves difficult. The bosom companions Nicanor and Simachus dare to lead a surprise assault on a mid-stream island, but, after some initial success, are overwhelmed by the enemy and share the same fate. Attalus, who bears a close resemblance to Alexander, is attired in the king's robes and made to stand in full view of the enemy, whilst Alexander, aided by a mist, effects a crossing downstream and surprises the enemy. The two armies clash, but a recent downpour gives the nimble Macedonians the advantage. Initially, the Indian elephants cause panic, but they are repulsed. As Alexander pursues Porus, his gallant horse Bucephalus is killed. Porus kills Taxiles' brother for daring to counsel submission. Alexander captures Porus, who urges the Macedonian to learn from his experience that Fortune's gifts are perishable and is generously pardoned. The victory encourages Alexander to extend his conquests, but he is almost killed when he leaps down from the walls into the city of the Sudracae. He is saved only by the arrival of Peucestes and the other Macedonians. On its capture, the city is severely punished. The wounded Alexander encourages the fearful Critobulus to remove the barbed arrow and refuses to be bound. Critobulus is successful, and the troops rejoice. When Alexander intends to scour the ocean and find the source of the Nile, Craterus urges him to spare himself, for the safety of all depends on him. Alexander, though grateful, insists on gaining further glory, even at the price of death. (Book 9)

Nature, indignant at Alexander's resolve to probe her inmost recesses, descends to the Underworld, where she is welcomed with due reverence by all its denizens. She complains to Leviathan, urging him to check Alexander's progress in case he should penetrate hell itself. Leviathan summons a general council and repeats Nature's warning, suggesting that Alexander may be the man long prophesied to overthrow the halls of hell. Thereupon, Treachery undertakes to remove Alexander through the agency of the disgruntled Antipater. Applauded by all, she wings her way to the upper world and instructs her favourite. Alexander proposes to return to Babylon and then conquer, in turn, Africa, Spain, Gaul, Germany, and Italy. The poet urges him to curb his greed and denounces Fortune for allowing Alexander's death, especially by poison. All the threatened countries seek to avert the king's wrath by sending envoys with placatory gifts. Alexander enters Babylon in triumph and, receiving these gifts, promises to show leniency to all who submit (323 BC). To his men he promises fresh rewards and new fields to conquer, beginning with rebellious Rome. Heaven sends portents to mark his death as it did his birth. The fatal day reluctantly dawns, and Alexander spends it entertaining the envoys. When the wine is carried round, the king drinks and collapses. Alexander, though conscious of his imminent death, reassures his army gathered at his couch. He is being summoned to heaven to direct the affairs of gods and men. Asked who is to succeed him, he gives his ring to Perdiccas and then dies, much lamented by his men. The poet from his own and Alexander's experience reflects on the variability of Fortune and offers the poem, now finished, to his patron William in the hope that it will achieve immortality for both poet and patron. (Book 10)

THE TRANSLATION

The translation here offered is based completely upon my own collation of a representative sample of *Alexandreis* manuscripts. In establishing the text, I have paid particular attention to the readings of four late twelfth- or very early thirteenth-century copies: Copenhagen, Det Kongelige Bibliotek, Gl. kgl. S. 2146; London, Lambeth Palace Library, 471; Oxford, Bodleian Library, Digby 52; Wolfenbüttel, Herzog August Bibliothek, Guelf. 28. I. Aug. 4°. I have also consulted the following thirteenth-century copies: Berlin, Deutsche Staatsbibliothek, Phill. 1799; Cambridge, Corpus Christi College, 406; Cambridge, Trinity College, 604; Erfurt, Wissenschaftliche Allgemeinbibliothek, Amplon. 8° 90; London, British Library, Royal 15 A. X; London, British Library, Add. 23891; Laon, Bibliothèque municipale, 401; Oxford, Bodleian Library, D'Orville 205; Oxford, Bodleian Library, Bod. 527. The readings which differ from those adopted by Colker are listed in the appendix.

Translating any poet is by common consent a well-nigh impossible task, for the translator has to steer a middle course between Scylla and Charybdis. A too literal prose translation exposes him to the charge of being wooden and lifeless; yet a freer poetic rendering, or even a prose version that puts elegance first, can often stray considerably from the original and totally deceive the reader. At the risk of being too literal at times, I have preferred to aim more at clarity than elegance, believing that this is what readers of the poem would find most helpful, whether they read it in conjunction with the Latin text or as students of other medieval disciplines.

If the task facing the editor of the *Alexandreis* is complicated by the fact that so many of our manuscripts bear signs of a distinct horizontal transmission, the task facing the poem's translator is little easier. This is due, in most part, to the poet's style which, in keeping with the scholastic traditions of his day, is highly rhetorical and erudite. Walter has all the embellishments of style at his fingertips, and he is not slow to use them. He delights in impassioned exclamations to some object or person to heighten the emotional effect by a show of feeling on his own part; he is fond of repeating both exact words and also the same idea in slightly different language in successive lines; he has many descriptive passages, embracing countries, races, nature, as well as people's physical and moral attributes; alliteration, *anaphora*, deliberative questions, simile, *sententia*, graphic use of present tense, all appear regularly. And the countless long speeches give him an excellent opportunity to display his rhetorical training.

Three characteristics, however, deserve special mention. Firstly, the poet is particularly fond of metaphorical language. Alexander, to give but one example out of many, is variously described as "the hammer of the world," "the wrath of heaven," "the scourge of all the lands." Closely linked with this use of metaphor is the poet's fondness for personification, whereby inanimate objects are given feelings and desires usually associated with human beings. A mountain laments the loss of its cedars; a sword is thirsty for slaughter; a hand threatens to fail. Such personifications are, of course, found in all literature, but the recurrent usage in Walter is noteworthy. I have, therefore, been very careful to retain both these characteristics in my translation. However, this was not possible in the case of the third of the poet's favourite devices—*adnominatio* or 'play on words,' which was so popular with twelfth-century authors and which appears frequently in the **Alexandreis,** e.g.:

> . . . captam captivis reddidit urbem
>
> (6.139)
>
> Sic quoque multa cupis que non capis . . .
>
> (8.385)
>
> . . . et qui graviore reatu
>
> Excessit gravius, graviorem sentiat ignem.
>
> (10.66-67)

In the case of proper names, the conventional Anglicized Latin forms have generally been adopted. Occasionally, however, as in the case of battle scenes where the manuscripts often reveal considerable confusion, especially if a name is a figment of Walter's own imagination, I have tended to retain the form suggested by the better manuscripts.

In conclusion, no translation can hope to do justice to the quality of this fine poem, nor catch the studied elegance of style and rhetorical flourishes of its highly talented author. Reading the **Alexandreis** dispenses once and for all with the popular myth of the poor Latinity of even the best medieval writers. To wrestle with the poet's meaning is to appreciate his profound knowledge and instant recall of the great classical Latin poets. One cannot but be surprised at the facility with which he handles the hexameter and observes its general rules, whether avoiding monosyllabic final words or deftly varying his pauses. His diction, too, is for the most part classical, and his vocabulary impressively wide-ranging. For him Latin is clearly the living language of culture with which he is completely at ease. Thus his obvious delight in his romantic subject, combined with his excellent Latinity and mastery of epic convention, resulted in a memorable poem which can, with some justification, be regarded as the best of all medieval Latin epics.

Notes

1. For the Latin side of the Renaissance, C. H. Haskins' *The Renaissance of the Twelfth Century*

(Cambridge: University Press, 1927) is still the fullest account.

2. Presumably Châtillon-sur-Marne since this belonged to the archbishopric of Reims.

3. Marvin L. Colker, *Galteri de Castellione Alexandreis* (Padua: Editrice Antenore, 1978), p.xv, quotes Paris Bibliothèque Nationale lat. 8358 for other reasons why Walter wrote the *Alexandreis.* One was to regain William's favour after quarreling over the archbishop's support for a certain Berterus. The second was to display his poetic superiority over Matthew of Vendôme.

4. J. Hellegouarc'h, "Un poète latin du XIIe siècle Gautier de Lille," *Bulletin de l'Association Guillaume Budé* (1967) 95-115, sees his canonry as a kind of disguised exile.

5. Cf. F. Châtillon, "Flagello sepe castigatus vitam terminavit: Contribution à l'étude des mauvais traitements infligés à Gautier de Châtillon," *Revue du moyen âge latin 7* 151 ff. for a discussion of this problem.

6. K. Strecker, *Moralisch-satirische Gedichte Walters von Châtillon,* (Heidelberg: Carl Winter, 1929), 17 and 18.

7. Cf. E. F. Wilson, "The *Georgica spiritualia* of John of Garland," *Speculum* 8 (1933) 358 ff.

8. E.g. *The Letters of John of Salisbury,* ed. W. J. Millor, S. J. and H. E. Butler, rev. C. N. L. Brooke (London: Nelson, 1955), letters 144 and 168.

9. Cf. K. Strecker, *Die Lieder Walters von Châtillon in der handschrift 351 von St. Omer* (Berlin: Wiedmannsche Buchhandlung 1925), 16, p.27.

10. Cf. J. R. Williams, "William of the White Hands and Men of Letters" in *Anniversary Essays in Mediaeval History by Students of C.H. Haskins* (Boston, 1929); R. A. Gauthier, "Pour l'attribution à Gauthier de Châtillon du Moralium dogma philosophorum," *Revue du moyen âge latin 7* (1951) 62, n.80.

11. His *I shall not be silent for the sake of Sion* (*Propter Sion non tacebo*) is an excellent example. See Strecker, *Moralisch-satirische Gedichte Walters,* 2.

12. It is possible, of course, that both authors were drawing on a book of epitaphs as a common source.

13. Tr. J. J. Sheridan (Toronto: Pontifical Institute of Mediaeval Studies, 1973), pp. 51-52. For Maevius or Mevius the poor Latin poet, cf. Vergil, *Eclogae* 3.90 and Horace, *Epistulae* 10.2. Yet not even

Alan could refrain from imitating parts of the poem, cf. K. Strecker, "Walter von Châtillon und seine Schule," *Zeitschrift für deutsches Altertum* 64 (1927) 164 ff.

14. M. Manitius, *Geschichte der lateinischen Literatur des Mittelalters* (Munich, 1931), 3.923.

15. Ed. J. B. Pitra, *Spicilegium Solesmense* (Paris: Firmin Didot, 1852-1858), 2.219; 3.235, 467.

16. E.g. Paris, Bibliothèque Nationale lat. 15155.

17. For this line's popularity, cf. E. Sandys, "Notes on Medieval Latin Authors," *Hermathena* 12 (1903) 438.

18. Cf. G. Cary, *The Medieval Alexander* (Cambridge: University Press, 1956), pp. 64 ff. and D. J. A. Ross, *Alexander Historiatus; a Guide to Medieval Illustrated Alexander Literature* (London, 1963), pp. 72 ff.

19. R. S. Willis, *The Relationship of the Spanish "Libro de Alexandre" to the "Alexandreis" of Gautier de Châtillon* (Princeton: University Press, 1934). This is also the conclusion of J. H. Michael in *The Treatment of Classical Material in the 'Libro de Alexandre'* (Manchester: University Press, 1971).

20. F. J. E. Raby, *A History of Secular Latin Poetry in the Middle Ages* (Oxford: Clarendon Press, 1934), 2.346. Cf. H. Christensen, *Das Alexanderlied Walters von Châtillon* (Halle, 1905), p. 166.

21. Cf. Christensen, p. 174.

22. A. Baumgarten, *Die lateinische und griechische Literatur der christlichen Völker* (Freiburg, 1905), p. 372. For Henry's dependence, cf. Strecker, "Henricus Septimellensis und die zeitgenössische Literatur," *Studi Medievali,* n.s. 2 (1929) 120. Cf. Christensen, p. 172.

23. Raby, 2.343. Cf. Christensen, p. 168.

24. For detailed examples of these similarities, cf. Christensen, c. 5.

25. Manitius, 3.922.

26. Cf. P. M. Clogan's useful remarks on commentaries in *The Medieval Achilleid of Statius* (Leiden: Brill, 1968), introduction; cf. also G. Paré, A. Brunet, P. Tremblay, *La Renaissance du XIIe siècle, Les Ecoles et l'Enseignement* (Paris and Ottawa, 1933), *passim.*

27. "A Note on the History of the Commentary on the Alexandreis." *Medium Aevum,* 28 (1959) 97-98. For transcriptions of glosses and commentaries on the *Alexandreis* see Colker's ed., pp. 275 ff.

28. Cf. Christensen, pp. 102 ff.

29. Cf. Cary, *The Medieval Alexander* and Ross, *Alexander Historiatus.*

30. Cf. J. E. Atkinson, *A Commentary on Q. Curtius Rufus' Historiae Alexandri Magni, Books 3 and 4,* (Amsterdam, 1980); J. Yardley and W. Heckel, *Quintus Curtius Rufus* (Penguin Classics, 1984).

31. Manitius 3.924. For Curtius' popularity in the Middle Ages, cf. S. Dosson, *Etude sur Quinte Curce, sa vie et son oeuvre* (Paris: Librairie Hachette, 1866), Appendix II, pp. 357 ff.

32. Cf. M. Bacherler's study, "Gualterus' Alexandreis in ihrem Verhältnis zum Curtius-Text," *Berliner philologische Wochenschrift,* 37 (1917) 663-672, 698-704, 730-736, 761-766.

33. Quintus Curtius Rufus, *Historiae Alexandri Magni,* 4.6.29.

34. Curtius, 5.7.3-10.

35. Curtius, 8.1.20-52.

36. Curtius, 8.6.7-8.8.20.

37. Curtius, 8.8.21-23.

38. Curtius, 6.6.1-10.

39. Curtius, 7.4.20 ff.; 7.5.1 ff.

40. Curtius, 5.2.8 ff.

41. Curtius, 6.6.21 ff.

42. Curtius, 8.3.1 ff.

43. Curtius, 4.2.1 ff.; Walter of Châtillon, *Alexandreis,* 3.278 ff.

44. Curtius, 6.7-11; Walter, 8.75 ff.

45. Curtius, 4.7.5 ff.; Walter, 3.370 ff.

46. Curtius, 3.9-11 and 4.15.1 ff.; Walter, 3.1 ff. and 5.1 ff.

47. Walter, 2.64-68.

48. Curtius, 5.11.1 ff.; Walter, 6.490 ff.

49. *Marci Iuniani Iustini Epitoma Historiarum Philippicarum Pompei Trogi,* ed. O. Seel (Leipzig: Teubner Press, 1935), 11.6.4-6; Walter, 1.249 ff.

50. Justin, 11.6.2; Walter, 1.246, 256, 357.

51. Justin, 11.6.3; Walter, 1.264 ff.

52. Justin, 11.2.7; Walter, 1.268 ff.

53. Justin, 11.5.3; Walter, 1.353 ff.

54. Justin, 11.5.10; Walter, 1.388 ff.

55. Justin, 11.5.5; Walter, 1.440 ff.

56. Justin, 11.6.1; Walter, 1.445 ff.

57. Justin, 11.15.5-15; Walter, 7.235 ff.

58. Justin, 12.13.1; Walter, 10.225 ff.

59. Justin, 11.3.1; Walter, 1.473, 9.545.

60. *Opera hactenus inedita Rogeri Baconi, Fasc. V, Secretum Secretorum*, ed. R. Steele (Oxford: Clarendon Press, 1920). See especially I, cap. 4-8, 10, 13-14, 19; III, cap. 17, 19.

61. *Julii Valerii Epitome*, ed. J. Zacher (Halle, 1867).

62. Walter, 1.46 ff.; 2.333; 3.167 ff.

63. *Epitome*, 1.23; Walter, 1.30 ff.

64. Justin, 11.3.6 ff.; *Epitome*, 1.46.

65. *Epitome*, 2.7; Walter, 1.378, 447.

66. Walter, 2.144.

67. Curtius, 3.5.12; *Epitome*, 1.36; Walter, 2.18 ff.

68. *Epitome*, 1.29; Walter, 10.322 ff.

69. *Isidori Hispalensis Episcopi Etymologiae sive Origines*, ed. W. M. Lindsay (Oxford: Clarendon Press, 1911).

70. *Isidori Iunioris episcopi Hispalensis chronica maiora*, ed. T. Mommsen (Berlin: Weidmann, 1894).

71. Josephus, *Jewish Antiquities*, trans. R. Marcus, Loeb Classical Library (London: William Heinemann, 1937), 11.5; Walter, 1.502 ff.

72. Walter, 10.340 ff.

73. Justin, 12.16.4-5.

74. *Pauli Orosii Historiae Adversum Paganos*, ed. C. Zangemeister (Leipzig: Teubner Press, 1889), 3.7.4.

75. *Epitome*, 1.11.

76. Isidore, *Chronica maiora, sub anno* 4427.

77. The repetition of this simile in Book 5. 313 ff. demonstrates its appeal to the poet himself.

78. A notable example, apart from Darius' shield, is the story of Nicanor and Simachus in Book 9, clearly modelled on that of Nisus and Euryalus (*Aeneid* 9.176-449).

Glynn Meter (essay date 1989)

SOURCE: Meter, Glynn. Introduction to *Walter of Châtillon's* Alexandreis *Book 10—A Commentary*, pp. 1-27. Frankfurt am Main, Germany: Peter Lang, 1991.

[*In the following introduction to his examination of Book 10 of the* Alexandreis, *originally published as a dissertation in 1989, Meter argues that Walter's purpose in writing his poem was to apply biblical and classical literary techniques to a secular work.*]

The purpose of this thesis is to present a commentary on Book 10 of the *Alexandreis* of Walter of Châtillon, who wrote in the last decades of the twelfth century in France. Underlying this commentary is a discussion of the inter-relationship of his Latin epic poem with the tradition of epic writing he had inherited from classical antiquity and the biblical epicists of the fifth and sixth centuries. I put forward the hypothesis that instead of being merely a learned epic written in the classical style with some moralising and anachronistic comments added in, Walter's poem reflects a conscious effort to adapt traditional methods of bliblical paraphrase and commentary to a secular rather than biblical text.[1] Walter has versified a history of Alexander the Great, using classical epic hexameter and vocabulary, themes and *topoi,* for the purpose of presenting a comment relevant to his age and times.

To understand the classical background to Walter's epic, his poetry should be seen in the context of the prevailing literary classicism of the twelfth century in France which saw a revival and transformation of classical forms of literary expression.[2] In this classicising tradition the *Alexandreis* exemplifies a number of the characteristics of the particular form classicism took in this period in France. This classicism is defined in terms of what the influence of the classical works on rhetoric was, works such as Cicero's *De inventione,* the *Rhetorica ad Herennium,* and Horace's *Ars poetica,* together with Augustine's *De doctrina christiana.*[3] Although the influence is immeasurable, it is apparent. It is well documented that manuals on the rhetoric of poetry proliferated in the twelfth century, as part of the systematization of writing practice.[4] The *artes dictandi* formalised letter-writing, the *artes poetriae* fulfilled the same function for poetry writing. The exact relation between the theory of literary composition and the practice of it in the twelfth century is difficult to pinpoint. When viewed from a twentieth century perspective there is a wide margin for difference of opinion in fitting the great variety of formal terms from the medieval handbooks to examples in the works of poets. However, in broad outline, concepts like *materia,* something already written and able to be used and reordered by the poet as suitable to his overall intention, are generally agreed upon.[5] The *inventio* involved in discovering the best *materia* is not without its dangers, as Walter remarks in his prefatory comment to the *Alexandreis:*

> siquid in uolumine reprehensibile seu satyra
> dignum inuenerint, considerent arti temporis
> breuitatem qua scripsimus et altitudinem materiae,
> quam nullum ueterum poetarum teste Seruio
> ausus fuit aggredi perscribendam; . . .
>
> (*Prol.*32-36)[6]

That the depth and extent, *altitudinem,* of interpretation necessary in reading his *materia* (and the brief time spent in writing) should result in readers finding the poem reprehensible and of satiric intent is just such a danger. The *materia* had not been re-worked by any ancient poet which would have sanctioned its validity as suitable to the purpose it must serve for Walter.[7] This purpose will become apparent in the discussion below, after the steps to literary composition are discussed. These steps include the disposition of the *materia,* and its embellishment. While scholars generally agree on the broad interpretation of these two concepts, in detailed explication there is argument.[8]

The *materia* used by Walter is the historiography written by Quintus Curtius Rufus, *De rebus gestis Alexandri Magni,* and it is disposed in the order in which the poet finds it. There are a few minor re-arrangements of the order of events and those in Book 10 will be discussed in the Commentary as paradeigmatic for the whole poem. Just as the historiography spans Alexander's career, so does the poem, from his childhood to death. The largest part of the first three books and of Book 10, the last book, of the Curtian text was missing even in the twelfth century (as in the twentieth).[9] This problem was overcome in a way typical of a medieval poet. Walter simply added material from elsewhere to point up his overall intention and to fill in the gaps left by the *lacunae* in his *materia.* The form of the work, epic hexameter in the style of Vergil, is a pointer to the great significance the poet wishes his readers to find in his poem. The epic dignifies the *materia.* The fact that there are ten books of the epic poem no doubt reflects the poet's decision to retain the ordering of the material after Curtius, as well as being a reminder of Lucan's ten books of the *Bellum civile.* But, the acrostic *GUILLERMUS* is also accommodated by 10 books. *Guillermus* refers to Walter's patron.

The actual means by which Walter transforms the prose of his material source, while keeping close to the precepts of the rhetorical practice of the day, as far as we can compare text and theoretical treatise on it, seems to have more in common with the writers of biblical epic than has been commonly supposed or suggested. That his epic has superficial similarities to Joseph of Exeter's *De bello Troiano* is not to be doubted.[10] But whether the themes of the *Alexandreis* are classical to the exclusion of all else is arguable. It seems more likely that although Walter has used a pagan history as his *materia,* and his verse paraphrase adheres to the classical text, yet his explication, comments on and about events, is strictly Christian. In this type of epic then, his work has more in common with Juvencus, Claudius Marius Victorius and Avitus. The poet paraphrases into verse the material which is in prose, and by the processes of abbreviation, omission, literal

paraphrase, modal variation, periphrasis, synonymic amplification and *interpretatio* he emphasises those points he would like his readers to take to heart while enjoying the edifying material presented.[11] The great facility and technical expertise which Walter displays in composing hexameter verse has caused critics perhaps to place undue emphasis on the classical themes he is supposed to treat at the expense of the Christian themes he quite plainly treats. That the form and structure of the poem is classical is not doubted, but the themes which are treated are not only classical but to a very large extent Christian.

The foremost scholar on the **Alexandreis,** Christensen (1905)[12] has noted that large portions of the Curtius text are simply versified without much change in Books 2 to 9 of the **Alexandreis.** The significantly marked changes in the presentation of the text occur in Books 1 and 10. In part this has to do with the absence of Books 1, 2, 3 and parts of 10 of the Curtian text, but it has more to do with the decision of the poet to emphasise themes that seemed important for his audience, particularly that excessive greed ends in a punishment in Hell and that there is little reward on earth that is lasting. Man should remember his Maker and that a proper relationship between creature and Creator is vital for ensuring a chance in the Life Hereafter. Also, the virtues of ancient moral philosophy are inadequate for the demands placed on a ruler in the postlapsarian world. These are the themes which the poet treats in the moralising comments he inserts between episodes in the narration of the events of Alexander's life and death. The poem is dedicated to William of Rheims (William of the White Hands)[13] who is described thus, 1.19-23:

> Quem partu effusum gremio suscepit alendum
> Phylosophia suo totumque Elycona propinans
> Doctrinae sacram patefecit pectoris aulam,
> Excoctumque diu studii fornace, fugata
> Rerum nube, dedit causas penetrare latentes:

> 'Whom Philosophy took onto her lap at your birth to nourish, for whom she opened the sacred chamber of your heart for learning, offering you all Helicon, for whom when you had been baked for a long time in the oven of studies, she dispersed the cloud of ignorance which covers the truth and allowed you to penetrate hidden matters . . .'[14]

The Archbishop William to whom these words are addressed is included in Walter's final admonition addressed to his readers, 10.433-434:

> O felix mortale genus si semper haberet
> Eternum pre mente bonum finemque timeret

> 'O mortal race, happy if it would always bear in mind the eternal good and death . . .'

Part, then, of what William is capable of understanding is the fundamental truth that man in the face of death, physical and spiritual, has to remember God. Poetry, even when it is 'all Helicon' is an allurement, 'modulamina vestra alliciant animas' (10.459-460), 'let the songs of the Muses entice minds', and should be merely the step that precedes the uncovering of the truth. The truth or 'doctrina' which is known to Walter is the promise of eternal life, granted to whose who are in a right relationship with God, referred to variously as the 'alium fontem' (10.459), the 'other fountain', and the cure for the thirst of death, 'sitis est medicina secundae' (10.460). This is what might be hidden from a man who is under a cloud of ignorance.

Allied to the idea of the resurrection and the promise of eternal life made available to man, is the doctrine of Hell which the poet describes at the beginning of Book 10. Then, of particular interest to the learned poets of the twelfth century was the cosmological speculation of the natural philosophers.[15] This is subsumed under the metaphor of the goddess *Natura,* who appears at the beginning of Book 10. Another essential fact relating to history, to which Walter refers for the edification of his readers, is the Antichrist. Alexander is compared with the Antichrist.[16] All these notions are used to expand and amplify the basic story of Alexander's death in Book 10.

Walter was much indebted to the classical writers who had preceded him and provided him with models. In the references to classical and biblical history his poem conforms to the medieval criteria of a classical epic, but the *altitudo* of Walter's poem lies in the weighty matters of Christian doctrine that it presents. To call it a classicising poem only, is to miss his point.

By setting the **Alexandreis** only in the context of classicising epics, critics like Manitius (1931) and Raby (1957)[17] seem to suggest that the poet was successful in creating a good or tolerably good imitation of a classical poem. What results then from such an emphasis is a certain insistence on the poet's reliance on classical forms. There is a consequent minimising of the poem's medieval setting. It must follow that if the poet deviates from strict classical norms of correctness his poem is not successful. Such a view as this does not take into consideration, sufficiently, the thousand year period intervening between Walter's time of writing and that of the so-called classical poets. The interest in the texts of classical antiquity and the re-appearance of certain ancient texts with their subsequent influence on the thinking of the twelfth century in France has led scholars this century into referring to the twelfth century as a Renaissance.[18] But the resurgence of the influence of the classical tradition in literature does not mean that the tradition of biblical epic was eclipsed. I suggest that there is no need to posit Christian and classical as mutually exclusive domains in literature in France in the

twelfth century. The classical forms and themes and all that they encompass in the way of shaping a narrative and managing the reader's response to the material, were pressed into service by a confident body of poets who could compare themselves to the ancients without any anxiety that their motives might be misconstrued as a falling back into paganism.

Medieval writers typically combined original material with that derived from a variety of authoritative sources; this is the contention of the German scholar Lausberg (1973:62).[19] Besides, the poetic genres had been legitimised very early in the middle ages, and through the inclusion by Jerome, of Juvencus' biblical epic, *Evangeliorum Libri IV,* into the canon of Christian literature, the classicising epic became a respectable mode for conveying Christian truths in verse. Biblical material with moralisations written in the style of classical epic was an acceptable tradition, which Walter inherited and turned to his own advantage. What is more unusual is Walter's choice of a secular history rather than a biblical story as the narrative into which he inserts his moral allegory. The significance given to the moral allegory (the *Natura* episode) which dominates Book 10 at the expense of the narrative, is also, in my opinion, original.

The harmonising of Christian and pagan imagery and allusion occurs in poems other than Walter's in the twelfth century, as for instance in the poems of Bernard Silvestris and Alan of Lille.[20] The same is true in the artistic representations in manuscripts and in sculpture, stained glass windows and in carvings. The iconographic schemes bequeathed to the middle ages through classical presentations of mythological subjects were used to treat Christian themes with equal success.[21] In Walter's poem the results achieved through the blending of classical form and language, usage and allusion, with orthodox Christian doctrine is a sought-after effect. Willis (1934:67-68) in assessing the poem in terms of one of its vernacular offshoots says: 'The atmosphere as well as the context of the **Alexandreis** is studiously classical and pagan, although the poem is not devoid of incidental Christian elements.' This remark typifies an attitude to the poem which was current in the earlier part of this century. The poem is naturally 'classical and pagan' in that it treats of a pagan, pre-Christian history, a historiography of a famous figure, Alexander, who was tremendously popular in the medieval world. But to suggest that the Christian elements are 'incidental' is, I feel, to have misunderstood the poem's literary milieu.[22] The poem, after all, is written by a cleric, is dedicated to a bishop, and the Christian allegory of the Vices, the souls of the damned, mention of the Antichrist, and especially Nature, in the prominent place in which they appear, are an integral and essential part of the poem. I believe it is *the essential* part of the poem. The audience to whom the poem was addressed shared the common assumption with Walter that Alexander as a mortal creature was subject to the same God-given laws as they were themselves. That Alexander jeopardised the life of his immortal soul because he sinned through being avaricious is the message of Book 10, perhaps not original from a twentieth century viewpoint, but a commonplace which was thought to express a basic truth in Walter's day. So, in a reading of the poem which emphasises the classical elements at the expense of the cultural milieu in which the poem was written, there is, I consider, the danger of falsely imputing to Walter a paganism by which he is not affected. A certain twentieth century self-consciousness and embarrassment at Walter's world-view shows itself in the critics' implication that the non-classical elements detract from the value of the poem, instead of the more balanced appreciation which I aim to give, which recognises that Walter is a twelfth century cleric first, who is manipulating the classical tradition to subserve a deeply moral Christian purpose.

The moral message is ostensibly directed at William, Archbishop of Rheims, as previously stated, but the poem could also have been written for reading in court circles where criticism of the ruling monarch would be veiled in a suitable moral allegory.[23] If the poem was directed at Frederick Barbarossa as a criticism of expansionist tendencies in Europe at the time, or at Philip Augustus of France, or at another important personage whom Walter does not directly mention, on another level it still has significance as a critique of the greed exhibited by all men.[24] Walter's allegory of the Vices represents human vice in the real world: *Avaritia* and her sisters are the metaphysical counterparts of man's greed and vice, in the same way as Alexander stands for everyman who is mortal and over-reaches himself. In the concluding lines of the epic, Walter reminds readers of the dangers of poetry as a species of worldly vanity: it can turn them away from properly Christian concerns. In the atmosphere of didacticism in which the poem was conceived, the poet warns his audience not to receive the poem as a superficial neo-pagan exercise as it has far deeper meaning (*Prol.* 32-34). By placing the poem firmly in a 'postlapsarian' world Walter clearly states that his poem is to be read as far more than a classicising epic. This is, I consider, contrary to the view expressed by those who like Willis would maintain that the Christian elements in the poem are 'incidental'.

A consideration of the biblical epic tradition which Walter inherited might aid our understanding of what Walter's models in epic were. Biblical epics of the fifth and sixth centuries formed part of the literary tradition inherited by Walter. Modelling their style on that of the classical writers to achieve dignity, the biblical epicists transformed parts of the Old and New Testaments into epic poetry. These biblical epics served as a powerful evangelising force in Western Europe where the Christian religion was being pressed on a pagan community. Juvencus, (early fourth century) the first writer of biblical epic to follow the requirements of classical prosody in imitation of the classical models, was given the stamp of approval by Jerome when his *Evangeliorum Libri IV* was included in the canon of Christian literature. Jerome legitimised Juvencus' work by including him in the *De viris illustribus*. Sedulius' work, the *Carmen paschale,* covers New Testament themes in epic verse and belongs to the early fifth century. In the middle years of the sixth century, Arator's poem on the New Testament appeared as a versification of the Acts of the Apostles. The above three poems all paraphrase parts of the New Testament in classical verse forms. The ancients' theory of paraphrase 'depends for its cogency on the belief that a work of literature contained a basic, underlying sense which should remain intact in any new version, but which might be overlaid with any amount of amplification and stylistic elaboration without altering the essential identity of the work' (Roberts, 1985:82-83). A distinction between grammatical and rhetorical paraphrase needs to be made. The word-for-word grammatical paraphrase is in no sense a literary work, whereas the rhetorical paraphrases of the Old and New Testament have literary intent and merit.

To show this literary intent and merit it is worthwhile to review the poets' own comments on their poems. In the dedicatory letters of the Old Testament poets the motives for writing and their procedures are alluded to. An early fifth century metrical version of the Bible, called by scholars the *Heptateuchos,* although it does not have a prefatory letter, appears to have been directed at a cultivated audience.[25] It preserves the ordering of the historical books of the Old Testament. In the preface to his Old Testament poem, the *Alethia,* Claudius Marius Victorius describes his poem as didactic, for the instruction of the young and as a biblical paraphrase. He refers to the procedures characteristic of paraphrase, namely, abbreviation, omission and transposition.[26] It is also a principle of paraphrase that the sense of the original be maintained, in contrast to a commentary. In the work of Alcimus Ecdicius Avitus (died about 518), *De spiritalis historiae gestis,* five of the six books do not follow the sequence of the chronological biblical narrative he is versifying. Instead the narrative is unified by the theme it treats, that of the Fall and Redemption, Christian salvation.[27] Three ideas predominate in the manipulation of the biblical text by the Old Testament poets and the success of the epic depends on the readers' agreement with the writer on these ideas: that a Vergilian type epic is an excellent means for teaching fundamental truths; that rhetorical paraphrase of the *materia* will ensure this, and that the stylistic freedom of paraphrase used on biblical narrative will point a message with profound implications even when the original order of the text is changed. Or as Roberts (1985:107) says it: 'the irreducible narrative core of the text to be paraphrased must be retained, but the omissions or amplifications, provided they leave this essential substratum untouched, are quite compatible with the requirement of fidelity to the original', and as such are an excellent means for enjoying the allurements of poetry and the edification of Christian theology.

The use of biblical epics at schools in the twelfth century in France is to be expected. Such a valuable tool for teaching fundamental Christian truths is unlikely to have been neglected in the Cathedral cloister schools. As models for the practice of epic-making, the biblical epics must have ranked high and can be accepted as familiar to Walter.[28]

In my commentary on Book 10 I have tried to stress the way in which classical and Christian elements are harmonised in the poem, to indicate where a didactic note is struck, showing how the poet retains an individual response to the material he is treating through the use of the rhetorical means at his disposal. These means include paraphrase, wordplay, figures of speech and thought, biting criticism of the foolishness of men, and a selfconscious delight in the author's own role as a poet. These means are used to manipulate the reader's response to the poem.

My commentary had to be detailed to be of some value, so it had to be limited in scope. Because Books 1 and 10 more than the others contain Walter's original material, which throws into relief the problem of the combination or conflict of Christian and classical material, one of these books was my necessary choice. In Book 10, with its allegory of Nature, the poet seems to me to express most clearly his concept of how the reader should interpret the material. The story with its didactic interpolations presented in Books 1 to 9 is interpreted in the moral allegory in the final book. In my commentary on Book 10 I hope to have shown that the poet has paraphrased his source using the methods familiar to him from biblical epic. He has amplified his basic narrative with twelfth century cosmological speculation in the episode of *Natura* and the excurses on the Vices in Hell and the coming of the Antichrist. This allegorical exegesis of history is, in my opinion, what Walter means when he refers to the *altitudo materiae* in the Prologue (34).

A brief review of critical opinions of the poem will show how important for an understanding of Walter's work a detailed commentary can be, particularly of his major work, the **Alexandreis.** Until the publication of Colker's critical edition of the poem in 1978, all work on it was hampered by the need for a modern critical

edition,[29] although the poem was held in high esteem. As Colker says, 'The renowned twelfth century Latin poet Gualterus de Castellione, or Walter of Châtillon has drawn the attention of such scholars as R. Peiper, B. Hauréau, F. Novati, H. Christensen, K. Strecker, M. Manitius, J. K. Williams, A. Wilmart, F. G. E. Raby, R. de Cesare and F. Châtillon. The poet has received in modern times very high praise.' (Colker, 1978:xi).

However, except for Christensen (1905), who offers a comprehensive overview of the poem in terms of its being a classical epic, none of the scholars mentioned above has given, in my opinion, a convincing interpretation of the poem as a whole, or addressed satisfactorily the questions inherent in the poem for a twentieth century audience. These questions include: some doubt concerning the person to whom the poem is actually addressed, even though it is dedicated to William of the White Hands; why there are so many moralisations within the narrative; to what extent Books 1 and 10 are the author's own invention; what the purpose of the *Natura* episode is in the final book of the poem.

Christensen's (1905) work goes back to the nineteenth century works by Mueldener (1859), Peiper (1869), Ivančić (1878) and Toischer (1880). It is not my intention to review the critics of the nineteenth century, but simply to report that the quality of their observations and work when reinterpreted in Christensen's fundamental study of the **Alexandreis** has not been bettered by twentieth century scholars.[30] But although Christensen provides a detailed study of the sources of the poem, antique and medieval, he does not treat the entire poem as a synthesised whole. Giordano (1917) is perhaps the only critic of the **Alexandreis** who does not go back to Christensen (the exigencies of World War I?). He sets the poem in its literary background, classical and contemporary, showing that common currents of thought in the twelfth century France reappear in poetry of the thirteenth and fourteenth centuries and especially in Dante's *Divine Comedy*. In his overall response to the poem he articulates a view which sets the medieval poem at a disadvantage when compared to Dante's inspired work:

> Sì, classicismo della peggiore forma, e, sotto un certo aspetto, alla stregua di quello, tramandatoci dalle infinite
> logomachie, tra classici e romantici, in tempi a noi più vicini; incetta di parole e di frasi; allitterazione; bisticci; uso ed abuso di mitologia; secentismo, infine.

(165)

Manitius (1931) in his encyclopedic review of medieval literature essentially summarises Christensen's arguments and finds the poem to fit into the classicising epic mould most perfectly. He says:

Und auch die Form ist alles Lobes wert. Wer die von
  Reimen
strotzenden Gedichte der Zeitgenossen auf sein Ohr
  hat wirken
lassen, der findet in diesem Epos einmal einen
  wohltätigen
Ruhepunkt und wird sich vom Zauber klassisch anmu-
  tender
Dichtung gern umspinnen lassen.

(Manitius, 1931:925)

Herkenrath's (1934) treatment of the poem as a whole echoes Christensen's observations, but is too brief to be of much consequence as a serious assessment of the poem's worth and meaning. Willis (1934) is primarily concerned with the Spanish *Libro del Alexandre* and so his focus on the *Alexandreis* is primarily as a source for the Spanish poem. What is valuable about Willis' work is that he points out the areas in which Walter had Christianised his pagan material, thus highlighting what I will call, not Christianisations but moralising comments. Willis is firmly biased towards the idea of a conflict of pagan and Christian ideas, ideals and responses. Hagendahl in his 1958 study of the Latin Fathers made the point quite clearly when he said:

'. . . the poets who had classical poetry for a pattern did not shrink from imitating and applying to Christian matters epithets and invocations belonging to pagan divinities or pictures of situations representing their activity. Thus we have to deal . . . with literary cli-chés, not with the real effect exercised on Christianity by pagan conceptions . . .'

(Hagendahl, 1958:382)

Willis is importing anachronistic difficulties into twelfth century literature.

Raby's (1957) works of reference on secular Latin poetry made the the *Alexandreis* accessible to English readers and they cover the narrative in some detail. He places the poem in a context of other Latin epics in Europe and especially France, and concurs with Chris-tensen's favourable response to the poem, but again, counts it as a classicising epic.[31]

Cary (1956, repr. 1964) in his invaluable treatment of the *Alexandreis* as part of a larger phenomenon, the spread of the Alexander story all over Europe in the middle ages, traces the influence of the poem on the literature of the centuries subsequent to the twelfth. Cary firmly establishes the importance and prestige of the *Alexandreis,* but because of the nature of his study he does not offer any comprehensive evaluation of the poem. Hellegouarc'h's (1967 and 1980) brief reviews of important stylistic points in the poem serve to show that the poem is successful as a poetic work in terms of rhetoric and aesthetics. What is topical is offset by the poet's individual manipulation of the tradition to produce an attractively coherent poetic work.[32]

Other studies of the *Alexandreis* address particular problems, not relating necessarily to an interpretation of the poem. Pfister's (1911) work on *Natura*'s complaint is very useful for a study of Book 10 as he discusses the correspondences between Alan of Lille's work, *De planctu Naturae* and Walter's moral allegory in Book 10 but without integrating the moral allegory into the whole poem. This is one of the few studies which relates the *Alexandreis* to contemporary works in such a specific and detailed fashion. Bacherler (1917) examines Walter's material source, Quintus Curtius Rufus' his-tory of Alexander the Great, in terms of the manuscripts available to writers of the twelfth century. He shows that substantially the same books, and parts of books, 1-3 and 10 are missing from the Curtian history in the twelfth century as today. This observation is important in substantiating Christensen's insight that Walter had used his own invention in Books 1 and 10. That he has amplified his material in these books in accordance with the artistic, aesthetic requirements of the audience to whom he addresses the poem is significant for my interpretation of the poem.

Spanke (1931) and Strecker (1924, 1927, 1930, 1963) are more concerned with Walter's lyrical poetry and in a general sense can be considered useful for an understanding of Walter's poetic method, but their works are not influential in respect of the *Alexandreis*. Colker (1959) has written briefly about the influence of the Prologue of the *Alexandreis*.[33] Pascal's (1964) observations of Walter's lyrical poetry are valuable for pointing out the complexities of interpretation possible for that poetry. The positing of a combination of classi-cal, medieval and topical reference in the lyrical poems, susceptible of complex and highly developed interpreta-tion is an extension of Strecker's poetic collection of Walter's lyrical poetry.[34] Rico (1977)[35] develops this interpretation, as does Taylor (1971). Allied to moral al-legorical interpretations is what Hegener (1971) calls the *zweite Sprache* in religious texts. Hegener's general study serves to remind the twentieth century reader of clerical poetry that events in history are seen by a twelfth century audience as part of God's developing plan for man. Alexander in such a context is a figural representative of the Antichrist. Dronke (1976) and Klopsch (1980), treating medieval poetry in general and fitting the *Alexandreis* into the overall pattern, call at-tention to the larger movements in literature in the twelfth century. Although Klopsch reports that Walter's poem is devoid of a deeper meaning present in Walter's contemporaries' works, the *Cosmographia* and the *Anti-claudianus,* yet he accords the poem a prominence it deserves. In terms of his dismissive approach to Walter's didactic intentions, a commentary on the poem detailing techniques and achievements seems urgent if the epic is to be addressed seriously.

Of the small studies on the *Alexandreis* Harich's (1985/6) treatment of Aristotle's advice in Book 1 is convincing. She suggests that Aristotle's advice is programmatic for the entire narrative. The advice revolves around the question of the relationship between master and servant. Harich says:

> Schon der Fragenkreis *dominus—servus* zeigt die Be-
> deutung
> des Spiegels, vor dem die Helden agieren. Nicht nur
> Alexander
> sondern auch Dareius und Poros werden am Tu-
> gendkatalog
> des Aristoteles gemessen. Dabei liefern Dareius und
> Poros
> die negative Kontrastfolie für Alexanders Handlungen.

But with her attention fixed on the opening book with its programmatic prince's mirror, she has nothing to say about the prologue and its enigmatic suggestions, or the frequent moralisations throughout the poem, or Book 10. She correctly maintains that the contrast between Christian and pagan morality as a central theme in the epic is untenable:

> Dabei ist ein Kontrast zwischen Christen- und Heiden-
> tum
> *in moralibus* nicht Zentralthema dieses *carmen epi-*
> *cum.*

(1985/6:168)

She addresses the questions the poem raises entirely in terms of 'die *Alexandreis* als ein an Antikem orientiertes Epos' (Harich, 1985/6: 168), indicating to some extent how the poem was influenced by the crusading fervour of the time. She criticises Kratz's (1980) ideas about 'mocking epic' as absurd, the result of an inadequate examination of such important excurses as the Daniel prophecy (5.6-10); 6.1-4), the shield of Darius (2.494-539) and the grave monument of Stateira (4.176-274). In this she does not go far enough: she does not raise the question of why Walter has such excurses at all.

An important tool which should facilitate working on the poem was published in 1985, namely *Verskonkordanz zur Alexander von Châtillon,* edited by Stiene and Grub; although it does not address the interpretation of the poem, it assists in facilitating research. In both translations produced to date, Jolly's (1968) and Pritchard's (1986) no interpretation is offered, despite the promise made by notes. Two studies, however, do address the interpretation of the poem, namely that of Kratz in his 1980 book and that of Zwierlein in 1987. Since they both rely extensively on Christensen's (1905) book I shall discuss these three studies together as being most important.

Christensen (1905) sought to set the poem in the context of the contemporary classicising epics of the twelfth

century in showing just how classical the poem was. He did this by providing detailed wordlists drawn from the poem, proving that despite Walter's use of innumerable words foreign to the classical corpus, his poem is classical. Christensen also listed the grammatical constructions common to medieval writers rather than classical poets noting unusual quantities in his versification.[36] An appendix of classical echoes and allusions demonstrated that Walter achieved a classical elegance and atmosphere in his epic. Christensen's assessment went a long way towards improving the ungenerous response of earlier critics to medieval works. Raby (1957:138), writing much later, speaks of certain poems as being 'imitations of classical tales or outworn moralisings'.

Christensen (1905) set in motion the critical approach in respect of the *Alexandreis* which cites the classical echoes and allusions from the best known classical epic poets, and in this way gives evidence of Walter's reliance on his classical models. Colker (1978) extended Christensen's observations by an exhaustive list of classical echoes and borrowings, in the *apparatus fontium* of his critical edition. 'Borrowings' from historians, medieval writers, the Bible and Boethius are also included. Some of these citations go back to Christensen but some are Colker's own observations. Zwierlein (1987) has expanded Christensen's and Colker's basic observations into a more detailed examination of the thematic echoes of classical authors in the *Alexandreis,* backing up his arguments with evidence of verbal echoes. He makes convincing arguments for re-inforcing the idea that Walter's use of the classical authors is extensive, reveals a deep knowledge and love of the material and has been expertly used. But Zwierlein concentrates on the *epic* parts of the poem and has little to say about Book 10's strange *Natura* episode, mentioning it only briefly.[37] Nor does he offer any persuasive reasons for the inclusion of moral allegory and what have been called 'Old Testament and Christian reference and even contemporary allusion to, for example, the murder of Becket or ecclesiastical abuses' (Hood, 1987:127). The authorial comments in the style of Lucan, to which Zwierlein alludes, are not seen in their Christian epic context as part of the exegetical tradition of the biblical epicists. But the value of Zwierlein's study is that it is part of a beginning of a literary analysis of the *Alexandreis* which develops and expands the work started by Christensen and continued by Colker.

That Walter's intention in his poem is to gain fame for himself and his patron is argued by Zwierlein (1987).[38] The poem holds up to that interpretation. As Dronke has reminded us, *Toposforschung* is a most essential study in medieval poetry, but as important is the consideration that 'questions of individuality of expression cannot be divorced from those of the poets' total intention in his poem' (Dronke, 1970:21).[39] So, Walter's poem is more than a poem about epic warfare which is so cleverly written that the poet and his patron will be remembered forever by it. Zwierlein does not address the problem of the moralisations in the poem in terms of their twelfth century context, nor does he examine Books 1 and 10 in any detail, passing them off as merely a species of contemporary and Christian allusion. Christensen had already shown convincingly in 1905 that the poem revealed an unmechanical classicising. So what is Zwierlein proving? How far and how completely Walter had assimilated his classical literature? But what about his medieval context? As Wisbey (1966:19) says in his study of Rudolf von Ems' Alexander:

> Mittelalterlichem Geschichtsdenken liegen vorwiegend drei heilsgeschichtliche Einteilungsschemata zugrunde: Das Schema der vier Weltreiche, das sowohl der jüdischen Exegese wie auch dem griechischen und römischen Altertum geläufig war, erlangte seine für das Mittelalter massgebende Bedeutung durch den im frühen 12. Jh. in die *Glossa Ordinaria* aufgenommenen Danielkommentar des Hieronymus. Das zweite Schema der sechs Weltzeitalter, entsprechend den sechs Tagen des Schöpfungswerks, liegt schon bei Irenäus voll ausgebildet vor und wird von Augustin dem Mittelalter zugeleitet. Gleichfalls ist es Augustin, der die Dreiteilung des dritten Schemas weitergibt: vor dem Gesetz, unter dem Gesetz, unter der Gnade. Im 12. Jh. ist diese Einteilung bereits allgemein bekannt.

In looking at the history of Alexander the Great, his story cannot be treated simply as a literary exercise; it also purports to be part of history as the frequent historical excurses in the *Alexandreis* show. Then, to treat the poem as a classicising exercise without reference to the medieval concepts of where the particular history fits into the medieval scheme of history is, I believe, a falsification of the poet's intention. The poem as history has to be understood in the broader context of history as the explication of God's plan for man.[40] The moral allegory of Book 10 with its reference to the Antichrist is a pointer to Walter's view of what the history of Alexander means. It is an essential point to consider when speaking about the poem.

Kratz (1980), following the lead given by Christensen (1905) in juxtaposing Christian and pagan ideals of language usage and outlook, suggests that the poet faced a problem in the poem which, I suggest, had been solved centuries before. He says:

> The attempts of medieval poets to use classical literary genres for the expression of Christian values often reveal an ambivalent attitude toward pagan culture. Those authors in particular, who composed epic poems in Latin modelled on the *Aeneid* and its successors were compelled to face the inherent conflict between the traditional concept of the epic hero and the standards of Christian ethics. In grappling with this

problem many tried to forge a new definition of heroic virtue and managed, with varying degrees of success, to reconcile classical and Christian elements within the portrait of a single protagonist. In two works, however, the *Waltharius* and *Alexandreis*, a radically different approach is taken to resolve the problem of transforming the epic into a Christian genre.

(1980: 1-2)

In my opinion, Walter nowhere reveals an 'ambivalent' attitude towards pagan culture' either by an ironic tone or by other means. Pagan concepts of heroic virtue in conflict with Christian concepts is not the central problem of the **Alexandreis.**

But, that Walter expresses through the means of the poem the values associated with Christian ethical standards of correct behaviour in an epic hero cannot be disputed. However, I contend that he does not do it by adopting an ironic stance vis-a-vis his hero and by praising him, blame him (Kratz, 1980:2).[41] Rather, the biblical epics of the fifth and sixth centuries had shown how a poet points out the underlying meaning of historical material: by moralisations and moral allegory. The glory Alexander seeks is a 'phantom' and a species of 'sinful greediness' as Kratz asserts (1980:162), but Walter is at pains to say this plainly, in moralisations at the conclusion of the narrative sections, not by ironic implication. There are certain dramatic ironies in the poem, exploited for effect, as when in Book 1 Alexander states that he needs no other area than Asia to satisfy his desires, but in Book 10 the poet comments that he has to be content with only a five foot tomb after his death.[42] But I do not consider that the overall tone of the poem is mocking and ironic. I believe the idea that Walter is being ironic goes back to Giordano's perception of something grotesque in the poem: 'C' è del grottesco . . . una certa scarsezza di gusto e discernimento . . .' (Giordano, 1917:147). Altogether, Kratz's hypothesis that by references to the *Bellum Civile* of Lucan, in which Caesar's glory is shown as worthless, and a constant interplay of allusions to Boethius' *De consolatione Philosophiae*, the poet achieves an ironic tone, seems to me to be an over-complicated twentieth century assessment of Walter's techniques of writing. When Walter modifies his sources, says Kratz, or 'inserts new material . . . the result almost invariably is an increased emphasis concerning *Fortuna*—whether it is her role in human events as Alexander and the other characters interpret them or Walter's attack on the foolishness of that view. In sum, while the narrative focus may shift from Alexander to other characters, *Fortuna* herself constantly occupies centre stage.' (Kratz, 1980:140). It is in what *Fortuna* stands for in medieval terms that Kratz is less clear. It may or may not be true that *Fortuna* occupies a central place in the poem, but it is true that unless we interpret *Fortuna* in the terms her twelfth century audience did, we come no nearer to an appreciation of the poem than if we say it is a classicising epic without further qualifications. This is a question which Kratz does not address.

To sum up, Christensen examines the disparate parts of the poem, showing the literary sources, both classical and medieval. In placing them side by side, he ignores the synthesis of all the material into a cohesive whole and has only this to say about the poet's reasons for writing, that he wished to make Alexander a central figure in the poem at the expense of all other figures in the history. In the examination of sources the stress placed on finding exact echoes and parallels must highlight the technical aspects of the poet's *poesis,* so that his creative effort evidenced in the poem as a whole is overshadowed. Even in the most recent study of the poem (Zwierlein 1987), the suggestion is made that Walter has used an ironic tone.[43] This is an importation of late nineteenth century ideas into a work which requires different criteria of judgement. Kratz (1980) ignores the strong didactic impact of the poem on the audience for whom it was meant by imputing to Walter a degree of playfulness which is not evident in the epic poem, in my opinion, however much it is apparent in Walter's lyric poetry. I find no hint of playful irony in Walter's condemnation of the follies of kings (Book 2) or in the depiction of the punishment of Vice in Hell, or the threat of the Antichrist. These didactic and moralising comments cast their shadow over the narrative: the poet demands that the poem be interpreted in their light.

To redress the balance in criticism accorded the poem to date, it is important to look at Walter's technique of paraphrase as well as his classicising inheritance and, out of a synthesis of these notions, there is a chance that something like the poet's intended meaning for his audience might appear. Such an exercise is possible through a detailed analysis of the poem.

In my commentary I aim to show i.a. that the classical hexameter is the vehicle Walter has used to express his Christian message; that Walter has adapted the method of paraphrasing together with the technique of inserting moralisations after narrative material used by the biblical epicists, although their material is of biblical not secular origin. The extent of moralisation used by Walter in Book 10, I suggest, goes far beyond the occasional remarks of previous criticism, and it is the importance of this that I hope to have shown in the body of my work: the moralising is of primary importance and not incidental.

Notes

1. I have understood 'style' to refer to the ordering and selection of language; as Martin (1982:563) puts it, 'The classicising features [of twelfth century Latin style] range from stylistically significant use of a single word, to larger effects of structure and pervasive verbal reminiscence, to (rarely) a multifaceted imitation'. See especially Ax (1976) who examines the problem of classical style in a detailed discussion of modern critics of style in Latin verse.

2. Numerous styles of writing, other than classical, also of course flourished in Europe. A succinct review of these styles has most recently been provided by Martin (1982:563-565); see especially her bibliographical note, pp. 566-568. Klopsch (1980) provides a longer and more comprehensive review.

3. For a convenient summary of the influence of classical poetics on the middle ages see Klopsch (1980:40-47). Aristotle's poetics only becomes available in the thirteenth century, too late to be influential for Walter. But, Horace's *Ars poetica,* referred to as *Poetria vetus* was most influential, both directly from the ninth century and indirectly through the commentary of Porphyrius in the third century, and other scholarly commentaries from that time onwards (see especially Klopsch 1980:42-43). Minor influences, namely Quintilian's *Institutio oratoria,* Diomedes' *Ars grammatica* and Isidore of Seville's chapter on poetry in his *Origines* were not systematically integrated into medieval poetic handbooks, but had a less easily traced history. As Klopsch (1980:47) says, 'Bis zum 12. Jh. wird das poetologische Gut der Antike nicht geordnet und systematisch dargestellt, sondern sporadisch und okkasionell verwendet. Die grösste Anhäufung poetologischer Trümmer und Spolien bietet der Accessus zur Ecloga Theoduli Bernhards von Utrecht'.

The complex development of poetics in the twelfth century, which included the questions of where poetry stood in relation to science, logic and philosophy, was summed up in Bernard Silvestris' *Aeneid* commentary which allowed Poetry a separate existence from Grammar and Rhetoric (Klopsch 1980:69-70). Gradually poetry came to have more dignity than prose, and was seen as a metaphor for the ordering faculty of the Creator. The close relationship between philosophy and poetry developed. Klopsch (p. 88) remarks, 'Während als Bezeichnungen für den Dichter in *poeta* und *vates* zwei Wörter zur Verfügung standen . . .'. Poetry became a means of gaining fame (of a personal kind), social status and an opportunity to outdo the ancient writers: the enormous confidence that twelfth century poets had in themselves was expressed through their vision of what poetry meant. Walter exemplifies this confidence.

4. For a convenient collection of the most important texts relating to the systematisation of poetic practice in the twelfth century, see Faral's *Les arts poétiques du XIIᵉ et du XIIIᵉ siècle,* Paris 1958. There is also the article by Sedgewick, *Notes and emendations on Faral's Les arts poétiques du XIIᵉ et du XIIIᵉ siècle,* in *Speculum* 2, 1927, 331-343, and his other article entitled *The style and vocabulary of the latin arts of poetry in the 12th and 13th centuries* in *Speculum* 3, 1928, 349-381.

5. Walter's *materia* would be labelled *illibata,* or 'nicht poetisch bearbeiteten Stoff' (Klopsch 1980:94) by Matthew of Vendôme (*Ars vers.* 4.3).

6. *Alexandreis, Prol.* 32-36: 'if anyone should find something reprehensible or worth satirising in this book, they should take into account the short time in which we wrote it and the depth of the material, which, worth writing in full, none of the ancient poets (according to the evidence of Servius) cared to attempt . . .' (Own translation.)

7. Walter adopts the traditional pose of humility in order to press home the value of his poem, purposely suggesting that as a twelfth century poet he would be able to invest his material with a significance available only to an initiated audience. He sees himself as a 'poeta doctus' (Knapp 1975:10).

8. 'The foundation for most scholarship and criticism touching on rhetoric in medieval French literature has been the work of E. Faral and E. R. Curtius' says Kelly (1978:231). See Faral (1958) and Curtius (1953). Kelly's assessment of their work is useful, (pp. 231-233). See also Knapp (1975:1-38) for a learned review of the most important work on medieval philology and rhetoric to 1975.

9. For the condition of the text, see Bacherler (1917) whose study covers Curtius in Walter in all ten books.

10. Both Walter and Joseph display an admirably pure classical style. See Martin 1982:565.

11. See Roberts (1985) for a recent study of biblical epic, especially pp. 61-74, in which he reviews the Christian reception of the paraphrase and appends a useful survey of the most important works on biblical epic from Joseph Golega's *Studien über die Evangeliendichtung des Nonnos von Panopolis: ein Beitrag zur Geschichte der Bibeldichtung im Altertum,* Breslau 1930, to Dieter Kartschoke's fundamental and learned work, *Bibeldichtung: Studien zur Geschichte der epischen Bibelparaphrase von Juvencus bis Otfrid von Weissenburg,* Munich 1975.

12. Medieval philology became a recognised discipline with the institution of 'die ersten Lehrstühle 1895 in Göttingen', (Langosch, 1975:13). Then followed chairs in Munich 1902 and Berlin 1904. Christensen belongs to these early, fundamental years of medieval scholarship at the close of the nineteenth century and the beginning of the twentieth century when German scholars moved into areas of study other than Classics, Germanistics, Romance and English Studies. Langosch (pp. 14-15) gives a succinct survey of primarily German philologists and philological studies from Strecker's *Einführung in das Mittellatein,* 1928, to important publications in the 1950's and 1960's, e.g. Southern's *The making of the middle ages,* 1953, and Lehmann's *Erforschung des Mittelalters* (Ausgew. Abhandlungen und Aufsätze 1/5, 1959/62 in I, 'Aufgaben und Anregungen der latein. Philologie des Mittelalters', 'Vom Leben des Lateinischen im Mittelalter', in III, 'Die Vielgestalt des 12. Jahrhunderdts').

For a survey of scholarship on the twelfth century, see Young (1977) especially his brief introduction pp. 1-5.

13. See Zwierlein (1987:5) for an accessible and neat tabulation of William's relationship to Philip Augustus, his nephew, through his mother Adelaide.

14. Trans. Jolly 1968:36.

15. Of recent studies on the cosmological epics, Chenu's important and illuminating work *La théologie au douzième siècle,* Paris 1957, is fundamental. Parts of it are translated by Taylor and Little in 1968 (see Chenu, 1968). For a comprehensive introduction to twelfth century Platonism and the pursuit of wisdom see Wetherbee (1972:3-73), who reviews the most essential works. Stock's (1972) study of Bernard Silvestris is important as is Dronke's (1978) edition because they make detailed studies of sources as well as providing excellent notes with their translations of Bernard's work. Gregory's (1955) study of William of Conches has served as an impetus to more studies on William, see Maurach (1980), and the forthcoming work of Ronca on William of Conches' *Dragmaticon* (in the press). See Flatten (1931) on the concept of *hyle,* and Economou (1972) on *Natura*'s meaning from antiquity to the high middle ages.

16. Alexander is referred to as the ram which will break the two kingdoms with its horns (6.3-4), the 'lues mundi' (6.1) after St Jerome's interpretation of Books 7, 8 and 11 of Daniel (*Commentarius in Danielem*, PL 25, 529-558), cited in Kloos (1983: 407 n.47). As Kloos, (p. 407) goes on to say, 'Neben diese im Sinne des Mittelalters geschichtliche Interpretation trat die allegorische Ausdeutung der Angaben im ersten Buch der Makkabäer. Hier ist Alexander als Vorgänger des Antiochus erwähnt, der schon früh als 'typus antichristi' gedeutet wurde. Von dieser Sicht her war es nur ein Schritt, Alexander als Teufel zu interpretieren, denn der Antichrist sollte ja vom Teufel gezeugt werden; dieser Schritt wurde offenbar erstmals von Hugo von St. Viktor im 12. Jahrhundert getan und machte rasch Schule, so etwa bei Gottfried von Admont und Rupert von Deutz. Bei Aegidius Diaconus schliesslich ist Alexander selbst zum Typus Antichristi geworden, doch scheint diese letzte Ausdeutung keine weitere Verbreitung gefunden zu haben.' It is interesting that Walter should amplify Alexander's last speech with material from Hildebert's versified *De Machabaeis* (PL 171, 1293) at 10.400-417, and that Satan should speak of Alexander as 'typus Antichristi' (10.131-133).

The secondary literature on twelfth and thirteenth century views of the Antichrist is extensive. But for a medieval statement about what and who the Antichrist was, see Adso of Montier's letter to Queen Gerberga, *De ortu et tempore Antichristi* (in Sackur 1898:104-113), written in the late eleventh century. In the early twelfth century Hugo of St Victor, (*Allegoriae in Vetus Testamentum* 11, in PL 175, 749 ff.) developed some of Adso's ideas, as did Godfrey of Admont (*Homilia in Maccabaeos* in PL 174, 1130 ff.) and Rupert of Deutz (*De victoria verbi Dei*, PL 169, 1397-1410). The late twelfth century work of Joachim of Fiore on the Antichrist has been studied in some depth by Reeves particularly. See, for example, Reeves 1969, and Williams 1980.

McGinn (1980:83-85) suggests that the *reason* for interest in the coming of the Antichrist was the result of a society which needed to come to terms with extremely violent and unstable conditions. The Antichrist 'would advance his cause under the banner of seeming goodness, even to the point of performing signs and wonders. To be forewarned was to be forearmed'. See Murray (1978) on the society in which the *Alexandreis* was written.

If Walter is writing to criticize the ruling party or for the reason of advancing the political ideology

of some party within the court (see 5.510-520) his exposé of Alexander is extremely critical. Political comment derived from the examination of historical *exempla* in John of Salisbury's *Policraticus* serves to alert readers to the mistakes leaders should avoid (see *Policraticus*, Prol.1, p.12.1, Webb's edition, quoted in Peter von Moos', *The use of 'exempla' in the 'Policraticus'* in *The world of John of Salisbury* ed. M. Wilks, Oxford 1984, 216). Alan of Lille longed for a 'novus homo', since although the final age in which the twelfth century writers found themselves to be 'also implied the discarding of all outward authority, both the Church and the State, . . . even the renewed world . . . [would] still need a ruler—blessed and idealistic, but a ruler nonetheless' (Dronke, 1986:10).

17. Manitius has been most important in medieval studies in collecting and elucidating the details of classical borrowings. His monumental work, *Geschichte der lateinischen Literatur des Mittelalters*, Munich 1911-1931 is fundamental for any study of a medieval poem, but as Dronke says, 'the evaluation of this evidence, the detailed literary study of the classical elements in medieval Latin verse, distinguishing their various functions, and assessing for each poet what the classical elements contribute to his poetic intentions, to his artistry, to the fabric of his verse' is the next stage necessary. (Quoted from Bolgar, 1969:159-164.)

Raby on the non-classical elements as detracting from the poem's success, says, 'where he followed his own inventions, as in the descriptions of the grave memorials, he was less successful than when he modelled himself on Vergil. But he deserves praise for providing a lively and progressive narrative, not too encumbered by rhetoric' (1957, vol.2, p.79). Raby usefully sets Walter's poem in the context of other epic and historical poems (pp. 69-83. For Walter, see pp. 72-79).

18. Wetherbee (1972: 13.n.4) remarks, 'Another application of Burckhardt's famous definition of the Renaissance to the twelfth century is the conclusion to Etienne Gilson's *Heloise and Abelard*, trans. L. K. Shook, Ann Arbor 1960: 124-144'. Haskins' (1927 repr. 1966) dramatic statement about the twelfth century has become something of a critical commonplace. The most useful recent collection of essays on ideas of renaissance and renewal in the twelfth century is Benson's (1982) book. His contributors seek to define the characteristics of the renaissance, discuss the problem of classicism, the sources of the renaissance, religious

elements within it, its social, economic and institutional setting and its chronological and regional framework, (p. xx).

19. Lausberg's learned reference work is one of the most comprehensive and useful examinations of medieval rhetoric.

20. This can also be seen in the 'Chartrian' (Christian) Platonism' in the natural philosophy of writers such as Thierry of Chartres and William of Conches.

21. See Hecksher (1937:8, quoted in Young, 1977:59): 'A clear-cut idea of Antiquity as a historical period of the past did not exist in the middle ages. Medieval thinkers were convinced that they themselves were still citizens of the emprie which had been founded by Augustus'. Hecksher also adduces evidence to prove this notion, as for instance in the ideas of historians about the 'principium unitatis': antiquity and medieval times were continuous in the age which had begun with Caesar Augustus and would end with the coming of the Antichrist, (St Jerome's 'Fourth Monarch') (Young 1977:59-60). The transformation and careful preservation of antiques and relics in the middle ages exemplifies this thinking. Hecksher (Young 1977:66-67) continues: 'often a simple inscription or a mere association sufficed to transform a whole pagan scene into a biblical event. An antique intaglio of Athena and Poseidon, with a tree standing between them, was interpreted, according to the inscription, as a representation of Adam and Eve. (The biblical words narrating the Fall of Man were added to the figures.)' Such examples can be multipied.

22. In Pritchard's recent translation of the poem he makes no attempt in his introduction to fit it into any sort of literary milieu, but he says, substantially repeating Raby's outlook, 'Walter's presentation of Alexander's death is imaginative with several original touches, even if there are distinct echoes of earlier Latin poets.' (Pritchard 1986:16).

23. See n. 12.

24. For a history of the time, I consulted J. B. Bell's *The medieval French monarchy,* Illinois, 1975, pp. 64-70; Z. N. Brooke's, *A history of Europe 911-1198,* London 1938 repr. 1969, pp. 458-478 on 'France and England in the second half of the twelfth century'. On Philip, see Brooke 1969:468-471. I also used Ch. Petit-Dutaillis, *The feudal monarchy in France and England from the tenth to the thirteenth century,* trans. B. A.Hunt, London 1936 repr. 1966, chapter 4, pp.76-96.

Yunck (1963) has made an interesting study of avarice in relation to English literature. More use-

ful for a study of the *Alexandreis* is Murray's chapter on avarice (1978:59-80), seen as the besetting sin of twelfth century society thanks to the gradual development of a money economy.

25. See Roberts 1985: 92-96 for a detailed discussion.

26. See Roberts 1985:98.

27. See Peiper's 1961 edition of Avitus' *Opera.*

28. Occasional echoes of material from the biblical epicists appears in Book 10 of the *Alexandreis,* but it is primarily in the style of paraphrase that their influence can be discerned in the epic. It remains for other readers of the *Alexandreis* to pursue closely the exact relationship between Walter's possible school texts and his paraphrastic technique.

29. Langosch (1975:86-89) summed up the state of affairs thus: 'Die Epik ist mit Ausgaben schlecht bestellt, was wohl mit am Umfang der Texte und Uberlieferung liegt; das ist bedauerlich, weil hier an künstlerisch hervorstechenden Leistungen, kein Mangel ist. Fur die 'Alexandreis' des Walter von Châtillon sind wir noch immer auf die zu den rarissima zählende, völlig unzulängliche Ausgabe von F. A. W. Mueldener 1863 angewiesen. . . .'

30. Christensen's notes bear out his dependence on earlier critics. I have not consulted J. Ivančić's, *Wie hat Walther von Castiglione Vergil nachgeahmt?* Mitterburg, 1878, or W. Toischer's *Uber die Alexandreis Ulrichs von Aschenbach,* Vienna, 1880.

31. See n. 17.

32. The emphasis in his criticism remains firmly on the *classical* aspects of the poem. So, for example, he reviews the conventional epic episodes in the poem, (Hellegouarc'h 1967:108) and notes that the form is 'très proche de Virgile' (Hellegouarc'h 1967:109). All he has to say about the moralisations in the poem is, 'il faut signaler le mélange aux éléments paiens de notations chrétiennes' (p. 109) and, 'Il faut signaler d'autre part que, suivant les exigences éthiques et esthétiques du temps, Gautier de Châtillon voit dans son poème un moyen d'exposer ses doctrines et de faire oeuvre d'apologie chrétienne; il veut *restaurare omnia in Christo,* il reprend les événements d'un point de vue moralisateur, clérical et religieux: ainsi, lorsqu'il trace un portrait conventionel d'Aristote (1.59-71) auquel il donne la figure d'un philosophe scolastique dans l'exhortation qu'il lui fait adresser à Alexandre (1.82-183). Il a voulu, en brodant sur le thème d'Alexandre, travailler à l'édification des consciences chrétiennes du XIIe siècle.

Malgré tous ces éléments, si défavorables finalement à la valeur esthétique du poème, il y a assez souvent dans l'*Alexandréide* des morceaux de vraie poésie.'

33. Colker (1970: 89-95) records Rigord of St Denis' 'capacious borrowing' from Walter. If this is true that Rigord's prologue imitates Walter's then the date for the completion of the *Alexandreis* seems to lie before 1189, and to be more likely in 1182 (see Colker 1978:92).

34. The dates of Strecker's editions are 1925 (*Die Lieder . . .*) and 1929 (*Moralisch-satirische. . .*); the date for his seminal article on the 1925 edition is the year before, 1924. His work on Walter and his school of poetry was published in 1927.

35. Rico's work is brief but useful and one of the rare works in English on Walter's lyrics.

36. See Christensen 1905: 14 ff.

37. See Zwierlein's (1987:65) discussion of Walter's imitation of the conventional epic divine machinery for his assessment of the function of *Nature* i.a. in the epic: 'Seit Homer ist es ein Kennzeichen des antiken Epos, dass das menschliche Handeln vom tätigen Eingreifen der Götter begleitet oder gar bestimmt wird', of *Proditio*. There is no attempt made by the critic to link Walter's allegory to cosmological investigation of the day.

38. See Zwierlein 1987:82-86. See also Lida da Malkiel's (1955) study of *glory* in twelfth century literature. I do not think, however, that Walter's reason for writing the poem is only to gain everlasting fame for Alexander, Darius, Archbishop William and himself (Zwierlein 1987:86).

39. The idea of poetry as a means of penetrating arcane matters of philosophy is enunciated by John of Salisbury: 'sc. ['Aeneid'] liber, in quo totius philosophiae rimatur archana.' (*Policrat.* 2.15, cited in Klopsch 1980:98).

40. See Sanford's (1944) useful survey of the medieval view of history, also Ray (1974) and Claasen (1982). I disagree with Claasen (p.387) when he says that 'in the twelfth century, the relationship to early Christian historiography lives on, while the classical authors—as in earlier periods—prove to be little more than stylistic models'. Rather the emphasis of the function of history changes in the middle ages to include an interpretation in line with fundamental Christian religious tenets. Claasen proposes that the best type of historical writing 'has always arisen from the experience of specific events' (p.387). In this statement there is much truth, but whether the classical authors were nothing more than stylistic models, seems to me arguable. I suggest that in deploying traditional literary means, the historiographer sought, i) to give weight to his history because by these traditional means he reinforced the idea of *auctoritas* which is so essential in medieval literature, and, ii) the very way in which historical authors may have perceived reality is inseparable from their rhetorical ability to represent it. On this see *Topos und Gedankengefüge bei Einhard* in H. Beumann, *Ideengeschichtliche Studien zu Einhard und anderen Geschichtschreibern des früheren Mittelalters,* Darmstadt 1962:1-14. Also see D. J. Wilcox, 1969, *The development of Florentine Humanist Historiography in the fifteenth century,* Cambridge.

41. When Walter does criticize Alexander he does so roundly in plain terms. See 10.433 ff.

42. See 10.448-450.

43. See Zwierlein 1987:35.

Bibliography

1. PRIMARY SOURCES

Alan of Lille. *Anticlaudianus,* ed. R. Bossuat. Paris 1955.

———. *Anticlaudianus or the good and perfect man,* trans. & comm. J. J. Sheridan. Toronto 1973.

———. *De planctu Naturae,* ed. N. M. Häring. Spoleto 1978. (Studi medievali, vol.19).

———. *The plaint of Nature,* trans. & comm. J. J. Sheridan. Toronto 1980.

Augustine, St. *De doctrina Christiana.* PL 34. 15ff.

———. *De civitate Dei libri XXII,* ed. E. Hoffman. 2 vols. 1898-1900. (CSEL vol. 40).

Bernard Silvestris. *Commentum super sex libros Eneidos Virgilii,* ed. W. Riedel. Greifswald 1924.

———. *De mundi universitate libri duo sive megacosmus et microcosmus (Cosmographia),* edd. C. S. Barach & J. Wrobel. Innsbruck 1876 repr. 1964.

———. *The Cosmographia of Bernardus Silvestris,* trans. W. Wetherbee. New York 1973.

———. *The commentary on the first six books of the 'Aeneid' of Vergil commonly attributed to Bernardus Silvestris,* edd. J. W. Jones & E. F. Jones. London 1977.

———. *Cosmographia,* ed. P. Dronke. Leiden 1978.

———. *Commentary on the first six books of Vergil's 'Aeneid',* trans. E. G. Shreiber & T. E. Maresca. Lincoln 1979.

Cicero. *De Inventione,* trans. H. M. Hubbell. London 1949. (Loeb Classical Library.)

Claudius Marius Victorius. *Alethia,* ed. P. F. Hovingh. Turnhout 1960. (CCL 128, 115-193.)

Curtius, Rufus Quintus. *De rebus gestis Alexandri Magni,* trans. J. C. Rolfe. 2 vols. London 1956. (Loeb Classical Library.)

————. *A commentary on Quintus Curtius Rufus Historiae Alexandri Magni, Books 3 and 4,* ed. J. E. Atkinson. Amsterdam 1980.

Dante. *La Commedia secondo l'antica vulgata,* ed. G. Petrocchi. 4 vols. Milan 1967.

————. *Opere minori* II, ed. P. Mengaldo et al. Milan-Naples 1979.

Horace. *Epistulae,* trans. H. R. Fairclough. London 1942. (Loeb Classical Library.)

————. *Sämtliche Werke,* edd H. Färber & W. Schöne. Munich 1960.

Joseph of Exeter. *The Iliad of Dares Phrygius,* trans. G. Roberts. Cape Town 1970.

Walter of Châtillon. *Alexandreis.* PL 209, 459-568.

————. *Moralium dogma philosophorum.* PL 171, 1007ff.

————. *Tractatus sive Dialogus contra Iudaeos.* PL 209, 423-458.

————. *Die Zehn Gedichte des Walther von Lille gennant von Châtillon,* ed. W. Mueldener. Hanover 1859.

————. *Alexandreis,* ed. F. A. W. Mueldener. Leipzig 1863.

————. *Die Lieder Walters von Châtillon in der Hs. 351 von St. Omer,* ed. K. Strecker. Berlin 1925.

————. *Moralisch-satirische Gedichte Walters von Châtillon aus deutschen, englischen, französischen und italienischen Handschriften,* ed. K. Strecker. Heidelberg 1929.

————. Poèmes de Gautier de Châtillon dans un manuscrit de Charleville, ed. A. Walmart. *Revue bénédictine* vol. 49, 1937, 121-169; 322-368.

————. *The 'Alexandreid' of Walter of Châtillon. A translation and commentary,* trans. W. T. Jolly. Tulane 1968. (Diss.)

————. *Alexandreis,* ed. M. L. Colker. Padua 1978. (Thesaurus Mundi. Bibliotheca Scriptorum Latinorum Mediae et recentioris aetatis.)

————. *Verskondordanz zur Alexandreis des Walter von Châtillon,* edd. H. E. Stiene & Grub. Hildesheim 1985. (Alpha- B.3.)

————. *Walter of Châtillon. The Alexandreis,* trans. R. T. Pritchard. Toronto 1986. (Medieval Sources in translation.)

2. Secondary Literature

Ax, W. 1976. *Probleme des Sprachstils als Gegenstand der lateinischen Philologie.* New York.

Bacherler, M. 1917. Gualterus' Alexandreis in ihrem Verhaltnis zum Curtiustext. *Berliner Philologische Wochenschrift,* vol. 37, 663-672; 698-704; 730-736; 761-766.

Benson, R. L. Constable. G. & Lanham, C. D. edd. 1982. *Renaissance and renewal in the twelfth century.* Oxford.

Bolgar, R. R. 1969. *Classical influences on European culture AD 500-1500;* Proceedings of an intrnational conference held at King's College, Cambridge.

Brooke, C. 1969. *The twelfth century Renaissance.* London.

Cary, G. 1964. *The medieval Alexander,* ed. D. J. A. Ross. Cambridge 1956 repr. 1964.

de Cesare, R. 1951. *Glosse latine e antico-francesi all' 'Alexandreis' di Gautier de Châtillon.* Milan. (Publicazioni dell' Università Cattolica del S. Cuore, NS 39.)

Chatillon, F. 1952. Raffaele de Cesare: Glosse latine e antico-francesi all' 'Alexandreis' di Gautier de Châtillon. *Revue du moyen âge latin,* vol. 8, 65-74.

————. 1952. 'Flagello sepe castigatus vitam terminavit': Contribution á l'étude des mauvais traitements infligés à Gautier de Châtillon. *Revue du moyen âge latin,* vol. 8, 151-174.

Chenu, M. D. 1958. *Nature, man and society in the twelfth century, essays on new theological perspectives in the Latin west,* trans. J. Taylor & L. K. Little. seleted chapters from *La théologie au douzieme siecle.* Chicago.

Christensen, H. 1883. *Beiträge zur Alexandersage.* Hamburg.

Christensen, H. 1905. *Das Alexanderlied Walters von Chatillon.* Halle.

————. 1909. Ein Alexanderepos aus der Zeit Barbarossas und sein Verfasser. *Preussische Jahrbücher,* vol. 137, 280-304.

Claason, P. 1902. *'Res gestee', universal history, apocalypse visions of past and future* in *Renaissance and renewal in the twelfth century,* edd. R. L. Benson, G. Constable & C. D. Lanham. Oxford. 387-417.

Colker, M. L. 1959. A note on the history of the commentary on the 'Alexandreis'. *Medium Aevum,* vol. 28, 97-98.

————. 1962. De nobilitate animi. *Medieval Studies,* vol. 23, 47-79.

————. 1970. Walter of Châtillon, Rigord of St. Denis, and an alleged quotation from Juvenal. *Classical Folia,* vol. 24, 1, 89-95.

Dronke, P. 1968. *Medieval latin and the rise of the European love lyric.* 2 vols. Oxford.

————. 1969. *The medieval lyric.* New York.

————. 1970. *Poetic individuality in the middle ages. New departures in poetry 1000-1500.* Oxford.

————. 1976. Peter of Blois and poetry at the court of Henry II. *Medieval studies,* vol. 38, 185-235.

————. 1986. *Dante and medieval latin traditions.* Cambridge.

Economou, G. D. 1972. *The goddess natural in medieval literature.* Cambridge Mass.

Faral, E. 1958. *Les arts poétiques du XIIe-et du XIIIe siecles.* Paris. (Bibliotheque de l'Ecole des Hautes Etudes fasc. 238.)

Flatten, H. 1931. Die 'materia primordialis' in der Schule von Chartres. *Archiv fur Geschichte der Philosophie,* vol. 40, 58-65.

Giordano, C. 1917. *Alexandreis: Poema di Gautier da Châtillon,* Naples.

Gregory, T. 1955. *Anima mundi. La filosofia di Guglielmo di Conches e la scuola di Chartres.* Florence.

Hagendahl, H. 1958. *Latin fathers and the classics. A study on the apologists Jerome and other Christian writers.* Goteborg. (Studia Graeca ex Latina Gothoburgensia G.)

Harich, H. 1985-1986. 'Parce humili, facilis oranti, frange superbum.' Aristoteles in der 'Alexandreis' Walters von Châtillon. *Grazer Beiträge,* vols. 12-13, 147-169.

Haskins, C. H. 1966. *The Renaissance of the twelfth century.* 11 ed. Cambridge 1927 repr. New York 1966.

Hauréau, B. 1858. Notice sur un manuscrit de la reine Christine à la Bibliothèque du Vatican. *Notices et extraits des manuscrits de la Bibliothèque Nationale,* vol. 29.2, 295-298.

Hecksher, W. S. 1937-1938. Relics of pagan antiquity in medieval settings. *Journal of the Warburg Institute,* vol. 1, 204-220.

Hegener, E. 1971. *Studien zur 'zweiten Sprache' in der religiosen Lyrik des zwolften Jahrunderts: Adam von St. Victor, Walter von Châtillon.* Ratingen u.a. (Beihefte zum Mittellateinischee Jahrbuch, vol. 6)

Hellegouarc'h, J. 1967. Un poète latin du XIIe siècle: Gautier de Châtillon. *Bulletin de l'Association Guillaume Budé,* vol. 4, 95-115.

————. 1980. *Gauthier de Châtillon, poete epique dans l' 'Alexandreide'* in *Alan de Lille, Gautier de Châtillon, Jakemart Giellée et leur temps,* edd. H. Roussel & F. Suard. Paris. 229-247.

Herkenrath, E. 1931. *Textkritisches zur Apokalypse des Golias, zu Hilarius, und zu Walter von Chatillon,* in *Studien zur lateinischen Dichtung des Mittelalters: Ehrengabe für Karl Strecker.* Dresden. 94-96.

————. 1934. Die Zeit der Alexandreis Walters von Châtillon. *Historische Vierteljahrsschrift,* vol. 29, 597-598.

Hood, A. 1988. Walter of Châtillon's 'Alexandreis' R. Telfryn Pritchard: Walter . . . Toronto 1986. Otto Zwierlein: Der pragende . . . Stuttgart 1987. *The Classical Review,* vol. 84, 127-128.

Kelly, D. 1978. *Topical inventions in medieval French literature,* in *Medieval Eloquence. Studies in the Theory and Practice of Medieval Rhetoric,* ed. J. J. Murphy, 231-251. Berkeley.

Kloos, R. M. 1983. Alexander der Grosse und Kaiser Frederich II. *Collectanea Franciscana,* vol. 53, 395-415.

Klopsch, P. 1972. *Einführung in die mittellateinische Verslehre.* Darmstadt.

————. 1980. *Einführung in die Dichtungslehren des lateinischen Mittelalters.* Darmstadt.

Knapp, F. P. 1975. *Similitude: Stil und Erzanlfunktion von Vergleich und Exempel in der lateinischen, franzosischen und deutschen Grossepik des Hochmittelalters.* Vienna. (Philologica Germanica 2, vol. 1)

Kratz, D. M. 1977. Knapp: Similitudo: Stil- und Erzählfunktion von Vergleich und Exempel in der lateinischen, französischen und deutschen Grossepik des Hochmittelalters. *Speculum,* vol. 52, 1010-1013.

————. 1980. *Mocking epic, Waltharius, Alexandreis and the problem of Christian heroes.* Madrid.

Langosch, K. 1975. *Lateinisches Mittelalter Einleitung in Sprache und Literatur.* Darmstadt.

Lausberg, H. 1973. *Handbuch der literarischen Rhetorik.* 2 vols. Munich.

Manitius, M. 1923; 1931. *Geschichte der lateinischen Literatur des Mittelalters,* vol. 2, 717; vol. 3, 920-936. Munich.

Martin, J. 1982. Classicism and style in latin literature in *Renaissance and renewal in the twelfth century,* ed. R. L. Benson, G. Constable & C. D. Lanham, 537-568. Oxford.

Maurach, G. 1983. *'Enchiridion poeticum'. Hilfsbuch zur lateinishcen Dichtersprache.* Darmstadt.

McGinn, B. 1980. *Apocalyptic spirituality. Treatises and letters of Lactantius, Adso of Montier-en-Der, Joachim of Fiore, the Franciscan Spirituals, Savanarolo.* London. (The Classics of Western Spirituality.)

Mueldener, F. A. W. 1854. *De vita magistri Philippi Gualtheri ab Insulis dicti de Castellione.* Göttingen. (Diss.)

Murray, A. 1978. *Reason and society in the middle ages.* Oxford.

Pascal, P. 1964. *Notes on 'missus sum in vineam' of Walter of Châtillon* in *Classical, medieval and Renaissance studies in honour of B. L. Ullmann,* vol. 2, 37-40. Rome.

Peiper, R. 1869. *Walter von Châtillon.* Breslau.

Pfister, F. 1911. Die Klage der Natur im Alexanderlied des Walter von Châtillon. *Neues Jahrbücher für das Klassische Altertum,* vol. 27, 520-524.

————. 1960. Cary: 'The medieval Alexander'. *Gnomon* 32, 360-365.

Raby, F. J. E. 1953. *A history of Christian Latin poetry from the beginnings to the close of the middle ages.* 2 ed. Oxford.

————. 1957. *A history of secular Latin poetry in the middle ages.* 2 vols. 2 ed. Oxford.

————. 1968. 'Nuda Natura' and 12th century cosmology. *Speculum,* vol. 43, 72-77.

Ray, R. D. 1974. *Orderic Vitalis on Henry 1: theocratic ideology and didactic narrative.* 119-134, in *Contemporary reflections on the medieval Christian tradition. Essays in honor of Ray C. Petry,* ed. G. H. Shriver. Durham.

Rico, F. 1977. *On source, meaning and form in Walter of Châtillon's 'versa est in luctum'.* Barcelona.

Robert, M. 1985. *Biblical epic and rhetorical paraphrase in late antiquity.* Liverpool.

Sanford, E. M. 1984. The study of ancient history in the middle ages. *Journal of the History of Ideas,* vol. 5, 21-43.

Spanke, H. 1931. Zu den Gedichten Walters von Châtillon. *Volkstum und Kultur der Romanen,* vol. 4, 197-220.

Stock, B. 1972. *Myth and science in the twelfth century: a study of Bernard Silvester.* Princeton.

Strecker, K. 1924. Zu den Gedichten Walters von Chatillon, der Dichter der Lieder von St. Omer, *Zeitschrift für deutsches Altertum,* vol. 61, 197-222.

————. 1927. Walter von Chatillon und seine Schule, ii. *Zeitschrift für deutsches Altertum und deutsche Literatur,* vol. 64, 97-125; 161-189.

————. 1930. Ein Gedicht Walters von Châtillon? *Atti dell' Accaemia degli Arcadi,* vols. 5-6, 47-55.

————. 1963. *Introduction to medieval latin,* trans. R. B. Palmer. Berlin.

Taylor, A. M. 1971. *Four poems of Walter of Châtillon.* Boston. (Ph.D.)

Wetherbee, W. 1972. *Platonism and poetry in the 12th century. The literary influence of the school of Chartres.* Princeton.

Williams, A. 1969. *Medieval allegory: an operational approach.* Iowa City. (Poetic theory/poetic practice: papers of the Midwest Modern Language Association.)

————. 1980. *Prophecy and millenarianism. Essays in honour of Marjorie Reeves.* Essex.

Williams, J. R. 1929. William of the white hands and men of letters, in *Anniversary essays in medieval history by students of Charles Homer Haskins,* ed. C. H. Taylor, 365-387. Boston.

————. 1931. The authorship of the 'Moralium Dogma Philosophorum'. *Speculum,* vol. 6, 392-411.

————. 1957. The quest for the author of the 'Moralium Dogma Philosophorum'. *Speculum,* vol. 32, 736-747.

Willis, R. S. Jr. 1934. *The relationship of the Spanish 'Libro de Alexandre' to the 'Alexandreis' of Gautier de Châtillon.* Princeton. (Elliott Monographs in the Romance Languages, 31.)

Wisbey, R. 1956. *Das Alexanderbild Rudolf van Ems.* Berlin. (Philologische Studien und Quellen, vol. 31.)

Young, C. R. 1977. *The twelfth century renaissance,* New York 1969, repr. 1977.

Yunck, J. 1963. *The lineage of Lady Meed: the culmination and significance of the theme.* Indiana.

Zwierlein, O. 1987. *Der prägende Einfluss des antiken Epos auf die 'Alexandreis' des Walter von Châtillon.* Mainz.

A. C. Dionisotti (essay date 1990)

SOURCE: Dionisotti, A. C. "Walter of Châtillon and the Greeks." In *Latin Poetry and the Classical Tradition: Essays in Medieval and Renaissance Literature,* edited by Peter Godman and Oswyn Murray, pp. 73-96. Oxford: Clarendon Press, 1990.

[*In the following essay, Dionisotti examines how Walter adapted the classical material that formed the basis of his* Alexandreis *to ensure a broad understanding among his medieval readers.*]

Few medieval poets present us so squarely with the problem of understanding classical influences as Walter of Châtillon. Readers of his ***Alexandreis,*** from Walter's time down to our own, have always felt that it is more like a classic than anything produced before it, or indeed after, at least until Petrarch's *Africa.* Moreover, the poem was an immediate and lasting success: upwards of 180 MSS survive, not counting excerpts. It may be tempting, especially for a classicist, to relate these two facts: the classical is good; the more classical, therefore, the better; so the ***Alexandreis*** was justly and deservedly successful, in the best of all possible worlds. Critics less sympathetic to the classical underline the scholastic success of the poem: schoolmasters liked it, because it exemplified classical diction and metre. But, on both counts, the very different fate of Petrarch's *Africa* shows that there are holes in such reasoning. Schoolmasters were not short of real classical poems, if diction and metre were all that mattered. And in any case the success of the ***Alexandreis*** was not confined to schools: it was quoted, quarried and imitated in all kinds of literature, both Latin and vernacular. Somehow, we must suppose, the argument of the ***Alexandreis*** made sense to contemporaries. What sort of sense, how and why, and what role its classicism played in this, are the questions I would like to consider.[1]

Walter himself, in a rare concession to the traditions of Christian epic, wrote a prose preface for his poem. This, however, does little to explain the nature and purposes of the work. It concentrates, conventionally enough, on pre-empting the criticism of envious tongues: such critics, Walter pleads, should bear in mind the short time spent on composition, some five years, and the grandiose subject-matter, *altitudinem materiae,* not attempted by any ancient poet. This last point, though it is given more specific meaning in the body of the poem, in itself only echoes the claims to originality made by ancient poets; it does not, any more than for ancient poets, adequately explain the choice of theme: the fact that a theme has not been treated before does not explain why there is any need to treat it now. But the last sentence of the preface abruptly introduces a surprising twist which may be significant (Prol. 39-42):

> Sed hec hactenus. nunc autem quod instat agamus; et ut facilius que quesierit quis possit invenire, totum opus per capitula distinguamus.

> So much for that, now let's get down to business; and so that the reader may more easily find what he's looking for, let's divide the whole work into chapter-headings.

What Walter means is the short verse summaries that precede each book, like the verse *argumenta* accompanying books of the *Aeneid.* But to call such summaries *capitula,* and explain them as designed for ease of reference, is to relate them to something quite different, namely to serious informative prose; suffice it to say that the archetype for this remark is the preface to Pliny's *Natural History.* Walter himself uses it again in the preface to his prose theological dialogue against the Jews. The work we are about to read, he seems to hint here, is no merely aesthetic or literary entertainment.

This is the only external clue we have. Early commentators, and some modern ones, observe that the poem is dedicated to William of the White Hands, Archbishop of Rheims from 1176, and convert that into the poem's *raison d'être*: the purpose of the poem is to please the Archbishop, or to win his favour. This is good Servian tradition, but it does not explain why the poem should be about Alexander the Great, why it is the kind of poem it is, or why it was so widely successful. In fact it explains nothing at all.

If we try to place the poem in the literary landscape of the time, we unearth a lot of questions but no ready answers. The history of Latin epic in the twelfth century still seems to be a subject in search of an author. In Manitius' monumental work there is no such concept; the ***Alexandreis*** is discussed in the chapter on 'Persönliche Dichtung', wafted there on the coat-tails of Walter's accentual lyric verse, which also rates twice as much space. It is indeed arguable, Romantic presuppositions apart, that Walter had a more assured and refined command of the more modern medium: on the level of style the ***Alexandreis*** can let one down with a bump; hyperbole, conceit, and word-play are sometimes misjudged, even by the generous standards of Lucan or Claudian. But epic is not only style. It requires scale, plot, character, speech and action, tradition and invention, all welded to create a large and imaginative and not merely individual view of the human condition. What immediate precedents had Walter for such an undertaking, if any? The poems that most readily spring to mind, the *Ligurinus,* Joseph of Exeter's *Ylias,* and (for all the differences) the *Anticlaudianus* and the *Architrenius,* were all composed after the ***Alexandreis***; soon after, within a generation: so did Walter's poem set a new standard, or was it itself just an early example of a wider trend? Large-scale narrative Latin poems of earlier date are not lacking, but it remains to be seen how far they constitute a developing tradition: one feature that most of them share is minimal diffusion.

Further questions arise if we peer over the linguistic fence to consider developments in the vernacular. One of the few bits of biographical information about Walter that cannot be a deduction from his poems is the statement that he was taught by Stephen of Beauvais, whom it is plausible to identify with the Stephen described by Helinand as 'de clericis Henrici comitis . . . exercitatissimus in omni genere facetiarum utriusque linguae, latinae et gallicae'. Count Henry of Champagne was the elder brother of William of the White Hands;[2] but in any case it is scarcely credible that Walter was unaware of the *romans antiques* composed in rather sudden profusion since the 1150s, including some about Alexander the Great. In what measure is the **Alexandreis** a response to these, and with what implications?

Such questions may offer us a framework, even if we cannot answer them. But the first essential is to look at the poem itself, and see what it can tell us. It is a poem of some five and half thousand lines, in ten books, giving a selective account of Alexander's career from his accession to his death. Of course it is a career of conquest. After rapid suppression of mutiny in Greece, Alexander crosses to Asia Minor, inflicts an initial defeat on the Persians, briefly sorts out Palestine and Egypt, then concentrates on the major business of wiping out the Persian Empire; in two great battles, Issus and Arbela, he defeats the Persian King Darius, who escapes only to be murdered by his own nobles. Alexander pursues the murderers eastwards, quickly conquers the Scythians (noble savages who had tried to suggest he might live and let live), then confronts the army of King Porus of India, and defeats that. At the beginning of Book 10, as Alexander sets out to impose his power on the ultimate Ocean that bounds the earth, personified Natura, aghast that this human creature threatens to overstep the limits of creation, goes to enlist the powers of hell against him. Personified Betrayal (Proditio) duly prepares the cup of poison that will kill him in Babylon, though not before he has received volunteered submission from the entire western world, from Spain to the Rhine.

Alexander, then, is the unrivalled central figure. But what kind of hero is he, and what is the purpose of telling his story?

The criteria by which Walter selected and adapted his sources may give us some bearings. By the late twelfth century, there was no shortage of Latin material about Alexander. Besides the brief accounts in Orosius and Josephus, digested in Peter Comestor's *Historia Scolastica,* there were the historians Justin and Curtius Rufus, and several texts deriving from the Greek Alexander romance, both handed down from late antique versions and more recently translated from Eastern sources.[3] Moreover, as Cary beautifully demonstrated, Alexander's character and the significance of his career had been much discussed by theologians in the wake of patristic judgements. There is evidence in the poem that Walter was familiar with most of this material, but his selection from it is single-minded and highly abstemious. A few examples will suffice.

From an early period, all manner of stories clustered round the birth and youth of Alexander—notably that

he was not really the son of Philip, but of an Egyptian astrologer-king Nectanebus, who seduced Philip's wife Olympias by visions and transformation into a serpent. This not only occupies much space in various versions of the romance, it is also referred to in Justin's history, as a story that the adult Alexander is at pains to quash by consulting the oracle of Jupiter Ammon. It gets no such showing in the **Alexandreis.** Early in the first book, the twelve-year-old Alexander dismisses it in all of four words (1. 46-7 'semperne putabor / Nectanebi proles?'), and thereafter it is only used for the odd bit of malicious innuendo on the part of Alexander's adversaries.[4]

Likewise, Walter's Alexander meets no basilisks, talking trees, or fire-breathing monsters on his eastern journey. When he gets to India he joyfully exclaims (9. 203-5):

> 'Inveni tandem dignumque stupore meoque
> par animo discrimen,' ait 'res ecce gerenda est
> cum monstris michi cumque viris illustribus una.'

—at last he has found a truly amazing contest worthy of himself, a battle with monsters and famous warriors all at once; but the monsters are in fact elephants, monstrous in their size, but otherwise portrayed as fully natural, and naturally vulnerable.

Walter evidently also knew the story of Alexander's journey to paradise, but he only alludes to it, and very cleverly, in the explicitly mythological tableau in Book 10, where Natura thus clinches her plea to Lucifer (10. 102-4):

> que tua laus, coluber, vel que tua gloria primum
> eiecisse hominem, si tam venerabilis hortus
> cedat Alexandro?

> Where's your pride and glory, snake, your expulsion of
> Adam, if that so venerable garden falls to Alexander?

Thus Walter alludes to the fabulous legends about Alexander, but systematically and rigorously excludes them from his narrative. Was it because he thought such stories were too folk-loreish, not suitable for epic style? But there are plenty of epic models for handling portents, visions, magic, and the like. Was it because he did not believe these stories to be true, and was concerned to give a bona fide historical account? This at first sight seems more plausible, fitting in with the fact that he chose Curtius, the fullest and most soberly historical account available to him, as his primary source, followed very closely indeed for large stretches of his narrative. But I do not think historicity is the whole answer either; for Walter both invents much quite un-historical matter, and omits or dismisses matter that was both acceptably historical and potentially heroic.

A revealing case is the very opening of the poem. The narrative proper begins, as I mentioned, with Alexander's accession to the throne, imagined by Walter as a peaceful coronation at Corinth. But before that, immediately following the dedication of the poem, there is a curious scene, a sort of play before the play, presenting the youth of Alexander. We hear nothing of the taming of Bucephalus, of the victory at the Olympic games, or of Philip's murder and Alexander's avenging of it. Instead, we are given two speeches, not prompted by any particular circumstance: a monologue by the twelve-year-old Alexander, exasperated by his own youth and impatient for action and victory; and then a long lecture to him by Aristotle, on the arts of power and rule. Whether for epic or history, the episode is strangely timeless, symbolic, adrift from narrative.[5] If we opened the book expecting the adventures of Alexander, or even a historical biography of him, this is clear warning that the poem will be neither. Kingly power is its theme; that is what governs the poet's choice and use of both history and imagination.

Turning to look at the poem as a whole, we see that Walter has taken pains to set his story into a very large historical and geographical perspective. Among the episodes entirely invented by him are two lengthy descriptions of tombs, those of Darius' wife and of Darius himself, both sculpted by a Jewish artist in Alexander's service called Apelles. The first tomb depicts the history of the world from the Creation down to Alexander, based, of course, on the Old Testament. The second has a canopy representing a map of the world with all its lands and peoples; it also has an epitaph for Darius and a date calculated from the Creation, which reassert the historical dimension.[6] Elaborate descriptions of work of art are a traditional feature of epic, and critics have rather dismissed Walter's tombs as artificial and anachronistic bits of epic machinery. Their purpose, however, is quite clear: Alexander is not just one epic hero among many, he is the culmination of human history to date, in its central development as established by the Old Testament, not in some side-show like the Trojan War. And the whole known world is his stage, extending from Arthur's Brittany to India.

But if the range of time and space is about as large as it could be, the range of human relationships depicted in the poem is extraordinarily narrow. Beyond the glimpse of the boy Alexander as pupil to Aristotle, we only ever see him as a commander of men. He inspires, and to a degree reciprocates, loyalty in his troops, and his dealings with his officers successively illustrate devotion and betrayal, on both sides. Alexander behaves with impeccable but distant courtesy towards Darius' mother, wife, and children, who are his prisoners of war. Darius is so touched by this that he offers Alexander peace, a share of his kingdom, and a daughter in marriage. Alexander rejects this: he is courteous to Darius' family, he

coldly explains, because he has not come to fight against women and children (4. 144-51). It is as if anyone who cannot fight, either with him or against him, scarcely exists.

Walter's Alexander is in fact much lonelier than the supposedly lonely hero Aeneas. He has no father-figure like Anchises or Evander. He not only has no wife or son, he never displays the slightest interest in acquiring any. Roxane is never mentioned. And, in this age of burgeoning romance, this poem has no romantic episode. Ancient tradition and modern versions offered the exotic Queen Candace, who lured Alexander to her castle and almost held him in thrall; Walter ignores the story. All we get is the Queen of the Amazons, who comes to meet Alexander, in full armour and with 200 of her cavalry, as he journeys east. Though initially disappointed with Alexander's physique, she none the less proceeds to a business-like proposal, monarch to monarch, for a bit of genetic planning (8. 36-48):

> ergo rogata semel ad quid regina veniret
> anne aliquid vellet a principe poscere magnum,
> se venisse refert ut pleno ventre regressa
> communem pariat cum tanto principe prolem,
> dignam se reputans de qua rex gignere regni
> debeat heredes. fuerit si femina partu
> prodita, maternis potietur filia regnis.
> si mas extiterit, patri reddetur alendus.
> querit Alexander sub eone vacare Talestris
> militiae velit. illa suum custode carere
> causatur regnum. tandem pro munere noctem
> ter deciesque tulit, et quod querebat adepta
> ad solium regni patriasque revertitur urbes.

She would like to have a child by him, preferably a girl: if it turns out a boy, he can keep it. Alexander reacts by suggesting she might like to join his army—presumably it would save time. When she objects that she cannot abandon her kingdom for so long, Alexander finally ('tandem'), agrees to spend some nights with her, thirteen to be precise, and the queen, having prosily got what she wanted ('quod querebat adepta') returns to her kingdom. Here Walter is simply versifying the dry account in Curtius. That is no answer, however, for he is quite capable of expanding and transforming Curtius when he wants to. Thus he turns a brief notice of an exploit by two officers into a complete rerun of the Nisus and Euryalus episode of *Aeneid* 9.[7] Clearly he wants no Dido and Aeneas, not even any Cornelia and Pompey, or Caesar and Cleopatra.

In the Alexander legend, Alexander's mother Olympias is a prominent figure to whom he is warmly devoted. In Walter's poem she is only rarely and dimly evoked, and one passage starkly redefines the relationship. In the thick of the battle of Arbela the twin gods of war, Mars and Bellona, observe that while Alexander is hell-bent on chasing Darius, his own best regiment is being badly hammered by one of Darius' generals. Bellona, in suitably horrendous Gorgonic attire, descends on Alexander to tell him that his chase is in vain, a different fate has been decreed for Darius, he should return to help his men. At this Alexander (5. 241-50):

> excutitur saltu Macedo profugamque secutus
> voce deam, 'quocumque venis, dea, cardine, vanum
> spernimus omen,' ait 'non me divellet ab armis
> et curru Darii licet impiger ales ab alto
> missus Atlantiades verax michi nuncius ipsas
> afferat a Persis raptas cum matre sorores.
> ex Dario pendet nostri spes unica voti,
> quem si perdidero, parvi michi cetera, parvi
> perdita momenti. solum si vicero, solus
> perdita restituet . . .'

> shakes himself with a jump and calls after the fleeing goddess 'Whatever corner of the world you come from, goddess, I scorn your empty omen: I'll not be dragged away from the arms and chariot of Darius, not even if the true messenger Mercury swoops down despatched from on high to tell me that my own mother and sisters have been raped by the Persians. On Darius depends my one hope and prayer; if I lose him, it little matters what else I lose, if I defeat only him, he alone will make up for any losses . . .'

and more in the same vein. The episode is of course entirely invented by Walter—most of his battle descriptions are freely invented in the epic manner. But we should note that Alexander here is in fact made to break all the rules for how to behave, in epic, when visited by a deity: normally your limbs freeze, your hair stands on end, and your voice sticks in your throat; and you do not proceed to tell the deity to get lost. Walter even seems to underline the abnormality, by the reference to Mercury flying down from on high, complete with verbal echoes of his most famous such flight, when he went to tell Aeneas to stop dallying in Carthage and think of his destiny, at least for the sake of his son. For Alexander, the pursuit of victory, as defined by himself, is all: to hell with what fate may have decreed, to hell with his mother and sisters.[8]

What then of Alexander's character? Are we supposed to admire, or abhor, this drastically single-minded pursuit of pre-eminence and victory, which is his dominant characteristic throughout the poem? It is of course a commonplace, in both biblical and pagan moralizing tradition, to condemn such vaulting ambition, such vanity of vanities. But we should hesitate before concluding that the poet devoted himself to writing ten books of highly original epic merely to reassert this commonplace. And in fact such a view fails to account for one of the poem's most striking novelties.

The entire Alexander tradition had always stressed the dramatic degeneration of Alexander's character: the virtues of courage and leadership that brought him suc-

cess were corrupted by that very success; oriental wealth and luxury bred self-indulgence, intemperate and tyrannical behaviour; Alexander had conquered the Persians, ran a much quoted epigram, only himself to be conquered by Persian vices. Curtius has several long disquisitions on this theme, and offers plenty of graphic evidence for it in Alexander's actions.

Walter does versify one such disquisition in Book 3, commenting on Alexander's generous treatment of Darius' family: if only he had continued like that, no one would have had cause to denigrate him; but Persian wealth and success corrupted him (3. 250-2):

> qui pius ergo prius erat hostibus, hostis amicis
> impius in caedes et bella domestica demum
> conversus, ratus illicitum nichil esse tyranno.[9]

> So whereas before he was saintly to his enemies, he became an evil enemy to his friends, and finally turned to murder and war against his own people, and thought like a tyrant that nothing was unlawful for him.

But in the remaining seven and a half books of the poem, Walter systematically omits all evidence for this transformation of Alexander's character. At the beginning of Book 6, Babylon is invited to admire her new king (6. 8-15):

> rex erit ille tuus a quo se posceret omnis
> rege regi tellus, si perduraret in illa
> indole virtutum qua ceperat ire potestas.
> aspice quam blandis victos moderetur habenis,
> aspice quam clemens inter tot prospera victor,
> aspice quam mitis dictet ius gentibus, ut quos
> hostes in bellis habuit cognoscat in urbe
> cives, et bello quos vicit vincat amore.

> Your king will be the sort of king by whom every land would wish to be ruled, if his power remained set in the virtuous nature in which it first grew. See with what gentle reins he governs the vanquished, see how merciful is the victor amidst all his success, see how in the city he recognizes as citizens those who were his enemies in war, and conquers with love those whom he conquered by war.

This is not in Curtius. Babylon is of course a pit of corruption, and the poet reverts to Curtius for a general statement that Babylonian luxury broke down Alexander's innate and acquired virtues. But in the following narrative it is not Alexander who is corrupted, but his troops; or rather, they would have been, except that Alexander promptly introduced a programme of moral re-armament, with a reform of military organization which Walter goes so far as to argue was a greater achievement than the whole of Roman Law. In Curtius' account the capture of Persepolis which follows is celebrated by a drunken orgy that gets out of hand and leads to the wholesale destruction and burning down of the famous city. In Walter's version the capture and the destruction are rolled into one, there is no mention of any orgy, and the city's fate is emotionally justified by only then recounting, as a flashback, Alexander's piteous meeting with a convoy of Greek prisoners, brutally mutilated by the Persians.

Famous among the crimes of Alexander were the murders of his friends, especially Clitus and the philosopher Callisthenes. Curtius describes them at length, underlining the corrupted Alexander's jealousy, intemperance, arrogance, and cruelty. Walter just registers their deaths in a couple of lines (9. 3-8):

> . . . quam [sc. Indiam] dum petit ille deorum
> aemulus in terris, Clytus, Ermolaus et eius
> doctor, Aristotili preter quem nemo secundus,
> extremum clausere diem, documenta futuris
> certa relinquentes: etenim testatur eorum
> finis amicitias regum non esse perennes

and draws a quite different moral: their end bears witness for future generations that the friendships of kings do not last. Not Alexander's character, then, but a general truth about kings.

As for tyranny, right at the end of the poem, when Alexander receives the homage of all Western peoples, Walter gives him an invented speech. These people have nothing to fear from his rule, says Alexander (10. 289-98):

> cui si se Darius posito diademate supplex
> commisisset, eo regnorum in parte recepto,
> sensisset nichil esse iugo mansuetius isto.
> Porus in exemplo est qua mansuetudine victis
> presideam victor, nedum parentibus ultro.
> quosque iugum nostrum vis nulla subire coegit
> subiectos michi mortales ita vivere salva
> libertate volo ut iam non sit servitus, immo
> libertas, servire michi. distinctio nulla
> libertatis erit inter quos nemo rebellis.

Had Darius surrendered, he would have had a share of the kingdom and found no yoke more gentle than Alexander's; Porus is an example of how gently he treats the conquered, never mind those who submit voluntarily. Such people will be subject to him in such a way as to retain their full freedom, it will be no servitude, indeed to serve him will itself be freedom; where there is no rebellion, all will be equally free. There is a disquieting sense of Antichrist here, of a demonic man usurping the role and language of the Christian god. But it is a far cry from the conventional picture of the corrupted tyrant. And Alexander goes on to make a speech of quite exemplary generosity to his soldiers.

In all this I do not think the poet's purpose is to glorify or whitewash Alexander: what he does is rather to isolate his single driving passion, his thirst for unchal-

lenged power, stripping it bare of the conventionally concomitant vices that would make moral judgement easy. Wealth, luxury, love, family, friends, one's own country, all these matter, for good or ill, to other men in the poem, not to Alexander. He is savagely ruthless against any disloyalty or opposition, real or supposed, but otherwise generous, just, courageous to a fault, and brilliant in the art of war. The upshot is a poem not so much about Alexander the Great but, as the preamble implied, about political and military power; power that requires a combination of passion and skill, and extremes of both self-obsession and self-denial.

Is such power a good or a bad thing? For us in the twentieth century, with our democratic traditions and autocratic realities, the notion of power like that of Walter's Alexander is rather automatically abhorrent; and the warrior heroism of epic tradition is now so alien to serious art that we may be tempted to interpret it away as ironic anti-heroism, or schematize it into a tussle between good and bad; either way, to seek a moral excuse for it. But Walter was no democrat, and the very stuff of his verse shows that he was steeped in the epic tradition. I think that if we respect his text, its tone, proportions and emphases, what is said and what is not, we can no more draw a simple moral from his poem than we can from the *Iliad* or the *Aeneid*; in other words it is truly an epic, not a didactic, poem: its aim is to explore a vision at the limits of human greatness and frailty, not to teach an orthodoxy.

This seems to me inherently true of the poem as a whole, but one passage makes the point as explicit as it could well be in epic poetry. Alexander's goddess is Victory, and Victory holds court in a palace (4. 408-32):

> ad limina prima susurrat
> introitumque tenet curarum sedula mater
> Ambitio pernox. solio sedet intus eburno
> diva, triumphales lauro mordente capillos,
> munifica munita manu, cinguntque sorores
> cius utrunque latus et regia tecta coronant
> perpetue comites: lirico modulamine carmen
> inmortale canens et in evum Gloria vivax,
> Maiestasque premens rugoso secula fastu,
> conciliansque sibi facilem Reverentia plebem,
> et dea que leges armat, que iura tuetur,
> Iustitia, in ncutram declinans munere partem.
> assidet hiis stabilitque deae Clementia regnum,
> sola docens miseris misereri et parcere victis.
> has inter locuples sed barbara moribus astat
> fomentum vicii genitrixque Pecunia luxus.
> pacifico reliquis prelibans oscula vultu
> inmemor est odii finis Concordia belli
> et Pax agricola et cum pleno Copia cornu.
> Applausus a fronte sedent, qui seria ludis
> miscentes vario divam oblectamine mulcent,
> et Favor ambiguus et bleso subdolus ore
> Risus adulator, commentaque Ludicra divae
> singula policronos aptant, et musica circum

instrumenta sonant numeros aptante camena.

At the first threshold sleepless Ambition, anxious mother of cares, whispering guards the entry. Within sits the goddess on an ivory throne, the laurel of triumph gripping her hair, her hand generous with gifts. Her sisters and constant companions surround her and adorn her royal palace: everliving Glory sings an immortal song of lyric melody, Majesty overawes the world with frowning pride, Reverence wins the people to her, and Justice arms the laws and defends rights, unswerving in her task. Sitting by them is Clemency, securing the goddess's kingdom, who alone can teach to take pity on the wretched and spare the defeated. Among them stands Money, rich and vulgar, the nurse of vice and mother of dissipation. Concord with her visage of peace snatches kisses from the rest, forgetting hatred and ending war, together with Peace the farmer and Plenty with her full horn. Before the goddess sits the crowd of Applause, soothing her with varied pleasure, serious and playful, fickle Favour, flattery's Smile and deceitful Shows, all ready to cry 'Vivat' for the goddess, while musical instruments sound to the rhythms of poetry.

The tableau has a long ancestry in classical and classicizing poetry, the personifications suggest moral discourse in epic dress. But this is no psychomachy of orderly virtues marshalled against opposing vices: Walter mythologizes a real world, in which victorious power depends upon both virtue and vice, truth and illusion. The style invokes the moralist, only to defy him in the substance.

Why should Walter have been so interested in such power? It is an immediately striking fact that this poem about military might and world rule is repeatedly and explicitly anti-Roman. This begins in the very first lines (1. 1-11):

Gesta ducis Macedum totum digesta per orbem,
quam large dispersit opes, quo milite Porum
vicerit et Darium, quo principe Grecia victrix
risit et a Persis rediere tributa Corintho
Musa refer. qui si senio non fractus inermi
pollice fatorum nostros vixisset in annos
Cesareos numquam loqueretur fama tryumphos,
totaque Romuleae squaleret gloria gentis:
preradiaret enim meriti fulgore caminus
igniculos, solisque sui palleret in ortu
Lucifer, et tardi languerent Plaustra Boete.

Alexander is the prince under whom 'Grecia victrix risit', victorious Greece smiled. Had he lived on, fame would have had nothing to say of the triumphs of the Caesars, the whole glory of the Roman race would be tarnished, for the furnace with the blaze of its merit would outshine the little flickers, and at the rising of their sun Lucifer would pale and the wagon of plodding Bootes would wane.

Now *Graecia victrix* was a concept that the Romans never really accepted this side of the Trojan War. *Grae-*

cia capta might indeed conquer her rough conqueror with the fine arts, statues of breathing bronze, and the like. But precisely on condition of being *capta*: the arts of conquest and rule were Roman. Alexander made the Romans nervous, but they coped by treating him as a flash in the pan, a monstrous individual, in any case a Macedonian, not a representative Greek. Many writers inveigh against his vices and folly; Virgil more tellingly, in the whole vast canvas of the *Aeneid* going from the Trojan War to Augustus, never once mentions him. But Walter is not merely protesting the importance of his subject against a literary tradition: time and again he uses Alexander to rob Rome of all it stands for. The Eusebian doctrine, that the Roman Empire had been ordained by God to further and maintain Christianity, was the common ground underlying even the most divergent theories of papal versus imperial power; it is excluded from Walter's vision. Instead, half-way through the poem, the peroration of Book 5 delineates a revealing alternative. Alexander's triumph after Arbela, says Walter, was greater than any ever seen by Rome, whether that of Augustus after Actium or Julius Caesar's after Pharsalus. And rightly so, since Alexander's success against such heavy odds and on such a scale makes the heroes sung by Lucan and Claudian look like mere *plebs*. The poet then turns to the future (5. 510-20):

si gemitu commota pio votisque suorum
flebilibus divina daret clementia talem
Francorum regem, toto radiaret in orbe
haut mora vera fides, et nostris fracta sub armis
Parthia baptismo renovari posceret ultro,
queque diu iacuit effusis menibus alta
ad nomen Christi Kartago resurgeret, et quas
sub Karolo meruit Hyspania solvere poenas
exigerent vexilla crucis, gens omnis et omnis
lingua Ihesum caneret et non invita subiret
sacrum sub sacro Remorum presule fontem.

If divine clemency, moved by the tearful prayers of her people, granted France a king like Alexander, then soon the true faith would shine over the whole world. Parthia, broken by French arms, would itself beg for baptism, Carthage long in ruins would rise up again in the Christian faith, and the standards of the cross would exact punishment from Spain for its defeat of Charlemagne. Every land and every people would sing of Christ and willingly seek baptism from the Archbishop of Rheims.

The text warrants a few glosses. Parthia, Carthage, and Spain represent points of the compass and also, of course, Islam. France's Alexander would be no ordinary Crusader setting out to rescue the Holy Places; his aim would be no less than a new world empire to be guardian of the Christian faith, in defiance of the established scheme of universal history which allotted that role to Rome. Moreover, 'Parthia' and 'Carthage' are no idle poetic archaisms. The new French empire would undo Roman history, ancient and modern: it would vanquish

Rome's one unvanquished enemy, and resuscitate the enemy that Rome had destroyed, as well as avenge the defeat of Rome's second founder, Charlemagne.

One might usefully compare the Archpoet's one public poem, a hymn to Barbarossa after the destruction of Milan in 1162.[10] It begins, 'Salve mundi domine, Caesar noster, ave!'; the emperor is 'princeps terrae principum', he will restore Roman sway:

> qui potenter sustinens sarcinam mundanam
> relevat in pristinum statum rem Romanam.

He is both a new Charlemagne in war, 'repraesentat Karolum dextera victrici', and a new Augustus in peace, the peace which heralded the Incarnation and was the cornerstone of the Eusebian doctrine:

> iterum describitur orbis ab Augusto,
> redditur res publica statui vetusto,
> pax terras ingreditur habitu venusto
> et iam non opprimitur iustus ab iniusto.

It is then only natural that Greece, ancient and modern, should be seen as an antithesis. The Greek emperor is admonished to take due warning from the defeat of Milan:

> interim precipio tibi, Constantine,
> iam depone dexteram, tue cessent mine . . .
> tantus erat populus atque locus ille,
> si venisset Grecia tota cum Achille
> in qua tot sunt menia, tot potentes ville,
> non eam subicere possent annis mille.[11]

Walter was no monk buried in some introspective cloister. His patron and perhaps employer was a scion of the house of Champagne, nephew of the ousted King Stephen of England and brother of the Queen of France. Walter travelled to Rome and Bologna, through an Italy scarred by the ravages of Barbarossa. His other poems reveal a keen eye for the events of his day, as do many passages of the *Alexandreis*. But when did he write it? It is generally said that the poem was composed between 1178 and 1182, and published shortly after. For various reasons I think we are much more probably in the early seventies.[12] The current king of France is then the ageing Louis VII, his only son is a sickly boy of between five and ten, who may or may not survive. Louis VII was famous for his great piety, but for little else. His crusade in 1147 had been an ignominious failure; he had lost both his wife and much of France to Henry Plantagenet, who repeatedly outmanoeuvred him. On the other side he was dwarfed by the ruthless conqueror all too like Alexander, the heir of the Caesars, Frederick Barbarossa. A Frenchman might well ponder the nature of political and military power.

The choice of Alexander as a theme gave scope for a poem simultaneously classical, secular, and anti-Roman. But the theme did not of itself necessitate such treat-ment. When Walter wrote, large-scale poems on ancient themes were all the rage, but written in the vernacular, utterly unclassical in manner and much of their matter, and especially associated with the Plantagenet court. One way to consider Walter's classicism would be as a deliberate challenge and antithesis to this vogue, an as-sertion of cultural superiority on a comparable scale and ground. Certainly, if one compares the *Alexandreis* with Stephen of Rouen's *Draco Normannicus,* com-pleted in honour of Henry II in 1169, one can see why the latter poem was left to lie discreetly uncopied at Bec: some 4500 elephantine Latin elegiacs, reeking of the schoolroom, yet innocent of any classical shape or style, it could be no epic advertisement for the patron of John of Salisbury and Peter of Blois. By the time Joseph of Exeter set about his *Ylias* (1188-90), it was an exercise in catching up: Joseph is clearly inspired and influenced by the *Alexandreis.*

In a different perspective, the secular and anti-Roman character of Walter's poem might also be seen as a literary concomitant to the increasingly secular, and increasingly Greek, philosophy burgeoning in the schools of Paris. Walter knew very little about the Greece whose world empire he conjured up to chal-lenge that of Rome and its heirs. But he knew, of course, that Athens is the immortal spring of science and philosophy. When Aristotle appears at the beginning of the poem (1. 59-62), wan and desiccated with study, he has just put the last full stop on his *Sophistici Elenchi:*

> forte macer pallens incompto crine magister
> (nec facies studio male respondebat) apertis
> exierat thalamis ubi nuper corpore toto
> perfecto logyces pugiles armarat elencos.

New translations of the logical works were being sought out by inquiring Westerners at this very time; still it is quite something that a text-book of advanced logic should figure in an epic poem, complete with title.[13] The speech that Walter gives Aristotle on the arts of rule is freely composed, and certainly it knows nothing of the *Ethics* and *Politics.* But, like the figure of Alexander himself, it breathes a remarkably secular spirit, irreduc-ibly of this world, the spirit that makes Aristotle so much more of a challenge to Christian thought than Plato. It was not till the next generation that men began to take up the challenge of the *Nicomachean Ethics* and size up the vast reaches of Greek philosophy that Rome, pagan and Christian, had failed to transmit.[14] By then, too, France was seeing an Alexander in Philip Augus-tus. These were changes in the habits of thought that required much intellectual openness and energy. The *Alexandreis* did not go uncontested; indeed the *Anti-claudianus* is one kind of answer to it. But it remained a classic of that new readiness to break out of the Western mould, to question the boundary and to declare, like Alexander, that one's own world is scarcely enough.

The starting-point for dating the **Alexandreis** has always been its dedication to William of the White Hands, who became archbishop of Rheims in 1176. That the dedication was no afterthought is shown by the first lines of the ten books, which together give the acrostic GUILLER-MUS, as contemporaries were quick to note. However, William was already William, and already a grand enough patron, when he was bishop of Chartres and also, from 1169, archbishop of Sens. In the poem there are just two references to him as archbishop of Rheims. First in the dedication itself, which is worth quoting in full (1. 12-26):

> at tu, cui maior genuisse Britannia reges
> gaudet avos, Senonum quo presule non minor urbi
> nupsit honos quam cum Romam Senonensibus armis
> fregit adepturus Tarpeiam Brennius arcem
> si non exciret vigiles argenteus anser,
> quo tandem regimen kathedrae Remensis adepto
> duriciae nomen amisit bellica tellus,
> quem partu effusum gremio suscepit alendum
> phylosophia suo totumque Elycona propinans
> doctrinae sacram patefecit pectoris aulam,
> excoctumque diu studii fornace, fugata
> rerum nube, dedit causas penetrare latentes:
> huc ades et mecum pelago decurre patenti,
> funde sacros fontes et crinibus imprime laurum
> ascribique tibi nostram paciare camenam.

Here we have: (*a*) a prefatory line about William's royal descent; (*b*) nearly four colourful lines on him as archbishop of Sens, including Virgilian echoes, anti-Roman slant continuing that of the opening lines 1-11, and vindication of Brennus as a local anti-Roman hero;[15] (*c*) just two lines prosily recording his elevation to Rheims, decorated only by etymological allusion to its ancient name of Durocortorum; (*d*) five highly poetic lines on his devotion to learning, which lead naturally into the poet's request for support. In style and in construction the passage runs much better without the two lines about Rheims; and if William had already risen to be archbishop of Rheims when Walter first wrote the passage, the focus on his earlier post is hard to explain. Moreover, there is uncertainty in the MSS about where those two lines should go: some slot them in after line 23 or 24.[16]

The other reference to Rheims is also problematic. It occurs at the end of the peroration of book 5 (quoted above, p. 86-7), 518-20:

> gens omnis et omnis
> lingua Ihesum caneret et non invita subiret
> sacrum sub sacro Remorum presule fontem.

Every people and every tongue would sing of Jesus and willingly submit to the holy font of the holy prelate of Rheims.

Presumably Walter imagined his patron accompanying his crusader king and baptizing infidels as he went along. But the lines risk conjuring up a vision of the entire Islamic world converging on Rheims that is little short of comic grotesque. I suspect that the last line was a belated and rather infelicitous substitute, born of a desire to salute the patron half way through the poem, once his elevation to Rheims allowed him a role in this context.

Apart from these two references to Rheims, the latest datable allusion in the poem is to the murder of Robert, archbishop of Cambrai in 1174. Of course the poem does not necessitate up-to-the-minute topical allusion. None the less, there is in fact enough of it to give substance to at least one argument from silence.

In November 1179 Walter's patron performed the office that the see of Rheims claimed as its special privilege: coronation of the king of France. The counter-claims of William's ex-see of Sens and the fact that the young king was his nephew gave the event a very personal significance, highlighted by Walter himself in a lyric poem.[17] The first book of the **Alexandreis** includes an elaborate account of the young Alexander's coronation at Corinth (1. 203-38). Corinth is described not only as the capital of Greece, but also as a city converted by St Paul; in any case Walter is not shy of modern comparisons (cf. especially 8. 168-71). If the coronation of a young king of France, 40 years since the last one and of particular significance to Walter's patron, had been a recent event, or was even on the cards, this passage was crying out for an allusion to it. There is none that I can see, not even implicit.

The same argument applies with greater force to the peroration of book 5 (510 ff.):

> si gemitu commota pio votisque suorum
> flebilibus divina *daret* clementia talem
> Francorum regem, toto *radiaret* in robe . . .

If divine clemency, moved by the devout lament and tearful prayers of its people, granted such a king of France, then in the whole world would shine . . .

The subjectives imply that divine clemency has not so far shown signs of obliging. If a young French king had just ascended the throne, even if he had not yet had time to prove himself an Alexander, it would not have required a sycophant to be just a little more optimistic. Indeed, the passage as it stands, with its emphasis on tears, could only be a senseless insult.

Yet it was also on the basis of this peroration that Christensen argued for the dating 1178-82 which has been generally accepted, though I do wonder how many have troubled to read the argument.[18] Briefly, it runs thus: (*a*) the final lines, 518-20, must refer to conversion of the Jews in France, since the archbishop of Rheims cannot be imagined baptizing the whole world; (*b*) the prayer in lines 510 ff. implies that Philip Augustus has not yet declared his crusade against the Jews, though it is hoped for by clerics like Walter who could have no other reason to wish for a bellicose king of France; (*c*) a crusade against the Jews was in fact declared in 1180, so this passage must have been written in the winter of 1179-80, and the rest of the poem either side of that date. But the fact is that neither in this passage, nor elsewhere in the poem, is there any suggestion of any crusade against the Jews;[19] and that, like it or not, it is 'gens omnis et omnis lingua' who will be baptized by the archbishop and these can only be the many peoples of Islam referred to in the preceding lines, which also amplify the prayer of 510 ff. The argument seems to me wholly unfounded.[20]

Moreover, there is independent evidence for dating the *Alexandreis,* which, instead of being deployed for this purpose, has itself been misinterpreted on the basis of the supposed date 1178-82. Among Walter's minor works there is a fascinating prosimetrum on the world of learning and its various branches. It presents itself as an address for the fourth Sunday in Lent to the assembled doctors and students of law at Bologna.[21] The first of the arts is introduced thus (7-8):

> inter artes igitur que   dicuntur trivium
> fundatrix grammatica   vendicat principium.
> sub hac chorus militat   metrice scribentium;
> inter quos sunt quatuor   rithmice dictantium
> qui super hoc retinent   sibi privilegium,
> Stephanus flos scilicet   Aurelianensium
> et Petrus, qui dicitur   de castro Blesensium.

> istis non inmerito   Berterus adicitur,
> set nec inter alios   quartus pretermittitur
> ille, quem Castellio   latere non patitur,
> in cuius opusculis   Alexander legitur.

So among the arts that are called the trivium, grammar the foundress claims first place. Under her banner campaigns the chorus of metrical poets, among whom there are four who are also pre-eminent in rhyme, that is Stephen, the pride of Orleans, and Peter, known as from Blois; Berterus is added with good reason, nor among others is a fourth forgotten, the one whom Châtillon proclaims, among whose works Alexander is read.

The date of this prosimetrum can be fixed with fair precision within the years 1174-6.[22] Starting from the premiss that the *Alexandreis* was written later, Strecker was reduced to supposing that the last line referred to lost and otherwise unknown poems that Walter had written about Alexander, taking 'in cuius opusculis' to mean 'in several of whose small works', and suggesting that these works should belong to the class of 'rithmice

dictata'. But the relative clause, like the preceding one 'quem Castellio . . .', serves to identify the poet; it does not need to refer to 'rhythmic' poems. Moreover, the diminutive is not to be pressed, since Walter in his own preface to the *Alexandreis* addresses 'lectores huius opusculi'; and the more natural sense of the line is that among his works there is one poem about Alexander, with the subject standing for the work as e.g. in Ovid, *Amores* 1. 15. 25 'Tityrus et segetes Aeneiaque arma legentur', or *Ars Amatoria* 3. 337-8 'et profugum Aenean, altac primordia Romae, / quo nullum Latio clarius exstat opus'. Above all, the line has no point unless it refers to something for which the poet was renowned; and it passes belief that the poet of the *Alexandreis* could have previously written famous poems on the same subject and no trace of them remain: it is just the sort of thing that accessus and scholia would have fastened on.

So I would conclude that the hypothesis is implausible and unnecessary, and that when Walter wrote these lines in 1174-6 he was already known to have written the *Alexandreis.*

But we have not yet finished with the prosimetrum. For further on, in part 14, we have twelve classical hexameter lines, the only ones in the work, capped by two rhyming ones, and the classical ones recur almost verbatim at *Alexandreis* 3. 140-57. Which is quoting which? Let us first look at the *Alexandreis* passage. In the think of the battle of the Issus Alexander is faced with a warrior-astrologer who knows he is about to die and hopes to make it a glorious death by provoking Alexander (the parts recurring in the prosimetrum are in italics and its variants listed below):

> stabat ab opposito niveis pretiosus in armis   140
> Memphites Zoroas, quo nemo peritior astris
> mundanas prenosse vices: *quo sydere frugis*
> *defectum patiatur ager, quis frugifer annus,*
> *unde nives producat hyemps, que veris in ortu*
> *temperies impregnet human, cur ardeat estas,*   145
> quid dedit autumpno maturis cingier uvis,
> *circulus an possit quadrari, an musica formet*
> *caelestes modulos,* vel quanta proportio rerum
> quatuor inter se. novit *quis sydera septem*
> *impetus oblique rapiat contraria mundo,*   150
> *quot distent a se gradibus, que stella nocivum*
> *inpediat sevire senem, quo sydere fiat*
> *obice propitius, Martem quis temperet ignis,*
> quam sibi quisque domum querat, quod sydus in isto
> regnet hemisperio. motus rimatur et horas   155
> colligit, eventus hominum perpendit in astris.
> *Parva loquor, totum claudit sub pectore caelum.*

142 esto secundus Atlas, dicas quo . . .

146 cur legat autumnus pregnantes ebrius uvas

148-9 c. m. dicas quis . . .

post 157 finge quod hec scieris, set et his maiora: quid ad rem? / tam cito descieris hec omnia, quod nihil ad rem.

Opposite him stood Zoroas of Memphis, sumptuous in snow-white armour, more skilled than any in foretelling the course of nature by the stars: by what star the crops would fail, what year would bring a full harvest, whence the winter produces snows, what warmth seeps into the soil at spring's rising, why the summer burns, what gave autumn a girdle of ripe grapes; whether the circle can be squared, whether music is a pattern of heavenly harmonies, or what is the proportion between the four elements of things. He knows what force rushes the seven planets cross-wise against the firmament, how many intervals there are between them, what star can prevent old man Saturn from raging, by what star's intervention he will become kind, what luminary can soften Mars, what home each planet seeks, what star rules in its hemisphere. He tracks each movement and reckons the hours, and weighs up the fortunes of men in the stars. I have said but a fraction: he encloses the whole sky in his mind.

The episode is invented by Walter, and it neatly balances the astrological episode at the end of the same book (501-25), which is freely elaborated from Curtius. For Zoroas, Walter found one starting-point in his favourite Lucan, where Nigidius Figulus is introduced as an astrologer (1. 639-41):

at Figulus, cui cura deos secretaque caeli
nosse fuit, quem non stellarum Aegyptia Memphis
aequaret visu numerisque moventibus astra,

followed by a speech in which some of the themes of the Zoroas description appear in catastrophic tone (failure of crops, planetary oppositions). And the concluding idiom in line 157, 'Parva loquor', is also a tag from Lucan (9. 783). But verbally the beginning of the passage draws on a different epic model, the prayer to Apollo at the end of the first book of Statius' *Thebaid* (1. 705-6):

tu doctus iniquas
parcarum *praenosse* manus fatumque quod ultra est
et summo placitura Iovi, *quis* let*ifer annus,*
bella quibus populis, quae mutent sceptra cometae.

Walter's combination of *praenosse* and *quis . . . 'fer annus,* both in the same metrical position and with neat inversion of sense in the second, can hardly be coincidental. But this shows that lines 142-3 in the *Alexandreis* passage were composed as a unit; the split found in the prosimetrum must be secondary.

This conclusion would in any case follow from comparing the functions of the two passages in context. In the *Alexandreis* the emphasis on astrology, confirmed in the concluding epigram, 'totum claudit sub pectore caelum', is integral to the scene.[23] In the prosimetrum,

the purpose of the passage is to take leave of the arts of the quadrivium, rather summarily treated in part 11. There was just enough general science in the Zoroas description to warrant its re-use in this sense, but even after the omissions the emphasis on astronomy/astrology is rather off key—contrast the careful balance in the parallel dismissal of the trivium that precedes. But on a literary level there is ample compensation for the imbalance if we read the passage as an elegantly adapted self-quotation, confirming with gentle irony the previous self-advertisement. The jingling couplet added at the end:

finge quod hec scieris, sed et his maiora: quid ad rem?
tam scito descieris hec omnia, quod nihil ad rem

gives a smooth transition back to medieval measures just at the point where the *Alexandreis* description switches back to narrative. On the opposite view, that the prosimetrum version was composed first, its combination of epic style and echoes, astrological emphasis and ironic flourishes seems to me hard to explain.[24]

I conclude then that the *Alexandreis* was largely complete before 1176 and probably published in that year with a couple of last-minute additions about Rheims. It was as fine a promotion-present as any patron could expect from his poet. But does it matter whether the *Alexandreis* was finished by 1176 or not till 1182/4? I think it does, and not just for the sake of getting details right rather than wrong. The *Alexandreis* is a historical poem on the most public and political of themes: conquest and rule. Properly to understand it will require more knowledge than I have of the political history and thought of the period. But it may be a start to determine just what period we are talking about.

Notes

1. Quotations are from Galteri de Castellione *Alexandreis,* ed. M. L. Colker (Padua, 1978). The best study of the poem remains H. Christensen, *Das Alexanderlied Walters von Châtillon* (Halle, 1905); see also the English translation by R. Telfryn Pritchard (Toronto, 1986) with useful bibliography, and H. Harich, *Alexander Epicus: Studien zur Alexandreis Walters von Châtillon* (Graz, 1987). Study of the poem will be much facilitated by H. E. Stiene and J. Grub, *Verskonkordanz zur Alexandreis des Walter von Châtillon* (Hildesheim, 1985), which only became available to me after this paper was written.

2. J. F. Benton, 'The Court of Champagne as a Literary Center', in *Speculum,* 36 (1961), 551-91. One of Walter's lyric poems (below, n. 17, poem 4) may have been dedicated to Count Henry.

3. Surveyed and discussed in G. Cary, *The Medieval Alexander* (Cambridge, 1956) and D. J. A. Ross, *Alexander Historiatus* (Warburg Institute Surveys, 1: London, 1963; 2nd edn., Frankfurt a.M., 1988).

4. 2. 333, 3. 167, cf. Christensen, 141 n. 1.

5. Walter may have taken a hint from Lambert Le Tort's Alexander poem, which also began with a protreptic speech by Aristotle, albeit more closely keyed into the narrative and focused on the dangers of promoting low-born servants (E. C. Armstrong et al. ed., *The Medieval French Roman d'Alexandre,* ii (Elliott Monographs, 37: Princeton, 1937), 143-5). Walter's scene as a whole owes more to Claudian (besides the references given by Colker cf. *Paneg. IV cons. Honorii* 358-78 with *Alexandreis* 1. 33-47, 198-9).

6. 4. 176-274, 7. 379-430; cf. also 1. 396-426, 2. 494-539.

7. 9. 77-147.

8. Cf. also 2. 381-7, 3. 280-1, 4. 361-6.

9. Cf. Curtius 3. 12. 18-21 and Justin 11. 11.

10. *Die Gedichte des Archipoeta,* ed. H. Watenphul and H. Krefeld (Heidelberg, 1958), 69-73, 127-38 (poem 9).

11. Cf. also stanza 31 'volat fama Cesaris velut velox equus, / hac audita trepidat imperator Grecus; / iam quid agat nescius, iam timore cecus, / timet nomen Cesaris ut lconem pecus'. And contrast *Alexandreis* 10. 182-4.

12. See [Dionisotti, A. C. "Walter of Chatillon and the Greeks." In *Latin Poetry and the Classical Tradition.* Oxford: Clarendon Press, 1990], Appendix.

13. Cf. also the scientific language at 1. 59-71, 415-17, 2. 166-70.

14. The more Aristotle was discovered, the more difficult it was to accommodate him in Western tradition and to explain his poor showing in Latin texts, especially in Augustine. Cf. the essentially hostile account in John of Salisbury's *Entheticus* 823-936 and in Alan of Lille's *Anticlaudianus*; a century later Roger Bacon could bluntly conclude that Augustine had just not read enough Aristotle.

15. Contrast John of Salisbury, *Policraticus* 6. 7.

16. Besides S as recorded by Colker, also at least London, BL Add. 23891, Novara Capit. N. 44, Oxford Bodl. 527; it should be noted that Colker's edition is based on a selection rather than a recension of the MSS.

17. *Die Lieder Walters von Châtillon,* ed. K. Strecker (Berlin, 1925), poem 30.

18. Christensen (n. 1 above), 4-13.

19. The Jews do figure in the poem, but as predecessors, not enemies, of Christianity, cf. 1. 420-1 'inde Palestinae cunctis supereminet una / unius Iudea Dei'. Alexander's dream and visit to Jerusalem (1. 499-554) are based on tradition, but the much-praised Jewish sculptor Apelles (Colker, *index nominum* s.v.) is Walter's creation and he includes Christian prophecy in his work (4. 256-67); the only note of criticism is 4. 242-5, which hardly suggests a crusade (cf. 2. 511-21). Walter's own dialogue *Adversus Iudaeos* is evangelizing, not bellicose.

20. E. Herkenrath, 'Die Zeit der *Alexandreis* Walters von Châtillon', *Historische Vierteljahrsschrift,* 29 (1935), 597-8, dates the passage to the crusading fervour of 1188/9, which would be plausible if 510 ff. could possibly mean: 'Machte Gottes Gnade den König der Franzosen so erfolgreich wie Alexander . . .'; they cannot.

21. *Moralisch-satirische Gedichte Walters von Châtillon,* ed. K. Strecker (Heidelberg, 1929), poem 3; cf. part 3: 'ante legum dominos et magistros artium / usurpare videor doctoris officium / ut sermonis epulo relevem ieiunium', and the MS rubrics: 'Galterus de Insula predicans scolaribus bon[oniensibus] in reditu suo a curia romana' and 'sermo recitatus Bononiae coram episcopo et scolaribus in dominica Letare Ierusalem'; since Bologna is not mentioned in the work, but Walter's presence there is independently attested in *Vita* 2 (Colker, p. xii), the rubrics seem trustworthy.

22. Strecker, pp. 36-7; I see no reason to suppose that the list of poets was a later addition (cf. E. Herkenrath's review of Strecker's edition, *Historische Vierteljahrsschrift,* 26 (1931), 856-7). There is independent evidence that both Stephen of Orleans and Peter of Blois performed publicly at Bologna; nothing is known of Berterus. The choice makes much better sense as a list of precedents (French poets addressing the university of Bologna) than as a list of famous poets in general; indeed I wonder whether the rather obscure line 'qui super hoc retinent sibi privilegium' should not be translated 'who in addition can claim this privilege', viz. of having addressed the law faculty at Bologna.

23. Manilius 2. 121 is curiously similar; it would be interesting to see whether there are any other parallels with this rare poet.

24. I would add that the prosimetrum version of l. 146 is a decided improvement on the other, completing the personification of Autumn as a

tipsy *vindemiator.* Strecker's argument from the variant reading *eclipsim* for *defectum* in l. 143 is invalid because the same variant is found in *Alexandreis* MSS and may well be a gloss.

Neil Adkin (essay date 1991)

SOURCE: Adkin, Neil. "The Proem of Walter of Châtillon's *Alexandreis*: 'Si . . . Nostros Uixisset in Annos.'" *Medium Ævum* 60, no. 2 (1991): 207-21.

[*In the following essay, Adkin attempts to explicate some puzzling lines in Walter's* Alexandreis *that appear to indicate that Alexander the Great lived for 1,500 years.*]

Walter opens his celebrated epic as follows:

> Gesta ducis Macedum totum digesta per orbem,
> Quam large dispersit opes, quo milite Porum
> Vicerit et Darium, quo principe Grecia uictrix
> Risit et a Persis rediere tributa Chorintum,
> Musa refer. Qui si senio non fractus inermi   (5)
> Pollice Fatorum nostros uixisset in annos,
> Cesareos numquam loqueretur fama tryumphos,
> Totaque Romuleae squaleret gloria gentis:
> Preradiaret enim meriti fulgore caminus
> Igniculos, solisque sui palleret in ortu   (10)
> Lucifer, et tardi languerent Plaustra Boete.[1]

The poem's most recent commentator gives the following rendering of lines 5-6:[2] 'Hätte dieser, nicht durch das wehrlose Alter gebrochen, mit der Befürwortung des Schicksals bis in unsere Jahre gelebt.' This is certainly the meaning that Walter's words appear to bear.[3] Yet the idea that Alexander might have lived for no less than 1,500 years has been a source of perplexity to expositors of the *Alexandreis* from the start. It is the intention of the present article to contribute towards an understanding of these puzzling lines.

Already the earliest extant manuscript of the poem contains a gloss on line 6, which runs as follows: 'nostros uixisset in annos: id est quantum nostrates uiuere solent'.[4] To set aside for the moment the other difficulties which this interpretation involves, there is a linguistic objection to it. The phrase 'nostros . . . in annos' also occurs in Ovid, *Ars Amatoria*, III.127: 'nec nostros mansit in annos / rusticitas'. Here the meaning is clearly 'to our day'.

In the first modern edition of the text, Mueldener proceeded to emend *nostros* to *iustos*.[5] He did not insert any punctuation:

> qui si senio non fractus inermi
> Pollice fatorum iustos uixisset in annos.

This conjecture was then accepted by Christensen.[6] There is, however, a serious objection to Mueldener's emendation. Whatever age he imagined his 'iustos . . . annos' to signify with reference to Alexander, they are at all events incompatible with 'senio non fractus inermi'. If 'just years' mean middle age, the specification that Alexander should not be 'broken by defenceless old age' is superfluous. If they denote old age themselves, as the parallels would suggest, then the lines are self-contradictory.[7]

There is a further reason why the solutions proposed by Mueldener and the Geneva gloss are unacceptable. Kratz[8] adopts Mueldener's text and paraphrases it as follows: 'In his proposition, Walter stresses not only the glory which Alexander won but also how much more he would have won had he lived longer (l. 1-8).' If this were so, Walter would again be guilty of self-contradiction. At the mid-point of the poem (v.491ff.) Walter states that Alexander's triumphal entry into Babylon, which has just been described, had no match in Roman history. He then continues:

> Et merito: nam si regum miranda recordans
> Laudibus et titulis cures attollere iustis,
> Si fide recolas quam raro milite contra   (500)
> Victores mundi tenero sub flore iuuente
> Quanta sit aggressus Macedo, quam tempore paruo
> Totus Alexandri genibus se fuderit orbis,
> Tota ducum series, uel quos Hyspana poesis
> Grandiloquo modulata stilo uel Claudius
> altis   (505)
> Versibus insignit, respectu principis
> Plebs erit ut pigeat tanto splendore Lucanum
> Cesareum cecinisse melos Romaeque ruinam
> Et Macedum claris succumbat Honorius armis.

Accordingly the entire world was already at Alexander's feet before he died (503).[9] Moreover, it was precisely because he achieved this at such a young age and in so short a time (501ff.) that he deserved to eclipse completely the subject-matter of Roman poetry. The idea of a 'normal' life-span for Alexander is therefore wholly out of place in the proem: instead of enhancing his glory, it would actually diminish it.

Walter is accordingly putting forward the serious proposition that Alexander might have lived on for a millennium and a half right down to the poet's own day, had the fates allowed it.[10] What then is Walter's purpose in propounding this remarkable idea?

No commentator has yet considered Walter's statement from the viewpoint of rhetorical theory. If the words 'nostros uixisset in annos' are examined in these terms, they present a clear case of hyperbole, for which the usual Latin term is *superlatio*. Hyperbole is regularly included in the *artes poeticae* produced during the twelfth and thirteenth centuries. It is customarily defined as: 'oratio superans ueritatem alicuius augendi minuendiue causa'.[11] Geoffrey of Vinsauf modifies this definition as follows: 'mirifice laudes . . . modus iste . . . auget'.[12] Such amplified praise of Alexander is of course just what Walter needs at the start of his poem. The fullest treatment of hyperbole is found in Quintilian.[13] His discussion concludes with the statement that hyperbole is most acceptable when the object to which we apply it is itself exceptional (VIII, vi, 76). This is unquestionably the case with Walter's depiction of Alexander.[14] In particular the review of Alexander's extraordinary feats in lines 1-4 forms a fitting prelude to the hyperbole in line 6.[15]

What made an effective proem was conveniently set out for the Middle Ages by the *Rhetorica ad Herennium*.[16] The prime function of the proem was to ensure that the audience was *attentus* (I, iv, 6): this could best be achieved by stressing the unique importance of the theme (I, iv, 7). We have noted that hyperbole was defined as transcendence of the truth 'alicuius augendi . . . causa'. Such a device for amplifying an object's importance was therefore ideally suited to the proem's function of *attentum parare*. The *Ad Herennium* goes on to say that we can achieve the same effect if we promise to speak 'de iis, quae . . . pertineant . . . ad eos ipsos, qui audient' (I, iv, 7). When Walter puts 'nostros uixisset in annos' in his proem, he is accordingly doing precisely what the standard handbook required. After the combination of hyperbole and this contemporary reference, the audience cannot have failed to be totally *attentus*.

A final point may be made. In his discussion of hyperbole Quintilian observes further that by its very nature it is incredible: 'est omnis hyperbole ultra fidem' (VIII, vi, 73). Moreover, the particular kind of hyperbole that Walter uses here is of the type κατὰ τὸ ἀδύνατον.[17] Accordingly the bewilderment expressed by Harich is quite out of place.[18]

If, then, lines 5-6, when seen in rhetorical terms, are simply an arresting example of hyperbole intended to capture the audience's attention, the question must still be asked why Walter chooses to express himself in these particular terms.[19] After stating her surprise, Harich endeavours to justify the idea that Alexander might have lived on for one and a half millennia with the following argument: 'Doch (der Gedanke) dient dem Epiker sehr wohl in einem wichtigen Auftrag. Durch diesen Wunsch schafft er sich nämlich ein Vehikel, zu zwei weiteren Motivkreisen seines Gedichtes, zur Kritik an Rom und zur Auseinandersetzung mit den Epikern der 'urbs aeterna' überzuleiten.'[20] If the notion of Alexander's phenomenal longevity were simply meant to facilitate a transition to anti-Roman polemic, it would be a

singularly inept way of doing it. In the first place, such longevity is superfluous, since the lines quoted above from the end of Book v (498ff.) state that consideration of Alexander's actual achievements is alone enough to show the massive superiority of Walter's subject-matter over that of the epic poets of Rome. Secondly, the idea entails a *non sequitur*: had Alexander lived to the present, it may be thought that he would not so much have eclipsed the Roman Emperors ('preradiaret' 9) as actually precluded their very existence.[21]

Harich is in fact wrong to interpret lines 7-8 ('Cesareos numquam loqueretur . . .') as an attack on Rome and its poets. Nor is Walter rebutting Lucan's abuse of Alexander in *Bellum Civile*, x.20ff.[22] Rather, these lines are just another instance of the *Überbietungstopos*:[23] the poet asserts that his own subject-matter surpasses all others and therefore has a unique claim to the audience's attention.[24] The ancient term for *Überbietung* is *hyperoche*; it is a form of hyperbole.[25] Walter has thus accommodated two consecutive cases of hyperbole in the space of four lines (5-8). Quintilian himself stresses the powerful impact that is produced by two successive occurrences of this rhetorical figure (VIII, vi, 70). However, the point was made above that for all its effectiveness this juxtaposition would appear to involve a *non sequitur*: an Alexander who had lived to the present would have left no room for the Roman Caesars.[26]

This brings us back to the question from which we set out: why does Walter say 'si . . . nostros uixisset in annos'? The answer is surely to be found in the very last lines of Book v. This passage stands at the central point of the entire poem[27] and therefore carries the utmost significance. It runs as follows:

> Si gemitu commota pio uotisque suorum   (510)
> Flebilibus diuina daret clementia talem
> Francorum regem, toto radiaret in orbe
> Haut mora uera fides, et nostris fracta sub armis
> Parthia baptismo renouari posceret ultro,
> Queque diu iacuit effusis menibus alta   (515)
> Ad nomen Christi Kartago resurgeret, et quas
> Sub Karolo meruit Hyspania soluere penas
> Exigerent uexilla crucis, gens omnis et omnis
> Lingua Ihesum caneret et non inuita subiret
> Sacrum sub sacro Remorum presule fontem.   (520)

'Talem/Francorum regem' (511-12) is generally recognized as a reference to Philip Augustus, who was crowned King of France on 1 November 1179[28] at the age of fourteen; the coronation was performed by the boy's uncle, Archbishop William of Rheims, who was Walter's patron. The remainder of the passage pictures the defeat and conversion of the Saracens.[29] Accordingly Walter is making the encomiastic assertion that Philip resembles Alexander and he will therefore be able to lead a final, overwhelming crusade.[30]

Lines 5-6 of the proem are surely to be seen as an adumbration of this idea, which is then made explicit in the centre of the poem. The concept of an Alexander who had 'lived to our day' is meant to suggest that France's own royal prince is himself a contemporary analogue of the great Macedonian.[31] Walter is therefore beginning his poem with an encomium of the new monarch which is very discreet but also extremely flattering. At the same time the identification suggests that the ensuing portrait of Alexander, which for the most part is highly favourable,[32] should be seen as providing a model for the young king.[33]

This interpretation is confirmed by the second half of line five: 'senio non fractus inermi'. Insofar as the words are applied to Alexander, they would appear to be supererogatory. Alexander himself had died young: old age was not his problem. If he were to live a further 1,500 years, he would obviously need to be exempt from its effects: a soldierly Tithonus would be no use. The stipulation accordingly seems pointless. On the other hand, the phrasing that Walter employs is not attested elsewhere.[34] It would seem therefore to be Walter's own: he evidently intends it to be significant. Moreover, the words occupy an extremely prominent position at the start of this long and very important sentence. Why, then, has Walter put them in?[35]

Philip Augustus was the offspring of Louis VII's third marriage; Louis's previous two wives had only given him daughters. Consequently, when Philip was born in 1165, chroniclers say this occurred when Louis was already 'in senectute sua'.[36] Likewise in William the Breton's *Philippeis* Louis describes himself as 'iam decrepito senioque labanti' at the time of his son's birth (1.318).[37] At all events by the beginning of 1179 Louis was ailing very seriously. Rigord says that in this year Louis was 'pene septuagenarius'.[38] He adds that the king was suffering from paralysis.[39] Later in the same year Louis suffered a stroke which deprived him of the use of his right side.[40] He was now completely incapacitated. He could neither walk[41] nor speak.[42] Under such circumstances the old king was naturally unable to attend his son's coronation. In connection with this event Louis is described by Roger of Hoveden as 'senio et morbo laborans paralytico',[43] while Gilbert of Mons speaks of him as being 'senio et corporis debilitate grauis'.[44] Some time before the coronation Louis's condition is twice characterized by Gerald of Wales: the terms he uses are 'morbo simul et senio ualde grauatus',[45] and 'senio iam et ualetudine confectus'.[46] Louis continued this helpless existence until he finally died on 19 September 1180.[47] Ralph Niger describes his end thus: 'martyrio igitur longae infirmitatis decoctus in sanctitate decessit'.[48]

The abundance of the foregoing evidence would suggest that Louis's senility had been a matter of the widest concern. Moreover, no fewer than five of the passages cited apply to him the word *senium*. Here we surely have the key to Walter's 'senio non fractus inermi'. These words will have been recognized immediately by contemporaries as a reference to the senile and paralytic king. The identification leads in turn to a correct understanding of the next line. If the senile wreck of line 5 is Louis VII,[49] then the present-day Alexander of line 6 can be none other than his dynamic young successor, Philip Augustus.

In rhetorical terms these two lines are an example of the figure which Quintilian calls 'emphasis'. He defines it as follows: 'est emphasis . . . cum ex aliquo dicto latens aliquid eruitur'.[50] The space which Quintilian allots to the treatment of 'emphasis' is very considerable.[51] In particular he lists three circumstances in which it is appropriate: 'eius triplex usus est: unus, si dicere palam parum tutum est, alter, si non decet, tertius, qui uenustatis modo gratia adhibetur et ipsa nouitate ac uarietate magis, quam si relatio sit recta, delectat'.[52] At the end of Book v Walter makes an explicit request for 'talem Francorum regem': it might seem therefore that his principal motive for using the figure here was the last of those enumerated by Quintilian. On the other hand, the early months of Philip Augustus' reign were marked by the ascendancy of the Count of Flanders and by a consequent eclipse of the house of Blois-Champagne; a reconciliation with the latter did not take place until June 1180.[53] One of the leading members of this house was Archbishop William of Rheims, to whom the *Alexandreis* is dedicated. Accordingly it would appear that Quintilian's first motive is the main factor involved here: 'si dicere palam parum tatum est'. Whereas in the middle of the work it was possible to be more explicit, discretion required the use of *emphasis* in the proem.

Instead of *emphasis* the *Rhetorica ad Herennium* use the term *significatio*.[54] This term was taken over by the mediaeval *artes poeticae*, which give a regular place to the figure.[55] The *Ad Herennium* enumerates five devices whereby *significatio* can be achieved. The first of them is *exsuperatio*: this is essentially the same as *superlatio*, which is the *Ad Herennium*'s basic term for hyperbole.[56] The prescription that *significatio* is achieved by hyperbole is also repeated by some of the mediaeval *artes*.[57] According to the *Ad Herennium*, hyperbole is an appropriate means of generating *significatio* because it can be used 'augendae suspicionis causa'. The point was made earlier that hyperbole is the figure which Walter employs in line 6. It would seem, therefore, that he is following the standard prescription to the letter.

The perception that line 6 refers to Philip Augustus also affects the reader's understanding of the following two lines. In particular it makes clear that Walter is not guilty of a *non sequitur* after all. If the Alexander who lives to the present is simply meant to suggest Philip Augustus, there is no inconsistency in affirming that such a figure would eclipse the Caesars: whereas an aeonian Alexander might have seemed to leave no room for them, a young Philip Augustus can easily be imagined as their rival. Favourable comparison with the Caesars is of course very emphatic encomium of the French monarch. At the same time it was argued above that this comparison also serves to establish the superiority of Walter's own work over classical Roman poetry. The point is no less valid when line 6 is understood as referring to Philip Augustus, for the same outstanding virtues which are to find their contemporary expression in Philip will be the subject-matter of Walter's poem: it is these that enable Walter to outdo the classics. The reader must admire the skill and economy with which Walter has here combined encomium of the ruler with *commendatio* of his own work.

One further point may be made in regard to this section. If lines 5-6 refer to contemporaries, it would appear legitimate to see a contemporary as well as a classical reference in lines 7-8. Here the combination of 'Cesareos' and 'Romuleae' is surely meant to call to mind the Holy Roman Emperor. He is regularly styled *Romanorum cesar.*[58] There are in fact a number of reasons why such a reference is *à propos* in Walter's proem. It is clear that Walter himself was a patrotic Frenchman.[59] Moreover, the rivalry of the kings of France *vis-à-vis* the Emperor was notorious in this period.[60] At the same time, Walter had his own good reason for hating the emperor: it was the Emperor Frederick who had been responsible for the schism which split the Church until 1177. In one of his short poems,[61] Walter compares Alexander the Great's triple victory over Darius to Pope Alexander III's triple victory over 'cesar rex tenebrarum' (4).[62] There is evidently a parallel here to the proem of the ***Alexandreis,*** in which a French king also eclipses the Caesars. It would therefore appear highly probable that alongside the reference to Roman poetry *cesareos* and *Romuleae* in lines 7-8 are indeed meant to contain an allusion to the Emperor Frederick Barbarossa.

The final lines of Book v form a counterpart to the proem insofar as they too combine an encomiastic reference to the young King of France with an assertion of the superiority of Walter's theme over those of Lucan and Claudian. Besides politics and poetics the two passages also have a third element in common: both conclude with praise of Walter's patron, the great Archbishop of Rheims. Accordingly the proem and the end of Book v are exactly parallel in content. It is not therefore surprising that the two passages should also be linked by a close verbal correlation. Since this feature has not been noted by previous commentators, it will be convenient to provide a full documentation.

In v.497, 'Tarpeiam Iulius arcem' clearly recalls 'Tarpeiam Brennius arcem' at 1.15. Similarly, 'quam raro milite' (v.500) recalls 'quo milite' (1.2). At v.508 'cesareum' is the first word of the line and is followed by 'Romae'; in 1.7, 'cesareos' stands first in the line and precedes 'Romuleae'. 'Radiaret' (v.512) matches 'preradiaret' (1.9); both verbs occur in the first of a series of parallel clauses *in apodosi*. Most significant of all is the manner in which 'nostris fracta sub armis' (v.513) echoes 'senio non fractus inermi' (1.5); both phrases occupy the final position in their respective lines. Here the parallel shows that *inermi* is to be understood quite literally: in contrast to the bedridden old king Walter wants Philip Augustus to be an effective fighter. Jolly and Pritchard are therefore wrong to render the word simply as 'weak'. The interpretation given by the gloss is also erroneous: 'inermi dicit quia senium humores siccat'.[63] A final parallel between the proem and the last lines of Book v may be cited. As 'sacros fontes' occurs in the penultimate line of the proem, so 'sacrum . . . fontem' encloses the final line of the fifth book and thereby rounds off the first half of the poem. On both occasions the words refer to Walter's patron, Archbishop William. It may be noted that an encomiastic reference to the archbishop also concludes the entire poem (x.469).

If, then, the proem and the end of Book v reveal a strict parallelism in regard to both content and language, the second of these two passages is distinctly more explicit. Whereas the proem speaks in general terms of 'cesareos . . . tryumphos', the fifth book makes specific mention of Lucan and Claudian along with the subjects of their respective poems. The same is true in regard to the King of France. While the proem does no more than hint by means of *significatio,* Walter refers explicitly in Book v to 'talem/Francorum regem' (511-12).[64] Moreover, the last lines of this book make clear that it is specifically as a crusader that Philip Augustus should model himself on Alexander. The appeal comes at the mid-point of the poem; by this time the audience has had plenty of opportunity to see Alexander in action. It is also noteworthy that along with this greater explicitness comes a shift from pagan to Christian: while the proem has 'pollice Fatorum' (6),[65] Book v speaks of 'diuina . . . clementia' (511).

As soon as the proem is over the audience receives its first glimpse of Alexander. He learns that his people are subject to the Persians and reacts to the news with anger. In this opening episode Alexander is introduced as 'arma puer sitiens' (30). The first two words are a clear echo of 'senio . . . inermi' in line 5 of the proem:

'inermi' is picked up by 'arma' and 'senio' by 'puer'.[66] It has been argued above that for contemporaries 'senio . . . inermi' was an unmistakable reference to Louis VII. Accordingly 'arma puer sitiens' must necessarily have put the audience in mind of Philip Augustus. It will be recalled that Philip was a boy of fourteen at the time of his coronation in November 1179.[67] The same collocation 'puer . . . arma' also rounds off this opening scene (56).[68] Walter has thereby exploited Alexander's very first appearance to establish his role as model for the young French king.

This exemplary function is confirmed by the following scene. In it Aristotle comes out and proceeds to give Alexander instruction on the art of virtuous kingship. For the first time Walter now refers to his hero by name; significantly he chooses the patronymic 'Philippida' (72). The name occurs nowhere else in the entire poem and requires explication by the glosses:[69] inevitably it calls to mind Philip Augustus. The next sentence contains an even clearer signal. When Aristotle asks why the face of his young ward is flushed with anger, Alexander replies that he is sorrowing for his father's old age: 'senium lugere parentis' (78). Colker's *apparatus fontium* cites no parallel for this phrase; it would therefore appear to be Walter's own deliberate formulation. The idea of a mere *puer* sorrowing for the *senium* of his father is very strange indeed.[70] It certainly does not fit Alexander: when he was twelve ('duodenni', 44), Philip of Macedon was only thirty-eight.[71] On the other hand, when Philip Augustus was twelve years old, his father Louis VII was fifty-seven; it was noted above that sources regularly speak of him as already an 'old man'. Hence the conclusion may be drawn that Walter has written these words with Philip Augustus in mind. The passage is therefore further evidence that 'senium' in line 5 refers to Louis.

Aristotle then begins his long speech of instruction on the virtues of a king. Its very first line significantly contains the juxtaposition 'puer, arma': 'Macedo puer, arma capesce' (82). This collocation has thus occurred three times within the first sixty lines of Walter's narrative.[72] Its presence in the opening line of this *Fürstenspiegel*[73] might therefore suggest that Aristotle's precepts are also meant to have some relevance for the young French king.[74] Such an application would seem to be all the more probable inasmuch as the ensuing scene depicting Alexander's coronation also calls to mind that of Philip Augustus in 1179.[75] For both Aristotle's speech and Alexander's coronation Walter was not following any source.[76] It would appear, therefore, that both these episodes have been composed with the young king of France in mind. After the clear signal in lines 5-6 of the proem, the audience would necessarily see them as having such a reference.

In conclusion some remarks may be made on the implications which the interpretation offered above has for the poem's date. The reference to *puer* would fit any time at which Philip Augustus was growing up. His coronation too was in prospect from the early 1170s onwards.[77] However, 'senio non fractus inermi' in line 5 of the proem must have been written after Louis VII had become a helpless and senile invalid. Though he had been ailing for some time already, the stroke which he suffered at the end of August or the very beginning of September 1179 incapacitated him completely, and he remained in much the same condition for more than a year until his death on 19 September 1180. It might, therefore, seem reasonable to suppose that line 5 was written at some time between the date of Louis's stroke and a date not much later than his decease, before his senility ceased to occupy people's minds.

If this is so, then it would appear that line 5 also supplies the key to the vexed question of the poem's date of publication.[78] Since the impression made by a proem is naturally crucial to any work's success, Walter will have been extremely anxious to ensure that his own opening words were not marred by any obscurity. In particular, it was argued above that line 5 provides the clue to the correct interpretation of the hyperbole in the following line. Accordingly 'senio non fractus inermi' needed to be immediately intelligible. These words must therefore have been highly topical at the time the poem was published.

Hitherto there has been a wide range of proposals for the date of publication. Peiper argued for 1177 or 1178;[79] however, his dating is open to the objection that in these years Louis was not yet bedridden.[80] Christensen postulated a date 'some years after 1182';[81] this cannot be right, since by then Louis had been dead too long for line 5 to be properly intelligible. The same objection applies all the more cogently to Herkenrath's proposed date of 'around 1189'.[82] We know that Louis was 'senio . . . fractus inermi' from the time of his stroke at the end of August or the start of September 1179 until his death on 19 September 1180. It would seem therefore to be a legitimate inference that the *Alexandreis* was published between these two dates, or very shortly afterwards.

Notes

1. *Galteri de Castellione Alexandreis*, ed. by M. L. Colker, Thesaurus Mundi, 17 (Padua, 1978), p. 7.

2. H. Harich, *Alexander Epicus. Studien zur 'Alexandreis' Walters von Châtillon* (Graz, 1987), p. 97.

3. A similar rendering is given in R. T. Pritchard, *Walter of Châtillon: the 'Alexandreis'; Translated with an Introduction and Notes* (Toronto, 1986),

p. 35 ('Had he been permitted by the thumbs of the fates to live on to our time, without being broken by weak senility').

4. Geneva, Bibliothèque publique et universitaire, MS lat. 98 (s. xii); see *Alexandreis,* ed. Colker, p. 277.

5. *M. Philippi Gualtheri ab Insulis dicti de Castellione Alexandreis,* ed. by F. A. W. Mueldener (Leipzig, 1863), p. 5.

6. H. Christensen, *Das Alexanderlied Walters von Châtillon* (Halle/S., 1905; repr. Hildesheim, 1969), p. 200. Christensen referred to Ovid, *Metamorphoses,* x.36: 'cum iustos matura peregerit annos'. Ovid uses the words in connection with Eurydice to denote an age at which death would not be untimely. In his commentary on this line, F. Bömer, *P. Ovidius Naso, 'Metamorphosen': Kommentar, Buch X-XI* (Heidelberg, 1980), p. 25, compared Ausonius, cccLxv.1-2 (ed. by R. Peiper (Leipzig, 1886), p. 93), where *iusta* refers to the age of ninety-six: 'ter binos deciesque nouem super exit in annos, iusta senescentum quos implet uita uirorum'. Bömer notes that Ovid's combination of *iustus* and *annus* is without parallel.

7. The same objections apply to the interpretation in the gloss mentioned above ('quantum nostrates uiuere solent'). Christensen was evidently aware of the problem; he therefore made the following modification to Mueldener's punctuation, though without any explicit comment (Christensen, *Das Alexanderlied,* p. 89):

> qui si senio, non fractus inermi
> Pollice fatorum iustos uixisset in annos.

This obviates the difficulty, but at the cost of immense awkwardness. The glosses on line 5 naturally take 'senio . . . inermi' as a single unit: so Erfurt, Wissenschaftliche Bibliothek, MS Amplon. 8° 17 (*Alexandreis,* ed. Colker, p. 304); Vienna, Nationalbibliothek, MS 568 (*Alexandreis,* ed. Colker, p. 354). It may be noted that Christensen's misgivings are not shared in W. T. Jolly, 'The *Alexandreid* of Walter of Châtillon: a translation and commentary' (unpub. diss., Tulane University, 1968), p. 35; he translates Mueldener's text thus: 'If, unbroken by weak old age, he had lived to a proper span of years with the approval of the fates'. Christensen's punctuation recurs in C. Giordano, *'Alexandreis', poema di Gautier da Châtillon* (Naples, 1917), p. 166: he cites 'fractus Pollice fatorum' (*sic*) as an example of *secentismo.*

8. D. M. Kratz, *Mocking Epic: 'Waltharius', 'Alexandreis' and the Problem of Christian Heroism* (Madrid, 1980), p. 79.

9. Cf. also x.216-17: 'Vt tamen ante diem extremum, quem fata parabant, / Omnia rex regum sibi subdita regna uideret . . .'; the passage is based on Justin, *Epitoma historiarum Philippicarum Pompei Trogi,* xii, xiii, 1-2.

10. The text in *PL,* CCIX, col. 464 punctuates thus:

> qui si senio non fractus inermi
> Pollice fatorum, nostros uixisset in annos.

However, it would seem a more fitting employment for the thumbs of the fates to multiply Alexander's life-span rather than merely to shield him from the effects of old age; cf. the Erfurt gloss (*Alexandreis,* ed. Colker, p. 304): 'pollice: quia Fata pollice suo uitam hominum dispensant'. Hence there is no place for a comma after 'fatorum'. Nonetheless the Migne punctuation recurs in J. Hellegouarc'h, 'Gautier de Châtillon, poète épique dans l'*Alexandréide.* Quelques observations', in *Alain de Lille, Gautier de Châtillon, Jakemart Giélée et leur temps,* ed. by H. Roussel and F. Suard (Lille, 1980), pp. 239-40.

11. So the anonymous Saint-Omer treatise, ed. by C. Fierville, *Notices et extraits des manuscrits,* XXXI:1 (1884), 107 (no. xliv); also John of Garland, *Parisiana Poetria,* ed. by T. Lawler (New Haven; London, 1974), p. 128 (vi.298-9). The definition is taken verbatim from *Rhetorica ad Herennium,* iv, xxxiii, 44.

12. Geoffrey of Vinsauf, *Poetria Nova,* ed. in e. Faral, *Les Arts poétiques du XIIᵉ et du XIIIᵉ siècle* (Paris, 1924; repr. 1962), p. 229 (line 1020).

13. *Institutio Oratoria,* viii, vi, 67-76. This passage did form part of the mutilated text current in France: cf. P. Lehmann, 'Die "Institutio oratoria" des Quintilianus im Mittelalter', *Philologus,* LXXXIX (1934), 355.

14. One might compare the following words from Alexander's final speech:

> summum deinceps recturus Olympum
> Ad maiora uocor, et me uocat arduus ether
> Vt solium regni et sedem sortitus in astris
> Cum loue disponam rerum secreta breuesque
> Euentus hominum superumque negocia tractem.
>
> (x.405-9)

15. Walter's hyperbole might seem somewhat less bold when set against Revelation xx.4: 'uixerunt . . . mille annis'. On mediaeval millenarianism, cf. N. Cohn, *The Pursuit of the Millennium,* 3rd edn (Oxford, 1970), esp. pp. 29ff. (p. 32 on the 'Sleeping Emperor' of the Pseudo-Methodius).

16. On the enormous importance of this work for the Middle Ages, cf. J. Brzoska, *Paulys Real-Encyclopädie,* IV (1901), coll. 1617ff.

17. According to the classification in Demetrius, *De Elocutione,* cxxiv.

18. Harich, *Alexander Epicus,* p. 99: 'Das Verspaar . . . bringt . . . eine interpretatorische Schwierigkeit mit sich, da man ja nicht annehmen kann, der Erzähler trage mit sich den Gedanken herum, Alexander hätte wirklich bis in seine Gegenwart leben können.'

19. It may be that the idea of 'living on' was initially suggested to Walter by Alexander's early death. However, it will be argued below that he had a much stronger reason for making Alexander live 'to our day'.

20. Harich, *Alexander Epicus,* p. 100.

21. F. P. Knapp, *Similitudo, Stil- und Erzählfunktion von Vergleich und Exempel in der lateinischen, französischen und deutschen Grossepik des Hochmittelalters* (Vienna, 1975), p. 225, glosses over the *non sequitur* with the following paraphrase: 'Walthers Voraussage . . . der durch sein Gedicht verbreitete Ruhm Alexanders des Grossen werde den Roms und seiner Caesaren verblassen lassen.'

22. So Christensen, *Das Alexanderlied,* p. 88 (cited in Harich, *Alexander Epicus,* p. 100 n. 1).

23. On *Überbietung* in general, cf. E. R. Curtius, 'Beiträge zur Topik der mittellateinischen Literatur', in *Corona Quernea, Festgabe Karl Strecker* (Stuttgart, 1941; repr. 1952), pp. 1ff. On the topos as a feature of the proem, cf. L. Arbusow, *Colores Rhetorici,* 2nd edn, rev. by H. Peter (Göttingen, 1963), p. 97.

24. It therefore belongs to the *commendatio,* which is one of the eight standard elements of the proem according to the classification in G. Engel, *De Antiquorum Epicorum Didacticorum Historicorum Prooemiis* (Marburg, 1910), p. 7.

25. So Curtius, 'Beiträge', p. 1; Arbusow, *Colores Rhetorici,* pp. 89-90.

26. Perhaps it is pertinent to refer in this connection to one particular variety of the *Überbietungstopos,* which takes the form: 'Had he lived in ancient times, he would have eclipsed the classics.' Examples in Baudry of Bourgueil are noted in E. R. Curtius, 'Die Musen im Mittelalter. Erster Teil: bis 1100', *Zeitschrift für romanische Philolgie,* LIX (1939), 177-8 (see *Baldricus Burgulianus Carmina,* ed. by K. Hilbert (Heidelberg, 1979), xxxvii.1-2; lxxxvii.14; xcix.67-8; cci.27-8). In Walter, of course, there is a reversal of the usual order: instead of a contemporary being placed in the past, the ancient hero is transposed to the present.

27. Cf. O. Zwierlein, *Der prägende Einfluss des antiken Epos auf die 'Alexandreis' des Walter von Châtillon* (Stuttgart, 1987), p. 8.

28. The composition of Walter's poem is placed variously between 1170 and 1182, its publication between 1177 and 1189: cf. Jolly, 'The *Alexandreid*', pp. 15ff. The question is reconsidered below.

29. So E. Herkenrath, 'Die Zeit der *Alexandreis* Walters von Châtillon', *Historische Vierteljahrschrift,* XXIX (1934), 597. The passage had previously been taken as referring to the Jews; cf. Christensen, *Das Alexanderlied,* p. 9 n. 1.

30. On Philip's early enthusiasm in the matter of a crusade, cf. A. Cartellieri, *Philipp II. August, König von Frankreich,* Vol. II (Leipzig, 1906; repr. Aalen, 1969), pp. 12ff.

31. The proem has thus made a transition from Greece ('Grecia uictrix', 3) to the poet's own country, France.

32. Cf. Harich, *Alexander Epicus,* pp. 206ff.

33. It might, therefore, be said that the poem has a similar function to Gilles de Paris's epic on Charlemagne, the *Karolinus,* which was written shortly after the *Alexandreis* for Philip Augustus' own son, the future Louis VIII; in Gilles of course the didactic intent is much more explicit. It accords with such a pedagogic purpose that both these poems eschew legendary elements. Similarly, it has been argued that the 'new man' of Alain de Lille's *Anticlaudianus* is meant to suggest Philip Augustus: cf. L. E. Marshall, 'The identity of the "new man" in the *Anticlaudianus* of Alan of Lille', *Viator,* X (1979), 77-94; M. Wilks, 'Alan of Lille and the new man', in *Renaissance and Renewal in Christian History,* ed. by D. Baker, Studies in Church History, 14 (Oxford, 1977), pp. 137-57.

34. Colker's *apparatus fontium* compares Lucan *Pharsalia,* viii.476: 'placidus senio fractisque modestior annis', which is hardly apposite. *Thesaurus Linguae Latinae, s.v.* 'inermis' gives no example of the collocation with *senium.*

35. The same question puzzled the glossators. Vienna MS 568, of the late thirteenth century, suggests: 'inermi senio: . . . a sene inermi, scilicet Antipatre, qui eum inuenenauit' (*Alexandreis,* ed. Colker, p. 354).

36. *Chronicon S. Medardi Suessionensis,* (L. d'Achéry, *Spicilegium sive Collectio Veterum aliquot Scriptorum,* Vol. II (Paris, 1723), p. 494); *Recueil des historiens des Gaules et de la France,* Vol. XII (Paris, 1877), p. 133 n. (a). Cartellieri, *Philipp II. August,* I, 7 n. 5 detects an echo of Luke i.36 ('in senecta sua').

37. *Oeuvres de Rigord et de Guillaume le Breton,* ed. by H.-F. Delaborde, 2 vols. (Paris, 1882-5), II, 20.

38. *Gesta Philippi Augusti,* II (*ibid.,* I, 9). Louis was seventy according to William the Breton, *Gesta Philippi Augusti,* XVI (*ibid.,* I, 179), and *Philippeis,* I, 361 (*ibid.,* I, 21). Since Louis was born in 1120, he was in fact not quite sixty; cf. Cartellieri, *Philipp II. August,* I, 29 and n. 4 ('obwohl er erst 60 Jahre alt war, sahen ihn seine Vertrauten als einen Greis an').

39. *Gesta Philippi Augusti,* II (*Oeuvres de Rigord . . .* , ed. Delaborde, I, 10).

40. *Gesta Regis Henrici Secundi Benedicti Abbatis,* ed. by W. Stubbs, Vol. I, Rolls Series (London, 1867), p. 243.

41. Rigord, *Gesta Philippi Augusti,* IV (*Oeuvres de Rigord . . .* , ed. Delaborde, I, 13): 'Ludouico . . . aduersa egritudine nimis grauato, uidelicet paralysi que ei gressum prorsus negauerat.' Cartellieri, *Philipp II. August,* I, 36 and *Beilagen,* p. 15, notes the devastating effect of such immobility in an age which required a ruler to be constantly on the move.

42. *Fragmentum Historicum Vitam Ludovici VII. summatim complectens* (*Recueil des historiens des Gaules et de la France,* Vol. XII (Paris, 1877), p. 286): 'percussus est paralysi in lingua et in toto corpore, sed maxime in lingua'.

43. *Chronica,* ed. by W. Stubbs, Vol. II, Rolls Series (London, 1869), p. 194.

44. *Chronicon Hanoniense,* XCII (ed. by L. Vanderkindere (Brussels, 1904), p. 127).

45. *De Invectionibus,* VI.26 (ed. by W. S. Davies, Y Cymmrodor, 30 (London, 1920), p. 230).

46. *De Principis Instructione,* III.1 (ed. by G. F. Warner, Vol. VIII, Rolls Series (London, 1891), p. 226). Gerald may be referring to an event of 1177: cf. *ibid., ad loc.*

47. Cf. Cartellieri, *Philipp II. August,* I, 89.

48. *Chronicon,* 1 (ed. by R. Anstruther, Publications of the Caxton Society, 13 (London, 1851; repr. New York, 1967), p. 93).

49. It may be recalled that Louis had favoured Count Philip of Flanders as adviser to Philip Augustus at the expense of the boy's uncle, Archbishop William of Rheims, who was Walter's patron: cf. Cartellieri, *Philipp II. August,* I, 38ff., and *Beilagen,* pp. 14ff. Accordingly a somewhat derogatory reference to Louis in the proem is perhaps not surprising.

50. *Institutio Oratoria,* IX, ii, 64. Cf. *ibid.,* IX, ii, 65 'per quandam suspicionem quod non dicimus accipi uolumus, non utique contrarium, ut in εἰρωνείᾳ, sed aliud latens et auditori quasi inueniendum'.

51. *Ibid.,* IX, ii, 64-99. This passage was part of the incomplete text circulating in France: cf. Lehmann, 'Die "Institutio oratoria"', p. 355.

52. *Ibid.,* IX, ii, 66.

53. Cf. Cartellieri, *Philipp II. Augustus,* I, 48ff. On renewed friction in 1181, cf. *ibid.,* I, 106.

54. *Rhetorica ad Herennium,* IV, liii, 67. Cf. G. Calboli, *Cornifici Rhetorica ad C. Herennium: Introduzione, Testo critico, Commento* (Bologna, 1969), p. 429 n. 300. The *Ad Herennium,* IV, liv, 67, describes the figure thus: 'haec exornatio plurimum festivitatis habet interdum et dignitatis; sinit enim quiddam tacito oratore ipsum auditorem suspicari'.

55. Anon. Saint-Omer (n. 11), 111 (nos. lxxiv-lxxviii); Geoffrey of Vinsauf, *Poetria Nova,* lines 1269-70, 1423-31, 1531-83 (Faral, *Les Arts poétiques,* pp. 236, 240-1, 244-5); Evrard the German, *Laborintus,* lines 561-70 (*ibid.,* p. 357); John of Garland, *Parisiana Poetria,* VI.385-7, and *Exempla Honestae Vitae,* lines 249-59 (ed. by E. Habel, *Romanische Forschungen,* XXIX (1911), 151).

56. Cf. Calboli, *Cornifici Rhetorica ad C. Herennium,* p. 431 n. 301.

57. Saint-Omer treatise (see n. 11 above), no. lxxiv (p. 111); Geoffrey of Vinsauf, *Poetria Nova,* lines 1538-44 (Faral, *Les Arts poétiques,* p. 244).

58. Cf. *Mittellateinisches Wörterbuch, s.v.* 'caesar', I, B.1 *passim.* For Walter's association of the two terms, cf. *Moralisch-satirische Gedichte,* ed. by K. Strecker (Heidelberg, 1929), xv, vii, 1 (p. 135): 'Si Roma cesar, si cesare Roma careret'.

59. Cf. *Alexandreis,* x.232-3.

60. Cf. P. E. Schramm, *Der König von Frankreich: das Wesen der Monarchie vom 9. zum 16. Jahrhundert,* 2nd edn, Vol. I (Darmstadt, 1960), pp. 180-1. It may be noted that Frederick Barbarossa was crowned King of Burgundy on 30 July 1178.

61. *Moralisch-satirische Gedichte,* ed. Strecker, p. 137 (xv.18). The poem was written some time before 29 August 1178 (*ibid.,* p. 132).

62. 'Federicus (*sic*) cesar', as author of the schism, is a precursor of Antichrist (*ibid.,* p. 144 (xvi.24)).

63. MS Amplon. 8° 17 (*Alexandreis,* ed. Colker, p. 304).

64. In the fifth book this topic comes after the theme of poetic rivalry. The reverse order occurs in the proem.

65. The phrase is taken from Claudian, *De Raptu Proserpinae,* I.52.

66. Julius Valerius, who is the source of this episode, places it just before Philip's assassination; cf. Christensen, *Das Alexanderlied,* p. 143. At the time of his father's death Alexander was twenty according to Justin, *Epitoma,* XI, i, 9. Walter's use of *puer* would therefore appear to be significant.

67. He was born on 21 August 1165.

68. 'Sic puer effrenus totus bachatur in arma'. The words frame the line emphatically.

69. I.e. Geneva MS lat. 98 (*Alexandreis,* ed. Colker, p. 278); MS Amplon. 8° 17 (*ibid.,* p. 307); Vienna MS 568 (*ibid.,* p. 359).

70. However, there is no comment in either Jolly, 'The *Alexandreid*', or Pritchard, *Walter of Châtillon.*

71. Philip's exact age will have been known to Walter from Justin, *Epitoma,* IX, viii, 1.

72. Harich omits it from her list of 'wichtige Leitmotive' (*Alexander Epicus,* pp. 16ff.). It may also be remarked how at the end of Book v, where the King of France is mentioned explicitly, Walter stresses that Alexander's conquests took place 'tenero sub flore iuuentae' (v.501).

73. The term is used loosely: cf. W. Berges, *Die Fürstenspiegel des hohen und späten Mittelalters* (Stuttgart, 1938), p. xiii.

74. Harich devotes a whole article to Aristotle's speech without considering this possibility: H. Harich, '*Parce humili, facilis oranti, frange superbum*: Aristoteles in der *Alexandreis* Walters von Châtillon', *Grazer Beiträge,* XII (1985/6), 147-69. It may be noted that the speech contains advice for a commander too young to fight: 'Si conferre manum, dum luditur alea Martis, / debilis et nondum matura refugerit etas . . .' (118ff.). The lines are certainly appropriate to Aristotle's young pupil. However, they might also seem to have been written with Philip Augustus in mind, especially as Walter makes Alexander's own military career start with the capture of Thebes, when he was already twenty-one.

75. On the mediaeval colouring of Walter's coronation scene, cf. Harich, *Alexander Epicus,* pp. 226-7. It may be noteworthy that before his description of this event Walter inserts the words: 'Ergo ubi que ferulae pueros emancipat etas /

aduenit' (194-5). Whereas Philip Augustus' coronation took place when he was only fourteen, Alexander was appointed successor to his father at the age of twenty. It would seem also that 'maioraque uiribus audet' (231) points to Philip.

76. Cf. Christensen, *Das Alexanderlied,* p. 212. Zwierlein, *Der prägende Einfluss,* pp. 21-3 suggests that the speech was influenced by Claudian, *Panegyricus de IV consulatu Honorii,* lines 214ff. Similarly, he would connect Alexander's indignation that his youthfulness disqualifies him from war with Claudian, *Panegyricus de III consulatu Honorii,* lines 73ff., and *Panegyricus de IV consulatu Honorii,* lines 353ff.; Ovid, *Ars Amatoria,* I.181ff. (*ibid.,* pp. 22ff.).

77. Cf. Cartellieri, *Philipp II. August,* I, 14ff.

78. When Walter affirms solemnly in his prologue that 'diu te, o mea Alexandrei, in mente habui semper supprimere' (14-15), he is merely employing a form of the 'modesty topos': cf. E. R. Curtius, 'Dichtung und Rhetorik im Mittelalter', *Deutsche Vierteljahrschrift,* XVI (1938), 456-7, citing as a 'Musterstück dieses Topos' the opening of Cicero's *Orator,* I: 'diu multumque . . . dubitaui'. Accordingly the scholars cited in nn. 79-82 below are wrong to suppose that Walter's *diu* has any bearing whatsoever on the question of date.

79. R. Peiper, *Walter von Châtillon* (Breslau, 1869), p. 9.

80. He was still capable of a pilgrimage to Canterbury in August 1179; he suffered his stroke on his return.

81. Christensen, *Das Alexanderlied,* pp. 10, 13. This dating has been accepted recently in Pritchard, *Walter of Châtillon,* p. 5; cf. also Zwierlein, *Der prägende Einfluss,* p. 5.

82. Herkenrath, 'Die Zeit der *Alexandreis*', p. 597.

David Townsend (essay date spring 1995)

SOURCE: Townsend, David. "Sex and the Single Amazon in Twelfth-Century Latin Epic." *University of Toronto Quarterly* 64, no. 2 (spring 1995): 255-73.

[*In the following essay, Townsend analyzes Walter's handling of gender—and, specifically, Alexander's sexuality—in the* Alexandreis.]

'I even made poor Louis take me on Crusade. How's that for blasphemy? I dressed my maids as Amazons and rode bare-breasted halfway to Damascus. Louis had a seizure and I damn near died of windburn, but the troops were dazzled.' This is Eleanor of Aquitaine speaking, not perhaps as she was, but as she is imagined in *The Lion in Winter.*[1] As a teenager going to summer stock in southern Indiana, I was shocked and delighted by Eleanor's reminiscences of the Second Crusade, as by the other Plantagenet perversities acted out that muggy July night. At sixteen, this became the twelfth century for me, soon to be reinforced by the film version of the play, and supplemented by Kenneth Clark's *Civilisation* episode on the age of the cathedrals.[2] But Clark, alas, offered neither Amazons nor homosexual heirs to the throne of Henry II.

When I was a child, I read as a child, but having become a medievalist, I put away childish interpretations. In the intervening twenty-three years, I have learned with a vengeance to distrust such popularizations. I now know that in regard to the image of Eleanor trotting through a bitterly contested Middle East done up as an Amazon, 'our caution . . . cannot be too extreme.' Eleanor indeed went East with female companions, and a Greek chronicler towards the end of the twelfth century likened her to a second Penthesilea, suggesting that her fellows 'behaved in an even more masculine way than the Amazons.' But not until we reach the Victorian account by a disapproving Agnes Strickland do we actually find the queen and her ladies themselves donning Amazon garb. So much for windburn and bedazzled troops.[3] Perhaps (I still cannot help thinking during occasional lapses) the twelfth century was poorer for the loss.

On the other hand, Eleanor surely knew an Amazon when she saw one. Benoît de Sainte-Maure would dedicate the massive *Roman de Troie* to her about ten years after the Crusade. There Penthesilea and her army appear with much pomp, and in considerable detail.[4] Maybe Eleanor, beholding her anachronistic representation, might approve: *si non è vero, è ben trovato.* I long for the imagined Eleanor's subversion of the rules others made for her. I remember the space her nostalgic recollection opened for me, as I churned through the void between my own anomalous desires and the brutally enforced norms of a respectable small town. Professionally, however, I have to settle for Amazons where I can find them.

Penthesilea, thee I invoke.

Walter of Châtillon's long Latin epic, the **Alexandreis,** dates from the last quarter of the twelfth century.[5] At the beginning of book VIII, after his victory over his nemesis Darius and before the Indian campaigns that will lead swiftly to his hybris-ridden downfall, Alexander the Great receives a visit from Talestris, Queen of the Amazons:

> Lamenting Memnon's death with endless grief,
> three times the Dawn had strewn her radiant beams

through all the earth, when earth's sole conqueror,
valiant and swiftly lunging toward all peril,
approached Hyrcania's boundaries with his
   host.   (5)
He'd scarcely gained the victory, or heard
the supplications of the lisping Bagoas
to grant bloodstained Narbazanes his life,
when Queen Talestris of the Amazons
approached the camp with virgin retinue,
aflame with her desire to see the king.   (10)
All peoples dwelling from the Caucasus
to rushing Phasis' wide-encircling stream
received this woman's laws. When once an audience
was granted to her with the king, she swiftly
descended from her horse, with quiver slung
from her left arm, and carrying two darts.   (15)
(The dress of Amazons does not obscure
their bodies wholly. On the left, their chests
are bared; their garments settle on the rest
and hide what must be hidden, though the soft
raiment doesn't fall below the knee-joint.
The left teat is preserved until adulthood
to nurse their infants of the female sex;
the other one receives an early searing
to ease their wielding of the pliant bow
and leave them unencumbered for the
   javelin.)   (23)
   Perusing, then, the king with wary eye,
Talestris marvelled that his meagre body
ill fit his fame, and silently she pondered
where the great virtue of the unvanquished prince
might lie concealed: the simple savage mind
respects and judges all according to
their bodies' beauty and their splendid raiment,
and thinks none capable of mighty deeds
save those whom nature has seen fit to bless
with shapely body and a charming form.
But sometimes mightier courage dwells inside
a middling body, and illustrious power
transgresses all the body's limbs to rule
somewhere within obscure and darkened
   members.   (35)
   And so the queen, asked once for what she'd come,
whether she sought some great boon of the king,
responded that she'd come to fill her womb
and leave again to bear an offspring shared
with such a prince: she judged herself as worthy
that from her he might sire a kingdom's heirs.
If from that birth a noble woman issued,
the daughter would attain her mother's realms;
if there came forth a male, he'd be returned
for nourishment under his father's tutelage.
The king inquired whether Talestris cared
to take up arms beneath him, but she pleaded
her realm now lacked a guardian. Finally
she took the gift of thirteen nights and gained
what she was seeking. Then she turned her steps
back to her realm's throne and ancestral
   cities.[6]   (48)

Some modern readers know Walter better for his lyrical and satirical poems in the accentual metres that appealed to post-romantic conceptions of medieval literature: these works are conducive to the wide appreciation of the 'Goliardic' Latin verse long associated with Helen Waddell's 'Wandering Scholars.'[7] Walter also wrote an extended prose treatise against the Jews.[8] But despite any relative inattention from modern students, his hexameter epic was his *magnum opus,* attested by some two hundred surviving manuscripts, many of them heavily and systematically glossed.[9] Nor was the popularity of the poem restricted to the thirteenth century's burgeoning academic culture. Vernacular adaptations testify to the breadth of its appeal.[10] The work's currency in circles of high political power was already presupposed by its dedication: Walter's patron William of the White Hands, bishop of Sens from 1169 to 1176 and archbishop of Reims from 1176 to 1202, was also the uncle of Philip Augustus.[11]

The poem draws on a Latin prose text of the early imperial period, the *Historiae Alexandri Magni Macedonis* of Quintus Curtius Rufus, as its principal source.[12] Walter sometimes follows Curtius very closely indeed, but at others he amply demonstrates his willingness to handle his principal source more freely: he modifies or omits episodes, adds digressions, often to provide epic coloration, and conflates the text with other sources.[13]

Twentieth-century criticism of the *Alexandreis* has in large part organized itself around several central topoi of traditional philological criticism. Treatments often focus on the epic's classicizing tendencies, so that Walter comes to be judged by his success or his failure at reproducing the aesthetic, and to some extent the ethos, of the Gold and Silver Latin epic.[14] Much attention is paid to Walter's use of Curtius and to his synthesis of this with other materials from the Alexander legend and from the Latin poetic tradition.[15] And extensive argument obtains over the engagement or withdrawal of the text from the pressing political issues of its day.[16]

In so far as the poem resonates against the controversies surrounding the French prosecution of the Crusades, we can read it as one of medieval high culture's principal monuments to the long history of Western Orientalism. Its literary constructions of the newly accessible East must necessarily evoke as intertexts other, more fantastic materials in the Alexander tradition, like the *Letter of Alexander to Aristotle* embedded in another vastly popular Latin text, the *Historia de preliis.*[17] Less foregrounded in the poem, and thus understandably bypassed in recent criticism, is the representation of gender: Walter generally presents Alexander as a sexless being in a homosocial environment, and indeed, Walter's practice of omitting many of the episodes in Curtius that cast a pall over Alexander's character covers the traces of gender and sexuality issues.[18] But the appearance of the Amazon queen affords a remarkably easy *entrée* into such concerns. A close reading of the passage reveals a deeply embedded problematic of

gender, a problematic that intersects the incipient Orientalism of this underread masterpiece of the twelfth century.

> Memnonis eterno deplorans funera luctu,
> Tercia luciferos terras Aurora per omnes
> Spargebat radios cum fortis et impiger ille
> Terrarum domitor, in cuncta pericula preceps,
> Hyrcanos subiit armato milite fines.   (5)

The opening lines of book VIII, with their conventional epic allusion to Aurora's grief at the tomb of Memnon, betray an immediate debt to Ovid's *Metamorphoses* and to the *Aeneid.*[19] But at the caesura of line 3 comes a first seam in the construction of the passage, as the text moves from mythological description to the representation of martial prowess. We can read this juxtaposition as entirely commonplace, a derivation from the previous epic tradition. Nevertheless, in the *Alexandreis* it reflects the amalgamation of two profoundly different kinds of source, namely the epics and the prose historiographical discourse of Curtius. Much criticism focuses upon the synthesis of these voices, but it is possible instead to read the poem as existing at the intersection of their dialogic tensions, as constituted precisely by the intertextual relays that the reader must negotiate to construe the text.[20] In the gap that opens up in the middle of the passage's third line, there arises, overlapping but not coinciding with the dialogue between these competing discourses, a gendered tension between the passivity of the female Dawn and the behaviour of the Macedonian conqueror. Although one could read this tension as purely conventional, verbal repetition militates against such a dismissal: *terras* of line 2 is set off against *terrarum* of line 4 in almost exactly symmetrical relation to the caesura of line 3: while Aurora scatters her tears through all lands, the still-unnamed Alexander appears as those lands' conqueror. Both gender and the militarist expansionism of Alexander's project thus become visible in this space.

> Quos ubi perdomuit uitamque cruentus ab ipso
> Narbazanes molli Bagoa supplicante recepit,
> Haut mora, uisendi succensa cupidine regis,
> Gentis Amazoniae uenit regina Talestris
> Castraque uirginibus subiit comitata ducentis.   (10)

Two lines of circumstantial detail now intervene between the opening of the book and the arrival of Talestris. Here we learn that Alexander spares the treasonous Persian general Narbazanes at the prompting of 'effeminate Bagoas.' With this reference, the text encodes an interpretive lack, depending as it does for comprehension on a network of references that undermine the work's self-sufficiency. A late-thirteenth-century gloss from Vienna, National Library 568 reflects the necessity of such supplementation:

Hic dicit quod Narbazanes reconciliatus fuit Alexandro per blanda uerba, sed auctor subticet ueritatem quoniam Narbazanes duos filios pulcerrimos habuit quibus abutebatur Alexander. Qui ab Alexandro inpetrauerunt pacem patri suo Narbazani, sed quoniam hoc Alexandro fuit dedecus, et ideo tacuit auctor.

Here he says that Narbazanes was reconciled to Alexander by pretty words, but the author hushes up the truth that Narbazanes had two very beautiful sons whom Alexander abused. They begged peace for their father Narbazanes from Alexander; but since this redounds to Alexander's dishonour, so, therefore, the author keeps quiet.[21]

Only by the recognition that the poem's ideal reader is already familiar with the material from Curtius and other sources can we recognize these lines as classic *praeteritio,* highlighting precisely that which they purport to omit. But if Walter is attempting to whitewash Alexander here, as this and other glosses in the same manuscript suggest,[22] and as some modern scholars have asserted on the more general issue of the hero's portrayal in the poem, we must concede that he has been singularly clumsy about it. Even given the choice of detail with which Walter contextualizes Talestris's arrival, he could have omitted Bagoas altogether; and even given Bagoas's presence, Walter surely could have spared him the epithet 'molly.' If we choose to ignore the text's signposts towards Alexander's gender and sexuality, we can only rescue Alexander's normative virility by casting aspersions on Walter's competence to produce the effects critics have proposed he intended.

> Omnibus hec populis, dorso quos Caucasus illinc
> Circuit, hinc rapidi circumdat Phasidos amnis,
> Iura dabat mulier. cui primo ut copia facta est
> Regis, equo rapide descendit, spicula dextra
> Bina ferens, leuo pharetram suspensa lacerto.   (15)

The text's immediate valorizations of gender and sexuality as interpretive issues do not easily allow us to dismiss details of Talestris's entrance as though they were inevitable in the representation of the Amazon queen, and so unworthy of sustained attention. Walter does indeed follow Curtius's account remarkably closely for the rest of the episode,[23] but details of his adaptation tellingly depart from mechanical versification of the source. The ensuing lines give particular emphasis to Talestris's gender by radically splitting the nominative subject between the demonstrative *hec* of line 11 and *mulier,* line 13, at the final position in its sentence. The victorious Alexander has just granted clemency to a parricide at the prompting of his catamite; now a ruler who governs a wide territory described in some geographical detail is emphatically asserted, at the last possible moment in the syntactical unit, to be a woman. She swiftly dismounts and carries two javelins and a quiver with her to her audience with the king.

> Vestis Amazonibus non totum corpus obumbrat.
> Pectoris a leua nudatur, cetera uestis
> Occupat et celat celanda, nichil tamen infra
> Iuncturam genuum descendit mollis amictus.
> Leua papilla manet et conseruatur adultis,   (20)
> Cuius lacte infans sexus muliebris alatur.
> Non intacta manet sed aduritur altera lentos
> Prompcius ut tendant arcus et spicula uibrent.   (23)

Lines 16-23 present something like an ethnographical description. If the attention to detail given the garb of the Amazons represents a kind of cultural tourism, the searing away of the right breast in childhood can be read as the inscription of their society's organization upon their bodies. In this context, Amazonian dress becomes a kind of gloss both supplementing and partially covering over the body-as-text. In that gloss, the dialectic of concealment and revelation, thematically announced in line 16—'the Amazons' garb does not veil the whole body'—unsettles any perceived naturalism of dress and its relation to the body's social meaning. The left breast—that left intact by Amazon society—is revealed; their garments cover 'the rest,' and particularly, we are told, 'conceal what ought to be concealed.'

Perhaps the phrase *celat celanda* merely provides a poetic variation on the preceding *cetera occupat*—Walter has added it to an otherwise close paraphrase of Curtius's corresponding sentence. But the nature of what must be concealed is here manifold. The exposure of the female breast already suggests that *celanda* means something significantly different to the Amazons than to the society of the West. *Celanda* clearly denotes the sexual organs and substitutes for another gerundive, *pudenda.* This imputes universality to the prohibition against exposing the sexual organs. But the indeterminacy of the relation of *cetera* to *celanda* leaves open the question of what, in the eyes of the Amazons themselves, must be concealed. At the end of line 19 we pass from the description of Amazon fashion to their practice of nursing children—females only, so that the boys both vanish from our sight and are the focus of our attention by yet another *praeteritio* (of which the missing term is this time not Curtius, but the reader's consciousness of gender as a binary opposition)—and so to the cauterization of the right breast. In the light of the sartorial gloss that has preceded the reading of the Amazon body, it is not clear whether the missing breast is simply part of the *cetera* which happen to be concealed, or of the *celanda* that must be rendered invisible. Nor, if the absence of the breast is indeed a *celandum,* is it self-evident in whose eyes it is a site for potential shame, in those of Walter and his readers, or in those of the Amazons themselves.[24]

I read these lines as thus implicated not only in a tension between concealment and revelation, but more deeply in the gendered dialectic of sexual organs as lack or possession of the phallic signifier of cultural power.[25] Under concealment and revelation there lies the more fundamental grid of the male and female genitalia and the divergent meanings of their concealment. If the male sexual organs must be concealed, it is in order to keep the phallus veiled, and so to protect it against challenges to what Kaja Silverman has called the 'dominant fiction' that the phallus as transcendent guarantor of power and cultural meaning is equivalent to the penis. Unveiling the phallus risks the beholder's recognition that phallic transcendence is hardly matched by 'the' male organ's limitation and mutability.[26] If the female genitalia must be concealed, according to that same dominant fiction it is because the scandal of lack must be covered over. The ideology of patriarchy demands that we must understand sexual difference as what the female body is deprived of.

But the seared breast of the Amazon queen introduces a third term of difference into the obsession with the phallus or its absence as the binary opposition upon which gender is founded. The seared breast represents the construction of social power not upon a naturalized lack, a 'castration' that is the always already given of female bodily existence, but rather upon a choice determined by the contingent norms of a given society, a choice by which the excision of the biologically natural effects not the deprivation of power, but an access to it. Talestris's cauterization *produces* the power of her socially determined subjectivity. Patriarchy maps its metaphor of 'castration' onto the female body in order to secure the dominant fiction; but the lack it imputes remains figurative. Amazon society, by contrast, demands a literal and physically exacted deprivation; but it offers inclusion in the social body as compensation for that introduction of lack into the subject. I want to suggest that enormous conceptual strain is thus placed on a continued patriarchal reading of Talestris's body: by juxtaposing the patriarchal imposition of a figurative lack onto the subject with the Amazons' imposition of a literal one, the text problematizes the very notion of 'castration' upon which the dominant fiction depends. Talestris's cauterization is not simply a reverse 'castration' by which the female aspires to hardness and is thus masculinized: Talestris remains very much a woman, coming to Alexander with the possibility of conception in mind, and capable of nurturing a child with the breast that her dress reveals. The concealment of the female *celanda* is refigured. No longer does that concealment mask an ontological 'lack.' It veils, rather, a socially determined lack that carries with it the consequence of socially constructed power. The bow and javelins wielded by the Amazons, those same weapons with which Talestris has already made her appearance before the Macedonian king, are the visible tokens of that power. Such weapons, in Alexander's eyes, might well stand for the phallus; but to Talestris,

they are rather the tokens of her status as a woman inducted into Amazon society; and it is to her perspective that we will be more compellingly guided in the lines that follow.

> Perlustrans igitur attento lumine regem,
> Mirata est fame non respondere Talestris
> Exiguum corpus, taciturnaque uersat apud se
> Principis indomiti uirtus ubi tanta lateret.
> Barbara simplicitas a maiestate uenusti
> Corporis atque habitu ueneratur et estimat omnes,
> Magnorumque operum nullos putat esse capaces
> Preter eos, conferre quibus natura decorum
> Dignata est corpus specieque beare uenusta.
> Sed modico prestat interdum corpore maior
> Magnipotens animus, transgressaque corporis artus
> Regnat   in   obscuris   preclara   potentia
>   membris.   (35)

The text now stands poised between a dominant fiction of male plenitude and a realization of Amazon 'castration' as a positive term effecting the possibility of being-in-society. It is at the same time poised between the dominant fiction (that phallus and penis are one) and a space in which Talestris's own subjective vision of her self becomes articulable. If the text has regarded Talestris, up to this point, as the object of its gaze, Talestris now gazes back. In line 24, she 'wanders over' the king with a careful eye and finds his scanty body lacking. In her silence she speculates—as she does not, explicitly, in Curtius's version—as to where the *virtus* of this man lies. In the Latin, even more than in the English of our own readings, the line between virtue and virility begins to blur as we ponder etymology, to say nothing of raw sound. Alexander's virtue, along with his power and his manliness, is hidden somewhere Talestris cannot lay eyes on it. Talestris's silent contemplation focuses our attention on the fact that the emperor is indeed clothed, and for good reason. Her unspoken speculations as to what he may, or may not, have under the hood throws the notion of the veiled power of the phallus back on itself. Her aporia ridicules the phallus precisely in its concealment. If Alexander's hidden parts are not more impressive than what he shows off, she has clearly decided, then he is hardly the eighth wonder of the world she came to inspect.

A medieval audience was if anything more likely than a modern one to have grasped the comic incongruities of Alexander's position. Thomas Laqueur has traced in much detail the dominance of a so-called 'one-sex' model of sexual difference in Western culture up until the late eighteenth century.[27] In a world where sexual difference, according to such a paradigm, signified greater or lesser perfection on a continuum, and where women were seen as beings possessing analogous sexual equipment to men's, but turned outside in as a sign of their inferior status, the signification of power by the phallus must have been even further valorized than it is for twentieth-century readers, who have simultaneous access to other conceptions of difference that have come to the fore since the Enlightenment—'two-sex' conceptions that, for better or worse, imagine sexual difference not as degrees of perfection ranking individuals along a single scale, but as a more fundamental dimorphism of somatic and psychological reality.

If the text allows such a rupture as I have delineated in the dominant fiction of phallic signification and power, if it opens such a space for the expression of Talestris's female subjectivity, it nevertheless moves immediately to contain the threat that this heterodox perspective represents. I am struck by the fact, however, that it does not circumscribe Talestris's alternatively gendered gaze as partial and inauthentic in terms of sex, but, rather, generalizes upon the barbarian simplicity that fails to recognize the distinction of inward power from external appearance. Walter has introduced the dangerous possibility that Talestris's female subjectivity signifies a construction of gender in society alternative to Alexander's normative *virtus*. Now Walter negates that possibility not by appeal to gender, much less to sex, but in terms of an ethnically marked distinction between hermeneutic sophistication and naïve observation. Talestris fails to read Alexander's *virtus* appreciatively not because she is a woman, but because she is a barbarian. This defence of Alexander strikes me as the lamest of apologiae. Certainly, my reaction reflects deep-seated personal inclination. But other passages in the *Alexandreis* also suggest a commingling of voices that undermines the privileging of any one among them. The indeterminacy of the poem's dialogic relations leaves the reader adrift to order their hierarchy, or not to do so, in the freedom of his or her own reception.[28] But more specifically, the baldness of this representation of the ethnic Other, reflective of the text's position in the history of modern xenophobia in the West, creates for itself in nine lines perhaps as many difficulties as it lays to rest, as the following paragraphs attempt to sketch.

These lines assimilate the evaluation of the relation between body and inner virtue to the typological interpretation of the text: inside the bodily *integumentum* resides the mighty spirit, a kernel of meaning that the barbarian cannot grasp, but in which lies the body's true significance.[29] Yet in order to accumulate its assertions of the invisibility of inner virtue, the passage focuses precisely on that body which it chides Talestris for regarding without reference to what lies hidden within it. In nine lines the body appears four times (*corporis,* line 29; *corpus,* line 32; *corpore,* line 33; *corporis,* line 34), returning repeatedly even as the text urges the reader's understanding to transcend it, lest he or she, too, turn out to be a barbarian. Nor has this

body yet escaped from the literal-minded gaze of Talestris against which Walter protests so profusely: the body is still represented as Talestris chooses to evaluate it, and the text merely reacts against this vision by negating it. Alexander's outward appearance lacks the *maiestas uenusti corporis,* the majesty of a lovely body; the positive term of this discourse remains the status of those 'upon whom nature has seen fit to bestow a seemly body of charming appearance.' Notably absent here is any assertion, in contradiction of Talestris's gaze, that Alexander's male body is to be judged by a male standard of appearance. The language the text uses to suggest that prettiness is not everything represents Alexander's physical reality in language more generally used of women: *venustas* is by both etymology and classical usage the property of Venus, not of Mars.[30] The defence of Alexander's inner majesty thus lands the king in an even worse situation than that in which Talestris' silent appraisal has left him. She does not merely find him lacking; she finds him lacking according to a standard by which women are judged, but here itself employed by a woman. Perhaps Talestris would be more favourably impressed by her fellow Amazons.

In terms aligned with post-Lacanian feminism, the defence attempts to shield the phallus from Talestris's single-mindedly physical, and so literal, gaze. If it succeeds in vindicating Alexander's possession of the phallus as the transcendent signifier of power, it does so by denying the unproblematic equivalence of the phallus with the penis, of power with the specificity of the male body. If Alexander's virtue is vindicated at the expense of that virtue's straightforward connection with his physical stature, a crack has opened in the dominant fiction. 'Mighty spirit' must 'transgress' the body's limbs in order to sustain its rule; 'illustrious power' has retreated to a habitation *in obscuris membris.* Thus the text leaves Alexander stuck on the horns of its dilemma.

It remains unclear, however, whether even here the phallus can rest safe from Talestris's scrutiny. Her evaluation, at once cool and salacious, may well continue to speculate as to just which obscure members have become the place of retreat. A hermeneutically informed understanding, of course, would recognize that these members are figurative, and that the body's types and shadows have their ending in the transcendent dwelling place of virtue. But for a moment, learned reader, give Talestris her way: like the queen she is, she will probably have it in any case. What if these obscure members are themselves still physical? *Obscurus* is, in fact, in this context a rather strange choice of words on Walter's part—and the entire sentence is his free elaboration of his source.[31] Its usual meanings run along the lines of 'gloomy, dark, obscure.' In Vergil, a grove is *obscurus*; the night is *obscura*; of language, the word can mean obscure or incomprehensible. The *obscurum* is imperfectly known, uncertain, concealed from knowledge. The word suggests only with some contortion the higher intelligibility of inward understanding. If these out-of-sight members are physical, they are indeed covered over, and so darkened. We are back to the organs, then, that earlier were described as universally *celanda,* requiring concealment. These may well be Alexander's private parts, the declared goal of Talestris's sojourn: she has after all come, as she will soon tell us, specifically in order to be inseminated by the universal conqueror.

Even so, these organs are more than concealed; potentially, they are unintelligible or indistinct, and with this my mind cannot help but run to Luce Irigaray's exploration of the indeterminacy of the female body.[32] Perhaps, if these *membra* are physical, they belong to Alexander and still point ahead to Talestris's imminent acquisition of what she has come for; but perhaps they represent an alternative somatic correlative of power altogether. Perhaps they are the organs of Talestris's own fecundity—not only obscure in their concealment, but *unheimlich* in the castration fear they engender in a patriarchal subjectivity constituted in terror of the potential loss of phallic power.[33] (Perhaps, indeed, this is an eruption of 'two-sex' thinking against the dominant ideology of the age.) Both these valuations come together, interpretively as well as at the literal narrative level, in the climax of Talestris's appearance.

> Ergo rogata semel ad quid regina ueniret,
> Anne aliquid uellet a principe poscere magnum,
> Se unenisse refert ut pleno uentre regressa
> Communem pariat cum tanto principe prolem,
> Dignam se reputans de qua rex gignere regni   (40)
> Debeat heredes. fuerit si femina partu
> Prodita, maternis pocietur filia regnis.
> Si mas extiterit, patri reddetur alendus.
> Querit Alexander sub eone uacare Talestris
> Miliciae uelit. illa suum custode carere   (45)
> Causatur regnum. tandem pro munere noctem
> Ter deciesque tulit, et quod querebat adepta
> Ad solium regni patriasque reuertitur urbes.

Alexander wants to know whether Talestris has come to ask for something big. She replies straightforwardly enough. She wants to go back home pregnant with a child sired by so great a prince. She judges *herself* worthy to mother the offspring of Alexander. Her proposal is thoroughgoingly contractual: if the issue of this union is a woman (and a woman of rank, *femina*, at that), she will inherit the 'maternal realms.' A male child will be returned to sender. The language is overwhelmingly loaded. Talestris's daughter will emerge into the world a gendered being, born into a matrix of social relations in which her standing is guaranteed by

her mother and her society.[34] Talestris's potential male offspring is scarcely even represented as her son: *mas* can apply to humans, animals, and even plants. This child awaits an identity which, if it is imparted at all, will be received at the hands of its father, to whom it will be restored 'for sustenance.'[35]

The fate of such a child is indeed precarious. Perhaps one can read the gerundive *alendus* straightforwardly as 'to be nourished.' But it emphasizes just as plausibly that the child is in a state of requiring nourishment, 'needing to be nourished.' How Alexander will accomplish this in the absence of the child's mother is unclear. Of course he will provide the boy with a wet nurse. But in the framework of the entire episode's continuous focus on the physical, I cannot but attend to the fact that here Talestris's own source of power, entirely outside the discourse of the phallus, comes to the margin of awareness. Talestris's left breast is capable of nurturing her daughter, as her right arm displays the prowess that will gurantee that daughter's position in Amazon society. Alexander must rely, for the nourishment of the male child that may come of this union, upon an unnamed and unacknowledged woman. That child will already have been born from Talestris's own *obscura membra*, whose power depends on no tenuous relay between the body and its concealment of *virtus*: her literal body is itself its own power, in need of no act of tropological alienation.

Talestris thus refuses to look beyond Alexander's physical stature for what she is seeking not out of arbitrarily and wilfully bad hermeneutics, but out of knowledge and choice. She knows what she wants from the start, and her search for a somatic *virtus* (a *muliertas*, if you will) will not be diverted, either by the defensive tactics of the (possibly disingenuous) narrator or by Alexander's own initial parry of her request: immediately following her proposal, Alexander changes the subject, in what looks very much like a counter-offer. Would the Amazon not like to make some time for warfare under *him* (*vacare sub eo*, where Curtius had read *cum ipso militare*, to fight *with* him)? Falling back once again on figurative language as a defence of his prowess, Alexander devises a way to make sure he remains on top, at least metaphorically: whether he will be able to maintain that relation in a more physically constituted relationship, like the one Talestris proposes, is perhaps a more open question. But Talestris, in a rather ladylike gesture allowing the gentleman to save face, pleads a previous engagement: her kingdom, without her, would lack a guardian. 'At last, as a gift, she carries the night thirteen times, and having gained what she was seeking, returns to her kingdom's throne and to the cities of her ancestors.'

Talestris has clearly won this combat for discursive space, which has rather unobtrusively raged for forty-eight lines of an epic generally read in the twentieth century, when read at all, as an inscription of the dominant cultural values of its time. Not merely does she receive the gift of thirteen nights; she carries them one by one, each encounter with Alexander an active exercise of her choice. Finally, with supreme irony, she returns to her *patrias urbes*. What can this (yet another detail Walter adds gratuitously to Curtius's version) possibly mean, in a society that is not merely matrilineal, but exclusively female? In both prose and verse, I have rendered *patrias* as 'ancestral'; R. Telfryn Pritchard, in his prose translation, gives his reader 'native.'[36] But how, in idiomatic English, might we capture the jarring incongruity of a term at the centre of whose connotation lies fatherhood as conceived by the tribes of Latium?

One answer is fairly straightforward, given the context: Talestris has it all. By biological fact, the Amazons all have fathers. That those fathers are rendered invisible and absent in Amazon society suggests that in Talestris's social discourse it is *she* who represents the Lacanian Name-of-the-Father and so wields the phallus that is its signifier. The fiction of any natural correspondence of the phallus to male anatomy is shattered. In its abjection from phallic signification, the penis has become the unspeakable term of human intercourse, as are the female genitalia in the patriarchal world into which she has made her brief counter-insurgence. Behind the catachresis of the notion that the Amazon cities could be 'paternal' lies another trope. By synecdoche the paternal function is here absorbed into the maternal, which is thereby universalized. In much the same way, though with reversed polarity, patriarchal discourse has long insisted that the universalizing language of 'man' incorporates the experience of women.

Under such an interpretation, Talestris would indeed bring forth her subjectivity out of a most unlikely context. But at what price of fulfilling, on another level, the deepest stereotypical fears of patriarchy that female power carries with it, inevitably, the threat of male castration? I see another possibility, born of my own desire in the first instance, but not at the expense, I'd still maintain, of the text's integrity. Talestris has indeed shattered the illusion of any natural correspondence between the Law of being-in-society and the particulars of male anatomy. But what she takes away appears as castration only from within that illusion of the equivalence of phallus and penis. In contrast to what the text fears that she threatens to take away, and to what Alexander himself seems to fear in his counter-offer to take the queen on as a sidekick in combat, she offers Alexander that same physicality with which she insists on regarding him. Taking away the phallus, she holds out to Alexander the reality of his body, and the pleasure of thirteen nights with a real woman whose spear stands

propped in the corner, and whose body itself bears the marks of her prestige. We have no indication in the text that he can or does recognize such an offer for what it is. He is perhaps too obsessed with *aliquid magnum,* some big thing he should be bestowing out of his own turgid sense of largesse. But Talestris resolutely puts forward what to patriarchy is as much a scandal as the threat of castration. She makes it clear that she has indeed come for what Alexander has below the belt, but on her terms, not his. In so doing, she ultimately unveils not the phallus, but rather the penis, the sign not of transcendent power but of the male body's partiality and contingency. She offers Alexander a freedom that he appears unable to accept.

But what she offers does suggest an alternative explanation for her return to the *patrias urbes.* Perhaps, by insisting on calling the body the body, and by resisting the metaphorical identifications that crush somatic reality under the weight of cultural significations, Amazon society offers a space for an alternative male subjectivity, one in which fatherhood signifies not power and disembodiment, but the body's real presence. The *Historia de preliis* describes the carefully controlled circumstances under which the Amazons come together with the men of their race.[37] Nothing in the account suggests the subjugation of the men. Though Walter chose here to follow Curtius instead, this alternative account remained within the horizon of his contemporaries, as surely as did Curtius at those points when Walter departed from him.

Still, in the *Historia de preliis* I cannot find the presence of men, and so my own presence as embodied reader, *within* Amazonia itself. Nor can I find it in later medieval accounts. In the late fourteenth century, in *The Book of the City of Ladies,* Christine de Pizan described the founding of the Amazon state as the reconstitution of a society in which men had previously made great slaughter.[38] Perhaps we should count Christine, one of the most erudite women of her day, among Walter of Châtillon's readers: by her time, the **Alexandreis** had been a standard of the literary curriculum for nearly two centuries. So I have to go still further afield in search of Amazon men.

I have to shift to my own horizons and leap from twelfth-century epic to twentieth-century feminist science fiction. In *The Gate to Women's Country,* Sheri S. Tepper constructs her own cities of women, peopled by the descendants of those who survived a nuclear holocaust. Beyond the town walls lie the garrisons—a militaristic, exclusively male culture where men in touch with the Warrior Within can chant and drum to their hearts' content.[39] In Women's Country only a few 'soft' males find a place. Reproduction is assured for both communities by carefully controlled periods of mating between the women's and men's societies, and mothers surrender the male offspring of these unions to their 'warrior fathers' at the age of five. At age fifteen, the boys choose whether to become warriors or to return through the Gate to Women's Country. But the zealously guarded secret of Women's Country is that the fathers of the children these unions ostensibly produce are not the testosterone-poisoning cases encountered at the semi-annual carnivals. The true fathers are the men harboured within Women's Country itself. Rejects and refugees of the dominant patriarchy that supposes itself the source of life, they are possessed of their own concealed and tenderer strengths.

Tepper's vision poses its own problems. Her women govern their cities by elitist meritocracy, and with very little humour. Her elimination of male aggression by sustained selective breeding explains sexual oppression by appeal to a crudely essentialist biologism. By that same blithe faith in genetics she dismisses diversity of sexual preference as treatable hormone imbalance. In any case, Talestris's society is of course not Women's Country. But it does appear to be a place where everyone knows what women want, and where men who learn the answer to that vexed question perhaps also find the reality of their own embodiment.

Walter of Châtillon was no feminist. The *Alexandreis* is no feminist text. But it *is* a work of remarkable and underappreciated subtlety, and its commingling of voices allows a great deal to slip through the gaps of its construction. If it celebrates Alexander, it does so with continuously ironic qualification. If it purports, however half-heartedly, to defend him from Talestris's momentary gaze, it creates room for her to speak in the gaps between its dialogically juxtaposed languages. How many medieval readers of the poem may have heard her voice? Perhaps no one can answer that question definitively. If the copious surviving glosses on the poem settle the matter, the answer lies in a manuscript I have not seen, and whose annotations are not printed. Clearly, at least some people in the twelfth century *were* capable of appreciating a dirty joke. Some could perceive the margins around normative masculine identity, as the copious eleventh- and twelfth-century literatures against and in favour of homosexual activity attest—margins that the literature of romance was also exploring in a generally heterosexual context.[40] Then, as now, such a reading might well have struggled against an orthodox reception of the text. Finally, the twelfth century I imagine as a modern reader includes, after all, Eleanor of Aquitaine (or at least, as on a palimpsest, the divine Katharine Hepburn in bogus Plantagenet drag) dressing her women as Amazons and riding bare-

breasted halfway to Damascus. If I write, wilfully enough, my own gloss on Walter, it will be covered over in its turn. Mine too is another voice in the margin of his text.

Notes

1. James Goldman, *The Lion in Winter* (New York: Random House 1966), 43.

2. Kenneth Clark, *Civilisation: A Personal View* (London: BBC 1969, 1970), ch 2.

3. D. D. R. Owen, *Eleanor of Aquitaine: Queen and Legend* (Oxford: Blackwell 1993), esp 148-52.

4. Ibid; Benoît de Sainte-Maure, *Le Roman de Troie,* ed Léopold Constans, 6 vols (Paris: Fermin Didot 1904-12), lines 23,357ff.

5. H. Christensen, *Das Alexanderlied Walters von Châtillon* (Halle: Buchhandlung des Waisenhauses 1905), 10, dates the composition of the poem to 1178-82; Carlotta Dionisotti, 'Walter of Châtillon and the Greeks,' in Peter Godman and Oswyn Murray, eds, *Latin Poetry and the Classical Tradition: Essays in Medieval and Renaissance Literature* (Oxford: Clarendon 1990), 90-6, argues for substantial completion by 1176. Neil Adkin argues for the first release of the poem between September 1179 and September 1180 in 'The Proem of Walter of Châtillon's *Alexandreis*: "Si . . . nostros uixisset in annos,"' *Medium Aevum* 60 (1991), 207-21.

6. The blank verse translation is my own. The present essay glosses not my translation, itself an interpretation of the text, but the Latin original of lines 1-48, as given below from Colker, *Alexandreis,* 199-201. My readings will suggest aspects of Walter's text from which the translation may be seen to diverge. The reader of the present essay will have to weigh my rendering dialogically against the exposition provided in the following pages. For easier cross-reference, I have provided line numbers against the verse translation, corresponding to the blocks of the Latin text as given below.

7. Helen Waddell, *The Wandering Scholars* (London: Constable 1927). Walter's rhythmical verses have been available in good editions for generations, thanks to Karl Strecker, ed, *Moralisch-satirische Gedichte Walters von Châtillon* (Heidelberg: Carl Winter 1929); the *Alexandreis,* however, waited fifty years for the services of Marvin Colker, who edited *Galteri de Castellione Alexandreis* (Padua: Antenore 1978).

8. *Tractatus contra Judaeos,* Patrilogia Latina 209, cols 459-574.

9. For a census of surviving manuscripts, see Colker, *Alexandreis,* xxxiii-xxxviii; for the glossing tradition, see R. DeCesare, *Glosse latine e antico-francesi all' 'Alexandreis' di Gautier de Châtillon* (Milan: Vita e Pensiero 1951). Colker, *Alexandreis,* 277-514, prints excerpts from the glosses of four manuscripts.

10. Colker, *Alexandreis,* xviii-xx.

11. J. R. Williams, 'William of the White Hands and Men of Letters,' in *Anniversary Essays in Medieval History by Students of C. H. Haskins* (Boston: Houghton Mifflin 1929), 365-87.

12. John C. Rolfe, trans and ed, *Quintus Curtius,* 2 vols (Cambridge, Mass: Harvard University Press 1946).

13. For Walter's sources, see the summary by R. Telfryn Pritchard in the introduction to his prose translation of the poem (Toronto: PIMS 1986), 11-14.

14. E.g. Max Manitius, *Geschichte der lateinischen Literatur des Mittelalters,* vol 3 (Munich: Beck 1931), 924-5; Otto Zwierlein, *Der Prägende Einfluss des antiken Epos auf die 'Alexandreis' des Walter von Châtillon* (Stuttgart: Steiner 1987), 87 et passim.

15. E.g. Christensen, *Das Alexanderlied,* 102-64.

16. F. J. E. Raby, *A History of Secular Latin Poetry in the Middle Ages,* 2nd ed, vol 2 (Oxford: Clarendon 1957), 79, denying any engagement with current affairs; asserting the resonance against contemporary events are Henriette Harich, *Alexander Epicus: Studien zur Alexandreis Walters von Châtillon* (Graz: Verlag für die Technische Universität Graz 1987), 2-3, and Maura Keyne Lafferty, 'Reading Latin Epic: Walter of Châtillon's *Alexandreis,*' diss Toronto 1992, 163-89.

17. R. Telfryn Pritchard, trans, *The History of Alexander's Battles: Historia de preliis—The J1 Version* (Toronto: PIMS 1992). George Cary, *The Medieval Alexander,* ed. D. J. A. Ross (Cambridge: Cambridge University Press 1956) provides an account of the rich and varied development of the Alexander tradition in the centuries before and after Walter.

18. Pritchard, *Alexandreis,* 10.

19. Cf. *Metamorphoses* XIII.578-9; *Aeneid* IV.584-5 and IX.459-60.

20. David Townsend, '*Mihi barbaries incognita linguae*: Other Voices and Other Visions in Walter of Châtillon's *Alexandreis,*' *Allegorica* 13 (1992), 21-37.

21. Gloss printed in Colker, *Alexandreis,* 458; the translation is mine.

22. The glossator of the Vienna manuscript in fact seems especially eager to point out the possibility of homosexual elements in the legend and then to commend Walter for his omissions. A gloss on II.437 is even plainer about it: '*conscius archanis quia simul peragebant uicium sodomiticum. Vel conscius aliis rebus archanis et melius secundum propositum auctoris quoniam auctor celat in hoc libro que sunt celanda*' (Colker, 384); '*conscious of his secrets* because at the time they were committing the vice of Sodom; or *conscious* of other secret matters, and better thus according to the author's intention, since in this book the author conceals those things which ought to be concealed.' On the resonance of the glossator's phrase *celat . . . celanda* with the passage I discuss here, see below.

23. Curtius VI.v.24-32.

24. At this juncture, I want to juxtapose with my reading the current politics of breast cancer and mastectomy. The *New York Times Magazine* for 15 August 1993 ran Susan Ferraro's essay 'The Anguished Politics of Breast Cancer' as its lead story, using for its cover illustration one of the poster-sized photographic self-portraits of New York artist Matuschka. Strongly sidelit, head swathed in white fabric blown by an off-camera fan, the subject looks to her left with some introspection and wistfulness, but holds her arms at an angle of self-assurance. The conventions are those of fashion photography. But the low-backed white dress is skewed to reveal the scar of a radical mastectomy, with the caption, 'You can't look away any more.'

I wrote this essay about the time a friend was struggling to decide on her treatment after a lumpectomy. At that time I remembered Matuschka's image as one of extraordinary courage, combined with uncompromising self-assertion. Perhaps I also respond to it because its shocking appropriation of a commercialized aesthetic employs the same tactic as the AIDS imagery collective Gran Fury: AIDS (unlike breast cancer) is a health risk in which I have a first-person stake. In any case, the scandal of the image exposes what Alexander, and perhaps Walter, would sooner drape in cloth.

25. Jacques Lacan, 'The Signification of the Phallus,' in *Écrits: A Selection,* trans Alan Sheridan (New York: Norton 1977), 281-91.

26. Kaja Silverman, *Male Subjectivity at the Margins* (New York: Routledge 1992), 15-51. See also

Charles Bernheimer, 'Penile Reference in Phallic Theory,' *Differences* 4:1 (1992), 116-32.

27. Thomas Laqueur, *Making Sex: Body and Gender from the Greeks to Freud* (Cambridge, Mass: Harvard University Press 1990).

28. Townsend, 'Other Voices,' 26-8.

29. Carolyn Dinshaw has been among the most recent to trace the conventionally gendered distinction of (carnal/feminine) letter and (spiritual/masculine) typology in the Pauline tradition: *Chaucer's Sexual Poetics* (Madison: University of Wisconsin Press 1989), 21-2 et passim.

30. Cicero, *De officiis* I.130: 'cum . . . pulchritudinis duo genera sint . . . uenustatem muliebrem ducere debemus, dignitatem uirilem' (*Oxford Latin Dictionary*, s.v. *uenustas*, def 2). Walter has heightened the effect of Curtius, who uses the word *corpus* only once in the source passage, and *venustas* not at all.

31. *Oxford Latin Dictionary*, s.v. *obscurus*.

32. Luce Irigaray, 'This Sex Which Is Not One,' trans Claudia Reeder, in Elaine Marks and Isabelle de Courtivron, eds, *New French Feminisms* (Brighton: Harvester 1980), 99-106.

33. Sigmund Freud, 'The Uncanny,' trans James Sheridan, Standard Edition, vol 17 (London: Hogarth Press 1955), 219-56.

34. I can't help recalling the ecstatic shouts of Joannie Caucus's daycare charge, Ellie, in *Doonesbury* in the early 1970s, on hearing the news of her sister's birth: 'It's a woman! It's a baby woman!' Garry Trudeau, *'And What Do We Have for the Witnesses, Johnnie?'* (New York: Holt, Rinehart and Winston 1973, 1975), n.p.

35. This problem of the indeterminate identity of the male child might well provide an *entrée* into a wider gendered reading of the poem as a whole, since it gathers into the discussion Alexander's own obsessions with parentage, often suppressed by Walter but abundantly present in the intertext against which the poem presses: plagued by the rumours of his own illegitimate status as the child of the sorceror Nectanabus, he compensates by his concern to gain the title 'son of Jove'—a title which by the end of the poem constitutes a principal indication of the hybris that will bring him to the unfavourable, and fatal, attention of the Goddess Natura.

36. Pritchard, *Alexandreis*, 180.

37. *The History of Alexander's Battles*, 77-9.

38. Christine de Pizan, *The Book of the City of Ladies*, trans Earl Jeffrey Richards (New York: Persea Books 1982), 40-1.

39. Sheri S. Tepper, *The Gate to Women's Country* (New York: Bantam Spectra 1988).

40. John Boswell, *Christianity, Social Tolerance, and Homosexuality* (Chicago: University of Chicago Press 1980), 207-302. The romances of Chrétien de Troyes are predicated on the double binds of masculine identity; in *Erec and Enide* in particular, the social perils of excessive sexual love, however licit its context, dominate the narrative: David Staines, trans, *The Complete Romances of Chrétien de Troyes* (Bloomington: Indiana University Press 1990), 31-5.

David Townsend (essay date 2007)

SOURCE: Townsend, David. Introduction to *The Alexandreis, A Twelfth-Century Epic; Walter of Châtillon*, pp. 11-22. Toronto: Broadview Press, 2007.

[*In the following introduction to his translation of the Alexandreis,* Townsend *discusses the textual history of the poem as well as its reception by Walter's contemporaries and modern readers.*]

THE POEM AND ITS AUTHOR

Walter of Châtillon's ten-book epic on the life of Alexander the Great is one of the high achievements of twelfth-century literature. It ranks among the finest works of Latin literature in a century that also produced Bernard Silvestris, Nigel of Canterbury, the *Ysengrimus* poet, Alan of Lille, Walter Map, and Joseph of Exeter. In artistry and intelligence it loses nothing by comparison to the first flowerings of European vernaculars. Yet Walter's work, while today better known and more widely read than it was before the appearance of Marvin Colker's critical edition in 1978, remains largely an object of specialist scrutiny. Most undergraduate students and committed amateurs of medieval literature have never read it. Scholars of vernacular literature, with some notable exceptions, refer to it more or less cursorily as a work of ancillary interest.

But to Walter's own generation and for several centuries following, the **Alexandreis** enjoyed undisputed pre-eminence. Over two hundred manuscripts survive, the majority of them dating from the thirteenth century, but significant numbers representing the fourteenth and fifteenth centuries as well.[1] The poem was printed in 1487 (Rouen), and again in 1513 (Strasbourg), 1541 (Ingolstadt), and 1558 (Lyons). Few works of medieval literature survive in such a copious transmission: the *Roman de la Rose* and Dante's *Divine Comedy* come down to us in roughly comparable numbers of manuscripts, while Chaucer's *Canterbury Tales* are extant in fewer than one hundred. Literary quality, and even influence, are of course not to be so easily measured as this; but Walter's poem certainly loomed as large in the literary milieux of Jean de Meun, Boccaccio, Dante, Chaucer, and Gower as do works by Chaucer, Milton, and even Shakesepare in ours. Its disappearance from the canon after a sustained popularity might suggest instead an analogy to *Orlando Furioso*. Nor was Walter's poem simply copied and read widely: it was studied intensively as a standard text of the literary curriculum, as copius glosses in many surviving manuscripts attests.[2]

If the poemertr only of historical interest—if it were simply a curious monument to the otherness of tastes that modern readers cannot share—its neglect today might be allowed to continue without intervention. But shifts in literary expectation have not rendered the signal qualities of the **Alexandreis** inaccessible. Readers today can still find in the poem an extraordinary subtlety, a keen intelligence, a beauty in turns lyrical and outlandish—and at times even an uncanny postmodernity. It rewards the reader as richly as do many of the better-known texts of medieval European literature. It deserves to be read alongside the medieval authors we receive as canonical, and to be read, by those without access to the original Latin, in a translation that allows the reader an experience of the work as poetry.

We know less than we might wish of Walter's life and the circumstances of the poem's composition. Walter was probably born around 1135. Various biiographical notices survive in the *accessus* (introductions) included among the glosses of some manuscripts,[3] but the details of these sketches are mutually contradictory. Walter seems to have been born in Lille. After studies in Paris and Reims, and after directing the school of Laon, he headed a school at one of the several towns of Châtillon in northeastern France—Châtillon-sur-Marne is the prime candidate. It is by his association with Châtillon that he is usually known. At Châtillon he composed *quedam ludicra*, "light verses," which presumably included love lyrics and moral satires in rhyming accentual meters in a form in which he also excelled.[4] Subsequent to a realization that the liberal arts don't pay, he may have gone on to study law in Bologna. Thereafter he entered into the service of Guillaume des Blanches Mains (William of the White Hands), brother-in-law of Louis VII, uncle of Philip Augustus, archbishop of Sens and subsequently of Reims.[5] The **Alexandreis** is dedicated to William, as the opening of Book One and the close of Books Five and Ten attest. The initial letters of the poem's ten books spell out GUILLERMUS, his patron's last name. One thirteenth-century

biographical gloss from Paris, Bibliothèque nationale, MS lat. 8358, fol. 91v suggests that Walter composed the poem to regain William's favor. According to the anecdote, Walter was jealous of William's sexual liaison with a cleric named Berterus, himself a poet of some reputation[6]; he took his revenge by contriving the recitation of a scurrilous jingle at the papal curia, thus effectively "outing" the archbishop (and himself) before the Pope:

> Some say that the work was begun in order to restore the love of Lord William of Reims for Master Walter, after the enmity that he had incurred with him because of Master Berterus. If one dare speak the truth, the Lord Archbishop William was using Berterus sexually, and Master Walter envied him. And eventually it happened that the archbishop sent Master Berterus to Rome to plead his case. Master Walter, thinking that he might there acquire some dignity under the guise of that affection, sent him these verses in letters close, indicating that he should not break the seal except in the presence of the Lord Pope, and this is how things turned out. Here are the verses:

> Sole head of the world, O Rome,
> you who've caused us to stray far from home
> and plunged all your pastors
> in stormy disasters,
> greet Walter, who comes here on loan,
> of women a wretched despiser.
> Let the Curia now be the wiser:
> to speak truth unriddled,
> his fair lord he diddled
> not once, as the young lad's adviser,
> while still Homer's verses brought tears
> to his eyes, but long since, in those years
> when a beard full and rough
> made him far tougher stuff,
> and the long march of days stilled his fears.

> When the archbishop learned of this, he cut Master Walter off from his company. Knowing that he had incurred his lord's wrath, Walter took thought how he might regain his love. He began and composed this book to his honor and praise, comparing his virtues to those of Alexander, and so this is the reason why he treated the narratives of Alexander rather than those of some other noble man. But some say that the reason for the work is that Master Matthew of Vendôme and Master Walter quarreled as to who wrote better poetry, and in contest with each other they composed the *Tobias* and the **Alexandreis**.[7]

William made Walter a canon, variously of Amiens, Beauvais, Reims, or Orléans, depending on the gloss one follows. Walter died of leprosy, or perhaps of self-flagellation; if of leprosy, perhaps contracted from a prostitute.[8]

In addition to the confusing and contradictory details drawn from the biographical notices, Walter is sometimes identified with a Walter of Lille who appears in the letters of John of Salisbury as a trusted emissary of King Henry II.[9] Colker, following Williams, denies this connection, while Pritchard is more equivocal on the matter.[10] Walter certainly wrote, in addition to his epic and his accentual poems, a long prose **Tractatus contra Judaeos,** a treatise of refutation against the Jews. Carsten Wollin has recently attributed to him several saints' lives in rhymed, rhythmical verse. From Walter's own prose prologue to the **Alexandreis,** we know that he worked on the poem for five years. The biographical glosses assert that he began it in the year of Thomas Becket's death, 1170, but as William became Archbishop of Reims only in 1176, this is impossible. The exact dating of the poem is probably beyond definitive establishment, despite recent and sometimes contentious attempts to do so.

The details of which we can be sure are as follows. (1) The poem cannot have been completed before 1176, when William was raised to the archbishopric of Reims. (2) The poem is referred to by John of Hauvilla in the *Architrenius,* which is securely datable to 1184.[11] (3) It was well enough known by 1189 for lines 10.448-50 (10.537-39 of the translation) to have served as the model for the epitaph of Henry II.[12] (4) A *prosimetrum* by Walter that was probably written between 1174 and 1176 refers to *opuscula* among which Alexander is a subject. Perhaps the *opuscula* on Alexander are in fact a draft of the **Alexandreis** still in progress. The *prosimetrum* contains twelve lines that recur virtually *verbatim* at 3.140-57 (3.169-89 of this translation), and there is reason, though not conclusive evidence, for believing that the epic's version of these lines is the earlier.[13] (5) Alan of Lille denigrates the **Alexandreis** in *Anticlaudianus* 1.166-70; but the usual date of Alan's poem, 1182 or 1183, is deduced from a presumed dating of the **Alexandreis** to 1181, and is of no use to us as evidence for the date of the latter.

We can say nothing with certainty beyond the fact that the poem was probably begun no earlier than 1171 and was finished by about 1181, though most scholars until twenty years ago followed Christensen's suggestion of 1178-82.[14] Carlotta Dionisotti has since argued for 1171-76, while Neil Adkin has insisted that the coronation of Alexander is intended to reflect the circumstances surrounding Philip Augustus' succession to the throne of France in late 1179.[15] Most recently, David Traill, building on the researches of Orlandi, argues persuasively for a precise date of 1178.[16]

RECEPTIONS OF THE TEXT

Alan of Lille's criticism of the poem, the 1184 reference in the *Architrenius,* and the imitation of lines from the end of Book Ten in the epitaph of Henry II testify to the speed with which Walter's poem began to

establish itself in the literary culture of its day. It created a vogue in the ensuing years for classicizing epics, notably the *Ylias* of Joseph of Exeter and the *Philippis* of Guillaume le Breton (as distinguished from the more allegorical or satirical epics that abounded in twelfth-century Latin literature). The explosion of manuscripts in the thirteenth century assured the work's wide availability up to the date of the first printed edition. In the thirteenth century, Eberhard's *Laborintus* and Hugo of Trimberg's *Registrum multorum auctorum* listed the poem among standard school texts, while Henry of Ghent compained that it had displaced the reading of the classical poets in grammatical study.[17] The influential Latin verse anthology known as the *Florilegium Gallicum,* a collection that began its life in northwestern France in the twelfth century, favors excerpts from the **Alexandreis** among its largely classical contents.[18] Henry of Avranches, arguably the most successful Latin poet of his generation, listed Walter alongside Homer and Lucan as one of the authors with whom he had to vie in order to give worthy honor to Oswald of Northumbria, the subject of a hexameter saint's life he wrote in the 1220s (lines 18-27). Walter's influence can be seen elsewhere in Henry's works: Henry closely models the prologue to his life of Guthlac on the invocation of Walter's poem; similarly, in Henry's *magnum opus*—a life of Francis—he uses the initials of his fourteen books to spell out the name of his patron, ("GREGORIUS NONUS"), in imitation of Walter's practice. He also prefaces each book with four lines of summary, just as Walter had provided ten lines of *capitula* for each of his ten books.[19] The **Alexandreis** was translated into Old Norse, Czech, Dutch, and Spanish; Ulrich von Eschenbach and Rudolf von Ems drew on it substanitally for their Alexander romances.[20] It has been suggested that Petrarch composed his *Africa* as a kind of literary rebuttal of Walter's work.[21] If far less obvious among the Latin texts referred to by Chaucer than the *Consolation of Philosophy* or the *Dissuasio Valerii,* the **Alexandreis** was nevertheless among those works that Chaucer expected a sophisticated reader to recognize in passing allusions. In the Wife of Bath's prologue, for example, Alisoun refers (lines 503-5) to the tomb of Darius, "which that Appelles wroghte subtilly," an unmistakable reference to the description of Darius' tomb in Book Seven.

SOURCES, STYLE, AND MEANING

As Walter's prose prologue reminds us, none of the classical poets had attempted a full epic treatment of Alexander's life and exploits, but Alexander texts of miscellaneous date and authorship had come down to the twelfth century.[22] Among these were several late imperial works: the narrative by Julius Valerius, freely adapted from the Greek Alexander Romance; a purported letter of Alexander to Aristotle on the marvels of

India, much expanded in the early Middle Ages; a report of Alexander's contacts with the Indian Brahmins; and another text representing his correspondence with their king. Julius Valerius was epitomized (i.e., reproduced in a condensed version) in the ninth century. The vastly popular version of the Romance most widely known as the *Historia de preliis* (The History of Alexander's Battles) was first translated into Latin in the tenth century, most widely known as the the history of Alexander's battles, was first produced, but by the late twelfth, in the course of its wide dissemination, it had undergone a series of subsequent recensions. There survives as well a twelfth-century Latin version of an eighth-century Syriac work, the *Secreta secretorum,* which purports to be Aristotle's advice to Alexander on the practice of kingship.

In addition to these fictionalized narratives and ancillary texts, more properly historical accounts had come down to Walter's day, including the relevant sections of Orosius' universal history. But Walter drew principally on the Alexander biography by the first-century Roman Quintus Curtius Rufus. Curtius's work was not as widely known as the *Historia de preliis,* and it survived in a defective version, lacking the first two of its ten books. Walter, however, had at his disposal an interpolated version that filled in for the missing two books amidst other innovations.[23]

Even a cursory comparison of the poem with his principal source reveals Walter's extensive debt to Curtius. (The apparatus of sources at the bottom of the page in Colker's edition gives a quick index of the correspondences.) Many details of the narravie go back directly to his model, and in long passages of the poem Walter does little more than tweak Curtius' word order and vocabulary according to the exigencies of the metre. Modern readers have often seen Walter's debts to Curtius and ohter sources as mitigating his artistry, but such judgments presuppose that creativity lies in an originality more absolute than twelfth-century literary culture expected or even esteemed. Medieval literary sensibilities were both more workmanly and more indebted to the classical rhetorical tradition, in which *inventio,* the discovery or appropriation of material, was only the first division of the poet's task: manuals of poetic practice that flourished in the generations just after the composition of the **Alexandreis** (notably the *Poetria nova* of Geoffrey of Vinsauf) give invention very short treatment indeed, compared to their voluminous attentions to arrangement and style.

Neither would medieval readers have been troubled—indeed, they would more likely have found it gratifying—that Walter frequently and without acknowledgement appropriates from the classical poets, most notably from Vergil, Ovid, and Lucan, but also from Horace,

Juvenal, and the fifth-century Claudian, among others.[24] Such splicing of voices from the long tradition of Latin verse was commonplace in medieval poetic practice. Walter's artistry is enabled, not compromised, by his interweavings of other texts into his own. For readers at the turn of the twenty-first century, this poetic practice, in which sampling and reappropriation play so large a part, is at once strange and strangely familiar. It challenges modernist notions of an unproblematic link between creativity and individual genius. For that very reason, though, it resonates with notions of intertextuality and postmodernism, notions that have percolated increasingly into our own sensibilities over the past twenty years. One might argue that Walter exploits the fertility of such recombinatory literary practice to the full. He produces his text as a tissue of other texts, in which his own voice emerges from the web of borrowed voices spun by his poem.[25]

Walter's recasting of a prose biography as epci is itself the most fundamental level at which this aesthetic of disjunction and juxtaposition operates. The consequent amalgamation of genres produces incongruities between form and content throughout the poem. Direct speech, for exaple, often closely reflects the extended, rhetorically balanced set pieces of prose historiography than it does the generally briefer and more focussed style of epic—though within the epic tradition, Walter's practice has more in common with Lucan's than with Vergil's. the speech of the doomed Darius to his men at 6.350-421 is an apogee of such ornate rhetoric. Darius's exhortations leave his men cold: he has just invited them to participate in a suicide mission. But their reaction is also an index of how unsatisfactorily such a style incites men to arms upon the battlefield of epic. At other points, tactical deliberations of strategy admit of too much practical warcraft, and of too little individual heroism, to fit within an epic ethos of individual combat.

Other splicings suggest still further voices, and sensibilities more characteristic of still other genres. A description of the Greeks plundering the Persian camp in Book Three includes some lines (267-72) whose tone and diction vividly suggest the Roman satire tradition and its medieval continuations. The text passes thence to a description of Persian women raped by their Greek captors, and here the graphic sexuality shocks both for its brutality and for its transgression of epic norms. In Book Two, the description of the hill that Darius climbs for a view of his vast army (351-67) rather peculiarly imports the imagery of pastoral into the immediate martial context.

While a modernist reader might feel dissatisfaction with such incongruities, the text actually goes out of its way to exploit them. The tomb description of Book Four (222-342) powerfully flouts the norms of epic diction.

The monument houses the body of Darius's wife, who has died. Apelles, an historical artist here identified by Walter as a Jew, designs the tomb and its decoration. At the beginning of the passage, we learn in passing that the names of Greek kings appear on the tomb, but the next hundred lines are offer an unadorned catalog of scenes from the Hebrew Bible that occupy the monument's surface. The passage's bald, paratactic style, so starkly at odds with the norms of classical ecphrasis (a formal extended description in literature of a material object), has earned the censure of a number of modern critics.[26] But precisely this same passage garnered an inordinate degree of attention from many of the poem's medieval glossators; mnemonic verses were even composed in order to help students remember the arrangement of the representation. These lines held clear pride of place in medieval receptions of Walter's work.[27] Modern readers tend to get stuck on the passage's transgression of epic style and sensibility; but in the twelfth and thirteenth centuries, the ecphrasis may have evoked a very different use of language, namely the captions that often accompanied the pictorial cycles of murals and tapestries. Similarly, the ecphrasis of another tomb decorated by Apelles, that of Darius himself in Book Seven, evokes the legends on the great *mappae mundi* of the thirteenth and fourteenth centuries, such as the Hereford Map.[28] If some passages in the poem evoke the norms of other literary genres, these ecphrases, and particularly the one in Book Four, stop behaving like high literature at all. They call into question the very boundaries by which we delineate "literature" from other culturally less prestigious uses of language.

Such effects are not merely a matter of style superficially conceived. Style, more profoundly, is the means by which the text, shaping us into the readers it requires, goes on thus to shape our vision of the world. The *Alexandreis* demands readers who can negotiate the leaps between its disparate conventions of language, in full wariness of the discrepancies between those conventions' conflicting truth-claims. At this level, the *Alexandreis* treats among its themes the very processes of reading and interpretation. Alexander himself interprets the world around him. In Book One, he reads flawlessly the crumbling traces of fallen Troy in the wastes of Asia Minor (530-70). But almost immediately thereafter, he betrays a very superficial and self-obsessed understanding indeed, as he reports to his troops of a vision of the Hebrew High Priest, who has appeared to him in a dream as he prepares to march against the Persian Empire. In Book Two, when he attempts to undo the Gordian Knot (84-101), he shows more concern about how those around him will interpret his failure than about the action itself. In Book Ten, Satan commits the greatest interpretive gaffe of all, imagining that Alexander's threatened invasion of the Antipodes will be the

fulfillment of the prophecy according to which some New Man will harrow Hell (154-59). In all these cases, interpreters of the Text that is the world around them fail to understand the signs confronting them because they insist on reading those signs according to inappropriate frames of reference.

But inadequate frames of reference are all the poem gives us as readers. There is no Final Say in the *Alexandreis*. Each of its voices, each of the textual frames it evokes, crosses the others, to the point that even its most straightforwardly moralizing asides, which ought to resolve our doubts and to reestablish us in comfortable certitude, become suspect. Ultimately, our attention wanders from the ostensible moral credibility of such pronouncements, toward the margins they form with respect to one another, and to the peripheries beyond them all. In Book Eight, toward the end of his wanderings, Alexander receives in turn the Queen of the Amazons and a messenger of the Scythians. His visitors' societies clearly remain beyond his comprehension. Alexander answers the Scythian's indictment of his rapacity is by invading and subduing the speaker's land. But what the Scythian has prophesied about such a conquest, we can well imagine coming true: the displaced Scythians will attack from the margins of the Greeks' awareness, appearing where their incursions are least expected. And ultimately, as readers of a Text they understand very imperfectly indeed, the Greeks will lose what they have gained.

Walter clearly intended his epic as a poem for ages to come, not merely for his own day. The tenor of his prose prologue bears this out, as does his decision to frame the text with ten lines of verse *capitula* at the head of each book. Such versified summaries were by Walter's day a fixture of manuscripts of the classical epics. By supplying them himself, Walter signals that this is a poem worthy of repeated reading and intense study. To limit the text's meaning to the concerns of its immediate historical milieu, however illuminating its original circumstances may be as a partial explication of the poem's significance, is thus finally an inadequate approach.

Walter lived amidst his culture's sustained dreams of a New World Order, as contradictory as those dreams were, and as violently as they conflicted with one another. The papacy was embarked upon a centuries-long campaign for sovereignty on earth as in heaven; the Holy Roman Emperor and the kings of France and England were just as determined to protect their own hegemony.[29] The text decries (7.360-63) the murder of Thomas Becket in 1170, one of the central symbols of that struggle between disparate dreams of mastery. The ideology of a Christendom united against an external enemy was shored up by the disastrous exploits of the

Crusades, which had reached a lull when Walter wrote, but which would soon erupt again, as the earliest manuscripts were copied, in the Third and Fourth Crusades of 1189-92 and 1200-1204, respectively.[30] At the end of Book Five, Walter effuses that a king of the Franks as effective as the uncorrupted Alexander might well assure the defeat of Islam. But in a poem like the **Alexandreis,** Walter's panegyric only invites a further question. At what point can we say that Alexander, bearer of the West's dream of mastery, is wholly uncorrupted? And why are we told that all the world *would* beg baptism at the hands of the Archbishop of Reims *if* the Franks had so worthy a king? Ultimately, Walter's text corrodes not only the hermeneutic certainty of our literary frames of reference, but also any illusions we might have about the unity of moral vision with which a great twelfth-century writer regarded the ideological certainties of his culture.

Notes

1. See the census of manuscripts on pp. xxxiii-xxxviii of Colker's edition.

2. On the glosses to the poem, see Colker 1959 and DeCesare.

3. For the biographical details that follow, see the Latin glosses in the introduction and on p. 494 of Colker's edition.

4. See the editions by Strecker of 1925 and 1929.

5. For William's biography, see J. R. Williams.

6. Traill, pp. 857-58.

7. For the Latin text, see Colker's edition, xv-xvi.

8. On the possible causes of Walter's death, see F. Châtillon.

9. Letters 161, 168, 180, ad 189.

10. Colker, ed.,*Alexandreis,* xvi-xvii; Williams, 374-76; Pritchard, trans., *The Alexandreis,* 2-3.

11. John of Hauville, xxx.

12. Christensen, 10.

13. Dionisotti, 90-96.

14. Christensen, 4-13.

15. Dionisotti; Adkin 1991 and 1992.

16. Traill, p. 861.

17. "The *Alexandreis* is today held in such honor in the grammar schools that on its account the reading of the ancient poets is neglected" (my translation). Cited by Colker, *Alexandreis,* xx.

18. Burton, with an index entry on p. 405 to further references.

19. For the prologue of Henry's life of Guthlac, see Adkin 1990.

20. Cary, 64-67.

21. See Bergin and Wilson's note on 8.186.

22. Cary, 24-70.

23. See the account of this version by Smits.

24. Christensen, 195-211; Zwieflein.

25. For the following paragraphs, see Townsend 1992 and 1998.

26. Townsend 1992, 21-22.

27. Ibid., 22-23. See the notes on 94-99, 4.176-274, below.

28. Ratkowitsch, 164-73. For the comprehensive and definitive account of the legends on the Hereford Map, see Westrem.

29. For introductions to the struggle of church and secular authority in the High Middle Ages, see Barraclough and Tierney.

30. For a general history of the Crusades, see Runciman; on the Fourth Crusade specifically, see Godfrey.

Bibliography

Adkin, Neil. "The Date of Walter of Châtillon's *Alexandreis.*" *Bolletino di Studi Latini* 22 (1992), 282-87.

———. "The Proem of Walter of Châtillon's *Alexandreis*: 'Si . . . nostros uixisset in annos.'" *Medium Aevum* 60 (1991), 207-21.

———. "The Proem of Henry of Avranches' *Vita S. Guthlaci.*" *Analecta Bollandiana* 108 (1990), 349-55.

Barraclough, Geoffrey. *The Medieval Papacy.* London: Thames and Hudson, 1968.

Bergin, Thomas G. and Alice S. Wilson, trans. *Petrarch's Africa.* New Haven, CT: Yale UP, 1977.

Cary, George. *The Medieval Alexander.* Ed. D. J. A. Ross. Cambridge: Cambridge University Press, 1956, repr. 1967.

Châtillon, F. "Flagello sepe castigatus vitam terminavit: Contribution à l'étude des mauvais traitements infligés à Gautier de Châtillon." *Révue du Moyen Âge Latin* 7 (1951), 151-74.

Christensen, Heinrich. *Das Alexanderlied Walters von Châtillon.* Halle: Waisenhaus, 1905. Repr. Hildesheim: Georg Olms, 1969.

Colker, Marvin. "Note on the History of the Commentary on the Alexandreis." *Medium Aevum* 28 (1959), 97-98.

DeCesare, R. *Glosse latine e antico-frances all "Alexandreis" di Gautier de Châtillon*. Milan: Vita e Pensiero, 1951.

Dionisotti, Carlotta. "Walter of Châtillon and the Greeks." In *Latin Poetry and the Classical Tradition: Essays in Medieval and Renaissance Literature*, 73-96. Ed. Peter Godman and Oswyn Murray. Oxford: Clarendon Press, 1990.

Godfrey, John. *1204, The Unholy Crusade*. Oxford: Oxford UP, 1980.

John of Hauville. *Architrenius*. Ed. and trans. Winthrop Wetherbee. Cambridge Medieval Classics 3. Cambridge: Cambridge UP, 1994.

Pritchard, R. Telfryn, trans. *The History of Alexander's Battles: Historia de preliis—The J1 Version*. Toronto: Pontificial Institute of Mediaeval Studies, 1992.

Ratkowitsch, Christine. *Descriptio picturae: Die literarische Funktion der Beschreibung von Kunstwerken in lateinischen Grossdichtung des 12. Jahrhunderts*. Vienna der Osterreichischen Academie der Wissenschaften, 1991.

Runciman, Stephen. *A History of the Crusades*. 3 vols. Cambridge: Cambridge UP, 1951-54. Repr. 1987.

Tierney, Brian. *The Crisis of the Church and State, 1050-1350*. Englewood Cliffs, N.J.: Prentice-Hall, 1964.

Smits, Edme R. "A Medieval Supplement to the Beginning of Curtius Rufus's *Historia Alexandri*: An Edition with Introduction." *Viator* 18 (1987), 89-124.

Townsend, David. "*Mihi barbaries incognita linguae*: Other Voices and Other Visions in Walter of Châtillon's *Alexandreis*." *Allegorica* 12 (1992), 21-37.

————. "Sex and the Single Amazon in Twelfth-Century Latin Epic." *University of Toronto Quarterly* 64 (1995), 255-73.

Traill, David A. "Walter of Châtillon's Prosimetron *In Domino confido* (W.3): Where and When Was It Performed?" In *Poesia Latina Medieval*, Actas del IV Congreso del "Internationales Mittellateinerkomittee," Santiago de Compostela, 12-15 de septiembre de 2002. Ed. Manuel C. Diaz y Diaz and Jose M. Diaz de Bustamente. Firenze: Edizioni del Galuzzo, 2005.

Walter of Châtillon. *Galteri de Castellione Alexandreis*. Ed. Marvin Colker. Padua: Antenore, 1978.

————. *The Alexandreis*. Trans. R. Telfryn Pritchard. Toronto: Pontifical Institute of Mediaeval Studies, 1986.

————. *Alexandreis. Das Lied von Alexander dem Grossen*. Trans. Gerhard Streckenbach. Heidelberg: Lambert Schneider, 1990.

————. *Tractatus contra Judaeos*. Patrologia Latina 209, cols. 459-574.

————. *Die Lieder Walters von Châtillon in der Handschrift 351 von St. Omer*. Ed. Karl Strecker. Berlin: Weidmann, 1925.

————. *Moralisch-satirische Gedichte Walters von Châtillon*. Ed. Karl Strecker. Heidelberg: Carl Winter, 1929.

Westrem, Scott D. *The Hereford Map*. Terrarum Orbis: History of the Representation of Space in Text and Image 1. Turnhout: Brepols, 2001.

Williams, J. R. "William of the White Hands and Men of Letters." In *Anniversary Essays in Medieval History by Students of Charles Homer Haskins*, 365-87. Ed. Charles Holt Taylor. Boston: Houghton Mifflin, 1929.

Zwierlein, Otto. *Der Pragende Einfluss des antiken Epos auf die "Alexandreis" des Walter von Châtillon*. Mainz: Akademie der Wissenschaften und der Literatur, 1987.

FURTHER READING

Criticism

Adkin, Neil. "'School' of Walter of Châtillon (*De avaricia et inordinata vita clericorum*)." *Giornale Italiano de Filologia* 44, no. 2 (15 November 1992): 293-97.

    Traces characteristics of Walter's poetry to prove that a recently found poem, *De avaricia et inordinata vita clericorum*, is in fact a work he wrote.

Kratz, Dennis M. "Mocking Heroism: Alexander the Great and the Pursuit of Glory." In *Mocking Epic: Waltharius*, Alexandreis, *and the Problem of Christian Heroism*, pp. 61-155. Madrid, Spain: José Porrúa Turanzas, S. A., 1980.

    Demonstrates how Walter adapted classical forms for his examinations of medieval Christian themes.

How to Use This Index

The main references

list all author entries in the following Gale Literary Criticism series:

AAL = *Asian American Literature*
BG = *The Beat Generation: A Gale Critical Companion*
BLC = *Black Literature Criticism*
BLCS = *Black Literature Criticism Supplement*
CLC = *Contemporary Literary Criticism*
CLR = *Children's Literature Review*
CMLC = *Classical and Medieval Literature Criticism*
DC = *Drama Criticism*
FL = *Feminism in Literature: A Gale Critical Companion*
GL = *Gothic Literature: A Gale Critical Companion*
HLC = *Hispanic Literature Criticism*
HLCS = *Hispanic Literature Criticism Supplement*
HR = *Harlem Renaissance: A Gale Critical Companion*
LC = *Literature Criticism from 1400 to 1800*
NCLC = *Nineteenth-Century Literature Criticism*
NNAL = *Native North American Literature*
PC = *Poetry Criticism*
SSC = *Short Story Criticism*
TCLC = *Twentieth-Century Literary Criticism*
WLC = *World Literature Criticism, 1500 to the Present*
WLCS = *World Literature Criticism Supplement*

The cross-references

list all author entries in the following Gale biographical and literary sources:

AAYA = *Authors & Artists for Young Adults*
AFAW = *African American Writers*
AFW = *African Writers*
AITN = *Authors in the News*
AMW = *American Writers*
AMWR = *American Writers Retrospective Supplement*
AMWS = *American Writers Supplement*
ANW = *American Nature Writers*
AW = *Ancient Writers*
BEST = *Bestsellers*
BPFB = *Beacham's Encyclopedia of Popular Fiction: Biography and Resources*
BRW = *British Writers*
BRWS = *British Writers Supplement*
BW = *Black Writers*
BYA = *Beacham's Guide to Literature for Young Adults*
CA = *Contemporary Authors*
CAAS = *Contemporary Authors Autobiography Series*
CABS = *Contemporary Authors Bibliographical Series*
CAD = *Contemporary American Dramatists*
CANR = *Contemporary Authors New Revision Series*
CAP = *Contemporary Authors Permanent Series*
CBD = *Contemporary British Dramatists*
CCA = *Contemporary Canadian Authors*
CD = *Contemporary Dramatists*
CDALB = *Concise Dictionary of American Literary Biography*

CDALBS = *Concise Dictionary of American Literary Biography Supplement*
CDBLB = *Concise Dictionary of British Literary Biography*
CMW = *St. James Guide to Crime & Mystery Writers*
CN = *Contemporary Novelists*
CP = *Contemporary Poets*
CPW = *Contemporary Popular Writers*
CSW = *Contemporary Southern Writers*
CWD = *Contemporary Women Dramatists*
CWP = *Contemporary Women Poets*
CWRI = *St. James Guide to Children's Writers*
CWW = *Contemporary World Writers*
DA = *DISCovering Authors*
DA3 = *DISCovering Authors 3.0*
DAB = *DISCovering Authors: British Edition*
DAC = *DISCovering Authors: Canadian Edition*
DAM = *DISCovering Authors: Modules*
   DRAM: *Dramatists Module;* **MST**: *Most-studied Authors Module;*
   MULT: *Multicultural Authors Module;* **NOV**: *Novelists Module;*
   POET: *Poets Module;* **POP**: *Popular Fiction and Genre Authors Module*
DFS = *Drama for Students*
DLB = *Dictionary of Literary Biography*
DLBD = *Dictionary of Literary Biography Documentary Series*
DLBY = *Dictionary of Literary Biography Yearbook*
DNFS = *Literature of Developing Nations for Students*
EFS = *Epics for Students*
EW = *European Writers*
EWL = *Encyclopedia of World Literature in the 20th Century*
EXPN = *Exploring Novels*
EXPP = *Exploring Poetry*
EXPS = *Exploring Short Stories*
FANT = *St. James Guide to Fantasy Writers*
FW = *Feminist Writers*
GFL = *Guide to French Literature,* Beginnings to 1789, 1798 to the Present
GLL = *Gay and Lesbian Literature*
HGG = *St. James Guide to Horror, Ghost & Gothic Writers*
HW = *Hispanic Writers*
IDFW = *International Dictionary of Films and Filmmakers: Writers and Production Artists*
IDTP = *International Dictionary of Theatre: Playwrights*
LAIT = *Literature and Its Times*
LAW = *Latin American Writers*
JRDA = *Junior DISCovering Authors*
MAICYA = *Major Authors and Illustrators for Children and Young Adults*
MAICYAS = *Major Authors and Illustrators for Children and Young Adults Supplement*
MAWW = *Modern American Women Writers*
MJW = *Modern Japanese Writers*
MTCW = *Major 20th-Century Writers*
NCFS = *Nonfiction Classics for Students*
NFS = *Novels for Students*
PAB = *Poets: American and British*
PFS = *Poetry for Students*
RGAL = *Reference Guide to American Literature*
RGEL = *Reference Guide to English Literature*
RGSF = *Reference Guide to Short Fiction*
RGWL = *Reference Guide to World Literature*
RHW = *Twentieth-Century Romance and Historical Writers*
SAAS = *Something about the Author Autobiography Series*
SATA = *Something about the Author*
SFW = *St. James Guide to Science Fiction Writers*
SSFS = *Short Stories for Students*
TCWW = *Twentieth-Century Western Writers*
WLIT = *World Literature and Its Times*
WP = *World Poets*
YABC = *Yesterday's Authors of Books for Children*
YAW = *St. James Guide to Young Adult Writers*

Literary Criticism Series
Cumulative Author Index

Author Index

Bean, Normal
See Burroughs, Edgar Rice
Beard, Charles A(ustin)
1874-1948 .... **TCLC 15**
See also CA 115; 189; DLB 17; SATA 18
Beardsley, Aubrey 1872-1898 .... **NCLC 6**
Beattie, Ann 1947- ..... **CLC 8, 13, 18, 40, 63, 146; SSC 11**
See also AMWS 5; BEST 90:2; BPFB 1; CA 81-84; CANR 53, 73, 128; CN 4, 5, 6, 7; CPW; DA3; DAM NOV, POP; DLB 218, 278; DLBY 1982; EWL 3; MAL 5; MTCW 1, 2; MTFW 2005; RGAL 4; RGSF 2; SSFS 9; TUS
Beattie, James 1735-1803 .... **NCLC 25**
See also DLB 109
Beauchamp, Kathleen Mansfield
1888-1923 . **SSC 9, 23, 38, 81; TCLC 2, 8, 39, 164; WLC 4**
See also BPFB 2; BRW 7; CA 104; 134; DA; DA3; DAB; DAC; DAM MST; DLB 162; EWL 3; EXPS; FW; GLL 1; MTCW 2; RGEL 2; RGSF 2; SSFS 2, 8, 10, 11; TEA; WWE 1
Beaumarchais, Pierre-Augustin Caron de
1732-1799 .... **DC 4; LC 61**
See also DAM DRAM; DFS 14, 16; DLB 313; EW 4; GFL Beginnings to 1789; RGWL 2, 3
Beaumont, Francis 1584(?)-1616 .. **DC 6; LC 33**
See also BRW 2; CDBLB Before 1660; DLB 58; TEA
Beauvoir, Simone de 1908-1986 .... **CLC 1, 2, 4, 8, 14, 31, 44, 50, 71, 124; SSC 35; WLC 1**
See also BPFB 1; CA 9-12R; 118; CANR 28, 61; DA; DA3; DAB; DAC; DAM MST, NOV; DLB 72; DLBY 1986; EW 12; EWL 3; FL 1:5; FW; GFL 1789 to the Present; LMFS 2; MTCW 1, 2; MTFW 2005; RGSF 2; RGWL 2, 3; TWA
Beauvoir, Simone Lucie Ernestine Marie Bertrand de
See Beauvoir, Simone de
Becker, Carl (Lotus) 1873-1945 ..... **TCLC 63**
See also CA 157; DLB 17
Becker, Jurek 1937-1997 .... **CLC 7, 19**
See also CA 85-88; 157; CANR 60, 117; CWW 2; DLB 75, 299; EWL 3; RGHL
Becker, Walter 1950- .... **CLC 26**
Becket, Thomas a 1118(?)-1170 .... **CMLC 83**
Beckett, Samuel 1906-1989 .. **CLC 1, 2, 3, 4, 6, 9, 10, 11, 14, 18, 29, 57, 59, 83; DC 22; SSC 16, 74; TCLC 145; WLC 1**
See also BRWC 2; BRWR 1; BRWS 1; CA 5-8R; 130; CANR 33, 61; CBD; CDBLB 1945-1960; CN 1, 2, 3, 4; DA; DA3; DAB; DAC; DAM DRAM, MST, NOV; DFS 2, 7, 18; DLB 13, 15, 233, 319, 321, 329; DLBY 1990; EWL 3; GFL 1789 to the Present; LATS 1:2; LMFS 2; MTCW 1, 2; MTFW 2005; RGSF 2; RGWL 2, 3; SSFS 15; TEA; WLIT 4
Beckford, William 1760-1844 .... **NCLC 16**
See also BRW 3; DLB 39, 213; GL 2; HGG; LMFS 1; SUFW
Beckham, Barry (Earl) 1944- .... **BLC 1:1**
See also BW 1; CA 29-32R; CANR 26, 62; CN 1, 2, 3, 4, 5, 6; DAM MULT; DLB 33
Beckman, Gunnel 1910- .... **CLC 26**
See also CA 33-36R; CANR 15, 114; CLR 25; MAICYA 1, 2; SAAS 9; SATA 6
Becque, Henri 1837-1899 .... **DC 21; NCLC 3**
See also DLB 192; GFL 1789 to the Present
Becquer, Gustavo Adolfo
1836-1870 .... **HLCS 1; NCLC 106**
See also DAM MULT

Beddoes, Thomas Lovell 1803-1849 .. **DC 15; NCLC 3, 154**
See also BRWS 11; DLB 96
Bede c. 673-735 .... **CMLC 20**
See also DLB 146; TEA
Bedford, Denton R. 1907-(?) .... **NNAL**
Bedford, Donald F.
See Fearing, Kenneth (Flexner)
Beecher, Catharine Esther
1800-1878 .... **NCLC 30**
See also DLB 1, 243
Beecher, John 1904-1980 .... **CLC 6**
See also AITN 1; CA 5-8R; 105; CANR 8; CP 1, 2, 3
Beer, Johann 1655-1700 .... **LC 5**
See also DLB 168
Beer, Patricia 1924- .... **CLC 58**
See also BRWS 14; CA 61-64; 183; CANR 13, 46; CP 1, 2, 3, 4, 5, 6; CWP; DLB 40; FW
Beerbohm, Max
See Beerbohm, (Henry) Max(imilian)
Beerbohm, (Henry) Max(imilian)
1872-1956 .... **TCLC 1, 24**
See also BRWS 2; CA 104; 154; CANR 79; DLB 34, 100; FANT; MTCW 2
Beer-Hofmann, Richard
1866-1945 .... **TCLC 60**
See also CA 160; DLB 81
Beg, Shemus
See Stephens, James
Begiebing, Robert J(ohn) 1946- .... **CLC 70**
See also CA 122; CANR 40, 88
Begley, Louis 1933- .... **CLC 197**
See also CA 140; CANR 98, 176; DLB 299; RGHL; TCLE 1:1
Behan, Brendan (Francis)
1923-1964 .... **CLC 1, 8, 11, 15, 79**
See also BRWS 2; CA 73-76; CANR 33, 121; CBD; CDBLB 1945-1960; DAM DRAM; DFS 7; DLB 13, 233; EWL 3; MTCW 1, 2
Behn, Aphra 1640(?)-1689 .. **DC 4; LC 1, 30, 42, 135; PC 13, 88; WLC 1**
See also BRWS 3; DA; DA3; DAB; DAC; DAM DRAM, MST, NOV, POET; DFS 16, 24; DLB 39, 80, 131; FW; TEA; WLIT 3
Behrman, S(amuel) N(athaniel)
1893-1973 .... **CLC 40**
See also CA 13-16; 45-48; CAD; CAP 1; DLB 7, 44; IDFW 3; MAL 5; RGAL 4
Bekederemo, J. P. Clark
See Clark Bekederemo, J.P.
See also CD 6
Belasco, David 1853-1931 .... **TCLC 3**
See also CA 104; 168; DLB 7; MAL 5; RGAL 4
Belcheva, Elisaveta Lyubomirova
1893-1991 .... **CLC 10**
See also CA 178; CDWLB 4; DLB 147; EWL 3
Beldone, Phil "Cheech"
See Ellison, Harlan
Beleno
See Azuela, Mariano
Belinski, Vissarion Grigoryevich
1811-1848 .... **NCLC 5**
See also DLB 198
Belitt, Ben 1911- .... **CLC 22**
See also CA 13-16R; CAAS 4; CANR 7, 77; CP 1, 2, 3, 4, 5, 6; DLB 5
Belknap, Jeremy 1744-1798 .... **LC 115**
See also DLB 30, 37
Bell, Gertrude (Margaret Lowthian)
1868-1926 .... **TCLC 67**
See also CA 167; CANR 110; DLB 174
Bell, J. Freeman
See Zangwill, Israel

Bell, James Madison 1826-1902 ..... **BLC 1:1; TCLC 43**
See also BW 1; CA 122; 124; DAM MULT; DLB 50
Bell, Madison Smartt 1957- ..... **CLC 41, 102, 223**
See also AMWS 10; BPFB 1; CA 111, 183; CAAE 183; CANR 28, 54, 73, 134, 176; CN 5, 6, 7; CSW; DLB 218, 278; MTCW 2; MTFW 2005
Bell, Marvin (Hartley) 1937- ...... **CLC 8, 31; PC 79**
See also CA 21-24R; CAAS 14; CANR 59, 102; CP 1, 2, 3, 4, 5, 6, 7; DAM POET; DLB 5; MAL 5; MTCW 1; PFS 25
Bell, W. L. D.
See Mencken, H(enry) L(ouis)
Bellamy, Atwood C.
See Mencken, H(enry) L(ouis)
Bellamy, Edward 1850-1898 ..... **NCLC 4, 86, 147**
See also DLB 12; NFS 15; RGAL 4; SFW 4
Belli, Gioconda 1948- .... **HLCS 1**
See also CA 152; CANR 143; CWW 2; DLB 290; EWL 3; RGWL 3
Bellin, Edward J.
See Kuttner, Henry
Bello, Andres 1781-1865 .... **NCLC 131**
See also LAW
Belloc, (Joseph) Hilaire (Pierre Sebastien Rene Swanton) 1870-1953 .... **PC 24; TCLC 7, 18**
See also CA 106; 152; CLR 102; CWRI 5; DAM POET; DLB 19, 100, 141, 174; EWL 3; MTCW 2; MTFW 2005; SATA 112; WCH; YABC 1
Belloc, Joseph Peter Rene Hilaire
See Belloc, (Joseph) Hilaire (Pierre Sebastien Rene Swanton)
Belloc, Joseph Pierre Hilaire
See Belloc, (Joseph) Hilaire (Pierre Sebastien Rene Swanton)
Belloc, M. A.
See Lowndes, Marie Adelaide (Belloc)
Belloc-Lowndes, Mrs.
See Lowndes, Marie Adelaide (Belloc)
Bellow, Saul 1915-2005 ...... **CLC 1, 2, 3, 6, 8, 10, 13, 15, 25, 33, 34, 63, 79, 190, 200; SSC 14, 101; WLC 1**
See also AITN 2; AMW; AMWC 2; AMWR 2; BEST 89:3; BPFB 1; CA 5-8R; 238; CABS 1; CANR 29, 53, 95, 132; CDALB 1941-1968; CN 1, 2, 3, 4, 5, 6, 7; DA; DA3; DAB; DAC; DAM MST, NOV, POP; DLB 2, 28, 299, 329; DLBD 3; DLBY 1982; EWL 3; MAL 5; MTCW 1, 2; MTFW 2005; NFS 4, 14, 26; RGAL 4; RGHL; RGSF 2; SSFS 12, 22; TUS
Belser, Reimond Karel Maria de
1929- .... **CLC 14**
See also CA 152
Bely, Andrey
See Bugayev, Boris Nikolayevich
Belyi, Andrei
See Bugayev, Boris Nikolayevich
Bembo, Pietro 1470-1547 .... **LC 79**
See also RGWL 2, 3
Benary, Margot
See Benary-Isbert, Margot
Benary-Isbert, Margot 1889-1979 .... **CLC 12**
See also CA 5-8R; 89-92; CANR 4, 72; CLR 12; MAICYA 1, 2; SATA 2; SATA-Obit 21
Benavente (y Martinez), Jacinto
1866-1954 .... **DC 26; HLCS 1; TCLC 3**
See also CA 106; 131; CANR 81; DAM DRAM, MULT; DLB 329; EWL 3; GLL 2; HW 1, 2; MTCW 1, 2

Benchley, Peter 1940-2006 .... **CLC 4, 8**
See also AAYA 14; AITN 2; BPFB 1; CA
17-20R; 248; CANR 12, 35, 66, 115;
CPW; DAM NOV, POP; HGG; MTCW 1,
2; MTFW 2005; SATA 3, 89, 164
Benchley, Peter Bradford
See Benchley, Peter
Benchley, Robert (Charles)
1889-1945 .... **TCLC 1, 55**
See also CA 105; 153; DLB 11; MAL 5;
RGAL 4
Benda, Julien 1867-1956 .... **TCLC 60**
See also CA 120; 154; GFL 1789 to the
Present
Benedict, Ruth 1887-1948 .... **TCLC 60**
See also CA 158; CANR 146; DLB 246
Benedict, Ruth Fulton
See Benedict, Ruth
Benedikt, Michael 1935- .... **CLC 4, 14**
See also CA 13-16R; CANR 7; CP 1, 2, 3,
4, 5, 6, 7; DLB 5
Benet, Juan 1927-1993 .... **CLC 28**
See also CA 143; EWL 3
Benet, Stephen Vincent 1898-1943 ..... **PC 64;
SSC 10, 86; TCLC 7**
See also AMWS 11; CA 104; 152; DA3;
DAM POET; DLB 4, 48, 102, 249, 284;
DLBY 1997; EWL 3; HGG; MAL 5;
MTCW 2; MTFW 2005; RGAL 4; RGSF
2; SSFS 22; SUFW; WP; YABC 1
Benet, William Rose 1886-1950 ..... **TCLC 28**
See also CA 118; 152; DAM POET; DLB
45; RGAL 4
Benford, Gregory 1941- .... **CLC 52**
See also BPFB 1; CA 69-72, 175, 268;
CAAE 175, 268; CAAS 27; CANR 12,
24, 49, 95, 134; CN 7; CSW; DLBY 1982;
MTFW 2005; SCFW 2; SFW 4
Benford, Gregory Albert
See Benford, Gregory
Bengtsson, Frans (Gunnar)
1894-1954 .... **TCLC 48**
See also CA 170; EWL 3
Benjamin, David
See Slavitt, David R.
Benjamin, Lois
See Gould, Lois
Benjamin, Walter 1892-1940 .... **TCLC 39**
See also CA 164; CANR 181; DLB 242;
EW 11; EWL 3
Ben Jelloun, Tahar 1944- .... **CLC 180**
See also CA 135, 162; CANR 100, 166;
CWW 2; EWL 3; RGWL 3; WLIT 2
Benn, Gottfried 1886-1956 .. **PC 35; TCLC 3**
See also CA 106; 153; DLB 56; EWL 3;
RGWL 2, 3
Bennett, Alan 1934- .... **CLC 45, 77**
See also BRWS 8; CA 103; CANR 35, 55,
106, 157; CBD; CD 5, 6; DAB; DAM
MST; DLB 310; MTCW 1, 2; MTFW
2005
Bennett, (Enoch) Arnold
1867-1931 .... **TCLC 5, 20, 197**
See also BRW 6; CA 106; 155; CDBLB
1890-1914; DLB 10, 34, 98, 135; EWL 3;
MTCW 2
Bennett, Elizabeth
See Mitchell, Margaret (Munnerlyn)
Bennett, George Harold 1930- .... **CLC 5**
See also BW 1; CA 97-100; CAAS 13;
CANR 87; DLB 33
Bennett, Gwendolyn B. 1902-1981 .... **HR 1:2**
See also BW 1; CA 125; DLB 51; WP
Bennett, Hal
See Bennett, George Harold
Bennett, Jay 1912- .... **CLC 35**
See also AAYA 10, 73; CA 69-72; CANR
11, 42, 79; JRDA; SAAS 4; SATA 41, 87;
SATA-Brief 27; WYA; YAW

Bennett, Louise 1919-2006 .... **BLC 1:1; CLC
28**
See also BW 2, 3; CA 151; 252; CDWLB
3; CP 1, 2, 3, 4, 5, 6, 7; DAM MULT;
DLB 117; EWL 3
Bennett, Louise Simone
See Bennett, Louise
Bennett-Coverley, Louise
See Bennett, Louise
Benoit de Sainte-Maure fl. 12th cent.
.... **CMLC 90**
Benson, A. C. 1862-1925 .... **TCLC 123**
See also DLB 98
Benson, E(dward) F(rederic)
1867-1940 .... **TCLC 27**
See also CA 114; 157; DLB 135, 153;
HGG; SUFW 1
Benson, Jackson J. 1930- .... **CLC 34**
See also CA 25-28R; DLB 111
Benson, Sally 1900-1972 .... **CLC 17**
See also CA 19-20; 37-40R; CAP 1; SATA
1, 35; SATA-Obit 27
Benson, Stella 1892-1933 .... **TCLC 17**
See also CA 117; 154, 155; DLB 36, 162;
FANT; TEA
Bentham, Jeremy 1748-1832 .... **NCLC 38**
See also DLB 107, 158, 252
Bentley, E(dmund) C(lerihew)
1875-1956 .... **TCLC 12**
See also CA 108; 232; DLB 70; MSW
Bentley, Eric 1916- .... **CLC 24**
See also CA 5-8R; CAD; CANR 6, 67;
CBD; CD 5, 6; INT CANR-6
Bentley, Eric Russell
See Bentley, Eric
ben Uzair, Salem
See Horne, Richard Henry Hengist
Beolco, Angelo 1496-1542 .... **LC 139**
Beranger, Pierre Jean de
1780-1857 .... **NCLC 34**
Berdyaev, Nicolas
See Berdyaev, Nikolai (Aleksandrovich)
Berdyaev, Nikolai (Aleksandrovich)
1874-1948 .... **TCLC 67**
See also CA 120; 157
Berdyayev, Nikolai (Aleksandrovich)
See Berdyaev, Nikolai (Aleksandrovich)
Berendt, John 1939- .... **CLC 86**
See also CA 146; CANR 75, 83, 151
Berendt, John Lawrence
See Berendt, John
Beresford, J(ohn) D(avys)
1873-1947 .... **TCLC 81**
See also CA 112; 155; DLB 162, 178, 197;
SFW 4; SUFW 1
Bergelson, David (Rafailovich)
1884-1952 .... **TCLC 81**
See Bergelson, Dovid
See also CA 220; DLB 333
Bergelson, Dovid
See Bergelson, David (Rafailovich)
See also EWL 3
Berger, Colonel
See Malraux, (Georges-)Andre
Berger, John 1926- .... **CLC 2, 19**
See also BRWS 4; CA 81-84; CANR 51,
78, 117, 163; CN 1, 2, 3, 4, 5, 6, 7; DLB
14, 207, 319, 326
Berger, John Peter
See Berger, John
Berger, Melvin H. 1927- .... **CLC 12**
See also CA 5-8R; CANR 4, 142; CLR 32;
SAAS 2; SATA 5, 88, 158; SATA-Essay
124

Berger, Thomas 1924- .... **CLC 3, 5, 8, 11, 18,
38, 259**
See also BPFB 1; CA 1-4R; CANR 5, 28,
51, 128; CN 1, 2, 3, 4, 5, 6, 7; DAM
NOV; DLB 2; DLBY 1980; EWL 3;
FANT; INT CANR-28; MAL 5; MTCW
1, 2; MTFW 2005; RHW; TCLE 1:1;
TCWW 1, 2
Bergman, Ernst Ingmar
See Bergman, Ingmar
Bergman, Ingmar 1918-2007 ..... **CLC 16, 72,
210**
See also AAYA 61; CA 81-84; 262; CANR
33, 70; CWW 2; DLB 257; MTCW 2;
MTFW 2005
Bergson, Henri(-Louis) 1859-1941 . **TCLC 32**
See also CA 164; DLB 329; EW 8; EWL 3;
GFL 1789 to the Present
Bergstein, Eleanor 1938- .... **CLC 4**
See also CA 53-56; CANR 5
Berkeley, George 1685-1753 .... **LC 65**
See also DLB 31, 101, 252
Berkoff, Steven 1937- .... **CLC 56**
See also CA 104; CANR 72; CBD; CD 5, 6
Berlin, Isaiah 1909-1997 .... **TCLC 105**
See also CA 85-88; 162
Bermant, Chaim (Icyk) 1929-1998 ... **CLC 40**
See also CA 57-60; CANR 6, 31, 57, 105;
CN 2, 3, 4, 5, 6
Bern, Victoria
See Fisher, M(ary) F(rances) K(ennedy)
Bernanos, (Paul Louis) Georges
1888-1948 .... **TCLC 3**
See also CA 104; 130; CANR 94; DLB 72;
EWL 3; GFL 1789 to the Present; RGWL
2, 3
Bernard, April 1956- .... **CLC 59**
See also CA 131; CANR 144
Bernard, Mary Ann
See Soderbergh, Steven
Bernard of Clairvaux 1090-1153 .. **CMLC 71**
See also DLB 208
Bernard Silvestris fl. c. 1130-fl. c.
1160 .... **CMLC 87**
See also DLB 208
Bernart de Ventadorn c. 1130-c.
1190 .... **CMLC 98**
Berne, Victoria
See Fisher, M(ary) F(rances) K(ennedy)
Bernhard, Thomas 1931-1989 ..... **CLC 3, 32,
61; DC 14; TCLC 165**
See also CA 85-88; 127; CANR 32, 57; CD-
WLB 2; DLB 85, 124; EWL 3; MTCW 1;
RGHL; RGWL 2, 3
Bernhardt, Sarah (Henriette Rosine)
1844-1923 .... **TCLC 75**
See also CA 157
Bernstein, Charles 1950- .... **CLC 142**
See also CA 129; CAAS 24; CANR 90; CP
4, 5, 6, 7; DLB 169
Bernstein, Ingrid
See Kirsch, Sarah
Beroul fl. c. 12th cent. - .... **CMLC 75**
Berriault, Gina 1926-1999 .... **CLC 54, 109;
SSC 30**
See also CA 116; 129; 185; CANR 66; DLB
130; SSFS 7,11
Berrigan, Daniel 1921- .... **CLC 4**
See also CA 33-36R, 187; CAAE 187;
CAAS 1; CANR 11, 43, 78; CP 1, 2, 3, 4,
5, 6, 7; DLB 5
Berrigan, Edmund Joseph Michael, Jr.
1934-1983 .... **CLC 37**
See also CA 61-64; 110; CANR 14, 102;
CP 1, 2, 3; DLB 5, 169; WP
Berrigan, Ted
See Berrigan, Edmund Joseph Michael, Jr.

Bontemps, Arna(ud Wendell)
1902-1973 ..... **BLC 1:1; CLC 1, 18; HR 1:2**
See also BW 1; CA 1-4R; 41-44R; CANR 4, 35; CLR 6; CP 1; CWRI 5; DA3; DAM MULT, NOV, POET; DLB 48, 51; JRDA; MAICYA 1, 2; MAL 5; MTCW 1, 2; SATA 2, 44; SATA-Obit 24; WCH; WP

Boot, William
See Stoppard, Tom

Booth, Irwin
See Hoch, Edward D.

Booth, Martin 1944-2004 .... **CLC 13**
See also CA 93-96, 188; 223; CAAE 188; CAAS 2; CANR 92; CP 1, 2, 3, 4

Booth, Philip 1925-2007 .... **CLC 23**
See also CA 5-8R; 262; CANR 5, 88; CP 1, 2, 3, 4, 5, 6, 7; DLBY 1982

Booth, Philip Edmund
See Booth, Philip

Booth, Wayne C. 1921-2005 .... **CLC 24**
See also CA 1-4R; 244; CAAS 5; CANR 3, 43, 117; DLB 67

Booth, Wayne Clayson
See Booth, Wayne C.

Borchert, Wolfgang 1921-1947 .... **TCLC 5**
See also CA 104; 188; DLB 69, 124; EWL 3

Borel, Petrus 1809-1859 .... **NCLC 41**
See also DLB 119; GFL 1789 to the Present

Borges, Jorge Luis 1899-1986 ... **CLC 1, 2, 3, 4, 6, 8, 9, 10, 13, 19, 44, 48, 83; HLC 1; PC 22, 32; SSC 4, 41, 100; TCLC 109; WLC 1**
See also AAYA 26; BPFB 1; CA 21-24R; CANR 19, 33, 75, 105, 133; CDWLB 3; DA; DA3; DAB; DAC; DAM MST, MULT; DLB 113, 283; DLBY 1986; DNFS 1, 2; EWL 3; HW 1, 2; LAW; LMFS 2; MSW; MTCW 1, 2; MTFW 2005; PFS 27; RGHL; RGSF 2; RGWL 2, 3; SFW 4; SSFS 17; TWA; WLIT 1

Borne, Ludwig 1786-1837 .... **NCLC 193**
See also DLB 90

Borowski, Tadeusz 1922-1951 .... **SSC 48; TCLC 9**
See also CA 106; 154; CDWLB 4; DLB 215; EWL 3; RGHL; RGSF 2; RGWL 3; SSFS 13

Borrow, George (Henry)
1803-1881 .... **NCLC 9**
See also BRWS 12; DLB 21, 55, 166

Bosch (Gavino), Juan 1909-2001 ..... **HLCS 1**
See also CA 151; 204; DAM MST, MULT; DLB 145; HW 1, 2

Bosman, Herman Charles
1905-1951 .... **TCLC 49**
See Malan, Herman
See also CA 160; DLB 225; RGSF 2

Bosschere, Jean de 1878(?)-1953 ... **TCLC 19**
See also CA 115; 186

Boswell, James 1740-1795 ... **LC 4, 50; WLC 1**
See also BRW 3; CDBLB 1660-1789; DA; DAB; DAC; DAM MST; DLB 104, 142; TEA; WLIT 3

Boto, Eza
See Biyidi, Alexandre

Bottomley, Gordon 1874-1948 ..... **TCLC 107**
See also CA 120; 192; DLB 10

Bottoms, David 1949- .... **CLC 53**
See also CA 105; CANR 22; CSW; DLB 120; DLBY 1983

Boucicault, Dion 1820-1890 .... **NCLC 41**
See also DLB 344

Boucolon, Maryse
See Conde, Maryse

Bourcicault, Dion
See Boucicault, Dion

Bourdieu, Pierre 1930-2002 .... **CLC 198**
See also CA 130; 204

Bourget, Paul (Charles Joseph)
1852-1935 .... **TCLC 12**
See also CA 107; 196; DLB 123; GFL 1789 to the Present

Bourjaily, Vance (Nye) 1922- .... **CLC 8, 62**
See also CA 1-4R; CAAS 1; CANR 2, 72; CN 1, 2, 3, 4, 5, 6, 7; DLB 2, 143; MAL 5

Bourne, Randolph S(illiman)
1886-1918 .... **TCLC 16**
See also AMW; CA 117; 155; DLB 63; MAL 5

Boursiquot, Dionysius
See Boucicault, Dion

Bova, Ben 1932- .... **CLC 45**
See also AAYA 16; CA 5-8R; CAAS 18; CANR 11, 56, 94, 111, 157; CLR 3, 96; DLBY 1981; INT CANR-11; MAICYA 1, 2; MTCW 1; SATA 6, 68, 133; SFW 4

Bova, Benjamin William
See Bova, Ben

Bowen, Elizabeth (Dorothea Cole)
1899-1973 . **CLC 1, 3, 6, 11, 15, 22, 118; SSC 3, 28, 66; TCLC 148**
See also BRWS 2; CA 17-18; 41-44R; CANR 35, 105; CAP 2; CDBLB 1945-1960; CN 1; DA3; DAM NOV; DLB 15, 162; EWL 3; EXPS; FW; HGG; MTCW 1, 2; MTFW 2005; NFS 13; RGSF 2; SSFS 5, 22; SUFW 1; TEA; WLIT 4

Bowering, George 1935- .... **CLC 15, 47**
See also CA 21-24R; CAAS 16; CANR 10; CN 7; CP 1, 2, 3, 4, 5, 6, 7; DLB 53

Bowering, Marilyn R(uthe) 1949- .... **CLC 32**
See also CA 101; CANR 49; CP 4, 5, 6, 7; CWP; DLB 334

Bowers, Edgar 1924-2000 .... **CLC 9**
See also CA 5-8R; 188; CANR 24; CP 1, 2, 3, 4, 5, 6, 7; CSW; DLB 5

Bowers, Mrs. J. Milton 1842-1914
See Bierce, Ambrose (Gwinett)

Bowie, David
See Jones, David Robert

Bowles, Jane (Sydney) 1917-1973 ..... **CLC 3, 68**
See Bowles, Jane Auer
See also CA 19-20; 41-44R; CAP 2; CN 1; MAL 5

Bowles, Jane Auer
See Bowles, Jane (Sydney)
See also EWL 3

Bowles, Paul 1910-1999 ..... **CLC 1, 2, 19, 53; SSC 3, 98; TCLC 209**
See also AMWS 4; CA 1-4R; 186; CAAS 1; CANR 1, 19, 50, 75; CN 1, 2, 3, 4, 5, 6; DA3; DLB 5, 6, 218; EWL 3; MAL 5; MTCW 1, 2; MTFW 2005; RGAL 4; SSFS 17

Bowles, William Lisle 1762-1850 . **NCLC 103**
See also DLB 93

Box, Edgar
See Vidal, Gore

Boyd, James 1888-1944 .... **TCLC 115**
See also CA 186; DLB 9; DLBD 16; RGAL 4; RHW

Boyd, Nancy
See Millay, Edna St. Vincent

Boyd, Thomas (Alexander)
1898-1935 .... **TCLC 111**
See also CA 111; 183; DLB 9; DLBD 16, 316

Boyd, William 1952- .... **CLC 28, 53, 70**
See also CA 114; 120; CANR 51, 71, 131, 174; CN 4, 5, 6, 7; DLB 231

Boyesen, Hjalmar Hjorth
1848-1895 .... **NCLC 135**
See also DLB 12, 71; DLBD 13; RGAL 4

Boyle, Kay 1902-1992 .... **CLC 1, 5, 19, 58, 121; SSC 5, 102**
See also CA 13-16R; 140; CAAS 1; CANR 29, 61, 110; CN 1, 2, 3, 4, 5; CP 1, 2, 3, 4, 5; DLB 4, 9, 48, 86; DLBY 1993; EWL 3; MAL 5; MTCW 1, 2; MTFW 2005; RGAL 4; RGSF 2; SSFS 10, 13, 14

Boyle, Mark
See Kienzle, William X.

Boyle, Patrick 1905-1982 .... **CLC 19**
See also CA 127

Boyle, T. C.
See Boyle, T. Coraghessan
See also AMWS 8

Boyle, T. Coraghessan 1948- ..... **CLC 36, 55, 90; SSC 16**
See Boyle, T. C.
See also AAYA 47; BEST 90:4; BPFB 1; CA 120; CANR 44, 76, 89, 132; CN 6, 7; CPW; DA3; DAM POP; DLB 218, 278; DLBY 1986; EWL 3; MAL 5; MTCW 2; MTFW 2005; SSFS 13, 19

Boz
See Dickens, Charles (John Huffam)

Brackenridge, Hugh Henry
1748-1816 .... **NCLC 7**
See also DLB 11, 37; RGAL 4

Bradbury, Edward P.
See Moorcock, Michael

Bradbury, Malcolm (Stanley)
1932-2000 .... **CLC 32, 61**
See also CA 1-4R; CANR 1, 33, 91, 98, 137; CN 1, 2, 3, 4, 5, 6, 7; CP 1; DA3; DAM NOV; DLB 14, 207; EWL 3; MTCW 1, 2; MTFW 2005

Bradbury, Ray 1920- ... **CLC 1, 3, 10, 15, 42, 98, 235; SSC 29, 53; WLC 1**
See also AAYA 15; AITN 1, 2; AMWS 4; BPFB 1; BYA 4, 5, 11; CA 1-4R; CANR 2, 30, 75, 125, 186; CDALB 1968-1988; CN 1, 2, 3, 4, 5, 6, 7; CPW; DA; DA3; DAB; DAC; DAM MST, NOV, POP; DLB 2, 8; EXPN; EXPS; HGG; LAIT 3, 5; LATS 1:2; LMFS 2; MAL 5; MTCW 1, 2; MTFW 2005; NFS 1, 22; RGAL 4; RGSF 2; SATA 11, 64, 123; SCFW 1, 2; SFW 4; SSFS 1, 20; SUFW 1, 2; TUS; YAW

Bradbury, Ray Douglas
See Bradbury, Ray

Braddon, Mary Elizabeth
1837-1915 .... **TCLC 111**
See also BRWS 8; CA 108; 179; CMW 4; DLB 18, 70, 156; HGG

Bradfield, Scott 1955- .... **SSC 65**
See also CA 147; CANR 90; HGG; SUFW 2

Bradfield, Scott Michael
See Bradfield, Scott

Bradford, Gamaliel 1863-1932 .... **TCLC 36**
See also CA 160; DLB 17

Bradford, William 1590-1657 .... **LC 64**
See also DLB 24, 30; RGAL 4

Bradley, David, Jr. 1950- ...... **BLC 1:1; CLC 23, 118**
See also BW 1, 3; CA 104; CANR 26, 81; CN 4, 5, 6, 7; DAM MULT; DLB 33

Bradley, David Henry, Jr.
See Bradley, David, Jr.

Bradley, John Ed 1958- .... **CLC 55**
See also CA 139; CANR 99; CN 6, 7; CSW

Bradley, John Edmund, Jr.
See Bradley, John Ed

Bradley, Marion Zimmer
1930-1999 .... **CLC 30**
See Chapman, Lee; Dexter, John; Gardner, Miriam; Ives, Morgan
See also AAYA 40; BPFB 1; CA 57-60; 185; CAAS 10; CANR 7, 31, 51, 75, 107; CPW; DA3; DAM POP; DLB 8; FANT;

FW; GLL 1; MTCW 1, 2; MTFW 2005; SATA 90, 139; SATA-Obit 116; SFW 4; SUFW 2; YAW

Bradshaw, John 1933- .... **CLC 70**
See also CA 138; CANR 61

Bradstreet, Anne 1612(?)-1672 .... **LC 4, 30, 130; PC 10**
See also AMWS 1; CDALB 1640-1865; DA; DA3; DAC; DAM MST, POET; DLB 24; EXPP; FW; PFS 6; RGAL 4; TUS; WP

Brady, Joan 1939- .... **CLC 86**
See also CA 141

Bragg, Melvyn 1939- .... **CLC 10**
See also BEST 89:3; CA 57-60; CANR 10, 48, 89, 158; CN 1, 2, 3, 4, 5, 6, 7; DLB 14, 271; RHW

Brahe, Tycho 1546-1601 .... **LC 45**
See also DLB 300

Braine, John (Gerard) 1922-1986 . **CLC 1, 3, 41**
See also CA 1-4R; 120; CANR 1, 33; CD-BLB 1945-1960; CN 1, 2, 3, 4; DLB 15; DLBY 1986; EWL 3; MTCW 1

Braithwaite, William Stanley (Beaumont) 1878-1962 ...... **BLC 1:1; HR 1:2; PC 52**
See also BW 1; CA 125; DAM MULT; DLB 50, 54; MAL 5

Bramah, Ernest 1868-1942 .... **TCLC 72**
See also CA 156; CMW 4; DLB 70; FANT

Brammer, Billy Lee
See Brammer, William

Brammer, William 1929-1978 .... **CLC 31**
See also CA 235; 77-80

Brancati, Vitaliano 1907-1954 .... **TCLC 12**
See also CA 109; DLB 264; EWL 3

Brancato, Robin F(idler) 1936- .... **CLC 35**
See also AAYA 9, 68; BYA 6; CA 69-72; CANR 11, 45; CLR 32; JRDA; MAICYA 2; MAICYAS 1; SAAS 9; SATA 97; WYA; YAW

Brand, Dionne 1953- .... **CLC 192**
See also BW 2; CA 143; CANR 143; CWP; DLB 334

Brand, Max
See Faust, Frederick (Schiller)

Brand, Millen 1906-1980 .... **CLC 7**
See also CA 21-24R; 97-100; CANR 72

Branden, Barbara 1929- .... **CLC 44**
See also CA 148

Brandes, Georg (Morris Cohen) 1842-1927 .... **TCLC 10**
See also CA 105; 189; DLB 300

Brandys, Kazimierz 1916-2000 .... **CLC 62**
See also CA 239; EWL 3

Branley, Franklyn M(ansfield) 1915-2002 .... **CLC 21**
See also CA 33-36R; 207; CANR 14, 39; CLR 13; MAICYA 1, 2; SAAS 16; SATA 4, 68, 136

Brant, Beth (E.) 1941- .... **NNAL**
See also CA 144; FW

Brant, Sebastian 1457-1521 .... **LC 112**
See also DLB 179; RGWL 2, 3

Brathwaite, Edward Kamau 1930- ..... **BLC 2:1; BLCS; CLC 11; PC 56**
See also BRWS 12; BW 2, 3; CA 25-28R; CANR 11, 26, 47, 107; CDWLB 3; CP 1, 2, 3, 4, 5, 6, 7; DAM POET; DLB 125; EWL 3

Brathwaite, Kamau
See Brathwaite, Edward Kamau

Brautigan, Richard (Gary) 1935-1984 .... **CLC 1, 3, 5, 9, 12, 34, 42; PC 94; TCLC 133**
See also BPFB 1; CA 53-56; 113; CANR 34; CN 1, 2, 3; CP 1, 2, 3, 4; DA3; DAM NOV; DLB 2, 5, 206; DLBY 1980, 1984; FANT; MAL 5; MTCW 1; RGAL 4; SATA 56

Brave Bird, Mary
See Crow Dog, Mary

Braverman, Kate 1950- .... **CLC 67**
See also CA 89-92; CANR 141; DLB 335

Brecht, (Eugen) Bertolt (Friedrich) 1898-1956 ..... **DC 3; TCLC 1, 6, 13, 35, 169; WLC 1**
See also CA 104; 133; CANR 62; CDWLB 2; DA; DA3; DAB; DAC; DAM DRAM, MST; DFS 4, 5, 9; DLB 56, 124; EW 11; EWL 3; IDTP; MTCW 1, 2; MTFW 2005; RGHL; RGWL 2, 3; TWA

Brecht, Eugen Berthold Friedrich
See Brecht, (Eugen) Bertolt (Friedrich)

Bremer, Fredrika 1801-1865 .... **NCLC 11**
See also DLB 254

Brennan, Christopher John 1870-1932 .... **TCLC 17**
See also CA 117; 188; DLB 230; EWL 3

Brennan, Maeve 1917-1993 ... **CLC 5; TCLC 124**
See also CA 81-84; CANR 72, 100

Brenner, Jozef 1887-1919 .... **TCLC 13**
See also CA 111; 240

Brent, Linda
See Jacobs, Harriet A(nn)

Brentano, Clemens (Maria) 1778-1842 .... **NCLC 1, 191; SSC 115**
See also DLB 90; RGWL 2, 3

Brent of Bin Bin
See Franklin, (Stella Maria Sarah) Miles (Lampe)

Brenton, Howard 1942- .... **CLC 31**
See also CA 69-72; CANR 33, 67; CBD; CD 5, 6; DLB 13; MTCW 1

Breslin, James
See Breslin, Jimmy

Breslin, Jimmy 1930- .... **CLC 4, 43**
See also CA 73-76; CANR 31, 75, 139, 187; DAM NOV; DLB 185; MTCW 2; MTFW 2005

Bresson, Robert 1901(?)-1999 .... **CLC 16**
See also CA 110; 187; CANR 49

Breton, Andre 1896-1966 .. **CLC 2, 9, 15, 54; PC 15**
See also CA 19-20; 25-28R; CANR 40, 60; CAP 2; DLB 65, 258; EW 11; EWL 3; GFL 1789 to the Present; LMFS 2; MTCW 1, 2; MTFW 2005; RGWL 2, 3; TWA; WP

Breton, Nicholas c. 1554-c. 1626 .... **LC 133**
See also DLB 136

Breytenbach, Breyten 1939(?)- .. **CLC 23, 37, 126**
See also CA 113; 129; CANR 61, 122; CWW 2; DAM POET; DLB 225; EWL 3

Bridgers, Sue Ellen 1942- .... **CLC 26**
See also AAYA 8, 49; BYA 7, 8; CA 65-68; CANR 11, 36; CLR 18; DLB 52; JRDA; MAICYA 1, 2; SAAS 1; SATA 22, 90; SATA-Essay 109; WYA; YAW

Bridges, Robert (Seymour) 1844-1930 .... **PC 28; TCLC 1**
See also BRW 6; CA 104; 152; CDBLB 1890-1914; DAM POET; DLB 19, 98

Bridie, James
See Mavor, Osborne Henry

Brin, David 1950- .... **CLC 34**
See also AAYA 21; CA 102; CANR 24, 70, 125, 127; INT CANR-24; SATA 65; SCFW 2; SFW 4

Brink, Andre 1935- .... **CLC 18, 36, 106**
See also AFW; BRWS 6; CA 104; CANR 39, 62, 109, 133, 182; CN 4, 5, 6, 7; DLB 225; EWL 3; INT CA-103; LATS 1:2; MTCW 1, 2; MTFW 2005; WLIT 2

Brinsmead, H. F.
See Brinsmead, H(esba) F(ay)

Brinsmead, H. F(ay)
See Brinsmead, H(esba) F(ay)

Brinsmead, H(esba) F(ay) 1922- ...... **CLC 21**
See also CA 21-24R; CANR 10; CLR 47; CWRI 5; MAICYA 1, 2; SAAS 5; SATA 18, 78

Brittain, Vera (Mary) 1893(?)-1970 . **CLC 23**
See also BRWS 10; CA 13-16; 25-28R; CANR 58; CAP 1; DLB 191; FW; MTCW 1, 2

Broch, Hermann 1886-1951 ... **TCLC 20, 204**
See also CA 117; 211; CDWLB 2; DLB 85, 124; EW 10; EWL 3; RGWL 2, 3

Brock, Rose
See Hansen, Joseph

Brod, Max 1884-1968 .... **TCLC 115**
See also CA 5-8R; 25-28R; CANR 7; DLB 81; EWL 3

Brodkey, Harold (Roy) 1930-1996 .. **CLC 56; TCLC 123**
See also CA 111; 151; CANR 71; CN 4, 5, 6; DLB 130

Brodskii, Iosif (Alexandrovich)
See Brodsky, Iosif Alexandrovich
See also CWW 2

Brodsky, Iosif Alexandrovich 1940-1996 . **CLC 4, 6, 13, 36, 100; PC 9**
See Brodskii, Iosif (Alexandrovich)
See also AAYA 71; AITN 1; AMWS 8; CA 41-44R; 151; CANR 37, 106; CWW 2; DA3; DAM POET; DLB 285, 329; EWL 3; MTCW 1, 2; MTFW 2005; RGWL 2, 3

Brodsky, Joseph
See Brodsky, Iosif Alexandrovich

Brodsky, Michael 1948- .... **CLC 19**
See also CA 102; CANR 18, 41, 58, 147; DLB 244

Brodsky, Michael Mark
See Brodsky, Michael

Brodzki, Bella .... **CLC 65**

Brome, Richard 1590(?)-1652 .... **LC 61**
See also BRWS 10; DLB 58

Bromell, Henry 1947- .... **CLC 5**
See also CA 53-56; CANR 9, 115, 116

Bromfield, Louis (Brucker) 1896-1956 .... **TCLC 11**
See also CA 107; 155; DLB 4, 9, 86; RGAL 4; RHW

Broner, E(sther) M(asserman) 1930- .... **CLC 19**
See also CA 17-20R; CANR 8, 25, 72; CN 4, 5, 6; DLB 28

Bronk, William (M.) 1918-1999 .... **CLC 10**
See also CA 89-92; 177; CANR 23; CP 3, 4, 5, 6, 7; DLB 165

Bronstein, Lev Davidovich
See Trotsky, Leon

Bronte, Anne
See Bronte, Anne

Bronte, Anne 1820-1849 ..... **NCLC 4, 71, 102**
See also BRW 5; BRWR 1; DA3; DLB 21, 199, 340; NFS 26; TEA

Bronte, (Patrick) Branwell 1817(1848) .... **NCLC 109**
See also DLB 340

Bronte, Charlotte
See Bronte, Charlotte

Bronte, Charlotte 1816-1855 ...... **NCLC 3, 8, 33, 58, 105, 155; WLC 1**
See also AAYA 17; BRW 5; BRWC 2; BRWR 1; BYA 2; CDBLB 1832-1890; DA; DA3; DAB; DAC; DAM MST, NOV; DLB 21, 159, 199, 340; EXPN; FL 1:2; GL 2; LAIT 2; NFS 4; TEA; WLIT 4

Bronte, Emily
See Bronte, Emily (Jane)

Bronte, Emily (Jane) 1818-1848 ... **NCLC 16, 35, 165; PC 8; WLC 1**
See also AAYA 17; BPFB 1; BRW 5; BRWC 1; BRWR 1; BYA 3; CDBLB 1832-1890; DA; DA3; DAB; DAC; DAM MST, NOV, POET; DLB 21, 32, 199, 340; EXPN; FL 1:2; GL 2; LAIT 1; TEA; WLIT 3

Brontes
See Bronte, Anne; Bronte, (Patrick) Branwell; Bronte, Charlotte; Bronte, Emily (Jane)

Brooke, Frances 1724-1789 .... **LC 6, 48**
See also DLB 39, 99

Brooke, Henry 1703(?)-1783 .... **LC 1**
See also DLB 39

Brooke, Rupert (Chawner)
1887-1915 .. **PC 24; TCLC 2, 7; WLC 1**
See also BRWS 3; CA 104; 132; CANR 61; CDBLB 1914-1945; DA; DAB; DAC; DAM MST, POET; DLB 19, 216; EXPP; GLL 2; MTCW 1, 2; MTFW 2005; PFS 7; TEA

Brooke-Haven, P.
See Wodehouse, P(elham) G(renville)

Brooke-Rose, Christine 1923(?)- ..... **CLC 40, 184**
See also BRWS 4; CA 13-16R; CANR 58, 118, 183; CN 1, 2, 3, 4, 5, 6, 7; DLB 14, 231; EWL 3; SFW 4

Brookner, Anita 1928- . **CLC 32, 34, 51, 136, 237**
See also BRWS 4; CA 114; 120; CANR 37, 56, 87, 130; CN 4, 5, 6, 7; CPW; DA3; DAB; DAM POP; DLB 194, 326; DLBY 1987; EWL 3; MTCW 1, 2; MTFW 2005; NFS 23; TEA

Brooks, Cleanth 1906-1994 . **CLC 24, 86, 110**
See also AMWS 14; CA 17-20R; 145; CANR 33, 35; CSW; DLB 63; DLBY 1994; EWL 3; INT CANR-35; MAL 5; MTCW 1, 2; MTFW 2005

Brooks, George
See Baum, L(yman) Frank

Brooks, Gwendolyn 1917-2000 .... **BLC 1:1, 2:1; CLC 1, 2, 4, 5, 15, 49, 125; PC 7; WLC 1**
See also AAYA 20; AFAW 1, 2; AITN 1; AMWS 3; BW 2, 3; CA 1-4R; 190; CANR 1, 27, 52, 75, 132; CDALB 1941-1968; CLR 27; CP 1, 2, 3, 4, 5, 6, 7; CWP; DA; DA3; DAC; DAM MST, MULT, POET; DLB 5, 76, 165; EWL 3; EXPP; FL 1:5; MAL 5; MBL; MTCW 1, 2; MTFW 2005; PFS 1, 2, 4, 6; RGAL 4; SATA 6; SATA-Obit 123; TUS; WP

Brooks, Mel 1926-
See Kaminsky, Melvin
See also CA 65-68; CANR 16; DFS 21

Brooks, Peter 1938- .... **CLC 34**
See also CA 45-48; CANR 1, 107, 182

Brooks, Peter Preston
See Brooks, Peter

Brooks, Van Wyck 1886-1963 .... **CLC 29**
See also AMW; CA 1-4R; CANR 6; DLB 45, 63, 103; MAL 5; TUS

Brophy, Brigid (Antonia)
1929-1995 .... **CLC 6, 11, 29, 105**
See also CA 5-8R; 149; CAAS 4; CANR 25, 53; CBD; CN 1, 2, 3, 4, 5, 6; CWD; DA3; DLB 14, 271; EWL 3; MTCW 1, 2

Brosman, Catharine Savage 1934- ..... **CLC 9**
See also CA 61-64; CANR 21, 46, 149

Brossard, Nicole 1943- .... **CLC 115, 169; PC 80**
See also CA 122; CAAS 16; CANR 140; CCA 1; CWP; CWW 2; DLB 53; EWL 3; FW; GLL 2; RGWL 3

Brother Antoninus
See Everson, William (Oliver)

Brothers Grimm
See Grimm, Jacob Ludwig Karl; Grimm, Wilhelm Karl

The Brothers Quay
See Quay, Stephen; Quay, Timothy

Broughton, T(homas) Alan 1936- ..... **CLC 19**
See also CA 45-48; CANR 2, 23, 48, 111

Broumas, Olga 1949- .... **CLC 10, 73**
See also CA 85-88; CANR 20, 69, 110; CP 5, 6, 7; CWP; GLL 2

Broun, Heywood 1888-1939 .... **TCLC 104**
See also DLB 29, 171

Brown, Alan 1950- .... **CLC 99**
See also CA 156

Brown, Charles Brockden
1771-1810 .... **NCLC 22, 74, 122**
See also AMWS 1; CDALB 1640-1865; DLB 37, 59, 73; FW; GL 2; HGG; LMFS 1; RGAL 4; TUS

Brown, Christy 1932-1981 .... **CLC 63**
See also BYA 13; CA 105; 104; CANR 72; DLB 14

Brown, Claude 1937-2002 ..... **BLC 1:1; CLC 30**
See also AAYA 7; BW 1, 3; CA 73-76; 205; CANR 81; DAM MULT

Brown, Dan 1964- .... **CLC 209**
See also AAYA 55; CA 217; MTFW 2005

Brown, Dee 1908-2002 .... **CLC 18, 47**
See also AAYA 30; CA 13-16R; 212; CAAS 6; CANR 11, 45, 60, 150; CPW; CSW; DA3; DAM POP; DLBY 1980; LAIT 2; MTCW 1, 2; MTFW 2005; NCFS 5; SATA 5, 110; SATA-Obit 141; TCWW 1, 2

Brown, Dee Alexander
See Brown, Dee

Brown, George
See Wertmueller, Lina

Brown, George Douglas
1869-1902 .... **TCLC 28**
See Douglas, George
See also CA 162

Brown, George Mackay 1921-1996 ... **CLC 5, 48, 100**
See also BRWS 6; CA 21-24R; 151; CAAS 6; CANR 12, 37, 67; CN 1, 2, 3, 4, 5, 6; CP 1, 2, 3, 4, 5, 6; DLB 14, 27, 139, 271; MTCW 1; RGSF 2; SATA 35

Brown, James Willie
See Komunyakaa, Yusef

Brown, James Willie, Jr.
See Komunyakaa, Yusef

Brown, Larry 1951-2004 .... **CLC 73**
See also CA 130; 134; 233; CANR 117, 145; CSW; DLB 234; INT CA-134

Brown, Moses
See Barrett, William (Christopher)

Brown, Rita Mae 1944- .... **CLC 18, 43, 79, 259**
See also BPFB 1; CA 45-48; CANR 2, 11, 35, 62, 95, 138, 183; CN 5, 6, 7; CPW; CSW; DA3; DAM NOV, POP; FW; INT CANR-11; MAL 5; MTCW 1, 2; MTFW 2005; NFS 9; RGAL 4; TUS

Brown, Roderick (Langmere) Haig-
See Haig-Brown, Roderick (Langmere)

Brown, Rosellen 1939- .... **CLC 32, 170**
See also CA 77-80; CAAS 10; CANR 14, 44, 98; CN 6, 7

Brown, Sterling Allen 1901-1989 ...... **BLC 1; CLC 1, 23, 59; HR 1:2; PC 55**
See also AFAW 1, 2; BW 1, 3; CA 85-88; 127; CANR 26; CP 3, 4; DA3; DAM MULT, POET; DLB 48, 51, 63; MAL 5; MTCW 1, 2; MTFW 2005; RGAL 4; WP

Brown, Will
See Ainsworth, William Harrison

Brown, William Hill 1765-1793 .... **LC 93**
See also DLB 37

Brown, William Larry
See Brown, Larry

Brown, William Wells 1815-1884 ... **BLC 1:1; DC 1; NCLC 2, 89**
See also DAM MULT; DLB 3, 50, 183, 248; RGAL 4

Browne, Clyde Jackson
See Browne, Jackson

Browne, Jackson 1948(?)- .... **CLC 21**
See also CA 120

Browne, Sir Thomas 1605-1682 .... **LC 111**
See also BRW 2; DLB 151

Browning, Robert 1812-1889 . **NCLC 19, 79; PC 2, 61; WLCS**
See also BRW 4; BRWC 2; BRWR 2; CDBLB 1832-1890; CLR 97; DA; DA3; DAB; DAC; DAM MST, POET; DLB 32, 163; EXPP; LATS 1:1; PAB; PFS 1, 15; RGEL 2; TEA; WLIT 4; WP; YABC 1

Browning, Tod 1882-1962 .... **CLC 16**
See also CA 141; 117

Brownmiller, Susan 1935- .... **CLC 159**
See also CA 103; CANR 35, 75, 137; DAM NOV; FW; MTCW 1, 2; MTFW 2005

Brownson, Orestes Augustus
1803-1876 .... **NCLC 50**
See also DLB 1, 59, 73, 243

Bruccoli, Matthew J. 1931-2008 .... **CLC 34**
See also CA 9-12R; 274; CANR 7, 87; DLB 103

Bruccoli, Matthew Joseph
See Bruccoli, Matthew J.

Bruce, Lenny
See Schneider, Leonard Alfred

Bruchac, Joseph 1942- .... **NNAL**
See also AAYA 19; CA 33-36R; 256; CAAE 256; CANR 13, 47, 75, 94, 137, 161; CLR 46; CWRI 5; DAM MULT; DLB 342; JRDA; MAICYA 2; MAICYAS 1; MTCW 2; MTFW 2005; SATA 42, 89, 131, 176; SATA-Essay 176

Bruin, John
See Brutus, Dennis

Brulard, Henri
See Stendhal

Brulls, Christian
See Simenon, Georges (Jacques Christian)

Brunetto Latini c. 1220-1294 .... **CMLC 73**

Brunner, John (Kilian Houston)
1934-1995 .... **CLC 8, 10**
See also CA 1-4R; 149; CAAS 8; CANR 2, 37; CPW; DAM POP; DLB 261; MTCW 1, 2; SCFW 1, 2; SFW 4

Bruno, Giordano 1548-1600 .... **LC 27**
See also RGWL 2, 3

Brutus, Dennis 1924- ...... **BLC 1:1; CLC 43; PC 24**
See also AFW; BW 2, 3; CA 49-52; CAAS 14; CANR 2, 27, 42, 81; CDWLB 3; CP 1, 2, 3, 4, 5, 6, 7; DAM MULT, POET; DLB 117, 225; EWL 3

Bryan, C(ourtlandt) D(ixon) B(arnes)
1936- .... **CLC 29**
See also CA 73-76; CANR 13, 68; DLB 185; INT CANR-13

Bryan, Michael
See Moore, Brian

Bryan, William Jennings
1860-1925 .... **TCLC 99**
See also DLB 303

Bryant, William Cullen 1794-1878 . **NCLC 6, 46; PC 20**
See also AMWS 1; CDALB 1640-1865; DA; DAB; DAC; DAM MST, POET; DLB 3, 43, 59, 189, 250; EXPP; PAB; RGAL 4; TUS

Butler, Octavia E. 1947-2006 .... **BLC 2:1; BLCS; CLC 38, 121, 230, 240**
See also AAYA 18, 48; AFAW 2; AMWS 13; BPFB 1; BW 2, 3; CA 73-76; 248; CANR 12, 24, 38, 73, 145, 240; CLR 65; CN 7; CPW; DA3; DAM MULT, POP; DLB 33; LATS 1:2; MTCW 1, 2; MTFW 2005; NFS 8, 21; SATA 84; SCFW 2; SFW 4; SSFS 6; TCLE 1:1; YAW

Butler, Octavia Estelle
See Butler, Octavia E.

Butler, Robert Olen, (Jr.) 1945- ...... **CLC 81, 162; SSC 117**
See also AMWS 12; BPFB 1; CA 112; CANR 66, 138; CN 7; CSW; DAM POP; DLB 173, 335; INT CA-112; MAL 5; MTCW 2; MTFW 2005; SSFS 11, 22

Butler, Samuel 1612-1680 . **LC 16, 43; PC 94**
See also DLB 101, 126; RGEL 2

Butler, Samuel 1835-1902 .... **TCLC 1, 33; WLC 1**
See also BRWS 2; CA 143; CDBLB 1890-1914; DA; DA3; DAB; DAC; DAM MST, NOV; DLB 18, 57, 174; RGEL 2; SFW 4; TEA

Butler, Walter C.
See Faust, Frederick (Schiller)

Butor, Michel (Marie Francois) 1926- .... **CLC 1, 3, 8, 11, 15, 161**
See also CA 9-12R; CANR 33, 66; CWW 2; DLB 83; EW 13; EWL 3; GFL 1789 to the Present; MTCW 1, 2; MTFW 2005

Butts, Mary 1890(?)-1937 .... **TCLC 77**
See also CA 148; DLB 240

Buxton, Ralph
See Silverstein, Alvin; Silverstein, Virginia B(arbara Opshelor)

Buzo, Alex
See Buzo, Alexander (John)
See also DLB 289

Buzo, Alexander (John) 1944- .... **CLC 61**
See also CA 97-100; CANR 17, 39, 69; CD 5, 6

Buzzati, Dino 1906-1972 .... **CLC 36**
See also CA 160; 33-36R; DLB 177; RGWL 2, 3; SFW 4

Byars, Betsy 1928- .... **CLC 35**
See also AAYA 19; BYA 3; CA 33-36R, 183; CAAE 183; CANR 18, 36, 57, 102, 148; CLR 1, 16, 72; DLB 52; INT CANR-18; JRDA; MAICYA 1, 2; MAICYAS 1; MTCW 1; SAAS 1; SATA 4, 46, 80, 163; SATA-Essay 108; WYA; YAW

Byars, Betsy Cromer
See Byars, Betsy

Byatt, Antonia Susan Drabble
See Byatt, A.S.

Byatt, A.S. 1936- .... **CLC 19, 65, 136, 223; SSC 91**
See also BPFB 1; BRWC 2; BRWS 4; CA 13-16R; CANR 13, 33, 50, 75, 96, 133; CN 1, 2, 3, 4, 5, 6; DA3; DAM NOV, POP; DLB 14, 194, 319, 326; EWL 3; MTCW 1, 2; MTFW 2005; RGSF 2; RHW; SSFS 26; TEA

Byrd, William II 1674-1744 .... **LC 112**
See also DLB 24, 140; RGAL 4

Byrne, David 1952- .... **CLC 26**
See also CA 127

Byrne, John Keyes 1926-2009 .... **CLC 19**
See also CA 102; CANR 78, 140; CBD; CD 5, 6; DFS 13, 24; DLB 13; INT CA-102

Byron, George Gordon (Noel) 1788-1824 ..... **DC 24; NCLC 2, 12, 109, 149; PC 16, 95; WLC 1**
See also AAYA 64; BRW 4; BRWC 2; CD-BLB 1789-1832; DA; DA3; DAB; DAC; DAM MST, POET; DLB 96, 110; EXPP; LMFS 1; PAB; PFS 1, 14, 29; RGEL 2; TEA; WLIT 3; WP

Byron, Robert 1905-1941 .... **TCLC 67**
See also CA 160; DLB 195

C. 3. 3.
See Wilde, Oscar

Caballero, Fernan 1796-1877 .... **NCLC 10**

Cabell, Branch
See Cabell, James Branch

Cabell, James Branch 1879-1958 .... **TCLC 6**
See also CA 105; 152; DLB 9, 78; FANT; MAL 5; MTCW 2; RGAL 4; SUFW 1

Cabeza de Vaca, Alvar Nunez 1490-1557(?) .... **LC 61**

Cable, George Washington 1844-1925 .... **SSC 4; TCLC 4**
See also CA 104; 155; DLB 12, 74; DLBD 13; RGAL 4; TUS

Cabral de Melo Neto, Joao 1920-1999 .... **CLC 76**
See Melo Neto, Joao Cabral de
See also CA 151; DAM MULT; DLB 307; LAW; LAWS 1

Cabrera Infante, G. 1929-2005 ... **CLC 5, 25, 45, 120; HLC 1; SSC 39**
See also CA 85-88; 236; CANR 29, 65, 110; CDWLB 3; CWW 2; DA3; DAM MULT; DLB 113; EWL 3; HW 1, 2; LAW; LAWS 1; MTCW 1, 2; MTFW 2005; RGSF 2; WLIT 1

Cabrera Infante, Guillermo
See Cabrera Infante, G.

Cade, Toni
See Bambara, Toni Cade

Cadmus and Harmonia
See Buchan, John

Caedmon fl. 658-680 .... **CMLC 7**
See also DLB 146

Caeiro, Alberto
See Pessoa, Fernando

Caesar, Julius .... **CMLC 47**
See Julius Caesar
See also AW 1; RGWL 2, 3; WLIT 8

Cage, John (Milton), (Jr.) 1912-1992 .... **CLC 41; PC 58**
See also CA 13-16R; 169; CANR 9, 78; DLB 193; INT CANR-9; TCLE 1:1

Cahan, Abraham 1860-1951 .... **TCLC 71**
See also CA 108; 154; DLB 9, 25, 28; MAL 5; RGAL 4

Cain, Christopher
See Fleming, Thomas

Cain, G.
See Cabrera Infante, G.

Cain, Guillermo
See Cabrera Infante, G.

Cain, James M(allahan) 1892-1977 .. **CLC 3, 11, 28**
See also AITN 1; BPFB 1; CA 17-20R; 73-76; CANR 8, 34, 61; CMW 4; CN 1, 2; DLB 226; EWL 3; MAL 5; MSW; MTCW 1; RGAL 4

Caine, Hall 1853-1931 .... **TCLC 97**
See also RHW

Caine, Mark
See Raphael, Frederic (Michael)

Calasso, Roberto 1941- .... **CLC 81**
See also CA 143; CANR 89

Calderon de la Barca, Pedro 1600-1681 . **DC 3; HLCS 1; LC 23, 136**
See also DFS 23; EW 2; RGWL 2, 3; TWA

Caldwell, Erskine 1903-1987 ... **CLC 1, 8, 14, 50, 60; SSC 117**
See also AITN 1; AMW; BPFB 1; CA 1-4R; 121; CAAS 1; CANR 2, 33; CN 1, 2, 3, 4; DA3; DAM NOV; DLB 9, 86; EWL 3; MAL 5; MTCW 1, 2; MTFW 2005; RGAL 4; RGSF 2; TUS

Caldwell, (Janet Miriam) Taylor (Holland) 1900-1985 .... **CLC 2, 28, 39**
See also BPFB 1; CA 5-8R; 116; CANR 5; DA3; DAM NOV, POP; DLBD 17; MTCW 2; RHW

Calhoun, John Caldwell 1782-1850 .... **NCLC 15**
See also DLB 3, 248

Calisher, Hortense 1911-2009 .... **CLC 2, 4, 8, 38, 134; SSC 15**
See also CA 1-4R; CANR 1, 22, 117; CN 1, 2, 3, 4, 5, 6, 7; DA3; DAM NOV; DLB 2, 218; INT CANR-22; MAL 5; MTCW 1, 2; MTFW 2005; RGAL 4; RGSF 2

Callaghan, Morley Edward 1903-1990 ..... **CLC 3, 14, 41, 65; TCLC 145**
See also CA 9-12R; 132; CANR 33, 73; CN 1, 2, 3, 4; DAC; DAM MST; DLB 68; EWL 3; MTCW 1, 2; MTFW 2005; RGEL 2; RGSF 2; SSFS 19

Callimachus c. 305B.C.-c. 240B.C. .... **CMLC 18**
See also AW 1; DLB 176; RGWL 2, 3

Calvin, Jean
See Calvin, John
See also DLB 327; GFL Beginnings to 1789

Calvin, John 1509-1564 .... **LC 37**
See Calvin, Jean

Calvino, Italo 1923-1985 .... **CLC 5, 8, 11, 22, 33, 39, 73; SSC 3, 48; TCLC 183**
See also AAYA 58; CA 85-88; 116; CANR 23, 61, 132; DAM NOV; DLB 196; EW 13; EWL 3; MTCW 1, 2; MTFW 2005; RGHL; RGSF 2; RGWL 2, 3; SFW 4; SSFS 12; WLIT 7

Camara Laye
See Laye, Camara
See also EWL 3

Cambridge, A Gentleman of the University of
See Crowley, Edward Alexander

Camden, William 1551-1623 .... **LC 77**
See also DLB 172

Cameron, Carey 1952- .... **CLC 59**
See also CA 135

Cameron, Peter 1959- .... **CLC 44**
See also AMWS 12; CA 125; CANR 50, 117; DLB 234; GLL 2

Camoens, Luis Vaz de 1524(?)-1580
See Camoes, Luis de
See also EW 2

Camoes, Luis de 1524(?)-1580 . **HLCS 1; LC 62; PC 31**
See Camoens, Luis Vaz de
See also DLB 287; RGWL 2, 3

Camp, Madeleine L'Engle
See L'Engle, Madeleine

Campana, Dino 1885-1932 .... **TCLC 20**
See also CA 117; 246; DLB 114; EWL 3

Campanella, Tommaso 1568-1639 .... **LC 32**
See also RGWL 2, 3

Campbell, Bebe Moore 1950-2006 . **BLC 2:1; CLC 246**
See also AAYA 26; BW 2, 3; CA 139; 254; CANR 81, 134; DLB 227; MTCW 2; MTFW 2005

Campbell, John Ramsey
See Campbell, Ramsey

Campbell, John W(ood, Jr.) 1910-1971 .... **CLC 32**
See also CA 21-22; 29-32R; CANR 34; CAP 2; DLB 8; MTCW 1; SCFW 1, 2; SFW 4

Campbell, Joseph 1904-1987 .... **CLC 69; TCLC 140**
See also AAYA 3, 66; BEST 89:2; CA 1-4R; 124; CANR 3, 28, 61, 107; DA3; MTCW 1, 2

Carter, Martin (Wylde) 1927- .... **BLC 2:1**
See also BW 2; CA 102; CANR 42; CD-
WLB 3; CP 1, 2, 3, 4, 5, 6; DLB 117;
EWL 3
Carter, Nick
See Smith, Martin Cruz
Carter, Nick
See Smith, Martin Cruz
Carver, Raymond 1938-1988 ..... **CLC 22, 36,
53, 55, 126; PC 54; SSC 8, 51, 104**
See also AAYA 44; AMWS 3; BPFB 1; CA
33-36R; 126; CANR 17, 34, 61, 103; CN
4; CPW; DA3; DAM NOV; DLB 130;
DLBY 1984, 1988; EWL 3; MAL 5;
MTCW 1, 2; MTFW 2005; PFS 17;
RGAL 4; RGSF 2; SSFS 3, 6, 12, 13, 23;
TCLE 1:1; TCWW 2; TUS
Cary, Elizabeth, Lady Falkland
1585-1639 .... **LC 30, 141**
Cary, (Arthur) Joyce (Lunel)
1888-1957 .... **TCLC 1, 29, 196**
See also BRW 7; CA 104; 164; CDBLB
1914-1945; DLB 15, 100; EWL 3; MTCW
2; RGEL 2; TEA
Casal, Julian del 1863-1893 .... **NCLC 131**
See also DLB 283; LAW
Casanova, Giacomo
See Casanova de Seingalt, Giovanni Jacopo
See also WLIT 7
Casanova, Giovanni Giacomo
See Casanova de Seingalt, Giovanni Jacopo
Casanova de Seingalt, Giovanni Jacopo
1725-1798 .... **LC 13, 151**
See also Casanova, Giacomo
Casares, Adolfo Bioy
See Bioy Casares, Adolfo
Casas, Bartolome de las 1474-1566
See Las Casas, Bartolome de
See also WLIT 1
Case, John
See Hougan, Carolyn
Casely-Hayford, J(oseph) E(phraim)
1866-1903 .... **BLC 1:1; TCLC 24**
See also BW 2; CA 123; 152; DAM MULT
Casey, John (Dudley) 1939- .... **CLC 59**
See also BEST 90:2; CA 69-72; CANR 23,
100
Casey, Michael 1947- .... **CLC 2**
See also CA 65-68; CANR 109; CP 2, 3;
DLB 5
Casey, Patrick
See Thurman, Wallace (Henry)
Casey, Warren (Peter) 1935-1988 .... **CLC 12**
See also CA 101; 127; INT CA-101
Casona, Alejandro
See Alvarez, Alejandro Rodriguez
Cassavetes, John 1929-1989 .... **CLC 20**
See also CA 85-88; 127; CANR 82
Cassian, Nina 1924- .... **PC 17**
See also CWP; CWW 2
Cassill, R(onald) V(erlin)
1919-2002 .... **CLC 4, 23**
See also CA 9-12R; 208; CAAS 1; CANR
7, 45; CN 1, 2, 3, 4, 5, 6, 7; DLB 6, 218;
DLBY 2002
Cassiodorus, Flavius Magnus c. 490(?)-c.
583(?) .... **CMLC 43**
Cassirer, Ernst 1874-1945 .... **TCLC 61**
See also CA 157
Cassity, (Allen) Turner 1929- .... **CLC 6, 42**
See also CA 17-20R; 223; CAAE 223;
CAAS 8; CANR 11; CSW; DLB 105
Cassius Dio c. 155-c. 229 .... **CMLC 99**
See also DLB 176
Castaneda, Carlos (Cesar Aranha)
1931(?)-1998 .... **CLC 12, 119**
See also CA 25-28R; CANR 32, 66, 105;
DNFS 1; HW 1; MTCW 1

Castedo, Elena 1937- .... **CLC 65**
See also CA 132
Castedo-Ellerman, Elena
See Castedo, Elena
Castellanos, Rosario 1925-1974 .... **CLC 66;
HLC 1; SSC 39, 68**
See also CA 131; 53-56; CANR 58; CD-
WLB 3; DAM MULT; DLB 113, 290;
EWL 3; FW; HW 1; LAW; MTCW 2;
MTFW 2005; RGSF 2; RGWL 2, 3
Castelvetro, Lodovico 1505-1571 .... **LC 12**
Castiglione, Baldassare 1478-1529 ...... **LC 12**
See Castiglione, Baldesar
See also LMFS 1; RGWL 2, 3
Castiglione, Baldesar
See Castiglione, Baldassare
See also EW 2; WLIT 7
Castillo, Ana 1953- .... **CLC 151**
See also AAYA 42; CA 131; CANR 51, 86,
128, 172; CWP; DLB 122, 227; DNFS 2;
FW; HW 1; LLW; PFS 21
Castillo, Ana Hernandez Del
See Castillo, Ana
Castle, Robert
See Hamilton, Edmond
Castro (Ruz), Fidel 1926(?)- .... **HLC 1**
See also CA 110; 129; CANR 81; DAM
MULT; HW 2
Castro, Guillen de 1569-1631 .... **LC 19**
Castro, Rosalia de 1837-1885 ... **NCLC 3, 78;
PC 41**
See also DAM MULT
Castro Alves, Antonio de
1847-1871 .... **NCLC 205**
See also DLB 307; LAW
Cather, Willa (Sibert) 1873-1947 . **SSC 2, 50,
114; TCLC 1, 11, 31, 99, 132, 152;
WLC 1**
See also AAYA 24; AMW; AMWC 1;
AMWR 1; BPFB 1; CA 104; 128; CDALB
1865-1917; CLR 98; DA; DA3; DAB;
DAC; DAM MST, NOV; DLB 9, 54, 78,
256; DLBD 1; EWL 3; EXPN; EXPS; FL
1:5; LAIT 3; LATS 1:1; MAL 5; MBL;
MTCW 1, 2; MTFW 2005; NFS 2, 19;
RGAL 4; RGSF 2; RHW; SATA 30; SSFS
2, 7, 16; TCWW 1, 2; TUS
Catherine II
See Catherine the Great
See also DLB 150
Catherine, Saint 1347-1380 .... **CMLC 27**
Catherine the Great 1729-1796 .... **LC 69**
See Catherine II
Cato, Marcus Porcius
234B.C.-149B.C. .... **CMLC 21**
See Cato the Elder
Cato, Marcus Porcius, the Elder
See Cato, Marcus Porcius
Cato the Elder
See Cato, Marcus Porcius
See also DLB 211
Catton, (Charles) Bruce 1899-1978 . **CLC 35**
See also AITN 1; CA 5-8R; 81-84; CANR
7, 74; DLB 17; MTCW 2; MTFW 2005;
SATA 2; SATA-Obit 24
Catullus c. 84B.C.-54B.C. .... **CMLC 18**
See also AW 2; CDWLB 1; DLB 211;
RGWL 2, 3; WLIT 8
Cauldwell, Frank
See King, Francis (Henry)
Caunitz, William J. 1933-1996 .... **CLC 34**
See also BEST 89:3; CA 125; 130; 152;
CANR 73; INT CA-130
Causley, Charles (Stanley)
1917-2003 .... **CLC 7**
See also CA 9-12R; 223; CANR 5, 35, 94;
CLR 30; CP 1, 2, 3, 4, 5; CWRI 5; DLB
27; MTCW 1; SATA 3, 66; SATA-Obit
149

Caute, (John) David 1936- .... **CLC 29**
See also CA 1-4R; CAAS 4; CANR 1, 33,
64, 120; CBD; CD 5, 6; CN 1, 2, 3, 4, 5,
6, 7; DAM NOV; DLB 14, 231
Cavafy, C(onstantine) P(eter)
See Kavafis, Konstantinos Petrou
Cavafy, Constantin
See Kavafis, Konstantinos Petrou
Cavalcanti, Guido c. 1250-c.
1300 .... **CMLC 54**
See also RGWL 2, 3; WLIT 7
Cavallo, Evelyn
See Spark, Muriel
Cavanna, Betty
See Harrison, Elizabeth (Allen) Cavanna
Cavanna, Elizabeth
See Harrison, Elizabeth (Allen) Cavanna
Cavanna, Elizabeth Allen
See Harrison, Elizabeth (Allen) Cavanna
Cavendish, Margaret Lucas
1623-1673 .... **LC 30, 132**
See also DLB 131, 252, 281; RGEL 2
Caxton, William 1421(?)-1491(?) .... **LC 17**
See also DLB 170
Cayer, D. M.
See Duffy, Maureen (Patricia)
Cayrol, Jean 1911-2005 .... **CLC 11**
See also CA 89-92; 236; DLB 83; EWL 3
Cela (y Trulock), Camilo Jose
See Cela, Camilo Jose
See also CWW 2
Cela, Camilo Jose 1916-2002 .... **CLC 4, 13,
59, 122; HLC 1; SSC 71**
See Cela (y Trulock), Camilo Jose
See also BEST 90:2; CA 21-24R; 206;
CAAS 10; CANR 21, 32, 76, 139; DAM
MULT; DLB 322; DLBY 1989; EW 13;
EWL 3; HW 1; MTCW 1, 2; MTFW
2005; RGSF 2; RGWL 2, 3
Celan, Paul
See Antschel, Paul
Celine, Louis-Ferdinand
See Destouches, Louis-Ferdinand
Cellini, Benvenuto 1500-1571 .... **LC 7**
See also WLIT 7
Cendrars, Blaise
See Sauser-Hall, Frederic
Centlivre, Susanna 1669(?)-1723 .... **DC 25;
LC 65**
See also DLB 84; RGEL 2
Cernuda (y Bidon), Luis
1902-1963 .... **CLC 54; PC 62**
See also CA 131; 89-92; DAM POET; DLB
134; EWL 3; GLL 1; HW 1; RGWL 2, 3
Cervantes, Lorna Dee 1954- ..... **HLCS 1; PC
35**
See also CA 131; CANR 80; CP 7; CWP;
DLB 82; EXPP; HW 1; LLW
Cervantes (Saavedra), Miguel de
1547-1616 .... **HLCS; LC 6, 23, 93; SSC
12, 108; WLC 1**
See also AAYA 56; BYA 1, 14; DA; DAB;
DAC; DAM MST, NOV; EW 2; LAIT 1;
LATS 1:1; LMFS 1; NFS 8; RGSF 2;
RGWL 2, 3; TWA
Cesaire, Aime
See Cesaire, Aime
Cesaire, Aime 1913-2008 .... **BLC 1:1; CLC
19, 32, 112; DC 22; PC 25**
See also BW 2, 3; CA 65-68; 271; CANR
24, 43, 81; CWW 2; DA3; DAM MULT,
POET; DLB 321; EWL 3; GFL 1789 to
the Present; MTCW 1, 2; MTFW 2005;
WP
Cesaire, Aime Fernand
See Cesaire, Aime
Chaadaev, Petr Iakovlevich
1794-1856 .... **NCLC 197**
See also DLB 198

Clark, Walter Van Tilburg
1909-1971 .... **CLC 28**
See also CA 9-12R; 33-36R; CANR 63, 113; CN 1; DLB 9, 206; LAIT 2; MAL 5; RGAL 4; SATA 8; TCWW 1, 2

Clark Bekederemo, J.P. 1935- .... **BLC 1:1; CLC 38; DC 5**
See Bekederemo, J. P. Clark; Clark, J. P.; Clark, John Pepper
See also AAYA 79; BW 1; CA 65-68; CANR 16, 72; DAM DRAM, MULT; DFS 13; EWL 3; MTCW 2; MTFW 2005

Clarke, Arthur
See Clarke, Arthur C.

Clarke, Arthur C. 1917-2008 .. **CLC 1, 4, 13, 18, 35, 136; SSC 3**
See also AAYA 4, 33; BPFB 1; BYA 13; CA 1-4R; 270; CANR 2, 28, 55, 74, 130; CLR 119; CN 1, 2, 3, 4, 5, 6, 7; CPW; DA3; DAM POP; DLB 261; JRDA; LAIT 5; MAICYA 1, 2; MTCW 1, 2; MTFW 2005; SATA 13, 70, 115; SATA-Obit 191; SCFW 1, 2; SFW 4; SSFS 4, 18; TCLE 1:1; YAW

Clarke, Arthur Charles
See Clarke, Arthur C.

Clarke, Austin 1896-1974 .... **CLC 6, 9**
See also CA 29-32; 49-52; CAP 2; CP 1, 2; DAM POET; DLB 10, 20; EWL 3; RGEL 2

Clarke, Austin C. 1934- .... **BLC 1:1; CLC 8, 53; SSC 45, 116**
See also BW 1; CA 25-28R; CAAS 16; CANR 14, 32, 68, 140; CN 1, 2, 3, 4, 5, 6, 7; DAC; DAM MULT; DLB 53, 125; DNFS 2; MTCW 2; MTFW 2005; RGSF 2

Clarke, Gillian 1937- .... **CLC 61**
See also CA 106; CP 3, 4, 5, 6, 7; CWP; DLB 40

Clarke, Marcus (Andrew Hislop)
1846-1881 .... **NCLC 19; SSC 94**
See also DLB 230; RGEL 2; RGSF 2

Clarke, Shirley 1925-1997 .... **CLC 16**
See also CA 189

Clash, The
See Headon, (Nicky) Topper; Jones, Mick; Simonon, Paul; Strummer, Joe

Claudel, Paul (Louis Charles Marie)
1868-1955 .... **TCLC 2, 10**
See also CA 104; 165; DLB 192, 258, 321; EW 8; EWL 3; GFL 1789 to the Present; RGWL 2, 3; TWA

Claudian 370(?)-404(?) .... **CMLC 46**
See also RGWL 2, 3

Claudius, Matthias 1740-1815 .... **NCLC 75**
See also DLB 97

Clavell, James 1925-1994 .... **CLC 6, 25, 87**
See also BPFB 1; CA 25-28R; 146; CANR 26, 48; CN 5; CPW; DA3; DAM NOV, POP; MTCW 1, 2; MTFW 2005; NFS 10; RHW

Clayman, Gregory .... **CLC 65**

Cleage, Pearl 1948- .... **DC 32**
See also BW 2; CA 41-44R; CANR 27, 148, 177; DFS 14, 16; DLB 228; NFS 17

Cleage, Pearl Michelle
See Cleage, Pearl

Cleaver, (Leroy) Eldridge
1935-1998 .... **BLC 1:1; CLC 30, 119**
See also BW 1, 3; CA 21-24R; 167; CANR 16, 75; DA3; DAM MULT; MTCW 2; YAW

Cleese, John (Marwood) 1939- .... **CLC 21**
See also CA 112; 116; CANR 35; MTCW 1

Cleishbotham, Jebediah
See Scott, Sir Walter

Cleland, John 1710-1789 .... **LC 2, 48**
See also DLB 39; RGEL 2

Clemens, Samuel Langhorne
1835-1910 .... **SSC 6, 26, 34, 87, 119; TCLC 6, 12, 19, 36, 48, 59, 161, 185; WLC 6**
See also AAYA 20; AMW; AMWC 1; BPFB 3; BYA 2, 3, 11, 14; CA 104; 135; CDALB 1865-1917; CLR 58, 60, 66; DA; DA3; DAB; DAC; DAM MST, NOV; DLB 12, 23, 64, 74, 186, 189, 11, 343; EXPN; EXPS; JRDA; LAIT 2; LMFS 1; MAICYA 1, 2; MAL 5; NCFS 4; NFS 1, 6; RGAL 4; RGSF 2; SATA 100; SFW 4; SSFS 1, 7, 16, 21; SUFW; TUS; WCH; WYA; YABC 2; YAW

Clement of Alexandria
150(?)-215(?) .... **CMLC 41**

Cleophil
See Congreve, William

Clerihew, E.
See Bentley, E(dmund) C(lerihew)

Clerk, N. W.
See Lewis, C.S.

Cleveland, John 1613-1658 .... **LC 106**
See also DLB 126; RGEL 2

Cliff, Jimmy
See Chambers, James

Cliff, Michelle 1946- .... **BLCS; CLC 120**
See also BW 2; CA 116; CANR 39, 72; CD-WLB 3; DLB 157; FW; GLL 2

Clifford, Lady Anne 1590-1676 .... **LC 76**
See also DLB 151

Clifton, Lucille 1936- ..... **BLC 1:1, 2:1; CLC 19, 66, 162; PC 17**
See also AFAW 2; BW 2, 3; CA 49-52; CANR 2, 24, 42, 76, 97, 138; CLR 5; CP 2, 3, 4, 5, 6, 7; CSW; CWP; CWRI 5; DA3; DAM MULT, POET; DLB 5, 41; EXPP; MAICYA 1, 2; MTCW 1, 2; MTFW 2005; PFS 1, 14, 29; SATA 20, 69, 128; WP

Clinton, Dirk
See Silverberg, Robert

Clough, Arthur Hugh 1819-1861 .. **NCLC 27, 163**
See also BRW 5; DLB 32; RGEL 2

Clutha, Janet Paterson Frame
See Frame, Janet

Clyne, Terence
See Blatty, William Peter

Cobalt, Martin
See Mayne, William (James Carter)

Cobb, Irvin S(hrewsbury)
1876-1944 .... **TCLC 77**
See also CA 175; DLB 11, 25, 86

Cobbett, William 1763-1835 .... **NCLC 49**
See also DLB 43, 107, 158; RGEL 2

Coben, Harlan 1962- .... **CLC 269**
See also CA 164; CANR 162

Coburn, D(onald) L(ee) 1938- .... **CLC 10**
See also CA 89-92; DFS 23

Cocteau, Jean 1889-1963 ... **CLC 1, 8, 15, 16, 43; DC 17; TCLC 119; WLC 2**
See also AAYA 74; CA 25-28; CANR 40; CAP 2; DA; DA3; DAB; DAC; DAM DRAM, MST, NOV; DFS 24; DLB 65, 258, 321; EW 10; EWL 3; GFL 1789 to the Present; MTCW 1, 2; RGWL 2, 3; TWA

Cocteau, Jean Maurice Eugene Clement
See Cocteau, Jean

Codrescu, Andrei 1946- .... **CLC 46, 121**
See also CA 33-36R; CAAS 19; CANR 13, 34, 53, 76, 125; CN 7; DA3; DAM POET; MAL 5; MTCW 2; MTFW 2005

Coe, Max
See Bourne, Randolph S(illiman)

Coe, Tucker
See Westlake, Donald E.

Coelho, Paulo 1947- .... **CLC 258**
See also CA 152; CANR 80, 93, 155

Coen, Ethan 1957- .... **CLC 108, 267**
See also AAYA 54; CA 126; CANR 85

Coen, Joel 1954- .... **CLC 108, 267**
See also AAYA 54; CA 126; CANR 119

The Coen Brothers
See Coen, Ethan; Coen, Joel

Coetzee, J.M. 1940- ...... **CLC 23, 33, 66, 117, 161, 162**
See also AAYA 37; AFW; BRWS 6; CA 77-80; CANR 41, 54, 74, 114, 133, 180; CN 4, 5, 6, 7; DA3; DAM NOV; DLB 225, 326, 329; EWL 3; LMFS 2; MTCW 1, 2; MTFW 2005; NFS 21; WLIT 2; WWE 1

Coetzee, John Maxwell
See Coetzee, J.M.

Coffey, Brian
See Koontz, Dean R.

Coffin, Robert P(eter) Tristram
1892-1955 .... **TCLC 95**
See also CA 123; 169; DLB 45

Cohan, George M. 1878-1942 .... **TCLC 60**
See also CA 157; DLB 249; RGAL 4

Cohan, George Michael
See Cohan, George M.

Cohen, Arthur A(llen) 1928-1986 ...... **CLC 7, 31**
See also CA 1-4R; 120; CANR 1, 17, 42; DLB 28; RGHL

Cohen, Leonard 1934- .... **CLC 3, 38, 260**
See also CA 21-24R; CANR 14, 69; CN 1, 2, 3, 4, 5, 6; CP 1, 2, 3, 4, 5, 6, 7; DAC; DAM MST; DLB 53; EWL 3; MTCW 1

Cohen, Leonard Norman
See Cohen, Leonard

Cohen, Matt(hew) 1942-1999 .... **CLC 19**
See also CA 61-64; 187; CAAS 18; CANR 40; CN 1, 2, 3, 4, 5, 6; DAC; DLB 53

Cohen-Solal, Annie 1948- .... **CLC 50**
See also CA 239

Colegate, Isabel 1931- .... **CLC 36**
See also CA 17-20R; CANR 8, 22, 74; CN 4, 5, 6, 7; DLB 14, 231; INT CANR-22; MTCW 1

Coleman, Emmett
See Reed, Ishmael

Coleridge, Hartley 1796-1849 .... **NCLC 90**
See also DLB 96

Coleridge, M. E.
See Coleridge, Mary E(lizabeth)

Coleridge, Mary E(lizabeth)
1861-1907 .... **TCLC 73**
See also CA 116; 166; DLB 19, 98

Coleridge, Samuel Taylor
1772-1834 ..... **NCLC 9, 54, 99, 111, 177, 197; PC 11, 39, 67; WLC 2**
See also AAYA 66; BRW 4; BRWR 2; BYA 4; CDBLB 1789-1832; DA; DA3; DAB; DAC; DAM MST, POET; DLB 93, 107; EXPP; LATS 1:1; LMFS 1; PAB; PFS 4, 5; RGEL 2; TEA; WLIT 3; WP

Coleridge, Sara 1802-1852 .... **NCLC 31**
See also DLB 199

Coles, Don 1928- .... **CLC 46**
See also CA 115; CANR 38; CP 5, 6, 7

Coles, Robert (Martin) 1929- .... **CLC 108**
See also CA 45-48; CANR 3, 32, 66, 70, 135; INT CANR-32; SATA 23

Colette, (Sidonie-Gabrielle)
1873-1954 .. **SSC 10, 93; TCLC 1, 5, 16**
See Willy, Colette
See also CA 104; 131; DA3; DAM NOV; DLB 65; EW 9; EWL 3; GFL 1789 to the Present; MTCW 1, 2; MTFW 2005; RGWL 2, 3; TWA

Collett, (Jacobine) Camilla (Wergeland)
1813-1895 .... NCLC 22

Collier, Christopher 1930- .... CLC 30
See also AAYA 13; BYA 2; CA 33-36R;
CANR 13, 33, 102; CLR 126; JRDA;
MAICYA 1, 2; SATA 16, 70; WYA; YAW
1

Collier, James Lincoln 1928- .... CLC 30
See also AAYA 13; BYA 2; CA 9-12R;
CANR 4, 33, 60, 102; CLR 3, 126; DAM
POP; JRDA; MAICYA 1, 2; SAAS 21;
SATA 8, 70, 166; WYA; YAW 1

Collier, Jeremy 1650-1726 .... LC 6, 157
See also DLB 336

Collier, John 1901-1980 . SSC 19; TCLC 127
See also CA 65-68; 97-100; CANR 10; CN
1, 2; DLB 77, 255; FANT; SUFW 1

Collier, Mary 1690-1762 .... LC 86
See also DLB 95

Collingwood, R(obin) G(eorge)
1889(?)-1943 .... TCLC 67
See also CA 117; 155; DLB 262

Collins, Billy 1941- .... PC 68
See also AAYA 64; CA 151; CANR 92; CP
7; MTFW 2005; PFS 18

Collins, Hunt
See Hunter, Evan

Collins, Linda 1931- .... CLC 44
See also CA 125

Collins, Merle 1950- .... BLC 2:1
See also BW 3; CA 175; DLB 157

Collins, Tom
See Furphy, Joseph
See also RGEL 2

Collins, (William) Wilkie
1824-1889 .... NCLC 1, 18, 93; SSC 93
See also BRWS 6; CDBLB 1832-1890;
CMW 4; DLB 18, 70, 159; GL 2; MSW;
RGEL 2; RGSF 2; SUFW 1; WLIT 4

Collins, William 1721-1759 ...... LC 4, 40; PC
72
See also BRW 3; DAM POET; DLB 109;
RGEL 2

Collodi, Carlo
See Lorenzini, Carlo

Colman, George
See Glassco, John

Colman, George, the Elder
1732-1794 .... LC 98
See also RGEL 2

Colonna, Vittoria 1492-1547 .... LC 71
See also RGWL 2, 3

Colt, Winchester Remington
See Hubbard, L. Ron

Colter, Cyrus J. 1910-2002 .... CLC 58
See also BW 1; CA 65-68; 205; CANR 10,
66; CN 2, 3, 4, 5, 6; DLB 33

Colton, James
See Hansen, Joseph

Colum, Padraic 1881-1972 .... CLC 28
See also BYA 4; CA 73-76; 33-36R; CANR
35; CLR 36; CP 1; CWRI 5; DLB 19;
MAICYA 1, 2; MTCW 1; RGEL 2; SATA
15; WCH

Colvin, James
See Moorcock, Michael

Colwin, Laurie (E.) 1944-1992 .... CLC 5, 13,
23, 84
See also CA 89-92; 139; CANR 20, 46;
DLB 218; DLBY 1980; MTCW 1

Comfort, Alex(ander) 1920-2000 .... CLC 7
See also CA 1-4R; 190; CANR 1, 45; CN
1, 2, 3, 4; CP 1, 2, 3, 4, 5, 6, 7; DAM
POP; MTCW 2

Comfort, Montgomery
See Campbell, Ramsey

Compton-Burnett, I(vy)
1892(?)-1969 .... CLC 1, 3, 10, 15, 34;
TCLC 180
See also BRW 7; CA 1-4R; 25-28R; CANR
4; DAM NOV; DLB 36; EWL 3; MTCW
1, 2; RGEL 2

Comstock, Anthony 1844-1915 ...... TCLC 13
See also CA 110; 169

Comte, Auguste 1798-1857 .... NCLC 54

Conan Doyle, Arthur
See Doyle, Sir Arthur Conan

Conde (Abellan), Carmen
1901-1996 .... HLCS 1
See also CA 177; CWW 2; DLB 108; EWL
3; HW 2

Conde, Maryse 1937- .... BLC 2:1; BLCS;
CLC 52, 92, 247
See also BW 2, 3; CA 110, 190; CAAE 190;
CANR 30, 53, 76, 171; CWW 2; DAM
MULT; EWL 3; MTCW 2; MTFW 2005

Condillac, Etienne Bonnot de
1714-1780 .... LC 26
See also DLB 313

Condon, Richard 1915-1996 ...... CLC 4, 6, 8,
10, 45, 100
See also BEST 90:3; BPFB 1; CA 1-4R;
151; CAAS 1; CANR 2, 23, 164; CMW
4; CN 1, 2, 3, 4, 5, 6; DAM NOV; INT
CANR-23; MAL 5; MTCW 1, 2

Condon, Richard Thomas
See Condon, Richard

Condorcet .... LC 104
See Condorcet, marquis de Marie-Jean-
Antoine-Nicolas Caritat
See also GFL Beginnings to 1789

Condorcet, marquis de
Marie-Jean-Antoine-Nicolas Caritat
1743-1794
See Condorcet
See also DLB 313

Confucius 551B.C.-479B.C. .... CMLC 19, 65;
WLCS
See also DA; DA3; DAB; DAC; DAM
MST

Congreve, William 1670-1729 ... DC 2; LC 5,
21; WLC 2
See also BRW 2; CDBLB 1660-1789; DA;
DAB; DAC; DAM DRAM, MST, POET;
DFS 15; DLB 39, 84; RGEL 2; WLIT 3

Conley, Robert J. 1940- .... NNAL
See also CA 41-44R; CANR 15, 34, 45, 96,
186; DAM MULT; TCWW 2

Connell, Evan S., Jr. 1924- .... CLC 4, 6, 45
See also AAYA 7; AMWS 14; CA 1-4R;
CAAS 2; CANR 2, 39, 76, 97, 140; CN
1, 2, 3, 4, 5, 6; DAM NOV; DLB 2, 335;
DLBY 1981; MAL 5; MTCW 1, 2;
MTFW 2005

Connelly, Marc(us Cook) 1890-1980 . CLC 7
See also CA 85-88; 102; CAD; CANR 30;
DFS 12; DLB 7; DLBY 1980; MAL 5;
RGAL 4; SATA-Obit 25

Connolly, Paul
See Wicker, Tom

Connor, Ralph
See Gordon, Charles William

Conrad, Joseph 1857-1924 ..... SSC 9, 67, 69,
71; TCLC 1, 6, 13, 25, 43, 57; WLC 2
See also AAYA 26; BPFB 1; BRW 6;
BRWC 1; BRWR 2; BYA 2; CA 104; 131;
CANR 60; CDBLB 1890-1914; DA; DA3;
DAB; DAC; DAM MST, NOV; DLB 10,
34, 98, 156; EWL 3; EXPN; EXPS; LAIT
2; LATS 1:1; LMFS 1; MTCW 1, 2;
MTFW 2005; NFS 2, 16; RGEL 2; RGSF
2; SATA 27; SSFS 1, 12; TEA; WLIT 4

Conrad, Robert Arnold
See Hart, Moss

Conroy, Pat 1945- .... CLC 30, 74
See also AAYA 8, 52; AITN 1; BPFB 1;
CA 85-88; CANR 24, 53, 129; CN 7;
CPW; CSW; DA3; DAM NOV, POP;
DLB 6; LAIT 5; MAL 5; MTCW 1, 2;
MTFW 2005

Constant (de Rebecque), (Henri) Benjamin
1767-1830 .... NCLC 6, 182
See also DLB 119; EW 4; GFL 1789 to the
Present

Conway, Jill K. 1934- .... CLC 152
See also CA 130; CANR 94

Conway, Jill Kathryn Ker
See Conway, Jill K.

Conybeare, Charles Augustus
See Eliot, T(homas) S(tearns)

Cook, Michael 1933-1994 .... CLC 58
See also CA 93-96; CANR 68; DLB 53

Cook, Robin 1940- .... CLC 14
See also AAYA 32; BEST 90:2; BPFB 1;
CA 108; 111; CANR 41, 90, 109, 181;
CPW; DA3; DAM POP; HGG; INT CA-
111

Cook, Roy
See Silverberg, Robert

Cooke, Elizabeth 1948- .... CLC 55
See also CA 129

Cooke, John Esten 1830-1886 .... NCLC 5
See also DLB 3, 248; RGAL 4

Cooke, John Estes
See Baum, L(yman) Frank

Cooke, M. E.
See Creasey, John

Cooke, Margaret
See Creasey, John

Cooke, Rose Terry 1827-1892 ...... NCLC 110
See also DLB 12, 74

Cook-Lynn, Elizabeth 1930- .... CLC 93;
NNAL
See also CA 133; DAM MULT; DLB 175

Cooney, Ray .... CLC 62
See also CBD

Cooper, Anthony Ashley 1671-1713 .. LC 107
See also DLB 101, 336

Cooper, Dennis 1953- .... CLC 203
See also CA 133; CANR 72, 86; GLL 1;
HGG

Cooper, Douglas 1960- .... CLC 86

Cooper, Henry St. John
See Creasey, John

Cooper, J. California (?)- .... CLC 56
See also AAYA 12; BW 1; CA 125; CANR
55; DAM MULT; DLB 212

Cooper, James Fenimore
1789-1851 .... NCLC 1, 27, 54, 203
See also AAYA 22; AMW; BPFB 1;
CDALB 1640-1865; CLR 105; DA3;
DLB 3, 183, 250, 254; LAIT 1; NFS 25;
RGAL 4; SATA 19; TUS; WCH

Cooper, Susan Fenimore
1813-1894 .... NCLC 129
See also ANW; DLB 239, 254

Coover, Robert 1932- .. CLC 3, 7, 15, 32, 46,
87, 161; SSC 15, 101
See also AMWS 5; BPFB 1; CA 45-48;
CANR 3, 37, 58, 115; CN 1, 2, 3, 4, 5, 6,
7; DAM NOV; DLB 2, 227; DLBY 1981;
EWL 3; MAL 5; MTCW 1, 2; MTFW
2005; RGAL 4; RGSF 2

Copeland, Stewart (Armstrong)
1952- .... CLC 26

Copernicus, Nicolaus 1473-1543 .... LC 45

Coppard, A(lfred) E(dgar)
1878-1957 .... SSC 21; TCLC 5
See also BRWS 8; CA 114; 167; DLB 162;
EWL 3; HGG; RGEL 2; RGSF 2; SUFW
1; YABC 1

Coppee, Francois 1842-1908 .... TCLC 25
See also CA 170; DLB 217

416

Diodorus Siculus c. 90B.C.-c.
　31B.C. .... **CMLC 88**
Diphusa, Patty
　See Almodovar, Pedro
Disch, Thomas M. 1940-2008 .... **CLC 7, 36**
　See also AAYA 17; BPFB 1; CA 21-24R;
　274; CAAS 4; CANR 17, 36, 54, 89; CLR
　18; CP 5, 6, 7; DA3; DLB 8, 282; HGG;
　MAICYA 1, 2; MTCW 1, 2; MTFW 2005;
　SAAS 15; SATA 92; SATA-Obit 195;
　SCFW 1, 2; SFW 4; SUFW 2
Disch, Thomas Michael
　See Disch, Thomas M.
Disch, Tom
　See Disch, Thomas M.
d'Isly, Georges
　See Simenon, Georges (Jacques Christian)
Disraeli, Benjamin 1804-1881 ... **NCLC 2, 39,
　79**
　See also BRW 4; DLB 21, 55; RGEL 2
Ditcum, Steve
　See Crumb, R.
Dixon, Paige
　See Corcoran, Barbara (Asenath)
Dixon, Stephen 1936- .... **CLC 52; SSC 16**
　See also AMWS 12; CA 89-92; CANR 17,
　40, 54, 91, 175; CN 4, 5, 6, 7; DLB 130;
　MAL 5
Dixon, Thomas, Jr. 1864-1946 ..... **TCLC 163**
　See also RHW
Djebar, Assia 1936- .... **BLC 2:1; CLC 182;
　SSC 114**
　See also CA 188; CANR 169; DLB 346;
　EWL 3; RGWL 3; WLIT 2
Doak, Annie
　See Dillard, Annie
Dobell, Sydney Thompson
　1824-1874 .... **NCLC 43**
　See also DLB 32; RGEL 2
Doblin, Alfred
　See Doeblin, Alfred
Dobroliubov, Nikolai Aleksandrovich
　See Dobrolyubov, Nikolai Alexandrovich
　See also DLB 277
Dobrolyubov, Nikolai Alexandrovich
　1836-1861 .... **NCLC 5**
　See Dobroliubov, Nikolai Aleksandrovich
Dobson, Austin 1840-1921 .... **TCLC 79**
　See also DLB 35, 144
Dobyns, Stephen 1941- .... **CLC 37, 233**
　See also AMWS 13; CA 45-48; CANR 2,
　18, 99; CMW 4; CP 4, 5, 6, 7; PFS 23
Doctorow, Edgar Laurence
　See Doctorow, E.L.
Doctorow, E.L. 1931- . **CLC 6, 11, 15, 18, 37,
　44, 65, 113, 214**
　See also AAYA 22; AITN 2; AMWS 4;
　BEST 89:3; BPFB 1; CA 45-48; CANR
　2, 33, 51, 76, 97, 133, 170; CDALB 1968-
　1988; CN 3, 4, 5, 6, 7; CPW; DA3; DAM
　NOV, POP; DLB 2, 28, 173; DLBY 1980;
　EWL 3; LAIT 3; MAL 5; MTCW 1, 2;
　MTFW 2005; NFS 6; RGAL 4; RGHL;
　RHW; TCLE 1:1; TCWW 1, 2; TUS
Dodgson, Charles L(utwidge)
　1832-1898 ...... **NCLC 2, 53, 139; PC 18,
　74; WLC 1**
　See also AAYA 39; BRW 5; BYA 5, 13; CD-
　BLB 1832-1890; CLR 18, 108; DA; DA3;
　DAB; DAC; DAM MST, NOV, POET;
　DLB 18, 163, 178; DLBY 1998; EXPN;
　EXPP; FANT; JRDA; LAIT 1; MAICYA
　1, 2; NFS 27; PFS 11; RGEL 2; SATA
　100; SUFW 1; TEA; WCH; YABC 2
Dodsley, Robert 1703-1764 .... **LC 97**
　See also DLB 95; RGEL 2

Dodson, Owen (Vincent)
　1914-1983 .... **BLC 1:1; CLC 79**
　See also BW 1; CA 65-68; 110; CANR 24;
　DAM MULT; DLB 76
Doeblin, Alfred 1878-1957 .... **TCLC 13**
　See also CA 110; 141; CDWLB 2; DLB 66;
　EWL 3; RGWL 2, 3
Doerr, Harriet 1910-2002 .... **CLC 34**
　See also CA 117; 122; 213; CANR 47; INT
　CA-122; LATS 1:2
Domecq, H(onorio) Bustos
　See Bioy Casares, Adolfo; Borges, Jorge
　Luis
Domini, Rey
　See Lorde, Audre
Dominic, R. B.
　See Hennissart, Martha
Dominique
　See Proust, (Valentin-Louis-George-Eugene)
　Marcel
Don, A
　See Stephen, Sir Leslie
Donaldson, Stephen R. 1947- ... **CLC 46, 138**
　See also AAYA 36; BPFB 1; CA 89-92;
　CANR 13, 55, 99; CPW; DAM POP;
　FANT; INT CANR-13; SATA 121; SFW
　4; SUFW 1, 2
Donleavy, J(ames) P(atrick) 1926- .... **CLC 1,
　4, 6, 10, 45**
　See also AITN 2; BPFB 1; CA 9-12R;
　CANR 24, 49, 62, 80, 124; CBD; CD 5,
　6; CN 1, 2, 3, 4, 5, 6, 7; DLB 6, 173; INT
　CANR-24; MAL 5; MTCW 1, 2; MTFW
　2005; RGAL 4
Donnadieu, Marguerite
　See Duras, Marguerite
Donne, John 1572-1631 ... **LC 10, 24, 91; PC
　1, 43; WLC 2**
　See also AAYA 67; BRW 1; BRWC 1;
　BRWR 2; CDBLB Before 1660; DA;
　DAB; DAC; DAM MST, POET; DLB
　121, 151; EXPP; PAB; PFS 2, 11; RGEL
　3; TEA; WLIT 3; WP
Donnell, David 1939(?)- .... **CLC 34**
　See also CA 197
Donoghue, Denis 1928- .... **CLC 209**
　See also CA 17-20R; CANR 16, 102
Donoghue, Emma 1969- .... **CLC 239**
　See also CA 155; CANR 103, 152; DLB
　267; GLL 2; SATA 101
Donoghue, P.S.
　See Hunt, E. Howard
Donoso (Yanez), Jose 1924-1996 ... **CLC 4, 8,
　11, 32, 99; HLC 1; SSC 34; TCLC 133**
　See also CA 81-84; 155; CANR 32, 73; CD-
　WLB 3; CWW 2; DAM MULT; DLB 113;
　EWL 3; HW 1, 2; LAW; LAWS 1; MTCW
　1, 2; MTFW 2005; RGSF 2; WLIT 1
Donovan, John 1928-1992 .... **CLC 35**
　See also AAYA 20; CA 97-100; 137; CLR
　3; MAICYA 1, 2; SATA 72; SATA-Brief
　29; YAW
Don Roberto
　See Cunninghame Graham, Robert
　(Gallnigad) Bontine
Doolittle, Hilda 1886-1961 . **CLC 3, 8, 14, 31,
　34, 73; PC 5; WLC 3**
　See also AAYA 66; AMWS 1; CA 97-100;
　CANR 35, 131; DA; DAC; DAM MST,
　POET; DLB 4, 45; EWL 3; FL 1:5; FW;
　GLL 1; LMFS 2; MAL 5; MBL; MTCW
　1, 2; MTFW 2005; PFS 6, 28; RGAL 4
Doppo, Kunikida .... **TCLC 99**
　See Kunikida Doppo
Dorfman, Ariel 1942- .... **CLC 48, 77, 189;
　HLC 1**
　See also CA 124; 130; CANR 67, 70, 135;
　CWW 2; DAM MULT; DFS 4; EWL 3;
　HW 1, 2; INT CA-130; WLIT 1

Dorn, Edward (Merton)
　1929-1999 .... **CLC 10, 18**
　See also CA 93-96; 187; CANR 42, 79; CP
　1, 2, 3, 4, 5, 6, 7; DLB 5; INT CA-93-96;
　WP
Dor-Ner, Zvi .... **CLC 70**
Dorris, Michael 1945-1997 .... **CLC 109;
　NNAL**
　See also AAYA 20; BEST 90:1; BYA 12;
　CA 102; 157; CANR 19, 46, 75; CLR 58;
　DA3; DAM MULT, NOV; DLB 175;
　LAIT 5; MTCW 2; MTFW 2005; NFS 3;
　RGAL 4; SATA 75; SATA-Obit 94;
　TCWW 2; YAW
Dorris, Michael A.
　See Dorris, Michael
Dorsan, Luc
　See Simenon, Georges (Jacques Christian)
Dorsange, Jean
　See Simenon, Georges (Jacques Christian)
Dorset
　See Sackville, Thomas
Dos Passos, John (Roderigo)
　1896-1970 ... **CLC 1, 4, 8, 11, 15, 25, 34,
　82; WLC 2**
　See also AMW; BPFB 1; CA 1-4R; 29-32R;
　CANR 3; CDALB 1929-1941; DA; DA3;
　DAB; DAC; DAM MST, NOV; DLB 4,
　9, 274, 316; DLBD 1, 15; DLBY 1996;
　EWL 3; MAL 5; MTCW 1, 2; MTFW
　2005; NFS 14; RGAL 4; TUS
Dossage, Jean
　See Simenon, Georges (Jacques Christian)
Dostoevsky, Fedor Mikhailovich
　1821-1881 .. **NCLC 2, 7, 21, 33, 43, 119,
　167, 202; SSC 2, 33, 44; WLC 2**
　See Dostoevsky, Fyodor
　See also AAYA 40; DA; DA3; DAB; DAC;
　DAM MST, NOV; EW 7; EXPN; NFS 28;
　RGSF 2; RGWL 2, 3; SSFS 8; TWA
Dostoevsky, Fyodor
　See Dostoevsky, Fedor Mikhailovich
　See also DLB 238; LATS 1:1; LMFS 1, 2
Doty, Mark 1953(?)- .... **CLC 176; PC 53**
　See also AMWS 11; CA 161, 183; CAAE
　183; CANR 110, 173; CP 7; PFS 28
Doty, Mark A.
　See Doty, Mark
Doty, Mark Alan
　See Doty, Mark
Doty, M.R.
　See Doty, Mark
Doughty, Charles M(ontagu)
　1843-1926 .... **TCLC 27**
　See also CA 115; 178; DLB 19, 57, 174
Douglas, Ellen 1921- .... **CLC 73**
　See also CA 115; CANR 41, 83; CN 5, 6,
　7; CSW; DLB 292
Douglas, Gavin 1475(?)-1522 .... **LC 20**
　See also DLB 132; RGEL 2
Douglas, George
　See Brown, George Douglas
　See also RGEL 2
Douglas, Keith (Castellain)
　1920-1944 .... **TCLC 40**
　See also BRW 7; CA 160; DLB 27; EWL
　3; PAB; RGEL 2
Douglas, Leonard
　See Bradbury, Ray
Douglas, Michael
　See Crichton, Michael
Douglas, Michael
　See Crichton, Michael
Douglas, (George) Norman
　1868-1952 .... **TCLC 68**
　See also BRW 6; CA 119; 157; DLB 34,
　195; RGEL 2
Douglas, William
　See Brown, George Douglas

du Maurier, Daphne 1907-1989 .. **CLC 6, 11, 59; SSC 18; TCLC 209**
See also AAYA 37; BPFB 1; BRWS 3; CA 5-8R; 128; CANR 6, 55; CMW 4; CN 1, 2, 3, 4; CPW; DA3; DAB; DAC; DAM MST, POP; DLB 191; GL 2; HGG; LAIT 3; MSW; MTCW 1, 2; NFS 12; RGEL 2; RGSF 2; RHW; SATA 27; SATA-Obit 60; SSFS 14, 16; TEA

Du Maurier, George 1834-1896 ..... **NCLC 86**
See also DLB 153, 178; RGEL 2

Dunbar, Paul Laurence
1872-1906 .... **BLC 1:1; PC 5; SSC 8; TCLC 2, 12; WLC 2**
See also AAYA 75; AFAW 1, 2; AMWS 2; BW 1, 3; CA 104; 124; CANR 79; CDALB 1865-1917; DA; DA3; DAC; DAM MST, MULT, POET; DLB 50, 54, 78; EXPP; MAL 5; RGAL 4; SATA 34

Dunbar, William 1460(?)-1520(?) .... **LC 20; PC 67**
See also BRWS 8; DLB 132, 146; RGEL 2

Duncan, Dora Angela
See Duncan, Isadora

Duncan, Isadora 1877(?)-1927 .... **TCLC 68**
See also CA 118; 149

Duncan, Lois 1934- .... **CLC 26**
See also AAYA 4, 34; BYA 6, 8; CA 1-4R; CANR 2, 23, 36, 111; CLR 29, 129; JRDA; MAICYA 1, 2; MAICYAS 1; MTFW 2005; SAAS 2; SATA 1, 36, 75, 133, 141; SATA-Essay 141; WYA; YAW

Duncan, Robert 1919-1988 ... **CLC 1, 2, 4, 7, 15, 41, 55; PC 2, 75**
See also BG 1:2; CA 9-12R; 124; CANR 28, 62; CP 1, 2, 3, 4; DAM POET; DLB 5, 16, 193; EWL 3; MAL 5; MTCW 1, 2; MTFW 2005; PFS 13; RGAL 4; WP

Duncan, Sara Jeannette
1861-1922 .... **TCLC 60**
See also CA 157; DLB 92

Dunlap, William 1766-1839 .... **NCLC 2**
See also DLB 30, 37, 59; RGAL 4

Dunn, Douglas (Eaglesham) 1942- .... **CLC 6, 40**
See also BRWS 10; CA 45-48; CANR 2, 33, 126; CP 1, 2, 3, 4, 5, 6, 7; DLB 40; MTCW 1

Dunn, Katherine 1945- .... **CLC 71**
See also CA 33-36R; CANR 72; HGG; MTCW 2; MTFW 2005

Dunn, Stephen 1939- .... **CLC 36, 206**
See also AMWS 11; CA 33-36R; CANR 12, 48, 53, 105; CP 3, 4, 5, 6, 7; DLB 105; PFS 21

Dunn, Stephen Elliott
See Dunn, Stephen

Dunne, Finley Peter 1867-1936 ...... **TCLC 28**
See also CA 108; 178; DLB 11, 23; RGAL 4

Dunne, John Gregory 1932-2003 ..... **CLC 28**
See also CA 25-28R; 222; CANR 14, 50; CN 5, 6, 7; DLBY 1980

Dunsany, Lord
See Dunsany, Edward John Moreton Drax Plunkett

Dunsany, Edward John Moreton Drax Plunkett 1878-1957 .... **TCLC 2, 59**
See also CA 104; 148; DLB 10, 77, 153, 156, 255; FANT; MTCW 2; RGEL 2; SFW 4; SUFW 1

Duns Scotus, John 1266(?)-1308 ... **CMLC 59**
See also DLB 115

du Perry, Jean
See Simenon, Georges (Jacques Christian)

Durang, Christopher 1949- .... **CLC 27, 38**
See also CA 105; CAD; CANR 50, 76, 130; CD 5, 6; MTCW 2; MTFW 2005

Durang, Christopher Ferdinand
See Durang, Christopher

Duras, Claire de 1777-1832 .... **NCLC 154**

Duras, Marguerite 1914-1996 .. **CLC 3, 6, 11, 20, 34, 40, 68, 100; SSC 40**
See also BPFB 1; CA 25-28R; 151; CANR 50; CWW 2; DFS 21; DLB 83, 321; EWL 3; FL 1:5; GFL 1789 to the Present; IDFW 4; MTCW 1, 2; RGWL 2, 3; TWA

Durban, (Rosa) Pam 1947- .... **CLC 39**
See also CA 123; CANR 98; CSW

Durcan, Paul 1944- .... **CLC 43, 70**
See also CA 134; CANR 123; CP 1, 5, 6, 7; DAM POET; EWL 3

d'Urfe, Honore
See Urfe, Honore d'

Durfey, Thomas 1653-1723 .... **LC 94**
See also DLB 80; RGEL 2

Durkheim, Emile 1858-1917 .... **TCLC 55**
See also CA 249

Durrell, Lawrence (George)
1912-1990 ..... **CLC 1, 4, 6, 8, 13, 27, 41**
See also BPFB 1; BRWS 1; CA 9-12R; 132; CANR 40, 77; CDBLB 1945-1960; CN 1, 2, 3, 4; CP 1, 2, 3, 4, 5; DAM NOV; DLB 15, 27, 204; DLBY 1990; EWL 3; MTCW 1, 2; RGEL 2; SFW 4; TEA

Durrenmatt, Friedrich
See Duerrenmatt, Friedrich

Dutt, Michael Madhusudan
1824-1873 .... **NCLC 118**

Dutt, Toru 1856-1877 .... **NCLC 29**
See also DLB 240

Dwight, Timothy 1752-1817 .... **NCLC 13**
See also DLB 37; RGAL 4

Dworkin, Andrea 1946-2005 ..... **CLC 43, 123**
See also CA 77-80; 238; CAAS 21; CANR 16, 39, 76, 96; FL 1:5; FW; GLL 1; INT CANR-16; MTCW 1, 2; MTFW 2005

Dwyer, Deanna
See Koontz, Dean R.

Dwyer, K.R.
See Koontz, Dean R.

Dybek, Stuart 1942- .... **CLC 114; SSC 55**
See also CA 97-100; CANR 39; DLB 130; SSFS 23

Dye, Richard
See De Voto, Bernard (Augustine)

Dyer, Geoff 1958- .... **CLC 149**
See also CA 125; CANR 88

Dyer, George 1755-1841 .... **NCLC 129**
See also DLB 93

Dylan, Bob 1941- .... **CLC 3, 4, 6, 12, 77; PC 37**
See also AMWS 18; CA 41-44R; CANR 108; CP 1, 2, 3, 4, 5, 6, 7; DLB 16

Dyson, John 1943- .... **CLC 70**
See also CA 144

Dzyubin, Eduard Georgievich 1895-1934
See Bagritsky, Eduard
See also CA 170

E. V. L.
See Lucas, E(dward) V(errall)

Eagleton, Terence (Francis) 1943- .. **CLC 63, 132**
See also CA 57-60; CANR 7, 23, 68, 115; DLB 242; LMFS 2; MTCW 1, 2; MTFW 2005

Eagleton, Terry
See Eagleton, Terence (Francis)

Early, Jack
See Scoppettone, Sandra
See also GLL 1

East, Michael
See West, Morris L(anglo)

Eastaway, Edward
See Thomas, (Philip) Edward

Eastlake, William (Derry)
1917-1997 .... **CLC 8**
See also CA 5-8R; 158; CAAS 1; CANR 5, 63; CN 1, 2, 3, 4, 5, 6; DLB 6, 206; INT CANR-5; MAL 5; TCWW 1, 2

Eastman, Charles A(lexander)
1858-1939 .... **NNAL; TCLC 55**
See also CA 179; CANR 91; DAM MULT; DLB 175; YABC 1

Eaton, Edith Maude 1865-1914 .... **AAL**
See Far, Sui Sin
See also CA 154; DLB 221, 312; FW

Eaton, (Lillie) Winnifred 1875-1954 .... **AAL**
See also CA 217; DLB 221, 312; RGAL 4

Eberhart, Richard 1904-2005 ...... **CLC 3, 11, 19, 56; PC 76**
See also AMW; CA 1-4R; 240; CANR 2, 125; CDALB 1941-1968; CP 1, 2, 3, 4, 5, 6, 7; DAM POET; DLB 48; MAL 5; MTCW 1; RGAL 4

Eberhart, Richard Ghormley
See Eberhart, Richard

Eberstadt, Fernanda 1960- .... **CLC 39**
See also CA 136; CANR 69, 128

Ebner, Margaret c. 1291-1351 ...... **CMLC 98**

Echegaray (y Eizaguirre), Jose (Maria Waldo) 1832-1916 .... **HLCS 1; TCLC 4**
See also CA 104; CANR 32; DLB 329; EWL 3; HW 1; MTCW 1

Echeverria, (Jose) Esteban (Antonino)
1805-1851 .... **NCLC 18**
See also LAW

Echo
See Proust, (Valentin-Louis-George-Eugene) Marcel

Eckert, Allan W. 1931- .... **CLC 17**
See also AAYA 18; BYA 2; CA 13-16R; CANR 14, 45; INT CANR-14; MAICYA 2; MAICYAS 1; SAAS 21; SATA 29, 91; SATA-Brief 27

Eckhart, Meister 1260(?)-1327(?) .. **CMLC 9, 80**
See also DLB 115; LMFS 1

Eckmar, F. R.
See de Hartog, Jan

Eco, Umberto 1932- .... **CLC 28, 60, 142, 248**
See also BEST 90:1; BPFB 1; CA 77-80; CANR 12, 33, 55, 110, 131; CPW; CWW 2; DA3; DAM NOV, POP; DLB 196, 242; EWL 3; MSW; MTCW 1, 2; MTFW 2005; NFS 22; RGWL 3; WLIT 7

Eddison, E(ric) R(ucker)
1882-1945 .... **TCLC 15**
See also CA 109; 156; DLB 255; FANT; SFW 4; SUFW 1

Eddy, Mary (Ann Morse) Baker
1821-1910 .... **TCLC 71**
See also CA 113; 174

Edel, (Joseph) Leon 1907-1997 .. **CLC 29, 34**
See also CA 1-4R; 161; CANR 1, 22, 112; DLB 103; INT CANR-22

Eden, Emily 1797-1869 .... **NCLC 10**

Edgar, David 1948- .... **CLC 42**
See also CA 57-60; CANR 12, 61, 112; CBD; CD 5, 6; DAM DRAM; DFS 15; DLB 13, 233; MTCW 1

Edgerton, Clyde (Carlyle) 1944- ...... **CLC 39**
See also AAYA 17; CA 118; 134; CANR 64, 125; CN 7; CSW; DLB 278; INT CA-134; TCLE 1:1; YAW

Edgeworth, Maria 1768-1849 ... **NCLC 1, 51, 158; SSC 86**
See also BRWS 3; DLB 116, 159, 163; FL 1:3; FW; RGEL 2; SATA 21; TEA; WLIT 3

Edmonds, Paul
See Kuttner, Henry

Elman, Richard (Martin)
1934-1997 .... **CLC 19**
See also CA 17-20R; 163; CAAS 3; CANR 47; TCLE 1:1

Elron
See Hubbard, L. Ron

El Saadawi, Nawal 1931- ...... **BLC 2:2; CLC 196**
See also al'Sadaawi, Nawal; Sa'adawi, al-Nawal; Sa'dawi, Nawal al-
See also CA 118; CAAS 11; CANR 44, 92; DLB 346; WLIT 2

El-Shabazz, El-Hajj Malik
See Little, Malcolm

Eluard, Paul
See Grindel, Eugene

Eluard, Paul
See Grindel, Eugene

Elyot, Thomas 1490(?)-1546 .... **LC 11, 139**
See also DLB 136; RGEL 2

Elytis, Odysseus 1911-1996 .... **CLC 15, 49, 100; PC 21**
See also CA 102; 151; CANR 94; CWW 2; DAM POET; DLB 329; EW 13; EWL 3; MTCW 1, 2; RGWL 2, 3

Emecheta, Buchi 1944- ... **BLC 1:2; CLC 14, 48, 128, 214**
See also AAYA 67; AFW; BW 2, 3; CA 81-84; CANR 27, 81, 126; CDWLB 3; CN 4, 5, 6, 7; CWRI 5; DA3; DAM MULT; DLB 117; EWL 3; FL 1:5; FW; MTCW 1, 2; MTFW 2005; NFS 12, 14; SATA 66; WLIT 2

Emerson, Mary Moody
1774-1863 .... **NCLC 66**

Emerson, Ralph Waldo 1803-1882 . **NCLC 1, 38, 98; PC 18; WLC 2**
See also AAYA 60; AMW; ANW; CDALB 1640-1865; DA; DA3; DAB; DAC; DAM MST, POET; DLB 1, 59, 73, 183, 223, 270; EXPP; LAIT 2; LMFS 1; NCFS 3; PFS 4, 17; RGAL 4; TUS; WP

Eminem 1972- .... **CLC 226**
See also CA 245

Eminescu, Mihail 1850-1889 .. **NCLC 33, 131**

Empedocles 5th cent. B.C.- .... **CMLC 50**
See also DLB 176

Empson, William 1906-1984 ... **CLC 3, 8, 19, 33, 34**
See also BRWS 2; CA 17-20R; 112; CANR 31, 61; CP 1, 2, 3; DLB 20; EWL 3; MTCW 1, 2; RGEL 2

Enchi, Fumiko (Ueda) 1905-1986 ..... **CLC 31**
See Enchi Fumiko
See also CA 129; 121; FW; MJW

Enchi Fumiko
See Enchi, Fumiko (Ueda)
See also DLB 182; EWL 3

Ende, Michael (Andreas Helmuth)
1929-1995 .... **CLC 31**
See also BYA 5; CA 118; 124; 149; CANR 36, 110; CLR 14, 138; DLB 75; MAICYA 1, 2; MAICYAS 1; SATA 61, 130; SATA-Brief 42; SATA-Obit 86

Endo, Shusaku 1923-1996 ..... **CLC 7, 14, 19, 54, 99; SSC 48; TCLC 152**
See Endo Shusaku
See also CA 29-32R; 153; CANR 21, 54, 131; DA3; DAM NOV; MTCW 1, 2; MTFW 2005; RGSF 2; RGWL 2, 3

Endo Shusaku
See Endo, Shusaku
See also CWW 2; DLB 182; EWL 3

Engel, Marian 1933-1985 .... **CLC 36; TCLC 137**
See also CA 25-28R; CANR 12; CN 2, 3; DLB 53; FW; INT CANR-12

Engelhardt, Frederick
See Hubbard, L. Ron

Engels, Friedrich 1820-1895 .. **NCLC 85, 114**
See also DLB 129; LATS 1:1

Enquist, Per Olov 1934- .... **CLC 257**
See also CA 109; 193; CANR 155; CWW 2; DLB 257; EWL 3

Enright, D(ennis) J(oseph)
1920-2002 .... **CLC 4, 8, 31; PC 93**
See also CA 1-4R; 211; CANR 1, 42, 83; CN 1, 2; CP 1, 2, 3, 4, 5, 6, 7; DLB 27; EWL 3; SATA 25; SATA-Obit 140

Ensler, Eve 1953- .... **CLC 212**
See also CA 172; CANR 126, 163; DFS 23

Enzensberger, Hans Magnus
1929- .... **CLC 43; PC 28**
See also CA 116; 119; CANR 103; CWW 2; EWL 3

Ephron, Nora 1941- .... **CLC 17, 31**
See also AAYA 35; AITN 2; CA 65-68; CANR 12, 39, 83, 161; DFS 22

Epicurus 341B.C.-270B.C. .... **CMLC 21**
See also DLB 176

Epinay, Louise d' 1726-1783 .... **LC 138**
See also DLB 313

Epsilon
See Betjeman, John

Epstein, Daniel Mark 1948- .... **CLC 7**
See also CA 49-52; CANR 2, 53, 90

Epstein, Jacob 1956- .... **CLC 19**
See also CA 114

Epstein, Jean 1897-1953 .... **TCLC 92**

Epstein, Joseph 1937- .... **CLC 39, 204**
See also AMWS 14; CA 112; 119; CANR 50, 65, 117, 164

Epstein, Leslie 1938- .... **CLC 27**
See also AMWS 12; CA 73-76, 215; CAAE 215; CAAS 12; CANR 23, 69, 162; DLB 299; RGHL

Equiano, Olaudah 1745(?)-1797 ..... **BLC 1:2; LC 16, 143**
See also AFAW 1, 2; CDWLB 3; DAM MULT; DLB 37, 50; WLIT 2

Erasmus, Desiderius 1469(?)-1536 ..... **LC 16, 93**
See also DLB 136; EW 2; LMFS 1; RGWL 2, 3; TWA

Erdman, Paul E. 1932-2007 .... **CLC 25**
See also AITN 1; CA 61-64; 259; CANR 13, 43, 84

Erdman, Paul Emil
See Erdman, Paul E.

Erdrich, Karen Louise
See Erdrich, Louise

Erdrich, Louise 1954- .... **CLC 39, 54, 120, 176; NNAL; PC 52; SSC 121**
See also AAYA 10, 47; AMWS 4; BEST 89:1; BPFB 1; CA 114; CANR 41, 62, 118, 138; CDALBS; CN 5, 6, 7; CP 6, 7; CPW; CWP; DA3; DAM MULT, NOV, POP; DLB 152, 175, 206; EWL 3; EXPP; FL 1:5; LAIT 5; LATS 1:2; MAL 5; MTCW 1, 2; MTFW 2005; NFS 5; PFS 14; RGAL 4; SATA 94, 141; SSFS 14, 22; TCWW 2

Erenburg, Ilya (Grigoryevich)
See Ehrenburg, Ilya (Grigoryevich)

Erickson, Stephen Michael
See Erickson, Steve

Erickson, Steve 1950- .... **CLC 64**
See also CA 129; CANR 60, 68, 136; MTFW 2005; SFW 4; SUFW 2

Erickson, Walter
See Fast, Howard

Ericson, Walter
See Fast, Howard

Eriksson, Buntel
See Bergman, Ingmar

Eriugena, John Scottus c.
810-877 .... **CMLC 65**
See also DLB 115

Ernaux, Annie 1940- .... **CLC 88, 184**
See also CA 147; CANR 93; MTFW 2005; NCFS 3, 5

Erskine, John 1879-1951 .... **TCLC 84**
See also CA 112; 159; DLB 9, 102; FANT

Erwin, Will
See Eisner, Will

Eschenbach, Wolfram von
See von Eschenbach, Wolfram
See also RGWL 3

Eseki, Bruno
See Mphahlele, Es'kia

Esekie, Bruno
See Mphahlele, Es'kia

Esenin, S.A.
See Esenin, Sergei
See also EWL 3

Esenin, Sergei 1895-1925 .... **TCLC 4**
See Esenin, S.A.
See also CA 104; RGWL 2, 3

Esenin, Sergei Aleksandrovich
See Esenin, Sergei

Eshleman, Clayton 1935- .... **CLC 7**
See also CA 33-36R, 212; CAAE 212; CAAS 6; CANR 93; CP 1, 2, 3, 4, 5, 6, 7; DLB 5

Espada, Martin 1957- .... **PC 74**
See also CA 159; CANR 80; CP 7; EXPP; LLW; MAL 5; PFS 13, 16

Espriella, Don Manuel Alvarez
See Southey, Robert

Espriu, Salvador 1913-1985 .... **CLC 9**
See also CA 154; 115; DLB 134; EWL 3

Espronceda, Jose de 1808-1842 ..... **NCLC 39**

Esquivel, Laura 1950(?)- .. **CLC 141; HLCS 1**
See also AAYA 29; CA 143; CANR 68, 113, 161; DA3; DNFS 2; LAIT 3; LMFS 2; MTCW 2; MTFW 2005; NFS 5; WLIT 1

Esse, James
See Stephens, James

Esterbrook, Tom
See Hubbard, L. Ron

Esterhazy, Peter 1950- .... **CLC 251**
See also CA 140; CANR 137; CDWLB 4; CWW 2; DLB 232; EWL 3; RGWL 3

Estleman, Loren D. 1952- .... **CLC 48**
See also AAYA 27; CA 85-88; CANR 27, 74, 139, 177; CMW 4; CPW; DA3; DAM NOV, POP; DLB 226; INT CANR-27; MTCW 1, 2; MTFW 2005; TCWW 1, 2

Etherege, Sir George 1636-1692 . **DC 23; LC 78**
See also BRW 2; DAM DRAM; DLB 80; PAB; RGEL 2

Euclid 306B.C.-283B.C. .... **CMLC 25**

Eugenides, Jeffrey 1960- .... **CLC 81, 212**
See also AAYA 51; CA 144; CANR 120; MTFW 2005; NFS 24

Euripides c. 484B.C.-406B.C. .... **CMLC 23, 51; DC 4; WLCS**
See also AW 1; CDWLB 1; DA; DA3; DAB; DAC; DAM DRAM, MST; DFS 1, 4, 6, 25; DLB 176; LAIT 1; LMFS 1; RGWL 2, 3; WLIT 8

Eusebius c. 263-c. 339 .... **CMLC 103**

Evan, Evin
See Faust, Frederick (Schiller)

Evans, Caradoc 1878-1945 ... **SSC 43; TCLC 85**
See also DLB 162

Evans, Evan
See Faust, Frederick (Schiller)

Evans, Marian
See Eliot, George

Evans, Mary Ann
See Eliot, George

Felski, Rita .... CLC 65

Fenelon, Francois de Pons de Salignac de la
        Mothe- 1651-1715 .... LC 134
    See also DLB 268; EW 3; GFL Beginnings
        to 1789

Fenno, Jack
    See Calisher, Hortense

Fenollosa, Ernest (Francisco)
        1853-1908 .... TCLC 91

Fenton, James 1949- .... CLC 32, 209
    See also CA 102; CANR 108, 160; CP 2, 3,
        4, 5, 6, 7; DLB 40; PFS 11

Fenton, James Martin
    See Fenton, James

Ferber, Edna 1887-1968 .... CLC 18, 93
    See also AITN 1; CA 5-8R; 25-28R; CANR
        68, 105; DLB 9, 28, 86, 266; MAL 5;
        MTCW 1, 2; MTFW 2005; RGAL 4;
        RHW; SATA 7; TCWW 1, 2

Ferdousi
    See Ferdowsi, Abu'l Qasem

Ferdovsi
    See Ferdowsi, Abu'l Qasem

Ferdowsi
    See Ferdowsi, Abu'l Qasem

Ferdowsi, Abolghasem Mansour
    See Ferdowsi, Abu'l Qasem

Ferdowsi, Abol-Qasem
    See Ferdowsi, Abu'l Qasem

Ferdowsi, Abolqasem
    See Ferdowsi, Abu'l Qasem

Ferdowsi, Abu'l Qasem
        940-1020(?) .... CMLC 43
    See Firdawsi, Abu al-Qasim
    See also CA 276; RGWL 2, 3

Ferdowsi, A.M.
    See Ferdowsi, Abu'l Qasem

Ferdowsi, Hakim Abolghasem
    See Ferdowsi, Abu'l Qasem

Ferguson, Helen
    See Kavan, Anna

Ferguson, Niall 1964- .... CLC 134, 250
    See also CA 190; CANR 154

Ferguson, Niall Campbell
    See Ferguson, Niall

Ferguson, Samuel 1810-1886 .... NCLC 33
    See also DLB 32; RGEL 2

Fergusson, Robert 1750-1774 .... LC 29
    See also DLB 109; RGEL 2

Ferling, Lawrence
    See Ferlinghetti, Lawrence

Ferlinghetti, Lawrence 1919(?)- .... CLC 2, 6,
        10, 27, 111; PC 1
    See also AAYA 74; BG 1:2; CA 5-8R; CAD;
        CANR 3, 41, 73, 125, 172; CDALB 1941-
        1968; CP 1, 2, 3, 4, 5, 6, 7; DA3; DAM
        POET; DLB 5, 16; MAL 5; MTCW 1, 2;
        MTFW 2005; PFS 28; RGAL 4; WP

Ferlinghetti, Lawrence Monsanto
    See Ferlinghetti, Lawrence

Fern, Fanny
    See Parton, Sara Payson Willis

Fernandez, Vicente Garcia Huidobro
    See Huidobro Fernandez, Vicente Garcia

Fernandez-Armesto, Felipe .... CLC 70
    See Fernandez-Armesto, Felipe Fermin
        Ricardo
    See also CANR 153

Fernandez-Armesto, Felipe Fermin Ricardo
        1950-
    See Fernandez-Armesto, Felipe
    See also CA 142; CANR 93

Fernandez de Lizardi, Jose Joaquin
    See Lizardi, Jose Joaquin Fernandez de

Ferre, Rosario 1938- ...... CLC 139; HLCS 1;
        SSC 36, 106
    See also CA 131; CANR 55, 81, 134; CWW
        2; DLB 145; EWL 3; HW 1, 2; LAWS 1;
        MTCW 2; MTFW 2005; WLIT 1

Ferrer, Gabriel (Francisco Victor) Miro
    See Miro (Ferrer), Gabriel (Francisco
        Victor)

Ferrier, Susan (Edmonstone)
        1782-1854 .... NCLC 8
    See also DLB 116; RGEL 2

Ferrigno, Robert 1947- .... CLC 65
    See also CA 140; CANR 125, 161

Ferron, Jacques 1921-1985 .... CLC 94
    See also CA 117; 129; CCA 1; DAC; DLB
        60; EWL 3

Feuchtwanger, Lion 1884-1958 .... TCLC 3
    See also CA 104; 187; DLB 66; EWL 3;
        RGHL

Feuerbach, Ludwig 1804-1872 ..... NCLC 139
    See also DLB 133

Feuillet, Octave 1821-1890 .... NCLC 45
    See also DLB 192

Feydeau, Georges (Leon Jules Marie)
        1862-1921 .... TCLC 22
    See also CA 113; 152; CANR 84; DAM
        DRAM; DLB 192; EWL 3; GFL 1789 to
        the Present; RGWL 2, 3

Fichte, Johann Gottlieb
        1762-1814 .... NCLC 62
    See also DLB 90

Ficino, Marsilio 1433-1499 .... LC 12, 152
    See also LMFS 1

Fiedeler, Hans
    See Doeblin, Alfred

Fiedler, Leslie A(aron) 1917-2003 ..... CLC 4,
        13, 24
    See also AMWS 13; CA 9-12R; 212; CANR
        7, 63; CN 1, 2, 3, 4, 5, 6; DLB 28, 67;
        EWL 3; MAL 5; MTCW 1, 2; RGAL 4;
        TUS

Field, Andrew 1938- .... CLC 44
    See also CA 97-100; CANR 25

Field, Eugene 1850-1895 .... NCLC 3
    See also DLB 23, 42, 140; DLBD 13; MAI-
        CYA 1, 2; RGAL 4; SATA 16

Field, Gans T.
    See Wellman, Manly Wade

Field, Michael 1915-1971 .... TCLC 43
    See also CA 29-32R

Fielding, Helen 1958- .... CLC 146, 217
    See also AAYA 65; CA 172; CANR 127;
        DLB 231; MTFW 2005

Fielding, Henry 1707-1754 .... LC 1, 46, 85,
        151, 154; WLC 2
    See also BRW 3; BRWR 1; CDBLB 1660-
        1789; DA; DA3; DAB; DAC; DAM
        DRAM, MST, NOV; DLB 39, 84, 101;
        NFS 18; RGEL 2; TEA; WLIT 3

Fielding, Sarah 1710-1768 .... LC 1, 44
    See also DLB 39; RGEL 2; TEA

Fields, W. C. 1880-1946 .... TCLC 80
    See also DLB 44

Fierstein, Harvey (Forbes) 1954- ..... CLC 33
    See also CA 123; 129; CAD; CD 5, 6;
        CPW; DA3; DAM DRAM, POP; DFS 6;
        DLB 266; GLL; MAL 5

Figes, Eva 1932- .... CLC 31
    See also CA 53-56; CANR 4, 44, 83; CN 2,
        3, 4, 5, 6, 7; DLB 14, 271; FW; RGHL

Filippo, Eduardo de
    See de Filippo, Eduardo

Finch, Anne 1661-1720 ..... LC 3, 137; PC 21
    See also BRWS 9; DLB 95

Finch, Robert (Duer Claydon)
        1900-1995 .... CLC 18
    See also CA 57-60; CANR 9, 24, 49; CP 1,
        2, 3, 4, 5, 6; DLB 88

Findley, Timothy (Irving Frederick)
        1930-2002 .... CLC 27, 102
    See also CA 25-28R; 206; CANR 12, 42,
        69, 109; CCA 1; CN 4, 5, 6, 7; DAC;
        DAM MST; DLB 53; FANT; RHW

Fink, William
    See Mencken, H(enry) L(ouis)

Firbank, Louis 1942- .... CLC 21
    See also CA 117

Firbank, (Arthur Annesley) Ronald
        1886-1926 .... TCLC 1
    See also BRWS 2; CA 104; 177; DLB 36;
        EWL 3; RGEL 2

Firdaosi
    See Ferdowsi, Abu'l Qasem

Firdausi
    See Ferdowsi, Abu'l Qasem

Firdavsi, Abulqosimi
    See Ferdowsi, Abu'l Qasem

Firdavsii, Abulqosim
    See Ferdowsi, Abu'l Qasem

Firdawsi, Abu al-Qasim
    See Ferdowsi, Abu'l Qasem
    See also WLIT 6

Firdosi
    See Ferdowsi, Abu'l Qasem

Firdousi
    See Ferdowsi, Abu'l Qasem

Firdousi, Abu'l-Qasim
    See Ferdowsi, Abu'l Qasem

Firdovsi, A.
    See Ferdowsi, Abu'l Qasem

Firdovsi, Abulgasim
    See Ferdowsi, Abu'l Qasem

Firdusi
    See Ferdowsi, Abu'l Qasem

Fish, Stanley
    See Fish, Stanley Eugene

Fish, Stanley E.
    See Fish, Stanley Eugene

Fish, Stanley Eugene 1938- .... CLC 142
    See also CA 112; 132; CANR 90; DLB 67

Fisher, Dorothy (Frances) Canfield
        1879-1958 .... TCLC 87
    See also CA 114; 136; CANR 80; CLR 71;
        CWRI 5; DLB 9, 102, 284; MAICYA 1,
        2; MAL 5; YABC 1

Fisher, M(ary) F(rances) K(ennedy)
        1908-1992 .... CLC 76, 87
    See also AMWS 17; CA 77-80; 138; CANR
        44; MTCW 2

Fisher, Roy 1930- .... CLC 25
    See also CA 81-84; CAAS 10; CANR 16;
        CP 1, 2, 3, 4, 5, 6, 7; DLB 40

Fisher, Rudolph 1897-1934 ...... BLC 1:2; HR
        1:2; SSC 25; TCLC 11
    See also BW 1, 3; CA 107; 124; CANR 80;
        DAM MULT; DLB 51, 102

Fisher, Vardis (Alvero) 1895-1968 .... CLC 7;
        TCLC 140
    See also CA 5-8R; 25-28R; CANR 68; DLB
        9, 206; MAL 5; RGAL 4; TCWW 1, 2

Fiske, Tarleton
    See Bloch, Robert (Albert)

Fitch, Clarke
    See Sinclair, Upton

Fitch, John IV
    See Cormier, Robert

Fitzgerald, Captain Hugh
    See Baum, L(yman) Frank

FitzGerald, Edward 1809-1883 ...... NCLC 9,
        153; PC 79
    See also BRW 4; DLB 32; RGEL 2

Fitzgerald, F(rancis) Scott (Key)
        1896-1940 ... SSC 6, 31, 75; TCLC 1, 6,
        14, 28, 55, 157; WLC 2
    See also AAYA 24; AITN 1; AMW; AMWC
        2; AMWR 1; BPFB 1; CA 110; 123;
        CDALB 1917-1929; DA; DA3; DAB;

Grayson, David
　　See Baker, Ray Stannard
Grayson, Richard (A.) 1951- .... **CLC 38**
　　See also CA 85-88, 210; CAAE 210; CANR
　　14, 31, 57; DLB 234
Greeley, Andrew M. 1928- .... **CLC 28**
　　See also BPFB 2; CA 5-8R; CAAS 7;
　　CANR 7, 43, 69, 104, 136, 184; CMW 4;
　　CPW; DA3; DAM POP; MTCW 1, 2;
　　MTFW 2005
Green, Anna Katharine
　　1846-1935 .... **TCLC 63**
　　See also CA 112; 159; CMW 4; DLB 202,
　　221; MSW
Green, Brian
　　See Card, Orson Scott
Green, Hannah
　　See Greenberg, Joanne (Goldenberg)
Green, Hannah 1927(?)-1996 .... **CLC 3**
　　See also CA 73-76; CANR 59, 93; NFS 10
Green, Henry
　　See Yorke, Henry Vincent
Green, Julian
　　See Green, Julien (Hartridge)
Green, Julien (Hartridge)
　　1900-1998 .... **CLC 3, 11, 77**
　　See also CA 21-24R; 169; CANR 33, 87;
　　CWW 2; DLB 4, 72; EWL 3; GFL 1789
　　to the Present; MTCW 2; MTFW 2005
Green, Paul (Eliot) 1894-1981 .... **CLC 25**
　　See also AITN 1; CA 5-8R; 103; CAD;
　　CANR 3; DAM DRAM; DLB 7, 9, 249;
　　DLBY 1981; MAL 5; RGAL 4
Greenaway, Peter 1942- .... **CLC 159**
　　See also CA 127
Greenberg, Ivan 1908-1973 .... **CLC 24**
　　See also CA 85-88; DLB 137; MAL 5
Greenberg, Joanne (Goldenberg)
　　1932- .... **CLC 7, 30**
　　See also AAYA 12, 67; CA 5-8R; CANR
　　14, 32, 69; CN 6, 7; DLB 335; NFS 23;
　　SATA 25; YAW
Greenberg, Richard 1959(?)- .... **CLC 57**
　　See also CA 138; CAD; CD 5, 6; DFS 24
Greenblatt, Stephen J(ay) 1943- ...... **CLC 70**
　　See also CA 49-52; CANR 115
Greene, Bette 1934- .... **CLC 30**
　　See also AAYA 7, 69; BYA 3; CA 53-56;
　　CANR 4, 146; CLR 2, 140; CWRI 5;
　　JRDA; LAIT 4; MAICYA 1, 2; NFS 10;
　　SAAS 16; SATA 8, 102, 161; WYA; YAW
Greene, Gael .... **CLC 8**
　　See also CA 13-16R; CANR 10, 166
Greene, Graham 1904-1991 .. **CLC 1, 3, 6, 9,**
　　14, 18, 27, 37, 70, 72, 125; SSC 29, 121;
　　WLC 3
　　See also AAYA 61; AITN 2; BPFB 2;
　　BRWR 2; BRWS 1; BYA 3; CA 13-16R;
　　133; CANR 35, 61, 131; CBD; CDBLB
　　1945-1960; CMW 4; CN 1, 2, 3, 4; DA;
　　DA3; DAB; DAC; DAM MST, NOV;
　　DLB 13, 15, 77, 100, 162, 201, 204;
　　DLBY 1991; EWL 3; MSW; MTCW 1, 2;
　　MTFW 2005; NFS 16; RGEL 2; SATA
　　20; SSFS 14; TEA; WLIT 4
Greene, Robert 1558-1592 .... **LC 41**
　　See also BRWS 8; DLB 62, 167; IDTP;
　　RGEL 2; TEA
Greer, Germaine 1939- .... **CLC 131**
　　See also AITN 1; CA 81-84; CANR 33, 70,
　　115, 133; FW; MTCW 1, 2; MTFW 2005
Greer, Richard
　　See Silverberg, Robert
Gregor, Arthur 1923- .... **CLC 9**
　　See also CA 25-28R; CAAS 10; CANR 11;
　　CP 1, 2, 3, 4, 5, 6, 7; SATA 36
Gregor, Lee
　　See Pohl, Frederik

Gregory, Lady Isabella Augusta (Persse)
　　1852-1932 .... **TCLC 1, 176**
　　See also BRW 6; CA 104; 184; DLB 10;
　　IDTP; RGEL 2
Gregory, J. Dennis
　　See Williams, John A(lfred)
Gregory of Nazianzus, St.
　　329-389 .... **CMLC 82**
Gregory of Rimini 1300(?)-1358 . **CMLC 109**
　　See also DLB 115
Grekova, I. .... **CLC 59**
　　See Ventsel, Elena Sergeevna
　　See also CWW 2
Grendon, Stephen
　　See Derleth, August (William)
Grenville, Kate 1950- .... **CLC 61**
　　See also CA 118; CANR 53, 93, 156; CN
　　7; DLB 325
Grenville, Pelham
　　See Wodehouse, P(elham) G(renville)
Greve, Felix Paul (Berthold Friedrich)
　　1879-1948 .... **TCLC 4**
　　See also CA 104; 141, 175; CANR 79;
　　DAC; DAM MST; DLB 92; RGEL 2;
　　TCWW 1, 2
Greville, Fulke 1554-1628 .... **LC 79**
　　See also BRWS 11; DLB 62, 172; RGEL 2
Grey, Lady Jane 1537-1554 .... **LC 93**
　　See also DLB 132
Grey, Zane 1872-1939 .... **TCLC 6**
　　See also BPFB 2; CA 104; 132; DA3; DAM
　　POP; DLB 9, 212; MTCW 1, 2; MTFW
　　2005; RGAL 4; TCWW 1, 2; TUS
Griboedov, Aleksandr Sergeevich
　　1795(?)-1829 .... **NCLC 129**
　　See also DLB 205; RGWL 2, 3
Grieg, (Johan) Nordahl (Brun)
　　1902-1943 .... **TCLC 10**
　　See also CA 107; 189; EWL 3
Grieve, C(hristopher) M(urray)
　　1892-1978 ... **CLC 2, 4, 11, 19, 63; PC 9**
　　See also BRWS 12; CA 5-8R; 85-88; CANR
　　33, 107; CDBLB 1945-1960; CP 1, 2;
　　DAM POET; DLB 20; EWL 3; MTCW 1;
　　RGEL 2
Griffin, Gerald 1803-1840 .... **NCLC 7**
　　See also DLB 159; RGEL 2
Griffin, John Howard 1920-1980 ..... **CLC 68**
　　See also AITN 1; CA 1-4R; 101; CANR 2
Griffin, Peter 1942- .... **CLC 39**
　　See also CA 136
Griffith, David Lewelyn Wark
　　See Griffith, D.W.
Griffith, D.W. 1875(?)-1948 .... **TCLC 68**
　　See also AAYA 78; CA 119; 150; CANR 80
Griffith, Lawrence
　　See Griffith, D.W.
Griffiths, Trevor 1935- .... **CLC 13, 52**
　　See also CA 97-100; CANR 45; CBD; CD
　　5, 6; DLB 13, 245
Griggs, Sutton (Elbert)
　　1872-1930 .... **TCLC 77**
　　See also CA 123; 186; DLB 50
Grigson, Geoffrey (Edward Harvey)
　　1905-1985 .... **CLC 7, 39**
　　See also CA 25-28R; 118; CANR 20, 33;
　　CP 1, 2, 3, 4; DLB 27; MTCW 1, 2
Grile, Dod
　　See Bierce, Ambrose (Gwinett)
Grillparzer, Franz 1791-1872 .... **DC 14;**
　　NCLC 1, 102; SSC 37
　　See also CDWLB 2; DLB 133; EW 5;
　　RGWL 2, 3; TWA
Grimble, Reverend Charles James
　　See Eliot, T(homas) S(tearns)

Grimke, Angelina (Emily) Weld
　　1880-1958 .... **HR 1:2**
　　See Weld, Angelina (Emily) Grimke
　　See also BW 1; CA 124; DAM POET; DLB
　　50, 54
Grimke, Charlotte L(ottie) Forten
　　1837(?)-1914 .... **BLC 1:2; TCLC 16**
　　See also BW 1; CA 117; 124; DAM MULT,
　　POET; DLB 50, 239
Grimm, Jacob Ludwig Karl
　　1785-1863 .... **NCLC 3, 77; SSC 36**
　　See Grimm Brothers
　　See also CLR 112; DLB 90; MAICYA 1, 2;
　　RGSF 2; RGWL 2, 3; SATA 22; WCH
Grimm, Wilhelm Karl 1786-1859 .. **NCLC 3,**
　　77; SSC 36
　　See Grimm Brothers
　　See also CDWLB 2; CLR 112; DLB 90;
　　MAICYA 1, 2; RGSF 2; RGWL 2, 3;
　　SATA 22; WCH
Grimm and Grim
　　See Grimm, Jacob Ludwig Karl; Grimm,
　　Wilhelm Karl
Grimm Brothers .... **SSC 88**
　　See Grimm, Jacob Ludwig Karl; Grimm,
　　Wilhelm Karl
　　See also CLR 112
Grimmelshausen, Hans Jakob Christoffel
　　von
　　See Grimmelshausen, Johann Jakob Christ-
　　offel von
　　See also RGWL 2, 3
Grimmelshausen, Johann Jakob Christoffel
　　von 1621-1676 .... **LC 6**
　　See Grimmelshausen, Hans Jakob Christof-
　　fel von
　　See also CDWLB 2; DLB 168
Grindel, Eugene 1895-1952 .... **PC 38; TCLC**
　　7, 41
　　See also CA 104; 193; EWL 3; GFL 1789
　　to the Present; LMFS 2; RGWL 2, 3
Grisham, John 1955- .... **CLC 84**
　　See also AAYA 14, 47; BPFB 2; CA 138;
　　CANR 47, 69, 114, 133; CMW 4; CN 6,
　　7; CPW; CSW; DA3; DAM POP; MSW;
　　MTCW 2; MTFW 2005
Grosseteste, Robert 1175(?)-1253 . **CMLC 62**
　　See also DLB 115
Grossman, David 1954- .... **CLC 67, 231**
　　See also CA 138; CANR 114, 175; CWW
　　2; DLB 299; EWL 3; RGHL; WLIT 6
Grossman, Vasilii Semenovich
　　See Grossman, Vasily (Semenovich)
　　See also DLB 272
Grossman, Vasily (Semenovich)
　　1905-1964 .... **CLC 41**
　　See Grossman, Vasilii Semenovich
　　See also CA 124; 130; MTCW 1; RGHL
Grove, Frederick Philip
　　See Greve, Felix Paul (Berthold Friedrich)
Grubb
　　See Crumb, R.
Grumbach, Doris 1918- .... **CLC 13, 22, 64**
　　See also CA 5-8R; CAAS 2; CANR 9, 42,
　　70, 127; CN 6, 7; INT CANR-9; MTCW
　　2; MTFW 2005
Grundtvig, Nikolai Frederik Severin
　　1783-1872 .... **NCLC 1, 158**
　　See also DLB 300
Grunge
　　See Crumb, R.
Grunwald, Lisa 1959- .... **CLC 44**
　　See also CA 120; CANR 148
Gryphius, Andreas 1616-1664 .... **LC 89**
　　See also CDWLB 2; DLB 164; RGWL 2, 3

Haines, John (Meade) 1924- .... **CLC 58**
See also AMWS 12; CA 17-20R; CANR 13, 34; CP 1, 2, 3, 4, 5; CSW; DLB 5, 212; TCLE 1:1

Ha Jin
See Jin, Xuefei

Hakluyt, Richard 1552-1616 .... **LC 31**
See also DLB 136; RGEL 2

Haldeman, Joe 1943- .... **CLC 61**
See also AAYA 38; CA 53-56, 179; CAAE 179; CAAS 25; CANR 6, 70, 72, 130, 171; DLB 8; INT CANR-6; SCFW 2; SFW 4

Haldeman, Joe William
See Haldeman, Joe

Hale, Janet Campbell 1947- .... **NNAL**
See also CA 49-52; CANR 45, 75; DAM MULT; DLB 175; MTCW 2; MTFW 2005

Hale, Sarah Josepha (Buell)
1788-1879 .... **NCLC 75**
See also DLB 1, 42, 73, 243

Halevy, Elie 1870-1937 .... **TCLC 104**

Haley, Alex(ander Murray Palmer)
1921-1992 ...... **BLC 1:2; CLC 8, 12, 76; TCLC 147**
See also AAYA 26; BPFB 2; BW 2, 3; CA 77-80; 136; CANR 61; CDALBS; CPW; CSW; DA; DA3; DAB; DAC; DAM MST, MULT, POP; DLB 38; LAIT 5; MTCW 1, 2; NFS 9

Haliburton, Thomas Chandler
1796-1865 .... **NCLC 15, 149**
See also DLB 11, 99; RGEL 2; RGSF 2

Hall, Donald 1928- ... **CLC 1, 13, 37, 59, 151, 240; PC 70**
See also AAYA 63; CA 5-8R; CAAS 7; CANR 2, 44, 64, 106, 133; CP 1, 2, 3, 4, 5, 6, 7; DAM POET; DLB 5, 342; MAL 5; MTCW 2; MTFW 2005; RGAL 4; SATA 23, 97

Hall, Donald Andrew, Jr.
See Hall, Donald

Hall, Frederic Sauser
See Sauser-Hall, Frederic

Hall, James
See Kuttner, Henry

Hall, James Norman 1887-1951 ..... **TCLC 23**
See also CA 123; 173; LAIT 1; RHW 1; SATA 21

Hall, Joseph 1574-1656 .... **LC 91**
See also DLB 121, 151; RGEL 2

Hall, Marguerite Radclyffe
See Hall, Radclyffe

Hall, Radclyffe 1880-1943 ...... **TCLC 12, 215**
See also BRWS 6; CA 110; 150; CANR 83; DLB 191; MTCW 2; MTFW 2005; RGEL 2; RHW

Hall, Rodney 1935- .... **CLC 51**
See also CA 109; CANR 69; CN 6, 7; CP 1, 2, 3, 4, 5, 6, 7; DLB 289

Hallam, Arthur Henry
1811-1833 .... **NCLC 110**
See also DLB 32

Halldor Laxness
See Gudjonsson, Halldor Kiljan

Halleck, Fitz-Greene 1790-1867 .... **NCLC 47**
See also DLB 3, 250; RGAL 4

Halliday, Michael
See Creasey, John

Halpern, Daniel 1945- .... **CLC 14**
See also CA 33-36R; CANR 93, 174; CP 3, 4, 5, 6, 7

Hamburger, Michael 1924-2007 ... **CLC 5, 14**
See also CA 5-8R, 196; 261; CAAE 196; CAAS 4; CANR 2, 47; CP 1, 2, 3, 4, 5, 6, 7; DLB 27

Hamburger, Michael Peter Leopold
See Hamburger, Michael

Hamill, Pete 1935- .... **CLC 10, 261**
See also CA 25-28R; CANR 18, 71, 127, 180

Hamill, William Peter
See Hamill, Pete

Hamilton, Alexander 1712-1756 .... **LC 150**
See also DLB 31

Hamilton, Alexander
1755(?)-1804 .... **NCLC 49**
See also DLB 37

Hamilton, Clive
See Lewis, C.S.

Hamilton, Edmond 1904-1977 .... **CLC 1**
See also CA 1-4R; CANR 3, 84; DLB 8; SATA 118; SFW 4

Hamilton, Elizabeth 1758-1816 ... **NCLC 153**
See also DLB 116, 158

Hamilton, Eugene (Jacob) Lee
See Lee-Hamilton, Eugene (Jacob)

Hamilton, Franklin
See Silverberg, Robert

Hamilton, Gail
See Corcoran, Barbara (Asenath)

Hamilton, (Robert) Ian 1938-2001 . **CLC 191**
See also CA 106; 203; CANR 41, 67; CP 1, 2, 3, 4, 5, 6, 7; DLB 40, 155

Hamilton, Jane 1957- .... **CLC 179**
See also CA 147; CANR 85, 128; CN 7; MTFW 2005

Hamilton, Mollie
See Kaye, M.M.

Hamilton, (Anthony Walter) Patrick
1904-1962 .... **CLC 51**
See also CA 176; 113; DLB 10, 191

Hamilton, Virginia 1936-2002 .... **CLC 26**
See also AAYA 2, 21; BW 2, 3; BYA 1, 2, 8; CA 25-28R; 206; CANR 20, 37, 73, 126; CLR 1, 11, 40, 127; DAM MULT; DLB 33, 52; DLBY 2001; INT CANR-20; JRDA; LAIT 5; MAICYA 1, 2; MAICYAS 1; MTCW 1, 2; MTFW 2005; SATA 4, 56, 79, 123; SATA-Obit 132; WYA; YAW

Hammett, (Samuel) Dashiell
1894-1961 .... **CLC 3, 5, 10, 19, 47; SSC 17; TCLC 187**
See also AAYA 59; AITN 1; AMWS 4; BPFB 2; CA 81-84; CANR 42; CDALB 1929-1941; CMW 4; DA3; DLB 226, 280; DLBD 6; DLBY 1996; EWL 3; LAIT 3; MAL 5; MSW; MTCW 1, 2; MTFW 2005; NFS 21; RGAL 4; RGSF 2; TUS

Hammon, Jupiter 1720(?)-1800(?) . **BLC 1:2; NCLC 5; PC 16**
See also DAM MULT, POET; DLB 31, 50

Hammond, Keith
See Kuttner, Henry

Hamner, Earl (Henry), Jr. 1923- ...... **CLC 12**
See also AITN 2; CA 73-76; DLB 6

Hampton, Christopher 1946- .... **CLC 4**
See also CA 25-28R; CD 5, 6; DLB 13; MTCW 1

Hampton, Christopher James
See Hampton, Christopher

Hamsun, Knut
See Pedersen, Knut

Hamsund, Knut Pedersen
See Pedersen, Knut

Handke, Peter 1942- .... **CLC 5, 8, 10, 15, 38, 134; DC 17**
See also CA 77-80; CANR 33, 75, 104, 133, 180; CWW 2; DAM DRAM, NOV; DLB 85, 124; EWL 3; MTCW 1, 2; MTFW 2005; TWA

Handler, Chelsea 1976(?)- .... **CLC 269**
See also CA 243

Handy, W(illiam) C(hristopher)
1873-1958 .... **TCLC 97**
See also BW 3; CA 121; 167

Hanley, James 1901-1985 ..... **CLC 3, 5, 8, 13**
See also CA 73-76; 117; CANR 36; CBD; CN 1, 2, 3; DLB 191; EWL 3; MTCW 1; RGEL 2

Hannah, Barry 1942- .. **CLC 23, 38, 90, 270; SSC 94**
See also BPFB 2; CA 108; 110; CANR 43, 68, 113; CN 4, 5, 6, 7; CSW; DLB 6, 234; INT CA-110; MTCW 1; RGSF 2

Hannon, Ezra
See Hunter, Evan

Hansberry, Lorraine (Vivian)
1930-1965 ... **BLC 1:2, 2:2; CLC 17, 62; DC 2; TCLC 192**
See also AAYA 25; AFAW 1, 2; AMWS 4; BW 1, 3; CA 109; 25-28R; CABS 3; CAD; CANR 58; CDALB 1941-1968; CWD; DA; DA3; DAB; DAC; DAM DRAM, MST, MULT; DFS 2; DLB 7, 38; EWL 3; FL 1:6; FW; LAIT 4; MAL 5; MTCW 1, 2; MTFW 2005; RGAL 4; TUS

Hansen, Joseph 1923-2004 .... **CLC 38**
See also BPFB 2; CA 29-32R; 233; CAAS 17; CANR 16, 44, 66, 125; CMW 4; DLB 226; GLL 1; INT CANR-16

Hansen, Karen V. 1955- .... **CLC 65**
See also CA 149; CANR 102

Hansen, Martin A(lfred)
1909-1955 .... **TCLC 32**
See also CA 167; DLB 214; EWL 3

Hanson, Kenneth O(stlin) 1922- .... **CLC 13**
See also CA 53-56; CANR 7; CP 1, 2, 3, 4, 5

Hardwick, Elizabeth 1916-2007 .... **CLC 13**
See also AMWS 3; CA 5-8R; 267; CANR 3, 32, 70, 100, 139; CN 4, 5, 6; CSW; DA3; DAM NOV; DLB 6; MBL; MTCW 1, 2; MTFW 2005; TCLE 1:1

Hardwick, Elizabeth Bruce
See Hardwick, Elizabeth

Hardwick, Elizabeth Bruce
See Hardwick, Elizabeth

Hardy, Thomas 1840-1928 . **PC 8, 92; SSC 2, 60, 113; TCLC 4, 10, 18, 32, 48, 53, 72, 143, 153; WLC 3**
See also AAYA 69; BRW 6; BRWC 1, 2; BRWR 1; CA 104; 123; CDBLB 1890-1914; DA; DA3; DAB; DAC; DAM MST, NOV, POET; DLB 18, 19, 135, 284; EWL 3; EXPN; EXPP; LAIT 2; MTCW 1, 2; MTFW 2005; NFS 3, 11, 15, 19; PFS 3, 4, 18; RGEL 2; RGSF 2; TEA; WLIT 4

Hare, David 1947- . **CLC 29, 58, 136; DC 26**
See also BRWS 4; CA 97-100; CANR 39, 91; CBD; CD 5, 6; DFS 4, 7, 16; DLB 13, 310; MTCW 1; TEA

Harewood, John
See Van Druten, John (William)

Harford, Henry
See Hudson, W(illiam) H(enry)

Hargrave, Leonie
See Disch, Thomas M.

Hariri, Al- al-Qasim ibn 'Ali Abu Muhammad al-Basri
See al-Hariri, al-Qasim ibn 'Ali Abu Muhammad al-Basri

Harjo, Joy 1951- ..... **CLC 83; NNAL; PC 27**
See also AMWS 12; CA 114; CANR 35, 67, 91, 129; CP 6, 7; CWP; DAM MULT; DLB 120, 175, 342; EWL 3; MTCW 2; MTFW 2005; PFS 15; RGAL 4

Harlan, Louis R(udolph) 1922- .... **CLC 34**
See also CA 21-24R; CANR 25, 55, 80

Harling, Robert 1951(?)- .... **CLC 53**
See also CA 147

Harmon, William (Ruth) 1938- .... **CLC 38**
See also CA 33-36R; CANR 14, 32, 35; SATA 65

Kesey, Ken 1935-2001 .... **CLC 1, 3, 6, 11, 46, 64, 184; WLC 3**
See also AAYA 25; BG 1:3; BPFB 2; CA 1-4R; 204; CANR 22, 38, 66, 124; CDALB 1968-1988; CN 1, 2, 3, 4, 5, 6, 7; CPW; DA; DA3; DAB; DAC; DAM MST, NOV, POP; DLB 2, 16, 206; EWL 3; EXPN; LAIT 4; MAL 5; MTCW 1, 2; MTFW 2005; NFS 2; RGAL 4; SATA 66; SATA-Obit 131; TUS; YAW

Kesselring, Joseph (Otto) 1902-1967 .... **CLC 45**
See also CA 150; DAM DRAM, MST; DFS 20

Kessler, Jascha (Frederick) 1929- ...... **CLC 4**
See also CA 17-20R; CANR 8, 48, 111; CP 1

Kettelkamp, Larry (Dale) 1933- .... **CLC 12**
See also CA 29-32R; CANR 16; SAAS 3; SATA 2

Key, Ellen (Karolina Sofia) 1849-1926 .... **TCLC 65**
See also DLB 259

Keyber, Conny
See Fielding, Henry

Keyes, Daniel 1927- .... **CLC 80**
See also AAYA 23; BYA 11; CA 17-20R, 181; CAAE 181; CANR 10, 26, 54, 74; DA; DA3; DAC; DAM MST, NOV; EXPN; LAIT 4; MTCW 2; MTFW 2005; NFS 2; SATA 37; SFW 4

Keynes, John Maynard 1883-1946 .... **TCLC 64**
See also CA 114; 162, 163; DLBD 10; MTCW 2; MTFW 2005

Khanshendel, Chiron
See Rose, Wendy

Khayyam, Omar 1048-1131 ... **CMLC 11; PC 8**
See Omar Khayyam
See also DA3; DAM POET; WLIT 6

Kherdian, David 1931- .... **CLC 6, 9**
See also AAYA 42; CA 21-24R, 192; CAAE 192; CAAS 2; CANR 39, 78; CLR 24; JRDA; LAIT 3; MAICYA 1, 2; SATA 16, 74; SATA-Essay 125

Khlebnikov, Velimir .... **TCLC 20**
See Khlebnikov, Viktor Vladimirovich
See also DLB 295; EW 10; EWL 3; RGWL 2, 3

Khlebnikov, Viktor Vladimirovich 1885-1922
See Khlebnikov, Velimir
See also CA 117; 217

Khodasevich, V.F.
See Khodasevich, Vladislav

Khodasevich, Vladislav 1886-1939 .... **TCLC 15**
See also CA 115; DLB 317; EWL 3

Khodasevich, Vladislav Felitsianovich
See Khodasevich, Vladislav

Kidd, Sue Monk 1948- .... **CLC 267**
See also AAYA 72; CA 202; MTFW 2005; NFS 27

Kielland, Alexander Lange 1849-1906 .... **TCLC 5**
See also CA 104

Kiely, Benedict 1919-2007 . **CLC 23, 43; SSC 58**
See also CA 1-4R; 257; CANR 2, 84; CN 1, 2, 3, 4, 5, 6, 7; DLB 15, 319; TCLE 1:1

Kienzle, William X. 1928-2001 .... **CLC 25**
See also CA 93-96; 203; CAAS 1; CANR 9, 31, 59, 111; CMW 4; DA3; DAM POP; INT CANR-31; MSW; MTCW 1, 2; MTFW 2005

Kierkegaard, Soren 1813-1855 ..... **NCLC 34, 78, 125**
See also DLB 300; EW 6; LMFS 2; RGWL 3; TWA

Kieslowski, Krzysztof 1941-1996 .... **CLC 120**
See also CA 147; 151

Killens, John Oliver 1916-1987 ...... **BLC 2:2; CLC 10**
See also BW 2; CA 77-80; 123; CAAS 2; CANR 26; CN 1, 2, 3, 4; DLB 33; EWL 3

Killigrew, Anne 1660-1685 .... **LC 4, 73**
See also DLB 131

Killigrew, Thomas 1612-1683 .... **LC 57**
See also DLB 58; RGEL 2

Kim
See Simenon, Georges (Jacques Christian)

Kincaid, Jamaica 1949- . **BLC 1:2, 2:2; CLC 43, 68, 137, 234; SSC 72**
See also AAYA 13, 56; AFAW 2; AMWS 7; BRWS 7; BW 2, 3; CA 125; CANR 47, 59, 95, 133; CDALBS; CDWLB 3; CLR 63; CN 4, 5, 6, 7; DA3; DAM MULT, NOV; DLB 157, 227; DNFS 1; EWL 3; EXPS; FW; LATS 1:2; LMFS 2; MAL 5; MTCW 2; MTFW 2005; NCFS 1; NFS 3; SSFS 5, 7; TUS; WWE 1; YAW

King, Francis (Henry) 1923- .... **CLC 8, 53, 145**
See also CA 1-4R; CANR 1, 33, 86; CN 1, 2, 3, 4, 5, 6, 7; DAM NOV; DLB 15, 139; MTCW 1

King, Kennedy
See Brown, George Douglas

King, Martin Luther, Jr. 1929-1968 ... **BLC 1:2; CLC 83; WLCS**
See also BW 2, 3; CA 25-28; CANR 27, 44; CAP 2; DA; DA3; DAB; DAC; DAM MST, MULT; LAIT 5; LATS 1:2; MTCW 1, 2; MTFW 2005; SATA 14

King, Stephen 1947- .... **CLC 12, 26, 37, 61, 113, 228, 244; SSC 17, 55**
See also AAYA 1, 17; AMWS 5; BEST 90:1; BPFB 2; CA 61-64; CANR 1, 30, 52, 76, 119, 134, 168; CLR 124; CN 7; CPW; DA3; DAM NOV, POP; DLB 143; DLBY 1980; HGG; JRDA; LAIT 5; MTCW 1, 2; MTFW 2005; RGAL 4; SATA 9, 55, 161; SUFW 1, 2; WYAS 1; YAW

King, Stephen Edwin
See King, Stephen

King, Steve
See King, Stephen

King, Thomas 1943- .... **CLC 89, 171; NNAL**
See also CA 144; CANR 95, 175; CCA 1; CN 6, 7; DAC; DAM MULT; DLB 175, 334; SATA 96

King, Thomas Hunt
See King, Thomas

Kingman, Lee
See Natti, (Mary) Lee

Kingsley, Charles 1819-1875 .... **NCLC 35**
See also CLR 77; DLB 21, 32, 163, 178, 190; FANT; MAICYA 2; MAICYAS 1; RGEL 2; WCH; YABC 2

Kingsley, Henry 1830-1876 .... **NCLC 107**
See also DLB 21, 230; RGEL 2

Kingsley, Sidney 1906-1995 .... **CLC 44**
See also CA 85-88; 147; CAD; DFS 14, 19; DLB 7; MAL 5; RGAL 4

Kingsolver, Barbara 1955- .... **CLC 55, 81, 130, 216, 269**
See also AAYA 15; AMWS 7; CA 129; 134; CANR 60, 96, 133, 179; CDALBS; CN 7; CPW; CSW; DA3; DAM POP; DLB 206; INT CA-134; LAIT 5; MTCW 2; MTFW 2005; NFS 5, 10, 12, 24; RGAL 4; TCLE 1:1

Kingston, Maxine Hong 1940- .... **AAL; CLC 12, 19, 58, 121, 271; WLCS**
See also AAYA 8, 55; AMWS 5; BPFB 2; CA 69-72; CANR 13, 38, 74, 87, 128; CDALBS; CN 6, 7; DA3; DAM MULT,

NOV; DLB 173, 212, 312; DLBY 1980; EWL 3; FL 1:6; FW; INT CANR-13; LAIT 5; MAL 5; MBL; MTCW 1, 2; MTFW 2005; NFS 6; RGAL 4; SATA 53; SSFS 3; TCWW 2

Kingston, Maxine Ting Ting Hong
See Kingston, Maxine Hong

Kinnell, Galway 1927- ..... **CLC 1, 2, 3, 5, 13, 29, 129; PC 26**
See also AMWS 3; CA 9-12R; CANR 10, 34, 66, 116, 138, 175; CP 1, 2, 3, 4, 5, 6, 7; DLB 5, 342; DLBY 1987; EWL 3; INT CANR-34; MAL 5; MTCW 1, 2; MTFW 2005; PAB; PFS 9, 26; RGAL 4; TCLE 1:1; WP

Kinsella, Thomas 1928- .... **CLC 4, 19, 138; PC 69**
See also BRWS 5; CA 17-20R; CANR 15, 122; CP 1, 2, 3, 4, 5, 6, 7; DLB 27; EWL 3; MTCW 1, 2; MTFW 2005; RGEL 2; TEA

Kinsella, W.P. 1935- .... **CLC 27, 43, 166**
See also AAYA 7, 60; BPFB 2; CA 97-100, 222; CAAE 222; CAAS 7; CANR 21, 35, 66, 75, 129; CN 4, 5, 6, 7; CPW; DAC; DAM NOV, POP; FANT; INT CANR-21; LAIT 5; MTCW 1, 2; MTFW 2005; NFS 15; RGSF 2

Kinsey, Alfred C(harles) 1894-1956 .... **TCLC 91**
See also CA 115; 170; MTCW 2

Kipling, (Joseph) Rudyard 1865-1936 . **PC 3, 91; SSC 5, 54, 110; TCLC 8, 17, 167; WLC 3**
See also AAYA 32; BRW 6; BRWC 1, 2; BYA 4; CA 105; 120; CANR 33; CDBLB 1890-1914; CLR 39, 65; CWRI 5; DA; DA3; DAB; DAC; DAM MST, POET; DLB 19, 34, 141, 156, 330; EWL 3; EXPS; FANT; LAIT 3; LMFS 1; MAICYA 1, 2; MTCW 1, 2; MTFW 2005; NFS 21; PFS 22; RGEL 2; RGSF 2; SATA 100; SFW 4; SSFS 8, 21, 22; SUFW 1; TEA; WCH; WLIT 4; YABC 2

Kircher, Athanasius 1602-1680 .... **LC 121**
See also DLB 164

Kirk, Russell (Amos) 1918-1994 .. **TCLC 119**
See also AITN 1; CA 1-4R; 145; CAAS 9; CANR 1, 20, 60; HGG; INT CANR-20; MTCW 1, 2

Kirkham, Dinah
See Card, Orson Scott

Kirkland, Caroline M. 1801-1864 . **NCLC 85**
See also DLB 3, 73, 74, 250, 254; DLBD 13

Kirkup, James 1918- .... **CLC 1**
See also CA 1-4R; CAAS 4; CANR 2; CP 1, 2, 3, 4, 5, 6, 7; DLB 27; SATA 12

Kirkwood, James 1930(?)-1989 .... **CLC 9**
See also AITN 2; CA 1-4R; 128; CANR 6, 40; GLL 2

Kirsch, Sarah 1935- .... **CLC 176**
See also CA 178; CWW 2; DLB 75; EWL 3

Kirshner, Sidney
See Kingsley, Sidney

Kis, Danilo 1935-1989 .... **CLC 57**
See also CA 109; 118; 129; CANR 61; CD-WLB 4; DLB 181; EWL 3; MTCW 1; RGSF 2; RGWL 2, 3

Kissinger, Henry A(lfred) 1923- ..... **CLC 137**
See also CA 1-4R; CANR 2, 33, 66, 109; MTCW 1

Kittel, Frederick August
See Wilson, August

Kivi, Aleksis 1834-1872 .... **NCLC 30**

Kizer, Carolyn 1925- ..... **CLC 15, 39, 80; PC 66**
See also CA 65-68; CAAS 5; CANR 24, 70, 134; CP 1, 2, 3, 4, 5, 6, 7; CWP; DAM

Krleza, Miroslav 1893-1981 .... **CLC 8, 114**
See also CA 97-100; 105; CANR 50; CD-WLB 4; DLB 147; EW 11; RGWL 2, 3

Kroetsch, Robert (Paul) 1927- .... **CLC 5, 23, 57, 132**
See also CA 17-20R; CANR 8, 38; CCA 1; CN 2, 3, 4, 5, 6, 7; CP 6, 7; DAC; DAM POET; DLB 53; MTCW 1

Kroetz, Franz
See Kroetz, Franz Xaver

Kroetz, Franz Xaver 1946- .... **CLC 41**
See also CA 130; CANR 142; CWW 2; EWL 3

Kroker, Arthur (W.) 1945- .... **CLC 77**
See also CA 161

Kroniuk, Lisa
See Berton, Pierre (Francis de Marigny)

Kropotkin, Peter (Aleksieevich)
1842-1921 .... **TCLC 36**
See Kropotkin, Petr Alekseevich
See also CA 119; 219

Kropotkin, Petr Alekseevich
See Kropotkin, Peter (Aleksieevich)
See also DLB 277

Krotkov, Yuri 1917-1981 .... **CLC 19**
See also CA 102

Krumb
See Crumb, R.

Krumgold, Joseph (Quincy)
1908-1980 .... **CLC 12**
See also BYA 1, 2; CA 9-12R; 101; CANR 7; MAICYA 1, 2; SATA 1, 48; SATA-Obit 23; YAW

Krumwitz
See Crumb, R.

Krutch, Joseph Wood 1893-1970 ..... **CLC 24**
See also ANW; CA 1-4R; 25-28R; CANR 4; DLB 63, 206, 275

Krutzch, Gus
See Eliot, T(homas) S(tearns)

Krylov, Ivan Andreevich
1768(?)-1844 .... **NCLC 1**
See also DLB 150

Kubin, Alfred (Leopold Isidor)
1877-1959 .... **TCLC 23**
See also CA 112; 149; CANR 104; DLB 81

Kubrick, Stanley 1928-1999 .... **CLC 16; TCLC 112**
See also AAYA 30; CA 81-84; 177; CANR 33; DLB 26

Kueng, Hans
See Kung, Hans

Kumin, Maxine 1925- .... **CLC 5, 13, 28, 164; PC 15**
See also AITN 2; AMWS 4; ANW; CA 1-4R, 271; CAAE 271; CAAS 8; CANR 1, 21, 69, 115, 140; CP 2, 3, 4, 5, 6, 7; CWP; DA3; DAM POET; DLB 5; EWL 3; EXPP; MTCW 1, 2; MTFW 2005; PAB; PFS 18; SATA 12

Kundera, Milan 1929- .. **CLC 4, 9, 19, 32, 68, 115, 135, 234; SSC 24**
See also AAYA 2, 62; BPFB 2; CA 85-88; CANR 19, 52, 74, 144; CDWLB 4; CWW 2; DA3; DAM NOV; DLB 232; EW 13; EWL 3; MTCW 1, 2; MTFW 2005; NFS 18, 27; RGSF 2; RGWL 3; SSFS 10

Kunene, Mazisi 1930-2006 .... **CLC 85**
See also BW 1, 3; CA 125; 252; CANR 81; CP 1, 6, 7; DLB 117

Kunene, Mazisi Raymond
See Kunene, Mazisi

Kunene, Mazisi Raymond Fakazi Mngoni
See Kunene, Mazisi

Kung, Hans
See Kung, Hans

Kung, Hans 1928- .... **CLC 130**
See also CA 53-56; CANR 66, 134; MTCW 1, 2; MTFW 2005

Kunikida Doppo 1869(?)-1908
See Doppo, Kunikida
See also DLB 180; EWL 3

Kunitz, Stanley 1905-2006 ..... **CLC 6, 11, 14, 148; PC 19**
See also AMWS 3; CA 41-44R; 250; CANR 26, 57, 98; CP 1, 2, 3, 4, 5, 6, 7; DA3; DLB 48; INT CANR-26; MAL 5; MTCW 1, 2; MTFW 2005; PFS 11; RGAL 4

Kunitz, Stanley Jasspon
See Kunitz, Stanley

Kunze, Reiner 1933- .... **CLC 10**
See also CA 93-96; CWW 2; DLB 75; EWL 3

Kuprin, Aleksander Ivanovich
1870-1938 .... **TCLC 5**
See Kuprin, Aleksandr Ivanovich; Kuprin, Alexandr Ivanovich
See also CA 104; 182

Kuprin, Aleksandr Ivanovich
See Kuprin, Aleksander Ivanovich
See also DLB 295

Kuprin, Alexandr Ivanovich
See Kuprin, Aleksander Ivanovich
See also EWL 3

Kureishi, Hanif 1954- .. **CLC 64, 135; DC 26**
See also BRWS 11; CA 139; CANR 113; CBD; CD 5, 6; CN 6, 7; DLB 194, 245; GLL 2; IDFW 4; WLIT 4; WWE 1

Kurosawa, Akira 1910-1998 ..... **CLC 16, 119**
See also AAYA 11, 64; CA 101; 170; CANR 46; DAM MULT

Kushner, Tony 1956- .... **CLC 81, 203; DC 10**
See also AAYA 61; AMWS 9; CA 144; CAD; CANR 74, 130; CD 5, 6; DA3; DAM DRAM; DFS 5; DLB 228; EWL 3; GLL 1; LAIT 5; MAL 5; MTCW 2; MTFW 2005; RGAL 4; RGHL; SATA 160

Kuttner, Henry 1915-1958 .... **TCLC 10**
See also CA 107; 157; DLB 8; FANT; SCFW 1, 2; SFW 4

Kutty, Madhavi
See Das, Kamala

Kuzma, Greg 1944- .... **CLC 7**
See also CA 33-36R; CANR 70

Kuzmin, Mikhail (Alekseevich)
1872(?)-1936 .... **TCLC 40**
See also CA 170; DLB 295; EWL 3

Kyd, Thomas 1558-1594 .. **DC 3; LC 22, 125**
See also BRW 1; DAM DRAM; DFS 21; DLB 62; IDTP; LMFS 1; RGEL 2; TEA; WLIT 3

Kyprianos, Iossif
See Samarakis, Antonis

L. S.
See Stephen, Sir Leslie

Labe, Louise 1521-1566 .... **LC 120**
See also DLB 327

Labrunie, Gerard
See Nerval, Gerard de

La Bruyere, Jean de 1645-1696 .... **LC 17**
See also DLB 268; EW 3; GFL Beginnings to 1789

LaBute, Neil 1963- .... **CLC 225**
See also CA 240

Lacan, Jacques (Marie Emile)
1901-1981 .... **CLC 75**
See also CA 121; 104; DLB 296; EWL 3; TWA

Laclos, Pierre-Ambroise Francois
1741-1803 .... **NCLC 4, 87**
See also DLB 313; EW 4; GFL Beginnings to 1789; RGWL 2, 3

Lacolere, Francois
See Aragon, Louis

La Colere, Francois
See Aragon, Louis

La Deshabilleuse
See Simenon, Georges (Jacques Christian)

Lady Gregory
See Gregory, Lady Isabella Augusta (Persse)

Lady of Quality, A
See Bagnold, Enid

La Fayette, Marie-(Madelaine Pioche de la Vergne) 1634-1693 .... **LC 2, 144**
See Lafayette, Marie-Madeleine
See also GFL Beginnings to 1789; RGWL 2, 3

Lafayette, Marie-Madeleine
See La Fayette, Marie-(Madelaine Pioche de la Vergne)
See also DLB 268

Lafayette, Rene
See Hubbard, L. Ron

La Flesche, Francis 1857(?)-1932 ...... **NNAL**
See also CA 144; CANR 83; DLB 175

La Fontaine, Jean de 1621-1695 .... **LC 50**
See also DLB 268; EW 3; GFL Beginnings to 1789; MAICYA 1, 2; RGWL 2, 3; SATA 18

LaForet, Carmen 1921-2004 .... **CLC 219**
See also CA 246; CWW 2; DLB 322; EWL 3

LaForet Diaz, Carmen
See LaForet, Carmen

Laforgue, Jules 1860-1887 . **NCLC 5, 53; PC 14; SSC 20**
See also DLB 217; EW 7; GFL 1789 to the Present; RGWL 2, 3

Lagerkvist, Paer (Fabian)
1891-1974 .. **CLC 7, 10, 13, 54; SSC 12; TCLC 144**
See also CA 85-88; 49-52; DA3; DAM DRAM, NOV; DLB 259, 331; EW 10; EWL 3; MTCW 1, 2; MTFW 2005; RGSF 2; RGWL 2, 3; TWA

Lagerkvist, Par
See Lagerkvist, Paer (Fabian)

Lagerloef, Selma (Ottiliana Lovisa)
See Lagerlof, Selma (Ottiliana Lovisa)

Lagerlof, Selma (Ottiliana Lovisa)
1858-1940 .... **TCLC 4, 36**
See also CA 108; 188; CLR 7; DLB 259, 331; MTCW 2; RGWL 2, 3; SATA 15; SSFS 18

La Guma, Alex 1925-1985 .. **BLCS; CLC 19; TCLC 140**
See also AFW; BW 1, 3; CA 49-52; 118; CANR 25, 81; CDWLB 3; CN 1, 2, 3; CP 1; DAM NOV; DLB 117, 225; EWL 3; MTCW 1, 2; MTFW 2005; WLIT 2; WWE 1

Lahiri, Jhumpa 1967- .... **SSC 96**
See also AAYA 56; CA 193; CANR 134, 184; DLB 323; MTFW 2005; SSFS 19

Laidlaw, A. K.
See Grieve, C(hristopher) M(urray)

Lainez, Manuel Mujica
See Mujica Lainez, Manuel

Laing, R(onald) D(avid) 1927-1989 . **CLC 95**
See also CA 107; 129; CANR 34; MTCW 1

Laishley, Alex
See Booth, Martin

Lamartine, Alphonse (Marie Louis Prat) de
1790-1869 .... **NCLC 11; PC 16**
See also DAM POET; DLB 217; GFL 1789 to the Present; RGWL 2, 3

Lamb, Charles 1775-1834 ..... **NCLC 10, 113; SSC 112; WLC 3**
See also BRW 4; CDBLB 1789-1832; DA; DAB; DAC; DAM MST; DLB 93, 107, 163; RGEL 2; SATA 17; TEA

Lamb, Lady Caroline 1785-1828 ... **NCLC 38**
See also DLB 116

Lamb, Mary Ann 1764-1847 ...... **NCLC 125; SSC 112**
See also DLB 163; SATA 17

Lame Deer 1903(?)-1976 .... **NNAL**
See also CA 69-72
Lamming, George (William)
1927- . **BLC 1:2, 2:2; CLC 2, 4, 66, 144**
See also BW 2, 3; CA 85-88; CANR 26,
76; CDWLB 3; CN 1, 2, 3, 4, 5, 6, 7; CP
1; DAM MULT; DLB 125; EWL 3;
MTCW 1, 2; MTFW 2005; NFS 15;
RGEL 2
L'Amour, Louis 1908-1988 .... **CLC 25, 55**
See also AAYA 16; AITN 2; BEST 89:2;
BPFB 2; CA 1-4R; 125; CANR 3, 25, 40;
CPW; DA3; DAM NOV, POP; DLB 206;
DLBY 1980; MTCW 1, 2; MTFW 2005;
RGAL 4; TCWW 1, 2
Lampedusa, Giuseppe (Tomasi) di
See Tomasi di Lampedusa, Giuseppe
Lampman, Archibald 1861-1899 .. **NCLC 25,**
194
See also DLB 92; RGEL 2; TWA
Lancaster, Bruce 1896-1963 .... **CLC 36**
See also CA 9-10; CANR 70; CAP 1; SATA
9
Lanchester, John 1962- .... **CLC 99**
See also CA 194; DLB 267
Landau, Mark Alexandrovich
See Aldanov, Mark (Alexandrovich)
Landau-Aldanov, Mark Alexandrovich
See Aldanov, Mark (Alexandrovich)
Landis, Jerry
See Simon, Paul
Landis, John 1950- .... **CLC 26**
See also CA 112; 122; CANR 128
Landolfi, Tommaso 1908-1979 .... **CLC 11, 49**
See also CA 127; 117; DLB 177; EWL 3
Landon, Letitia Elizabeth
1802-1838 .... **NCLC 15**
See also DLB 96
Landor, Walter Savage
1775-1864 .... **NCLC 14**
See also BRW 4; DLB 93, 107; RGEL 2
Landwirth, Heinz
See Lind, Jakov
Lane, Patrick 1939- .... **CLC 25**
See also CA 97-100; CANR 54; CP 3, 4, 5,
6, 7; DAM POET; DLB 53; INT CA-97-
100
Lane, Rose Wilder 1887-1968 ...... **TCLC 177**
See also CA 102; CANR 63; SATA 29;
SATA-Brief 28; TCWW 2
Lang, Andrew 1844-1912 .... **TCLC 16**
See also CA 114; 137; CANR 85; CLR 101;
DLB 98, 141, 184; FANT; MAICYA 1, 2;
RGEL 2; SATA 16; WCH
Lang, Fritz 1890-1976 .... **CLC 20, 103**
See also AAYA 65; CA 77-80; 69-72;
CANR 30
Lange, John
See Crichton, Michael
Langer, Elinor 1939- .... **CLC 34**
See also CA 121
Langland, William 1332(?)-1400(?) .... **LC 19,**
120
See also BRW 1; DA; DAB; DAC; DAM
MST, POET; DLB 146; RGEL 2; TEA;
WLIT 3
Langstaff, Launcelot
See Irving, Washington
Lanier, Sidney 1842-1881 . **NCLC 6, 118; PC**
50
See also AMWS 1; DAM POET; DLB 64;
DLBD 13; EXPP; MAICYA 1; PFS 14;
RGAL 4; SATA 18
Lanyer, Aemilia 1569-1645 .... **LC 10, 30, 83;**
PC 60
See also DLB 121
Lao-Tzu
See Lao Tzu

Lao Tzu c. 6th cent. B.C.-3rd cent.
B.C. .... **CMLC 7**
Lapine, James (Elliot) 1949- .... **CLC 39**
See also CA 123; 130; CANR 54, 128; DFS
25; DLB 341; INT CA-130
Larbaud, Valery (Nicolas)
1881-1957 .... **TCLC 9**
See also CA 106; 152; EWL 3; GFL 1789
to the Present
Larcom, Lucy 1824-1893 .... **NCLC 179**
See also AMWS 13; DLB 221, 243
Lardner, Ring
See Lardner, Ring(gold) W(ilmer)
Lardner, Ring W., Jr.
See Lardner, Ring(gold) W(ilmer)
Lardner, Ring(gold) W(ilmer)
1885-1933 ..... **SSC 32, 118; TCLC 2, 14**
See also AMW; BPFB 2; CA 104; 131;
CDALB 1917-1929; DLB 11, 25, 86, 171;
DLBD 16; MAL 5; MTCW 1, 2; MTFW
2005; RGAL 4; RGSF 2; TUS
Laredo, Betty
See Codrescu, Andrei
Larkin, Maia
See Wojciechowska, Maia (Teresa)
Larkin, Philip (Arthur) 1922-1985 ... **CLC 3,**
5, 8, 9, 13, 18, 33, 39, 64; PC 21
See also BRWS 1; CA 5-8R; 117; CANR
24, 62; CDBLB 1960 to Present; CP 1, 2,
3, 4; DA3; DAB; DAM MST, POET;
DLB 27; EWL 3; MTCW 1, 2; MTFW
2005; PFS 3, 4, 12; RGEL 2
La Roche, Sophie von
1730-1807 .... **NCLC 121**
See also DLB 94
La Rochefoucauld, Francois
1613-1680 .... **LC 108**
See also DLB 268; EW 3; GFL Beginnings
to 1789; RGWL 2, 3
Larra (y Sanchez de Castro), Mariano Jose
de 1809-1837 .... **NCLC 17, 130**
Larsen, Eric 1941- .... **CLC 55**
See also CA 132
Larsen, Nella 1893(?)-1963 ... **BLC 1:2; CLC**
37; HR 1:3; TCLC 200
See also AFAW 1, 2; AMWS 18; BW 1;
CA 125; CANR 83; DAM MULT; DLB
51; FW; LATS 1:1; LMFS 2
Larson, Charles R(aymond) 1938-... **CLC 31**
See also CA 53-56; CANR 4, 121
Larson, Jonathan 1960-1996 .... **CLC 99**
See also AAYA 28; CA 156; DFS 23;
MTFW 2005
La Sale, Antoine de c. 1386-1460(?) . **LC 104**
See also DLB 208
Las Casas, Bartolome de
1474-1566 .... **HLCS; LC 31**
See Casas, Bartolome de las
See also DLB 318; LAW
Lasch, Christopher 1932-1994 .... **CLC 102**
See also CA 73-76; 144; CANR 25, 118;
DLB 246; MTCW 1, 2; MTFW 2005
Lasker-Schueler, Else 1869-1945 ... **TCLC 57**
See Lasker-Schuler, Else
See also CA 183; DLB 66, 124
Lasker-Schuler, Else
See Lasker-Schueler, Else
See also EWL 3
Laski, Harold J(oseph) 1893-1950 . **TCLC 79**
See also CA 188
Latham, Jean Lee 1902-1995 .... **CLC 12**
See also AITN 1; BYA 1; CA 5-8R; CANR
7, 84; CLR 50; MAICYA 1; SATA 2,
68; YAW
Latham, Mavis
See Clark, Mavis Thorpe
Lathen, Emma
See Hennissart, Martha

Lathrop, Francis
See Leiber, Fritz (Reuter, Jr.)
Lattany, Kristin
See Lattany, Kristin (Elaine Eggleston)
Hunter
Lattany, Kristin (Elaine Eggleston) Hunter
1931- .... **CLC 35**
See Hunter, Kristin
See also AITN 1; BW 1; BYA 3; CA 13-
16R; CANR 13, 108; CLR 3; CN 7; DLB
33; INT CANR-13; MAICYA 1, 2; SAAS
10; SATA 12, 132; YAW
Lattimore, Richmond (Alexander)
1906-1984 .... **CLC 3**
See also CA 1-4R; 112; CANR 1; CP 1, 2,
3; MAL 5
Laughlin, James 1914-1997 .... **CLC 49**
See also CA 21-24R; 162; CAAS 22; CANR
9, 47; CP 1, 2, 3, 4, 5, 6; DLB 48; DLBY
1996, 1997
Laurence, Jean Margaret Wemyss
See Laurence, Margaret
Laurence, Margaret 1926-1987 ..... **CLC 3, 6,**
13, 50, 62; SSC 7
See also BYA 13; CA 5-8R; 121; CANR
33; CN 1, 2, 3, 4; DAC; DAM MST; DLB
53; EWL 3; FW; MTCW 1, 2; MTFW
2005; NFS 11; RGEL 2; RGSF 2; SATA-
Obit 50; TCWW 2
Laurent, Antoine 1952- .... **CLC 50**
Lauscher, Hermann
See Hesse, Hermann
Lautreamont 1846-1870 .... **NCLC 12, 194;**
SSC 14
See Lautreamont, Isidore Lucien Ducasse
See also GFL 1789 to the Present; RGWL
2, 3
Lautreamont, Isidore Lucien Ducasse
See Lautreamont
See also DLB 217
Lavater, Johann Kaspar
1741-1801 .... **NCLC 142**
See also DLB 97
Laverty, Donald
See Blish, James (Benjamin)
Lavin, Mary 1912-1996 . **CLC 4, 18, 99; SSC**
4, 67
See also CA 9-12R; 151; CANR 33; CN 1,
2, 3, 4, 5, 6; DLB 15, 319; FW; MTCW
1; RGEL 2; RGSF 2; SSFS 23
Lavond, Paul Dennis
See Kornbluth, C(yril) M.; Pohl, Frederik
Lawes, Henry 1596-1662 .... **LC 113**
See also DLB 126
Lawler, Ray
See Lawler, Raymond Evenor
See also DLB 289
Lawler, Raymond Evenor 1922- .... **CLC 58**
See Lawler, Ray
See also CA 103; CD 5, 6; RGEL 2
Lawrence, D(avid) H(erbert Richards)
1885-1930 .... **PC 54; SSC 4, 19, 73;**
TCLC 2, 9, 16, 33, 48, 61, 93; WLC 3
See also BPFB 2; BRW 7; BRWR 2; CA
104; 121; CANR 131; CDBLB 1914-
1945; DA; DA3; DAB; DAC; DAM MST,
NOV, POET; DLB 10, 19, 36, 98, 162,
195; EWL 3; EXPP; EXPS; GLL 1; LAIT
2, 3; MTCW 1, 2; MTFW 2005; NFS 18,
26; PFS 6; RGEL 2; RGSF 2; SSFS 2, 6;
TEA; WLIT 4; WP
Lawrence, T(homas) E(dward)
1888-1935 .... **TCLC 18, 204**
See also BRWS 2; CA 115; 167; DLB 195
Lawrence of Arabia
See Lawrence, T(homas) E(dward)

Lawson, Henry (Archibald Hertzberg)
1867-1922 .... **SSC 18; TCLC 27**
See also CA 120; 181; DLB 230; RGEL 2;
RGSF 2

Lawton, Dennis
See Faust, Frederick (Schiller)

Laxness, Halldor (Kiljan)
See Gudjonsson, Halldor Kiljan
See also CWW 2; DLB 331

Layamon fl. c. 1200- .... **CMLC 10, 105**
See also DLB 146; RGEL 2

Laye, Camara 1928-1980 .. **BLC 1:2; CLC 4,
38**
See Camara Laye
See also AFW; BW 1; CA 85-88; 97-100;
CANR 25; DAM MULT; MTCW 1, 2;
WLIT 2

Layton, Irving 1912-2006 ..... **CLC 2, 15, 164**
See also CA 1-4R; 247; CANR 2, 33, 43,
66, 129; CP 1, 2, 3, 4, 5, 6, 7; DAC; DAM
MST, POET; DLB 88; EWL 3; MTCW 1,
2; PFS 12; RGEL 2

Layton, Irving Peter
See Layton, Irving

Lazarus, Emma 1849-1887 ...... **NCLC 8, 109**

Lazarus, Felix
See Cable, George Washington

Lazarus, Henry
See Slavitt, David R.

Lea, Joan
See Neufeld, John (Arthur)

Leacock, Stephen (Butler)
1869-1944 .... **SSC 39; TCLC 2**
See also CA 104; 141; CANR 80; DAC;
DAM MST; DLB 92; EWL 3; MTCW 2;
MTFW 2005; RGEL 2; RGSF 2

Lead, Jane Ward 1623-1704 .... **LC 72**
See also DLB 131

Leapor, Mary 1722-1746 .... **LC 80; PC 85**
See also DLB 109

Lear, Edward 1812-1888 ..... **NCLC 3; PC 65**
See also AAYA 48; BRW 5; CLR 1, 75;
DLB 32, 163, 166; MAICYA 1, 2; RGEL
2; SATA 18, 100; WCH; WP

Lear, Norman (Milton) 1922- .... **CLC 12**
See also CA 73-76

Least Heat-Moon, William
See Trogdon, William (Lewis)
See also ANW

Leautaud, Paul 1872-1956 .... **TCLC 83**
See also CA 203; DLB 65; GFL 1789 to the
Present

Leavis, F(rank) R(aymond)
1895-1978 .... **CLC 24**
See also BRW 7; CA 21-24R; 77-80; CANR
44; DLB 242; EWL 3; MTCW 1, 2;
RGEL 2

Leavitt, David 1961- .... **CLC 34**
See also CA 116; 122; CANR 50, 62, 101,
134, 177; CPW; DA3; DAM POP; DLB
130; GLL 1; INT CA-122; MAL 5;
MTCW 2; MTFW 2005

Leblanc, Maurice (Marie Emile)
1864-1941 .... **TCLC 49**
See also CA 110; CMW 4

Lebowitz, Fran(ces Ann) 1951(?)- ... **CLC 11,
36**
See also CA 81-84; CANR 14, 60, 70; INT
CANR-14; MTCW 1

Lebrecht, Peter
See Tieck, (Johann) Ludwig

le Carre, John
See le Carre, John

le Carre, John 1931- .... **CLC 9, 15**
See also AAYA 42; BEST 89:4; BPFB 2;
BRWS 2; CA 5-8R; CANR 13, 33, 59,
107, 132, 172; CDBLB 1960 to Present;
CMW 4; CN 1, 2, 3, 4, 5, 6, 7; CPW;
DA3; DAM POP; DLB 87; EWL 3; MSW;
MTCW 1, 2; MTFW 2005; RGEL 2; TEA

Le Clezio, J. M.G. 1940- .... **CLC 31, 155**
See also CA 116; 128; CANR 147; CWW
2; DLB 83; EWL 3; GFL 1789 to the
Present; RGSF 2

Le Clezio, Jean Marie Gustave
See Le Clezio, J. M.G.

Leconte de Lisle, Charles-Marie-Rene
1818-1894 .... **NCLC 29**
See also DLB 217; EW 6; GFL 1789 to the
Present

Le Coq, Monsieur
See Simenon, Georges (Jacques Christian)

Leduc, Violette 1907-1972 .... **CLC 22**
See also CA 13-14; 33-36R; CANR 69;
CAP 1; EWL 3; GFL 1789 to the Present;
GLL 1

Ledwidge, Francis 1887(?)-1917 .... **TCLC 23**
See also CA 123; 203; DLB 20

Lee, Andrea 1953- .... **BLC 1:2; CLC 36**
See also BW 1, 3; CA 125; CANR 82;
DAM MULT

Lee, Andrew
See Auchincloss, Louis

Lee, Chang-rae 1965- .... **CLC 91, 268**
See also CA 148; CANR 89; CN 7; DLB
312; LATS 1:2

Lee, Don L.
See Madhubuti, Haki R.

Lee, George W(ashington)
1894-1976 .... **BLC 1:2; CLC 52**
See also BW 1; CA 125; CANR 83; DAM
MULT; DLB 51

Lee, Harper 1926- ... **CLC 12, 60, 194; WLC
4**
See also AAYA 13; AMWS 8; BPFB 2;
BYA 3; CA 13-16R; CANR 51, 128;
CDALB 1941-1968; CSW; DA; DA3;
DAB; DAC; DAM MST, NOV; DLB 6;
EXPN; LAIT 3; MAL 5; MTCW 1, 2;
MTFW 2005; NFS 2; SATA 11; WYA;
YAW

Lee, Helen Elaine 1959(?)- .... **CLC 86**
See also CA 148

Lee, John .... **CLC 70**

Lee, Julian
See Latham, Jean Lee

Lee, Larry
See Lee, Lawrence

Lee, Laurie 1914-1997 .... **CLC 90**
See also CA 77-80; 158; CANR 33, 73; CP
1, 2, 3, 4, 5, 6; CPW; DAB; DAM POP;
DLB 27; MTCW 1; RGEL 2

Lee, Lawrence 1941-1990 .... **CLC 34**
See also CA 131; CANR 43

Lee, Li-Young 1957- .... **CLC 164; PC 24**
See also AMWS 15; CA 153; CANR 118;
CP 6, 7; DLB 165, 312; LMFS 2; PFS 11,
15, 17

Lee, Manfred B. 1905-1971 .... **CLC 11**
See also CA 1-4R; 29-32R; CANR 2, 150;
CMW 4; DLB 137

Lee, Manfred Bennington
See Lee, Manfred B.

Lee, Nathaniel 1645(?)-1692 .... **LC 103**
See also DLB 80; RGEL 2

Lee, Nelle Harper
See Lee, Harper

Lee, Shelton Jackson
See Lee, Spike

Lee, Sophia 1750-1824 .... **NCLC 191**
See also DLB 39

Lee, Spike 1957(?)- .... **BLCS; CLC 105**
See also AAYA 4, 29; BW 2, 3; CA 125;
CANR 42, 164; DAM MULT

Lee, Stan 1922- .... **CLC 17**
See also AAYA 5, 49; CA 108; 111; CANR
129; INT CA-111; MTFW 2005

Lee, Tanith 1947- .... **CLC 46**
See also AAYA 15; CA 37-40R; CANR 53,
102, 145, 170; DLB 261; FANT; SATA 8,
88, 134, 185; SFW 4; SUFW 1, 2; YAW

Lee, Vernon
See Paget, Violet

Lee, William
See Burroughs, William S.

Lee, Willy
See Burroughs, William S.

Lee-Hamilton, Eugene (Jacob)
1845-1907 .... **TCLC 22**
See also CA 117; 234

Leet, Judith 1935- .... **CLC 11**
See also CA 187

Le Fanu, Joseph Sheridan
1814-1873 .... **NCLC 9, 58; SSC 14, 84**
See also CMW 4; DA3; DAM POP; DLB
21, 70, 159, 178; GL 3; HGG; RGEL 2;
RGSF 2; SUFW 1

Leffland, Ella 1931- .... **CLC 19**
See also CA 29-32R; CANR 35, 78, 82;
DLBY 1984; INT CANR-35; SATA 65;
SSFS 24

Leger, Alexis
See Leger, (Marie-Rene Auguste) Alexis
Saint-Leger

**Leger, (Marie-Rene Auguste) Alexis
Saint-Leger** 1887-1975 .. **CLC 4, 11, 46;
PC 23**
See Perse, Saint-John
See also CA 13-16R; 61-64; CANR 43;
DAM POET; EW 10; EWL 3; GFL 1789
to the Present; MTCW 1; RGWL 2

Leger, Saintleger
See Leger, (Marie-Rene Auguste) Alexis
Saint-Leger

Le Guin, Ursula K. 1929- ...... **CLC 8, 13, 22,
45, 71, 136; SSC 12, 69**
See also AAYA 9, 27; AITN 1; BPFB 2;
BYA 5, 8, 11, 14; CA 21-24R; CANR 9,
32, 52, 74, 132; CDALB 1968-1988; CLR
3, 28, 91; CN 2, 3, 4, 5, 6, 7; CPW; DA3;
DAB; DAC; DAM MST, POP; DLB 8,
52, 256, 275; EXPS; FANT; FW; INT
CANR-32; JRDA; LAIT 5; MAICYA 1,
2; MAL 5; MTCW 1, 2; MTFW 2005;
NFS 6, 9; SATA 4, 52, 99, 149, 194;
SCFW 1, 2; SFW 4; SSFS 2; SUFW 1, 2;
WYA; YAW

Lehmann, Rosamond (Nina)
1901-1990 .... **CLC 5**
See also CA 77-80; 131; CANR 8, 73; CN
1, 2, 3, 4; DLB 15; MTCW 2; RGEL 2;
RHW

Leiber, Fritz (Reuter, Jr.)
1910-1992 .... **CLC 25**
See also AAYA 65; BPFB 2; CA 45-48; 139;
CANR 2, 40, 86; CN 2, 3, 4, 5; DLB 8;
FANT; HGG; MTCW 1, 2; MTFW 2005;
SATA 45; SATA-Obit 73; SCFW 1, 2;
SFW 4; SUFW 1, 2

Leibniz, Gottfried Wilhelm von
1646-1716 .... **LC 35**
See also DLB 168

Leino, Eino
See Lonnbohm, Armas Eino Leopold

Leiris, Michel (Julien) 1901-1990 ..... **CLC 61**
See also CA 119; 128; 132; EWL 3; GFL
1789 to the Present

Leithauser, Brad 1953- .... **CLC 27**
See also CA 107; CANR 27, 81, 171; CP 5,
6, 7; DLB 120, 282

le Jars de Gournay, Marie
See de Gournay, Marie le Jars

Lelchuk, Alan 1938- .... **CLC 5**
See also CA 45-48; CAAS 20; CANR 1,
70, 152; CN 3, 4, 5, 6, 7

Lem, Stanislaw 1921-2006 ..... **CLC 8, 15, 40, 149**
See also AAYA 75; CA 105; 249; CAAS 1;
CANR 32; CWW 2; MTCW 1; SCFW 1,
2; SFW 4

Lemann, Nancy (Elise) 1956- .... **CLC 39**
See also CA 118; 136; CANR 121

Lemonnier, (Antoine Louis) Camille
1844-1913 .... **TCLC 22**
See also CA 121

Lenau, Nikolaus 1802-1850 .... **NCLC 16**

L'Engle, Madeleine 1918-2007 .... **CLC 12**
See also AAYA 28; AITN 2; BPFB 2; BYA
2, 4, 5, 7; CA 1-4R; 264; CANR 3, 21,
39, 66, 107; CLR 1, 14, 57; CPW; CWRI
5; DA3; DAM POP; DLB 52; JRDA;
MAICYA 1, 2; MTCW 1, 2; MTFW 2005;
SAAS 15; SATA 1, 27, 75, 128; SATA-
Obit 186; SFW 4; WYA; YAW

L'Engle, Madeleine Camp Franklin
See L'Engle, Madeleine

Lengyel, Jozsef 1896-1975 .... **CLC 7**
See also CA 85-88; 57-60; CANR 71;
RGSF 2

Lenin 1870-1924 .... **TCLC 67**
See also CA 121; 168

Lenin, N.
See Lenin

Lenin, Nikolai
See Lenin

Lenin, V. I.
See Lenin

Lenin, Vladimir I.
See Lenin

Lenin, Vladimir Ilyich
See Lenin

Lennon, John (Ono) 1940-1980 .. **CLC 12, 35**
See also CA 102; SATA 114

Lennox, Charlotte Ramsay
1729(?)-1804 .... **NCLC 23, 134**
See also DLB 39; RGEL 2

Lentricchia, Frank, Jr.
See Lentricchia, Frank

Lentricchia, Frank 1940- .... **CLC 34**
See also CA 25-28R; CANR 19, 106, 148;
DLB 246

Lenz, Gunter .... **CLC 65**

Lenz, Jakob Michael Reinhold
1751-1792 .... **LC 100**
See also DLB 94; RGWL 2, 3

Lenz, Siegfried 1926- .... **CLC 27; SSC 33**
See also CA 89-92; CANR 80, 149; CWW
2; DLB 75; EWL 3; RGSF 2; RGWL 2, 3

Leon, David
See Jacob, (Cyprien-)Max

Leonard, Dutch
See Leonard, Elmore

Leonard, Elmore 1925- .... **CLC 28, 34, 71, 120, 222**
See also AAYA 22, 59; AITN 1; BEST 89:1,
90:4; BPFB 2; CA 81-84; CANR 12, 28,
53, 76, 96, 133, 176; CMW 4; CN 5, 6, 7;
CPW; DA3; DAM POP; DLB 173, 226;
INT CANR-28; MSW; MTCW 1, 2;
MTFW 2005; RGAL 4; SATA 163;
TCWW 1, 2

Leonard, Elmore John, Jr.
See Leonard, Elmore

Leonard, Hugh
See Byrne, John Keyes

Leonov, Leonid (Maximovich)
1899-1994 .... **CLC 92**
See Leonov, Leonid Maksimovich
See also CA 129; CANR 76; DAM NOV;
EWL 3; MTCW 1, 2; MTFW 2005

Leonov, Leonid Maksimovich
See Leonov, Leonid (Maximovich)
See also DLB 272

Leopardi, (Conte) Giacomo
1798-1837 .... **NCLC 22, 129; PC 37**
See also EW 5; RGWL 2, 3; WLIT 7; WP

Le Reveler
See Artaud, Antonin (Marie Joseph)

Lerman, Eleanor 1952- .... **CLC 9**
See also CA 85-88; CANR 69, 124, 184

Lerman, Rhoda 1936- .... **CLC 56**
See also CA 49-52; CANR 70

Lermontov, Mikhail Iur'evich
See Lermontov, Mikhail Yuryevich
See also DLB 205

Lermontov, Mikhail Yuryevich
1814-1841 .... **NCLC 5, 47, 126; PC 18**
See Lermontov, Mikhail Iur'evich
See also EW 6; RGWL 2, 3; TWA

Leroux, Gaston 1868-1927 .... **TCLC 25**
See also CA 108; 136; CANR 69; CMW 4;
MTFW 2005; NFS 20; SATA 65

Lesage, Alain-Rene 1668-1747 .... **LC 2, 28**
See also DLB 313; EW 3; GFL Beginnings
to 1789; RGWL 2, 3

Leskov, N(ikolai) S(emenovich) 1831-1895
See Leskov, Nikolai (Semyonovich)

Leskov, Nikolai (Semyonovich)
1831-1895 ... **NCLC 25, 174; SSC 34, 96**
See Leskov, Nikolai Semyonovich

Leskov, Nikolai Semenovich
See Leskov, Nikolai (Semyonovich)
See also DLB 238

Lesser, Milton
See Marlowe, Stephen

Lessing, Doris 1919- .. **CLC 1, 2, 3, 6, 10, 15, 22, 40, 94, 170, 254; SSC 6, 61; WLCS**
See also AAYA 57; AFW; BRWS 1; CA
9-12R; CAAS 14; CANR 33, 54, 76, 122,
179; CBD; CD 5, 6; CDBLB 1960 to
Present; CN 1, 2, 3, 4, 5, 6, 7; CWD; DA;
DA3; DAB; DAC; DAM MST, NOV;
DFS 20; DLB 15, 139; DLBY 1985; EWL
3; EXPS; FL 1:6; FW; LAIT 4; MTCW 1,
2; MTFW 2005; NFS 27; RGEL 2; RGSF
2; SFW 4; SSFS 1, 12, 20, 26; TEA;
WLIT 2, 4

Lessing, Doris May
See Lessing, Doris

Lessing, Gotthold Ephraim
1729-1781 .... **DC 26; LC 8, 124, 162**
See also CDWLB 2; DLB 97; EW 4; RGWL
2, 3

Lester, Julius 1939- .... **BLC 2:2**
See also AAYA 12, 51; BW 2; BYA 3, 9,
11, 12; CA 17-20R; CANR 8, 23, 43, 129,
174; CLR 2, 41; JRDA; MAICYA 1, 2;
MAICYAS 1; MTFW 2005; SATA 12, 74,
112, 157; YAW

Lester, Richard 1932- .... **CLC 20**

Levenson, Jay .... **CLC 70**

Lever, Charles (James)
1806-1872 .... **NCLC 23**
See also DLB 21; RGEL 2

Leverson, Ada Esther
1862(?)-1933(?) .... **TCLC 18**
See also CA 117; 202; DLB 153; RGEL 2

Levertov, Denise 1923-1997 .. **CLC 1, 2, 3, 5, 8, 15, 28, 66; PC 11**
See also AMWS 3; CA 1-4R, 178; 163;
CAAE 178; CAAS 19; CANR 3, 29, 50,
108; CDALBS; CP 1, 2, 3, 4, 5, 6; CWP;
DAM POET; DLB 5, 165, 342; EWL 3;
EXPP; FW; INT CANR-29; MAL 5;
MTCW 1, 2; PAB; PFS 7, 17; RGAL 4;
RGHL; TUS; WP

Levi, Carlo 1902-1975 .... **TCLC 125**
See also CA 65-68; 53-56; CANR 10; EWL
3; RGWL 2, 3

Levi, Jonathan .... **CLC 76**
See also CA 197

Levi, Peter (Chad Tigar)
1931-2000 .... **CLC 41**
See also CA 5-8R; 187; CANR 34, 80; CP
1, 2, 3, 4, 5, 6, 7; DLB 40

Levi, Primo 1919-1987 ...... **CLC 37, 50; SSC 12; TCLC 109**
See also CA 13-16R; 122; CANR 12, 33,
61, 70, 132, 171; DLB 177, 299; EWL 3;
MTCW 1, 2; MTFW 2005; RGHL;
RGWL 2, 3; WLIT 7

Levin, Ira 1929-2007 .... **CLC 3, 6**
See also CA 21-24R; 266; CANR 17, 44,
74, 139; CMW 4; CN 1, 2, 3, 4, 5, 6, 7;
CPW; DA3; DAM POP; HGG; MTCW 1,
2; MTFW 2005; SATA 66; SATA-Obit
187; SFW 4

Levin, Ira Marvin
See Levin, Ira

Levin, Ira Marvin
See Levin, Ira

Levin, Meyer 1905-1981 .... **CLC 7**
See also AITN 1; CA 9-12R; 104; CANR
15; CN 1, 2, 3; DAM POP; DLB 9, 28;
DLBY 1981; MAL 5; RGHL; SATA 21;
SATA-Obit 27

Levine, Albert Norman
See Levine, Norman
See also CN 7

Levine, Norman 1923-2005 .... **CLC 54**
See Levine, Albert Norman
See also CA 73-76; 240; CAAS 23; CANR
14, 70; CN 1, 2, 3, 4, 5, 6; CP 1; DLB 88

Levine, Norman Albert
See Levine, Norman

Levine, Philip 1928- .. **CLC 2, 4, 5, 9, 14, 33, 118; PC 22**
See also AMWS 5; CA 9-12R; CANR 9,
37, 52, 116, 156; CP 1, 2, 3, 4, 5, 6, 7;
DAM POET; DLB 5; EWL 3; MAL 5;
PFS 8

Levinson, Deirdre 1931- .... **CLC 49**
See also CA 73-76; CANR 70

Levi-Strauss, Claude 1908- .... **CLC 38**
See also CA 1-4R; CANR 6, 32, 57; DLB
242; EWL 3; GFL 1789 to the Present;
MTCW 1, 2; TWA

Levitin, Sonia 1934- .... **CLC 17**
See also AAYA 13, 48; CA 29-32R; CANR
14, 32, 79, 182; CLR 53; JRDA; MAI-
CYA 1, 2; SAAS 2; SATA 4, 68, 119, 131,
192; SATA-Essay 131; YAW

Levon, O. U.
See Kesey, Ken

Levy, Amy 1861-1889 .... **NCLC 59, 203**
See also DLB 156, 240

Lewees, John
See Stockton, Francis Richard

Lewes, George Henry 1817-1878 ... **NCLC 25**
See also DLB 55, 144

Lewis, Alun 1915-1944 .... **SSC 40; TCLC 3**
See also BRW 7; CA 104; 188; DLB 20,
162; PAB; RGEL 2

Lewis, C. Day
See Day Lewis, C(ecil)

Lewis, Cecil Day
See Day Lewis, C(ecil)

Lewis, Clive Staples
See Lewis, C.S.

Lewis, C.S. 1898-1963 ... **CLC 1, 3, 6, 14, 27, 124; WLC 4**
See also AAYA 3, 39; BPFB 2; BRWS 3;
BYA 15, 16; CA 81-84; CANR 33, 71,
132; CDBLB 1945-1960; CLR 3, 27, 109;
CWRI 5; DA; DA3; DAB; DAC; DAM
MST, NOV, POP; DLB 15, 100, 160, 255;
EWL 3; FANT; JRDA; LMFS 2; MAI-

Author Index

Malthus, Thomas Robert
1766-1834 .... **NCLC 145**
See also DLB 107, 158; RGEL 2

Malzberg, Barry N(athaniel) 1939- ... **CLC 7**
See also CA 61-64; CAAS 4; CANR 16;
CMW 4; DLB 8; SFW 4

Mamet, David 1947- .. **CLC 9, 15, 34, 46, 91,**
166; DC 4, 24
See also AAYA 3, 60; AMWS 14; CA 81-
84; CABS 3; CAD; CANR 15, 41, 67, 72,
129, 172; CD 5, 6; DA3; DAM DRAM;
DFS 2, 3, 6, 12, 15; DLB 7; EWL 3;
IDFW 4; MAL 5; MTCW 1, 2; MTFW
2005; RGAL 4

Mamet, David Alan
See Mamet, David

Mamoulian, Rouben (Zachary)
1897-1987 .... **CLC 16**
See also CA 25-28R; 124; CANR 85

Mandelshtam, Osip
See Mandelstam, Osip (Emilievich)
See also EW 10; EWL 3; RGWL 2, 3

Mandelstam, Osip (Emilievich)
1891(?)-1943(?) .... **PC 14; TCLC 2, 6**
See Mandelshtam, Osip
See also CA 104; 150; MTCW 2; TWA

Mander, (Mary) Jane 1877-1949 ... **TCLC 31**
See also CA 162; RGEL 2

Mandeville, Bernard 1670-1733 .... **LC 82**
See also DLB 101

Mandeville, Sir John fl. 1350- ...... **CMLC 19**
See also DLB 146

Mandiargues, Andre Pieyre de
See Pieyre de Mandiargues, Andre

Mandrake, Ethel Belle
See Thurman, Wallace (Henry)

Mangan, James Clarence
1803-1849 .... **NCLC 27**
See also BRWS 13; RGEL 2

Maniere, J.-E.
See Giraudoux, Jean(-Hippolyte)

Mankiewicz, Herman (Jacob)
1897-1953 .... **TCLC 85**
See also CA 120; 169; DLB 26; IDFW 3, 4

Manley, (Mary) Delariviere
1672(?)-1724 .... **LC 1, 42**
See also DLB 39, 80; RGEL 2

Mann, Abel
See Creasey, John

Mann, Emily 1952- .... **DC 7**
See also CA 130; CAD; CANR 55; CD 5,
6; CWD; DLB 266

Mann, (Luiz) Heinrich 1871-1950 ... **TCLC 9**
See also CA 106; 164, 181; DLB 66, 118;
EW 8; EWL 3; RGWL 2, 3

Mann, (Paul) Thomas 1875-1955 . **SSC 5, 80,**
82; TCLC 2, 8, 14, 21, 35, 44, 60, 168;
WLC 4
See also BPFB 2; CA 104; 128; CANR 133;
CDWLB 2; DA; DA3; DAB; DAC; DAM
MST, NOV; DLB 66, 331; EW 9; EWL 3;
GLL 1; LATS 1:1; LMFS 1; MTCW 1, 2;
MTFW 2005; NFS 17; RGSF 2; RGWL
2, 3; SSFS 4, 9; TWA

Mannheim, Karl 1893-1947 .... **TCLC 65**
See also CA 204

Manning, David
See Faust, Frederick (Schiller)

Manning, Frederic 1882-1935 .... **TCLC 25**
See also CA 124; 216; DLB 260

Manning, Olivia 1915-1980 .... **CLC 5, 19**
See also CA 5-8R; 101; CANR 29; CN 1,
2; EWL 3; FW; MTCW 1; RGEL 2

Mannyng, Robert c. 1264-c.
1340 .... **CMLC 83**
See also DLB 146

Mano, D. Keith 1942- .... **CLC 2, 10**
See also CA 25-28R; CAAS 6; CANR 26,
57; DLB 6

Mansfield, Katherine
See Beauchamp, Kathleen Mansfield

Manso, Peter 1940- .... **CLC 39**
See also CA 29-32R; CANR 44, 156

Mantecon, Juan Jimenez
See Jimenez (Mantecon), Juan Ramon

Mantel, Hilary 1952- .... **CLC 144**
See also CA 125; CANR 54, 101, 161; CN
5, 6, 7; DLB 271; RHW

Mantel, Hilary Mary
See Mantel, Hilary

Manton, Peter
See Creasey, John

Man Without a Spleen, A
See Chekhov, Anton (Pavlovich)

Manzano, Juan Franciso
1797(?)-1854 .... **NCLC 155**

Manzoni, Alessandro 1785-1873 ... **NCLC 29,**
98
See also EW 5; RGWL 2, 3; TWA; WLIT 7

Map, Walter 1140-1209 .... **CMLC 32**

Mapu, Abraham (ben Jekutiel)
1808-1867 .... **NCLC 18**

Mara, Sally
See Queneau, Raymond

Maracle, Lee 1950- .... **NNAL**
See also CA 149

Marat, Jean Paul 1743-1793 .... **LC 10**

Marcel, Gabriel Honore 1889-1973 . **CLC 15**
See also CA 102; 45-48; EWL 3; MTCW 1,
2

March, William .... **TCLC 96**
See Campbell, William Edward March
See also CA 216; DLB 9, 86, 316; MAL 5

Marchbanks, Samuel
See Davies, Robertson

Marchi, Giacomo
See Bassani, Giorgio

Marcus Aurelius
See Aurelius, Marcus
See also AW 2

Marcuse, Herbert 1898-1979 .... **TCLC 207**
See also CA 188; 89-92; DLB 242

Marguerite
See de Navarre, Marguerite

Marguerite d'Angouleme
See de Navarre, Marguerite
See also GFL Beginnings to 1789

Marguerite de Navarre
See de Navarre, Marguerite
See also RGWL 2, 3

Margulies, Donald 1954- .... **CLC 76**
See also AAYA 57; CA 200; CD 6; DFS 13;
DLB 228

Marias, Javier 1951- .... **CLC 239**
See also CA 167; CANR 109, 139; DLB
322; HW 2; MTFW 2005

Marie de France c. 12th cent. - ...... **CMLC 8,**
111; PC 22
See also DLB 208; FW; RGWL 2, 3

Marie de l'Incarnation 1599-1672 ...... **LC 10**

Marier, Captain Victor
See Griffith, D.W.

Mariner, Scott
See Pohl, Frederik

Marinetti, Filippo Tommaso
1876-1944 .... **TCLC 10**
See also CA 107; DLB 114, 264; EW 9;
EWL 3; WLIT 7

Marivaux, Pierre Carlet de Chamblain de
1688-1763 .... **DC 7; LC 4, 123**
See also DLB 314; GFL Beginnings to
1789; RGWL 2, 3; TWA

Markandaya, Kamala
See Taylor, Kamala

Markfield, Wallace (Arthur)
1926-2002 .... **CLC 8**
See also CA 69-72; 208; CAAS 3; CN 1, 2,
3, 4, 5, 6, 7; DLB 2, 28; DLBY 2002

Markham, Edwin 1852-1940 .... **TCLC 47**
See also CA 160; DLB 54, 186; MAL 5;
RGAL 4

Markham, Robert
See Amis, Kingsley

Marks, J.
See Highwater, Jamake (Mamake)

Marks-Highwater, J.
See Highwater, Jamake (Mamake)

Markson, David M. 1927- .... **CLC 67**
See also AMWS 17; CA 49-52; CANR 1,
91, 158; CN 5, 6

Markson, David Merrill
See Markson, David M.

Marlatt, Daphne (Buckle) 1942- .... **CLC 168**
See also CA 25-28R; CANR 17, 39; CN 6,
7; CP 4, 5, 6, 7; CWP; DLB 60; FW

Marley, Bob
See Marley, Robert Nesta

Marley, Robert Nesta 1945-1981 ...... **CLC 17**
See also CA 107; 103

Marlowe, Christopher 1564-1593 . **DC 1; LC**
22, 47, 117; PC 57; WLC 4
See also BRW 1; BRWR 1; CDBLB Before
1660; DA; DA3; DAB; DAC; DAM
DRAM, MST; DFS 1, 5, 13, 21; DLB 62;
EXPP; LMFS 1; PFS 22; RGEL 2; TEA;
WLIT 3

Marlowe, Stephen 1928-2008 .... **CLC 70**
See also CA 13-16R; 269; CANR 6, 55;
CMW 4; SFW 4

Marmion, Shakerley 1603-1639 .... **LC 89**
See also DLB 58; RGEL 2

Marmontel, Jean-Francois 1723-1799 .. **LC 2**
See also DLB 314

Maron, Monika 1941- .... **CLC 165**
See also CA 201

Marot, Clement c. 1496-1544 .... **LC 133**
See also DLB 327; GFL Beginnings to 1789

Marquand, John P(hillips)
1893-1960 .... **CLC 2, 10**
See also AMW; BPFB 2; CA 85-88; CANR
73; CMW 4; DLB 9, 102; EWL 3; MAL
5; MTCW 2; RGAL 4

Marques, Rene 1919-1979 .. **CLC 96; HLC 2**
See also CA 97-100; 85-88; CANR 78;
DAM MULT; DLB 305; EWL 3; HW 1,
2; LAW; RGSF 2

Marquez, Gabriel Garcia
See Garcia Marquez, Gabriel

Marquis, Don(ald Robert Perry)
1878-1937 .... **TCLC 7**
See also CA 104; 166; DLB 11, 25; MAL
5; RGAL 4

Marquis de Sade
See Sade, Donatien Alphonse Francois

Marric, J. J.
See Creasey, John

Marryat, Frederick 1792-1848 .... **NCLC 3**
See also DLB 21, 163; RGEL 2; WCH

Marsden, James
See Creasey, John

Marsh, Edward 1872-1953 .... **TCLC 99**

Marsh, (Edith) Ngaio 1895-1982 .. **CLC 7, 53**
See also CA 9-12R; CANR 6, 58; CMW 4;
CN 1, 2, 3; CPW; DAM POP; DLB 77;
MSW; MTCW 1, 2; RGEL 2; TEA

Marshall, Allen
See Westlake, Donald E.

Marshall, Garry 1934- .... **CLC 17**
See also AAYA 3; CA 111; SATA 60

22; DLB 10, 36, 77, 100, 162, 195; EWL 3; LAIT 3; MTCW 1, 2; MTFW 2005; NFS 23; RGEL 2; RGSF 2; SATA 54; SSFS 17

Maugham, William Somerset
See Maugham, W(illiam) Somerset

Maupassant, (Henri Rene Albert) Guy de 1850-1893 . **NCLC 1, 42, 83; SSC 1, 64; WLC 4**
See also BYA 14; DA; DA3; DAB; DAC; DAM MST; DLB 123; EW 7; EXPS; GFL 1789 to the Present; LAIT 2; LMFS 1; RGSF 2; RGWL 2, 3; SSFS 4, 21; SUFW; TWA

Maupin, Armistead 1944- .... **CLC 95**
See also CA 125; 130; CANR 58, 101, 183; CPW; DA3; DAM POP; DLB 278; GLL 1; INT CA-130; MTCW 2; MTFW 2005

Maupin, Armistead Jones, Jr.
See Maupin, Armistead

Maurhut, Richard
See Traven, B.

Mauriac, Claude 1914-1996 .... **CLC 9**
See also CA 89-92; 152; CWW 2; DLB 83; EWL 3; GFL 1789 to the Present

Mauriac, Francois (Charles) 1885-1970 .... **CLC 4, 9, 56; SSC 24**
See also CA 25-28; CAP 2; DLB 65, 331; EW 10; EWL 3; GFL 1789 to the Present; MTCW 1, 2; MTFW 2005; RGWL 2, 3; TWA

Mavor, Osborne Henry 1888-1951 .. **TCLC 3**
See also CA 104; DLB 10; EWL 3

Maxwell, Glyn 1962- .... **CLC 238**
See also CA 154; CANR 88, 183; CP 6, 7; PFS 23

Maxwell, William (Keepers, Jr.) 1908-2000 .... **CLC 19**
See also AMWS 8; CA 93-96; 189; CANR 54, 95; CN 1, 2, 3, 4, 5, 6, 7; DLB 218, 278; DLBY 1980; INT CA-93-96; MAL 5; SATA-Obit 128

May, Elaine 1932- .... **CLC 16**
See also CA 124; 142; CAD; CWD; DLB 44

Mayakovski, Vladimir (Vladimirovich) 1893-1930 .... **TCLC 4, 18**
See Maiakovskii, Vladimir; Mayakovsky, Vladimir
See also CA 104; 158; EWL 3; MTCW 2; MTFW 2005; SFW 4; TWA

Mayakovsky, Vladimir
See Mayakovski, Vladimir (Vladimirovich)
See also EW 11; WP

Mayhew, Henry 1812-1887 .... **NCLC 31**
See also DLB 18, 55, 190

Mayle, Peter 1939(?)- .... **CLC 89**
See also CA 139; CANR 64, 109, 168

Maynard, Joyce 1953- .... **CLC 23**
See also CA 111; 129; CANR 64, 169

Mayne, William (James Carter) 1928- .... **CLC 12**
See also AAYA 20; CA 9-12R; CANR 37, 80, 100; CLR 25, 123; FANT; JRDA; MAICYA 1, 2; MAICYAS 1; SAAS 11; SATA 6, 68, 122; SUFW 2; YAW

Mayo, Jim
See L'Amour, Louis

Maysles, Albert 1926- .... **CLC 16**
See also CA 29-32R

Maysles, David 1932-1987 .... **CLC 16**
See also CA 191

Mazer, Norma Fox 1931- .... **CLC 26**
See also AAYA 5, 36; BYA 1, 8; CA 69-72; CANR 12, 32, 66, 129; CLR 23; JRDA; MAICYA 1, 2; SAAS 1; SATA 24, 67, 105, 168; WYA; YAW

Mazzini, Guiseppe 1805-1872 .... **NCLC 34**

McAlmon, Robert (Menzies) 1895-1956 .... **TCLC 97**
See also CA 107; 168; DLB 4, 45; DLBD 15; GLL 1

McAuley, James Phillip 1917-1976 .. **CLC 45**
See also CA 97-100; CP 1, 2; DLB 260; RGEL 2

McBain, Ed
See Hunter, Evan

McBrien, William (Augustine) 1930- .... **CLC 44**
See also CA 107; CANR 90

McCabe, Patrick 1955- .... **CLC 133**
See also BRWS 9; CA 130; CANR 50, 90, 168; CN 6, 7; DLB 194

McCaffrey, Anne 1926- .... **CLC 17**
See also AAYA 6, 34; AITN 2; BEST 89:2; BPFB 2; BYA 5; CA 25-28R, 227; CAAE 227; CANR 15, 35, 55, 96, 169; CLR 49, 130; CPW; DA3; DAM NOV, POP; DLB 8; JRDA; MAICYA 1, 2; MTCW 1, 2; MTFW 2005; SAAS 11; SATA 8, 70, 116, 152; SATA-Essay 152; SFW 4; SUFW 2; WYA; YAW

McCaffrey, Anne Inez
See McCaffrey, Anne

McCall, Nathan 1955(?)- .... **CLC 86**
See also AAYA 59; BW 3; CA 146; CANR 88, 186

McCann, Arthur
See Campbell, John W(ood, Jr.)

McCann, Edson
See Pohl, Frederik

McCarthy, Charles
See McCarthy, Cormac

McCarthy, Charles, Jr.
See McCarthy, Cormac

McCarthy, Cormac 1933- .... **CLC 4, 57, 101, 204**
See also AAYA 41; AMWS 8; BPFB 2; CA 13-16R; CANR 10, 42, 69, 101, 161, 171; CN 6, 7; CPW; CSW; DA3; DAM POP; DLB 6, 143, 256; EWL 3; LATS 1:2; MAL 5; MTCW 2; MTFW 2005; TCLE 1:2; TCWW 2

McCarthy, Mary (Therese) 1912-1989 .. **CLC 1, 3, 5, 14, 24, 39, 59; SSC 24**
See also AMW; BPFB 2; CA 5-8R; 129; CANR 16, 50, 64; CN 1, 2, 3, 4; DA3; DLB 2; DLBY 1981; EWL 3; FW; INT CANR-16; MAL 5; MBL; MTCW 1, 2; MTFW 2005; RGAL 4; TUS

McCartney, James Paul
See McCartney, Paul

McCartney, Paul 1942- .... **CLC 12, 35**
See also CA 146; CANR 111

McCauley, Stephen (D.) 1955- .... **CLC 50**
See also CA 141

McClaren, Peter .... **CLC 70**

McClure, Michael (Thomas) 1932- ... **CLC 6, 10**
See also BG 1:3; CA 21-24R; CAD; CANR 17, 46, 77, 131; CD 5, 6; CP 1, 2, 3, 4, 5, 6, 7; DLB 16; WP

McCorkle, Jill (Collins) 1958- .... **CLC 51**
See also CA 121; CANR 113; CSW; DLB 234; DLBY 1987; SSFS 24

McCourt, Frank 1930- .... **CLC 109**
See also AAYA 61; AMWS 12; CA 157; CANR 97, 138; MTFW 2005; NCFS 1

McCourt, James 1941- .... **CLC 5**
See also CA 57-60; CANR 98, 152, 186

McCourt, Malachy 1931- .... **CLC 119**
See also SATA 126

McCoy, Edmund
See Gardner, John

McCoy, Horace (Stanley) 1897-1955 .... **TCLC 28**
See also AMWS 13; CA 108; 155; CMW 4; DLB 9

McCrae, John 1872-1918 .... **TCLC 12**
See also CA 109; DLB 92; PFS 5

McCreigh, James
See Pohl, Frederik

McCullers, (Lula) Carson (Smith) 1917-1967 .... **CLC 1, 4, 10, 12, 48, 100; SSC 9, 24, 99; TCLC 155; WLC 4**
See also AAYA 21; AMW; AMWC 2; BPFB 2; CA 5-8R; 25-28R; CABS 1, 3; CANR 18, 132; CDALB 1941-1968; DA; DA3; DAB; DAC; DAM MST, NOV; DFS 5, 18; DLB 2, 7, 173, 228; EWL 3; EXPS; FW; GLL 1; LAIT 3, 4; MAL 5; MBL; MTCW 1, 2; MTFW 2005; NFS 6, 13; RGAL 4; RGSF 2; SATA 27; SSFS 5; TUS; YAW

McCulloch, John Tyler
See Burroughs, Edgar Rice

McCullough, Colleen 1937- ...... **CLC 27, 107**
See also AAYA 36; BPFB 2; CA 81-84; CANR 17, 46, 67, 98, 139; CPW; DA3; DAM NOV, POP; MTCW 1, 2; MTFW 2005; RHW

McCunn, Ruthanne Lum 1946- .... **AAL**
See also CA 119; CANR 43, 96; DLB 312; LAIT 2; SATA 63

McDermott, Alice 1953- .... **CLC 90**
See also AMWS 18; CA 109; CANR 40, 90, 126, 181; CN 7; DLB 292; MTFW 2005; NFS 23

McElroy, Joseph 1930- .... **CLC 5, 47**
See also CA 17-20R; CANR 149; CN 3, 4, 5, 6, 7

McElroy, Joseph Prince
See McElroy, Joseph

McEwan, Ian 1948- ... **CLC 13, 66, 169, 269; SSC 106**
See also BEST 90:4; BRWS 4; CA 61-64; CANR 14, 41, 69, 87, 132, 179; CN 3, 4, 5, 6, 7; DAM NOV; DLB 14, 194, 319, 326; HGG; MTCW 1, 2; MTFW 2005; RGSF 2; SUFW 2; TEA

McEwan, Ian Russell
See McEwan, Ian

McFadden, David 1940- .... **CLC 48**
See also CA 104; CP 1, 2, 3, 4, 5, 6, 7; DLB 60; INT CA-104

McFarland, Dennis 1950- .... **CLC 65**
See also CA 165; CANR 110, 179

McGahern, John 1934-2006 .... **CLC 5, 9, 48, 156; SSC 17**
See also CA 17-20R; 249; CANR 29, 68, 113; CN 1, 2, 3, 4, 5, 6, 7; DLB 14, 231, 319; MTCW 1

McGinley, Patrick (Anthony) 1937- . **CLC 41**
See also CA 120; 127; CANR 56; INT CA-127

McGinley, Phyllis 1905-1978 .... **CLC 14**
See also CA 9-12R; 77-80; CANR 19; CP 1, 2; CWRI 5; DLB 11, 48; MAL 5; PFS 9, 13; SATA 2, 44; SATA-Obit 24

McGinniss, Joe 1942- .... **CLC 32**
See also AITN 2; BEST 89:2; CA 25-28R; CANR 26, 70, 152; CPW; DLB 185; INT CANR-26

McGivern, Maureen Daly
See Daly, Maureen

McGivern, Maureen Patricia Daly
See Daly, Maureen

McGrath, Patrick 1950- .... **CLC 55**
See also CA 136; CANR 65, 148; CN 5, 6, 7; DLB 231; HGG; SUFW 2

Millin, Sarah Gertrude 1889-1968 ... **CLC 49**
See also CA 102; 93-96; DLB 225; EWL 3
Milne, A. A. 1882-1956 .... **TCLC 6, 88**
See also BRWS 5; CA 104; 133; CLR 1,
26, 108; CMW 4; CWRI 5; DA3; DAB;
DAC; DAM MST; DLB 10, 77, 100, 160;
FANT; MAICYA 1, 2; MTCW 1, 2;
MTFW 2005; RGEL 2; SATA 100; WCH;
YABC 1
Milne, Alan Alexander
See Milne, A. A.
Milner, Ron(ald) 1938-2004 .. **BLC 1:3; CLC
56**
See also AITN 1; BW 1; CA 73-76; 230;
CAD; CANR 24, 81; CD 5, 6; DAM
MULT; DLB 38; MAL 5; MTCW 1
Milnes, Richard Monckton
1809-1885 .... **NCLC 61**
See also DLB 32, 184
Milosz, Czeslaw 1911-2004 .... **CLC 5, 11, 22,
31, 56, 82, 253; PC 8; WLCS**
See also AAYA 62; CA 81-84; 230; CANR
23, 51, 91, 126; CDWLB 4; CWW 2;
DA3; DAM MST, POET; DLB 215, 331;
EW 13; EWL 3; MTCW 1, 2; MTFW
2005; PFS 16, 29; RGHL; RGWL 2, 3
Milton, John 1608-1674 ..... **LC 9, 43, 92; PC
19, 29; WLC 4**
See also AAYA 65; BRW 2; BRWR 2; CD-
BLB 1660-1789; DA; DA3; DAB; DAC;
DAM MST, POET; DLB 131, 151, 281;
EFS 2; EXPP; LAIT 1; PAB; PFS 3, 17;
RGEL 2; TEA; WLIT 3; WP
Min, Anchee 1957- .... **CLC 86**
See also CA 146; CANR 94, 137; MTFW
2005
Minehaha, Cornelius
See Wedekind, Frank
Miner, Valerie 1947- .... **CLC 40**
See also CA 97-100; CANR 59, 177; FW;
GLL 2
Minimo, Duca
See D'Annunzio, Gabriele
Minot, Susan (Anderson) 1956- ...... **CLC 44,
159**
See also AMWS 6; CA 134; CANR 118;
CN 6, 7
Minus, Ed 1938- .... **CLC 39**
See also CA 185
Mirabai 1498(?)-1550(?) .... **LC 143; PC 48**
See also PFS 24
Miranda, Javier
See Bioy Casares, Adolfo
Mirbeau, Octave 1848-1917 .... **TCLC 55**
See also CA 216; DLB 123, 192; GFL 1789
to the Present
Mirikitani, Janice 1942- .... **AAL**
See also CA 211; DLB 312; RGAL 4
Mirk, John (?)-c. 1414 .... **LC 105**
See also DLB 146
Miro (Ferrer), Gabriel (Francisco Victor)
1879-1930 .... **TCLC 5**
See also CA 104; 185; DLB 322; EWL 3
Misharin, Alexandr .... **CLC 59**
Mishima, Yukio
See Hiraoka, Kimitake
Mishima Yukio
See Hiraoka, Kimitake
Miss C. L. F.
See Grimke, Charlotte L(ottie) Forten
Mister X
See Hoch, Edward D.
Mistral, Frederic 1830-1914 .... **TCLC 51**
See also CA 122; 213; DLB 331; GFL 1789
to the Present
Mistral, Gabriela
See Godoy Alcayaga, Lucila

Mistry, Rohinton 1952- ... **CLC 71, 196; SSC
73**
See also BRWS 10; CA 141; CANR 86,
114; CCA 1; CN 6, 7; DAC; DLB 334;
SSFS 6
Mitchell, Clyde
See Ellison, Harlan; Silverberg, Robert
Mitchell, Emerson Blackhorse Barney
1945- .... **NNAL**
See also CA 45-48
Mitchell, James Leslie 1901-1935 .... **TCLC 4**
See also BRWS 14; CA 104; 188; DLB 15;
RGEL 2
Mitchell, Joni 1943- .... **CLC 12**
See also CA 112; CCA 1
Mitchell, Joseph (Quincy)
1908-1996 .... **CLC 98**
See also CA 77-80; 152; CANR 69; CN 1,
2, 3, 4, 5, 6; CSW; DLB 185; DLBY 1996
Mitchell, Margaret (Munnerlyn)
1900-1949 .... **TCLC 11, 170**
See also AAYA 23; BPFB 2; BYA 1; CA
109; 125; CANR 55, 94; CDALBS; DA3;
DAM NOV, POP; DLB 9; LAIT 2; MAL
5; MTCW 1, 2; MTFW 2005; NFS 9;
RGAL 4; RHW; TUS; WYAS 1; YAW
Mitchell, Peggy
See Mitchell, Margaret (Munnerlyn)
Mitchell, S(ilas) Weir 1829-1914 .... **TCLC 36**
See also CA 165; DLB 202; RGAL 4
Mitchell, W(illiam) O(rmond)
1914-1998 .... **CLC 25**
See also CA 77-80; 165; CANR 15, 43; CN
1, 2, 3, 4, 5, 6; DAC; DAM MST; DLB
88; TCLE 1:2
Mitchell, William (Lendrum)
1879-1936 .... **TCLC 81**
See also CA 213
Mitford, Mary Russell 1787-1855 ... **NCLC 4**
See also DLB 110, 116; RGEL 2
Mitford, Nancy 1904-1973 .... **CLC 44**
See also BRWS 10; CA 9-12R; CN 1; DLB
191; RGEL 2
Miyamoto, (Chujo) Yuriko
1899-1951 .... **TCLC 37**
See Miyamoto Yuriko
See also CA 170, 174
Miyamoto Yuriko
See Miyamoto, (Chujo) Yuriko
See also DLB 180
Miyazawa, Kenji 1896-1933 .... **TCLC 76**
See Miyazawa Kenji
See also CA 157; RGWL 3
Miyazawa Kenji
See Miyazawa, Kenji
See also EWL 3
Mizoguchi, Kenji 1898-1956 .... **TCLC 72**
See also CA 167
Mo, Timothy (Peter) 1950- .... **CLC 46, 134**
See also CA 117; CANR 128; CN 5, 6, 7;
DLB 194; MTCW 1; WLIT 4; WWE 1
Modarressi, Taghi (M.) 1931-1997 ... **CLC 44**
See also CA 121; 134; INT CA-134
Modiano, Patrick (Jean) 1945- .... **CLC 18,
218**
See also CA 85-88; CANR 17, 40, 115;
CWW 2; DLB 83, 299; EWL 3; RGHL
Mofolo, Thomas (Mokopu)
1875(?)-1948 .... **BLC 1:3; TCLC 22**
See also AFW; CA 121; 153; CANR 83;
DAM MULT; DLB 225; EWL 3; MTCW
2; MTFW 2005; WLIT 2
Mohr, Nicholasa 1938- .... **CLC 12; HLC 2**
See also AAYA 8, 46; CA 49-52; CANR 1,
32, 64; CLR 22; DAM MULT; DLB 145;
HW 1, 2; JRDA; LAIT 5; LLW; MAICYA
2; MAICYAS 1; RGAL 4; SAAS 8; SATA
8, 97; SATA-Essay 113; WYA; YAW

Moi, Toril 1953- .... **CLC 172**
See also CA 154; CANR 102; FW
Mojtabai, A(nn) G(race) 1938- ..... **CLC 5, 9,
15, 29**
See also CA 85-88; CANR 88
Moliere 1622-1673 ..... **DC 13; LC 10, 28, 64,
125, 127; WLC 4**
See also DA; DA3; DAB; DAC; DAM
DRAM, MST; DFS 13, 18, 20; DLB 268;
EW 3; GFL Beginnings to 1789; LATS
1:1; RGWL 2, 3; TWA
Molin, Charles
See Mayne, William (James Carter)
Molnar, Ferenc 1878-1952 .... **TCLC 20**
See also CA 109; 153; CANR 83; CDWLB
4; DAM DRAM; DLB 215; EWL 3;
RGWL 2, 3
Momaday, N. Scott 1934- ...... **CLC 2, 19, 85,
95, 160; NNAL; PC 25; WLCS**
See also AAYA 11, 64; AMWS 4; ANW;
BPFB 2; BYA 12; CA 25-28R; CANR 14,
34, 68, 134; CDALBS; CN 2, 3, 4, 5, 6,
7; CPW; DA; DA3; DAB; DAC; DAM
MST, MULT, NOV, POP; DLB 143, 175,
256; EWL 3; EXPP; INT CANR-14;
LAIT 4; LATS 1:2; MAL 5; MTCW 1, 2;
MTFW 2005; NFS 10; PFS 2, 11; RGAL
4; SATA 48; SATA-Brief 30; TCWW 1,
2; WP; YAW
Monette, Paul 1945-1995 .... **CLC 82**
See also AMWS 10; CA 139; 147; CN 6;
GLL 1
Monroe, Harriet 1860-1936 .... **TCLC 12**
See also CA 109; 204; DLB 54, 91
Monroe, Lyle
See Heinlein, Robert A.
Montagu, Elizabeth 1720-1800 .... **NCLC 7,
117**
See also FW
Montagu, Mary (Pierrepont) Wortley
1689-1762 .... **LC 9, 57; PC 16**
See also DLB 95, 101; FL 1:1; RGEL 2
Montagu, W. H.
See Coleridge, Samuel Taylor
Montague, John (Patrick) 1929- ..... **CLC 13,
46**
See also CA 9-12R; CANR 9, 69, 121; CP
1, 2, 3, 4, 5, 6, 7; DLB 40; EWL 3;
MTCW 1; PFS 12; RGEL 2; TCLE 1:2
Montaigne, Michel (Eyquem) de
1533-1592 .... **LC 8, 105; WLC 4**
See also DA; DAB; DAC; DAM MST;
DLB 327; EW 2; GFL Beginnings to
1789; LMFS 1; RGWL 2, 3; TWA
Montale, Eugenio 1896-1981 ... **CLC 7, 9, 18;
PC 13**
See also CA 17-20R; 104; CANR 30; DLB
114, 331; EW 11; EWL 3; MTCW 1; PFS
22; RGWL 2, 3; TWA; WLIT 7
Montesquieu, Charles-Louis de Secondat
1689-1755 .... **LC 7, 69**
See also DLB 314; EW 3; GFL Beginnings
to 1789; TWA
Montessori, Maria 1870-1952 ...... **TCLC 103**
See also CA 115; 147
Montgomery, (Robert) Bruce
1921(?)-1978 .... **CLC 22**
See also CA 179; 104; CMW 4; DLB 87;
MSW
Montgomery, L(ucy) M(aud)
1874-1942 .... **TCLC 51, 140**
See also AAYA 12; BYA 1; CA 108; 137;
CLR 8, 91; DA3; DAM MST; DLB
92; DLBD 14; JRDA; MAICYA 1, 2;
MTCW 2; MTFW 2005; RGEL 2; SATA
100; TWA; WCH; WYA; YABC 1
Montgomery, Marion, Jr. 1925- .... **CLC 7**
See also AITN 1; CA 1-4R; CANR 3, 48,
162; CSW; DLB 6

Montgomery, Marion H. 1925-
See Montgomery, Marion, Jr.

Montgomery, Max
See Davenport, Guy (Mattison, Jr.)

Montherlant, Henry (Milon) de
1896-1972 .... **CLC 8, 19**
See also CA 85-88; 37-40R; DAM DRAM;
DLB 72, 321; EW 11; EWL 3; GFL 1789
to the Present; MTCW 1

Monty Python
See Chapman, Graham; Cleese, John
(Marwood); Gilliam, Terry; Idle, Eric;
Jones, Terence Graham Parry; Palin,
Michael

Moodie, Susanna (Strickland)
1803-1885 .... **NCLC 14, 113**
See also DLB 99

Moody, Hiram
See Moody, Rick

Moody, Hiram F. III
See Moody, Rick

Moody, Minerva
See Alcott, Louisa May

Moody, Rick 1961- .... **CLC 147**
See also CA 138; CANR 64, 112, 179;
MTFW 2005

Moody, William Vaughan
1869-1910 .... **TCLC 105**
See also CA 110; 178; DLB 7, 54; MAL 5;
RGAL 4

Mooney, Edward 1951- .... **CLC 25**
See also CA 130

Mooney, Ted
See Mooney, Edward

Moorcock, Michael 1939- ...... **CLC 5, 27, 58,**
236
See also AAYA 26; CA 45-48; CAAS 5;
CANR 2, 17, 38, 64, 122; CN 5, 6, 7;
DLB 14, 231, 261, 319; FANT; MTCW 1,
2; MTFW 2005; SATA 93, 166; SCFW 1,
2; SFW 4; SUFW 1, 2

Moorcock, Michael John
See Moorcock, Michael

Moorcock, Michael John
See Moorcock, Michael

Moore, Al
See Moore, Alan

Moore, Alan 1953- .... **CLC 230**
See also AAYA 51; CA 204; CANR 138,
184; DLB 261; MTFW 2005; SFW 4

Moore, Brian 1921-1999 ... **CLC 1, 3, 5, 7, 8,**
19, 32, 90
See also BRWS 9; CA 1-4R; 174; CANR 1,
25, 42, 63; CCA 1; CN 1, 2, 3, 4, 5, 6;
DAB; DAC; DAM MST; DLB 251; EWL
3; FANT; MTCW 1, 2; MTFW 2005;
RGEL 2

Moore, Edward
See Muir, Edwin

Moore, G. E. 1873-1958 .... **TCLC 89**
See also DLB 262

Moore, George Augustus
1852-1933 .... **SSC 19; TCLC 7**
See also BRW 6; CA 104; 177; DLB 10,
18, 57, 135; EWL 3; RGEL 2; RGSF 2

Moore, Lorrie
See Moore, Marie Lorena

Moore, Marianne (Craig)
1887-1972 .... **CLC 1, 2, 4, 8, 10, 13, 19,**
47; PC 4, 49; WLCS
See also AMW; CA 1-4R; 33-36R; CANR
3, 61; CDALB 1929-1941; CP 1; DA;
DA3; DAB; DAC; DAM MST, POET;
DLB 45; DLBD 7; EWL 3; EXPP; FL 1:6;
MAL 5; MBL; MTCW 1, 2; MTFW 2005;
PAB; PFS 14, 17; RGAL 4; SATA 20;
TUS; WP

Moore, Marie Lorena 1957- ...... **CLC 39, 45,**
68, 165
See also AMWS 10; CA 116; CANR 39,
83, 139; CN 5, 6, 7; DLB 234; MTFW
2005; SSFS 19

Moore, Michael 1954- .... **CLC 218**
See also AAYA 53; CA 166; CANR 150

Moore, Thomas 1779-1852 .... **NCLC 6, 110**
See also DLB 96, 144; RGEL 2

Moorhouse, Frank 1938- .... **SSC 40**
See also CA 118; CANR 92; CN 3, 4, 5, 6,
7; DLB 289; RGSF 2

Mora, Pat 1942- .... **HLC 2**
See also AMWS 13; CA 129; CANR 57,
81, 112, 171; CLR 58; DAM MULT; DLB
209; HW 1, 2; LLW; MAICYA 2; MTFW
2005; SATA 92, 134, 186

Moraga, Cherríe 1952- ... **CLC 126, 250; DC**
22
See also CA 131; CANR 66, 154; DAM
MULT; DLB 82, 249; FW; GLL 1; HW 1,
2; LLW

Morand, Paul 1888-1976 .... **CLC 41; SSC 22**
See also CA 184; 69-72; DLB 65; EWL 3

Morante, Elsa 1918-1985 .... **CLC 8, 47**
See also CA 85-88; 117; CANR 35; DLB
177; EWL 3; MTCW 1, 2; MTFW 2005;
RGHL; RGWL 2, 3; WLIT 7

Moravia, Alberto
See Pincherle, Alberto

Morck, Paul
See Rolvaag, O.E.

More, Hannah 1745-1833 ...... **NCLC 27, 141**
See also DLB 107, 109, 116, 158; RGEL 2

More, Henry 1614-1687 .... **LC 9**
See also DLB 126, 252

More, Sir Thomas 1478(?)-1535 ... **LC 10, 32,**
140
See also BRWC 1; BRWS 7; DLB 136, 281;
LMFS 1; RGEL 2; TEA

Moreas, Jean
See Papadiamantopoulos, Johannes

Moreton, Andrew Esq.
See Defoe, Daniel

Moreton, Lee
See Boucicault, Dion

Morgan, Berry 1919-2002 .... **CLC 6**
See also CA 49-52; 208; DLB 6

Morgan, Claire
See Highsmith, Patricia

Morgan, Edwin 1920- .... **CLC 31**
See also BRWS 9; CA 5-8R; CANR 3, 43,
90; CP 1, 2, 3, 4, 5, 6, 7; DLB 27

Morgan, Edwin George
See Morgan, Edwin

Morgan, (George) Frederick
1922-2004 .... **CLC 23**
See also CA 17-20R; 224; CANR 21, 144;
CP 2, 3, 4, 5, 6, 7

Morgan, Harriet
See Mencken, H(enry) L(ouis)

Morgan, Jane
See Cooper, James Fenimore

Morgan, Janet 1945- .... **CLC 39**
See also CA 65-68

Morgan, Lady 1776(?)-1859 .... **NCLC 29**
See also DLB 116, 158; RGEL 2

Morgan, Robin (Evonne) 1941- .... **CLC 2**
See also CA 69-72; CANR 29, 68; FW;
GLL 2; MTCW 1; SATA 80

Morgan, Scott
See Kuttner, Henry

Morgan, Seth 1949(?)-1990 .... **CLC 65**
See also CA 185; 132

Morgenstern, Christian (Otto Josef
Wolfgang) 1871-1914 .... **TCLC 8**
See also CA 105; 191; EWL 3

Morgenstern, S.
See Goldman, William

Mori, Rintaro
See Mori Ogai

Mori, Toshio 1910-1980 .... **AAL; SSC 83**
See also CA 116; 244; DLB 312; RGSF 2

Moricz, Zsigmond 1879-1942 .... **TCLC 33**
See also CA 165; DLB 215; EWL 3

Morike, Eduard (Friedrich)
1804-1875 .... **NCLC 10, 201**
See also DLB 133; RGWL 2, 3

Mori Ogai 1862-1922 .... **TCLC 14**
See Ogai
See also CA 110; 164; DLB 180; EWL 3;
RGWL 3; TWA

Moritz, Karl Philipp 1756-1793 .... **LC 2, 162**
See also DLB 94

Morland, Peter Henry
See Faust, Frederick (Schiller)

Morley, Christopher (Darlington)
1890-1957 .... **TCLC 87**
See also CA 112; 213; DLB 9; MAL 5;
RGAL 4

Morren, Theophil
See Hofmannsthal, Hugo von

Morris, Bill 1952- .... **CLC 76**
See also CA 225

Morris, Julian
See West, Morris L(anglo)

Morris, Steveland Judkins (?)-
See Wonder, Stevie

Morris, William 1834-1896 . **NCLC 4; PC 55**
See also BRW 5; CDBLB 1832-1890; DLB
18, 35, 57, 156, 178, 184; FANT; RGEL
2; SFW 4; SUFW

Morris, Wright (Marion) 1910-1998 . **CLC 1,**
3, 7, 18, 37; TCLC 107
See also AMW; CA 9-12R; 167; CANR 21,
81; CN 1, 2, 3, 4, 5, 6; DLB 2, 206, 218;
DLBY 1981; EWL 3; MAL 5; MTCW 1,
2; MTFW 2005; RGAL 4; TCWW 1, 2

Morrison, Arthur 1863-1945 .... **SSC 40;**
TCLC 72
See also CA 120; 157; CMW 4; DLB 70,
135, 197; RGEL 2

Morrison, Chloe Anthony Wofford
See Morrison, Toni

Morrison, James Douglas
1943-1971 .... **CLC 17**
See also CA 73-76; CANR 40

Morrison, Jim
See Morrison, James Douglas

Morrison, John Gordon 1904-1998 ... **SSC 93**
See also CA 103; CANR 92; DLB 260

Morrison, Toni 1931- . **BLC 1:3, 2:3; CLC 4,**
10, 22, 55, 81, 87, 173, 194; WLC 4
See also AAYA 1, 22, 61; AFAW 1, 2;
AMWC 1; AMWS 3; BPFB 3; BW 2, 3;
CA 29-32R; CANR 27, 42, 67, 113, 124;
CDALB 1968-1988; CLR 99; CN 3, 4, 5,
6, 7; CPW; DA; DA3; DAB; DAC; DAM
MST, MULT, NOV, POP; DLB 6, 33, 143,
331; DLBY 1981; EWL 3; EXPN; FL 1:6;
FW; GL 3; LAIT 2, 4; LATS 1:2; LMFS
2; MAL 5; MBL; MTCW 1, 2; MTFW
2005; NFS 1, 6, 8, 14; RGAL 4; RHW;
SATA 57, 144; SSFS 5; TCLE 1:2; TUS;
YAW

Morrison, Van 1945- .... **CLC 21**
See also CA 116; 168

Morrissy, Mary 1957- .... **CLC 99**
See also CA 205; DLB 267

Mortimer, John 1923-2009 .... **CLC 28, 43**
See also CA 13-16R; CANR 21, 69, 109,
172; CBD; CD 5, 6; CDBLB 1960 to
Present; CMW 4; CN 5, 6, 7; CPW; DA3;
DAM DRAM, POP; DLB 13, 245, 271;
INT CANR-21; MSW; MTCW 1, 2;
MTFW 2005; RGEL 2

Musil, Robert (Edler von)
1880-1942 ... **SSC 18; TCLC 12, 68, 213**
See also CA 109; CANR 55, 84; CDWLB 2; DLB 81, 124; EW 9; EWL 3; MTCW 2; RGSF 2; RGWL 2, 3

Muske, Carol
See Muske-Dukes, Carol

Muske, Carol Anne
See Muske-Dukes, Carol

Muske-Dukes, Carol 1945- .... **CLC 90**
See also CA 65-68, 203; CAAE 203; CANR 32, 70, 181; CWP; PFS 24

Muske-Dukes, Carol Ann
See Muske-Dukes, Carol

Muske-Dukes, Carol Anne
See Muske-Dukes, Carol

Musset, Alfred de 1810-1857 . **DC 27; NCLC 7, 150**
See also DLB 192, 217; EW 6; GFL 1789 to the Present; RGWL 2, 3; TWA

Musset, Louis Charles Alfred de
See Musset, Alfred de

Mussolini, Benito (Amilcare Andrea)
1883-1945 .... **TCLC 96**
See also CA 116

Mutanabbi, Al-
See al-Mutanabbi, Ahmad ibn al-Husayn Abu al-Tayyib al-Jufi al-Kindi
See also WLIT 6

My Brother's Brother
See Chekhov, Anton (Pavlovich)

Myers, L(eopold) H(amilton)
1881-1944 .... **TCLC 59**
See also CA 157; DLB 15; EWL 3; RGEL 2

Myers, Walter Dean 1937- ...... **BLC 1:3, 2:3; CLC 35**
See also AAYA 4, 23; BW 2; BYA 6, 8, 11; CA 33-36R; CANR 20, 42, 67, 108, 184; CLR 4, 16, 35, 110; DAM MULT, NOV; DLB 33; INT CANR-20; JRDA; LAIT 5; MAICYA 1, 2; MAICYAS 1; MTCW 2; MTFW 2005; SAAS 2; SATA 41, 71, 109, 157, 193; SATA-Brief 27; WYA; YAW

Myers, Walter M.
See Myers, Walter Dean

Myles, Symon
See Follett, Ken

Nabokov, Vladimir (Vladimirovich)
1899-1977 .... **CLC 1, 2, 3, 6, 8, 11, 15, 23, 44, 46, 64; SSC 11, 86; TCLC 108, 189; WLC 4**
See also AAYA 45; AMW; AMWC 1; AMWR 1; BPFB 2; CA 5-8R; 69-72; CANR 20, 102; CDALB 1941-1968; CN 1, 2; CP 2; DA; DA3; DAB; DAC; DAM MST, NOV; DLB 2, 244, 278, 317; DLBD 3; DLBY 1980, 1991; EWL 3; EXPS; LATS 1:2; MAL 5; MTCW 1, 2; MTFW 2005; NCFS 4; NFS 9; RGAL 4; RGSF 2; SSFS 6, 15; TUS

Naevius c. 265B.C.-201B.C. .... **CMLC 37**
See also DLB 211

Nagai, Kafu 1879-1959 .... **TCLC 51**
See also CA 117; 276; DLB 180; EWL 3; MJW

Nagai, Sokichi
See Nagai, Kafu

Nagai Kafu
See Nagai, Kafu

na gCopaleen, Myles
See O Nuallain, Brian

na Gopaleen, Myles
See O Nuallain, Brian

Nagy, Laszlo 1925-1978 .... **CLC 7**
See also CA 129; 112

Naidu, Sarojini 1879-1949 .... **TCLC 80**
See also EWL 3; RGEL 2

Naipaul, Shiva 1945-1985 .... **CLC 32, 39; TCLC 153**
See also CA 110; 112; 116; CANR 33; CN 2, 3; DA3; DAM NOV; DLB 157; DLBY 1985; EWL 3; MTCW 1, 2; MTFW 2005

Naipaul, Shivadhar Srinivasa
See Naipaul, Shiva

Naipaul, V.S. 1932- .. **CLC 4, 7, 9, 13, 18, 37, 105, 199; SSC 38, 121**
See also BPFB 2; BRWS 1; CA 1-4R; CANR 1, 33, 51, 91, 126; CDBLB 1960 to Present; CDWLB 3; CN 1, 2, 3, 4, 5, 6, 7; DA3; DAB; DAC; DAM MST, NOV; DLB 125, 204, 207, 326, 331; DLBY 1985, 2001; EWL 3; LATS 1:2; MTCW 1, 2; MTFW 2005; RGEL 2; RGSF 2; TWA; WLIT 4; WWE 1

Nakos, Lilika 1903(?)-1989 .... **CLC 29**

Napoleon
See Yamamoto, Hisaye

Narayan, R.K. 1906-2001 ...... **CLC 7, 28, 47, 121, 211; SSC 25**
See also BPFB 2; CA 81-84; 196; CANR 33, 61, 112; CN 1, 2, 3, 4, 5, 6, 7; DA3; DAM NOV; DLB 323; DNFS 1; EWL 3; MTCW 1, 2; MTFW 2005; RGEL 2; RGSF 2; SATA 62; SSFS 5; WWE 1

Nash, Fredric Ogden
See Nash, Ogden

Nash, Ogden 1902-1971 ...... **CLC 23; PC 21; TCLC 109**
See also CA 13-14; 29-32R; CANR 34, 61, 185; CAP 1; CP 1; DAM POET; DLB 11; MAICYA 1, 2; MAL 5; MTCW 1, 2; RGAL 4; SATA 2, 46; WP

Nashe, Thomas 1567-1601(?) . **LC 41, 89; PC 82**
See also DLB 167; RGEL 2

Nathan, Daniel
See Dannay, Frederic

Nathan, George Jean 1882-1958 .... **TCLC 18**
See also CA 114; 169; DLB 137; MAL 5

Natsume, Kinnosuke
See Natsume, Soseki

Natsume, Soseki 1867-1916 .... **TCLC 2, 10**
See Natsume Soseki; Soseki
See also CA 104; 195; RGWL 2, 3; TWA

Natsume Soseki
See Natsume, Soseki
See also DLB 180; EWL 3

Natti, (Mary) Lee 1919- .... **CLC 17**
See also CA 5-8R; CANR 2; CWRI 5; SAAS 3; SATA 1, 67

Navarre, Marguerite de
See de Navarre, Marguerite

Naylor, Gloria 1950- . **BLC 1:3; CLC 28, 52, 156, 261; WLCS**
See also AAYA 6, 39; AFAW 1, 2; AMWS 8; BW 2, 3; CA 107; CANR 27, 51, 74, 130; CN 4, 5, 6, 7; CPW; DA; DA3; DAC; DAM MST, MULT, NOV, POP; DLB 173; EWL 3; FW; MAL 5; MTCW 1, 2; MTFW 2005; NFS 4, 7; RGAL 4; TCLE 1:2; TUS

Neal, John 1793-1876 .... **NCLC 161**
See also DLB 1, 59, 243; FW; RGAL 4

Neff, Debra .... **CLC 59**

Neihardt, John Gneisenau
1881-1973 .... **CLC 32**
See also CA 13-14; CANR 65; CAP 1; DLB 9, 54, 256; LAIT 2; TCWW 1, 2

Nekrasov, Nikolai Alekseevich
1821-1878 .... **NCLC 11**
See also DLB 277

Nelligan, Emile 1879-1941 .... **TCLC 14**
See also CA 114; 204; DLB 92; EWL 3

Nelson, Alice Ruth Moore Dunbar
1875-1935 .... **HR 1:2**
See also BW 1, 3; CA 122; 124; CANR 82; DLB 50; FW; MTCW 1

Nelson, Willie 1933- .... **CLC 17**
See also CA 107; CANR 114, 178

Nemerov, Howard 1920-1991 .... **CLC 2, 6, 9, 36; PC 24; TCLC 124**
See also AMW; CA 1-4R; 134; CABS 2; CANR 1, 27, 53; CN 1, 2, 3; CP 1, 2, 3, 4, 5; DAM POET; DLB 5, 6; DLBY 1983; EWL 3; INT CANR-27; MAL 5; MTCW 1, 2; MTFW 2005; PFS 10, 14; RGAL 4

Nepos, Cornelius c. 99B.C.-c. 24B.C. .... **CMLC 89**
See also DLB 211

Neruda, Pablo 1904-1973 .. **CLC 1, 2, 5, 7, 9, 28, 62; HLC 2; PC 4, 64; WLC 4**
See also CA 19-20; 45-48; CANR 131; CAP 2; DA; DA3; DAB; DAC; DAM MST, MULT, POET; DLB 283, 331; DNFS 2; EWL 3; HW 1; LAW; MTCW 1, 2; MTFW 2005; PFS 11, 28; RGWL 2, 3; TWA; WLIT 1; WP

Nerval, Gerard de 1808-1855 ... **NCLC 1, 67; PC 13; SSC 18**
See also DLB 217; EW 6; GFL 1789 to the Present; RGSF 2; RGWL 2, 3

Nervo, (Jose) Amado (Ruiz de)
1870-1919 .... **HLCS 2; TCLC 11**
See also CA 109; 131; DLB 290; EWL 3; HW 1; LAW

Nesbit, Malcolm
See Chester, Alfred

Nessi, Pio Baroja y
See Baroja, Pio

Nestroy, Johann 1801-1862 .... **NCLC 42**
See also DLB 133; RGWL 2, 3

Netterville, Luke
See O'Grady, Standish (James)

Neufeld, John (Arthur) 1938- .... **CLC 17**
See also AAYA 11; CA 25-28R; CANR 11, 37, 56; CLR 52; MAICYA 1, 2; SAAS 3; SATA 6, 81, 131; SATA-Essay 131; YAW

Neumann, Alfred 1895-1952 .... **TCLC 100**
See also CA 183; DLB 56

Neumann, Ferenc
See Molnar, Ferenc

Neville, Emily Cheney 1919- .... **CLC 12**
See also BYA 2; CA 5-8R; CANR 3, 37, 85; JRDA; MAICYA 1, 2; SAAS 2; SATA 1; YAW

Newbound, Bernard Slade 1930- .... **CLC 11, 46**
See also CA 81-84; CAAS 9; CANR 49; CCA 1; CD 5, 6; DAM DRAM; DLB 53

Newby, P(ercy) H(oward)
1918-1997 .... **CLC 2, 13**
See also CA 5-8R; 161; CANR 32, 67; CN 1, 2, 3, 4, 5, 6; DAM NOV; DLB 15, 326; MTCW 1; RGEL 2

Newcastle
See Cavendish, Margaret Lucas

Newlove, Donald 1928- .... **CLC 6**
See also CA 29-32R; CANR 25

Newlove, John (Herbert) 1938- .... **CLC 14**
See also CA 21-24R; CANR 9, 25; CP 1, 2, 3, 4, 5, 6, 7

Newman, Charles 1938-2006 .... **CLC 2, 8**
See also CA 21-24R; 249; CANR 84; CN 3, 4, 5, 6

Newman, Charles Hamilton
See Newman, Charles

Newman, Edwin (Harold) 1919- ...... **CLC 14**
See also AITN 1; CA 69-72; CANR 5

Newman, John Henry 1801-1890 . **NCLC 38, 99**
See also BRWS 7; DLB 18, 32, 55; RGEL 2

Nye, Robert 1939- .... **CLC 13, 42**
See also BRWS 10; CA 33-36R; CANR 29,
67, 107; CN 1, 2, 3, 4, 5, 6, 7; CP 1, 2, 3,
4, 5, 6, 7; CWRI 5; DAM NOV; DLB 14,
271; FANT; HGG; MTCW 1; RHW;
SATA 6

Nyro, Laura 1947-1997 .... **CLC 17**
See also CA 194

Oates, Joyce Carol 1938- .. **CLC 1, 2, 3, 6, 9,
11, 15, 19, 33, 52, 108, 134, 228; SSC 6,
70, 121; WLC 4**
See also AAYA 15, 52; AITN 1; AMWS 2;
BEST 89:2; BPFB 2; BYA 11; CA 5-8R;
CANR 25, 45, 74, 113, 129, 165; CDALB
1968-1988; CN 1, 2, 3, 4, 5, 6, 7; CP 5,
6, 7; CPW; CWP; DA; DA3; DAB; DAC;
DAM MST, NOV, POP; DLB 2, 5, 130;
DLBY 1981; EWL 3; EXPS; FL 1:6; FW;
GL 3; HGG; INT CANR-25; LAIT 4;
MAL 5; MBL; MTCW 1, 2; MTFW 2005;
NFS 8, 24; RGAL 4; RGSF 2; SATA 159;
SSFS 1, 8, 17; SUFW 2; TUS

O'Brian, E.G.
See Clarke, Arthur C.

O'Brian, Patrick 1914-2000 .... **CLC 152**
See also AAYA 55; BRWS 12; CA 144; 187;
CANR 74; CPW; MTCW 2; MTFW 2005;
RHW

O'Brien, Darcy 1939-1998 .... **CLC 11**
See also CA 21-24R; 167; CANR 8, 59

O'Brien, Edna 1932- ..... **CLC 3, 5, 8, 13, 36,
65, 116, 237; SSC 10, 77**
See also BRWS 5; CA 1-4R; CANR 6, 41,
65, 102, 169; CDBLB 1960 to Present;
CN 1, 2, 3, 4, 5, 6, 7; DA3; DAM NOV;
DLB 14, 231, 319; EWL 3; FW; MTCW
1, 2; MTFW 2005; RGSF 2; WLIT 4

O'Brien, E.G.
See Clarke, Arthur C.

O'Brien, Fitz-James 1828-1862 ..... **NCLC 21**
See also DLB 74; RGAL 4; SUFW

O'Brien, Flann
See O Nuallain, Brian

O'Brien, Richard 1942- .... **CLC 17**
See also CA 124

O'Brien, Tim 1946- .... **CLC 7, 19, 40, 103,
211; SSC 74**
See also AAYA 16; AMWS 5; CA 85-88;
CANR 40, 58, 133; CDALBS; CN 5, 6,
7; CPW; DA3; DAM POP; DLB 152;
DLBD 9; DLBY 1980; LATS 1:2; MAL
5; MTCW 2; MTFW 2005; RGAL 4;
SSFS 5, 15; TCLE 1:2

Obstfelder, Sigbjoern 1866-1900 .... **TCLC 23**
See also CA 123

O'Casey, Brenda
See Haycraft, Anna

O'Casey, Sean 1880-1964 .... **CLC 1, 5, 9, 11,
15, 88; DC 12; WLCS**
See also BRW 7; CA 89-92; CANR 62;
CBD; CDBLB 1914-1945; DA3; DAB;
DAC; DAM DRAM, MST; DFS 19; DLB
10; EWL 3; MTCW 1, 2; MTFW 2005;
RGEL 2; TEA; WLIT 4

O'Cathasaigh, Sean
See O'Casey, Sean

Occom, Samson 1723-1792 .... **LC 60; NNAL**
See also DLB 175

Occomy, Marita (Odette) Bonner
1899(?)-1971
See Bonner, Marita
See also BW 2; CA 142; DFS 13; DLB 51,
228

Ochs, Phil(ip David) 1940-1976 .... **CLC 17**
See also CA 185; 65-68

O'Connor, Edwin (Greene)
1918-1968 .... **CLC 14**
See also CA 93-96; 25-28R; MAL 5

O'Connor, (Mary) Flannery
1925-1964 .... **CLC 1, 2, 3, 6, 10, 13, 15,
21, 66, 104; SSC 1, 23, 61, 82, 111;
TCLC 132; WLC 4**
See also AAYA 7; AMW; AMWR 2; BPFB
3; BYA 16; CA 1-4R; CANR 3, 41;
CDALB 1941-1968; DA; DA3; DAB;
DAC; DAM MST, NOV; DLB 2, 152;
DLBD 12; DLBY 1980; EWL 3; EXPS;
LAIT 5; MAL 5; MBL; MTCW 1, 2;
MTFW 2005; NFS 3, 21; RGAL 4; RGSF
2; SSFS 2, 7, 10, 19; TUS

O'Connor, Frank 1903-1966
See O'Donovan, Michael Francis

O'Dell, Scott 1898-1989 .... **CLC 30**
See also AAYA 3, 44; BPFB 3; BYA 1, 2,
3, 5; CA 61-64; 129; CANR 12, 30, 112;
CLR 1, 16, 126; DLB 52; JRDA; MAI-
CYA 1, 2; SATA 12, 60, 134; WYA; YAW

Odets, Clifford 1906-1963 ..... **CLC 2, 28, 98;
DC 6**
See also AMWS 2; CA 85-88; CAD; CANR
62; DAM DRAM; DFS 3, 17, 20; DLB 7,
26, 341; EWL 3; MAL 5; MTCW 1, 2;
MTFW 2005; RGAL 4; TUS

O'Doherty, Brian 1928- .... **CLC 76**
See also CA 105; CANR 108

O'Donnell, K. M.
See Malzberg, Barry N(athaniel)

O'Donnell, Lawrence
See Kuttner, Henry

O'Donovan, Michael Francis
1903-1966 .... **CLC 14, 23; SSC 5, 109**
See also BRWS 14; CA 93-96; CANR 84;
DLB 162; EWL 3; RGSF 2; SSFS 5

Oe, Kenzaburo 1935- .. **CLC 10, 36, 86, 187;
SSC 20**
See Oe Kenzaburo
See also CA 97-100; CANR 36, 50, 74, 126;
DA3; DAM NOV; DLB 182, 331; DLBY
1994; LATS 1:2; MJW; MTCW 1, 2;
MTFW 2005; RGSF 2; RGWL 2, 3

Oe Kenzaburo
See Oe, Kenzaburo
See also CWW 2; EWL 3

O'Faolain, Julia 1932- .... **CLC 6, 19, 47, 108**
See also CA 81-84; CAAS 2; CANR 12,
61; CN 2, 3, 4, 5, 6, 7; DLB 14, 231, 319;
FW; MTCW 1; RHW

O'Faolain, Sean 1900-1991 ...... **CLC 1, 7, 14,
32, 70; SSC 13; TCLC 143**
See also CA 61-64; 134; CANR 12, 66; CN
1, 2, 3, 4; DLB 15, 162; MTCW 1, 2;
MTFW 2005; RGEL 2; RGSF 2

O'Flaherty, Liam 1896-1984 .... **CLC 5, 34;
SSC 6, 116**
See also CA 101; 113; CANR 35; CN 1, 2,
3; DLB 36, 162; DLBY 1984; MTCW 1,
2; MTFW 2005; RGEL 2; RGSF 2; SSFS
5, 20

Ogai
See Mori Ogai
See also MJW

Ogilvy, Gavin
See Barrie, J(ames) M(atthew)

O'Grady, Standish (James)
1846-1928 .... **TCLC 5**
See also CA 104; 157

O'Grady, Timothy 1951- .... **CLC 59**
See also CA 138

O'Hara, Frank 1926-1966 .... **CLC 2, 5, 13,
78; PC 45**
See also CA 9-12R; 25-28R; CANR 33;
DA3; DAM POET; DLB 5, 16, 193; EWL
3; MAL 5; MTCW 1, 2; MTFW 2005;
PFS 8, 12; RGAL 4; WP

O'Hara, John (Henry) 1905-1970 . **CLC 1, 2,
3, 6, 11, 42; SSC 15**
See also AMW; BPFB 3; CA 5-8R; 25-28R;
CANR 31, 60; CDALB 1929-1941; DAM
NOV; DLB 9, 86, 324; DLBD 2; EWL 3;
MAL 5; MTCW 1, 2; MTFW 2005; NFS
11; RGAL 4; RGSF 2

O'Hehir, Diana 1929- .... **CLC 41**
See also CA 245; CANR 177

O'Hehir, Diana F.
See O'Hehir, Diana

Ohiyesa
See Eastman, Charles A(lexander)

Okada, John 1923-1971 .... **AAL**
See also BYA 14; CA 212; DLB 312; NFS
25

Okigbo, Christopher 1930-1967 ..... **BLC 1:3;
CLC 25, 84; PC 7; TCLC 171**
See also AFW; BW 1, 3; CA 77-80; CANR
74; CDWLB 3; DAM MULT, POET; DLB
125; EWL 3; MTCW 1, 2; MTFW 2005;
RGEL 2

Okigbo, Christopher Ifenayichukwu
See Okigbo, Christopher

Okri, Ben 1959- .... **BLC 2:3; CLC 87, 223**
See also AFW; BRWS 5; BW 2, 3; CA 130;
138; CANR 65, 128; CN 5, 6, 7; DLB
157, 231, 319, 326; EWL 3; INT CA-138;
MTCW 2; MTFW 2005; RGSF 2; SSFS
20; WLIT 2; WWE 1

Old Boy
See Hughes, Thomas

Olds, Sharon 1942- .. **CLC 32, 39, 85; PC 22**
See also AMWS 10; CA 101; CANR 18,
41, 66, 98, 135; CP 5, 6, 7; CPW; CWP;
DAM POET; DLB 120; MAL 5; MTCW
2; MTFW 2005; PFS 17

Oldstyle, Jonathan
See Irving, Washington

Olesha, Iurii
See Olesha, Yuri (Karlovich)
See also RGWL 2

Olesha, Iurii Karlovich
See Olesha, Yuri (Karlovich)
See also DLB 272

Olesha, Yuri (Karlovich) 1899-1960 . **CLC 8;
SSC 69; TCLC 136**
See Olesha, Iurii; Olesha, Iurii Karlovich;
Olesha, Yury Karlovich
See also CA 85-88; EW 11; RGWL 3

Olesha, Yury Karlovich
See Olesha, Yuri (Karlovich)
See also EWL 3

Oliphant, Mrs.
See Oliphant, Margaret (Oliphant Wilson)
See also SUFW

Oliphant, Laurence 1829(?)-1888 .. **NCLC 47**
See also DLB 18, 166

Oliphant, Margaret (Oliphant Wilson)
1828-1897 .... **NCLC 11, 61; SSC 25**
See Oliphant, Mrs.
See also BRWS 10; DLB 18, 159, 190;
HGG; RGEL 2; RGSF 2

Oliver, Mary 1935- ... **CLC 19, 34, 98; PC 75**
See also AMWS 7; CA 21-24R; CANR 9,
43, 84, 92, 138; CP 4, 5, 6, 7; CWP; DLB
5, 193, 342; EWL 3; MTFW 2005; PFS
15

Olivier, Laurence (Kerr) 1907-1989 . **CLC 20**
See also CA 111; 150; 129

O.L.S.
See Russell, George William

Olsen, Tillie 1912-2007 .... **CLC 4, 13, 114;
SSC 11, 103**
See also AAYA 51; AMWS 13; BYA 11;
CA 1-4R; 256; CANR 1, 43, 74, 132;
CDALBS; CN 2, 3, 4, 5, 6, 7; DA; DA3;
DAB; DAC; DAM MST; DLB 28, 206;

Pa Chin
See Jin, Ba

Pack, Robert 1929- .... **CLC 13**
See also CA 1-4R; CANR 3, 44, 82; CP 1, 2, 3, 4, 5, 6, 7; DLB 5; SATA 118

Packer, Vin
See Meaker, Marijane

Padgett, Lewis
See Kuttner, Henry

Padilla (Lorenzo), Heberto
1932-2000 .... **CLC 38**
See also AITN 1; CA 123; 131; 189; CWW 2; EWL 3; HW 1

Paerdurabo, Frater
See Crowley, Edward Alexander

Page, James Patrick 1944- .... **CLC 12**
See also CA 204

Page, Jimmy 1944-
See Page, James Patrick

Page, Louise 1955- .... **CLC 40**
See also CA 140; CANR 76; CBD; CD 5, 6; CWD; DLB 233

Page, P(atricia) K(athleen) 1916- ...... **CLC 7, 18; PC 12**
See also CA 53-56; CANR 4, 22, 65; CCA 1; CP 1, 2, 3, 4, 5, 6, 7; DAC; DAM MST; DLB 68; MTCW 1; RGEL 2

Page, Stanton
See Fuller, Henry Blake

Page, Thomas Nelson 1853-1922 .... **SSC 23**
See also CA 118; 177; DLB 12, 78; DLBD 13; RGAL 4

Pagels, Elaine
See Pagels, Elaine Hiesey

Pagels, Elaine Hiesey 1943- .... **CLC 104**
See also CA 45-48; CANR 2, 24, 51, 151; FW; NCFS 4

Paget, Violet 1856-1935 .. **SSC 33, 98; TCLC 5**
See also CA 104; 166; DLB 57, 153, 156, 174, 178; GLL 1; HGG; SUFW 1

Paget-Lowe, Henry
See Lovecraft, H. P.

Paglia, Camille 1947- .... **CLC 68**
See also CA 140; CANR 72, 139; CPW; FW; GLL 2; MTCW 2; MTFW 2005

Pagnol, Marcel (Paul)
1895-1974 .... **TCLC 208**
See also CA 128; 49-52; DLB 321; EWL 3; GFL 1789 to the Present; MTCW 1; RGWL 2, 3

Paige, Richard
See Koontz, Dean R.

Paine, Thomas 1737-1809 .... **NCLC 62**
See also AMWS 1; CDALB 1640-1865; DLB 31, 43, 73, 158; LAIT 1; RGAL 4; RGEL 2; TUS

Pakenham, Antonia
See Fraser, Antonia

Palamas, Costis
See Palamas, Kostes

Palamas, Kostes 1859-1943 .... **TCLC 5**
See Palamas, Kostis
See also CA 105; 190; RGWL 2, 3

Palamas, Kostis
See Palamas, Kostes
See also EWL 3

Palazzeschi, Aldo 1885-1974 .... **CLC 11**
See also CA 89-92; 53-56; DLB 114, 264; EWL 3

Pales Matos, Luis 1898-1959 .... **HLCS 2**
See Pales Matos, Luis
See also DLB 290; HW 1; LAW

Paley, Grace 1922-2007 ... **CLC 4, 6, 37, 140; SSC 8**
See also AMWS 6; CA 25-28R; 263; CANR 13, 46, 74, 118; CN 2, 3, 4, 5, 6, 7; CPW; DA3; DAM POP; DLB 28, 218; EWL 3;

EXPS; FW; INT CANR-13; MAL 5; MBL; MTCW 1, 2; MTFW 2005; RGAL 4; RGSF 2; SSFS 3, 20

Paley, Grace Goodside
See Paley, Grace

Palin, Michael 1943- .... **CLC 21**
See also CA 107; CANR 35, 109, 179; SATA 67

Palin, Michael Edward
See Palin, Michael

Palliser, Charles 1947- .... **CLC 65**
See also CA 136; CANR 76; CN 5, 6, 7

Palma, Ricardo 1833-1919 .... **TCLC 29**
See also CA 168; LAW

Pamuk, Orhan 1952- .... **CLC 185**
See also CA 142; CANR 75, 127, 172; CWW 2; NFS 27; WLIT 6

Pancake, Breece Dexter 1952-1979 . **CLC 29; SSC 61**
See also CA 123; 109; DLB 130

Pancake, Breece D'J
See Pancake, Breece Dexter

Panchenko, Nikolai .... **CLC 59**

Pankhurst, Emmeline (Goulden)
1858-1928 .... **TCLC 100**
See also CA 116; FW

Panko, Rudy
See Gogol, Nikolai (Vasilyevich)

Papadiamantis, Alexandros
1851-1911 .... **TCLC 29**
See also CA 168; EWL 3

Papadiamantopoulos, Johannes
1856-1910 .... **TCLC 18**
See also CA 117; 242; GFL 1789 to the Present

Papadiamantopoulos, Yannis
See Papadiamantopoulos, Johannes

Papini, Giovanni 1881-1956 .... **TCLC 22**
See also CA 121; 180; DLB 264

Paracelsus 1493-1541 .... **LC 14**
See also DLB 179

Parasol, Peter
See Stevens, Wallace

Pardo Bazan, Emilia 1851-1921 .... **SSC 30; TCLC 189**
See also EWL 3; FW; RGSF 2; RGWL 2, 3

Paredes, Americo 1915-1999 .... **PC 83**
See also CA 37-40R; 179; DLB 209; EXPP; HW 1

Pareto, Vilfredo 1848-1923 .... **TCLC 69**
See also CA 175

Paretsky, Sara 1947- .... **CLC 135**
See also AAYA 30; BEST 90:3; CA 125; 129; CANR 59, 95, 184; CMW 4; CPW; DA3; DAM POP; DLB 306; INT CA-129; MSW; RGAL 4

Paretsky, Sara N.
See Paretsky, Sara

Parfenie, Maria
See Codrescu, Andrei

Parini, Jay (Lee) 1948- .... **CLC 54, 133**
See also CA 97-100, 229; CAAE 229; CAAS 16; CANR 32, 87

Park, Jordan
See Kornbluth, C(yril) M.; Pohl, Frederik

Park, Robert E(zra) 1864-1944 ..... **TCLC 73**
See also CA 122; 165

Parker, Bert
See Ellison, Harlan

Parker, Dorothy (Rothschild)
1893-1967 . **CLC 15, 68; PC 28; SSC 2, 101; TCLC 143**
See also AMWS 9; CA 19-20; 25-28R; CAP 2; DA3; DAM POET; DLB 11, 45, 86; EXPP; FW; MAL 5; MBL; MTCW 1, 2; MTFW 2005; PFS 18; RGAL 4; RGSF 2; TUS

Parker, Robert B. 1932- .... **CLC 27**
See also AAYA 28; BEST 89:4; BPFB 3; CA 49-52; CANR 1, 26, 52, 89, 128, 165; CMW 4; CPW; DAM NOV, POP; DLB 306; INT CANR-26; MSW; MTCW 1; MTFW 2005

Parker, Robert Brown
See Parker, Robert B.

Parker, Theodore 1810-1860 .... **NCLC 186**
See also DLB 1, 235

Parkin, Frank 1940- .... **CLC 43**
See also CA 147

Parkman, Francis, Jr. 1823-1893 .. **NCLC 12**
See also AMWS 2; DLB 1, 30, 183, 186, 235; RGAL 4

Parks, Gordon 1912-2006 . **BLC 1:3; CLC 1, 16**
See also AAYA 36; AITN 2; BW 2, 3; CA 41-44R; 249; CANR 26, 66, 145; DA3; DAM MULT; DLB 33; MTCW 2; MTFW 2005; SATA 8, 108; SATA-Obit 175

Parks, Suzan-Lori 1964(?)- ..... **BLC 2:3; DC 23**
See also AAYA 55; CA 201; CAD; CD 5, 6; CWD; DFS 22; DLB 341; RGAL 4

Parks, Tim(othy Harold) 1954- ...... **CLC 147**
See also CA 126; 131; CANR 77, 144; CN 7; DLB 231; INT CA-131

Parmenides c. 515B.C.-c.
450B.C. .... **CMLC 22**
See also DLB 176

Parnell, Thomas 1679-1718 .... **LC 3**
See also DLB 95; RGEL 2

Parr, Catherine c. 1513(?)-1548 .... **LC 86**
See also DLB 136

Parra, Nicanor 1914- ... **CLC 2, 102; HLC 2; PC 39**
See also CA 85-88; CANR 32; CWW 2; DAM MULT; DLB 283; EWL 3; HW 1; LAW; MTCW 1

Parra Sanojo, Ana Teresa de la
1890-1936 .... **HLCS 2**
See de la Parra, (Ana) Teresa (Sonojo)
See also LAW

Parrish, Mary Frances
See Fisher, M(ary) F(rances) K(ennedy)

Parshchikov, Aleksei 1954- .... **CLC 59**
See Parshchikov, Aleksei Maksimovich

Parshchikov, Aleksei Maksimovich
See Parshchikov, Aleksei
See also DLB 285

Parson, Professor
See Coleridge, Samuel Taylor

Parson Lot
See Kingsley, Charles

Parton, Sara Payson Willis
1811-1872 .... **NCLC 86**
See also DLB 43, 74, 239

Partridge, Anthony
See Oppenheim, E(dward) Phillips

Pascal, Blaise 1623-1662 .... **LC 35**
See also DLB 268; EW 3; GFL Beginnings to 1789; RGWL 2, 3; TWA

Pascoli, Giovanni 1855-1912 .... **TCLC 45**
See also CA 170; EW 7; EWL 3

Pasolini, Pier Paolo 1922-1975 .. **CLC 20, 37, 106; PC 17**
See also CA 93-96; 61-64; CANR 63; DLB 128, 177; EWL 3; MTCW 1; RGWL 2, 3

Pasquini
See Silone, Ignazio

Pastan, Linda (Olenik) 1932- .... **CLC 27**
See also CA 61-64; CANR 18, 40, 61, 113; CP 3, 4, 5, 6, 7; CSW; CWP; DAM POET; DLB 5; PFS 8, 25

Pasternak, Boris 1890-1960 ... **CLC 7, 10, 18, 63; PC 6; SSC 31; TCLC 188; WLC 4**
See also BPFB 3; CA 127; 116; DA; DA3; DAB; DAC; DAM MST, NOV, POET; DLB 302, 331; EW 10; MTCW 1, 2; MTFW 2005; NFS 26; RGSF 2; RGWL 2, 3; TWA; WP

Patchen, Kenneth 1911-1972 .... **CLC 1, 2, 18**
See also BG 1:3; CA 1-4R; 33-36R; CANR 3, 35; CN 1; CP 1; DAM POET; DLB 16, 48; EWL 3; MAL 5; MTCW 1; RGAL 4

Patchett, Ann 1963- .... **CLC 244**
See also AAYA 69; AMWS 12; CA 139; CANR 64, 110, 167; MTFW 2005

Pater, Walter (Horatio) 1839-1894 . **NCLC 7, 90, 159**
See also BRW 5; CDBLB 1832-1890; DLB 57, 156; RGEL 2; TEA

Paterson, A(ndrew) B(arton) 1864-1941 .... **TCLC 32**
See also CA 155; DLB 230; RGEL 2; SATA 97

Paterson, Banjo
See Paterson, A(ndrew) B(arton)

Paterson, Katherine 1932- .... **CLC 12, 30**
See also AAYA 1, 31; BYA 1, 2, 7; CA 21-24R; CANR 28, 59, 111, 173; CLR 7, 50, 127; CWRI 5; DLB 52; JRDA; LAIT 4; MAICYA 1, 2; MAICYAS 1; MTCW 1; SATA 13, 53, 92, 133; WYA; YAW

Paterson, Katherine Womeldorf
See Paterson, Katherine

Patmore, Coventry Kersey Dighton 1823-1896 .... **NCLC 9; PC 59**
See also DLB 35, 98; RGEL 2; TEA

Paton, Alan 1903-1988 ..... **CLC 4, 10, 25, 55, 106; TCLC 165; WLC 4**
See also AAYA 26; AFW; BPFB 3; BRWS 2; BYA 1; CA 13-16; 125; CANR 22; CAP 1; CN 1, 2, 3, 4; DA; DA3; DAB; DAC; DAM MST, NOV; DLB 225; DLBD 17; EWL 3; EXPN; LAIT 4; MTCW 1, 2; MTFW 2005; NFS 3, 12; RGEL 2; SATA 11; SATA-Obit 56; TWA; WLIT 2; WWE 1

Paton Walsh, Gillian
See Paton Walsh, Jill
See also AAYA 47; BYA 1, 8

Paton Walsh, Jill 1937- .... **CLC 35**
See Paton Walsh, Gillian
See also AAYA 11; CA 262; CAAE 262; CANR 38, 83, 158; CLR 2, 6, 128; DLB 161; JRDA; MAICYA 1, 2; SAAS 3; SATA 4, 72, 109, 190; SATA-Essay 190; WYA; YAW

Patsauq, Markoosie 1942- .... **NNAL**
See also CA 101; CLR 23; CWRI 5; DAM MULT

Patterson, (Horace) Orlando (Lloyd) 1940- .... **BLCS**
See also BW 1; CA 65-68; CANR 27, 84; CN 1, 2, 3, 4, 5, 6

Patton, George S(mith), Jr. 1885-1945 .... **TCLC 79**
See also CA 189

Paulding, James Kirke 1778-1860 ... **NCLC 2**
See also DLB 3, 59, 74, 250; RGAL 4

Paulin, Thomas Neilson
See Paulin, Tom

Paulin, Tom 1949- .... **CLC 37, 177**
See also CA 123; 128; CANR 98; CP 3, 4, 5, 6, 7; DLB 40

Pausanias c. 1st cent. - .... **CMLC 36**

Paustovsky, Konstantin (Georgievich) 1892-1968 .... **CLC 40**
See also CA 93-96; 25-28R; DLB 272; EWL 3

Pavese, Cesare 1908-1950 .... **PC 13; SSC 19; TCLC 3**
See also CA 104; 169; DLB 128, 177; EW 12; EWL 3; PFS 20; RGSF 2; RGWL 2, 3; TWA; WLIT 7

Pavic, Milorad 1929- .... **CLC 60**
See also CA 136; CDWLB 4; CWW 2; DLB 181; EWL 3; RGWL 3

Pavlov, Ivan Petrovich 1849-1936 . **TCLC 91**
See also CA 118; 180

Pavlova, Karolina Karlovna 1807-1893 .... **NCLC 138**
See also DLB 205

Payne, Alan
See Jakes, John

Payne, Rachel Ann
See Jakes, John

Paz, Gil
See Lugones, Leopoldo

Paz, Octavio 1914-1998 . **CLC 3, 4, 6, 10, 19, 51, 65, 119; HLC 2; PC 1, 48; TCLC 211; WLC 4**
See also AAYA 50; CA 73-76; 165; CANR 32, 65, 104; CWW 2; DA; DA3; DAB; DAC; DAM MST, MULT, POET; DLB 290, 331; DLBY 1990, 1998; DNFS 1; EWL 3; HW 1, 2; LAW; LAWS 1; MTCW 1, 2; MTFW 2005; PFS 18; RGWL 2, 3; SSFS 13; TWA; WLIT 1

p'Bitek, Okot 1931-1982 . **BLC 1:3; CLC 96; TCLC 149**
See also AFW; BW 2, 3; CA 124; 107; CANR 82; CP 1, 2, 3; DAM MULT; DLB 125; EWL 3; MTCW 1, 2; MTFW 2005; RGEL 2; WLIT 2

Peabody, Elizabeth Palmer 1804-1894 .... **NCLC 169**
See also DLB 1, 223

Peacham, Henry 1578-1644(?) .... **LC 119**
See also DLB 151

Peacock, Molly 1947- .... **CLC 60**
See also CA 103, 262; CAAE 262; CAAS 21; CANR 52, 84; CP 5, 6, 7; CWP; DLB 120, 282

Peacock, Thomas Love 1785-1866 .... **NCLC 22; PC 87**
See also BRW 4; DLB 96, 116; RGEL 2; RGSF 2

Peake, Mervyn 1911-1968 .... **CLC 7, 54**
See also CA 5-8R; 25-28R; CANR 3; DLB 15, 160, 255; FANT; MTCW 1; RGEL 2; SATA 23; SFW 4

Pearce, Ann Philippa
See Pearce, Philippa

Pearce, Philippa 1920-2006 .... **CLC 21**
See also BYA 5; CA 5-8R; 255; CANR 4, 109; CLR 9; CWRI 5; DLB 161; FANT; MAICYA 1; SATA 1, 67, 129; SATA-Obit 179

Pearl, Eric
See Elman, Richard (Martin)

Pearson, Jean Mary
See Gardam, Jane

Pearson, Thomas Reid
See Pearson, T.R.

Pearson, T.R. 1956- .... **CLC 39**
See also CA 120; 130; CANR 97, 147, 185; CSW; INT CA-130

Peck, Dale 1967- .... **CLC 81**
See also CA 146; CANR 72, 127, 180; GLL 2

Peck, John (Frederick) 1941- .... **CLC 3**
See also CA 49-52; CANR 3, 100; CP 4, 5, 6, 7

Peck, Richard 1934- .... **CLC 21**
See also AAYA 1, 24; BYA 1, 6, 8, 11; CA 85-88; CANR 19, 38, 129, 178; CLR 15; INT CANR-19; JRDA; MAICYA 1, 2; SAAS 2; SATA 18, 55, 97, 110, 158, 190; SATA-Essay 110; WYA; YAW

Peck, Richard Wayne
See Peck, Richard

Peck, Robert Newton 1928- .... **CLC 17**
See also AAYA 3, 43; BYA 1, 6; CA 81-84, 182; CAAE 182; CANR 31, 63, 127; CLR 45; DA; DAC; DAM MST; JRDA; LAIT 3; MAICYA 1, 2; SAAS 1; SATA 21, 62, 111, 156; SATA-Essay 108; WYA; YAW

Peckinpah, David Samuel
See Peckinpah, Sam

Peckinpah, Sam 1925-1984 .... **CLC 20**
See also CA 109; 114; CANR 82

Pedersen, Knut 1859-1952 .. **TCLC 2, 14, 49, 151, 203**
See also AAYA 79; CA 104; 119; CANR 63; DLB 297, 330; EW 8; EWL 8; MTCW 1, 2; RGWL 2, 3

Peele, George 1556-1596 .... **DC 27; LC 115**
See also BRW 1; DLB 62, 167; RGEL 2

Peeslake, Gaffer
See Durrell, Lawrence (George)

Peguy, Charles (Pierre) 1873-1914 .... **TCLC 10**
See also CA 107; 193; DLB 258; EWL 3; GFL 1789 to the Present

Peirce, Charles Sanders 1839-1914 .... **TCLC 81**
See also CA 194; DLB 270

Pelecanos, George P. 1957- .... **CLC 236**
See also CA 138; CANR 122, 165; DLB 306

Pelevin, Victor 1962- .... **CLC 238**
See Pelevin, Viktor Olegovich
See also CA 154; CANR 88, 159

Pelevin, Viktor Olegovich
See Pelevin, Victor
See also DLB 285

Pellicer, Carlos 1897(?)-1977 .... **HLCS 2**
See also CA 153; 69-72; DLB 290; EWL 3; HW 1

Pena, Ramon del Valle y
See Valle-Inclan, Ramon (Maria) del

Pendennis, Arthur Esquir
See Thackeray, William Makepeace

Penn, Arthur
See Matthews, (James) Brander

Penn, William 1644-1718 .... **LC 25**
See also DLB 24

PEPECE
See Prado (Calvo), Pedro

Pepys, Samuel 1633-1703 ... **LC 11, 58; WLC 4**
See also BRW 2; CDBLB 1660-1789; DA; DA3; DAB; DAC; DAM MST; DLB 101, 213; NCFS 4; RGEL 2; TEA; WLIT 3

Percy, Thomas 1729-1811 .... **NCLC 95**
See also DLB 104

Percy, Walker 1916-1990 .... **CLC 2, 3, 6, 8, 14, 18, 47, 65**
See also AMWS 3; BPFB 3; CA 1-4R; 131; CANR 1, 23, 64; CN 1, 2, 3, 4; CPW; CSW; DA3; DAM NOV, POP; DLB 2; DLBY 1980, 1990; EWL 3; MAL 5; MTCW 1, 2; MTFW 2005; RGAL 4; TUS

Percy, William Alexander 1885-1942 .... **TCLC 84**
See also CA 163; MTCW 2

Perdurabo, Frater
See Crowley, Edward Alexander

Perec, Georges 1936-1982 .... **CLC 56, 116**
See also CA 141; DLB 83, 299; EWL 3; GFL 1789 to the Present; RGHL; RGWL 3

Pereda (y Sanchez de Porrua), Jose Maria de 1833-1906 .... **TCLC 16**
See also CA 117

Pereda y Porrua, Jose Maria de
See Pereda (y Sanchez de Porrua), Jose Maria de

Peregoy, George Weems
See Mencken, H(enry) L(ouis)
Perelman, S(idney) J(oseph)
1904-1979 .. **CLC 3, 5, 9, 15, 23, 44, 49; SSC 32**
See also AAYA 79; AITN 1, 2; BPFB 3; CA 73-76; 89-92; CANR 18; DAM DRAM; DLB 11, 44; MTCW 1, 2; MTFW 2005; RGAL 4
Peret, Benjamin 1899-1959 .... **PC 33; TCLC 20**
See also CA 117; 186; GFL 1789 to the Present
Peretz, Isaac Leib
See Peretz, Isaac Loeb
See also CA 201; DLB 333
Peretz, Isaac Loeb 1851(?)-1915 ...... **SSC 26; TCLC 16**
See Peretz, Isaac Leib
See also CA 109
Peretz, Yitzkhok Leibush
See Peretz, Isaac Loeb
Perez Galdos, Benito 1843-1920 ..... **HLCS 2; TCLC 27**
See also CA 125; 153; EW 7; EWL 3; HW 1; RGWL 2, 3
Peri Rossi, Cristina 1941- .. **CLC 156; HLCS 2**
See also CA 131; CANR 59, 81; CWW 2; DLB 145, 290; EWL 3; HW 1, 2
Perlata
See Peret, Benjamin
Perloff, Marjorie G(abrielle) 1931- .... **CLC 137**
See also CA 57-60; CANR 7, 22, 49, 104
Perrault, Charles 1628-1703 .... **LC 2, 56**
See also BYA 4; CLR 79, 134; DLB 268; GFL Beginnings to 1789; MAICYA 1, 2; RGWL 2, 3; SATA 25; WCH
Perrotta, Tom 1961- .... **CLC 266**
See also CA 162; CANR 99, 155
Perry, Anne 1938- .... **CLC 126**
See also CA 101; CANR 22, 50, 84, 150, 177; CMW 4; CN 6, 7; CPW; DLB 276
Perry, Brighton
See Sherwood, Robert E(mmet)
Perse, St.-John
See Leger, (Marie-Rene Auguste) Alexis Saint-Leger
Perse, Saint-John
See Leger, (Marie-Rene Auguste) Alexis Saint-Leger
See also DLB 258, 331; RGWL 3
Persius 34-62 .... **CMLC 74**
See also AW 2; DLB 211; RGWL 2, 3
Perutz, Leo(pold) 1882-1957 .... **TCLC 60**
See also CA 147; DLB 81
Peseenz, Tulio F.
See Lopez y Fuentes, Gregorio
Pesetsky, Bette 1932- .... **CLC 28**
See also CA 133; DLB 130
Peshkov, Alexei Maximovich 1868-1936 .... **SSC 28; TCLC 8; WLC 3**
See Gor'kii, Maksim
See also CA 105; 141; CANR 83; DA; DAB; DAC; DAM DRAM, MST, NOV; DFS 9; DLB 295; EW 8; EWL 3; MTCW 2; MTFW 2005; TWA
Pessoa, Fernando 1888-1935 .... **HLC 2; PC 20; TCLC 27**
See also CA 125; 183; CANR 182; DAM MULT; DLB 287; EW 10; EWL 3; RGWL 2, 3; WP
Pessoa, Fernando Antonio Nogueira
See Pessoa, Fernando
Peterkin, Julia Mood 1880-1961 ...... **CLC 31**
See also CA 102; DLB 9
Peters, Joan K(aren) 1945- .... **CLC 39**
See also CA 158; CANR 109

Peters, Robert L(ouis) 1924- .... **CLC 7**
See also CA 13-16R; CAAS 8; CP 1, 5, 6, 7; DLB 105
Peters, S. H.
See Porter, William Sydney
Petofi, Sandor 1823-1849 .... **NCLC 21**
See also RGWL 2, 3
Petrakis, Harry Mark 1923- .... **CLC 3**
See also CA 9-12R; CANR 4, 30, 85, 155; CN 1, 2, 3, 4, 5, 6, 7
Petrarch 1304-1374 .... **CMLC 20; PC 8**
See also DA3; DAM POET; EW 2; LMFS 1; RGWL 2, 3; WLIT 7
Petronius c. 20-66 .... **CMLC 34**
See also AW 2; CDWLB 1; DLB 211; RGWL 2, 3; WLIT 8
Petrov, Eugene
See Kataev, Evgeny Petrovich
Petrov, Evgenii
See Kataev, Evgeny Petrovich
See also DLB 272
Petrov, Evgeny
See Kataev, Evgeny Petrovich
Petrovsky, Boris
See Beauchamp, Kathleen Mansfield
Petry, Ann (Lane) 1908-1997 .. **CLC 1, 7, 18; TCLC 112**
See also AFAW 1, 2; BPFB 3; BW 1, 3; BYA 2; CA 5-8R; 157; CAAS 6; CANR 4, 46; CLR 12; CN 1, 2, 3, 4, 5, 6; DLB 76; EWL 3; JRDA; LAIT 1; MAICYA 1, 2; MAICYAS 1; MTCW 1; RGAL 4; SATA 5; SATA-Obit 94; TUS
Petursson, Halligrimur 1614-1674 .... **LC 8**
Peychinovich
See Vazov, Ivan (Minchov)
Phaedrus c. 15B.C.-c. 50 .... **CMLC 25**
See also DLB 211
Phelge, Nanker
See Richards, Keith
Phelps (Ward), Elizabeth Stuart
See Phelps, Elizabeth Stuart
See also FW
Phelps, Elizabeth Stuart 1844-1911 .... **TCLC 113**
See Phelps (Ward), Elizabeth Stuart
See also CA 242; DLB 74
Pheradausi
See Ferdowsi, Abu'l Qasem
Philippe de Remi c. 1247-1296 ... **CMLC 102**
Philips, Katherine 1632-1664 ..... **LC 30, 145; PC 40**
See also DLB 131; RGEL 2
Philipson, Ilene J. 1950- .... **CLC 65**
See also CA 219
Philipson, Morris H. 1926- .... **CLC 53**
See also CA 1-4R; CANR 4
Phillips, Caryl 1958- ..... **BLCS; CLC 96, 224**
See also BRWS 5; BW 2; CA 141; CANR 63, 104, 140; CBD; CD 5, 6; CN 5, 6, 7; DA3; DAM MULT; DLB 157; EWL 3; MTCW 2; MTFW 2005; WLIT 4; WWE 1
Phillips, David Graham 1867-1911 .... **TCLC 44**
See also CA 108; 176; DLB 9, 12, 303; RGAL 4
Phillips, Jack
See Sandburg, Carl (August)
Phillips, Jayne Anne 1952- .... **CLC 15, 33, 139; SSC 16**
See also AAYA 57; BPFB 3; CA 101; CANR 24, 50, 96; CN 4, 5, 6, 7; CSW; DLBY 1980; INT CANR-24; MTCW 1, 2; MTFW 2005; RGAL 4; RGSF 2; SSFS 4
Phillips, Richard
See Dick, Philip K.

Phillips, Robert (Schaeffer) 1938- .... **CLC 28**
See also CA 17-20R; CAAS 13; CANR 8; DLB 105
Phillips, Ward
See Lovecraft, H. P.
Philo c. 20B.C.-c. 50 .... **CMLC 100**
See also DLB 176
Philostratus, Flavius c. 179-c. 244 .... **CMLC 62**
Phiradausi
See Ferdowsi, Abu'l Qasem
Piccolo, Lucio 1901-1969 .... **CLC 13**
See also CA 97-100; DLB 114; EWL 3
Pickthall, Marjorie L(owry) C(hristie) 1883-1922 .... **TCLC 21**
See also CA 107; DLB 92
Pico della Mirandola, Giovanni 1463-1494 .... **LC 15**
See also LMFS 1
Piercy, Marge 1936- .... **CLC 3, 6, 14, 18, 27, 62, 128; PC 29**
See also BPFB 3; CA 21-24R, 187; CAAE 187; CAAS 1; CANR 13, 43, 66, 111; CN 3, 4, 5, 6, 7; CP 1, 2, 3, 4, 5, 6, 7; CWP; DLB 120, 227; EXPP; FW; MAL 5; MTCW 1, 2; MTFW 2005; PFS 9, 22; SFW 4
Piers, Robert
See Anthony, Piers
Pieyre de Mandiargues, Andre 1909-1991 .... **CLC 41**
See also CA 103; 136; CANR 22, 82; DLB 83; EWL 3; GFL 1789 to the Present
Pil'niak, Boris
See Vogau, Boris Andreyevich
See also RGSF 2; RGWL 2, 3
Pil'niak, Boris Andreevich
See Vogau, Boris Andreyevich
See also DLB 272
Pilnyak, Boris 1894-1938
See Vogau, Boris Andreyevich
Pinchback, Eugene
See Toomer, Jean
Pincherle, Alberto 1907-1990 .. **CLC 2, 7, 11, 27, 46; SSC 26**
See also CA 25-28R; 132; CANR 33, 63, 142; DAM NOV; DLB 127; EW 12; EWL 3; MTCW 2; MTFW 2005; RGSF 2; RGWL 2, 3; WLIT 7
Pinckney, Darryl 1953- .... **CLC 76**
See also BW 2, 3; CA 143; CANR 79
Pindar 518(?)B.C.-438(?)B.C. .... **CMLC 12; PC 19**
See also AW 1; CDWLB 1; DLB 176; RGWL 2
Pineda, Cecile 1942- .... **CLC 39**
See also CA 118; DLB 209
Pinero, Arthur Wing 1855-1934 .... **TCLC 32**
See also CA 110; 153; DAM DRAM; DLB 10, 344; RGEL 2
Pinero, Miguel (Antonio Gomez) 1946-1988 .... **CLC 4, 55**
See also CA 61-64; 125; CAD; CANR 29, 90; DLB 266; HW 1; LLW
Pinget, Robert 1919-1997 .... **CLC 7, 13, 37**
See also CA 85-88; 160; CWW 2; DLB 83; EWL 3; GFL 1789 to the Present
Pink Floyd
See Barrett, (Roger) Syd; Gilmour, David; Mason, Nick; Waters, Roger; Wright, Rick
Pinkney, Edward 1802-1828 .... **NCLC 31**
See also DLB 248
Pinkwater, D. Manus
See Pinkwater, Daniel Manus
Pinkwater, Daniel
See Pinkwater, Daniel Manus
Pinkwater, Daniel M.
See Pinkwater, Daniel Manus

Poquelin, Jean-Baptiste
  See Moliere
Porete, Marguerite (?)-1310 .... **CMLC 73**
  See also DLB 208
Porphyry c. 233-c. 305 .... **CMLC 71**
Porter, Connie (Rose) 1959(?)- .... **CLC 70**
  See also AAYA 65; BW 2, 3; CA 142;
  CANR 90, 109; SATA 81, 129
Porter, Gene(va Grace) Stratton
  See Stratton-Porter, Gene(va Grace)
Porter, Katherine Anne 1890-1980 ... **CLC 1,
  3, 7, 10, 13, 15, 27, 101; SSC 4, 31, 43,
  108**
  See also AAYA 42; AITN 2; AMW; BPFB
  3; CA 1-4R; 101; CANR 1, 65; CDALBS;
  CN 1, 2; DA; DA3; DAB; DAC; DAM
  MST, NOV; DLB 4, 9, 102; DLBD 12;
  DLBY 1980; EWL 3; EXPS; LAIT 3;
  MAL 5; MBL; MTCW 1, 2; MTFW 2005;
  NFS 14; RGAL 4; RGSF 2; SATA 39;
  SATA-Obit 23; SSFS 1, 8, 11, 16, 23;
  TCWW 2; TUS
Porter, Peter (Neville Frederick)
  1929- .... **CLC 5, 13, 33**
  See also CA 85-88; CP 1, 2, 3, 4, 5, 6, 7;
  DLB 40, 289; WWE 1
Porter, William Sydney 1862-1910 ..... **SSC 5,
  49, 117; TCLC 1, 19; WLC 3**
  See also AAYA 41; AMWS 2; CA 104; 131;
  CDALB 1865-1917; DA; DA3; DAB;
  DAC; DAM MST; DLB 12, 78, 79; EXPS;
  MAL 5; MTCW 1, 2; MTFW 2005;
  RGAL 4; RGSF 2; SSFS 2, 18; TCWW
  1, 2; TUS; YABC 2
Portillo (y Pacheco), Jose Lopez
  See Lopez Portillo (y Pacheco), Jose
Portillo Trambley, Estela
  1927-1998 .... **HLC 2; TCLC 163**
  See also CA 77-80; CANR 32; DAM
  MULT; DLB 209; HW 1; RGAL 4
Posey, Alexander (Lawrence)
  1873-1908 .... **NNAL**
  See also CA 144; CANR 80; DAM MULT;
  DLB 175
Posse, Abel .... **CLC 70**
  See also CA 252
Post, Melville Davisson
  1869-1930 .... **TCLC 39**
  See also CA 110; 202; CMW 4
Postman, Neil 1931(?)-2003 .... **CLC 244**
  See also CA 102; 221
Potok, Chaim 1929-2002 ... **CLC 2, 7, 14, 26,
  112**
  See also AAYA 15, 50; AITN 1, 2; BPFB 3;
  BYA 1; CA 17-20R; 208; CANR 19, 35,
  64, 98; CLR 92; CN 4, 5, 6; DA3; DAM
  NOV; DLB 28, 152; EXPN; INT CANR-
  19; LAIT 4; MTCW 1, 2; MTFW 2005;
  NFS 4; RGHL; SATA 33, 106; SATA-Obit
  134; TUS; YAW
Potok, Herbert Harold -2002
  See Potok, Chaim
Potok, Herman Harold
  See Potok, Chaim
Potter, Dennis (Christopher George)
  1935-1994 .... **CLC 58, 86, 123**
  See also BRWS 10; CA 107; 145; CANR
  33, 61; CBD; DLB 233; MTCW 1
Pound, Ezra (Weston Loomis)
  1885-1972 .. **CLC 1, 2, 3, 4, 5, 7, 10, 13,
  18, 34, 48, 50, 112; PC 4, 95; WLC 5**
  See also AAYA 47; AMW; AMWR 1; CA
  5-8R; 37-40R; CANR 40; CDALB 1917-
  1929; CP 1; DA; DA3; DAB; DAC; DAM
  MST, POET; DLB 4, 45, 63; DLBD 15;
  EFS 2; EWL 3; EXPP; LMFS 2; MAL 5;
  MTCW 1, 2; MTFW 2005; PAB; PFS 2,
  8, 16; RGAL 4; TUS; WP
Povod, Reinaldo 1959-1994 .... **CLC 44**
  See also CA 136; 146; CANR 83

Powell, Adam Clayton, Jr.
  1908-1972 .... **BLC 1:3; CLC 89**
  See also BW 1, 3; CA 102; 33-36R; CANR
  86; DAM MULT; DLB 345
Powell, Anthony 1905-2000 ... **CLC 1, 3, 7, 9,
  10, 31**
  See also BRW 7; CA 1-4R; 189; CANR 1,
  32, 62, 107; CDBLB 1945-1960; CN 1, 2,
  3, 4, 5, 6; DLB 15; EWL 3; MTCW 1, 2;
  MTFW 2005; RGEL 2; TEA
Powell, Dawn 1896(?)-1965 .... **CLC 66**
  See also CA 5-8R; CANR 121; DLBY 1997
Powell, Padgett 1952- .... **CLC 34**
  See also CA 126; CANR 63, 101; CSW;
  DLB 234; DLBY 01; SSFS 25
Power, Susan 1961- .... **CLC 91**
  See also BYA 14; CA 160; CANR 135; NFS
  11
Powers, J(ames) F(arl) 1917-1999 ..... **CLC 1,
  4, 8, 57; SSC 4**
  See also CA 1-4R; 181; CANR 2, 61; CN
  1, 2, 3, 4, 5, 6; DLB 130; MTCW 1;
  RGAL 4; RGSF 2
Powers, John J(ames) 1945- .... **CLC 66**
  See also CA 69-72
Powers, John R.
  See Powers, John J(ames)
Powers, Richard 1957- .... **CLC 93**
  See also AMWS 9; BPFB 3; CA 148;
  CANR 80, 180; CN 6, 7; MTFW 2005;
  TCLE 1:2
Powers, Richard S.
  See Powers, Richard
Pownall, David 1938- .... **CLC 10**
  See also CA 89-92; 180; CAAS 18; CANR
  49, 101; CBD; CD 5, 6; CN 4, 5, 6, 7;
  DLB 14
Powys, John Cowper 1872-1963 ... **CLC 7, 9,
  15, 46, 125**
  See also CA 85-88; CANR 106; DLB 15,
  255; EWL 3; FANT; MTCW 1, 2; MTFW
  2005; RGEL 2; SUFW
Powys, T(heodore) F(rancis)
  1875-1953 .... **TCLC 9**
  See also BRWS 8; CA 106; 189; DLB 36,
  162; EWL 3; FANT; RGEL 2; SUFW
Pozzo, Modesta
  See Fonte, Moderata
Prado (Calvo), Pedro 1886-1952 ... **TCLC 75**
  See also CA 131; DLB 283; HW 1; LAW
Prager, Emily 1952- .... **CLC 56**
  See also CA 204
Pratchett, Terence David John
  See Pratchett, Terry
Pratchett, Terry 1948- .... **CLC 197**
  See also AAYA 19, 54; BPFB 3; CA 143;
  CANR 87, 126, 170; CLR 64; CN 6, 7;
  CPW; CWRI 5; FANT; MTFW 2005;
  SATA 82, 139, 185; SFW 4; SUFW 2
Pratolini, Vasco 1913-1991 .... **TCLC 124**
  See also CA 211; DLB 177; EWL 3; RGWL
  2, 3
Pratt, E(dwin) J(ohn) 1883(?)-1964 . **CLC 19**
  See also CA 141; 93-96; CANR 77; DAC;
  DAM POET; DLB 92; EWL 3; RGEL 2;
  TWA
Premacanda
  See Srivastava, Dhanpat Rai
Premchand
  See Srivastava, Dhanpat Rai
Premchand, Munshi
  See Srivastava, Dhanpat Rai
Prem Chand, Munshi
  See Srivastava, Dhanpat Rai
Prescott, William Hickling
  1796-1859 .... **NCLC 163**
  See also DLB 1, 30, 59, 235
Preseren, France 1800-1849 .... **NCLC 127**
  See also CDWLB 4; DLB 147

Preussler, Otfried 1923- .... **CLC 17**
  See also CA 77-80; SATA 24
Prevert, Jacques (Henri Marie)
  1900-1977 .... **CLC 15**
  See also CA 77-80; 69-72; CANR 29, 61;
  DLB 258; EWL 3; GFL 1789 to the
  Present; IDFW 3, 4; MTCW 1; RGWL 2,
  3; SATA-Obit 30
Prevost, (Antoine Francois)
  1697-1763 .... **LC 1**
  See also DLB 314; EW 4; GFL Beginnings
  to 1789; RGWL 2, 3
Price, Edward Reynolds
  See Price, Reynolds
Price, Reynolds 1933- .. **CLC 3, 6, 13, 43, 50,
  63, 212; SSC 22**
  See also AMWS 6; CA 1-4R; CANR 1, 37,
  57, 87, 128, 177; CN 1, 2, 3, 4, 5, 6, 7;
  CSW; DAM NOV; DLB 2, 218, 278;
  EWL 3; INT CANR-37; MAL 5; MTCW
  2005; NFS 18
Price, Richard 1949- .... **CLC 6, 12**
  See also CA 49-52; CANR 3, 147; CN 7;
  DLBY 1981
Prichard, Katharine Susannah
  1883-1969 .... **CLC 46**
  See also CA 11-12; CANR 33; CAP 1; DLB
  260; MTCW 1; RGEL 2; RGSF 2; SATA
  66
Priestley, J(ohn) B(oynton)
  1894-1984 .... **CLC 2, 5, 9, 34**
  See also BRW 7; CA 9-12R; 113; CANR
  33; CDBLB 1914-1945; CN 1, 2, 3; DA3;
  DAM DRAM, NOV; DLB 10, 34, 77,
  100, 139; DLBY 1984; EWL 3; MTCW
  1, 2; MTFW 2005; RGEL 2; SFW 4
Prince 1958- .... **CLC 35**
  See also CA 213
Prince, F(rank) T(empleton)
  1912-2003 .... **CLC 22**
  See also CA 101; 219; CANR 43, 79; CP 1,
  2, 3, 4, 5, 6, 7; DLB 20
Prince Kropotkin
  See Kropotkin, Peter (Aleksieevich)
Prior, Matthew 1664-1721 .... **LC 4**
  See also DLB 95; RGEL 2
Prishvin, Mikhail 1873-1954 .... **TCLC 75**
  See Prishvin, Mikhail Mikhailovich
Prishvin, Mikhail Mikhailovich
  See Prishvin, Mikhail
  See also DLB 272; EWL 3
Pritchard, William H(arrison)
  1932- .... **CLC 34**
  See also CA 65-68; CANR 23, 95; DLB
  111
Pritchett, V(ictor) S(awdon)
  1900-1997 ... **CLC 5, 13, 15, 41; SSC 14**
  See also BPFB 3; BRWS 3; CA 61-64; 157;
  CANR 31, 63; CN 1, 2, 3, 4, 5, 6; DA3;
  DAM NOV; DLB 15, 139; EWL 3;
  MTCW 1, 2; MTFW 2005; RGEL 2;
  RGSF 2; TEA
Private 19022
  See Manning, Frederic
Probst, Mark 1925- .... **CLC 59**
  See also CA 130
Procaccino, Michael
  See Cristofer, Michael
Proclus c. 412-c. 485 .... **CMLC 81**
Prokosch, Frederic 1908-1989 ...... **CLC 4, 48**
  See also CA 73-76; 128; CANR 82; CN 1,
  2, 3, 4; CP 1, 2, 3, 4; DLB 48; MTCW 2
Propertius, Sextus c. 50B.C.-c.
  16B.C. .... **CMLC 32**
  See also AW 2; CDWLB 1; DLB 211;
  RGWL 2, 3; WLIT 8
Prophet, The
  See Dreiser, Theodore

Rabinovitch, Sholem 1859-1916 .... **SSC 33;**
　　TCLC 1, 35
　　See also CA 104; DLB 333; TWA
Rabinovitsh, Sholem Yankev
　　See Rabinovitch, Sholem
Rabinowitz, Sholem Yakov
　　See Rabinovitch, Sholem
Rabinowitz, Solomon
　　See Rabinovitch, Sholem
Rabinyan, Dorit 1972- .... **CLC 119**
　　See also CA 170; CANR 147
Rachilde
　　See Vallette, Marguerite Eymery; Vallette,
　　Marguerite Eymery
　　See also EWL 3
Racine, Jean 1639-1699 .. **DC 32; LC 28, 113**
　　See also DA3; DAB; DAM MST; DLB 268;
　　EW 3; GFL Beginnings to 1789; LMFS
　　1; RGWL 2, 3; TWA
Radcliffe, Ann (Ward) 1764-1823 ... **NCLC 6,**
　　55, 106
　　See also DLB 39, 178; GL 3; HGG; LMFS
　　1; RGEL 2; SUFW; WLIT 3
Radclyffe-Hall, Marguerite
　　See Hall, Radclyffe
Radiguet, Raymond 1903-1923 ...... **TCLC 29**
　　See also CA 162; DLB 65; EWL 3; GFL
　　1789 to the Present; RGWL 2, 3
Radishchev, Aleksandr Nikolaevich
　　1749-1802 .... **NCLC 190**
　　See also DLB 150
Radishchev, Alexander
　　See Radishchev, Aleksandr Nikolaevich
Radnoti, Miklos 1909-1944 .... **TCLC 16**
　　See also CA 118; 212; CDWLB 4; DLB
　　215; EWL 3; RGHL; RGWL 2, 3
Rado, James 1939- .... **CLC 17**
　　See also CA 105
Radvanyi, Netty 1900-1983 .... **CLC 7**
　　See also CA 85-88; 110; CANR 82; CD-
　　WLB 2; DLB 69; EWL 3
Rae, Ben
　　See Griffiths, Trevor
Raeburn, John (Hay) 1941- .... **CLC 34**
　　See also CA 57-60
Ragni, Gerome 1942-1991 .... **CLC 17**
　　See also CA 105; 134
Rahv, Philip
　　See Greenberg, Ivan
Rai, Navab
　　See Srivastava, Dhanpat Rai
Raimund, Ferdinand Jakob
　　1790-1836 .... **NCLC 69**
　　See also DLB 90
Raine, Craig 1944- .... **CLC 32, 103**
　　See also BRWS 13; CA 108; CANR 29, 51,
　　103, 171; CP 3, 4, 5, 6, 7; DLB 40; PFS 7
Raine, Craig Anthony
　　See Raine, Craig
Raine, Kathleen (Jessie) 1908-2003 .. **CLC 7,**
　　45
　　See also CA 85-88; 218; CANR 46, 109;
　　CP 1, 2, 3, 4, 5, 6, 7; DLB 20; EWL 3;
　　MTCW 1; RGEL 2
Rainis, Janis 1865-1929 .... **TCLC 29**
　　See also CA 170; CDWLB 4; DLB 220;
　　EWL 3
Rakosi, Carl
　　See Rawley, Callman
Ralegh, Sir Walter
　　See Raleigh, Sir Walter
　　See also BRW 1; RGEL 2; WP
Raleigh, Richard
　　See Lovecraft, H. P.
Raleigh, Sir Walter 1554(?)-1618 .... **LC 31,**
　　39; PC 31
　　See Ralegh, Sir Walter
　　See also CDBLB Before 1660; DLB 172;
　　EXPP; PFS 14; TEA

Rallentando, H. P.
　　See Sayers, Dorothy L(eigh)
Ramal, Walter
　　See de la Mare, Walter (John)
Ramana Maharshi 1879-1950 .... **TCLC 84**
Ramoacn y Cajal, Santiago
　　1852-1934 .... **TCLC 93**
Ramon, Juan
　　See Jimenez (Mantecon), Juan Ramon
Ramos, Graciliano 1892-1953 .... **TCLC 32**
　　See also CA 167; DLB 307; EWL 3; HW 2;
　　LAW; WLIT 1
Rampersad, Arnold 1941- .... **CLC 44**
　　See also BW 2, 3; CA 127; 133; CANR 81;
　　DLB 111; INT CA-133
Rampling, Anne
　　See Rice, Anne
Ramsay, Allan 1686(?)-1758 .... **LC 29**
　　See also DLB 95; RGEL 2
Ramsay, Jay
　　See Campbell, Ramsey
Ramuz, Charles-Ferdinand
　　1878-1947 .... **TCLC 33**
　　See also CA 165; EWL 3
Rand, Ayn 1905-1982 ...... **CLC 3, 30, 44, 79;**
　　SSC 116; WLC 5
　　See also AAYA 10; AMWS 4; BPFB 3;
　　BYA 12; CA 13-16R; 105; CANR 27, 73;
　　CDALBS; CN 1, 2, 3; CPW; DA; DA3;
　　DAC; DAM MST, NOV, POP; DLB 227,
　　279; MTCW 1, 2; MTFW 2005; NFS 10,
　　16; RGAL 4; SFW 4; TUS; YAW
Randall, Dudley (Felker)
　　1914-2000 .... **BLC 1:3; CLC 1, 135; PC**
　　86
　　See also BW 1, 3; CA 25-28R; 189; CANR
　　23, 82; CP 1, 2, 3, 4, 5; DAM MULT;
　　DLB 41; PFS 5
Randall, Robert
　　See Silverberg, Robert
Ranger, Ken
　　See Creasey, John
Rank, Otto 1884-1939 .... **TCLC 115**
Rankin, Ian 1960- .... **CLC 257**
　　See also BRWS 10; CA 148; CANR 81,
　　137, 171; DLB 267; MTFW 2005
Rankin, Ian James
　　See Rankin, Ian
Ransom, John Crowe 1888-1974 .. **CLC 2, 4,**
　　5, 11, 24; PC 61
　　See also AMW; CA 5-8R; 49-52; CANR 6,
　　34; CDALBS; CP 1, 2; DA3; DAM POET;
　　DLB 45, 63; EWL 3; EXPP; MAL 5;
　　MTCW 1, 2; MTFW 2005; RGAL 4; TUS
Rao, Raja 1908-2006 . **CLC 25, 56, 255; SSC**
　　99
　　See also CA 73-76; 252; CANR 51; CN 1,
　　2, 3, 4, 5, 6; DAM NOV; DLB 323; EWL
　　3; MTCW 1, 2; MTFW 2005; RGEL 2;
　　RGSF 2
Raphael, Frederic (Michael) 1931- ... **CLC 2,**
　　14
　　See also CA 1-4R; CANR 1, 86; CN 1, 2,
　　3, 4, 5, 6, 7; DLB 14, 319; TCLE 1:2
Raphael, Lev 1954- .... **CLC 232**
　　See also CA 134; CANR 72, 145; GLL 1
Ratcliffe, James P.
　　See Mencken, H(enry) L(ouis)
Rathbone, Julian 1935-2008 .... **CLC 41**
　　See also CA 101; 269; CANR 34, 73, 152
Rathbone, Julian Christopher
　　See Rathbone, Julian
Rattigan, Terence (Mervyn)
　　1911-1977 .... **CLC 7; DC 18**
　　See also BRWS 7; CA 85-88; 73-76; CBD;
　　CDBLB 1945-1960; DAM DRAM; DFS
　　8; DLB 13; IDFW 3, 4; MTCW 1, 2;
　　MTFW 2005; RGEL 2

Ratushinskaya, Irina 1954- .... **CLC 54**
　　See also CA 129; CANR 68; CWW 2
Raven, Simon (Arthur Noel)
　　1927-2001 .... **CLC 14**
　　See also CA 81-84; 197; CANR 86; CN 1,
　　2, 3, 4, 5, 6; DLB 271
Ravenna, Michael
　　See Welty, Eudora
Rawley, Callman 1903-2004 .... **CLC 47**
　　See also CA 21-24R; 228; CAAS 5; CANR
　　12, 32, 91; CP 1, 2, 3, 4, 5, 6, 7; DLB
　　193
Rawlings, Marjorie Kinnan
　　1896-1953 .... **TCLC 4**
　　See also AAYA 20; AMWS 10; ANW;
　　BPFB 3; BYA 3; CA 104; 137; CANR 74;
　　CLR 63; DLB 9, 22, 102; DLBD 17;
　　JRDA; MAICYA 1, 2; MAL 5; MTCW 2;
　　MTFW 2005; RGAL 4; SATA 100; WCH;
　　YABC 1; YAW
Ray, Satyajit 1921-1992 .... **CLC 16, 76**
　　See also CA 114; 137; DAM MULT
Read, Herbert Edward 1893-1968 ..... **CLC 4**
　　See also BRW 6; CA 85-88; 25-28R; DLB
　　20, 149; EWL 3; PAB; RGEL 2
Read, Piers Paul 1941- .... **CLC 4, 10, 25**
　　See also CA 21-24R; CANR 38, 86, 150;
　　CN 2, 3, 4, 5, 6, 7; DLB 14; SATA 21
Reade, Charles 1814-1884 .... **NCLC 2, 74**
　　See also DLB 21; RGEL 2
Reade, Hamish
　　See Gray, Simon
Reading, Peter 1946- .... **CLC 47**
　　See also BRWS 8; CA 103; CANR 46, 96;
　　CP 5, 6, 7; DLB 40
Reaney, James 1926-2008 .... **CLC 13**
　　See also CA 41-44R; CAAS 15; CANR 42;
　　CD 5, 6; CP 1, 2, 3, 4, 5, 6, 7; DAC;
　　DAM MST; DLB 68; RGEL 2; SATA 43
Reaney, James Crerar
　　See Reaney, James
Rebreanu, Liviu 1885-1944 .... **TCLC 28**
　　See also CA 165; DLB 220; EWL 3
Rechy, John 1934- ..... **CLC 1, 7, 14, 18, 107;**
　　HLC 2
　　See also CA 5-8R, 195; CAAE 195; CAAS
　　4; CANR 6, 32, 64, 152; CN 1, 2, 3, 4, 5,
　　6, 7; DAM MULT; DLB 122, 278; DLBY
　　1982; HW 1, 2; INT CANR-6; LLW;
　　MAL 5; RGAL 4
Rechy, John Francisco
　　See Rechy, John
Redcam, Tom 1870-1933 .... **TCLC 25**
Reddin, Keith 1956- .... **CLC 67**
　　See also CAD; CD 6
Redgrove, Peter (William)
　　1932-2003 .... **CLC 6, 41**
　　See also BRWS 6; CA 1-4R; 217; CANR 3,
　　39, 77; CP 1, 2, 3, 4, 5, 6, 7; DLB 40;
　　TCLE 1:2
Redmon, Anne
　　See Nightingale, Anne Redmon
Reed, Eliot
　　See Ambler, Eric
Reed, Ishmael 1938- . **BLC 1:3; CLC 2, 3, 5,**
　　6, 13, 32, 60, 174; PC 68
　　See also AFAW 1, 2; AMWS 10; BPFB 3;
　　BW 2, 3; CA 21-24R; CANR 25, 48, 74,
　　128; CN 1, 2, 3, 4, 5, 6, 7; CP 1, 2, 3, 4,
　　5, 6, 7; CSW; DA3; DAM MULT; DLB
　　2, 5, 33, 169, 227; DLBD 8; EWL 3;
　　LMFS 2; MAL 5; MSW; MTCW 1, 2;
　　MTFW 2005; PFS 6; RGAL 4; TCWW 2
Reed, John (Silas) 1887-1920 .... **TCLC 9**
　　See also CA 106; 195; MAL 5; TUS
Reed, Lou
　　See Firbank, Louis

Rubens, Bernice (Ruth) 1923-2004 . **CLC 19, 31**
See also CA 25-28R; 232; CANR 33, 65, 128; CN 1, 2, 3, 4, 5, 6, 7; DLB 14, 207, 326; MTCW 1
Rubin, Harold
See Robbins, Harold
Rudkin, (James) David 1936- .... **CLC 14**
See also CA 89-92; CBD; CD 5, 6; DLB 13
Rudnik, Raphael 1933- .... **CLC 7**
See also CA 29-32R
Ruffian, M.
See Hasek, Jaroslav (Matej Frantisek)
Rufinus c. 345-410 .... **CMLC 111**
Ruiz, Jose Martinez
See Martinez Ruiz, Jose
Ruiz, Juan c. 1283-c. 1350 .... **CMLC 66**
Rukeyser, Muriel 1913-1980 . **CLC 6, 10, 15, 27; PC 12**
See also AMWS 6; CA 5-8R; 93-96; CANR 26, 60; CP 1, 2, 3; DA3; DAM POET; DLB 48; EWL 3; FW; GLL 2; MAL 5; MTCW 1, 2; PFS 10, 29; RGAL 4; SATA-Obit 22
Rule, Jane 1931-2007 .... **CLC 27, 265**
See also CA 25-28R; 266; CAAS 18; CANR 12, 87; CN 4, 5, 6, 7; DLB 60; FW
Rule, Jane Vance
See Rule, Jane
Rulfo, Juan 1918-1986 .. **CLC 8, 80; HLC 2; SSC 25**
See also CA 85-88; 118; CANR 26; CD-WLB 3; DAM MULT; DLB 113; EWL 3; HW 1, 2; LAW; MTCW 1, 2; RGSF 2; RGWL 2, 3; WLIT 1
Rumi, Jalal al-Din 1207-1273 ...... **CMLC 20; PC 45**
See also AAYA 64; RGWL 2, 3; WLIT 6; WP
Runeberg, Johan 1804-1877 .... **NCLC 41**
Runyon, (Alfred) Damon
1884(?)-1946 .... **TCLC 10**
See also CA 107; 165; DLB 11, 86, 171; MAL 5; MTCW 2; RGAL 4
Rush, Norman 1933- .... **CLC 44**
See also CA 121; 126; CANR 130; INT CA-126
Rushdie, Salman 1947- .... **CLC 23, 31, 55, 100, 191; SSC 83; WLCS**
See also AAYA 65; BEST 89:3; BPFB 3; BRWS 4; CA 108; 111; CANR 33, 56, 108, 133; CLR 125; CN 4, 5, 6, 7; CPW 1; DA3; DAB; DAC; DAM MST, NOV, POP; DLB 194, 323, 326; EWL 3; FANT; INT CA-111; LATS 1:2; LMFS 2; MTCW 1, 2; MTFW 2005; NFS 22, 23; RGEL 2; RGSF 2; TEA; WLIT 4
Rushforth, Peter 1945-2005 .... **CLC 19**
See also CA 101; 243
Rushforth, Peter Scott
See Rushforth, Peter
Ruskin, John 1819-1900 .... **TCLC 63**
See also BRW 5; BYA 5; CA 114; 129; CD-BLB 1832-1890; DLB 55, 163, 190; RGEL 2; SATA 24; TEA; WCH
Russ, Joanna 1937- .... **CLC 15**
See also BPFB 3; CA 25-28; CANR 11, 31, 65; CN 4, 5, 6, 7; DLB 8; FW; GLL 1; MTCW 1; SCFW 1, 2; SFW 4
Russ, Richard Patrick
See O'Brian, Patrick
Russell, George William
1867-1935 .... **TCLC 3, 10**
See A.E.
See also BRWS 8; CA 104; 153; CDBLB 1890-1914; DAM POET; EWL 3; RGEL 2
Russell, Jeffrey Burton 1934- .... **CLC 70**
See also CA 25-28R; CANR 11, 28, 52, 179

Russell, (Henry) Ken(neth Alfred)
1927- .... **CLC 16**
See also CA 105
Russell, William Martin 1947-
See Russell, Willy
See also CA 164; CANR 107
Russell, Willy .... **CLC 60**
See Russell, William Martin
See also CBD; CD 5, 6; DLB 233
Russo, Richard 1949- .... **CLC 181**
See also AMWS 12; CA 127; 133; CANR 87, 114; NFS 25
Rutebeuf fl. c. 1249-1277 .... **CMLC 104**
See also DLB 208
Rutherford, Mark
See White, William Hale
Ruysbroeck, Jan van 1293-1381 ... **CMLC 85**
Ruyslinck, Ward
See Belser, Reimond Karel Maria de
Ryan, Cornelius (John) 1920-1974 ..... **CLC 7**
See also CA 69-72; 53-56; CANR 38
Ryan, Michael 1946- .... **CLC 65**
See also CA 49-52; CANR 109; DLBY 1982
Ryan, Tim
See Dent, Lester
Rybakov, Anatoli (Naumovich)
1911-1998 .... **CLC 23, 53**
See Rybakov, Anatolii (Naumovich)
See also CA 126; 135; 172; SATA 79; SATA-Obit 108
Rybakov, Anatolii (Naumovich)
See Rybakov, Anatoli (Naumovich)
See also DLB 302; RGHL
Ryder, Jonathan
See Ludlum, Robert
Ryga, George 1932-1987 .... **CLC 14**
See also CA 101; 124; CANR 43, 90; CCA 1; DAC; DAM MST; DLB 60
Rymer, Thomas 1643(?)-1713 .... **LC 132**
See also DLB 101, 336
S. H.
See Hartmann, Sadakichi
S. L. C.
See Clemens, Samuel Langhorne
S. S.
See Sassoon, Siegfried (Lorraine)
Sa'adawi, al- Nawal
See El Saadawi, Nawal
See also AFW; EWL 3
Saadawi, Nawal El
See El Saadawi, Nawal
Saadiah Gaon 882-942 .... **CMLC 97**
Saba, Umberto 1883-1957 .... **TCLC 33**
See also CA 144; CANR 79; DLB 114; EWL 3; RGWL 2, 3
Sabatini, Rafael 1875-1950 .... **TCLC 47**
See also BPFB 3; CA 162; RHW
Sabato, Ernesto 1911- ... **CLC 10, 23; HLC 2**
See also CA 97-100; CANR 32, 65; CD-WLB 3; CWW 2; DAM MULT; DLB 145; EWL 3; HW 1, 2; LAW; MTCW 1, 2; MTFW 2005
Sa-Carneiro, Mario de 1890-1916 . **TCLC 83**
See also DLB 287; EWL 3
Sacastru, Martin
See Bioy Casares, Adolfo
Sacher-Masoch, Leopold von
1836(?)-1895 .... **NCLC 31**
Sachs, Hans 1494-1576 .... **LC 95**
See also CDWLB 2; DLB 179; RGWL 2, 3
Sachs, Marilyn 1927- .... **CLC 35**
See also AAYA 2; BYA 6; CA 17-20R; CANR 13, 47, 150; CLR 2; JRDA; MAI-CYA 1, 2; SAAS 2; SATA 3, 68, 164; SATA-Essay 110; WYA; YAW
Sachs, Marilyn Stickle
See Sachs, Marilyn

Sachs, Nelly 1891-1970 .. **CLC 14, 98; PC 78**
See also CA 17-18; 25-28R; CANR 87; CAP 2; DLB 332; EWL 3; MTCW 2; MTFW 2005; PFS 20; RGHL; RGWL 2, 3
Sackler, Howard (Oliver)
1929-1982 .... **CLC 14**
See also CA 61-64; 108; CAD; CANR 30; DFS 15; DLB 7
Sacks, Oliver 1933- .... **CLC 67, 202**
See also CA 53-56; CANR 28, 50, 76, 146, 187; CPW; DA3; INT CANR-28; MTCW 1, 2; MTFW 2005
Sacks, Oliver Wolf
See Sacks, Oliver
Sackville, Thomas 1536-1608 .... **LC 98**
See also DAM DRAM; DLB 62, 132; RGEL 2
Sadakichi
See Hartmann, Sadakichi
Sa'dawi, Nawal al-
See El Saadawi, Nawal
See also CWW 2
Sade, Donatien Alphonse Francois
1740-1814 .... **NCLC 3, 47**
See also DLB 314; EW 4; GFL Beginnings to 1789; RGWL 2, 3
Sade, Marquis de
See Sade, Donatien Alphonse Francois
Sadoff, Ira 1945- .... **CLC 9**
See also CA 53-56; CANR 5, 21, 109; DLB 120
Saetone
See Camus, Albert
Safire, William 1929- .... **CLC 10**
See also CA 17-20R; CANR 31, 54, 91, 148
Sagan, Carl 1934-1996 .... **CLC 30, 112**
See also AAYA 2, 62; CA 25-28R; 155; CANR 11, 36, 74; CPW; DA3; MTCW 1, 2; MTFW 2005; SATA 58; SATA-Obit 94
Sagan, Francoise
See Quoirez, Francoise
Sahgal, Nayantara (Pandit) 1927- .... **CLC 41**
See also CA 9-12R; CANR 11, 88; CN 1, 2, 3, 4, 5, 6, 7; DLB 323
Said, Edward W. 1935-2003 .... **CLC 123**
See also CA 21-24R; 220; CANR 45, 74, 107, 131; DLB 67, 346; MTCW 2; MTFW 2005
Saikaku, Ihara 1642-1693 .... **LC 141**
See also RGWL 3
Saikaku Ihara
See Saikaku, Ihara
Saint, H(arry) F. 1941- .... **CLC 50**
See also CA 127
St. Aubin de Teran, Lisa 1953- .... **CLC 36**
See also CA 118; 126; CN 6, 7; INT CA-126
Saint Birgitta of Sweden c.
1303-1373 .... **CMLC 24**
St. E. A. of M. and S
See Crowley, Edward Alexander
Sainte-Beuve, Charles Augustin
1804-1869 .... **NCLC 5**
See also DLB 217; EW 6; GFL 1789 to the Present
Saint-Exupery, Antoine de
1900-1944 .... **TCLC 2, 56, 169; WLC**
See also AAYA 63; BPFB 3; BYA 3; CA 108; 132; CLR 10; DA3; DAM NOV; DLB 72; EW 12; EWL 3; GFL 1789 to the Present; LAIT 3; MAICYA 1, 2; MTCW 1, 2; MTFW 2005; RGWL 2, 3; SATA 20; TWA
Saint-Exupery, Antoine Jean Baptiste Marie Roger de
See Saint-Exupery, Antoine de
St. John, David
See Hunt, E. Howard

Schwob, Marcel (Mayer Andre)
1867-1905 .... **TCLC 20**
See also CA 117; 168; DLB 123; GFL 1789
to the Present

Sciascia, Leonardo 1921-1989 .. **CLC 8, 9, 41**
See also CA 85-88; 130; CANR 35; DLB
177; EWL 3; MTCW 1; RGWL 2, 3

Scoppettone, Sandra 1936- .... **CLC 26**
See Early, Jack
See also AAYA 11, 65; BYA 8; CA 5-8R;
CANR 41, 73, 157; GLL 1; MAICYA 2;
MAICYAS 1; SATA 9, 92; WYA; YAW

Scorsese, Martin 1942- .... **CLC 20, 89, 207**
See also AAYA 38; CA 110; 114; CANR
46, 85

Scotland, Jay
See Jakes, John

Scott, Duncan Campbell
1862-1947 .... **TCLC 6**
See also CA 104; 153; DAC; DLB 92;
RGEL 2

Scott, Evelyn 1893-1963 .... **CLC 43**
See also CA 104; 112; CANR 64; DLB 9,
48; RHW

Scott, F(rancis) R(eginald)
1899-1985 .... **CLC 22**
See also CA 101; 114; CANR 87; CP 1, 2,
3, 4; DLB 88; INT CA-101; RGEL 2

Scott, Frank
See Scott, F(rancis) R(eginald)

Scott, Joan .... **CLC 65**

Scott, Joanna 1960- .... **CLC 50**
See also AMWS 17; CA 126; CANR 53,
92, 168

Scott, Joanna Jeanne
See Scott, Joanna

Scott, Paul (Mark) 1920-1978 ...... **CLC 9, 60**
See also BRWS 1; CA 81-84; 77-80; CANR
33; CN 1, 2; DLB 14, 207, 326; EWL 3;
MTCW 1; RGEL 2; RHW; WWE 1

Scott, Ridley 1937- .... **CLC 183**
See also AAYA 13, 43

Scott, Sarah 1723-1795 .... **LC 44**
See also DLB 39

Scott, Sir Walter 1771-1832 .... **NCLC 15, 69,**
110, 209; PC 13; SSC 32; WLC 5
See also AAYA 22; BRW 4; BYA 2; CD-
BLB 1789-1832; DA; DAB; DAC; DAM
MST, NOV, POET; DLB 93, 107, 116,
144, 159; GL 3; HGG; LAIT 1; RGEL 2;
RGSF 2; SSFS 10; SUFW 1; TEA; WLIT
3; YABC 2

Scribe, (Augustin) Eugene 1791-1861 . **DC 5;**
NCLC 16
See also DAM DRAM; DLB 192; GFL
1789 to the Present; RGWL 2, 3

Scrum, R.
See Crumb, R.

Scudery, Georges de 1601-1667 .... **LC 75**
See also GFL Beginnings to 1789

Scudery, Madeleine de 1607-1701 .. **LC 2, 58**
See also DLB 268; GFL Beginnings to 1789

Scum
See Crumb, R.

Scumbag, Little Bobby
See Crumb, R.

Seabrook, John
See Hubbard, L. Ron

Seacole, Mary Jane Grant
1805-1881 .... **NCLC 147**
See also DLB 166

Sealy, I(rwin) Allan 1951- .... **CLC 55**
See also CA 136; CN 6, 7

Search, Alexander
See Pessoa, Fernando

Sebald, W(infried) G(eorg)
1944-2001 .... **CLC 194**
See also BRWS 8; CA 159; 202; CANR 98;
MTFW 2005; RGHL

Sebastian, Lee
See Silverberg, Robert

Sebastian Owl
See Thompson, Hunter S.

Sebestyen, Igen
See Sebestyen, Ouida

Sebestyen, Ouida 1924- .... **CLC 30**
See also AAYA 8; BYA 7; CA 107; CANR
40, 114; CLR 17; JRDA; MAICYA 1, 2;
SAAS 10; SATA 39, 140; WYA; YAW

Sebold, Alice 1963- .... **CLC 193**
See also AAYA 56; CA 203; CANR 181;
MTFW 2005

Second Duke of Buckingham
See Villiers, George

Secundus, H. Scriblerus
See Fielding, Henry

Sedges, John
See Buck, Pearl S(ydenstricker)

Sedgwick, Catharine Maria
1789-1867 .... **NCLC 19, 98**
See also DLB 1, 74, 183, 239, 243, 254; FL
1:3; RGAL 4

Sedulius Scottus 9th cent. -c. 874 .. **CMLC 86**

Seebohm, Victoria
See Glendinning, Victoria

Seelye, John (Douglas) 1931- .... **CLC 7**
See also CA 97-100; CANR 70; INT CA-
97-100; TCWW 1, 2

Seferiades, Giorgos Stylianou
1900-1971 .... **CLC 5, 11; TCLC 213**
See also CA 5-8R; 33-36R; CANR 5, 36;
DLB 332; EW 12; EWL 3; MTCW 1;
RGWL 2, 3

Seferis, George
See Seferiades, Giorgos Stylianou

Segal, Erich (Wolf) 1937- .... **CLC 3, 10**
See also BEST 89:1; BPFB 3; CA 25-28R;
CANR 20, 36, 65, 113; CPW; DAM POP;
DLBY 1986; INT CANR-20; MTCW 1

Seger, Bob 1945- .... **CLC 35**

Seghers
See Radvanyi, Netty

Seghers, Anna
See Radvanyi, Netty

Seidel, Frederick 1936- .... **CLC 18**
See also CA 13-16R; CANR 8, 99, 180; CP
1, 2, 3, 4, 5, 6, 7; DLBY 1984

Seidel, Frederick Lewis
See Seidel, Frederick

Seifert, Jaroslav 1901-1986 . **CLC 34, 44, 93;**
PC 47
See also CA 127; CDWLB 4; DLB 215,
332; EWL 3; MTCW 1, 2

Sei Shonagon c. 966-1017(?) ..... **CMLC 6, 89**

Sejour, Victor 1817-1874 .... **DC 10**
See also DLB 50

Sejour Marcou et Ferrand, Juan Victor
See Sejour, Victor

Selby, Hubert, Jr. 1928-2004 ..... **CLC 1, 2, 4,**
8; SSC 20
See also CA 13-16R; 226; CANR 33, 85;
CN 1, 2, 3, 4, 5, 6, 7; DLB 2, 227; MAL
5

Selzer, Richard 1928- .... **CLC 74**
See also CA 65-68; CANR 14, 106

Sembene, Ousmane
See Ousmane, Sembene

Senancour, Etienne Pivert de
1770-1846 .... **NCLC 16**
See also DLB 119; GFL 1789 to the Present

Sender, Ramon (Jose) 1902-1982 ...... **CLC 8;**
HLC 2; TCLC 136
See also CA 5-8R; 105; CANR 8; DAM
MULT; DLB 322; EWL 3; HW 1; MTCW
1; RGWL 2, 3

Seneca, Lucius Annaeus c. 1B.C.-c.
65 .... **CMLC 6, 107; DC 5**
See also AW 2; CDWLB 1; DAM DRAM;
DLB 211; RGWL 2, 3; TWA; WLIT 8

Senghor, Leopold Sedar
1906-2001 .. **BLC 1:3; CLC 54, 130; PC**
25
See also AFW; BW 2; CA 116; 125; 203;
CANR 47, 74, 134; CWW 2; DAM
MULT, POET; DNFS 2; EWL 3; GFL
1789 to the Present; MTCW 1, 2; MTFW
2005; TWA

Senior, Olive (Marjorie) 1941- .... **SSC 78**
See also BW 3; CA 154; CANR 86, 126;
CN 6; CP 6, 7; CWP; DLB 157; EWL 3;
RGSF 2

Senna, Danzy 1970- .... **CLC 119**
See also CA 169; CANR 130, 184

Sepheriades, Georgios
See Seferiades, Giorgos Stylianou

Serao, Ramon Gomez de la
See Gomez de la Serna, Ramon

Serpieres
See Guillevic, (Eugene)

Service, Robert
See Service, Robert W(illiam)

Service, Robert W(illiam)
1874(?)-1958 ... **PC 70; TCLC 15; WLC**
5
See also BYA 4; CA 115; 140; CANR 84;
DA; DAB; DAC; DAM MST, POET;
DLB 92; PFS 10; RGEL 2; SATA 20

Seth, Vikram 1952- .... **CLC 43, 90**
See also BRWS 10; CA 121; 127; CANR
50, 74, 131; CN 6, 7; CP 5, 6, 7; DA3;
DAM MULT; DLB 120, 271, 282, 323;
EWL 3; INT CA-127; MTCW 2; MTFW
2005; WWE 1

Setien, Miguel Delibes
See Delibes Setien, Miguel

Seton, Cynthia Propper 1926-1982 .. **CLC 27**
See also CA 5-8R; 108; CANR 7

Seton, Ernest (Evan) Thompson
1860-1946 .... **TCLC 31**
See also ANW; BYA 3; CA 109; 204; CLR
59; DLB 92; DLBD 13; JRDA; SATA 18

Seton-Thompson, Ernest
See Seton, Ernest (Evan) Thompson

Settle, Mary Lee 1918-2005 ...... **CLC 19, 61**
See also BPFB 3; CA 89-92; 243; CAAS 1;
CANR 44, 87, 126, 182; CN 6, 7; CSW;
DLB 6; INT CA-89-92

Seuphor, Michel
See Arp, Jean

Sevigne, Marie (de Rabutin-Chantal)
1626-1696 .... **LC 11, 144**
See Sevigne, Marie de Rabutin Chantal
See also GFL Beginnings to 1789; TWA

Sevigne, Marie de Rabutin Chantal
See Sevigne, Marie (de Rabutin-Chantal)
See also DLB 268

Sewall, Samuel 1652-1730 .... **LC 38**
See also DLB 24; RGAL 4

Sexton, Anne (Harvey) 1928-1974 ..... **CLC 2,**
4, 6, 8, 10, 15, 53, 123; PC 2, 79; WLC
5
See also AMWS 2; CA 1-4R; 53-56; CABS
2; CANR 3, 36; CDALB 1941-1968; CP
1, 2; DA; DA3; DAB; DAC; DAM MST,
POET; DLB 5, 169; EWL 3; EXPP; FL
1:6; FW; MAL 5; MBL; MTCW 1, 2;
MTFW 2005; PAB; PFS 4, 14; RGAL 4;
RGHL; SATA 10; TUS

Shaara, Jeff 1952- .... **CLC 119**
See also AAYA 70; CA 163; CANR 109,
172; CN 7; MTFW 2005

Shaara, Michael 1929-1988 .... **CLC 15**
See also AAYA 71; AITN 1; BPFB 3; CA
102; 125; CANR 52, 85; DAM POP;
DLBY 1983; MTFW 2005; NFS 26

Shackleton, C.C.
See Aldiss, Brian W.

Shacochis, Bob
See Shacochis, Robert G.

Shacochis, Robert G. 1951- .... **CLC 39**
See also CA 119; 124; CANR 100; INT CA-
124

Shadwell, Thomas 1641(?)-1692 .... **LC 114**
See also DLB 80; IDTP; RGEL 2

Shaffer, Anthony 1926-2001 .... **CLC 19**
See also CA 110; 116; 200; CBD; CD 5, 6;
DAM DRAM; DFS 13; DLB 13

Shaffer, Anthony Joshua
See Shaffer, Anthony

Shaffer, Peter 1926- ... **CLC 5, 14, 18, 37, 60;
DC 7**
See also BRWS 1; CA 25-28R; CANR 25,
47, 74, 118; CBD; CD 5, 6; CDBLB 1960
to Present; DA3; DAB; DAM DRAM,
MST; DFS 5, 13; DLB 13, 233; EWL 3;
MTCW 1, 2; MTFW 2005; RGEL 2; TEA

Shakespeare, William 1564-1616 . **PC 84, 89;
WLC 5**
See also AAYA 35; BRW 1; CDBLB Before
1660; DA; DA3; DAB; DAC; DAM
DRAM, MST, POET; DFS 20, 21; DLB
62, 172, 263; EXPP; LAIT 1; LATS 1:1;
LMFS 1; PAB; PFS 1, 2, 3, 4, 5, 8, 9;
RGEL 2; TEA; WLIT 3; WP; WS; WYA

Shakey, Bernard
See Young, Neil

Shalamov, Varlam (Tikhonovich)
1907-1982 .... **CLC 18**
See also CA 129; 105; DLB 302; RGSF 2

Shamloo, Ahmad
See Shamlu, Ahmad

Shamlou, Ahmad
See Shamlu, Ahmad

Shamlu, Ahmad 1925-2000 .... **CLC 10**
See also CA 216; CWW 2

Shammas, Anton 1951- .... **CLC 55**
See also CA 199; DLB 346

Shandling, Arline
See Berriault, Gina

Shange, Ntozake 1948- .. **BLC 1:3, 2:3; CLC
8, 25, 38, 74, 126; DC 3**
See also AAYA 9, 66; AFAW 1, 2; BW 2;
CA 85-88; CABS 3; CAD; CANR 27, 48,
74, 131; CD 5, 6; CP 5, 6, 7; CWD; CWP;
DA3; DAM DRAM, MULT; DFS 2, 11;
DLB 38, 249; FW; LAIT 4, 5; MAL 5;
MTCW 1, 2; MTFW 2005; NFS 11;
RGAL 4; SATA 157; YAW

Shanley, John Patrick 1950- .... **CLC 75**
See also AAYA 74; AMWS 14; CA 128;
133; CAD; CANR 83, 154; CD 5, 6; DFS
23

Shapcott, Thomas W(illiam) 1935- .. **CLC 38**
See also CA 69-72; CANR 49, 83, 103; CP
1, 2, 3, 4, 5, 6, 7; DLB 289

Shapiro, Jane 1942- .... **CLC 76**
See also CA 196

Shapiro, Karl 1913-2000 ... **CLC 4, 8, 15, 53;
PC 25**
See also AMWS 2; CA 1-4R; 188; CAAS
6; CANR 1, 36, 66; CP 1, 2, 3, 4, 5, 6;
DLB 48; EWL 3; EXPP; MAL 5; MTCW
1, 2; MTFW 2005; PFS 3; RGAL 4

Sharp, William 1855-1905 .... **TCLC 39**
See Macleod, Fiona
See also CA 160; DLB 156; RGEL 2

Sharpe, Thomas Ridley 1928- .... **CLC 36**
See also CA 114; 122; CANR 85; CN 4, 5,
6, 7; DLB 14, 231; INT CA-122

Sharpe, Tom
See Sharpe, Thomas Ridley

Shatrov, Mikhail .... **CLC 59**

Shaw, Bernard
See Shaw, George Bernard

Shaw, G. Bernard
See Shaw, George Bernard

Shaw, George Bernard 1856-1950 ..... **DC 23;
TCLC 3, 9, 21, 45, 205; WLC 5**
See also AAYA 61; BRW 6; BRWC 1;
BRWR 2; CA 104; 128; CDBLB 1914-
1945; DA; DA3; DAB; DAC; DAM
DRAM, MST; DFS 1, 3, 6, 11, 19, 22;
DLB 10, 57, 190, 332; EWL 3; LAIT 3;
LATS 1:1; MTCW 1, 2; MTFW 2005;
RGEL 2; TEA; WLIT 4

Shaw, Henry Wheeler 1818-1885 .. **NCLC 15**
See also DLB 11; RGAL 4

Shaw, Irwin 1913-1984 .... **CLC 7, 23, 34**
See also AITN 1; BPFB 3; CA 13-16R; 112;
CANR 21; CDALB 1941-1968; CN 1, 2,
3; CPW; DAM DRAM, POP; DLB 6,
102; DLBY 1984; MAL 5; MTCW 1, 21;
MTFW 2005

Shaw, Robert (Archibald)
1927-1978 .... **CLC 5**
See also AITN 1; CA 1-4R; 81-84; CANR
4; CN 1, 2; DLB 13, 14

Shaw, T. E.
See Lawrence, T(homas) E(dward)

Shawn, Wallace 1943- .... **CLC 41**
See also CA 112; CAD; CD 5, 6; DLB 266

Shaykh, al- Hanan
See al-Shaykh, Hanan

Shchedrin, N.
See Saltykov, Mikhail Evgrafovich

Shea, Lisa 1953- .... **CLC 86**
See also CA 147

Sheed, Wilfrid 1930- .... **CLC 2, 4, 10, 53**
See also CA 65-68; CANR 30, 66, 181; CN
1, 2, 3, 4, 5, 6, 7; DLB 6; MAL 5; MTCW
1, 2; MTFW 2005

Sheed, Wilfrid John Joseph
See Sheed, Wilfrid

Sheehy, Gail 1937- .... **CLC 171**
See also CA 49-52; CANR 1, 33, 55, 92;
CPW; MTCW 1

Sheldon, Alice Hastings Bradley
1915(?)-1987 .... **CLC 48, 50**
See also CA 108; 122; CANR 34; DLB 8;
INT CA-108; MTCW 1; SCFW 1, 2; SFW
4

Sheldon, John
See Bloch, Robert (Albert)

Sheldon, Raccoona
See Sheldon, Alice Hastings Bradley

Shelley, Mary Wollstonecraft (Godwin)
1797-1851 .... **NCLC 14, 59, 103, 170;
SSC 92; WLC 5**
See also AAYA 20; BPFB 3; BRW 3;
BRWC 2; BRWS 3; BYA 5; CDBLB
1789-1832; CLR 133; DA; DA3; DAB;
DAC; DAM MST, NOV; DLB 110, 116,
159, 178; EXPN; FL 1:3; GL 3; HGG;
LAIT 1; LMFS 1, 2; NFS 1; RGEL 2;
SATA 29; SCFW 1, 2; SFW 4; TEA;
WLIT 3

Shelley, Percy Bysshe 1792-1822 .. **NCLC 18,
93, 143, 175; PC 14, 67; WLC 5**
See also AAYA 61; BRW 4; BRWR 1; CD-
BLB 1789-1832; DA; DA3; DAB; DAC;
DAM MST, POET; DLB 96, 110, 158;
EXPP; LMFS 1; PAB; PFS 2, 27; RGEL
2; TEA; WLIT 3; WP

Shepard, James R.
See Shepard, Jim

Shepard, Jim 1956- .... **CLC 36**
See also AAYA 73; CA 137; CANR 59, 104,
160; SATA 90, 164

Shepard, Lucius 1947- .... **CLC 34**
See also CA 128; 141; CANR 81, 124, 178;
HGG; SCFW 2; SFW 4; SUFW 2

Shepard, Sam 1943- .... **CLC 4, 6, 17, 34, 41,
44, 169; DC 5**
See also AAYA 1, 58; AMWS 3; CA 69-72;
CABS 3; CAD; CANR 22, 120, 140; CD
5, 6; DA3; DAM DRAM; DFS 3, 6, 7,
14; DLB 7, 212, 341; EWL 3; IDFW 3, 4;
MAL 5; MTCW 1, 2; MTFW 2005;
RGAL 4

Shepherd, Jean (Parker)
1921-1999 .... **TCLC 177**
See also AAYA 69; AITN 2; CA 77-80; 187

Shepherd, Michael
See Ludlum, Robert

Sherburne, Zoa (Lillian Morin)
1912-1995 .... **CLC 30**
See also AAYA 13; CA 1-4R; 176; CANR
3, 37; MAICYA 1, 2; SAAS 18; SATA 3;
YAW

Sheridan, Frances 1724-1766 .... **LC 7**
See also DLB 39, 84

Sheridan, Richard Brinsley
1751-1816 . **DC 1; NCLC 5, 91; WLC 5**
See also BRW 3; CDBLB 1660-1789; DA;
DAB; DAC; DAM DRAM, MST; DFS
15; DLB 89; WLIT 3

Sherman, Jonathan Marc 1968- .... **CLC 55**
See also CA 230

Sherman, Martin 1941(?)- .... **CLC 19**
See also CA 116; 123; CAD; CANR 86;
CD 5, 6; DFS 20; DLB 228; GLL 1;
IDTP; RGHL

Sherwin, Judith Johnson
See Johnson, Judith (Emlyn)

Sherwood, Frances 1940- .... **CLC 81**
See also CA 146, 220; CAAE 220; CANR
158

Sherwood, Robert E(mmet)
1896-1955 .... **TCLC 3**
See also CA 104; 153; CANR 86; DAM
DRAM; DFS 11, 15, 17; DLB 7, 26, 249;
IDFW 3, 4; MAL 5; RGAL 4

Shestov, Lev 1866-1938 .... **TCLC 56**

Shevchenko, Taras 1814-1861 .... **NCLC 54**

Shiel, M(atthew) P(hipps)
1865-1947 .... **TCLC 8**
See Holmes, Gordon
See also CA 106; 160; DLB 153; HGG;
MTCW 2; MTFW 2005; SCFW 1, 2;
SFW 4; SUFW

Shields, Carol 1935-2003 .. **CLC 91, 113, 193**
See also AMWS 7; CA 81-84; 218; CANR
51, 74, 98, 133; CCA 1; CN 6, 7; CPW;
DA3; DAC; DLB 334; MTCW 2; MTFW
2005; NFS 23

Shields, David 1956- .... **CLC 97**
See also CA 124; CANR 48, 99, 112, 157

Shields, David Jonathan
See Shields, David

Shiga, Naoya 1883-1971 .... **CLC 33; SSC 23;
TCLC 172**
See Shiga Naoya
See also CA 101; 33-36R; MJW; RGWL 3

Shiga Naoya
See Shiga, Naoya
See also DLB 180; EWL 3; RGWL 3

Shilts, Randy 1951-1994 .... **CLC 85**
See also AAYA 19; CA 115; 127; 144;
CANR 45; DA3; GLL 1; INT CA-127;
MTCW 2; MTFW 2005

Shimazaki, Haruki 1872-1943 .... **TCLC 5**
See also CA 105; 134; CANR 84; DLB 180;
EWL 3; MJW; RGWL 3

Simpson, N(orman) F(rederick)
1919- .... **CLC 29**
See also CA 13-16R; CBD; DLB 13; RGEL 2

Sinclair, Andrew (Annandale) 1935- . **CLC 2, 14**
See also CA 9-12R; CAAS 5; CANR 14, 38, 91; CN 1, 2, 3, 4, 5, 6, 7; DLB 14; FANT; MTCW 1

Sinclair, Emil
See Hesse, Hermann

Sinclair, Iain 1943- .... **CLC 76**
See also BRWS 14; CA 132; CANR 81, 157; CP 5, 6, 7; HGG

Sinclair, Iain MacGregor
See Sinclair, Iain

Sinclair, Irene
See Griffith, D.W.

Sinclair, Julian
See Sinclair, May

Sinclair, Mary Amelia St. Clair (?)-
See Sinclair, May

Sinclair, May 1865-1946 .... **TCLC 3, 11**
See also CA 104; 166; DLB 36, 135; EWL 3; HGG; RGEL 2; RHW; SUFW

Sinclair, Roy
See Griffith, D.W.

Sinclair, Upton 1878-1968 ...... **CLC 1, 11, 15, 63; TCLC 160; WLC 5**
See also AAYA 63; AMWS 5; BPFB 3; BYA 2; CA 5-8R; 25-28R; CANR 7; CDALB 1929-1941; DA; DA3; DAB; DAC; DAM MST, NOV; DLB 9; EWL 3; INT CANR-7; LAIT 3; MAL 5; MTCW 1, 2; MTFW 2005; NFS 6; RGAL 4; SATA 9; TUS; YAW

Sinclair, Upton Beall
See Sinclair, Upton

Singe, (Edmund) J(ohn) M(illington)
1871-1909 .... **WLC**

Singer, Isaac
See Singer, Isaac Bashevis

Singer, Isaac Bashevis 1904-1991 .. **CLC 1, 3, 6, 9, 11, 15, 23, 38, 69, 111; SSC 3, 53, 80; WLC 5**
See also AAYA 32; AITN 1, 2; AMW; AMWR 2; BPFB 3; BYA 1, 4; CA 1-4R; 134; CANR 1, 39, 106; CDALB 1941-1968; CLR 1; CN 1, 2, 3, 4; CWRI 5; DA; DA3; DAB; DAC; DAM MST, NOV; DLB 6, 28, 52, 278, 332, 333; DLBY 1991; EWL 3; EXPS; HGG; JRDA; LAIT 3; MAICYA 1, 2; MAL 5; MTCW 1, 2; MTFW 2005; RGAL 4; RGHL; RGSF 2; SATA 3, 27; SATA-Obit 68; SSFS 2, 12, 16; TUS; TWA

Singer, Israel Joshua 1893-1944 .... **TCLC 33**
See also CA 169; DLB 333; EWL 3

Singh, Khushwant 1915- .... **CLC 11**
See also CA 9-12R; CAAS 9; CANR 6, 84; CN 1, 2, 3, 4, 5, 6, 7; DLB 323; EWL 3; RGEL 2

Singleton, Ann
See Benedict, Ruth

Singleton, John 1968(?)- .... **CLC 156**
See also AAYA 50; BW 2, 3; CA 138; CANR 67, 82; DAM MULT

Siniavskii, Andrei
See Sinyavsky, Andrei (Donatevich)
See also CWW 2

Sinibaldi, Fosco
See Kacew, Romain

Sinjohn, John
See Galsworthy, John

Sinyavsky, Andrei (Donatevich)
1925-1997 .... **CLC 8**
See Siniavskii, Andrei; Sinyavsky, Andrey Donatovich
See also CA 85-88; 159; RGSF 2

Sinyavsky, Andrey Donatovich
See Sinyavsky, Andrei (Donatevich)
See also EWL 3

Sirin, V.
See Nabokov, Vladimir (Vladimirovich)

Sissman, L(ouis) E(dward)
1928-1976 .... **CLC 9, 18**
See also CA 21-24R; 65-68; CANR 13; CP 2; DLB 5

Sisson, C(harles) H(ubert)
1914-2003 .... **CLC 8**
See also BRWS 11; CA 1-4R; 220; CAAS 3; CANR 3, 48, 84; CP 1, 2, 3, 4, 5, 6, 7; DLB 27

Sitting Bull 1831(?)-1890 .... **NNAL**
See also DA3; DAM MULT

Sitwell, Dame Edith 1887-1964 ..... **CLC 2, 9, 67; PC 3**
See also BRW 7; CA 9-12R; CANR 35; CDBLB 1945-1960; DAM POET; DLB 20; EWL 3; MTCW 1, 2; MTFW 2005; RGEL 2; TEA

Siwaarmill, H. P.
See Sharp, William

Sjoewall, Maj 1935- .... **CLC 7**
See also BPFB 3; CA 65-68; CANR 73; CMW 4; MSW

Sjowall, Maj
See Sjoewall, Maj

Skelton, John 1460(?)-1529 ..... **LC 71; PC 25**
See also BRW 1; DLB 136; RGEL 2

Skelton, Robin 1925-1997 .... **CLC 13**
See Zuk, Georges
See also AITN 2; CA 5-8R; 160; CAAS 5; CANR 28, 89; CCA 1; CP 1, 2, 3, 4, 5, 6; DLB 27, 53

Skolimowski, Jerzy 1938- .... **CLC 20**
See also CA 128

Skram, Amalie (Bertha)
1847-1905 .... **TCLC 25**
See also CA 165

Skvorecky, Josef 1924- . **CLC 15, 39, 69, 152**
See also CA 61-64; CAAS 1; CANR 10, 34, 63, 108; CDWLB 4; CWW 2; DA3; DAC; DAM NOV; DLB 232; EWL 3; MTCW 1, 2; MTFW 2005

Slade, Bernard 1930-
See Newbound, Bernard Slade

Slaughter, Carolyn 1946- .... **CLC 56**
See also CA 85-88; CANR 85, 169; CN 5, 6, 7

Slaughter, Frank G(ill) 1908-2001 ... **CLC 29**
See also AITN 2; CA 5-8R; 197; CANR 5, 85; INT CANR-5; RHW

Slavitt, David R. 1935- .... **CLC 5, 14**
See also CA 21-24R; CAAS 3; CANR 41, 83, 166; CN 1, 2; CP 1, 2, 3, 4, 5, 6, 7; DLB 5, 6

Slavitt, David Rytman
See Slavitt, David R.

Slesinger, Tess 1905-1945 .... **TCLC 10**
See also CA 107; 199; DLB 102

Slessor, Kenneth 1901-1971 .... **CLC 14**
See also CA 102; 89-92; DLB 260; RGEL 2

Slowacki, Juliusz 1809-1849 .... **NCLC 15**
See also RGWL 3

Smart, Christopher 1722-1771 .... **LC 3, 134; PC 13**
See also DAM POET; DLB 109; RGEL 2

Smart, Elizabeth 1913-1986 .... **CLC 54**
See also CA 81-84; 118; CN 4; DLB 88

Smiley, Jane 1949- ...... **CLC 53, 76, 144, 236**
See also AAYA 66; AMWS 6; BPFB 3; CA 104; CANR 30, 50, 74, 96, 158; CN 6, 7; CPW 1; DA3; DAM POP; DLB 227, 234; EWL 3; INT CANR-30; MAL 5; MTFW 2005; SSFS 19

Smiley, Jane Graves
See Smiley, Jane

Smith, A(rthur) J(ames) M(arshall)
1902-1980 .... **CLC 15**
See also CA 1-4R; 102; CANR 4; CP 1, 2, 3; DAC; DLB 88; RGEL 2

Smith, Adam 1723(?)-1790 .... **LC 36**
See also DLB 104, 252, 336; RGEL 2

Smith, Alexander 1829-1867 .... **NCLC 59**
See also DLB 32, 55

Smith, Alexander McCall 1948- ..... **CLC 268**
See also CA 215; CANR 154; SATA 73, 179

Smith, Anna Deavere 1950- ...... **CLC 86, 241**
See also CA 133; CANR 103; CD 5, 6; DFS 2, 22; DLB 341

Smith, Betty (Wehner) 1904-1972 .... **CLC 19**
See also AAYA 72; BPFB 3; BYA 3; CA 5-8R; 33-36R; DLBY 1982; LAIT 3; RGAL 4; SATA 6

Smith, Charlotte (Turner)
1749-1806 .... **NCLC 23, 115**
See also DLB 39, 109; RGEL 2; TEA

Smith, Clark Ashton 1893-1961 .... **CLC 43**
See also AAYA 76; CA 143; CANR 81; FANT; HGG; MTCW 2; SCFW 1, 2; SFW 4; SUFW

Smith, Dave
See Smith, David (Jeddie)

Smith, David (Jeddie) 1942- .... **CLC 22, 42**
See also CA 49-52; CAAS 7; CANR 1, 59, 120; CP 3, 4, 5, 6, 7; CSW; DAM POET; DLB 5

Smith, Iain Crichton 1928-1998 .... **CLC 64**
See also BRWS 9; CA 21-24R; 171; CN 1, 2, 3, 4, 5, 6; CP 1, 2, 3, 4, 5, 6; DLB 40, 139, 319; RGSF 2

Smith, John 1580(?)-1631 .... **LC 9**
See also DLB 24, 30; TUS

Smith, Johnston
See Crane, Stephen (Townley)

Smith, Joseph, Jr. 1805-1844 .... **NCLC 53**

Smith, Kevin 1970- .... **CLC 223**
See also AAYA 37; CA 166; CANR 131

Smith, Lee 1944- .... **CLC 25, 73, 258**
See also CA 114; 119; CANR 46, 118, 173; CN 7; CSW; DLB 143; DLBY 1983; EWL 3; INT CA-119; RGAL 4

Smith, Martin
See Smith, Martin Cruz

Smith, Martin Cruz 1942- .. **CLC 25; NNAL**
See Smith, Martin Cruz
See also BEST 89:4; BPFB 3; CA 85-88; CANR 6, 23, 43, 65, 119, 184; CMW 4; CPW; DAM MULT, POP; HGG; INT CANR-23; MTCW 2; MTFW 2005; RGAL 4

Smith, Patti 1946- .... **CLC 12**
See also CA 93-96; CANR 63, 168

Smith, Pauline (Urmson)
1882-1959 .... **TCLC 25**
See also DLB 225; EWL 3

Smith, R. Alexander McCall
See Smith, Alexander McCall

Smith, Rosamond
See Oates, Joyce Carol

Smith, Seba 1792-1868 .... **NCLC 187**
See also DLB 1, 11, 243

Smith, Sheila Kaye
See Kaye-Smith, Sheila

Smith, Stevie 1902-1971 .... **CLC 3, 8, 25, 44; PC 12**
See also BRWS 2; CA 17-18; 29-32R; CANR 35; CAP 2; CP 1; DAM POET; DLB 20; EWL 3; MTCW 1, 2; PAB; PFS 3; RGEL 2; TEA

Smith, Wilbur 1933- .... **CLC 33**
See also CA 13-16R; CANR 7, 46, 66, 134, 180; CPW; MTCW 1, 2; MTFW 2005

Smith, Wilbur Addison
See Smith, Wilbur

Smith, William Jay 1918- .... **CLC 6**
See also AMWS 13; CA 5-8R; CANR 44,
106; CP 1, 2, 3, 4, 5, 6, 7; CSW; CWRI
5; DLB 5; MAICYA 1, 2; SAAS 22;
SATA 2, 68, 154; SATA-Essay 154; TCLE
1:2

Smith, Woodrow Wilson
See Kuttner, Henry

Smith, Zadie 1975- .... **CLC 158**
See also AAYA 50; CA 193; DLB 347;
MTFW 2005

Smolenskin, Peretz 1842-1885 .... **NCLC 30**

Smollett, Tobias (George) 1721-1771 ... **LC 2, 46**
See also BRW 3; CDBLB 1660-1789; DLB
39, 104; RGEL 2; TEA

Snodgrass, Quentin Curtius
See Clemens, Samuel Langhorne

Snodgrass, Thomas Jefferson
See Clemens, Samuel Langhorne

Snodgrass, W. D. 1926-2009 .... **CLC 2, 6, 10, 18, 68; PC 74**
See also AMWS 6; CA 1-4R; CANR 6, 36,
65, 85, 185; CP 1, 2, 3, 4, 5, 6, 7; DAM
POET; DLB 5; MAL 5; MTCW 1, 2;
MTFW 2005; PFS 29; RGAL 4; TCLE
1:2

Snodgrass, William De Witt
See Snodgrass, W. D.

Snorri Sturluson 1179-1241 .... **CMLC 56**
See also RGWL 2, 3

Snow, C(harles) P(ercy) 1905-1980 ... **CLC 1, 4, 6, 9, 13, 19**
See also BRW 7; CA 5-8R; 101; CANR 28;
CDBLB 1945-1960; CN 1, 2; DAM NOV;
DLB 15, 77; DLBD 17; EWL 3; MTCW
1, 2; MTFW 2005; RGEL 2; TEA

Snow, Frances Compton
See Adams, Henry (Brooks)

Snyder, Gary 1930- . **CLC 1, 2, 5, 9, 32, 120; PC 21**
See also AAYA 72; AMWS 8; ANW; BG
1:3; CA 17-20R; CANR 30, 60, 125; CP
1, 2, 3, 4, 5, 6, 7; DA3; DAM POET; DLB
5, 16, 165, 212, 237, 275, 342; EWL 3;
MAL 5; MTCW 2; MTFW 2005; PFS 9,
19; RGAL 4; WP

Snyder, Zilpha Keatley 1927- .... **CLC 17**
See also AAYA 15; BYA 1; CA 9-12R, 252;
CAAE 252; CANR 38; CLR 31, 121;
JRDA; MAICYA 1, 2; SAAS 2; SATA 1,
28, 75, 110, 163; SATA-Essay 112, 163;
YAW

Soares, Bernardo
See Pessoa, Fernando

Sobh, A.
See Shamlu, Ahmad

Sobh, Alef
See Shamlu, Ahmad

Sobol, Joshua 1939- .... **CLC 60**
See Sobol, Yehoshua
See also CA 200; RGHL

Sobol, Yehoshua 1939-
See Sobol, Joshua
See also CWW 2

Socrates 470B.C.-399B.C. .... **CMLC 27**

Soderberg, Hjalmar 1869-1941 ...... **TCLC 39**
See also DLB 259; EWL 3; RGSF 2

Soderbergh, Steven 1963- .... **CLC 154**
See also AAYA 43; CA 243

Soderbergh, Steven Andrew
See Soderbergh, Steven

Sodergran, Edith (Irene) 1892-1923
See Soedergran, Edith (Irene)

Soedergran, Edith (Irene)
1892-1923 .... **TCLC 31**
See also CA 202; DLB 259; EW 11; EWL
3; RGWL 2, 3

Softly, Edgar
See Lovecraft, H. P.

Softly, Edward
See Lovecraft, H. P.

Sokolov, Alexander V(sevolodovich)
1943- .... **CLC 59**
See also CA 73-76; CWW 2; DLB 285;
EWL 3; RGWL 2, 3

Sokolov, Raymond 1941- .... **CLC 7**
See also CA 85-88

Sokolov, Sasha
See Sokolov, Alexander V(sevolodovich)

Solo, Jay
See Ellison, Harlan

Sologub, Fedor
See Teternikov, Fyodor Kuzmich
See also DLB 295

Sologub, Feodor
See Teternikov, Fyodor Kuzmich

Sologub, Fyodor
See Teternikov, Fyodor Kuzmich

Solomons, Ikey Esquir
See Thackeray, William Makepeace

Solomos, Dionysios 1798-1857 .... **NCLC 15**

Solwoska, Mara
See French, Marilyn

Solzhenitsyn, Aleksandr 1918-2008 ... **CLC 1, 2, 4, 7, 9, 10, 18, 26, 34, 78, 134, 235; SSC 32, 105; WLC 5**
See Solzhenitsyn, Aleksandr Isayevich
See also AAYA 49; AITN 1; BPFB 3; CA
69-72; CANR 40, 65, 116; DA; DA3;
DAB; DAC; DAM MST, NOV; DLB 302,
332; EW 13; EXPS; LAIT 4; MTCW 1,
2; MTFW 2005; NFS 6; RGSF 2; RGWL
2, 3; SSFS 9; TWA

Solzhenitsyn, Aleksandr I.
See Solzhenitsyn, Aleksandr

Solzhenitsyn, Aleksandr Isayevich
See Solzhenitsyn, Aleksandr
See also CWW 2; EWL 3

Somers, Jane
See Lessing, Doris

Somerville, Edith Oenone
1858-1949 .... **SSC 56; TCLC 51**
See also CA 196; DLB 135; RGEL 2; RGSF
2

Somerville & Ross
See Martin, Violet Florence; Somerville,
Edith Oenone

Sommer, Scott 1951- .... **CLC 25**
See also CA 106

Sommers, Christina Hoff 1950- ...... **CLC 197**
See also CA 153; CANR 95

Sondheim, Stephen 1930- .. **CLC 30, 39, 147; DC 22**
See also AAYA 11, 66; CA 103; CANR 47,
67, 125; DAM DRAM; DFS 25; LAIT 4

Sondheim, Stephen Joshua
See Sondheim, Stephen

Sone, Monica 1919- .... **AAL**
See also DLB 312

Song, Cathy 1955- .... **AAL; PC 21**
See also CA 154; CANR 118; CWP; DLB
169, 312; EXPP; FW; PFS 5

Sontag, Susan 1933-2004 ... **CLC 1, 2, 10, 13, 31, 105, 195**
See also AMWS 3; CA 17-20R; 234; CANR
25, 51, 74, 97, 184; CN 1, 2, 3, 4, 5, 6, 7;
CPW; DA3; DAM POP; DLB 2, 67; EWL
3; MAL 5; MBL; MTCW 1, 2; MTFW
2005; RGAL 4; RHW; SSFS 10

Sophocles 496(?)B.C.-406(?)B.C. .... **CMLC 2, 47, 51, 86; DC 1; WLCS**
See also AW 1; CDWLB 1; DA; DA3;
DAB; DAC; DAM DRAM, MST; DFS 1,
4, 8, 24; DLB 176; LAIT 1; LATS 1:1;
LMFS 1; RGWL 2, 3; TWA; WLIT 8

Sordello 1189-1269 .... **CMLC 15**

Sorel, Georges 1847-1922 .... **TCLC 91**
See also CA 118; 188

Sorel, Julia
See Drexler, Rosalyn

Sorokin, Vladimir .... **CLC 59**
See Sorokin, Vladimir Georgievich
See also CA 258

Sorokin, Vladimir Georgievich
See Sorokin, Vladimir
See also DLB 285

Sorrentino, Gilbert 1929-2006 .... **CLC 3, 7, 14, 22, 40, 247**
See also CA 77-80; 250; CANR 14, 33, 115,
157; CN 3, 4, 5, 6, 7; CP 1, 2, 3, 4, 5, 6,
7; DLB 5, 173; DLBY 1980; INT
CANR-14

Soseki
See Natsume, Soseki
See also MJW

Soto, Gary 1952- ... **CLC 32, 80; HLC 2; PC 28**
See also AAYA 10, 37; BYA 11; CA 119;
125; CANR 50, 74, 107, 157; CLR 38;
CP 4, 5, 6, 7; DAM MULT; DLB 82;
EWL 3; EXPP; HW 1, 2; INT CA-125;
JRDA; LLW; MAICYA 2; MAICYAS 1;
MAL 5; MTCW 2; MTFW 2005; PFS 7;
RGAL 4; SATA 80, 120, 174; WYA; YAW

Soupault, Philippe 1897-1990 .... **CLC 68**
See also CA 116; 147; 131; EWL 3; GFL
1789 to the Present; LMFS 2

Souster, (Holmes) Raymond 1921- .... **CLC 5, 14**
See also CA 13-16R; CAAS 14; CANR 13,
29, 53; CP 1, 2, 3, 4, 5, 6, 7; DA3; DAC;
DAM POET; DLB 88; RGEL 2; SATA 63

Southern, Terry 1924(?)-1995 .... **CLC 7**
See also AMWS 11; BPFB 3; CA 1-4R;
150; CANR 1, 55, 107; CN 1, 2, 3, 4, 5,
6; DLB 2; IDFW 3, 4

Southerne, Thomas 1660-1746 .... **LC 99**
See also DLB 80; RGEL 2

Southey, Robert 1774-1843 .... **NCLC 8, 97**
See also BRW 4; DLB 93, 107, 142; RGEL
2; SATA 54

Southwell, Robert 1561(?)-1595 .... **LC 108**
See also DLB 167; RGEL 2; TEA

Southworth, Emma Dorothy Eliza Nevitte
1819-1899 .... **NCLC 26**
See also DLB 239

Souza, Ernest
See Scott, Evelyn

Soyinka, Wole 1934- .. **BLC 1:3; 2:3; CLC 3, 5, 14, 36, 44, 179; DC 2; WLC 5**
See also AFW; BW 2, 3; CA 13-16R;
CANR 27, 39, 82, 136; CD 5, 6; CDWLB
3; CN 6, 7; CP 1, 2, 3, 4, 5, 6 ,7; DA;
DA3; DAB; DAC; DAM DRAM, MST,
MULT; DFS 10; DLB 125, 332; EWL 3;
MTCW 1, 2; MTFW 2005; PFS 27; RGEL
2; TWA; WLIT 2; WWE 1

Spackman, W(illiam) M(ode)
1905-1990 .... **CLC 46**
See also CA 81-84; 132

Spacks, Barry (Bernard) 1931- .... **CLC 14**
See also CA 154; CANR 33, 109; CP 3, 4,
5, 6, 7; DLB 105

Spanidou, Irini 1946- .... **CLC 44**
See also CA 185; CANR 179

Strand, Mark 1934- .. CLC 6, 18, 41, 71; PC 63
See also AMWS 4; CA 21-24R; CANR 40, 65, 100; CP 1, 2, 3, 4, 5, 6, 7; DAM POET; DLB 5; EWL 3; MAL 5; PAB; PFS 9, 18; RGAL 4; SATA 41; TCLE 1:2

Stratton-Porter, Gene(va Grace) 1863-1924 .... **TCLC 21**
See also ANW; BPFB 3; CA 112; 137; CLR 87; CWRI 5; DLB 221; DLBD 14; MAICYA 1, 2; RHW; SATA 15

Straub, Peter 1943- .... **CLC 28, 107**
See also BEST 89:1; BPFB 3; CA 85-88; CANR 28, 65, 109; CPW; DAM POP; DLBY 1984; HGG; MTCW 1, 2; MTFW 2005; SUFW 2

Straub, Peter Francis
See Straub, Peter

Strauss, Botho 1944- .... **CLC 22**
See also CA 157; CWW 2; DLB 124

Strauss, Leo 1899-1973 .... **TCLC 141**
See also CA 101; 45-48; CANR 122

Streatfeild, Mary Noel
See Streatfeild, Noel

Streatfeild, Noel 1897(?)-1986 .... **CLC 21**
See also CA 81-84; 120; CANR 31; CLR 17, 83; CWRI 5; DLB 160; MAICYA 1, 2; SATA 20; SATA-Obit 48

Stribling, T(homas) S(igismund) 1881-1965 .... **CLC 23**
See also CA 189; 107; CMW 4; DLB 9; RGAL 4

Strindberg, (Johan) August 1849-1912 ... DC 18; TCLC 1, 8, 21, 47; WLC 6
See also CA 104; 135; DA; DA3; DAB; DAC; DAM DRAM, MST; DFS 4, 9; DLB 259; EW 7; EWL 3; IDTP; LMFS 2; MTCW 2; MTFW 2005; RGWL 2, 3; TWA

Stringer, Arthur 1874-1950 .... **TCLC 37**
See also CA 161; DLB 92

Stringer, David
See Roberts, Keith (John Kingston)

Stroheim, Erich von 1885-1957 ..... **TCLC 71**

Strugatskii, Arkadii (Natanovich) 1925-1991 .... **CLC 27**
See Strugatsky, Arkadii Natanovich
See also CA 106; 135; SFW 4

Strugatskii, Boris (Natanovich) 1933- .... **CLC 27**
See Strugatsky, Boris (Natanovich)
See also CA 106; SFW 4

Strugatsky, Arkadii Natanovich
See Strugatskii, Arkadii (Natanovich)
See also DLB 302

Strugatsky, Boris (Natanovich)
See Strugatskii, Boris (Natanovich)
See also DLB 302

Strummer, Joe 1952-2002 .... **CLC 30**

Strunk, William, Jr. 1869-1946 ... **TCLC 92**
See also CA 118; 164; NCFS 5

Stryk, Lucien 1924- .... **PC 27**
See also CA 13-16R; CANR 10, 28, 55, 110; CP 1, 2, 3, 4, 5, 6, 7

Stuart, Don A.
See Campbell, John W(ood, Jr.)

Stuart, Ian
See MacLean, Alistair (Stuart)

Stuart, Jesse (Hilton) 1906-1984 ... CLC 1, 8, 11, 14, 34; SSC 31
See also CA 5-8R; 112; CANR 31; CN 1, 2, 3; DLB 9, 48, 102; DLBY 1984; SATA 2; SATA-Obit 36

Stubblefield, Sally
See Trumbo, Dalton

Sturgeon, Theodore (Hamilton) 1918-1985 .... **CLC 22, 39**
See also AAYA 51; BPFB 3; BYA 9, 10; CA 81-84; 116; CANR 32, 103; DLB 8; DLBY 1985; HGG; MTCW 1, 2; MTFW 2005; SCFW; SFW 4; SUFW

Sturges, Preston 1898-1959 .... **TCLC 48**
See also CA 114; 149; DLB 26

Styron, William 1925-2006 .. CLC 1, 3, 5, 11, 15, 60, 232, 244; SSC 25
See also AMW; AMWC 2; BEST 90:4; BPFB 3; CA 5-8R; 255; CANR 6, 33, 74, 126; CDALB 1968-1988; CN 1, 2, 3, 4, 5, 6, 7; CPW; CSW; DA3; DAM NOV, POP; DLB 2, 143, 299; DLBY 1980; EWL 3; INT CANR-6; LAIT 2; MAL 5; MTCW 1, 2; MTFW 2005; NCFS 1; NFS 22; RGAL 4; RGHL; RHW; TUS

Styron, William Clark
See Styron, William

Su, Chien 1884-1918 .... **TCLC 24**
See also CA 123; EWL 3

Suarez Lynch, B.
See Bioy Casares, Adolfo; Borges, Jorge Luis

Suassuna, Ariano Vilar 1927- .... **HLCS 1**
See also CA 178; DLB 307; HW 2; LAW

Suckert, Kurt Erich
See Malaparte, Curzio

Suckling, Sir John 1609-1642 . LC 75; PC 30
See also BRW 2; DAM POET; DLB 58, 126; EXPP; PAB; RGEL 2

Suckow, Ruth 1892-1960 .... **SSC 18**
See also CA 193; 113; DLB 9, 102; RGAL 4; TCWW 2

Sudermann, Hermann 1857-1928 .. **TCLC 15**
See also CA 107; 201; DLB 118

Sue, Eugene 1804-1857 .... **NCLC 1**
See also DLB 119

Sueskind, Patrick 1949- .... **CLC 182**
See Suskind, Patrick
See also BPFB 3; CA 145; CWW 2

Suetonius c. 70-c. 130 .... **CMLC 60**
See also AW 2; DLB 211; RGWL 2, 3; WLIT 8

Su Hsuan-ying
See Su, Chien

Su Hsuean-ying
See Su, Chien

Sukenick, Ronald 1932-2004 ..... CLC 3, 4, 6, 48
See also CA 25-28R; 209; 229; CAAE 209; CAAS 8; CANR 32, 89; CN 3, 4, 5, 6, 7; DLB 173; DLBY 1981

Suknaski, Andrew 1942- .... **CLC 19**
See also CA 101; CP 3, 4, 5, 6, 7; DLB 53

Sullivan, Vernon
See Vian, Boris

Sully Prudhomme, Rene-Francois-Armand 1839-1907 .... **TCLC 31**
See Prudhomme, Rene Francois Armand
See also DLB 332; GFL 1789 to the Present

Su Man-shu
See Su, Chien

Sumarokov, Aleksandr Petrovich 1717-1777 .... **LC 104**
See also DLB 150

Summerforest, Ivy B.
See Kirkup, James

Summers, Andrew James
See Summers, Andy

Summers, Andy 1942- .... **CLC 26**
See also CA 255

Summers, Hollis (Spurgeon, Jr.) 1916- .... **CLC 10**
See also CA 5-8R; CANR 3; CN 1, 2, 3; CP 1, 2, 3, 4; DLB 6; TCLE 1:2

Summers, (Alphonsus Joseph-Mary Augustus) Montague 1880-1948 .... **TCLC 16**
See also CA 118; 163

Sumner, Gordon Matthew
See Sting

Sun Tzu c. 400B.C.-c. 320B.C. ...... **CMLC 56**

Surdas c. 1478-c. 1583 .... **LC 163**
See also RGWL 2, 3

Surrey, Henry Howard 1517-1574 ... LC 121; PC 59
See also BRW 1; RGEL 2

Surtees, Robert Smith 1805-1864 .. **NCLC 14**
See also DLB 21; RGEL 2

Susann, Jacqueline 1921-1974 .... **CLC 3**
See also AITN 1; BPFB 3; CA 65-68; 53-56; MTCW 1, 2

Su Shi
See Su Shih
See also RGWL 2, 3

Su Shih 1036-1101 .... **CMLC 15**
See Su Shi

Suskind, Patrick .... **CLC 182**
See Sueskind, Patrick
See also BPFB 3; CA 145; CWW 2

Suso, Heinrich c. 1295-1366 .... **CMLC 87**

Sutcliff, Rosemary 1920-1992 .... **CLC 26**
See also AAYA 10; BYA 1, 4; CA 5-8R; 139; CANR 37; CLR 1, 37, 138; CPW; DAB; DAC; DAM MST, POP; JRDA; LATS 1:1; MAICYA 1, 2; MAICYAS 1; RHW; SATA 6, 44, 78; SATA-Obit 73; WYA; YAW

Sutherland, Efua (Theodora Morgue) 1924-1996 .... **BLC 2:3**
See also AFW; BW 1; CA 105; CWD; DLB 117; EWL 3; IDTP; SATA 25

Sutro, Alfred 1863-1933 .... **TCLC 6**
See also CA 105; 185; DLB 10; RGEL 2

Sutton, Henry
See Slavitt, David R.

Su Yuan-ying
See Su, Chien

Su Yuean-ying
See Su, Chien

Suzuki, D. T.
See Suzuki, Daisetz Teitaro

Suzuki, Daisetz T.
See Suzuki, Daisetz Teitaro

Suzuki, Daisetz Teitaro 1870-1966 .... **TCLC 109**
See also CA 121; 111; MTCW 1, 2; MTFW 2005

Suzuki, Teitaro
See Suzuki, Daisetz Teitaro

Svareff, Count Vladimir
See Crowley, Edward Alexander

Svevo, Italo
See Schmitz, Aron Hector

Swados, Elizabeth 1951- .... **CLC 12**
See also CA 97-100; CANR 49, 163; INT CA-97-100

Swados, Elizabeth A.
See Swados, Elizabeth

Swados, Harvey 1920-1972 .... **CLC 5**
See also CA 5-8R; 37-40R; CANR 6; CN 1; DLB 2, 335; MAL 5

Swados, Liz
See Swados, Elizabeth

Swan, Gladys 1934- .... **CLC 69**
See also CA 101; CANR 17, 39; TCLE 1:2

Swanson, Logan
See Matheson, Richard

Swarthout, Glendon (Fred) 1918-1992 .... **CLC 35**
See also AAYA 55; CA 1-4R; 139; CANR 1, 47; CN 1, 2, 3, 4, 5; LAIT 5; SATA 26; TCWW 1, 2; YAW

Taylor, Peter (Hillsman) 1917-1994 .. **CLC 1, 4, 18, 37, 44, 50, 71; SSC 10, 84**
See also AMWS 5; BPFB 3; CA 13-16R; 147; CANR 9, 50; CN 1, 2, 3, 4, 5; CSW; DLB 218, 278; DLBY 1981, 1994; EWL 3; EXPS; INT CANR-9; MAL 5; MTCW 1, 2; MTFW 2005; RGSF 2; SSFS 9; TUS

Taylor, Robert Lewis 1912-1998 .... **CLC 14**
See also CA 1-4R; 170; CANR 3, 64; CN 1, 2; SATA 10; TCWW 1, 2

Tchekhov, Anton
See Chekhov, Anton (Pavlovich)

Tchicaya, Gerald Felix 1931-1988 .. **CLC 101**
See also CA 129; 125; CANR 81; EWL 3

Tchicaya U Tam'si
See Tchicaya, Gerald Felix

Teasdale, Sara 1884-1933 .... **PC 31; TCLC 4**
See also CA 104; 163; DLB 45; GLL 1; PFS 14; RGAL 4; SATA 32; TUS

Tecumseh 1768-1813 .... **NNAL**
See also DAM MULT

Tegner, Esaias 1782-1846 .... **NCLC 2**

Teilhard de Chardin, (Marie Joseph) Pierre 1881-1955 .... **TCLC 9**
See also CA 105; 210; GFL 1789 to the Present

Temple, Ann
See Mortimer, Penelope (Ruth)

Tennant, Emma 1937- .... **CLC 13, 52**
See also BRWS 9; CA 65-68; CAAS 9; CANR 10, 38, 59, 88, 177; CN 3, 4, 5, 6, 7; DLB 14; EWL 3; SFW 4

Tenneshaw, S.M.
See Silverberg, Robert

Tenney, Tabitha Gilman 1762-1837 .... **NCLC 122**
See also DLB 37, 200

Tennyson, Alfred 1809-1892 ... **NCLC 30, 65, 115, 202; PC 6; WLC 6**
See also AAYA 50; BRW 4; CDBLB 1832-1890; DA; DA3; DAB; DAC; DAM MST, POET; DLB 32; EXPP; PAB; PFS 1, 2, 4, 11, 15, 19; RGEL 2; TEA; WLIT 4; WP

Teran, Lisa St. Aubin de
See St. Aubin de Teran, Lisa

Terence c. 184B.C.-c. 159B.C. ...... **CMLC 14; DC 7**
See also AW 1; CDWLB 1; DLB 211; RGWL 2, 3; TWA; WLIT 8

Teresa de Jesus, St. 1515-1582 .... **LC 18, 149**

Teresa of Avila, St.
See Teresa de Jesus, St.

Terkel, Louis
See Terkel, Studs

Terkel, Studs 1912-2008 .... **CLC 38**
See also AAYA 32; AITN 1; CA 57-60; 278; CANR 18, 45, 67, 132; DA3; MTCW 1, 2; MTFW 2005; TUS

Terkel, Studs Louis
See Terkel, Studs

Terry, C. V.
See Slaughter, Frank G(ill)

Terry, Megan 1932- .... **CLC 19; DC 13**
See also CA 77-80; CABS 3; CAD; CANR 43; CD 5, 6; CWD; DFS 18; DLB 7, 249; GLL 2

Tertullian c. 155-c. 245 .... **CMLC 29**

Tertz, Abram
See Sinyavsky, Andrei (Donatevich)

Tesich, Steve 1943(?)-1996 .... **CLC 40, 69**
See also CA 105; 152; CAD; DLBY 1983

Tesla, Nikola 1856-1943 .... **TCLC 88**

Teternikov, Fyodor Kuzmich 1863-1927 .... **TCLC 9**
See Sologub, Fedor
See also CA 104; EWL 3

Tevis, Walter 1928-1984 .... **CLC 42**
See also CA 113; SFW 4

Tey, Josephine
See Mackintosh, Elizabeth

Thackeray, William Makepeace 1811-1863 ...... **NCLC 5, 14, 22, 43, 169; WLC 6**
See also BRW 5; BRWC 2; CDBLB 1832-1890; DA; DA3; DAB; DAC; DAM MST, NOV; DLB 21, 55, 159, 163; NFS 13; RGEL 2; SATA 23; TEA; WLIT 3

Thakura, Ravindranatha
See Tagore, Rabindranath

Thames, C. H.
See Marlowe, Stephen

Tharoor, Shashi 1956- .... **CLC 70**
See also CA 141; CANR 91; CN 6, 7

Thelwall, John 1764-1834 .... **NCLC 162**
See also DLB 93, 158

Thelwell, Michael Miles 1939- .... **CLC 22**
See also BW 2; CA 101

Theo, Ion
See Theodorescu, Ion N.

Theobald, Lewis, Jr.
See Lovecraft, H. P.

Theocritus c. 310B.C.- .... **CMLC 45**
See also AW 1; DLB 176; RGWL 2, 3

Theodorescu, Ion N. 1880-1967 .... **CLC 80**
See also CA 167; 116; CDWLB 4; DLB 220; EWL 3

Theriault, Yves 1915-1983 .... **CLC 79**
See also CA 102; CANR 150; CCA 1; DAC; DAM MST; DLB 88; EWL 3

Therion, Master
See Crowley, Edward Alexander
See also GLL 1

Theroux, Alexander 1939- .... **CLC 2, 25**
See also CA 85-88; CANR 20, 63; CN 4, 5, 6, 7

Theroux, Alexander Louis
See Theroux, Alexander

Theroux, Paul 1941- .... **CLC 5, 8, 11, 15, 28, 46, 159**
See also AAYA 28; AMWS 8; BEST 89:4; BPFB 3; CA 33-36R; CANR 20, 45, 74, 133, 179; CDALBS; CN 1, 2, 3, 4, 5, 6, 7; CP 1; CPW 1; DA3; DAM POP; DLB 2, 218; EWL 3; HGG; MAL 5; MTCW 1, 2; MTFW 2005; RGAL 4; SATA 44, 109; TUS

Theroux, Paul Edward
See Theroux, Paul

Thesen, Sharon 1946- .... **CLC 56**
See also CA 163; CANR 125; CP 5, 6, 7; CWP

Thespis fl. 6th cent. B.C.- .... **CMLC 51**
See also LMFS 1

Thevenin, Denis
See Duhamel, Georges

Thibault, Jacques Anatole Francois 1844-1924 .... **TCLC 9**
See also CA 106; 127; DA3; DAM NOV; DLB 123, 330; EWL 3; GFL 1789 to the Present; MTCW 1, 2; RGWL 2, 3; SUFW 1; TWA

Thiele, Colin 1920-2006 .... **CLC 17**
See also CA 29-32R; CANR 12, 28, 53, 105; CLR 27; CP 1, 2; DLB 289; MAICYA 1, 2; SAAS 2; SATA 14, 72, 125; YAW

Thiong'o, Ngugi Wa
See Ngugi wa Thiong'o

Thistlethwaite, Bel
See Wetherald, Agnes Ethelwyn

Thomas, Audrey (Callahan) 1935- .... **CLC 7, 13, 37, 107; SSC 20**
See also AITN 2; CA 21-24R; 237; CAAE 237; CAAS 19; CANR 36, 58; CN 2, 3, 4, 5, 6, 7; DLB 60; MTCW 1; RGSF 2

Thomas, Augustus 1857-1934 .... **TCLC 97**
See also MAL 5

Thomas, D.M. 1935- ..... **CLC 13, 22, 31, 132**
See also BPFB 3; BRWS 4; CA 61-64; CAAS 11; CANR 17, 45, 75; CDBLB 1960 to Present; CN 4, 5, 6, 7; CP 1, 2, 3, 4, 5, 6, 7; DA3; DLB 40, 207, 299; HGG; INT CANR-17; MTCW 1, 2; MTFW 2005; RGHL; SFW 4

Thomas, Dylan (Marlais) 1914-1953 .... **PC 2, 52; SSC 3, 44; TCLC 1, 8, 45, 105; WLC 6**
See also AAYA 45; BRWS 1; CA 104; 120; CANR 65; CDBLB 1945-1960; DA; DA3; DAB; DAC; DAM DRAM, MST, POET; DLB 13, 20, 139; EWL 3; EXPP; LAIT 3; MTCW 1, 2; MTFW 2005; PAB; PFS 1, 3, 8; RGEL 2; RGSF 2; SATA 60; TEA; WLIT 4; WP

Thomas, (Philip) Edward 1878-1917 . **PC 53; TCLC 10**
See also BRW 6; BRWS 3; CA 106; 153; DAM POET; DLB 19, 98, 156, 216; EWL 3; PAB; RGEL 2

Thomas, J.F.
See Fleming, Thomas

Thomas, Joyce Carol 1938- .... **CLC 35**
See also AAYA 12, 54; BW 2, 3; CA 113; 116; CANR 48, 114, 135; CLR 19; DLB 33; INT CA-116; JRDA; MAICYA 1, 2; MTCW 1, 2; MTFW 2005; SAAS 7; SATA 40, 78, 123, 137; SATA-Essay 137; WYA; YAW

Thomas, Lewis 1913-1993 .... **CLC 35**
See also ANW; CA 85-88; 143; CANR 38, 60; DLB 275; MTCW 1, 2

Thomas, M. Carey 1857-1935 .... **TCLC 89**
See also FW

Thomas, Paul
See Mann, (Paul) Thomas

Thomas, Piri 1928- .... **CLC 17; HLCS 2**
See also CA 73-76; HW 1; LLW

Thomas, R(onald) S(tuart) 1913-2000 .... **CLC 6, 13, 48**
See also BRWS 12; CA 89-92; 189; CAAS 4; CANR 30; CDBLB 1960 to Present; CP 1, 2, 3, 4, 5, 6, 7; DAB; DAM POET; DLB 27; EWL 3; MTCW 1; RGEL 2

Thomas, Ross (Elmore) 1926-1995 .. **CLC 39**
See also CA 33-36R; 150; CANR 22, 63; CMW 4

Thompson, Francis (Joseph) 1859-1907 .... **TCLC 4**
See also BRW 5; CA 104; 189; CDBLB 1890-1914; DLB 19; RGEL 2; TEA

Thompson, Francis Clegg
See Mencken, H(enry) L(ouis)

Thompson, Hunter S. 1937(?)-2005 .. **CLC 9, 17, 40, 104, 229**
See also AAYA 45; BEST 89:1; BPFB 3; CA 17-20R; 236; CANR 23, 46, 74, 77, 111, 133; CPW; CSW; DA3; DAM POP; DLB 185; MTCW 1, 2; MTFW 2005; TUS

Thompson, James Myers
See Thompson, Jim

Thompson, Jim 1906-1977 .... **CLC 69**
See also BPFB 3; CA 140; CMW 4; CPW; DLB 226; MSW

Thompson, Judith (Clare Francesca) 1954- .... **CLC 39**
See also CA 143; CD 5, 6; CWD; DFS 22; DLB 334

Thomson, James 1700-1748 .... **LC 16, 29, 40**
See also BRWS 3; DAM POET; DLB 95; RGEL 2

Thomson, James 1834-1882 .... **NCLC 18**
See also DAM POET; DLB 35; RGEL 2

Tournier, Michel Edouard
See Tournier, Michel

Tournimparte, Alessandra
See Ginzburg, Natalia

Towers, Ivar
See Kornbluth, C(yril) M.

Towne, Robert (Burton) 1936(?)- ..... **CLC 87**
See also CA 108; DLB 44; IDFW 3, 4

Townsend, Sue .... **CLC 61**
See Townsend, Susan Lilian
See also AAYA 28; CA 119; 127; CANR
65, 107; CBD; CD 5, 6; CPW; CWD;
DAB; DAC; DAM MST; DLB 271; INT
CA-127; SATA 55, 93; SATA-Brief 48;
YAW

Townsend, Susan Lilian 1946-
See Townsend, Sue

Townshend, Pete
See Townshend, Peter

Townshend, Peter 1945- .... **CLC 17, 42**
See also CA 107

Townshend, Peter Dennis Blandford
See Townshend, Peter

Tozzi, Federigo 1883-1920 .... **TCLC 31**
See also CA 160; CANR 110; DLB 264;
EWL 3; WLIT 7

Trafford, F. G.
See Riddell, Charlotte

Traherne, Thomas 1637(?)-1674 .. **LC 99; PC 70**
See also BRW 2; BRWS 11; DLB 131;
PAB; RGEL 2

Traill, Catharine Parr 1802-1899 .. **NCLC 31**
See also DLB 99

Trakl, Georg 1887-1914 .... **PC 20; TCLC 5**
See also CA 104; 165; EW 10; EWL 3;
LMFS 2; MTCW 2; RGWL 2, 3

Trambley, Estela Portillo
See Portillo Trambley, Estela

Tranquilli, Secondino
See Silone, Ignazio

Transtroemer, Tomas Gosta
See Transtromer, Tomas

Transtromer, Tomas (Gosta)
See Transtromer, Tomas
See also CWW 2

Transtromer, Tomas 1931- .... **CLC 52, 65**
See also CA 117; 129; CAAS 17; CANR
115, 172; DAM POET; DLB 257; EWL
3; PFS 21

Transtromer, Tomas Goesta
See Transtromer, Tomas

Transtromer, Tomas Gosta
See Transtromer, Tomas

Transtromer, Tomas Gosta
See Transtromer, Tomas

Traven, B. 1882(?)-1969 .... **CLC 8, 11**
See also CA 19-20; 25-28R; CAP 2; DLB
9, 56; EWL 3; MTCW 1; RGAL 4

Trediakovsky, Vasilii Kirillovich
1703-1769 .... **LC 68**
See also DLB 150

Treitel, Jonathan 1959- .... **CLC 70**
See also CA 210; DLB 267

Trelawny, Edward John
1792-1881 .... **NCLC 85**
See also DLB 110, 116, 144

Tremain, Rose 1943- .... **CLC 42**
See also CA 97-100; CANR 44, 95, 186;
CN 4, 5, 6, 7; DLB 14, 271; RGSF 2;
RHW

Tremblay, Michel 1942- .... **CLC 29, 102, 225**
See also CA 116; 128; CCA 1; CWW 2;
DAC; DAM MST; DLB 60; EWL 3; GLL
1; MTCW 1, 2; MTFW 2005

Trevanian .... **CLC 29**
See Whitaker, Rod

Trevisa, John c. 1342-c. 1402 .... **LC 139**
See also BRWS 9; DLB 146

Trevor, Glen
See Hilton, James

Trevor, William 1928- ... **CLC 1, 2, 3, 4, 5, 6, 7; SSC 21, 58**
See also BRWS 4; CA 9-12R; CANR 4, 37,
55, 76, 102, 139; CBD; CD 5, 6; DAM
NOV; DLB 14, 139; EWL 3; INT CANR-
37; LATS 1:2; MTCW 1, 2; MTFW 2005;
RGEL 2; RGSF 2; SSFS 10; TCLE 1:2;
TEA

Trifonov, Iurii (Valentinovich)
See Trifonov, Yuri (Valentinovich)
See also DLB 302; RGWL 2, 3

Trifonov, Yuri (Valentinovich)
1925-1981 .... **CLC 45**
See Trifonov, Iurii (Valentinovich); Trifonov, Yury Valentinovich
See also CA 126; 103; MTCW 1

Trifonov, Yury Valentinovich
See Trifonov, Yuri (Valentinovich)
See also EWL 3

Trilling, Diana (Rubin) 1905-1996 . **CLC 129**
See also CA 5-8R; 154; CANR 10, 46; INT
CANR-10; MTCW 1, 2

Trilling, Lionel 1905-1975 ..... **CLC 9, 11, 24; SSC 75**
See also AMWS 3; CA 9-12R; 61-64;
CANR 10, 105; CN 1, 2; DLB 28, 63;
EWL 3; INT CANR-10; MAL 5; MTCW
1, 2; RGAL 4; TUS

Trimball, W. H.
See Mencken, H(enry) L(ouis)

Tristan
See Gomez de la Serna, Ramon

Tristram
See Housman, A(lfred) E(dward)

Trogdon, William (Lewis) 1939- .... **CLC 29**
See Least Heat-Moon, William
See also AAYA 9, 66; CA 115; 119; CANR
47, 89; CPW; INT CA-119

Trollope, Anthony 1815-1882 .... **NCLC 6, 33, 101; SSC 28; WLC 6**
See also BRW 5; CDBLB 1832-1890; DA;
DA3; DAB; DAC; DAM MST, NOV;
DLB 21, 57, 159; RGEL 2; RGSF 2;
SATA 22

Trollope, Frances 1779-1863 .... **NCLC 30**
See also DLB 21, 166

Trollope, Joanna 1943- .... **CLC 186**
See also CA 101; CANR 58, 95, 149; CN
7; CPW; DLB 207; RHW

Trotsky, Leon 1879-1940 .... **TCLC 22**
See also CA 118; 167

Trotter (Cockburn), Catharine
1679-1749 .... **LC 8**
See also DLB 84, 252

Trotter, Wilfred 1872-1939 .... **TCLC 97**

Troupe, Quincy 1943- .... **BLC 2:3**
See also BW 2; CA 113; 124; CANR 43,
90, 126; DLB 41

Trout, Kilgore
See Farmer, Philip Jose

Trow, George William Swift
See Trow, George W.S.

Trow, George W.S. 1943-2006 .... **CLC 52**
See also CA 126; 255; CANR 91

Troyat, Henri 1911-2007 .... **CLC 23**
See also CA 45-48; 258; CANR 2, 33, 67,
117; GFL 1789 to the Present; MTCW 1

Trudeau, Garretson Beekman
See Trudeau, G.B.

Trudeau, Garry
See Trudeau, G.B.

Trudeau, Garry B.
See Trudeau, G.B.

Trudeau, G.B. 1948- .... **CLC 12**
See also AAYA 10, 60; AITN 2; CA 81-84;
CANR 31; SATA 35, 168

Truffaut, Francois 1932-1984 ... **CLC 20, 101**
See also CA 81-84; 113; CANR 34

Trumbo, Dalton 1905-1976 .... **CLC 19**
See also CA 21-24R; 69-72; CANR 10; CN
1, 2; DLB 26; IDFW 3, 4; YAW

Trumbull, John 1750-1831 .... **NCLC 30**
See also DLB 31; RGAL 4

Trundlett, Helen B.
See Eliot, T(homas) S(tearns)

Truth, Sojourner 1797(?)-1883 ...... **NCLC 94**
See also DLB 239; FW; LAIT 2

Tryon, Thomas 1926-1991 .... **CLC 3, 11**
See also AITN 1; BPFB 3; CA 29-32R; 135;
CANR 32, 77; CPW; DA3; DAM POP;
HGG; MTCW 1

Tryon, Tom
See Tryon, Thomas

Ts'ao Hsueh-ch'in 1715(?)-1763 .... **LC 1**

Tsurayuki Ed. fl. 10th cent. - .... **PC 73**

Tsvetaeva (Efron), Marina (Ivanovna)
1892-1941 .... **PC 14; TCLC 7, 35**
See also CA 104; 128; CANR 73; DLB 295;
EW 11; MTCW 1, 2; PFS 29; RGWL 2, 3

Tuck, Lily 1938- .... **CLC 70**
See also AAYA 74; CA 139; CANR 90

Tuckerman, Frederick Goddard
1821-1873 .... **PC 85**
See also DLB 243; RGAL 4

Tu Fu 712-770 .... **PC 9**
See Du Fu
See also DAM MULT; TWA; WP

Tulsidas, Gosvami 1532(?)-1623 .... **LC 158**
See also RGWL 2, 3

Tunis, John R(oberts) 1889-1975 ..... **CLC 12**
See also BYA 1; CA 61-64; CANR 62; DLB
22, 171; JRDA; MAICYA 1, 2; SATA 37;
SATA-Brief 30; YAW

Tuohy, Frank
See Tuohy, John Francis

Tuohy, John Francis 1925- .... **CLC 37**
See also CA 5-8R; 178; CANR 3, 47; CN
1, 2, 3, 4, 5, 6, 7; DLB 14, 139

Turco, Lewis 1934- .... **CLC 11, 63**
See also CA 13-16R; CAAS 22; CANR 24,
51, 185; CP 1, 2, 3, 4, 5, 6, 7; DLBY
1984; TCLE 1:2

Turco, Lewis Putnam
See Turco, Lewis

Turgenev, Ivan (Sergeevich)
1818-1883 ..... **DC 7; NCLC 21, 37, 122;
SSC 7, 57; WLC 6**
See also AAYA 58; DA; DAB; DAC; DAM
MST, NOV; DFS 6; DLB 238, 284; EW
6; LATS 1:1; NFS 16; RGSF 2; RGWL 2,
3; TWA

Turgot, Anne-Robert-Jacques
1727-1781 .... **LC 26**
See also DLB 314

Turner, Frederick 1943- .... **CLC 48**
See also CA 73-76, 227; CAAE 227; CAAS
10; CANR 12, 30, 56; DLB 40, 282

Turton, James
See Crace, Jim

Tutu, Desmond M(pilo) 1931- .... **BLC 1:3;
CLC 80**
See also BW 1, 3; CA 125; CANR 67, 81;
DAM MULT

Tutuola, Amos 1920-1997 .... **BLC 1:3, 2:3;
CLC 5, 14, 29; TCLC 188**
See also AAYA 76; AFW; BW 2, 3; CA
9-12R; 159; CANR 27, 66; CDWLB 3;
CN 1, 2, 3, 4, 5, 6; DA3; DAM MULT;
DLB 125; DNFS 2; EWL 3; MTCW 1, 2;
MTFW 2005; RGEL 2; WLIT 2

Twain, Mark
See Clemens, Samuel Langhorne

Twohill, Maggie
See Angell, Judie
Tyler, Anne 1941- . **CLC 7, 11, 18, 28, 44, 59, 103, 205, 265**
See also AAYA 18, 60; AMWS 4; BEST 89:1; BPFB 3; BYA 12; CA 9-12R; CANR 11, 33, 53, 109, 132, 168; CDALBS; CN 1, 2, 3, 4, 5, 6, 7; CPW; CSW; DAM NOV, POP; DLB 6, 143; DLBY 1982; EWL 3; EXPN; LATS 1:2; MAL 5; MBL; MTCW 1, 2; MTFW 2005; NFS 2, 7, 10; RGAL 4; SATA 7, 90, 173; SSFS 17; TCLE 1:2; TUS; YAW
Tyler, Royall 1757-1826 .... **NCLC 3**
See also DLB 37; RGAL 4
Tynan, Katharine 1861-1931 ... **TCLC 3, 217**
See also CA 104; 167; DLB 153, 240; FW
Tyndale, William c. 1484-1536 .... **LC 103**
See also DLB 132
Tyutchev, Fyodor 1803-1873 .... **NCLC 34**
Tzara, Tristan 1896-1963 .... **CLC 47; PC 27; TCLC 168**
See also CA 153; 89-92; DAM POET; EWL 3; MTCW 2
Uc de Saint Circ c. 1190B.C.-13th cent.
B.C. .... **CMLC 102**
Uchida, Yoshiko 1921-1992 .... **AAL**
See also AAYA 16; BYA 2, 3; CA 13-16R; 139; CANR 6, 22, 47, 61; CDALBS; CLR 6, 56; CWRI 5; DLB 312; JRDA; MAICYA 1, 2; MTCW 1, 2; MTFW 2005; NFS 26; SAAS 1; SATA 1, 53; SATA-Obit 72
Udall, Nicholas 1504-1556 .... **LC 84**
See also DLB 62; RGEL 2
Ueda Akinari 1734-1809 .... **NCLC 131**
Uhry, Alfred 1936- .... **CLC 55; DC 28**
See also CA 127; 133; CAD; CANR 112; CD 5, 6; CSW; DA3; DAM DRAM, POP; DFS 11, 15; INT CA-133; MTFW 2005
Ulf, Haerved
See Strindberg, (Johan) August
Ulf, Harved
See Strindberg, (Johan) August
Ulibarri, Sabine R(eyes) 1919-2003 .... **CLC 83; HLCS 2**
See also CA 131; 214; CANR 81; DAM MULT; DLB 82; HW 1, 2; RGSF 2
Ulyanov, V. I.
See Lenin
Ulyanov, Vladimir Ilyich
See Lenin
Ulyanov-Lenin
See Lenin
Unamuno (y Jugo), Miguel de 1864-1936 .. **HLC 2; SSC 11, 69; TCLC 2, 9, 148**
See also CA 104; 131; CANR 81; DAM MULT, NOV; DLB 108, 322; EW 8; EWL 3; HW 1, 2; MTCW 1, 2; MTFW 2005; RGSF 2; RGWL 2, 3; SSFS 20; TWA
Uncle Shelby
See Silverstein, Shel
Undercliffe, Errol
See Campbell, Ramsey
Underwood, Miles
See Glassco, John
Undset, Sigrid 1882-1949 .... **TCLC 3, 197; WLC 6**
See also AAYA 77; CA 104; 129; DA; DA3; DAB; DAC; DAM MST, NOV; DLB 293, 332; EW 9; EWL 3; FW; MTCW 1, 2; MTFW 2005; RGWL 2, 3
Ungaretti, Giuseppe 1888-1970 ... **CLC 7, 11, 15; PC 57; TCLC 200**
See also CA 19-20; 25-28R; CAP 2; DLB 114; EW 10; EWL 3; PFS 20; RGWL 2, 3; WLIT 7

Unger, Douglas 1952- .... **CLC 34**
See also CA 130; CANR 94, 155
Unsworth, Barry 1930- .... **CLC 76, 127**
See also BRWS 7; CA 25-28R; CANR 30, 54, 125, 171; CN 6, 7; DLB 194, 326
Unsworth, Barry Forster
See Unsworth, Barry
Updike, John 1932-2009 .... **CLC 1, 2, 3, 5, 7, 9, 13, 15, 23, 34, 43, 70, 139, 214; PC 90; SSC 13, 27, 103; WLC 6**
See also AAYA 36; AMW; AMWC 1; AMWR 1; BPFB 3; BYA 12; CA 1-4R; CABS 1; CANR 4, 33, 51, 94, 133; CDALB 1968-1988; CN 1, 2, 3, 4, 5, 6, 7; CP 1, 2, 3, 4, 5, 6, 7; CPW 1; DA; DA3; DAB; DAC; DAM MST, NOV, POET, POP; DLB 2, 5, 143, 218, 227; DLBD 3; DLBY 1980, 1982, 1997; EWL 3; EXPP; HGG; MAL 5; MTCW 1, 2; MTFW 2005; NFS 12, 24; RGAL 4; RGSF 2; SSFS 3, 19; TUS
Updike, John Hoyer
See Updike, John
Upshaw, Margaret Mitchell
See Mitchell, Margaret (Munnerlyn)
Upton, Mark
See Sanders, Lawrence
Upward, Allen 1863-1926 .... **TCLC 85**
See also CA 117; 187; DLB 36
Urdang, Constance (Henriette) 1922-1996 .... **CLC 47**
See also CA 21-24R; CANR 9, 24; CP 1, 2, 3, 4, 5, 6; CWP
Urfe, Honore d' 1567(?)-1625 .... **LC 132**
See also DLB 268; GFL Beginnings to 1789; RGWL 2, 3
Uriel, Henry
See Faust, Frederick (Schiller)
Uris, Leon 1924-2003 .... **CLC 7, 32**
See also AITN 1, 2; BEST 89:2; BPFB 3; CA 1-4R; 217; CANR 1, 40, 65, 123; CN 1, 2, 3, 4, 5, 6; CPW 1; DA3; DAM NOV, POP; MTCW 1, 2; MTFW 2005; RGHL; SATA 49; SATA-Obit 146
Urista (Heredia), Alberto (Baltazar) 1947- .... **HLCS 1; PC 34**
See also CA 45-48R; CANR 2, 32; DLB 82; HW 1; LLW
Urmuz
See Codrescu, Andrei
Urquhart, Guy
See McAlmon, Robert (Menzies)
Urquhart, Jane 1949- .... **CLC 90, 242**
See also CA 113; CANR 32, 68, 116, 157; CCA 1; DAC; DLB 334
Usigli, Rodolfo 1905-1979 .... **HLCS 1**
See also CA 131; DLB 305; EWL 3; HW 1; LAW
Usk, Thomas (?)-1388 .... **CMLC 76**
See also DLB 146
Ustinov, Peter (Alexander) 1921-2004 .... **CLC 1**
See also AITN 1; CA 13-16R; 225; CANR 25, 51; CBD; CD 5, 6; DLB 13; MTCW 2
U Tam'si, Gerald Felix Tchicaya
See Tchicaya, Gerald Felix
U Tam'si, Tchicaya
See Tchicaya, Gerald Felix
Vachss, Andrew 1942- .... **CLC 106**
See also CA 118, 214; CAAE 214; CANR 44, 95, 153; CMW 4
Vachss, Andrew H.
See Vachss, Andrew
Vachss, Andrew Henry
See Vachss, Andrew
Vaculik, Ludvik 1926- .... **CLC 7**
See also CA 53-56; CANR 72; CWW 2; DLB 232; EWL 3

Vaihinger, Hans 1852-1933 .... **TCLC 71**
See also CA 116; 166
Valdez, Luis (Miguel) 1940- ..... **CLC 84; DC 10; HLC 2**
See also CA 101; CAD; CANR 32, 81; CD 5, 6; DAM MULT; DFS 5; DLB 122; EWL 3; HW 1; LAIT 4; LLW
Valenzuela, Luisa 1938- .... **CLC 31, 104; HLCS 2; SSC 14, 82**
See also CA 101; CANR 32, 65, 123; CDWLB 3; CWW 2; DAM MULT; DLB 113; EWL 3; FW; HW 1, 2; LAW; RGSF 2; RGWL 3
Valera y Alcala-Galiano, Juan 1824-1905 .... **TCLC 10**
See also CA 106
Valerius Maximus .... **CMLC 64**
See also DLB 211
Valery, (Ambroise) Paul (Toussaint Jules) 1871-1945 .... **PC 9; TCLC 4, 15**
See also CA 104; 122; DA3; DAM POET; DLB 258; EW 8; EWL 3; GFL 1789 to the Present; MTCW 1, 2; MTFW 2005; RGWL 2, 3; TWA
Valle-Inclan, Ramon (Maria) del 1866-1936 .... **HLC 2; TCLC 5**
See del Valle-Inclan, Ramon (Maria)
See also CA 106; 153; CANR 80; DAM MULT; DLB 134; EW 8; EWL 3; HW 2; RGSF 2; RGWL 2, 3
Vallejo, Antonio Buero
See Buero Vallejo, Antonio
Vallejo, Cesar (Abraham) 1892-1938 .... **HLC 2; TCLC 3, 56**
See also CA 105; 153; DAM MULT; DLB 290; EWL 3; HW 1; LAW; PFS 26; RGWL 2, 3
Valles, Jules 1832-1885 .... **NCLC 71**
See also DLB 123; GFL 1789 to the Present
Vallette, Marguerite Eymery 1860-1953 .... **TCLC 67**
See Rachilde
See also CA 182; DLB 123, 192
Valle Y Pena, Ramon del
See Valle-Inclan, Ramon (Maria) del
Van Ash, Cay 1918-1994 .... **CLC 34**
See also CA 220
Vanbrugh, Sir John 1664-1726 .... **LC 21**
See also BRW 2; DAM DRAM; DLB 80; IDTP; RGEL 2
Van Campen, Karl
See Campbell, John W(ood, Jr.)
Vance, Gerald
See Silverberg, Robert
Vance, Jack 1916- .... **CLC 35**
See also CA 29-32R; CANR 17, 65, 154; CMW 4; DLB 8; FANT; MTCW 1; SCFW 1, 2; SFW 4; SUFW 1, 2
Vance, John Holbrook
See Vance, Jack
Van Den Bogarde, Derek Jules Gaspard Ulric Niven 1921-1999 .... **CLC 14**
See also CA 77-80; 179; DLB 14
Vandenburgh, Jane .... **CLC 59**
See also CA 168
Vanderhaeghe, Guy 1951- .... **CLC 41**
See also BPFB 3; CA 113; CANR 72, 145; CN 7; DLB 334
van der Post, Laurens (Jan) 1906-1996 .... **CLC 5**
See also AFW; CA 5-8R; 155; CANR 35; CN 1, 2, 3, 4, 5, 6; DLB 204; RGEL 2
van de Wetering, Janwillem 1931-2008 .... **CLC 47**
See also CA 49-52; 274; CANR 4, 62, 90; CMW 4
Van Dine, S. S.
See Wright, Willard Huntington

Van Doren, Carl (Clinton)
   1885-1950 .... **TCLC 18**
   See also CA 111; 168
Van Doren, Mark 1894-1972 .... **CLC 6, 10**
   See also CA 1-4R; 37-40R; CANR 3; CN
   1; CP 1; DLB 45, 284, 335; MAL 5;
   MTCW 1, 2; RGAL 4
Van Druten, John (William)
   1901-1957 .... **TCLC 2**
   See also CA 104; 161; DLB 10; MAL 5;
   RGAL 4
Van Duyn, Mona 1921-2004 .... **CLC 3, 7, 63,
   116**
   See also CA 9-12R; 234; CANR 7, 38, 60,
   116; CP 1, 2, 3, 4, 5, 6, 7; CWP; DAM
   POET; DLB 5; MAL 5; MTFW 2005;
   PFS 20
Van Dyne, Edith
   See Baum, L(yman) Frank
van Herk, Aritha 1954- .... **CLC 249**
   See also CA 101; CANR 94; DLB 334
van Itallie, Jean-Claude 1936- .... **CLC 3**
   See also CA 45-48; CAAS 2; CAD; CANR
   1, 48; CD 5, 6; DLB 7
Van Loot, Cornelius Obenchain
   See Roberts, Kenneth (Lewis)
van Ostaijen, Paul 1896-1928 .... **TCLC 33**
   See also CA 163
Van Peebles, Melvin 1932- .... **CLC 2, 20**
   See also BW 2, 3; CA 85-88; CANR 27,
   67, 82; DAM MULT
van Schendel, Arthur(-Francois-Emile)
   1874-1946 .... **TCLC 56**
   See also EWL 3
Van See, John
   See Vance, Jack
Vansittart, Peter 1920-2008 .... **CLC 42**
   See also CA 1-4R; 278; CANR 3, 49, 90;
   CN 4, 5, 6, 7; RHW
Van Vechten, Carl 1880-1964 ... **CLC 33; HR
   1:3**
   See also AMWS 2; CA 183; 89-92; DLB 4,
   9, 51; RGAL 4
van Vogt, A(lfred) E(lton) 1912-2000 . **CLC 1**
   See also BPFB 3; BYA 13, 14; CA 21-24R;
   190; CANR 28; DLB 8, 251; SATA 14;
   SATA-Obit 124; SCFW 1, 2; SFW 4
Vara, Madeleine
   See Jackson, Laura (Riding)
Varda, Agnes 1928- .... **CLC 16**
   See also CA 116; 122
Vargas Llosa, Jorge Mario Pedro
   See Vargas Llosa, Mario
Vargas Llosa, Mario 1936- .. **CLC 3, 6, 9, 10,
   15, 31, 42, 85, 181; HLC 2**
   See also BPFB 3; CA 73-76; CANR 18, 32,
   42, 67, 116, 140, 173; CDWLB 3; CWW
   2; DA; DA3; DAB; DAC; DAM MST,
   MULT, NOV; DLB 145; DNFS 2; EWL
   3; HW 1, 2; LAIT 5; LATS 1:2; LAW;
   LAWS 1; MTCW 1, 2; MTFW 2005;
   RGWL 2, 3; SSFS 14; TWA; WLIT 1
Varnhagen von Ense, Rahel
   1771-1833 .... **NCLC 130**
   See also DLB 90
Vasari, Giorgio 1511-1574 .... **LC 114**
Vasilikos, Vasiles
   See Vassilikos, Vassilis
Vasiliu, George
   See Bacovia, George
Vasiliu, Gheorghe
   See Bacovia, George
Vassa, Gustavus
   See Equiano, Olaudah
Vassilikos, Vassilis 1933- .... **CLC 4, 8**
   See also CA 81-84; CANR 75, 149; EWL 3
Vaughan, Henry 1621-1695 .... **LC 27; PC 81**
   See also BRW 2; DLB 131; PAB; RGEL 2

Vaughn, Stephanie .... **CLC 62**
Vazov, Ivan (Minchov) 1850-1921 . **TCLC 25**
   See also CA 121; 167; CDWLB 4; DLB
   147
Veblen, Thorstein B(unde)
   1857-1929 .... **TCLC 31**
   See also AMWS 1; CA 115; 165; DLB 246;
   MAL 5
Vega, Lope de 1562-1635 ... **HLCS 2; LC 23,
   119**
   See also EW 2; RGWL 2, 3
Veldeke, Heinrich von c. 1145-c.
   1190 .... **CMLC 85**
Vendler, Helen (Hennessy) 1933- ... **CLC 138**
   See also CA 41-44R; CANR 25, 72, 136;
   MTCW 1, 2; MTFW 2005
Venison, Alfred
   See Pound, Ezra (Weston Loomis)
Ventsel, Elena Sergeevna 1907-2002
   See Grekova, I.
   See also CA 154
Verdi, Marie de
   See Mencken, H(enry) L(ouis)
Verdu, Matilde
   See Cela, Camilo Jose
Verga, Giovanni (Carmelo)
   1840-1922 .... **SSC 21, 87; TCLC 3**
   See also CA 104; 123; CANR 101; EW 7;
   EWL 3; RGSF 2; RGWL 2, 3; WLIT 7
Vergil 70B.C.-19B.C. .. **CMLC 9, 40, 101; PC
   12; WLCS**
   See Virgil
   See also AW 2; DA; DA3; DAB; DAC;
   DAM MST, POET; EFS 1; LMFS 1
Vergil, Polydore c. 1470-1555 .... **LC 108**
   See also DLB 132
Verhaeren, Emile (Adolphe Gustave)
   1855-1916 .... **TCLC 12**
   See also CA 109; EWL 3; GFL 1789 to the
   Present
Verlaine, Paul (Marie) 1844-1896 .. **NCLC 2,
   51; PC 2, 32**
   See also DAM POET; DLB 217; EW 7;
   GFL 1789 to the Present; LMFS 2; RGWL
   2, 3; TWA
Verne, Jules (Gabriel) 1828-1905 ... **TCLC 6,
   52**
   See also AAYA 16; BYA 4; CA 110; 131;
   CLR 88; DA3; DLB 123; GFL 1789 to
   the Present; JRDA; LAIT 2; LMFS 2;
   MAICYA 1, 2; MTFW 2005; RGWL 2, 3;
   SATA 21; SCFW 1, 2; SFW 4; TWA;
   WCH
Verus, Marcus Annius
   See Aurelius, Marcus
Very, Jones 1813-1880 .... **NCLC 9; PC 86**
   See also DLB 1, 243; RGAL 4
Very, Rev. C.
   See Crowley, Edward Alexander
Vesaas, Tarjei 1897-1970 .... **CLC 48**
   See also CA 190; 29-32R; DLB 297; EW
   11; EWL 3; RGWL 3
Vialis, Gaston
   See Simenon, Georges (Jacques Christian)
Vian, Boris 1920-1959(?) .... **TCLC 9**
   See also CA 106; 164; CANR 111; DLB
   72, 321; EWL 3; GFL 1789 to the Present;
   MTCW 2; RGWL 2, 3
Viator, Vacuus
   See Hughes, Thomas
Viaud, (Louis Marie) Julien
   1850-1923 .... **TCLC 11**
   See also CA 107; DLB 123; GFL 1789 to
   the Present
Vicar, Henry
   See Felsen, Henry Gregor
Vicente, Gil 1465-c. 1536 .... **LC 99**
   See also DLB 318; IDTP; RGWL 2, 3

Vicker, Angus
   See Felsen, Henry Gregor
Vico, Giambattista .... **LC 138**
   See Vico, Giovanni Battista
   See also WLIT 7
Vico, Giovanni Battista 1668-1744
   See Vico, Giambattista
   See also EW 3
Vidal, Eugene Luther Gore
   See Vidal, Gore
Vidal, Gore 1925- ..... **CLC 2, 4, 6, 8, 10, 22,
   33, 72, 142**
   See also AAYA 64; AITN 1; AMWS 4;
   BEST 90:2; BPFB 3; CA 5-8R; CAD;
   CANR 13, 45, 65, 100, 132, 167; CD 5,
   6; CDALBS; CN 1, 2, 3, 4, 5, 6, 7; CPW;
   DA3; DAM NOV, POP; DFS 2; DLB 6,
   152; EWL 3; GLL 1; INT CANR-13;
   MAL 5; MTCW 1, 2; MTFW 2005;
   RGAL 4; RHW; TUS
Viereck, Peter 1916-2006 .... **CLC 4; PC 27**
   See also CA 1-4R; 250; CANR 1, 47; CP 1,
   2, 3, 4, 5, 6, 7; DLB 5; MAL 5; PFS 9,
   14
Viereck, Peter Robert Edwin
   See Viereck, Peter
Vigny, Alfred (Victor) de
   1797-1863 .... **NCLC 7, 102; PC 26**
   See also DAM POET; DLB 119, 192, 217;
   EW 5; GFL 1789 to the Present; RGWL
   2, 3
Vilakazi, Benedict Wallet
   1906-1947 .... **TCLC 37**
   See also CA 168
Vile, Curt
   See Moore, Alan
Villa, Jose Garcia 1914-1997 ... **AAL; PC 22;
   TCLC 176**
   See also CA 25-28R; CANR 12, 118; CP 1,
   2, 3, 4; DLB 312; EWL 3; EXPP
Villard, Oswald Garrison
   1872-1949 .... **TCLC 160**
   See also CA 113; 162; DLB 25, 91
Villarreal, Jose Antonio 1924- .... **HLC 2**
   See also CA 133; CANR 93; DAM MULT;
   DLB 82; HW 1; LAIT 4; RGAL 4
Villaurrutia, Xavier 1903-1950 ...... **TCLC 80**
   See also CA 192; EWL 3; HW 1; LAW
Villaverde, Cirilo 1812-1894 .... **NCLC 121**
   See also LAW
Villehardouin, Geoffroi de
   1150(?)-1218(?) .... **CMLC 38**
Villiers, George 1628-1687 .... **LC 107**
   See also DLB 80; RGEL 2
**Villiers de l'Isle Adam, Jean Marie Mathias
   Philippe Auguste** 1838-1889 ... **NCLC 3;
   SSC 14**
   See also DLB 123, 192; GFL 1789 to the
   Present; RGSF 2
Villon, Francois 1431-1463(?) . **LC 62; PC 13**
   See also DLB 208; EW 2; RGWL 2, 3;
   TWA
Vine, Barbara
   See Rendell, Ruth
Vinge, Joan (Carol) D(ennison)
   1948- .... **CLC 30; SSC 24**
   See also AAYA 32; BPFB 3; CA 93-96;
   CANR 72; SATA 36, 113; SFW 4; YAW
Viola, Herman J(oseph) 1938- .... **CLC 70**
   See also CA 61-64; CANR 8, 23, 48, 91;
   SATA 126
Violis, G.
   See Simenon, Georges (Jacques Christian)
Viramontes, Helena Maria 1954- .... **HLCS 2**
   See also CA 159; CANR 182; DLB 122;
   HW 2; LLW

4, 5, 6; CP 1, 2, 3, 4, 5, 6; CSW; DAM
MULT; DLB 76, 152; EXPP; FW; MAL
5; MTCW 1, 2; MTFW 2005; RGAL 4;
RHW

Walker, Ted
See Walker, Edward Joseph

Wallace, David Foster 1962-2008 .... **CLC 50,
114, 271; SSC 68**
See also AAYA 50; AMWS 10; CA 132;
277; CANR 59, 133; CN 7; DA3; MTCW
2; MTFW 2005

Wallace, Dexter
See Masters, Edgar Lee

Wallace, (Richard Horatio) Edgar
1875-1932 .... **TCLC 57**
See also CA 115; 218; CMW 4; DLB 70;
MSW; RGEL 2

Wallace, Irving 1916-1990 .... **CLC 7, 13**
See also AITN 1; BPFB 3; CA 1-4R; 132;
CAAS 1; CANR 1, 27; CPW; DAM NOV,
POP; INT CANR-27; MTCW 1, 2

Wallant, Edward Lewis 1926-1962 ... **CLC 5,
10**
See also CA 1-4R; CANR 22; DLB 2, 28,
143, 299; EWL 3; MAL 5; MTCW 1, 2;
RGAL 4; RGHL

Wallas, Graham 1858-1932 .... **TCLC 91**

Waller, Edmund 1606-1687 .... **LC 86; PC 72**
See also BRW 2; DAM POET; DLB 126;
PAB; RGEL 2

Walley, Byron
See Card, Orson Scott

Walpole, Horace 1717-1797 ..... **LC 2, 49, 152**
See also BRW 3; DLB 39, 104, 213; GL 3;
HGG; LMFS 1; RGEL 2; SUFW 1; TEA

Walpole, Hugh (Seymour)
1884-1941 .... **TCLC 5**
See also CA 104; 165; DLB 34; HGG;
MTCW 2; RGEL 2; RHW

Walrond, Eric (Derwent) 1898-1966 . **HR 1:3**
See also BW 1; CA 125; DLB 51

Walser, Martin 1927- .... **CLC 27, 183**
See also CA 57-60; CANR 8, 46, 145;
CWW 2; DLB 75, 124; EWL 3

Walser, Robert 1878-1956 ..... **SSC 20; TCLC
18**
See also CA 118; 165; CANR 100; DLB
66; EWL 3

Walsh, Gillian Paton
See Paton Walsh, Jill

Walsh, Jill Paton
See Paton Walsh, Jill

Walter, Villiam Christian
See Andersen, Hans Christian

Walter of Chatillon c. 1135-c.
1202 .... **CMLC 111**

Walters, Anna L(ee) 1946- .... **NNAL**
See also CA 73-76

Walther von der Vogelweide c.
1170-1228 .... **CMLC 56**

Walton, Izaak 1593-1683 .... **LC 72**
See also BRW 2; CDBLB Before 1660;
DLB 151, 213; RGEL 2

Walzer, Michael (Laban) 1935- ...... **CLC 238**
See also CA 37-40R; CANR 15, 48, 127

Wambaugh, Joseph, Jr. 1937- ...... **CLC 3, 18**
See also AITN 1; BEST 89:3; BPFB 3; CA
33-36R; CANR 42, 65, 115, 167; CMW
4; CPW 1; DA3; DAM NOV, POP; DLB
6; DLBY 1983; MSW; MTCW 1, 2

Wambaugh, Joseph Aloysius
See Wambaugh, Joseph, Jr.

Wang Wei 699(?)-761(?) . **CMLC 100; PC 18**
See also TWA

Warburton, William 1698-1779 .... **LC 97**
See also DLB 104

Ward, Arthur Henry Sarsfield
1883-1959 .... **TCLC 28**
See also CA 108; 173; CMW 4; DLB 70;
HGG; MSW; SUFW

Ward, Douglas Turner 1930- .... **CLC 19**
See also BW 1; CA 81-84; CAD; CANR
27; CD 5, 6; DLB 7, 38

Ward, E. D.
See Lucas, E(dward) V(errall)

Ward, Mrs. Humphry 1851-1920
See Ward, Mary Augusta
See also RGEL 2

Ward, Mary Augusta 1851-1920 ... **TCLC 55**
See Ward, Mrs. Humphry
See also DLB 18

Ward, Nathaniel 1578(?)-1652 .... **LC 114**
See also DLB 24

Ward, Peter
See Faust, Frederick (Schiller)

Warhol, Andy 1928(?)-1987 .... **CLC 20**
See also AAYA 12; BEST 89:4; CA 89-92;
121; CANR 34

Warner, Francis (Robert Le Plastrier)
1937- .... **CLC 14**
See also CA 53-56; CANR 11; CP 1, 2, 3, 4

Warner, Marina 1946- .... **CLC 59, 231**
See also CA 65-68; CANR 21, 55, 118; CN
5, 6, 7; DLB 194; MTFW 2005

Warner, Rex (Ernest) 1905-1986 ...... **CLC 45**
See also CA 89-92; 119; CN 1, 2, 3, 4; CP
1, 2, 3, 4; DLB 15; RGEL 2; RHW

Warner, Susan (Bogert)
1819-1885 .... **NCLC 31, 146**
See also AMWS 18; DLB 3, 42, 239, 250,
254

Warner, Sylvia (Constance) Ashton
See Ashton-Warner, Sylvia (Constance)

Warner, Sylvia Townsend
1893-1978 .. **CLC 7, 19; SSC 23; TCLC
131**
See also BRWS 7; CA 61-64; 77-80; CANR
16, 60, 104; CN 1, 2; DLB 34, 139; EWL
3; FANT; FW; MTCW 1, 2; RGEL 2;
RGSF 2; RHW

Warren, Mercy Otis 1728-1814 ..... **NCLC 13**
See also DLB 31, 200; RGAL 4; TUS

Warren, Robert Penn 1905-1989 .. **CLC 1, 4,
6, 8, 10, 13, 18, 39, 53, 59; PC 37; SSC
4, 58; WLC 6**
See also AITN 1; AMW; AMWC 2; BPFB
3; BYA 1; CA 13-16R; 129; CANR 10,
47; CDALB 1968-1988; CN 1, 2, 3, 4;
CP 1, 2, 3, 4; DA; DA3; DAB; DAC;
DAM MST, NOV, POET; DLB 2, 48, 152,
320; DLBY 1980, 1989; EWL 3; INT
CANR-10; MAL 5; MTCW 1, 2; MTFW
2005; NFS 13; RGAL 4; RGSF 2; RHW;
SATA 46; SATA-Obit 63; SSFS 8; TUS

Warrigal, Jack
See Furphy, Joseph

Warshofsky, Isaac
See Singer, Isaac Bashevis

Warton, Joseph 1722-1800 ... **LC 128; NCLC
118**
See also DLB 104, 109; RGEL 2

Warton, Thomas 1728-1790 .... **LC 15, 82**
See also DAM POET; DLB 104, 109, 336;
RGEL 2

Waruk, Kona
See Harris, (Theodore) Wilson

Warung, Price .... **TCLC 45**
See Astley, William
See also DLB 230; RGEL 2

Warwick, Jarvis
See Garner, Hugh

Washington, Alex
See Harris, Mark

Washington, Booker T(aliaferro)
1856-1915 .... **BLC 1:3; TCLC 10**
See also BW 1; CA 114; 125; DA3; DAM
MULT; DLB 345; LAIT 2; RGAL 4;
SATA 28

Washington, George 1732-1799 .... **LC 25**
See also DLB 31

Wassermann, (Karl) Jakob
1873-1934 .... **TCLC 6**
See also CA 104; 163; DLB 66; EWL 3

Wasserstein, Wendy 1950-2006 . **CLC 32, 59,
90, 183; DC 4**
See also AAYA 73; AMWS 15; CA 121;
129; 247; CABS 3; CAD; CANR 53, 75,
128; CD 5, 6; CWD; DA3; DAM DRAM;
DFS 5, 17; DLB 228; EWL 3; FW; INT
CA-129; MAL 5; MTCW 2; MTFW 2005;
SATA 94; SATA-Obit 174

Waterhouse, Keith (Spencer) 1929- . **CLC 47**
See also BRWS 13; CA 5-8R; CANR 38,
67, 109; CBD; CD 6; CN 1, 2, 3, 4, 5, 6,
7; DLB 13, 15; MTCW 1, 2; MTFW 2005

Waters, Frank (Joseph) 1902-1995 .. **CLC 88**
See also CA 5-8R; 149; CAAS 13; CANR
3, 18, 63, 121; DLB 212; DLBY 1986;
RGAL 4; TCWW 1, 2

Waters, Mary C. .... **CLC 70**

Waters, Roger 1944- .... **CLC 35**

Watkins, Frances Ellen
See Harper, Frances Ellen Watkins

Watkins, Gerrold
See Malzberg, Barry N(athaniel)

Watkins, Gloria Jean
See hooks, bell

Watkins, Paul 1964- .... **CLC 55**
See also CA 132; CANR 62, 98

Watkins, Vernon Phillips
1906-1967 .... **CLC 43**
See also CA 9-10; 25-28R; CAP 1; DLB
20; EWL 3; RGEL 2

Watson, Irving S.
See Mencken, H(enry) L(ouis)

Watson, John H.
See Farmer, Philip Jose

Watson, Richard F.
See Silverberg, Robert

Watts, Ephraim
See Horne, Richard Henry Hengist

Watts, Isaac 1674-1748 .... **LC 98**
See also DLB 95; RGEL 2; SATA 52

Waugh, Auberon (Alexander)
1939-2001 .... **CLC 7**
See also CA 45-48; 192; CANR 6, 22, 92;
CN 1, 2, 3; DLB 14, 194

Waugh, Evelyn 1903-1966 ... **CLC 1, 3, 8, 13,
19, 27, 44, 107; SSC 41; WLC 6**
See also AAYA 78; BPFB 3; BRW 7; CA
85-88; 25-28R; CANR 22; CDBLB 1914-
1945; DA; DA3; DAB; DAC; DAM MST,
NOV, POP; DLB 15, 162, 195; EWL 3;
MTCW 1, 2; MTFW 2005; NFS 13, 17;
RGEL 2; RGSF 2; TEA; WLIT 4

Waugh, Evelyn Arthur St. John
See Waugh, Evelyn

Waugh, Harriet 1944- .... **CLC 6**
See also CA 85-88; CANR 22

Ways, C.R.
See Blount, Roy, Jr.

Waystaff, Simon
See Swift, Jonathan

Webb, Beatrice (Martha Potter)
1858-1943 .... **TCLC 22**
See also CA 117; 162; DLB 190; FW

Webb, Charles (Richard) 1939- .... **CLC 7**
See also CA 25-28R; CANR 114

Webb, Frank J. .... **NCLC 143**
See also DLB 50

Webb, James, Jr.
See Webb, James

Wilbur, Richard 1921- .. **CLC 3, 6, 9, 14, 53, 110; PC 51**
See also AAYA 72; AMWS 3; CA 1-4R; CABS 2; CANR 2, 29, 76, 93, 139; CDALBS; CP 1, 2, 3, 4, 5, 6, 7; DA; DAB; DAC; DAM MST, POET; DLB 5, 169; EWL 3; EXPP; INT CANR-29; MAL 5; MTCW 1, 2; MTFW 2005; PAB; PFS 11, 12, 16, 29; RGAL 4; SATA 9, 108; WP

Wilbur, Richard Purdy
See Wilbur, Richard

Wild, Peter 1940- .... **CLC 14**
See also CA 37-40R; CP 1, 2, 3, 4, 5, 6, 7; DLB 5

Wilde, Oscar 1854(?)-1900 ... **DC 17; SSC 11, 77; TCLC 1, 8, 23, 41, 175; WLC 6**
See also AAYA 49; BRW 5; BRWC 1, 2; BRWR 2; BYA 15; CA 104; 119; CANR 112; CDBLB 1890-1914; CLR 114; DA; DA3; DAB; DAC; DAM DRAM, MST, NOV; DFS 4, 8, 9, 21; DLB 10, 19, 34, 57, 141, 156, 190, 344; EXPS; FANT; GL 3; LATS 1:1; NFS 20; RGEL 2; RGSF 2; SATA 24; SSFS 7; SUFW; TEA; WCH; WLIT 4

Wilde, Oscar Fingal O'Flahertie Willis
See Wilde, Oscar

Wilder, Billy .... **CLC 20**
See Wilder, Samuel
See also AAYA 66; DLB 26

Wilder, Samuel 1906-2002
See Wilder, Billy
See also CA 89-92; 205

Wilder, Stephen
See Marlowe, Stephen

Wilder, Thornton (Niven)
1897-1975 .. **CLC 1, 5, 6, 10, 15, 35, 82; DC 1, 24; WLC 6**
See also AAYA 29; AITN 2; AMW; CA 13-16R; 61-64; CAD; CANR 40, 132; CDALBS; CN 1, 2; DA; DA3; DAB; DAC; DAM DRAM, MST, NOV; DFS 1, 4, 16; DLB 4, 7, 9, 228; DLBY 1997; EWL 3; LAIT 3; MAL 5; MTCW 1, 2; MTFW 2005; NFS 24; RGAL 4; RHW; WYAS 1

Wilding, Michael 1942- ...... **CLC 73; SSC 50**
See also CA 104; CANR 24, 49, 106; CN 4, 5, 6, 7; DLB 325; RGSF 2

Wiley, Richard 1944- .... **CLC 44**
See also CA 121; 129; CANR 71

Wilhelm, Kate .... **CLC 7**
See Wilhelm, Katie
See also AAYA 20; BYA 16; CAAS 5; DLB 8; INT CANR-17; SCFW 2

Wilhelm, Katie 1928-
See Wilhelm, Kate
See also CA 37-40R; CANR 17, 36, 60, 94; MTCW 1; SFW 4

Wilkins, Mary
See Freeman, Mary E(leanor) Wilkins

Willard, Nancy 1936- .... **CLC 7, 37**
See also BYA 5; CA 89-92; CANR 10, 39, 68, 107, 152, 186; CLR 5; CP 2, 3, 4, 5; CWP; CWRI 5; DLB 5, 52; FANT; MAI-CYA 1, 2; MTCW 1; SATA 37, 71, 127, 191; SATA-Brief 30; SUFW 2; TCLE 1:2

William of Malmesbury c. 1090B.C.-c.
1140B.C. .... **CMLC 57**

William of Moerbeke c. 1215-c.
1286 .... **CMLC 91**

William of Ockham 1290-1349 ..... **CMLC 32**

Williams, Ben Ames 1889-1953 ..... **TCLC 89**
See also CA 183; DLB 102

Williams, Charles
See Collier, James Lincoln

Williams, Charles (Walter Stansby)
1886-1945 .... **TCLC 1, 11**
See also BRWS 9; CA 104; 163; DLB 100, 153, 255; FANT; RGEL 2; SUFW 1

Williams, C.K. 1936- .... **CLC 33, 56, 148**
See also CA 37-40R; CAAS 26; CANR 57, 106; CP 1, 2, 3, 4, 5, 6, 7; DAM POET; DLB 5; MAL 5

Williams, Ella Gwendolen Rees
See Rhys, Jean

Williams, (George) Emlyn
1905-1987 .... **CLC 15**
See also CA 104; 123; CANR 36; DAM DRAM; DLB 10, 77; IDTP; MTCW 1

Williams, Hank 1923-1953 .... **TCLC 81**
See Williams, Hiram King

Williams, Helen Maria
1761-1827 .... **NCLC 135**
See also DLB 158

Williams, Hiram Hank
See Williams, Hank

Williams, Hiram King
See Williams, Hank
See also CA 188

Williams, Hugo (Mordaunt) 1942- ... **CLC 42**
See also CA 17-20R; CANR 45, 119; CP 1, 2, 3, 4, 5, 6, 7; DLB 40

Williams, J. Walker
See Wodehouse, P(elham) G(renville)

Williams, John A(lfred) 1925- .... **BLC 1:3; CLC 5, 13**
See also AFAW 2; BW 2, 3; CA 53-56, 195; CAAE 195; CAAS 3; CANR 6, 26, 51, 118; CN 1, 2, 3, 4, 5, 6, 7; CSW; DAM MULT; DLB 2, 33; EWL 3; INT CANR-6; MAL 5; RGAL 4; SFW 4

Williams, Jonathan 1929-2008 .... **CLC 13**
See also CA 9-12R; 270; CAAS 12; CANR 8, 108; CP 1, 2, 3, 4, 5, 6, 7; DLB 5

Williams, Jonathan Chamberlain
See Williams, Jonathan

Williams, Joy 1944- .... **CLC 31**
See also CA 41-44R; CANR 22, 48, 97, 168; DLB 335; SSFS 25

Williams, Norman 1952- .... **CLC 39**
See also CA 118

Williams, Roger 1603(?)-1683 .... **LC 129**
See also DLB 24

Williams, Sherley Anne
1944-1999 .... **BLC 1:3; CLC 89**
See also AFAW 2; BW 2, 3; CA 73-76; 185; CANR 25, 82; DAM MULT, POET; DLB 41; INT CANR-25; SATA 78; SATA-Obit 116

Williams, Shirley
See Williams, Sherley Anne

Williams, Tennessee 1911-1983 . **CLC 1, 2, 5, 7, 8, 11, 15, 19, 30, 39, 45, 71, 111; DC 4; SSC 81; WLC 6**
See also AAYA 31; AITN 1, 2; AMW; AMWC 1; CA 5-8R; 108; CABS 3; CAD; CANR 31, 132, 174; CDALB 1941-1968; CN 1, 2, 3; DA; DA3; DAB; DAC; DAM DRAM, MST; DFS 17; DLB 7, 341; DLBD 4; DLBY 1983; EWL 3; GLL 1; LAIT 4; LATS 1:2; MAL 5; MTCW 1, 2; MTFW 2005; RGAL 4; TUS

Williams, Thomas (Alonzo)
1926-1990 .... **CLC 14**
See also CA 1-4R; 132; CANR 2

Williams, Thomas Lanier
See Williams, Tennessee

Williams, William C.
See Williams, William Carlos

Williams, William Carlos
1883-1963 .... **CLC 1, 2, 5, 9, 13, 22, 42, 67; PC 7; SSC 31; WLC 6**
See also AAYA 46; AMW; AMWR 1; CA 89-92; CANR 34; CDALB 1917-1929; DA; DA3; DAB; DAC; DAM MST, POET; DLB 4, 16, 54, 86; EWL 3; EXPP; MAL 5; MTCW 1, 2; MTFW 2005; NCFS 4; PAB; PFS 1, 6, 11; RGAL 4; RGSF 2; TUS; WP

Williamson, David (Keith) 1942- ..... **CLC 56**
See also CA 103; CANR 41; CD 5, 6; DLB 289

Williamson, Jack .... **CLC 29**
See Williamson, John Stewart
See also CAAS 8; DLB 8; SCFW 1, 2

Williamson, John Stewart 1908-2006
See Williamson, Jack
See also AAYA 76; CA 17-20R; 255; CANR 23, 70, 153; SFW 4

Willie, Frederick
See Lovecraft, H. P.

Willingham, Calder (Baynard, Jr.)
1922-1995 .... **CLC 5, 51**
See also CA 5-8R; 147; CANR 3; CN 1, 2, 3, 4, 5; CSW; DLB 2, 44; IDFW 3, 4; MTCW 1

Willis, Charles
See Clarke, Arthur C.

Willis, Nathaniel Parker
1806-1867 .... **NCLC 194**
See also DLB 3, 59, 73, 74, 183, 250; DLBD 13; RGAL 4

Willy
See Colette, (Sidonie-Gabrielle)

Willy, Colette
See Colette, (Sidonie-Gabrielle)
See also GLL 1

Wilmot, John 1647-1680 .... **LC 75; PC 66**
See Rochester
See also BRW 2; DLB 131; PAB

Wilson, A.N. 1950- .... **CLC 33**
See also BRWS 6; CA 112; 122; CANR 156; CN 4, 5, 6, 7; DLB 14, 155, 194; MTCW 2

Wilson, Andrew Norman
See Wilson, A.N.

Wilson, Angus (Frank Johnstone)
1913-1991 . **CLC 2, 3, 5, 25, 34; SSC 21**
See also BRWS 1; CA 5-8R; 134; CANR 21; CN 1, 2, 3, 4; DLB 15, 139, 155; EWL 3; MTCW 1, 2; MTFW 2005; RGEL 2; RGSF 2

Wilson, August 1945-2005 .... **BLC 1:3, 2:3; CLC 39, 50, 63, 118, 222; DC 2, 31; WLCS**
See also AAYA 16; AFAW 2; AMWS 8; BW 2, 3; CA 115; 122; 244; CAD; CANR 42, 54, 76, 128; CD 5, 6; DA; DA3; DAB; DAC; DAM DRAM, MST, MULT; DFS 3, 7, 15, 17, 24; DLB 228; EWL 3; LAIT 4; LATS 1:2; MAL 5; MTCW 1, 2; MTFW 2005; RGAL 4

Wilson, Brian 1942- .... **CLC 12**

Wilson, Colin (Henry) 1931- .... **CLC 3, 14**
See also CA 1-4R; CAAS 5; CANR 1, 22, 33, 77; CMW 4; CN 1, 2, 3, 4, 5, 6; DLB 14, 194; HGG; MTCW 1; SFW 4

Wilson, Dirk
See Pohl, Frederik

Wilson, Edmund 1895-1972 .. **CLC 1, 2, 3, 8, 24**
See also AMW; CA 1-4R; 37-40R; CANR 1, 46, 110; CN 1; DLB 63; EWL 3; MAL 5; MTCW 1, 2; MTFW 2005; RGAL 4; TUS

Wilson, Ethel Davis (Bryant)
1888(?)-1980 .... **CLC 13**
See also CA 102; CN 1, 2; DAC; DAM POET; DLB 68; MTCW 1; RGEL 2

Wilson, Harriet
See Wilson, Harriet E. Adams
See also DLB 239

Wilson, Harriet E.
See Wilson, Harriet E. Adams
See also DLB 243
Wilson, Harriet E. Adams
1827(?)-1863(?) ...... **BLC 1:3; NCLC 78**
See Wilson, Harriet; Wilson, Harriet E.
See also DAM MULT; DLB 50
Wilson, John 1785-1854 .... **NCLC 5**
See also DLB 110
Wilson, John (Anthony) Burgess
See Burgess, Anthony
Wilson, Katharina .... **CLC 65**
Wilson, Lanford 1937- .. **CLC 7, 14, 36, 197; DC 19**
See also CA 17-20R; CABS 3; CAD; CANR 45, 96; CD 5, 6; DAM DRAM; DFS 4, 9, 12, 16, 20; DLB 7, 341; EWL 3; MAL 5; TUS
Wilson, Robert M. 1941- .... **CLC 7, 9**
See also CA 49-52; CAD; CANR 2, 41; CD 5, 6; MTCW 1
Wilson, Robert McLiam 1964- .... **CLC 59**
See also CA 132; DLB 267
Wilson, Sloan 1920-2003 .... **CLC 32**
See also CA 1-4R; 216; CANR 1, 44; CN 1, 2, 3, 4, 5, 6
Wilson, Snoo 1948- .... **CLC 33**
See also CA 69-72; CBD; CD 5, 6
Wilson, William S(mith) 1932- .... **CLC 49**
See also CA 81-84
Wilson, (Thomas) Woodrow
1856-1924 .... **TCLC 79**
See also CA 166; DLB 47
Winchester, Simon 1944- .... **CLC 257**
See also AAYA 66; CA 107; CANR 90, 130
Winchilsea, Anne (Kingsmill) Finch
1661-1720
See Finch, Anne
See also RGEL 2
Winckelmann, Johann Joachim
1717-1768 .... **LC 129**
See also DLB 97
Windham, Basil
See Wodehouse, P(elham) G(renville)
Wingrove, David 1954- .... **CLC 68**
See also CA 133; SFW 4
Winnemucca, Sarah 1844-1891 .... **NCLC 79; NNAL**
See also DAM MULT; DLB 175; RGAL 4
Winstanley, Gerrard 1609-1676 .... **LC 52**
Wintergreen, Jane
See Duncan, Sara Jeannette
Winters, Arthur Yvor
See Winters, Yvor
Winters, Janet Lewis .... **CLC 41**
See Lewis, Janet
See also DLBY 1987
Winters, Yvor 1900-1968 .. **CLC 4, 8, 32; PC 82**
See also AMWS 2; CA 11-12; 25-28R; CAP 1; DLB 48; EWL 3; MAL 5; MTCW 1; RGAL 4
Winterson, Jeanette 1959- .... **CLC 64, 158**
See also BRWS 4; CA 136; CANR 58, 116, 181; CN 5, 6, 7; CPW; DA3; DAM POP; DLB 207, 261; FANT; FW; GLL 1; MTCW 2; MTFW 2005; RHW; SATA 190
Winthrop, John 1588-1649 .... **LC 31, 107**
See also DLB 24, 30
Winthrop, Theodore 1828-1861 ... **NCLC 210**
See also DLB 202
Winton, Tim 1960- .... **CLC 251; SSC 119**
See also AAYA 34; CA 152; CANR 118; CN 6, 7; DLB 325; SATA 98
Wirth, Louis 1897-1952 .... **TCLC 92**
See also CA 210
Wiseman, Frederick 1930- .... **CLC 20**
See also CA 159

Wister, Owen 1860-1938 ..... **SSC 100; TCLC 21**
See also BPFB 3; CA 108; 162; DLB 9, 78, 186; RGAL 4; SATA 62; TCWW 1, 2
Wither, George 1588-1667 .... **LC 96**
See also DLB 121; RGEL 2
Witkacy
See Witkiewicz, Stanislaw Ignacy
Witkiewicz, Stanislaw Ignacy
1885-1939 .... **TCLC 8**
See also CA 105; 162; CDWLB 4; DLB 215; EW 10; EWL 3; RGWL 2, 3; SFW 4
Wittgenstein, Ludwig (Josef Johann)
1889-1951 .... **TCLC 59**
See also CA 113; 164; DLB 262; MTCW 2
Wittig, Monique 1935-2003 .... **CLC 22**
See also CA 116; 135; 212; CANR 143; CWW 2; DLB 83; EWL 3; FW; GLL 1
Wittlin, Jozef 1896-1976 .... **CLC 25**
See also CA 49-52; 65-68; CANR 3; EWL 3
Wodehouse, P(elham) G(renville)
1881-1975 .. **CLC 1, 2, 5, 10, 22; SSC 2, 115; TCLC 108**
See also AAYA 65; AITN 2; BRWS 3; CA 45-48; 57-60; CANR 3, 33; CDBLB 1914-1945; CN 1, 2; CPW 1; DA3; DAB; DAC; DAM NOV; DLB 34, 162; EWL 3; MTCW 1, 2; MTFW 2005; RGEL 2; RGSF 2; SATA 22; SSFS 10
Woiwode, L.
See Woiwode, Larry (Alfred)
Woiwode, Larry (Alfred) 1941- ... **CLC 6, 10**
See also CA 73-76; CANR 16, 94; CN 3, 4, 5, 6, 7; DLB 6; INT CANR-16
Wojciechowska, Maia (Teresa)
1927-2002 .... **CLC 26**
See also AAYA 8, 46; BYA 3; CA 9-12R, 183; 209; CAAE 183; CANR 4, 41; CLR 1; JRDA; MAICYA 1, 2; SAAS 1; SATA 1, 28, 83; SATA-Essay 104; SATA-Obit 134; YAW
Wojtyla, Karol (Josef)
See John Paul II, Pope
Wojtyla, Karol (Jozef)
See John Paul II, Pope
Wolf, Christa 1929- ...... **CLC 14, 29, 58, 150, 261**
See also CA 85-88; CANR 45, 123; CD-WLB 2; CWW 2; DLB 75; EWL 3; FW; MTCW 1; RGWL 2, 3; SSFS 14
Wolf, Naomi 1962- .... **CLC 157**
See also CA 141; CANR 110; FW; MTFW 2005
Wolfe, Gene 1931- .... **CLC 25**
See also AAYA 35; CA 57-60; CAAS 9; CANR 6, 32, 60, 152; CPW; DAM POP; DLB 8; FANT; MTCW 2; MTFW 2005; SATA 118, 165; SCFW 2; SFW 4; SUFW 2
Wolfe, Gene Rodman
See Wolfe, Gene
Wolfe, George C. 1954- .... **BLCS; CLC 49**
See also CA 149; CAD; CD 5, 6
Wolfe, Thomas (Clayton)
1900-1938 .... **SSC 33, 113; TCLC 4, 13, 29, 61; WLC 6**
See also AMW; BPFB 3; CA 104; 132; CANR 102; CDALB 1929-1941; DA; DA3; DAB; DAC; DAM MST, NOV; DLB 9, 102, 229; DLBD 2, 16; DLBY 1985, 1997; EWL 3; MAL 5; MTCW 1, 2; NFS 18; RGAL 4; SSFS 18; TUS
Wolfe, Thomas Kennerly, Jr.
1931- .... **CLC 147**
See Wolfe, Tom
See also CA 13-16R; CANR 9, 33, 70, 104; DA3; DAM POP; DLB 185; EWL 3; INT CANR-9; MTCW 1, 2; MTFW 2005; TUS

Wolfe, Tom .... **CLC 1, 2, 9, 15, 35, 51**
See Wolfe, Thomas Kennerly, Jr.
See also AAYA 8, 67; AITN 2; AMWS 3; BEST 89:1; BPFB 3; CN 5, 6, 7; CPW; CSW; DLB 152; LAIT 5; RGAL 4
Wolff, Geoffrey 1937- .... **CLC 41**
See also CA 29-32R; CANR 29, 43, 78, 154
Wolff, Geoffrey Ansell
See Wolff, Geoffrey
Wolff, Sonia
See Levitin, Sonia
Wolff, Tobias 1945- .... **CLC 39, 64, 172; SSC 63**
See also AAYA 16; AMWS 7; BEST 90:2; BYA 12; CA 114; 117; CAAS 22; CANR 54, 76, 96; CN 5, 6, 7; CSW; DA3; DLB 130; EWL 3; INT CA-117; MTCW 2; MTFW 2005; RGAL 4; RGSF 2; SSFS 4, 11
Wolitzer, Hilma 1930- .... **CLC 17**
See also CA 65-68; CANR 18, 40, 172; INT CANR-18; SATA 31; YAW
Wollstonecraft, Mary 1759-1797 .... **LC 5, 50, 90, 147**
See also BRWS 3; CDBLB 1789-1832; DLB 39, 104, 158, 252; FL 1:1; FW; LAIT 1; RGEL 2; TEA; WLIT 3
Wonder, Stevie 1950- .... **CLC 12**
See also CA 111
Wong, Jade Snow 1922-2006 .... **CLC 17**
See also CA 109; 249; CANR 91; SATA 112; SATA-Obit 175
Wood, Ellen Price
See Wood, Mrs. Henry
Wood, Mrs. Henry 1814-1887 ...... **NCLC 178**
See also CMW 4; DLB 18; SUFW
Wood, James 1965- .... **CLC 238**
See also CA 235
Woodberry, George Edward
1855-1930 .... **TCLC 73**
See also CA 165; DLB 71, 103
Woodcott, Keith
See Brunner, John (Kilian Houston)
Woodruff, Robert W.
See Mencken, H(enry) L(ouis)
Woodward, Bob 1943- .... **CLC 240**
See also CA 69-72; CANR 31, 67, 107, 176; MTCW 1
Woodward, Robert Upshur
See Woodward, Bob
Woolf, (Adeline) Virginia 1882-1941 .. **SSC 7, 79; TCLC 1, 5, 20, 43, 56, 101, 123, 128; WLC 6**
See also AAYA 44; BPFB 3; BRW 7; BRWC 2; BRWR 1; CA 104; 130; CANR 64, 132; CDBLB 1914-1945; DA; DA3; DAB; DAC; DAM MST, NOV; DLB 36, 100, 162; DLBD 10; EWL 3; EXPS; FL 1:6; FW; LAIT 3; LATS 1:1; LMFS 2; MTCW 1, 2; MTFW 2005; NCFS 2; NFS 8, 12, 28; RGEL 2; RGSF 2; SSFS 4, 12; TEA; WLIT 4
Woollcott, Alexander (Humphreys)
1887-1943 .... **TCLC 5**
See also CA 105; 161; DLB 29
Woolman, John 1720-1772 .... **LC 155**
See also DLB 31
Woolrich, Cornell .... **CLC 77**
See Hopley-Woolrich, Cornell George
See also MSW
Woolson, Constance Fenimore
1840-1894 .... **NCLC 82; SSC 90**
See also DLB 12, 74, 189, 221; RGAL 4
Wordsworth, Dorothy 1771-1855 . **NCLC 25, 138**
See also DLB 107

Wordsworth, William 1770-1850 .. **NCLC 12, 38, 111, 166, 206; PC 4, 67; WLC 6**
See also AAYA 70; BRW 4; BRWC 1; CD-BLB 1789-1832; DA; DA3; DAB; DAC; DAM MST, POET; DLB 93, 107; EXPP; LATS 1:1; LMFS 1; PAB; PFS 2; RGEL 2; TEA; WLIT 3; WP

Wotton, Sir Henry 1568-1639 .... **LC 68**
See also DLB 121; RGEL 2

Wouk, Herman 1915- .... **CLC 1, 9, 38**
See also BPFB 2, 3; CA 5-8R; CANR 6, 33, 67, 146; CDALBS; CN 1, 2, 3, 4, 5, 6; CPW; DA3; DAM NOV, POP; DLBY 1982; INT CANR-6; LAIT 4; MAL 5; MTCW 1, 2; MTFW 2005; NFS 7; TUS

Wright, Charles 1932-2008 ... **BLC 1:3; CLC 49**
See also BW 1; CA 9-12R; 278; CANR 26; CN 1, 2, 3, 4, 5, 6, 7; DAM MULT, POET; DLB 33

Wright, Charles 1935- ... **CLC 6, 13, 28, 119, 146**
See also AMWS 5; CA 29-32R; CAAS 7; CANR 23, 36, 62, 88, 135, 180; CP 3, 4, 5, 6, 7; DLB 165; DLBY 1982; EWL 3; MTCW 1, 2; MTFW 2005; PFS 10

Wright, Charles Penzel, Jr.
See Wright, Charles

Wright, Charles Stevenson
See Wright, Charles

Wright, Frances 1795-1852 .... **NCLC 74**
See also DLB 73

Wright, Frank Lloyd 1867-1959 .... **TCLC 95**
See also AAYA 33; CA 174

Wright, Harold Bell 1872-1944 .... **TCLC 183**
See also BPFB 3; CA 110; DLB 9; TCWW 2

Wright, Jack R.
See Harris, Mark

Wright, James (Arlington)
1927-1980 .... **CLC 3, 5, 10, 28; PC 36**
See also AITN 2; AMWS 3; CA 49-52; 97-100; CANR 4, 34, 64; CDALBS; CP 1, 2; DAM POET; DLB 5, 169, 342; EWL 3; EXPP; MAL 5; MTCW 1, 2; MTFW 2005; PFS 7, 8; RGAL 4; TUS; WP

Wright, Judith 1915-2000 ... **CLC 11, 53; PC 14**
See also CA 13-16R; 188; CANR 31, 76, 93; CP 1, 2, 3, 4, 5, 6, 7; CWP; DLB 260; EWL 3; MTCW 1, 2; MTFW 2005; PFS 8; RGEL 2; SATA 14; SATA-Obit 121

Wright, L(aurali) R. 1939- .... **CLC 44**
See also CA 138; CMW 4

Wright, Richard (Nathaniel)
1908-1960 ...... **BLC 1:3; CLC 1, 3, 4, 9, 14, 21, 48, 74; SSC 2, 109; TCLC 136, 180; WLC 6**
See also AAYA 5, 42; AFAW 1, 2; AMW; BPFB 3; BW 1; BYA 2; CA 108; CANR 64; CDALB 1929-1941; DA; DA3; DAB; DAC; DAM MST, MULT, NOV; DLB 76, 102; DLBD 2; EWL 3; EXPN; LAIT 3, 4; MAL 5; MTCW 1, 2; MTFW 2005; NCFS 1; NFS 1, 7; RGAL 4; RGSF 2; SSFS 3, 9, 15, 20; TUS; YAW

Wright, Richard B. 1937- .... **CLC 6**
See also CA 85-88; CANR 120; DLB 53

Wright, Richard Bruce
See Wright, Richard B.

Wright, Rick 1945- .... **CLC 35**

Wright, Rowland
See Wells, Carolyn

Wright, Stephen 1946- .... **CLC 33**
See also CA 237

Wright, Willard Huntington
1888-1939 .... **TCLC 23**
See also CA 115; 189; CMW 4; DLB 306; DLBD 16; MSW

Wright, William 1930- .... **CLC 44**
See also CA 53-56; CANR 7, 23, 154

Wroth, Lady Mary 1587-1653(?) .... **LC 30, 139; PC 38**
See also DLB 121

Wu Ch'eng-en 1500(?)-1582(?) .... **LC 7**

Wu Ching-tzu 1701-1754 .... **LC 2**

Wulfstan c. 10th cent. -1023 .... **CMLC 59**

Wurlitzer, Rudolph 1938(?)- .. **CLC 2, 4, 15**
See also CA 85-88; CN 4, 5, 6, 7; DLB 173

Wyatt, Sir Thomas c. 1503-1542 . **LC 70; PC 27**
See also BRW 1; DLB 132; EXPP; PFS 25; RGEL 2; TEA

Wycherley, William 1640-1716 .... **LC 8, 21, 102, 136**
See also BRW 2; CDBLB 1660-1789; DAM DRAM; DLB 80; RGEL 2

Wyclif, John c. 1330-1384 .... **CMLC 70**
See also DLB 146

Wylie, Elinor (Morton Hoyt)
1885-1928 .... **PC 23; TCLC 8**
See also AMWS 1; CA 105; 162; DLB 9, 45; EXPP; MAL 5; RGAL 4

Wylie, Philip (Gordon) 1902-1971 ... **CLC 43**
See also CA 21-22; 33-36R; CAP 2; CN 1; DLB 9; SFW 4

Wyndham, John .... **CLC 19**
See Harris, John (Wyndham Parkes Lucas) Beynon
See also BRWS 13; DLB 255; SCFW 1, 2

Wyss, Johann David Von
1743-1818 .... **NCLC 10**
See also CLR 92; JRDA; MAICYA 1, 2; SATA 29; SATA-Brief 27

Xenophon c. 430B.C.-c. 354B.C. ... **CMLC 17**
See also AW 1; DLB 176; RGWL 2, 3; WLIT 8

Xingjian, Gao 1940-
See Gao Xingjian
See also CA 193; DFS 21; DLB 330; RGWL 3

Yakamochi 718-785 .... **CMLC 45; PC 48**

Yakumo Koizumi
See Hearn, (Patricio) Lafcadio (Tessima Carlos)

Yamada, Mitsuye (May) 1923- .... **PC 44**
See also CA 77-80

Yamamoto, Hisaye 1921- .... **AAL; SSC 34**
See also CA 214; DAM MULT; DLB 312; LAIT 4; SSFS 14

Yamauchi, Wakako 1924- .... **AAL**
See also CA 214; DLB 312

Yanez, Jose Donoso
See Donoso (Yanez), Jose

Yanovsky, Basile S.
See Yanovsky, V(assily) S(emenovich)

Yanovsky, V(assily) S(emenovich)
1906-1989 .... **CLC 2, 18**
See also CA 97-100; 129

Yates, Richard 1926-1992 .... **CLC 7, 8, 23**
See also AMWS 11; CA 5-8R; 139; CANR 10, 43; CN 1, 2, 3, 4, 5; DLB 2, 234; DLBY 1981, 1992; INT CANR-10; SSFS 24

Yau, John 1950- .... **PC 61**
See also CA 154; CANR 89; CP 4, 5, 6, 7; DLB 234, 312; PFS 26

Yearsley, Ann 1753-1806 .... **NCLC 174**
See also DLB 109

Yeats, W. B.
See Yeats, William Butler

Yeats, William Butler 1865-1939 . **DC 33; PC 20, 51; TCLC 1, 11, 18, 31, 93, 116; WLC 6**
See also AAYA 48; BRW 6; BRWR 1; CA 104; 127; CANR 45; CDBLB 1890-1914; DA; DA3; DAB; DAC; DAM DRAM, MST, POET; DLB 10, 19, 98, 156, 332;

EWL 3; EXPP; MTCW 1, 2; MTFW 2005; NCFS 3; PAB; PFS 1, 2, 5, 7, 13, 15; RGEL 2; TEA; WLIT 4; WP

Yehoshua, A.B. 1936- .... **CLC 13, 31, 243**
See also CA 33-36R; CANR 43, 90, 145; CWW 2; EWL 3; RGHL; RGSF 2; RGWL 3; WLIT 6

Yehoshua, Abraham B.
See Yehoshua, A.B.

Yellow Bird
See Ridge, John Rollin

Yep, Laurence 1948- .... **CLC 35**
See also AAYA 5, 31; BYA 7; CA 49-52; CANR 1, 46, 92, 161; CLR 3, 17, 54, 132; DLB 52, 312; FANT; JRDA; MAICYA 1, 2; MAICYAS 1; SATA 7, 69, 123, 176; WYA; YAW

Yep, Laurence Michael
See Yep, Laurence

Yerby, Frank G(arvin) 1916-1991 . **BLC 1:3; CLC 1, 7, 22**
See also BPFB 3; BW 1, 3; CA 9-12R; 136; CANR 16, 52; CN 1, 2, 3, 4, 5; DAM MULT; DLB 76; INT CANR-16; MTCW 1; RGAL 4; RHW

Yesenin, Sergei Aleksandrovich
See Esenin, Sergei

Yevtushenko, Yevgeny (Alexandrovich)
1933- ...... **CLC 1, 3, 13, 26, 51, 126; PC 40**
See also CA 81-84; CANR 33, 54; CWW 2; DAM POET; EWL 3; MTCW 1; PFS 29; RGHL; RGWL 2, 3

Yezierska, Anzia 1885(?)-1970 .... **CLC 46; TCLC 205**
See also CA 126; 89-92; DLB 28, 221; FW; MTCW 1; RGAL 4; SSFS 15

Yglesias, Helen 1915-2008 .... **CLC 7, 22**
See also CA 37-40R; 272; CAAS 20; CANR 15, 65, 95; CN 4, 5, 6, 7; INT CANR-15; MTCW 1

Y.O.
See Russell, George William

Yokomitsu, Riichi 1898-1947 .... **TCLC 47**
See also CA 170; EWL 3

Yolen, Jane 1939- .... **CLC 256**
See also AAYA 4, 22; BPFB 3; BYA 9, 10, 11, 14, 16; CA 13-16R; CANR 11, 29, 56, 91, 126, 185; CLR 4, 44; CWRI 5; DLB 52; FANT; INT CANR-29; JRDA; MAICYA 1, 2; MTFW 2005; SAAS 1; SATA 4, 40, 75, 112, 158, 194; SATA-Essay 111; SFW 4; SUFW 2; WYA; YAW

Yonge, Charlotte (Mary)
1823-1901 .... **TCLC 48**
See also CA 109; 163; DLB 18, 163; RGEL 2; SATA 17; WCH

York, Jeremy
See Creasey, John

York, Simon
See Heinlein, Robert A.

Yorke, Henry Vincent 1905-1974 ...... **CLC 2, 13, 97**
See also BRWS 2; CA 85-88; 175; 49-52; DLB 15; EWL 3; RGEL 2

Yosano, Akiko 1878-1942 ... **PC 11; TCLC 59**
See also CA 161; EWL 3; RGWL 3

Yoshimoto, Banana .... **CLC 84**
See Yoshimoto, Mahoko
See also AAYA 50; NFS 7

Yoshimoto, Mahoko 1964-
See Yoshimoto, Banana
See also CA 144; CANR 98, 160; SSFS 16

Young, Al(bert James) 1939- .... **BLC 1:3; CLC 19**
See also BW 2, 3; CA 29-32R; CANR 26, 65, 109; CN 2, 3, 4, 5, 6, 7; CP 1, 2, 3, 4, 5, 6, 7; DAM MULT; DLB 33

Young, Andrew (John) 1885-1971 ...... **CLC 5**
    See also CA 5-8R; CANR 7, 29; CP 1;
    RGEL 2
Young, Collier
    See Bloch, Robert (Albert)
Young, Edward 1683-1765 .... **LC 3, 40**
    See also DLB 95; RGEL 2
Young, Marguerite (Vivian)
    1909-1995 .... **CLC 82**
    See also CA 13-16; 150; CAP 1; CN 1, 2,
    3, 4, 5, 6
Young, Neil 1945- .... **CLC 17**
    See also CA 110; CCA 1
Young Bear, Ray A. 1950- ... **CLC 94; NNAL**
    See also CA 146; DAM MULT; DLB 175;
    MAL 5
Yourcenar, Marguerite 1903-1987 ... **CLC 19,**
    38, 50, 87; TCLC 193
    See also BPFB 3; CA 69-72; CANR 23, 60,
    93; DAM NOV; DLB 72; DLBY 1988;
    EW 12; EWL 3; GFL 1789 to the Present;
    GLL 1; MTCW 1, 2; MTFW 2005;
    RGWL 2, 3
Yuan, Chu 340(?)B.C.-278(?)B.C. . **CMLC 36**
Yurick, Sol 1925- .... **CLC 6**
    See also CA 13-16R; CANR 25; CN 1, 2,
    3, 4, 5, 6, 7; MAL 5
Zabolotsky, Nikolai Alekseevich
    1903-1958 .... **TCLC 52**
    See Zabolotsky, Nikolay Alekseevich
    See also CA 116; 164
Zabolotsky, Nikolay Alekseevich
    See Zabolotsky, Nikolai Alekseevich
    See also EWL 3
Zagajewski, Adam 1945- .... **PC 27**
    See also CA 186; DLB 232; EWL 3; PFS
    25
Zakaria, Fareed 1964- .... **CLC 269**
    See also CA 171; CANR 151
Zalygin, Sergei -2000 .... **CLC 59**
Zalygin, Sergei (Pavlovich)
    1913-2000 .... **CLC 59**
    See also DLB 302
Zamiatin, Evgenii
    See Zamyatin, Evgeny Ivanovich
    See also RGSF 2; RGWL 2, 3
Zamiatin, Evgenii Ivanovich
    See Zamyatin, Evgeny Ivanovich
    See also DLB 272
Zamiatin, Yevgenii
    See Zamyatin, Evgeny Ivanovich
Zamora, Bernice (B. Ortiz) 1938- .. **CLC 89;**
    HLC 2
    See also CA 151; CANR 80; DAM MULT;
    DLB 82; HW 1, 2
Zamyatin, Evgeny Ivanovich
    1884-1937 .... **SSC 89; TCLC 8, 37**
    See Zamiatin, Evgenii; Zamiatin, Evgenii
    Ivanovich; Zamyatin, Yevgeny Ivanovich
    See also CA 105; 166; SFW 4

Zamyatin, Yevgeny Ivanovich
    See Zamyatin, Evgeny Ivanovich
    See also EW 10; EWL 3
Zangwill, Israel 1864-1926 ... **SSC 44; TCLC
    16**
    See also CA 109; 167; CMW 4; DLB 10,
    135, 197; RGEL 2
Zanzotto, Andrea 1921- .... **PC 65**
    See also CA 208; CWW 2; DLB 128; EWL
    3
Zappa, Francis Vincent, Jr. 1940-1993
    See Zappa, Frank
    See also CA 108; 143; CANR 57
Zappa, Frank .... **CLC 17**
    See Zappa, Francis Vincent, Jr.
Zaturenska, Marya 1902-1982 ..... **CLC 6, 11**
    See also CA 13-16R; 105; CANR 22; CP 1,
    2, 3
Zayas y Sotomayor, Maria de 1590-c.
    1661 .... **LC 102; SSC 94**
    See also RGSF 2
Zeami 1363-1443 .... **DC 7; LC 86**
    See also DLB 203; RGWL 2, 3
Zelazny, Roger 1937-1995 .... **CLC 21**
    See also AAYA 7, 68; BPFB 3; CA 21-24R;
    148; CANR 26, 60; CN 6; DLB 8; FANT;
    MTCW 1, 2; MTFW 2005; SATA 57;
    SATA-Brief 39; SCFW 1, 2; SFW 4;
    SUFW 1, 2
Zephaniah, Benjamin 1958- .... **BLC 2:3**
    See also CA 147; CANR 103, 156, 177; CP
    5, 6, 7; DLB 347; SATA 86, 140, 189
Zhang Ailing
    See Chang, Eileen
Zhdanov, Andrei Alexandrovich
    1896-1948 .... **TCLC 18**
    See also CA 117; 167
Zhukovsky, Vasilii Andreevich
    See Zhukovsky, Vasily (Andreevich)
    See also DLB 205
Zhukovsky, Vasily (Andreevich)
    1783-1852 .... **NCLC 35**
    See Zhukovsky, Vasilii Andreevich
Ziegenhagen, Eric .... **CLC 55**
Zimmer, Jill Schary
    See Robinson, Jill
Zimmerman, Robert
    See Dylan, Bob
Zindel, Paul 1936-2003 ...... **CLC 6, 26; DC 5**
    See also AAYA 2, 37; BYA 2, 3, 8, 11, 14;
    CA 73-76; 213; CAD; CANR 31, 65, 108;
    CD 5, 6; CDALBS; CLR 3, 45, 85; DA;
    DA3; DAB; DAC; DAM DRAM, MST,
    NOV; DFS 12; DLB 7, 52; JRDA; LAIT
    5; MAICYA 1, 2; MTCW 1, 2; MTFW
    2005; NFS 14; SATA 16, 58, 102; SATA-
    Obit 142; WYA; YAW
Zinger, Yisroel-Yehoyshue
    See Singer, Israel Joshua

Zinger, Yitskhok
    See Singer, Isaac Bashevis
Zinn, Howard 1922- .... **CLC 199**
    See also CA 1-4R; CANR 2, 33, 90, 159
Zinov'Ev, A.A.
    See Zinoviev, Alexander
Zinov'ev, Aleksandr
    See Zinoviev, Alexander
    See also DLB 302
Zinoviev, Alexander 1922-2006 .... **CLC 19**
    See Zinov'ev, Aleksandr
    See also CA 116; 133; 250; CAAS 10
Zinoviev, Alexander Aleksandrovich
    See Zinoviev, Alexander
Zizek, Slavoj 1949- .... **CLC 188**
    See also CA 201; CANR 171; MTFW 2005
Zobel, Joseph 1915-2006 .... **BLC 2:3**
Zoilus
    See Lovecraft, H. P.
Zola, Emile (Edouard Charles Antoine)
    1840-1902 ...... **SSC 109; TCLC 1, 6, 21,
    41; WLC 6**
    See also CA 104; 138; DA; DA3; DAB;
    DAC; DAM MST, NOV; DLB 123; EW
    7; GFL 1789 to the Present; IDTP; LMFS
    1, 2; RGWL 2; TWA
Zoline, Pamela 1941- .... **CLC 62**
    See also CA 161; SFW 4
Zoroaster 628(?)B.C.-551(?)B.C. ... **CMLC 40**
Zorrilla y Moral, Jose 1817-1893 .... **NCLC 6**
Zoshchenko, Mikhail 1895-1958 ...... **SSC 15;
    TCLC 15**
    See also CA 115; 160; EWL 3; RGSF 2;
    RGWL 3
Zoshchenko, Mikhail Mikhailovich
    See Zoshchenko, Mikhail
Zuckmayer, Carl 1896-1977 .... **CLC 18;
    TCLC 191**
    See also CA 69-72; DLB 56, 124; EWL 3;
    RGWL 2, 3
Zuk, Georges
    See Skelton, Robin
    See also CCA 1
Zukofsky, Louis 1904-1978 ... **CLC 1, 2, 4, 7,
    11, 18; PC 11**
    See also AMWS 3; CA 9-12R; 77-80;
    CANR 39; CP 1, 2; DAM POET; DLB 5,
    165; EWL 3; MAL 5; MTCW 1; RGAL 4
Zweig, Arnold 1887-1968 .... **TCLC 199**
    See also CA 189; 115; DLB 66; EWL 3
Zweig, Paul 1935-1984 .... **CLC 34, 42**
    See also CA 85-88; 113
Zweig, Stefan 1881-1942 .... **TCLC 17**
    See also CA 112; 170; DLB 81, 118; EWL
    3; RGHL
Zwingli, Huldreich 1484-1531 .... **LC 37**
    See also DLB 179

Literary Criticism Series
Cumulative Topic Index

This index lists all topic entries in Gale's *Children's Literature Review* (CLR), *Classical and Medieval Literature Criticism* (CMLC), *Contemporary Literary Criticism* (CLC), *Drama Criticism* (DC), *Literature Criticism from 1400 to 1800* (LC), *Nineteenth-Century Literature Criticism* (NCLC), *Short Story Criticism* (SSC), and *Twentieth-Century Literary Criticism* (TCLC). The index also lists topic entries in the Gale Critical Companion Collection, which includes the following publications: *The Beat Generation* (BG), *Feminism in Literature* (FL), *Gothic Literature* (GL), and *Harlem Renaissance* (HR).

Topic Index

Topic Index

CMLC Cumulative Nationality Index

CMLC Cumulative Title Index

CLASSICAL AND MEDIEVAL LITERATURE CRITICISM

Commentaries on the Sentences (Gregory of Rimini)
See *Lectura super Primum et Secundum Librum Sententiarum*
Commentarii (Caesar) **47**:149-52, 156-57, 159-60, 195, 218, 221, 259
Commentarii (Xenophon)
See *Memorabilia*
Commentarioli in Psalmos (Jerome) **30**:89
Commentarius (Caesar) **47**:157
Commentarius in Evangelium Iohannis (Eriugena) **65**:281, 313
Commentarius in Ezechiel (Jerome) **30**:67
Commentarius in Ezechielem (Hrabanus Maurus) **78**:184
Commentarius in Joannem (Cyril of Alexandria) **59**:11
Commentarius in Micheam (Jerome) **30**:67
Commentarius quo medetu filio, servis, familiaribus (Cato) **21**:21
Commentarius in symbolum Apostolorum (Rufinus) **111**:249, 251, 257, 270, 312-13
Commentary (Augustine)
See *Epistolae ad Galatas expositio*
Commentary (Eriugena)
See *Commentarius in Evangelium Iohannis*
Commentary (Marsilius of Inghen)
See *Quaestiones super quattuor libros Sententiarum*
Commentary on 1 Corinthians: (Cyril of Alexandria) **59**:27-8
Commentary on Apollonius Pergaeus Conics (Hypatia)
See *On the Comics of Apollonius*
Commentary on Aristotle's De Generatione et de Coruptione (Averroes) **7**:30
Commentary on Aristotle's "De Interpretatione" (al-Farabi)
See *Sharḥ al-Fārābī li Kitāb Arisṭūṭālīs fī 'l- 'Ibāra*
Commentary on Aristotle's Nichomachean Ethics (Averroes) **7**:43
Commentary on Aristotle's Meteorology (Albert the Great) **16**:97
Commentary on Aristotle's Poetics (Averroes) **104**:73
Commentary on Bhagavadgita (Sankara)
See *Bhagavadgita-bhasya*
Commentary on Book I of the Sentences (Aquinas)
See *Commentaries on Aristotle*
Commentary on Brahmasutra (Sankara)
See *Brahma-sutra-bhasya*
Commentary on Brhadaranyaka (Sankara)
See *Brhadaranyaka Upanisad*
The Commentary of Commentaries (Saadiah Gaon)
See *Tafsir al-Tafsir*
Commentary on Daniel (Jerome) **30**:60, 107, 113, 117
The Commentary on Ecclesiastes (Bonaventure)
See *Commentary on Ecclesiasticus*
Commentary on Ecclesiastes (Jerome) **30**:86, 119
Commentary on Ecclesiasticus (Bonaventure) **79**:147, 283
Commentary on Ephesians (Jerome) **30**:56-57, 119
Commentary on Exodus (Eckhart) **80**:245, 249, 251-52
Commentary on Ezechiel 42:13f (Jerome) **30**:92, 119, 121
Commentary on Galatians (Augustine)
See *Epistolae ad Galatas expositio*
Commentary on Galatians (Jerome) **30**:56, 59, 108, 111, 119
Commentary on Genesis (Origen) **19**:186, 201, 246

Commentary on the Apostle's Creed (Rufinus)
See *Commentarius in symbolum Apostolorum*
A Commentary on the Benedictions of the 12 Patriarchs (Rufinus)
See *De benedictionibus XII patriarchum libri II*
Commentary on the Creed (Rufinus)
See *Commentarius in symbolum Apostolorum*
Commentary on the De generatione animalium (Averroes) **104**:49, 51, 53-4
Commentary on III de Anima (Averroes) **7**:24
Commentary on Isaiah (Cyril of Alexandria) **59**:51, 74, 77
Commentary on Isaiah (Eusebius) **103**:131
Commentary on Isaias (Jerome) **30**:112-113, 121
Commentary on Jeremiah (Jerome) **30**:67
The Commentary on John (Bonaventure)
See *Commentary on St. John*
Commentary on John (Cyril of Alexandria)
See *Commentary on St. John*
Commentary on John (Eckhart)
See *Commentary on John's Gospel*
Commentary on John (Eriugena)
See *Commentarius in Evangelium Iohannis*
Commentary on John's Gospel (Eckhart) **80**:219, 223, 228, 249-50, 256, 262, 293
Commentary on Lamentations (William of Malmesbury) **57**:330, 332
Commentary on Logic (Gersonides) **49**:196-97
Commentary on Luke (Cyril of Alexandria) **59**:74
Commentary on Matthew (Cyril of Alexandria)
See *Commentary on St. Matthew*
Commentary on Osee (Jerome) **30**:99
Commentary on Paul's Epistle to the Romans (Abelard)
See *Commentaria in Epistolam Pauli ad Romanos*
Commentary on Plato's Cratylus (Proclus)
See *In Platonis Cratylum commentarii*
Commentary on Plato's Parmenides (Proclus)
See *In Platonis Parmenidem commentarii*
Commentary on Plato's Republic (Averroes) **7**:30, 38, 40-3
Commentary on Plato's Republic (Proclus)
See *In Platonis Rem publicam commentarii*
Commentary on Romans (Abelard)
See *Commentaria in Epistolam Pauli ad Romanos*
Commentary on Scipio's Dream (Macrobius)
See *Commentary on the Somnium Scipionis*
Commentary on St. John (Bonaventure) **79**:238
Commentary on St. John (Cyril of Alexandria) **59**:18, 25, 47, 74-9, 83, 85-7
Commentary on St. John (Origen) **19**:186-88, 209, 247, 257, 260, 262-63
Commentary on St Luke (Albert the Great) **16**:29
Commentary on St. Matthew (Cyril of Alexandria) **59**:18, 74
Commentary on St. Matthews's Gospel (Jerome) **30**:88
Commentary on s. al-falaq (Avicenna) **110**:141
Commentary on the Book of the Sentences (Albert the Great) **16**:6-7, 14, 16, 26, 31, 44, 66, 68, 76, 86, 93-4
Commentary on the Book of Creation (Saadiah Gaon)
See *Commentary on the Sefer Yezirah*
Commentary on the Book of Wisdom (Bonaventure) **79**:152-53
Commentary on the Books of Dionysius (Grosseteste) **62**:112

Commentary on the Categories (Gersonides) **49**:147, 199
Commentary on the De Anima (Buridan)
See *Quaestiones in De Anima*
Commentary on the Divine Names (Albert the Great) **16**:28-9
Commentary on the Dream of Scipio (Macrobius)
See *Commentary on the Somnium Scipionis*
Commentary on the Epistle of the Greek, Zeno the Great (al-Farabi)
See *Sharḥ Risālat Zīnūn al-Kabīr al-Yūnānī*
Commentary on the Epistle to the Galatians (Jerome)
See *Commentary on Galatians*
A Commentary on the First Book of Euclid's Elements (Proclus)
See *In primum Euclida elementarum librum commentarii*
Commentary on the De generatione animalium (Averroes) **104**:49, 51
Commentary on the Gospel According to John (Eckhart)
See *Commentary on John's Gospel*
Commentary on the Gospel according to Matthew (Origen) **19**:187, 240, 246
Commentary on the Gospel of Saint Luke (Bonaventure) **79**:149, 151
Commentary on the Letter of Saint Paul to the Romans (Abelard)
See *Commentaria in Epistolam Pauli ad Romano*
Commentary on the Lord's Prayer (Abelard)
See *Expositio orationis dominicae*
Commentary on the Metaphysics (Buridan)
See *Quaestiones in Aristotelis Metaphysicam*
Commentary on the Minor Prophets (Cyril of Alexandria) **59**:17-18, 51
Commentary on the Mishnah (Maimonides)
See *Commentary to the Mishnah*
Commentary on the Parmenides (Proclus)
See *In Platonis Parmenidem commentarii*
Commentary on the Perihermenias (William of Ockham) **32**:210
Commentary on the Physics (Buridan)
See *Quaestiones super octo libros Physicorum Aristotelis*
Commentary on the Posterior Analytics (Grosseteste) **62**:140
Commentary on the Prophet Daniel (Jerome)
See *Commentary on Daniel*
Commentary on the Psalms (Athanasius) **48**:28
Commentary on the Psalms (Cassiodorus) **43**:264-65
Commentary on the Psalms (Origen) **19**:202
Commentary on the Psalms and Canticles of the Old Testament (Rolle) **21**:273, 279, 284, 294, 362
Commentary on the Sefer Yeṣīrah (Saadiah Gaon)
See *Commentary on the Sefer Yezirah*
Commentary on the Sefer Yezirah (Saadiah Gaon) **97**:287-89, 298
Commentary on the Sentences (Gregory of Rimini)
See *Lectura super Primum et Secundum Librum Sententiarum*
Commentary on the Sentences (William of Ockham) **32**:209-10
Commentary on the Sentences of Peter Lombard (Albert the Great)
See *Commentary on the Book of the Sentences*
Commentary on the Somnium Scipionis (Macrobius) **48**:289, 293-96, 299, 307, 312-16, 318-31, 333, 337-39, 342-45, 350, 357, 360-69
Commentary on the Song of Songs (Origen) **19**:210, 212, 240, 255-62

(Title Index)

Title Index

"On the Study of Sacred Scripture" (Jerome) **30**:89

On the Subjects of Learning (Protagoras)
See *Peri tôn Mathêmatôn*

On the Sublime (Longinus)
See *Peri Hysos*

On the Superiority of the Belly to the Back (Al-Jahiz)
See *Fi Tafdil-al-bafn ala l-zahr*

On the Symmories (Demosthenes) **13**:145, 148, 159, 163-4, 171, 197

On the Synods (Athanasius) **48**:10, 67

On the Temptations of the Enemy, Which She First Endured, and Her Subsequently Divinely Revealed Visions (Elisabeth of Schönau)
See *Liber Visionum Primus*

On the Thrice Holy Hymn (St. John) **95**:311, 313

On the Treaties with Alexander (Demosthenes) **13**:166

On the Trinity (Boethius)
See *De trinitate*

On the True, First, Perfect Agent and the Deficient Agent which is (an Agent) Metaphorically (al-Kindi) **80**:134

On the Truth (Antiphon)
See *On Truth*

"On the twelfth night" (Su Shih) **15**:398

On the Two Wills and Operations (St. John)
See *De duabus in Christo voluntatibus*

On the Two Wills in Christ; or, Against the Monothelites (St. John)
See *De duabus in Christo voluntatibus*

"On the Unity of God and the Finiteness of the Body of the World" (al-Kindi)
See *On the Bowing of the Outermost Sphere and its Obeisance to God*

On the Unchangeableness of God (Philo)
See *Quod Deus sit immutabiulis*

On the Unity of Study (Philo)
See *De congressu eruditionis gratia*

On the Unity of the Intellect: against Averroes (Augustine) **16**:57

On the Universe (Apuleius)
See *De mundo*

On the Usefulness of Mathematics (Bacon)
See *De utilitate mathematicae*

On the Vanities of Courtiers and the Footsteps of the Philosophers (John of Salisbury)
See *Policraticus: De Nugis Curialium et Vestigiis Philosophorum*

"On the Vestiments of the High Priest" (Jerome) **30**:89

On the Vices Contracted in the Study of Theology (Bacon) **14**:92

On the Virtues (Philo)
See *De virtutibus*

On the Virtues and Vices (Alcuin) **69**:3, 10

On The Virtues and Vices of the Soul and Body (St. John) **95**:310, 314

On the Virtues of the Turk (Al-Jahiz)
See *Kitab Manaqib al-Turkwa-ammat jund al-khilafah*

"On the Voluntary and the Will of the One" (Plotinus) **46**:269

On Times (Bede)
See *De temporibus*

On True Religion (Augustine)
See *De vera religione*

On Truth (Antiphon) **55**:25, 27-30

On Types of Style (Hermogenes) **6**:158, 170, 185-92, 196, 200-02, 204

On the Unity of God (al-Kindi)
See "On the Unity of God and the Finiteness of the Body of the World"

On Truth (Protagoras)
See *Tês Alêtheia*

On Universals (Wyclif)
See *De Universalibus*

On Veiling Virgins (Tertullian) **29**:311-12,377

On Virginity (Ambrose)
See *De virginitate*

On Virtues (Philo)
See *De virtutibus*

"On Virtues" (Plotinus) **46**:297

On Vision (Epicurus) **21**:73

"On Visiting a Village" (Wang Wei) **100**:291

On Widows (Ambrose)
See *De viduis*

"On Wisdom" (Petrarch) **20**:286

On Witches (St. John) **95**:313

On words of insult (Suetonius) **60**:321-23

One the Art of Metre (Bede)
See *De arte metrica*

The One Thousand and One Nights (Anonymous)
See *Alf Layla wa-Layla*

1001 Nights (Anonymous)
See *Alf Layla wa-Layla*

Onomasticon (Eusebius) **103**:234, 239

Onomasticum (Jerome) **30**:88, 111

Onos (Lucian) **32**:23-28

Opera (Hrotsvit of Gandersheim) **29**:121, 140

Opera omnia (Bonaventure) **79**:151-52

Opera omnia (Duns Scotus)
See *Ioannis Duns Scoti opera omnia, . . . studio et cura Commissionis Scotisticae ad fidem codicum edita, praeside Carolo Balic, O.F.M*

Opera omnia (Euclid) **25**:1-86, 212

De opificio mundi (Philo)
See *De Opificio Mundi*

De Opificio Mundi (Philo) **100**:67-9, 152-54, 160, 162, 173

The Opinions (al-Farabi)
See *Kitāb Ārā' Ahl al-Madīna al-Fāḍila*

Opinions of the Inhabitants of the Virtuous City (al-Farabi)
See *Kitāb Ārā' Ahl al-Madīna al-Fāḍila*

The Opinions of the People of the Virtuous City (al-Farabi)
See *Kitāb Ārā' Ahl al-Madīna al-Fāḍila*

Opposed Arguments (Protagoras)
See *Antilogiai*

Opposing Arguments (Protagoras)
See *Antilogiai*

Optica (Euclid)
See *Optics*

Optica, Liber de visu (Euclid)
See *Optics*

Optics (Bacon) **14**:20

Optics (Biruni) **28**:130

Optics (Euclid) **25**:1-86, 90, 98, 110, 148-62, 199-205, 231, 261-62, 264

De Optimo (Cicero)
See *De optimo genere oratorum*

De optimo genere dicendi (Cicero) **3**:188, 193, 199, 201, 217-18, 259-63, 288

De Optimo Genere Interpretandi (Jerome) **30**:56

De optimo genere oratorum (Cicero) **3**:201, 261; **81**:179, 253

Opus evangelicum (Wyclif) **70**:279

Opus imperfectum contra Julianum (Augustine) **6**:149

Opus Maius (Bacon)
See *Opus Majus*

Opus Majus (Bacon) **14**:3-5, 7-8, 15, 18, 20, 22-23, 29-31, 34-35, 37, 40, 42, 47, 49-50, 53-54, 59, 61-65, 68-70, 73, 76-77, 80, 82, 84, 86, 92-94, 100, 102, 106-15; **108**:3-5, 32-9, 55-62

Opus Minus (Bacon) **14**:15, 18-20, 29, 40, 48, 52, 54, 62-63, 66-68, 80, 100, 102-03; **108**:37

Opus nonaginta duierum (William of Ockham) **32**:199

Opus Oxoniense (Duns Scotus) **59**:142, 144, 149, 165, 197-98, 200, 202, 204

Opus Prophetale (Jerome) **30**:89

Opus Quaestionum (Eckhart) **80**:228

Opus Sermonum (Eckhart) **9**:57

Opus Tertium (Bacon) **14**:15, 19-21, 29-30, 40, 47-48, 52, 54, 58-59, 62-63, 65, 67-68, 80, 83, 86, 100-05, 108; **108**:3, 33, 36-7

Opus Tripartitum (Eckhart) **9**:55; **80**:219-20, 228, 255-56, 292

O quanta qualia (Abelard) **77**:97

"The Orange Tree" (Yuan) **36**:81

Oratio (Ausonius) **88**:9, 12, 16, 89, 91

Oratio (St. John) **95**:336

Oratio (St. Anselm)
See *Orationes sive Meditationes*

Oratio ad Christum (St. Anselm) **67**:90-91

Oratio contra Gentes (Athanasius) **48**:15, 28, 68-70

Oratio de incarnatione Verbi (Athanasius) **48**:11-13, 16-17, 19-20, 28, 39, 68-71, 73, 76

Oratio Lepidi (Sallust) **68**:235-36

Oration 5 (St. Gregory of Nazianzus) **82**:131

Oration 41 (St. Gregory of Nazianzus) **82**:71-2

Oration 4 (St. Gregory of Nazianzus) **82**:131-32

Oration 34 (St. Gregory of Nazianzus) **82**:71

Oration 22 (St. Gregory of Nazianzus) **82**:72

Oration II (St. Gregory of Nazianzus) **82**:104, 130-31

Oration 2 (St. Gregory of Nazianzus)
See *Oration II*

An Oration Against the Heathen (Athanasius) **48**:11-12, 19-21, 73

De oratione (Tertullian) **29**:374

De Oratione Moysi (Aelfric) **46**:61

Orationes (St. Anselm)
See *Orationes sive Meditationes*

Orationes (St. Gregory of Nazianzus)
See *Orationes theologicae*

Orationes contra Arianos (Athanasius) **48**:10, 14, 16-17, 28, 68, 70-1

Orationes sive Meditationes (St. Anselm) **67**:56-58, 89-92

Orationes theologicae (St. Gregory of Nazianzus) **82**:71-3, 84, 95, 97, 104, 127, 130

Orations against the Arians (Athanasius)
See *Orationes contra Arianos*

Orations against Those Who Attack the Divine Images (St. John)
See *Contra imaginum calumniatores orationes tres*

Orator (Cicero) **81**:196, 219-20, 234, 253, 268

The Orator (Cicero)
See *De optimo genere dicendi*

Orator ad M. Brutum (Cicero)
See *De optimo genere dicendi*

The Orator: To Marcus Brutus (Cicero)
See *De optimo genere dicendi*

De oratore (Cicero) **3**:186, 193, 200-01, 207-11, 217-18, 227, 246, 258-59, 261, 263, 270, 288; **81**:179, 181, 195, 219-20, 227-29, 231-34, 238-42, 253-56, 259-60, 262, 264-69

De oratore ad filium (Cato) **21**:21

Oratorio contra Gentes (Athanasius)
See *Oratio contra Gentes*

Order of Battle against the Alani (Arrian) **43**:25, 36, 44, 46-8, 52, 61, 64, 69

The Order of Famous Cities (Ausonius)
See *Ordo urbium nobilium*

Ordinatio (Duns Scotus) **59**:165, 176, 178, 190, 197, 200-05, 210, 212-13, 218-19, 221-22

Ordinatio (William of Ockham) **32**:138, 145

De ordine (Augustine) **6**:5, 102; **95**:56, 180-189, 192

Ordo generis Cassiodororum (Cassiodorus) **43**:277-79

Ordo nobilium (Ausonius)
See *Ordo urbium nobilium*

Ordo Representacionis Ade (Anonymous) **4**:182-221

Pytine (Cratinus) **54**:120-21, 131-40
Qabl Ta'allum al-Falsafah (al-Farabi) **58**:93, 95
Qāfiyya (Ibn Zaydūn) **89**:57-8
"Qamar al-Zamān" (Anonymous) **62**:66-7
Qarīḏiyya (al-Hamadhānī) **93**:33, 60
Qāsim al-surūr wa'ayn al-hayāt (Biruni) **28**:176
Qawā'id al'Aqā'id (Al-Ghazali) **50**:10, 53, 92-3
Qisṭās (Al-Ghazali) **50**:8
Quaestio de Aeternitae Munid (Siger of Brabant) **69**:168
Quaestio de Necessitate et Contingentia Causarum (Siger of Brabant) **69**:168, 175, 177-78, 205-7, 210-12, 214-17, 219, 221-22
Quaestio utrum haec sit vera (Siger of Brabant) **69**:168
Quaestiones (Isidore of Seville) **101**:79, 101
Quaestiones ad Thalassium (Eriugena) **65**:313
Quaestiones altere supra libros Prime Philosophiae (Bacon) **108**:16, 18, 20-1, 24
Quaestiones circa logicum (Albert of Saxony) **110**:55-7
Quaestiones Disputatae de Mysterio Trinitatis (Bonaventure) **79**:159, 163-65, 167, 238-39
Quaestiones Disputatae de Scientia Christi (Bonaventure) **79**:287
Quaestiones disputatas de veritate (Aquinas)
   See *Disputed Questions*
Quaestiones Elenchorum (Buridan) **97**:159
Quaestiones et Solutiones in Exodum (Philo)
   See *Questiones in Exodium*
Quaestiones evangeliorum (Augustine) **6**:68, 94; **95**:15
Quaestiones in Analytica Priora (Buridan) **97**:133-34
Quaestiones in Aristotelis Metaphysicam (Buridan) **97**:12, 15-16, 159
Quaestiones in artem veterem (Albert of Saxony) **110**:25-7, 29-30, 56, 74-5
Quaestiones in De Anima (Buridan) **97**:159
Quaestiones in Libros Priorum Analiticorum (Buridan) **97**:159
Quaestiones in Metaphysicam (Siger of Brabant) **69**:168, 172-73, 176-78, 184-85, 204, 206-8, 210-11, 214-18, 229, 234-35, 243, 245, 247-48, 250-52
Quaestiones in Physicam (Siger of Brabant) **69**:168, 172-73, 175-78, 206
Quaestiones in Tertium de Anima (Siger of Brabant) **69**:167-68, 172, 193-95
Quaestiones logicales (Albert of Saxony) **110**:25, 50
Quaestiones Logicales (Siger of Brabant) **69**:168-69
Quaestiones Longae super Librum Peri Hermeneias (Buridan) **97**:159
Quaestiones **69**:169
Quaestiones Morales (Siger of Brabant) **69**:169
Quaestiones Naturales (Seneca)
   See *Naturales quaestiones*
Quaestiones Naturales (Siger of Brabant) **69**:168
Quaestiones on De caelo (Albert of Saxony) **110**:18-20, 23
Quaestiones on the Physics (Albert of Saxony) **110**:18, 23, 38
Quaestiones Parisienses (Eckhart) **9**:69; **80**:195, 250, 292
Quaestiones Subtilissime super Libros posteriorum analyticorum Aristotelis (Albert of Saxony) **110**:69
Quaestiones super artem veterem (Albert of Saxony)
   See *Quaestiones in artem veterem*
Quaestiones super decem libros Ethicorum Aristotelis ad Nichomachum (Buridan) **97**:11-12, 15-16. 104, 180

Quaestiones super librio de Caelo et Mundo (Buridan)
   See *Quaestiones super libris quattuor de Caelo et Mundo*
Quaestiones super libris quattuor de Caelo et Mundo (Buridan) **97**:4
Quaestiones super libros i-vi Physicorum Aristotelis (Bacon) **14**:49, 66
Quaestiones super Libros Posteriorum analyticorum Aristotelis (Albert of Saxony) **110**:57
Quaestiones super Librum de causis (Siger of Brabant) **69**:193, 195, 206-7, 234, 236, 244, 248-51, 260
Quaestiones super logicam (Albert of Saxony)
   See *25 Quaestiones super logicam*
Quaestiones super Metaphysicam (Duns Scotus) **59**:204, 210-12
Quaestiones super librum Metaphysicorum (Marsilius of Inghen) **106**:170
Quaestiones super octo libros Physicorum Aristotelis (Buridan) **97**:4, 151
Quaestiones super octos libros Physicorum (William of Ockham) **32**:145, 150
Quaestiones super octo libros Policorum Aristotelis (Buridan) **97**:15
Quaestiones super quattuor libros Sententiarum (Marsilius of Inghen) **106**:171, 180
Quaestiones veteris artis (Marsilius of Inghen) **106**:170
"Quando t'alegri" (Jacopone) **95**:230, 238
De quantitate animae (Augustine) **6**:68
Quaestiones et Solutiones in Genesium (Philo)
   See *Questione in Genesin (Exodum)*
"Les Quatre Deuils" (Marie de France)
   See "Le Chaitivel"
"Quatre Dols" (Marie de France)
   See "Le Chaitivel"
Quatuor oraciones (Saint Birgitta of Sweden) **24**:93, 97, 101, 158
"De lo que contesçió al árvol de la Mentira" (Juan Manuel) **88**:284
"De lo que contesçió al Bien e al Mal" (Juan Manuel)
   See "De lo que contesçió al Bien e al Mal, e al Cuerdo con el Loco"
"De lo que contesçió al Bien e al Mal, e al Cuerdo con el Loco" (Juan Manuel) **88**:233, 284
"De lo que contesçió al león et al toro" (Juan Manuel) **88**:233
"De lo que contesçió al que echaron en la ysla desnuyo quandol tomaron el señorío que teníe" (Juan Manuel) **88**:284
"De lo que contesçió los cuervos con los buhos" (Juan Manuel) **88**:232
"De lo [que] contesçió a don Lorenço Suárez sobre la çerca de Sevilla" (Juan Manuel) **88**:233
"De lo que contesçió a los dos cavallos con el león" (Juan Manuel) **88**:233
"De lo que contesçió a un mançebo que casó con una [muger] muy fuerte et muy brava" (Juan Manuel) **88**:318
"De lo que contesçió a un rey con los burladores que fizieron el paño" (Juan Manuel) **88**:233
"De lo que contesçió a un rey con un su privado" (Juan Manuel) **88**:234
"De lo que contesçió a un rey moço con un muy grant philósopho a qui lo acomendara su padre" (Juan Manuel) **88**:233
"De lo que contesçió a un rey que quería provar a tres sus fijos" (Juan Manuel) **88**:296
"De lo que contesçió a uno que provava sus amigos" (Juan Manuel) **88**:234, 284
"De lo que facen las formigas para se mantener" (Juan Manuel) **88**:294

Queen Arsinoe (Callimachus) **18**:5-6
"Quel c'ha nostra natura in se piu degno" (Petrarch) **20**:333
Questio de dependentiis, diversitatibus, et convenientiis (Buridan) **97**:93-4, 101-02
Questio Quodlibetis (Aquinas)
   See *Quodlibets*
Questione in Genesin (Exodum) (Philo) **100**:69, 82, 84, 111, 186, 198
Questiones altere supra libros prime philosophie Aristotelis (Bacon)
   See *Quaestiones altere supra libros Prime Philosophiae*
Questiones de nomine (Albert of Saxony) **110**:30
Questiones in Exodium (Philo) **100**:69-70, 78, 111, 161
Questiones supra libros prime philosophie Aristotelis (Bacon) **108**:16, 19-22, 24-5
"Questioning Heaven" (Yuan)
   See *T'ien-wen*
"Questioning the Soothsayer" (Yuan)
   See *Pu-Ku*
Questions (Isidore of Seville)
   See *Quaestiones*
Questions (Porphyry)
   See *The Homeric Questions*
Questions and Answers on Genesis (Philo)
   See *Questione in Genesin (Exodum)*
Questions and Answers on Renga (Nijō Yoshimoto)
   See *Tsukuba mondō*
Questions and Answers on the Subject of Knowledge (Al-Jahiz)
   See *Kitab al-Masail wa l-jawabat fi l-marifah*
Questions and Answers on the way of Tsukuba (Nijō Yoshimoto)
   See *Tsukuba mondō*
Questions of Truth (Aquinas) **33**:56, 60
Questions on Aristotle (Bacon)
   See *Quaestiones super libros i-vi Physicorum Aristotelis*
Questions on Aristotle's Ethics (Buridan)
   See *Quaestiones super decem libros Ethicorum Aristotelis ad Nichomachum*
Questions on Aristotle's Metaphysics (Duns Scotus)
   See *Quaestiones super Metaphysicam*
Questions on Aristotle's Parva naturalia (Buridan) **97**:4
Questions on Aristotle's Physics (Bacon)
   See *Quaestiones super libros i-vi Physicorum Aristotelis*
Questions on Aristotle's Physics (Buridan)
   See *Quaestiones super octo libros Physicorum Aristotelis*
Questions on De cælo (Albert of Saxony)
   See *Quaestiones on De caelo*
Questions on De generatione et corruptione (Albert of Saxony) **110**:18, 23
Questions on Generation and Corruption (Albert of Saxony)
   See *Questions on De generatione et corruptione*
Questions on Genesis (Jerome)
   See *Liber Hebraicarum Quaestionum in Genesim*
Questions on Genesis and Exodus (Philo)
   See *Questione in Genesin (Exodum)*
Questions on the De Caelo et Mundo (Buridan)
   See *Quaestiones super libris quattuor de Caelo et Mundo*
Questions on the De generatione et corruptione (Buridan) **97**:4
Questions on the Metaphysics (Duns Scotus)
   See *Quaestiones super Metaphysicam*
Questions on the Physics (Albert of Saxony)
   See *Quaestiones on the Physics*
Questions on the Physiognomy Ascribed to Aristotle (Buridan) **97**:7

Sanctorum Septem Dormientium (Aelfric) **46**:119-20, 122, 124-25

Sanctus Servatius (Veldeke)
See *Servatius*

Sanka-shū (Saigyō)
See *Sankashū*

Sankashū (Saigyō) **77**:351, 355, 357-61, 363-64, 374, 381, 384, 402

Sannyâsa (Anonymous) **69**:272, 277

"Sappho" (Alcaeus) **65**:11

Sāriyya (al-Hamadhānī) **93**:32

Sarva-darsana-siddhantasangraha (Sankara) **32**:390

Sarvopanishatsâra (Anonymous) **69**:272, 277

Satira (Petronius)
See *Satyricon*

Satirarium libri (Petronius)
See *Satyricon*

"Satire Agaimst Three Disinherited Lords" (Sordello) **15**:276

Satire 5 (Persius)
See *Saturae*

Satire 4 (Persius)
See *Saturae*

Satire 1 (Persius)
See *Saturae*

Satire 6 (Persius)
See *Saturae*

Satire 3 (Persius)
See *Saturae*

Satire 2 (Persius)
See *Saturae*

Satires (Horace) **39**:141-42, 146, 171, 175-76, 189, 191-93, 202-04, 277-82

Satires (Juvenal) **8**:7, 14, 19, 22, 27-8, 59-60, 66, 68-9, 73-8

Satires (Lucilius)
See *C. Lucilii saturarum*

Satires (Persius)
See *Saturae*

Satiricon (Petronius)
See *Satyricon*

Satiricum (Petronius)
See *Satyricon*

Satura (Lucilius)
See *C. Lucilii saturarum*

Saturae (Lucilius)
See *C. Lucilii saturarum*

Saturae (Persius) **74**:295-380

Saturicon (Petronius)
See *Satyricon*

Saturnalia (Lucan) **33**:422

Saturnalia (Lucian) **32**:8, 15, 18, 48

Saturnalia (Macrobius) **48**:280, 283-84, 288-90, 293-94, 296, 299, 312-14, 320-22, 326, 331, 333, 337-46, 353-54, 356-58

Satyra (Petronius)
See *Satyricon*

Satyrici libri (Petronius)
See *Satyricon*

Satyricon (Petronius) **34**:248-427

Satyroi (Cratinus) **54**:119

"Saying Farewell to the Children at Nanling as I Leave for the Capital" (Li Po) **2**:174

"Saying Goodbye to Ping Danran, Overseer" (Wang Wei) **100**:326

Sayings of the High One (Anonymous)
See *Hávamál*

Scala perfectionis (Hilton) **58**:158, 160-61, 166-67, 169, 172-76, 178, 180, 182-84, 188-99, 207, 217-20, 222-24, 233-38, 243-47, 250-51, 253-54, 256

Scale (Hilton)
See *Scala perfectionis*

Scandals of the Esoterics (Al-Ghazali)
See *Faḍā'iḥ al-bāṭiniyya*

"The Scavenger and the Noble Lady" (Anonymous) **2**:40

De schematibus et tropis sacrae scripturae (Bede) **20**:42,93

Schionatulander (Wolfram von Eschenbach)
See *Titurel*

"The Schism of the Popes" (Wyclif) **70**:300

Scholia de incarnatione Unigeniti (Cyril of Alexandria) **59**:74, 85, 87

Scholia on the Incarnation (Cyril of Alexandria)
See *Scholia de incarnatione Unigeniti*

Die Schwänke des Pfaffen Amis (Der Stricker) **75**:330, 381-84

Scientia (Aquinas) **33**:114

De scientia experimentali (Bacon) **14**:5, 80

De Scientia Perspectiva (Bacon) **14**:20, 47; **108**:55

Scipio's Dream (Cicero)
See *Somnium Scipionis*

Scírnismál (Anonymous)
See *Skírnismál*

Scite Teipsum (Abelard)
See *Ethica seu liber dictus Scito Teipsum*

Scito Te Ipsum (Abelard)
See *Ethica seu liber dictus Scito Teipsum*

Scivias (Hildegard von Bingen) **20**:132-33, 135-37, 143, 153, 161-63, 168, 172-75, 178, 182-86

Scorpiace (Tertullian) **29**:312, 329-30, 332, 334-38

Scripta Super Sententias (Albert the Great)
See *Commentary on the Book of the Sentences*

Scriptum Principale (Bacon) **14**:15

The Sea Captain (Menander) **51**:227

The Seafarer (Anonymous) **94**:234-388

"The Sealed Vessel" (Ibn Arabi) **105**:138

Seals of Wisdom (Ibn Arabi)
See *Tarjuman al-ashwaq*

The Seasons (Kālidāsa)
See *Rtusamhāra*

Second Action against Verres (Cicero) **81**:180, 197

Second Alcibiades (Plato)
See *Alcibiades II*

Second Book of Visions (Elisabeth of Schönau)
See *Liber Visionum Secundus*

"Second Canticle of the Nativity" (Jacopone) **95**:249

"Second Idyll" (Theocritus)
See "Idyll 2"

The Second Lay of Gudrun (Anonymous)
See *Guðrúnarqviða önnor*

The Second Lay of Helgi Hunding's Bane (Anonymous)
See *Helgaqviða Hundingsbana II*

"Second Letter" (Hadewijch of Antwerp)
See "Letter 2"

"Second Mendicant" (Anonymous) **62**:23

Second Olympian (Pindar)
See *Olympian 2*

Second Olynthiac (Demosthenes)
See *Olynthiac II*

Second Philippic (Cicero)
See *Phillipicae*

Second Philippic (Demosthenes)
See *Philippic II*

Second Pythian (Pindar)
See *Pythian 2*

Second Satire (Persius)
See *Saturae*

The Second Sermon on the Nativity (Bonaventure) **79**:283

Second Tetralogy (Antiphon)
See *Tetralogies*

A Secret Treatise on Renga Principles (Nijō Yoshimoto)
See *Renri Hishō*

De secreto conflictu curarum mearum (Petrarch) **20**:318

Secretum (Petrarch) **20**:212, 214, 243-44, 246, 250, 258, 261-63, 266, 272, 279, 287, 290, 294, 299, 303, 323, 326-27

Secretum secretorum cum glossis et notulis Fratris Rogeri (Bacon) **108**:57, 59-60

Secretum secretorum (Bacon)
See *Secretum secretorum cum glossis et notulis Fratris Rogeri*

Sectio Canonis (Euclid) **25**:1-86, 99, 110, 205-20, 245-258

Secular Hymn (Horace) **39**:143, 171

"Secundum Lucam" (Wulfstan) **59**:330-31

"Seeing Off the Spring" (Po Chu-i) **24**:347

"Seeing off Wei Wan, Recluse of Wang-wu Mountain, on His Trip Home" (Li Po) **2**:168

"Seeing Someone Off" (Wang Wei) **100**:287

"Seeing Yuan off on His Official Trip to Anxi" (Wang Wei) **100**:326

"Seeing Zu off at Qizhon" (Wang Wei) **100**:325

Sefer 'Elleh Shemot (Anonymous)
See *Exodus*

Sefer ha-'Emūnōt we-ha-Deōt (Saadiah Gaon)
See *Commentary on the Sefer Yezirah*

Sefer ha-Emunoth ve De'ot (Saadiah Gaon) **97**:276-81, 283-84, 286-90, 292, 298-300, 303-05, 307-09, 313-15, 317-18, 320, 322-23, 325-26, 335

Sefer ha-Galui (Saadiah Gaon) **97**:335

Sefer haMada (Maimonides) **76**:224

"Segnore, damme la morte" (Jacopone) **95**:220

"Segrek Son of Ushun Koja" (Anonymous) **8**:103

Sei Shōnagon ga Makura-no-Sōshi (Sei Shonagon)
See *Makura no sōshi*

Sei Shōnagon's Pillow Book (Sei Shonagon)
See *Makura no sōshi*

Sei Shōnagon shū (Sei Shonagon) **89**:328

Seishu (Izumi Shikibu)
See *Izumi Shikibu seishu*

"Seizure" (Sappho)
See "Ode to Anactoria"

Select Apophthegums (Epicurus) **21**:122

Select Odes (Hafiz) **34**:56

The Selected Aphorisms (al-Farabi) **58**:46, 129-31

Selected Sayings (Confucius)
See *Lun Yü*

Self-Punishment (Terence)
See *Heautontimoreumenos*

"Self-Realization" (Po Chu-i) **24**:346

The Self-Tormentor (Terence)
See *Heautontimoreumenos*

"Se li maus c'amours envoie" (Adam de la Halle) **80**:21

"Selpwahsen kint, dû bist zu krump" (Walther von der Vogelweide) **56**:361

De senectute (Cicero) **3**:193, 195, 202, 204, 227, 231, 288; **81**:182, 203-04, 227, 229, 231-32, 241

Sengohyakuban utaawase (Teika) **73**:361

"Senh' En Sordel mandamen" (Sordello) **15**:362

De Sensu (Aristotle) **31**:65, 332, 359

De sensu et sensato (Albert the Great) **16**:61, 106, 110

Sente Servas (Veldeke)
See *Servatius*

Sentence Commentary (Bonaventure)
See *Commentaria in Quartuor Libros Sententiarum*

Sentence Commentary (Gregory of Rimini)
See *Lectura super Primum et Secundum Librum Sententiarum*

The Sentence of Evagrius Ponticus (Rufinus) **111**:250

Sentences (Albert the Great)
See *Commentary on the Book of the Sentences*

Sentences (Isidore of Seville)
See *Sententiarum libri tres*

Sentences (Lombard)
See *Sententiarum Quatuor Libri*

Title Index